The **Rough Guide** to

Central America

written and researched by

Peter Eltringham, Joe Fullman, Brendon Griffin, Jean McNeil, Toby Nortcliffe, Paul Smith, Iain Stewart and **Andy Symington**

NEW YORK • LONDON • DELHI

www.roughguides.com

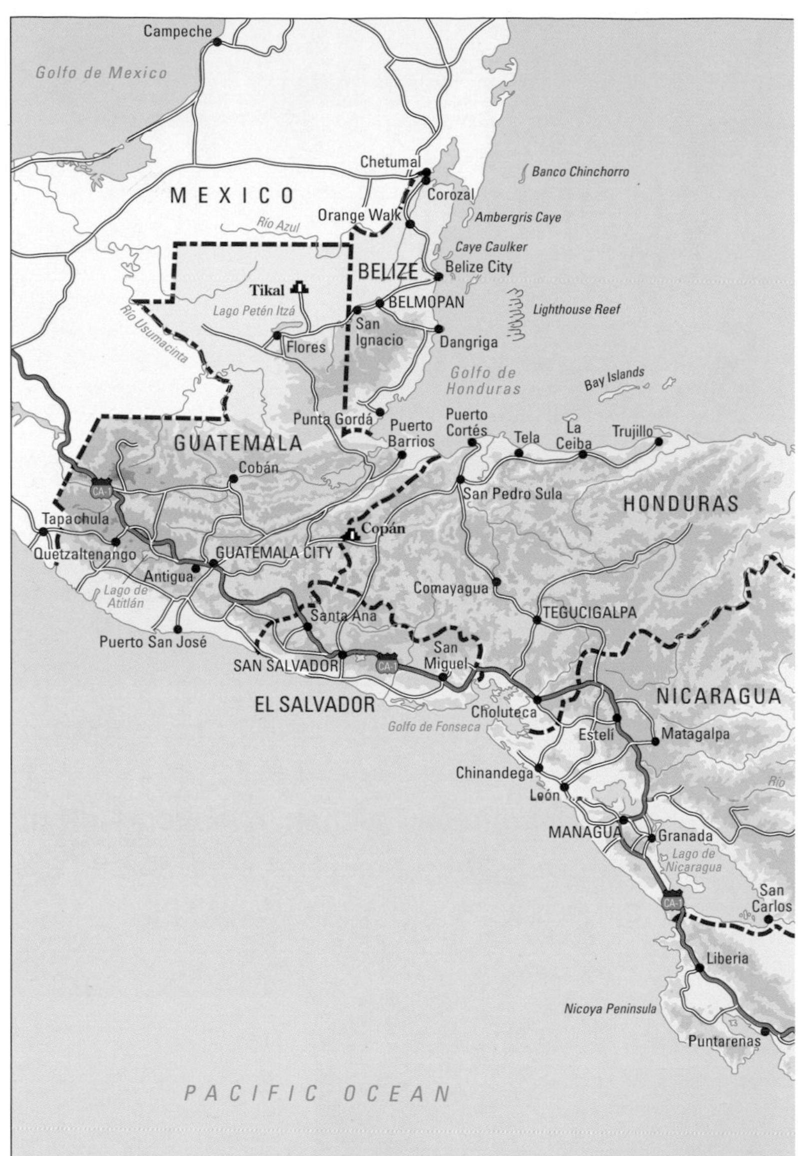

Campeche
Golfo de Mexico
MEXICO
Chetumal
Banco Chinchorro
Corozal
Orange Walk
Río Azul
Ambergris Caye
Caye Caulker
BELIZE
Belize City
Tikal
BELMOPAN
Lago Petén Itzá
Lighthouse Reef
Río Usumacinta
San Ignacio
Flores
Dangriga
Golfo de Honduras
Bay Islands
Punta Gordá
Puerto Barrios
Puerto Cortés
Tela
La Ceiba
Trujillo
GUATEMALA
Cobán
San Pedro Sula
HONDURAS
CA-1
Tapachula
Copán
Quetzaltenango
GUATEMALA CITY
Antigua
Lago de Atitlán
Comayagua
Santa Ana
TEGUCIGALPA
Puerto San José
San Miguel
SAN SALVADOR
EL SALVADOR
NICARAGUA
Choluteca
Golfo de Fonseca
Estelí
Matagalpa
Chinandega
León
Río
MANAGUA
Granada
Lago de Nicaragua
San Carlos
Liberia
Nicoya Peninsula
Puntarenas
PACIFIC OCEAN
0
200 km

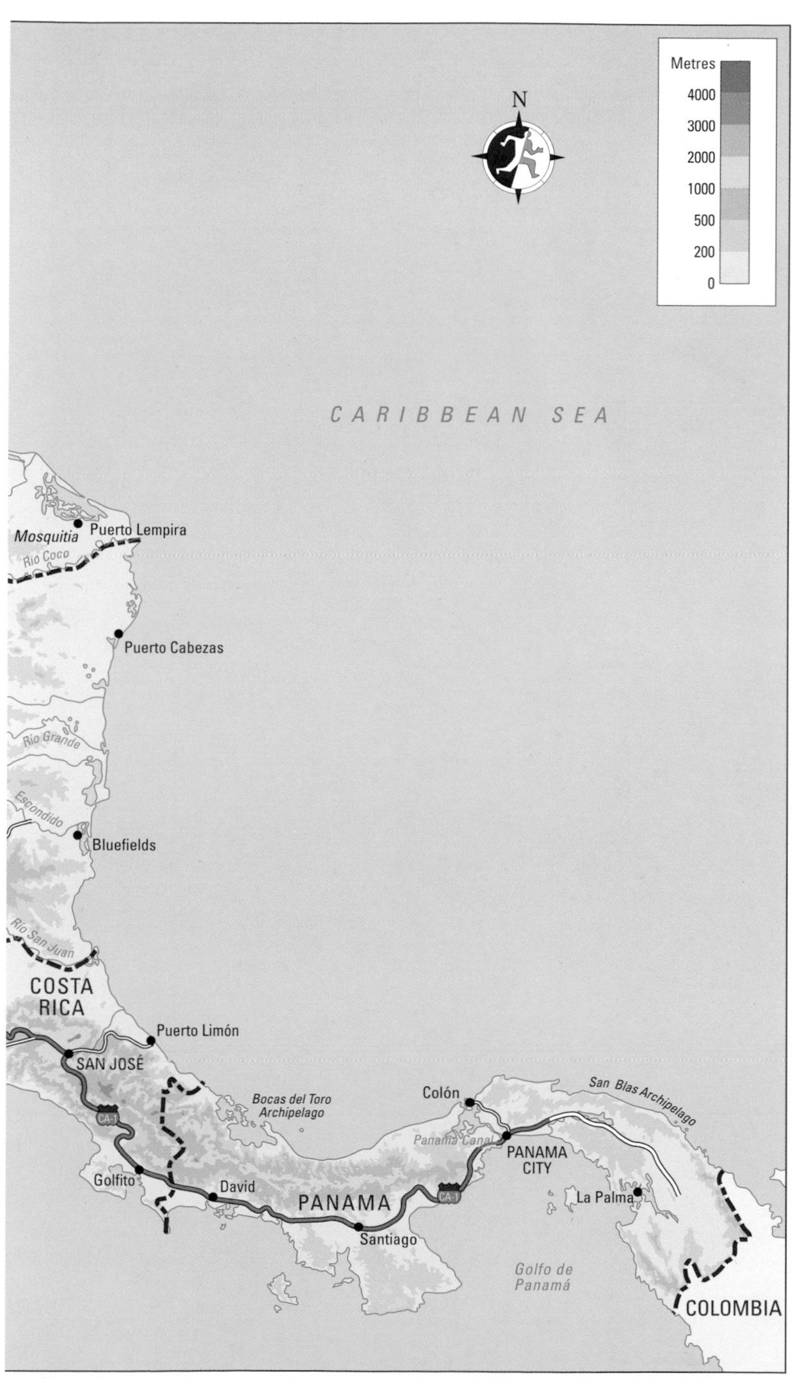
Metres
4000
3000
2000
1000
500
200
0
N
CARIBBEAN SEA
Mosquitia
Puerto Lempira
Río Coco
Puerto Cabezas
Río Grande
Escondido
Bluefields
Río San Juan
COSTA RICA
Puerto Limón
SAN JOSÉ
CA-1
Bocas del Toro Archipelago
Colón
San Blas Archipelago
Panama Canal
PANAMA CITY
Golfito
David
PANAMA
CA-1
La Palma
Santiago
Golfo de Panamá
COLOMBIA

Introduction to

Central America

Hemmed in by the Pacific and Atlantic oceans, the slender land bridge of Central America stretches from Mexico to South America – seven piecemeal nations stacked on top of each other in a narrowing isthmus. Its geography is in many ways its destiny: a small but distinctive region which for millennia has been the meeting point of the plants, animals and people of the giant continents to the north and the south. Although Central America has receded in the general public consciousness following the resolution of the conflicts which convulsed it during the 1980s, the region's new-found stability has resulted in something of a tourism renaissance, as thousands of visitors have come to experience its startling natural beauty and biodiversity at first hand, along with a range of man-made attractions ranging from the Maya ruins and traditional highland communities of Guatemala to the modernist skyline of Panama City.

Central America's position at the volcanic cusp between North and South America, and at the meeting point of tropical and temperate climatic zones, has created a startling, often surreal landscape, ranging from the rugged, mountainous

cloudforests of **Costa Rica** and **Panama** to the impenetrable swamp-jungles of Mosquitia in eastern **Honduras** and **Nicaragua**. Beaches, coves, cayes and island archipelagos hem the coral-laced coasts, while volcanoes – some active – form a backbone of fire that stretches the length of the isthmus. Not surprisingly, given its biological diversity and pivotal geographical position, Central America seems to have been designed for the **ecotourist**, with a complex system of interlocking terrains, from pristine rainforest to rare mangrove, which are home to a fascinating range of birdlife and wildlife, including tropical, temperate and hybrid species. And along with ecotourism go more traditional pleasures: lolling on Costa Rica's palm-draped Caribbean beaches, diving and snorkelling off the coral atolls of Belize, or exploring the sand-fringed islands of Panama's San Blas archipelago.

Amidst all the hype about the region's natural beauty it's easy to forget that this part of the world was home to one of the Americas' most sophisticated pre-Columbian cultures, the **Maya**, whose splendid civilization flourished in **Guatemala** – and to a lesser extent in modern-day **Belize**, Honduras and **El Salvador** – between 300 and 900 AD. During this period the region was made up of independent and often mutually antagonistic city-states – Tikal in Guatemala, Copán in Honduras and San Andrés in El Salvador being three of the more prominent – which fought each other for prestige and economic dominance while their architects and craftsmen fashioned fabulous cities and stelae, and their scientists created the famous Maya calendar, one of the most complex systems of measuring time ever devised.

The high point of Maya civilization had already passed, however, when Central America was "discovered" by the Spanish during **Christopher Columbus**'s fourth and last voyage to the Americas in 1502–04. Columbus himself barely set foot in Central America, however, preferring to anchor offshore and write florid letters back home to his sovereign, packed with references to maidens and gold (of which the Spaniards unhappily discovered very little). Nearly ten years later, in 1513, the conquistador **Vasco Nuñez de Balboa** slashed and clambered his way over the scaly

Maya ruins

War and wildlife aside, Central America has long been known for its enigmatic and majestic **Maya ruins**. These physical remnants of one of the Americas' most sophisticated and spiritual pre-Columbian peoples are scattered across the northwest part of the region. Recent advances in deciphering Maya hieroglyphics have led to a more accurate picture of the rulers' genealogy and the often fraught relations between the various city-states, most of which flourished during the Classic era of 300–900 AD and which were subsequently – and still rather mysteriously – abandoned. The grey-white pyramids of Tikal (see p.267) rising smokily above the rainforest canopy remains the archetypal image of Central America and few travellers leave the region without visiting them; northern Guatemala's Petén department – once the centre of the Maya world – also houses the relatively inaccessible but equally intoxicating El Mirador (see p.275). Copán (see p.418), in western Honduras, is Central America's other great site, and while it lacks the exotic atmospherics and setting of Tikal, its stelae are stunningly well preserved. Lesser-known sites include Caracol (see p.111) in Belize and Joya de Cerén (see p.319) in El Salvador.

Diving

Central America's world-class **dive sites** are a result of the isthmus's unique geological formation and evolution – the coasts of Belize and Honduras are home to the second largest coral-reef system on earth. With 185 miles of barrier reef and three atolls to choose from in Belize alone, divers of all levels come to snorkel in Shark-Ray Alley (see p.92) or plumb the mesmerizing depths of the Great Blue Hole (a vast collapsed cave, originally made famous by a 1970s Jacques Cousteau documentary; see p.98). While diving tuition is available in Belize, the famously low-priced PADI courses in Honduras's Bay Islands (see p.460), together with a psychedelic abundance of marine life, magnificent wrecks and plunging coral shelves, have long made them a magnet for travellers. Great diving and snorkelling can also be had in the San Blas and Bocas del Toro archipelagos in Panama, while competitively priced PADI courses are available on Nicaragua's idyllic Corn Islands (see p.565).

mountain spine of Panama, becoming the first European to set eyes on the American side of the Pacific Ocean.

Within a few years, in 1519, the Spanish had established Panama City; the city of León, in present-day Nicaragua, followed in 1524; and in 1541, in Guatemala, they established their most important capital, Antigua, from which the region was administered. Still, Central America remained a backwater of the Spanish Empire in the New World: poor in gold and stuffed with venomous snakes, impenetrable jungles and often hostile natives. In human terms, the ensuing **colonial period** was characterized by the arrival of waves of yeoman farmers from Spain, and the deaths of countless thousands of indigenous people from diseases to which they had no immunity, while many others were taken as slaves to work the mines in Peru.

In the early 1800s, nearly 300 years after Spain's first incursions in the isthmus, the region was caught up in a fervour of **independence**, in part fuelled by the growing anger of the *criollos* (Spanish people born in the New World), who were barred from advancement and political office by Spain's snobbish insistence on promoting only those born on Spanish soil. By 1823 the collective drive towards autonomy was strong enough for all the Central American states to declare themselves independent, forming a loose federation (with the exception of Panama, by then part of Colombia, and Belize, which was effectively a British colony). In many of the countries, separate but eerily similar internal conflicts erupted between educated, Europhile liberals demanding egalitarianism and a form of democracy and the monied, land-owning conservatives – a rift between the right and the left which even today remains the most divisive and destructive presence in Central American **politics**.

It was these tensions that sparked the ravaging **wars** of the 1970s and 1980s. Nicaragua's Sandinistas succeeded in shaking off their country's dictator, Anastasio Somoza, though their revolution ultimately failed as a result of the US-sponsored Civil War (1981–1990), while US-fuelled internal conflicts also devastated El Salvador and Guatemala for much of the same decade. Now peace seemingly reigns, although less conspicuous conflicts persist, as in Guatemala, where the state's long-running campaign of repression against its own (mostly indigenous) inhabitants shows signs of continuing, despite the signing of official peace accords.

Nowadays, most citizens want to forget about the past and look towards the future. Increasingly, that future is to be found in the overwhelming presence of **North American culture**, whether it be four-wheel-drives, shopping malls, fast-food outlets or credit-card spending. American culture has been wholeheartedly embraced by the urban upper middle classes, and trickles down into the poorer echelons in the form of much-prized baseball hats and Nike trainers – any *ropa americana* is better than the homespun equivalent. This relatively new yen for the good life and consumer desirables is one reason why Central American society is described – at least by economists – as "modernizing", and times have changed from when countries like Honduras and Costa Rica were bona fide banana republics, little more than hosts providing land and cheap labour for the huge, US-owned fruit companies. Manufacturing and service industries are increasingly investing in the region, while piecework factories churning out cheap goods for the US market, called *maquiladoras*, still provide many people – particularly women – with employment.

Despite this, there's not much evidence that this new-found investment is trickling down into the pockets of the poorest Central Americans:

income differentials here are still among the widest in the world, and much of the population lives in poverty, sometimes abjectly so – you don't need to look further than the faces of begging children on street corners or at border crossings, asking to relieve you of your surplus small change. One product of this widespread deprivation are the high rates of common **crimes** like pickpocketing and burglary, while violent crime against tourists is becoming more common, especially in Guatemala. Certain cities, like Managua, Guatemala City and Panama City, have always had bad reputations, and it has to be said travelling in Central America is hardly risk-free, and visitors should read up on the various dangers before arriving. Fortunately, where dangers are real – mostly in cities – they are well-publicized, and locals will often volunteer warnings and advice.

When it comes to relations between the countries, Central America is rather like a family where there's little love lost, but they recognize that sticking together is their best chance for economic survival. Amongst themselves, the nations have oscillated between surprising regional solidarity to outright war, sometimes in the form of incomprehensible conflicts, such as El Salvador's and Honduras's infamous "Football War" of 1969, a five-day border conflict ostensibly sparked by a soccer match. National **stereotypes** are bandied back and forth with relish (Costa Ricans think Nicaraguans are intrinsically violent, Nicaraguans think Costa Ricans are placid opportunists, virtually everybody thinks the Hondurans wrote the book on corruption) even while the region's politicians describe neighbour nations as *hermanos* (brothers) and put their collective signatures to the new Central American Free Trade Agreement.

Central America is rather like a family where there's little love lost...

Wherever you go, it's easy to get around. **Travel networks** in the region are well-developed, with reliable air- and road-transport systems. Flying from Guatemala City to San José or Panama City can save you a lot of time, as what looks like a short hop on the map is often a lengthy road journey thanks to the (often bad) state of the highways and the effects of weather. In the riverine waterways of Mosquitia, boats are the only way to get around, along with light planes. Most of the time, though, you'll be going by **bus** – cheap, frequent, cheerful, and the quintessential Central American experience, where you'll find yourself seated among knitting grandmothers, travelling evangelists, gum-popping teenagers and perhaps the odd chicken.

Ecotourism

Ecotourism is a concept pioneered in – and now inextricably linked with – Central America. While the word itself continues to be hijacked by unscrupulous industry operators, it boils down to responsible tourism that seeks to conserve the natural environment and empower local communities. Costa Rica remains the best-known ecotourism destination in the western hemisphere, with a network of easily accessible national parks, like the Monteverde cloudforest reserve (see p.658), providing the main draw. Belize, long recognized as an innovator in creating sustainable, community-led tourism, boasts some of the most stunning marine reserves in the isthmus along with several protected areas inland. More adventurous travellers may prefer Panama's remote – and often dangerous – Parque Nacional Darién (see p.791), a swathe of dense rainforest that is home to wonderfully varied flora and fauna. Similarly, Nicaragua's isolated Indio-Maíz reserve (see p.559) is one of the largest and most naturally diverse stretches of primary rainforest in Central America. Facilities in both countries are still quite rudimentary. For more in-depth discussion of ecotourism and its implications as well as examples of community-based eco-initiatives, see Contexts, p.844.

Where to go

Despite their modest dimensions, each of the seven countries of Central America is distinctively different, and one of the pleasures of a trip through the region is to experience such a diverse range of peoples and culture within a relatively small area. **Costa Rica** draws nature-lovers by the planeload to its unsurpassed system of national parks and reserves, while English-speaking **Belize**, for much of its history a forgotten fragment of the British Empire, has reinvented itself as a prime diving and snorkelling destination thanks to its offshore national treasury: the second-longest barrier reef in the world. The best place to experience the region's pre-conquest culture is **Guatemala**, which has the strongest indigenous traditions, not to mention a stunning landscape of soaring volcanoes and amethyst lakes, while **Panama** and **Honduras** are just waking up to the tourist potential of their rainforests, rugged mountain cloudforests, mangroves and beaches. Tourists still tend to avoid **Nicaragua** and **El Salvador** – a misguided manoeuvre, as neither is more dangerous for visitors than its neighbours, and despite considerable poverty, the people are welcoming and the basic tourist infrastructure good; plus, they too have the volcanoes, beaches and rainforests that draw travellers to their more popular neighbours.

One of the pleasures of a trip through the region is to experience such a diverse range of peoples and culture within a relatively small area.

Even if you don't visit the region's **Maya ruins** at glorious places like Copán and Tikal, everywhere in the isthmus you can appreciate the craftsmanship of the Maya peoples, in their technicolour textiles (not just decorative, but a visually encoded social history), exquisite wood carvings and jewellery made from local or imported jade, turquoise and silver.

For **wildlife** enthusiasts, Guatemala's Biotopo del Quetzal and the Monteverde Reserve in Costa Rica will be high on the itinerary. In the pristine forests of Nicaragua's Matagalpa region, the shimmering quetzal, the sacred bird of the Maya, is still abundant; while in Costa Rica's Tortuguero region you can take steamy boat journeys along mirror-still canals, and watch sea turtles nest by night. Commentators struggle to represent this staggering biodiversity in spiralling numbers: 3000 species of moth in Costa Rica's Guanacaste province alone, 850 species of bird (more than in the whole of North America) and literally millions of plants, some as yet uncatalogued.

Life on the **Caribbean coast** of Central America is a shock for those who are used to the formal code of good manners and appearance that are so dear to the highland *ladino* culture. The atmosphere in these slightly rancid coastal towns – Lívingston, Bluefields, Limón and Colón, to name a few – can be raffish; certainly the machete-feuds and drug-running are real. On the Caribbean coast it's Marley, not marimba, you'll hear; English, cricket and herbal teas make an appearance, too. Immigration from Jamaica and Barbados to work on banana plantations and railroads in the late nineteenth and early twentieth centuries transformed this coast into an area which is more Caribbean than Latin American, dominated by West Indian accents, subsistence agriculture, and a quaint allegiance to the Queen (even if they don't always know which Queen is in at the moment).

For most travellers the **cities** of Central America are not much of a draw in themselves, with their potholed, traffic-choked streets, cheap skyscrapers and gutters full of soapy water and rotting fruits. Yet in each of them, if you can get beyond the initial ugliness you'll find a vibrant, if hectic, urban life with enough cafés, bars, galleries and museums to keep you busy for at least a few days. True city-lovers will want to indulge in spates of salsa dancing, join ice-cream-eating teenagers lolling on the benches of the local park, or improve their Spanish by watching the latest subtitled blockbuster American movie in a theatre filled with sighing matrons and buzzing boys.

When to go

Although located firmly within the tropics, altitude, rather than latitude, governs **climate** in Central America. Covering terrain which ranges between sea level and 3000m, the temperature can vary by as much as twenty degrees. The year is divided into just two seasons: a **rainy season**, which lasts roughly from May to October and is often called "winter" (*invierno*), and a **dry season** – or "summer" (*verano*) – from November to April, although the distinction between the two varies wildly, even within small areas. In the highlands of Guatemala or Costa Rica, rainy-season downpours (*aguaceros*) are common in September and October. Meanwhile, on the Caribbean coastline, you'll find it's mostly wet year-round and almost supernaturally humid.

Where there is a rainy season, don't assume it will rain all the time; a common pattern is a fine, sunny dry morning until about noon or 1pm, then a clouding over and an afternoon downpour that sometimes extends into evening showers. It's true that **travelling** in the rainy season can be a little more problematic, due to washed-out roads and swollen creeks on some of the more backroad routes, but the advantages of coming to Central America in the rainy season are many, including lower accommodation prices (especially in heavily touristed areas like Costa Rica), fewer tourists, and the relief of a cooling shower or two.

Yearly average **temperatures** in the region change little, with daytime temperatures in the lowlands the hottest, averaging anywhere from 28 to 32°C. The coastal areas or the low inland plains are where you will feel the heat most uncomfortably. In the mountains the weather can be cooler, fresh, and surprisingly like a fine late spring day in the temperate zone, with temperatures more like 22 to 25°C. For more specific climate details, see the individual country introductions.

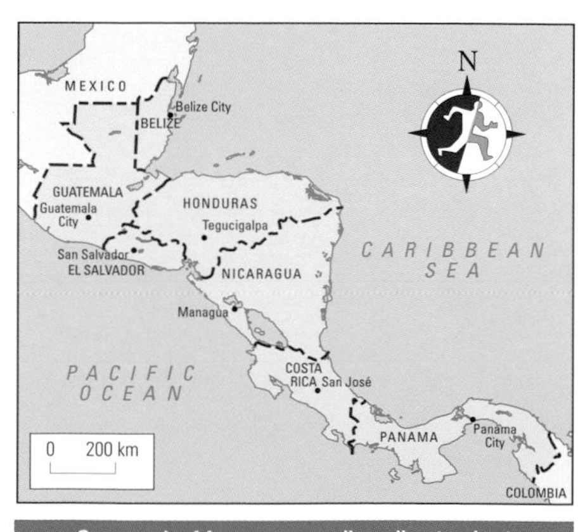

See overleaf for corresponding climate chart

Average temperatures and monthly rainfall

	Jan	Feb	Mar	Apr	May	Jun	Jul	Aug	Sep	Oct	Nov	Dec
Belize (Belize City)												
Max °C	27	28	29	30	31	31	31	31	31	30	28	27
Min °C	19	21	22	23	24	24	24	24	23	22	20	20
Rainfall (mm)	137	61	38	56	109	196	163	170	244	305	226	185
Guatemala (Guatemala City)												
Max °C	23	25	27	28	29	27	26	26	26	24	23	22
Min °C	12	12	14	14	16	16	16	16	16	16	14	13
Rainfall (mm)	8	3	13	31	152	274	203	198	231	173	23	8
El Salvador (San Salvador)												
Max °C	32	33	34	34	33	31	32	32	31	31	31	32
Min °C	16	16	17	18	19	19	18	19	19	18	17	16
Rainfall (mm)	8	5	10	43	196	328	292	297	307	241	41	10
Honduras (Tegucigalpa)												
Max °C	25	27	29	30	30	28	27	28	28	27	26	25
Min °C	14	14	15	17	18	18	18	17	17	17	16	15
Rainfall (mm)	12	2	1	26	180	177	70	74	151	87	38	14
Nicaragua (Managua)												
Max °C	31	32	34	34	34	31	31	31	31	31	31	31
Min °C	20	21	22	23	23	23	22	22	22	22	21	20
Rainfall (mm)	5	1	5	5	76	296	134	130	182	243	59	5
Costa Rica (San José)												
Max °C	24	24	26	26	27	26	25	26	26	25	25	24
Min °C	14	14	15	17	17	17	17	16	16	16	16	14
Rainfall (mm)	15	5	20	46	229	241	211	241	305	300	145	41
Panama (Panama City)												
Max °C	32	33	33	34	31	30	31	31	30	30	30	31
Min °C	23	23	24	24	24	23	23	23	23	22	22	23
Rainfall (mm)	30	10	20	55	200	210	205	200	205	245	250	120

things not to miss

It's not possible to see everything Central America has to offer in one trip – and we don't suggest you try. What follows is a selective and subjective taste of the region's highlights: magnificent ruins, spectacular landscapes, thrilling ecotourist activities and rich cultural traditions. They're arranged in five colour-coded categories, so you can browse through to find the very best things to see, do, and experience. All highlights have a page reference to take you straight into the Guide, where you can find out more.

01 **Caye Caulker** Page **94** • Relax at sunset after a hard day's snorkelling at Belize's budget-traveller's paradise.

02 Parque Nacional Corcovado Page **722** • Costa Rica's ecological wonderland boasts a biodiversity to rival the Amazon Basin, with a vast array of wildlife that includes jaguars, pumas, tapirs and peccaries.

03 León Page **516** • The intellectual heart and artistic soul of Nicaragua, with a legacy of revered poetry, revolutionary fervour and striking colonial architecture.

04 Pipeline Road Page **778** • On every birdwatcher's must-see list, this Panamanian trail provides even the most casual spectator an opportunity to spot a profusion of bird life.

05 Lago de Atitlán Page **201** • Described by Aldous Huxley as "really too much of a good thing", the shores of this stunning lake in Guatemala's western highlands are ringed by three volcanoes and dotted with Maya villages.

06 Volcán Arenal Page **708** • Listen to the grumbling lava belches at one of Costa Rica's star attractions – there's no more active volcano in Central America.

07 Bay Islands Page **460** • Whether you've come for the inexpensive diving and watersports or just the beach lifestyle, you'll find the Caribbean flavour of these Honduran islands infectious.

08 Azuero Peninsula Page **808** • Festival time kick-starts this sleepy agricultural region in Panama into a folkloric fusion of elaborate costumes, chaotic parades and traditional dance.

09 The Pacuaré and Reventazón rivers Page **629** • Costa Rica's rivers have some of the best whitewater rafting and kayaking in the entire region, combining exhilarating action with opportunities for wildlife-spotting.

10 Tikal Page **267** • Central America's most breathtaking Maya site, Tikal boasts soaring temples, palaces and pyramids in a rainforest reserve that's teeming with wildlife.

11 Antigua Page **180** • Guatemala's most graceful, civilized city has an incredible legacy of colonial-era Baroque churches, convents and mansions, plus terrific hotels, cafés and restaurants.

12 Sámara and Nosara Pages **697–701** • Enjoy a fine meal before watching the sun set in all its glory over the Pacific Ocean from one of the beaches on Costa Rica's Nicoya Peninsula.

13 Ruta de la Paz Page **341** • A reminder of El Salvador's recent violent past, the Ruta de la Paz is a haunting testimony to those that lost their lives during the Civil War.

14 Copán Page **418** • Though relatively small in scale, the magnificent ruins at Copán in Honduras hold the finest examples of ornate stelae and intricate stonework in the Maya world.

15 Flor de Caña rum Page **484** • The standard-bearer for Nicaraguan rum is an essential Central American tipple, usually served up by the bottle with a handful of deep green limes and a huge bucket of ice.

16 Lighthouse Reef Page **98** • Pristine Lighthouse Reef is the most easterly of Belize's three coral atolls, where the collapsed cavern of the Great Blue Hole acts as a magnet for divers and snorkellers.

17 Coffee Page **626** • Still a vital export crop throughout Central America and, at plantations such as the Café Britt Finca in Costa Rica's Valle Central, you can tour the rolling fields and find out how the modern coffee industry works.

18 Monteverde Page **658** • Get up close and personal with the top of the Costa Rican cloudforest in these lush highlands.

19 Chiriquí Highlands Page **818** • Panama's mountain villages make great bases for exploring mist-swathed cloud-forests, which are laced with superb hiking trails flanked by rare flora.

20 Lago Yojoa Page **406** • Surrounded by forest in Honduras's central highlands, this shimmering lake makes for a perfect retreat.

21 Sandinista murals Page **516** • Among Nicaragua's few surviving revolutionary murals, this much-photographed painting of Sandino is one of the most vibrant and compelling.

22 Finca El Paraíso waterfall Page 242 • Wallow away a day at the idyllic hot-spring waterfall and natural pools near the Finca El Paraíso in eastern Guatemala.

23 Panama Canal Page 772 • Just minutes from the nation's capital one of man's greatest engineering triumphs carves its path through steaming tropical rainforest.

24 Belize Zoo Page 99 • Although the country has one of the highest concentrations of jaguars anywhere in their range, you're only guaranteed close-up shots at this superb zoo.

25 La Mosquitia Page **455** • Poised along the coast of Honduras and Nicaragua, but inaccessible by road, is one of Central America's last true wildernesses.

26 Santa Ana Page **352** • Bordered on three sides by architectural gems like the cream-coloured Alcaldía, Santa Ana's Parque Central is without a doubt El Salvador's finest square.

27 Mountain Pine Ridge Forest Reserve Page **108** • Within this dazzling landscape in western Belize tumble the 1000 Foot Falls (also known as Hidden Valley Falls), the tallest waterfall in Central America.

28 San Salvador Page **304** • El Salvador's modern capital provides a refreshing counterpoint to the colonial cities throughout the region.

Contents

Using this Rough Guide

We've tried to make this Rough Guide a good read and easy to use. The book is divided into six main sections, and you should be able to find whatever you want in one of them.

Colour section

The front colour section offers a quick tour of Central America. The **introduction** aims to give you a feel for the place, with suggestions on where to go. We also tell you what the weather is like and include a basic country fact file. Next, our authors round up their favourite aspects of Central America in the **things not to miss** section – whether it's great food, amazing sights or a special hotel. Right after this comes a full **contents** list.

Basics

The Basics section covers all the **pre-departure** nitty-gritty to help you plan your trip. This is where to find out which airlines fly to your destination, what paperwork you'll need, what to do about money and insurance, about Internet access, security, public transport, car rental – in fact just about every piece of **general practical information** you might need.

Guide

This is the heart of the Rough Guide, divided into user-friendly chapters, each of which covers a specific country. Every chapter starts with a list of **highlights** and an **introduction** that helps you to decide where to go, followed by every other piece or **practical information** you might need, plus a country **history**. Introductions to the various towns and smaller regions within each chapter should also help you plan your itinerary. We start most town accounts with information on arrival and accommodation, followed by a tour of the sights, and finally reviews of places to eat and drink, and details of nightlife. Longer accounts also have a directory of practical listings. Each chapter concludes with **public transport** details for that region.

Contexts

Read Contexts to get a deeper understanding of what makes Central America tick. We include articles about **wildlife** and **ecotourism**, and a detailed further reading section that reviews dozens of **books** relating to the region.

Language

The **Language** section gives useful guidance for speaking Spanish and pulls together all the vocabulary you might need on your trip, including a comprehensive menu reader. Here you'll also find a glossary of words and terms peculiar to the region.

small print and Index

Apart from a **full index**, which includes maps as well as places, this section covers publishing information, credits and acknowledgements, and also has our contact details in case you want to send in updates and corrections to the book – or suggestions as to how we might improve it.

Map and chapter list

- Colour section
- B Basics
- 1 Belize
- 2 Guatemala
- 3 El Salvador
- 4 Honduras
- 5 Nicaragua
- 6 Costa Rica
- 7 Panama
- C Contexts
- L Language
- I Index

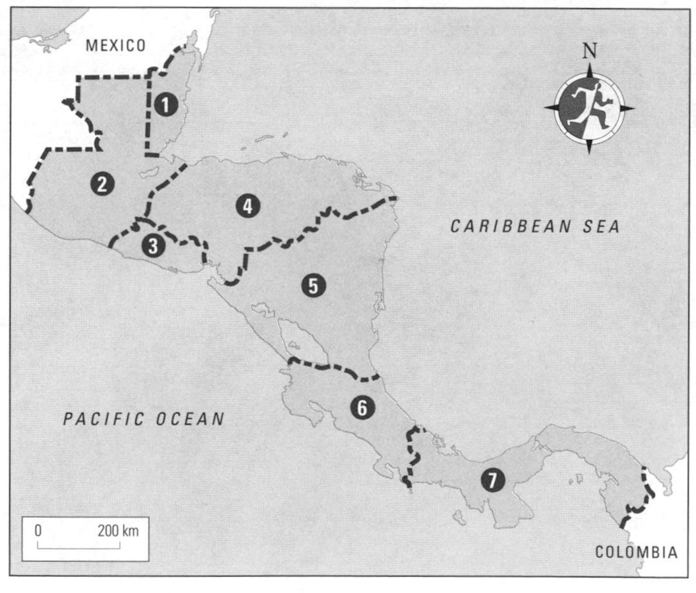

△ Trombone player at Semana Santa

Contents

Colour section i–xxiv

Colour map of Central America ii
Where to go xii
When to go xv
28 Things not to miss xvii

Basics 9–44

Getting there 11
Red tape and visas 20
Information, websites and maps 22
Insurance 25
Health 26
Costs, money and banks 31
Getting around 33
Accommodation 36
Communications 38
Work, volunteering and study 40
Crime and personal safety 43

The Guide 45–833

1 Belize 47–132
- Highlights 48
- Introduction and Basics 49
- History 61
- Belize City 66
- Corozal, Orange Walk and the north 77
- The northern cayes and atolls 87
- Cayo and the west 99
- The south 114
- Travel details 131

2 Guatemala 133–282
- Highlights 134
- Introduction and Basics 135
- History 151
- Guatemala City 161
- The western highlands 176
- The Pacific coast 225
- East to the Caribbean 233
- Cobán and the Verapaces 246
- Petén 259
- Travel details 280

3 El Salvador 283–366
Highlights......284
Introduction and Basics......285
History......296
San Salvador and around......304
The Pacific coast......322
The east......333
The west......345
The north......360
Travel details......366

4 Honduras......367–474
Highlights......368
Introduction and Basics......369
History......378
Tegucigalpa and the south......385
The central and western highlands......403
Olancho......426
The north coast and Mosquitia......432
The Bay Islands......460
Travel details......474

5 Nicaragua......475–570
Highlights......476
Introduction and Basics......477
History......487
Managua and around......496
The north......516
The southwest......534
Lago de Nicaragua......550
The Atlantic Coast......560
Travel details......570

6 Costa Rica......571–726
Highlights......572
Introduction and Basics......573
History......588
San José......594
The Valle Central and the Highlands......616
Limón Province and the Caribbean coast......631
The Central Pacific and Southern Nicoya......650
Guanacaste......680
The Zona Norte......702
The Zona Sur......715
Travel details......725

7 Panama......727–834
Highlights......728
Introduction and Basics......729
History......741
Panama City......747
The Canal and Colón Province......772
Eastern Panama: Darién and Kuna Yala......787
Western Panama......803
Bocas del Toro......823
Travel details......833

Contexts **835–862**
Wildlife......837
Ecotourism......844
Books......850

Language 863–876

English 865
Spanish 865
Words and phrases 868
A Spanish menu reader 870
Glossary 874

Small print and Index 877–891

A rough guide to Rough Guides 878
Rough Guide credits 879
Publishing information 879
Help us update 879
Acknowledgements 880
Readers' letters 881
Photo credits 881
Full index 883

△ Beach, Belize

Basics

Basics

Getting there 11

Red tape and visas 20

Information, websites and maps 22

Insurance 25

Health 26

Costs, money and banks 31

Getting around 33

Accommodation 36

Communications 38

Work, volunteering and study 40

Crime and personal safety 43

Getting there

The simplest and most convenient way to get to Central America is by air. If coming from the US, however, you might want to consider travelling overland; it's a long haul, but definitely worthwhile should you want to take in something of Mexico en route.

When flying, the price you pay for a ticket to any of the Central American countries generally depends more on how and when you book your flight and how long you plan to stay than on a particular season. However, prices to most destinations do go up in the **high seasons** of July and August (due mainly to the cost of flights within the US; ironically, this is the rainy season in much of Central America), and Easter and Christmas. Regardless of when you go, it pays to book ahead: with the airlines having cut back their capacity post 9/11, cut-price seats are unsurprisingly selling faster. The airlines' cheapest published fares generally allow for a maximum stay of three months, with higher prices for stays of up to six months and higher prices again for tickets lasting a year. Being a student or under 26 can also help, though you may be subject to eccentric booking conditions.

You can cut costs further by going through a **specialist flight agent** – either a consolidator, who buys up blocks of tickets from the airlines and sells them at a discount, or **a discount agent**, who in addition to dealing with discounted flights may also offer special student and youth fares and a range of other travel-related services such as car rentals, tours and the like. Bear in mind, though, that penalties for changing your plans can be stiff. Some agents specialize in **charter flights**, which may be cheaper than scheduled flights, but again departure dates are fixed and withdrawal penalties are high (check the refund policy).

For countries such as Costa Rica, Belize and Panama you may even find it cheaper to pick up a bargain **package deal** from a travel agent in North America and then find alternative accommodation when you get there. A further possibility is to see if you can arrange a **courier flight** although you'll need a flexible schedule, and preferably be travelling alone with very little luggage. In return for shepherding a parcel through customs, you can expect to get a deeply discounted ticket. You'll probably also be restricted in the duration of your stay. Although the number of air-courier flights to Latin America has decreased dramatically in recent times you should still be able to pick up a cheap fare to Mexico City from the US.

Open-jaw tickets, where you fly into one city and out of another, are readily available and, depending on which airline you use, often cost little more than a return to one city, particularly if combined with an airpass (for more on which, see p.33).

Lastly, if you're combining a trip to Central America with travels elsewhere in the world you might want to consider a **Round-The-World** (RTW) ticket. While "off-the-shelf" RTW tickets from the likes of One World and Star Alliance don't normally include Central America in their itineraries (although Sky Team do include Mexico), you could easily make a side trip from Los Angeles at a cost of around US$600. There's also increasing scope for creating your own itinerary although this will cost more than the standard RTW fare which currently comes in at around US$3000/£1500/A$3600/NZ$4200.

Booking flights online

Most airlines and discount travel websites offer you the opportunity to book your tickets, hotels and holiday packages **online**, cutting out the costs of agents and middlemen; these are worth going for, as long as you don't mind the inflexibility of non-refundable, non-changeable deals. There are some bargains to be had on auction sites too, if you're prepared to bid keenly.

Online booking agents and general travel sites

Ⓦ**www.cheapflights.com**, Ⓦ**www.cheapflights.co.uk** (in UK & Ireland), Ⓦ**www.cheapflights.ca** (in Canada), Ⓦ**www.cheapflights.com.au** (in Australia). Flight deals, both chartered and scheduled, plus links to travel agents and other travel sites.
Ⓦ**www.cheaptickets.com** American discount flight specialists. Also 24hr toll free-number: Ⓣ1-888/922-8849.
Ⓦ**www.expedia.com** (in US), Ⓦ**www.expedia.co.uk** (in UK), Ⓦ**www.expedia.ca** (in Canada). Discount airfares, reliable all-airline search engine and daily deals.
Ⓦ**www.flyaow.com** "Airlines of the Web" – online air-travel info and reservations.
Ⓦ**www.gaytravel.com** US gay travel agent, offering accommodation, tours and more, including cruises on the Panama Canal. Also at Ⓣ1-800/GAY-TRAVEL.
Ⓦ**www.geocities.com/thavery2000** An extensive list of airline websites and US toll-free numbers.
Ⓦ**www.hotwire.com** Bookings from the US only. Last-minute savings of up to forty percent on regular published fares. Travellers must be at least 18 and there are no refunds, transfers or changes allowed. Log-in required.
Ⓦ**www.lastminute.com** (in UK), Ⓦ**www.lastminute.com.au** (in Australia), Ⓦ**www.lastminute.co.nz** (in New Zealand), Ⓦ**www.site59.com** (in US). Good last-minute holiday package and flight-only deals.
Ⓦ**www.opodo.co.uk** Popular and reliable source of low UK airfares. Owned by, and run in conjunction with, nine major European airlines.
Ⓦ**www.priceline.com** (in US), Ⓦ**www.priceline.co.uk** (in UK). Name-your-own-price website that has deals at around forty percent off standard fares. You cannot specify flight times (although you can specify dates) and tickets are non-refundable, non-transferable and non-changeable.
Ⓦ**www.skyauction.com** Bookings from the US only. Auctions tickets and travel packages to destinations worldwide with bids starting from US$1 and no minimum reserve price. Log-in required.
Ⓦ**www.studentuniverse.com** Online travel agency offering exclusive student discounts on mainly US departures. Also on Ⓣ1-800/272-9676.
Ⓦ**www.travel.com.au**, Ⓦ**www.travel.co.nz** Comprehensive online travel company, with discounted fares. Also on Australia Ⓣ1300/130 482 or 02/9249 5444 and New Zealand Ⓣ0800/468 332.
Ⓦ**www.travelocity.co.uk** (in UK), Ⓦ**www.travelocity.com** (in US), Ⓦ**www.travelocity.ca** (in Canada), Ⓦ**www.zuji.com.au** (in Australia). Sources great deals on the usual range of travel products with flight bookings via the world's most comprehensive travel reservations system and low-price, money-back guarantees on hotel rooms.
Ⓦ**www.travelshop.com.au** Australian site offering discounted flights, packages, insurance and online bookings. Also on Ⓣ1800/108 108.

Flights from the US and Canada

The main US and Central American airlines have daily **scheduled flights** to all Central American capitals from their primary US gateways. The great variety of possible destinations, routes and prices makes any comprehensive listing virtually impossible, but most non-stop flights leave from Miami, Houston, Dallas, LA, Atlanta and New Orleans; airlines serving these hubs have excellent connections throughout the US and Canada (where gateways are Toronto, Montréal and Vancouver). In addition, several Mexican airlines – and most US airlines – fly direct from more than twenty cities in the US and Canada to Mexico (the most frequent destination obviously being Mexico City), with onward connections to Central America – it's particularly easy and cheap to fly to Cancún and continue from there.

Excluding taxes (US$50–90), the cheapest flights to Central America are generally from **Miami**, costing around US$300–500 while flights from **Houston**, **Atlanta** and **New Orleans** tend to cost an extra US$50–100. Departures from **New York**, **Chicago**, **LA** and **San Francisco** cost more again, roughly around US$450–700. Unless you are flying on an airline with 'hub' in the particular city you're departing from, it's likely you'll have to change planes. For example, American and Continental have hubs in Miami and Houston respectively, with non-stop flights to all Central American capitals. Taca has the best deals from Miami and Houston although you'll have to change planes in San Salvador.

The only non-stop flights from **Canada** to Central America are operated by Air Canada who fly twice weekly to San José, Costa Rica, from Toronto for around CAN$1000. For other destinations, your best bet is to fly to Miami or Houston and change there. Non-stop flights from Toronto to Miami can go as low as CAN$150, while flights from Vancouver to Houston can drop to around CAN$250. Canadian charter company Air Transat also operate seasonal flights to the region.

Airlines

Aeromexico ⓣ1-800/237-6639, ⓦwww.aeromexico.com. Direct flights from many US gateway cities to Mexico City, for connections on Mexicana Airlines to Guatemala City, San José and Panama City.
Air Canada ⓣ1-800/247-2262, ⓦwww.aircanada.ca. Twice weekly direct from Toronto to San José and daily flights direct to Mexico City from Vancouver with next-day connections to San José. Very competitive daily flights from Toronto to Miami and Vancouver to Houston.
Air Transat ⓣ1-866/847-1112, ⓦwww.airtransat.com. Canadian charter airline with seasonal flights from Toronto to Panama and Costa Rica.
American ⓣ1-800/433-7300, ⓦwww.aa.com. Daily non-stop flights from Miami, Dallas and Fort Worth to all Central American capitals as well as less frequent flights to San Pedro Sula in Honduras and Liberia in Costa Rica. Non-stop from Toronto to Miami and Vancouver to Dallas for connections.
Continental ⓣ1-800/231-0856, ⓦwww.continental.com. Daily non-stop flights from Houston and Newark to all Central American capitals, and to San Pedro Sula, Honduras.
Copa ⓣ1-800/359-2672, ⓦwww.copaair.com. Daily non-stop flights from Miami to Panama City, with connections to other Central American capitals. Also fly from Newark and Houston through an alliance with Continental.
Delta ⓣ1-800/241-4141, ⓦwww.delta.com. Non-stop discounted daily flights from Atlanta to San Salvador, Guatemala City, San José, Liberia and Panama City.
Iberia ⓣ1-800/772-4642, ⓦwww.iberia.com. Daily non-stop flights from Miami to all Central American capitals except Belize City and Tegucigalpa (although they do service San Pedro Sula in Honduras).
Mexicana ⓣ1-800/531-7921, ⓦwww.mexicana.com. Frequent flights from Chicago, Denver, LA, Newark, San Antonio, San Francisco, Miami, Vancouver, Montréal and Toronto (in tandem with Air Canada) to Mexico City, with connections to Guatemala City, San José and San Salvador. Tickets can be linked to flights on subsidiary airline Aerocaribe from airports in Yucatán to Flores, Guatemala and Belize City.
Taca ⓣ1-800/535-8780, ⓦwww.taca.com. Information and reservations for four of the national airlines of Central America: Aviateca (Guatemala), Lacsa (Costa Rica), Taca (El Salvador) and Taca Honduras. Regular flights from Houston, Miami, New York, Boston, Chicago, New Orleans, LA, San Francisco and Toronto to all Central American capitals and many other cities. One of the cheapest airlines although many flights are via hubs in San Salvador and San José.
United ⓣ1-800/538-2929, ⓦwww.united.com. Daily non-stop flights from Chicago, Washington, LA and San Francisco to Guatemala City, San Salvador, San José and Liberia.

Courier flights

Air Courier Association ⓣ1-800/280-5973, ⓦwww.aircourier.org. Courier flight broker. Membership (US$35 for a year). Lowest fare money-back guarantee plus last-minute and discounted non-courier flights, all departing from the US. Good prices for Mexico.
International Association of Air Travel Couriers ⓣ308/632-3273, ⓦwww.courier.org. Long-established courier flight broker with twice daily updates (wait until last minute for best prices). One year's membership costs US$45 in the US or Canada (US$50 elsewhere).

Travel agents

Airtech ⓣ212/219-7000, ⓦwww.airtech.com. Standby seat broker; also deals in consolidator fares.
Airtreks ⓣ1-877/AIRTREKS, ⓦwww.airtreks.com. Round-The-World tickets. The website features an interactive database that lets you build and price your own itinerary.
Educational Travel Center ⓣ1-800/747-5551 or 608/256-5551, ⓦwww.edtrav.com. Low-cost fares, student/youth discount offers, car rental and tours.
eXito ⓣ1-800/655-4053, ⓦwww.wonderlink.com/exito. Excellent Latin American independent

travel specialists – their website has a particularly useful air-fare finder and lots of other invaluable information.
Flightcentre US ⓣ1-866/WORLD-51, ⓦwww.flightcentre.us, Canada ⓣ1-888/WORLD-55, ⓦwww.flightcentre.ca. Rock-bottom fares worldwide.
Fly Latin America ⓣ1-888/246-1431, ⓦwww.flylatinamerica.com. Costa Rica-based travel agent with huge selection of discount flights and package deals to all Central American countries.
STA Travel US ⓣ1-800/329-9537, Canada ⓣ1-888/427-5639, ⓦwww.statravel.com. Worldwide specialists in independent travel; also student IDs, travel insurance, car rental, and more.
Student Flights ⓣ1-800/255-8000 or 480/951-1177, ⓦwww.isecard.com/studentflights. Student/youth fares, plus student IDs.
TFI Tours ⓣ1-800/745-8000 or 212/736-1140, ⓦwww.lowestairprice.com. Well-established consolidator with a wide variety of global fares.
Travel Avenue ⓣ1-800/333-3335, ⓦwww.travelavenue.com. Full-service travel agent that offers discounts in the form of rebates.
Travel Cuts US ⓣ1-800/592-CUTS, Canada ⓣ1-888/246-9762, ⓦwww.travelcuts.com. Popular, long-established student-travel organization, with worldwide offers.
Travelers Advantage ⓣ1-877/259-2691, ⓦwww.travelersadvantage.com. Discount travel club, with cash-back deals and discounted car rental. Membership required ($1 for 3 months' trial).
Travelosophy US ⓣ1-800/332-2687, ⓦwww.itravelosophy.com. Good range of discounted and student fares worldwide.
Worldtek Travel ⓣ1-800/243-1723, ⓦwww.worldtek.com. Discount travel agency for worldwide travel.

Tour operators

Abercrombie & Kent ⓣ1-800/554-7016 or 630/954-2944, ⓦwww.abercrombiekent.com. Luxury travel specialists with nine-day Costa Rica trips led by Masters-level naturalists.
Adventure Center ⓣ1-800/228-8747 or 510/654-1879, ⓦwww.adventurecenter.com. Hiking and "soft-adventure" specialists with a bulging portfolio of Central American trips taking in Belize, Guatemala, Costa Rica and Panama, both individually and together, including a month-long journey from Cancún to San José. Accommodation options include hotels, lodges and camping.
Adventures Abroad ⓣ1-800/665-3998, ⓦwww.adventures-abroad.com. Excellent one- to four-week small-group tours focusing on archeology, culture, nature and relaxation. A 17-day tour of Belize and Costa Rica costs CAN$3709 excluding air fare.
Backroads ⓣ1-800/GO-ACTIVE or 510/527-1555, ⓦwww.backroads.com. Cycling, hiking, snorkelling and multi-sport tours designed for the young at heart, with the emphasis on going at your own pace. Accommodation ranges from campsites to luxury hotels. Also family-friendly options and singles trips. CA destinations include Belize and Costa Rica, with a six-day trip to the latter costing US$2498 including air fare.
Ecosummer Expeditions ⓣ1-800/465-8884 or ⓣ 250/674-0102, ⓦwww.ecosummer.com. Wildlife tours, snorkelling and sailing in Belize; around US$1300 a week. Recommended.
Elderhostel ⓣ1-877/426-8056 or 426-2166, ⓦwww.elderhostel.org. Twelve-day natural study trips and two-week educational trips studying environment and history in Costa Rica, plus Maya-related tours in Honduras, Guatemala and Belize. Must be over 55 (companions may be younger).
Far Horions ⓣ1-800/552-4575, ⓦwww.farhorizon.com. Superb yearly archeological trips to remote Maya sites in Guatemala and Honduras, led by the archeologists directing the projects or renowned experts in the field. Recommended.
Gap Adventures ⓣ1-800/465-5600 or 416/260-0999, ⓦwww.gap.ca. Canadian company with good group trips (some camping) featuring cultural and nature activities, diving and kayaking in Guatemala, Belize, Honduras, Nicaragua and Costa Rica – a 32-day journey from Cancún to San José, taking in the main archeological sites, costs around CAN$1785 (excluding air fare). Individual trips are also available to Panama and all trips can be mixed and matched.
Global Exchange ⓣ415/255-7296, ⓦwww.globalexchange.org. Human rights organization offering "Reality Tours" (all subject to political stability) to meet local activists, visit areas of poverty and/or strife and participate in educational workshops. Occasional tours to Costa Rica, Guatemala, Honduras and Nicaragua.
Green Tortoise Adventure Travel ⓣ1-800/867-8647 or 415/956-7500, ⓦwww.greentortoise.com. Tours from November through April (except Costa Rica trips which run all year) on converted buses with sleeping space. The "Southern Migration" (leaving in December; US$1200 including food) is a very popular 28-day journey from San Francisco to Antigua, Guatemala.
Guatemala Unlimited ⓣ1-800/733-3350, ⓦwww.guatemalaunlimited.com. Eight-day comprehensive tours or shorter one- to three-day tours of Maya ruins both obscure and well known, as

well as jungle-trekking, river-rafting, mountain-biking and volcano tours. Their website also has cultural and economic info on Guatemala including details of Spanish schools.

Journeys International ⓣ1-800/255-8735 or 734/655-4407, ⓕ655-2945, ⓦwww.journeys-intl.com. Prestigious operator focusing on ecotourism and small-group trips worldwide. Superb nature- and culture-oriented week-long tours of Belize (around US$2295), Guatemala (US$2495), Costa Rica (US$2195) and Panama (US$2495). Also specializes in woman-only and family travel. Recommended.

Latin American Escapes ⓣ1-800/510-5999, ⓦwww.latinamericanescapes.com. Extensive range of fully escorted, customized or "hosted" independent tours to all Central American countries incorporating natural history, cultural and adventure packages. Prices start at US$425 for a six-day tour of the Guatemalan Highlands.

Nature Expeditions International ⓣ1-800/869-0639, ⓦwww.naturexp.com. Excellent small-group and independent 'soft' adventure tours to Costa Rica, with biking, canoeing, canopy walks and lecture options, aimed at the more mature traveller. The eleven-day wildlife expedition costs US$3750 excluding air fare.

Slickrock Adventures ⓣ1-800/390-5715, ⓦwww.slickrock.com. One of the very best Central American operators, offering sea kayaking, caving, diving, and jungle and river trips in Belize which usually include a stint on their own private island. Their renowned 'Belize Adventure Week' costs around US$2195.

South American Fiesta ⓣ1-800/334-3782, ⓦwww.southamericanfiesta.com or www.hondurastours.com. Trips to Belize, Costa Rica, Panama, Honduras, and one of the few North American operators to offer tours in Nicaragua. The seven-day San Juan River trip includes hiking in the pristine Indio-Maíz Biological Reserve with prices starting at US$955 for a group of 12–14 people.

Toucan Adventure Tours ⓣ805/927-5885, ⓦwww.toucanadventures.com. Inexpensive camping tours through northern Central America such as the three-week "Ruta Maya" trip through Mexico, Guatemala, Honduras and Belize, which concentrates on ruins and rainforest.

Tropical Travel ⓣ1-800/451-8017 or 281/367-3386, ⓦwww.tropicaltravel.com. Tailor-made trips to Belize, Costa Rica, Guatemala and Honduras, taking in ruins and rainforests. Diving packages also available.

Wildland Adventure ⓣ1-800/345-4453, ⓦwww.wildland.com. Highly respected ecotourism leader with pioneering approach to conservation of the environment and traditional cultures. Cultural and natural history-oriented trips to Guatemala (with leading archeologists), Belize, Costa Rica and Panama with prices from around US$1500.

Flights from the UK and Ireland

There are no non-stop flights **from the UK** to Central America – as a rule, the journey will involve changing aircraft (and sometimes airline), usually in the US. That said, it's possible to reach most of the Central American capitals (except Belize City and Tegucigalpa) in one day from London – the best connections are on Continental and American. Obviously you'll have the widest range of options if you fly out of London, though most of the main carriers to the US have two or three regional options available, often at the same fares as you would pay from the capital.

Fares to Central America are almost always higher than those to Mexico, so you might want to consider travelling down overland from Mexico City (see p.19). Aeromexico (in tandem with Air France) and several European airlines fly there, although the only direct flights from London are on British Airways. It's also worth checking if your transatlantic carrier has an airpass which links flights in the US and Mexico (usually only Mexico City); for details of Taca and Copa's airpasses, see p.33.

Another option for same-day arrival is to fly on one of the main **European carriers**: KLM (via Amsterdam) has good connections from throughout the UK and Ireland, with flights to Mexico City, while Iberia from London (via Madrid and Miami) flies daily to all the capitals except Belize City and Tegucigalpa.

As for **ticket prices**, expect to pay around £650–£750 high season (£470–590 at other times) for scheduled return flights from London or Manchester to Guatemala City or San José. To Mexico City prices are lower, ranging from £400 to £500.

There are no direct flights from **Ireland** to Central America. The cheapest way to get to Central America is to take one of the numerous daily flights from Dublin or Belfast to London, and then connect with a transatlantic flight there. Ryanair and easyJet have daily (often very cheap) flights to London from Dublin and Belfast respectively. Alternatively, you can take a direct flight from Ireland to the US or Europe for easy onward connections to Mexico and Central America. Delta and Continental have the widest range of direct flights from Dublin (and several from Shannon) to JFK and Atlanta, and Newark and Houston respectively, with daily connections to Mexico City and many Central American capitals.

Airlines

Aer Lingus UK ⓣ0845/084 4444, Republic of Ireland ⓣ0818/365 000, ⓦwww.aerlingus.com.
Aeroflot UK ⓣ020/7355 2233, ⓦwww.aeroflot.co.uk.
Aeromexico UK ⓣ020/7801 6234, ⓦwww.aeromexico.com.
American UK ⓣ0845/789789, Republic of Ireland ⓣ01/602 0550, ⓦwww.aa.co.com.
British Airways UK ⓣ0870/850 9850, Republic of Ireland ⓣ1800/626 747, ⓦwww.britishairways.com.
British Midland ⓣ01332/854854, ⓦwww.britishmidland.co.uk.
Continental UK ⓣ0845/607 6760, Republic of Ireland ⓣ1890/925 252, ⓦwww.contintental.com.
Delta UK ⓣ0800/414767, Republic of Ireland ⓣ1800/768 080 or 01/407 3165, ⓦwww.delta.com.
easyJet UK ⓣ0871/750 0100, ⓦwww.easyjet.com.
Grupo Taca UK ⓣ0870/608 0737, ⓦwww.grupotaca.com.
Iberia UK ⓣ0845/601 2854, ⓦwww.iberiaairlines.co.uk.
KLM UK ⓣ0870/507 4074, ⓦwww.klm.com.
Ryanair UK ⓣ0871/246 0000, Republic of Ireland ⓣ0818/303 030, ⓦwww.ryanair.com.
United UK ⓣ0845/844 4777, ⓦwww.ual.com.
Virgin Atlantic UK ⓣ0870/380 2007, ⓦwww.virgin-atlantic.com.

Travel agents

UK

Bridge the World ⓣ0870/443 2399, ⓦwww.bridgetheworld.com. Specialists in long-haul travel and RTW tickets targeted at the backpacker market.
Co-op Travel Care ⓣ0870/112 0085, ⓦwww.travelcareonline.com. Flights and holidays around the world from the UK's largest independent travel agent. Non-partisan and informed advice.
Flightcentre ⓣ0870/890 8099, ⓦwww.flightcentre.co.uk. Rock-bottom fares worldwide.
Flights4Less ⓣ0871/222 3423, ⓦwww.flights4less.co.uk. Good discount airfares. Part of Lastminute.com.
Flightbookers ⓣ0870/010 7000, ⓦwww.ebookers.com. Leading online flight agency with a huge range of discounted fares.
Journey Latin America ⓣ020/8747 3108 or 0161/832 1441, ⓦwww.journeylatinamerica.co.uk. The leaders in the field on air fares and tours to Latin America, with some of the best prices on high-season flights and a very useful quarterly magazine.
North South Travel ⓣ01245/608291, ⓦwww.northsouthtravel.co.uk. Friendly, competitive travel agency, offering discounted fares worldwide. Profits are used to support projects in the developing world, especially the promotion of sustainable tourism.
Rosetta Travel ⓣ028/9064 4996, ⓦwww.rosettatravel.com. Flight and holiday agent, specializing in deals direct from Belfast.
STA Travel ⓣ0870/160 0599, ⓦwww.statravel.co.uk. World's leading student/youth travel specialists with an international travel help network if you have problems while abroad; just under twenty branches in London alone, dozens of branches throughout the UK, and many more worldwide.
Trailfinders ⓣ020/7938 3939, ⓦwww.trailfinders.com. Well-informed air-fare specialists who also offer tailor-made packages for independent travellers. Offices throughout London, the UK and Australia. Also one branch in Dublin.
Travelbag ⓣ0870/890 1456, ⓦwww.travelbag.co.uk. Veteran discount flight specialists, geared towards Australia but selling cheap flights worldwide.
USIT ⓣ 028/9032 7111, ⓦwww.usitnow.com. Established, all Ireland student-travel specialist with more than twenty branches (most located on student campuses) in the North.

Republic of Ireland

Apex Travel ⓣ01/241 8000, ⓦwww.apextravel.ie. Specialists in transatlantic flights and consolidators for both BA and American.
ebookers ⓣ01/241 5689, ⓦwww.ebookers.ie.

Extensive selection of scheduled flights with lowest price guarantees.

Joe Walsh Tours ⓣ01/676 0991, ⓦ**www.joewalshtours.ie.** Long-established general budget fares agent.

Maxwell's Travel ⓣ01/679 5700, ⓔ**sales@worldwideadventure.ie.** Veteran Latin American operator, and the Irish representative for many of the British specialist tour operators listed below.

Trailfinders ⓣ01/677 7888, ⓦ**www.trailfinders.ie.** One of the best-informed and most efficient agents for independent travellers.

USIT ⓣ0818/200 020, ⓦ**www.usit.ie.** Specialists in student, youth and independent travel – flights, study tours, TEFL, visas and more.

World Travel Centre Republic of Ireland ⓣ01/416 7007, ⓦ**www.worldtravel.ie.** Excellent fares to Europe and worldwide.

Courier flights

International Association of Air Travel Couriers UK ⓣ0800/0746 481 or 01291/625 656, ⓦ**www.aircourier.co.uk.** UK branch of this company which acts as an agent for courier firms. £32 registration fee with flights from London to New York and Miami.

Tour operators

Abercrombie & Kent ⓣ020/7730 9600, ⓦ**www.abercrombiekent.co.uk.** Luxury tours to Guatemala, Belize and Costa Rica run in tandem with British Airways and utilising upmarket resorts, spas and private hideaways.

Birdfinders ⓣ01258/839066, ⓦ**www.birdfinders.co.uk.** Two-week specialist bird-watching tours in Costa Rica.

Dragoman ⓣ0870/499 4475, ⓦ**www.dragoman.co.uk.** Eight-week overland camping expeditions through Mexico to Panama for around £1600, plus food kitty. Transport in the shape of purpose-built expedition vehicles.

Exodus ⓣ020/8673 0859, ⓦ**www.exodus.co.uk.** Respected adventure tours with emphasis on environmental and cultural awareness. Fifteen-day escorted tours, staying at hotels, through the Maya region (around £1050) and Costa Rica (£1050). Prices include air fare. In Republic of Ireland contact Worldwide Adventures ⓣ01/679 5700.

Explore Worldwide ⓣ01252/760000, ⓦ**www.explore.co.uk.** Another very professional operator offering a variety of small-group tours to Central America (except El Salvador), some of which run year-round and most of which maintain a measured balance between comfort and adventure. About £1349 for 15 days in Guatemala and Belize; £1249 for a 16-day tour of volcanoes and rainforest in Costa Rica and Nicaragua, including air fare.

Global Travel Club ⓣ01268/541732, ⓕ01268/541363, ⓦ**www.global-travel.co.uk.** Small Central American specialist offering individually arranged tours (including diving trips and wedding/honeymoon holidays) to all countries in the region apart from El Salvador.

Guerba ⓣ01373/826611, ⓦ**www.guerba.co.uk.** Award-winning adventure specialist with proven commitment to responsible tourism. Their "Volcano Trail" overland tour covers the highlights of Guatemala, Honduras, Nicaragua and Costa Rica.

Journey Latin America ⓣ020/8747 3108 or 0161/832 1441, ⓦ**www.journeylatinamerica.co.uk.** Wide range of high-quality tours and individual itineraries from the acknowledged experts. Around £1700 (fully inclusive) for 11 days' superb wildlife and birdwatching in Costa Rica.

Kumuka Expeditions ⓣ0800/068 8855, ⓦ**www.kumuka.co.uk.** Central American tours taking in Belize, Guatemala, Costa Rica, Honduras and Nicaragua, and using local transport.

Reef and Rainforest Tours ⓣ0180/386 6965, ⓦ**www.reefandrainforest.co.uk.** Individual itineraries from a very experienced company, focusing on nature reserves, research projects and diving in Belize, Honduras and Costa Rica.

Responsible Travel ⓦ**www.responsibletravel.com.** Pioneering operation promoting tours, ecolodges and voluntary projects, all of which have been screened to ensure their benefits for both the environment and local community. Central American trips include turtle watching and luxury honeymoon packages in Costa Rica.

Wildlife Worldwide UK ⓣ020/8667 9158, ⓦ**www.wildlifeworldwide.com.** Tailor-made trips for wildlife and wilderness enthusiasts with Costa Rica and combined Belize and Guatemala itineraries coming in at around £1500 for two weeks. Accommodation consisting largely of jungle lodges and biological stations.

Flights from Australia and New Zealand

There are no direct flights from **Australasia** to Central America, but it's easy enough to get there via the US or Mexico. Low-season prices run from mid-January to the end of February, and October to the end of November; high season comprises mid-May to the end of August, and December to mid-January. Count on paying between A$200 and A$400 more at peak season than the fares quoted below.

The cheapest fares and most direct flights from Australia and New Zealand at the time of writing are with Qantas/Taca Group who fly to Mexico City via LA from Sydney for around A$2000/NZ$2300. Alternatively, you could travel to Mexico City via Asia on Japan Airlines (JAL) or Singapore Airlines, and then on to Central America with the relevant national airline; JAL charge around A$2150/NZ$2500, while Singapore are a little more expensive at around A$2350/NZ$2700. Add-on return fares to Central America for all these routes cost in the region of A$600/NZ$700.

Airlines

Air New Zealand Australia ⓣ13/2476, New Zealand ⓣ0800/737 000 or 09/357 3000, ⓦwww.airnz.com. Daily flights from Sydney and Auckland to Guatemala City, San Salvador and San José in tandem with United Airlines.

American Airlines Australia ⓣ1300/130 757, New Zealand ⓣ0800/887 997, ⓦwww.aa.com. Daily flights from Melbourne, Sydney and Auckland to LA with onward connections to Miami for Central American destinations.

Japan Airlines Australia ⓣ02/9272 1111, New Zealand ⓣ09/379 9906, ⓦwww.japanair.com. Daily flights from Sydney, Brisbane and Cairns to Dallas–Fort Worth (stopover in Tokyo or Osaka) with onward connections to Mexico City on American Airlines.

Qantas Australia ⓣ13/1313, New Zealand ⓣ0800/808 767 or 09/357 8900, ⓦwww.qantas.com.au. Daily flights to Dallas–Fort Worth from major Australasian cities with onward connections to most Central American capitals.

Singapore Airlines Australia ⓣ13/1011, New Zealand ⓣ09/303 2129, ⓦwww.singaporeair.com. Daily to LA from Auckland and major Australian cities via Singapore.

Taca & Aviateca Australia ⓣ03/9329 5211 (no NZ office). Airpasses from LA to Guatemala City and San José.

United Airlines Australia ⓣ13/1777, New Zealand ⓣ09/379 3800, ⓦwww.united.com. Daily direct to LA from Sydney, Melbourne and Auckland with onward connections to all Central American capitals; also sells airpasses.

Travel agents

Backpackers Travel Centre Australia ⓣ02/9215 2400, ⓦwww.backpackerstravel.com.au.

Budget Travel New Zealand ⓣ0800/808 040, ⓦwww.budgettravel.co.nz.

Destinations Unlimited New Zealand ⓣ09/414 1680, ⓦwww.travel-nz.com.

Flight Centre Australia ⓣ13 31 33, ⓦwww.flightcentre.com.au, New Zealand ⓣ0800 243 544, ⓦwww.flightcentre.co.nz. Lowest-fare guarantees on flights to the USA.

Holiday Shoppe New Zealand ⓣ0800/808 480, ⓦwww.holidayshoppe.co.nz. Great deals on flights, hotels and holidays.

OTC Australia ⓣ1300/855 118, ⓦwww.otctravel.com.au. Deals on flights, hotels and holidays.

STA Travel Australia ⓣ1300/733 035, New Zealand ⓣ0508/782 872, ⓦwww.statravel.com.

Student Uni Travel Australia ⓣ02/9232 8444, ⓦwww.sut.com.au, New Zealand ⓣ09/379 4224, ⓦwww.sut.co.nz.

Trailfinders Australia ⓣ02/9247 7666, ⓦwww.trailfinders.com.au.

Tour operators

Adventure Associates Australia ⓣ02/9389 7466, ⓦwww.adventureassociates.com. Two- to five-day jungle, archeological and cultural tours in Guatemala and Honduras; diving, fishing, snorkelling and windsurfing on Belize's Ambergris Caye and week-long tours of Costa Rica's national parks.

Adventure Travel Company New Zealand ⓣ09/379 9755, ⓦwww.adventuretravel.co.nz. Agent for industry leaders such as Exodus, Explore and Dragoman.

Adventure World Australia ⓣ02/89130755, ⓦwww.adventureworld.com.au, New Zealand ⓣ09/524 5118, ⓦwww.adventureworld.co.nz. Tours include trips to Tikal and Chichicastenango from Guatemala City, reef and river cruises in Belize, and five-day packages and rainforest tours in Costa Rica.

Intrepid Travel Australia ⓣ1300/360 887 or 03/9473 2626, ⓦwww.intrepidtravel.com, New Zealand ⓣ0800/174 043. Asian specialists with a small selection of Central American small-group tours. Seventeen-day "Volcano Trail" takes in Guatemala, Honduras, Nicaragua and Costa Rica.

Kumuku Worldwide Australia ⓣ1800/804 277 or 02/9279 0491, ⓦwww.kumuku.com.au, New Zealand ⓣ0800/440 499. One-week to two-month tours of Central America using local transport and encompassing Mexico, Belize, Guatemala, Nicaragua and Costa Rica.

Peregrine Adventures ⓣ03/9663 8611 or 1300/854 444, ⓦwww.peregrineadventures.com.

Australian agent for the likes of Exodus. Sixteen-day tours of Maya ruins and Guatemalan Highlands or twelve-day wildlife-orientated excursions to Costa Rica. Also have a programme of budget tours for younger, more independent-minded travellers; check out the website Ⓦwww.geckosadventures.com.

South America Travel Centre Australia Ⓣ1800/655 051 or 03/9642 5353, Ⓦwww.satc.com.au. Small selection of short, upmarket tours to the Tortuguero and Monteverde national parks in Costa Rica and a week-long Best of Guatemala excursion.

World Expeditions Australia Ⓣ1300/720 000, Ⓦwww.worldexpeditions.com.au, New Zealand Ⓣ0800/350 354, Ⓦwww.worldexpeditions.co.nz. Australian-owned adventure company offering a programme of Central American destinations including Guatemala, Honduras, Costa Rica and Nicaragua. A 17-day trip taking in the best of Costa Rica's national parks and Nicaragua's volcanoes costs $A3990.

Overland from Mexico

You can reach Central America inexpensively and relatively comfortably overland by bus from **Mexico**, though this can take between two and four days. From Tapachula and Chetumal, in southern Mexico, buses for Guatemala and Belize take you safely across the border. For those needing a visa to visit Central America there are Guatemalan consulates in Tapachula, Ciudad Hidalgo and Comitán and a Belizean consulate in Chetumal; for more on entry requirements see overleaf.

From the US, **Greyhound** (Ⓣ1-800/229-9424, Ⓦwww.greyhound.com) runs regularly to all the major border crossings; some of their buses will take you over the frontier and into the Mexican bus station and in many cases you can reserve tickets with their Mexican counterparts. **Green Tortoise** (see p.14) run cheap and cheerful long-haul trips through Mexico to Guatemala using buses dubbed "hostels-on-wheels".

There are constant buses to Mexico City from every Mexican–US border crossing (generally a journey of around 18–24 hours), and beyond Mexico City there are good connections to all the main Guatemalan and Belizean border crossings. Probably the best **route into Guatemala** is along the Carretera Interamericana through Oaxaca to San Cristóbal de las Casas, and then on to Huehuetenango in Guatemala. The other main road crossings are on the Pacific coast, through Tapachula, from where you can take an international bus to Guatemala City, and on the Caribbean coast from Chetumal into Belize. You could also travel overland to Mexico City, and from there **fly** to Flores or Belize City on Aerocaribe. Also, if you are considering heading overland via Chiapas it's advisable to check on the current security situation in the region before setting off.

Driving south may give you a lot more freedom, but it does entail a great deal of **bureaucracy**. You need separate **car insurance**, which you can either purchase beforehand or from one of the many companies located in the vicinity of the US–Mexican border. Sanborns (Ⓣ1-800/222-0158, Ⓦwww.sanbornsinsurance.com) is probably the most established and arranges insurance for Mexico and Central America, although they can be expensive. Mexico Insurance Professionals (Ⓣ1-888/INS-4-MEX or 928/214-9750, Ⓦwww.mexpro.com) are another experienced operator. Note that the minimum lawful requirement is civil liability cover, which is what most companies will offer you, although some also include physical damage.

In addition to a Mexican tourist card for yourself, you'll need to acquire a **vehicle entry permit** from customs. For this you'll need one original plus two copies of the following: your vehicle registration certificate, your passport, your driver's licence, the tourist card and a credit card in your own name (if you're renting then you'll also need the leasing contract). Your credit card will then be charged an equivalent of US$15. If you don't have a credit card, you'll have to post a hefty bond running into hundreds of dollars. There are strict controls everywhere to make sure you're not importing the vehicle to sell – if you attempt to leave without it you'll face a massive duty bill. US, Canadian, EU, Australian and New Zealand **driving licences** are valid in Mexico and throughout Central America, but it's a good idea to arm yourself with an International Driving Licence

– available for a nominal fee from the American Automobile Association (☎1-800/222-4357). If you run into problems with a traffic cop, show that first, and if they abscond with it you at least still have your own licence. For more on driving around Central America, see p.34.

Red tape and visas

Information on the entry requirements of the seven Central American countries is liable to sudden change, and it's crucial to contact a consulate before travelling to check what's required of you. Even when you've checked and armed yourself with the correct paperwork you may find the requests of the immigration officer at variance with the official policy.

That said, **visas** (with a few notable exceptions) are usually not needed by citizens of EU countries, the US, Canada, Australia and New Zealand to enter Central America as tourists, although you may be required to purchase a **tourist card** on entry. Visitors are usually permitted a stay from thirty to ninety days, depending on the country; again, check with your consulate.

All the Central American countries have consulates in **Mexico City**; there are also Guatemalan consulates in Comitán and Ciudad Hidalgo; Guatemalan and El Salvadorean consulates in Tapachula; and a Belizean consulate in Chetumal.

If you're flying in on a **one-way ticket** (providing the airline lets you board – some countries, Costa Rica for example, refuse travellers with no return tickets) you may have to prove your intention to leave the country; additionally you may have to show "sufficient funds" for your stay, though these conditions are rarely enforced.

Even if you don't officially require a visa or tourist card to enter a particular country, the immigration official may ask you to "buy" one, or pay some form of unspecified "fee" – usually equivalent to a dollar or five (exceptions are Belize and El Salvador, where you'll never be asked for illegal entry or exit fees). How you deal with this depends on how good your Spanish is, the amount of hassle you're willing to put up with and the attitude of the official. It's certainly annoying to have to pay these **bribes** and, if you know the rules, and stick to the "won't pay" line, you'll probably get waved through – eventually. Asking for a receipt is another ploy that may put your official off although you could well be levied with an additional charge to cover the receipt. This is especially true in places like Guatemala and Honduras, where there's a semi-institutionalized requirement to pay officials Q10/L20 (around US$1.50); it's usually more bother than it's worth to kick up a fuss. Once you get your stamp (and visa/tourist card if required) you should keep your **passport** with you at all times, or at the very least carry a photocopy, as you may be asked to show it.

Extensions to the permitted period of stay – whether you need a visa/tourist card or not – can be obtained at the immigration department (**migración**) in the country concerned, sometimes only in the capital. The process often takes a full day, so you may prefer to use the services of a *tramitador*, an agency that, for a fee, will deal with the red tape. In many cases it's often easier to leave the country for a few days and re-enter with a new stamp.

If you need a **visa** it's always best to get one well in advance; don't bank on picking one up at the border. That said, the only country which currently requires visas for citizens of the US, Canada, Australia and New Zealand is **El Salvador** (citizens of Ireland need a visa for **Panama**). US citizens are strongly advised to check Ⓦwww.travel.state.gov for any changes in visa requirements or travel warnings before making travel plans.

Finally, it's worth noting that citizens of countries participating in the US visa waiver programme – UK, Ireland, Australia and New Zealand – must use a machine-readable passport **when travelling to or transiting the USA**. In the unlikely event your passport isn't of the machine-readable variety, you'll either have to apply for a new one, or apply for a non-immigrant US visa at a hefty cost of US$100. Citizens of Canada are not affected by these changes.

Central American embassies and consulates

In the US and Canada

Belize 2535 Massachusetts Ave NW, Washington DC 20008 Ⓣ202/332-9636, Ⓕ332-6888, Ⓦwww.embassyofbelize.org; Honorary Consul, Suite 3800, South Tower, Royal Bank Plaza, Toronto, ON M5J 2JP Ⓣ416/865-7000; in Québec Ⓣ514/288-1687.
Costa Rica 2114 S St NW, Washington DC 20008 Ⓣ202/234-2945, Ⓕ234-2946, Ⓦwww.costarica-embassy.org.
El Salvador 2308 California St NW, Washington DC 20008 Ⓣ202/265-9671, Ⓦwww.elsalvador.org; Consulate, 1724 20th St NW, Washington DC 20009 Ⓣ202/331-4032; 1087 Hornby St, Vancouver BC V6Z 2S5 Ⓣ604/732-8142.
Guatemala 2220 R St NW, Washington DC 20008 Ⓣ202/745 4952, Ⓦwww.guatemala-embassy.org.
Honduras 3007 Tilden St NW, Washington DC 20008 Ⓣ202/966-7702, Ⓦwww.hondurasemb.org.
Nicaragua 1627 New Hampshire Ave NW, Washington DC 20009 Ⓣ202/939-6570, Ⓕ939-6532.
Panama 2862 McGill Terrace NW, Washington DC 20009 Ⓣ202/483-1407, Consulate Ⓣ202/387-6154.

In the UK

Belize Third Floor, 45 Crawford Place W1H 4LP Ⓣ020/7723 3603, Ⓦwww.bzhc-lon.co.uk.
Costa Rica Flat 1, 14 Lancaster Gate, London W2 3LH Ⓣ020/7706 8844, Ⓦwww.embcrlon.demon.co.uk.
El Salvador 3rd Floor, Mayfair House, 39 Great Portland St, London W1N 7JZ Ⓣ020/7436 8282, Ⓔembasalondres@netscapeonline.co.uk.
Guatemala 13 Fawcett St, London SW10 9HN Ⓣ020/7351 3042, Ⓕ7376 5708.
Honduras 115 Gloucester Place, London W1H 3PJ Ⓣ020/7486 4880, Ⓔhondurasuk@lineone.net.
Nicaragua Suite 12, Vicarage House, 58–60 Kensington Church St, London W8 4DB Ⓣ020/7938 2373, Ⓔemb.ofnicaragua@virgin.net.
Panama Panama House, 40 Hertford St, London W1J 7SH Ⓣ020/7943 4646, Ⓔemb.pan@lineone.net.

In Australia and New Zealand

Belize Consulate, 5/1 Oliver Rd, Roseville, NSW 2069 Ⓣ 02/9880 7160.
Costa Rica Consulate-General, 30 Clarence St, Sydney Ⓣ02/9261 1177, Ⓕ9261 2953.
El Salvador The nearest representative is in South Korea Ⓣ82/2753 3432.
Guatemala Consulate, 41 Blarney Ave, Kilarney Heights, NSW 2087 Ⓣ02/9451 3018, Ⓔconquasydney@optusnet.com.au.
Honduras Consulate, 43 Carpenter St, Brighton Beach VIC 3186 Ⓣ03/9593 1595.
Nicaragua The nearest representative is in the US.
Panama Consulate-General, 14/46 Slade Rd, Bardwell Park NSW 2207 Ⓣ02/9567 2347, Ⓕ9567 1539, Ⓔpanaconsul.sydney@bigpond.com.au; Consulate, Level 8, 61 High Street, Auckland Ⓣ09/379 8550, Ⓔgthwaite@iprolink.co.nz.

Information, websites and maps

Information about Central America is available from a number of sources, though much of the promotional puff provided by the official tourist offices is pretty to look at but of little practical use. However, the quality of such information is improving, and if you have specific questions you could try contacting some of the official organizations listed below.

Information

In Central America itself, you'll find government **tourism offices** in each capital city, and sometimes in the main tourist centres. At the least they can usually provide a city map, a bus timetable and perhaps a list of hotels. Below we've listed contact details for tourism offices in the US and UK, along with the web addresses for each country's tourist board. It's difficult to find information about Central America in Australia or New Zealand; your best bet is to have a look at the websites listed below or contact the specialist tour operators listed on p.18.

Central American tourist offices

Belize Ⓦwww.travelbelize.org
Costa Rica Ⓦwww.tourism-costarica.com
El Salvador Ⓦwww.elsalvadorturismo.gob.sv
Guatemala Ⓦwww.mayaspirit.com.gt
Honduras Ⓦwww.hondurasinfo.hn
Nicaragua Ⓦwww.intur.gob.ni
Panama Ⓦwww.panamatravel.com

In North America

Belize US Ⓣ1-800/624-0686, Ⓦwww.travelbelize.org.
Costa Rica (Ⓦwww.tourism-costarica.com) No tourist office in the US or Canada.
El Salvador US Ⓣ202/265-9671, Canada Ⓣ613/238-2939.
Guatemala US Ⓣ1-800/464 8281.
Honduras US Ⓣ202/966-7702, Ⓦwww.letsgohonduras.com.
Nicaragua US Ⓣ202/939-6571.
Panama US Ⓣ507/315-0609, Ⓦwww.panamainfo.com.

In the UK

Belize Ⓣ020/7499 9728
Costa Rica Ⓣ020/7706 8844
Guatemala Ⓣ020/7349 0346
EL Salvador Ⓣ020/7436 8282
Honduras Ⓣ020/7486 4880
Nicaragua Ⓣ020/7938 2373
Panama Ⓣ020/7943 4646

Useful websites

The following government **websites** provide current information on the security situation in the respective Central American countries. The news and information sites listed encompass a wealth of information on Central America in general; for individual country websites see Basics in the relevant chapter.

Governmental travel advisories

Australian Department of Foreign Affairs Ⓦwww.dfat.gov.au.
British Foreign & Commonwealth Office Ⓦwww.fco.gov.uk.
Canadian Department of Foreign Affairs Ⓦwww.dfait-maeci.gc.ca.
Irish Department of Foreign Affairs Ⓦwww.irlgov.ie/iveagh.
New Zealand Ministry of Foreign Affairs Ⓦwww.mft.govt.nz.
US State Department Ⓦtravel.state.gov.

News and general information

Central America Panorama Ⓦwww.elpanorama.net. Bilingual – if not always up to date – Central American news and info platform.
Centramerica Ⓦwww.centramerica.com. Country by country links for business, government, education, news and media, society and culture, many of which are in Spanish.

Latin America Links
ⓦwww.latinamericalinks.com. Comprehensive site primarily aimed at travellers and featuring links on everything from art, music and archeology to business and international trade, as well as travel and tourism.
Latin America Press
ⓦwww.latinamericapress.org. Hard-hitting alternative news, analysis and info with an emphasis on human rights and social justice.
Latin American Information Center (LANIC)
ⓦwww.lanic.utexas.edu. This site's comprehensive and logically laid-out homepage has a seemingly never-ending series of superb links for each country. From here you can reach almost anywhere and anything in Central America connected to the Net.
Latin American Newsletters
ⓦwww.latinnews.com. Veteran leader in political, economic and business intelligence and analysis.
Latin American Travel Advisor
ⓦwww.amerispan.com/lata. Comprehensive information on every Central American country, covering safety, health, politics, culture and the economy. The site also provides general advice on travelling in the region.
Mesoweb ⓦwww.mesoweb.com. Intriguing site focusing on the cultures of ancient Mesoamerica with learned articles on history, archeology and anthropolgy as well as links to newspaper articles on human rights, the environment etc.
Travel Latin America
ⓦwww.travellatinamerica.com. Offers a selection of news, features and information about travelling in the region, along with a currency converter, consulate details and an impressive selection of Web links for each country.
Zona Latina ⓦwww.zonalatina.com. Excellent site with both articles from the US press on Latin American issues and links to the homepages of all Latin America's newspapers, magazines and other media.

Libraries and resource centres

In-depth, specialist and academic analysis and information on Central America can be sourced from the **organizations** and **libraries** listed below.

In the US

California Cooperative Latin America Collection Development Group (CALAFIA) University of Stanford ⓦwww-sul.stanford.edu/depts/hasrg/latinam/calafia/index.html.
Center for Latin American Studies University of California at Berkeley
ⓦwww.clas.berkeley.edu/clas.
David Rockefeller Center for Latin American Studies Harvard University
ⓦwww.fas.harvard.edu/~drclas.

In the UK

Canning House Library 2 Belgrave Square, London SW1X 8PJ ⓣ020/7235 2303, ⓦwww.canninghouse.com. The UK's largest publicly accessible collection of books and periodicals on Latin America – anyone can visit, but you have to be a member to take books out and receive the twice-yearly Bulletin, a review of recently published books on Latin America.
Latin America Bureau 1 Amwell St, London EC1R 1UL ⓣ020/7278 2829, ⓦwww.lab.org.uk. Independent, non-profit group centring on issues of social justice and human rights. Their excellent In Focus series offers interesting and informative overviews of politics, society, the economy and environment of various Central American countries. Their website and annual catalogue are also great sources of inspiration for other on-the-road reading material, featuring Latin novels, as well as works on Latin American music and folklore.

Maps and map outlets

The best overall **map of Central America**, covering the region at a scale of 1:1,100,000, is produced by Canada's International Travel Maps and Books (see overleaf). They also publish **individual maps** of each country at various scales, but these tend to have a few mistakes. You can buy them direct from the publisher or from most specialist map shops and it's wise to try to get what you need before you go, although they are available in many Central American capitals. Equally recommended is Rough Guides' *Guatemala and Belize* map, which also covers a sizeable part of western Honduras and most of northern El Salvador. Again, you can either purchase it direct via the Rough Guides website (ⓦwww.roughguides.com/store) or from one of the retailers listed below.

In the US and Canada

Book Passage 51 Tamal Vista Blvd, Corte Madera, CA 94925 and in the historic San

Francisco Ferry Building ⓣ1-800/999-7909 or ⓣ415/927-0960, ⓦwww.bookpassage.com.
California Map and Travel Center 3312 Pico Blvd, Santa Monica CA 90405 ⓣ310/396-6277.
Distant Lands 56 S Raymond Ave, Pasadena CA 91105 ⓣ1-800/310-3220.
International Travel Maps and Books 530 W Broadway, Vancouver, BC V5Z IE9 ⓣ604/879-3621, ⓦwww.itmb.com.
Longitude Books 115 W 30th St #1206, New York, NY 10001 ⓣ1-800/342-2164, ⓦwww.longitudebooks.com.
Open Air Books and Maps 25 Toronto St, Toronto, ON M5R 2C1 ⓣ416/363-0719.
Travel Bug Bookstore 3065 W Broadway, Vancouver, BC V6K 2G9 ⓣ604/737-1122, ⓦwww.travelbugbooks.ca.
Traveler's Bookstore 22 W 52nd St, New York, NY 10019 ⓣ212/664-0995.
Ulysses Travel Bookshop 4176 St-Denis, Montréal, PQ ⓣ514/843-9447, ⓦwww.ulyssesguides.com.
World of Maps 1235 Wellington St, Ottawa, ON K1Y 3A3 ⓣ1-800/214-8524 or ⓣ613/724-6776, ⓦwww.worldofmaps.com.

In the UK and Ireland

Blackwell's Map Centre 50 Broad St, Oxford OX1 3BQ ⓣ01865/793 550, ⓦmaps.blackwell.co.uk. Branches in Bristol, Cambridge, Cardiff, Leeds, Liverpool, Newcastle, Reading and Sheffield.
Daunt Books 83 Marylebone High St, London W1M 3DE ⓣ020/7224 2295; 193 Haverstock Hill, London NW3 4QL ⓣ020/7794 4006.
The Map Shop 15 High St, Upton upon Severn, Worcs WR8 0HJ ⓣ01684/593146, ⓦwww.themapshop.co.uk.
National Map Centre 22–24 Caxton St, London SW1H 0QU ⓣ020/7222 2466, ⓦwww.mapsnmc.co.uk.
National Map Centre 34 Aungier St, Dublin ⓣ01/476 0471, ⓦwww.mapcentre.ie.
Newcastle Map Centre 55 Grey St, Newcastle-upon-Tyne NE1 6EF ⓣ0191/261 5622.
Stanfords 12–14 Long Acre, London WC2E 9LP ⓣ020/7836 1321, ⓦwww.stanfords.co.uk. Also at 29 Corn St, Bristol BS1 1HT ⓣ0117/929 9966 and 39 Spring Gardens, Manchester M2 2BG, ⓣ0161/831 0250.
The Travel Bookshop 13–15 Blenheim Crescent, London W11 2EE ⓣ020/7229 5260, ⓦwww.thetravelbookshop.co.uk.
Traveller 55 Grey St, Newcastle-upon-Tyne NE1 6EF ⓣ0191/261 5622, ⓦwww.newtraveller.com.

In Australia and New Zealand

Map Centre ⓦwww.mapcentre.co.nz.
Mapland 372 Little Bourke St, Melbourne ⓣ03/9670 4383, ⓦwww.mapland.com.au.
The Map Shop 6–10 Peel St, Adelaide ⓣ08/8231 2033, ⓦwww.mapshop.net.au.
Map World 371 Pitt St, Sydney ⓣ02/9261 3601, ⓦwww.mapworld.net.au. Also at 900 Hay St, Perth ⓣ08/9322 5733, Jolimont Centre, Canberra ⓣ02/6230 4097 and 1981 Logan Rd, Brisbane ⓣ07/3349 6633.
Mapworld 173 Gloucester St, Christchurch ⓣ0800/627 967, ⓦwww.mapworld.co.nz.
Specialty Maps 46 Albert St, Auckland ⓣ09/307 2217, ⓦwww.wise5maps.co.nz.

Insurance

You'd do well to take out an insurance policy before travelling to cover against theft, loss, illness or injury. Before paying for a new policy, however, it's worth checking whether you are already covered: some all-risks home insurance policies may cover your possessions when overseas, and many private medical schemes include cover when abroad. In Canada, provincial health plans usually provide partial cover for medical mishaps overseas, while holders of official student/teacher/youth cards in Canada and the US are entitled to meagre accident coverage and hospital in-patient benefits. Students will often find that their student health coverage extends during vacations and for one term beyond the date of last enrolment.

After checking out the possibilities above, you might want to contact a specialist travel insurance company, or consider the travel insurance deal we offer (see box below). A typical **travel insurance policy** usually provides cover for the loss of baggage, tickets and – up to a certain limit – cash or cheques, as well as cancellation or curtailment of your journey. Most of them exclude so-called **dangerous sports** unless an extra premium is paid: in Central America this can mean scuba-diving, whitewater rafting, windsurfing and trekking. Many policies can be chopped and changed to exclude coverage you don't need – for example, sickness and accident benefits can often be excluded or included at will. If you do take medical coverage, ascertain whether benefits will be paid as treatment proceeds or only after you return home, and if there is a 24-hour medical emergency number. When securing **baggage cover**, make sure that the per-article limit – typically under £500/$750 and sometimes as little as £250/$400 – will cover your most valuable possession. If you need to make a claim, you should keep receipts for medicines and medical treatment, and in the event you have anything stolen, you must obtain a *denuncia* from the police.

Health

It's always easier to become ill in a country with a different climate, food and germs, still more so in a poor country with lower standards of sanitation than you might be used to. Most visitors, however, get through Central America without catching anything more serious than a dose of "traveller's diarrhoea", and the most important precaution is to be aware of health risks posed by poor hygiene, untreated water, insect bites, undressed open cuts and unprotected sex.

Above all, it's vital to get the best **health advice** you can before you set off: pay a visit to your doctor or a travel clinic as far in advance of travel as possible. Many clinics also sell travel-related accessories, malaria tablets, mosquito nets, water filters and the like. Regardless of how well-prepared you are medically, you will still want the security of medical insurance (see overleaf).

Vaccinations, inoculations and malaria precautions

If possible, all **inoculations** should be sorted out at least ten weeks before departure. The only obligatory jab for certain Central American countries is a **yellow fever** vaccination if you're arriving from a "high-risk" area – northern South America and much of central Africa – in which case you need to carry your vaccination certificate. A yellow fever jab is also highly recommended if travelling in Panama south of the canal. Long-term travellers should look at the combined **hepatitis A and B** and the **rabies** vaccines (see p.29). And all travellers should check that they are up to date with **polio**, **diphtheria**, **tetanus**, **typhoid** and **hepatitis A** jabs.

North Americans can get inoculations at any immunization centre or at most local clinics, and will have to pay a fee. Most GPs in the **UK** have a travel surgery where you can get advice and certain vaccines on prescription, though they may not administer some of the less common immunizations. Note too that though some jabs (diphtheria, typhoid) are free, others will incur quite a hefty charge, and it can be worth checking out a travel clinic. These offer immediate access to all vaccinations, in particular the likes of rabies, which GPs rarely carry due to its short shelf life. They can also offer up-to-the-minute advice on malaria regimes for the particular area in which you'll be travelling. Prices have been rising in recent years however, and in many cases your local doctor will still be the cheapest option, especially for hepatitis A and B. In **Australasia**, vaccination centres are always less expensive than doctors' surgeries.

Malaria is endemic in many parts of Central America, especially in the rural lowlands. The recommended prophylactic west of the Panama Canal is Chloroquine; Mefloquine to the east of the canal, including the San Blas Islands. However, as Mefloquine (also known as Larium) can have upsetting side effects, it's worth checking with a medical practitioner as to its suitability for you. Malarone is a better, less controversial alternative for the malignant P falciparum strain of malaria, with minimal side effects, although its cost (around £20 per week) can be prohibitive. Another alternative to Mefloquine is Doxycycline, which is cheaper but can cause increased skin sensitivity to sunlight. You should still take precautions to avoid getting bitten by insects altogether: sleep in screened rooms or under nets, burn mosquito coils containing permethrin (available everywhere), cover up arms and legs, especially around dawn and dusk when the mosquitoes are most active, and use insect repellent containing over 35 percent Deet. Also prevalent – and on the increase – throughout Central America (usually occurring in epidemic outbreaks) is **dengue fever**, a viral infection transmitted by mosquitoes active during the day. There's no vaccine or specific treatment, so you need to pay great attention to avoiding bites. If you do become ill after returning home, consult your doctor and be sure to inform him or her that you've been in a malarial risk area.

Other simple precautions

What you **eat or drink** while you're travelling is crucial: a poor diet lowers your resistance. Be sure to drink clean water and eat a good balanced diet. Washing your hands before meals is another obvious precaution, as is the avoidance of shared water bottles. Eating plenty of peeled fresh fruit helps keep up your vitamin and mineral intake, but it might be worth taking daily multi-vitamin and mineral tablets with you. It is also important to eat enough and get enough **rest**, as it's easy to become run down if you're on the move a lot, especially in a hot climate. Don't try anything too exotic in the first few days, before your body has had a chance to adjust to local microbes, and avoid food that has been on display for a while and is not freshly cooked. You should also steer clear of raw shellfish, salads, and don't eat anywhere that is obviously dirty. In addition to the hazards mentioned under "Intestinal troubles", below, contaminated food and water will also transmit the hepatitis A virus, which can lay a victim low for several months with exhaustion, fever, diarrhoea, and can even cause liver damage. For advice on **water**, see p.29.

More serious are **hepatitis B**, and **HIV** and **AIDS**, all transmitted through blood or sexual contact; you should take all the usual, well-publicized precautions to avoid them. To contemplate casual sex without a condom would be madness; condoms also offer protection from other sexually transmitted infections.

Two other common causes of problems are **altitude** and the **sun**. The answer in both cases is to take it easy; allow yourself time to acclimatize before you start running up volcanoes, and build up exposure to the sun gradually – only a few minutes on the first day. Use a strong sunscreen and, if you're walking during the day, wear a hat and try to keep in the shade. Avoid dehydration by drinking enough – water or fruit juice rather than beer or coffee. Overheating can cause heatstroke, which is potentially fatal. Lowering body temperature (by taking a tepid shower, for example) is the first step in treatment.

Travellers should also take account of **DVT** or Deep Vein Thrombosis, an ailment misleadingly connected – largely through recent high-profile media reports – solely to air travel. In fact DVT – clotting of blood, usually occurring in the lower legs – is caused by inactivity and cramped spaces, and passengers in cars, buses and trains may all be at risk. People with heart disease, diabetes, pregnant women and women taking the oral contraceptive pill are among those considered at moderate risk (high risk being stroke and heart patients) while people over the age of forty and those suffering from varicose veins are considered low risk. In addition to the basic guidelines such as drinking adequate fluids, avoiding alcohol, walking around the cabin and regularly flexing the ankle and calf muscles, those at increased risk may consider wearing special support stockings aimed specifically at travellers.

Finally you might want to consider carrying a **travel medical kit**. These range from a box of band-aids to a full compact sterilized kit, complete with syringes and sutures.

Intestinal troubles

A bout of **diarrhoea** is the medical problem you're most likely to encounter, and no one, however cautious, seems to avoid it altogether. Its main cause is simply the change of diet: the food in Central America contains a whole new set of bacteria, as well as perhaps rather more of them than you're used to. The best cure is the simplest one: take it easy for a day or two and make sure you rehydrate yourself. It's a good idea to carry sachets of rehydration salts although you can make up your own solution by dissolving five teaspoons of sugar or honey and half a teaspoon of salt in a litre of water. Replace lost fluids by drinking lots of bottled water, and eat only the blandest of foods – papaya is good for soothing the stomach, and is also crammed with vitamins. Diarrhoea remedies like Imodium and Lomotil should be reserved for emergencies, like if you need to travel immediately. Only if the symptoms last more than four or five days do you need to worry. If you can't get to a doctor for an exact diagnosis, a last resort would be a course of Ciproxin (ciprofloxacin), which you may want to consider carrying in your medical kit. **Cholera** is an acute bacterial infection, recognizable by watery diarrhoea and vomiting, though many victims may have only mild or even no symptoms. However, risk of infection is considered low as Central America was recently declared a cholera-free zone by the Pan American Health Organisation.

If you're spending any time in rural areas you also run the risk of picking up various **parasitic infections**: protozoa – amoeba and giardia – and intestinal worms. These sound (and can be) hideous, but they're easily treated once detected. If you suspect you have an infestation take a stool sample to a good pathology lab and go to a doctor or pharmacist with the test results (see "Getting medical help", opposite). More serious is **amoebic dysentery**, which is endemic in many parts of the region. The symptoms are more or less the same as a bad dose of diarrhoea, but include bleeding. On the whole, a course of Flagyl (metronidazole or tinidozole) will cure it; if you plan to visit the far-flung corners of Central America then it's worth carrying these, just in case. If possible get some, and some advice on their usage, from a doctor before you go.

Bites and stings

Taking steps to avoid getting bitten by insects, particularly mosquitoes, is always good practice. **Sandflies**, often present on beaches, are tiny but their bites, usually on feet and ankles, itch like hell and last for days. They can also spread cutaneous leishmaniasis, an extremely unpleasant disease characterised by skin lesions that can take months and even years to heal if left untreated. Head or body lice can be picked up from people or bedding, and are best treated with medicated soap or shampoo; very occasionally, they may spread typhus, characterized by fever, muscle aches, headaches and eventually a measles-like rash. If you think you have it, seek treatment. Chiggers (coloradillas) are also a nuisance, small red mites which bite around the waist band.

Scorpions are common: mostly nocturnal, they hide during the heat of the day under rocks and in crevices. If you're camping, or sleeping in a village cabaña, shake your shoes out before putting them on and try not to wander round barefoot. Their sting is painful (occasionally fatal) and can become infected, so you should seek medical treatment. You're less likely to be bitten by a **spider**, but the advice is the same as for scorpions and venomous insects – seek medical treatment if the pain persists or increases.

You're unlikely to see a **snake**, and most are harmless in any case. Wearing boots and long trousers will go a long way towards preventing a bite – walk heavily and they will usually slither away. Exceptions are the fer-de-lance (which lives in both wet and dry environments, in both forest and open country but rarely emerges during the day) and the bushmaster (which can be found in places with heavy rainfall, or near streams and rivers), both of which can be aggressive, and whose venom can be fatal. If you do get bitten remember what the snake looked like (kill it if it's safe to do so), wrap a lightly restrictive crepe bandage above and below the bite area, but don't apply enough pressure to restrict the blood flow and never use a tourniquet. Use a commercial bite suction device on the wound (in the likely event you don't have one, disinfect the bite area and apply hard pressure with a gauze pad, taped in place) and immobilize the bitten limb as far as possible. Seek medical help immediately: antivenins are available in most hospitals.

Swimming and snorkelling might bring you into contact with potentially dangerous or venomous **sea creatures**. You're extremely unlikely to be a victim of shark attack (though the dubious practice of shark-feeding as a tourist attraction is growing, and could lead to an accidental bite), but jellyfish are common and all corals will sting. Some jellyfish, like the Portuguese man-o'-war, with its distinctive purple, bag-like sail, have very long tentacles with stinging cells, and an encounter will result in raw, red welts. Equally painful is a brush against fire coral: in each case clean the wound with vinegar or iodine and seek medical help if the pain persists or infection develops.

Rabies does exist in Central America; the best advice is to give dogs a wide berth, and not to play with animals at all, no matter how cuddly they may look. Treat any bite or scratch as suspect: wash any wound immediately with soap or detergent and running water for five minutes and apply alcohol or iodine if possible. Act immediately to get treatment – rabies is fatal once symptoms appear. If you're going to be working with animals, or planning a long stay, especially in rural areas far from medical help, you may well want to consider a pre-exposure vaccination, despite the hefty cost. Although this won't give you complete immunity, it will give you a window of 24–48 hours to seek treatment and reduce the amount of post-exposure vaccine you'll need if bitten.

Water safety

Contaminated water is a major cause of sickness in Central America, and even if it looks clean, all drinking water should be regarded with caution (a point to bear in mind when cleaning teeth and showering). That said, however, it's also essential to increase fluid intake to prevent dehydration. Bottled water is widely available, but stick with known brands and always check that the seal is intact, since refilling empties with tap water for resale is not unknown (carbonated water is generally a safer bet in this respect). Many restaurants use purified water (*agua purificada*), but always check; many hotels have a supply and will often provide bottles in your room. There are various methods of treating water while you are travelling, whether your source is from a tap or a river: boiling for a minimum of five minutes is the most effective method of sterilization, but it is not always practical, and will not remove unpleasant tastes.

Water filters remove visible impurities and larger pathogenic organisms (most bacteria and parasites). The Swiss-made Katadyn filter is expensive but extremely useful (various sizes are available from outdoor equipment stores). To be really sure your filtered water is also purified however, **chemical sterilization**, using either chlorine or iodine tablets, or a tincture of iodine liquid, is advisable. Both chlorine and iodine leave a nasty aftertaste (though it can be masked with lemon or lime juice), and iodine is more effective in destroying amoebic cysts. Pregnant women or people with thyroid problems should consult their doctor before using iodine sterilizing tablets or iodine-based purifiers. Inexpensive iodine removal filters are recommended if treated water is being used continuously for more than a month or is being given to babies.

Any good outdoor equipment shop will stock a range of **water treatment products**; their staff will give you the best advice for your particular needs.

Getting medical help

For minor medical problems, head for the **farmacia** – look for a green cross. Pharmacists are knowledgeable and helpful, and many may speak some English. They can also sell drugs over the counter (if necessary) which are only available by prescription at home. Most large cities have **doctors and dentists**, many trained in the US, who are experienced in treating visitors and speak good English. Your embassy will always have a list of recommended doctors, and we've included some in our "Listings" for the main towns. Medical insurance (see p.25) is essential, and for anything serious you should go to the best **private hospital** you can reach; again, these are located mainly in the capital cities. If you suspect something is amiss with your insides, it might be worth heading straight for the local **pathology lab** (*laboratorio médico*), found in all main towns, before seeing a doctor, as the doctor will probably send you there anyway. Many rural communities have a **health centre** (*centro de salud* or *puesto de salud*), where healthcare is free, although there may be only a nurse or health-worker available and you can't rely on finding an English-speaking doctor. Should you need an injection or transfusion, make sure that the equipment is sterile (it might be worth bringing a sterile kit from home) and ensure any blood you receive is screened.

Medical resources for travellers

Websites

Ⓦ www.cdc.gov The US government's official site for travel health.

Ⓦwww.fitfortravel.scot.nhs.uk Scottish NHS website carrying information about travel-related diseases and how to avoid them.

Ⓦwww.istm.org The website of the International Society for Travel Medicine, with a full list of clinics specializing in international travel health. Publishes outbreak warnings, suggested inoculations, precautions and other background information for travellers.

Ⓦwww.nativeplanet.org NGO working for indigenous rights whose useful website covers disease in Central America country by country with recommended treatment drugs.

Ⓦwww.TravelHealth.gc.ca Canadian government website with comprehensive list of travel clinics throughout the country.

In the US and Canada

American Society of Tropical Medicine and Hygiene 60 Revere Drive, Suite 500, Northbrook, IL 60062 Ⓣ847/480-9282, Ⓦwww.astmh.org. Scoiety of tropical medicine specialists with a comprehensive online directory of travel clinics (many part of universities) throughout the USA complete with opening hours, descriptions etc.

Canadian Society for International Health 1 Nicholas St, Suite 1105, Ottawa, ON K1N 7B7 Ⓣ613/241-5785, Ⓦwww.csih.org. Distributes a free pamphlet, "Health Information for Canadian Travellers", containing an extensive list of travel health centres in Canada.

Centers for Disease Control 1600 Clifton Rd NE, Atlanta, GA 30333 Ⓣ1-800/311-3435 or 404/639-3534, Ⓦwww.cdc.gov. Publishes outbreak warnings, suggested inoculations, precautions and other background information for travellers. Useful website plus International Travelers Hotline on Ⓣ1-877/FYI-TRIP.

International Association for Medical Assistance to Travellers (IAMAT) 417 Center St, Lewiston, NY 14092 Ⓣ716/754-4883, Ⓦwww.iamat.org, and 1287 St Clair Ave W, Suite #1, Toronto, ON M6E 1B8 Ⓣ416/652-0137. A non-profit organization supported by donations, it can provide a list of English-speaking doctors in Central America, with detailed online world malaria and immunization charts.

In the UK and Ireland

British Airways Travel Clinics 156 Regent St, London W1 (Mon–Fri 9.30am–6pm, Sat 10am–5pm no appointment necessary; Ⓣ0845/600 2236); 101 Cheapside, London EC2 (Mon–Fri 9am–4.45pm appointment required; Ⓣ0845/600 2236); Ⓦwww.britishairways.com/travel/healthclinintro. Vaccinations, tailored advice from an online database and a complete range of travel healthcare products.

Edinburgh Travel Health Clinic 14 East Preston St, Edinburgh EH8 9QA Ⓣ0131/667 1030, Ⓦwww.healthytrip.co.uk. Friendly, expert medical advice and very competitive rates on all major vaccinations and malaria prophylaxis.

Hospital for Tropical Diseases Travel Clinic 2nd floor, Mortimer Market Centre, off Capper St, London WC1E 6AU (Mon–Fri 9am–5pm by appointment only; Ⓣ020/7388 9600, Ⓦwww.masta.org). A consultation costs £15, which is waived if you have your injections here. A recorded Health Line (Ⓣ0906/133 7733; 50p per min) gives hints on hygiene and illness prevention as well as listing appropriate immunizations.

MASTA (Medical Advisory Service for Travellers Abroad) 40 regional clinics (call Ⓣ0870/606 2782 for nearest). Also operates a pre-recorded 24-hour Travellers' Health Line (UK Ⓣ0906/822 4100; 60p per min), giving written information tailored to your journey by return of post.

Nomad Pharmacy surgeries 40 Bernard St, London WC1N 1LE and 3–4 Wellington Terrace, Turnpike Lane, London N8 0PX (Mon–Fri 9.30am–6pm, Ⓣ020/7833 4114 to book vaccination appointment). They give advice free if you go in person, or their telephone helpline is Ⓣ0906/863 3414 (60p per min). They can give information tailored to your travel needs.

Travel Medicine Services PO Box 254, 16 College St, Belfast DT1 6BT Ⓣ028/9031 5220. Operates a travel clinic (Mon 9–11am & Wed 2–4pm) which can give inoculations after a GP referral, but primarily administers yellow fever vaccine.

Tropical Medical Bureau Grafton Buildings, 34 Grafton St, Dublin 2 Ⓣ1850/487 674, Ⓦwww.tmb.ie. Branches throughout Dublin and rest of Eire, offering all-in consultations covering everything from DVT to malaria prophylaxis.

In Australia and New Zealand

Travellers' Medical and Vaccination Centres 27–29 Gilbert Place, Adelaide, SA 5000 Ⓣ08/8212 7522, Ⓦwww.tmvc.com.au; 1/170 Queen St, Auckland Ⓣ09/373 3531, 5/247 Adelaide St, Brisbane, Qld 4000 Ⓣ07/3221 9066, 5/8–10 Hobart Place, Canberra, ACT 2600 Ⓣ02/6257 7156, 270 Sandy Bay Rd, Sandy Bay Tas, Hobart 7005 Ⓣ03/6223 7577, 2/393 Little Bourke St, Melbourne, Vic 3000 Ⓣ03/9602 5788, Level 7, Dymocks Bldg, 428 George St, Sydney, NSW 2000 Ⓣ02/9221 7133, Shop 15, Grand Arcade, 14–16 Willis St, Wellington Ⓣ04/473 0991.

Costs, money and banks

Life in Central America is generally cheaper than in North America and Europe although it's difficult to generalise since costs vary significantly between different countries. Although it's not as cheap as it was even a few years ago, Nicaragua is probably still the best-value destination while travellers are often surprised by the expense of Belize, Costa Rica and Panama, where prices are not that different from the US. As a general rule, locally produced goods are cheap, and anything imported is overpriced.

To an extent, what you spend will also obviously depend on where, when and how you choose to travel. During **peak tourist seasons**, such as Christmas and Easter, hotel prices tend to rise, and certain tourist centres are notably more expensive. **Public transport**, geared to locals, is invariably a bargain – though bear in mind that in some places foreigners are routinely charged more in what's effectively an institutionalized two-tier price system. Travelling by car is expensive, and the cost of renting a car (for prices see "Getting around", p.34) is higher in Central America than it is in the US, as is the cost of fuel – although this is still cheaper than in Europe. **Student cards** may sometimes get you small reductions on standard prices, although Central America isn't really geared up for such discounts (apart from anything else, prices in many countries are already very cheap); unless you're trying to obtain a reduced air fare at home, it's not worth buying one for the trip.

The **US dollar** is the most widely accepted foreign currency in Central America – Panama's unit of currency, the balboa, *is* the US dollar, and El Salvador switched over to the greenback in 2003. All prices quoted in the *Guide* are in US dollars.

Cash and travellers' cheques

You may want to carry some dollar **travellers' cheques** as a standby though these aren't accepted everywhere, and there's also the added hassle of waiting in (often huge) bank queues, not to mention paying a commission once the cheque is cashed. Nevertheless they are a safe way to carry money, offering the security of a refund if stolen. To facilitate this, make sure that you have cheques issued by one of the big names such as **American Express** or **Thomas Cook**, which are also more readily accepted. It pays to get a selection of denominations. Make sure to keep the purchase agreement, contact details of the issuing company and a record of cheque serial numbers safe and separate from the

Exchange rates

The following exchange rates were correct at time of going to press, though rates will inevitably vary over the course of this edition of the *Guide* in those countries whose currency is not pegged to the dollar; we've also given equivalents in British pounds.

Belize (Belizean dollar) Bz$1.97 = US$1 / Bz $3.5 = £1
Costa Rica (colón) 418.63c = US$1 / 770c = £1
Guatemala (quetzal) Q7.89 = US$1 / Q14=£1
Honduras (lempira) L17.9 = US$1 / L32=£1
Nicaragua (córdoba) C$15,65 = US$1 / C$28=£1
Panama (dollar/balboa) $1 = US$1 / $1.8 = £1

cheques themselves. In the event that cheques are lost or stolen, the issuing company will expect you to report the loss forthwith. Most companies claim to replace lost or stolen cheques within 24 hours.

A supply of **cash dollars** is probably a better bet, extremely useful if you run short of local currency a long way from the nearest bank. You'll get the best rate for your dollars if you change them for local currency in the country you're in or entering. Most international airports have a bank for currency exchange, while at the main land border crossings there might be a bank, or more likely a swarm of moneychangers, who'll give fair rates for cash and occasionally travellers' cheques. At even the most remote border crossing you can usually depend on finding some entrepreneur willing to change dollars, though rates worsen the further you are from a bank.

Small change, or rather the lack of it, is also a serious problem in many Central American countries and sometimes it's nigh on impossible to find anyone willing to accept the kind of large (often ridiculously so) denomination notes routinely churned out by ATMs. It's therefore advisable to take any opportunity to break these bills – the kind of places which usually accept them are more upmarket restaurants, hotels, supermarkets, gas stations etc.

Credit and debit cards

Credit/debit cards are probably the most convenient method of financing yourself in Central America and are at the very least a handy backup source of funds. They're widely used in Central America and although you shouldn't rely on them too much in Nicaragua or Honduras, are becoming increasingly accepted even in smaller hotels and restaurants. While MasterCard and American Express are widely accepted, Visa is the most useful; it's probably best to carry at least two brands out of the three. You can use your card to get cash (except when crossing land borders, which is where travellers' cheques and especially cash dollars come in handy) from ATMs, of which there are an increasing number in the region, and over the counter at banks; but remember that all cash advances are treated as loans, with interest accruing daily from the date of withdrawal; there may be a transaction fee on top of this. However, you may also be able to make withdrawals from ATMs using your debit card, which is not liable to interest payments, and the flat transaction fee is usually quite small – your bank will be able to advise on this. Yet another option is to "credit" (ie pay money into) your credit-card account before travelling in order to avoid interest charges. Make sure you have a personal identification number (PIN) that's designed to work overseas and if your card has been issued in the USA or Canada, make sure it's cleared for international cash withdrawal.

A compromise between travellers' cheques and plastic is Visa TravelMoney, a disposable pre-paid debit card with a PIN that works in all ATMs that take Visa cards. You load up your account with funds before leaving home, and when they run out, you simply throw the card away. For more information, check Ⓦwww.usa.visa.com.

Wiring money

Having money **wired from home** using one of the companies listed below is never convenient or cheap, and should be considered a last resort. It's also possible to have money wired directly from a bank in your home country to a bank in Central America, although this is somewhat less reliable because it involves two separate institutions. If you go this route, your home bank will need the address of the branch bank where you want to pick up the money and the address and telex number of the nearest head office, which will act as the clearing house; money wired this way normally takes two working days to arrive, and costs around £25/US$40/CAN$54/A$52/NZ$59 per transaction.

Money-wiring companies

Travelers Express/MoneyGram US Ⓣ1-800/444-3010, Canada Ⓣ1-800/933-3278, UK, Ireland and New Zealand Ⓣ00800/6663 9472, Australia Ⓣ0011800/6663 9472, Ⓦwww.moneygram.com.

Western Union US and Canada Ⓣ1-800/CALL-CASH, Australia Ⓣ1800/501 500, New Zealand Ⓣ0800/005 253, UK Ⓣ0800/833 833, Republic of Ireland Ⓣ66/947 5603; Ⓦwww.westernunion.com (Customers in the US and Canada can send money online.)

Getting around

Travel within Central America is as varied as the region itself. Since most locals don't own a car, buses are the most common form of public transport, and if you're travelling independently without your own vehicle you'll be spending a lot of time in (and waiting for) them. Although they can often be cramped and baking hot, the compact geography of Central America means that most of your journeys will be relatively short and certainly nothing like the endurance-testing routes further south.

The following is a general guide to Central American transport. More specific information on the transport infrastructure can be found in the "Getting around" section of each country's introductory chapter.

By bus

Cheap, convenient, often crowded and sometimes wildly entertaining, Central American **buses** come in a variety of forms, from first-class, air-conditioned luxury liners with videos and reclining seats, to ramshackle, third-class, third-hand, recycled US schoolbuses. Buses ply the main routes regularly, and some form of service connects the most remote villages to the provincial and national capitals – provided even a rudimentary road exists. Central American bus stations can be daunting places, noisy, crowded and utterly confusing. Sometimes there may be timetable boards but more often than not you'll have to ask around to find the bus you're after. Given the keen competition between the various operators, however, chances are that their touts will find you before you find them. Also, you really don't want to be separated from your luggage on any bus journey and in this respect it's definitely worth thinking about bringing a smaller pack or bag – one which you can carry on your lap or at your feet.

There are also an increasing number of **minibus** operators plying the busier routes and while these may be faster, they're often more expensive and more crowded than the normal buses.

The most popular **international bus service** is Ticabus, which runs from Tapachula in Mexico to Panama City, calling at Guatemala City, San Salvador, Managua (with connections to Tegucigalpa and San Pedro Sula in Honduras) and San José. The whole journey takes three and a half days, including overnights (at your own expense) at San Salvador and Managua. There are, in addition, a number of other international bus services, such as those run by King Quality, which offer comfortable bus services between the region's capital cities.

At many **land borders** buses from the adjacent country will cross the border to drop off and pick up passengers in the other country's terminal, which simplifies transport and immigration, especially if the immigration posts and terminals are some distance apart.

Flights

Each country has at least one domestic **airline**; fares are usually relatively inexpensive, and flying will often save hours of road travel over the region's difficult terrain, especially in eastern Nicaragua and Honduras. If covering a lot of territory, or if you want to visit the whole region in a fairly short time, an airpass offers great value and can cut costs considerably. Both **Grupo Taca** and **Copa** offer similar schemes linking the various Central American countries, with the routing Miami–San José–Managua–Guatemala City–LA costing US$740, a significant saving on a normal ticket for the same journey. Both passes link North American gateways with all the capitals and some other cities in Central America, plus some destinations in South America and the Caribbean; the possible routes are mind-boggling. You have to buy the pass before leaving home and book your route in advance.

The "Mexipass International" combines the extensive networks of Aeroméxico and Mexicana, linking destinations throughout Mexico with several Central and South American cities as well as Canada and the USA. The best way to find out how (or if) an airpass will benefit you is to call JLA in the UK (ⓣ020/8747 3018 or 0161/832 1551, ⓦwww.journeylatinamerica.co.uk); or contact eXito in the US (ⓣ1-800/655-4053 or 510/655-4566, ⓦwww.wonderlink.com/exito).

By car

Taxis are readily available in all the main towns; some routes (from airports to city centres for example) have set prices, but meters are a rarity – always fix a price before you set off. Taxis can also be a good substitute for a rental car; you have the advantage of your own transport without the responsibility, and it could even work out cheaper. Agreeing a fare before you get in is probably even more important if you're hiring a taxi for the day or are being driven to a distant location: make sure the price agreed is for both the outward *and* return legs of the journey.

Prices vary for **car rental** throughout Central America. The most expensive country is Belize – the cheapest weekly rate, excluding taxes, is around US$410 for an economy four-door. Car rental in Honduras is also quite pricey: expect to pay around US$210 a week for the cheapest car, or US$300 for 4WD. Other countries are considerably cheaper, ranging from around US$90 in Nicaragua, US$120 in Guatemala and US$130 in El Salvador to US$160 in Panama and US$180 in Costa Rica. Organising car rental before you travel is probably a better guarantee that there will be a car waiting when you get there although it won't necessarily get you the cheapest prices. If you do plan to rent a car make sure you get a good **map** (see p.23). Having succeeded in getting your own car to Central America, any further problems you face are likely to seem fairly minor.

Security is a major headache – always park in a safe place and never leave your car in the street overnight. If you're renting a car, some agencies may expect you to keep the vehicle in guarded car parks when not in use. **Fuel** is marginally more expensive than in the US and cheap by European standards, and filling stations are plentiful throughout Central America, even in the countryside.

There's no **breakdown service** in Central America and unless you're renting (in which case you can call the agency) you'll have to rely on the goodwill of local people for assistance and local mechanics for repairs. In general, most garages are fairly cheap, but always get an idea of cost before you agree to the work and don't be scared to negotiate when the job's done.

Rules of the road

Road conditions vary from country to country although, in general, their state of repair worsens the further you go from major centres of population. Look out for potholes, rocks, and people and animals in the road, especially if you're driving at night (not exactly advisable in any case) or in rural areas; most local vehicles have poor headlights and often no rear lights at all. All of Central America **drives on the right** although the state of the roads means that cars often steer the best route through the obstacles until they have to overtake. If the road is particularly bad, drivers (especially of express buses) will have their hazard lights on warning you not to overtake as they could be swerving at any moment to avoid a pothole. **Police checkpoints** are common in the vicinity of provincial and national borders, and you should always slow down and stop if requested to do so; it's unlikely they'll keep you any longer than it takes to check your documentation. Piles of branches in the road indicate that there's a breakdown ahead or that there *was* a breakdown and the driver neglected to remove them. Watch out also for drunk drivers at weekends and around carnival time–Central America suffers some of the highest **accident rates** in the world and as a foreigner any collision is likely to be construed as your fault, so always take full-cover insurance (see p.25).

Car rental agencies

Alamo US ⓣ1-800/462-5266, ⓦ**www.alamo.com**. Offices in Honduras, El Salvador, Nicaragua and Panama.

Avis US ⓣ1-800/230-4898, Canada ⓣ1-800/272-5871, UK ⓣ0870/606 0100, Northern Ireland ⓣ028/9024 0404, Republic of Ireland ⓣ021/428 1111, Australia ⓣ13 63 33 or 02/9353 9000, New Zealand ⓣ09/526 2847 or 0800/655 111, ⓦwww.avis.com. All of Central America covered; particularly strong on Honduras.
Budget US ⓣ1-800/527-0700, Canada ⓣ1-800/472-3325, UK ⓣ01442/276266, Republic of Ireland ⓣ09/0662 7711, Australia ⓣ1300/362 848, New Zealand ⓣ09/976 2222 or 0800/652-227, ⓦwww.budget.com. Comprehensive coverage throughout Central America.
Dollar US ⓣ1-800/800-3665, ⓦwww.dollar.com. Offices in every country except Belize.
Hertz US ⓣ1-800/654-3131, Canada ⓣ1-800/263-0600, UK 0870/536 5365, Australia ⓣ13 30 39 or 03/9698 2555, New Zealand ⓣ0800/654 321, ⓦwww.hertz.com. Comprehensive coverage in every country.
National US ⓣ1-800/962-7070, ⓦwww.nationalcar.com. Offices in El Salvador, Honduras, Nicaragua, Costa Rica and Panama.
Thrifty US and Canada ⓣ1-800/847-4389, UK ⓣ01494/751600, Republic of Ireland ⓣ1800/515 800, Australia ⓣ1300/367 227, New Zealand ⓣ09/309 0111, ⓦwww.thrifty.com. All countries except Nicaragua.

Motoring organizations

In the US and Canada

AAA ⓣ1-800/AAA-HELP, ⓦwww.aaa.com. Each state has its own club – check the phone book for local address and phone number.
CAA ⓣ613/247-0117, ⓦwww.caa.ca. Each region has its own club – check the phone book for local address and phone number.

In the UK and Ireland

AA UK ⓣ0870/600 0371, ⓦwww.theaa.com.
AA Ireland Dublin ⓣ01/617 9999, ⓦwww.aaireland.ie.
RAC UK ⓣ0800/550 055, ⓦwww.rac.co.uk.

In Australia and New Zealand

AAA Australia ⓣ02/6247 7311, ⓦwww.aaa.asn.au.
New Zealand AA New Zealand ⓣ0800/500 444, ⓦwww.nzaa.co.nz.

Other transport

While buses are the chief form of public transport in Central America, you're also likely to travel by **boat** at some point – out to and between islands, along rivers, and as the main form of transport in areas like the northern coast of Honduras and Nicaragua. The crafts themselves range from precarious-looking dugout canoes and old tubs for ferries, to fast, modern launches capable of long-distance sea travel. While there are some regular scheduled services such as the ferries on Lake Nicaragua and the regular boats between the Corn Islands, the majority of transport operates on an informal supply-and-demand basis.

Bicycles are very common in Central America, and increasing numbers of visitors bring their own. If you do (or if you rent a bike) you'll find a repair shop in every town. Some buses can carry bikes on the roof, giving greater flexibility. In the UK, membership of the Cyclists' Touring Club (69 Meadrow, Godalming, Surrey GU7 3HS ⓣ01483/417217, ⓦwww.ctc.org.uk) allows you access to trip reports from and information geared to cyclists who've taken bikes to the region.

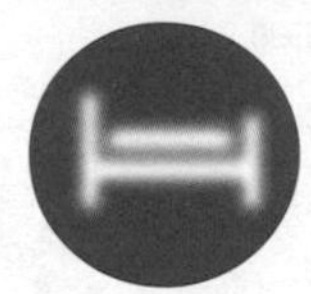

Accommodation

Central American hotels come in all shapes and sizes and it's usually not hard to find somewhere reasonable. Accommodation comes under a bewildering range of names; *hotel*, obviously, but you'll frequently see *pensión*, *casa de huéspedes*, *hospedaje*, *posada*, *alojamiento*, *rancho* and *campamento* – the last two usually refer to some form of camping. The different names don't always mean a great deal: in theory a *casa de huéspedes* is less formal than a *hotel* but in reality the main difference will be the price. You'll soon get used to finding what's on offer in your preferred price range.

Most countries have some form of price (and, in theory, quality) regulation and there's sometimes also a **hotel tax** to pay: always check if this is included in the rate you're quoted. It's a good idea to have a look at the room before you take it; make sure the light and fan work, and if you've been told there's hot water, see just what that means.

Budget hotels

There's so much variety in standards even among budget hotels that to list every possible permutation of types and furnishings would be impossible. However, a **basic room** in a town will have a light and a fan in addition to the bed, though don't expect a reading light or anywhere to put clothes, and all but the rock-bottom places will also supply a towel, soap and toilet paper. You'll often have the option of a private bathroom (ie a toilet and a basic shower), which is usually worth the small extra cost. If the **price** seems a little high for the type of establishment it's worth asking if there's a less expensive room (*¿Tiene un cuarto más barato, por favor?*) – you'll often get the same room at a lower price. It's always better to get a room at the back, away from the noise of the street, and upstairs you're more likely to benefit from a breeze. Most small hotels will be family run, and the owners usually take pride in the cleanliness of the rooms. There will usually be a place to hand-wash clothes (a *pila*); ask first before you use it.

In **lowland areas** a fan (*ventilador*) will be more important than hot water (*agua caliente*), but in the mountains you'd probably prefer a hot shower, though there will rarely be any form of heating (*calefacción*); make sure you have enough blankets. The term "hot shower" in Central America can be a bit misleading; the water temperature may just be tepid rather than really hot. And sometimes the "heating element" will be a couple of wires running into a contraption above the shower nozzle – touching this is likely to give you an electric shock.

As a rule budget hotels in the capital cities tend to be less attractive than those in smaller towns and tourist areas, though we've listed the exceptions in the relevant chapters. In the bigger cities it's worth paying a little more, or even moving to one grade of

Accommodation price codes

All accommodation reviewed in this guide has been graded according to the following price scales, which represent the cost of a **double room in high season**, excluding any taxes.

- ❶ up to US$5
- ❷ US$5–10
- ❸ US$10–15
- ❹ US$15–25
- ❺ US$25–40
- ❻ US$40–60
- ❼ US$60–80
- ❽ US$80–100
- ❾ US$100 and over

hotel higher than you might otherwise, to stay in a more secure place – particularly for your first night. Cheap hotels are often crowded around bus stations and markets; some of these can be very dismal, many of them being used by prostitutes and their clients. However, in every capital there are at least one or two hotels where other travellers congregate (as well as plenty where they don't) to offer company and perhaps security.

Budget hotels in **rural areas** or **coastal locations** that are not touristy are often quite basic; a ramshackle building or perhaps a stick and thatch cabaña. These can be delightful – you'll be less of a guest and more an extra member of the family – but they can also be very uncomfortable, with lumpy mattresses and poor ventilation. This is where serviceable insect-proofing can make the difference between misery and a good night's sleep.

Booking ahead for a budget room is not usually necessary (and often not possible, because of the difficulty of paying in advance and the fact that many such establishments don't have a telephone), though it might be worth trying at busy times like Christmas and Easter. Otherwise arriving early at your destination will give you a better selection.

Resorts and lodges

Bigger hotels in cities will have similar facilities to those at home, though often in a more attractive setting and sometimes in a wonderfully restored colonial building. They will almost certainly have air conditioning (*aire acondicionado*); a feature which is also increasingly offered in less expensive places. You'll pay a good deal more for this than you would for a room with a fan and, other things being equal, it may not be worth the extra, especially given that the air is often so cold as to be unpleasant. Some of the best accommodation in the region, however, is offered by the **resorts** in beach areas and the **jungle lodges**, often in beautiful, remote locations in or near national parks. Here you'll often have a private thatched cabaña, with a balcony overlooking the forest, lake, beach or other natural attraction. Obviously you'll be paying extra for this, but the experience of a rainforest dawn chorus and the chance of getting close to wildlife make it worthwhile. These lodges are often used by the adventure and nature tour operators and occupancy varies with the season – if the lodge is open out of season, ask about possible discounts.

Youth hostels and camping

In a region so full of inexpensive hotels you need rarely consider staying in **youth hostels**. In any case, only Costa Rica has a useful hostel network, with many located near national parks. The situation is similar with respect to **camping** and few places outside Costa Rica offer formal campsites. Elsewhere, you'll usually only need a tent if you're hiking really off the beaten track – though you'll probably have a guide who knows where there are shelters to hang a hammock, a tent offers better protection from rain and, more importantly, from insects. Some volcanoes are too high to climb and descend in one day, and if camping at the top you'll need some protection from the cold as well; a good sleeping bag is essential.

Communications

Mail and telecommunication services in Central America run the gamut from extremely efficient to chronically temperamental. Postal services are generally inexpensive, and postcards and letters mailed home do usually get through. Local calls (and many long-distance internal calls) from payphones are fairly cheap, but standard international calls are comparatively more expensive than at home. The increasing availability of Internet phones has been a godsend for travellers, offering incredibly cheap calls worldwide.

Mail

Throughout the region the best way to ensure the speedier delivery of your mail is to use the **main post office** in a capital city; this will also be the best place to send parcels. **Post-boxes** are rare – you'll find them in the lobbies of big hotels and some tourist shops – but the best bet is to take mail to a post office. As a rule of thumb, an **airmail letter** to the US takes about a week; to Europe, about ten days. **Receiving mail** is less certain, but the service in main post offices is usually reliable. Letters should be sent to you (with your surname underlined) followed by *Lista de Correos* (or "General Delivery" in Belize), *Correo Central*, name of city, country, and finishing with "Central America". When looking to see if mail has arrived ask to see the *Lista de Correos*, which is usually typed up each day, and search for your name (check under both your forename and surname). You'll need identification; a passport is best.

Always use some form of registration for **parcels** (the exact name differs from country to country); it won't cost much extra and you'll get a certificate to give you some peace of mind. You can send parcels via surface mail but this literally takes months. Be prepared for the parcel to undergo some form of inspection, and there may be some quaint labelling and wrapping regulations to observe.

Telephones

Although Central America's **telephone system** is gradually improving, and telephone charge and calling cards are widely accepted, much of it still leaves a lot to be desired. Sending a fax from a public telephone office is often easier than making a phone call. **Calling home collect** (*llamar por cobrar*) is simple to those countries which receive collect calls from the country you're in – but not all do. Before leaving home, it's worth checking whether a phone company in your country has a number to call abroad to connect you with the operator – this is usually the easiest way to call home collect. That said, the increasing number of **Internet phone facilities** (and the invariably great value such facilities offer) is fast making conventional telephone systems obsolete, at least as far as travellers are concerned.

Calling home from abroad

Another alternative for phoning home from abroad is via a **telephone charge card** from your phone company back home. Using a PIN number, you can make calls from most hotels, public and private phones that will be charged to your account. Since most major charge cards are free to obtain, it's certainly worth getting one at least for emergencies; enquire first though whether your destination is covered, and bear in mind that rates aren't necessarily cheaper than calling from a public phone.

In the **US and Canada**, AT&T, MCI, Sprint, Canada Direct and other North American long-distance companies all enable their customers to make credit-card calls while overseas, billed to your home number. In the **UK and Ireland**, British Telecom (☎0800/345 144) will issue free to all BT customers the BT Charge Card; AT&T (dial

Calling home from overseas

Note that the initial zero is omitted from the area code when dialling the UK, Ireland, Australia and New Zealand from abroad.

USA and Canada international access code + 1 + area code.
Australia international access code + 61 + city code.
New Zealand international access code + 64 + city code.
UK international access code + 44 + city code.
Republic of Ireland international access code + 353 + city code.

International access codes

Belize ⓣ501
Costa Rica ⓣ506
El Salvador ⓣ503
Guatemala ⓣ502
Honduras ⓣ504
Nicaragua ⓣ505
Panama ⓣ507

ⓣ0800/890 011, then 888/641-6123 when you hear the AT&T prompt to be transferred to the Florida Call Centre, free 24 hours) has the Global Calling Card.

Mobile phones

Using your **mobile phone** in Central America is a question of contacting your network provider to find out if they've got coverage in the country you're headed to. Although over 70 percent of the world's mobile phones – including most western phones – use GSM (Global System for Mobile Communications) networks, most countries in Central America use non-GSM standard networks that are incompatible with most, if not all, western phones. The exception is El Salvador where mobiles are tuned to operate as tri-band, in common with most phones in the USA. Given that the situation is likely to change dramatically during the lifetime of this guide, it's worth having a look at the website ⓦwww.gsmworld.com/roaming which has a worldwide directory of coverage and 'roaming' partners.

Email

One of the best (and cheapest) ways to keep in touch while travelling is to sign up for a free **Internet** email address – if you haven't already done so – that can be accessed from anywhere, for example Yahoo! (ⓦmail.yahoo.com) or Hotmail (ⓦwww.hotmail.com). Once you've set up your account, you'll be able to pick up and send mail from any Internet café, Web kiosk or hostel or hotel with Internet access. Central America is now well connected, and many travellers eschew telephone and fax communication altogether in favour of **email**. Most of the big towns, and many smaller ones, now have at least one **cybercafé**, usually in a central location. Most of these cafés have at least one Internet phone (usually far from private and with a queue behind it) although some are beginning to install conventional booths. Check ⓦwww.kropla.com for details of how to plug your laptop in when abroad, phone country codes around the world, and information about electrical systems in different countries.

Work, volunteering and study

High unemployment and bureaucratic hurdles make the possibility of finding paid work in Central America very unlikely, although there are limited opportunities to teach English, especially in wealthier countries like Costa Rica. Wages from this kind of work aren't going to make you rich, but can allow you to extend your stay if travel funds are running low. Voluntary opportunities are far greater with a wide range of projects, operated largely by NGOs, which rely on volunteer staff. Opportunities for studying Spanish are also relatively plentiful and often fairly cheap, with a number of congenial Central American locations drawing students from all over the world. General details on all of this are listed below; check the introduction to each country in the *Guide* for more specific information.

Teaching English

There are two options for teaching English in Central America: find work before you go, or just wing it and see what you come up with after arriving, particularly if you already have a degree and/or teaching experience. Teaching English – often abbreviated as **ELT** (English Language Teaching) – is the way many people finance their way around the greater part of the world; you can get a **CELTA** (Certificate in English Language Teaching to Adults), a **TEFL** (Teaching English as a Foreign Language) or a **TESOL** (Teaching English to Speakers of Other Languages) qualification before you leave home or even while you're abroad. **International House** (ⓦwww.ihworld.com) has branches in many countries, including the US, Australia and most of Europe, which offer at least one – and often two – out of the three courses listed above. Strictly speaking, a university degree is not needed to do the course, but you'll certainly find it easier to get a job with the degree/certificate combination. Certified by the RSA, the course is very demanding and costs about £1025/US$2250–2500/A$2550 for the month's full-time tuition; you'll be thrown in at the deep end and expected to teach right away. In **Canada**, try the Vancouver English Centre (ⓣ604/687-1600, ⓦwww.vec.ca) where the four-week TEFL Certificate course costs CAN$1440, with occasional deals in the winter. New Zealand's Communicative Language Training International (ⓣ03/377 8157, ⓦwww.clt-intl.com) offer a six-week TEFL course for NZ$3720. The **British Council**'s website, ⓦwww.britishcouncil.org/work/job, and the **TEFL** website, ⓦwww.tefl.com, both have a list of English-teaching vacancies.

Places like Guatemala City and San José in Costa Rica are your best bet for teaching in Central America although colonial, tourist-orientated towns like Antigua in Guatemala and Granada in Nicaragua are also likely spots.

If you have any kind of talent for writing, another option is working for one of the English-language newspapers based in Central America. One of the most established is San José's *Tico Times* (ⓦwww.ticotimes.net), offering four-month internships with a small monthly stipend.

Volunteering

In addition to teaching English, there are a number of **voluntary positions** available, including everything from conservation work in Costa Rica to accompanying human-rights workers in Guatemala. If you have a useful skill or specialisation, you might just have your room and board paid for and perhaps even a little pocket money, although more often than not you'll have to fund yourself. If you don't have any particular skills, you'll almost definitely have to pay for the privilege of volunteering and in many cases – particularly in conservation work – this doesn't come cheap: some voluntary schemes oblige you to undertake fundraising at home in order to finance your placement. While many positions are organised prior to arrival, it's also possible to fix something up on the ground through word of mouth. Notice boards in the more popular backpacker hostels are always good sources of info.

Studying Spanish

Some people travel to Central America solely to **learn Spanish** and there are many cities and towns with highly respected schools. Antigua and Quetzaltenango in Guatemala, San José in Costa Rica and to a lesser extent, Estelí in Nicaragua are all noted centres of language activity, with Estelí probably cheapest at around US$150 per week. This figure includes room and board with a local family, a standard feature of many Spanish courses and great for full cultural immersion. There's also the possibility of booking a pre-paid language course holiday, an increasingly popular option among people whose travel time is limited.

Useful publications and websites

Another pre-planning strategy for working abroad, whether teaching English or otherwise, is to get hold of one of the books on summer jobs abroad and how to work your way around the world published by Vacation Work; call ⓣ01865/241978 or visit ⓦwww.vacationwork.co.uk for their catalogue. Travel magazines like the reliable *Wanderlust* (every two months; £2.80) have a Job Shop section that often advertises job opportunities with tour companies. Another useful source is ⓦwww.studyabroad.com, loaded with listings and links to study and work programmes worldwide.

Useful contacts

In the US and Canada

AFS Intercultural Programs ⓣ1-800/876-2377 or 212/299-9000, ⓦwww.afs.org/usa; ⓣ1-800/361-7248, ⓦwww.afscanada.org. Cultural immersion programmes for high school students and graduates in Costa Rica, Guatemala, Honduras and Panama.

Alliances Abroad ⓣ1-888/6-ABROAD or 512/457-8062, ⓦwww.alliancesabroad.com. Combined language and conservation-themed voluntary placements in Costa Rica lasting two weeks to one year. Intermediate Spanish ability required.

AmeriSpan ⓣ1-800/879-6640, ⓦwww.amerispan.com. Language programmes, volunteer/internship placements (English teaching, healthcare, environment, social work, etc) and academic study-abroad courses throughout Central America.

Amigos de las Américas ⓣ1-800/231-7796 or 713/782-5290, ⓦwww.amigoslink.org. Veteran non-profit organisation placing high school- and college-age students in child health promotion and other community projects in Costa Rica, Honduras, Nicaragua and Panama.

Council on International Educational Exchange (CIEE) ⓣ1-800/2COUNCIL, ⓦwww.ciee.org. Semester and summer study programmes in Costa Rica with subjects ranging from agriculture and agroecology to Spanish language. Also publishes *Work, Study, Travel Abroad* and *Volunteer! The Comprehensive Guide to Voluntary Service in the US and Abroad.*

Earthwatch Institute ⓣ1-800/776-0188, ⓦwww.earthwatch.org. Voluntary positions throughout Central America assisting scientists in the field.

Experiment in International Living ⓣ1-800/345-2929 or 802/257-7751, ⓦwww.usexperiment.org. Month-long community/environmental placements in Costa Rica and Belize for high school students.

Learn Spanish ⓦwww.studyspanish.com. Details of agencies and schools in Costa Rica and Guatemala.

Peace Corps ⓣ1-800/424-8580, ⓦwww.peacecorps.gov. US institution which recruits volunteers of all ages (18 being the lower limit) and from all walks of professional life for two-year postings throughout Central America. All applicants must be US citizens.

School for International Training ⓣ1-800/336-1616, ⓦwww.sit.edu. Accredited college semesters abroad. The large Latin American studies programme includes an ecology/conservation course in Belize and a politically-themed course in Nicaragua.

In the UK and Ireland

AFS UK ⓦwww.afsuk.org. Six-month community volunteer placements for young people aged 18 to 34 in Costa Rica, Guatemala, Honduras and Panama.

British Council ⓣ020/7930 8466. Produces a free leaflet which details study opportunities abroad. The Council's Central Management of Direct

Teaching (Ⓣ020/7389 4931) recruits TEFL teachers for posts worldwide (check Ⓦwww.britishcouncil.org/work/jobs for a current list of vacancies). It also publishes a book, *Year Between*, aimed principally at gap-year students detailing volunteer programmes and schemes abroad.

Earthwatch Institute Ⓣ01865/318 838, Ⓦ**www.uk.earthwatch.org.** International non-profit organisation dedicated to environmental sustainability. Voluntary positions assisting archeologists, biologists and even ethnomusicologists in the field – CA destinations include Costa Rica and Guatemala.

Cactus Languages Ⓣ0845/130 4775, Ⓦ**www.cactuslanguage.co.uk.** Brighton-based language-holiday specialist with wide range of courses in Costa Rica, Guatemala, Nicaragua and Panama. Prices often lower than applying directly to the schools.

Caledonia Languages Abroad Ⓣ0131/621 7721/2, Ⓦ**www.caledonialanguages.co.uk.** Competitively priced, intensive language courses and combined language and voluntary work packages (community- or environmental-based) in Costa Rica.

i to i International Projects Ⓣ0870/333 2332, Ⓦ**www.i-to-i.com.** Award-winning company offering pricey voluntary placements in Costa Rica, El Salvador, Guatemala and Honduras. Contact Deirdre O'Sullivan. Options include conservation, building, journalism, health, teaching English and community development with pre-trip TEFL courses included in the price for the latter two.

Peace Brigades International Ⓣ0207/561 9141, Ⓦ**www.peacebrigades.org.** NGO dedicated to protecting human rights with placements accompanying human-rights workers in Guatemala. Costs (incuding a small monthly stipend) are covered although fundraising is encouraged and applicants need to be aged 25 or over and fluent in Spanish.

Raleigh International Ⓣ020/7371 8585, Ⓦ**www.raleigh.org.uk.** Long-established youth-development charity working on community and environmental projects worldwide. Opportunities for both young volunteers (17–25) and older skilled staff (25+). Central American projects in Costa Rica and Nicaragua.

In Australia and New Zealand

Australian Volunteers International Ⓣ03/9279 1788, Ⓦ**www.ozvol.org.au.** Postings of up to two years in Costa Rica, Guatemala, El Salvador and Nicaragua with shorter-term, team-based assignments for younger volunteers.

Earthwatch Australia Ⓣ03/9682 6828, Ⓦ**www.earthwatch.org/australia.** Australian branch of this non-profit organisation which places prospective volunteers with an array of scientists from various fields in locations throughout Central America.

Global Volunteer Network Ⓣ04/569 9080, Ⓦ**www.volunteer.org.nz.** Voluntary placements on community projects worldwide. No Central American destinations at the time of writing, although new programmes are being researched all the time and it's worth having a check on the website.

International Exchange Programs Ⓣ0800/443 769, Ⓦ**www.iepnz.co.nz.** A variety of work, teach and study abroad programs for New Zealanders wishing to go to Costa Rica.

Crime and personal safety

While political violence has decreased over recent years, crime rates in Central America are rising alarmingly, and in many popular tourist locations determined thieves will target you or your belongings. The majority of crime is petty theft – bag-snatching or pickpocketing, for example – but some criminals operate in gangs and are prepared to use extreme violence to rob you.

Though it is commonly accepted that **Guatemala** tops the list for tourist crime, it's closely followed by the north of **Honduras** and **El Salvador** – and given the relatively small number of tourists in these countries, the probability of coming across trouble is that bit higher. Recent years have also seen a rise in crime in **Costa Rica**, especially in San José and increasingly in rural areas. Outside of Managua, **Nicaragua** is one of the safer countries in Central America and **Panama**'s reputation as a dangerous destination is somewhat exaggerated. Wherever you go you should take commonsense precautions; relax, but don't get complacent. If you've got valuables, insure them properly (see p.25).

Avoiding crime

You're more likely to be a **victim** of crime when you've just arrived, especially when you're looking for a room after dark – getting to your hotel in daylight will add greatly to your safety. Keep your most valuable possessions on you (but don't wear expensive jewellery) in a moneybelt under your outer clothes, though this isn't as easy as it sounds, as you'll have to get your passport and money out at border crossings. Trousers with zipped pockets are an idea to deter pickpockets. Border crossings, where you'll often have to change money, surprisingly enough aren't that dangerous; the money-changer is unlikely to short-change you (though getting the right exchange rate is another matter), and the presence of armed officials generally discourages thieves in the immediate area of the immigration post. Do the transaction and put your money away out of sight of other people if at all possible. Once away from the post however, you need to be on your guard; beware of people "helping" you find a bus and offering to carry your luggage. In many cases they will genuinely be offering a service in return for a tip, but at times like this you're easily distracted and you should never put your belongings down or let them out of sight unless you're confident they're in a safe place.

You can always register at your **embassy** when (or even before) you arrive – we've listed phone numbers in the *Guide*. This is advisable if you're spending a long time in or travelling to remote areas of the region, though it's not necessary if you're on an organized tour. Always take photocopies of your passport and insurance documents and try to leave them in a secure place; leave a copy with someone at home too. A second credit card, kept in a very safe location and only to be used in emergencies, will be invaluable if your other cards or funds get stolen.

Travel and hotels

When travelling on **public transport**, particularly by bus, you'll often be separated from your main bag – it will go either in the luggage compartment underneath or in the rack on top. This is generally safe enough (and you'll probably have little option in any case) but keep an eye on it whenever you can. Although the theft of the bag itself is uncommon, opportunist thieves may dip into zippers and outer pockets. It's seriously worth considering cutting back on your luggage and taking a holdall-type bag (the older and more worthless-looking the better) instead of a huge, flashy backpack. That way, you'll be able to put your bag at your feet or on your lap during bus trips, you'll be less easily identified as a tourist target and you'll simply have far less hassle carrying the thing around. If you must take a backpack, you can usually get small padlocks for them, although for greater security you can put your pack into a coffee or flour sack (*costal*) and put that into a net (*red*). It might look a little outlandish but it's the way the locals transport goods and keeps it clean and dry too – sacks and nets are sold in any market. Once on the bus it's best to keep at least your small bag on your lap. If you do put it on the inside luggage rack keep it in sight and tie it (or preferably clip it with a carabineer) onto the rack to deter thieves who may try to snatch it and throw it out of the window to an accomplice.

In your **hotel**, make sure the lock on your door works: from the inside as well as out. In many budget hotels the lock will be a small padlock on the outside, and it's a good idea to buy your own (*candado* – readily available on street stalls) so you're the only one with keys. Many hotels will have a safe or secure area for valuables. It's up to you whether you use this; most of the time it will be fine, but make sure whatever you do put in is securely and tightly wrapped; a spare, lockable moneybelt is good for this.

You're less likely to be a victim of a mugging or armed robbery, but when it happens there's little you can do about it, so prevention is essential. Avoid obviously dangerous areas – deserted city centres and bus stations late at night – and wherever possible take taxis after dark. One ploy to watch out for is someone who surreptitiously throws an obnoxious liquid over your pack or clothes – a "passerby" kindly offers to clean it up while another member of the gang snatches your bag. Much worse are the frequent **armed robberies** of tourist minibuses and other similar violent crimes in Guatemala; usually the robbers will go through the passengers collecting money and valuables, but occasionally victims are taken away and assaulted, or even raped. For this reason some tour groups in Guatemala are accompanied by an armed guard.

Police

If you have anything stolen, report the incident immediately to the **police** – if there is a tourist police force, try them first – if only to get a copy of the report (*denuncia*) which you'll need for insurance purposes. The police in Central America are poorly paid and you can't expect them to do much more than make out the report – and often you'll have difficulty getting them to do even this. You may have to dictate it to them (and sometimes they'll demand a fee for their services); unless you're fluent, try to take someone along who speaks better Spanish than you do. And if you can, also report the crime to your **embassy** – it helps the consular staff build up a higher-level case for the better protection of tourists.

Obviously you want to avoid any **trouble** with the police whatsoever. Practically every capital city has foreigners incarcerated for drug offences who'd never do it again if they knew what the punishment was like. **Drugs** of all kinds are readily available but if you indulge be very discreet: the pusher may have a sideline reporting clients to the police (he may also try and convince you that the police turn a blind eye to smoking dope; while this may be true for him, it certainly won't be true for you), and catching "international drug smugglers" gives the country concerned brownie points with the DEA. If you are arrested your embassy will probably send someone to visit you, and maybe find an English-speaking lawyer, but they certainly can't get you out of jail.

Guide

Guide

1. Belize 47–132
2. Guatemala 133–282
3. El Salvador 283–366
4. Honduras 367–474
5. Nicaragua 475–570
6. Costa Rica 571–726
7. Panama 727–834

1

Belize

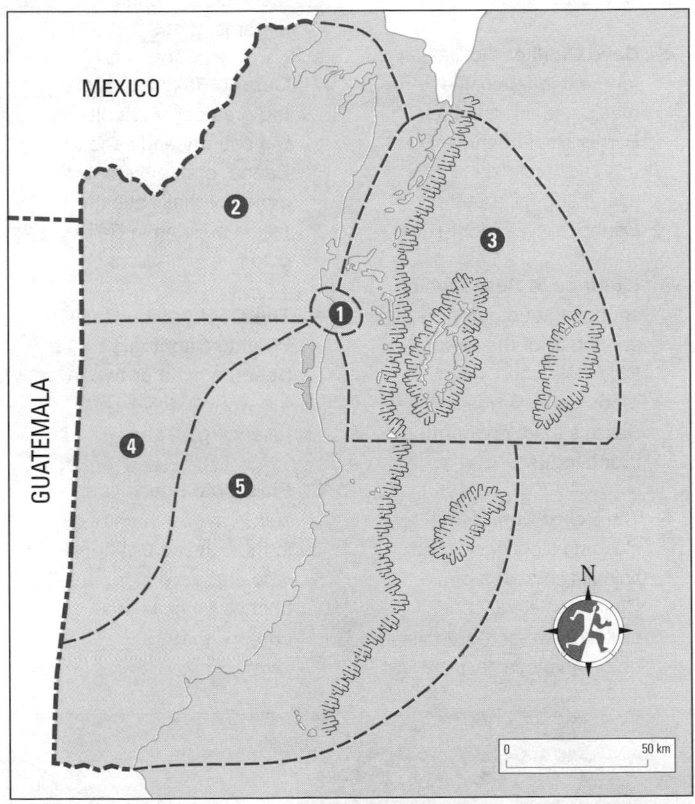

Highlights 48
Introduction and Basics 49
1.1 Belize City 66
1.2 Corozal, Orange Walk and the north 77
1.3 The northern cayes and atolls 87
1.4 Cayo and the west 99
1.5 The south 114
Travel details 131

Belize Highlights

* **Museum of Belize** Marvel at the astonishing quality of Maya treasures on display in this museum, housed in a former colonial prison in Belize City. **p.71**

* **Caye Caulker** Go barefoot, eat inexpensive meals and snorkel the Barrier Reef offshore; this laid-back island has everything for a perfect Caribbean vacation. **p.94**

* **Lighthouse Reef** Dive or snorkel the unique splendour of the Great Blue Hole, then visit Half Moon Caye, arguably Belize's most enchanting island. **p.98**

* **The Belize Zoo** Enjoy close-up sightings of the animals and birds of Central America, especially the awesome power of the harpy eagle. **p.99**

* **Mountain Pine Ridge Forest Reserve** Escape the humidity of the jungle to enjoy the cooler air of the pine forest and take a dip in one of many clear mountain streams. **p.108**

* **Caracol** Take a trip to the greatest Maya city in the country and ascend Caana, a 1200-year-old complex that's still the tallest building in Belize. **p.111**

* **The Cockscomb Basin Wildlife Sanctuary** Spend a night or two in the world's only jaguar reserve. **p.121**

* **Placencia** Rouse yourself from your hammock in this relaxed fishing village and stroll along the best beaches in the country. **p.123**

Introduction and Basics

Wedged into the northeastern corner of Central America between Mexico's Yucatán peninsula and the Petén forests of Guatemala, **Belize** offers some of the most breathtaking scenery anywhere in the Caribbean. The country actually consists of marginally more sea than land, with the dazzling turquoise shallows and cobalt depths of the longest **barrier reef** in the Americas just offshore. Here, beneath the surface, a brilliant, technicolour world of fish and corals awaits divers and snorkellers. Scattered along the reef, a chain of islands – known as **cayes** – protect the mainland from the ocean swell and offer more than a hint of tropical paradise. Beyond the reef lie the real jewels in Belize's natural crown – three of only four **coral atolls** in the Caribbean.

Belizeans recognize the importance of conservation and their country boasts a higher proportion of protected land (over 45 percent) than any other. This has allowed the **densely forested interior** to remain relatively untouched, home to abundant natural attractions, including the highest waterfall in Central America and the world's only **jaguar reserve**. Rich tropical forests support a tremendous range of wildlife, including howler and spider monkeys, tapirs and pumas, jabiru storks and scarlet macaws; spend any time inland and you're sure to see the national bird, the very visible keel-billed toucan.

Despite being the only Central American country without a volcano, Belize does have some rugged uplands in the south-central region, where the **Maya Mountains** rise to over 1100m. The country's main rivers rise here, flowing north or east to the Caribbean, forming along the way some of the largest **cave systems** in the Americas, few of which have been fully explored. These caves often bear traces of the **Maya civilization** that dominated the area from around 2000 BC until the arrival of the Spanish. The most obvious remains of this fascinating culture are the remains of dozens of **ancient cities** rising out of the rainforest.

Officially **English-speaking**, and only gaining full independence from Britain in 1981, Belize is as much a Caribbean nation as a Latin one, but one with plenty of distinctively Central American features, above all a blend of cultures and races that includes Maya, mestizo, African and European. Spanish is at least as widely spoken as English, but the rich, lilting **Creole** is the spoken language understood and used by almost every Belizean, whatever their first tongue. You'll hear this everywhere – and though based on English, it's less comprehensible to outsiders than you might expect.

With far less of a language barrier to overcome than elsewhere in the region, uncrowded Belize is the ideal first stop on a tour of the isthmus. And, although it's the second-smallest country in Central America (slightly larger than El Salvador), the wealth of national parks and reserves, the numerous small hotels and restaurants, together with plenty of reliable public transport make Belize an ideal place to travel independently, giving visitors plenty of scope to explore little-visited Caribbean islands as well as the heartland of the ancient Maya.

Where to go

Almost every visitor will have to spend at least some time in **Belize City** even if only passing through, as it's the hub of the country's transport system. First-time visitors may find the crowded streets and polluted river alarming, but it's possible to spend many pleasant hours in this former outpost of the British Empire, visiting the splendid new museums and galleries. In contrast, Belize's capital, **Belmopan**, is primarily an administrative centre with little to offer visitors.

Northern Belize is relatively flat and often swampy, with a large proportion of agricultural land, though as everywhere in Belize there are Maya ruins and nature reserves.

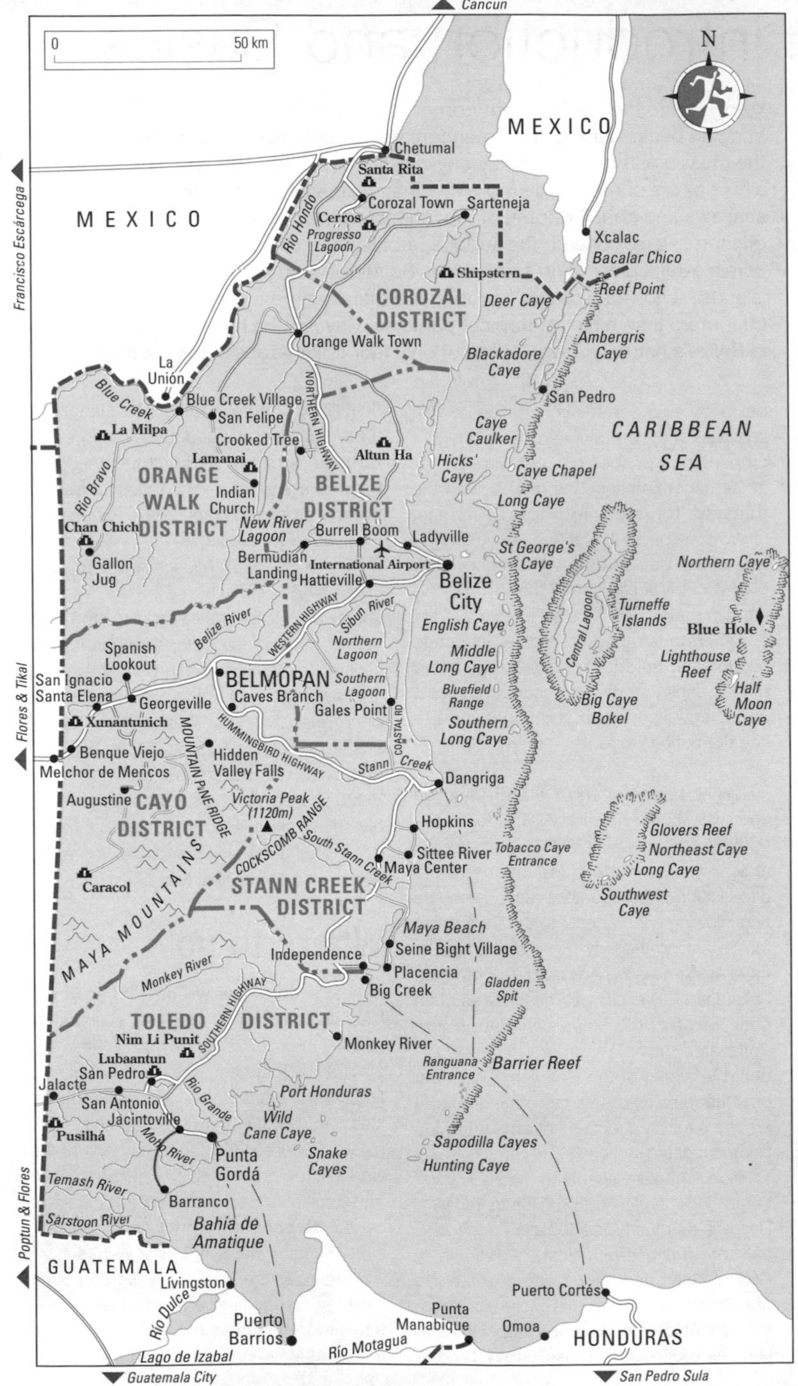

Cancun
0
50 km
N
MEXICO
MEXICO
Francisco Escárcega
Chetumal
Santa Rita
Corozal Town
Sarteneja
Rio Hondo
Cerros
Progresso Lagoon
Xcalac
Bacalar Chico
Shipstern
Reef Point
COROZAL DISTRICT
Deer Caye
Orange Walk Town
Ambergris Caye
Blackadore Caye
La Unión
San Pedro
Blue Creek
Blue Creek Village
San Felipe
La Milpa
NORTHERN HIGHWAY
CARIBBEAN SEA
Crooked Tree
Caye Caulker
Altun Ha
Lamanai
Hicks' Caye
Caye Chapel
ORANGE WALK DISTRICT
Indian Church
BELIZE DISTRICT
Rio Bravo
Long Caye
Chan Chich
New River Lagoon
Burrell Boom
Ladyville
St George's Caye
Northern Caye
Gallon Jug
Bermudian Landing
International Airport
Hattieville
Belize City
Central Lagoon
Turneffe Islands
Belize River
WESTERN HIGHWAY
Sibun River
English Caye
Blue Hole
Spanish Lookout
Northern Lagoon
Middle Long Caye
Lighthouse Reef
San Ignacio
Santa Elena
BELMOPAN
Caves Branch
Southern Lagoon
Bluefield Range
Half Moon Caye
Flores & Tikal
Georgeville
Gales Point
Big Caye Bokel
Xunantunich
HUMMINGBIRD HIGHWAY
COASTAL RD
Southern Long Caye
Benque Viejo
Hidden Valley Falls
MOUNTAIN PINE RIDGE
Melchor de Mencos
Stann Creek
Dangriga
Augustine
CAYO DISTRICT
Victoria Peak (1120m)
COCKSCOMB RANGE
Hopkins
Glovers Reef
South Stann Creek
Sittee River
Tobacco Caye Entrance
Northeast Caye
Maya Center
Long Caye
Caracol
MAYA MOUNTAINS
STANN CREEK DISTRICT
Southwest Caye
Maya Beach
Seine Bight Village
Independence
Placencia
Monkey River
Gladden Spit
Big Creek
SOUTHERN HIGHWAY
TOLEDO DISTRICT
Nim Li Punit
Monkey River
Lubaantun
San Pedro
Ranguana Entrance
Barrier Reef
Jalacte
San Antonio
Rio Grande
Port Honduras
Jacintoville
Wild Cane Caye
Pusilhá
Moho River
Punta Gordá
Snake Cayes
Sapodilla Cayes
Hunting Caye
Temash River
Poptun & Flores
Barranco
Sarstoon River
Bahía de Amatique
GUATEMALA
Lívingston
Puerto Cortés
Río Dulce
Punta Manabique
Omoa
Puerto Barrios
Río Motagua
HONDURAS
Lago de Izabal
Guatemala City
San Pedro Sula

Lamanai, near Orange Walk, is one of the most impressive Maya sites in the country, and the lagoons here and at **Sarteneja** and **Crooked Tree** offer a superb protected habitat for wildlife. Adjacent to the Guatemalan border is the vast **Rio Bravo Conservation Area**.

The largest of the cayes, **Ambergris Caye**, draws more than half of all tourists to Belize, their main destination being the resort town of **San Pedro**. To the south, **Caye Caulker** is the most popular of the islands amongst independent travellers. Many of the less-developed cayes are becoming easier to reach, and organized trips are readily available to the atolls of **Lighthouse Reef** and **Glover's Reef**.

In the west, the **Cayo District** has everything for the ecotourist: Maya ruins and rainforest, rivers and caves, with excellent accommodation in every price range in the main town of **San Ignacio**. **Caracol**, the largest Maya site in Belize, is now a routine day-trip from San Ignacio, while the magnificent ruin of **Xunantunich** is even easier to reach.

Dangriga, the main town of the south-central region, serves as a jumping-off point for the little-visited central cayes and **Glover's Reef** atoll, as well as for trips to the **Cockscomb Basin Wildlife Sanctuary**. On the coast, the quiet Garífuna village of **Hopkins** sees more visitors every year, while further south the delightful and laid-back **Placencia Peninsula** has some of the country's best **beaches**. Most visitors to **Punta Gorda**, the main town in the far south of Belize, are on their way to or from Puerto Barrios in Guatemala. If you venture inland, however, you'll come across the **villages** of the Mopan and Kekchí Maya, set in some of the most stunning countryside in Belize and surrounded by the only true **rainforest** in the country, dotted with caves, rivers and ruins.

When to go

Belize lies in a **subtropical** latitude, so the weather is generally warm by European standards. Local climates are largely determined by **altitude**, with the Maya Mountains pleasantly cool and the lowland jungles usually steamy and humid, no matter what the time of year. The coast and offshore cayes can be sweltering, but most of the time the heat is tempered by cooling ocean breezes. Humidity is most marked in the **rainy season** – officially from May to November – when mornings are generally clear and afternoons often drenched by downpours. The worst of the rain falls in September to November, when in the more remote southern parts of the country roads can be flooded and journeys delayed, though the rains can continue through to January, when **cold fronts** push down from the north, occasionally lowering temperatures to around 10°C. The **best** time of year to visit is from December to March, when the vegetation is lush and the skies are generally clear. This coincides with the peak tourist season, though many people also visit during the summer. Late March to May, before the onset of the first rains, can be stiflingly hot.

Perhaps the most serious weather threat is from **hurricanes**, which occasionally sweep through the Caribbean in the late summer and autumn. If you're on the coast or the cayes, you'll hear about it long before the storm hits. Wind speeds can exceed 120km per hour, but rest assured that the country has an efficient warning system and a network of shelters. The best advice, once you hear a hurricane is forming, is to **head inland** to Cayo District immediately.

Getting around

Despite having just four main all-weather highways connecting the main towns, Belize is well served by **public transport**. The highways, and even most unpaved side roads, are generally kept in good repair and are usually passable except in the very worst rainstorms. Anywhere you can't get to by bus, you can generally reach by water-taxi or light aircraft, which can be less expensive than you might expect.

Buses

Regular **bus services** connect all towns in Belize (and cross the border to Chetumal in Mexico), but for villages off the main highways you'll have to rely on slower local

Land and sea crossings to and from Belize

Belize has only two **land routes** to the adjacent countries: the northern border crossing over the Rio Hondo to Mexico (see p.77) and the western border crossing to Melchor in Guatemala (see p.112); both have very frequent services during daylight hours.

The main **sea crossing** is from Punta Gorda to Puerto Barrios or Lívingston in Guatemala (see p.127), with at least two daily boats in either direction. In addition there are weekly boats to and from Dangriga (see p.119) and Placencia (see p.123) to Puerto Cortés in Honduras.

services, often with just one bus a day and running Monday to Saturday only. The majority of buses are **second-class**, although all the main towns are served by faster and more comfortable **express buses** which stop only in the terminals; regular buses will pick up and drop off anywhere along the roadside. The most frequent services operate along the Western Highway, with buses every 30 minutes to San Ignacio and Benque Viejo (near the Guatemalan border) and the Northern Highway, with hourly buses to Orange Walk, Corozal and Chetumal. The Hummingbird and Southern highways, to Dangriga, Placencia and Punta Gorda, are not quite so well provided for, though there are at least a dozen daily buses to Dangriga, two to Placencia and seven to Punta Gorda. On all of these routes tickets can be bought in advance from the offices in Belize City; pay the conductor if you get on along the route. **Fares** are very reasonable (roughly US$4 from Belize City to San Ignacio, US$6 to Chetumal and US$12 to Punta Gorda).

Taxis

All **taxis** in Belize are licensed and easily identifiable by their green licence plates. They operate from special ranks in the centre of all mainland towns and, particularly in Belize City, drivers will call out to anyone they suspect is a foreigner. There are no meters, so you'll need to establish the fare in advance, though within the towns a US$3 **fixed rate** should apply.

Driving and hitching

Driving in Belize is subject to the same limitations as bus travel. The Northern, Western, Hummingbird and Southern highways offer easy motoring and smooth roads (though watch out for frequent **speed bumps**), but off these main roads the surface can be rough at times. If you want to head off the beaten track you'll need high clearance and 4WD. **Unleaded gas/petrol** is easily available, but expensive at US$3.85 per gallon for premium. **Insurance** (around US$7–10 a day for your own car) is available from an agent just inside either of the land border crossings or in Belize City. Under Belize's **seatbelt law** you'll be fined US$12.50 for not belting up. Distances are measured in miles.

All the main **car rental companies** offer cars, Jeeps and 4WDs for between US$65 and US$125 a day, plus up to US$15 per day for insurance. You'll usually have to be over 25 and will need to leave either a credit card, travellers' cheques or a large cash deposit. Many outfits do not offer comprehensive insurance, so the renter is likely to be held liable for any damage to the vehicle, however caused. Note that some companies consider driving a car on minor dirt roads (especially in the south) to be taking the vehicle "off-road", which may invalidate your insurance. Check carefully before signing anything.

In the more remote parts of Belize the bus service will probably only operate once a day, if at all, and unless you have your own transport, **hitching** is the only option. The main drawback is the shortage of traffic, but if cars or, more likely, pick-up trucks, do pass they'll usually offer you a lift, though you may be expected to offer the driver some money.

Cycling

Seeing Belize from a **bike** is fairly straightforward and you'll find repair shops in all the towns. Bikes are increasingly available for

rent, especially in San Ignacio and Placencia. Belizean buses don't have the roof racks that are such a familiar sight in Guatemala; if there's room, the driver *might* let you take your bike onto the bus.

Boats

Most **boats** you're likely to use will be fast **skiffs**, usually open boats with two powerful outboard motors (though some are covered, it's advisable to carry a light raincoat just in case). Carrying about 30 passengers, skiffs run from Belize City and mainland destinations out to the **cayes**, and also cover **international routes** from Punta Gorda to Puerto Barrios and Lívingston in Guatemala and from Dangriga and Placencia to Puerto Cortés in Honduras – times and destinations are covered in the text. Services are fast, reliable and safe; all registered boats should carry lifejackets and most also carry marine radios. It's worth buying your ticket the day before for early departures from the cayes and on international services if you want to be sure of a place, though there's usually plenty of room.

Planes

Maya Island Air (⊕223-1140, ⓦwww.mayaislandair.com) and Tropic Air (⊕224-5671, ⓦwww.tropicair.com) offer a **scheduled service** from Belize International Airport and Belize City's municipal airport to all the country's main towns and out to San Pedro and Caye Caulker; there are also several **charter airlines**. A flight from Belize City to San Pedro or Caye Caulker costs around US$26; to Punta Gorda, US$77. The domestic airlines also have several daily flights to **Flores** in Guatemala (for Tikal; US$88) and there are daily departures to regional destinations such as **San Salvador** and **San Pedro Sula** and **Roatán** in the Bay Islands, Honduras. There are currently no flights between Belize and Mexico.

Costs, money and banks

Belize has a generally well-deserved reputation as being one of the more **expensive** countries in Central America, and even on a tight budget you'll spend at least forty percent more than in, say, Guatemala. Perhaps as compensation for the general cost of living you can at least travel in the sure knowledge that you'll be paying the same fares as the locals, and you'll never be subjected to mysterious (and sometimes illegal) border crossing charges; the existing ones are already the highest in the region.

Currency, exchange and banks

The national currency is the **Belize dollar**, which is conveniently fixed at two to one with the US dollar (**US$1=Bz$2**); US dollars are also widely accepted (sometimes preferred), either in cash or travellers' cheques. This apparently simple **dual-currency system** can be problematic: it's all too easy to assume the price of your hotel room or trip, for example, is in Belize dollars, only to find payment is demanded in the same number of US dollars – a common cause of misunderstanding and aggravation. All Belizean notes (divided into 100 cents) and coins carry the British imperial legacy in the form of a portrait of Queen Elizabeth, while quarters are called "shillings".

You'll find at least one **bank** (generally open Mon–Thurs 8am–2.30pm, Fri 8am–4pm) in every town, and also in the main seaside destinations of San Pedro, Caye Caulker and Placencia. Although the exchange rate is fixed, banks in Belize will give slightly less than Bz$2 for US$1 for both cash and travellers' cheques; on the other hand, **moneychangers** at the borders will often give slightly higher rates, especially for larger sums; anywhere else beware of rip-offs. You can usually buy US dollars from licensed *casas de cambio*, located in most towns or from banks, though you'll often have to show an onward ticket – difficult if you're leaving by bus and don't already have a ticket. Technically, buying US dollars other than from a licensed moneychanger or *casa de cambio* is illegal but there's usually a shop or restaurant where the locals go; just ask discreetly.

Credit and debit cards are widely used in Belize, with Visa being the best option, and are increasingly accepted even in smaller hotels and restaurants, though you might pay an extra five or even seven percent for the privilege – check before you pay. Although any bank can give you a Visa/MasterCard **cash advance** over the counter, First Caribbean Bank (formerly Barclays) and the Belize Bank are the only banks with **ATMs** accepting foreign-issued cards.

Costs

Even travelling as a couple it's difficult to survive on less than US$18/£10 a day per person – though it can be done – but US$25–30/£15 a day each will cover a decent budget hotel, meals and drinks, bus travel, a short taxi ride and an occasional tour, for example. For a **simple, shared-bath room** you can expect to pay at least US$15/£9 for a double, whereas a night in an upmarket lodge will set you back anything from US$65/£35 to US$175/£95 (though it's always worth asking for a discount out of season). Food and drink are fairly pricey too, with an average dinner costing around US$6–8/£5.

Bus travel is much more reasonable, with the longest journey in the country, from Belize City to Punta Gorda, costing US$12/£7. A **taxi** ride within a town costs US$3/£2 for one or two people; for more passengers and longer rides agree a price beforehand.

Hotel rooms are subject to a seven percent **tax**, usually added separately (and many of the more expensive places will also impose a **service charge** of around ten percent). There's also a nine percent **sales tax**, which applies to most goods and services (including meals in restaurants, though not to drinks). It doesn't apply to hotel rooms, though some package operators may slap it on anyway; check carefully to see what you're paying.

Leaving Belize you must pay a US$15 **exit tax**, plus the **PACT conservation fee** of US$3.75, at all departure points; flying out of the International Airport will add a further US$15 to these taxes.

Information

The country's official source of tourist information is the **Belize Tourism Board** (BTB; in North America ⓣ1-800/624-0686, ⓦwww.travelbelize.org), with an information booth at the airport and an office in Belize City. The best places to search for links to tourism-related **websites** are ⓦwww.belize.net and ⓦwww.belizenet.com. The travel advice in ⓦwww.belizefirst.com, the best online magazine dedicated to the country, is definitely worth checking out before you go, featuring accurate reviews and articles about hotels, restaurants and destinations.

The **Belize Tourism Industry Association** (BTIA; ⓦwww.btia.org) also has numerous offices and representatives around the country and, although they are really an industry organization, staff can help with information and will deal with complaints about hotel standards or service. Perhaps more usefully, most of the **hotels** and all the **travel agents** mentioned in this guide can recommend local guides and attractions.

For the latest information on the growing number of reserves, national parks and associated visitor centres, call or visit the **Belize Audubon Society** in Belize City (ⓦwww.belizeaudubon.org), which administers many of the country's protected areas. For in-depth information on social, cultural, political and economic matters concerning Belize, the place to look is the **SPEAR** website (Society for the Promotion of Education and Research) at ⓦwww.spearbelize.org.

Accommodation

Most Belizean **accommodation** is expensive by Central American standards, though fortunately there are budget hotels in all towns, and the most popular tourist destinations, like Caye Caulker, San Ignacio and Placencia, have a great deal of choice.

A **simple double** room in Belize usually costs around US$15 (US$9 single) for facilities only a little better than a Guatemalan budget hotel; for the luxury of a private bathroom expect to pay at least US$19. If you have more money to spend you could try one of the delightful, often family-run **lodges**, most of which are set in a spectacular natural location, with rooms in the house or in private cabañas. Some of these offer

bed and breakfast, an increasingly popular style of accommodation.

Finding a room is no problem in Belizean towns: even in Belize City most options are within ten minutes' walk of the main points of arrival. On the whole there's always accommodation available, though during the **peak season**, from December to April (and especially at Christmas and Easter when booking ahead is advisable), you may have to look a little longer and prices in resort areas may rise even higher; booking by phone or email is easy.

See p.36 for an explanation of the accommodation price codes.

Camping

Although there are few proper **campsites** in Belize, it's easy to find somewhere to pitch a tent or sling a hammock in rural areas and coastal villages like Placencia and Hopkins. Camping is not really possible (or recommended) on Caye Caulker or in San Pedro. You can also camp in the area around San Ignacio and in the Mountain Pine Ridge, where several lodges have campsites, some very economical, some surprisingly expensive. Down south a tent will enable you to spend some time wandering inland, around the Maya villages and ancient sites.

Food and drink

Belizean food is a distinctive mix of Latin America and the Caribbean, with Creole "rice and beans" dominating the scene in local restaurants, but with plenty of other important influences. Central American *empanadas* are as common as pizza, chow mein and hamburgers. In most places Belizean food is a real treat, with particularly good seafood, but in a few it's a neglected art.

Where to eat

The quality of the food in Belize rarely bears much relation to the appearance of the restaurant it's served in, whether you're eating in a bar, a café or a smart-looking restaurant. Out on the islands and in small seashore villages some restaurants are little more than thatched shelters, with open sides and sand floors, while in other places you'll find upmarket hotels with polished floors, tablecloths and napkins. Most places, however, are somewhere between the two, serving up good food without too much concern for presentation. You'll soon become accustomed to the fact that **lunch hour** (noon–1pm) is observed with almost religious devotion – abandon any hope of getting anything else done and tuck in with the locals. Belize City and the main tourist destinations have plenty of choice, with several surprisingly elegant restaurants and with fast-food and snack bars sprouting on street corners.

Travelling, you'll find that food sometimes comes to you, as street traders offer up *tamales*, *empanadas*, hamburgers (literally a slice of canned ham served in a bun) and fruit to waiting bus passengers, although the practice isn't nearly as common as elsewhere in Central America.

What to eat

The basis of any Creole main meal is **rice and beans**, and this features heavily in smaller restaurants. The white rice and red beans are cooked together in coconut oil and flavoured with *recado* (a mild ground red spice) – often with a chunk of salted pork thrown in for extra taste – and usually served with stewed chicken or beef, or fried fish. If you like your flavours full on, there's always a bottle of hot sauce on the table for extra spice. Vegetables are scarce in Creole food but there's often a side dish of potato salad and fried plantains, and sometimes flour tortillas (the maize tortillas so common in Guatemala are rarely served here).

Seafood is almost always excellent. **Red snapper** or **grouper** is invariably fantastic, and you might also try a **barracuda** steak, **conch fritters** or a plate of fresh (though usually farmed) **shrimp**. In San Pedro, Caye Caulker, San Ignacio and Placencia the food can be exceptional, and the only concern is that you might get bored with **lobster**, which is served in an amazing range of dishes: pasta with lobster sauce, lobster and scrambled eggs, lobster chow mein or even lobster curry. The **closed season** for lobster (when it will not be served) is from mid-February to mid-June. **Turtle** is still on the menu in a few places, in theory only during the short open season, but note that this is a threatened species, and by even tasting it – or any other wild animal – you'll be contributing to its extinction.

There are few specifically **vegetarian** restaurants, but in the main tourist resorts many places offer a couple of vegetarian dishes. Otherwise, you're likely to be offered chicken or ham if you say you don't eat meat. The fruit is good and there are usually plenty of locally produced vegetables, though they're rarely served in restaurants. Your best bet for a vegetarian meal outside the main tourist areas may well be one of Belize's scores of **Chinese** restaurants. Other Belizean ethnic minorities have entered the restaurant trade: several places serve **Garífuna** dishes, and there are **Indian** restaurants in Belize City and San Ignacio (where there's also a **Sri Lankan** restaurant), serving superb curries.

Drinks

The most basic **drinks** to accompany food are water, beer and the usual soft drinks. Belikin, Belize's main **beer**, comes in several varieties: regular, a lager-type bottled and draught beer; bottled **stout** (a rich, dark beer); and Lighthouse and Premium, more expensive bottled beers and often all you'll be able to get in upmarket hotels and restaurants. The Belikin brewery also produces bottled **Guinness**. Cashew-nut and berry **wines**, rich and full-bodied, are bottled and sold in some villages, and you can also get hold of imported and locally bottled wine, though it's far from cheap. Local **rum**, in both dark and clear varieties, is the best deal in Belizean alcohol. The locally produced gin, brandy and vodka are poor imitations – cheap and fairly nasty. It's worth noting that the **legal age for drinking** alcohol in Belize is 18.

Non-alcoholic alternatives include the predictable array of oversweet soft drinks. Despite the number of citrus plantations, **fruit juices** are rarely available, though you can usually get orange juice. *Licuados*, the thirst-quenching blended fruit drinks, ubiquitous throughout Mexico and the rest of Central America, are only rarely served in Belize. **Tap water**, in the towns at least, is safe but highly chlorinated, and many villages (though not Caye Caulker) now have a potable water system. Pure **rainwater** is usually available in the countryside and on the cayes. Filtered **bottled water** and mineral water are sold everywhere.

Tea, due to the British influence, is a popular hot drink, and **coffee**, except in the best establishments, will almost certainly be instant. One last drink that deserves a mention is **seaweed**, a strange blend of seaweed, milk, cinnamon, sugar and cream. If you see someone selling this on a street corner, give it a try.

Opening hours, holidays and festivals

It's difficult to be specific about **opening hours** in Belize but in general most **shops** are open 8am–noon and 1–8pm. The **lunch hour** – noon to 1pm – is almost universally observed and it's hopeless trying to get anything done then. Some shops and businesses work a half-day on Saturday, and everything is liable to close early on Friday. **Banks** (generally Mon–Thurs 8am–2.30pm, Fri 8am–4.30pm) and government offices are only open Monday to Friday. Watch out for Sundays, when everybody takes it easy; shops, and sometimes restaurants, are closed, and fewer bus services and internal flights operate. Archeological sites, however, are open every day.

The main **public holidays**, when virtually everything will be closed, are listed in the box opposite, though note that in most cases the actual holiday is observed on the following Monday, to give a longer weekend.

You'll generally find plenty of entertainment at any time, as Belizeans are great party people, and **music** and **dance** are crucial to the country's culture. All national celebrations – above all the **Carnival** and **Independence Day**, both in September, and marked by parades and open-air dances – are the excuse for a fantastic, day-long party, with the rhythms of the Caribbean dominating the proceedings and visitors will be welcome to dance and drink

Public holidays

January 1 New Year's Day
March 9 Baron Bliss Day
Good Friday
Holy Saturday
Easter Monday
May 1 Labour Day
May 24 Commonwealth Day
September 10 St George's Caye Day/National Day
September 21 Independence Day
October 12 Columbus Day (Pan America Day)
November 19 Garífuna Settlement Day
December 25 & 26 Christmas

with the locals. Belize also has a fantastically talented and energetic **National Dance Company**, and a live performance is an unforgettable highlight.

Traditional dance is still practised by two ethnic groups in Belize: the Maya and the Garífuna, but it's generally only in the outlying areas, such as around San Ignacio and Corozal, and in the Maya villages of the south, that you'll find traditional village fiestas. The best time to see **Garífuna drumming** and dancing is November 19, Garífuna Settlement Day, in either Dangriga or Hopkins.

Communications

Belizean postal services are perhaps the most efficient (and most expensive) in Central America. **Sending letters**, cards and parcels home is straightforward: a normal airmail letter takes around four days to reach the US, under eight days to Europe, and up to two weeks to Australia.

Belize has a modern (albeit expensive) phone system with payphones found throughout the country. **Payphones** can only be used with **phonecards** (which can also be used on any touch-tone phone), widely available from BTL (Belize Telecommunications Limited) offices, hotels, shops and gas stations. There are **no area codes** in Belize; so you need to dial all seven digits. Some rural areas are served by **community telephones** (nowadays often fixed cellular phones), typically located in a private house, and used with a phonecard. Calling home collect is easy using the Home Country Direct service, available at BTL offices, most payphones and larger hotels. Simply dial the access code (printed on some payphones and in the phone book) to connect with an operator in your home country. Calling Belize from abroad, the **international country code** is ⓣ501.

Belizeans are also avid users of **email** and the **Internet**, and Web access is readily available in all the main towns and for guests at many hotels. **Fax** numbers are listed in the pink pages in the telephone directory and BTL offices will have a public fax you can use.

The media

Although Belize's English-language media can make a welcome break in a world of Spanish, this doesn't necessarily mean that it's easy to keep in touch with what's happening in the rest of the world. Local news takes pride of place in the **national newspapers** (published weekly on Friday) and international stories receive very little attention. In Belize City, San Pedro and some other main towns you should be able to get hold of **foreign publications**, including *The Miami Herald*, *Time* and *Newsweek*.

There are two national **television** stations, channels 5 and 7, which broadcast mainly imported American shows, with a few local news programmes. Cable TV, however, is the nation's preferred viewing medium, giving saturation coverage of American soaps, CNN and sports. Love FM has the widest coverage of any of the country's **radio stations**, offering easy listening, news and current affairs, while More FM plays youth-oriented music. Another major station is KREM FM with the emphasis on talk, reggae and punta rock. Each district town also has a local radio station and there's a British forces radio station, BFBS.

Shops and markets

Compared to its neighbours, Belize has less to offer in terms of traditional **crafts** or

Suspect souvenirs

Some souvenirs you'll see in Belize are the result of reef and wildlife destruction, so think twice before you buy – they include black coral, often made into jewellery, turtle shells, which look far better on their rightful owners, and indeed marine curios of any kind. Many of the animal and plant souvenirs you may be offered are **illegal** in Belize and may also be listed in Appendix 1 to CITES (the Convention on International Trade in Endangered Species; ⓦwww.cites.org), so you won't be allowed to bring them into the US, Canada or Europe, and will face a fine – or worse – for even trying. Just as illegal are **archeological artefacts**; all such items belong to Belize and theft or trade in them is strictly prohibited; anyone attempting to smuggle such items out of the country could end up in jail in Belize or at home.

neighbourhood **markets**. The latter are purely food markets, but in several places you'll come across some impressive local crafts. **Wood and slate carvers** are often to be found at the Maya sites, and their work, especially the reproductions of glyphs and stelae on slate, is high quality; **ceramics** are less good, but improving. In the Maya villages in southern Belize you'll come across some attractive **embroidery**, though it has to be said that the quality of both the cloth and the work is better in Guatemala. Garífuna and Creole villages produce good basketware and superb **drums**; Dangriga, Hopkins and Gales Point are the places to visit for these.

The excellent **National Handicrafts Center** in Belize City (see p.71) is the best place to buy souvenirs if time is short, with a wide range of genuine Belizean crafts, including paintings, prints and music recordings as well as the items mentioned above, and the craftspeople are paid fair prices for their work. There are often exhibitions by Belizean artists here too, but the best place for contemporary **Belizean art** is The Image Factory in Belize City (see p.71). For superb **videos** of Belizean wildlife, culture or history, have a look at the series produced by Great Belize Productions, which can be purchased from gift shops. Belize's wildly colourful **stamps**, often featuring the animals and plants of the country, are relatively cheap and certainly easy to post home. One tasty souvenir everyone likes to take home is a bottle (or three) of **Marie Sharp's Pepper Sauce**, made from Belizean *habañeros* in various strengths, ranging from "mild" to "fiery hot".

For everyday necessities you'll find some kind of shop in every village in Belize, however small, and most of the things you'd find at home are available in Belize, though you may have to hunt around for them. Luxury items, such as electrical goods and cameras, tend to be very expensive, as do other imported goods. **Camera film** is a little more expensive than at home, but easy to get hold of.

Safety and the police

Belize has a bad reputation for **crime**, but while it's true that Belize City has a relatively high crime rate, it certainly doesn't live up to some of the stories you might hear, while crime against tourists in the country as a whole is very low, especially in comparison to other Central American countries. **Violent crime** against tourists is very rare, even in Belize City.

In **Belize City**, theft is now fairly common, the majority of cases involving **break-ins** at hotels: bear this in mind when you're searching for a room. Out and about there's always a slight danger of **pickpockets**, but certainly no greater than in the surrounding countries, and with a bit of common sense you've nothing to fear. The atmosphere on the streets is much less intimidating since the introduction of the **tourism police**, but nevertheless it pays to be aware of the dangers. There's also a chance of something more serious happening, such as a **mugging**. During the daytime there's little to worry about. However, at night you should stick to the main streets and avoid going out alone, especially if you're a woman. If you arrive in Belize City at night, take a taxi to a hotel, as the bus stations are in a fairly derelict part of town – though not bad enough to worry about for daylight arrivals. Having said all this, muggings are really not that common, and your greatest fear is likely to be the mood of intimidation on the streets, which makes Belize City feel far more dangerous than it actually is. If you do need to **report a crime**, your first stop should be the tourism police, where they exist – crime against tourists is taken very seriously in Belize. The **police emergency number** in Belize is ⓣ90; to contact the tourism police in Belize City call ⓣ227-2222.

Verbal abuse is not uncommon, especially in Belize City, where there are always plenty of people hanging out on the streets, commenting on all that passes by. At first it can all seem very threatening, but if you take the time to stop and talk, you'll find the vast majority of these people simply want to know where you're from, and where you're heading – and perhaps try to bum a dollar or two. Once you realize that they mean no harm the whole experience of Belize City will be infinitely more enjoyable. Obviously, the situation can be a little more serious for women, and the abuse can be more offensive, but once again it's unlikely that anything will come of it, and it's usually possible to talk your way out of a dodgy situation without anyone losing face.

Homosexuality is still illegal in Belize and some recent prosecutions have resulted in convictions and even prison. Although no visitors have been prosecuted (or even warned) it's obviously sensible to be very discreet. And given the legal position, it's no surprise to learn that there's no openly gay community and no exclusively gay bars in Belize.

Drugs

Belize has long been an important link in the chain of supply between the drugs producers in South America and the users in North America, with minor players often being paid in kind, creating a deluge of illegal drugs. Marijuana, cocaine and crack are all readily available in Belize, and whether you like it or not you'll receive regular offers. Never attempt to buy drugs on the street. All such substances are **illegal**, and despite the fact that dope is smoked openly in the streets, the police do arrest people for possession of marijuana and they particularly enjoy catching tourists. If you're caught you'll probably end up spending a couple of days in jail and paying a fine of several hundred US dollars: expect no sympathy from your embassy.

Work and study

There's virtually no chance of finding paid temporary **work** in Belize. Work permits are only on offer to those who can prove their ability to support themselves without endangering the job of a Belizean, or to wealthy investors.

There are, however, a growing number of opportunities for **voluntary work** – mainly as a fee-paying member of a conservation expedition or an archeological group. These options generally mean raising at least a thousand dollars and committing yourself to weeks – or months – of hard work, often in difficult conditions. The rewards are personal satisfaction and (sometimes) a genuine contribution to scientific research. Many **conservation expeditions**, aimed at gap-year students, work on rural infrastructure projects such as schools and health centres, or building trails and visitor centres in nature reserves. In addition, at least twenty academic **archeological groups** undertake research in Belize each year, and many of them take paying students (and non-students); see below for a short list of contacts and have a look at *Archaeology Fieldwork Opportunities Bulletin* (ⓦwww.archaeological.org) or in *Archaeology Magazine* (ⓦwww.archaeology.org).

If you find the initial cost of such programmes a deterrent, you could always **volunteer independently** – many conservation organizations in Belize have volunteer programmes. You'll need to be self-motivated and self-supporting, since no funding will be available, though you'll probably get food and accommodation. Further details are given below.

Voluntary work and study contacts

The website ⓦ**www.gapyear.com** has a vast amount of information on volunteering, including organizations dealing with Belize, plus a huge, invaluable database on travel and living abroad. In addition, the comprehensive range of books and information published by *Vacation Work* (@www.vacationwork.co.uk) is well worth looking at – titles include *Directory of Summer Jobs Abroad*, *Taking a Gap Year* and *Work Your Way Around the World*; most are updated annually and include work and volunteer opportunities in Central America. The Council on International Educational Exchange (@www.ciee.org) also arranges and administers volunteer and study programmes and has information on Belize.

In Belize

Cornerstone Foundation 90 Burns Ave, San Ignacio, Cayo District, Belize ①501/824-2373, @www.peacecorner.org/cornerstone.htm. Belize-based NGO offering placements in environmental and youth education and HIV/AIDS outreach. A three-month stay (which can be extended) costs around US$1000, including accommodation.

In USA

Earthwatch ①1-800/776-0188, @www.earthwatch.org; also offices in the UK, Australia and Japan. Earthwatch matches paying volunteers with scientists working on marine conservation projects in Belize. The cost for two weeks is around US$2150/£1295.

Ecologic Development Fund ①617/441-6300, @www.ecologic.org. Internship programmes for volunteers in resource management in partnership with local NGOs.

Peace Corps ①1-800/424-8580, @www.peacecorps.gov. Sends American volunteers to Belize to train teachers in rural areas and to work in environmental education and health-related fields.

Western Belize Regional Cave Project contact Cameron Griffith on ①812/855-1041 or visit @www.indiana.edu/~belize. Cave archeology research in Cayo District. Prior field-school or caving experience preferred and students must be in excellent physical condition.

In UK

Trekforce Expeditions 34 Buckingham Palace Rd, London SW1 0RE ①020/7828 2275, @www.trekforceexpeditions.org.uk. Runs projects in Belize ranging from surveys of remote Maya sites to infrastructure projects in national parks and village communities. Expeditions (starting at £2750) last from two to five months; the longer programmes also involve learning Spanish in Guatemala and teaching in rural schools.

World Challenge Expeditions Black Arrow House, 2 Chandros Rd, London NW10 6NE ①020/8728 7274, @www.world-challenge.co.uk. Send 18–24-year-olds to Belize for three- or six-month placements. Tasks could include teaching in a primary school or working on a conservation project. Around £2000, plus £135 per month for food and accommodation.

History

Belize is the youngest nation in Central America, gaining **full independence** from Britain only in 1981, and its history has been markedly different from the Latin republics in the isthmus since at least the mid-seventeenth century. Although all the Central American countries were colonized by European powers from the early sixteenth century, it was the colonial entanglement with Britain that has given Belize its present cultural, social and political structures.

After crossing the **Bering land bridge** the early peoples of the Americas rapidly spread southwards, developing into the so-called **Clovis** hunter-gatherer culture by 11,000 BC. Worked stone flakes from this era have been found at Richmond Hill, in northern Belize. Gradually the hunters turned to more intensive use of plants, particularly the newly domesticated **maize** and **beans**, settling into primarily agricultural societies in Belize during the **Archaic** or **Proto-Maya** period, lasting from around 7500 BC until later than 2000 BC. Few visible remains from this period can be seen today, however, and it was only during the subsequent **Preclassic** period (1500 BC–300 AD) that the culture that we recognize as **Maya** emerged distinctly.

City-states emerged, with larger and more elaborate buildings. Temples and palaces were built of stone, using the famous Maya corbelled arch, and characteristic stepped pyramids rose above enormous plazas. Ceramics found at **Cuello**, near Orange Walk, dating from around 1000 BC, are amongst the earliest in the Maya lowlands. **Cerros**, at the mouth of the New River, and **Lamanai**, on the New River Lagoon, expanded into great trading centres, probably continuing in this role right through the Classic period into the Postclassic era.

The Classic and Postclassic periods

Whatever the original construction dates of the Maya sites in Belize, most of what you can see today dates from the **Classic period** (300–900 AD), the greatest phase of Maya achievement. Elaborately carved **stelae** bearing dates and emblem-glyphs tell of actual rulers and of historical events, such as battles, marriages, and the dynastic succession. The best example in the country is at **Nim Li Punit**, north of Punta Gorda.

Developments in the Maya area were powerfully influenced by cultures to the north, above all that of **Teotihuacán**, which dominated central Mexico during the early Classic period until its collapse in the seventh century, an event which sent shockwaves throughout Mesoamerica. However, as the new Maya rulers in Belize gradually established dynasties free of Teotihuacán's military or political control, their cities flourished as never before.

The entire Belize River valley was thickly populated during Classic times, with powerful cities such as **El Pilar** and **Xunantunich** in the west controlling this important trade route. Many Maya centres were much larger than contemporary western European cities: **Caracol** had an estimated 150,000 people. Exactly how the various cities related to one another is unclear, but it appears that three or four main centres dominated the Maya region through an uncertain process of alliances. **Calakmul**, in Campeche, Mexico, and **Tikal** in Petén, Guatemala, were the nearest of these "**superstates**" to Belize, but in 562 AD Caracol defeated Tikal, as shown by a Caracol ball-court marker. Detailed carvings on wooden lintels and stone monuments at the site depict elaborately costumed lords trampling on bound captives.

The end of the Classic Maya civilization, when it came, was abrupt. By 750 AD political and social changes began to be felt; alliances and trade links broke down, wars increased and stelae were carved less frequently. Most cities rapidly became depopulated and new construction ceased over much of Belize after about 830 AD. By the end of the Classic period there appears to have been strife and disorder throughout Mesoamerica. But not all Maya cities were deserted: those in northern Belize, in particular, survived and indeed prospered, with Lamanai and other cities in the area remaining occupied throughout the **Postclassic** period (900–1540 AD). In the years leading up to the Spanish Conquest, the Yucatán and northern Belize consisted of over a dozen rival provinces, bound up in a cycle of competition and conflict.

The Conquest

When the conquistadors arrived in Yucatán from the 1530s onwards, Maya towns and provinces were still vigorously independent, as the Spanish found to their cost on several occasions. Northern Belize was part of the wealthy Maya province of **Chactemal** (the name lives on today as Chetumal, in Quintana Roo, Mexico), with its capital probably at **Santa Rita**, near Corozal. Trade, alliances and wars kept Chetumal in contact with surrounding Maya states up to and beyond the Spanish conquest of Aztec Mexico. Further south was the province known to the Maya of Chetumal as Dzuluinicob – "land of foreigners" – whose capital was **Tipu**, located at Negroman, on the Macal River south of San Ignacio. The Maya here controlled the upper Belize River valley and put up strenuous resistance to attempts by the Spanish to subdue and convert them. The struggle was to continue with simmering resentment until 1707, when the population of Tipu was forcibly removed to Lago de Petén Itzá, near Tikal.

The first **Europeans** to set eyes on the mainland of Belize were Spanish sailors in the early 1500s, but they didn't attempt a landing. In 1511 a small group of shipwrecked Spanish sailors managed to reach land on the southern coast of Yucatán: five were immediately sacrificed but the others were taken as slaves. One of them, **Gonzalo Guerrero**, later married the daughter of Nachankan, the chief of Chetumal, and became a crucial military adviser to the Maya in their subsequent resistance to Spanish domination. The archeologist Eric Thompson calls him the first European to make Belize his home.

By 1544 however, **Gaspar Pacheco** had subdued Maya resistance sufficiently to found a town on Lake Bacalar, and a mission was established at Lamanai in 1570. Maya resentment was always present beneath the surface, however, and boiled over into open rebellion in 1638, forcing Spain to abandon the area. The whole region from southern Yucatán to Honduras was never completely pacified by the Spanish, nor were administrative boundaries clearly defined, but it is likely that the Maya of Belize were influenced by the Spanish, even if they were not ruled by them.

The arrival of the British

The failure of the Spanish authorities to clearly delineate the southern boundary of Yucatán subsequently allowed **buccaneers** or pirates (primarily British) preying on the Spanish treasure fleets to find refuge along the coast of Belize. When Spain attempted to take action on various occasions to expel the British there was confusion over which Spanish captain-general maintained jurisdiction in the area. Consequently the pirates were able to flee before the Spanish arrived and could return in the absence of any permanent Spanish outposts.

Treasure wasn't always easy to come by and sometimes pirates would plunder piles of **logwood** which had been cut and were awaiting shipment to Europe. Worth £90–110 a ton, the hard and extremely heavy wood was used in the expanding British textile industry to dye woollens black, red and grey. The various treaties signed between Britain and Spain from the late seventeenth to mid-eighteenth centuries, initially designed to outlaw the buccaneers, eventually allowed the British to establish logwood camps along the rivers in northern Belize, though they were never intended to permit permanent British settlement of a territory which Spain clearly regarded as falling within its imperial domain. Thus the **British settlements** in Belize and the Bay of Honduras periodically came under attack whenever Spain sought to defend its interests. But the attention of the European powers rarely rested upon the humid, insect-ridden swamps where the logwood cutters, who became known as **Baymen**, worked and lived. The British government, while wishing to profit from the trade in logwood, preferred to avoid the question of whether or not the Baymen were British subjects, and for the most part they were left to their own devices.

Spanish attacks on the settlements in Belize occurred throughout the eighteenth century, with the Baymen being driven out on several occasions. Increasingly, though, Britain began to admit a measure of responsibility for the protection of the settlers and occasionally sent troops to aid the Baymen. Decades of Spanish attacks had fostered in the settlers a spirit of defiance and self-reliance, along with the belief that British rule was preferable to Spanish.

The final showdown between the waning Spanish Empire and the Bay settlers (supported this time by a British warship and troops), the **Battle of St George's Caye**, came as a result of the outbreak of war between Britain and Spain in 1796. The governor of Yucatán assembled ships and troops, determined to drive out the British settlers and occupy Belize. But this time the Baymen had time to prepare and voted (by a small margin) to stay and fight. **Lieutenant-Colonel Barrow** was despatched to Belize as Superintendent, to command the settlers in the event of hostilities, and the Baymen, now under martial law, prepared for war, albeit grudgingly. A few companies of troops were sent from Jamaica and **slaves** were released from woodcutting to be armed and trained. The sloop **HMS Merlin** was stationed in the bay, local vessels were armed and gun rafts built in preparation for the attack, which was expected at any time.

The **Spanish fleet**, comprising sixteen heavily armed men-of-war and 12,000 troops, arrived just north of St George's Caye in early September 1798, making several attempts to capture the caye and force a passage to Belize. Each time they were beaten back by the Baymen with their small but highly manoeuvrable fleet, with the Baymen's slaves at least as eager to fight the Spanish as their masters were. During the final attack, on the morning of **September 10**, the Spanish fleet, already weakened by desertions and yellow fever, suffered heavy losses before sailing for Yucatán.

From settlement to British colony

Though a victory was won, the Battle of St George's Caye was not by itself decisive. Nor did it bring any change to the life of the slaves: even though they had fought valiantly alongside the Baymen, their owners expected them to go back to cutting mahogany – and also enabled them to claim that the slaves were willing to fight on behalf of their masters. Emancipation came no earlier than elsewhere in the British Empire. What the battle did show, however, was that the strength of the Spanish Empire was waning, while British power was expanding. Spain never again attempted to gain control of Belize, and the battle created the conditions for the settlement to become an integral part of the British Empire, with Britain gradually assuming a greater role in its government. Government House, built in Belize Town (later City) in 1814, housed the **Superintendent** (always an army officer) until 1862, when Belize became the colony of **British**

Honduras, after which it served as home to the Governor, head of government under British colonial policy.

Towards independence

By 1900 Belize had become an integral, though very minor, colony of the British Empire. Complacency set in amongst the predominantly white property-owners, while the black workers in the forests and on the estates – the descendants of former slaves, known as "creoles" – continued to suffer low wages and restricted freedom of movement. Despite this, Belizeans rushed to defend the "Mother Country" in both **world wars**, but each time the returning soldiers faced humiliation and poverty. In 1919 veterans rioted in Belize City, an event that marked the onset of black consciousness and the beginning of the **independence movement**. Despite this, little changed, and even after World War II political power still lay with a wealthy elite and with the governor, a Foreign Office appointee, while the devaluation of the British Honduras dollar at the end of 1949 caused additional hardship. The days of the British Empire were numbered, however, and in 1954 elections were held in which all literate adults over the age of 21 could vote. These elections were won with an overwhelming majority by the **Peoples' United Party** (PUP), led by **George Price**.

However, **Guatemala**, as the inheritor of the Spanish colonial territory of that name, had never entirely let go of its claim to the territory of Belize, regarding colonial treaties giving the British settlers rights to cut wood but not to own the land as still applicable in law. These interminable disputes, particularly the 1859 treaty which Britain, despite failing to fulfil the provision to build a road allowing Guatemala access to the Caribbean, regarded as the final settlement of the boundary dispute, rumbled on in the background. The British government never took the Guatemalan claim very seriously and Belize was allowed to proceed down the road to full independence by becoming an **internally self-governing** colony in 1964.

Ethnic Belize

Belize has a very mixed cultural background, with the two largest ethnic groups, **creoles**, descendants of enslaved Africans and early British settlers, and **mestizos**, descended from Amerindians and Spanish colonial settlers, forming about 75 percent of the population. The **Maya** in Belize are from three separate groups: **Yucatec**, who fled from the Caste Wars in the mid-nineteenth century; **Mopan**, who arrived in southern and western Belize from Petén in the 1880s; and **Kekchí**, who came to Toledo in southern Belize from Alta Verapaz from the late nineteenth century onwards. Together they form around 11 percent of the total population. The **Garífuna**, or **Caribs**, descended from enslaved Africans shipwrecked on St Vincent who mingled with the last Caribs there, settled in Belize in the nineteenth century, and now form around 7 percent of the population.

Since the 1980s, the arrival of an estimated 40,000 **Central American immigrants**, refugees from war and poverty, have helped boost Belize's population to around 265,000. These refugees, together with the existing population of predominantly Spanish-speaking mestizos, have dramatically altered the demographic balance, and are now the majority ethnic group in Belize. Though they are treated with tolerance and encouraged to integrate into Belizean society, the recent arrivals are the source of slight racial tension, often referred to as "aliens" and blamed for a disproportionate amount of crime. Some Creoles feel marginalized now that Spanish is the most widely spoken first language, though English, taught in all schools, is certain to remain the official language for the foreseeable future.

The prospect of what was (notionally at least) the department of "Belice" becoming independent outraged Guatemalan national pride and at least twice, in 1972 and 1977, Guatemala moved troops to the border and threatened to invade, but prompt British reinforcements offered an effective dissuasion. The situation remained tense but international opinion shifted gradually in favour of Belizean independence.

The most important demonstration of the worldwide endorsement of Belize's right to self-determination was the **UN resolution** passed in 1980, which demanded secure independence, with all territory intact, before the next session. Further negotiations with Guatemala began but complete agreement could not be reached: Guatemala still insisted on some territorial concessions. On March 11, 1981, Britain, Guatemala and Belize released the "Heads of Agreement", a document which would, they hoped, eventually result in a peaceful solution of the dispute. Accordingly, on September 21, 1981, Belize became an **independent member of the British Commonwealth**, with Queen Elizabeth II as its head of state.

The territorial dispute remains a stumbling block in relations between Belize and Guatemala, despite a bilateral agreement signed in 2002 to finally settle it – subject to successful referenda in each country. No dates for these referenda have even been proposed and it's unlikely they will be held in the foreseeable future.

Modern Belize

Belize's **democratic credentials** are beyond dispute: at each general election since independence (until the most recent) the voters have kicked out the incumbent government and replaced it with the opposition. This has meant that the nominally left-of-centre **People's United Party** (PUP) has alternated with the more market-led **United Democratic Party** (UDP). At the general election of March 2003, however, the PUP under the leadership of Prime Minister **Said Musa** won an unprecedented second term in a second consecutive landslide victory.

The booming **tourist industry**, bringing in around US$200 million a year out of Belize's US$1 billion GDP and employing almost a third of the country's workforce, is now the mainstay of Belize's **economy**, pushing agriculture and fisheries into a close second place. Figures are obviously not available for Belize's income from the lucrative drug transhipment business, but this illicit economy is probably half as large as the official one. **Per capita** income is high for Central America, at over US$2500, boosted by the remittances many Belizeans receive from relatives abroad, mainly in the US. This apparent advantage is offset, however, by the fact that many of the brightest and most highly trained citizens leave Belize, fitting in well in English-speaking North America.

Though traditional links with Britain and the Commonwealth countries in the West Indies remain relatively strong, Belize, together with all the other Central American countries, was a signatory to the negotiations held early in 2001 to establish a **Free Trade Area of the Americas**, with December 2005 set as the target date for the agreement to come into force. This step is viewed with alarm by many Belizean workers, who fear that an end to all tariffs will further depress agricultural prices and drive the small manufacturing base into bankruptcy. Even worse, in many people's eyes such proposals might signal an end to the **fixed rate of exchange** with the US dollar, leading to a potentially catastrophic devaluation of the Belize dollar. Regardless of the populist rhetoric of the PUP, however, Belize is already firmly linked to the US-dominated world of international finance, and is likely to face increasing challenges from global competitors in the early years of this century.

1.1

Belize City

The narrow, crowded streets of **BELIZE CITY** can initially be daunting to anyone who has been prepared by the usual tales of crime-ridden urban decay. Admittedly, at first glance the city is unprepossessing and chaotic. Its buildings – many of them dilapidated wooden structures – stand right at the edge of the road, and few sidewalks offer refuge to pedestrians from the ever-increasing numbers of vehicles. The hazards of Belize City, however, are often reported by those who have never been here. If you approach the city with an open mind and take some precautions with your belongings, you may well be pleasantly surprised. The city has a distinguished history, a world-class **museum** and an astonishing energy. The 75,000 people of Belize City represent every ethnic group in the country, with the **Creole** descendants of former slaves and Baymen forming the dominant element, generating an easy-going Caribbean atmosphere.

One of the very best times to visit is in fact during the "low season", when the **September Celebrations**, commemorating St George's Caye Day and Independence Day, fill the streets with music, dancing and parades, and the highlight, **Carnival**, sees gorgeously costumed dancers shimmer and gyrate through the city to electrifying Caribbean rhythms.

Belize City is divided neatly into north and south halves by **Haulover Creek**, a branch of the Belize River. The pivotal point of the city centre is the **Swing Bridge**, always busy with traffic and opened twice a day to allow larger vessels up and down the river. **North** of the Swing Bridge is the slightly more upmarket part of town, home to the most expensive hotels. **South** of the Swing Bridge is the market and commercial zone, the location of all the city's banks and a couple of supermarkets. The city is small enough to make **walking** the easiest way to get around.

Some history

Exactly how Belize came by its name is something of a mystery; it could be a corruption of the name Wallace, a Scotsman and probably a pirate, reputed to have settled here in 1620. Those preferring a more ancient origin believe the name to be derived from *beliz*, a Maya word meaning "muddy", or from the Maya term *belekin*, meaning "towards the east".

What *is* known is that by the late seventeenth century, buccaneers were cutting **logwood** (used for textile dyes in Europe) in the region, and had settled in a mangrove swamp consolidated with wood chips, loose coral and rum bottles at the mouth of today's Haulover Creek. The settlement became known as **Belize Town**, and by the 1700s it was well established as a centre for logwood cutters, their families and their slaves. The seafront contained the houses of the **Baymen**, as the settlers called themselves; the slaves lived in cabins on the south side of Haulover Creek, with various tribal groups occupying separate areas. After the rains had floated the logs downriver the men returned here to drink and brawl, with riotous Christmas celebrations going on for weeks.

Spain was the dominant colonial power in the region, and mounted several expeditions aimed at demonstrating control over the territory. These raids continued until the **Battle of St George's Caye** in 1798, when the settlers achieved victory

Hassle

Walking in Belize City **in daylight** is perfectly safe if you observe common-sense rules. Specially trained **tourism police** (☎227-2222), together with the legal requirement for all tour guides to be licensed, generally keep the hustlers away. In the city centre you can always ask the tourism police for advice or directions. They're instantly recognizable by their uniforms and caps emblazoned with "Tourism Police" – they'll even walk you back to your hotel if it's near their patrol route. That said, it's still sensible to proceed with caution: most people are friendly and chatty, but quite a few may want to sell you drugs or bum a dollar or two. The best advice is to stay cool. Be civil, don't provoke trouble by arguing too forcefully, and never show large sums of money on the street. Women wearing short shorts or skirts will attract mild verbal abuse from local studs.

Even though the chances of being mugged do increase **after dark**, you'll find you can walk around the centre – say from the *Hotel Mopan* to the Swing Bridge and along to the *Downtown* or *Freddie's* guesthouses or the Fort George area – in relative safety and you'll certainly encounter tourism police in this area. If you're venturing further afield, or if you've just arrived by bus at night, you'd be wise to travel by taxi.

with British naval help. British influence increased during the nineteenth century: in 1862 Belize became the colony of **British Honduras**, with Belize City as the administrative centre, and in 1871 Belize was officially declared a Crown Colony, with a resident governor appointed by Britain. Despite frequent fires and epidemics throughout the nineteenth century, the town grew with immigration from the West Indies and refugees from the Caste Wars in the Yucatán.

On September 10, 1931, the city was celebrating the anniversary of the Battle of St George's Caye when it was hit by a massive **hurricane** that uprooted houses, flooded the entire city and killed about a thousand people – ten percent of the population. In 1961 the city was again ravaged by a hurricane: 262 people died, and the damage was so serious that plans were made to relocate the capital inland to Belmopan. (Hattieville, on the Western Highway, began life as a refuge for those fleeing the hurricane.) The official attitude was that Belize City would soon become a redundant backwater as Belmopan grew, but in fact few people chose to leave for the sterile "new town" atmosphere of Belmopan, and Belize City remains by far the most populous place in the country. Since independence the rise of foreign investment and tourism has made an impact, and Belize City is now experiencing a major construction boom.

Arrival and information

International flights land at the **Phillip Goldson International Airport**, 17km northwest of the city; taxis into town cost US$20. There's a branch of the Belize Bank (with ATM) if you need to get Belize dollars on arrival. Domestic flights come and go from the **municipal airport**, a few kilometres north of town on the edge of the sea; taxis from here to the city centre charge US$4. The **bus terminal** is in a fairly derelict section on the western side of the city, along the West Collet Canal, but it's only 1km or so from the centre and you can easily walk – or, especially at night, take a taxi – to any of the recommended hotels. **Taxis**, identified by green licence plates, charge US$3 for one or two passengers within the city limits. **Boats** departing to/arriving from the cayes pull in at the Marine Terminal (see p.89) on the north side of the Swing Bridge, or at Courthouse Wharf on the south side.

The **Belize Tourism Board** (BTB; Mon–Fri 8am–5pm; ☎0223-1913) is in the Central Bank building, behind the Museum of Belize; it's not an essential point of call but you can pick up a hotel guide and city map, nature reserve brochures and copies of the (sometimes free) **tourist newspapers**. Inside the Marine Terminal, the *Mundo Maya Deli* has reliable information on **bus and boat schedules**, and sells tickets for the **express buses to Chetumal and Flores**. You can change US

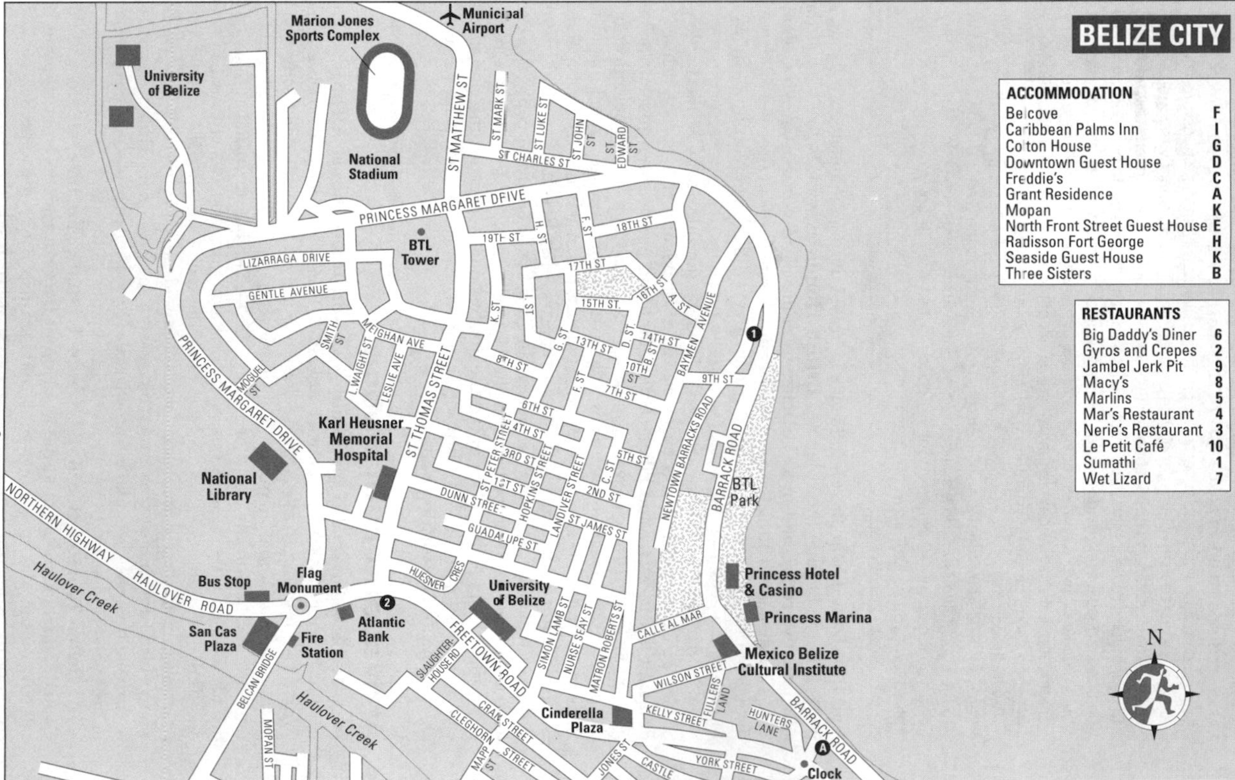
BELIZE CITY
ACCOMMODATION
Belcove F
Caribbean Palms Inn I
Colton House G
Downtown Guest House D
Freddie's C
Grant Residence A
Mopan K
North Front Street Guest House E
Radisson Fort George H
Seaside Guest House K
Three Sisters B
RESTAURANTS
Big Daddy's Diner 6
Gyros and Crepes 2
Jambel Jerk Pit 9
Macy's 8
Marlins 5
Mar's Restaurant 4
Nerie's Restaurant 3
Le Petit Café 10
Sumathi 1
Wet Lizard 7
N
Municipal Airport
Marion Jones Sports Complex
University of Belize
National Stadium
BTL Tower
Karl Heusner Memorial Hospital
National Library
Orange Walk & Corozal
Flag Monument
Bus Stop
San Cas Plaza
Fire Station
Atlantic Bank
University of Belize
Cinderella Plaza
Princess Hotel & Casino
Princess Marina
Mexico Belize Cultural Institute
BTL Park
Clock
Haulover Creek
NORTHERN HIGHWAY
HAULOVER ROAD
PRINCESS MARGARET DRIVE
ST MATTHEW ST
ST MARK ST
ST LUKE ST
ST JOHN ST
EDWARD ST
ST CHARLES ST
ST THOMAS STREET
BARRACK ROAD
NEWTOWN BARRACKS ROAD
BAYMEN AVENUE
FREETOWN ROAD
BELCAN BRIDGE
MOPAN ST
CALLE AL MAR
WILSON STREET
KELLY STREET
FULLERS LAND
HUNTERS LANE
YORK STREET
CASTLE
JONES ST
MATRON ROBERTS ST
NURSE SEAY ST
SIMON LAMB ST
CRAIG STREET
CLEGHORN STREET
MAPP ST
SLAUGHTER-HOUSE RD
HUESNER CRES
DUNN STREET
GUADALUPE ST
ST PETER STREET
HOPKINS STREET
LANDIVIER STREET
ST JAMES ST
LESLIE AVE
MEIGHAN AVE
L. WAIGHT ST
SMITH ST
LIZARRAGA DRIVE
GENTLE AVENUE
MOGUEL ST

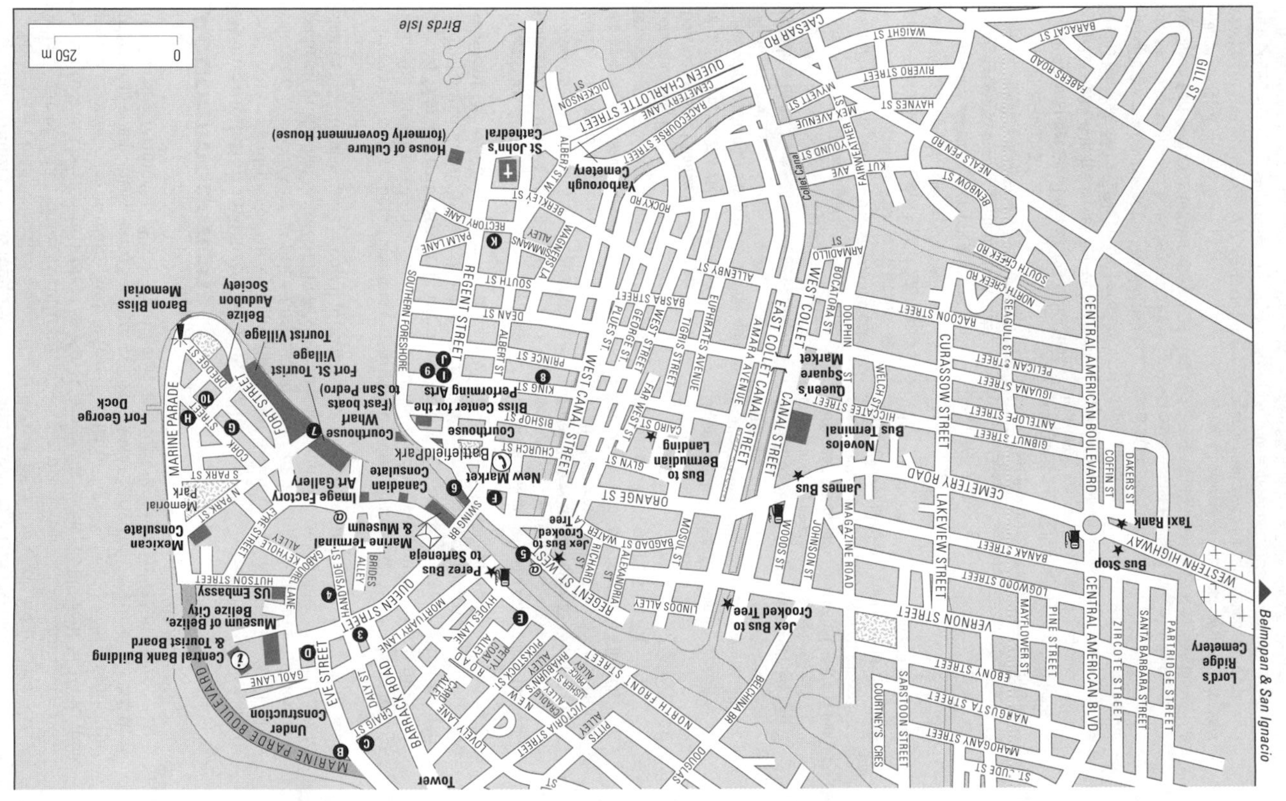
0
250 m
Birds Isle
House of Culture
(formerly Government House)
St John's
Cathedral
Yarborough
Cemetery
Baron Bliss
Memorial
Belize
Audubon
Society
Tourist Village
Fort St. Tourist
Village
Courthouse
Wharf
(Fast boats
to San Pedro)
Fort George
Dock
MARINE PARADE
Memorial
Park
Mexican
Consulate
Image Factory
Art Gallery
Canadian
Consulate
BattlefieldPark
Courthouse
Bliss Center for the
Performing Arts
New Market
Marine Terminal
& Museum
Perez Bus
to Sarteneja
Jex Bus to
Crooked
Tree
US Embassy
Museum of Belize,
Belize City
Central Bank Building
& Tourist Board
Under
Construction
Tower
MARINE PARDE BOULEVARD
FORT STREET
REGENT STREET
WEST CANAL STREET
EAST COLLET CANAL STREET
CANAL STREET
QUEEN CHARLOTTE STREET
CAESAR RD
Collet Canal
CENTRAL AMERICAN BOULEVARD
CENTRAL AMERICAN BLVD
CEMETERY ROAD
LAKEVIEW STREET
CURASSOW STREET
VERNON STREET
NORTH FRONT STREET
REGENT ST WEST
BARRACK ROAD
EVE STREET
QUEEN STREET
WESTERN HIGHWAY
GILL ST
Bus to
Bermudian
Landing
Novelos
Bus Terminal
James Bus
Queen's
Square
Market
Jex Bus to
Crooked Tree
Bus Stop
Taxi Rank
Lord's
Ridge
Cemetery
Belmopan & San Ignacio

dollars, Guatemalan quetzales and Mexican pesos here or in the Kaisa International shop; the terminal also has luggage lockers and reasonably clean toilets.

There aren't many places to access the **Internet** in Belize City and finding somewhere out of office hours is difficult, although many hotels have computers for guests to use. The cheapest place is Ray Communications, 15 Regent St West, just past the *Belcove Hotel* (8am–7pm Mon–Fri, 8am–1pm Sat; US$2/hr), while the most convenient place in the centre is Mail Boxes Etc., 166 North Front St, near the Marine Terminal (7.30am–6pm Mon–Fri, 9am–2pm Sat; US$3.80/hr).

Accommodation

Accommodation in Belize City is generally more expensive than elsewhere in the country, and prices for even budget rooms can come as quite a shock. The selection below covers all price ranges and you can be confident of cleanliness and security in the hotels listed. There's usually no need to book unless you're eager to stay in a particular hotel – you'll always be able to get something in the price range you're looking for.

Most of the city's hotels are located **north of the river**, and so are a little further from the bus terminal but closer to the Marine Terminal, with budget places mostly on or near **North Front Street** and **Queen Street**. The more upmarket hotels are generally located in the historic **Fort George area**, just north of the river, or along the **seafront** either side of the river mouth, where guests can benefit from sea breezes.

North of the river

Colton House 9 Cork St ⓣ203-4666, ⓦwww.coltonhouse.com. The best guesthouse in Belize, this beautifully kept colonial building has a/c rooms (all non-smoking) with balcony and immaculate private bathrooms; very popular with honeymooners. ❼

Downtown Guest House 5 Eve St, near the end of Queen Street ⓣ223-2057. Basic but friendly place with secure rooms (some with private bath, a/c and TV) and a balcony over the street. ❸

Freddie's Guest House 86 Eve St, on the city's edge near the waterfront ⓣ233-3851. Three clean, comfortable and secure fan-cooled rooms; the best value in this price range. One room has immaculate private bath and the shared bathroom gleams. ❺

Grant Residence 126 Barrack Rd ⓣ223-0926, ⓦwww.grantbedandbreakfast.com. Four very spacious and extremely comfortable rooms in an impressively maintained guesthouse, in a quiet seafront location just north of the city centre. Breakfast included. ❽

North Front Street Guest House 124 North Front St ⓣ227-7595, ⓔthoth@btl.net. Two blocks from Marine Terminal, rooms in this budget travellers' favourite are small and basic but they are clean and secure; all share cold-water showers. ❸

Radisson Fort George Hotel and Marina 2 Marine Parade ⓣ223-3333, ⓦwww.radisson.com/belizecitybz. Luxurious and well-run flagship of the city's hotels. The very well-furnished rooms have a huge cable TV, fridge and minibar, and many also have sea views. Two excellent restaurants and a café, and all the services you'd expect of a great hotel. ❾

Three Sisters Guest House 55 Eve St ⓣ203-5729. Three large, clean rooms (one with private bath) in a wooden building run by a friendly, mainly Spanish-speaking family. ❹

South of the river

Belcove Hotel 9 Regent St West ⓣ227-3054, ⓦwwwbelcove.com. Recently renovated rooms, some with a/c and most with private bath. Although it's on the edge of the dangerous part of town, the hotel itself is quite secure. ❹–❺

Caribbean Palms Inn Corner of Regent and King streets ⓣ227-0472, ⓔcpalms@hotmail.com. Wonderful new hotel with very comfortable, good-value, a/c rooms with private bath and TV. Meals can be arranged and there's Internet access and laundry service. Also a shared budget room for US$15 per person. ❸.

Hotel Mopan 55 Regent St ⓣ227-7351, ⓦwww.hotelmopan.com. Wood-fronted building with recently renovated rooms, all with private bath and some with a/c, near the colonial House of Culture. Restaurant serves good-value breakfasts (other meals can be ordered) and there's Internet access for guests. ❻

Seaside Guest House 3 Prince St, half a block from the southern foreshore ⓣ227-8339, ⓔseasidebelize@btl.net. Clean, well-run and very secure hotel. Good for information, there's a payphone and Internet access and you get your own front-door key. Dorm beds (with hot shared showers) US$12 per person, private rooms ❺.

The City

Richard Davies, a British traveller in the mid-nineteenth century, wrote of the city: "There is much to be said for Belize, for in its way it was one of the prettiest ports at which we touched, and its cleanliness and order…were in great contrast to the ports we visited later as to make them most remarkable."

Many of the features that elicited this praise have now gone, but several of the city's **colonial buildings** have been saved as heritage showpieces, as museums or galleries or by conversion into a hotel or restaurant. The central **Swing Bridge** was made in Liverpool and opened in 1923 – today it's the only manually operated swing bridge left in the Americas. Every day at 5.30am and 5.30pm the parade of vehicles and people is halted and the process of turning begins: using long poles inserted into a capstan, four men gradually lever the bridge around until it's pointing in the direction of the harbour mouth.

The north side

Immediately on the **north side** of the Swing Bridge is the **Marine Terminal**, housed inside the beautifully restored former Belize City Fire Station of 1923. The terminal is the departure point for boats to the northern cayes (see box, p.89), and is also home to a couple of superbly designed museums (both Mon–Sat 8am–4.30pm; US$2 for a combined ticket). Downstairs, the **Coastal Zone Museum** contains displays and explanations of reef ecology, the highlight being a 3-D model of the entire reef system; upstairs, the **Maritime Museum** exhibits a collection of models and documents relating to Belize's seafaring heritage. A block east of the Marine Terminal, at 91 North Front St, **The Image Factory** (Mon–Fri 9am–6pm; free but donations welcome) hosts Belize's hottest contemporary artists. The gallery puts on outstanding, frequently provocative exhibitions and you often get a chance to chat to the artists themselves.

Continuing east along North Front Street you'll encounter the advance guard of trinket sellers, street musicians, hustlers and hair-braiders, announcing you're near the **Tourist Village**, Belize's new **cruise ship terminal**. The Village itself is little more than a dock for the cruise ships to disembark their passengers, which can number in thousands, with an attached shopping mall.

Beyond the Tourist Village, the road follows the north shore of the river mouth, reaching the point marked by the **Fort George Lighthouse**, a memorial to **Baron Bliss**, Belize's greatest benefactor (see overleaf). On the seafront, **Memorial Park** honours the Belizean dead of the world wars and in the streets around the park you'll find several colonial mansions, many of the best-preserved now taken over by upmarket hotels and embassies. At 2 Park St, on the south side of the park, is the **National Handicraft Center** (Mon–Fri 8am–5pm), which sells high-quality Belizean crafts and art at fair prices. A little beyond here, at the corner of Hutson Street and Gabourel Lane a block from the sea, is the **US Embassy**: a superb "colonial" building actually constructed in New England in the nineteenth century then dismantled and shipped to Belize.

Marine Parade, the seaward edge of Memorial Park, marks the beginning of the biggest civil engineering project in the city's history. A massive **seawall**, stretching for hundreds of metres along the shore to Barrack Road, encloses over six hectares of shallow sea, now in the process of being pumped dry. Soon this seawall will combine a new boulevard for traffic and a pedestrian promenade, leading north for over a kilometre to the enormous *Princess Hotel*.

The Museum of Belize, Belize City

South of the centre of this new development, in front of the Central Bank building, the Victorian former colonial prison built in 1857 has undergone a remarkable transformation to become the **Museum of Belize, Belize City** (Mon–Fri 9am–5pm; US$5). The lower floor has echoes of the original jail, with plenty of exposed brickwork and bars on the windows – and a gruesome reconstruction of the condemned cell – together with photographs and items celebrating the city's history. Fascinating though this is, the star attractions are upstairs, in the **Maya Masterpieces** gallery, a first-class collection of the best of Belize's Maya artefacts, including some of the finest painted Maya ceramics anywhere. One of the most striking is the **Buenavista Vase**, depicting the mythical Hero Twins dressed as the young Maize Gods after defeating the Lords of Death – the central theme of the Maya creation story, the Popol Vuh. Other treasures include a replica of the famous **Jade Head** from Altun Ha (see p.84), jade masks and pendants, and several gorgeous jade necklaces.

The south side

The **south side** is the older half of Belize City: in the early days the elite lived in the seafront houses while the backstreets were home to slaves and labourers. These days it's the city's commercial centre, containing the ugly new market building just over the Swing Bridge, the main shopping streets, banks and travel agencies. **Albert Street**, running south from the Swing Bridge, is the main commercial thoroughfare. On the parallel **Regent Street** are the former colonial administration and court buildings, collectively known as the **Court House**. These well-preserved examples of colonial architecture, completed in 1926, with columns and fine wrought iron, overlook **Battlefield Park** (named to commemorate the noisy political meetings that took place there before independence), a patch of grass and trees with a dry ornamental fountain in the centre.

A block behind the Court House, on the waterfront, is the magnificent new **Bliss Centre for the Performing Arts** (☎227-2110), hosting exhibitions, concerts and plays. The original Bliss Institute here was funded by the legacy of **Baron Bliss**, an eccentric Englishman with a Portuguese title. A keen fisherman, he arrived off the coast of Belize in 1926 after hearing about the tremendous game fishing in local waters. Unfortunately, he became ill and died without ever having been ashore. Despite this he left most of his considerable estate to the colony and, in gratitude, the authorities declared March 9, the date of his death, Baron Bliss Day.

At the end of Albert Street is **St John's Cathedral**, the oldest Anglican cathedral in Central America and one of the oldest buildings in Belize. Looking like a large English parish church, it was begun in 1812, its red bricks being brought over as ballast in British ships. Here, between 1815 and 1845, the kings of the Mosquito Coast were crowned amid great pomp, taking the title to a British Protectorate that extended along the coast of Honduras and Nicaragua.

On the way to the seafront from the cathedral you'll come to the beautifully renovated, white-painted, green-lawned Government House, now renamed the **House of Culture** (daily 9am–4pm; US$5). You enter under the columned portico and inside a plush red carpet leads down the hall to the great mahogany staircase. In the main room a panoramic painting of Belize City in the early 1900s overlooks the collection of **colonial silverware**, glasses and furniture, and one wall is lined with prints of sombre past governors. The building's new role as the House of Culture means it also hosts painting, dance and drumming workshops, art exhibitions and musical performances.

Eating, drinking and nightlife

Belize City's selection of **restaurants** is becoming gradually more varied, though the tasty **Creole** fare of rice and beans still predominates at the lower end. There's plenty of seafood and steaks, and a preponderance of **Chinese** restaurants – usually the best bet for **vegetarians** – and very good **Lebanese** and **Indian** restaurants. The big **hotels** have their own restaurants, naturally quite expensive but with varied menus and good service. Be warned that many restaurants are closed on Sunday. In the listings below we have quoted a phone number in places where it is recommended you should reserve a table or for those places that offer a delivery service.

Restaurants north of the river

Gyros and Crepes 164 Freetown Rd. The finest Lebanese food in the city, with delicious tahini, falafel, hummus and kebabs at good prices.

Le Petit Café Cork Street, at the *Radisson Hotel*. The outdoor tables here make *Le Petit* the top place in the city to enjoy a genuine café atmosphere, with good coffee and baked treats, including croissants, at reasonable prices.

Mar's Restaurant 11 Handyside St. Tasty Belizean food at great prices in a spacious, clean restaurant.

Nerie's Restaurant corner of Queen and Daly streets. The best Belizean food north of the river, and fantastically good value; always a daily special. The conch soup is a meal in itself.

Sumathi 190 Newtown Barracks Rd ⓣ223-1172. Extremely good North Indian and tandoori food, but it's a long way from the centre, so you'll need to take a taxi, or call to order a delivery. Closed Mon.

Wet Lizard Fort Street, on the waterfront, next to the Tourist Village. Capture the feeling of the cayes as you eat on a deck overlooking the sea. Features an eclectic range of well-prepared and very tasty dishes, including tangy spring rolls, Thai and Mexican specialities, with great deserts.

Restaurants and cafés south of the river

Big Daddy's Diner upstairs in the new market, south side of the Swing Bridge. Excellent breakfasts and Belizean dishes, with a daily lunch special, served cafeteria-style in clean surroundings. Open Mon–Sat 7am–4pm.

Jambel Jerk Pit 2B King St ⓣ227-6080. Very tasty Jamaican-influenced dishes at reasonable prices. Specialities include the obvious jerk chicken, but also delicious, spicy fish and other seafood dishes, soups and salads or the daily special.

Macy's 18 Bishop St. Long-established, reasonably priced Creole restaurant that's popular with locals and very busy at lunchtimes.

Marlins 11 Regent St West, next to the *Belcove Hotel*. Good, inexpensive local food in large portions – and you can eat on the veranda overlooking the river. Great breakfasts, but closes by 8pm.

Drinking, nightlife and entertainment

Belize City's more sophisticated, air-conditioned **bars** are found in the most expensive establishments, and there aren't many of those. At the lowest end of the scale are dimly lit dives, effectively men-only, where, though there's the possibility that you'll be offered drugs or be robbed, it's more likely that you'll have a thoroughly enjoyable time meeting easy-going, hard-drinking locals. There are several places between the two extremes however; on Friday evenings try *La Bodega Lounge* upstairs at *Nerie's Restaurant* on the corner of Queen and Daly streets, or across the road at *Copacabana*, a karaoke bar with pool tables, or any night at *Nu Fenders Bar*, just opposite. A few of the top-end hotels tempt the after-work crowd with Friday evening **happy hours** (usually 5–7pm), where you can relax with the city's business elite. The liveliest is the poolside bar of the *Biltmore Plaza Hotel*, 5km out of town on the Northern Highway, accompanied by a fantastic steel band. Other Friday happy hour venues include the *Radisson Fort George* (see p.70) and the *Smokey Mermaid Restaurant*, across the street.

Belize City's **nightlife** really comes into its own at weekends, and there are plenty of venues, playing anything from techno to Latin grooves or punta, soca and reggae. If you go clubbing don't arrive much before midnight or you'll find many places empty. A relatively safe area of town with a variety of bars/clubs is the strip of the Barrack Road from the *Princess Hotel* to *Caesar's Palace* bar. The latter is a lively bar at weekends and next door is the relatively upmarket *Eden* nightclub, while further along is the slightly less salubrious *MJ's* nightclub. *Paradise 21* (formerly the *Lumba Yard*), on the riverbank just out of town on the Northern Highway, is another good place to catch current bands.

The *Princess Hotel* has Belize City's only **casino**: you'll need a passport or photo ID to gain temporary membership (free) and keep to the dress code – no shorts or sandals. Officially you have to change US$25 into tokens to feed the slot machines or play at the blackjack and roulette tables, but any unused tokens are changed back. The *Princess* also has the city's only cinema, and it's also the venue for Belize's **Film Festival**, held annually in March.

Listings

Airlines American, corner of New Road and Queen Street ⓣ223-2522; Continental, 80 Regent St ⓣ227-8309; Maya Island Air, Municipal Airport ⓣ223-1140 or 226-2345; Taca, in Belize Global Travel, 41 Albert St ⓣ227-7363; Tropic Air, Municipal Airport ⓣ224-5671 or 226-2012; US Airways toll free to USA office ⓣ0800/872-4700.
Banks and exchange The main banks all have branches on Albert Street (usually Mon–Thurs 8am–2pm, Fri 8am–4.30pm). Only the Belize and First Caribbean banks have ATMs that accept foreign-issued cards; others will process cash advances over the counter. At times cash US$ may only be available from the banks if you can show a ticket (plane, bus or boat) to leave the country. *Casas de cambio*, shops, hotels and restaurants change US$ travellers' cheques and everyone accepts US$. For Guatemalan quetzales and Mexican pesos try Kaisa International in the Marine Terminal.
Books Both the Book Center, 2 Church St, opposite the BTL office (ⓣ227-7457), and Angelus Press, 10 Queen St (ⓣ223-5777), have a wide range of Belize-related books and maps.
Car rental The following companies are in Belize City and will arrange vehicle pick-up and drop-off anywhere in the city or at the Municipal or International airports at no extra charge: Avis (ⓣ225-2385, ⓔavisbelize@btl.net); Budget 2 1/2 Miles Northern Highway and International Airport (ⓣ223-2435, ⓦwww.budget-belize.com); Crystal 4 1/2 Miles Northern Highway, in the Tourism Village and International Airport (ⓣ223-1600 or toll free in Belize ⓣ0800/777-7777, ⓦwww.crystal-belize.com). Crystal has the largest rental fleet in the country and is the only one that allows cars over the Guatemalan border.
Embassies and consulates Though the official capital is at Belmopan, some consulates remain in Belize City; they're normally open Mon–Fri mornings. Current addresses and phone numbers can be checked under "Diplomatic Listings" in the green pages of the telephone directory: Canada ⓣ223-1060; Costa Rica ⓣ223-6525; Guatemala ⓣ223-3150; Honduras ⓣ224-5889; Mexico ⓣ223-0194; Nicaragua ⓣ224-4488; Panama ⓣ222-4551; and USA ⓣ224-5563.
Immigration Belize Immigration is in the Government Complex on Mahogany Street, near the junction of Central American Blvd and the Western Highway (Mon–Thurs 8.30am–4pm, Fri 8.30am–3.30pm; ⓣ222-4620). Thirty-day extensions of stay (the maximum allowed) cost US$12.50.
Laundry Central America Coin Laundry, 114 Barrack Rd (Mon–Sat 8.30am–9pm, reduced hours on Sun).
Medical care Dr Gamero, Myo-On Clinic, 40 Eve St ⓣ224-5616; Karl Huesner Memorial Hospital, Princess Margaret Drive, near junction with the Northern Highway ⓣ223-1548.
Photography For prints, slides and fast passport photos, try Spooners, 89 North Front St.
Police The main police station is on Queen Street, a block north of the Swing Bridge ⓣ227-2210; Emergency ⓣ90 nationwide. Alternatively, contact the Tourism Police (see box on p.67).
Post office North Front St, opposite the Marine Terminal (Mon–Fri 8am–4.30pm).
Telecommunications There are payphones (operated using pre-paid cards only) dotted all around the city, or visit the main BTL office, 1 Church St (Mon–Sat 8am–6pm), which also has fax and email service.
Travel and tour agents The following travel agents are the best for information and bookings on flights and connections throughout the region; all can arrange tours within Belize: Belize Global Travel, 41 Albert St (ⓣ227-7363, ⓦwww.belize-global.com), agents for most of the international airlines operating in Belize; Belize Trips (ⓣ223-0376 or 610-1923, ⓦwww.belize-trips.com), very experienced Belize travel specialist; Maya Travel Services, 42 Cleghorn St (ⓣ223-1623, ⓦwww.mayatravelservices.com), inbound travel experts, very knowledgeable about tours and hotels within Belize; Mopan Travels, in the *Hotel Mopan* (ⓣ227-7351, ⓦwww.hotelmopan.com), arranges natural history tours throughout Belize.

Moving on from Belize City

Moving on from Belize City is easy, with regular departures **by bus** to all parts of the country, across the border to Chetumal in Mexico, and to Benque Viejo in Cayo, for the Guatemalan border; the box on p.76 lists all routes and frequencies. **Boats** to the northern cayes leave from the Marine Terminal (see p.89 for times and prices). **Domestic flights** (see p.53) to all main towns leave from the Municipal Airport.

△ Fly-fishing for snook, Belize

Bus services from Belize City

The main **bus company** in Belize is Novelos – with divisions called Northern, Western and Southern Transport – operating the most services within the country from the large terminal at West Collet Canal. There are several smaller bus companies with regular departures, and most operate from the streets near the terminal; the ones listed below are marked on the city map (pp.68–69). Services operate seven days a week unless otherwise stated; when available, **Express services** (Exp) are faster and more expensive than regular services. The abbreviations we've used for the bus companies in the bus services box are as follows:

James Bus (JA) ☎702-2049. For Dangriga and Punta Gorda (via Belmopan); leaves from Shell station, Cemetery Road, near Novelo's terminal at 5.30am, 10am and 2.30pm daily.
Jex Bus (SX) ☎225-7017. Leaves for Crooked Tree from Regent Street West (10.50am) and Pound Yard, Collet Canal.
McFadzean's Bus (MF). For Bermudian Landing (via Burrell Boom); leaves from Euphrates Avenue, off Orange Street, near the Novelo's bus depot, at noon and 5pm.
Northern Transport (NT) ☎207-2025. For the Northern Highway, Orange Walk, Corozal and Chetumal.
Perez Bus (PE) For Sarteneja; leaves from the Thunderbolt dock, North Front Street at noon & 1pm; also from Courthouse Wharf at 5pm.
Russell's Bus (RU) For Bermudian Landing; leaves from Cairo Street, near the corner of Cemetery Road and Euphrates Avenue at noon & 4pm.
Southern Transport (ST) ☎502-2160. For the Hummingbird and Southern highways and Coastal Road to Dangriga, Placencia and Punta Gorda.
Western Transport (WT) ☎227-1160. For the Western Highway, Belmopan, San Ignacio and Benque Viejo for the Guatemalan border.

Bus services from Belize City

Destination	Frequency	Bus Co	Duration
Belmopan	half-hourly 5am–9pm (Exp)	JA, WT, ST	1hr 15min
Benque Viejo	half-hourly 5am–9pm (Exp)	NV	3hr 30min (for the Guatemalan border)
Bermudian Landing	Mon–Sat noon, 4.30pm & 5.30pm	MR, RU	1hr 15min
Chetumal, Mexico	hourly 4am–7pm (Exp)	NT	3hr 30min
Corozal	hourly 4am–7pm (Exp)	NT	2hr 30min
Crooked Tree	Mon–Sat 10.30am, 4.30pm, 5.30pm	JX	1hr 30min
Dangriga	12 daily 6am–5pm (Exp)	JA, ST	2hr via Coastal Rd; 3hr 30min via Belmopan
Gales Point	Mon–Sat 5pm	ST	1hr 40min
Maskall	Mon–Sat 4pm	NT	1hr 30min (for Altun Ha)
Orange Walk	hourly 5am–7pm (Exp)	NT	1hr 30min
Placencia	2–3 daily, all via Belmopan; change at Dangriga	ST	6–7hr
Punta Gorda	6–7 daily, all via Dangriga (Exp)	JA, ST	6–8hr
San Ignacio	every 30min 5am–9pm (Exp), all via Belmopan	NT	2hr 30min
Sarteneja	3–4 daily, via Orange Walk noon, 1pm & 5pm	PE	3hr 30min

1.2

Corozal, Orange Walk and the north

The level expanses of northern Belize are a mixture of farmland and rainforest, dotted with swamps, savannas and lagoons. The largest settlement in the region is **Orange Walk**, the country's main centre for sugar production. Further north, just 15 minutes from the border with Mexico, **Corozal** is a small and peaceful Caribbean town, strongly influenced by Maya and mestizo culture. Most of the original settlers in the north were refugees from the nineteenth-century Caste Wars in Yucatán, and thus Spanish is more widely spoken than Creole.

Most visitors to northern Belize come to see the **Maya ruins** and **wildlife reserves**. The largest site, **Lamanai**, served by regular boat tours along the **New River Lagoon**, features some of the most impressive pyramids in the country. East of Lamanai, **Altun Ha**, reached via the Old Northern Highway, is usually visited as part of a day-trip from Belize City or San Pedro. The smaller Maya sites include **Santa Rita** and **Cerros**, both near Corozal.

The most northerly of the wildlife reserves is the **Shipstern Nature Reserve**, close to the village of Sarteneja. Further south, at the **Crooked Tree Wildlife Sanctuary**, a network of rivers and lagoons offers protection to a range of migratory birds, and at the **Bermudian Landing Community Baboon Sanctuary** a group of farmers have combined agriculture with conservation to the benefit of the black howler monkey. By far the largest and most ambitious conservation project, however, is the **Rio Bravo Conservation Area**, comprising one thousand square kilometres of tropical forest and river systems in the west of Orange Walk district.

Travelling around the north is fairly straightforward if you stick to the main Northern Highway, covered by bus services every hour from 5am to 7pm between Belize City and **Chetumal** in Mexico, calling at Orange Walk and Corozal on the way.

Crossing from Mexico

It's less than a four-hour bus journey along the Northern Highway from **Chetumal** in Mexico to Belize City. Entering Belize, Mexican **immigration and customs** posts are on the northern bank of the Rio Hondo at the **Santa Elena** border crossing, 12km from Chetumal; when you're finished there, the bus will pick you up again to take you across to Belizean immigration. Border formalities take just a matter of minutes. If **leaving Belize**, you'll have to pay an exit tax of US$15 and the PACT conservation fee of US$3.75. **Moneychangers** on the Belize side won't rip you off; you get the standard rate of Bz$2 for US$1.

Corozal and around

South from the Mexican border, the road meets the sea at **COROZAL**, near the mouth of the New River. The **ancient Maya** prospered here by controlling river

and seaborne trade, and two sites, **Santa Rita** and **Cerros**, are both within easy reach. Present-day Corozal was founded in 1849 by refugees from the massacre in Bacalar, Mexico, during the Caste Wars, although today's grid-pattern town, a neat mix of Mexican and Caribbean, is largely due to reconstruction in the wake of Hurricane Janet in 1955. There's little to do in Corozal, but it's an agreeable place to spend the day on the way to or from the border, and is hassle free, even at night. The breezy shoreline park is good for a stroll, while on the tree-shaded main plaza, the **town hall** is worth a look inside for a vivid depiction of local history in a mural by Manuel Villamar Reyes. In the block west of the plaza you can see the remains of **Fort Barlee**, built to ward off Maya attacks in the 1870s.

Practicalities

All **buses** between Belize City and Chetumal pass through Corozal, roughly hourly in each direction. The Northern Transport depot (Ⓣ402-3034) is near the northern edge of town, opposite the Shell station. Buses for surrounding villages (including Copper Bank, see opposite) leave from the market area; for the Linea Dorada express bus to Flores see *Hotel Maya* entry, below. The *Thunderbolt* provides a **fast boat service** to San Pedro, Ambergris Caye, leaving daily from the dock by the market at 7am (US$22.50; 1hr 30min; Ⓣ226-2904). Maya Island Air and Tropic Air operate several daily **flights** between Corozal and San Pedro on Ambergris Caye. Jal's **travel agency** (Ⓣ422-2163), at the southern end of town, beyond *Tony's Inn*, can organize **international flights**. There's no tourist office but Corozal's well-designed **website** (Ⓦwww.corozal.com) is worth a look. The **post office** is on the west side of the plaza (Mon–Fri 8.30am–4.30pm) and the Belize Bank, on the north side of the plaza, has an ATM.

For **Internet access** visit Charlotte's Web Cyber Café and Book Exchange (Mon–Sat 8.30am–6pm), 78 Fifth Ave, a few blocks south of the centre, where there's also good coffee, maps and books for sale along with a bulletin board. For organized **tours** to local nature reserves and archeological sites, contact Henry Menzies (ⓣ422-2725); he's also an expert on travel to Mexico and can arrange tours to the Maya sites in Quintana Roo, the state immediately over the border.

Accommodation and restaurants

Corozal has plenty of **accommodation** and you shouldn't have any problems finding a suitable room should you need to stay overnight. At the north end of town *TJ's International Cozy Corner Guest House*, 2nd Street North (ⓣ422-0150, ⓦwww.corozal.bz/tj; ❻), has six blissfully comfortable, great-value rooms with private bathroom and a/c, set in beautiful gardens. *Nestor's*, on 5th Avenue South, between 4th and 5th streets (ⓣ422-2354, ⓔnestorshotel@belizemail.net; ❺), has private showers; no single rates. *Mavirton Guest House*, 16 2nd Street North (ⓣ422-3365, ⓔmavirton@btl.net; ❹), is a quiet, family-run hotel with basic rooms, most with private bathroom, and a small bar and restaurant. *Hok'ol K'in Guest House*, facing the sea at the end of 4th Street (ⓣ422-3329, ⓔmaya@btl.net; ❻), has modern rooms (plus a shared-bath budget room for US$12.50 per person) with large, tiled private bathrooms and hammocks on the balcony. The *Hotel Maya*, on the main road at the south end of town and also facing the sea (ⓣ422-2082, ⓔstay@hotel-maya.com; ❻), is well run, with private bathrooms and some new rooms with a/c; this is also the place to buy tickets for the express bus to Flores.

With few exceptions the best **meals** in Corozal are to be found in the hotels. The popular bar at *Nestor's* serves American and Belizean food, while the *Hotel Maya* serves very good Belizean dishes in a quieter environment, while *TJ's* serves great American, Belizean and Mexican meals to appreciative locals and expats. The *Lonchería Barrera*, just off the southwest corner of the plaza, serves tasty, inexpensive Mexican-style dishes, and there are several good Belizean restaurants in the market. The best restaurant in town is *Le Café Kelá*, on the seafront just north of the centre, serving authentic, delicious and good-value French cuisine, cooked to order and well worth the wait.

Around Corozal: Santa Rita and Cerros

Of the two small Maya sites within reach of Corozal, the closest is **Santa Rita** (daily 8am–5pm; US$5), about fifteen minutes' walk northwest of town. To get there, follow the main road in the direction of the border and where it divides take the left-hand fork. Founded around 1500 BC, Santa Rita was in all probability the powerful Maya city known as Chactemal. It was still a thriving settlement in 1531 AD, when the conquistador Alonso Davila entered the town, only to be driven out almost immediately by Na Chan Kan, the Maya chief, and his Spanish adviser Gonzalo Guerrero. The main remaining building is a small pyramid, and excavations here have uncovered the burial sites of an elaborately bejewelled elderly woman and a Classic-period warlord. Some of these artefacts are on display in the Museum of Belize (see p.71).

The remains of the late Preclassic centre of **Cerros** (daily 8am–5pm; US$5) are just 5km across the bay from Corozal and, while they can be reached by **boat** with a guide from the town, a new road from **Copper Bank** village allows inexpensive access by bike (20min; rent one from *The Last Resort*) along a level road. Built in a strategic position at the mouth of the New River, this was one of the earliest places in the Maya world to adopt the rule of kings. Despite initial success, however, Cerros had been abandoned by the Classic period. The site includes three large acropolis structures, ball courts and plazas flanked by pyramids. The largest building is a 22-metre-high temple, whose intricate stucco masks represent the rising and setting sun.

To reach Cerros by road from Corozal (via Copper Bank) take the road, signed just behind *Tony's Inn*, and cross the New River on a chain-winched ferry (daily 6am–9pm; free). **Buses** to Copper Bank (Mon–Sat 11.30am; 30min) leave from the market in Corozal, returning at 6.30am. In Copper Bank, *The Last Resort* (Ⓣ606-1585, Ⓔdonnaflores25@yahoo.ca; ④) has great budget **accommodation** and camping on the shore of the tranquil Laguna Seca. The simple, whitewashed thatched cabins (some with private showers) have electricity and mosquito-netted beds. There's also a **restaurant**, Internet access, bikes and canoes for rent and a library/paperback exchange.

Sarteneja and Shipstern Nature Reserve

Across Chetumal Bay from Corozal, the largely uninhabited **Sarteneja peninsula** is covered with dense forests and swamps that support an amazing array of wildlife. The only village is **SARTENEJA**, a quiet, Spanish-speaking lobster-fishing centre. Though there's little to see in the village itself, a couple of new hotels have been built and **guides** are available to take you to the lagoons and beyond. All buses to here also pass the entrance to **Shipstern Nature Reserve** (daily 8am–5pm; US$5 including guided walk), 5km before the village. The bulk of the eighty square kilometre reserve is made up of what's technically known as "tropical moist forest", and includes some wide belts of savanna – covered in coarse grasses, palms and broad-leaved trees – and a section of the shallow Shipstern Lagoon, dotted with mangrove islands. Taking the superb guided walk along the **Chiclero Trail**, you'll encounter more named plant species in an hour than on any other trail in Belize. Shipstern is also a birdwatcher's paradise: the lagoon system supports blue-winged teal, American coot and huge flocks of lesser scaup, while the forest is home to keel-billed toucans and at least five species of parrot. Other wildlife in the reserve includes crocodiles, jaguars, peccaries, and an abundance of wonderful butterflies.

Practicalities

From Belize, buses (Mon–Sat only; US$6) head to Sarteneja from the Thunderbolt Dock (Sarteneja Bus Company) on North Front Street at noon and 4pm, Novelo's main bus terminal at 1pm, and from Perez Bus stop at the Courthouse Wharf at 5pm. They all pass through Orange Walk ninety minutes later, stopping at Zeta's store on Main Street. Buses return to Belize City from Sarteneja at 4am, 5am and 6am. The *Thunderbolt*, a **skiff** running between Corozal and San Pedro on Ambergris Caye, can call at Sarteneja if there's sufficient demand (call Ⓣ226-2904 to check). The best **place to stay** is *Fernando's Seaside Guest House* (Ⓣ423-2085, Ⓔsartenejabelize@hotmail.com; ⑤), on the seafront and with very comfortable rooms with private hot-water showers and a thatched rooftop cabaña. *Fernando's* **restaurant** is open if there are enough guests, and several more small bars and restaurants are dotted around the village.

Orange Walk and around

Like Corozal, **ORANGE WALK**, the largest town in the north of Belize, was founded by mestizo refugees fleeing from the Caste Wars in Yucatán, who chose as their site an area that had long been used for logging camps and was already occupied by the local Icaiché (Chichanha) Maya. The area around Orange Walk has long had some of the most productive arable farmland in Belize – aerial surveys have revealed evidence of raised fields and a network of irrigation canals dating from ancient Maya times. In the Postclassic era this region controlled the trade in **cacao** beans (used as currency by the Maya), grown in the Hondo and New river valleys. For a while the Maya here were even able to resist the conquistadors, and Maya

Mennonites in Belize

Members of Belize's **Mennonite** community, easily recognizable in their denim dungarees, can be seen trading their produce and buying supplies every day in Orange Walk and Belize City. The Mennonites, a Protestant group often noted for their rejection of modern advancements and governmental objections to their pacifist beliefs, arose from the radical Anabaptist movement of the sixteenth century and are named after the Dutch priest Menno Simons, leader of the community in its formative years. Recurring government restrictions on their lifestyle, especially regarding their pacifist objection to military service, forced them to move repeatedly. Having firstly moved to Switzerland, they then travelled on to Prussia, and in 1663 a group emigrated to North America. After World War I they migrated from Canada to Mexico, eventually arriving in Belize in 1958. Perseverance and hard work made them successful farmers, and in recent years prosperity has caused drastic changes in their lives. The Mennonite Church in Belize is increasingly split between a modernist section – who use electricity and power tools, and drive trucks, tractors and even cars – and the traditionalists, who prefer a stricter interpretation of their beliefs.

rebellions continued long after nominal Spanish rule had been established in 1544. For the last 150 years Orange Walk has depended on the sugar and citrus industries, but a fall in sugar prices has seen it come to depend more heavily on profits from marijuana growing and shipping – though pressure from the US government has forced the Belizean authorities to destroy many of the marijuana fields and landing strips.

The centre of town is marked by a distinctly Mexican-style formal plaza, and the town hall across the main road is actually called the Palacio Municipal, reinforcing the town's strong historical links to Mexico. The tranquil, slow-moving **New River**, a few blocks east of the centre, was a busy commercial waterway during the logging days. Now, however, it's a lovely starting point for visiting the ruins of **Lamanai**, the area's main attraction. Also worth a look is the **Banquitas House of Culture**, on the riverbank near the bridge (Mon–Fri 8.30am–4pm, Sat 8.30am–1pm; free; ⓣ322-0517). Along with a charming park and amphitheatre, the centre's main building houses a permanent exhibition charting the history of Orange Walk District, from Maya times to the present. Glass cases contain superb artefacts from local Maya sites alongside maps and drawings of the sites themselves.

Practicalities

Hourly **buses** from Belize City and Corozal pull up on the main road in the centre of town, officially Queen Victoria Avenue but always referred to as the Belize–Corozal Road. Services to and from Sarteneja stop at Zeta's Store on Main Street, two blocks to the east, while local buses to the surrounding villages leave from the **market** area, behind the town hall and fire station. The **post office** right in the centre of town. **Internet access** is cheap and plentiful; *K &N Printshop*, on the Belize–Corozal Road a block south of the post office, is the most convenient.

The main road is lined with hotels and restaurants, so there's no need to walk far if sticking around. The best **place to stay** is the *St Christopher's Hotel*, 10 Main St (ⓣ322-2420, ⓔrowzbze@btl.net; ❻), which has rooms (some a/c) with private bath, set in grounds sweeping down to the New River. The only recommended budget hotel, *Lucia's Guest House*, 68 San Antonio Rd (ⓣ322-2244; ❸), has rooms ranging from basic shared bath to private bath with a/c. The majority of **restaurants** are Chinese, though there are a few Belizean-style places serving simple Creole or "Mexican" food, including *Juanita's*, on Santa Ana Street, by the Shell station towards the south end of town; there are also **food stalls** around the park behind the town hall.

Lamanai

Extensive restoration and a spacious new museum make **Lamanai** (Mon–Fri 8am–5pm, Sat, Sun & holidays 8am–4pm; US$5) easily the most impressive Maya site in northern Belize. Lamanai is one of the few sites whose original Maya name *Lama'an ayin* – "Submerged Crocodile" – is known, hence the numerous representations of crocodiles on stucco carvings and artefacts found here. *Lamanai*, however, is a seventeenth-century mis-transliteration, which actually means "Drowned Insect" – unfortunately it's this erroneous name that has survived in common usage. The site was continually occupied from around 1500 BC up until the sixteenth century, when Spanish missionaries built a church alongside to lure the Indians from their heathen ways.

As striking as the ruins themselves is Lamanai's setting, perched on the bank of the New River Lagoon inside a 950-acre Archeological Reserve containing the only jungle for miles around. The surroundings give the site a special quality that's long gone from sites served by a torrent of tourist buses – though increasing numbers of speed boats now carry cruise-ship visitors here. Over a dozen troops of **black howler monkeys** make Lamanai their home and you'll certainly see them peering down through the branches as you wander the trails; mosquitoes too, will be ever-present, so bring repellent.

Within the ruins, the most remarkable feature is the prosaically named N10-43 (informally the "High Temple"), a massive **Late Preclassic pyramid** over 37m tall, the largest structure from the period in the Maya region. The view across the surrounding forest and along the lagoon from the top of the temple is magnificent, and well worth the daunting climb. On the way to the High Temple you pass N10-27, a much smaller pyramid, at the base of which stands a replica of Stela 9, depicting the splendidly attired **Lord Smoking Shell** participating in a ceremony dating from around 625 AD. North from here is N9-56, a **sixth-century pyramid** with two stucco masks of a glorified ruler represented as a deity, probably Kinich Ahau, the sun god. The lower mask, four metres high, is particularly well-preserved, showing a clearly humanized face bordered by decorative columns, wearing a crocodile headdress.

The spacious new **archeological museum** at the site houses an impressive collection of artefacts, mostly figurines depicting gods and animals, particularly crocodiles. The most beautiful exhibits are the delicate **eccentric flints** – star and sceptre-shaped symbols of office – skilfully chipped from a single stone. Traces of later settlers can be seen around the site: immediately to the south of the museum are the ruins of two churches built by Spanish missionaries, and a short trail behind the museum leads west to the remains of a nineteenth-century sugar mill, built by **Confederate refugees** from the American Civil War.

Practicalities

The easiest, most pleasant way to get to Lamanai is by **river**, along which guides point out lurking crocodiles and dozens of species of bird, including snail kites and even nesting jabiru storks. A number of operators organize **day-trips** for US$40–50 per person from Orange Walk, departing around 9am; the price will usually include picnic lunch at the site. The most informative are Jungle River Tours (ⓣ302-2293, ⓔlamanaimayatour@btl.net), run by Antonio and Herminio Novelo and based at the *Lover's Restaurant*, which, unfortunately, is now one of Orange Walk's many brothels. Another good operator is Reyes River Tours (ⓣ322-3327), departing from the Tower Hill Toll Bridge, 11km south of Orange Walk. To get to the bridge independently, take the Northern Transport bus that leaves Belize City at 7am for Chetumal (the driver will drop you at the right place in good time for the 9am start); doing this part on your own for either tour saves you at least US$30 on the price of a tour from Belize City.

The second option for reaching Lamanai from Orange Walk is by local **bus** (Mon, Wed & Fri 3.30pm) to tiny **Indian Church**, located 2km from the site.

The bus is based in the village, leaving for Orange Walk at 5.30am on the same days, so you'll have to stay overnight. There are a couple of obvious places offering **rooms** (❹) in Indian Church, though they're rather overpriced for what you get. Instead, try asking in the new **Artisan Center** if someone can rent you a room or let you **camp**. Luxury accommodation is available nearby in the thatched cabañas at *Lamanai Outpost Lodge* (Ⓣ223-3578, Ⓦwww.lamanai.com; ❾), set in extensive gardens sweeping down to the lagoon; rooms start at US$120 per night.

Rio Bravo Conservation Area

In the far northwest of Orange Walk district is the **Rio Bravo Conservation Area**, a 1000-square-kilometre tract designated for tropical forest conservation, research and sustained-yield forest harvests. This conservation success story actually began with a disastrous plan in the mid-1980s to clear the forest, initially to fuel a wood-fired power station and later to provide Coca-Cola with frost-free land to grow citrus.

An imaginative project to save the threatened forest, the **Programme for Belize**, was initiated by the Massachusetts Audubon Society in 1988. Funds were raised from corporate donors and conservation organizations, but the most widespread support was generated through an ambitious "adopt-an-acre" scheme. Coca-Cola itself, anxious to distance itself from the charge of rainforest destruction, has donated more than 360 square kilometres. Today, rangers patrol the area to prevent illegal logging and to stop farmers encroaching onto the reserve with *milpas* (slash and burn fields). Thanks to the ban on hunting, the forest teems with **wildlife**, including all five of Belize's cat species, plus more than 300 types of bird. The guarded boundaries also protect dozens of **Maya sites**, most of them unexcavated and unrestored, though many have been looted.

There's no **public transport** to Rio Bravo, but if you're staying at La Milpa Field Station (see below) you can get a bus (Mon–Sat at 10am) from the side of the fire station in Orange Walk to San Felipe, 37km away, and arrange to be picked up there.

La Milpa Field Station

Set in a former *milpa* clearing in the forest, **La Milpa Field Station** offers comfortable dorm and cabaña **accommodation** in a tranquil, studious atmosphere (dorms US$88, cabañas US$103 per person, including three meals and two excursions or lectures a day). Guests are mainly students on tropical ecology courses, though everyone is welcome, and the facilities all use the latest green technology, while deer and ocellated turkeys feed contentedly around the cabins. Five kilometres west of the station is the huge Classic Maya city of **La Milpa**, the third largest in Belize, where several royal tombs have been uncovered. A day visit, which includes a guided tour, costs US$20. For **information**, bookings and transport for the station, contact the PFB office, 1 Eyre St, Belize City (Ⓣ227-5616, Ⓔpfbel@btl.net).

Crooked Tree

Some 38km south of Orange Walk a branch road heads west to **Crooked Tree Wildlife Sanctuary**, a reserve that takes in a vast area of wetlands, covering four separate lagoons. Designated Belize's first Ramsar site (to protect wetlands of international importance) the sanctuary provides an ideal resting place for thousands of **migrating and resident birds**, such as snail kites, tiger herons, snowy egrets, ospreys and black-collared hawks. The reserve's most famous visitor is the **jabiru stork**, the largest flying bird in the New World, with a wingspan of 2.5m. Belize has the biggest nesting population of jabiru storks and Crooked Tree boasts the largest concentration at any site in the country: they arrive in November and the young hatch in April or May. The **best months** for birdwatching are late February to June, when the lagoons shrink to a string of pools, forcing wildlife to congregate for food and water.

In the middle of the reserve, straggling around the shores of a lagoon, 5km from the main road, is the village of **CROOKED TREE** – linked to the mainland by a **causeway**. At the end of the causeway is the **Sanctuary Visitor Centre** (daily; 8am–5pm), where you pay the US$4 entrance fee. One of the oldest inland villages in the country, Crooked Tree's existence is based on fishing and farming – some of the mango and cashew trees here are reckoned to be more than a hundred years old – though the main attraction for visitors is simply strolling through the sandy, tree-lined lanes, and along the lakeshore, where you'll see plenty of birds.

Practicalities

There are at least four daily **buses** to Crooked Tree from Belize City. The Jex service (☎225-7017) leaves from Regent Street West (Mon–Sat 10.45am), and from the Pound Yard bridge (Mon–Fri 4.30pm, 5.15pm & 8pm). Sunday services are unpredictable but there's enough traffic along the side road from the Northern Highway to make hitching a viable option at any time – any non-express bus along the highway will drop you off at the junction with the Northern Highway. Returning buses leave early for Belize City (Mon–Sat between 5.30 & 7am).

Most of the **accommodation** at Crooked Tree is in mid-priced hotels, often with meals included (most also have **camping** space); there are also some inexpensive bed and breakfast rooms (❸) – ask at the Sanctuary Visitor Centre. *Bird's Eye View Lodge* (☎205-7027, ⓦwww.birdseyeviewlodge.com; ❻), on the lakeshore at the south end of the village, has comfortable private rooms in two concrete buildings; there's also a dorm room (US$15 per person) and camping (US$5). Though not on the lake, the good-value *Sam Tillet's Hotel* (☎220-7026 or ☎614-7920, ⓔsamhotel@btl.net; ❹–❻) has comfortable rooms, private thatched suites and camping (US$5); the garden attracts a variety of birds. *Paradise Inn* (☎225-7044, ⓦwww.adventurecamera.com/paradise; ❻) has beautiful thatched cabins in a quiet location, just steps from the lagoon at the north end of the village. Anyone offering accommodation can also arrange boats for **tours**, and should also be able to set you up with one of the village's supremely knowledgeable **guides**.

Altun Ha

Fifty-five kilometres north of Belize City and just 9km from the sea is the impressive Maya site of **Altun Ha** (daily 8am–5pm; US$5), which was occupied for around twelve hundred years until abandoned around 900 AD. Its position close to the Caribbean coast suggests that it was sustained as much by trade as by agriculture – a theory upheld by the discovery of trade objects such as obsidian and jade, neither of which occurs naturally in Belize, though both were very important in Maya ceremony. The jade would have come from the Motagua valley in Guatemala and much of it would probably have been shipped onwards to the north.

The core of Altun Ha is clustered around two Classic period plazas, both dotted with palm trees. Entering from the road, you come first to Plaza A. Large temples enclose it on all four sides, and a magnificent tomb has been discovered beneath Temple A-1, the **Temple of the Green Tomb**. Dating from 550 AD, this yielded a total of three hundred pieces, including jade, jewellery, stingray spines, skin, flints and the remains of a Maya book. The adjacent Plaza B is dominated by the site's largest temple, the **Temple of the Masonry Altars**. Several tombs have been uncovered within the main structure, though only two were found intact. In one, archeologists discovered a carved jade head of **Kinich Ahau**, the Maya sun god. Standing just under 15cm high, it is the largest carved jade to be found anywhere in the Maya world; a replica is on display in the Museum of Belize (see p.71).

Outside these two main plazas are several other areas of interest, though little else has yet been restored. A short trail leads south to **Rockstone Pond**, a reservoir in Maya times and today home to a large crocodile, at the eastern edge of which stands another mid-sized temple. Built in the second century AD, this contained offerings from the great city of Teotihuacán in the Valley of Mexico.

Practicalities

Altun Ha is fairly difficult to reach independently as the 3km track to the site is located along the Old Northern Highway – turn off the Northern Highway at Sand Hill village, Mile 18. In theory there are **buses** (Mon–Sat 4pm) from the Belize City terminal to the village of **Maskall** (call the community phone ⓣ209-1058 to check bus times), passing the turn-off to the site at the village of **Lucky Strike** (community phone ⓣ209-1017), but the service is erratic. Any travel agent in Belize City can arrange a **tour** (see p.74) and increasing numbers visit as part of a day-trip from San Pedro and Caye Caulker.

The nearest **accommodation** to the site are the delightful thatched, screen-sided cabins at *Pueblo Escondido*, Lucky Strike Village (ⓣ614-1458, ⓦwww.pueblo-escondido.net; ❺; camping US$10), three kilometres from the turn-off to the site – look for the *Fyah Haat* ("Fire Hearth" in Creole) **restaurant**. The owners offer **horse riding** on jungle trails and **bike rental**: a great way to get to Altun Ha.

The Community Baboon Sanctuary

West off the Northern Highway, 43km from Belize City, the **Community Baboon Sanctuary** (ⓦwww.howlermonkeys.org) is one of the most interesting conservation projects in Belize. It was established in 1985 by Dr Rob Horwich and a group of local farmers (with help from the World Wide Fund for Nature), who adopted a voluntary code of practice to harmonize their own needs with those of the wildlife. A mixture of farmland and broad-leaved forest along the banks of the Belize River, the sanctuary coordinates several villages and more than a hundred landowners in a project combining conservation, education and tourism.

The main focus of attention is the **black howler monkey** (known locally as a "baboon"). They generally live in groups of between four and eight, and spend the day wandering through the leaf canopy feasting on leaves, flowers and fruits. At dawn and dusk they let rip with the famous howl: a deep and rasping roar that carries for miles. The sanctuary is also home to over two hundred bird species, plus iguanas, peccaries and coatis. The **visitor centre** (US$5, includes a short guided walk), at the west end of Bermudian Landing, is home to Belize's first natural history museum, with exhibits and information on the riverside habitats and animals you're likely to see.

Practicalities

The sanctuary comprises eight villages along the Belize River, from Flowers Bank to Big Falls. All of them welcome visitors and you'll find plenty of places where you can rent canoes or horses. The most convenient base is the village of **Bermudian Landing** at the heart of the area, an old logging centre that dates back to the seventeenth century. At least two **buses** daily (Mon–Sat), leaving early afternoon, run between Belize City and the village, a journey of an hour and a quarter – see the Belize City section, pp.74–76 for departure points and times; returning buses leave between 5.30–6.30am.

You can **camp** at the visitor centre (US$5), while a number of local families offer **bed and breakfast** (❹), but the best accommodation option is *Nature Resort* (Ⓣ610-1378, Ⓔnaturer@btl.net; ❹–❻), with beautiful cabins (some thatched) and most with private hot-water shower, fridge, fan or a/c, coffee maker and hammocks on the porch; one has a full kitchen. The **community restaurant** behind the visitor centre, run by the village's women's group, serves delicious Creole meals. Another good choice is *Russell's Restaurant*, in the village centre (also the place where the one of the buses parks for the night), with tables overlooking the river. There's a **payphone** and **Internet** access in the visitor centre.

1.3

The northern cayes and atolls

Belize's spectacular **Barrier Reef**, with its dazzling variety of underwater life and string of exquisite islands – known as **cayes** (pronounced "keys") – is the country's main attraction for most first-time visitors. Forming part of the Western Caribbean Barrier Reef, it runs the entire length of the coastline, 15 to 40km from the mainland, and most of the cayes lie in shallow water behind the shelter of the reef. Though the 450 cayes themselves form only a tiny proportion of the country's total land area, and relatively few have any kind of tourism development, Belize has more territorial water than it does land, and the islands' tourism and lobster fishing accounts for a substantial amount of foreign currency earnings.

The town of **San Pedro** on **Ambergris Caye** has been transformed from a predominantly fishing community to one dominated by tourism. There are still some beautiful spots here, however, notably the protected sections of reef at either end of the caye: the **Bacalar Chico National Park** to the north and **Hol Chan Marine Reserve** to the south. South of Ambergris Caye, **Caye Caulker** is less developed and popular with budget travellers.

Beyond the barrier reef are two of Belize's three **atolls**, the **Turneffe Islands** and **Lighthouse Reef**, regularly visited on day-trips from San Pedro and Caye Caulker. Here the coral reaches the surface, enclosing a shallow lagoon, with some cayes lying right on top of the encircling reef. Lighthouse Reef encompasses two of the most spectacular diving and snorkelling sites in the country – **Half Moon Caye Natural Monument** and the **Great Blue Hole**, an enormous collapsed cave.

A brief history of the cayes

The earliest inhabitants of the cayes were **Maya** peoples or their ancestors. By the Classic period (300–900 AD) the Maya had developed an extensive trade network stretching from the Yucatán to Honduras, with evidence of settlements and trading centres on several of the islands. The most infamous residents of the cayes, however, were the **buccaneers**, predominately British, who lived here in the seventeenth and eighteenth centuries, taking refuge in the shallow waters after plundering Spanish treasure ships. In time the pirates, now calling themselves **Baymen**, settled more or less permanently, establishing their first capital on St George's Caye. In 1779 a Spanish force sacked the caye and imprisoned 140 of the Baymen and 250 of their slaves. The Baymen returned in 1783 and took revenge on the Spanish fleet in 1798, during the celebrated **Battle of St George's Caye**.

Fishermen and turtlers continued to use the cayes as a base for their operations, and refugees fleeing the Caste Wars in the Yucatán towards the end of the nineteenth century also settled on the islands in small numbers. During the twentieth century the island population increased steadily, and the establishment of the **fishing cooperatives** in the 1960s brought improved traps, ice plants, and access to the export market. At around the same time another boom began, as the cayes of

Safeguarding the coral reef

Coral reefs are among the most complex and **fragile** ecosystems on earth. Colonies have been growing at a rate of less than 5cm a year for thousands of years; once damaged, the coral is far more susceptible to bacterial infection, which can quickly lead to large-scale irreversible damage. Unfortunately, a great deal of damage has already been caused on Belize's Barrier Reef by snorkellers standing on the coral or holding onto outcrops for a better look – on all the easily accessible areas of the reef you will clearly see the white, dead patches, especially on the large brain-coral heads. All **tour guides** in Belize are trained in reef ecology before being granted a licence (which must be displayed as they guide), and if you go on an organized trip, as most people do, the guide will brief you on the following precautions to avoid damage to the reef.

- Never anchor boats on the reef – use the permanently secured buoys.
- Never touch or stand on corals – protective cells are easily stripped away from the living polyps on their surface, destroying them and thereby allowing algae to enter. Coral also stings and can cause agonizing burns – even brushing against it causes cuts that are slow to heal.
- Don't remove shells, sponges or other creatures from the reef, or buy reef products from souvenir shops.
- Avoid disturbing the seabed around corals – quite apart from spoiling visibility, clouds of sand settle over corals, smothering them.
- If you're a beginner or an out-of-practice diver, practise away from the reef first.
- Don't use suntan lotion in reef areas – the oils remain on the water's surface. Wear a T-shirt instead to protect your skin from sunburn.
- Check you're not in one of the marine reserves before fishing.
- Don't feed or interfere with fish or marine life; this can harm not only sea creatures and the food chain, but snorkellers too – large fish may attack, trying to get their share.

Belize, particularly Caye Caulker, became a hangout on the hippy trail and a new-found prosperity began to transform life on the cayes.

Ambergris Caye and San Pedro

The most northerly and, at almost forty kilometres long, by far the largest of the cayes is **Ambergris Caye**, separated from Mexico by the narrow **Bacalar Chico channel**, dug by the ancient Maya. The island's main attraction is the former fishing village of **SAN PEDRO**, facing the reef just a few kilometres from the caye's southern tip, 58km northeast of Belize City. If you fly into San Pedro the views are breathtaking: the sea appears so clear and shallow as to barely cover the sandy bed, while the pure white line of the reef crest dramatically separates the vivid blue of the open sea from the turquoise water on its leeward side.

San Pedro is a small town, but its population of several thousand is the biggest of any of the cayes. Although you're never more than a stone's throw from the Caribbean – the town takes up the whole width of the island at this point – in the built-up area most of the palms have died or been cut down, and traffic has increased in recent years, creating deep ruts (which become mud holes after rain) in the sandy streets. Despite rapid development, San Pedro just about manages to retain its feeling of Caribbean charm and is the main destination for most visitors to Belize. The tourist industry here caters mainly for North Americans – almost all prices are quoted in US dollars. Some of the most exclusive hotels, restaurants and bars in Belize are here; the only budget places are in the original village of San Pedro.

Getting to Ambergris Caye from Belize City is simple. As well as very frequent **flights**, there are regular **fast boats**, leaving the Marine Terminal in Belize City at

Water-taxis to and from Ambergris Caye and Caye Caulker

Most boats from Belize City to **Ambergris Caye** (1hr 20min; US$14 one way/US$25 return) and **Caye Caulker** (45min; US$9/15) are operated by the Caye Caulker Water Taxi Association (☎226-0992, Ⓦwww.cayecaulkerwatertaxi.com) and leave from the Marine Terminal at 8am, 9am, 10.30am, noon, 1.30pm, 3pm, 4.30pm and 5.30pm (this last service calls at Caye Caulker only). The *Thunderbolt* (☎226-2904) leaves from the dock opposite the Holy Redeemer church on North Front Street, half a block upriver from the Marine Terminal at 8am, 1pm and 4pm, and the *Triple J* (US$6.50 to Caye Caulker) leaves from Courthouse Wharf, south side of the Swing Bridge at 9am. Most boats to San Pedro call at Caye Caulker on the way.

Boats leave from **San Pedro to Caye Caulker and Belize City** every hour from 7am until 3.30pm (until 5.30pm on weekends and holidays). From **Caye Caulker to Belize City** they leave every hour from 6.30am to 4pm (until 5pm on weekends and holidays). Fares between Caye Caulker and Ambergris Caye are US$9/15.

The *Thunderbolt* also operates from **San Pedro to Corozal** (daily at 3pm; 1hr 30min) and from **Corozal to San Pedro** (daily at 7am).

least every couple of hours between 8am and 4.30pm, taking around ninety minutes to reach San Pedro; full transport details are given in the box above.

Arrival and information

Arriving boats usually dock at the *Coral Beach* pier on the front (reef) side of the island, though the *Thunderbolt* docks at *Cesario's* at the back of the island at the end of Black Coral Street. Arriving at either **dock**, you're pretty much in the centre. If you land at the **airport**, there are golf buggies and taxis to take you to your hotel, though it's only a short walk to anywhere in town. Formerly called Front, Middle and Back streets, the town's three **main streets**, running parallel to the beach, have been given names in keeping with the new upmarket image – Barrier Reef Drive, Pescador Drive and Angel Coral Street – but in any case, it's impossible to get lost.

There's no official tourist office, but **information** is easy to find. For starters, Ambergris Caye has one of the best **websites** in the country (Ⓦwww.ambergriscaye.com), with links to most of the businesses on the island. It's also worth picking up a copy of *The San Pedro Sun* or *Ambergris Today*, the island's **tourist newspapers** (US$0.50), available from most hotels and restaurants. Two **Internet cafés** on Barrier Reef Drive offer high-speed access: Caribbean Connection, next to the *Coral Beach Hotel*, with the best coffee, and Coconet, a few blocks north, next to *Fido's Courtyard*, which also has a lively bar.

To arrange international flights and trips throughout the country, visit Travel and Tour Belize (☎226-2031, Ⓦwww.traveltourbelize.com), on Coconut Drive just north of the airstrip. You needn't worry about **changing money**, as travellers' cheques and US dollars are accepted – even preferred – everywhere; the Belize Bank on Barrier Reef Drive has an ATM and the others will give **cash advances**. San Pedro's **post office** (Mon–Fri 8am–4.30pm) is in the Alijua building opposite the Atlantic Bank. There are two **laundries** on Pescador Drive.

Accommodation

Most of the **hotels** in San Pedro are just a short walk or taxi ride from the airport and all but a few are outside the reach of budget travellers. It's risky turning up at Christmas or Easter unless you've booked a room; at other times you should be fine, though if you do book in advance you might get a discount.

Caribbean Villas Hotel just over 1km along Coconut Drive, the road heading south from town ☎226-2715, Ⓦwww.caribbeanvillashotel.com. Great, small hotel set on a lovely beach, with spacious rooms and suites. All rooms have sea views, and the secluded location guarantees plenty

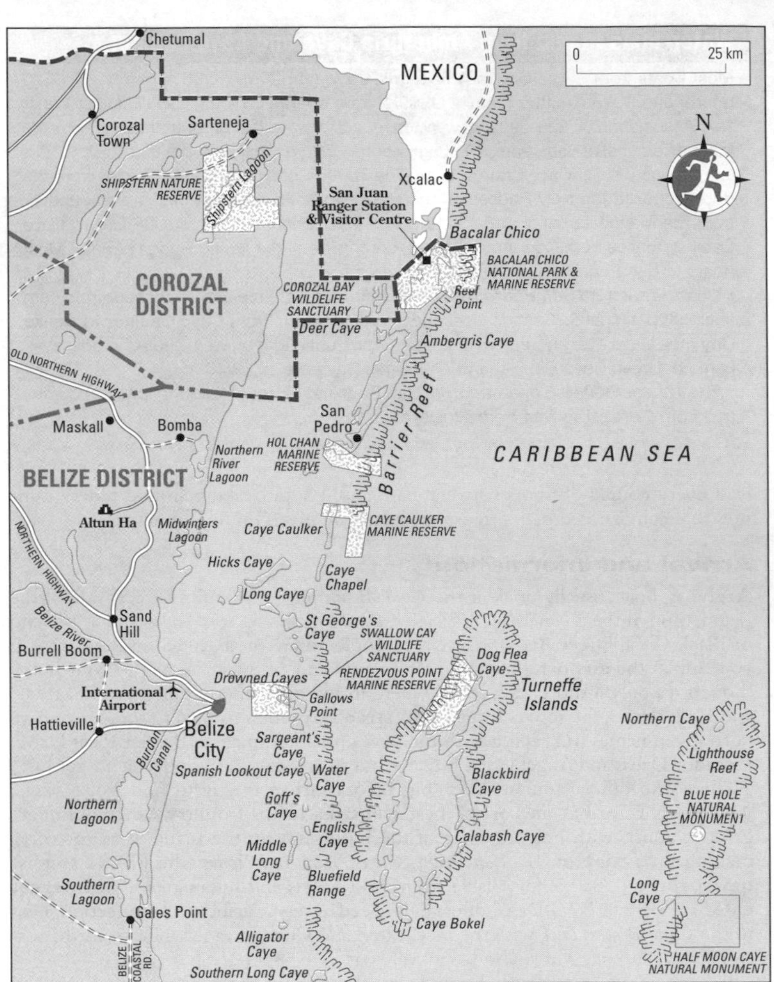

of peace and quiet. 8

Changes in Latitudes Coconut Drive, 1km south of town, near the Belize Yacht Club ⓣ 226-2986, ⓔ latitudesbelize@yahoo.com. Friendly B&B located half a block from the beach, with immaculately clean a/c rooms, and a communal kitchen. Canadian owner, Lori Reed, is a mine of information. 7

Coral Beach Hotel corner of Barrier Reef Drive and Black Coral Street. Nineteen recently renovated rooms with private bath, fan and a/c in a modern building with balconies front and back. Good packages for dive groups. 7

Corona del Mar On the beach a kilometre south of town ⓣ 226-2025, ⓔ corona@btl.net. Beautiful, well-equipped, spacious and very well-run apartments and suites (with full kitchens) with lots of extras. All have a/c, TV, phone and fridge and represent excellent value. Rates include rum punch all day and a full breakfast. 7–9

Martha's Hotel Pescador Drive, across from *Elvi's Kitchen* ⓣ 226-2053, ⓔ miguelperez@btl.net. A great-value hotel in the centre of town with clean, comfortable fan-cooled rooms with private bath. Free iced water in the rooms and laundry service available. 5

Pedro's Backpacker Inn Coconut Drive, 1km south of town ⓣ226-3825, ⓔpedroback2000@yahoo.com. Basic and rather bare budget rooms with two single beds with lockers underneath and shared showers, but the cheapest single rate on the island (though you could end up sharing if it's full), and there's even a small pool. US$12.50 per person; camping US$5 per person. ❺

Ruby's Barrier Reef Drive, a short walk from the airstrip ⓣ226-2063, ⓔrubys@btl.net. Clean, comfortable, family-run hotel on the seafront; rooms on the higher floors cost more, but all are good value, especially those located in the annex on the lagoon. ❺–❻

San Pedrano corner of Barrier Reef Drive and Caribeña Street ⓣ226-2054. Quiet, clean family-run hotel in a wooden building set back slightly from the sea, with comfortable, private-bath rooms (some with a/c) and breezy verandas. ❺–❻

Sunbreeze Hotel south end of Barrier Reef Drive ⓣ226-2191, ⓦwww.sunbreezehotel.com. Superbly run beachfront hotel with spacious, very comfortable a/c rooms (some with Jacuzzi bath) curving around a sandy courtyard and a pool. ❾

Victoria House three kilometres south of town ⓣ226-2027, in USA ⓣ1-800/247-5159, ⓦwww.victoria-house.com. Award-winning hotel with a stunning beachfront location and an obvious hit with honeymooners. The luxury a/c hotel rooms, thatched cabañas, suites and multi-room villas and houses with superbly equipped kitchens are set in spacious grounds resembling a botanical garden. Service is excellent and there's a pool and a fine restaurant. Prices start at US$195 for a double ("state") room in high season, and go up to US$825 for a two-bed villa. ❾

Exploring the caye

San Pedro's main streets are only half a dozen blocks long and the town doesn't boast any particular sights, though in a place so dedicated to tourist pleasure you're never far from a bar or gift shop. The main focus of daytime entertainment on Ambergris Caye is the **sea and the reef**, from sunbathing on the docks to windsurfing, sailing, fishing, diving, snorkelling and glass-bottomed boat rides. **Beaches** on the caye are narrow and the sea immediately offshore is shallow, with a lot of seagrass, so in town you'll usually need to walk to the end of a dock or take a boat trip to the reef if you want to swim. A word of warning: there have been a number of accidents in San Pedro where speeding boats have hit people swimming off the docks. A line of buoys, clearly visible, indicates the "safe area", but speedboat drivers can be a bit macho, so be careful where you swim.

Bikes, **mopeds** and expensive **golf carts** can be rented for exploring the caye on the rough tracks that run north and south from town; for bikes, try Joe's Bike Rental, corner of Pescador Drive and Caribeña ($12 per day). Heading south, you could ride at least part of the way to **Marco Gonzalez**, a Maya ruin near the southernmost tip of the island, though there's not much to see. After about ten minutes' walk north you'll come up against the **Boca del Rio** channel, crossed by a tiny ferry (free), on the other side of which are some secluded resorts and beaches. A **fast ferry**, the *Island Express* (US$5 each way), runs to the resorts in the north of the caye several times a day from Fido's dock, in the centre of town.

Diving and snorkelling

Before going snorkelling or diving, whet your appetite with a visit to the excellent **Hol Chan Marine Reserve office** (Mon–Sat 8.30am–5pm) on the lagoon side on Caribeña Street. Here you'll find plenty of photographs, maps and displays on the reserve, and the staff is happy to answer any questions. The most central snorkelling spot is the **reef** opposite San Pedro, a heavily used area that's been subject to intensive fishing and souvenir hunting. You're better off heading north, to **Mexico Rocks** for example, or south to Hol Chan (see overleaf), as the reef is in much better condition, with fascinating spur and groove formations. Marine life in these areas can include **large sharks** (hammerhead and tiger, as well as the common and harmless nurse sharks), turtles and spotted eagle rays, and even **manta rays** and **whale sharks**. That said, to experience the best diving in Belize you really need to take a trip out to one of the **atolls** (see p.98), for high-voltage excitement in a relatively pristine environment.

Diving and snorkelling operators

From Ambergris Caye, **open water certification**, which takes novices up to the standard of a qualified sport diver, costs around US$350, while a more basic, single-dive **resort course** ranges from US$90–125; both including equipment. For qualified divers a two-tank local dive costs around US$55, including tanks, weights, air and boat; fins, mask and regulator will be extra. Most dive shops in San Pedro recommend you make a voluntary contribution of US$1 per tank to help fund the town's **hyperbaric chamber** – though this may be included in the quoted price. Several dive centres now rent digital or film **cameras**; expect to pay at least US$25 a day for a basic model. The Protech **gear shop** in the centre of town (Ⓣ226-4660, Ⓦwww.protechbelize.com), the only such shop in Belize, also sells basic models, along with a wide range of other scuba and snorkel gear, spares and accessories.

The best **dive operators** are Amigos Del Mar, just north of the centre (Ⓣ226-2706, Ⓔamigosdive@btl.net), and Blue Hole Dive Center, just south of the centre (Ⓣ226-2982, Ⓔbluehole@btl.net). They both also have fast, comfortable boats for day-trips to the **atolls**: the Blue Hole and Half Moon Caye on Lighthouse Reef (US$185) and Turneffe Islands (US$165). Protech Belize (1km south of town, at the *Yacht Club* dock Ⓣ226-4690, Ⓔrg@protechbelize.com) offer all the regular dive trips in small groups, with the best rental gear. They're the only **technical dive centre** in Belize, offering IANTD rebreather technical diving and other courses, with oxygen and helium always in stock (they produce all nitrox on the island). Protech also operate an air-conditioned six-berth **live-aboard boat** for overnight trips to the outer atolls. A typical two-day trip costs US$275, including meals and five dives; on a three-day trip you can also reach Glover's Reef (see p.121).

All the dive shops in San Pedro also offer **snorkelling** trips, costing around US$20–30 for two to three hours, plus about US$5 or so to rent equipment. Snorkelling guides here (who must also be licensed tour guides) have lots of experience and will show you how to use the equipment before you set off. Two of the best **local guides** are Alfonso Graniel (Ⓣ226-3537) and Dino Gonzalez (Ⓣ600-0161).

The **Hol Chan Marine Reserve** (US$5), 8km south of San Pedro, at the southern tip of the caye, takes its name from the Mayan for "little channel", and it is this break in the reef that forms the focus of the reserve. Its three zones preserve a comprehensive cross-section of the marine environment, from the open sea beyond the reef crest through seagrass beds to mangroves. These habitats are closely linked: many reef fish feed on the seagrass beds, and the mangroves are a nursery area for juvenile fish. At **Shark-Ray Alley** (US$5, combined ticket US$8), now actually part of the reserve, you can swim in shallow water with three-metre **nurse sharks** and enormous **stingrays** – an extremely popular (but controversial) attraction. Watching these creatures glide effortlessly around you is an exhilarating experience and, despite their reputations, swimming here poses almost no danger to snorkellers, as humans are not part of their normal diet. Biologists, however, claim that the practice of feeding the fish to attract them alters their natural behaviour, and at times the area is so crowded that any hope of communing with nature is completely lost amongst the flailing bodies of other snorkellers.

Sailing and guided day-trips

While snorkelling and diving are easily the most popular watersports, **windsurfing** and **sailing** draw in visitors as well. The best rental and instruction for both is offered by SailSports Belize (Ⓣ226-4488, Ⓦwwwsailsportsbelize.com), on the beach in front of the *Holiday Hotel*. Sailboard rentals cost US$20–25 an hour, US$65–75 for a seven-hour day; sailboat rental US$25–45 an hour, again discounts for multiple hours. They also offer **kite-surfing** lessons; you'll need two 3-hour sessions (US$150 each) to really get going, as learning kite control is the hardest part.

Several large **sailboats** take snorkellers to Mexico Rocks and Hol Chan, or for a day-trip to **Caye Caulker**, employing a mix of motor and sail and returning to San Pedro around sunset. A popular one is *Rum Punch II* (☎226-2340; US$50), a ten-metre sailboat, while large groups can charter the 22-metre, motor-powered *Winnie Estelle* (☎226-2934), with a spacious, shaded deck and an open bar; both supremely relaxing experiences.

You could also take a **guided day-trip** to some of the **Maya sites** on the north-west coast of the island. On **San Juan** beach you'll be scrunching over literally thousands of pieces of Maya pottery, but perhaps the most spectacular site is **Chac Balam**, a ceremonial and administrative centre with deep burial chambers. On the way back, you navigate **Bacalar Chico**, the channel separating Belize from Mexico, now a **national park** and marine reserve with a visitor centre and some great snorkelling. At the mouth of the channel the reef is close to the shore; the boat has to cross into the open sea, re-entering the lagoon as you approach San Pedro and so completing a circumnavigation of the island. Tanisha, on Pescador between Pelican and Caribeña (☎226-2314 or 606-7814, Ⓦwww.tanishatours.com), and Excalibur, south end of Barrier Reef Drive (☎226-3235 or 606-8162), have the best tours and guides.

Day-trips from San Pedro to the ruins of **Altun Ha** (see p.84; US$80) or **Lamanai** (see p.82; US$125) are increasingly popular. Rounding the southern tip of the island in a fast skiff, you head for the mainland at the mouth of the Northern River, cross the lagoon and travel up the river to the tiny village of Bomba, where a van waits to take you to the sites. With a good guide this is an excellent way to spot wildlife, including crocodiles and manatees, and the riverbank trees are often adorned with orchids. Tanisha (above) and Seaduced (☎226-3221, Ⓔseabelize@btl.net) offer the best tours, led by naturalist guides.

Eating, drinking and nightlife

There are plenty of places to eat in San Pedro, and you'll usually get good service, though **prices** are generally higher than elsewhere in Belize. **Seafood** is prominent at most restaurants, and you can also rely on plenty of steak, shrimp, chicken, pizza and salads. There are several **Chinese** restaurants too, and in the evening several inexpensive **fast-food stands** open for business along the front of Central Park. **Buying your own food** isn't much of a bargain: there's no market and the supermarkets are stocked with expensive imported canned goods.

El Patio Black Coral Street, near the *Coral Beach Hotel*. Fine dining on seafood and steaks at very reasonable prices in a lovely thatched courtyard.

Elvi's Kitchen across the road from *Martha's* hotel. The place for seafood, burgers and fries, accompanied by delicious, *licuado*-like fruit drinks. Slick service and upmarket prices.

George's Kitchen south of town, behind the *Corona del Mar* hotel. Large portions of good seafood, Tex-Mex and Belizean dishes, and always a great daily special; a bargain for the island.

JamBel on the park, next to *Big Daddy's Disco*. A good-value place serving a very tasty blend of Jamaican and Belizean specialities, such as jerk chicken, pork, fish and curry, washed down with Belikin or Red Stripe.

The Reef near the north end of Pescador. Good Belizean food, including delicious seafood, at great prices; free cocktail with dinner.

Ruby's Café Barrier Reef Drive, next to *Ruby's Hotel*. Delicious homemade cakes, pies and sandwiches, and freshly brewed coffee. Opens at 6am, so it's a good place to order a packed lunch if you're going on a trip.

The Stained Glass Pub towards the north end of Barrier Reef Drive, opposite the Belize Bank. A friendly and successful blend of an American bar and grill and a British pub. The extensive menu includes soups, salads, meat loaf, fish and chips and a range of creative seafood dishes.

Waraguma towards the south end of Pescador Drive. A tiny, very inexpensive restaurant serving wonderful Creole, Garífuna, Mexican and Salvadorean dishes to locals and savvy travellers.

Bars and clubs

San Pedro is the tourist entertainment capital of Belize and if you check locally you'll find **live music** on somewhere every night of the week; *Fido's* just north of the park has a band most nights. Some of the hotels have fancy bars, several of which offer **happy hours**, while back from the main street are a couple of small **cantinas** where you can buy a beer or a bottle of rum and drink with the locals. For the best beachside happy hour (5–7pm), head for *Crazy Canuk Bar* at the *Exotic Caye Beach Resort*, where the resident band will get you in the party mood.

Big Daddy's **disco**, in and around a beach bar near the park, has the longest happy hour on the island, running from 5 to 9pm. *Jaguar's Temple*, opposite the park, has the top dancefloor, while the new, air-conditioned *Barefoot Iguana*, on Coconut Drive just south of the Yacht Club, is home to San Pedro's biggest disco. A few hundred metres beyond here to the right, the tiny *Black and White Reggae Bar* is the focal point for the island's Garífuna community and a good place to enjoy **drumming and punta**.

Caye Caulker

South of Ambergris Caye and 35km northeast of Belize City, **Caye Caulker** is even more relaxed and easy-going than San Pedro, and more affordable for the budget traveller. Until recently, tourism existed almost as a sideline to the island's main source of income, **lobster fishing**, and there's always plenty of lobster for the annual **Lobster Fest**, held in the third weekend of June to celebrate the opening of the season. **Flights** on the San Pedro run stop at Caye Caulker's airstrip, though most visitors still arrive on the regular **boats** leaving from the Marine Terminal or Courthouse Wharf in Belize City (for full details, see box on p.89).

Arrival and information

The **airstrip** is about 1km south of the centre, within easy walk of the hotels south of the main dock or you can take a **golf-cart taxi**. If you arrive at either the main "front" dock or the "back" docks, simply walk ahead one block and you're in the centre of the village. There's no official tourist office, but you may want to check the island's **website** (Ⓦwww.gocayecaulker.com) before arriving. Caye Caulker's **travel agency**, Treasured Travels (Ⓣ226-0083, Ⓦwww.staycayecaulker.com), is also a good source of information and can also book domestic and international flights. **Leaving for Belize City**, boats depart roughly every two hours from 6.30am to 4pm (5pm on weekends).

There are no street names in Caye Caulker village, but the street running along the shore at the front of the island is effectively "**Front Street**", with just one or two streets running behind it in the centre of the island. The **post office** is in the health-centre building, south of the centre, and the **BTL** office on the street leading to the back dock. There's **Internet** access at *Cyber Café*, just north of the *Sandbox Restaurant*. The Atlantic Bank, just south of the centre, gives Visa **cash advances** (US$5 fee), and most businesses accept plastic. Note that **tap water** on the caye should be regarded as unfit to drink; rainwater and bottled water are widely available.

Accommodation

Caye Caulker has an abundance of simply furnished and inexpensive shared-bath rooms in clapboard hotels, and there are plenty of more comfortable places with private bathrooms, but to arrive at Christmas or New Year without a **reservation** could leave you stranded. Even the furthest **hotels** are no more than ten minutes' walk from the front dock and places are easy to find. As yet there is little air conditioning on the island (though all rooms have fans), which is fine most of the time, when a cooling breeze blows in from the sea, but **sandflies and mosquitoes** can

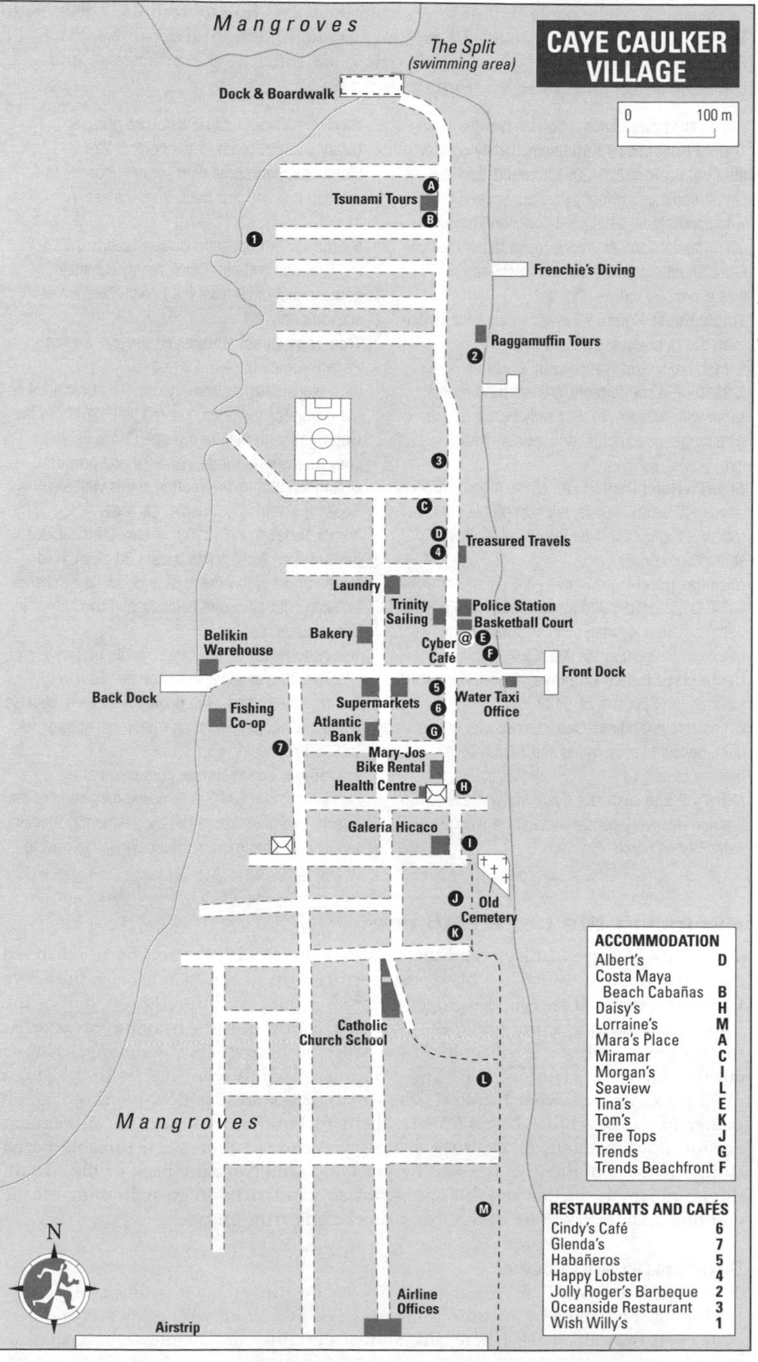
CAYE CAULKER VILLAGE
0
100 m
Mangroves
The Split
(swimming area)
Dock & Boardwalk
Tsunami Tours
Frenchie's Diving
Raggamuffin Tours
Treasured Travels
Laundry
Trinity Sailing
Police Station
Basketball Court
Bakery
Belikin Warehouse
Cyber Café
Front Dock
Back Dock
Fishing Co-op
Supermarkets
Water Taxi Office
Atlantic Bank
Mary-Jos Bike Rental
Health Centre
Galería Hicacao
Old Cemetery
Catholic Church School
Mangroves
Airline Offices
Airstrip
N
Barrier Reef (1.5km)
ACCOMMODATION
Albert's D
Costa Maya Beach Cabañas B
Daisy's H
Lorraine's M
Mara's Place A
Miramar C
Morgan's I
Seaview L
Tina's E
Tom's K
Tree Tops J
Trends G
Trends Beachfront F
RESTAURANTS AND CAFÉS
Cindy's Café 6
Glenda's 7
Habañeros 5
Happy Lobster 4
Jolly Roger's Barbeque 2
Oceanside Restaurant 3
Wish Willy's 1

cause almost unbearable irritation on calm days. For **house rentals**, check with Vacation Rentals (Ⓣ226-0029, Ⓦwww.cayecaulkerrentals.com) or M & N Apartments (Ⓣ226-0229). The hotels below are listed in the order you approach them, heading north or south from the front dock.

North from the front dock

Trends Beachfront Hotel immediately right of the front dock. Ⓣ226-0094, Ⓔtrendsbze@btl.net. Large rooms in a brightly painted wooden building with comfortable beds, tiled floors and balconies. (❻). There's another *Trends* round the corner on Front Street (left at *Habañeros Restaurant*) with less expensive rooms (❹). ❻

Tina's Guest House 75 metres along the beach from the front dock Ⓣ226-0351, Ⓔrastatinabelize@yahoo.com. Dorm beds (US$10) and comfortable, shared-bath rooms, some with balcony, in a friendly beach house with communal kitchen and garden with hammocks. ❺

Albert's Hotel Front Street, above Albert's grocery store Ⓣ226-0277. Basic but acceptable wooden rooms – the cheapest on the island – all with shared shower. ❸

Miramar Hotel Front Street, past *Albert's* Ⓣ206-0357. Basic good-value rooms, some with private bathroom, in a wooden building with a large balcony, overlooking the sea. ❹

Costa Maya Beach Cabañas 400m further north, towards the Split Ⓣ226-0432, Ⓔcostamaya@btl.net. Clean rooms with private bath, bedside lights, fridge and TV, run by a friendly family. ❺

Mara's Place Just past *Costa Maya* Ⓣ226-0156. Comfortable, very good-value cabins with private bath, TV and porch. ❺

South from the front dock

Daisy's 250m south of the dock Ⓣ226-0150. Simple budget rooms with shared showers in a wooden building just back from the sea, run by a friendly family. ❹

Morgan's Inn opposite Galería Hicaco Ⓣ226-0178, Ⓔsbf@btl.net. Quiet, roomy cabins in gardens just back from the beach. Cold-water showers only. ❺

Tree Tops Guest House just beyond *Tropical Paradise* restaurant Ⓣ226-0240, Ⓔtreetopsbelize@direcway.com. The best hotel on the island for the price, located just 50m from the water and with helpful owners. Chose between cosy rooms with fridge, cable TV and powerful ceiling fan and luxury rooftop suites with a/c. Booking ahead is advisable. ❺ & ❼

Tom's Hotel Ⓣ226-0102, Ⓔtoms@btl.net. Just beyond *Tree Tops*, *Tom's* boasts 20 clean, tiled rooms (most with private bathrooms) in a concrete building with all-round balcony, and five cabins in the grounds. ❺

Seaview Hotel on the beach, south of *Tom's* Ⓣ226-0205, Ⓔseaviewcc@btl.net. Four very comfortable rooms, with private bathroom, bedside lights and fridge, plus a one-bedroom cottage for US$350 per week. ❻

Lorraine's Guest House 75m south of the *Seaview* Ⓣ206-0162. A fantastic bargain near the beach, this guesthouse run by the friendly Alamilla family has simple but restful cabins with private hot showers. ❹

Exploring the caye and reef

The island of Caye Caulker is a little over 8km long, with the southern, inhabited end curving away west like a hook; the northern tip of the island forms the **Caye Caulker Forest Reserve**, designated to protect the caye littoral forest, one of the scarcest habitats in Belize, while the reef 1.5km offshore is a **marine reserve**. At the northern end of the village is "**The Split**", a narrow (but widening) channel cut by Hurricane Hattie in 1961 and a popular place to relax and swim. It's also a glaring example of what happens when mangroves are cut down – the original owner of the beach bar here removed them to build a dock, and the subsequent erosion now threatens to wash the bar away. Although there's a reasonable beach along the front of the caye (created by pumping sand from the back of the island), the sea nearby is shallow and full of seagrass, so you'll need to go swimming off the end of a dock or take one of the many snorkelling trips on offer.

Snorkelling and Diving

The **reef** is certainly an experience not to be missed, swimming along coral canyons accompanied by an astonishing range of fish, along with eagle rays and perhaps even the odd shark (these will almost certainly be harmless nurse sharks).

Here, as everywhere, snorkellers should be aware of the fragility of the reef and be careful not to touch any coral; see the box on p.88 for reef etiquette.

Snorkelling trips are easily arranged by the island's many snorkel and dive shops; expect to pay US$20–25 per person, plus US$5 for equipment rental. Some day-trips also go to **Hol Chan Marine Reserve** (see p.92), calling for lunch at San Pedro on Ambergris Caye, but they're more expensive and you're actually better off going to the local sites. Highly recommended operators include: Anwar Snorkel Tours (ⓣ226-0327); Carlos Tours (ⓣ226-1654, ⓔcarlosayala@hotmail.com); Tsunami Adventures, at the *Costa Maya Cabañas* (ⓣ226-0462, ⓦwww.tsunamiadventures.com); and the outstanding outings offered by Ras Creek, in his dory *Heritage* (US$15), which sails from the main dock in the morning.

Diving instruction and trips can be fractionally cheaper here than on San Pedro. Paradise Down, at the *Oceanside Bar* (ⓣ226-0437, ⓦwww.paradisedown.com), and Frenchie's, towards the northern end of the village (ⓣ226-0234, ⓔfrenchies@btl.net), both offer enthusiastic, knowledgeable local trips, with some great reef diving and coral gardens. They also offer regular fast boat trips to **Lighthouse Reef and The Blue Hole** (see overleaf), mainly for divers, but Seagull Adventures (ⓣ226-0384, ⓔseagulladventures@hotmail.com), on the street leading to the back dock, specialize in arranging Blue Hole trips for snorkellers, leaving at 6.30am (US$90). Other destinations include **Swallow Caye Wildlife Sanctuary**, on a mangrove caye near Belize City to view the **manatees**; contact Chocolate's Manatee Tours (ⓣ226-0151; US$40).

Sailing and other day-trips

An even better, more romantic way to enjoy the sea and the reef is to spend the best part of the day on one of the **sailboat trips**, costing around US$30–40 and usually including several snorkelling stops and lunch, arriving back as the sun goes down; there are also some **sunset cruises**. The most tranquil, run by a very experienced skipper, is aboard *Trinity*; check at the house across from the basketball court (ⓣ226-0414). Other day-trips are offered by Ragamuffin Tours, near the north end of Front Street (ⓣ226-0348, ⓦwww.raggamuffintours.com), who also run overnight trips to Lighthouse Reef and even down to Placencia (see p.123). For **sailboat rental** see Sail King, on the beach just north of the centre (ⓣ226-0489, ⓦwww.sailking.com), where you can rent boats from US$10–20 per hour. **Kayaks** are available too: try *Daisy's* hotel or ask at the Galería Hicaco (ⓣ226-0178), where you can also rent a **sailboard**. The Galería's owner, marine biologist Ellen McRae, also gives well-informed **wildlife tours** (US$15–25).

Eating and drinking

Good home-cooking, large portions and very reasonable prices are features of the island's many restaurants. **Lobster** (in season) is served in every imaginable dish, from curry to chow mein and **seafood** is generally good value. Some bars have **live music**; otherwise, evening entertainment mostly consists of relaxing in a restaurant over dinner or a drink, or gazing at the tropical night sky. You can buy food at several **shops** and supermarkets on the island and children walk around selling home-baked banana bread, coconut cakes and other goodies; there's also a good **bakery** on the street leading to the football field.

Cindy's Café, on Front Street just south of the centre, is the best place for filling Continental-style **breakfasts**, serving homemade bread and bagels, granola, fruit and excellent coffee; at the back of the island, *Glenda's* is another favourite breakfast meeting place, featuring great cinnamon rolls. The island's best restaurant, *Habañeros* (closed Mon & Tues; ⓣ226-0487), on Front Street near the main dock, serves fantastic and creative gourmet meals, with fine wine and slick bar service; it's usually packed, so call for reservations. The *Happy Lobster*, just north of the centre, serves good-value local dishes, while further north the *Oceanside Restaurant* has good food and service and occasional live music. Further on, *Jolly Roger's Barbeque*, on a beachfront deck, serves the island's best grilled lobster and fish. Follow the signs just past here to *Wish Willy's*, a friendly restaurant in a ramshackle building at the back of the island, for some of the most delicious seafood in Belize.

The northern atolls

Although Caye Caulker and San Pedro are the only villages anywhere on the reef, there are a couple of dozen other inhabited islands, some of them supporting fishing camps or upmarket resorts and lodges. The virtually uninhabited **Turneffe Islands**, 40km from Belize City and south of cayes Caulker and Ambergris, comprise an oval archipelago of low-lying mangrove islands around a shallow lagoon 60km long, enclosed by a beautiful coral reef. You can visit the archipelago as part of a day-trip from San Pedro and Caye Caulker. The construction of resorts on this remote and fragile island has resulted in the controversial destruction of mangroves, while a proposed marine reserve has yet to be established.

About 80km east of Belize City is Belize's outermost atoll, **Lighthouse Reef**, home to the underwater attractions of the Great Blue Hole and Half Moon Caye Natural Monument, while there are also several **shipwrecks** that have formed artificial reefs. The **Blue Hole**, technically a karst-eroded sinkhole, is a shaft over 300m in diameter and 135m deep, which drops through the bottom of the lagoon and opens out into a complex network of caves and crevices; its depth gives it an astonishing deep blue colour. You can visit the atoll either as a day or overnight trip from San Pedro or Caye Caulker.

The **Half Moon Caye Natural Monument**, the first marine conservation area in Belize, was declared a national park in 1982 and became one of Belize's first World Heritage Sites in 1996. The 180,000-square-metre caye is divided into two distinct ecosystems. In the west, guano from thousands of seabirds fertilizes the soil, allowing the growth of dense vegetation, while the eastern half has mostly coconut palms growing in the sand. A total of 98 bird species has been recorded here, including frigate birds, ospreys, and a resident population of four thousand **red-footed boobies**, one of only two such nesting colonies in the Caribbean. The boobies came by their name because they display no fear of humans, moving only reluctantly when visitors stroll among them – their nesting area is viewable from a platform. The resident reserve wardens will collect the US$5 **visitor fee** and can give permission to **camp** (US$5per person).

1.4

Cayo and the west

Heading west from Belize City towards the Guatemalan border 130km away, you travel through a wide range of landscapes, from open grassland to rolling hills and dense tropical forest. A fast, paved road, the **Western Highway**, runs the entire route, taking you from the heat and humidity of the coast to the lush foothills of the Maya Mountains.

Before reaching Belize's tiny capital, **Belmopan**, the road passes two worthwhile attractions, the **Belize Zoo** and the **Monkey Bay Wildlife Sanctuary**. West of Belmopan, following the Belize River valley, the road skirts the foothills of the **Maya Mountains**, a beautiful area where the air is clear and the land astonishingly fertile. You're now in **Cayo District**, the largest of Belize's six districts and arguably the most beautiful – a sentiment enthusiastically endorsed by the inhabitants who like to declare "the west is the best". South of the road, the **Mountain Pine Ridge** is a pleasantly cool region of hills and pine woods traversed by good dirt roads. **San Ignacio**, on the Macal River, is the ideal base for exploring the forests, rivers and ruins of western Belize. South of San Ignacio, deep in the jungle of the Vaca plateau, lie the ruins of **Caracol**, the largest Maya site in Belize.

Between San Ignacio and the Guatemalan border, the road climbs past the hilltop ruins of **Cahal Pech** then descends, following the valley of the Mopan River 15km to the frontier bridge. A few kilometres before the border, at the village of **San José Succotz**, an ancient ferry crosses the river, allowing access to the Maya site of **Xunantunich**, from the top of which you can look out over the Guatemalan department of Petén.

Belize City to San Ignacio

Leaving Belize City, the Western Highway cuts through the Lord's Ridge cemetery then skirts the shoreline, running behind a tangle of mangrove swamps. After 26km the road passes through **Hattieville** (named after the 1961 hurricane), where a paved road north to Burrell Boom provides a short cut to the Northern Highway, bypassing Belize City. If time permits you should allow an hour or two to visit the **Belize Zoo**, but you'd need to stay at least overnight to fully appreciate the nearby **Monkey Bay Wildlife Sanctuary**. For most people the capital, **Belmopan**, is no more than a break in the bus ride, though if heading south for Dangriga or Placencia this is the place to change buses. Beyond Belmopan the landscape becomes hilly, and unpaved **side roads** head south into the uplands, leading to some of Belize's most spectacular scenery. Once across the gorgeous **Macal River** you're in the delightful riverside town of **San Ignacio**.

The Belize Zoo and Monkey Bay Wildlife Sanctuary

The first point of interest along the highway is the **Belize Zoo**, at Mile 29 (daily 8.30am–5pm; US$7.50; ⓦwww.belizezoo.org), easily visited on a half-day trip from Belize City or as a stop on the way west. Probably the finest zoo in the Americas south of the USA, and long recognized as a phenomenal conservation achievement, the zoo originally opened in 1983 after an ambitious wildlife film (*Path of the Raingods*) left Sharon Matola (the film's production assistant, now zoo director),

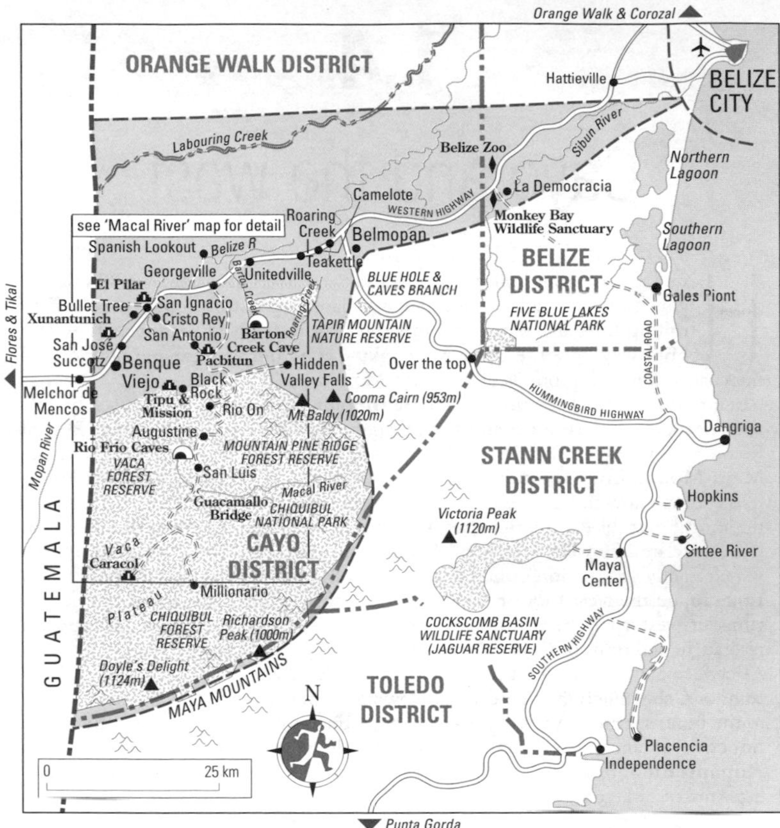

with a collection of semi-tame animals no longer able to fend for themselves in the wild. The zoo is organized around the theme of "a walk through Belize", and offers the chance to see the country's native animals at close quarters, housed in spacious enclosures closely resembling their natural habitat – residents include all the Belizean cats, some of which, including the jaguars, have bred successfully here. To **get to the zoo** take any bus between Belize City and Belmopan and ask the driver to drop you at the signed turn-off, a 200-metre walk from the entrance and visitor centre.

One kilometre past the zoo, the **Coastal Road** (served by only one daily bus in each direction) provides an unpaved short cut, marked by a sign and a couple of bars, to Gales Point (see p.116) and Dangriga. A kilometre or so past the junction is *Cheers*, a friendly **restaurant** with good food at reasonable prices, and reliable information. Half a kilometre past here and 300m off the Western Highway, **Monkey Bay Wildlife Sanctuary** (Ⓣ820-3032, Ⓦwww.monkeybaybelize.org; free), is a 44-square-kilometre protected area extending to the Sibun River, which offers birding and nature trails through five distinct types of vegetation and habitat. Adjoining the sanctuary is the **Monkey Bay National Park**, enclosing a biological corridor that runs south through karst limestone hills to connect with the Manatee Forest Reserve. Facilities include a field research station for student groups, with an excellent library and small museum. Apart from being a relaxing place **to stay**, either in a room in the Field Station (❺), a bed in the bunkhouse

(US$7.50) or camp (US$5) under thatched shelters, Monkey Bay is a viable experiment in sustainable living, using solar power, rainwater catchment and biogas fuel for cooking; the food (some of it grown in the station's organic gardens) is plentiful and delicious. *Amigos Bar* next to Monkey Bay has great food, a daily happy hour and Internet access.

Belmopan

Beyond here the Western Highway pushes on towards **BELMOPAN**, where the **Hummingbird Highway** (see p.114) heads south to Dangriga. Belmopan was founded in 1970 after Hurricane Hattie swept much of Belize City into the sea. The government decided to use the disaster as a chance to move to higher ground and, in a Brasília-style bid to focus development on the interior, chose a site in the geographical heart of the country. The name of the city combines the words "Belize" and "Mopan", the language spoken by the Maya of Cayo. The layout of the main government buildings is modelled loosely on a Maya city, grouped around a central plaza, and Belmopan was meant to symbolize the dawn of a new era, with tree-lined avenues, banks, embassies and communications worthy of a world centre. The city's population continues to grow slowly, but for now there's still little reason to stay any longer than it takes your bus to leave.

Practicalities

Buses from Belize City to San Ignacio, Benque Viejo, Dangriga and Punta Gorda all pass through Belmopan, so there's at least one service every thirty minutes in either direction – the last bus from Belmopan to Belize City leaves at 7pm; to San Ignacio, at 10pm. **Heading south** along the Hummingbird Highway, buses leave roughly every hour from 7am until 6pm. Most buses stop in the Novelo's terminal but the James bus pulls up across the parking lot, in front of the **market** – which has good fruit and food stands. The best **restaurant** is the *Caladium*, beside the Novelo's terminal, serving good Belizean food with an inexpensive daily special.

The **banks** (with ATMs) are close to where the buses stop and **Internet** access is available at Techno Hub (Mon–Sat 8am–8.30pm) at the front of the Novelo's terminal, and at PC Com, next to the *Caladium*. The **immigration** office is in the main government building by the fire station, and the **British High Commission** (Ⓣ822-2146) is on the North Ring Road.

Belmopan to San Ignacio

Beyond Belmopan the scenery becomes more rugged, with thickly forested ridges rising to the south. The road stays close to the valley of the Belize River, passing through a series of villages along with a string of cottage-style **lodges**. One of the best is *Pook's Hill Jungle Lodge* (Ⓣ820-2017, Ⓦwww.pookshilllodge.com; ❾), 9km along a signposted track from Teakettle village, 8km beyond the Belmopan junction. The lodge comprises cabañas set in a small clearing above a hillside terraced by the Maya, overlooking the thickly forested Roaring River valley, with breathtaking views across to the Mountain Pine Ridge. Another overnight option off the Western Highway, 23km west of Belmopan, is *Caesar's Place* (Ⓣ824-2341, Ⓔblack-rock@btl.net; ❻), a café and guesthouse with comfortable rooms, trailer hookups, space for camping and a fabulous gift shop on the banks of Barton Creek. A few kilometres further west, the **Chiquibul Road** heads south from the highway at **Georgeville** to the **Mountain Pine Ridge Forest Reserve** (see p.108), reaching deep into the forest and crossing the Macal River at the Guacamallo Bridge, eventually leading to **Caracol** (see p.111). Twelve kilometres along the Chiquibul Road, **Green Hills Butterfly Ranch** (daily 8am–5pm; US$4) has Belize's biggest and best collection of butterflies. The Western Highway continues for 9km to **Santa Elena**, San Ignacio's sister town on the eastern bank of the Macal River, which is crossed by the Hawkesworth Bridge, built in 1949 and still the only road

△ The Macal River, Cayo District

suspension bridge in Belize. Traffic from Belize City crosses the river on a low bridge (covered in high water) a little downstream; the Hawkesworth Bridge is only used by eastbound traffic.

San Ignacio and Cayo district

On the west bank of the Macal River, about 35km from Belmopan, **SAN IGNACIO** is a friendly, relaxed town that draws together the best of inland Belize. Surrounded by fast-flowing rivers and forested hills, it's an ideal base from which to explore the region, offering good food, inexpensive hotels and frequent bus connections. The evenings here are relatively cool and the days fresh – a welcome break from the sweltering heat of Belize City.

San Ignacio town is usually referred to as **Cayo** by locals (this is also the name usually seen on buses), the same word that the Spanish use to describe the offshore islands – an apt description of the area, which is set in a peninsula between two converging rivers. The early wave of the Spanish Conquest in 1544 made little impact here, and the area was a centre of rebellion in the following decades. **Tipu**, a Maya city on the Macal River about 9km south of the present-day town, was the capital of the province of Dzuluinicob, where for years the Maya resisted attempts to convert them to Christianity. **Spanish friars** arrived in 1618, but the population continued to practise idolatry and in 1641 Maya priests threw out some visiting Spanish clerics. Tipu retained a measure of independence until 1707, when the population was forcibly removed to Lago de Petén Itzá in Guatemala.

Around this time **British loggers** (Baymen) arrived, seeking mahogany – like many places in modern Belize, San Ignacio probably started life as a logging camp. Spanish influence, never great, was by now in permanent decline, and the British were not interested in converting the remaining Maya – a map of 1787 simply states that the Maya of this general area were "in friendship with the Baymen". Later, in addition to logging, San Ignacio became a centre for the shipment of **chicle**, the sap of the sapodilla tree and the basis of chewing gum. The self-reliant *chicleros*, as the collectors of chicle were called, knew the forest intimately, including the location of most, if not all, Maya ruins. When the demand for **Maya artefacts** sent black-market prices rocketing, some of them turned to looting.

Until the Western Highway was built in the 1930s local transport was by mule or water. It could take ten days of paddling to reach San Ignacio from Belize City, though small steamers later began to make the trip. Nowadays river traffic, which had almost died out, is enjoying something of a revival thanks to the increasing numbers of tourists. Indeed, a good time to visit San Ignacio is at the start of **La Ruta Maya canoe race**, held annually in early March, when teams of paddlers race all the way to Belize City. Anyone can enter, but local teams always win.

Practicalities

Novelo's Western Transport **buses** run regular services from Belize City to San Ignacio, continuing to Benque Viejo, for the Guatemalan border (35min total); a shared **taxi** to the border from San Ignacio costs US$2 per person. Buses stop in the terminal on Burns Avenue, the town's main street. As there's no official tourist office, the best stop for local **information** is the long-established *Eva's Bar* on Burns Avenue, whose owner knows almost everything about Cayo. *Eva's* also has **Internet access**, but for better value try the *Green Dragon Café* or *Tradewinds*, both on Hudson Street. Most other facilities can also be found on Burns Avenue, including **banks** (the Belize Bank has an ATM) and the **post office** is next to Courts furniture store in the centre of town. **Laundry** can be done at *Martha's* on West Street. For domestic and international **air tickets** go to Exodus Travel, 2 Burns Ave (☎824-4400).

Independent tour operators in San Ignacio

Numerous independent local operators offer superb guided trips to attractions around San Ignacio and the list below covers a range of adventurous options; there are many more. As always in Belize, make sure anyone offering you a guided trip is a **licensed tour guide** – they should display their photo-card guide licence. All the guides named below are either based in San Ignacio or will pick you up there. Not all have an office; if you can't contact them directly then go to the *Green Dragon Café* (see p.106), where they'll do it for you. For **bike rental**, check at the *Tropicool* Hotel; for **canoes**, see Snooty Fox, listed below.

David's Adventure Tours at the far side of the park, near the market ⓣ804-3674, ⓦwww.davidtours.com. Multilingual David Simpson, the original guide to Barton Creek Cave, also leads overnight jungle trips and tours to Caracol. See also *Guacamallo Jungle Camp*, p.108.

Easy Rider in Arts and Crafts, on Burns Avenue just past *Eva's* ⓣ824-2253, ⓔeasyrider@btl.net. Charlie Collins organizes the best-value horse-riding packages in San Ignacio (US$25 for a half-day, US$40 for a full day).

Everald's Caracol Shuttle at *Crystal Paradise Resort* (see p.108) ⓣ820-4014. Everald Tut runs inexpensive daily van trips to Caracol (US$50).

Mayawalk Adventures 19 Burns Ave ⓣ824-3070, ⓦwww.mayawalk.com. Aaron Juan leads trips to the astonishing sacrificial cave of Actun Tunichil Muknal (US$75) and overnight caving and rock-climbing expeditions.

River Rat ⓣ832-7013, ⓔriverratbelize@btl.net. Gonzalo Pleitez lives up the Macal River and arranges excellent whitewater kayak floats and jungle trips (US$45–80).

Snooty Fox Tours corner of West Street and Waight's Avenue, opposite *Martha's* ⓣ824-2720, ⓔsnootyfox@btl.net. Michael Waight has the best-value canoe rental in Cayo (US$30/day), and offers drop-off and shuttle service to points along the Macal River.

Toni's River Adventures at *Eva's Bar* ⓣ824-3292, ⓔevas@btl.net. Toni Santiago runs the longest-established and best-value guided canoe trip on the Macal River; under US$25 for an expert paddle upriver to the Rainforest Medicine Trail (see p.107). Also organizes fantastic overnight camping trips along the river.

Accommodation

San Ignacio has some of the best-value **budget accommodation** in the country and you'll almost always find space; most of the upmarket hotels and lodges are located in the countryside around the town and are covered on pp.107–108. For **camping**, try *Cosmos* or *Midas*.

Casa Blanca Guest House 10 Burns Ave ⓣ824-2080, ⓔcasablanca@btl.net. A new hotel with immaculate en-suite rooms, all with TV (some with a/c) and a comfortable sitting area with fridge, coffee and tea. Very friendly service and excellent value; booking is advisable. ❺–❻

Central O'tel 24 Burns Ave ⓣ824-3734, ⓔeasyrider@btl.net. Simple, clean, good-value budget hotel with shared bathrooms; the balcony with hammocks is a great place from which to watch the street below. ❸

Cosmos Campground 1km along the Branch Mouth Road ⓣ824-2116. Campsite with showers, flush toilets and a kitchen (US$3.50 per person) and simple rooms with shared hot-water showers. ❷

Hi-Et Hotel West Street, behind *Eva's* ⓣ824-2828. A popular and very good-value hotel, with shared-bath rooms upstairs in a beautiful old wooden building, each with a tiny balcony, and larger rooms with private bath in a new concrete building. ❸–❹

Martha's Guest House West Street, behind *Eva's* ⓣ824-3647, ⓔmarthas@btl.net. Very comfortable and good-value rooms in a homely atmosphere, most with private bathroom and balcony. New suites are also available. A popular option – the onsite restaurant is a favourite meeting place – so book ahead. ❺–❼

Midas Resort Branch Mouth Road, 500m from town ⓣ824-3172, ⓔmidas@btl.net. Cosy and good-value Maya-style thatched cabañas and newer wooden cabins, all with private bath, set in spacious grounds on the riverbank. Camping available for US$5 per person. ⑤

PACZ Hotel 4 Far West St, two blocks behind *Eva's* ⓣ 824-4538, ⓔ paczghouse@btl.net. Five clean, comfortable rooms at bargain rates, some with private hot-water showers; good local restaurant below. ⑤

Tropicool Hotel Burns Avenue, 75m past *Eva's* ⓣ 824-3052, ⓔ tropicool@btl.net. Bright, clean budget rooms with shared hot-water bathrooms, a sitting room with TV and a laundry area, and wooden cabins with private showers. ③–⑤

Venus Hotel 29 Burns Ave ⓣ 823-3203, ⓔ venus@btl.net. Two-storey hotel, the biggest in town, with very good rates and recently renovated rooms, most with tiled bathrooms, a/c and TV. ④–⑤

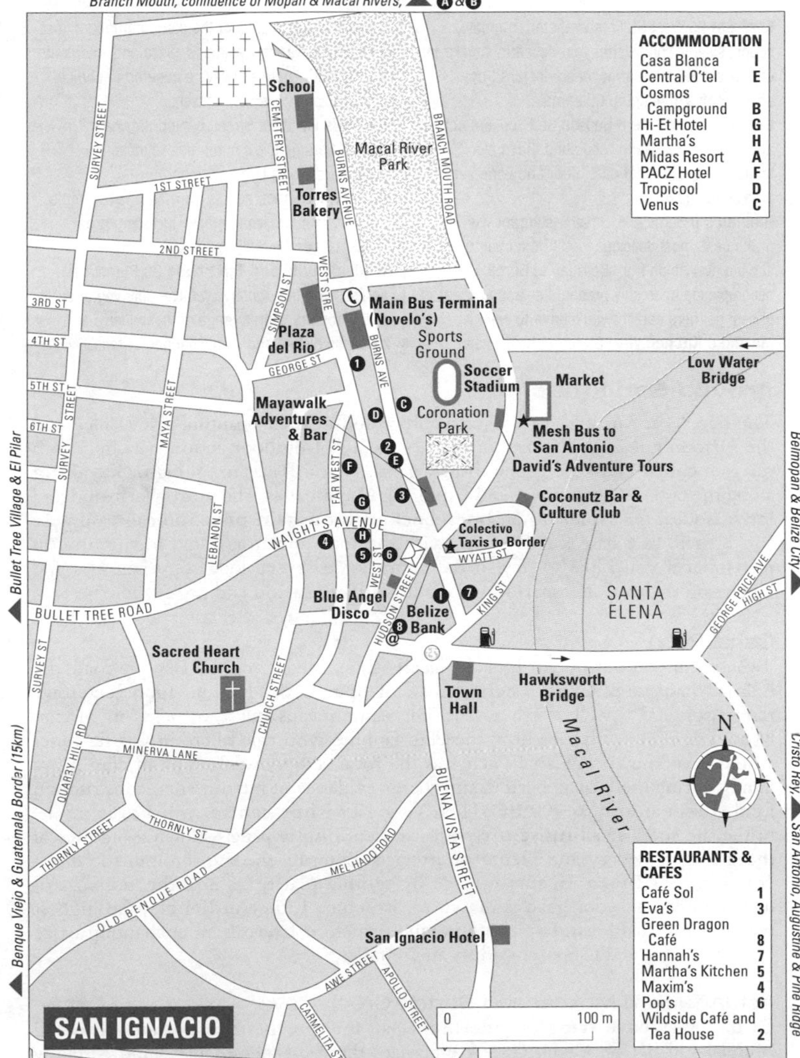

Eating, drinking and nightlife

San Ignacio has an abundance of good, inexpensive **restaurants**, and you can pick up good **bread** and snacks at the Torres Bakery on West Street. The Saturday **market** is also the best in Belize, with local farmers bringing in freshly harvested produce. For getting a drink, best bet is *Eva's*, a good local **bar** and a great place to meet other travellers and tour guides. As San Ignacio is a popular weekend spot for Belizeans, there's a range of **live music and dancing** on offer. The *Culture Club* (above *Coconutz* sports bar), near the riverbank market, is a typically Belizean **club**, with Latin and Afro-Cuban sounds mixing with Belizean beats. The *Blue Angel* disco, on Hudson Street, has bands at weekends, but has lost its pre-eminent position in the local music scene to the *Cahal Pech Tavern*, on the hilltop next to Cahal Pech Maya site.

Café Sol 25 West St. Fresh vegetarian meals, soups, salads, sandwiches and desserts, and great coffee, served in an atmosphere inspired by similar cafés in Antigua, Guatemala.

Green Dragon Café 8 Hudson St. Excellent coffee and snacks in a health-food shop that's also San Ignacio's best Internet café. Beer and wine served on a shady patio.

Hannah's 5 Burns Ave. Small restaurant with some of the best, most delicious food in the country, serving everything from Belizean to Burmese, accompanied by freshly prepared salads at great prices; get here early or you'll have to wait.

Martha's Kitchen West Street, behind *Eva's*. Under the guesthouse of the same name, and just as well-run. Great breakfasts, pizza and traditional Creole food. There's always a vegetarian choice, and delicious cakes for dessert.

Maxim's Far West Street, behind *Martha's*. The best of San Ignacio's numerous Chinese restaurants, with large portions.

Pop's West Street, across from *Martha's*. Simple but very tasty Belizean meals, including great breakfasts and a daily special.

Wildside Café and Tea House 30 Burns Ave, across from the *Venus Hotel*. The only vegan café in the country, with a range of inexpensive and delicious dishes and medicinal herbal teas.

Around San Ignacio

The people of San Ignacio are justifiably proud of their beautiful river valley and the surrounding countryside, and there's plenty of outdoor action on offer, from relaxing **canoe trips** along the mostly gentle Macal River to tubing or **kayaking** along the faster Mopan River and exploring **Maya caves**. The nearby farmland and forest is ideal for exploring on **horseback** or **mountain bike**. You can easily use San Ignacio as a base for day-trips with the tour operators listed in the box on p.104, but if you'd like to stay in the countryside, several lodges, guesthouses and ranches in the area offer **cottage-style accommodation** and organized trips.

Cahal Pech

Twenty minutes out of San Ignacio, clearly signposted along the Benque road, the hilltop Maya site of **Cahal Pech** (daily 8am–5pm; US$5) has undergone extensive restoration and is well worth a visit. The name means "place of ticks" in Mopan Maya, and is certainly not how the elite families who ruled here in Classic times would have known it. Cahal Pech was the royal acropolis-palace of an elite Maya family during the Classic period, and there's evidence of monumental construction from at least as early as 400 BC. There's a great **visitor centre** with a scale model of the site and a small **museum** with excellent display panels showing pictures of the site in its heyday and plenty of artefacts. Entering the site through the forest you arrive at **Plaza B**, surrounded by temple platforms and the remains of dwellings, where your gaze is drawn to Structure 1, the **Audiencia**, the highest building at Cahal Pech. Exploring behind Structure 1 reveals an enchanting maze of recently restored plazas, corridors and temples.

Actun Tunichil Muknal and Barton Creek Cave

Of the many **cave trips** on offer from San Ignacio, the trips to Actun Tunichil Muknal and Barton Creek Cave are perhaps the most memorable – and certainly the most popular. Both are registered archeological sites, and you must only enter with a licensed guide; nothing must be touched or removed. **Actun Tunichil Muknal** ("Cave of the Stone Sepulchre"; entry US$15, tours around US$75), in Roaring Creek valley, is named for the astonishingly well-preserved skeletons of Maya human sacrifices found here. You'll need to be pretty fit and able to swim to do the trip – for much of the time you're wading knee- or even chest-deep in water – but the artefacts in the cave are truly spellbinding. At one point an enormous stingray spine and a huge obsidian blade lean upright against each other, encircled by stones. These metre-long representations of **bloodletting implements**, carved in slate, are an indisputable indication of the sacred ceremonies performed here over 1000 years ago. Perhaps the most dramatic sight, however, is the skeleton of a young woman lying below a rock wall – and nearby the stone axe that may have killed her.

Barton Creek Cave (entry US$10, tours around $30) is also accessible only by river, but this time via canoe. Framed by jungle, the cave's entrance is at the far side of a jade-green pool, and inside the river is navigable for about 1600m – in a couple of places the roof comes so low you have to crouch right down in the canoe – before ending in a gallery blocked by a huge rockfall. If it's been raining a subterranean waterfall cascades over the rocks, making for a truly unforgettable sight. The clear, slow-moving river fills most of the cave width, though the roof soars 100m above in places, the way ahead illuminated by a powerful lamp. Several **Maya burials** and pottery vessels line the banks, the most awe-inspiring indicated by a skull set in a natural rock bridge used by the Maya to reach the sacred site.

The Macal River

Steep limestone cliffs and forested hills edge the lower **Macal River**, whose main tributaries rise in the Mountain Pine Ridge Forest Reserve and the Chiquibul Forest. In the upper reaches the water is sometimes fast and deep enough for whitewater kayaking, though you'll need an expert guide for this (see box on p.104). A canoe trip is by far the best way to visit one of the river's top sights, the **Rainforest Medicine Trail** (daily 8am–5pm; US$5), in the grounds of *The Lodge at Chaa Creek*, 5km upriver from San Ignacio. The medical knowledge of the Maya was extensive, and the trail, dedicated to a Maya bush doctor (*curandero*), is fascinating: among the almost 100 named plants here you'll see the negrito tree, whose bark was once sold in Europe for its weight in gold as a cure for dysentery. The more mundane but equally effective products of the forest range from herbal teas to blood tonic; Traveller's Tonic, a preventative for diarrhoea, really works. The **Chaa Creek Natural History Centre**, next to the Medicine Trail (daily 8am–5pm; US$5), offers a marvellous introduction to Cayo's history, geography and wildlife, with displays on the region's flora and fauna, vivid archeological and geological maps, and a scale model of the Macal Valley – if you're spending more than a couple of days in the area try to see this first. A combined ticket for both the above is US$8.

Located at *du Plooy's* resort, a few kilometres upstream from *Chaa Creek*, the ambitious **Belize Botanic Gardens** (daily 8am–5pm; US$5) aim to conserve many of Belize's native plant species in small areas representative of their natural habitats. The gardens already house four hundred tree species, two ponds with bird hides, several kilometres of interpretive **trails** and a magnificent, specially designed **orchid house**, the only one in Belize, containing 160 species.

Most **accommodation** on the Macal River is in beautifully located upmarket resorts, though there are some budget options (and most places will give discounts to Rough Guide readers, especially out of season). We've listed them in the order of distance upriver from San Ignacio; all are also accessible by road and all offer tours within Cayo and across to Tikal.

Hummingbird Cabañas entrance to Cristo Rey village ⓣ614-7446, ⓔecojungletours@hotmail.com. Simple thatched cabins with private bath, plus an inexpensive restaurant and canoe rental. For here and *Crystal Paradise* (below) you can get the San Antonio village bus to Cristo Rey. ❹

Crystal Paradise Resort Cristo Rey village, on the east bank of the river ⓣ824-2772, ⓦwww.crystalparadise.com. Beautiful thatched cabañas and cheaper rooms in wooden buildings, all with private bathrooms; rates include two delicious meals a day. Excellent guided birdwatching and horse-riding tours offered. ❼–❾

The Lodge at Chaa Creek ⓣ824-2037, ⓦwww.chaacreek.com. Whitewashed wood and stucco thatched cabañas and beautiful suites and villas in gorgeous grounds high above the Macal River, with a justly deserved reputation for luxury and ambience. There's also a spa. Just downstream, the *Camp at Chaa Creek* (US$55 per person, including breakfast and dinner), is "camping" in comfort, in delightful wooden cabins with shared hot showers in tiled bathrooms. ❽–❾

du Plooy's ⓣ824-3101, ⓦwww.duplooys.com. Private luxury bungalows and jungle lodge rooms, each with a private porch. The less expensive "Pink House" has seven rooms and can be rented by groups. A great choice for birdwatching. ❼–❾

Guacamallo Jungle Camp ⓣ804-3674, ⓔdavidtours@belizemail.net. Simple cabins high above the river (which you cross in a canoe) on the edge of a huge Maya site. US$25 per person, including transport, dinner and breakfast. ❻

Martz Farm ⓣ614-6142, ⓔmartzfarm@hotmail.com. Much further upriver from the other places on the Macal, but well worth the effort, with comfortable thatched cabins perched in trees above a rushing, crystal-clear creek. There's plenty of home-cooked food, plus great horse-riding in the forest across the river. ❺–❻

The Mopan River

Rushing down from the Guatemalan border, the **Mopan River** offers some attractive and not too serious **whitewater rapids**. All of the resorts below can arrange kayak or rafting trips; *Clarissa Falls* or *Trek Stop* (p.112) are best. There's less **accommodation** along the Mopan branch of the Belize River than there is along the Macal, but what's available is more within reach of the budget traveller. The resorts below are listed in order of distance from San Ignacio.

Iguana Junction Bullet Tree Falls village centre, 5km west of San Ignacio ⓣ829-4021, ⓦwww.Iguanajunction.com. Four wooden cabins with private bath and simple rooms with washbasins and shared showers in a riverside setting. Excellent home-cooked meals. ❺

Parrot Nest Bullet Tree Falls, at the end of the track just before the bridge ⓣ820-4058, ⓔparrot@btl.net. Six thatched cabins (two sitting very securely up a tree), set in beautiful gardens on the riverbank, with shared, hot-water bathrooms. Good, filling meals are available, and there's a free morning and afternoon shuttle for guests from *Eva's* in San Ignacio. ❻

Clarissa Falls along a signed track to the right off the Benque Road, just before the Chaa Creek turn-off ⓣ824-3916, ⓔclarissafalls@btl.net. Restful place on the riverbank with simple, clean stick-and-thatch cabins with private bathrooms, plus a dorm room (US$15 per person) and camping (US$7.50) with shared hot-water showers. Good home-cooking. ❻

Nabitunich off the Benque Road, down a track on the right, 2km before San José Succotz ⓣ823-2309, ⓔrudyjuan@btl.net. Stone-and-thatch cabins set in beautiful gardens on a working farm, featuring spectacular views of El Castillo at Xunantunich (see p.112). US$40 per person including dinner and breakfast; student rate US$20 per person (ID needed). ❻–❼

The Mountain Pine Ridge Forest Reserve

South of San Ignacio, running parallel to the border with Guatemala, the **Mountain Pine Ridge Forest Reserve** comprises a spectacular range of rolling hills, jagged peaks and gorges interspersed by areas of grassland and pine forest growing in nutrient-poor, sandy soil. In the warmth of the river valleys the vegetation is thicker gallery forest, giving way to rainforest south of the Guacamallo Bridge, which crosses the upper Macal River. One of the most scenic of the many small rivers in the Pine Ridge is the **Río On**, rushing over cataracts and on into a gorge – a sight of tremendous natural beauty. On the

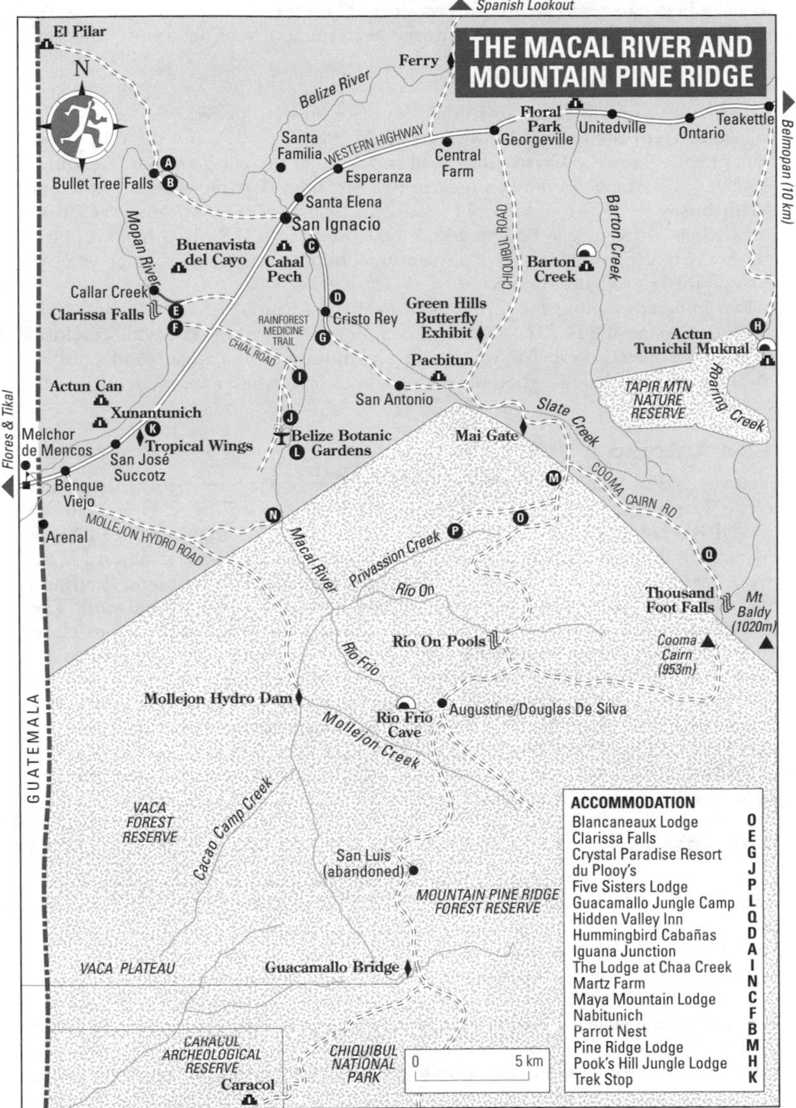

northern side of the ridge are the **Thousand-Foot Falls**, actually over 1600ft (488m) and the highest in Central America. The reserve also includes limestone areas riddled with caves, the most accessible being the **Río Frio Cave** near Augustine/Douglas Silva.

The area is virtually uninhabited but for a few tourist lodges and one small settlement, **Augustine/Douglas Silva**, site of the reserve headquarters. The whole area is perfect for **hiking** and **mountain biking**, but **camping** is allowed only at Augustine/Douglas Silva. The road through the reserve is currently being upgraded to allow better access to the great Maya site of **Caracol** (see opposite), but if you're **driving**, always check road conditions and heed the advice of the forestry officials.

Getting to the reserve

There are two **entrance roads** to the Mountain Pine Ridge reserve, one from the village of **Georgeville**, on the Western Highway (see p.101), and the other from Santa Elena, along the **Cristo Rey** road and through the village of **San Antonio**. Tours can be arranged from San Ignacio (see box on p.104) and there are also four Mesh **buses** a day (Mon–Sat only) from San Ignacio to San Antonio via Cristo Rey, where there's some budget accommodation (see p.108). If you're very fit a good way to get around is to rent a **mountain bike** in San Ignacio, which you can take on the bus to San Antonio.

Two kilometres along the Cristo Rey road from Santa Elena you'll pass *Maya Mountain Lodge* (ⓣ824-2164, ⓦwww.mayamountain.com; ❻–❽), with comfortable private thatched cabañas, some with a/c, and rooms in a large wooden cabin, ideal for groups. There's a good restaurant, a pool, and families are particularly welcome.

San Antonio

The villagers of **SAN ANTONIO** are descendants of Maya refugees who fled the Caste Wars in Yucatán in 1847 and some people still speak Yucatec. Nestled in the Macal River valley, surrounded by scattered farms, with the forested Maya Mountains in the background, this is a superb place to learn about traditional Maya ways. San Antonio was the home of the famous Maya healer Don Eligio Panti, and there's a small, informal museum in the village, dedicated to his life and work. The Garcia sisters, nieces of Don Eligio, run the **Tanah Museum** at the approach to the village (buses from San Ignacio stop outside). The sisters are also renowned for their slate carvings, and their **gift shop** has become a favourite tour-group stop. They also serve traditional meals and offer courses in the gathering and use of medicinal plants. Maria Garcia has played a prominent role in the establishment of the nearby **Elijio Panti National Park**, part of a project to allow the Maya to manage a protected area for conservation and tourism, and you can find out here about guided trips to the park.

The reserve

Not far beyond San Antonio, the roads meet and begin a steady climb to the **reserve**. One kilometre beyond the junction is a **campsite** (US$3.50 per person) run by Fidencio and Petronila Bol, who also operate Bol's Nature Tours; Fidencio can guide you to several nearby caves. About 5km uphill from the campsite is the **Mai Gate**, a forestry checkpoint with information about the reserve as well as toilets and drinking water. Though there are plans to levy an **entrance fee**, for the moment all the guard will do is write your name or that of the tour group in the visitors' book (to ensure there's no illegal camping).

Once in the reserve, the dense, leafy forest is quickly replaced by pine trees. After 3km a branch road heads off to the left, running for 16km to a point overlooking the **Thousand-Foot Falls** (US$2.50). The setting is spectacular, with rugged, thickly forested slopes across the steep valley – almost a gorge. The waterfall itself is about 1km from the viewpoint, but try to resist the temptation to climb around for a closer look as the slope is a lot steeper than it first appears.

Around 11km further on from the junction to the falls lies one of the reserve's main attractions, the **Río On Pools** – a gorgeous spot for a swim – where the river forms pools between huge granite boulders before plunging into a gorge. Another 8km from here and you reach the reserve headquarters at **Augustine/Douglas Silva**. If you're heading for Caracol, check road conditions with the Forestry Department here. You can **camp** here and the village store has a few basic supplies. The huge **Río Frio Caves** are a twenty-minute walk from Augustine/Douglas Silva, following the signposted track from the parking area through the forest to the main cave, beneath a small hill. Sandy beaches and rocky cliffs line the Río Frio on both sides as it flows right through the cave. Entering the foliage-framed cave mouth, you can scramble over limestone terraces the entire way under the hill.

Accommodation

The resorts in Mountain Pine Ridge include some of the most luxurious **accommodation** in the interior of Belize. These lodges – mostly cabins set amongst the pines and surrounded by the undisturbed natural beauty of the forest reserve, with quiet paths to secluded waterfalls – also provide ideal places to stay if you're visiting Caracol. Three kilometres beyond the Mai Gate, the **Cooma Cairn Road** heads left for 8km to *Hidden Valley Inn* (ⓣ822-3320, ⓦwww.hiddenvalleyinn.com; ❾), featuring twelve spacious, well-designed cottages with log fireplaces, set in thirty square kilometres of private reserve. There's also a pool and miles of trails to mountain overlooks and tranquil pools. Back on the main (Chiquibul) road to Augustine/Douglas Silva, just past the Cooma Cairn junction, *Pine Ridge Lodge* (ⓣ606-4557, ⓦwww.pineridgelodge.com; ❼), on the banks of Little Vaqueros Creek, has accommodation in thatched or tiled-roof cabins. The grounds and trees are full of orchids and trails lead to pristine waterfalls. A kilometre beyond here, a side road heads right 2km to *Blancaneaux Lodge* (ⓣ824-4912, ⓦwww.blancaneauxlodge.com; ❾), owned by Francis Ford Coppola, and the most luxurious place to stay in the Mountain Pine Ridge. Sumptuous rooms, cabins and villas decorated with Guatemalan and Mexican textiles are set in lovely gardens overlooking Privassion Creek. At the end of the road past *Blancaneaux*, *Five Sisters Lodge* (ⓣ820-4005, ⓦwww.fivesisterslodge.com; rooms, some with shared bath ❼, cabañas and suites ❾) has the finest location in Mountain Pine Ridge, with very comfortable palmetto-and-thatch cabañas and lodge rooms set in gardens on a forested hillside. The dining-room deck gives tremendous views of the Five Sisters waterfalls cascading over granite rocks, and if you don't fancy the climb down – or back up – you can ride in a funicular tram.

Caracol

Beyond Augustine/Douglas Silva the ridges of the Maya Mountains rise up to the south, while to the west is the wilderness of Vaca plateau. Here the ruins of **Caracol**, the most magnificent Maya site in Belize, and one of the largest in the Maya world, were lost for over a thousand years until their rediscovery in 1936. Two years later they were explored by A.H. Anderson, who named the site Caracol – Spanish for "snail" – because of the large numbers of snail shells found there. In 1985 the first detailed, full-scale excavation of the site, the "Caracol Project", began, and research and restoration continues today, unearthing artefacts relating to everyday life at all levels of Maya society.

The site is open daily (8am–4pm; US$7.50) and you'll be guided on your visit by one of the guards or, if excavation is in progress, by an archeology student. The **visitor centre** is one of the best at any Maya site in Belize and an essential first stop. There's a map of the centre of the site and some excellent display panels, as well as artefacts from the site. Only the core of the city, comprising thirty-two large structures and twelve smaller ones grouped round five main plazas, is open to visitors – though even this is far more than you can effectively see in a day. At its greatest extent, around 700 AD, during the Late Classic period, Caracol covered 88 square kilometres, with a population estimated to be around 150,000. The most massive structure, **Caana** ("Sky Place") is 42m high and still the tallest building in Belize. It is simply enormous, surmounted by a plaza with three sizeable pyramids on top. Opposite Caana is another large temple with monumental stucco masks of jaguars and monsters. Over 100 **tombs** have been found, some with painted texts decorating the walls, along with ceremonially buried caches containing items as diverse as a quantity of mercury and amputated human fingers. Hieroglyphic inscriptions here have enabled epigraphers to piece together a virtually complete dynastic record of Caracol's rulers from 599 AD, and glyphs carved on altars tell of war between Caracol and Tikal, when control over a vast area alternated between the two great cities. One altar records a victory of Caracol over Tikal at 562 AD – a triumph that set the seal on the city's rise to power. Caracol is also a haven for **wildlife** (including tapirs, jaguars and ocelots) and birds, among them the orange-breasted falcon and the very rare harpy eagle.

Xunantunich

Back on the Western Highway, around 12km west of San Ignacio on the bank of the Mopan River, the quiet village of **San José Succotz** is home to the ruins of **Xunantunich** (pronounced Shun-an-tun-ich), "the Stone Maiden", a Classic-period Maya centre (daily 8am–5pm; US$5). An old cable-winched ferry crosses the river (daily 8am–5pm; free) and a steep road leads through the forest for a couple of kilometres to the site.

Your first stop should be the **visitor centre**, with a superb scale model of the city. The site, located on top of an artificially flattened hill, includes five plazas, although the surviving structures are grouped around just three of them. Recent investigations have found evidence of Xunantunich's role in the power politics of the Classic period, during which it probably joined Caracol and the regional superpower Calakmul in an alliance against Tikal. By the Terminal Classic period, Xunantunich was already in decline, though still apparently inhabited until around 1000 AD, after the Classic Maya "collapse" in most other areas.

The track from the entrance brings you out into plaza A-2, with large structures on three sides. Plaza A-1, to the left, is dominated by **El Castillo**, at 40m the city's tallest structure. This is ringed by a decorative stucco frieze, now extensively restored, showing abstract designs, human faces and jaguar heads. The climb up El Castillo can be daunting, but the views from the top are superb, with the forest stretching out all around and the rest of the ancient city mapped out beneath you.

Practicalities

Just before San José Succotz (signed on the left) there's a wonderful budget **place to stay**, *Trek Stop* (☎823-2265, Ⓦwww.thetrekstop.com; ❹), with eight simple, clean, non-smoking cabins with comfortable beds (US$10 per person) and a **campsite** (US$5 per person). The restaurant serves some of the best-value food and largest portions in Cayo, with good vegetarian choices, and there's a self-catering kitchen, while bikes, kayaks and tubes are available for rent at reasonable rates. *Trek Stop* also runs the well-designed **Tropical Wings Butterfly House** (daily 8am–5pm; US$2.50, including guided tour), an enchanting world full of tropical colour.

Benque Viejo and the Guatemalan border

The final town in Belize, 2km before the Guatemalan border, is **BENQUE VIEJO DEL CARMEN**, where Guatemala and Belize combine in almost equal proportions and Spanish is the dominant language. It's a quiet place but served by a constant stream of **buses** (which terminate here); to get to the border you'll need to take a **shared taxi** (*colectivo*; US$1). The Belize border is open from 6am to midnight – though you're best advised to cross in daylight – and Guatemalan *migración* closes at around 8pm.

There's no charge to enter the country, but **leaving Belize** you pay an exit tax of US$15, plus the PACT Conservation fee of US$3.75. There's no charge to enter Guatemala for North Americans or EU, Australian and New Zealand citizens; if you do require a visa (US$10) they can sometimes be issued here, but you might have to go back to the embassy in Belize City, so it's best to equip yourself with one in advance. The Guatemalan border town of Melchor de Mencos has little to recommend it, so your best bet is to continue as soon as you're ready. **Moneychangers** will be waiting either side of the border, and there's no ATM until you reach Santa Elena or Flores, so if you need quetzales get them here.

You'll certainly be approached by drivers of the **minibuses** (US$10–15) that shuttle between the border and **Flores** or **Tikal** (see pp.261 & 267); *colectivo* minibuses to Flores will be waiting just over the bridge at the border and regular second-class buses pass the junction just beyond the bridge.

1.5

The south

To the **south of Belmopan**, Belize is at its wildest. Here the central area is dominated by the **Maya Mountains**, which slope down towards the coast through a series of forested ridges and valleys carved by sparkling rivers. As you head further south, the climate becomes more humid, promoting the growth of dense rainforest, rich in wildlife. Population density in this part of Belize is low, with most of the towns and villages located on the coast. **Dangriga**, the largest settlement, is home to the **Garífuna** people, descended from Native American Caribs and shipwrecked, enslaved Africans. The villages of **Gales Point**, north of Dangriga, and **Hopkins**, on the coast to the south, are worth visiting to experience their tranquil way of life, while offshore, the beautiful cayes of **Glover's Reef** offer budget and luxury accommodation in Belize's largest marine reserve. Further down the coast, **Placencia** is the focus of coastal tourism in southern Belize, and the departure point for yet more idyllic cayes, some of which sit right on the top of the Barrier Reef.

Inland, the Maya Mountains form a solid barrier to land travel except on foot or horseback. The Belize government, showing supreme foresight, has placed practically all the thickly forested mountain massif under some form of protection. The most accessible area of rainforest, though still little-visited by tourists, is the **Cockscomb Basin Wildlife Sanctuary**, a reserve designed to protect the area's sizeable jaguar population. The Southern Highway comes to an end in **Punta Gorda**, from where you can take a **boat to Guatemala** or head inland to visit **ancient Maya sites** or present-day **Maya villages** in the southern foothills of the Maya Mountains.

The Hummingbird Highway

Southeast from Belmopan, the **Hummingbird Highway** heads towards Dangriga, passing through magnificent scenery as it climbs over hills and through lush forest. On the right the eastern slopes of the **Maya Mountains** become visible, forming part of a ridge of limestone mountains riddled with underground rivers and **caves**, several of which are accessible.

St Herman's Cave to Five Blues Lake National Park

About 18km out of Belmopan the road crosses the **Caves Branch River**, a tributary of the Sibun River. Just beyond, by the roadside on the right, is **St Herman's Cave** (daily 8am–4pm; US$4, includes entrance to the Blue Hole National Park). A ten-minute walk on the marked trail behind the visitor centre leads to the cave entrance, located beneath a dripping rock face; you'll need a flashlight to enter, heading down steps that were originally cut by the Maya. Inside, you clamber over the rocks and splash through the river for about thirty minutes, admiring the stunning natural formations, before the accessible section of the cave ends. Two kilometres past the cave, signed from the roadside, is the **Blue Hole National Park**, centred on a beautiful pool whose cool turquoise waters, surrounded by dense forest and overhung with vines, mosses and ferns, are perfect for a refreshing dip. The "Hole" is actually a short stretch of underground river, whose course is revealed by a collapsed cavern. Trails lead through the dense surrounding forest and there's a **campsite** 4km from the visitor centre.

All buses between Belmopan and Dangriga can drop you at the cave or the Blue Hole, but to fully appreciate caving in Belize considering **staying** at the wonderful *Caves Branch Jungle Lodge* (☎822-2800, Ⓦwww.cavesbranch.com; bungalows ❾, cabañas ❼, bunkhouse US$15 per person, camping US$5 per person), located between St Herman's Cave and the Blue Hole and about 1km from the highway. The **guided cave and rappelling trips** run by the lodge aren't cheap (about US$75 per person), but well worth it for the experience. All the caves contain Maya artefacts – burials, ceramics and carvings – furnishing abundant evidence of the Classic-period ceremonies that were held in them. The best independent guide to the area is Marcos Cucul, based in Belmopan (☎600-3116, Ⓦwww.mayaguide.bz).

Beyond here, the Hummingbird Highway undulates smoothly through the hilly landscape, eventually crossing a low pass. The downhill slope is appropriately called Over the Top. On the way down, the road passes through **St Margaret's Village**, where a women's co-operative arranges B&B accommodation in private houses (community phone ☎809-2005; ❸). *Over the Top Restaurant* stands on a hill at Mile

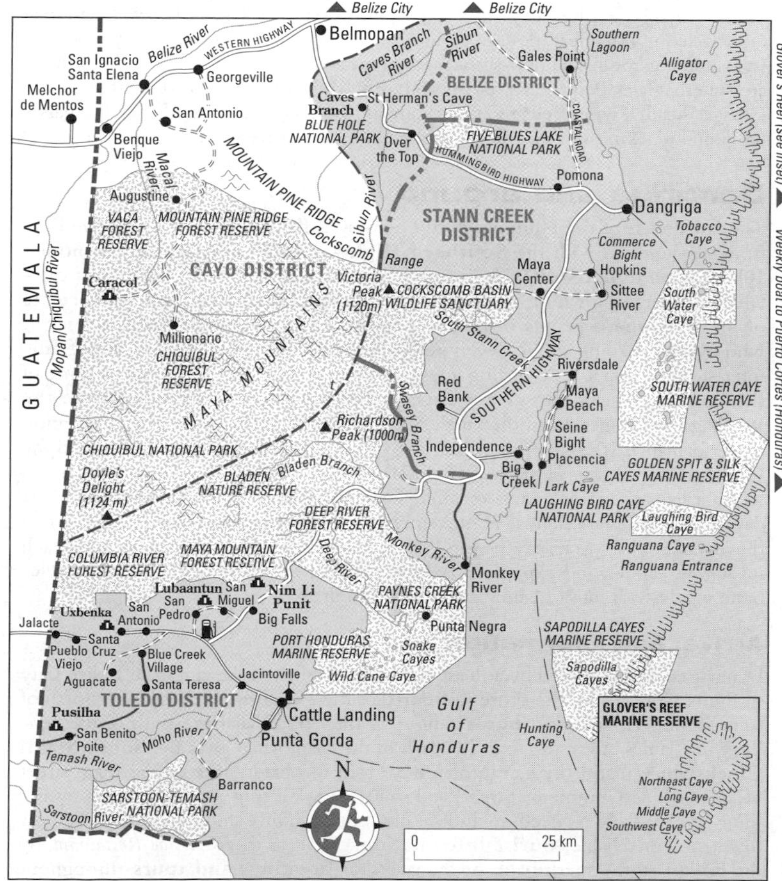

32, overlooking the junction of the track to **Five Blues Lake National Park**, seventeen square kilometres of luxuriantly forested karst scenery, centred on the lake named for its constantly changing colours. Beyond here is the start of the **Stann Creek valley**, renowned for its delicious citrus fruit.

Gales Point and the Southern Lagoon

At Melinda, 14km from Dangriga, an unpaved road heads north to the small Creole village of **GALES POINT**. The village straggles along a narrow peninsula jutting into the **Southern Lagoon**, a large body of shallow water which – along with **Northern Lagoon**, to which it's connected by creeks – comprise **Gales Point Wildlife Sanctuary**, an essential breeding ground for rare wildlife, including jabiru storks, turtles, manatee and crocodiles. The area is bounded on the west by the limestone Peccary Hills, riddled with caves, and the shores of the lagoons are cloaked with mangroves. Gales Point is also a centre of **traditional drum-making**; you can learn to make and play drums at the Maroon Creole Drum School (ⓔmethos_drums@hotmail.com), run by Emmeth Young and Randolph (Boombay) Andrewin.

Several houses offer simple **bed and breakfast rooms** (❸; check with Ionie at Martha's store), while *Gentle's Cool Spot* restaurant has basic but charming rooms (❸) and *Metho's Coconut Camping* (US$3.50 per person) has space in a sandy spot. *Manatee Lodge*, at the very tip of the peninsula (ⓣ220-8040, ⓦwww.manateelodge.com; ❼), offers more luxurious accommodation in a two-storey colonial-style building; rooms (all non-smoking) are spacious and comfortable and the meals are superb. Gales Point is served by only one daily **bus** in each direction on the Coastal Road, leaving Belize City at 5pm and Dangriga at 5am; other traffic passes the junction, 4km from the village, and hitching is relatively easy.

Dangriga and around

The last stretch of the Hummingbird Highway is flat and relatively uninteresting; from the junction with the **Southern Highway to Punta Gorda**, it's another 10km further to **DANGRIGA** (formerly known as Stann Creek), the district capital and the largest town in southern Belize. Though Dangriga is the cultural centre of the **Garífuna**, a people of mixed indigenous Caribbean and African descent, who overall make up about eleven percent of the country's population, it's of little interest unless you're here during a festival. However, the town is home to some of the country's most popular artists, including painters, drum-makers, the Waribagabaga Dancers and the Turtle Shell Band, and you may catch an exhibition or performance. It's also a useful base for visiting **Tobacco Caye** offshore and the **Jaguar Reserve** near Hopkins (see p.121).

Dangriga is a Garífuna word meaning "standing waters", and the most important day in the Garífuna calendar is November 19, **Garífuna Settlement Day**, when the arrival from Roatán (see box, p.118) is re-enacted with a landing on the beach in dugout canoes, and expatriate Belizeans return en masse to the town to celebrate wildly with music, drumming, dance and drink.

Arrival and information

Dangriga's airstrip, served by at least eight daily flights on the run from Belize City to Punta Gorda, is on the shore just north of the *Pelican Beach Hotel* 2km north of town. Southern Transport **buses** pull up at their terminal 1km south of the centre, while James buses stop slightly north of the road bridge over the **South Stann Creek** which marks the centre of town. From this bridge, the town's main street heads north (as Commerce Street) and south (as St Vincent Street) – almost everything you're likely to need, including hotels, restaurants and banks, is on or near this road. For reliable **tourist information**, call in at the *Riverside Restaurant*, by the bridge on the south bank of the river; for **bookings and tours** throughout

Belize contact Debbie Jones of Aquamarine Adventures (☎523-3262, djones@btl.net). The **post office** is on Caney Street, in the southern half of town, a block back from the sea and, across the street, Val's Laundry also has high-speed **Internet access**.

Accommodation

Dangriga has plenty of **places to stay**, with some real bargains, so there's no need to stay in a cheap dive – though there are a few of these, too.

Bluefield Lodge 6 Bluefield Rd ☎522-2742, ⓔbluefield@btl.net. By far the best budget hotel in town, with secure, comfortable and tidy rooms, some with private baths. ❹.

Chaleanor Hotel 35 Magoon St ☎522-2587, ⓔchaleanor@btl.net. Good-value hotel with well-kept, spacious rooms with tiled private bath, and some budget, shared-bath rooms. ❹–❺

Pelican Beach Resort on the beach, north of the town next to the airstrip ☎522-2044, ⓦwww.pelicanbeachbelize.com. Dangriga's most expensive hotel, though rates do drop out of season – ask for a discount. Rooms at the front are in a wooden colonial-style building; those at the rear are in a two-storey concrete building – most have TV and a/c. ❽

A brief history of the Garífuna

The Garífuna trace their history back to the island of **St Vincent**, in the eastern Caribbean, when two Spanish ships, carrying slaves from Nigeria to their colonies in America, were wrecked off the coast in 1635. The survivors took refuge on the island, which was already inhabited by **Caribs**, themselves recent arrivals from South America, who had subdued the original natives, the **Kalipuna**, from whom the Garífuna may have derived their own name. At first there was conflict between the Native Americans and the Africans, but the Caribs had been weakened by wars and disease, and eventually the predominant race was black with some indigenous blood, becoming known by the English as the **Black Caribs**.

For most of the seventeenth and eighteenth centuries St Vincent was nominally under British control, though in practice it belonged to the Caribs, who successfully fended off British attempts to gain full control of the island until 1796. The British colonial authorities, however, could not allow a free black society to survive amongst slave-owning European settlers, so the Carib population was hunted down and transported to **Roatán**, off the coast of Honduras (see p.467), where the British abandoned them. The Spanish Commandante of Trujillo, on the Honduran mainland, took the 1700 surviving Black Caribs to Trujillo, where they became in demand as free labourers, fishermen and soldiers. Their intimate knowledge of the rivers and coast also made them expert smugglers, evading the Spanish laws that forbade trade with the British in Belize.

In the early **nineteenth century** small numbers of Garífuna moved up the coast to Belize, establishing themselves in the area before the first European settlers arrived in Stann Creek in 1823. The largest single migration to Belize took place in 1832 when thousands fled from Honduras (then part of the Central American Republic) after they supported the wrong side in a failed revolution to overthrow the Republican government. It is this arrival that is today celebrated as **Garífuna Settlement Day**.

Riverside Hotel beside the bridge ☎522-2168. Clean rooms, with views over the river, and good rates for singles. ❹

Ruthie's Cabañas 31 Southern Foreshore ☎502-3184. Bargain thatched cabañas on the beach with private bath and porch. Ruthie will cook delicious meals by arrangement. ❹

Eating and drinking

Despite Dangriga's central position in Garífuna culture, there's no **restaurant** specializing in Garífuna food – you'll find it's generally more readily available in Hopkins (see opposite). The restaurant at the *Pelican Beach* is the top place in town, with staff skilled in preparing Belizean specialities, including Garífuna dishes. The *Riverside Restaurant*, on the south bank of the river by the bridge, is easily the best place in the town centre, serving tasty Creole food, including great breakfasts and a daily special. *King Burger* under the *Riverside Hotel* serves good rice, chicken, fish and burgers. Of the several Chinese restaurants on the main street, the *Starlight* is the probably the best.

Tobacco Caye

About 20km offshore from Dangriga is **Columbus Reef**, a superb section of the Barrier Reef with **Tobacco Caye** perched on its southern tip. Ideally situated in the middle of the reef, Tobacco Caye is easy to reach and has good-value accommodation. The island is tiny: stand in the centre and you're only a couple of minutes from the shore in any direction, with the unbroken reef stretching north for miles. Sunsets can be breathtakingly beautiful, outlining the distant Maya Mountains with a purple and orange aura.

Boats (40min; US$17.50) leave daily from near the bridge in Dangriga, though there are no scheduled departures; ask at your hotel or find Captain Buck at the

Moving on from Dangriga

If returning **to Belize City** (2–3hr), Southern Transport **buses** (☎502-2160; some express services) leave every hour or so from 5am to 5pm; most go via **Belmopan** (1hr 45min), though the 5am departure travels the Coastal Road, calling at **Gales Point**. James Bus Line doesn't have a terminal, but departing buses (currently 3–4 daily in each direction) pass along the main street. If you're **continuing south**, bear in mind that buses to **Punta Gorda** (4hr; up to eight daily) don't necessarily originate here and delays are possible. All buses to Punta Gorda stop at **Independence** (under 2hr) – also known as **Mango Creek** – where you can pick up boats to Placencia (see p.123). There are usually two daily Southern services from Dangriga to **Placencia** (2–3hr), but departure times are continually changing (they currently leave daily at noon & 5pm, sometimes also at 3.30pm); most call at **Hopkins** (30min) and **Sittee River**. Hopkins also has its own bus, leaving at 10.30am Mon–Sat from near the *Riverside Restaurant*. Dangriga is also served by **flights** on Tropic Air and Maya Island Air every couple of hours to and from Belize City, and south to Placencia and Punta Gorda.

For Puerto Cortés in Honduras (see p.440) a fast **skiff** leaves each Saturday at 9am (US$50; 3hr) from the north bank of the river, two blocks up from the bridge; be there an hour before departure with your passport so that the skipper, Carlos Reyes (☎522-3227), can take care of the formalities.

Riverside Restaurant; owners of the resorts on the caye may give guests a discount on the boat fare. Rates at all the following **places to stay** include three meals. The best-value choices are *Gaviota Coral Reef Resort* (☎509-5032; ❻), which offers cabins on the sand and less expensive rooms in the main building, all with shared bath, and *Tobacco Caye Paradise* (☎520-5101; ❻–❼), with simple rooms in a wooden house and cabañas overlooking the sea. For more comfort try *Reef's End Lodge* (☎522-2419, Ⓦwww.reefsendlodge.com; ❼–❾) which has rooms in a wooden building, cabañas and a suite on the beach, and a restaurant by the sea serving delicious meals; there's also a **dive shop**. *Tobacco Caye Lodge* (☎520-5033, Ⓦwww.tclodgebelize.com; ❾) has the largest area of any hotel on the island, spreading out from the reef at the front to the lagoon at the back – accommodations are in spacious two-room houses with deck and hammocks, and there's a good **beach bar** by the dock.

South to Placencia

To the **south of Dangriga** the country becomes more mountainous, with development restricted to the coastal lowlands. The only road heading in this direction is the recently paved **Southern Highway**, which ends in Punta Gorda, 170km away. For its entire length the road is set back from the coast, running beneath the peaks of the Maya Mountains, passing through pine forest and vast citrus and banana plantations. Branch roads lead off to settlements including **Hopkins**, a Garífuna village on the coast, and the nearby Creole village of **Sittee River**, from where boats head to the idyllic cayes of **Glover's Reef**. From the village of **Maya Centre**, 36km south of Dangriga, a road leads west into the Cockscomb Basin Wildlife Sanctuary, usually referred to as the **Jaguar Reserve**.

Hopkins

Stretching for more than 3km along a shallow, gently curving bay, the village of **HOPKINS** is home to upwards of a thousand Garífuna people. Garífuna Settlement Day, on November 19, is celebrated enthusiastically here, and at other times it's a pleasant place to spend a few days relaxing, with food and accommodation in all price ranges. You can rent **kayaks** at *Tipple Tree*, windsurf boards at Oliver's (☎601-7818) on the south beach (also has **Internet access**), and **bicycles**

(US$10/day) from Tina's Bike Rental, on the road toward the south end. Many hotels can arrange trips to the reef and cayes further out.

Arrival and accommodation

The **bus** service to Hopkins has improved recently, with KC's Bus leaving from the near dock outside the *Riverside Restaurant* in Dangriga (10.30am Mon–Sat, returning at 7am; US$2.50). Most Southern Transport services to Placencia pass through the village, continuing south via Sittee River. There are no street names in Hopkins; the main point of reference is where the road from the Southern Highway enters the village – dividing Hopkins into north and south – and signs point the way to the many hotels and restaurants.

All Seasons Guest House across from the beach at the south end of the village ⓣ608-3243, ⓦallseasonsbelize.com. Three beautifully decorated rooms, all with private bath, coffeemaker and fridge (a/c option), set in a lovely garden with a tranquil patio. Scooter rental (US$39/day) also available. ❻

Hopkins Inn on the beach, 300m south of the centre ⓣ523-7013, ⓦwww.hopkinsinn.com. Four immaculate and very comfortable white cabins with hot showers and fridge. Rate includes breakfast. ❻

Sandy Beach Lodge south end of village, on the beach ⓣ523-7006. Simple, spacious rooms in wood-and-thatch cabins with private bath. ❹

Seagull's Nest Guest House on the beach south of the centre ⓣ523-7015, ⓔjc_seagulls@yahoo.com. Great-value rooms with shared hot-water shower, in a wooden house with porch. ❹

Tania's Guest House on the right side of the road as you head south ⓣ523-7058. Bargain rooms, although not directly on the beach, all with private bath. ❸

Tipple Tree Beya south end, on the beach ⓣ520-7006, ⓦwww.tippletree.com. Fairly priced rooms (one with shared bath) in an attractive wooden building, plus a furnished house with fridge and microwave (US$50 per day) and camping space (US$5 per person). ❹–❺

Eating and drinking

Though the choice can be limited out of the tourist season, the village has enough good **restaurants** and **bars** and you'll always find good, simple Garífuna and Creole meals. Garífuna dishes frequently feature fish and vegetables such as yam, plantain, okra and cassava, often served in a rich sauce containing coconut milk (similar in consistency to a chowder), called "sere", usually accompanied by rice, but above all by the cultural staple of thin, crispy **cassava bread**. In the north try the *Hideaway*, while *Iris's Restaurant*, south of the centre, serves great, inexpensive breakfasts. Also south of the centre, the *Watering Hole* is one of the best restaurants in the village, serving great seafood. For a **drink** with the locals try either the *Tropical Bar* or *Lebeya* in the north, and for **live music** at weekends check the *King Casava Restaurant* where the road from the highway enters the village. The Women's Dance Group sometimes give performances and if lucky you'll enjoy **Garífuna drumming and dancing** – certainly around the 19 November – and often also at other times.

Sittee River and Glover's Reef

The 5km sandy road heading south from Hopkins is the "back way" to **SITTEE RIVER** village. Most visitors here are on their way to *Glover's Atoll Resort*, but there are a couple of good-value **places to stay**, right on the riverbank. The best option is *Toucan Sittee* (ⓣ523-7039, ⓔbirdcity@btl.net; ❹–❻), with comfortable rooms and apartments in neat wooden cabins; there's also a dorm room (US$9.50 per person) and **camping** (US$5 per person). Meals are really good, with lots of fresh fruit and vegetables. Nearby, *Glover's Guest House* (ⓣ520-2016, ⓔinfo@glovers.com.bz; ❹) has dorm beds for US$8 as well as double rooms. There's a restaurant on the riverbank and the boat heading to Glover's Reef ties up outside. If you need to stock up on supplies for your trip to the atoll, the well-stocked Reynold's Store has groceries and you can go **online** nearby at Sittee

River Internet. To organize a **diving trip**, check with Second Nature Divers (☎523-7038, Ⓔdivers@starband.net).

Glover's Reef

The southernmost of Belize's three coral atolls, **Glover's Reef** lies around 40km off the coast from Sittee River. Named after a British pirate, the reef is roughly oval in shape, stretching 35km north to south and with a handful of cayes in its southeastern section. The entire atoll is a **marine reserve** (US$10 entry fee), with a research station on Middle Caye. What makes Glover's Reef so unusual among the remote atolls is that it offers **accommodation** within the reach of budget travellers at *Glover's Atoll Resort* (☎614-8351, Ⓦwww.glovers.com.bz) on **Northeast Caye**. Here there are twelve simple, thatched beach cabins (US$199 per person per week) overlooking the reef, along with dorm beds in a wooden house (US$149) and **camping** space (US$99 per week); the weekly rates include transport from Sittee River in the resort's boat (leaves Sunday morning, returns following Saturday; 3hr). Unless here on a group package you'll need to bring most of your own food (some supplies are available) and cook meals on a kerosene stove or campfire. While here you're pretty much left to your own devices and you can choose either to enjoy the simple desert-island experience or take part in activities (paid for separately), including sailing, sea kayaking, fishing, snorkelling and scuba diving, which is spectacular, thanks to a huge underwater cliff and some tremendous wall-diving.

Two other cayes at Glover's Reef have more **upmarket resorts**, offering superb sea kayaking, diving and fishing, where guests are usually on all-inclusive packages, staying in thatched wooden cabins or spacious tents. **Long Caye**, just south of Northeast Caye, is the base camp for both *Slickrock Adventures* from Utah (see p.15) and *Off the Wall Dive Center* (☎614-6348, Ⓦwww.offthewallbelize.com). Further south again, **Southwest Caye** is the base for Vancouver-based *Island Expeditions* (☎1-800/667-1630, Ⓦwww.islandexpeditions.com) and the locally owned *Isla Marisol Resort* (☎520-2056, Ⓦwww.islamarisol.com; ⑨).

The Cockscomb Basin Wildlife Sanctuary

Back on the mainland the jagged peaks of the **Maya Mountains** rise to the west of the Southern Highway, their lower slopes covered in dense rainforest. The tallest summits are those of the Cockscomb range, which includes **Victoria Peak** (1120m), the second highest mountain in Belize. Beneath the ridges is a vast bowl of rainforest, over four hundred square kilometres of which is protected by the **Cockscomb Basin Wildlife Sanctuary** – better known as the **Jaguar Reserve**. The basin's luxuriant vegetation is home to a sizeable percentage of Belize's plant and animal species, including tapirs, otters, anteaters, armadillos and, of course, jaguars. Over 290 species of **birds** have also been recorded, including the endangered scarlet macaw, the great curassow and the king vulture, and there's an abundance of amphibians and reptiles, including the red-eyed tree frog and the deadly fer-de-lance.

The sanctuary is reached via a rough ten-kilometre track that branches off the main highway at the Mopan Maya village of **MAYA CENTRE**, running through towering forest and fording a couple of fresh, clear streams before crossing the Cabbage Hall Gap and entering the Cockscomb Basin. This area was inhabited in Maya times, and the ruins of **Kuchil Balam**, a small Classic-period ceremonial centre, still lie hidden in the forest. Trails have been cut to give visitors a taste of the forest's diversity, leading along the riverbanks, through the forest and even, if you're suitably prepared, on a three-day hike to Victoria Peak. The basin could be home to as many as sixty of Belize's 800-strong **jaguar population**, and though you'll almost certainly come across their tracks, your chances of actually seeing one are very slim.

Practicalities

All **buses** between Dangriga and Punta Gorda pass Maya Centre; if visiting the reserve you'll need to sign in and pay the **entrance fee** (US$5) at the craft centre at the junction of the road leading up to the Cockscomb. Julio's Store just beyond here sells basic supplies and cold drinks (there's no restaurant or shop in the reserve), and it's also a **bar** with **Internet access**. The owner also runs Cockscomb Maya Tours (ⓣ520-3042, ⓔjulio_saqui@hotmail.com) and can arrange guides and transport into the reserve.

Maya Centre has some inexpensive and good-value **places to stay**, and all can arrange meals, tours, guides and transport; a **taxi** or truck to the reserve headquarters will cost about US$18 for up to 5 people. On the highway just before the junction, *Tutzil Nah Cottages* (ⓣ520-3044, ⓔtutzilnah@btl.net, ⓦwww.mayacenter.com; ❹) has neat rooms with shared showers in a wooden building. It's run by the Chun brothers, excellent guides who set up memorable kayak trips through the reserve. *Mejen Tz'il Lodge* (ⓣ520-3032, ⓔlsaqui@btl.net; ❹), set in lovely gardens just behind the craft centre, has rooms in a thatched cabaña with private bathroom and a large wooden cabin with dorm rooms for US$8 per person. Some 500m up the track to the reserve, the *Nu'uk Che'il Cottages* (ⓣ520-3033 or 615-2091, ⓔnuukcheil@btl.net; ❹–❺) offer simple but delightful cabañas with private bath, rooms with shared showers, plus dorm beds (US$8). Owner Aurora Saqui is a Maya healer and she has a medical plant garden and the best **restaurant** in the village.

At the reserve headquarters there's an excellent **visitor centre** and a range of **accommodation**: a private furnished cabin (❻); purpose-built wooden dorm rooms (US$17 per person); simple but comfortable dorm beds in more basic "rustic" cabins (US$8 per person); and **camping** space (US$5 per person, with tents available). You'll have to bring your own food, but the cabins do have a kitchen with a gas stove. Camping at designated sites on the trails is US$2.50 per person and you'll need to get a permit from the reserve warden at the headquarters.

The Placencia Peninsula

Sixteen kilometres south of Maya Centre, a good dirt road cuts east from the Southern Highway, heading through pine forest and banana plantations, eventually reaching the sea at Riversdale, then snaking south down the narrow, sandy **Placencia Peninsula**.

The road first passes through a beautiful stretch of coast called **Maya Beach**, located halfway along the peninsula and home to several **restaurants** and a range of **accommodation**. *The Hungry Gecko* serves good Belizean dishes and seafood at great prices, while *Mangos* is a thatched bar on the beach with occasional live music. *Barnacle Bill's Beach Bungalows* (ⓣ523-8010,ⓔtaylors@btl.net; ❽) comprises two large, very well-equipped wooden houses on stilts on a gorgeous sandy beach. Five hundred metres further south, *Maya Playa* (ⓣ520-8020, ⓔmayaplaya@btl.net; ❼), has four palmetto-and-thatch cabañas on a similarly beautiful beachfront location. The friendly owner has built a very tall *palapa* (thatched hut) on the beach for his kitchen and dining room, and guests are welcome to cook and eat their meals there.

Some 3km further, the small Garífuna village of **Seine Bight** is worth a visit even if you're not staying: you can listen to Garífuna music and Western rock in the *White Sand Tiki Bar*, a distinctive bamboo-and-thatch building on the beach near the centre of the village, and check out Lola Delgado's superb (and affordable) oil and acrylic paintings of village life at *Lola's Art Gallery and Cat's Claw Bar and Café*, further south behind the soccer field. Lola is also a great entertainer and a wonderful cook. She serves superb Creole and Garífuna meals most days and dinners are often followed by **music and drumming** – call ⓣ601-1923 to check if she's cooking that evening – and Lola can arrange a taxi to pick you up in Placencia, a few more kilometres to the south.

Placencia village

Shaded by palm trees and cooled by the sea breeze, **Placencia**, perched at the tip of the peninsula, is one of the few places on mainland Belize with real beaches, and this, together with the abundant and inexpensive accommodation and food, makes it a great place to relax. Placencia's famous **Sidewalk** – the narrowest street in the world, according to the *Guinness Book of World Records* – running the length of the village, was built to enable easier walking in the heavy, gritty sand. Apart from simply relaxing, Placencia's a good base for snorkelling and diving trips to the southern cayes, particularly to the beautiful **Laughing Bird Caye National Park** and **Gladden Spit and Silk Cayes Marine Reserve**; you can also take a boat ride along the **Monkey River** and hike a jungle trail.

Arrival and information

The easiest way to get to Placencia is on one of the regular **flights** from Belize City (about 45min). The airstrip is about 3km north of the village; taxis are usually waiting – or it's a five-minute walk to *Kitty's Place* (see below), where you can phone for one. There are usually at least two direct **buses** a day from Dangriga, which terminate at the beachfront gas station, right at the end of the peninsula. Alternatively you can reach Placencia on the *Hokey Pokey* **ferry** from Independence/Mango Creek, a twenty-minute skiff ride across the lagoon. Independence is on the Dangriga–Punta Gorda bus route and the ferry meets all buses; for details of onward travel from Independence, see p.126. The fast boat *Gulf Cruza* leaves Placencia for **Puerto Cortés** in Honduras (Ⓣ523-4045 or Ⓣ202-4506; US$50; under 4hr), every Friday at 9.30am, returning to Placencia on Monday around 2pm.

The **Placencia Tourism Center** (Mon–Fri 9–11.30am & 1–5pm; Ⓣ523-4045, Ⓦwww.placencia.com) is Belize's best tourist office; call in to find out what's going on locally and call hotels from the payphone here. It's also worth picking up a copy of the *Placencia Breeze* (US$.50), the excellent local **newspaper** filled with comprehensive local listings and transport schedules, and a good map of the village and peninsula. The **post office** is upstairs in the wooden building on the right at the end of the sidewalk; the **BTL office** is by the sidewalk in the centre of the village, and there are several payphones around. The *Purple Space Monkey*, in a large thatched building on the roadside opposite the soccer field, provides decent **Internet connection**. The Atlantic **bank** (Mon–Fri 8am–2pm), across from the main dock by the filling station, deals swiftly with cash advances.

Accommodation

There's a wide choice of **accommodation** in Placencia and you shouldn't have a problem finding a room except at Christmas, New Year or Easter. Possibilities begin at the **Sidewalk**, and as you wend your way down it seems as though every family is offering **rooms**; you'll also see signs for **houses to rent**.

Coconut Cottage on the beach south of the centre Ⓣ523-3234, Ⓔkwplacencia@yahoo.com. A well-decorated and deservedly popular wooden cabin on the beach, with full kitchen. ❻

Deb & Dave's Last Resort on the road, near the centre Ⓣ523-3207, Ⓔdebanddave@btl.net. The best budget place in the village, offering lovely rooms with shared hot-water bathroom. Kayaks for rent and excellent tours arranged. ❹

Dianni's Guest House on the south beach Ⓣ523-3159, Ⓔdiannis@btl.net. New hotel with restful, clean and well-furnished rooms with private bathrooms and wide, breezy verandas. Internet access and kayaks for rent. ❻

Kitty's Place due south of the airstrip Ⓣ523-3227, Ⓦwww.kittysplace.com. One of the best upmarket options in the region, *Kitty's*, located 3km north of the village, offers a variety of accommodation, including apartments, beach cabañas and garden rooms. The restaurant serves delicious Belizean and international food and there's a wonderful small pool and adjacent beach bar. *Kitty's* also offers secluded overnight stays on the pristine French Louis Caye, 12km offshore. ❻–❾

Lydia's Guest House near the north end of the

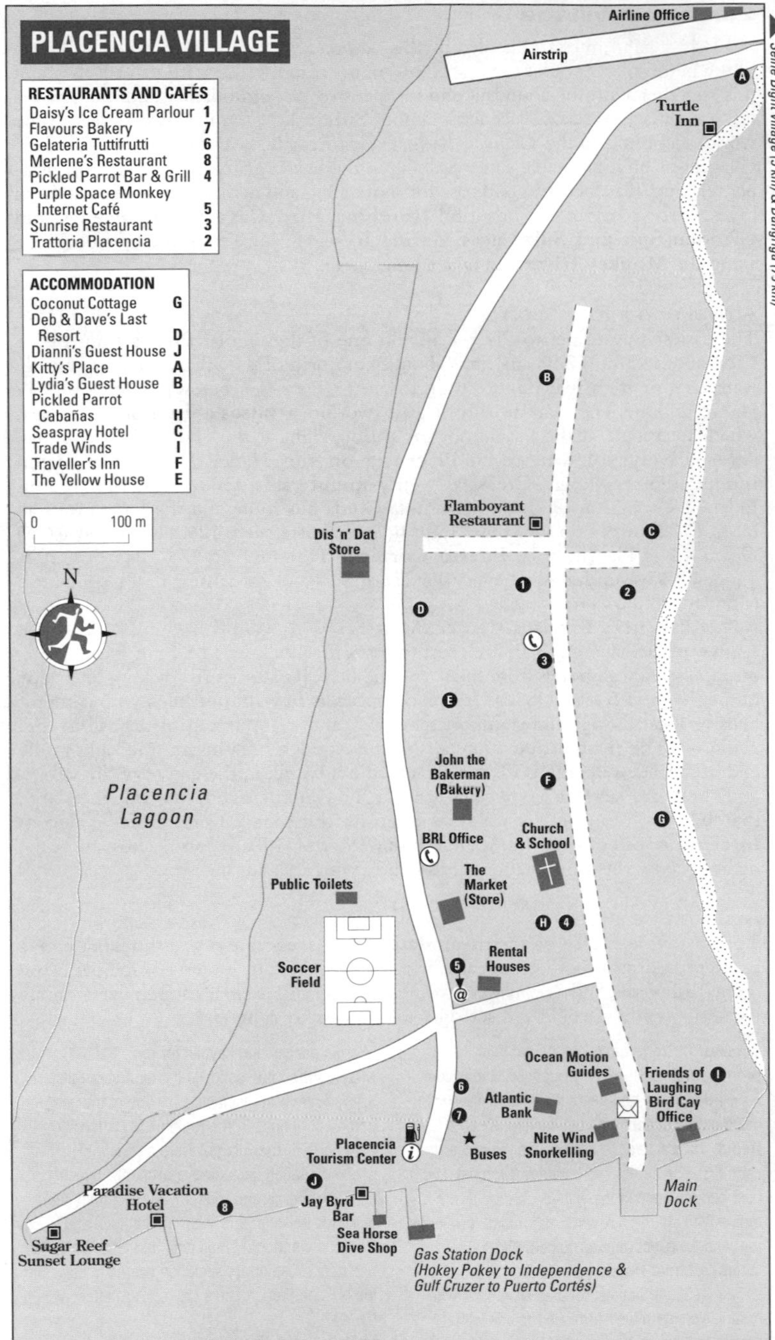
PLACENCIA VILLAGE
RESTAURANTS AND CAFÉS
Daisy's Ice Cream Parlour 1
Flavours Bakery 7
Gelateria Tuttifrutti 6
Merlene's Restaurant 8
Pickled Parrot Bar & Grill 4
Purple Space Monkey Internet Café 5
Sunrise Restaurant 3
Trattoria Placencia 2
ACCOMMODATION
Coconut Cottage G
Deb & Dave's Last Resort D
Dianni's Guest House J
Kitty's Place A
Lydia's Guest House B
Pickled Parrot Cabañas H
Seaspray Hotel C
Trade Winds I
Traveller's Inn F
The Yellow House E
0 100 m
N
Airline Office
Airstrip
Seine Bight village (5 km) & Dangriga (75 km)
Turtle Inn
Flamboyant Restaurant
Dis 'n' Dat Store
Placencia Lagoon
John the Bakerman (Bakery)
BRL Office
Church & School
The Market (Store)
Public Toilets
Soccer Field
Rental Houses
Ocean Motion Guides
Friends of Laughing Bird Cay Office
Atlantic Bank
Nite Wind Snorkelling
Placencia Tourism Center
Buses
Main Dock
Paradise Vacation Hotel
Jay Byrd Bar
Sea Horse Dive Shop
Sugar Reef Sunset Lounge
Gas Station Dock (Hokey Pokey to Independence & Gulf Cruzer to Puerto Cortés)

sidewalk ⓣ523-3117, ⓔlydias@btl.net. Clean, secure and affordable rooms in a great location, all sharing immaculate bathrooms; also several very good houses on the beach for rent. Lydia will cook breakfast on request and rents kayaks. ❹

Paradise Vacation Hotel on the south beach ⓣ523-3179, ⓔpvh@btl.net. Very good-value rooms, most with private bath and some with a/c, in a two-storey wooden building with spacious upstairs deck; no single rates. ❹–❺

Pickled Parrot Cabañas towards the south end of the village ⓣ604-0278, ⓔpickledparrotbelize@yahoo.com. Well-priced wooden cabins with private bathroom, fridge and coffee maker, and a deck with lounge chairs and a hammock. ❻

Seaspray Hotel on the beach in the centre of the village ⓣ & ⓕ523-3148, ⓦwww.seasprayhotel.com. Popular and well-run hotel in a great location, with a variety of excellent accommodation, all with private bath and some with fridge, kitchenette and balcony. ❹–❻

Trade Winds on the beach at the south point ⓣ523-3122, ⓔtrdewndpla@btl.net. Brightly painted cabins and rooms with private bath, fridge and porch on a spacious and secluded plot facing the sea. ❺–❻

Traveller's Inn on the sidewalk, just south of the centre ⓣ523-3190. Five basic rooms – the cheapest in the village – with shared bath and a tiny communal porch, plus some comfortable rooms with private bath in a separate building. ❸–❹

The Yellow House centre of the village, between the road and the beach ⓣ523-3481, ⓔctbze@btl.net. Bargain rooms with private bathroom (2 with kitchenette) in a bright yellow wooden building with balcony and hammocks. ❹

Eating, drinking and nightlife

There are plenty of good **restaurants** in Placencia, but establishments change management fast, so it's worth asking locally for the latest recommendations. Most places close early and you'll certainly have a better choice if you're at the table by 8pm. The central *Pickled Parrot Bar & Grill* is consistently the best restaurant in the village, serving fresh seafood, pizza and international dishes, and fantastic blended cocktails. On the sidewalk to the north, the *Sunrise Restaurant* serves the best-value Belizean meals in the village. At the south end of the village (turn right past the gas station), *Merlene's Restaurant* (ⓣ503-3153) is usually the first to open, serving great breakfasts with good coffee; lunch and dinner are equally good, especially for fish, but the place is tiny so you may want to book. The Italian-run *Trattoria Placencia*, on the beach near the centre of the village, serves great salads and hand-made pasta accompanied by good wines in a relaxed atmosphere. Towards the end of the road the *Purple Space Monkey Internet Café*, which opens early and closes late, offers good coffee, breakfasts, burgers and full meals under a huge thatched roof. Fresh **bread** is available from *John The Bakerman*, signed from the sidewalk, and there's an even greater range at *Flavours Bakery* (which also has a small restaurant), near the end of the road. *Daisy's Ice Cream Parlour*, set back from the sidewalk, just south of the *Seaspray Hotel*, is deservedly popular for its ice cream, cakes and snacks, and also serves full meals, but for the best ice cream in Belize taste the authentic Italian variety, available in literally dozens of flavours, at *Gelateria Tuttifrutti*, near the end of the road.

Although most of the restaurants also serve drinks there are a few places with more of a lively **bar** atmosphere: *J-Byrd's Bar*, by the south dock, is a great place to meet local characters and sometimes has **live music**, while further on from here the *Sugar Reef Sunset Lounge* features a daily **happy hour**, a regular DJ, bar games and karaoke.

Around Placencia

Trips from Placencia can include anything from an afternoon on or under the water to a week of camping, fishing, snorkelling and sailing. Placencia's **lagoon** is ideal for exploring in a **canoe or kayak** (US$15–30 per day from Dave Vernon, who runs Toadal Adventure ⓣ523-3207, ⓦwww.toadaladventure.com), where it's possible to spot a manatee. Several other hotels and the *Sugar Reef Sunset Lounge* also rent kayaks; some hotels also have **bikes** or you could rent one from *Flavours Bakery* for around US$15 per day.

Diving options from Placencia are excellent, with fringing and patch reefs, but bear in mind that the distance to most dive sites means that trips here are more expensive than elsewhere. Advanced Diving, on the sidewalk (☎523-4037, Ⓦwww.beautifulbelize.com), and Sea Horse Dive Shop, on the south dock (☎523-3166, Ⓦbelizescuba.com), offer the best diving instruction, excursions and equipment rental. For **snorkelling** or **manatee-watching**, check with Nite Wind Guides (☎523-3847) or Ocean Motion Guides (☎523-3336), both at the southern end of the sidewalk. Trips cost around US$35–45, depending on where you go, and most usually include lunch. You could visit uninhabited **Laughing Bird Caye National Park**, beyond which lie the exquisite **Silk Cayes**, where the Barrier Reef begins to break into several smaller reefs and cayes, or nearby **Gladden Spit**, now a marine reserve created to protect the seasonal visitation of the enormous yet graceful **whale shark**.

One of the best inland day-trips from Placencia takes you by boat 20km south-west to the almost pristine **Monkey River**, which teems with fish, birdlife, iguanas and, naturally enough, howler monkeys: a thirty-minute dash through the waves is followed by a leisurely glide up the river and a walk along forest trails. The tour operators above can all arrange trips (US$40), or you could contact Evaristo Muschamp, a very experienced local guide, at Trip and Travel, near the south end of the village (☎532-3433). You can get a meal in *Alice's Restaurant* in Monkey River village, and if you want **to stay** there's the *Sunset Inn* (❸) on a tiny bay at the back of the village, a two-storey wooden hotel with comfortable beds, private bath and fan.

Independence/Mango Creek

Just across the lagoon from Placencia, **Independence** (also called Mango Creek) is a useful travel hub. The *Hokey Pokey* ferry runs between here to Placencia at least four times a day (20min; US$5), connecting with most north-and southbound buses. Between them, Southern Transport and James **buses** have at least six departures daily in each direction, heading north to **Dangriga** (under 2hr), Belmopan and Belize City between 6am and 2.30pm, and south to **Punta Gorda** (2hr) from 11am to 7.30pm. Catch the bus where the bus crews take their meal break: Southern Transport at the *Café Hello* and the James Bus at *Shirl's Restaurant*; both serve inexpensive Belizean dishes and snacks.

The far south

Beyond Independence, the Southern Highway leaves the banana plantations, first twisting through pine forests, and crossing numerous creeks and rivers, then passing through new citrus plantations, their neat ranks of trees marching over the hills. **Red Bank**, on the northern edge of Toledo District, is home to one of the largest concentrations of scarlet macaws in Central America; for details on staying or visiting contact the Programme for Belize in Belize City (☎227-5616) or call the Red Bank community telephone (☎503-2233).

About 73km from the Placencia junction lies **Nim Li Punit** (daily 8am–4pm; US$5), a Late-Classic Maya site, possibly allied to nearby Lubaantun and to Quiriguá in Guatemala (see p.234). The ruins stand on top of a ridge, surrounded by the fields of the nearby Maya village of **Indian Creek**. The **visitor centre** has a good map of the site and explanations of some of the carved texts found there, which include eight stelae, among them **Stela 15**, at over 9m the tallest yet found in Belize. Carvings on this great sandstone slab depict a life-sized figure in the act of dropping an offering – perhaps *copal* incense or kernels of corn – into an elaborately carved burning brazier supported on the back of a monster. If you get off the bus here to visit the site, hitching on to Punta Gorda is relatively easy.

Eighteen kilometres further south, at a village with the unfortunate name of **Dump,** a road branches off west to **San Antonio** (see p.130), from where you can explore the southern foothills of the Maya Mountains, dotted with ruins and some delightful Maya villages. At the time of writing, paving of this road is about to begin and eventually it will lead to a **new border crossing** point into Guatemala; until this happens the existing unofficial crossing is not a legal exit point for Belize.

From Dump, it's only 22 kilometres to Punta Gorda, but there are a couple of good-value **places to stay** along the route should you want to stop. At **Sun Creek**, 2km south of the junction, *Sun Creek Lodge* (ⓣ604-2124, ⓔibtm@btl.net; ❺, including breakfast) has two beautiful thatched cabañas with electricity but no private bathroom. The owner organizes tours throughout Toledo and Belizem, and his website (ⓦwww.belizenet.de) is a great source of information for German-speakers. At **Jacintoville**, 7km past Sun Creek, *Tranquility Lodge* (no phone, ⓔmisspennyl@yahoo.com; ❻ including breakfast), set in orchid-laden gardens on the bank of Jacinto Creek, offers air-conditioned comfort in spacious, tiled, en-suite rooms. The thatched restaurant above has good views of the grounds and the creek is perfect for swimming. The highway reaches the sea 10km beyond Jacintoville, and continues along the attractive shoreline for the last few kilometres to Punta Gorda.

Punta Gorda

The Southern Highway comes to an end in **PUNTA GORDA**, the last town in Belize and the heart of the still isolated **Toledo District**, though access is much easier now the Southern Highway is paved. The town is populated by a mixture of Creoles, Garífuna and Maya – who make up more than half the population of the district – and is the focal point for a large number of villages and farming settlements. The busiest day is Saturday, when people from the surrounding villages come into town to trade. Despite a recent minor building boom, Punta Gorda remains a small, unhurried and hassle-free town, known to locals simply as "PG". Its position on low cliffs means that cooling sea breezes reduce the worst of the heat, though there's no escaping the rain – this is the wettest part of Belize and the trees here are heavy with mosses and bromeliads.

Arrival

Buses from Belize City (all via Dangriga) take around seven hours to reach Punta Gorda; Southern Transport (ⓣ702-5628) has a terminal at the south end of José María Nuñez Street, while James Bus (ⓣ722-2625) is based at an office near the dock. Buses (some express services) leave for Independence and Dangriga from 4am to noon, with the possibility of an additional bus at 3pm. Maya Island Air (ⓣ722-2856) and Tropic Air (ⓣ722-2008) each operate four or five **flights** to and from Belize City, landing at the small airstrip five blocks west of the main dock; all flights call at Dangriga and Placencia.

Skiffs to and from Puerto Barrios (see p.236) and Lívingston in Guatemala use the main dock, roughly in the centre of the seafront; the **immigration** office is nearby. Boats leave daily to Puerto Barrios (US$12.50; 1hr in good weather) at 9am and 4pm and there's usually a boat to Lívingston on Tuesday and Friday at 10am. Just turn up at the dock half an hour or so before departure so the skipper can get the paperwork ready, when you'll have to pay the **exit tax** of US$3.25.

Information

Despite having relatively few visitors, Punta Gorda has two **information** centres: the Toledo Visitors Information Center (TVIC; ⓣ722-2470), by the ferry dock, and the Belize Tourism Board on Front Street (ⓣ722-2531) – staff at either office can help with transportation schedules and assist in setting up **tours** of the interior of the Toledo District along with the outlying cayes. The local TIDE (Toledo Institute for Development and the Environment; ⓣ722-2192, ⓦwww.tidetours.org) is involved with many practical conservation projects and also offer **mountain-bike**

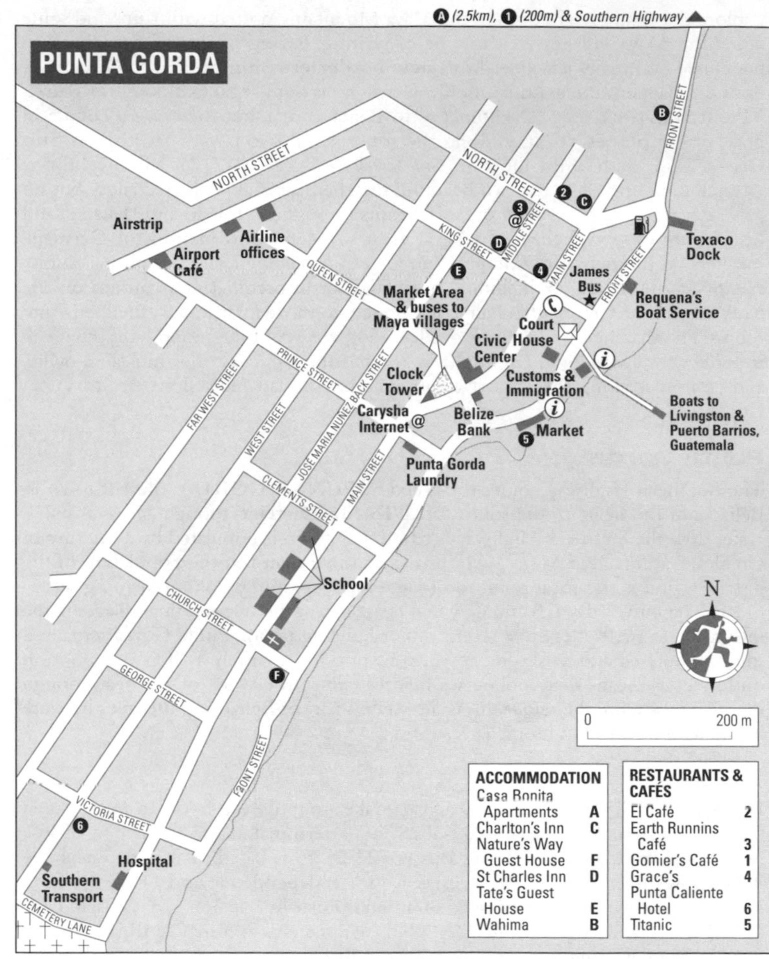

and kayak tours and camping trips to **Payne's Creek National Park**, north of Punta Gorda.

The only **bank** is the Belize Bank (with ATM), on the main square across from the Civic Center (Mon–Fri 8am–2pm), but there will usually be a **money-changer** outside the immigration office when international boats are coming and going and you can change money in *Grace's Restuarant*; it's best to get rid of your Belize dollars before you leave the country. The **post office** is in the government buildings a block back from the ferry dock and the **BTL office** is across the parking lot. For **Internet access** head to *Earth Runnins'* at 11 Main Street (daily 7am–11pm).

Accommodation

There has been a spate of **hotel-building** in town during the last few years and there are plenty of bargains to be had. For an alternative to staying in town contact *Nature's Way Guest House* (listed below), which operates an award-winning programme of guesthouse accommodation in surrounding villages in conjunction with the Toledo Ecotourism Association.

Casa Bonita Apartments Cattle Landing, three kilometres along the road out of town ⓣ722-2270, ⓔcba4cnn@btl.net. A good range of furnished, private apartments in a concrete building facing the sea for longer stays; from around US$125–300 per week; discounts for students and meals can be arranged.

Charlton's Inn 9 Main St ⓣ722-2197, ⓔcharlstin@btl.net. Rooms with hot-water showers – some also have a/c – in a two-storey concrete building with safe parking. Car rental available. ❺

Nature's Way Guest House 65 Front St ⓣ702-2119. The best budget place in Punta Gorda and a good place to meet other travellers and get information. Accommodation is in private rooms or dorms overlooking the sea (no private baths), and the onsite restaurant does good, healthy meals. Dorms US$10, rooms ❹

St Charles Inn 23 King St ⓣ722-2149. One of Punta Gorda's smartest options, with clean and quiet carpeted rooms with TV in a charming building at bargain rates. ❹

Tate's Guest House 34 José María Nuñez St, two blocks west of the town centre ⓣ722-0007. Quiet, friendly family-run hotel with some a/c rooms. ❹–❻

Wahima Hotel Front Street, just north of the Texaco gas station ⓣ722-2542. Good, inexpensive rooms with private bath, right on the seafront; also some apartments around US$150 per week. ❹

Eating

Restaurants in Punta Gorda have improved in recent years and it's certainly easy to get a good, filling meal for a reasonable price. *El Café*, behind *Charlton's Inn*, has good coffee and opens for breakfast at 6am. The *Punta Caliente Hotel* (closed Sat & Sun), next to the Southern Transport depot, has one of the best restaurants in town, serving Creole and Garífuna dishes and a daily special. In the centre of town *Grace's Restaurant*, opposite the BTL office, serves typical Belizean dishes in very clean surroundings. Behind here, on the corner of Middle Main and North streets, *Earth Runnins Café* (closed Tues) is perhaps the most sophisticated dining option, with a changing menu always featuring good breakfasts, fresh seafood, pasta and good vegetarian meals. A few hundred metres further north, *Gomier's Café* (closed Sun & Mon) serves delicious organic and soy meals, with a daily special. The *Titanic Restaurant*, above the market with fantastic sea and mountain views, serves good breakfasts and Belizean dishes, and the 6am to noon **happy hour** is the longest in the country.

The cayes and the coast

Four hundred square kilometres of the bay and coast north of Punta Gorda are now protected as the **Port Honduras Marine Reserve**, partly to safeguard the many **manatees** living and breeding in this shallow-water habitat. There are hundreds of tiny islands in the mouth of a large bay, whose shoreline is a complex maze of mangrove swamps. The cayes and reefs here mark the southern end of Belize's barrier reef, and the main reef has started to break up, leaving several clusters of islands, each surrounded by a small independent reef. The closest of these to Punta Gorda are the **Snake Cayes**, idyllic and uninhabited Caribbean islands. Farther out in the Gulf of Honduras are the **Sapodilla Cayes**, now a **marine reserve** (entry fee US$10), of which the largest caye, **Hunting Caye**, is frequented by Guatemalan as well as Belizean day-trippers. Some of these islands already have accommodation, and more resorts are planned, though at present the cayes and reserve receive relatively few foreign visitors and are fascinating to explore.

South of Punta Gorda the coastline is flat and sparsely populated, with rivers meandering across a coastal plain covered in thick tropical rainforest. These include the Temash River, lined with the tallest mangrove forest in the country, and the Sarstoon River, which forms the border with Guatemala. The only village here is **Barranco**, a small, traditional Garífuna settlement of two hundred people that you can visit through the village guesthouse programme arranged by *Nature's Way* (see above).

Towards the mountains: Maya villages and ruins

The area inland from Punta Gorda towards the foothills of the Maya Mountains is home to the uniquely Belizean mix of **Mopan Maya** with **Kekchí** speakers from the Verapaz highlands of Guatemala. For the most part each group keeps to its own villages, language and traditions, although both are partially integrated into modern Belizean life and most people speak English. The region's villages are connected to Punta Gorda by road, but while there's a **basic bus service** to and from Punta Gorda on Monday, Wednesday, Friday and Saturday (the market days, when buses all leave PG between 11.30 and noon; check with the information offices for exact times), getting around isn't that easy: in many places you'll have to rely on hitching – and traffic is sparse – or walking. The easiest village to reach is **San Antonio**, served by regular daily buses (Mon–Sat only) from Punta Gorda.

Blue Creek, San Antonio and Uxbenka

About 4km before San Antonio, at *Roy's Cool Spot* (where you can get a meal and a drink), a branch road heads off west to the village of **BLUE CREEK**, whose main attraction is a beautiful stretch of water that runs through magnificent rainforest. Whether you're walking or driving you won't miss the river, as the road crosses it just before it enters the village. The best swimming spot is a lovely turquoise pool about ten minutes' walk upriver along the right-hand bank (facing upstream). The source, the **Hokeb Ha** cave, is about another fifteen minutes' walk upriver through the privately owned **Blue Creek Rainforest Reserve**. A guide can take you to Maya altars deep in the cave.

Perched on a small hilltop, the Mopan Maya village of **SAN ANTONIO** has the advantage of *Bol's Hill Top Hotel* (community phone ☎702-2144; ❸), which offers basic **rooms** and superb views, and is a good place to get information on local natural history and archeology. The area is rich in wildlife, surrounded by jungle-clad hills and swift-flowing rivers. Further south and west are the villages of the **Kekchí Maya**. The founders of San Antonio were from the village of San Luis, just across the border in Guatemala, and they maintain many age-old traditions, including their patron saint, San Luis Rey, whose church stands opposite *Bol's* hotel. The Maya also adhere to their own pre-Columbian traditions and fiestas – the main one takes place on June 13, and features marimba music, masked dances and much heavy drinking.

Seven kilometres west from San Antonio, towards the village of **Santa Cruz**, are the ruins of **Uxbenka**, a small Maya site, superbly positioned on an exposed hilltop with great views towards the coast. As you climb the hill before the village you'll be able to make out the shape of two tree-covered mounds and a plaza, and there are several badly eroded stelae protected by thatched shelters. If you do make it out here you can enjoy some wonderful **waterfalls** within easy reach of the road. Between Santa Cruz and Santa Elena the **Rio Blanco Falls** tumble over a rocky ledge into a deep pool, and at **Pueblo Viejo**, 7km further on, an impressive series of cascades provides a spectacular sight. Trucks and buses continue 13km further west to **Jalacte**, at the Guatemalan border, used regularly as a crossing point by nationals of both countries, though it's not currently a legal entry or exit point for tourists.

Lubaantun

To visit the ruins of **Lubaantun** (daily 8am–5pm; US$5) from San Antonio, head back along the road to Punta Gorda and after 8km turn left at the track leading to **San Pedro Columbia**, a Kekchí village 4km along the road. Head through the village, cross the Columbia River and just beyond you'll see the track to the ruins, a few hundred metres away on the left. Some of the finds made at the site are displayed in glass cases at the **visitor centre**: astonishing, eccentric flints (symbols of a ruler's power), ceramics and ocarinas – clay whistles in the shape of animal effigies.

Lubaantun ("Place of the Fallen Stones") was a major Maya centre, though it was occupied only briefly, from 700 to 890 AD, very near the end of the Classic period. The city stands on a series of ridges which Maya architects shaped and filled, building retaining walls up to 10m high. There are no stelae or sculpted monuments other than ball-court markers, and the whole site is essentially a single acropolis, with five main plazas, eleven major structures, three ball courts and some impressive pyramids surrounded by forest. A recent restoration has confirmed that the famous Maya corbelled arch was never used here; buildings were instead constructed by laying stone blocks carved with great precision and fitted together, Inca-style, with nothing to bind them. This technique, and the fact that most of the main buildings have rounded corners, give Lubaantun an elegance sometimes missing from larger and more manicured sites.

Perhaps Lubaantun's most enigmatic find came in 1926, when the famous **Crystal Skull** was unearthed here. Carved from pure rock crystal, the skull was apparently found beneath an altar by Anna Mitchell-Hedges (who still has it in her possession), the adopted daughter of the British Museum expedition's leader, F.A. Mitchell-Hedges. The skull was given to the local Maya, who in turn presented it to Anna's father as a token of their gratitude for the help he had given them.

Travel details

Buses

Addresses and times of bus services from Belize City are given in the box on p.76. Express services, which may cut the journey times given below, operate to all main towns.

Belmopan to: Belize City (every 20min; 1hr 15min); Dangriga (every 2hrs; 1hr 40min); Punta Gorda (every 2hrs; 6hr); San Ignacio (1hr 15min) and Benque Viejo (for the Guatemala border, 15min past San Ignacio; every 30min).

Chetumal to: Belize City via Corozal and Orange Walk (hourly; 3hr 30min); Sarteneja via Orange Walk (1 daily at 1pm; 3hr 30min).

Corozal to: Belize City (hourly; 2hr 30min); Chetumal (hourly; 1hr); Orange Walk (hourly; 1hr).

Dangriga to: Belize City, mostly via Belmopan with one service via Gales Point (every 2hr; 2–3hr); Placencia via Hopkins and Sittee River (2–3 daily; 2hr); Punta Gorda (6–8 daily; 4hr).

Orange Walk to: Belize City (hourly; 1hr 30min); Chetumal (hourly; 2hr); Corozal (hourly; 1hr); Sarteneja (4 daily Mon–Sat; 2hr).

Placencia to: Dangriga, most via Hopkins and Sittee River (2–3 daily; 2hr).

Punta Gorda to: Belize City via Dangriga and Belmopan (at least 6 daily; around 7hr).

San Ignacio to: Belize City via Belmopan (every 30min from 5am–5pm; 3hr); Benque Viejo (for the Guatemala border every 30min; 15min).

Sarteneja to: Belize City (3 daily; 3hr 30min); Chetumal (1daily; 3hr 30min). All buses to and from Sarteneja operate Mon–Sat only, and all pass through Orange Walk.

Flights

Maya Island Air (☎226-2345) and **Tropic** (☎226-2012) each operate flights from Belize International Airport and Belize Municipal Airport to San Pedro, Ambergris Caye (calling at Caye Caulker on request), every hour from 7am to 6pm (20min). They also each operate 3–4 daily flights between San Pedro and Corozal (25min) and operate flights every couple of hours to Dangriga (8–10 daily; 20min), Placencia (40min) and Punta Gorda (60min).

International boats

For information on water-taxis from Belize City to Ambergris Caye and Caye Caulker, see the box on p.89.

Dangriga to Puerto Cortés, Honduras (1 weekly on Sat; 3hr).

Placencia to Puerto Cortés, Honduras (1 weekly on Fri; 3hr).

Punta Gorda to Puerto Barrios, Guatemala (2–3 daily; 1hr); also usually boats from Punta Gorda to **Lívingston** on Tuesday and Friday mornings.

2

Guatemala

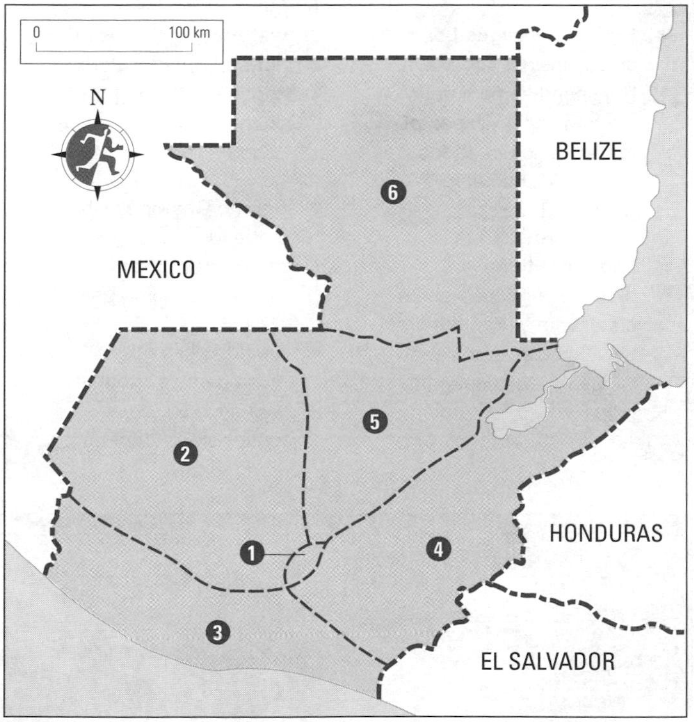

Highlights 134
Introduction and Basics 135
2.1 Guatemala City 161
2.2 The western highlands 176
2.3 The Pacific coast 225
2.4 East to the Caribbean 233
2.5 Cobán and the Verapaces 246
2.6 Petén..259
Travel details 280

Guatemala Highlights

* **Antigua** The former capital boasts a wonderful UNESCO-listed collection of churches, elegant municipal buildings and graceful plazas. **p.180**

* **Highland villages** For a unique insight into Maya life, spend some time in the traditional villages of the Ixil region or Todos Santos Cuchumatán. **p.198** and **p.222**

* **Lago de Atitlán** A breathtaking steep-sided crater lake, surrounded by volcanoes and sleepy indigenous settlements. **p.201**

* **Monterrico** A sweeping, almost undeveloped Pacific beach visited by sea turtles, plus extensive mangrove wetlands to explore. **p.231**

* **Finca El Paraíso waterfall** An exquisite hot-spring-fed waterfall and jungle-fringed pools on the north bank of Lago de Izabal. **p.242**

* **Semuc Champey** Chill in the turquoise waters of this idyllic riverside natural wonder. **p.254**

* **Tikal** Explore this incomparable site that was once the great metropolis of the Maya world. **p.267**

Introduction and Basics

Spread across a verdant and mountainous chunk of land, Guatemala is endowed with simply staggering natural, historical and cultural interest. Though the giant Maya temples and rainforest cities have been long abandoned, ancient traditions remain very much alive throughout the Guatemalan highlands. Uniquely in Central America, at least half the country's population is Native American, and this rural indigenous culture is far stronger than anywhere else in the region. Countering this is a powerful ladino society, characteristically urban and commercial in its outlook. All over the country you'll come across remnants of Guatemala's colonial past, nowhere more so than in the graceful former capital, Antigua.

It's this outstanding cultural legacy, combined with Guatemala's natural beauty, that makes the country so compelling for the traveller. The Maya temples of **Tikal** would be magnificent in any arena but set inside the pristine jungle of the Maya Biosphere Reserve, with attendant toucans and howler monkeys, they are bewitching. Similarly, the genteel cobbled streets and plazas of colonial **Antigua** gain an extra dimension from their proximity to the looming volcanoes that encircle the town. This architectural wealth is scattered to a lesser degree throughout the country – almost every large village or town boasts a giant whitewashed colonial church and a classic Spanish-style plaza. Though most of the really dramatic Maya ruins lie deep in the jungles of **Petén**, interesting sites are scattered throughout the land, along the Pacific coast and in the foothills of the highlands.

The diversity of the Guatemalan **landscape** is astonishing. Perhaps most obviously arresting is the chain of **volcanoes** (some still smoking) that divides the flat, steamy **Pacific coast** from the cool air and pine trees of the largely indigenous western highlands, with their green, sweeping valleys, tiny cornfields, gurgling streams and sleepy traditional villages. Further east towards the **Caribbean**, the scenery and the people have more of a tropical feel and at Lívingston, life beside the mango and coconut trees swings to reggae rhythms and punta rock.

The **rainforests** of Petén, among the best preserved in Latin America, harbour a tremendous array of **wildlife**, including jaguars, tapirs, spider and howler monkeys, jabiru storks and scarlet macaws. Further south, you may be lucky and catch a glimpse of the elusive quetzal in the cloudforests close to Cobán. On the Pacific coast three types of sea turtle nest in the volcanic sand beaches of Monterrico.

All of this exists against the nagging background of Guatemala's turbulent and bloody **history**. Over the years, the huge gulf between the rich and the poor, between indigenous and ladino culture, and the political left and right, has produced bitter conflict. With the signing of the **1996 peace accords** between the government and the ex-guerrillas, Latin America's longest running civil war ceased, though many of the country's deep-rooted inequalities remain. Land distribution remains woefully skewed in favour of agribusiness – it's estimated that close to seventy percent of the cultivable land is still owned by less than five percent of the population. Crime levels have soared in the absence of a functional **justice system**, leading to public lynchings of suspected criminals across the country, and an increase in drug smuggling and gang violence. At the same time the **economy** remains chronically weak, as income from the key coffee crop has plummeted and corruption remains endemic. Guatemala has very little industry except the (largely tax-exempt) foreign-owned *maquila* factories which produce goods for export and typically pay their assembly-line workers under US$6 for a twelve-hour day. Poverty levels are some of the worst in the hemisphere, malnutrition is rife in rural areas and there's general discontent with the high cost of living.

Yet despite these problems you'll find that most Guatemalans are extraordinarily courteous, and eager to help a lost foreigner

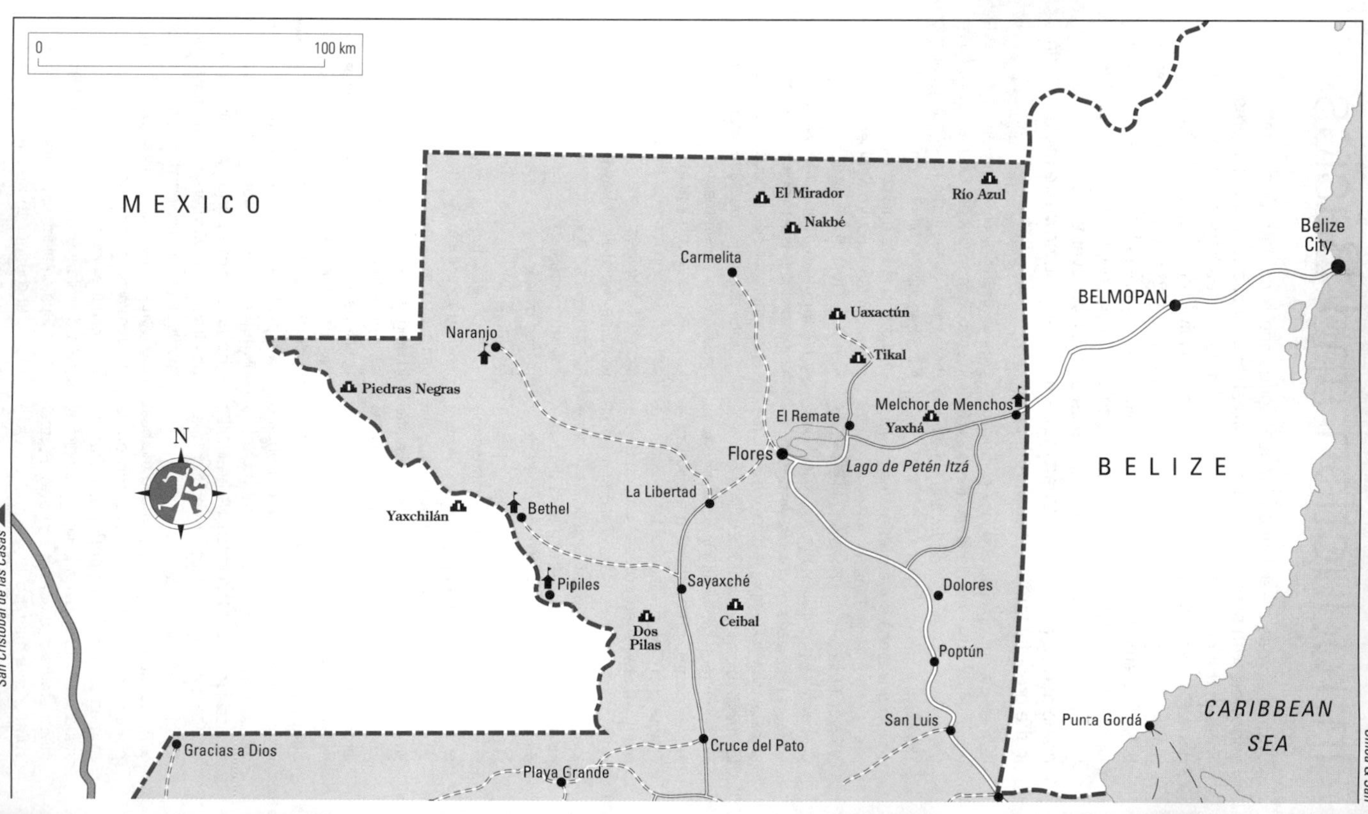
0
100 km
MEXICO
BELIZE
CARIBBEAN SEA
Belize City
BELMOPAN
El Mirador
Río Azul
Nakbé
Carmelita
Uaxactún
Tikal
Naranjo
Piedras Negras
Melchor de Menchos
El Remate
Yaxhá
Flores
Lago de Petén Itzá
N
La Libertad
Yaxchilán
Bethel
Sayaxché
Pipiles
Ceibal
Dos Pilas
Dolores
Poptún
San Luis
Punta Gordá
Gracias a Dios
Cruce del Pato
Playa Grande
San Cristóbal de las Casas
Omoa & San

Pedro Sula
San Pedro Sula
San Salvador
HONDURAS
EL SALVADOR
GUATEMALA
PACIFIC OCEAN
GUATEMALA CITY
Puerto Barrios
Santo Tomás
Livingston
El Golfete
Río Dulce
Entre Ríos
Tegucigalpita
Corinto
La Ruidosa
Morales
Bananera
Lago de Izabal
El Estor
Mariscos
Quiriguá
CARRETERA AL ATLÁNTICO
La Entrada
Copán
El Florido
Jocotán
Comotán
Zacapa
Río Hondo
Chiquimula
Esquipulas
Ipala
Ascunción Mita
Modesto Méndez
Fray Bartolomé de la Casas
Cahabón
Panzós
Telemán
Senahú
Lanquín
Sebol
Raxruhá
Chisec
Pajal
San Pedro Carchá
Cobán
Tactic
Tamahú
Tucurú
Purulhá
Salamá
Rabinal
Cubulco
El Chol
Granados
Pachalum
San Cristóbal Verapaz
Uspantán
Chajul
San Juan Cotzal
Nebaj
Sacapulas
Aguacatán
Salquil Grande
San Juan Ixcoy
Soloma
Santa Eulalia
Barillas
Altamirano
Mayalan
San Mateo Ixtatán
San Miguel Acatán
Nentón
Todos Santos Cuchumatán
La Mesilla
Chiantla
Zaculeu
Huehuetenango
CA-1
Cuilco
Tacaná
Momostenango
San Francisco el Alto
Santa Cruz del Quiché
Chinique
Zacualpa
Joyabaj
Chichicastenango
San Martín Jilotepeque
San Juan Sacatepéquez
El Rancho
El Progreso
Jalapa
Morazán
Monjas
Jutiapa
Cuilapa
San José Pinula
Antigua
Lago de Amatitlán
Palín
Escuintla
Chimaltenango
Panajachel
Sololá
Totonicapán
Lago de Atitlán
San Lucas Tolimán
Santiago Atitlán
Zunil
Quetzaltenango
Cuyotenango
Mazatenango
Santa Lucía Cotzumalguapa
Cocales
CARRETERA AL PACÍFICO
San Pedro
San Marcos
Retalhuleu
Talismán
Tecún Umán
Ocos
Tilapa
Champerico
El Tulate
Tecojate
Sipacate
Puerto San José
Iztapa
Taxisco
Monterrico
Chiquimulilla
Las Lisas
Valle Nuevo
Ciudad Pedro de Alvarado

catch the right bus or find a hotel. Guatemalans tend to be less extrovert than other Central Americans and are quite formal in social situations. Many will automatically assume you are wealthy, since very few Guatemalans ever get to visit another country. Though decades of dictatorship and misgovernment have brought despair to many, somehow a sense of hopefulness endures that the country will one day turn the corner.

Where to go

Perhaps the most fascinating part of the entire country is the **western highlands**, where not only is the scenery wildly beautiful, but you'll also find the most interesting Maya villages and amazing fiestas and markets. **Lago de Atitlán** is unmissable, a large highland lake, ringed by sentinel-like volcanoes, whose shores are dotted with some of the most traditional indigenous villages in the entire country. **Panajachel** is a booming lakeside town with some excellent restaurants, cafés and shops, while **San Pedro La Laguna** on the other side of the lake has a more bohemian travellers' scene. For handicrafts, the famous twice-weekly **Chichicastenango** market is unrivalled, with an incredible selection of weavings for sale.

Further scenic excesses lie around the country's second city of **Quetzaltenango** (Xela), an excellent base for a series of day-trips to nearby hot springs, market towns, pagan shrines and volcanoes. Finally, there are the isolated and traditional villages deep in the mountains of the Cuchumatanes: perhaps the two best places to head for are **Nebaj** in the Ixil triangle and **Todos Santos Cuchumatán** to the north of Huehuetenango. Both are intensely rewarding places to visit, with superb scenery, excellent walking and cheap guesthouses.

The **Pacific coast** is generally hot and dull, a strip of black volcanic sand with a smattering of mangrove swamps behind it that blend into the country's most productive farmland. The area is devoted to commercial agriculture and dotted with bustling urban centres; points of interest are thin on the ground. The beaches are not as you imagine Pacific beaches to be, except at the wildlife reserve of **Monterrico**, where there is a fine stretch of sand and a maze of mangrove swamps to explore.

If it's real adventure and exploration you seek, nothing can compete with the hidden archeological wonders of **Petén**, which is dotted with dozens of Maya ruins. Though large tracts of this unique lowland area, which makes up about a third of the country, have been cleared by settlers, cattle ranchers and loggers, pristine areas remain that are alive with wildlife. From the genteel town of **Flores** you can easily reach **Tikal**, the most impressive of all Maya sites. Other dramatic ruins like the monumental **El Mirador** require days of tough travel to reach.

In the east of the country are the spectacular gorge systems of the **Río Dulce**, the ruins of **Quiriguá** and on the Caribbean coast the funky town of **Lívingston**, home to Guatemala's only black community. Dividing this eastern area from the Petén is another highland region, the Verapaces, where there is more stunning alpine scenery and the sleepy coffee centre of **Cobán**.

Guatemala City is of little interest to the traveller except for its museums; it's much better to stay in the stunning colonial capital **Antigua**, just an hour away, where there are great hotels, restaurants and cafés for every budget.

When to go

The bulk of Guatemala enjoys one of the most pleasant **climates** on earth, with typically warm or hot days and mild or cool evenings all year round – only in the lowlands does it get really uncomfortably hot and humid.

The immediate climate is largely governed by **altitude**. The Guatemala tourist board calls the country "the land of eternal spring", and since most places of interest are between 1300 and 1600m (including Antigua, Lago de Atitlán and Cobán) there's some justification in this. However, in Quetzaltenango and the Cuchumatanes mountains the climate can be cool and damp and nights distinctly cold. In low-lying Petén it's a different world, with sticky, steamy conditions most of the year. The Pacific and Caribbean coasts are equally hot and humid, but here at least you can usually rely on the welcome relief of sea breezes.

There is also a **rainy season**, roughly from May to October, which Guatemalans call winter, though the rain is usually confined to the late afternoon and the rest of the day is often warm and pleasant. As a rule it's only in remote parts that rain can affect your travel plans. This is especially so in Petén, where the rainy season extends into December and it's advisable to delay any real exploration until February.

The **busiest time** for tourism is between December and March, when many North Americans seek respite from the cold; and again in July and August – this is also the busiest time for the language schools.

Getting around

For most people, travelling in Guatemala means using the anarchic fume-belching **bus system** – a chaotic mix of fun, frustration and discomfort – supplemented by cramped microbuses and pick-ups in rural areas. While it's possible to remove yourself from this chaos to a certain degree by taking **tourist shuttles** and flights, you risk missing out on one of Guatemala's essential experiences. Though in remote areas many buses leave in the dead of night in order to reach the morning markets, we strongly recommend **not travelling after dark** if you can avoid it, due to the greater risk of robbery.

Guatemala's road network has improved in recent years, but remains pretty overloaded in many areas and you'll constantly find yourself stuck behind smoking trucks as you climb up the Carretera Interamericana to Lago de Atitlán or drive down to the Caribbean. Fortunately, whatever the pace of your journey, you always have the Guatemalan countryside to wonder at.

Buses

Buses are cheap and convenient, and can be hugely entertaining. There are two types of service. **Second-class buses** – known as *camionetas* to Guatemalans and "chicken buses" to foreigners – are by far the most numerous, and easily distinguished by their trademark clouds of thick black fumes. If they look familiar to North Americans that's because they're old school buses (mainly Bluebirds). Second-class buses will usually stop for every possible passenger, cramming their seats, aisles and occasionally roofs: journeys are certainly never dull. Chickens cluck,

Land and sea routes to Guatemala

Crossing Guatemalan **borders** is usually always very straightforward, though you will most likely have to pay a **"fee"** of US$1–2 to enter or exit the country; this is an unofficial bribe, but difficult to avoid unless you have plenty of patience and good persuasive skills.

The borders with **Mexico** are at Ciudad Hidalgo–Tecún Umán (see p.226) and Talismán–El Carmen (see p.226), both close to the Mexican border city of Tapachula; and La Mesilla–Ciudad Cuauhtémoc (see p.224), convenient for San Cristóbal de Las Casas.

Heading to and from **El Salvador**, traffic from Guatemala City uses the Valle Nuevo–Las Chinamas border (see p.231), while the Ciudad Pedro de Alvarado–La Hachadura (see p.231) route is convenient for the Pacific coast. There are also two border crossings to the north at Anguiatú–Anjiatú and at Agua Caliente (see p.230) that both access the town of Esquipulas and the eastern highlands.

The two borders with **Honduras** are at El Florido (see p.244), which connects Chiquimula with Copán, and Entre Ríos–Corinto (see p.237), which links Puerto Barrios with Puerto Cortés. It's also possible to get between Lívingston and Omoa by boat (see p.238), but only when there is sufficient demand (minimum of six).

Travelling to **Belize**, there's either the land crossing in Petén at Melchor de Menchos–Benque Viejo (see p.279) or two boat routes: twice daily between Puerto Barrios and Punta Gorda (see p.236), and also Lívingston–Punta Gorda (see p.238), again only when there's enough people.

merengue assaults your eardrums, snack vendors tout for business and the locals gossip and laugh. Almost all second-class buses operate out of **bus terminals**, often adjacent to the local market. Tickets are bought on board and cost around US$0.75 per hour's travelling, though rip-offs do happen – check out what the locals are paying.

First-class or **pullman** buses, usually old Greyhounds, are faster and more expensive (around $1 an hour) than regular buses and make fewer stops. Each passenger will be sure of a seat to him- or herself, and tickets can be bought in advance. They only serve the main routes such as the Carretera al Atlántico and Interamericana, but they will usually stop for you en route if they have space aboard. Pullmans usually leave from the bus company's office rather than the main bus terminal.

Minibuses

All the main tourist routes are also served by minibus **shuttle buses** that will whisk you between destinations in a lot more comfort, for a price. Tickets are usually booked (best the day before) through a travel agent or your hotel and you'll be picked up from your accommodation and dropped off where you want, too. Between Antigua and Lago de Atitlán a ticket is around US$12, between Flores and Tikal it's US$5. More and more new shuttle routes are opening up all the time, and now operate around the Quetzaltenango and Cobán regions.

Non-tourist **minibuses** (microbuses) are becoming much more common in Guatemala as well. These cost the same as the larger public "chicken bus" services, and tend to be a bit quicker. They only tend to operate where there are paved roads, such as the Santa Elena–Poptún and Chiquimula–Honduran border routes. They usually operate from a private terminal near the main bus station.

Taxis

Taxis are available in all the main towns and rates are fairly low, around US$3 for a 3km trip. Except in Guatemala City, meters are nonexistent, so it's essential to **fix a price** before you set off. Local taxi drivers will almost always be prepared to negotiate a price for a half-day or day's excursion to nearby villages or sites.

Driving and hitching

Driving inside Guatemala is pretty straightforward and it certainly offers unrivalled freedom as traffic is rarely heavy apart from in the capital and on the main highways. **Parking and security** are the main problems, and in the larger towns you should always get your car shut away in a guarded car park. The main routes are paved but minor roads are often extremely rough. **Petrol (gas)** is around US$2 a gallon, **diesel** about US$1.50. If you plan to head up into the mountains or along any of the smaller roads in Petén, you'll need high clearance and 4WD.

Renting a car costs around US$40 a day (around US$230 a week) for a small vehicle by the time you've added the extras. If you do rent, make sure to check the details of the insurance, which often won't cover any damage to your vehicle.

If you plan to visit the more remote parts of the country then it's almost inevitable that you will **hitch a ride** with a pick-up or truck from time to time. You'll usually have to pay for your lift – around the same as the bus fare.

Bikes and motorbikes

Bikes are pretty common in Guatemala and cycling is a popular sport, so you'll be well received and should be able to find a repair shop in most towns. Though cycling is the most exhilarating way to see Guatemala, the country is very mountainous and roads are poor. Most buses will carry bikes on the roof if it all gets a bit too much. You can rent mountain bikes in Antigua, Flores and Panajachel: see the relevant listings.

Motorbike rental is not really recommended as it's relatively expensive, and insurance is rarely included. That said there are rental outlets in Panajachel, Antigua and Flores charging around US$8–10 per hour or from US$30 a day.

Boats

Small speedy motorized boats called **lanchas** are the main form of water transport, though there's still a slow ferry service between Puerto Barrios and Lívingston. The two definitive boat trips in Guatemala are through the Río Dulce gorge system, starting in either Lívingston or the town of Río Dulce, and across Lago de Atitlán, usually beginning in Panajachel.

Planes

The only internal **flight** most people are likely to take is from Guatemala City to Flores (from US$110 return), with four airlines offering rival services. Virtually any travel agent in the country can book you a ticket.

Costs, money and banks

The Guatemalan currency is the **quetzal**; the exchange rate at the time of writing was Q8.05 to US$1 (Q14.42 to £1). Though an attempt to make the US dollar an official currency fell through in 2001, US bills can be used in many of the main tourist centres.

Guatemala is an extremely cheap country to travel in. It's certainly possible for **budget travellers** to survive on around US$120/£70 a week in Guatemala by sleeping in simple hospedajes, eating at comedores, travelling by local bus and going easy on the beers. Your wallet will suffer in tourist towns like Antigua and Panajachel, and you'll pay for any indulgences like wine, taxis or shuttle buses. The extremely self-disciplined or fiscally challenged could survive in somewhere like San Pedro La Laguna (see p.208) on as little as US$75/£45 a week. If you can afford to burn a few more quetzales, however, and desire a hotel room with private bath, more varied food and want to take the odd shuttle bus, reckon on US$220/125 a week. Guatemala has some spectacular hotels at the luxury end of the market – to travel in **real style**, reckon on paying around US$95/£55 a day, for which you can expect accommodation with period character (plus modern amenities), shuttle buses and the best food in town. Remember that leaving the country you'll be charged an **airport tax** of US$30, payable in cash (either dollars or quetzales) only.

Credit or debit cards are the easiest and most convenient way to get money, using the country's relatively comprehensive network of ATMs. Visa/Plus cards are the best option, with the most machines, though MasterCard/Cirrus ATMs are becoming more widespread. Most banks will give you a cash advance at the till with your card if there's no hole in the wall.

Travellers' cheques are an alternative, though you'll spend a lot more time waiting around in banks. American Express, Thomas Cook, MasterCard and Citibank cheques are accepted in most banks; try to check first before you queue up. Note it's not a sensible idea to take cheques issued in any currency other than US$. If you do have euros, Banco Uno, 18 C 5–56, Zona 10 in Guatemala City will cash them at poor rates, while Lloyds TSB Bank (branches in Guatemala City, Antigua, Puerto Barrios and Escuintla) may cash sterling travellers' cheques, also at poor rates.

Information

The national tourist board, **Inguat** (@www.mayaspirit.com.gt), give out glossy brochures and will try to help you with your trip, but don't expect too much independent travel advice – branches can be found in Guatemala City, Panajachel, Antigua, Flores and Quetzaltenango. In **Petén**, the Flores-based organization CINCAP provides essential support for jungle trekking (see p.262).

Websites

Guatemala is well wired to the Internet, though it currently lacks a good English language news **website**.

@www.americas.org/guatemala Best bet for Guatemala-related news stories, with some in-depth analysis of the issues.

@www.fhrg.org The US-based Foundation for Human Rights in Guatemala site has news of current campaigns and news items.

@www.guatemalaweb.com Decent all-rounder with information as diverse as the latest Visa requirements to ATM locations.

@http://lanic.utexas.edu/la/ca/guatemala/ The University of Texas provides the most comprehensive Guatemala portal.

@www.revuemag.com The *Revue's* website has fully downloadable files of the monthly magazine, including back copies.

Accommodation

Accommodation in Guatemala comes in a multitude of different guises: pensiones, casas de huéspedes, posadas, hospedajes and hoteles. The names don't actually mean that much, though most hotels tend to be towards the top end of the price scale and most hospedajes and pensiones towards the bottom. Breakfast is almost never included in the price. As most small towns have a hospedaje or two, staying in peoples' houses is rare, but at fiesta time many families rent out rooms for a little extra cash.

All **room prices** are fixed by Inguat, the tourist board; there should be a tariff posted behind the door of your room. At the **top end** of the scale (above US$80 a night) you'll find magnificent colonial-style hotels with authentic interiors in most of the main tourist centres, especially Antigua. In the **mid-range** bracket (US$25–80) there are some brilliant deals available: you can still expect character and comfort, and a private bathroom, but perhaps without any extra facilities. Even at the **budget** (under US$10) end of the scale you should be able to find a clean double room in any town in the country (though you may have to look hard in Guatemala City). In some places room prices fall to as low as US$2.50 a person. It's woll worth trying to haggle a little, or asking if there are any cheaper rooms at quiet times of the year. There are no official youth hostels in Guatemala, but you will find the odd dormitory.

It's only on the Pacific and Caribbean coasts and in Petén that you'll need a **fan** or **air conditioning**; in the highlands you'll sometimes find a logwood fire in the luxury hotels, and heavy-duty blankets in the cheaper places. **Mosquito nets** are very rarely provided, even in the lowland areas, so if you plan to spend some time in Petén or on either coast, it's well worth investing in one, and essential if you plan to do some jungle trekking.

Campsites are extremely thin on the ground in Guatemala. The main cities certainly don't have them and the only places with any decent formal provision for camping are in Panajachel, Lanquín, Poptún and Tikal. However, if you decide to set off into the wilds then a tent is certainly a good idea, although even here it's by no means essential as most villages have a simple hospedaje – if not, ask for the mayor (*alcalde*), who should allow you to sleep in the town hall (*municipalidad*).

See p.36 for an explanation of the accommodation price codes.

Food and drink

Generally, **food** doesn't come high on the list of reasons to visit Guatemala. However, most of the towns most popular with tourists boast a variety of cuisine and you'll be able to feast on French, Italian, Asian, all-American and even Middle Eastern dishes. Up in the highland villages it's a different story and many menus consist of little more than grilled meat and rice, or a soup.

Traditionally, Guatemalans eat a **breakfast** of tortillas and eggs, accompanied by the inevitable beans. **Lunch** is the main meal of the day, and this is the best time to fill up as restaurants often offer **comidas corridas**, a set two- or three-course meal that sometimes costs as little as a couple of dollars. It's always filling and occasionally delicious. **Evening meals** are generally more expensive.

A Spanish **menu reader** can be found on p.870.

Where to eat

The first distinction in Guatemala is between the **restaurant** and the **comedor**. Comedores are basic eateries that serve simple food at cheap prices – expect to pay around US$2.50 for a good feed. In contrast, restaurants are more formal and expensive (US$5 a head and upwards). There are, however, plenty of restaurants with comedor-like menus, and vice versa.

In the larger towns you'll also find **fast-food** joints, modelled on the American originals and often part of the same chains. When travelling you'll also come across the local version of fast food: at junctions, buses are besieged by vendors offering a huge selection of drinks, sweets, local specialities and complete meals in a box. Many of these are delicious but you do need to treat this kind of food with a degree of caution and bear in mind the general lack of hygiene.

In most towns there's some kind of pizzeria and a Chinese restaurant: they can make a welcome break from eggs and beans but don't expect anything very authentic. Cakes and pastries are also widely available but tend to be pretty dull and dry.

Vegetarians are hardly catered for specifically, except in the tourist restaurants of Antigua and Panajachel and at a handful of places in Guatemala City. It is, however, fairly easy to get by eating plenty of beans and eggs, which are always on the menu, accompanied by freshly made tortillas. The **markets** also offer plenty of superb fruit and snacks like *tostadas* and *pupusas* (see below).

What to eat

Maya cuisine is at the heart of Guatemalan cooking. Maize is an essential – in Maya legend, humankind was originally created from corn – and it appears most commonly as a thin pancake, the **tortilla**. The maize is traditionally ground by hand and shaped by clapping it between two hands then toasted on a **comal**, a flat pan of clay or metal placed over the fire. Tortillas are eaten while warm and are usually brought to the table wrapped in cloth. The very best have a slightly smoky taste and a pliable texture. Mexican-style **tamales** (steamed cornmeal often stuffed with meat, wrapped in a banana leaf) are not that common, but when you can get them are usually delicious.

Beans (*frijoles*) are served as they are in the rest of Central America, either refried (*volteados*) or whole (*parados*) in their own black juice. Almost all truly Guatemalan meals include a portion of beans. In the highlands you'll come across **mosh** (porridge) from time to time. To a lesser extent, **chillies**, usually served in the form of a spicy sauce (salsa picante), are the final ingredient in a Maya meal.

Along with this essentially Maya culinary style, you'll find **ladino food** everywhere, often on the same menu. *Bistek* (steak), *pollo frito* (fried chicken) and *hamburguesas* are popular with all Guatemalans, though they do tend to be greasy. *Chiles rellenos* (stuffed peppers) make a healthy change from other cholesterol-saturated dishes and *pepián* (meat stew with vegetables) and *caldos* (meat broths) are usually excellent.

Popular **market snacks** include *pupusas* (thick stuffed tortillas topped with crunchy grated salad vegetables) and *tostadas* (corn crisps smeared with avocado, cheese and other toppings).

On the Caribbean coast there is a distinct **Creole cuisine**, heavily based on fish, seafood, coconuts, plantain and banana. *Tapado* (a coconut-based fish or shellfish soup) is the signature dish in these parts.

Healthy-eating Western-style food is also available anywhere where tourists travel in numbers, so many places geared to gringo tastes will have muesli and fruit for breakfast, vegetarian dishes and treats like carrot cake and brownies.

Drinks

To start off the day most Guatemalans drink a cup of weak **coffee**, which is usually loaded with sugar. It's becoming much easier to get a decent cup in tourist-oriented towns, but you're much more likely to be served brown-coloured slops rather than anything resembling the real thing elsewhere. Through the day locals drink water or *refresco*, a thirst-quenching water-based drink with some fruit flavour added. Coca-Cola, Pepsi, Sprite or Fanta (all called *aguas*) are also common and popular. For a healthy treat, order a *licuado*: a thick, fruit-based drink with either water or milk (milk is safer). Bottled water (*agua mineral* or *agua pura*) is available almost everywhere.

Until 2002 one bland beer – **Gallo** – had an almost total monopoly in Guatemala. Then **Brahma**, a Brazilian brewer, muscled in (they even flew the footballer Ronaldo over to promote the brand), adding some much needed variety. Gallo is a medium-strength lager-style beer that comes in 33cl or litre bottles (around US$1 and US$2 respectively in a bar; much less in a supermarket). Brahma comes in 33cl bottles and has a slightly spicy finish. Moza, a dark brew with a slight caramel flavour is worth trying but rarely available. Other brands (all lagers) rarely encountered include the premium beer Montecarlo, Dorada Draft and Cabro. Imported brands are rare.

As for spirits, **rum** (*ron*) and **aguardiente**, a clear and lethal sugarcane spirit, are very popular and correspondingly cheap. The finest rum is Ron Centenario Zacapa, costing around US$25 a bottle; Ron Botran Añejo is an acceptable, much cheaper, alternative at around $4 a bottle). Hard drinkers will soon get to know Quezalteca, a local *aguardiente* sold and drunk everywhere, whose power is at the heart of many a fiesta.

Guatemalan **wine** does exist but it bears little resemblance to the real thing. Chilean wines are the best value, with decent bottles available from around US$5 in supermarkets and double that in restaurants.

Opening hours, holidays and festivals

Most offices, shops, post offices and museums are **open** between 8.30am and 5pm, though some take a break for lunch. **Bank**

Guatemalan Festivals

January

1–5 Santa María de Jesús, near Antigua (main days 1st and 2nd)

19–24 Rabinal, in the Verapaces (main days 23rd and 24th)

22–26 San Pablo La Laguna, Lago de Atitlán (main day 25th)

March

Second Friday in Lent Chajul, in the Ixil triangle

April

24 San Jorge La Laguna, Lago de Atitlán

25 San Marcos La Laguna, Lago de Atitlán

May

6–10 Uspantán (main day 8th)

8–10 Santa Cruz La Laguna (main day 10th)

June

12–14 San Antonio Palopó, near Panajachel (main day 13th)

21–25 Olintepeque, near Quetzaltenango

22–25 San Juan Cotzal, near Nebaj

22–26 San Juan Atitán (main day 24th)

27–30 San Pedro La Laguna (main day 29th)

28–30 Almolongo, near Quetzaltenango (main day 29th)

July

21–Aug 4 Momostenango (most interesting on July 25 and Aug 1)

23–27 Santiago Atitlán (main day 25th)

25 Antigua

25 Cubulco, in the Verapaces

31–Aug 6 Cobán

August

1–4 Sacapulas (main day 4th)

9–15 Joyabaj, west of Santa Cruz del Quiché (main day 15th)

12–15 Nebaj (main day 15th)

15 Guatemala City

September

12–18 Quetzaltenango (main day 15th)

17–21 Salamá (main day 17th)

24–30 Totonicapán (main day 29th)

October

1–6 San Francisco El Alto (main day 4th)

2–6 Panajachel (main day 4th)

29–Nov 1 Todos Santos Cuchumatán

November

1 All Saints' Day Celebrations all over, but most dramatic in Todos Santos Cuchumatán and Santiago Sacatepéquez, where massive paper kites are flown

23–26 Nahualá (main day 25th)

22–26 Zunil (main day 25th)

25 Santa Catarina Palopó, Lago de Atitlán

30 San Andrés Xecul, near Quetzaltenango

30 San Andrés Iztapa, near Antigua

December

7 Bonfires (the Burning of the Devil) throughout the country

7 Ciudad Vieja, near Antigua

13–21 Chichicastenango (main day 21st)

hours are extremely convenient, with many opening until 7pm (and some as late as 8pm) from Monday to Friday and until 12.30pm or 1pm on Saturdays.

Archeological sites are open every day, usually from 8am to 5pm, though Tikal is open from 6am to 6pm. The principal public holidays, when almost all businesses close down, are listed in the box below; in villages, most shops shut during fiestas.

Fiestas

Traditional **fiestas** are one of the great excitements of a trip to Guatemala, and every town and village, however small, devotes at least one day a year to celebration.

Guatemalan fiestas can be divided into two basic models: ladino and Maya. **Ladino** towns and villages celebrate with daytime processions, beauty contests and perhaps the odd marching band, with dance-hall discos at night. In the highlands, however, where the bulk of the population is **Maya**, you'll see a blend of religious and pre-Columbian celebration. The very finest ceremonial costumes are usually dusted down and worn, and you can expect to see some hugely symbolic traditional dancing, including the *Baile de la Conquista*, which re-enacts the Spanish victory over the Maya. Whether ladino or Maya, festivals tend to be chaotic, drunken affairs with plenty of dancing and fireworks. If you can join in the mood, there's no doubt that fiestas are wonderfully entertaining as well as offering a real insight into both sides of Guatemalan culture.

Many of the best fiestas include some specifically local element, such as the giant kites at **Santiago Sacatepéquez**, the religious processions in Antigua and the horse race in **Todos Santos Cuchumatán**. At certain times virtually the whole country erupts simultaneously: **Easter Week** is perhaps the most important, particularly in Antigua and Santiago Atitlán, but **All Saints' Day** (November 1), when people gather in cemeteries to honour the dead, and **Christmas** are also marked by celebrations across the land. The **festivals** listed in the box opposite are the pick of the lot.

Public holidays

January 1 New Year's Day
Semana Santa Easter Week
May 1 Labour Day
June 30 Army Day, anniversary of 1871 revolution
August 15 Guatemala City fiesta (capital only)
September 15 Independence Day
October 12 Discovery of America (only banks closed)
October 20 Revolution Day
November 1 All Saints' Day
December 25 Christmas

Communications

The cheapest way to make an **international phone call** is usually from a cybercafé or a privately owned communications business. Prices start at US$0.15 per minute to the USA or US$0.25 to Europe using web-phone facilities, though these connections can be crackle- and delay-prone.

In many places (including Antigua, Flores, Panajachel and Quetzaltenango) shops, hotels or travel agencies advertise pretty competitive rates using conventional phone lines: typically around US$0.30 to North America or US$0.50 to Europe. Otherwise, to make an international call it's best to purchase either a Telgua or Telefónica **phonecard** (both available in many shops) and use one of the many cardphones common in virtually every town.

Local calls in Guatemala are very cheap, and it pays to get a phonecard if you plan to make a number of them. **Faxes** can be sent or received from any Telgua branch in the country, or (often more cheaply) through travel agencies, some shops and language schools. From Guatemala you can only make **collect calls** (reverse charges) to the USA, Canada, Mexico, Italy, Spain, Japan, Switzerland and other Central American countries – not to the UK. Dial ☎171 for the international operator. Calling Guatemala from abroad, the **country code** is ☎502.

Outgoing Guatemalan **postal services** are fairly efficient by Latin American standards, and you can send mail easily from even the smallest of towns – though it's probably safer to send anything of importance through a private firm. Airmail letters generally take around a week to the US, a couple of weeks or so to Europe. Alternatively, UPS, DHL and Federal Express all operate in Guatemala. **Sending parcels** through the standard mail service is very expensive, so for items more than 2kg, you may want to use a specialized shipping agency instead. See the Antigua and Panajachel listings for recommended companies.

Post coming into Guatemala is reliable, though note that the **poste restante** (Lista de Correos) method of holding mail is no longer operational. American Express will hold mail for cardholders; they are based in Guatemala City inside the Clark Tours office, 12 C 0-93, Zona 9, Centro Comercial Montúfar (Mon–Fri 8.30am–5pm; ⓣ331 7422). Alternatively, if you've studied with a language school they'll usually keep your mail for you.

Email and the Internet

For a developing country, Guatemala is very well wired to the **Internet**. Most towns have at least two or three **cybercafés**, while there are over a dozen in Antigua and Quetzaltenango. In more remote areas Guatemala's creaky power network can cause connection problems, but in the main towns connection speeds are rapid and reliable. Rates vary between US$0.80 and US$4 an hour. Virtually all language schools are online; many offer students discount Internet rates when they enrol for classes.

A vast number of hotels and businesses now have email (and websites). Additionally, some towns and regions now boast community websites, replete with information on accommodation, restaurants, culture and entertainment.

The media

Guatemala has a number of daily **newspapers** with extensive national coverage and a more limited international perspective. Best of the dailies are the *Siglo Veintiuno* and the forthright and outspoken *El Periódico*, which can be tricky to find. The most popular paper is the *Prensa Libre*, a fairly conservative business-orientated institution, with a reasonable sports section. Look out for a good weekly paper called *El Regional*, published in both Spanish and Maya languages. As for the **periodicals**, *La Crónica* is usually a decent read, concentrating on Guatemalan current political affairs and business news with a smattering of foreign coverage.

In theory the nation's newspapers are not subject to restrictions, though pressures and threats are still exerted by criminal gangs, the military and those in authority. Being an investigative journalist in Guatemala is a dangerous profession and there have been several contract killings in recent years.

Slightly surprisingly for a country so dependent on tourism, the **English-language** press is pretty limited. The only publication that's widely available is the *Revue* magazine, published in Antigua, which carries interesting articles about Guatemala and some coverage of Belize, El Salvador and Honduras. It doesn't cover politics but there's often some cultural or historical coverage, plus plenty of accommodation, restaurant and shopping advertisements. For really reliable, in-depth reporting, the *Central America Report* excels, with proper journalistic investigation of controversial news stories and political analysis. It's published by Inforpress Centroamericana and is available by subscription only at ⓦwww.inforpressca.com.

As for **foreign publications**, *Newsweek* and *Time* are available in quality bookstores around the country and in some luxury hotel gift shops.

Radio and TV

Guatemala has an abundance of **radio stations**, though variety is not their strong point. Most transmit a turgid stream of Latin dance and rock and cheesy merengue, which you're sure to hear plenty of on the buses. There is a host of religious stations, too, broadcasting an onslaught of rabid evangelical lectures, services, "miracles", and so on. If you're visiting Guatemala City, it's worth twiddling your FM dial – there can be some interesting stuff broadcast over the capital's airwaves at weekends.

Television stations are also in plentiful supply. Viewers can choose from over a dozen local cable stations, and some American programming. Many upmarket hotels and some bars in tourist areas also have direct satellite links to US stations, which can be handy for catching up with the news on CNN.

Shops and markets

Guatemalan craft traditions, locally known as **artesanías**, are very much a part of modern Maya culture, stemming from practices that in most cases predate the arrival of the Spanish. Many of these traditions are highly localized, with different regions and even different villages specializing in particular crafts. It's worth visiting as many **markets** as possible, particularly in the highland villages, where the colour and spectacular settings are like nowhere else in Central America.

You'll find that both slide and print **film** is available in most towns in the country, though monochrome is much less common. Camcorder videotapes are also widely on sale, though digital videotapes are more tricky to find.

Crafts

The best place to buy Guatemalan **crafts** is in their place of origin, where prices are reasonable and the craftsmen and women get a greater share of the profit. If you haven't the time to travel to remote highland villages, the best places to head for are Chichicastenango on market days (Thurs & Sun) and the shops and street hawkers in Antigua and Panajachel.

The greatest craft in Guatemala has to be **textile weaving**. Each Maya village has its own traditional designs, woven in fantastic patterns and with superbly vivid colours. All the finest weaving is done on the **backstrap loom**, using complex weft float and wrapping techniques. Chemical dyes have been dominant in Guatemala for over a century now, but interest in natural colourings has revived recently and they are being used again in some of the villages around Lago de Atitlán.

One of the best places to start looking at textiles is in Antigua's Nim Po't, 5 Av Norte 29 (daily 9am–9pm; Ⓣ & Ⓕ832 2681, Ⓦwww.nimpot.com), a large store with an excellent collection of styles and designs. Guatemala City's Museo Ixchel (see p.169) is another essential visit.

You should bear in mind that while most Maya are proud that foreigners find their textiles attractive, for them clothing has a spiritual significance – so it's not wise for women travellers to wear men's shirts or men to wear *huipiles*.

Alongside Guatemalan weaving most other crafts suffer by comparison. However, if you hunt around you'll also find good ceramics, baskets, mats, silver and jade. Antigua has the most comprehensive collection of shops, followed by Panajachel.

Markets

For shopping – or simply sightseeing – the **markets** of Guatemala are some of the finest anywhere in the world. The large markets of Chichicastenango, Sololá and San Francisco El Alto are all well worth a visit, but equally fascinating are the tiny weekly gatherings in remote villages like San Juan Atitán and Chajul, where the atmosphere is hushed and unhurried. In these isolated settlements market day is as much a social event as a commercial affair, providing the chance for villagers to catch up on local news, and perhaps enjoy a tipple or two, as well as selling some vegetables and buying a few provisions. Most towns and villages have at least one weekly event; for a comprehensive list, see pp.177 and 247.

Safety and the police

Personal safety is a serious problem in Guatemala, partly due to a recent nationwide rise in crime, but also because some criminal gangs have actively targeted visitors, including tourist shuttle buses. There is little pattern to these attacks, but some areas can be considered safer than others. It's wise to register with your embassy on arrival, try to keep informed of events, and avoid travelling at night.

Though relatively few tourists have any trouble, it's essential that you try to minimize the chance of becoming a victim. **Petty theft** and **pickpocketing** are likely to be your biggest worry. Theft is most common in Zona 1 and the bus stations of Guatemala City, but you should also take extra care when visiting markets popular with tourists (like Chichicastenango) and during fiestas. Avoid wearing flashy jewellery and keep your money well hidden. When **travelling**, there is actually little danger to your pack when it's on top of a bus; it's the conductor's responsibility alone to go up on the roof and collect luggage.

Muggings and violent crime are of particular concern in Guatemala City. There's not too much danger in the daylight hours but don't amble around at night, when it's much safer to use a taxi. There have also been a few cases of armed robbery in Antigua and around Lago de Atitlán too. The Pacaya volcano is now considered safe, though there have been occasional robberies on other volcanoes.

If you are robbed you'll have to report it to the police, which can be a very long process and may seem like little more than a symbolic gesture; however, most insurance companies will only pay up if you can produce a police statement.

Machismo is very much a part of Latin American culture, and many Guatemalan men consider it their duty to put on a bit of a show to impress the Western *gringas*. It's usually best to ignore any such hassle. Ladino towns and *cantinas* are the worst places. Indigenous society is more deferential so you're unlikely to experience any trouble in the western highlands. **Homosexuality** is not illegal, but can be publicly frowned upon by some so it's sensible to be discreet. There's a small gay community in Guatemala City (see p.171) but few clubs or public meeting places.

The police

Guatemala's civilian **police** force, introduced in 1997, has a poor reputation. Corruption is rampant and inefficiency the norm, so don't expect that much help if you experience any trouble. In Antigua, there's a well-established **tourist police** force (see p.180), a scheme which has been recently extended to Panajachel and Tikal.

If for any reason you do find yourself in **trouble with the law**, be as polite as possible. Remember that bribery is a way of life here, and that corruption is widespread. Officially you should **carry your passport** (or a photocopy) at all times.

Drugs

Drugs (particularly marijuana and cocaine) are quite widely available as Guatemala is a big transit country. Remember that **drug offences** are dealt with severely. Even the possession of marijuana could land you in jail – a sobering experience in Guatemala. If you do get into a problem with drugs, it may be worth enquiring with the first policeman if there is a "fine" (*multa*) to pay, to save expensive arbitration later. At the first possible opportunity, get in touch with your embassy and negotiate through them: they will understand the situation better than you. The addresses of embassies and consulates in Guatemala City are listed on p.173.

Work and study

Guatemala is one of the best – and most popular – places in the continent to **study Spanish**. The language school industry is big business, with over sixty well-established schools and many more less reliable setups. Thousands of foreigners from all over the world study each year in Guatemala – mainly travellers and college students, but also airline crew and business people.

As for **work**, teaching English is the best bet, though there are always opportunities for committed **volunteers**.

Studying Spanish

Most **language schools** offer a weekly deal that includes four or five hours one-on-one tuition a day, plus full board with a local family. This all-inclusive package works out at between US$85 and US$210 a week depending on the school and location – most are in the US$120–US$150 bracket. It's important to bear in mind that the success of the exercise is dependent both on your personal commitment to study and on the enthusiasm and aptitude of your teacher – if you are not happy with the teacher you've been allocated, ask for another. Insist on knowing the number of other students that will be sharing your family house; some schools (mainly in Antigua) pack as many as ten foreigners in with one family. Virtually all schools have a student liaison officer, usually an English-speaking foreigner who acts as a go-between for students and teachers, so if you're a complete beginner there will usually be someone around with whom you can communicate.

Recommended language schools

Many of the schools below have academic accreditation agreements with North American and European universities; some also have US offices – consult the schools' websites for more information. The websites ⓦwww.123teachme.com and ⓦwww.guatemala365.com have reports and some good tips about the relative advantages of different study centres.

Antigua

APPE 6 C Pte 40 ⓣ832 0720, ⓦwww.appeschool.com

Centro America Spanish Academy inside La Fuente, 4 C Ote 14 ⓣ832 3297, ⓦwww.quik.guate.com/spanishacademy

Centro Lingüístico de la Fuente 1 C Pte 27 ⓣ832 2711, ⓦwww.delafuenteschool.com

Centro Lingüístico Maya 5 C Pte 20 ⓣ832 0656, ⓦwww.travellog.com/guatemala/antigua/clmaya/school.html

Christian Spanish Academy 6 Av Nte 15 ⓣ832 3922, ⓦwww.learncsa.com

Los Capitanes Generales 5 Av Sur 4 ⓣ832 8769, ⓦwww.loscapitanes.com

Probigua 6 Av Nte 41B ⓣ832 2998, ⓦwww.probigua.conexion.com

Projecto Lingüístico Francisco Marroquín 7 C Pte 31 ⓣ832 2886, ⓦwww.plfm-antigua.org. Also offers classes in Maya languages.

San José El Viejo 5 Av Sur 34 ⓣ832 3028, ⓦwww.sanjoseelviejo.com

Sevilla 1 Av Sur 8 ⓣ832 5101, ⓦwww.sevillantigua.com

Tecún Umán 6 C Pte 34 A ⓣ831 2792, ⓦwww.escuelatecun.com

La Unión 1 Av Sur 21 ⓣ832 7337, ⓦwww.launion.conexion.com

Quetzaltenango

Casa de Español Xelajú Callejón 15, Diagonal 13–02, Zona 1 ⓣ761 5954, ⓦwww.casaxelaju.com

Celas Maya 6 C 14–55, Zona 1 ⓣ761 4342, ⓦwww.celasmaya.com

Centro Bilingüe Amerindía (CBA) 12 Av 8–21, Zona 1 ⓣ761 5260, ⓦwww.xelapages.com/cba

Centro Maya de Idiomas 21 Av 5–69, Zona 3 ⓣ767 0352 ⓦwww.centromaya.org. Also offers classes in Maya languages.

Educación para Todos 12 Av 1–78, Zona 3 ⓣ765 0715, ⓦwww.spanishschools.biz

English Club International Language School Diagonal 4 9–71, Zona 9 ⓣ763 2198. Also offers classes in K'iche' and Mam.

Escuela Juan Sisay 15 Av 8–38, Zona 1 ⓣ763 1318, ⓦwww.juansisay.co

Guatemalensis 19 Av 2–14, Zona 1 ⓦwww.guatemalensis.com

Inepas 15A Av 4–59 ⓣ765 1308, ⓦwww.inepas.org

La Paz Diagonal 11 7–38, Zona 1 ⓣ761 2159, ⓦwww.xelapages.com/lapaz

Kie–Balam, Diagonal 12 4–46, Zona 1 ⓣ761 1636, ⓦwww.kiebalam.com

Pop Wuj 1 C 17–72, Zona 1 ⓣ761 8286, ⓦwww.pop-wuj.org

Proyecto Lingüístico Quetzalteco de Español 5 C 2–40, Zona 1 ⓣ763 1061, ⓦwww.hermandad.com. Also has sister schools on the Pacific slope and in Todos Santos Cuchumatán.

Sakribal 6 C 7–42, Zona 1 ⓣ763 0717, ⓦwww.sakribal.com

Lago de Atitlán

Escuela Jabel Tinamit off c/Santander, Panajachel ⓣ762 0238, ⓦwww.jabeltinamit.com

Jardín de América C 14 de Febrero, Panajachel ⓣ762 2637, ⓦwww.jardindeamerica.com

Casa Rosario south of Santiago Atitlán dock, San Pedro La Laguna ⓣ613 6401, ⓦwww.casarosario.com

Mayab' between the docks, San Pedro La Laguna ⓣ815 7722, ⓦwww.mayabspanishschool.com

Corazón Maya south of Santiago dock, San Pedro La Laguna ⓣ721 8160, ⓦwww.corazonmaya.com

San Pedro Spanish School between the piers, San Pedro La Laguna ⓣ715 4604, ⓦwww.sanpedrospanishschool.com

continued overleaf

Recommended language schools (cont.)

Huehuetenango

Xinabajul 6 Av 0–69 ⓣ764 1518, ⓔacademyxinabajul@hotmail.com

Cobán

Active Spanish School 3 C 6–12, Zona 1 ⓣ952 1432, ⓦwww.spanish-schools.com/coban/city/ce.htm

School of Arts and Language Finca Tzalampec, 16 Av 2–50, Zona 1 ⓣ953-9062, ⓔalfonsotujab@yahoo.com.mx

Monterrico

Proyecto Lingüístico Monterrico ⓣ619 8200, ⓦwww.espanol.netfirms.com

Todos Santos Cuchumatán

Hispano Maya opposite Hotelito Todos Santos (no phone).

Nuevo Amanacer ⓔescuela_linguistica@yahoo.com

Proyecto Lingüístico Mam contact the Proyecto Lingüístico Quetzalteco de Español (see overleaf).

Petén

Eco-Escuela San Andrés, Lago de Petén Itzá ⓣ926 3202, ⓦwww.ecomaya.com

Nueva Juventud San Andrés, Lago de Petén Itzá ⓣ711 0040, ⓦwww.volunteerpeten.com

Escuela Bio–Itzá San José, Lago de Petén Itzá ⓣ926 1363, ⓦwww.conservation.org/ecoescuela

Mundo Maya ⓣ928 8321, ⓦwww.mundomayaguatemala.com

The first decision to make is to choose where you want to study. By far the most popular choices are the towns of Antigua and Quetzaltenango, though Lago de Atitlán is also starting to become an established language centre. Beautiful **Antigua** is undoubtedly an excellent place to study Spanish: though the major drawback is that there are so many other students and tourists here that you'll probably end up spending your evenings speaking English. **Quetzaltenango** (Xela) has a different atmosphere, with a stronger "Guatemalan" character and far fewer tourists, though as its popularity has grown the city's gringo scene has inevitably mushroomed. The third most popular location is now **San Pedro La Laguna** on Lago de Atitlán, which has around a dozen schools and very cheap prices (with plenty offering a full homestay/tuition package for less than US$100 per week). As yet standards are only average in San Pedro; however, Guatemala City, Panajachel, Flores, San Andrés and San José in Petén, Huehuetenango, Todos Santas Cuchumatán, Nebaj, Chichicastenango and Monterrico also have schools.

Many schools lay on **after-school activities** like salsa classes, cooking, visits to villages, films and lectures and even trips to the coast. In Quetzaltenango most schools have a social ethos and fund development projects in the region; some offer volunteer opportunities on these projects.

Volunteer and paid work

In **Antigua**, the Project Mosaic Guatemala, 3 Av Norte 3 (ⓣ832 0955, ⓦwww.promosaico.org), has links to over fifty groups, including education, health and environmental projects. The best place to head for in **Quetzaltenango** is Entre Mundos, 6 C 7–31, Zona 1 (ⓣ761-2179, ⓦwww.entremundos.org), which also has excellent contacts with dozens of development projects.

As for **paid work**, teaching English is the best bet: check the English schools in Guatemala City (listed in the phone book). In addition, all Spanish language schools employ student coordinators to liaise between staff and pupils – but you'll need near-fluent Spanish. In Antigua, there are always a few vacancies for staff in the gringo bars and occasionally sales positions in jade showrooms. The *Revue* magazine and noticeboards in the popular bars and restaurants in Antigua and Quetzaltenango also occasionally advertise vacancies.

History

The very first humans to inhabit the area now known as Guatemala were nomadic hunters. By around 1500 BC these nomads had settled into agricultural communities, farming maize, beans, squash and chillies – the staples of today's Central American diet – making pottery and building villages of thatched-roofed houses on the Pacific coast. These early farmers are regarded as the first of the **Maya**, and it's thought that most people spoke a proto-Maya language. In the period after 1500 BC, known as the **Preclassic**, the population began to increase steadily throughout the Maya area.

By the beginning of the **Middle Preclassic** (1000–300 BC), Olmec influence, Mesoamerica's "mother culture", began to filter through to the Maya region introducing the Long Count calendar, an early writing system and a polytheistic religion. It's now known that Maya civilization first took root in the Guatemalan Petén, and the earliest known settlement of **Nakbé** was flourishing by 750 BC. By 400 BC Nakbé boasted over eighty structures, including pyramids and the earliest recorded stelae. Ceremonial buildings also began to emerge at **Tikal** and **Cival** around this time.

Real advances in architecture came in the **Late Preclassic** (300 BC–300 AD), when large pyramids and temple platforms were built throughout Guatemala in an explosion of Maya culture. The principal centres at this time were the cities of **Kaminaljuyú**, which dominated the central highlands, and the great early settlements in Petén: El Mirador, Nakbé, Uaxactún and Tikal.

Of all the sites dating from this era, it is the colossal triadic structures of **El Mirador** that are the most astounding. Though almost entirely Late Preclassic, the temples are the highest ever built in the Maya world, rising over seventy metres above the forest and connected by a complex system of raised causeways to distant settlements. The scale of El Mirador – covering around sixteen square kilometres – was immense, and the city undoubtedly supported tens of thousands of inhabitants. This first great Maya city traded with centres as far away as the Gulf of Mexico, the Pacific and Caribbean coasts and the Guatemalan highlands.

In the south of Guatemala the settlements around Santa Lucía Cotzumalguapa and Takalik Abaj, showing strong Olmec influence, were also emerging and at the great urban centre of Kaminaljuyú, on the outskirts of Guatemala City, substantial Preclassic temple mounds and granite stelae were erected.

The Classic Maya

The development that separates the Late Preclassic from the early **Classic period** (300–900 AD) is the introduction of the Long Count calendar in the Petén lowlands and the development of a recognizable form of writing, which included phonetic glyphs. This appears to have taken place by the third century AD and marks the beginning of the greatest phase of Maya achievement.

During the Classic period all the cities we now know as ruined or restored sites were built, almost always over earlier structures. Elaborately carved **stelae**, bearing dates and emblem-glyphs, were erected at regular intervals. These tell of actual rulers and of historical events in their lives – battles, marriages, dynastic succession and so on.

Developments in the Maya area were still powerfully influenced by events to the north. The presence of the Olmecs was replaced by that of **Teotihuacán**, which dominated central Mexico during the Early Classic period. Armed merchants, called *pochteca*, operated at this time, spreading the influence of Teotihuacán as far as Petén and the Yucatán. They brought new styles of ceramics and alternative religious beliefs. By 400 AD, the overwhelming power of Teotihuacán had radically altered life in Maya lands. Influence spread south, via the Pacific coast, first to Kaminaljuyú and then to Petén, particularly at **Tikal** which was closely allied with Teotihuacán. Both cities prospered greatly, and Kaminaljuyú was rebuilt in the style of Teotihuacán.

For much of the Middle Classic era the two most important players, **Calakmul** and **Tikal**, dominated the Maya region, using a system of alliances with a second tier of cities that included Copán, Palenque and Caracol, and dozens of smaller centres. Detailed carvings on wooden lintels and stone monuments depict elaborately costumed lords trampling on captives and spilling their own blood at propitious festivals, staged according to the dictates of the intricate Maya calendar, while attacks were also launched on auspicious dates known as "star wars". After Tikal was overrun by Caracol (backed by Calakmul) in a 562 AD star war, a period ensued when many smaller centres, once under the control of Tikal, became independent city-states while no stelae commemorating events were erected.

However, as the new kings established dynasties, the Maya cities grew to flourish as never before. Architecture, astronomy and art reached degrees of sophistication unequalled by any other pre-Columbian society. Trade prospered and populations swelled. Many Maya centres were larger than contemporary Western European cities, then in their "Dark Ages".

The prosperity and grandeur of the **Late Classic** (600–800 AD) reached all across the Maya lands: from Bonampak and Palenque in the west, to Labná, Sayil, Calakmul and Uxmal in the north, Altun Ha and Cerros in the east, and Copán and Quiriguá in the south, as well as hundreds of smaller centres. Masterpieces of painted pottery and carved jade (their most precious material) were created, often to be used as funerary offerings. Shell, bone and, rarely, marble were also exquisitely carved; temples were painted in brilliant colours, inside and out.

The Maya in decline

The glory days were not to last very long, however, and by 750 AD political and social changes began to be felt: alliances and trade links broke down, warring increased and stelae were carved less frequently. Cities gradually became depopulated and new **construction ceased** (in present-day Guatemala) after about 830 AD. The exact factors that precipitated the downfall of the Maya are still extremely contentious but it is now known that a prolonged drought preceded the decline, putting great strains on food production. Some experts suggest there may also have been peasant revolts against the ruling elite. But by the tenth century, the Maya had abandoned their cities in Petén and those few Maya that remained were reduced to a fairly primitive state.

By the **Postclassic** period (900 AD to the Spanish Conquest) all the city-states in Guatemala had collapsed. The decline of Maya civilization in the heartland of Petén brought about a rapid depopulation that prompted an influx of people into the Guatemalan highlands to the south. Along with the Yucatán, this area, formerly a peripheral region of relatively little development, now contained the last vestiges of Maya culture. Small settlements remained scattered throughout the highlands, usually built on open valley floors and supporting large populations with the use of terraced farming and irrigation. Little was to change in this basic village structure for several hundred years.

Pre-conquest: the highland tribes

Towards the end of the thirteenth century the central Guatemalan highlands were invaded by a group of **Toltec**

Maya, who had controlled the Yucatán until this time. Their numbers were probably small but their impact was profound, and following their arrival life in the highlands was radically altered.

It's thought that a relatively settled society became, under the influence of the Toltecs, fundamentally secular, aggressive and militaristic. The well-organized Toltec quickly established themselves as a ruling elite, presiding over a series of competing tribes. The greatest of these were the **K'iche'**, who dominated the central highlands, with their capital at **Utatlán**. Next in line were the **Kaqchikel**, centred around **Iximché**. On the slopes of the San Pedro volcano on Lago de Atitlán were the **Tz'utujil**, while in the west the **Mam** occupied the area around the modern town of Huehuetenango, with their capital at **Zaculeu**. A number of smaller tribes controlled the high Cuchumatanes mountain region.

To the east, around the modern city of Cobán, were the notoriously fierce **Achi** nation with the **Q'eqchi'** to their north, while around the modern site of Guatemala City the land was controlled by the **Poqomam**. Finally, the **Pipil** occupied the stretch along the Pacific coast. The sheer number of these tribes gives an impression of the extent to which the area was fragmented, and it's these same divisions, now surviving on the basis of language alone, that still shape the highlands today.

It was the K'iche' tribe that grew to become the dominant power in the highlands, conquering the neighbouring Mam and Kaqchikel under their great ruler, **K'ikab**. After his death in 1475, their empire lost much of its authority and for the next fifty years the tribes were in a state of almost perpetual conflict, and when the Spanish arrived the highlands were in crisis. The population had grown so fast that it had outstripped the food supply, leaving a situation that could hardly have been more favourable to the conquistadors.

The Spanish Conquest

While the tribes of highland Guatemala were warring amongst themselves to the north, in what is now Mexico, the Spanish conquistadors had captured the Aztec capital at Tenochtitlán. Even amidst the horrors of the Conquest there was one man whose evil stood out: **Pedro de Alvarado**. Ambitious, cunning, intelligent and ruthlessly cruel, he was perfectly suited for the job of subduing Guatemala.

In 1523, Alvarado arrived via the Pacific coast with a very modest force of a few hundred horsemen, soldiers and Mexican allies. After some minor skirmishes Alvarado confronted the K'iche' army, said to be 30,000-strong, at **Xelajú** (present-day Quetzaltenango). Despite the huge disparity in numbers, slingshot and foot soldiers were no match for cavalry and gunpowder, and the Spanish were able to wade through the Maya ranks. Legend has it that the battle was brought to a close when Alvarado himself slew the K'iche' leader **Tecún Umán** in hand-to-hand combat.

By a series of tactical alliances and brilliant, utterly ruthless military maneuvers, Alvarado's small Spanish force had overpowered all the main highland tribes by 1525. Dealing with the more remote tribes proved more difficult and it wasn't until the 1530s that Alvarado managed to assert control over the Ixil and Uspantenko. In 1526, the Kaqchikel also revolted and waged a guerrilla war against their former partners, forcing the Spanish to a site near the modern town of Antigua (now called Ciudad Vieja). Here, at the base of the Volcán de Agua, they established their first permanent capital on November 22, 1527.

Meanwhile, one thorny problem remained. Despite all his efforts, Alvarado had been unable to conquer the **Achi** and **Q'eqchi'** tribes, who occupied what are now the Verapaz highlands. In the end, Dominican priests under Fray Bartolomé de Las Casas succeeded where gunpowder had failed, and in 1540 the last of the highland tribes were brought under colonial control. Thus did the area earn its name of Verapaz – "true peace".

Colonial rule

The early years of colonial rule were tumultuous, marked by uprisings, political wrangling and natural disaster. In 1541, following a massive earthquake, a great wall of mud and water swept down the side of Agua volcano, burying the capital. The surviving colonial authorities moved up the valley to a new site (at present-day Antigua), where a new city was established. The new capital controlled the provinces of the **Audiencia de Guatemala** (Costa Rica, Nicaragua, El Salvador, Honduras, Guatemala and Chiapas in Mexico) and was the region's centre of political and religious power for two hundred years. By the mid-eighteenth century its population had reached some 80,000 and the city boasted several of the finest buildings in the hemisphere, until another huge earthquake destroyed the city in 1773 and the capital was moved again to its present-day site.

Colonial society was rigidly structured along racial lines, with pure-blood Spaniards at the top, indigenous slaves at the bottom, and a host of carefully defined racial strata in between. There was very little in the way of instant plunder in Central America – certainly none of the gold and silver of Mexico and Peru – and the **economy** was based on agriculture: livestock, cacao, tobacco, cotton and, most valuable of all, indigo were all farmed. At the heart of the colonial economy was the system of *repartamientos*, whereby the ruling classes were granted the right to extract labour from the indigenous population.

Perhaps the greatest power in colonial times was the **Church**, whose wealth from sugar, wheat and indigo concessions, based on the exploitation of a Maya labour force, fostered the construction of some eighty churches, plus schools, convents, hospitals, hermitages, craft centres and colleges. In the countryside, scattered native communities were merged into new Spanish-style towns and villages, making exploitation that much easier. Though Maya social structures were also profoundly altered, in the distant corners of the highlands priests were few and far between and *cofradía* (brotherhood) groups and *principales* (village elders) developed a religion of Catholic and Maya traditions that has persisted to this day.

Even more brutal than the social changes were the **diseases** that arrived with the conquistadors. Waves of plague, typhoid and smallpox swept through a people lacking any natural resistance to them. It was the devastating impact of these diseases that ensured that the small Spanish invading force was able to maintain control in Guatemala: around ninety percent of the Maya population was wiped out within a few years of the arrival of Alvarado.

Two centuries of colonial rule totally reshaped the structure of Guatemalan society, giving it new cities, a new religion, a transformed economy and a hierarchy based on racism. Nevertheless, the impact of colonial rule was perhaps less marked than in many other parts of Latin America and indigenous culture was never eradicated. In the relative isolation of the highlands, the Maya simply absorbed the symbols and ideas of the new Spanish ideology, fusing Maya and Catholic traditions to create a unique synthesis of Old and New World beliefs.

Independence

The apartheid-style nature of colonial rule had created deep dissatisfaction amongst many groups in Central America. A fundamental issue was Spain's determination to keep wealth and power in the hands of those born in the motherland, a policy that left growing numbers of subjects hungry for power and change. The spark that precipitated independence was Napoleon's invasion of Spain, after which a mood of reform swept through the colonies.

Brigadier Don Gabino Gainza, the Captain General of Central America, bowed to liberal demands for independence but still hoped to preserve the colonial power structure when he signed the **Act of Independence** on September 15, 1821. Mexico promptly sent troops to annex Guatemala but by 1823 Guatemala had joined a **Central American federation** with a US-style liberal constitution. Religious orders were abolished, the death penalty and slavery done away with, and trial by jury, a general school system, civil marriage and the Lívingston law code were all instituted.

The liberal era was soon overthrown by a revolt from the mountains. The indigenous population, hit hard by a cholera epidemic and seething with discontent, marched on Guatemala City behind a charismatic leader, the 23-year-old **Rafael Carrera**. Carrera respected no authority other than that of the Church, and upon seizing power he reversed all the liberal reforms with the support of conservative religious and landowning lobbies. Carrera then fought a bitter war against the rest of the Central American federation and Guatemala declared itself an **independent republic** in 1847. Carrera died in 1865, at the age of 50, leaving the country ravaged by the chaos of his tyranny and inefficiency.

Coffee and bananas

A major turning point in Guatemalan politics came in 1871, when **Rufino Barrios** arrived from Mexico with an army of just 45 men and started a **liberal revolution**. Barrios was a charismatic leader with tyrannical tendencies (monuments throughout the country testify to his sense of his own importance), who regarded himself as the great reformer and was intent on making sweeping changes. He was undoubtedly a man of action: he restructured the education system, attacked the power of the Church and modernized the University of San Carlos in Guatemala City. Underneath the new liberal perspective lay a deep arrogance, however. Barrios would tolerate no opposition and developed a network of secret police and an army academy that became an essential part of his political power base.

Alongside all this, Barrios set about reforming agriculture, particularly **coffee farming**. Cultivation had increased fivefold by 1884, creating an economic boom. The railway network was expanded, ports developed and a national bank established. Between 1870 and 1900 the volume of foreign trade increased twenty times. Much of the coffee trade was bound for Germany and many of the plantations were owned by an immigrant German elite – reflecting Barrios's perspective that foreign ideas were superior to indigenous ones.

Maya society was also deeply affected by the coffee boom as Barrios instituted a system of **forced labour** to safeguard harvests. Up to a quarter of the male population was despatched to work on the fincas, where conditions were appalling and the workforce treated with utter contempt. Many lost not only their freedom but also their land. From 1873, the government began confiscating land and selling it to the highest bidder, sparking village revolts throughout the western highlands that continued into the twentieth century. The loss of their most productive land also ensured that the Maya became dependent on seasonal labour.

By the early twentieth century, a new and exceptionally powerful player was becoming involved in Guatemala: the **United Fruit Company**. It first moved into Guatemala in 1901 after previous successes in Costa Rica and initially bought a small tract of land on which to grow **bananas**. Soon after, it was awarded railway contracts and built its own port, Puerto Barrios, giving it a virtual monopoly over transport. Large-scale banana cultivation took off and United Fruit got very rich very quickly.

The company's power was by no means restricted to agriculture, and its influence was so pervasive that it earned itself the nickname "El Pulpo" (The Octopus). In 1919, President Carlos Herrera threatened to terminate United Fruit Company contracts. He lasted barely more than a year.

Jorge Ubico became president in 1930 and embarked on a radical programme of reform, including a sweeping drive against corruption and a massive road-building effort which won him great popularity in the provinces. Despite his liberal pretensions, however, Ubico sided firmly with big business when the chips were down, always offering his assistance to the United Fruit Company and other sections of the land-owning elite.

But while Ubico tightened his grip on every aspect of government through internal security and repression, the rumblings of opposition grew louder. In 1944 discontent erupted in a wave of student violence, and Ubico was finally forced to resign after 14 years of tyrannical rule.

Ten years of "spiritual socialism"

The overthrow of Jorge Ubico released a wave of opposition as students, professionals and young military officers demanded democracy and freedom. The transformation of Guatemalan politics was so extreme a contrast to previous governments that the handover was dubbed the **1944 revolution**. A new constitution was drawn up, the vote given to all adults and the president prevented from running for a second term.

Juan José Arévalo, a teacher, won the 1945 presidential elections with 85 percent of the vote. His political doctrine was dubbed **"spiritual socialism"** and he immediately set about effecting much-needed structural reforms. Extensive social welfare programmes were introduced: schools and hospitals were built, an ambitious literary campaign launched, the vagrancy law was abolished, and workers were granted the right to union representation and to strike. Some state-owned fincas were turned into co-operatives, and there were other policies to stimulate industrial and agricultural development, though land reform was not seriously tackled.

The next president, **Jacobo Arbenz**, won the election with ease and immediately set out **land reform** proposals in a direct challenge to the US corporations that dominated the economy. Arbenz enlisted the support of peasants, students and unions to break the foreign dominance and began a series of suits against foreign corporations, seeking unpaid taxes.

In July 1952, the **law of agrarian reform** was passed, stating that idle and state-owned land would be distributed to the landless. The big landowners were outraged. Between 1953 and 1954, around 8840 square kilometres was redistributed to the benefit of some 100,000 peasant families. The United Fruit Company lost about half of its property, provoking the US government to accuse the new Guatemalan government of being a communist beachhead in Central America.

In 1954, the CIA (whose director was on the United Fruit Company's board) set up a small **military invasion** of Guatemala to depose Arbenz and install an alternative administration more suited to US tastes. A ragtag invasion army of exiles and mercenaries was put together in Honduras and, under CIA supervision, invaded the country, prompting Arbenz to resign after failing to get the support of the Guatemalan military. The US approved a new "government" and flew it to Guatemala aboard a US Air Force plane. Guatemala's experiment with "spiritual socialism" had ended.

Military rule and guerrilla war

Following the overthrow of Arbenz, it was **the army** that rose to fill the power vacuum, with US support; they were to dominate politics for the next thirty years, sending the country into a spiral of violence and economic decline.

Castillo Armas, the new president, immediately swept away all the reforms of the previous ten years: the 1945 constitution was revoked, all illiterates were disenfranchised, left-wing parties were outlawed, and large numbers of unionists and agrarian reformers were simply executed. All the land that had been confiscated was returned to its previous owners, hitting the indigenous population particularly hard.

In the following years, corruption, incompetence, outrageous patronage, and economic decline caused by a fall in coffee prices brought Guatemala to its knees, provoking the start of **guerrilla warfare**, and subsequent army reprisals. Political assassination became commonplace as "death squads" operated with impunity, killing peasant leaders, students, unionists and academics.

In the 1970 elections the power of the military and the far right was confirmed as **Colonel Arana Osorio**, elected president with the support of just four percent of the population, set about eradicating armed opposition, declaring that "if it is necessary to turn the country into a cemetery in order to pacify it, I will not hesitate to do so". The reign of terror reached unprecedented levels. Then on February 4, 1976, a massive **earthquake** struck the country, leaving around 23,000 dead, 77,000 injured and a million homeless. During the process of reconstruction, many of the victims felt the time had come to take action, and trade unions and a new guerrilla organization, the EGP, emerged. The army's response was predictable, with daily disappearances, murders and atrocities. In 1977, US President Carter suspended all military aid to Guatemala because of the country's appalling human rights record. At the same time, Guatemala continued to press its long-standing claim to **Belize**, but failed to gain international support.

In 1978 **Lucas García**, the most murderous of all Guatemala's leaders, took over and all opposition groups met with severe repression: protesters were gunned down in Panzós and massacred in Guatemala City, political opponents assassinated while several guerrilla armies started developing strongholds. In the highlands the rural war intensified, as 6000 rebel combatants scored hit-and-run successes, and the demand for conscripts grew rapidly. Peasants were slaughtered in their thousands, while in the towns victims included students, journalists, academics, politicians, priests, lawyers, teachers and unionists. Tens of thousands fled to Mexico, and the Catholic Church withdrew all its clergy from Quiché after a number of priests were murdered. It's estimated that around 25,000 Guatemalans were killed during the four years of the García regime.

In 1982 a successful coup was engineered by **Efraín Ríos Montt**, an evangelical Christian who declared he would restore law and order, eradicate corruption, and defeat the guerrillas by any means. Villagers were organized into Civil Defence Patrols (PACs), armed with ancient rifles, and told to patrol the countryside. The guerrilla's support infrastructure was immediately undermined and villagers were forced to take sides, caught between the guerrilla's propaganda and the sheer brutality and "scorched earth" tactics of the armed forces. Significant gains were made against the guerrillas, but as fighting intensified thousands of highland Maya fled into Mexico.

Little progress was made towards democratic reform, however. The Catholic Church had become alienated and in 1983 Ríos Montt was overthrown by yet another military coup – this one backed by a US government keen to see Guatemala set on the road to democracy. Although the rural repression, death squads and disappearances continued under the new president, **General Mejía Víctores**, elections were held for an 88-member Constituent Assembly in July 1984.

GAM, a new mutual support group for families of the "disappeared", brought the human rights abuses in Guatemala to international media attention. In November 1985, the first legitimate elections in thirty years were held.

Civilian rule

The elections were won by **Vinicio Cerezo**, a Christian Democrat who once in office declared that the army still held 75 percent of power. Throughout his six-year rule he adopted a non-confrontational approach, avoiding upsetting big business interests, landowners and generals. Political killings did drop but murder was still a daily event in Guatemala in the late 1980s and the guerrilla war continued to rage in remote corners of the highlands.

By the time the decade drew to a close it was clear that the army was still actively controlling political opposition. The fate of the disappeared remained unsolved, death squads still operated and 65 percent of the population remained below the poverty line. Acknowledging that his greatest achievement had been to survive, in 1990 Cerezo organized the country's first civilian transfer of power for thirty years.

The 1990 elections were won by **Jorge Serrano**, another evangelical with a centre-right economic position. His ineffectual administration once again proved both incapable of producing any real reform as the civil war rumbled on. The level of Human rights abuses remained high and the economy remained weak with most Guatemalans having little access to health care or education.

Guatemala's dispossessed and poor continued to clamour for change. Maya peasants became increasingly organized and influential, denouncing the continued bombardment of villages and rejecting the presence of the army and the system of civil patrols. Matters were brought into sharp focus in 1992 when **Rigoberta Menchú** was awarded the **Nobel Peace Prize** for her campaigning work on behalf of Guatemala's indigenous population.

Small groups of refugees began to return from exile in Mexico and start civil communities, though an estimated 45,000 still remained abroad. The territorial dispute with **Belize** was officially resolved when the two countries established full diplomatic relations in 1991. By early 1993 Serrano's reputation had plummeted following a series of corruption scandals, and in May 1993 he responded to a wave of popular protests with a self-coup, declaring he would rule by decree. The US suspended its annual US$67 million of aid and Serrano was quickly removed from office. Congress finally appointed **Ramiro León de Carpio**, the country's human rights ombudsman, as the new president. Though he reshuffled the senior military command, he rejected calls for revenge, declaring that stability was the main goal. Public frustration quickly grew as the new government failed to address fundamental issues: crime, land ownership, tax and constitutional reform. Some progress was made in peace negotiations with the URNG guerrilla leadership, but the question of indigenous rights remained unsolved.

Arzú and the peace accords

The 1996 presidential elections were won by **Álvaro Arzú** of the right-wing PAN (National Advancement Party), a party with strong oligarchic roots committed to private-sector-led growth and the free market. Nevertheless, he quickly adopted a relatively progressive stance, working to bring an end to the 36-year civil war. The **peace accords**, signed on December 29, 1996, terminated a conflict that had claimed 150,000 lives and resulted in the "disappearance" of another 50,000. The core purposes of the peace accords were to investigate previous human rights violations through a Truth Commission overseen by MINUGUA (the UN mission to Guatemala), to recognize the identity of indigenous people, and to eliminate discrimination and promote socioeconomic development for all Guatemalans. Progress was slow on all these issues during the Arzú years.

Though Arzú presided over a token reduction in armed forces numbers, their influence remained unchallenged throughout his term, and despite being blamed for over 90 percent of the civil war atrocities no prosecutions of army personnel were implemented. Then, in April 1998, two days after publishing a long-awaited investigation into wartime slaughters, **Bishop Juan Geradi** was bludgeoned to death in his own garage in Guatemala City, an event which stunned the nation. Though Guatemalans had long been accustomed to horrific levels of political violence, most thought the days of disappearances and death squads were over – as one newspaper put it, "This wasn't supposed to happen. Not any more."

The acute fragility of the nascent Guatemalan democracy was revealed – most observers immediately recognizing Geradi's assassination as the work of a vengeful military intent on preserving its power base. Despite international and domestic outrage – hundreds of thousands attended a silent protest in the capital days after the killing – the Arzú government failed to bring the perpetrators of the murder to justice and terrified judges, prosecutors and key witnesses fled abroad after threats and intimidation.

Despite this horrific killing, levels of political violence fell in the Arzú years, though there was an alarming upsurge in the **crime rate**, with soaring incidences of petty theft, muggings, robberies, drug- and gang-related incidents and murders. In 1997, despite its relatively small population, Guatemala had the fourth-highest rate of kidnapping in the world, with over 1000 people being abducted. A new police force, the PNC, quickly gained a reputation for corruption and ineffectualness as bad as its predecessor. Not surprisingly, law and order became the key issue of the 1999 election campaign.

The Portillo years

Former lawyer and professor **Alfonso Portillo** won Guatemala's 1999 presidential elections on a populist platform with a mandate to implement the peace accords and tackle the impunity of both the military and criminal gangs. In the grossest of ironies, Portillo sought to boost his ratings during the presidential campaign by confessing to killing two men during a brawl in Mexico in 1982, declaring, "a man who defends his life will defend the lives of his people". The decisive factor in his victory was the support of his political mentor, the highly contentious former general **Ríos Montt** and founder of the FRG, charged with genocide in the 1980s, and widely perceived as the real power behind Portillo.

Portillo unveiled a fairly diverse cabinet, though most key positions were filled by right-wing FRG politicians and pro-business monetarists. He moved quickly to solve the **Geradi murder** – another key campaign pledge. Prosecutors arrested three senior military personnel and a priest: in June 2001 they were finally brought to trial and found guilty of plotting Geradi's murder. Despite intense pressure on the prosecution, and a bomb exploding outside the home of one judge on the first day of the trial, justice prevailed, breaking the historically almost complete impunity of the armed forces.

The Geradi case aside, Portillo lurched from crisis to crisis, and after four years of catastrophic presidency he departed office leaving Guatemala virtually bankrupt. The stench of **corruption** pervaded his entire term as a series of scandals were unearthed and public coffers were emptied, including an allegation that hundreds of millions of dollars were transferred from the social security fund into Panamanian bank accounts.

Virtually nothing was done to implement the terms of the peace accords.

Crime levels soared during his term, as near-complete impunity reigned. Human rights workers, journalists and environmentalists who dared to challenge powerful political interests were threatened and killed, while gangs terrorized the city suburbs. Hardly a week seemed to pass without an armed bank robbery or a public lynching of a suspected thief. Seventy of the country's most notorious criminals – murderers, rapists, kidnappers and gang leaders – blasted their way out of jail in 2001 and Portillo even dispatched his own family to Canada after threats from a kidnapping gang. Guatemala was even decertified as a partner country in the US's "war against drugs" in 2002.

Meanwhile, the economy continued to falter, as the quetzal remained weak and traditional exports (principally coffee, sugar and bananas) were hit by low commodity prices, and the nation's high interest rates affected investment.

With Guatemala seemingly teetering on the brink, **Ríos Montt** declared he would stand as the FRG candidate for the 2003 elections, busing in thousands of supporters who rioted in the capital in July 2003 demanding a constitutional change that would allow him to stand. The constitutional court yielded to this demand, but mercifully the subsequent campaign was not tainted with more than isolated incidents of violence. Montt fell at the first hurdle in November 2003, polling less than 20 percent of the vote, and dropped out of the race. Most Guatemalans heaved a collective sigh of relief as the enigma of the Montt legend, which had cast a shadow over Guatemala for over 20 years, at last seemed extinguished.

Guatemala today

Oscar Berger, inaugurated as president in January 2004, got off to an encouraging start. A former mayor of Guatemala City from the right-wing GANA coalition, he declared that the country was near broke and his goal would be to govern in an austere, cost-conscious manner that would bring long-term prosperity. Financial and industrial members of Guatemala's oligarchy were sworn in to his cabinet, but he also made several progressive appointments, most notably appointing Nobel laureate and Maya rights campaigner Rigoberta Menchú as a goodwill ambassador with a brief to implement the peace accords.

He attempted to deal with Guatemala's appalling security problems by supporting the establishment of CICIACS, a UN-backed commission to strengthen the judiciary in the fight against organized crime – though this move was initially rejected as unconstitutional by Congress. But most significantly, Berger signalled a commitment to curb the power of the armed forces by announcing sweeping cuts to military spending that would reduce it to 0.66 percent of the national budget, slash army numbers from 27,000 to 15,500, and close 13 military bases.

Arrests warrants were issued for former president Portillo on money-laundering charges – he fled to Mexico the day it was served – while Ríos Montt, was accused of inciting the riots in Guatemala City in June 2003 that led to the death of a journalist and placed under house arrest.

Berger's challenges are immense. Politically he faces difficulties, as his three-party GANA coalition is comprised of such disparate elements. And it's hard to see how the links between rogue elements of the military, drug mafia and urban gangs that have seen a horrific rise in violence can be confronted given the resources at Berger's disposal. Economically, Guatemala needs to attract much more inward investment. Living standards remain desperately low for most Guatemalans, and especially the Maya who continue to be subject to institutionalized discrimination. Huge obstacles remain, and the country certainly faces many more difficult years ahead.

2.1

Guatemala City

Chaotic, congested and polluted, **GUATEMALA CITY** is in many ways the antithesis of the rest of the country. The capital was moved here in 1776, after the destruction of Antigua, but the site had been of importance long before the arrival of the Spanish. Now the largest city in Central America, its shapeless and swelling metropolitan mass, ringed by shantytowns, is home to over three million people – about a quarter of Guatemala's population – and is the undisputed centre of the country's politics, power and wealth.

Sprawling across a sweeping highland basin, surrounded on three sides by a horseshoe of jagged hills and volcanic cones, the city has an intensity and vibrancy that are both its fascination and its horror. Indeed, for many travellers a trip to the capital is an exercise in damage limitation, struggling through a swirling mass of bus fumes and crowds. Despite efforts by conservationists to regenerate the run-down historic quarters of the city, aside from a smattering of cafés and bohemian bars in Zona 1 and the arty enclave of Quatro Grados Norte in Zona 4, its cultural appeal is pretty limited.

Like it or not – and most travellers don't – Guatemala City is the crossroads of the country, and you'll probably end up here at some time, if only to hurry between bus terminals or to catch an early flight. Once you get used to the pace, it can offer a welcome break from life on the road, with restaurants, cinemas, shopping plazas, and Guatemala's best museums. But with Antigua only an hour away, it's also easy to visit the capital as a day-trip.

Some history

The Maya city of **Kaminaljuyú**, whose ruins are still scattered amongst Guatemala City's western suburbs, was well established here two thousand years ago. As a result of an alliance with the great northern power of Teotihuacán (near present-day Mexico City) in early Classic times (250–550 AD), Kaminaljuyú came to dominate the highlands and eventually provided the political and commercial backing that fostered the rise of Tikal (see p.267). The city was situated at the crossroads of two trade routes, and at the height of its prosperity was home to a population of some fifty thousand. However, following the decline of Teotihuacán, Kaminaljuyú's fortunes slumped and by 700 AD it was virtually abandoned.

When Alvarado entered the country in 1523, the fractured tribes of the west controlled the highlands and preoccupied the conquistadors. The Spanish ignored the possibility of settling here until the devastating **1773 earthquake** forced them to flee Antigua and establish a new capital. The new city was named Nueva Guatemala de la Asunción by royal decree and was officially inaugurated on January 1, 1776, though the new capital's growth was by no means dramatic. An 1863 census listed just 1206 residences and the earliest photographs show the city was still little more than a large village with a theatre, a government palace and a fort. One of the factors restricting the city's growth was the existence of a major rival, Quetzaltenango, though when it too was razed to the ground by a massive earthquake in 1902, many wealthy families moved to the capital, finally establishing it as the country's primary city.

Since 1918, Guatemala City has grown at an incredible rate, mainly due to an influx of rural immigrants, the flight from the fields escalating in the 1970s and

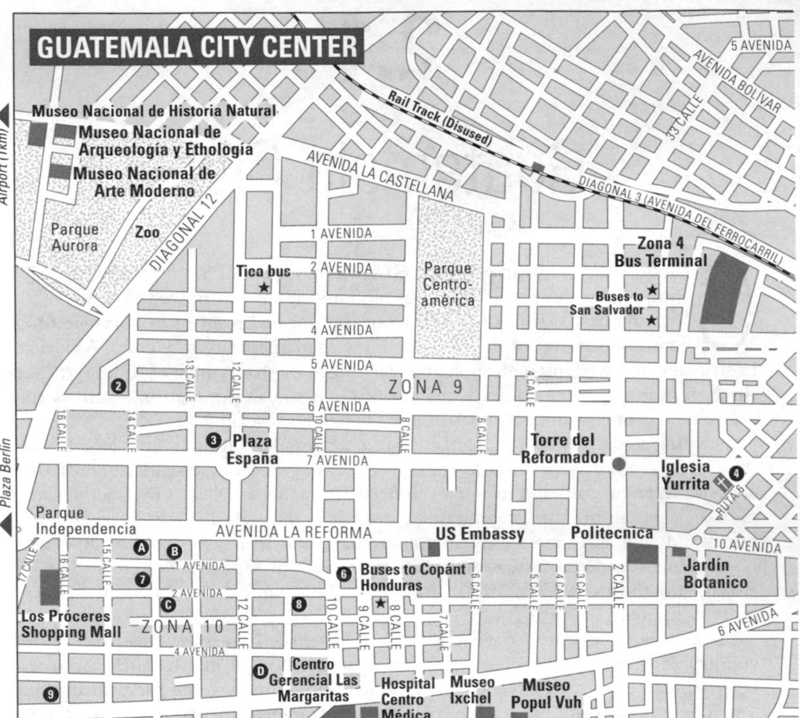

1980s as waves of internal refugees sought an escape from the violence in the countryside. Today the divisions that cleave Guatemalan society are at their most acute in the capital's crumbling streets, as glass skyscrapers rise alongside colonial churches and shoeless widows peddle cigarettes and sweets to designer-clad nightclubbers. While the wealthy elite sip coffee in air-conditioned shopping malls and plan their next visit to Miami, swathes of the city have been left to disintegrate into a threatening, treeless tangle of fume-choked streets, largely devoid of any kind of life after dark. A small army of **street children** live rough, scratching a living from begging, prostitution and petty crime, while brutal gangs terrorize the outer suburbs. Guatemala City has, in many ways, much more in common with São Paolo or Bogotá than with the rest of the country.

Arrival and orientation

Arriving in Guatemala City for the first time, it's easy to feel overwhelmed by its scale, with suburbs sprawling across some 17 **zones**. Fortunately the central area is really quite small. Broadly speaking, the city divides into two distinct halves. The northern section, centred on **Zona 1**, is the old part of town, containing the **Parque Central**, shops, fast-food joints, cinemas, the main post office, and many of the bus companies' offices. This part of the city is cramped, congested, polluted and bustling with activity in the day when the two main streets, 5 and 6 avenidas, are thick with street traders. Security is an issue after dark in Zona 1, when it's best to get around by taxi (see p.164).

To the south, acting as a buffer between the two halves of town, is **Zona 4**, home to the Centro Cívico administrative centre, the **tourist and immigration offices**, the Teatro Nacional and the arty enclave of Quatro Grados Norte. The other great landmark is the Zona 4 **bus terminal**, a crazy world of peripatetic humanity and exhaust fumes.

The southern half of the city, **Zona 9** and **Zona 10**, is the modern, wealthy part of town, split in two by **Avenida la Reforma**. Here you'll find exclusive offices, apartment blocks, hotels and shops, and Guatemala's most expensive nightclubs, restaurants and cafés. Many of the embassies and two of the country's finest museums are also here. Continuing south, the neighbouring zonas 13 and 14 are rich leafy suburbs and home to the airport, zoo, more museums and small guesthouses.

By air

Aurora international airport (☎334 7680) is on the edge of the city in Zona 13, some way from the centre. The **domestic terminal** is in the same complex, but with a separate entrance on Av Hincapié. There's a Banco del Quetzal (Mon–Fri 6am–8pm, Sat & Sun 8am–6pm) for US dollar cash and travellers' cheques (it does not change euros), plus 24-hour cashpoints which accept Visa, MasterCard, Cirrus and Plus cards. There are **tourist information desks** (both daily 6am–9pm; ☎331 4256) on the (upper) departures and (lower) arrivals floors, as well as a Telgua phone office and a post office (both Mon–Sat 7am–9pm).

Much the easiest way to get to and from the airport is by **taxi**: use the official desk with authorized tariffs in the arrivals hall. The fare to Zona 1 is around

US$12, and closer to $10 to zonas 9 and 10. **Buses** also depart from directly outside the terminal, across the concrete plaza: take a #83 marked "Terminal" which heads through Zona 9 and Zona 4, passing the Antigua bus terminal at 5 Av and 18 Calle in Zona 1. (Confusingly, a bus #83 marked "Bolívar" heads to a completely different part of town.) Virtually all Guatemala City's four- and five-star hotels, and the guesthouses in Zona 13, offer free pick-ups from the airport if you let them know when you're arriving.

If heading to **Antigua**, there are regular shuttle-bus services from the airport (US$8) until about 10pm, though they don't run to a fixed schedule and only leave when they have at least three passengers. A taxi from the airport is US$25.

By bus

Travelling by **first-class** (Pullman) **bus**, you'll arrive at the private terminal of whichever company you're using – there are about a dozen in total, most of them in Zona 1, including most services to Petén and Mexico. If you've come by second-class "chicken bus" **from Antigua**, you'll arrive in Zona 1 at the junction of 18 Calle, between 4 and 5 avenidas. The **Zona 4 terminal** is where second-class buses to the western highlands, the Pacific coast and some towns in the eastern highlands arrive and depart; the Melva terminal for San Salvador is very close by on 3 Avenida and 1 Calle.

Information

The Inguat **tourist office** (Mon–Fri 8am–4pm; ⓣ331 1333, ⓔinformacion@inguat.gob.gt) is at 7 Av 1–17, Zona 4. At the information desk on the ground floor they have plenty of material and there's always someone around who speaks English. There's another Inguat desk inside the Palacio Municipal on the Parque Central (same hours as above). For detailed hiking maps, go to the Instituto Geográfico Militar (Mon–Fri 8am–4pm), Av las Américas 5–76, Zona 13.

Addresses in Guatemala City

The system of street numbering in the capital may seem a little confusing at first and it is complicated by the fact that the same calles and avenidas can exist in several different zones. Always check the zone first and then the street. For example "4 Av 9–14, Zona 1" is in Zona 1, on 4 Avenida between 9 and 10 calles, house number 14.

City transport

Even locals can be bamboozled by Guatemala's seemingly anarchic web of city **bus routes**: for the most useful see the box opposite. Destinations are posted on the front of the bus, and routes are run from around 6.30am until about 9.30pm. Guatemala City has a ferocious **rush hour** and many roads throughout the city are jammed between 7 and 9am and from 4 to 7.30pm. All bus **fares** are US$0.15. Information on private bus companies and their **routes to other destinations in Guatemala** (and Mexico and Central America) is given in the box on pp.174–175.

There are currently both metered and non-metered **taxis**. If you can't face the complexities of the bus system, or it's late at night, the excellent metered taxis are comfortable and cheap; Amarillo (ⓣ332 1515) is highly recommended and will pick you up from anywhere in the city; Blanco y Azul (ⓣ360 0903) is also reliable. The fare from Zona 1 to Zona 10 is about US$5. There are plenty of non-metered taxis around too – you'll have to use your bargaining skills with these and fix the price beforehand.

Useful bus routes

83 Bolívar Airport–Av Bolívar–5 Av–Zone 1

83 Terminal Airport–7Av Zone 9–Zone 4 bus terminal–9 Av, Zone 1

101 6 Av Zone 1–Av la Reforma–20 C Zone 10. This route passes many of the embassies, the Popol Vuh and Ixchel museums and the Los Próceres mall.

76 6 Av Zone 1–Zone 9–Obelisco–20 C Zone 10

Terminal Any bus marked "terminal", and there are plenty of these on 4 Av in Zona 1, will take you to the main bus terminal in Zona 4.

Bolívar/Trébol Any bus marked "Bolívar" or "Trébol" will take you along the western side of the city, down Av Bolívar and to the Trébol junction, for connections to the western highlands.

Accommodation

Most budget and mid-range hotels are in noisy **Zona 1**. Be warned: it's not a safe neighbourhood at night, or a great place for wandering around in search of a room. Many travellers are now choosing to stay close to the airport, in **Zona 13**, where there are some good options – all offer free airport pick-ups and drop-offs, though be sure to book ahead. The disadvantage with this quiet, suburban location is that there are very few restaurants and cafés. Guatemala City's luxury hotels are clustered in a relatively safe part of town, in **Zona 10**, the "Zona Viva", where there's a glut of dining options, bars and nightclubs.

Zona 1

Chalet Suizo 14 C 6–82 ⓣ251 3786, ⓕ232 0429. This efficient and comfortable place is opposite the police headquarters, so it should be safe enough. The Swiss-hostel-style, well-designed rooms are spotlessly clean, and there's a left luggage facility. Private or shared bath; no double beds. ❹–❺

Hotel Colonial 7 Av 14–19 ⓣ232 6722, ⓕ232 8671, ⓦwww.hotelcolonial.net. Attractive hotel set in a historic building with a pleasingly formal dark wood and wrought iron interior. The accommodation offered is comfortable, but slightly old-fashioned; all rooms are fairly large and come with or without private bathroom. ❹–❺

Hotel Fénix 7 Av 15–81 ⓣ251 6625. Venerable place, but still one of the better budget bets in the central area. Friendly owners, and the rooms, some with private bath, are kept clean. There's a quirky café downstairs too. ❷

Hotel PanAmerican 9 C 5–63 ⓣ232 6807, ⓕ251 8749, ⓦwww.hotelpanamerican.com. Historic hotel, set in the heart of town with a formal, civilized air. The rooms all boast cable TV and private bathrooms. Airport transfer is included. Restaurant is brilliant for Sunday breakfast. ❻

Hotel Posada Belén 13 C A 10–30 ⓣ253 4530, ⓕ251 3478, ⓦwww.guateweb.com. A peaceful refuge from the fervour of the city's streets, the *Belén* occupies a beautiful old building, with a gorgeous little garden patio. The hosts can organize excursions and offer good cooking in the hotel restaurant. No children under 5. ❺

Hotel San Martín 16 C 7–65 ⓣ238 0319. Nothing fancy, but very cheap, clean rooms, some with private bath. Represents one of the best deals at the lower end of the scale. ❷–❸

Hotel Spring 8 Av 12–65 ⓣ232 2858, ⓕ232 0107. An excellent deal and a safe location, though it's perennially popular so book ahead. Spacious rooms, with or without private bath, all come with cable TV and are set around a pretty colonial courtyard. Breakfast is available, plus free mineral water. ❸–❹

Pensión Meza 10 C 10–17 ⓣ232 3177 or 253 4576. Legendary travellers' hangout, with plenty of 1960s-style decadence (and guests). Che Guevara stayed here back in the days. The dorms (US$3 per person) and doubles (some with private shower) are not too clean, but remain popular. There's a nice courtyard at the rear, a useful noticeboard, ping-pong, and the helpful owner speaks English. ❷

Zona 13

El Aeropuerto Guest House 15 C A 7–32 ⓣ332 3086, ⓕ362 1264, ⓦwww.hotelaeropuerto.centroamerica.com. A convenient and comfortable place a stone's throw from the international airport (call for a free pick-up). Nine spotless rooms, with or without private bathroom and featuring Maya textile bedspreads,

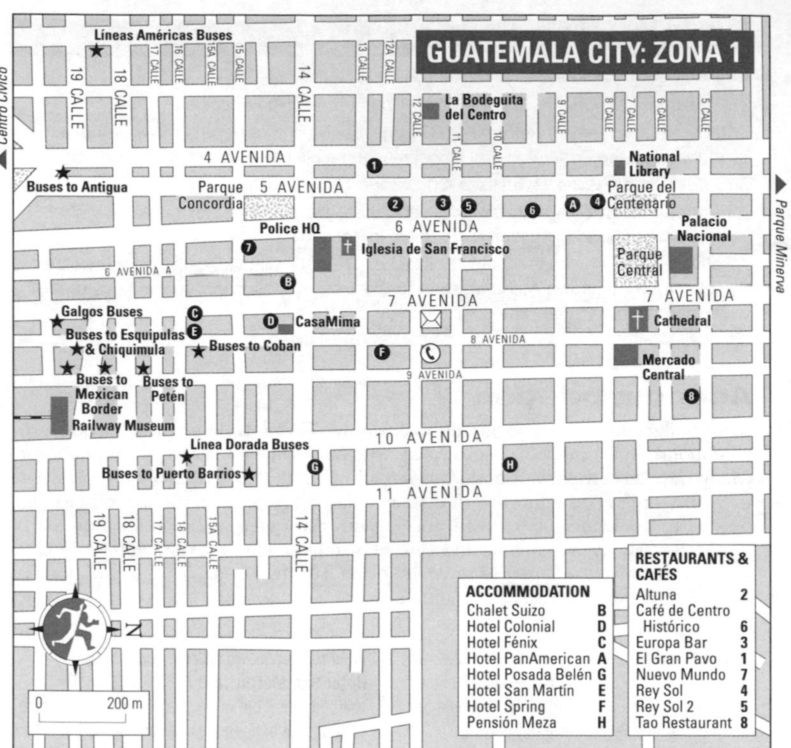

are on offer. The English-speaking management serve up a free continental breakfast along with email and fax facilities. ⑤

Dos Lunas 21 C 10–92 ⓣ & ⓕ 334 5264, ⓦ www.xelapages.com/doslunas. Extremely well-run guesthouse located on a safe, quiet suburban street close to the airport, with a second location in a suburban house around the corner. Free pick-up, drop-off and breakfast. The young Guatemalan owner speaks fluent English and offers reliable travel advice, and can arrange shuttle buses and taxis. Very popular, so it's essential to book well ahead. US$10 per bed, double with bath ⑤

Economy Dorms 8 Av 17–74, Col Aurora I ⓣ 331 8029. This friendly guesthouse is within a short ride of the airport, and offers four private rooms in a family's house – guests are welcome to mingle in the living room with the owners. A basic breakfast and airport transfers are included. ④

Hostal Los Volcanes 16a C 8–00 ⓣ 360 3232, ⓦ www.hostallosvolcanos.com. Decent B&B, close to the airport, with seven clean rooms and a pleasant sitting area. The management can also arrange transport connections. ⑤

Zona 10

Camino Real 14 C 0–20 ⓣ 333 3000, ⓕ 337 4313, ⓦ www.caminoreal.com.gt. Guatemala's first 5-star hotel, long favoured by visiting heads of state, though the chintzy decor now looks rather dated. Excellent location in the heart of the Zona Viva, plus bars, shops, business and sports facilities – including two pools, a spacious gym, and floodlit tennis courts. Rooms from US$190. ⑨

Holiday Inn 1 Av 13–22 ⓣ 332 2555, ⓕ 332 2584, ⓦ www.holidayinn.com.gt. In the heart of the Zona Viva, the *Holiday Inn* boasts 204 commodious rooms and suites, and an excellent buffet breakfast is included. Amenities include restaurant, bar, business centre and in-house Internet café. Rooms from US$120. ⑨

Hotel Casa Santa Clara 12 C 4–51 ⓣ 339 1811, ⓕ 332 0775, ⓦ www.hotelcasasantaclara.com. Attractive hotel where the 14 stylish modern rooms all have parquet wood floors, bedside lights and cable TV; there's also a quality restaurant. Free shuttle from airport. ❻

Hotel Inter-Continental 14 C 2–51 ⓣ379 4444, ⓕ379 4445, ⓦwww.interconti.com. Unquestionably the city's most stylish and sumptuous five-star address. A monumental lobby featuring fine art and modern sculpture sets the tone, and there's also a modish bar, two good restaurants and a heated outdoor pool to go along with the 239 wonderful rooms. Rooms from US$150. ❾

The City

Though few people come to Guatemala City for the sights, there are some places that are well worth visiting while you're here. The capital attractions include three superb **museums**: the Ixchel, Popol Vuh and Museo Nacional de Arqueología y Etnología. There's also the odd impressive historic building in **Zona 1**, and in the southern half of the city, some striking modern structures.

Zona 1: the old city

The hub of the old city is **Zona 1**: a squalid world of low-slung, crumbling nineteenth-century townhouses and faceless modern concrete blocks, broken pavements, parking lots and plenty of squalor. Though left to rot for decades, tentative signs of regeneration are evident in places as colonial-style facades are scrubbed and clusters of new bars and cafés open in historic buildings. However, pollution and noise from fume-belching buses are omnipresent and Zona 1 remains beset by social problems. Having said all this, the zona's streets do possess a certain brutal fascination and are undeniably the most exciting part of the capital.

The Parque Central

Towards the north of Zone 1 sits the country's political and religious centre, the windswept **Parque Central**, from where all distances in Guatemala are measured. Despite its importance, the Parque is a fairly soulless place, patronized by bored taxi drivers, *lustradores* (shoeshiners) and pigeons; the square only really comes alive on Sundays (when there's a good *huipil* market) and public holidays, when a tide of Guatemalans come to stroll, gossip and snack. Next to the giant Guatemalan flag in the Parque's centre is a small monument dedicated to "the anonymous heroes for peace" – its glass case has been cracked by vandals and the "eternal flame" hasn't flickered for years.

The Parque's most striking building is the **Palacio Nacional** (entrance by guided tour only, conducted in Spanish or English; Mon–Fri 9am–4.30pm, Sat & Sun tours 9am–4.30pm; free), a grandiose stone-faced structure started in 1939 under President Ubico. For decades it housed the executive branch of the government, and from time to time its steps have been fought over by assorted coupsters. It's worth a look inside for its most imposing features – two Moorish-style interior courtyards and the stained-glass windows of the former **Salas de Recepción** on the second floor.

On the east side of the plaza is the blue domed **Cathedral** (daily 7am–1pm & 3–7pm), completed in 1868. Its solid, squat design was intended to resist the force of earthquakes and has, for the most part, succeeded. Inside there are three main aisles, all lined with arching pillars, austere colonial paintings and intricate altars housing an array of saints. The cathedral's most poignant aspect is outside, however: etched into the twelve pillars that support the entrance railings are the names of thousands of the dead and "disappeared", victims of the civil war, including an astonishing number from the department of Quiché.

Around the back of the cathedral is the **Mercado Central**, housed in three sickly blue-and-yellow layers of sunken concrete; a structure which the architect apparently modelled on a nuclear bunker, sacrificing any aesthetic concerns to the need for strength. Inside, the top floor sells textiles, leatherware and jewellery, the middle floor has flowers, fruit and vegetables, and the bottom has **handicrafts** – mainly basketry and típica clothing.

South of the Parque Central

Heading south from the Parque Central are **6 and 7 avenidas**, thick with clothes shops, fast-food joints and neon signs. On the corner of 6 Av and 13 C is the **Iglesia de San Francisco**, dating from 1780 and famous for its carving of the Sacred Heart. It's said that cane syrup, egg whites and cow's milk were mixed with the mortar to enhance its resistance to earthquakes. Another block to the south is the **police headquarters**, an outlandish-looking mock castle with imitation medieval battlements.

Just 300m east of the police headquarters along 14 Calle, at the corner with 8 Avenida, **Casa Mima** (Mon–Fri 9am–12.30pm & 2–6pm, Sat 9am–5pm; US$2.50) is an immaculately restored late nineteenth-century townhouse with original furnishings from various periods, including Moderne, Art Deco and French neo-Rococo, offering a fascinating glimpse into a wealthy middle-class household of that era. There are excellent explanatory leaflets, and usually an English-speaking guide on hand, plus a delightful little **café** on the rear patio, with good coffee and cookies.

As you head south from Casa Mima, along 8 Avenida, things go into a slow but steady decline, until you finally emerge in the madness of **18 Calle**, a distinctly sleazy part of town that is definitely best avoided at night. If you have half an hour to kill you could take a look at the former **train station**, at the junction of 18 Calle and 9 Avenida, which has recently been converted into a well-presented **railway museum** (Tues–Sat 9am–5pm; US$1.30) with some wonderful old steam trains and information about the history of the Guatemalan railroads.

At the southern end of the old city, separating it from the newer parts of town, the distinctively 1960s architecture of the **Centro Cívico** area marks the boundary between zonas 1 and 4. Looming over 7 Avenida is the **Banco de Guatemala** building, bedecked with bold modern murals and stylized glyphs designed by Dagoberto Vásquez – the images recount the history of Guatemala and the conflict between Spanish and Maya. Just to the south you'll find the main office of **Inguat** (see p.164) and opposite is the lofty landmark **Teatro Nacional**, one of the city's most prominent and unusual structures, completed in 1978. Designed along the lines of an ocean liner, painted blue and white with portholes as windows, it has superb views across the city and hosts regular cultural events in its auditorium and the adjoining open-air space. There's also a little-visited **museum** dedicated to the Guatemalan military here, though it's really only of interest to would-be *comandantes.*

The new city

The more spacious southern half of the city, with its broader streets, is, roughly speaking, divided into two by 7 Avenida. To the south of the Centro Cívico, at the junction of 7 Av and 2 C, in Zona 4, is the landmark **Torre del Reformador**, Guatemala's answer to the Eiffel Tower. The steel structure was built in honour of President Barrios, whose liberal reforms transformed the country between 1871 and 1885. Unfortunately you can't go up it. Just to the north on the junction with Ruta 6 is the **Yurrita Church** (Tues–Sun 8am–noon & 3–6pm), built in an outlandish neo-Gothic style more reminiscent of a horror-movie set than the streets of Guatemala City.

A block east from the Torre is **Avenida la Reforma**, the new city's main transport artery, which divides zonas 9 and 10. It's best appreciated on Sundays when this tree-lined boulevard is closed to motor traffic, and pedestrians, cyclists, skateboarders and bladers reclaim the street. Many of the city's important sites and buildings are to be found on (or just off) the Reforma, including the **Jardín Botanico** (Mon–Fri 8am–3pm, Sat 9am–noon; US$1.20) of the San Carlos University. Inside you'll find a beautiful little garden with quite a selection of species, all neatly labelled in Spanish or Latin. In the grounds, there's also an anachronistic **natural**

history museum, with a collection of mouldy stuffed birds, including a quetzal and curios including a llama skeleton and swordfish swords.

Far more worthwhile are the two privately owned **museums** in the campus of the University Francisco Marroquín, reached by following 6 C Final off Av la Reforma to the east. The **Museo Ixchel** (Mon–Fri 8am–5pm, Sat 9am–12.50pm; US$2.50) is strikingly housed in its own purpose-built cultural centre. Probably the capital's best museum, the Ixchel is dedicated to Maya culture, with particular emphasis on traditional weaving. There's a stunning collection of hand-woven fabrics, including some very impressive examples of ceremonial costumes, with explanations in English, plus information about the techniques, dyes, fibres and weaving tools used and the way in which costumes have changed over the years. Don't miss the miniature *huipil* collection next to the basement café.

Right next door, on the third floor of the *auditorio* building, is the city's other private museum, the excellent **Museo Popol Vuh** (Mon–Fri 9am–5pm, Sat 9am–1pm; US$2.50), home to an outstanding collection of artefacts from sites all over the country. The small museum is divided into Preclassic, Classic, Postclassic and Colonial rooms, and all the exhibits are top quality. In the Preclassic room are some stunning ceramics and stone masks. The Classic room has an altar from Naranjo, some bizarre-looking incense burners, and a model of Tikal; the Postclassic contains a replica of the Dresden codex. The colonial era is represented with some ecclesiastical relics and processional crosses.

Back on Av la Reforma, heading south brings you to the smart part of town, a collection of leafy streets filled with boutiques, travel agents, banks, office blocks and sleek hotels. A little to the east, around 10 C and 3 Av, is the so-called **Zona Viva**, some ten small city blocks housing upmarket hotels, restaurants, nightclubs and, at the bottom of La Reforma, the Los Próceres shopping mall. To get to Av la Reforma from Zona 1, take bus #82, which runs along 10 Av in Zona 1, past the Yurrita Church and all the way along Av la Reforma.

West of 7 Avenida

West of 7 Avenida it's quite another story, and while there are still small enclaves of upmarket housing, and several expensive shopping areas, things are really dominated by commerce and transport, including the infamous **Zona 4 bus terminal**, at 1 C and 4 Av. This area is probably the country's most impenetrable and intimidating jungle, a brutish swirl of petty thieves, hardware stores, bus fumes and sleeping vagrants. Around the terminal the largest **market** in the city spreads across several blocks. To get to the bus terminal from Zona 1, take any of the buses marked "Terminal" from 4 Av or 9 Av, all of which pass within a block or two.

Some 2km further to the south in Zona 13, reachable by bus #63 from 4 Avenida or #83 from 10 Avenida, **Parque Aurora** houses the city's **zoo** (Tues–Sun 9am–5pm; US$1.50), home to African lions, Bengal tigers, crocodiles, giraffes, Indian elephants, hippos, monkeys and all the Central and South American big cats, including some well-fed jaguars.

On the other side of Parque Aurora is a collection of three state-run **museums** (all Tues–Fri 9am–4pm, Sat & Sun 9am–noon & 2–4pm). The best of these is the **Museo Nacional de Arqueología y Etnología** (US$5), which has a world-class selection of Maya treasures, though the design and displays are somewhat antiquated. The collection includes sections on prehistoric archeology and ethnology and features some wonderful stelae and panels from Machaquilá and Dos Pilas, spectacular jade masks from Abaj Takalik and a stunning wooden temple-top lintel from Tikal. However, it's the exhibits collected from Piedras Negras, one of the remotest sites in Petén, that are most impressive. Stela 12, dating from 672 AD, brilliantly depicts a cowering captive king begging for mercy, and there's a monumental carved stone throne from the same site, richly engraved with superb glyphs and decorated with a twin-faced head.

Right opposite the archeological museum, the city's **Museo Nacional de Arte Moderno** (US$1.70) also suffers from poor presentation and layout but can boast some imaginative geometric paintings by Dagoberto Vásquez, and a collection of startling exhibits by Efraín Recinos, including a colossal marimba-cum-tank sculpture. There's also a permanent collection of bold Cubist art and massive murals by Carlos Mérida, Guatemala's most celebrated artist, which draw strongly on ancient Maya tradition. The most neglected of the three museums, the **Museo Nacional de Historia Natural** (US$1.70), features a range of miserable stuffed animals from Guatemala and elsewhere and a few mineral samples. Close by on 11 Avenida is a touristy **handicraft market**, while to the south is Aurora airport.

Kaminaljuyú and Museo Miraflores

Way out west on the edge of the city is the long thin arm of Zona 7, which wraps around the ruins of **Kaminaljuyú** (daily 9am–4pm; US$4). Archeological digs have uncovered more than three hundred mounds and thirteen ball courts, though unlike the massive temples of the lowlands, these structures were built of adobe, and most of them have been lost to centuries of erosion and a few decades of urban sprawl. Today, the archeological site (incorporating only a tiny fraction of the original city) is little more than a series of earth-covered mounds, and though it's now a favourite spot for football and smooching teenagers, it's virtually impossible to get any impression of Kaminaljuyú's former scale and splendour. To **get to** the ruins, take **bus #35** from 4 Av in Zona 1. Alternatively, any bus from the Parque Central that has a small "Kaminaljuyú" sign in the windscreen passes within a block or two.

To gain a greater insight into the ancient city, visit the excellent new **Museo Miraflores** (Tues–Sun 9am–7pm; US$5), a ten-minute walk south of the ruins inside the upmarket Miraflores shopping mall on Calzada Roosevelt. The history of the city, and its importance as a trading centre is explained and there are some striking stone sculptures and stelae pieces, ceramics, impressive jade jewellery and obsidian flints.

Eating

Guatemala City isn't a great place for indulging in hedonistic pleasures. Most of the population hurry home after dark and only Zona 10 and Zona 4's Quatro Grados Norte have much life after dark. There are, however, **restaurants** everywhere in the city, invariably reflecting the type of neighbourhood they're in. For budget eats, **Zona 1** has some good comedores and dozens of fast-food chains. In the smarter parts of town, particularly **zonas 9** and **10**, the emphasis is more on upmarket cafés and refined dining, and there's also more choice, including Mexican, Middle Eastern, Chinese and Japanese options.

Zona 1

Altuna 5 Av 12–31. Elegant, formal and expensive Spanish/Basque restaurant that's something of a private club for Guatemala's old-money elite. Majors in fish and seafood, including paella and good *calamares* but also serves *ceviche*, pasta and Castilian treats like *bacalao* and *jamón serrano.*

Café de Centro Histórico 6 Av 9–50. Unashamedly nostalgic café on the upper floor of a beautifully restored 1930s building, replete with original tiles, wood panelling and monochrome photographs. Breakfasts, inexpensive Guatemalan dishes and set meals, pies and salads, plus great coffee. No smoking room.

Europa Bar 11 C 5–16. Long-running, popular expat hangout, set inauspiciously beneath a multi-storey car park. Primarily a bar, with CNN and sports on screen, but there are also cheap (though bland) eats including sandwiches and spaghetti. Closed Sun.

El Gran Pavo 13 C 4–41. Fairly authentic Mexican food, at moderate prices. Things really kick off on weekends when mariachi bands prowl the tables – you'll have to put up with piped ranchero music at other times, though the long tequila list helps ease the pain. Other branches at 6 C 3–09, Zona 9; 15 Av 16–72, Zona 10; 13 C and 6 Av, Zona 10.

Nuevo Mundo 6 Av 14–79. Centrally located Chinese restaurant, with kitsch-rich interior festooned with garish dragons, and a tooth-loosening jukebox. Try the *arroz frito a la cantonesa* washed down with *té verde*.

Rey Sol south side of Parque Centenario. Vegetarian café-restaurant with wholemeal bread sandwiches, *tamales*, salads, "Aerobic" breakfasts, juices and *licuados*. Also sells good bread, granola, herb teas and veggie snacks. There's a second branch at 11 C 5–51.

Tao Restaurant 5 C 9–70. The city's best-value three-course veggie lunch. There's no menu; you just eat the meal of the day at tiny tables around a plant-filled courtyard.

Zona 4

Arguileh Vía 5, Cuatro Grados Norte. Hip, popular Arabic-style restaurant where you sit on cushions and eat from a moderately priced Middle Eastern menu. Hubble-bubble pipes are available and some tables overlook the pedestrianized street below.

Café Restaurant Pereira inside the Gran Centro Comercial mall, 6 Av and 24 C. Inexpensive, popular comedor-cum-restaurant just a couple of blocks west of Inguat. Big portions and good-value set meals.

Sucré Salé Ruta 6 8–52. Terrific, friendly little café located in the ground floor of Casa Yurrita, which adjoins the church of the same name (see p.168). All the dishes (including great soups, breakfasts, set lunches and desserts) are freshly prepared every day and there's a shady garden. Daily 7am–3pm.

Zonas 9 and 10

Los Alpes 10 C 1–09, Zona 10. Tranquil garden café with great pastries, pies and crepes, and a relatively inexpensive breakfast menu considering the smart location. Closed Mon.

China Queen 6 Av 14–04, Zona 9. Excellent-value, good-quality Chinese restaurant that offers huge portions of tasty grub; fried rice with shrimp is US$10.

Piccadilly Plaza España, 7 Av 12–00, Zona 9. Clean, family-orientated restaurant with decent range of pasta and pizza, served along with huge jugs of beer. Moderate prices. There's another branch in Zona 1 on 6 Av and 11 C.

Tacontento 2 Av & 14 C, Zona 10. One of the cheapest places for a filling feed in the Zona Viva, with tasty tacos, *sopa azteca* and other Mexican standards.

Tamarindos 11 C 2–19 A, Zona 10. Guatemala's most urbane restaurant, with seriously stylish furnishings, a Japanese-style garden patio, electronica on the sound system and a fusion menu of creatively prepared Asian and Italian food. Expect to pay $15–20 a head.

El Tapeo 6 Av 16–01. Enjoyable, authentic Spanish restaurant, with gingham tablecloths, posters of Almería, and excellent tapas and mains. Moderate prices.

Nightlife and entertainment

It may be the capital, but Guatemala City is not renowned for its nightlife. Personal safety is a concern, especially in Zona 1, and it's best to get around by taxi, even if you're only moving a few blocks. There are three main areas – zonas 1, 4 and 10 – where people congregate, each with their own atmosphere. **Zona 1** has a grungy appeal and is popular with students. In **Zona 4**, the vibrant new enclave of Quatro Grados Norte (occupying a couple of pedestrianized streets) is a good bridge between zonas 1 and 10, with an arty, bohemian scene. It's very lively at night here with people darting between the cosmopolitan restaurants, hip bars and boutiques. There's often an arthouse film or exhibition worth catching at the Cultura Hispánica in the heart of the area on Vía 5. Zona Viva in **Zona 10** is where the wealthy go to have fun. Here there's a surplus of American-style bars, upmarket restaurants and clubs playing Latino and European house music, pop hits and salsa. Guatemala City's small **gay nightlife** scene is mostly underground. The key venue is the (almost exclusively male) club: *Pandora's Box*, Vía 3 and Ruta 3, Zona 4 (two blocks from Quatro Grados Norte). There are no specifically lesbian clubs or bars in the city.

Movie-watching is popular and there is a good selection of **cinemas**, most showing films in English with Spanish subtitles; there are four on 6 Av between the Parque Central and the police HQ. Elsewhere, the very best for sound quality include the Miraflores and neighbouring Cine Tikal Futura, Calzada Roosevelt, Zona 11, and Magic Place on Av las Américas, Zona 13. Programmes are listed in the main national newspapers including the *Prensa Libre*.

Bars and clubs

La Bodeguita del Centro 12 C 3–55, Zona 1. Large, left-field venue with live music, comedy, poetry and all manner of arty events. Free entry during the week, with a cover around US$4 at weekends. Definitely worth a visit for the Che

Guevara memorabilia alone. Closed Mon.

Café La Otra Puerta Pasaje Aycinema, 9 C between 6 and 7 Av, Zona 1. Agreeable, informal place in a crumbling historic building that serves good coffee, wine and food including pasta.

Las Cien Puertes Pasaje Aycinema, 9 C between 6 and 7 Av, Zone 1. Ever-popular bohemian bar in a beautiful run-down colonial arcade popular with artists, students and political activists. Graffiti-splattered walls, good Latin sounds and moderate prices.

Dos Continentes 10 Av 10–17, Zona 1. Sociable bar, next door to the *Pensión Mesa*, with draught Moza and Gallo beer, eclectic music and a good US$1.50 food menu.

El Establo 14 C 5–08, Zona 10. European-owned bar that attracts a middle-aged crowd. There's a large, polished wood interior, good food and a soundtrack of decent jazz and Western music.

Porai 4 Av & 12 C, Zona 10. The capital's most happening club, with its dancefloor semi-open to the elements, positioned under an expansive canvas canopy. Guatemalan and international DJs spin house, techno and trance, and there are occasional rock concerts too. No dress restrictions; Thurs, Fri and Sat nights only.

Rattle & Hum 4 Av & 16 C, Zona 10. Snug and stylish Australian-owned bar, popular with both expats and locals, with lively atmosphere and rock music on the stereo.

Suae Vía 5, Quatro Grados Norte, Zona 4. Lounge-style bar with arresting decor, modish electronic tunes and a hip clientele. Barstaff are well connected to the capital's underground rave scene.

Listings

Airlines Airline offices are scattered throughout the city, with many along Avenida la Reforma. It's fairly straightforward to phone them and there's nearly always someone in the office who speaks English. Aeroméxico, Av Reforma 7–62, Zona 9 ⓣ361 7171; Aerocaribe (see Mexicana, below); Aerovías, Av Hincapié 18 C, Zona 13 ⓣ332 5686; American Airlines, *Hotel El Dorado*, Av la Reforma 15–45, Zona 9 ⓣ337 1177; British Airways, 1 Av 10–81, Zona 10, 6th floor of Edificio Inexa ⓣ332 7402; Continental, 18 C 5–56, Zona 10 ⓣ366 9985, airport ⓣ331 2051; Copa, 1 Av 10–1, Zona 10 ⓣ385 5500, airport ⓣ385 0658; Delta, 15 C 3–20, Zona 10, Centro Ejecutivo building ⓣ337 0642; Iberia, Av la Reforma 8–60, Zona 9 ⓣ332 0911, airport ⓣ332 5517; Jungle Flying, Av Hincapié & 18 C, domestic terminal, Hangar L-16, Zona 13 ⓣ360 4917; KLM, 6 Av 20–25, Zona 10, 5th floor of Edificio Plaza Marítima ⓣ367 6179; Mexicana, 13 C 8–44, Zona 10, Edificio Edyma Plaza ⓣ366 4543; Taca, Av Hincapié 12–22, Zona 13 ⓣ470 8222; Racsa, airport ⓣ361 5703; Tapsa, Av Hincapié 18–00, Zona 13 ⓣ331 9180; Tikal Jets, Av Hincapié, Hangar J-6, Zona 13 ⓣ332 5070; United Airlines, Av la Reforma 1–50, Zona 9, Edificio el Reformador ⓣ336 9923.

American Express office inside Clark Tours office, 12 C 0–93, Zona 9, Centro Comercial Montúfar (Mon–Fri 8.30am–5pm; ⓣ331 7422).

Banks and exchange At the airport, Banco del Quetzal (Mon–Fri 6am–8pm, Sat & Sun 8am–6pm) gives good rates; there are also several 24hr MasterCard/Cirrus and Visa/Plus ATMs. You can exchange euros (at poor rates) at Banco Uno, 18 C 5–56, Zona 10. In Zona 1, Credomatic, 5 Av & 11 C, gives Visa and MasterCard cash advances (Mon–Fri 8.30am–7pm, Sat 9am–1pm) and will cash travellers' cheques. In Zona 10, head for the Centro Gerencial Las Margaritas, at Diagonal 6 10–01, where there are several 24hr cashpoints, and banks where you can cash travellers' cheques.

Books Sopho's on Av la Reforma 13–89, Zona 10 and Vía 5, Quatro Grados Norte, Zona 4, are the best bookshops for English-language fiction and literature and also have coffee bars. Géminis, 3 Av 17–05, Zona 14, is worth a visit if you're in the south of the city.

Car rental Renting a car in Guatemala is fairly expensive and it's essential to check out the terms of the contract as there are usually large penalties if you damage the vehicle. Jeeps can be rented for around US$50 a day and cars start from US$28. About a dozen companies have desks at the airport. Adaesa Renta Autos, 4 C A 16–57, Zona 1 (ⓣ220 2180) is recommended, a small Honda or Hyundai costing US$28 per day (with a US$440 accident deductible clause). Other companies include: Avis, 6 Av 7–64, Zona 9 ⓣ339 3248, ⓦwww.avisenlinea.com; Hertz, 7 Av 14–76, Zona 9 ⓣ332 2242, ⓦwww.hertz.com.gt; Tabarini, 2 C A 7–30, Zona 10 ⓣ331 6108; and Thrifty, 6 Av 11–57, Zona 9 ⓣ332 1456.

City tours Guided tours of the historic centre and museums are organized by Clark Tours (see "Travel agents", opposite). Prices start at US$25 for a half-day tour.

Embassies Most of the embassies are in the southeastern quarter of the city, along Avenida la Reforma and Avenida las Américas, and they tend to open weekday mornings only, unless otherwise indicated. Belize, Av la Reforma 1–50, 8th floor, Suite 803, Edificio el Reformador, Zona 9 (Mon–Fri 9am–1pm & 2–5pm; ☎334 5531 or 331 1137); Canada, 13 C 8–44, 6th floor, Edificio Edyma Plaza, Zona 10 (Mon–Thurs 8am–4.30pm, Fri 8am–1.30pm; ☎333 6102); Colombia, 5 Av 5–55, Edificio Europlaza Torre I, Zona 14 (☎385 3432); Costa Rica, 1 Av 15–52, Zona 10 (Mon–Fri 9am–4pm; ☎363 1345); El Salvador, 5 Av 8–15, Zona 9 (☎360 7660); Honduras, 19 Av A 20–19, Zona 10 (☎366 5640); México, 15 C 3–20, Zona 10 (Mon–Fri 9am–1pm & 3–5pm; ☎333 7254 or 333 7255); Nicaragua, 10 Av 14–72, Zona 10 (☎368 0785); Panama, 10 Av 18–53, Zona 14 (☎368 2805); United Kingdom, 16 C 0–55, 11th floor, Torre Internacional, Zona 10 (Mon–Fri 9am–noon & 2–4pm; ☎367 5425); United States, Av la Reforma 7–01, Zona 10 (Mon–Fri 8am–5pm; ☎331 1541).
Immigration The main immigration office (*migración*) is conveniently located on the second floor of the Inguat HQ at 7 Av 1–17, Zona 4 (Mon–Fri 9am–3pm; ☎634 8476).
Internet There are plenty of cybercafés in Zona 1 including Coffee Net at 5 Av 11–70, and several options in Zona 10 including Web Station at 2 Av 14–63. Rates are around US$1.75 per hour.
Laundry Lavandería Obelisco, Av la Reforma 16–30, charges around US$3 for a self-service wash and dry, and there's also a self-service laundry at 4 Av 13–89, Zona 1.
Libraries The best library for English books is in the IGA (Guatemalan American Institute) at Ruta 1 and Vía 4, Zona 4. There's also the National Library on the west side of Parque del Centenario, and specialist collections at the Ixchel and Popol Vuh museums.
Medical care Your embassy should have a list of bilingual doctors, but for emergency medical assistance dial ☎125 for the Red Cross, or head for the Centro Médico, a private hospital with 24hr cover, at 6 Av 3–47, Zona 10 (☎332 3555). Central Dentist de Especialistas, 20 C 11–17, Zona 10 (☎337 1773), is the best dental clinic in the country, and superb in emergencies.
Pharmacies Farmacia Osco, 16 C and 4 Av, Zona 10. There are dozens in Zona 1.
Photography Print film is very widely available; for transparency and monochrome film there are several camera shops on 6 Avenida in Zona 1. Foto Sittler, 12 C 6–20, Zona 1, and La Perla, 9 C and 6 Av, Zona 1, repair cameras and offer a guarantee on their work.
Police The main police station is on the corner of 6 Av and 14 C, Zona 1. In an emergency dial ☎120.
Post office The main post office is at 7 Av and 12 C, Zona 1 (Mon–Fri 8.30am–5pm, Sat 8.30am–1.30pm).
Telephone It's best to use phonecards for international and long-distance calls; there are plentiful cardphones all over the city. You can also make calls and send faxes from Telgua, one block east of the post office (daily 7am–midnight).
Travel agents Flights to Petén can be booked through any of the agents along Avenida la Reforma in zonas 9 and 10 including Servisa, Av la Reforma 8–33, Zona 10 (☎332 7526). Clark Tours, Diagonal 6, 10–01, 7th floor, Torre II, Las Margaritas, Zona 10 (☎470 4700, ⓦwww.clarktours.com.gt), organizes trips to many parts of the country; Viajes Tivoli, 6 Av 8–41, Zona 9 (☎339 2260, ⓦwww.tivoli.com), is a good all-round agent with competitive rates for international flights.
Work Hard to come by. The best bet is teaching at one of the English schools; check the classified sections of the *Guatemala Post* and *Revue*.

Moving on from Guatemala City

There are frequent **international** flights from Guatemala City's Aurora airport to Mexico, Central America, Cuba, the USA and Canada. Four airlines fly daily to Flores – most of these leave early in the morning, between 6 and 9am, enabling day-trippers to visit Tikal and get back to the capital. Tickets for the fifty-minute flight can be bought from virtually any travel agent, and cost around US$110 return in a small plane or US$130 in the larger Tikal Jets aircraft. To get to the international terminal of Aurora airport from Zona 1, either take bus #83 from 10 Av (30min) or a taxi (around US$10); from Zona 10, a taxi costs around US$7. There's a US$30 departure tax on all international flights (though this is included in the price of many tickets) and a US$3 security tax; both are payable in either quetzales or dollars.

Note that all Taca and Tikal Jets internal flights leave from the international terminal. For the **domestic terminal**, in the same complex as the international

Buses from Guatemala City

The abbreviations we've used for the bus companies are as follows:

ADN	ADN Mayan World	**SJ**	San Juanera
HA	Hedman Alas	**TA**	Transportes Alamo
KQ	King Quality	**TB**	Ticabus
L	Lituega	**TD**	Transportes Dulce María
LA	Líneas Américas	**TE**	Transportes Escobar y Monja Blanca
LD	Línea Dorada	**TGG**	Transportes Galgos
LH	Los Halcones	**TGR**	Transportes Guerra
M	Monarcas	**TM**	Transportes Marquensita
MI	Melva Internacional	**TR**	Transportes Rebuli
P	Pulmantur	**TV**	Transportes Velásquez
RO	Rutas Orientales		
RZ	Rápidos Zacaleu		

To	Company	Terminal	Frequency	Journey time
Antigua	various (2nd)	18 C & 4 Av, Zona 1	15min	1hr
Chichicastenango	various (2nd)	Zona 4 terminal	30min	3hr 15min
Chiquimula	RO (1st)	19 C 8–18, Zona 1	20 daily	3hr 30min
	TGR (1st)	19 C 8–39, Zona 1	20 daily	3hr 30min
Cobán	TE (1st)	8 Av 15–16, Zona 1	16 daily	4hr 30min
Copán	HA (1st)	2 Av 8–73, Zona 10	1 daily	5hr
	M (1st)	pick up from hotel	1 daily	5hr
Cubulco	TD (2nd)	19 C & 9 Av, Zona 1	8 daily	5hr
Escuintla	various (2nd)	Zona 4 terminal	30min	1hr 15min
Esquipulas	RO (1st)	19 C & 9 Av, Zona 1	15 daily	4hr
Flores	various (1st/2nd)	17 C & 8 Av, Zona 1	19 daily	8–9hr
	LD (1st)	16 C 10–55, Zona 1	4 daily	8hr
	ADN (1st)	15C 9–18A, Zona 1	2 daily	8hr
Huehuetenango	LH (1st)	7 Av 15–27, Zona 1	3 daily	5hr 30min
	TV (1st)	20 C 1–37, Zona 1	9 daily	5hr 30min
	RZ (1st)	9C 11–42, Zona 1	3 daily	5hr 30min
La Ceiba	HA (1st)	2 Av 8–73, Zona 10	1 daily	12hr
La Mesilla	TV (1st)	20 C 1–37, Zona 1	7 daily	7hr
Monterrico	various (2nd)	Zona 4 terminal	4 daily	4hr
Panajachel	TR (2nd)	21 C 1–54, Zona 1	11 daily	3hr
Puerto Barrios	L (1st)	15 C 10–40, Zona 1	16 daily	5hr 30min
Quetzaltenango	LA (1st)	2 Av 18–74, Zona 1	6 daily	4hr
	TA (1st)	21 C 1–14, Zona 1	6 daily	4hr
	TG (1st)	7 Av 19–44, Zona 1	7 daily	4hr
	SJ (2nd)	Zona 4 terminal	10 daily	4hr 15min
Rabinal	TD (2nd)	19 C & 9 Av, Zona 1	10 daily	4hr 30min
Salamá	TD (2nd)	19 C & 9 Av, Zona 1	12 daily	3hr 30min

To	Company	Terminal	Frequency	Journey time
San Salvador	MI (1st)	3 Av 1–38, Zona 9	14 daily	5hr
	TB (1st)	11 C 2–72, Zona 9	1 daily	5hr
	KQ (1st)	Col Vista Hermosa II, Zona 15	4 daily	5hr
	P (1st)	*Holiday Inn*, 1 Av 13–22, Zona 10	2 daily	5hr
Santa Cruz del Quiché	various (2nd)	Zona 4 terminal	20min	4hr
San Pedro Sula	HA (1st)	2 Av 8–73, Zona 10	1 daily	8hr
Tecún Umán	various (1st)	19 Av & 8 C, Zona 1	30min	5hr
Talismán	various (1st)	19 Av & 8 C, Zona 1	30min	5hr 30min
Tapachula	LD (1st)	16 C 10–55, Zona 1	2 daily	6hr 30min
	TB (1st)	11 C 2–72, Zona 9	1 daily	6hr 30min
	TG (1st)	7 Av 19–44, Zona 1	3 daily	6hr 30min

terminal but only accessible from Av Hicapié, you'll need to take a taxi; the domestic departure tax is US$0.80.

If leaving by **first-class bus**, departures are all from the offices of the relevant bus company. The **Zona 1 terminal**, spread out around the streets surrounding the old train station at 18 C and 9 Av, is the most important transit point, with departures to Puerto Barrios, Cobán, the Pacific highway, the Mexican border and Petén. If moving on by **second-class bus**, the main centre is the chaotic **Zona 4 terminal**, where services run to all parts of the country. To get there take any city bus marked "Terminal"; you'll find these heading south along 4 Av in Zona 1.

2.2

The western highlands

Guatemala's **western highlands**, stretching from Guatemala City to the Mexican border, are perhaps the most captivating and beautiful part of the entire country. The area is defined by two main features: the chain of awesome volcanoes that lines its southern side, and the high mountain ranges that dominate its northern boundaries, the greatest being the **Cuchumatanes**, whose granite peaks rise to over 3800m. Between the two is a bewitching pattern of twisting, pine-forested ridges, lakes, gushing streams and deep valleys.

It's an astounding landscape, blessed with tremendous fertility but cursed by instability. The hills are regularly shaken by earthquakes and occasionally showered by volcanic eruptions. Of the thirteen cones that loom over the western highlands, four volcanoes are still active. Two major **fault lines** also cut through the area, making earthquakes a regular occurrence. But despite its sporadic ferocity, the atmosphere here is calm and welcoming, with irrigated valleys and terraced hillsides carefully crafted to yield the maximum potential farmland.

The highland landscape is shaped by many factors, all of which affect its appearance. Perhaps the most important is **altitude**. At lower elevations the vegetation is almost tropical, supporting dense forests and plantations of coffee, cotton, bananas and cacao, while higher up the hills are often wrapped in cloud and the ground is sometimes hard with frost. Here trees are stunted by the cold, and maize and potatoes are grown alongside grazing land for herds of sheep and goats. The **seasons** also play their part. In the rainy season, from May to October, the land is superbly green, with young crops and lush forests of pine, cedar and oak, while during the dry winter months the hillsides gradually turn to a dusty yellow.

Some history

The western highlands are home to one of the American continent's largest groups of indigenous people, the **Maya**, who have lived in this land continuously for over two thousand years. Despite the catastrophe of the Spanish Conquest, their society, languages and traditions remain largely intact, and they continue to form the vast majority of the population in the western highlands.

The highlands are still divided up along traditional tribal lines. The **K'iche'** language is spoken by the largest number of people, centred on the town of Santa Cruz del Quiché and reaching west into the Quetzaltenango valley. The highlands around Huehuetenango are **Mam**-speaking, while the **Tz'utujil** occupy the southern shores of Lago de Atitlán, and the **Kaqchikel** the east. **Smaller tribal groups**, with distinct languages and costumes, such as the Ixil and the Awakateko, also occupy clearly defined areas in the Cuchumatán mountains.

Though pre-conquest life was certainly hard, the **arrival of the Spanish** in 1523 was a total disaster for the Maya population. In the early stages, **Alvarado** and his army met with a force of K'iche' warriors in the Quetzaltenango basin and defeated them in open warfare. The Spanish made their first permanent base at **Iximché**, the capital of their Kaqchikel Maya allies, but Alvarado soon moved to a site near the modern town of Antigua, from where the Spanish gradually brought the rest of the highlands under a degree of control. The damage done by Spanish swords, however, was nothing when compared to that of the **diseases** they introduced. Waves of

Market days

Make an effort to catch as many market days as possible – they're second only to local fiestas in offering a glimpse of the traditional Guatemalan way of life.

Monday: Antigua; San Juan Atitán; Zunil.

Tuesday: Chajul; Patzún; San Lucas Tolimán; San Marcos; Totonicapán.

Wednesday: Cotzal; Huehuetenango; Momostenango; Sacapulas.

Thursday: Aguacatán; Antigua; Chichicastenango; Jacaltenango; Nebaj; Panajachel; Sacapulas; San Pedro Sacatepéquez; Santa Cruz del Quiché; Soloma; Totonicapán; Uspantán.

Friday: Chajul; San Francisco El Alto; Santiago Atitlán; Sololá.

Saturday: Antigua; Cotzal; Santa Clara La Laguna; Santa Cruz del Quiché; Todos Santos Cuchumatán; Totonicapán.

Sunday: Aguacatán; Chichicastenango; Huehuetenango; Jacaltenango; Joyabaj; Momostenango; Nebaj; Nahualá; Panajachel; Sacapulas; San Juan Comalapa; San Pedro Sacatepéquez; Santa Cruz del Quiché; Santa Eulalia; Soloma; Uspantán.

smallpox, typhus, plague and measles swept through the indigenous population, reducing their numbers by as much as ninety percent in the worst-hit areas.

In the long term, the **Spanish administration** of the western highlands was no gentler than the Conquest, as indigenous labour became the backbone of the Spanish Empire. Guatemala offered little of the gold and silver that was available in Peru or Mexico, but there was still money to be made from **cacao** and **indigo**. As well as being at the heart of Spanish Guatemala, **Antigua** also served as the administrative centre for the whole of Central America and Chiapas (now in Mexico). In 1773, however, the city was destroyed by a massive earthquake and the capital was subsequently moved to its modern site. The departure of the Spanish in 1821 and subsequent **independence** brought little change at village level. *Ladino* authority replaced that of the Spanish, but Maya were still required to work the coastal plantations and, when labour supplies dropped off, they were simply press-ganged to work, often in horrific conditions. It's a state of affairs that has changed little even today, and remains a major burden on the *indígena* population.

In the late 1970s, **guerrilla movements** began to develop in opposition to military rule, seeking support from the highland population and establishing themselves in the western highlands. The Maya became the victims in this process, caught between the guerrillas and the army. A total of 440 villages were destroyed; around 200,000 people died and thousands more fled the country, seeking refuge in Mexico. Most of these villagers returned from exile in the 1990s to a region where burgeoning population increase has put intense pressure on scant land resources. Today, facing such limited opportunity at home, many Maya have fled the mountains in search of work in the United States. Dozens of North American–based **evangelical churches** have moved the other way, establishing themselves in the highlands, their presence disrupting local hierarchies and threatening ancient religious traditions. Yet despite these changes, many facets of Maya culture remain intact. Traditional costume is still worn in many areas (particularly by women), a plethora of indigenous languages still spoken and some remote areas even still observe the 260-day Tzolkin calendar.

Where to go

Large swathes of the western highlands are of terrific interest to the traveller. **Antigua**, the former capital, is unmissable: a beautiful colonial city nestling in the shadow of giant volcanoes, it also has the most cosmopolitan restaurant scene in Central America. **Lago de Atitlán** is another jewel – a lake of astounding natural

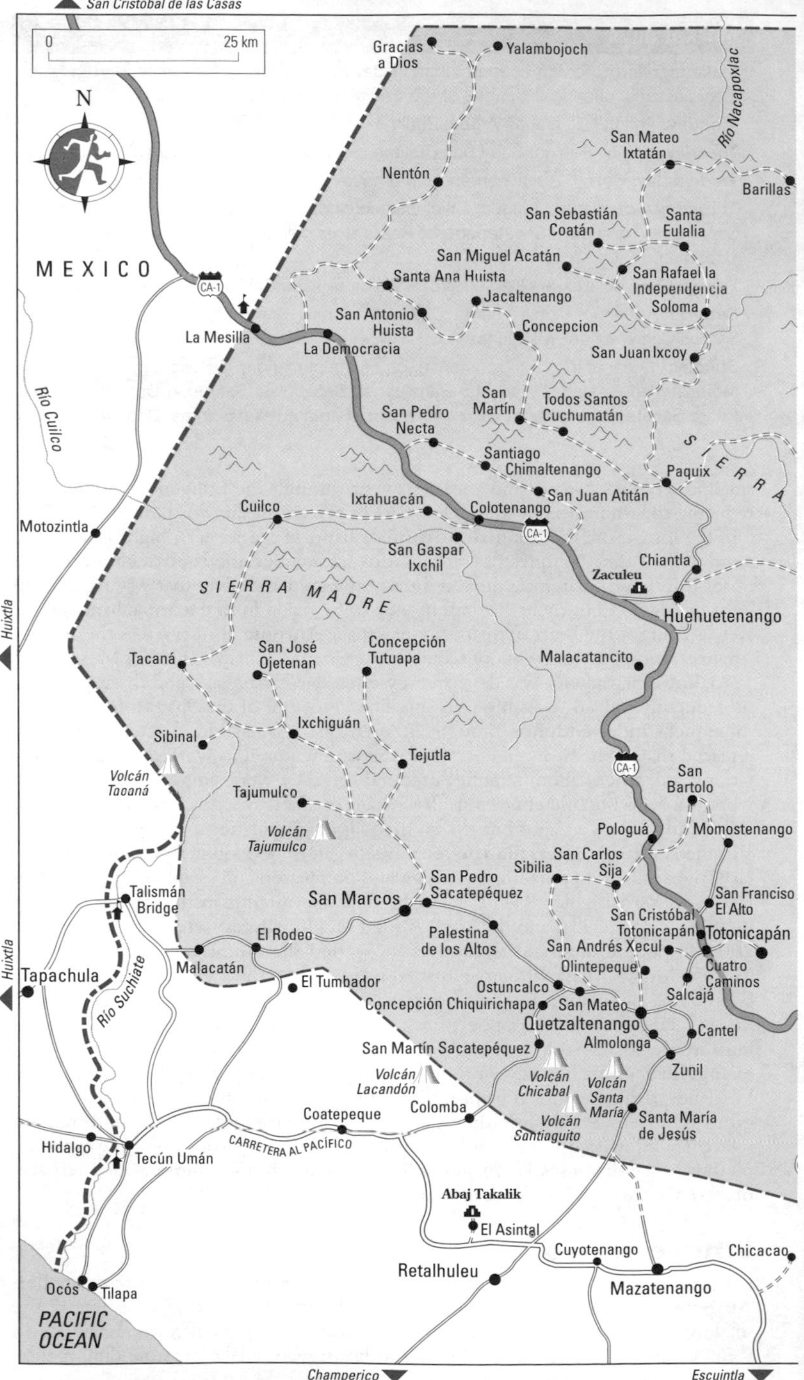
San Cristóbal de las Casas
0
25 km
N
MEXICO
Gracias a Dios
Yalambojoch
Río Nacapoxlac
San Mateo Ixtatán
Barillas
Nentón
San Sebastián Coatán
Santa Eulalia
San Miguel Acatán
San Rafael la Independencia
Santa Ana Huista
Jacaltenango
Soloma
San Antonio Huista
Concepcion
CA-1
La Mesilla
La Democracia
San Juan Ixcoy
Río Cuilco
San Martín
Todos Santos Cuchumatán
San Pedro Necta
Santiago Chimaltenango
SIERRA
Paquix
San Juan Atitán
Cuilco
Ixtahuacán
Colotenango
Motozintla
San Gaspar Ixchil
Chiantla
Zaculeu
SIERRA MADRE
Huehuetenango
Huixtla
Concepción Tutuapa
San José Ojetenan
Malacatancito
Tacaná
Ixchiguán
Sibinal
Tejutla
Volcán Tacaná
San Bartolo
Tajumulco
Volcán Tajumulco
Pologuá
Momostenango
San Carlos Sija
Sibilia
San Pedro Sacatepéquez
Talismán Bridge
San Marcos
San Francisco El Alto
San Cristóbal Totonicapán
Totonicapán
Palestina de los Altos
El Rodeo
San Andrés Xecul
Huixtla
Tapachula
Malacatán
Olintepeque
Cuatro Caminos
El Tumbador
Ostuncalco
Salcajá
Río Suchiate
Concepción Chiquirichapa
San Mateo
Quetzaltenango
Cantel
Almolonga
San Martín Sacatepéquez
Zunil
Volcán Lacandón
Volcán Chicabal
Volcán Santa María
Colomba
Coatepeque
Volcán Santiaguito
Santa María de Jesús
Hidalgo
Tecún Umán
CARRETERA AL PACÍFICO
Abaj Takalik
El Asintal
Cuyotenango
Chicacao
Retalhuleu
Mazatenango
Ocós
Tilapa
PACIFIC OCEAN
Champerico
Escuintla

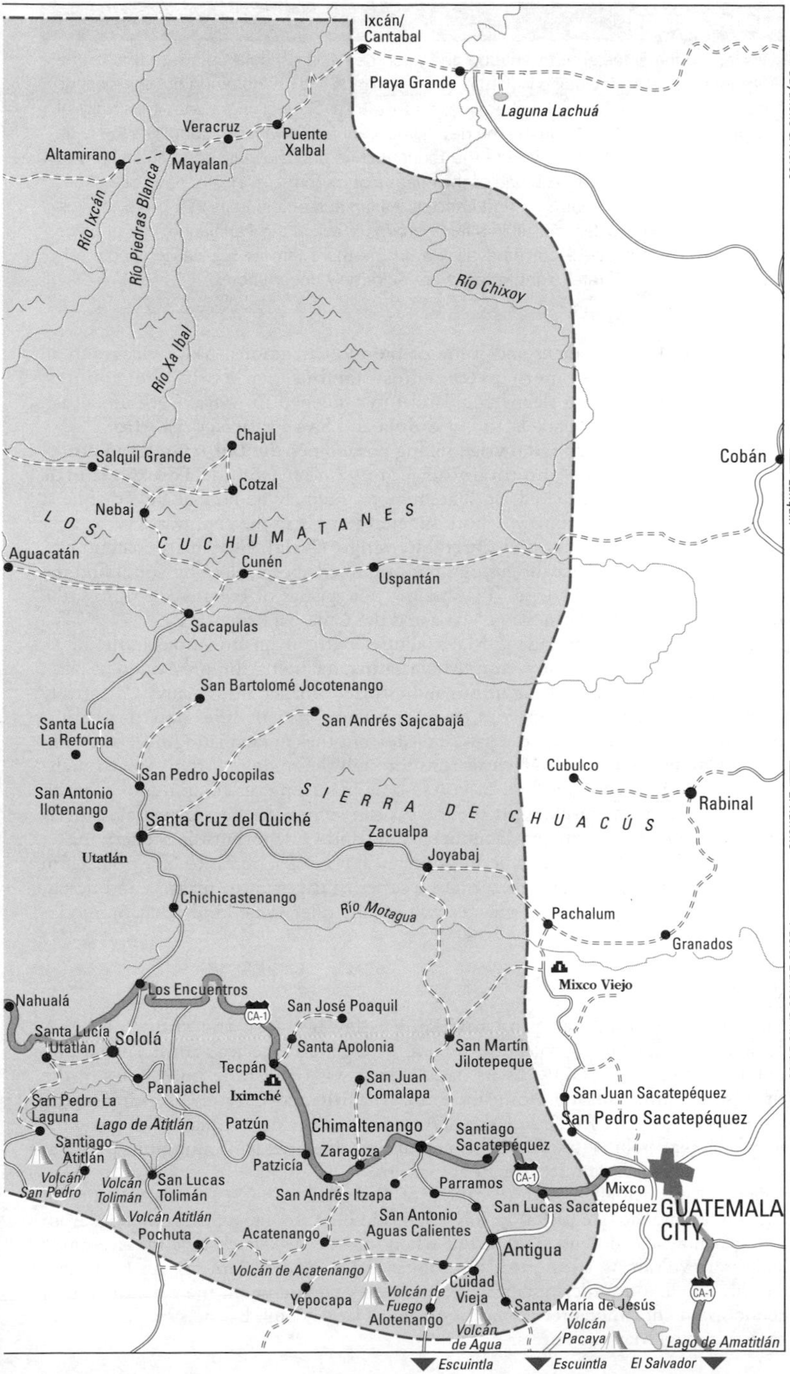

Ixcán/
Cantabal
Playa Grande
Sayaxché & Flores
Laguna Lachuá
Veracruz
Puente
Xalbal
Altamirano
Mayalan
Río Ixcán
Río Piedras Blanca
Río Chixoy
Río Xa Ibal
Chajul
Salquil Grande
Cotzal
Cobán
Lanquín
Nebaj
LOS CUCHUMATANES
Aguacatán
Cunén
Uspantán
Sacapulas
San Bartolomé Jocotenango
San Andrés Sajcabajá
Santa Lucía
La Reforma
Cubulco
San Pedro Jocopilas
Rabinal
El Rancho
San Antonio
Ilotenango
SIERRA DE CHUACÚS
Santa Cruz del Quiché
Utatlán
Zacualpa
Joyabaj
Chichicastenango
Río Motagua
Pachalum
Granados
Puerto Barrios & Río Dulce
Mixco Viejo
Los Encuentros
Nahualá
San José Poaquil
CA-1
Santa Lucía
Utatlán
Sololá
Santa Apolonia
San Martín
Jilotepeque
Tecpán
Iximché
San Juan
Comalapa
Panajachel
San Juan Sacatepéquez
San Pedro La
Laguna
Lago de Atitlán
Patzún
Chimaltenango
Santiago
Sacatepéquez
San Pedro Sacatepéquez
Santiago
Atitlán
Zaragoza
Patzicía
Volcán
San Pedro
Volcán
Tolimán
San Lucas
Tolimán
San Andrés Itzapa
Parramos
CA-1
Mixco
Volcán Atitlán
San Antonio
Aguas Calientes
San Lucas Sacatepéquez
GUATEMALA
CITY
Pochuta
Acatenango
Antigua
Volcán de Acatenango
Yepocapa
Volcán de
Fuego
Alotenango
Cuidad
Vieja
Santa María de Jesús
CA-1
Volcán
de Agua
Volcán
Pacaya
Lago de Amatitlán
Escuintla
Escuintla
El Salvador

Tourist crime

Visitors to the areas around Antigua and Lago de Atitlán should be aware that **crime against tourists** – including violent robbery and rape – is not common but does occur. Keep informed by taking local advice, and try to avoid walking alone, especially at night or to isolated spots during the day. If you want to visit viewing spots like the large cross overlooking Antigua, inform the tourist police and they will accompany you or even give you a ride there on one of their Jeeps or motorbikes. Hikers have been sporadically attacked on paths around Lago de Atitlán and on the trails that climb the volcanoes. It's much safer to walk in a large group, or ask in the Panajachel Inguat office (see p.205) if a police escort is available. In the more remote highlands, where foreigners are a much rarer sight, attacks are extremely uncommon.

beauty, ringed by volcanoes and some of the most traditional Maya villages in all Guatemala. Home to perhaps the most famous market in the country, **Chichicastenango** is a sleepy highland town steeped in Maya/Catholic ritual. There are tremendous markets, too, at **Sololá** and **San Francisco El Alto**.

For spectacular scenery and myriad hiking possibilities, the **Ixil triangle** in northern Quiché and the mountainous countryside around **Todos Santos Cuchumatán** are unmatched. Both are remote, intensely traditional areas that lie at the end of tortuous bus journeys; both suffered terribly in the civil war. Much easier to get to are the villages around **Quetzaltenango (Xela)**, Guatemala's second city. Though Xela itself is pleasant enough but of limited appeal, close by you'll find the villages of Zunil, San Francisco El Alto, the hot springs of Fuentes Georginas, the near-perfect cone ofVolcán Santa María and the Chicabal crater lake.

The scenery, villages and living Maya culture are the main attractions in the highlands, but there are also interesting **Maya ruins**, including the pre-conquest cities of **Iximché**, **Utatlán** and **Zaculeu**, and assorted smaller sites, many still actively used for Maya religious ritual and ceremony. These ancient cities don't bear comparison to Tikal, Copán and the lowland sites, but they're fascinating nevertheless.

The **Carretera Interamericana** runs through the middle of the western highlands, served by a constant flow of buses, some branching off along minor roads to more remote areas. Travelling in these areas can sometimes be a gruelling experience, particularly in northern Huehuetenango and Quiché, but the scenery makes it well worth the discomfort. The most practical plan of action is to base yourself in one of the larger places and then make a series of day-trips to markets and fiestas, although even the smallest of villages will usually offer some kind of accommodation.

Antigua

Superbly sited in a sweeping highland valley between the cones of Agua, Acatenango and Fuego volcanoes is one of Central America's most enchanting colonial cities: **ANTIGUA**. In its day, Antigua was one of the great cities of the Spanish Empire, ranking alongside Lima and Mexico City and serving as the administrative centre for all of Central America and Mexican Chiapas. The magnificent colonial architecture from this era ensures the city's continuing prosperity as one of Guatemala's premier tourist attractions.

Antigua was actually the third capital of Guatemala. The Spanish settled first at the site of Iximché (see p.193) in July 1524, and then at a site a few kilometres from Antigua, now called Ciudad Vieja, but when this was devastated by a massive mudslide from Volcán Agua in 1541, the capital was moved to Antigua. Antigua grew steadily as religious orders established themselves, competing in the construction of schools, churches, monasteries and hospitals, all largely built by the sweat and blood of conscripted Maya labourers.

The city reached its peak in the middle of the eighteenth century, after the 1717 earthquake prompted an unprecedented building boom, and the population rose to around fifty thousand. But, as is so often the case in Guatemala, **earthquakes** brought all of this to an abrupt end. For the best part of a year the city was shaken by tremors, with the final blows delivered by two severe shocks on September 7 and December 13, 1773. The damage was so bad that the decision was made to abandon the city in favour of the modern capital. Fortunately, despite endless official decrees, many refused to leave and Antigua was never completely deserted.

Since then, the city has been gradually repopulated, particularly in the last hundred years or so, and as Guatemala City has become increasingly congested, some of the capital's middle classes have moved to Antigua. They've been joined by a large number of resident and visiting foreigners, attracted by the relaxed and sophisticated atmosphere, cultural life, the benign climate and largely traffic-free cobbled streets.

Efforts have been made to preserve Antigua's grand architectural legacy, especially after it was listed as a UNESCO World Heritage Site in 1979 – local conservation laws protect the streets from overhanging signs, and house extensions are severely restricted. Though many colonial buildings lie in splendidly atmospheric ruin or else are steadily decaying, many more have been impeccably restored and sympathetically converted into hotels or restaurants.

Thanks to its relaxed atmosphere, Antigua is a favoured hangout for jaded travellers. The bar scene can get lively (though periodically the authorities clamp down on this) and there's a rich choice of restaurants. Antigua's **language schools**, some of the best and cheapest in all Latin America, are another attraction, drawing students from around the globe. Expats from Europe, North and South America and even Asia contribute to the town's cosmopolitan air, mingling with the Guatemalans who come here from the capital city at weekends to eat, drink and enjoy themselves. The downside of this settled, comfortable affluence is a certain loss of vitality – this civilized, isolated world can seem almost a little too smug and comfortable compared to the rest of the country. And after a few days sipping lattes and munching cake, it's easy to forget that you're in Central America at all.

Semana Santa in Antigua

Antigua's **Semana Santa (Holy Week) celebrations** are perhaps the most extravagant and impressive in all Latin America. The celebrations start with a procession on Palm Sunday, representing Christ's entry into Jerusalem, and continue through to the really big processions and pageants on Good Friday. On Thursday night the streets are carpeted with meticulously drawn patterns of coloured sawdust, and on Friday morning a series of processions re-enacts the progress of Christ to the Cross, accompanied by poignant music from local brass bands. Setting out from La Merced, Escuela de Cristo and the village of San Felipe, teams of penitents wearing peaked hoods and accompanied by solemn dirges and clouds of incense carry images of Christ and the Cross on massive platforms. The pageants set off at around 8am, with the penitents dressed in either white or purple. After 3pm, the hour of the Crucifixion, they change into black.

It is a great honour to be involved in the procession, but no easy task as the great cedar block carried from La Merced weighs some 3.5 tonnes, and needs eighty men to lift it. Some of the images displayed date from the seventeenth century and the procession itself is thought to have been introduced by Alvarado in the early years of the Conquest, imported directly from Spain.

Check the exact details of events with the tourist office, who should be able to provide you with a map detailing the routes of the processions. During Holy Week hotels in Antigua are virtually all full, and the entire town is always packed on Good Friday.

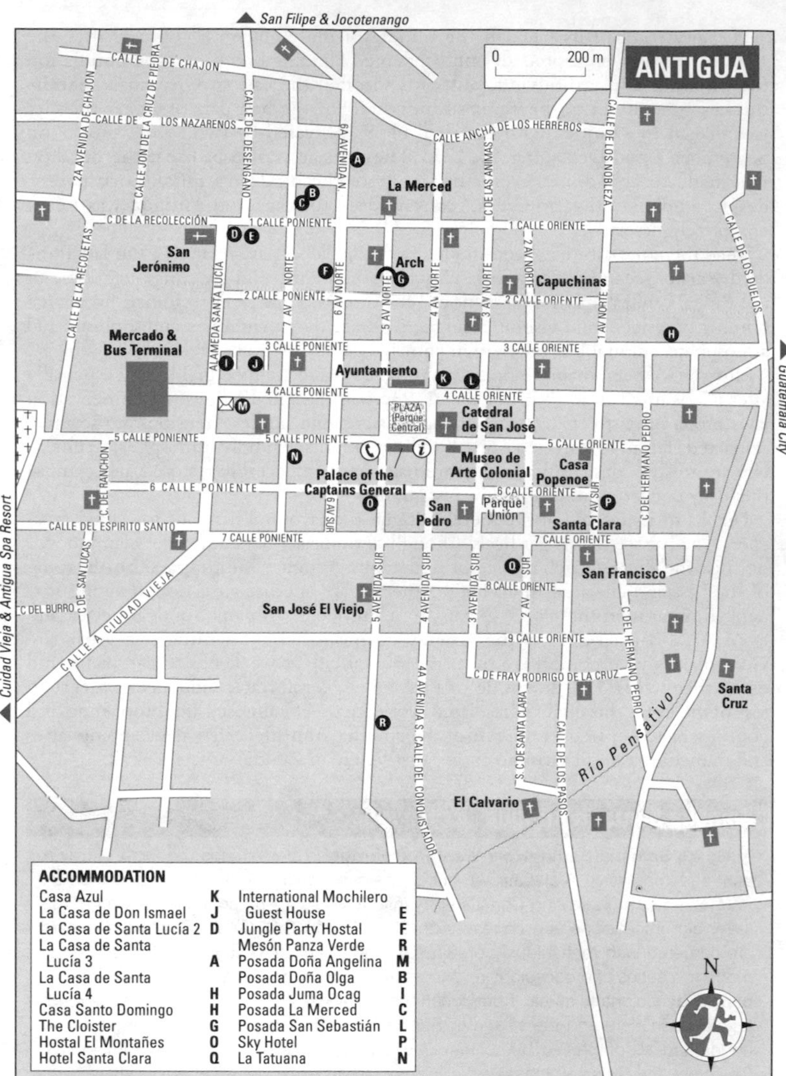

Arrival and information

Antigua is laid out on the traditional grid system, with avenidas running north–south, and calles east–west. Each street is numbered and has two halves, either a north (*norte/nte*) and south (*sur*) or an east (*oriente/ote*) and west (*poniente/pte*), with a plaza, the **Parque Central**, at the centre. Despite this apparent simplicity, poor street lighting and the lack of street signs combine to ensure that most people get lost here at some stage. If you get confused, remember that Volcán Agua, the one that looms most immediately over the town, is to the south.

Arriving by bus, you'll end up in the main **bus terminal** beside the market; shuttle buses will drop you off at your hotel or address in town. The street opposite (4 C Pte) leads directly to the plaza. Antigua is easy to get around on foot, but should you need a **taxi** you'll find one on the east side of the plaza close to the cathedral; alternatively you can call one on ⓣ832 0479. Mountain bikes and cars can also be rented – see p.189.

The well-informed **tourist office** (daily 8am–6pm; ⓣ & ⓕ832 0763) on the south side of the plaza provides reliable information. You'll find the **tourist police** (ⓣ832 7290) just off the Parque Central on 4 Avenida Norte; officers escort visitors twice daily up to the Cerro de la Cruz, from where there's a panoramic view of Antigua and the surrounding volcanoes. **Noticeboards** in various tourist venues advertise everything from haircuts, massage, private language tuition and apartments – probably the most read are those at *Doña Luisa's* restaurant, 4 C Ote 12, and the *Rainbow Reading Room*, 7 Av Sur 8. For **tours** of the city, Elizabeth Bell, at 3 C Ote 28 (ⓣ832 5821, ⓦwww.antiguatours.com) offers excellent historical walking tours of the town, while Geovany at Monarcas, Calzada Santa Lucía 7 (ⓣ832 1939), leads enjoyable walks looking at Maya influence on Antiguan architecture, also commenting on the flora around the city.

Antigua is an extremely popular place to **study Spanish**. For a full list of recommended schools, see p.149.

Accommodation

There's a plentiful supply of **hotels** in all price ranges in Antigua, and the steep competition means many are very good value. Be warned that rooms can get scarce (and prices increase) in July and August, and book well ahead for Semana Santa.

Budget

La Casa de Don Ismael 3 C Pte 6 ⓣ832 1932, ⓦwww.casadonismael.com. Hidden down a quiet side street, this is an excellent option with seven rooms (none with private bathroom) grouped around a lovely little garden. The communal bathrooms are kept spotless, and breakfasts are available. ❸

La Casa de Santa Lucía 2 Alameda Santa Lucía Nte 21 ⓣ832 6189. Popular place with secure, spacious rooms with private hot-water baths, plus a roof terrace. There are two other near-identical alternatives: branch *#4*, Alameda Santa Lucía Sur 5 (ⓣ832 3302) is two blocks to the south, and *#3*, at 6 Av Nte 43 A (ⓣ831 1386). ❸

Hostal El Montañes 6 C Pte & 5 Av Sur ⓣ832 8804. This inexpensive hostal has a nice feel, with a wonderful colonial courtyard, several large dorms (US$5pp) and clean shared bathrooms. Private rooms are planned too. ❷

International Mochilero Guest House 1C Pte 33 ⓣ832 0520, ⓔinternacional_mochilero@yahoo.com. Well-priced singles, doubles and a dorm (US$5pp) in a pleasant house with a lovely patio garden. There's a kitchen for guests. ❷

Jungle Party Hostal 6 Av Nte 20 ⓣ832 0463. Decent three- and five-bed dorms, with solid wood bunk beds. There's also a chill-out area with hammocks, and a café with an inexpensive menu. ❷

Posada Doña Angelina 4 C Pte 33 ⓣ832 5173. Long-running place where many of the 42 rooms are a bit gloomy, but there's usually space available, and there's a secure storeroom where you can leave your baggage. ❷–❸

Posada Doña Olga Callejón Campo Seco 3A ⓣ832 0623, ⓔhotelolga@yahoo.com. Family-run guesthouse, with very clean rooms, all with private bath, and a rooftop sun terrace. ❷–❸

Posada Juma Ocag Alameda Santa Lucía Nte 13 ⓣ832 3109. A welcoming, first-class budget hotel. The eight spotless, comfortable rooms all have a wardrobe or storage space and private bath, and are draped with local fabrics. Grassy patio, roof terrace and free drinking water. Book ahead. ❸

Sky Hotel 1 Av Sur 15 ⓣ832 3383. Well-run place with a sociable ambiance and brightly painted, tile-floored rooms (all with lockers). Pretty garden at the rear has some shade from orange trees, and *Café Sky* is upstairs. Breakfast included. ❸

Moderate

Hotel Santa Clara 2 Av Sur 20 ⓣ832 0342. Tranquil location and spacious, clean rooms, most with two double beds and all with private bath (some have tubs) set around a pleasant little courtyard. Parking available. ❹

Posada La Merced 7 Av Nte 43a ⓣ832 3197, ⓦwww.merced-landivar.com. Excellent

Kiwi-owned hotel with a good choice of cheerful, attractive rooms (some set around a garden patio), all with spotless private bathrooms and nice decorative touches. Family-friendly environment, and a kitchen for guests. Discounts outside peak season. ❹–❻, suite ❼

Posada San Sebastián 3 Av Nte 4 Ⓣ & Ⓕ 832 2621, Ⓔ snsebast@hotmail.com. Charming establishment where each of the nine rooms are decorated with antiques. There's a gorgeous little bar, a roof terrace and the location is very convenient. Breakfast is included. ❻

La Tatuana 7 Av Sur 3 Ⓣ 832 1223. Small hotel with bright rooms, all with private bath, and decent-quality beds. Book well ahead as it's good value and always popular. ❺

Expensive

Casa Azul 4 Av Nte 5 Ⓣ 832 0961, Ⓦ www.casazu.guate.com. Modish, elegant hotel, just off the plaza, with huge stylish rooms in a converted colonial mansion. Extras include a sauna, hot tub and a delightful pool. ❽

Casa Santo Domingo 3 C Ote 28 Ⓣ 832 0140, Ⓦ www.casasantodomingo.com.gt. One of Central America's most impressive hotels – a converted colonial-era convent where the rooms and corridors are bedecked in ecclesiastical art and paraphernalia and there's no lack of luxury. High-season rates start at US$132, but there are substantial discounts at quiet times of the year. ❾

The Cloister 5 Av Nte 23 Ⓣ 832 0712, Ⓦ www.thecloister.com. Set almost under Antigua's famous arch, this tasteful upmarket B&B has seven beautifully furnished rooms around a flowering courtyard. There's a real air of tranquillity here, plus a well-stocked private library and reading room. ❽–❾

Mesón Panza Verde 5 Av Sur 19 Ⓣ 832 2925, Ⓦ www.panzaverde.com. Intimate, immaculately furnished hotel with wonderful doubles and sumptuous suites spread across two colonial-style buildings. Also home to one of Antigua's premier restaurants and an art gallery; and there's a lap pool. A healthy breakfast is included. ❼–❾

The City

Antigua has an incredible number of ruined and restored **colonial buildings**, and although these constitute only a fraction of the city's original splendour, they do give an idea of its former extravagance. If the prospect of visiting all the sights listed below is too overwhelming, make La Merced, Las Capuchinas, Casa Popenoe and San Francisco your targets.

The Parque Central

Antigua's focal point is its central plaza, the **Parque Central**. For centuries it was the hub of the city, bustling with constant activity, while a huge market spilled out across it, being cleared only for bullfights, military parades, floggings and public hangings. The calm of today's shady square, with its risqué fountain, is relatively recent.

Of the structures that surround the plaza, the **Catedral de San José**, on its eastern side, is the most imposing. The city's first cathedral was begun in 1545 but an earthquake brought down much of the roof and, in 1670, it was decided to start on a new place of worship worthy of the town's role as a capital city. The scale was astounding – a vast dome, five aisles, eighteen chapels and an altar inlaid with mother-of-pearl, ivory and silver – but in 1773, the new cathedral was destroyed by an earthquake. Today, two of the chapels have been restored, and there's a figure of Christ by the colonial sculptor Quirio Cataño inside. Behind the church, entered from 5 C Oriente, are the **ruins** (entrance fee US$0.40) of the rest of the original structure – a mass of fallen masonry and rotting beams, broken arches and hefty pillars. Buried beneath the floor are some of the great names of the Conquest, including Alvarado, his wife Beatriz de la Cueva, Bishop Marroquín and the historian Bernal Díaz del Castillo. At the very rear of the original nave, steps lead down to a burial vault that's regularly used for Maya religious ceremonies – an example of the coexistence of pagan and Catholic beliefs that's so characteristic of Guatemala.

Along the entire south side of the square runs the squat two-storey facade of the **Palace of the Captains General**, originally constructed in 1558, but rebuilt after earthquake damage. The palace was home to the colonial rulers and also housed the barracks of the dragoons, the stables, the royal mint, law courts, tax offices, great ballrooms, a large bureaucracy, and a lot more besides. Today it contains the local government offices, the headquarters of the Sacatepéquez police department and the tourist office. Directly opposite is the **Ayuntamiento** (City Hall), which dates from 1740 and survived undamaged until the 1976 earthquake. It now holds a couple of minor museums: the **Museo de Santiago** (Tues–Sun 9am–4pm; US$1.20), housed in the old city jail and containing a collection of colonial artefacts, and the **Museo del Libro Antiguo** (same hours; US$1.20), in the rooms that held the first printing press in Central America. A replica of the press is on display, alongside some copies of the works produced on it. From the upper floor of the Ayuntamiento there's a wonderful **view** of the three volcanoes that ring the city that's especially fine at sunset.

Southeast of the Parque Central

Across the street from the ruined cathedral is the **Museo de Arte Colonial** (Tues–Fri 9am–4pm, Sat & Sun 9am–noon & 2–4pm; US$3), located on the site of a former university, whose ornate Moorish-style arcades make it one of the finest architectural survivors in Antigua. The museum contains a good collection of dark and brooding religious art, sculpture, furniture and murals depicting life on the colonial campus.

Further down 5 Calle Oriente, at the corner with 1 Avenida Sur, is the **Casa Popenoe** (Mon–Sat 2–4pm; US$1.20), a colonial mansion which was painstakingly restored by Dr Wilson Popenoe, a United Fruit Company scientist. Its paintings include portraits of Bishop Marroquín and a menacing-looking Alvarado himself. It also offers an interesting insight into domestic life in colonial times: the kitchen and servants' quarters have been carefully renovated and you can see the original bread ovens, the herb garden and the pigeon loft, which would have provided the mansion's occupants with their mail service. Go up to the roof for great views over the city and Volcán Agua.

A little further down 1 Avenida Sur is the imposing **church of San Francisco** (daily 8am–6pm). One of the oldest churches in Antigua, dating from 1579, it grew into a vast religious and cultural centre that included a school, a hospital, music rooms, a printing press and a monastery. All of it was lost, though, in the 1773 earthquake. Inside the church is the tomb of **Hermano Pedro de Betancourt**, a Franciscan from the Canary Islands who founded the Hospital of Belén in Antigua, and is credited powers of miraculous intervention by the faithful. Pope John Paul II made him Central America's first saint in 2002. The **ruins** of the monastery are among the most impressive in Antigua, and you're welcome to picnic next to the colossal fallen arches and pillars on the pleasant grassy verges.

One block west and one block north of San Francisco is **Parque Unión**, where two churches face each other at opposite ends of the Parque: at the western end is **San Pedro Church**, dating from 1680; at the eastern end is **Santa Clara**, a former convent with a fine ornate facade which in colonial times was a popular place for aristocratic ladies to take the veil – the hardships were not too extreme, and the nuns gained a reputation for their fine cooking. In front of Santa Clara is a large *pila* (washhouse) where women gather to scrub, rinse and gossip.

North and west of the Parque Central

At the junction of 2 C Ote and 2 Av Nte are the remains of **Las Capuchinas** (Tues–Sun 9am–5pm; US$3.75), dating from 1726, the largest and most impressive of the city's convents, whose ruins are some of the best preserved but least understood in Antigua. The Capuchin nuns who lived here were not allowed any visual contact with the outside world: food was passed to them by means of a turntable and they could only speak to visitors through a grille. The ruins are the most beautiful in Antigua, with fountains, courtyards, massive earthquake-proof pillars, and a unique tower, or "retreat", with eighteen tiny cells set into the walls on the top

Volcano tours from Antigua

Volcán Pacaya near Guatemala City is a spectacular and very active volcano, which regularly spews towering plumes of smoke and brilliant orange sludge – though such fire 'n' brimstone shows only happen sporadically. Depending on the activity of the volcano, you may be able to gaze down into the smoking cone, but sulfurous fumes and very high winds can make this ascent impossible some days. The safety issues that once plagued the mountain seem to have been cleared up, as there have been no reports of attacks for several years. Gran Jaguar Tours, 4 C Pte 30 (Ⓣ832 2712, Ⓦwww.granjaguar.com), offer basic trips for US$5–7 per person, while Old Town Outfitters (see p.189) charge US$25–30 per person, using comfortable minibuses and including a packed lunch. Entrance to the Pacaya National Park is an additional US$3.

floor and a cellar supported by a massive pillar, that probably functioned as a meat storage room. The exterior of the tower is also interesting, ringed with small stone recesses representing the Stations of the Cross.

A couple of blocks to the west, spanning 5 Avenida Norte, the arch of **Santa Catalina** is all that remains of the original convent founded here in 1609. The arch was built so that the nuns could walk between the two halves of the establishment without being exposed to the pollution of the outside world. At the end of the street the church of **La Merced** boasts one of the most intricate and impressive facades in the entire city. Look closely and you'll see the outline of a corn cob, a motif not normally used by the Catholic Church and probably added by the original Maya labourers. The church is still in use, but the cloisters and gardens (entrance US$0.35), including a monumental tiered fountain, lie in ruins exposed to the sky.

Eating

Antigua boasts a terrific array of **cafés** and **restaurants**, with most types of global cuisine represented. It's possible to snack well for a few bucks or dine in style for around US$12 a head. The only thing that seems hard to come by is authentic Guatemalan comedor food – which will be quite a relief if you've been subsisting on eggs and beans in the mountains.

Cafés

Café Condesa west side of Parque Central – go through the Casa del Conde bookshop. Refined, bourgeois but enjoyable place to enjoy an excellent (if pricey) breakfast, coffee and cake or lunch. The cobbled patio and period charm create a nice tone for the long, lazy Sunday brunches (US$7.50) favoured by Antiguan society.

Fernando's Kaffee 7 Av Norte 43. Unquestionably some of the finest coffee – ground, roasted and served by a friendly, English-speaking Guatemalan perfectionist – in Antigua. The homemade pastries and cakes are equally splendid.

La Fuente 4 C Ote 14. Attractive, moderately priced courtyard restaurant/café where you can eat a decent plate of pasta or a sandwich and sip good coffee. On Saturdays indigenous women set up a *huipil* market around the central fountain.

Peroleto Alameda Santa Lucía Nte 36. Hole-in-the-wall cabin with cheap, healthy breakfasts, fruit juices and delectable cakes.

Rainbow Reading Room 7 Av Sur 8. Long-standing, ever popular café-restaurant with a bohemian atmosphere and a great menu of imaginative salads and vegetarian choices. There's live music most nights (around a campfire when weather permits). Also home to one of Antigua's best travel agents and a good secondhand bookshop.

Restaurants

Beijing 5 C Pte 15C. Fairly pricey Chinese and East Asian food, with good noodle and rice dishes, and Vietnamese spring rolls prepared with a few imaginative twists. Inexpensive set-lunch menu.

Café Panchoy 6 Av Norte 1B. Good-value cooking with a real Guatemalan flavour, served around an open kitchen. Dishes include top steaks and *chiles rellenos*. Excellent margaritas too. Closed Tues.

Casa de las Mixtas 1 Callejón, off 3 C Poniente. Clean, better-than-average comedor, with bright, attractive decor and excellent breakfast and lunch selections.

Comedor Típico Antigüeño Alameda Santa Lucía Sur 5. Canteen-like comedor opposite the bus terminal and market, with cheap breakfasts and US$2 set lunches (such as *pollo a la carbón*, *pepián* and *adobado*) that all include a soup starter.

La Casserole Callejón de la Concepción 7. Elegant restaurant, in a pretty garden patio, that consistently delivers first-rate French cuisine. Leave some room for the epic desserts. Closed Mon.

The Dish 4 Av Sur 4. Stylish UK-US-owned place with a large courtyard and inexpensive

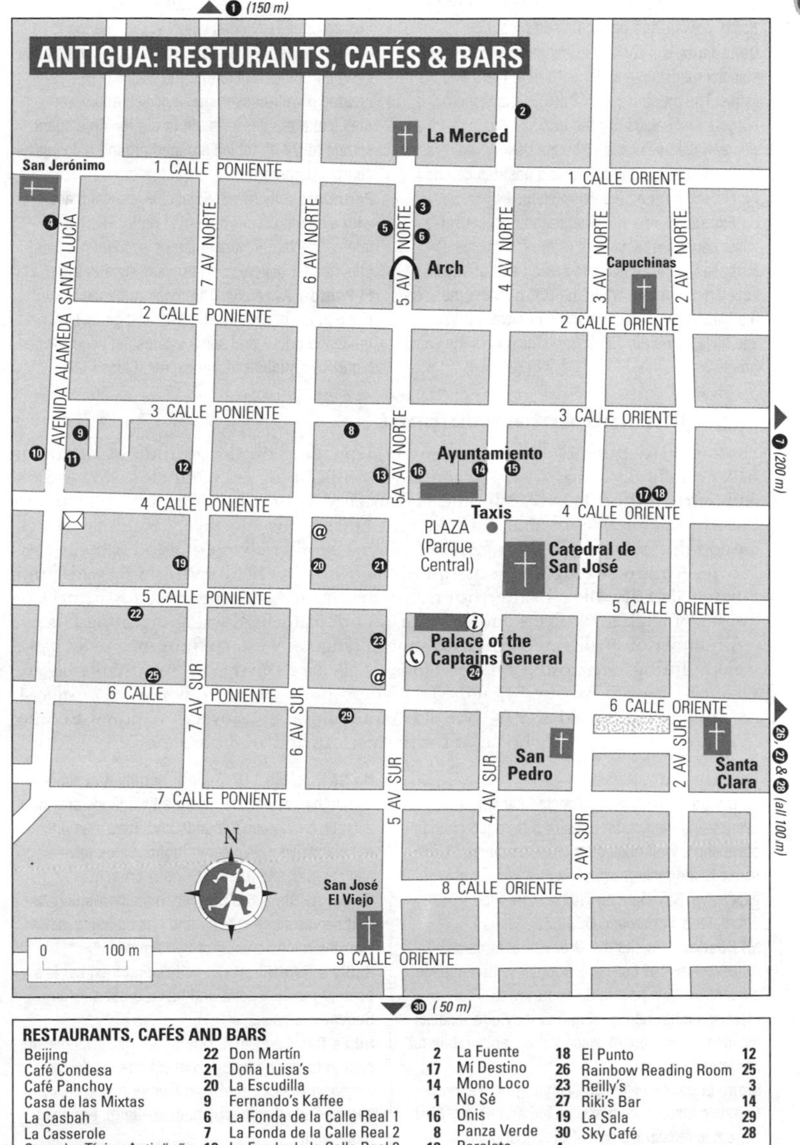

RESTAURANTS, CAFÉS AND BARS

Beijing	22	Don Martín	2	La Fuente	18	El Punto	12
Café Condesa	21	Doña Luisa's	17	Mí Destino	26	Rainbow Reading Room	25
Café Panchoy	20	La Escudilla	14	Mono Loco	23	Reilly's	3
Casa de las Mixtas	9	Fernando's Kaffee	1	No Sé	27	Riki's Bar	14
La Casbah	6	La Fonda de la Calle Real 1	16	Onis	19	La Sala	29
La Casserole	7	La Fonda de la Calle Real 2	8	Panza Verde	30	Sky Café	28
Comedor Típico Antigüeño	10	La Fonda de la Calle Real 3	13	Peroleto	4		
The Dish	24	Frida's	6	Perú Café	15		

well-presented food (all dishes cost US$2.50). There are magazines to browse and good electronic, lounge and jazzy tunes on the stereo.

Don Martín 5 C Pte 15C. Smallish, slightly out of the way place that nevertheless offers some of the most creative and appetizing Guatemalan food-with-a-twist in Antigua. The classically trained chef's moderately priced menu includes a *plato típico*, *pepián*, and pasta. Closed Mon.

Doña Luisa's 4 C Ote 12. Two-storey converted colonial mansion, popular with foreigners and locals. The menu is pretty basic: sandwiches, burgers and salads (try the *ensalada taco guatelmalteco*) but the in-house bakery really is the best in town, and bread and pastries can be purchased from an adjoining shop.

La Escudilla 4 Av Nte 4. Agreeable, excellent-value courtyard restaurant offering a choice of European dishes (including salads and plenty of vegetarian options) while the US$2.75 set meal is a steal. Always busy, but you can have a drink if you have to wait in *Riki's Bar*, which is in the same premises.

La Fonda de la Calle Real three branches: upstairs at 5 Av Nte 5; 5 Av Nte 12; and a third (the nicest location) at 3 C Pte 7. Excellent for authentic Guatemalan specialities including *caldo real* (chicken soup), *pepián* (spicy meat stew) or charcoal grilled meats. Closed Wed.

Frida's 5 Av Nte 29. Lively atmosphere, especially at weekends, with great Mexican food served up in surrounds festooned with 1950s Americana.

Panza Verde 5 Av Sur 19. Stylish and consistently good European restaurant; the Swiss chef has created a well-chosen menu of fish and meat mains and the desserts are to die for. An elegant setting too, with tables grouped around a delightful courtyard garden.

Perú Café 4 Av Nte 7. Enjoyable, casual place with a dining room off a small patio. There's interesting fare including *sausa seco de res* (beef in coriander sauce) and Peruvian-style *ceviche*.

El Punto 7 Av Nte 8A. The most authentic Italian place in town, with meat, pasta and gnocchi at moderate prices and some interesting wines. Rated highly by Antigua's foodie expats. Closed Mon.

Nightlife and entertainment

Evening activity tends to wax and wane depending on the attitude of the town hall; periodically a mayor will clamp down on licensing laws and close down **bars** and restrict **nightlife**, which is officially curtailed anyway by a "dry law" which forbids the sale of alcohol after 1am. Antigua's main *zona viva* (lively zone) is centred around the arch on 5 Av Norte, though there's another clutch of good bars on 1 Av Norte. Antigua's club scene is fairly small but lively, drawing a crowd from Guatemala City. Illegal "after hours" parties are held most weekends in private houses, publicized by flyers and word-of-mouth featuring local and visiting DJs.

A number of small video **cinemas** show a range of Western films on a daily basis; weekly listings are posted on noticeboards all over town. The main cinemas are Cinema Bistro (5 Av Sur 14) and Maya Moon (6 Av Nte 1A), while *Mi Destino*, 1 Av Sur and *Café 2000* at 6 Av Nte also show films. The Proyecto Cultural El Sitio (5 C Pte 15) has a good choice of Latin American and art-house movies.

Bars and clubs

La Casbah 5 Av Nte 30. Spectacular venue overlooking the floodlit ruins of a baroque church, attracting a well-heeled crowd. Commercial Latin house is the main musical flavour; drinks are expensive. Gay night on Thurs. Mon–Wed free, Thurs, Fri & Sat around US$3.50.

Mí Destino 1 Av Sur 17. Groovy Guatemalan-American-owned bar-café, popular with language students, with a pool table and movies. There's often some hip-hop playing and they offer snacks, inexpensive salads, Mexican dishes and wonderful homemade cakes.

Mono Loco 2 Av Nte 6B. Clichéd gringo sports-bar-style place, with bland music and dreary food. For some reason it's one of the most popular places in town.

No Sé 1 Av Nte 11C. Superb, scruffy American-owned bar, where the owner's twin iPods provide eclectic background sounds and there's an open mike and live music some nights. Drink specials like sangría, and a great Sunday brunch.

Onis 7 Av Nte & 6 C Pte. Hip, boho two-storey bar that serves some snacks and has stunning views over the ruined church of San Agustín.

Reilly's 5 Av Nte 31. The city's first Irish bar is a popular meeting point and has a great quiz on Sunday evenings.

Riki's Bar 4 Av Nte 4. One of the most happening bars in town due to its excellent site inside *La Escudilla*, eclectic funk and lounge music policy, and an unrivalled happy hour (7–9pm). Rammed most nights.

La Sala 6 C Pte 9. Spacious, sociable bar, with a

good drinks list and a mix of locals and foreigners. It's heaving every weekend.

Sky Café 1 Av Nte. Terrific views from the upper deck, great tunes and an infectious sociable vibe ensure this is one of *the* in destinations, from around sunset onwards.

Listings

Adventure sports Maya Mountain Bike Tours, 1 Av Sur 15 (Ⓣ832 3383), have an excellent range of trips, plus bike rental; Old Town Outfitters, 6 C Pte 7 (Ⓣ832 4243, Ⓦwww.bikeguatemala.com), run mountain bike excursions and rock climbing trips for all levels, and offer tent, sleeping bag, pack and bike rental.

Banks and exchange Banco Industrial, 5 Av Sur 4, just south of the plaza, has a 24hr ATM for Visa/Plus cardholders; Banco del Quetzal on north side of the plaza has a MasterCard/Cirrus ATM.

Bike rental Maya Mountain Bike Tours and Old Town Outfitters (see "Adventure sports" above) rent mountain bikes from around US$8 a day, US$28 weekly.

Bookstores Casa del Conde and Un Poco de Todo are both on the west side of the plaza. The *Rainbow Reading Room*, 7 Av Sur 8, has by far the largest selection of secondhand books.

Car and motorbike rental Avis, 5 Av Nte 22 (Ⓣ & Ⓕ832 2692), and Tabarini, 6 Av Sur 22 (Ⓣ832 8107, Ⓦwww.tabarini.com), both have cars from around US$35 a day and Jeeps from US$50, including unlimited mileage and insurance, though check the waiver clause. La Ceiba, 6 C Pte 6 (Ⓣ832 4168), rent out 250cc motorbikes for US$8 per hour or US$30 a day.

Horse-riding Ravenscroft Stables, 2 Av Sur 3, in the village of San Juan del Obispo (Ⓣ832 6229). It's on the road up to Santa María de Jesús.

Internet There are dozens of cybercafés; rates are set at around US$1.25 an hour. Conexión, in La Fuente at 4 C Ote 14 (daily 8.30am–7pm), is probably the best set up, with flat screens and fast connections. Funky Monkey, 5 Av Sur 6 (next to *Mono Loco*), is another good place.

Laundry Rainbow Laundry, 6 Av Sur 15 (Mon–Sat 7am–7pm). A wash typically costs around US$3.

Libraries and cultural institutes El Sitio, 5 C Pte 15 (Ⓣ832 3037), has an active theatre, library and art gallery, and regularly hosts exhibitions and concerts; see the *Revue* or *Guatemala Post* for listings.

Medical care There's a 24hr emergency service at the Santa Lucía Hospital, Calzada Santa Lucía Sur 7 (Ⓣ832 3122). Dr Aceituno, who speaks good English, has a surgery at 2 C Pte 7 (Ⓣ832 0512).

Pharmacies Farmacia Santa María, west side of the plaza (daily 8am–10pm).

Police The police HQ is on the south side of the plaza, next to the tourist office (Ⓣ & Ⓕ832 0251). The tourist police are just off the plaza on 4 Avenida Norte (Ⓣ832 7290).

Post office Alameda de Santa Lucía, opposite the bus terminal (Mon–Fri 8am–4.30pm). Federal Express, 2 C Pte 3.

Supermarket La Bodegona at 4 C Pte and Alameda Santa Lucía.

Taxis On the east side of the plaza, by the market or call Ⓣ832 0479. For a female cab driver call Chiqui on Ⓣ715 5720.

Telephones The Telgua office is just south of the plaza on 5 Av Sur (7am–10pm), but rates are higher here than anywhere else and you'll have to queue. You can netcall on good lines at the cybercafés Conexión and Funky Monkey (see "Internet" above) for around US$0.30 to North America, US$0.40 per hour to Europe, and US$0.50 per hour to Australia, New Zealand and the rest of the world.

Travel agents Of the dozens of travel agents in Antigua, these are some of the most professional: The Rainbow Travel Center, 7 Av Sur 8 (Ⓣ & Ⓕ832 4202, Ⓦwww.rainbowtravelcenter.com), is very efficient; Viajes Tivoli, at 4 C Ote 10, on the west side of the plaza (Ⓣ832 4274, Ⓔantigua@tivoli.com.gt), is a recommended all-rounder; Monarcas, Alameda de Santa Lucía 7 (Ⓣ832 1939, Ⓔmorarcas@conexion.com.gt), organizes direct daily buses to Copán and Maya culture and ecology tours; Adventure Travel Center Viareal, 5 Av Nte 25B (Ⓣ832 0162, Ⓔviareal@guate.net), is good for adventure and sailing trips.

Around Antigua

The countryside **around Antigua** is superbly fertile and breathtakingly beautiful. The valley is dotted with small villages, ranging from the *ladino* coffee centre of Jocotenango to the traditional *indígena* village of Santa María de Jesús. None of them is more than an hour or two away and all make interesting day-trips. For the more adventurous, the volcanic peaks of Agua, Acatenango and Fuego offer strenuous but superb hiking, best done through a specialist agency.

Santa María de Jesús and Volcán Agua

Up above Antigua, a smooth paved road snakes through the coffee bushes and past the village of San Juan del Obispo before arriving in **SANTA MARÍA DE JESÚS**, starting point for the ascent of Volcán Agua. Perched high on the shoulder of the volcano, the village is some 500m above Antigua, with magnificent views over the Panchoy valley and east towards the smoking cone of Pacaya. The village was founded at the end of the sixteenth century and is of minimal interest, though the women wear beautiful purple *huipiles*. There's also a good little hospedaje here, *El Oasis* (☎832 0130; ❶), just below the plaza, if you want to make an early start. **Buses** run from Antigua to Santa María every 30 minutes or so from 6am to 6pm, and the trip takes thirty minutes.

Volcán Agua is the easiest and by far the most popular of Guatemala's big cones to climb – on some Saturday nights dozens of people spend the night at the top. The trail starts in Santa María de Jesús: head straight across the plaza, between the two ageing pillars, and up the street opposite the church doors. Take a right turn just before the end, and then continue past the cemetery and out of the village. From here it's a fairly simple climb on a clear though trash-filled path, cutting across the road that goes some of the way up. The climb takes around six hours, and the peak, at 3766m, is always cold at night. There is shelter (though not always room) in a small chapel at the summit.

Jocotenango and San Andrés Itzapa

Just 2km north of Antigua, the unappealing suburb of **JOCOTENANGO**, "place of bitter fruit", set around a huge, dusty plaza and long notorious for its sleazy bars, boasts a couple of interesting attractions grouped in the **Centro La Azotea** cultural centre (daily 9am–5pm; US$3.50 including tour in English). **Casa K'ojom**, which forms one half of the centre, is a purpose-built museum dedicated to Maya culture, especially music. The history of indigenous musical traditions is clearly presented from its pre-Columbian origins, through sixteenth-century Spanish and African influences – which brought the marimba, bugles and drums – to the present day, with audiovisual documentaries of fiestas and ceremonies. Other rooms are dedicated to the village weavings of the Sacatepéquez department and the cult of Maximón (see below). Next door, the **Museo de Café** is a 34-hectare plantation dating from 1883, offering the chance to look around a working organic coffee farm. All the technicalities of husking, sieving and roasting are clearly explained, and you're served a cup of the aromatic homegrown brew after your tour. Buses from the Antigua terminal pass Jocotenango every thirty minutes on their way to Chimaltenango; the museums are about 500m west of the plaza.

The road from Antigua to Chimaltenango continues beyond Jocotenango, ascending the Panchoy valley, past dusty farming villages, before a dirt track branches off to **SAN ANDRÉS ITZAPA**, one of the many villages badly hit by the 1976 earthquake. San Andrés is home to the cult of **San Simón** (or Maximón), the "evil saint" – a kind of womanizing and rapacious combination of Judas Iscariot and the conquistador Pedro de Alvarado – who is housed in his own pagan chapel. Despite San Andrés being just 18km from Antigua, few tourists visit this shrine, and you may feel less intrusive and more welcome here than at his other places of abode, which include Zunil (see p.218) and Santiago Atitlán (p.207). Uniquely in Guatemala, this San Simón attracts a largely *ladino* congregation and is particularly popular with prostitutes. To reach the saint's "house" ("Casa de San Simón") head for the central plaza from the dirt road into the village, turn right when you reach the church, walk two blocks, then up a little hill and you should spot street vendors selling charms, incense and candles. You can only visit the saint between sunrise and sunset, as the Maya believe he sleeps at other times. Once you've tracked down the dimly lit shrine, you'll find that Maximón lives in a fairly strange world, his image surrounded by drunken men, cigar-smoking women and hundreds of burning candles, each symbolizing a request: red for love, white for health, and so on. You may

△ Masks hanging at a Guatemalan market

be offered a *limpia*, or soul cleansing, which, for a small fee, involves being beaten by one of the resident women workers with a bushel of herbs. A bottle of the firewater *aguardiente* is also demolished: some is offered to San Simón, some of it you'll have to drink yourself and the rest is consumed by the attendant, who may spray you with alcohol (from her mouth) for your sins – all in all, quite an experience.

To **get to** San Andrés Itzapa from Antigua, there are direct buses from the terminal every two hours (8am–6pm).

The Carretera Interamericana

Leaving Guatemala City to the west, the serpentine **Carretera Interamericana** cuts right through the central highlands as far as the border with Mexico. In its entirety, this road stretches from Alaska to Chile (with a short break in southern Panama), and here in Guatemala it forms the backbone of transport in the highlands. As you travel around, the highway and its junctions will inevitably become an all too familiar scene.

Heading west from the capital, you climb steadily up a three-lane highway to **San Lucas Sacatepéquez**, from where a well-maintained side road descends to Antigua. The next main junction is **Chimaltenango**, an important town and capital of its own department, from where you can also make connections to or from Antigua. Continuing west, you'll come to **Los Encuentros**, where one road heads off to the north for Chichicastenango and another branches south to Panajachel and Lago de Atitlán. Beyond this, the highway climbs high over a mountainous ridge before dropping to **Cuatro Caminos**, from where side roads lead to Quetzaltenango, Totonicapán and San Francisco El Alto. The Interamericana continues on to Huehuetenango before reaching the Mexican border at La Mesilla. Virtually every bus travelling along the highway will stop at all of these junctions and you'll be able to buy fruit, drink and fast food from a resident army of vendors.

Leaving Guatemala City, the first place of interest is **SANTIAGO SACATEPÉQUEZ**, 1km or so to the north of the highway. The road branches off from San Lucas Sacatepéquez and buses shuttle back and forth along the branch road. The best time to visit Santiago is on November 1, for a famous local fiesta to honour the **Day of the Dead**. Massive kites made from paper and bamboo are flown in the cemetery to release the souls of the dead from their agony. Teams of young men struggle to get the kites aloft while the crowd looks on with bated breath, rushing for cover if a kite comes crashing to the ground. There's also a **market** in Santiago on Tuesday and Sunday.

Chimaltenango

Founded by Pedro de Portocarrero in 1526, on the site of the Kaqchikel centre of Bokoh, **CHIMALTENANGO** was later considered as a possible location for the new capital. It has the misfortune, however, of being positioned on the continental divide and suffered terribly from the earthquake in 1976 which flattened much of the surrounding area. Today's town (its relatively tranquil centre is just to the north of the main road) is still suffering from that disaster, with dirt streets, breeze-block buildings and an air of weary desperation. The town extracts what little business it can from the stream of traffic on the Interamericana, and the roadside is crowded with cheap comedores, mechanics' workshops, and sleazy bars that become brothels by night. **Buses** passing through Chimaltenango run to all points along the Carretera Interamericana. For Antigua they leave every twenty minutes between 5am and 7pm from the turn-off on the highway.

Tecpán and Iximché

Further west along a fast section of the Carretera Interamericana is the small town of **TECPÁN**, ninety minutes or so from Guatemala City. Tecpán may well have been the site chosen by Alvarado as the first Spanish capital, to which the Spanish forces retreated in August 1524, after they'd been driven out of Iximché. Today it's a place of no great interest, though it has a substantial number of restaurants and guesthouses catering to a mainly Guatemalan clientele.

On a beautiful exposed hillside about 5km south of Tecpán are the ruins of **Iximché** (daily 8am–5pm; US$3.25), the pre-conquest capital of the Kaqchikel, protected on three sides by steep slopes and surrounded by pine forests. The Kaqchikel allied themselves with the conquistadors from the early days of the Conquest, so the structures here suffered less than most at the hands of the Spanish. Since then, however, time and weather have taken their toll, and the majority of the buildings that once housed a population of ten thousand have disappeared, leaving only a few stone-built pyramids, plazas and a couple of ball courts. Nevertheless, the site is strongly atmospheric and its grassy plazas, ringed with pine trees, are marvellously peaceful and a perfect picnic spot, especially during the week, when you may well have the place to yourself. The ruins are still actively used as a focus for Maya worship: sacrifices and offerings take place down a small trail through the pine trees behind the final plaza.

To get there, take any bus travelling along the Carretera Interamericana between Chimaltenango and Los Encuentros and ask to be dropped at Tecpán. Regular buses to the ruins leave from Tecpán 's plaza. There's **camping** at the site, but bring your own food as the small shop here sells little more than drinks. If you're not planning to camp, be back on the Carretera Interamericana before 6pm to be sure of a bus.

Chichicastenango

The road for Chichicastenango and the **department of El Quiché** leaves the Carretera Interamericana at the **Los Encuentros** junction, thirty kilometres past the Iximché turn-off. Heading north from Los Encuentros, the highway drops down through dense, aromatic pine forests, plunging into a deep ravine before bottoming out by a tributary of the Río Motagua.

Continuing upwards around endless switchbacks, the road eventually reaches **CHICHICASTENANGO**, Guatemala's "mecca del turismo". If it's market day, you may get embroiled in one of the country's rare traffic jams as traders, tourists and locals all struggle to reach the town centre. In this compact and traditional town of cobbled streets where old adobe houses sit alongside modern concrete structures, the calm of day-to-day life is shattered on a twice-weekly basis by the **Sunday and Thursday markets** – Sunday is the busiest. The market attracts myriad tourists and commercial traders, as well as Maya weavers from throughout the central highlands.

The market is by no means all that sets Chichicastenango apart, however. For the local Maya population it's an important centre of culture and religion. The area was inhabited by the Kaqchikel long before the arrival of the Spanish, and over the years Maya culture and folk Catholicism have been treated with a rare degree of respect – although inevitably this blessing has been mixed with waves of arbitrary persecution and exploitation. Today, the town has an incredible collection of Maya artefacts, parallel *indígena* and *ladino* governments, and a church that makes no effort to disguise its acceptance of unconventional pagan worship. Traditional weaving is also adhered to here and the women wear superb, heavily embroidered *huipiles*. The men's costume of short trousers and jackets of black wool embroidered with silk is highly distinguished, although it's very expensive to make and these days most men opt for Western dress. However, for the town's fiesta (December 14–21) and on Sundays, a handful of *cofrades* (elders of the religious hierarchy) still wear traditional clothing and carry spectacular silver processional crosses and incense burners.

Arrival and information

There's no bus station in Chichi, but the corner of 5 C and 5 Av operates loosely as a terminal. **Buses** heading between Guatemala City and Santa Cruz del Quiché pass through Chichicastenango about every twenty minutes, stopping in town for a few minutes to load up with passengers. In Guatemala City, buses leave from the terminal in Zona 4, from 4am to about 5pm. Coming from Antigua, there are no direct buses but you can pick up a bus easily in Chimaltenango; or catch a shuttle from Antigua (market days only). From Panajachel, you can take any bus up to Los Encuentros and change there; on market days there are also several direct buses, and special tourist shuttles.

At the time of research there was no Inguat **tourist information office** in Chichi. If you're bitten by market fever and need to **change money**, there's a glut of banks, with plenty open on Sundays: Banrural on 6 Calle (Tues–Sun 9am–5pm) also has a MasterCard/Cirrus ATM, or, almost opposite, Banco Industrial (Mon 10am–2pm, Wed–Sun 10am–5pm) has an ATM for Visa/Plus card holders. For **Internet** access try Acses at 6 C 4–52 (US$1.80 per hour).

Accommodation

Hotels can be in short supply on Saturday nights before the Sunday market, but you shouldn't have a problem on other days. Prices can also rise on market days, though at other times you can usually negotiate a good deal.

Hospedaje El Salvador 5 Av 10–09 ☎756 1329. Venerable budget hotel, with a vast warren of bare but fairly neat rooms, a bizarre external colour scheme and cheap prices. The hot water can be erratic. ❷

Hotel Chalet House 3C C 7–44 ☎756 1360,

Ⓕ756 1793. Welcoming hotel set on a quiet street with 13 double rooms (all with private bathrooms and some have a tub). Highland wool blankets and textiles add a pleasing decorative touch and the beds are comfortable. Breakfast is available. ❹

Hotel Chugüilá 5 Av 5–24 Ⓣ756 1134, Ⓕ756 1279. Rambling hotel, with a selection of spacious if slightly shabby rooms, all on different levels and some with fireplaces. The owners were planning some renovation work, so comfort levels may have improved by the time you read this. Secure parking. ❺

Hotel Posada Belen 12 C 5–55 Ⓣ & Ⓕ756 1244. Large place with plenty of space, but not overtly attractive rooms. However, some have private bath and many have stunning views. ❷–❸

Hotel Posada El Telefono 8 C 1–64 Ⓣ756 1197. Friendly guesthouse with small, clean, bare rooms scattered up and down steep staircases. The communal bathroom is kept tidy. ❷

Hotel Santo Tomás 7 Av 5–32 Ⓣ756 1061, Ⓕ756 1306. Spacious, modern well-appointed rooms set around two colonial-style courtyards and a (heated) swimming pool. The hotel is block booked by huge tour groups on market days, however. ❼

Mayan Inn 8 C and 3 Av Ⓣ756 1176, Ⓕ756 1212, Ⓦwww.mayaninn.com.gt. Echoing tradition and stability, Chichi's longest-established hotel offers very comfortable rooms with colonial-style furniture and fireplaces. Pity the staff are decked out in mock-traditional dress. ❽

Posada El Arco 4 C 4–36 Ⓣ756 1255. Excellent guesthouse, run by friendly English-speaking brothers, with seven large, attractive rooms with good wooden beds and reading lights. Rooms 6 and 7 have access to a pleasant terrace, and there's also a beautiful garden and stunning countryside views. ❹

The Town

Most visitors come here for the **market**, which fills the central plaza and all its surrounding streets. Fruit and vegetable vendors congregate inside the covered Centro Comerical (which adjoins the plaza), while most of the other stalls sell textiles and souvenirs geared to the tourist trade. Chichicastenango, though, also offers an unusual insight into traditional religious practices in the highlands. At the main **Iglesia de Santo Tomás**, in the southeast corner of the plaza, the K'iche' Maya have been left to adopt their own style of worship, blending pre-Columbian and Catholic rituals. The church was built in 1540 on the site of a Maya altar, and rebuilt in the eighteenth century. It's said that indigenous locals became interested in worshipping here after Francisco Ximénez, the priest from 1701 to 1703, started reading their holy book, the Popul Vuh.

Before entering the church, it's customary to make offerings in a fire at the base of the steps or to burn incense in perforated cans, a practice that leaves a cloud of thin, sweet smoke hanging over the entrance. Inside is an astonishing scene of avid worship. A soft hum of constant murmuring fills the air as the faithful kneel to place candles on low-level stone platforms for their ancestors and the saints. For these people, the entire building is alive with the souls of the dead, each located in a specific part of the church. Don't enter the building by the front door, which is reserved for *cofrades* and senior church officials; use the side door instead and be warned that taking photographs inside the building is considered **deeply offensive** – don't even contemplate it.

Beside the church is a former monastery, now used by the parish administration. It was here that the Spanish priest Francisco Ximénez became the first outsider to be shown the Popol Vuh. His copy of the manuscript is now housed in the Newberry Library in Chicago: the original was lost some time later in the eighteenth century. The text itself was written just to the north of here, in Utatlán, shortly after the arrival of the Spanish, and is a brilliant poem of over nine thousand lines that details the cosmology, mythology and traditional history of the K'iche'.

On the south side of the plaza, often hidden by stalls on market day, the **Rossbach Museum** (Tues, Wed, Fri & Sat 8am–noon & 2–4pm, Thurs 8am–4pm & Sun 8am–2pm; US$0.75) houses a wide-ranging collection of pre-Columbian artefacts, mostly small pieces of ceramics (including some demonic-looking incense burners), jade necklaces and earrings, and stone carvings (some 2000 years old). Also on show are some interesting old photographs of Chichi and local weavings, masks and carvings.

Pascual Abaj

The church is certainly not the only scene of Maya religious activity: many of the hills that surround the town, like so many throughout the country, are topped with shrines. The closest of these, **Pascual Abaj**, is less than a kilometre from the plaza and regularly visited by tourists, but it's important to remember that any ceremonies you may witness are deeply serious – you should keep your distance and be sensitive about taking photographs. The shrine comprises small altars facing a stern pre-Columbian sculpture. Offerings are usually overseen by a shaman, and range from flowers to sacrificed chickens, always incorporating plenty of incense, alcohol and incantations. To get to Pascual Abaj, walk down the hill beside Santo Tomás, take the first right, 9 Calle, and follow this as it winds its way out of town. You'll soon cross a stream and then a well-signposted route takes you past a mask workshop, continuing uphill for ten minutes through a pine forest.

Eating

There's little fancy cuisine in Chichi, but plenty of good-value Guatemalan comedor food. The plaza on **market day** is the place to come for authentic highland eating: try one of the makeshift food stalls, where you'll find cauldrons of stews and broths.

Buenadventura upper floor, inside the Centro Comercial. Offers a terrific view of the vegetable market and simple, no-nonsense food – the breakfasts are the cheapest in town.

Café-Restaurant La Villa de Los Cofrades 6 C and 5 Av, first floor. Good set meals – soup, a main dish and salad, fries and bread – for under US$4, plus great *churrascos*, and breakfasts. Real coffee and wine is available.

Casa San Juan beside El Calvario church. Modish bar-restaurant with a stylish interior and plenty of artwork on display. Imaginatively prepared sandwiches and Guatemalan cooking including *pepián de pollo* and chorizo.

La Fonda del Tzijolaj upper floor of the Centro Comercial. The name may be unpronounceable, but the food is moderately priced, tasty and reliable and the balcony views of the church of Santo Tomás are unrivalled. Try the delicious *chiles rellenos*.

Tu Café west side of plaza. Unpretentious place run by a friendly Guatemalan who worked as a cab driver in New York for many years. There's plenty of breakfast choice, *antojitos*, sandwiches, *carne adobada* and all lunchtime mains come with rice, salad and soup.

Santa Cruz del Quiché and around

The capital of the department of El Quiché, **SANTA CRUZ DEL QUICHÉ** is half an hour north of Chichicastenango. A good paved road connects the two towns, running through pine forests and ravines, and past the **Laguna Lemoa**, a lake which, according to local legend, was originally filled with tears wept by the wives of K'iche' kings after their husbands had been slaughtered by the Spanish. The Catholic Church suffered terribly in El Quiché in the late 1970s and early 1980s, when priests were singled out and murdered by the army for their connections with the co-operative movement. The situation was so serious that Bishop Juan Geradi withdrew all his priests from the department in 1981. They have since returned to their posts, but the bishop himself was later assassinated in April 1998. The town's large army base was finally closed down by Oscar Berger in 2004.

In the recently remodelled central **plaza**, there's a large colonial **church**, built by the Dominicans with stone from the ruins of Utatlán. In the middle of the plaza, a defiant **statue** of the K'iche' hero, Tecún Umán, stands prepared for battle. His position is undermined somewhat by an ugly urban tangle of hardware stores, bakeries and trash that surrounds this corner of the square and the looming, spectacularly ugly **market** building.

Practicalities

The **bus terminal**, a large, scruffy affair, is about four blocks south and a couple east of the central plaza. Connections are generally excellent from Quiché. There's a constant stream of second-class **buses** to Guatemala City, going every twenty minutes between 3.30am and 5pm (3hr 30min); all pass through Chichicastenango (30min) and Los Encuentros (1hr). There are also regular services to Nebaj between 8am and 5pm (7 daily; 2hr 45min), to Uspantán seven times daily between 8am and 4pm (3hr 30min), and to Quetzaltenango (10 daily; 3hr). The street directly north of the terminal is **1 Avenida**, which takes you up into the heart of the town. Several **banks** will change your travellers' cheques, including Banrural (Mon–Fri 8.30am–6.30pm, Sat 9am–1pm) which has a MasterCard ATM, and Bancafé (Mon–Fri 8.30am–6pm, Sat 8.30am–1pm) with a Visa ATM; both are located at the northwest corner of the plaza.

There's a limited range of **hotels** in Quiché and nothing luxurious. Try either the *Hotel Maya Quiché*, 3 Av 4–19, Zona 1 (☎755 1464, ❷), which is a friendly place with big clean rooms, some with bathroom, or the *Hotel Rey K'iche*, 8 C 0–39, Zona 5 (☎755 0824; ❷), home to a profusion of spotless rooms, most with cable TV and private bath, plus a good comedor. Most **restaurants** in Quiché are grouped around the plaza. The large *El Torito Steakhouse*, 7 C 1–73, just southwest of the plaza, is one of the smartest places, with kitsch cowboy decor and a menu that's a real carnivore's delight – try the sausages or *chuletas*. On the west side of the plaza, *La Pizza de Ciro* dispenses fairly uninspiring pizzas while close by are several so-so bakeries with dry pastries and cakes. For a no-nonsense comedor meal, try *Restaurante Las Rosas*, 1 Av 1–28.

Utatlán (K'umarkaaj)

Early in the fifteenth century, riding on a wave of successful conquests, the K'iche' king Gucumatz (Feathered Serpent) founded a new capital, K'umarkaaj. A hundred years later, the Spanish arrived, renamed the city **Utatlán**, and then destroyed it. Today you can visit the ruins, about 4km to the west of Santa Cruz del Quiché.

According to the Popol Vuh, Gucumatz was a lord of great genius, assisted by powerful spirits, and there's no doubt that his capital was once a substantial city, housing the nine dynasties of the tribal elite, including the four main K'iche' lords, and a total of 23 palaces. The splendour of the city embodied the strength of the K'iche' empire, which at its height boasted a population of around a million. By the time of the Conquest, however, the K'iche' had been severely weakened. They first made contact with the Spanish on the Pacific coast, suffering a heavy defeat at the hands of Alvarado's forces near Quetzaltenango, with the loss of their leader, Tecún Umán. The K'iche' then invited the Spanish to their capital, but the suspicious Alvarado captured the K'iche' leaders, burnt them alive and then destroyed the city.

Exploring the site

The site (8am–5pm; US$1.80) is not as dramatic as some of the ruins in Guatemala, but impressive nonetheless, surrounded by deep ravines and pine forests. There has been little restoration since the Spanish destroyed the city and only a few of the main structures are still recognizable, most buried beneath grassy mounds and shaded by pine trees. The small **museum** has a scale model of what the original city may once have looked like.

The central plaza is almost certainly where Alvarado burned alive the two K'iche' leaders in 1524. Nowadays, it's where you'll find the surviving three **temple buildings** of Tohil, Auilix and Hacauaitz, all of which were simple pyramids topped by thatched shelters. In the middle of the plaza there used to be a circular **tower**, the Temple of the Sovereign Plumed Serpent, and its foundations can still be made out. The only other feature that is still vaguely recognizable is the **ball court**, which lies beneath grassy banks to the south of the plaza.

Beneath the plaza is a long **tunnel** that runs underground for about 100m. Inside are nine **shrines**, perhaps signifying the nine levels of the Maya underworld, Xibalbá. Each is the subject of prayer and devotion, but it is the ninth, housed inside a chamber, that is the most actively used for sacrifice and offerings of incense and alcohol. Why the tunnel was constructed remains uncertain, but some local legends have it that it was dug by the K'iche' to hide their women and children from the advancing Spanish, whom they planned to ambush at Utatlán.

Perhaps the most interesting thing about the site today is that *costumbristas*, traditional Maya priests, still come here to perform **religious rituals**. The entire area is covered in small burnt circles – the ashes of incense – and chickens are regularly sacrificed in and around the plaza. If a ceremony is taking place you'll hear the murmurings of prayers and smell incense smoke as you enter the tunnel, in which case it's wise not to disturb the proceedings by approaching too closely.

A **taxi** from Santa Cruz del Quiché's plaza with an hour at the ruins costs around US$8. To **walk**, head south from the plaza along 2 Av, and then turn right down 10 C, which will take you all the way out to the site – it's a pleasant forty-minute hike. You're welcome to **camp** close to the ruins, but there are no facilities or food.

To the Cuchumatanes: Sacapulas and Uspantán

The land to the north of Santa Cruz del Quiché is sparsely inhabited and dauntingly hilly. About 10km out of town, the paved road passes through San Pedro Jocopilas, and from there presses on through parched mountains, eventually dropping to the isolated town of **SACAPULAS**, just over an hour from Quiché. In a spectacular position on the Río Negro, beneath the foothills of the Cuchumatanes, Sacapulas has a small colonial church, and a good market every Thursday and Sunday beneath two huge ceiba trees in the plaza.

Getting to Sacapulas is straightforward – catch any bus from Santa Cruz del Quiché heading to Uspantán or Nebaj. Leaving can be a bit more tricky in the late afternoon when buses south to Quiché are fewer, the last around 4pm. There are seven daily buses to Nebaj (1hr 45min), two daily buses to Huehuetenango at 4.30am and 5.30am (2hr) and seven buses to Uspantán (2hr), plus regular pick-ups on all routes. However if you do get stuck here there are two good, but basic hospedajes: *Hospedaje y Restaurant Río Negro* (☎410 8168) and *Comedor y Hospedaje Tujaal* (both ❷); neither place has private bathrooms, but both serve good food.

East of Sacapulas, a dirt road rises steeply, clinging to the mountainside and quickly leaving the Río Negro far below. As it climbs, the views are superb, with tiny Sacapulas dwarfed by the sheer enormity of the landscape. Eventually the road reaches a high valley and arrives in **USPANTÁN**, a small town lodged in a chilly gap in the mountains and often soaked in steady drizzle. Rigoberta Menchú, the K'iche' Maya woman who won the 1992 Nobel Peace Prize, is from Chimel, a tiny village in this region. But probably the only reason you'll end up here is in order to get somewhere else. With the **buses for Cobán** and San Pedro Carchá leaving at around 3am and 5am, the best thing to do is go to bed (unless you can get a ride in a pick-up). Uspantán has several friendly pensiones, all basic but clean and very cheap: *Galindo* (❶) on 5 Calle, and *La Uspanteka* (❶) on 4 Calle are two of the best. There are seven daily buses between Uspantán and Quiché via Sacapulas, and regular pick-ups too.

The Ixil triangle

High up on the spine of the Cuchumatanes, in a landscape of steep hills, bowl-shaped valleys and gushing rivers, is the **Ixil triangle**. Here the three small towns of **Nebaj**, **Chajul** and **Cotzal**, remote and extremely traditional, share a language spoken nowhere else in the country. This triangle of towns forms the hub of the **Ixil-speaking region**, a massive highland area that drops away towards the Mexican border and contains at least 100,000 inhabitants. These lush and rain-drenched hills are hard to reach and notoriously difficult to control, and today's relaxed atmosphere and highland charm conceal a bitter history of protracted conflict. It's an area that embodies some of the very best and the very worst characteristics of the Guatemalan highlands.

Before the arrival of the Spanish, Nebaj was a sizeable centre, producing large quantities of jade; but the Conquest was particularly brutal in these parts. After many setbacks, the Spanish managed to take Nebaj in 1530, and by then they were so enraged that not only was the town burnt to the ground but the survivors were condemned to slavery as punishment for their resistance. Things didn't improve with the coming of independence, when the Ixil people were regarded as a source of cheap labour and forced to work on the coastal plantations. Many never returned. Even today large numbers of local people are forced to migrate in search of work, though many now head north to the USA instead of the coast. In the late 1970s and early 1980s, the area was hit by waves of horrific violence as it became the main theatre of operation for the **EGP** (the Guerrilla Army of the Poor). Caught up in the conflict, the people suffered enormous losses, with the majority of the smaller villages destroyed by the army and their inhabitants herded into "protected" settlements. With the peace accords, a degree of normality has returned to the area and new villages are being rebuilt on the old sites.

Despite this terrible legacy, the fresh green hills are some of the most beautiful in the country and the three towns are friendly and accommodating, with a relaxed and distinctive atmosphere.

Nebaj

NEBAJ is the centre of Ixil country, a beautiful old town, by far the largest of the three, with white adobe walls and cobbled streets juxtaposed against new concrete structures. The weaving done here is unusual and intricate, the finest examples being the women's *huipiles*, which are an artistic tangle of complex geometrical designs in superb greens, yellows, reds and oranges, usually worn with brilliant red *cortes* (skirts). On their heads, the women wear headcloths decorated with pompom tassels that they pile up above their heads. Most men no longer wear traditional dress.

The small **market**, a block east of the church, is worth investigating. On Thursday and Sunday the numbers swell as traders visit from out of town with secondhand clothing from the USA, stereos from Taiwan and Korea, and chickens, eggs, fruit and vegetables from the highlands. The town **church** is also worth a look – inside its door on the left are dozens of crosses, forming a memorial to those killed in the civil war. If you're here for the second week in August, you'll witness the **Nebaj fiesta**, which includes processions, dances, drinking, fireworks and a marimba-playing marathon.

Arrival and information

The **plaza** is the focal point for the community with the major shops, municipal buildings and police station around the square. The market and **bus terminal** are two blocks to the southeast. Banrural on the north side of the plaza has a 5B ATM for MasterCard/Cirrus cards while Bancafé near the market on 2 Av has a Visa/Plus ATM and exchanges both cash and travellers' cheques. The best place for **information** is *El Descanso* restaurant, two blocks north of the plaza on 3C, where an excellent community tourism initiative has been established and numerous treks (from US$6 per day) can be arranged. You can surf the **Internet** here too, and they are behind the Ⓦwww.nebaj.org **website** (Spanish only) and affiliated with the **Nebaj Language School**, in the same building.

Getting to Nebaj is straightforward with seven daily **buses** from Santa Cruz del Quiché between 8am and 5pm (2hr 45min). For Huehuetenango or Uspantán you'll have to change in Sacapulas. Buses leave Nebaj for Quiché at 1am, 2am, 3am,

4am, 5.30am, 8am and the last is at 11am; there's also a direct service to Guatemala City at 11pm. Arrive early to grab a seat. **Pick-ups and trucks** supplement the buses; the best place to hitch south is on the road out of town, a little further past the *Hotel Ixil*.

Accommodation

You'll find little in the way of luxury in Nebaj, though standards have improved considerably recently and what there is does have an inimitable charm. There are few street signs, so you'll probably have to rely on the gang of children who act as guides – none of the hotels is more than a few minutes' walk from the terminal.

Hospedaje Ilebal Tenam five minutes' walk from the plaza on the road to Chajul/Cotzal ☎755 8039. Well-run hospedaje with decent, very clean rooms, some with TV and private bathroom, reliably hot showers and safe parking. ❷–❸

Hotel Ixil on the main road south out of town ☎756 0036. Some of the large, bare rooms are a little damp, though there's a pleasant setting around a courtyard. Warmish shower. ❷

Hotel Turansa one block west of the plaza ☎715 7803. Two-storey green-and-white block with smallish but neat rooms with pine furnishings, comfortable beds, cable TV and private bathrooms. Safe parking. ❸

Hotel Villa Nebaj two minutes' walk north of the plaza ☎715 1651. Garishly painted new four-storey construction that's something of a blot on the landscape, though the accommodation is extremely comfortable – all rooms have quality beds, TV and bathroom. ❹

Eating

The best places to eat are the *Maya-Inca* on 5 C, owned by a friendly Peruvian-Guatemalan couple which serves tasty Peruvian and local dishes, and *El Descanso*, which has well-prepared, inexpensive Guatemalan food. For a meat feast, *Asados el Pasabien* on the road to Sacapulas excels for *churrascos*, while *Cesar's* on 2 Av opposite Bancafé serves up reasonable pizzas. For entertainment, most of the raving in town is courtesy of Nebaj's burgeoning evangelical church scene, with four-hour services involving much wailing and gnashing of teeth.

Walks around Nebaj

There are several beautiful **walks** in the hills surrounding Nebaj, with one of the most interesting taking you to the village of **ACUL**, two hours away. Starting from the church in Nebaj, cross the plaza and head along 5 C past *Hotel Turansa*. At the bottom of the dip it divides after *Tienda y Comedor El Oasis*: take the right-hand fork and head out of town along a dirt road. The track switchbacks up a steep hillside, and heads over a narrow pass into the next valley, where it drops down into Acul. The village was one of the original so-called "model villages" into which people were herded after their homes had been destroyed by the army. If you walk on through the village and out the other side, you arrive at the alpine-lodge-like *Finca San Antonio* (☎599 3352), run by an Italian-Guatemalan family who have lived here for more than fifty years, making some of the country's best cheese, which they sell at pretty reasonable prices. They also rent out delightful **chalets** (❹).

Sadly, a second, shorter walk to a beautiful little **waterfall**, La Cascada de Plata, is so strewn with trash that it's not worth the effort unless a clean-up has been undertaken (check in *El Descanso*). Take the road to Chajul and turn left just before it crosses the bridge, a kilometre or two outside Nebaj. Don't be fooled by the smaller version you'll come to shortly before the main set of falls.

San Juan Cotzal and Chajul

To visit the other two towns in the Ixil triangle, it's best to time your visit to coincide with **market days**, when there's more traffic around: Cotzal is on Wednesday and Saturday, and Chajul on Tuesday and Friday. **Buses** run to an irregular schedule, but on Sunday transport returns to both Cotzal and Chajul from Nebaj after

10am. Pick-ups supplement the buses. It's certainly possible to visit both towns in one day from Nebaj if you get an early start.

SAN JUAN COTZAL is closer to Nebaj, about 45 minutes away, depending on the state of the road. The town is set in a gentle dip in the valley, sheltered somewhat beneath the Cuchumatanes and often wrapped in a damp blanket of mist. Cotzal attracts very few Western travellers, so you may find that many people assume you're an aid worker or attached to an evangelical church. Intricate turquoise *huipiles* are worn by the Maya women here, who also weave bags and rope from the fibres of the maguey plant. There's little to do in the town itself but there is some great hill-walking close by. **Buses** should return to Nebaj daily at 6am and 1am; at other times you'll have to hitch.

Last but by no means least of the Ixil settlements is **CHAJUL**. Made up mainly of old adobe houses, with wooden beams and red-tiled roofs blackened by the smoke of cooking fires, it is also the most determinedly traditional and least bilingual of the Ixil towns. The women of Chajul wear earrings made of old coins strung up on lengths of wool and dress in bright reds and blues, filling the streets with colour – you'll see them washing their scarlet *cortes* and *huipiles* at the stream that cuts through the middle of the village. Here boys still use blowpipes to hunt small birds, a skill that dates from the earliest of times but is now little used elsewhere.

The colonial church, a massive structure with huge wooden beams and gold-leaf decoration, is home to the **Christ of Golgotha** and the target of a large pilgrimage on the second Friday of Lent, a particularly good time to be here. If you want to **stay**, the very basic, pretty filthy *Hospedaje Cristina* (❶) is two blocks south of the church. The best place to eat is the clean *Comedor Las Gemelitas* two blocks downhill from the church. Local families also rent out beds in their houses to the steady trickle of travellers now coming to Chajul; you won't have to look for them, they will find you. A number of unscheduled trucks bump along the hour-long route between Nebaj and Chajul, and on **market** days (Tues & Fri) there are regular morning **buses** at 5.30am and 6am, returning at 11.30am and noon. You can also **walk** here from San Juan Cotzal, two to three hours away through the spectacular Ixil countryside. Follow the unpaved road that branches off to the main Nebaj–Cotzal road just before you enter Cotzal.

Lago de Atitlán

Lake Como, it seems to me, touches the limit of the permissibly picturesque; but Atitlán is Como with the additional embellishments of several immense volcanoes. It is really too much of a good thing. After a few days of this impossible landscape one finds oneself thinking nostalgically of the English Home Counties.

Aldous Huxley, *Beyond the Mexique Bay* (1934)

Whether or not you share Huxley's refined sensibilities, there's no doubt that **Lago de Atitlán** is astonishingly beautiful. Most people find themselves captivated by its scenic excesses – indeed, the effect is so overwhelming that a handful of gringo devotees have been rooted to its shores since the 1960s. Atitlán's waters shift through an astonishing range of blues, steely greys and greens as the sun moves across the sky. Measuring 18km by 12km, it's hemmed in on all sides by steep hills and three volcanoes, and is some 320m (nearly 1000 feet) deep.

Another astonishing aspect of Atitlán is the strength of Maya culture evident in its lakeside settlements, still some of the most intensely traditional villages in Guatemala, despite the thousands of tourists that pour in here from Europe and North America every year. **San Antonio Palopó**, **Santiago Atitlán** and, above the lake, **Sololá** are some of the few villages in the entire country where Maya men still wear traditional costume, and two languages, **Tz'utujil** and **Kaqchikel**, are spoken.

There are thirteen villages on the shores of the lake, with many more in the hills behind, ranging from the cosmopolitan resort-style **Panajachel** to tiny, isolated

Tzununá. The villages are mostly subsistence farming communities and it's easy to hike and boat around the lake staying in a different one each night. The area has only recently attracted large numbers of tourists and for the moment things are still fairly undisturbed, but some of the new pressures are decidedly threatening. The increase in population has also had a damaging impact on the shores of the lake, as the desperate need to cultivate more land leads to deforestation and accompanying soil erosion.

You'll probably reach the lake through Panajachel, which makes a good base for exploring the surrounding area. "Pana" has an abundance of cheap hotels and restaurants and is well served by buses. To get a real sense of a more typical Atitlán village, however, travel by boat to Santiago Atitlán or San Antonio Palopó. **San Pedro La Laguna** is now the village with the most established travellers' "scene", with a surplus of extremely cheap hotels and cheaper beer. **Santa Cruz** and **San Marcos** are the places to head for if you're seeking real peace and quiet, and there are good hikes on this side of the lake.

Sololá

Perched on a natural balcony overlooking the lake, **SOLOLÁ** is a fascinating town, largely ignored by the majority of travellers. In common with only a few other

Transport on the lake

All lakeside villages are served by small fast boats called **lanchas**. Lanchas do not run to a fixed schedule but depart when the owner has enough passengers to cover fuel costs. Normally you don't have to wait around too long, but at quiet times of year you may have to wait half an hour or so.

There are two **piers** in Panajachel. The main pier at the end of Calle del Embarcadero, is for all villages on the northern side of the lake: Santa Cruz (about 15min), Jaibalito (25min), Tzununá (30min) and San Marcos (40min). Direct (15min) and non-direct (50min) San Pedro boats also depart from here, from where you can easily get to San Juan and San Pablo. The second pier at the end of Calle Rancho Grande is for Santiago Atitlán (1hr by ferry or 20min by lancha) and lake tours. The last boats on all these routes leave around 6.30pm.

A semi-official fare system operates: tourists pay US$1.30 for a short trip, US$2–2.50 for a longer journey. Local pay less. Some lancheros try to charge more for the last boat of the day. **Tours of the lake** (US$8), visiting San Pedro, Santiago Atitlán and San Antonio Palopó, can be booked in virtually any travel agent (see p.207); all leave around 9am and return by 4pm.

places, it has parallel *indígena* and *ladino* governments and is probably the largest Maya town in the country, with the vast majority of the people still wearing traditional costume.

Sololá itself isn't much to look at: a wide central plaza with a clock tower on one side and a modern church on the other. However, its **Friday market** is one of Central America's finest – a mesmeric display of colour and commerce. From as early as 5am the plaza is packed, drawing traders from all over the highlands, as well as thousands of local Maya, the women covered in striped red cloth and the men in their outlandish "space cowboy" shirts, woollen aprons and wildly embroidered trousers. There's another, smaller, market on Tuesday. Another interesting time to visit Sololá is on Sunday, when the *cofrades*, the elders of the Maya religious hierarchy, parade through the streets in ceremonial costume to attend the mid-morning Mass.

Panajachel

Ten kilometres beyond Sololá, from which it's separated by a precipitous descent, is **PANAJACHEL**. Over the years, what was once a small Maya village has become something of a resort, with a sizeable population of long-term foreign residents whose numbers are swollen in the winter by an influx of North American seasonal migrants. Panajachel was a premier hippie hangout back in the 1960s and 1970s and developed a bad reputation amongst some sections of Guatemalan society as a haven for drug-taking gringo drop-outs. Today "Pana" is much more integrated into the tourism mainstream and is as popular with Guatemalans and other Central Americans as Westerners. The lotus-eaters and crystal-gazers have not all deserted Panajachel, however. Many have re-invented themselves as (vaguely) conscientious capitalists who own restaurants and export típica clothing. In many ways, it's this **gringo** crowd that gives the town its modern character and identity.

Not so long ago Panajachel was a quiet little village of **Kaqchikel** Maya, whose ancestors were settled here after the Spanish crushed a force of Tz'utujil warriors on the site. Today the old village has been enveloped by the new building boom, but it still retains a traditional feel, while the river delta behind the town continues to be farmed. The Sunday market, bustling with people from all around the lake, remains oblivious to the tourist invasion.

For travellers, Panajachel is one of those inevitable destinations. It's a comfortable base for exploring the area, and, although no one ever owns up to actually liking it, most people stay for a while. The old village is still attractive and, although most of

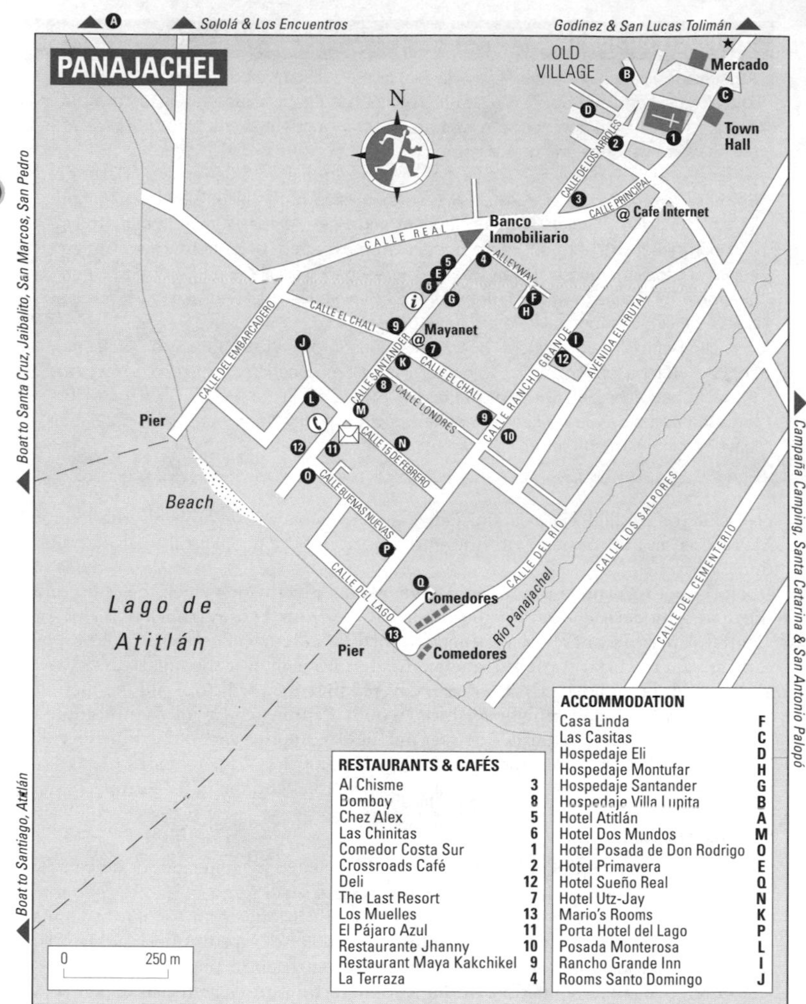

the new buildings are fairly nondescript, its lakeside setting is superb. The main **daytime activity** is either shopping – weaving from all over Guatemala is sold with daunting persistence in the streets here – or simply hanging out. There's an amazing selection of places to eat and drink or surf the Net, though it's probably best to swim elsewhere as the lake water is not that clean close to town. You could rent a kayak (available on the lakeshore between the piers) for a few hours – mornings are usually much calmer. Alternatively, if you're seduced by the bohemian ambiance and easy-going pace of lakeside life, Panajachel also boasts a couple of **language schools** (see p.149).

Arrival, information and accommodation

The bus drops you beside the Banco Inmobiliario, very close to the main drag, Calle Santander, which runs down to the lakeshore. Straight ahead, up C Principal, is the old village. The **tourist office** (daily 9am–5pm; ⓣ762 1392) on C Santander has English-speaking staff, limited hotel information, and boat and bus schedules. There are a dozen or more **Internet** cafés in Pana and rates are very cheap, at around US$1.25 an hour; try *Café Internet* on C Principal or *Mayanet* midway along Calle Santander.

There's no shortage of cheap and mid-range **hotels** in Pana, and there are plenty of "**rooms**". If you have a tent, first choice is the *Campana* **campsite** (ⓣ762 2479; US$1.50 per person), 1km east of the centre along the road to Santa Catarina, over the river bridge. Here, happy campers will find kitchen and storage facilities and there are also sleeping bags and tents for rent. Don't bother camping at the public beach: your stuff will be ripped off.

Budget

Casa Linda down an alley off the top of Calle Santander ⓣ762 0386. Not the cheapest hospedaje, but the central garden is undeniably beautiful, and the management friendly. Some rooms have private bath. ❷–❸

Las Casitas Calle Principal, near the market ⓣ762 1224, ⓦwww.hotellascasitas.net. Clean, friendly and safe, with tastefully decorated rooms sporting quality beds and reading lamps; most also have private bath. ❹

Hospedaje Montufar down an alley off the top of Calle Santander ⓣ762 040. Very clean, secure accommodation and a quiet location make this a good choice. Triples also available. ❷

Hospedaje Santander Calle Santander ⓣ762 1304. Agreeable place with a leafy courtyard and clean, inexpensive rooms, some with private bath. ❷–❸

Hospedaje Villa Lupita Callejón El Tino ⓣ762 1201. Excellent-value family-run place on a quiet lane in the old village. Sixteen rooms, all with bedside lights, rugs and mirrors, some with private bath. There's also a sun terrace and free purified water and coffee. ❷

Hotel Sueño Real Calle Ramós ⓣ762 0608, ⓕ762 1097. Welcoming little hotel, close to the lakeshore in a quiet location and run by a friendly family. The ten attractive rooms all have private bath and TV. ❹

Mario's Rooms Calle Santander ⓣ762 131. Appealing, clean rooms – some airy and light with private bath, others more basic. ❷–❸

Posada Monterosa Calle Monterrey ⓣ762 0055. Neat little hotel with attractive, recently renovated en-suite rooms. Secure car parking. ❸

Rooms Santo Domingo down a path off Calle Monterrey ⓣ762 0236. Very inexpensive, age-old place, set well away from the bustle of C Santander. Clapboard, super-basic rooms all face a charming little garden, with more expensive options with private bath upstairs. ❶–❸

Moderate to expensive

Hotel Atitlán on the lakeside, 1km west of the centre ⓣ762 1441 or 762 1416, ⓦwww.hotelatitlan.com. A wonderful lakeside location, and the luxurious rooms (from US$130) have all mod cons and volcano views. Highlights include extensive, beautifully maintained gardens and a swimming pool. ❾

Hotel Dos Mundos Calle Santander ⓣ762 2078, ⓕ762 0127. Just off the main drag, this Italian-owned hotel has comfortable rooms set to one side of a private garden, where there's also a small swimming pool. Breakfast is included; and there's an authentic in-house Italian restaurant. ❻

Hotel Posada de Don Rodrigo Calle Santander, facing the lake ⓣ & ⓕ762 2322 or 762 2329, ⓦwww.hotelposadadedonrodrigo.com. Colonial-style hotel by the lakeside, where most of the accommodation is a little on the small side; though the new wing (rooms 301–311) offers better value and much more space for a few dollars more. Large outdoor pool, sauna and squash court. ❽

Hotel Primavera C Santander ⓣ762 2052, ⓦwww.primaveraatitlan.com. A sparse, classy minimalist-style place where the rooms boast magnolia walls, pale wood and a notable absence of típica textiles. The smart restaurant downstairs, *Chez Alex*, is highly acclaimed too. ❺

Hotel Utz-Jay Calle 15 de Febrero ⓣ762 0217, ⓔutzjay_garcia@yahoo.com. An atmospheric place with very stylish adobe-and-stone *casitas* (all with private bath) in a large, tranquil garden. In-house *tuj* herbal sauna, plus a selection of excellent tours available. ❹

Rancho Grande Inn Calle Rancho Grande ⓣ762 2255, ⓦwww.ranchograndeinn.com. Attractive, large and nicely appointed bungalows bedecked with local textiles in spacious gardens with a swimming pool. A filling breakfast is included. ❺–❻

Eating, drinking and entertainment

Panajachel has an abundance of **restaurants**, all catering to the cosmopolitan tastes of its population. You'll have no trouble finding tasty Chinese, Italian, Mexican and Mediterranean dishes. For really cheap and authentically Guatemalan food there are plenty of comedores on and just off the beach promenade and close to the market.

Al Chisme Calle de los Árboles. Stylish café-restaurant with a menu including snacks (bagels and crepes) plus pasta and veggie options and fish and meat mains. Not cheap though. Closed Wed.

Bombay halfway along Calle Santander. Interesting vegetarian menu which, despite the name, has little Indian about it, instead featuring offerings such as Indonesian *gado-gado,* fried rice, falafel and organic coffee.

Chez Alex halfway along Calle Santander. Probably the flashest place in town, majoring in European classics, with trout and lobster on the menu. The wine list is pretty basic however. Expensive.

Las Chinitas towards the northern end of Calle Santander. Superb pan-Asian cuisine: Nonyan (Malay-Chinese) curries and stir-fries are the main draw, plus Thai and Chinese choices at moderate prices. Closed Mon.

Comedor Costa Sur near the church in the old town. Pana's best comedor: clean and inexpensive and great for breakfast or lunch. Bargain US$2 fried-fish set menu some days.

Crossroads Café Calle del Campanario 0–27. Easily the finest coffee in town: selected, blended and roasted by a South African barista, with plenty of combinations and flavourings available, plus herbal teas, real hot chocolate and fresh pastries. Closed Sun and Mon and for siesta 1–4pm.

Deli southern end of Calle Santander. Healthy meals, snacks and drinks in a pretty garden setting. Salads, sandwiches, pastries, bagels, cakes, wine and tea. Service is friendly, but can be a little lethargic.

Los Muelles lakeside by the Santiago Pier. Right above the water, with stunning views, this simple place is one of the best of several lakeside choices. Menu includes fish (including mojarra), *caldos* and sandwiches.

El Pájaro Azul Calle Santander. Elegant French-style brasserie with good sweet and savoury crepes, salads and sandwiches.

Restaurante Jhanny halfway down Calle Rancho Grande. Reliable, flavoursome and filling Guatemalan food; the tables are nicely arranged around a little garden.

La Terraza northern end of Calle Santander. Formal, expensive European restaurant, but with a few Asian-style dishes and a tapas menu too.

Nightlife

Panajachel buzzes at weekends and during the main holiday season, when many young Guatemalans (and some Mexicans and Salvadoreans) head to the lake to drink and flirt. Things are quieter at other times. Most bars and clubs are located around the southern end of Calle de los Árboles, where you find the *Circus Bar* for **live music** and *El Aleph*, plus the *Chapiteau* **nightclub**. Close by on C Principal, *Socrates* is a mainstream disco-club where a young local crowd gather to dance to Latin pop and merengue. Alternatively, *Ubu's Cosmic Cantina*, on Calle de los Árboles, is a more relaxed US-style bar with a big screen for sports fans and movie buffs. **Movies** are also shown at the Carrot Chic and Turquoise Buffalo cinemas on Calle de los Árboles, and there's a **pool hall** in the old village, near the post office.

Listings

Banks and exchange Banco Inmobiliario, at C Santander and C Principal (Mon–Fri 9.30am–5pm, Sat 9am–12.30pm); there's a 5B ATM opposite for MasterCard/Cirrus cards; Banco Industrial, Calle Santander, has a Visa/Plus ATM.

Bicycle and motorbike rental Moto Servicio Queche, C de los Árboles and C Principal (☎762 2089), rents mountain bikes for US$1 an hour, US$6 a day, and 200cc bikes for US$8 an hour, US$28 a day.

Bookstores The Gallery, Calle de los Árboles, stocks a reasonable choice of secondhand titles and a few interesting new books in English. Libería Libros del Lago, C Santander 9, has a good selection of books on Maya culture, maps and guidebooks.

Laundry Lavandería Automatico, C de los Árboles 0–15 (Mon–Sat 7.30am–6.30pm), US$3.50 for a full load washed, dried and folded.

Medical care Dr Edgar Barreno speaks good English; his surgery is down the first street that branches to the right off Calle de los Árboles

(☎762 1008).
Pharmacy Farmacia La Unión, Calle Santander.
Police On the plaza in the old village (☎762 1120).
Post office Calle Santader and 15 de Febrero or try Get Guated Out on Calle de los Árboles (☎762 0595) for bigger shipments.
Telephone Many of the businesses and cybercafés on Calle Santander offer the best rates to call long-distance; *Café Internet*, C Principal charges US$0.30 per minute to North America and US$0.50 to Europe. Otherwise, Telgua (daily 7am–midnight) is near the junction of C Santander and C 15 de Febrero.
Travel agents Unión Travel, C Santander & Calle El Chali (☎762 2426, Ⓦwww.igoguate.com); Servicios Turisticos Atitlán, C Santander, near C 14 de Febrero (☎762 2075, Ⓦwww.atitlan.com).

Panajachel to San Antonio Palopó

On the eastern shore of the lake, backed up against the slopes, are a couple of villages, the first of which, **SANTA CATARINA PALOPÓ**, is just 4km from Panajachel. The people of Santa Catarina used to live almost entirely by fishing and trapping crabs, but the introduction of black bass into the lake to create a sport-fishing industry has put an end to all that, as the bass eat the smaller fish. They've now turned to farming and migratory work, with many of the women travelling to Panajachel and Antigua to peddle their weaving. Much of the shoreline as you leave Santa Catarina has been bought and developed, and great villas, ringed by impenetrable walls and razor wire, have come to dominate the lakeside.

Some 8km from Santa Catarina, **SAN ANTONIO PALOPÓ** is a larger and more traditional village, squeezed in beneath a steep hillside. Because it is on the tour-group itinerary, the villagers have become a bit pushy in selling their weavings, but despite this, the village is quite interesting. The hillsides above San Antonio are well irrigated and terraced, reminiscent of rice paddies, and most men wear the village *traje* of red shirts with vertical stripes and short woollen kilts. Women wear almost identical shirts, made of the same fabric with subtle variations to the collar design. The whitewashed central church is also worth a look; just to the left of the entrance are two ancient bells. Regular **pick-ups** run between Panajachel and San Antonio, passing through Santa Catarina and leaving approximately every thirty minutes (the last one returns to Panajachel from San Antonio at 5pm). There's no regular boat service.

Santiago Atitlán

On the opposite side of the lake from Panajachel, **SANTIAGO ATITLÁN** is set to one side of a sheltered horseshoe inlet, overshadowed by the cones of the San Pedro, Atitlán and Tolimán volcanoes. It's the largest and most important of the lakeside villages, and also one of the most traditional, being the main centre of the Tz'utujil-speaking Maya. At the time of the Conquest, the Tz'utujil had their fortified capital, **Chuitinamit**, on the slopes of San Pedro, while the bulk of the population lived spread out around the site of today's village. Alvarado and his crew, needless to say, destroyed the capital and massacred its inhabitants, assisted this time by a force of Kaqchikel Maya, who arrived at the scene in some three hundred canoes.

The traditional **costume** of Santiago, still worn a fair amount, is both striking and unusual. The men wear long shorts which, like the women's *huipiles*, are striped white and purple and intricately embroidered with birds and flowers. The women also wear a *xk'ap*, a band of red cloth approximately 10m long, wrapped around their heads, which has the honour of being depicted on the 25 centavo coin. Sadly this head cloth is going out of use and on the whole you'll probably only see it at fiestas and on market days, and then worn mainly by older women.

Exploring Santiago Atitlán

Today, Santiago is an industrious but relaxed sort of place. During the day the town becomes fairly commercial, its **main street**, which runs from the dock to the plaza, lined with weaving shops and souvenir stands. There's nothing like the Panajachel overkill here, but the persistence of underage street vendors is daunting on market days (Friday and a smaller event on Sunday). By mid-afternoon, once the boats have left, the whole village becomes a lot more friendly. There's not that much to do other than stroll around soaking up the atmosphere, but you could drop into the new weaving museum, **Museo Cojolya** (Mon–Fri 9am–4pm, Sat 9am–1pm; free), about 100m up the main drag from the dock, on the left. Here you'll find excellent displays (in English and Spanish) about the tradition of backstrap weaving in Santiago, and you can see some of the weavers in action at 11am and 1pm.

The old whitewashed baroque Catholic **church** is also well worth a look. Inside, the huge central altarpiece, carved when the church was under *cofradía* control, culminates in the shape of a mountain peak and a cross. The cross symbolizes the Maya world tree. On the right as you enter, there's also a stone memorial commemorating Father Stanley Rother, an American priest who served in the parish from 1968 to 1981. Father Rother was a committed defender of his parishioners in an era when, in his own words, "shaking hands with an Indian has become a political act". Branded a Communist by President García, he was assassinated by a paramilitary death squad like hundreds of his parishioners before and after him. His body was returned to his native Oklahoma for burial but his heart was removed and buried in the church.

Folk Catholicism plays an important role in the life of Santiago and the town is one of the few places where Maya still pay homage to **Maximón**, the "evil" saint, known locally as Rilej Mam. Any child will take you to see him: just ask for the "Casa de Maximón". It costs US$0.25 to enter his abode and US$1.30 to take his picture.

Practicalities

Boats to Santiago leave from the beach in Panajachel at 8.35am, 10.30am, 1pm and 4.30pm – the trip takes about an hour but there are also unscheduled, much faster (20min) lancha services at other times. The village is well connected by **bus** with almost everywhere except Panajachel. **Leaving Santiago**, buses depart from the central plaza and head via Cocales to Guatemala City (7 daily between 3am and 3pm). For Panajachel, there are four daily boats at 6am, 11.45pm, 1.30pm and 3pm (plus supplementary lanchas). Nine daily boats for San Pedro La Laguna leave between 6am and 5pm (40min); and there are regular pick-ups from a stop by the *Hotel Chi-Nim-Ya*.

As for **accommodation**, two backpackers' favourites are the basic, clean and friendly *Hotel Chi-Nim-Ya* (ⓣ721 7131; ❷–❸), on the left uphill from the dock, where some rooms have private bath, and the good-value *Hotel Tzutuhil*, in the centre of town (ⓣ721 7174; ❷). For something special, there are a couple of good options which can be reached by road or water-taxi from the dock. The *Posada de Santiago*, 1km south of the town (ⓣ & ⓕ721 7167, ⓦwww.posadadesantiago.com; ❺), is a luxury lakeside American-owned B&B, with rooms in stone cabins, each with its own log fire, a few budget rooms, a fine restaurant and a pool. About a ten-minute walk north of the dock, *Hotel Bambú* (ⓣ416 2122; ❺) has beautiful thatch-roofed stone bungalows and rooms, all with lake views, plus an excellent restaurant here with Spanish specialities and fine wines.

Of the **restaurants** in town, the inexpensive *Wach'alal*, about 400m up from the dock is a good option for grilled meats, fish or soup, while *Restaurant El Pescador*, a bit further on, is a formal place with good views of Santiago's street life and a menu that includes black bass and *churrascos* for around US$5–7.

San Pedro La Laguna

Around the other side of Volcán San Pedro is the village of **SAN PEDRO LA LAGUNA**, which has usurped Panajachel as the pivotal centre of Guatemala's travelling "scene". It isn't Goa, but it does have a distinctively bohemian feel about it, with plenty of bongo-bashing and bong-smoking counterculture in evidence. Yet despite the obvious culture clash between locals (most of whom are evangelical Christians) and travellers, everyone seems to get on reasonably well. In recent years San Pedro has also established itself as a **language school** centre, the beautiful location drawing increasing numbers of students, though the quality of tuition is pretty variable (see p.149). There's a decent little beach just southeast of town, below the road to San Juan and some **thermal pools** between the two docks offer a further opportunity to relax.

Volcán San Pedro, which towers above the village to a height of some 3020m, is largely coated with thick forest and can be climbed in four to five hours. Unfortunately, there have been occasional attacks on tourists on its slopes, but if you do decide to do the hike take a guide, as the foliage is dense and the route near impossible to find. Samuel Cumatz Batzin (☎762 2487), who can often be found at *Casa Elena* (see below), is recommended. Get an early start in order to see the views at their best and avoid the worst of the heat. Alternatively, **Excursion Big Foot** (☎204 6267), just left of the Panajachel dock, organize hikes to a *mirador* nicknamed 'Indian Nose' from where there's a great view of the lake for US$4 per person (for a group of five). They also rent out **horses** for US$2 an hour (guide included), **bicycles** for US$8 a day and **canoes** for US$1.30 per hour. To unwind with a **massage**, see Ada at the *Hotel Villa Sol.*

Arrival, information and accommodation

There are two docks in San Pedro. All **boats** from Panajachel and villages on the north side of the lake, including Santa Cruz and San Marcos, arrive and depart from the Panajachel dock on the north side of town, while boats from Santiago Atitlán use a separate dock to the southeast, a ten-minute walk away. **Buses** connect San Pedro with Quetzaltenango (six daily; 2hr 15min) and Guatemala City's Zona 4 terminal (four daily; 3hr 15 min), or speak to Excursion Big Foot (see above) about **shuttle buses** which can be arranged to Chichicastenango, Quetzaltenango, Antigua and the Mexican border. In the centre of town you'll find the marketplace (busiest on Thurs and Sun), post office and, a block to the south, Banrural **bank** (Mon–Fri 9am–5.30pm, Sat 9am–12.30pm), which will change travellers' cheques. Of the several Internet places, the best set-up is located above *D'noz* by the Panajachel dock, where you can also burn photos to disk.

San Pedro has some of the cheapest **accommodation** in all Latin America, with a number of basic, clean guesthouses – most charge less than US$3 a person per night. There's nothing in the way of luxury.

Casa Elena left after *Nick's Place* ☎310 9243. Not the very cheapest place, but the nine tidy rooms are clean and there's a dock for swimming. ❷

Hotel Mansión del Lago right above the Panajachel dock ☎811 8172. The most comfortable place in San Pedro, where the spotless, good-value rooms all have nice pine beds, private bath and balcony areas with lake views. ❷

Hotel Nahual Maya turn left after *Nick's Place* ☎721 8158. Well-run, friendly new place with neat, clean tidy rooms (with bathrooms) facing a lawn. ❷

Hotel Ti'Kaaj near the Santiago dock. Very basic rooms, but a lovely shady garden with hammocks. ❶

Hotel Valle Azul turn right at the Panajachel dock ☎207 7292. Vaguely Soviet-style concrete monster of a hotel, but clean bare rooms (some with private bath) are reasonable enough. ❶–❷

Hotelito El Amanecer Sakcari between the docks ☎812 1113. Friendly, family-run place with ten attractive rooms, all with private bath, and most with wonderful lake views. ❷

Posada Casa Domingo between the docks. Six attractive, clean new rooms, all with private bath and good mattresses, facing Volcán San Pedro. Also has some ultra basic cell-like accommodation in a separate block. ❶–❸

Eating and drinking

San Pedro's **cafés** and **restaurants** have a decidedly international flavour, and most places are also excellent value for money. Vegetarians are well catered for, and there are also a few typical Guatemalan comedores in the centre of the village and by the Santiago dock. For a **drink**, there's a cluster of places close to the Pana dock: *D'Noz* is a great place to hear some electronic tunes; they also show a **film** nightly at 7.30pm. Just behind here the *Alegre Pub* has Premiership football and English grub like fish 'n' chips. *D'Noz* also organize DJ-driven **parties** on full moons and other occasions.

Freedom turn left at Panajachel dock. Popular at all times of day, the place has an inexpensive menu and great views of the lake from its terrace. Live music some nights.
El Iglú between the docks. Good ice cream and shakes, though the coffee is very pricey.
Matahari turn right from the Santiago dock. The best comedor in San Pedro, this clean place has good Guatemalan grub and amazingly good fries.
Munchies between the docks. Veggie stronghold where you can tuck into a healthy soup or salad in a pleasant patio setting
Nick's Place by the Panajachel dock. Popular, locally owned restaurant. Superb-value menu (most meals cost around US$2) and a fine lakefront location.
Pinocchio between the two docks. Pretty decent Italian, where you can feast on lake fish, pizza or pasta in a pretty garden setting.

San Juan La Laguna

From San Pedro it's just 2km to **SAN JUAN LA LAGUNA**, at the back of a sweeping bay surrounded by shallow beaches. The village specializes in the weaving of *petates*, mats made from lake reeds, and there are two large weaving co-ops, Las Artesanías de San Juan, signposted on the left from the dock and the Asociación de Mujeres de Color, on the right – both have plenty of goods for sale. Next to the latter is the simple *Hospedaje Estrella del Lago* (❶–❷) with eleven secure rooms (and eleven more on the way), none with private bath, and a guests' kitchen. Uphill, in the centre of the village, you'll find a quiet comedor, *Restaurant Chi'nimaya*, and almost next door, a shrine to **Maximón** (see p.190), the evil saint, dressed in local garb, though this shrine attracts fewer visitors here than those elsewhere, so you may want to bring him some liquor or a cigar. Regular pick-ups run between San Pedro and San Juan. Leaving the village by footpath, you'll pass below the Tz'utujil settlement of **San Pablo La Laguna**, perched high above the lake a fifteen-minute walk away, and connected to the Carratera Interamericana by a steep road. After this, the villages start shrinking considerably.

San Marcos La Laguna

Guatemala's premier New Age centre, the tiny village of **SAN MARCOS LA LAGUNA**, is about a two-hour walk from San Pedro, or a twenty-minute ride in one of the regular pick-ups that bump along the road between the villages. The land close to the lakeshore – densely wooded with banana, mango, jocote and avocado trees – is where San Marcos' bohemian hotels and guesthouses have been sensitively established, while the Maya village is centred on higher ground away from the shore. Relationships between the two communities remain a little distant. Apart from a huge new stone **church**, built to replace a colonial original destroyed in the 1976 earthquake, there are no sights in the Maya village.

San Marcos has a decidedly tranquil appeal – there's little in the way of partying and no bar scene at all. One of the main draws is the *Las Pirámides* yoga and meditation retreat (see opposite), and there's a surplus of auxiliary practitioners and masseurs, plus the requisite organic bakery and a healing centre – San Marcos Holistic Center – offering acupuncture, reflexology and natural remedies; it's located next to the *Unicornio*. There's excellent swimming from a number of wooden jetties by the lakeshore, and a mesmerizing view of Atitlán's three volcanoes, including a perspective of the double-coned summit of Tolimán, plus glimpses of the grey 3975m peak of Acatenango, over 50km to the east.

Accommodation

To **get to** any of the places listed below, get off at the westernmost of San Marcos' two docks, where *Posada Schumann* and *Las Pirámides* have jetties (look out for the mini pyramid): all accommodation is signposted from there. Avoid the *Hotel Jivana*.

Aaculaax ⓔniecolass@hotmail.com. An astonishing labour of love, this fantasy ecohotel was built by an (eccentric) German visionary craftsman from thousands of recycled bottles and wood, with stained glass detailing and giant glass butterflies doubling as lampshades. It has to be seen. ❹

Hotel La Paz ⓣ702 9168. Comfortable, rustic rooms and an excellent dorm (US$4.50) set in spacious grounds, and home cooking is often available. The Guatemalan owner once ran a restaurant in Liverpool. ❹

Hotel San Marcos Cheap, bare but clean rooms in a concrete block, none with private bath. ❷

El Paco Real ⓣ918 7215. Attractive, well-constructed stone bungalows, some sleeping up to four, set in a shady garden. No private bathrooms, but the communal facilities are kept spotless, and there's a good in-house Mexican restaurant (closed Mon). ❸

Las Pirámides ⓣ205 7151, ⓦwww.laspiramides.com.gt. Meditation retreat centre set in leafy grounds, where monthly courses beginning the day after the full moon (though you can also enrol on a daily or weekly basis) include hatha yoga, healing and meditation techniques, plus days of fasting and silence and plenty of esoteric pursuits. All accommodation is in comfortable pyramid cabañas, and there's delicious vegetarian food. US$10–12 per person per day includes all courses but not food. ❹

Posada Schumann ⓣ202 2216. Wonderful solar-powered lakeside hotel with rooms and stone bungalows (sleeping between two and six); numbers 8 and 10 have stupendous volcano views. There's also a great restaurant (the US$10 dinner includes a drink, breakfast is US$3.50), a private wooden jetty for sunbathing and swimming, and Maya-style sauna. ❹–❺

Unicornio ⓦwww.hotelunicornio.com. Inexpensive, idiosyncratic English-Guatemalan-owned place with small A-frame huts and rooms (none with bath) in a nice garden, with a kitchen and sauna. ❷

Eating

There's a limited choice of places to eat in San Marcos. Inexpensive Guatemalan food is available at the *Comedor Marquensita* and *Sonoma* close to the church and great meat dishes at *Jeff's Burger Shack* on the road to San Pablo. Closer to the lakeshore, you can get wonderful Italian and Latin American food at *Il Giardino*, while some of the hotels have restaurants attached, with superb Mexican food at *El Paco Real*. *Posada Schumann* also has a good menu. There's also excellent healthy eating (including delicious sandwiches and salads) at *Las Pirámides*, and the fairly expensive French-owned *Tul y Sol* right by the lake has views, good cooking and fine sandwiches.

Tzununá to Paxanax

Continuing east from San Marcos, it's about 3km to the next lakeside village, **TZUNUNÁ**, where the women still sometimes run from oncoming strangers, sheltering behind the nearest tree in giggling groups. Here the road indisputably ends, giving way to a narrow path cut out of the steep hillside, which can be a little hard to follow as it descends to cross small streams and then climbs up again around the rocky outcrops. The next, slightly ragged-looking place is **JAIBALITO**, an isolated lakeside settlement nestling between soaring *milpa*-clad slopes. The village remains resolutely Kaqchikel – very little Spanish is spoken, and few women have ever journeyed much beyond Lago de Atitlán – though the opening of two new hotels means that outside influence is growing. Almost lost amongst the coffee bushes, 70m north of the main pathway, the Norwegian-owned *Vulcano Lodge* (ⓣ410 2237, ⓔvulcanolodge@hotmail.com) occupies a tranquil spot, though it does not have lake views, with a well-tended garden bursting with flowering shrubs and scattered with sun loungers and hammocks. There's good European and Guatemalan food in the restaurant and a choice of spotless, comfortable rooms (❹) or a very stylish two-bedroomed suite (❻).

Heading west, it's a steep five-minute walk up along the cliff path to the spectacularly sited *La Casa del Mundo* (ⓣ218 2237, ⓦwww.lacasademundo.com; ❹–❺). It's an astounding place, perched above the lake water, the culmination of twelve years' work by the warm American host family, with a range of atmospheric accommodation including budget room, doubles (rooms 1 and 3 have the best views), detached stone cabins and a suite. There's also a great restaurant (dinner is US$9 per person) and guests can rent kayaks and use the lakeside hot tub (US$35 for up to 10 people). From Jaibalito it's around an hour to Santa Cruz along a glorious, easy-to-follow path that parallels the steep hillside. Set well back from the lake on a shelf 100m or so above the water, **SANTA CRUZ LA LAGUNA** is the largest in this line of villages with a population of around 4000. If you arrive here by boat it may appear to be just a collection of **hotels**, as the village is much higher up above the lake. There isn't much to see in the village, apart from a fine sixteenth-century church, and most people spend their time by the lake swimming or just chilling out with a book. Alternatively, there's some excellent **hiking**, including a walk to a waterfall above the village football pitch, and another to Sololá along a spectacular path that takes around three hours.

On the shore, you'll find the *Iguana Perdida* (Ⓔlaiguanaperdida@itelgua.com; ❷–❸), owned by an English-American couple, with one of the most convivial atmospheres in Lago de Atitlán. The rooms are fairly basic, with dorms (US$3), singles and twin-bedded doubles (the "Jerry Garcia" room has its own balcony with views) but it's the gorgeous, peaceful site overlooking the lake that really makes this place. Dinner (US$4.50) is a wholesome three-course communal affair. The *Iguana* is also home to a professional PADI **dive school**, ATI Divers (in Panajachel Ⓣ762 2646). Next door is another good place, the slightly more expensive and comfortable *Hotel Arca de Noé* (Ⓣ306 4352, Ⓔthearca@yahoo.com; ❸–❺), with attractive rooms, most with private bath, and uninterrupted views of the lake from the spacious terraced gardens, plus good home cooking.

Beyond Santa Cruz a lakeside path wriggles past luxury villas for a kilometre to the small bay of **Paxanax**, ringed by about twenty holiday homes, where a superb-value American-owned luxury guesthouse, *Villa Sumaya* (Ⓣ762 0488, Ⓦwww.villasumaya.com; ❺), enjoys stupendous lake views. All the seven rooms and one suite have plush beds, stylish decor and balconies with hammocks, and there's a restaurant, a hot tub and sauna.

Quetzaltenango and around

To the west of Lago de Atitlán, the highlands rise to form a steep-sided ridge topped by a string of forested peaks. On the far side of this is the **Quetzaltenango basin**, a sweeping expanse of level ground that forms the natural hub of the western highlands. It was here that the conquistador Pedro de Alvarado first struggled up into the highlands and came upon the abandoned city of Xelajú (near Quetzaltenango), entering it without any resistance. Six days later he and his troops fought the K'iche' in a decisive battle on the nearby plain, massacring the Maya warriors. Legend has it that Alvarado himself killed the K'iche' king, Tecún Umán, in hand-to-hand combat.

Guatemala's second city, **QUETZALTENANGO** (**Xela**, pronounced "Shay-La"), has the subdued provincial atmosphere that you might expect in the capital of the highlands, its edges gently giving way to corn and maize fields. Bizarre though it may seem, the city's character and appearance is vaguely reminiscent of an industrial town in northern England – grey, cool and culturally quite conservative. Ringed by high mountains and distinctly chilly in the early mornings, the city wakes slowly, only getting going once the warmth of the sun has made its mark. There aren't that many sights in the city itself, but if you have an hour or two to spare then it's worth wandering through the streets, soaking up the atmosphere and taking in the museum in the **Casa de la Cultura**.

Some history

Under colonial rule, Quetzaltenango flourished as a commercial centre, benefiting from the fertility of the surrounding farmland and good connections to the port at

Champerico. When the prospect of independence eventually arose, the city was set on deciding its own destiny and Quetzaltenango declared itself the capital of the independent state of **Los Altos**. The separatist movement was unsuccessful, however, and the city has had to accept provincial status ever since, although during the coffee boom at the end of the last century Quetzaltenango's wealth and population grew so rapidly that it began to rival the capital in status.

All this, however, came to an abrupt end when the city was almost totally destroyed by the massive **1902 earthquake**. Rebuilding took place in a mood of high optimism: all the grand Neoclassical architecture dates from this period. A new rail line was built to connect the city with the coast, but after this was washed out in 1932–33 the town never regained its former glory, gradually falling further and further behind the capital.

Today Quetzaltenango has all the trappings of wealth and self-importance: the grand architecture, the great banks, and a list of famous sons. But it is completely devoid of the rampant energy that so defines the capital, retaining a calm and dignified air, while its inhabitant Quetzaltecos have a reputation for formality and politeness.

Arrival and information

Unhelpfully for the traveller, virtually all buses arrive and depart Quetzaltenango from nowhere near the centre of town. If you arrive by **second-class bus** you'll almost certainly end up in the chaotic **Minerva Bus Terminal** on the city's north-western edge. Walk 300m through the market stalls to 4 C and catch a microbus marked "Parque" to get to the plaza from there. Three main companies operate **first-class buses** to and from the capital, each with their own private terminal: the

Líneas Américas terminal is just off Calzada Independencia at 7 Av 3–33, Zona 2 (ⓣ761 2063), Alamo is at 14 Av 5–15, Zona 3 (ⓣ767 7117), and Galgos is at C Rodolfo Robles 17–43, Zona 1 (ⓣ761 2248).

Quetzaltenango is divided up into **zones**, although for the most part you'll only be interested in zonas 1 and 3, which contain the central plaza area and the Minerva Bus Terminal respectively. When it comes to **getting around**, most places are within easy walking distance (except the terminal). To get to the Minerva terminal there are regular microbuses from the junction of 4 C and 13 Av, at the back of the Pasaje Enríquez. The **tourist office**, on the main plaza (Mon–Fri 8am–1pm & 2–5pm, Sat 8am–1pm; ⓣ761 4931), has maps and local information. Xela is also an excellent place to **study Spanish**, with dozens of language schools (see p.149), many of a high standard.

Accommodation

Most **accommodation** in Quetzaltenango tends to be a little dark and old-fashioned, but a few bright new places have opened in recent years. Once you've made it to the plaza, all the places listed below are within a ten-minute walk.

Casa Argentina 12 Diagonal 8–37 ⓣ761 2470. Xela's definitive budget choice, with a myriad (43 at the last count) of comfortable single rooms, a large dorm (US$2.50 a bed), a kitchen, sun terrace, and a café. It's also the home of Quetzaltrekkers (see p.217). ❷

Casa Kaehler 13 Av 3–33 ⓣ761 2091. Attractive guesthouse with seven spotless rooms (one with bathroom) set around a patio. Good value, secure and always popular. ❸

Casa Mañen 9 Av 4–11 ⓣ765 0786, ⓦwww.comeseeit.com. Immaculate American-owned boutique-style hotel, that's good value for money. Spacious rooms with fireplaces and cable TV, plus two huge suites with sofas and fridges. Wonderful rooftop terrace and a large breakfast is included. Rooms ❼, suites ❾

Hostal Don Diego 7 C 15–20 ⓣ761 6497, ⓔdondiegoxela@hotmail.com. Good new option with a pleasant courtyard, guests' kitchen and 12 basic cheap rooms. Very inexpensive weekly and monthly rates. ❷

Hotel Casa Florencia 12 Av 3–61 ⓣ761 2811, ⓦwww.xelapages.com/florencia/index.htm. Just north of the main plaza, this place has nine pretty comfortable, large rooms with wood-panelled walls and fitted carpets; all have private bath. ❹

Hotel Modelo 14 Av A 2–31 ⓣ761 2529, ⓕ763 1376. A fine mid-range choice, this historic hotel has a civilized, classy air. The rooms are spacious though tend to lack natural light. Most face a small garden courtyard, and there are cheaper options in a separate annexe. ❹–❺

Hotel Virginia 11 Av 8–11 ⓣ761 7355. New place where the good-value rooms have nice wooden beds and decent mattresses, desks and TV; though the design of the building – it's above a basement car park – is bizarre. ❺

Pensión Andina 8 Av 6–07 ⓣ761 4012. Very cheap, bare and fairly clean rooms – some have private bath (hot water 6–9am only). ❶–❷

Pensión Bonifaz northeast corner of the plaza ⓣ761 2182, ⓔbonifaz@intel.net.gt. The hotel, founded in 1935, has character, comfort and a well-regarded (though overpriced) restaurant. Retains an air of faded upper-class pomposity, but still one of the better places in town, and has a pool. ❼

The City

Xela's hub is its central plaza, officially known as the **Parque Centro América**, whose mass of mock-Greek columns and imposing bank facades exude an atmosphere of dignified calm. There's none of the buzz of business that you'd expect, except on the first Sunday of the month when the plaza hosts a good artesanía market with blankets, basketry and piles of típica weavings for sale. On the west side is Bancafé and the impressive but crumbling **Pasaje Enríquez**, planned as a sparkling arcade of upmarket shops but left derelict for many years, though it has now been partially revived. Inside you'll find the *Salón Tecún Bar*, the hippest place in town, and a good place for meeting other travellers and locals.

At the bottom end of the plaza, next to the tourist office, is the **Casa de la Cultura** (Mon–Fri 8am–noon & 2–6pm, Sat 9am–1pm; US$0.75), the city's most

blatant impersonation of a Greek temple. On the ground floor you'll find a display of assorted documents, photographs and pistols from the liberal revolution and the State of Los Altos (see p.213), along with sports trophies and a room dedicated to the marimba. Upstairs there are some modest Maya artefacts, historic photographs and a bizarre natural history room. Amongst the dusty displays of stuffed bats, pickled snakes and animal skins are the macabre remains of assorted freaks of nature, including a sheep born with eight legs and a four-horned goat.

Away from the plaza, the city spreads out, a mixture of the old and new. The commercial heart is 14 Avenida, complete with pizza restaurants and neon signs. At the top of 14 Avenida, at the junction with 1 Calle, stands the **Teatro Municipal**, another spectacular Neoclassical edifice. Further afield, Xela's role as a regional centre of trade is more in evidence. Out in Zona 3 is the **Mercado La Democracia**, a vast covered complex with stalls spilling out onto the streets. There's another Greek-style structure right out on the edge of town, the **Minerva Temple**, built to honour President Barrios's enthusiasm for education and making no pretence at serving any practical purpose. Beside the temple is the fairly miserable **zoo** (Tues–Sun 9am–5pm; free) and a children's playground. Below the temple are the sprawling **market** and **Minerva Bus Terminal**, and it's here that you can really sense the city's role as the centre of the western highlands, with *indígena* traders from all over the area doing business. Just behind the market, the spanking new shopping plaza **La Pradera** boasts over 100 stores and a multiplex cinema.

Eating, drinking and entertainment

Quetzaltenango has a fairly moderate choice of restaurants, suiting its character as a fairly modest, unpretentious city. Almost nowhere opens before 8am in the morning, so forget early **breakfasts**. After dark, things are generally quiet in the week, but there are a number of lively **bars** that fill up at the weekend, plus a small **club** scene. The most popular drinking den in town is *Salón Tecún*, inside the Pasaje Enríquez on the west side of the plaza, with good tunes and a raucous buzz most evenings. The main area for nightlife in central Quetzaltenango is 14 Av A where there are several bars, some with dancing, including *El Duende* (Thursdays is salsa and merengue night) and *Fratta's* (Fridays and Saturdays for Latin house and groove). If electronic dance is more your scene, the excellent *Hektisch* club at 15 Av 3–64 is an "after hours" place that plays fearsome techno and trance till dawn. For a quieter drink, try *Bajo La Luna* on 8 Av and 4 C.

Quetzaltenango is a good place to catch the **movies**. In the centre of town Cine Paraíso, 1 C 12–20, shows a variety of interesting Latin and western films, while there's a new multi-screen by La Pradera mall near the Minerva terminal. To find **what's on** in Xela, pick up a copy of the free listings magazine, *Fin de Semana*, available in many of the popular bars and cafés.

Bake Shop 18 Av and 1 C. Fine Mennonite-run bakery with tasty pastries and breads that are used by Xela's best restaurants. Tues & Fri only, 9am–6pm.

Blue Angel Video Café 7 C 15–19. Popular, sociable hangout with a daily video programme; plus great salads and sandwiches.

Café Baviera 5 C 12–50, a block from the plaza. Anachronistic, pine-panelled coffeehouse, with photographic nostalgia on the walls. This place is mainly about the coffee, but the cakes and sandwiches are fine too.

Cardinali's 14 Av 3–41. Fine, reliable Italian food (and huge portions) at reasonable prices. For pizza delivery call ⓣ761 0924.

Casa Babilón 13 Av and 5 C. Friendly French-Guatemalan-owned place that dispenses wonderful, very filling sandwiches, tacos and crepes. Recommended. Closed Sun.

La Luna 8 Av 4–11. Crammed with curios and antiques, *La Luna* has wonderful drinking chocolate with seven different varieties, though the food is mediocre.

Pensión Bonifaz in the hotel of the same name, corner of the plaza. Worth a visit, as it's a pleasingly civilized spot for a cup of tea, a cake, and the chance to rub shoulders with the town's elite, though the restaurant is expensive and the cooking only average.

El Rincón de los Antojitos 15 Av and 5. Another French-Guatemalan place, this friendly little restaurant has specialities such as *hilachas* (beef in tomato sauce) and some French dishes.

Royal Paris 14 Av A 3–06. Authentic, enjoyable French-owned restaurant with a winsome menu of really flavoursome dishes, plus snacks like *croque monsieur*. Moderate prices given the quality of the cuisine.

Sagrado Corazón 9 C 9–00. Agreeable comedor, with great-value breakfasts, a huge US$2.50 set lunch and friendly service.

La Taquería 8 Av 5 C. Enjoyable Mexican food, moderately priced and fairly authentic.

Ut'z Hua 12 Av & 3 C. Excellent choice specializing in Guatemalan cuisine, including *jocon*, *quichom* and seven kinds of soup. Always a daily special too.

Listings

Banks and exchange There are several banks on the main plaza that will change travellers' cheques including Banrural (Mon–Fri 9am–7pm, Sat 9am–1pm) with a MasterCard/Cirrus ATM, and Banco Industrial (Mon–Fri 9.30am–6.30pm, Sat 9.30am–1.30pm) with a Visa/Plus ATM.

Bike and car rental Vrisa bookstore (see below) has bikes for US$3.50 per day, US$9 per week and US$19 per month.

Bookstore Vrisa, 15 Av 3–64, has over 5000 used titles. El Libro Abierto, 15 Av A 1–56, Zona 1, has political, social and anthropological books on Guatemala, guidebooks and some used titles.

Consulates Mexican Consulate, 9 Av 6–19, Zona 1 (Mon–Fri 9am–noon & 2–3pm). Most nationalities do not need a visa or tourist card, but if you do, hand in your paperwork in the morning and collect it in the afternoon.

Email and Internet access There are at least two dozen places in Xela where you can surf the

Net, including Maya Communications, above Salón Tecún in the Plaza Central, and Alternativa's at 16 Av 3–35, Zona 3 (all open until 9pm or later; around US$1.25/hr).
Laundry MiniMax, 4 Av and 1 C, Zona 1 (Mon–Sat 7am–7pm); US$2.50 for a full-load wash and dry.
Medical care Hospital San Rafael, 9 C 10–41, Zona 1 ⓣ761 4414.
Post office 15 Av and 4 C.
Telephone Alternativa's (see "Internet" above) has the best rates: webcalls on clear lines are US$0.10 per minute to the USA and Canada, US$0.25 to Europe. You'll pay much more at the main Telgua office, 15 Av and 4 C.
Tours and travel agencies Adrenalina Tours, inside Pasaje Enríquez, Plaza Central (ⓣ761 4509, ⓦwww.adrenalinatours.com), offers various tours of the region around Xela including trips to Zunil and Fuentes Georginas, San Andrés Xecul, shuttle buses, volcano climbs (Volcán Santa María costs from US$15 per person) and sells airline tickets. Casa Iximulew, 15 Av and 5 C, Zona 1 (ⓣ761 5057, ⓦwww.mayaexplor.com), run organized trips to most of the volcanoes and sights around Xela. Quetzaltrekkers inside *Casa Argentina* (see "Accommodation", p.214; ⓣ761 4520, ⓦwww.quetzalventures.com) offers cultural tours and hiking trips to volcanoes with all profits going to a charity for street children.

Around Quetzaltenango

It's easy to spend a week or two exploring this part of the country – making day-trips to the markets and fiestas, basking in hot springs, or trekking in the mountains – and Quetzaltenango is the obvious place to base yourself, with bus connections to all parts of the western highlands. The valley is heavily populated and there are numerous smaller towns and villages in the surrounding hills, mostly indigenous agricultural communities and weaving centres. The area also offers excellent **hiking**. The most obvious climbs are **Volcán Santa María**, towering above Quetzaltenango itself, and up **Volcán Chicabal** to a sublime crater lake. Straddling the coast road to the south is **Zunil** and the hot springs of **Fuentes Georginas**, overshadowed by breathtaking volcanic peaks. To the north are **Totonicapán**, capital of the department of the same name, and **San Francisco El Alto**, a small town perched on an outcrop overlooking the valley. Beyond that lies **Momostenango**, the country's principal wool-producing centre and a centre of Maya culture. For organized **tours** to all these places, contact the travel agents in Quetzaltenango listed on above.

Volcán Santa María

Due south of Quetzaltenango, the perfect cone of **Volcán Santa María** rises to a height of 3772m. From the town only the peak is visible, but seen from the rest of the valley the entire cone seems to lord it over everything around. The view from the top is, as you might expect, truly spectacular, with nine other cones visible on clear days, including the smoking summit of Santiaguito directly below. It's possible to climb the volcano as a day-trip, but to really see it at its best you need to be on top at dawn, either sleeping on the freezing peak, or camping at the site below and climbing the final section in the dark by torchlight. Either way you need to bring enough food and water for the entire trip; and make sure you're acclimatized to the altitude for a few days before attempting the climb.

Laguna Chicabal

Southeast of Xela, the road to the coast passes through a gusty pass before winding down to **SAN MARTÍN SACATEPÉQUEZ**, also known as San Martín Chile Verde, an isolated Mam-speaking village set in the base of a natural bowl, 23km away. The men of San Martín wear a particularly unusual costume, a long white tunic with thin red stripes, ornately embroidered around the cuffs and tied around the middle with a red sash; the women wear beautiful red *huipiles* and blue *cortes*.

A two-hour hike from San Martín brings you to **Laguna Chicabal**, a spectacular lake set in the cone of the Chicabal volcano that is the site of Maya religious rituals. To get there, get the bus to drop you off the stop for "la laguna", head down to a small bridge, then uphill to a yellow-and-red church, where you bear left. The dirt track climbs steeply uphill for 40 minutes before levelling out before the entrance to the Chicabal reserve (US$1.80 entrance) where there's a football field and some *palapas*, each with four bunk beds (❶), a comedor and a shop.

A signposted route then ascends again through a forest, winding around the cone to the rim, from where there are two routes to the lake: either to the left via a *mirador* (from where there are stunning views of the emerald lake, and the volcanoes of Santa María and Santiaguito, Tajamulco and Tacaná), or alternatively via precipitous steps straight down to the shore. At the water's edge, you come into a different world, eerily still, disturbed only by the soft buzz of a hummingbird's wings or the screech of parakeets. Small sandy bays bear charred crosses and bunches of fresh-cut flowers mark the site of ritual sacrifice. On May 3 every year *costumbristas* gather here for ceremonies to mark the fiesta of the Holy Cross: at any time, but on this date especially, you should take care not to disturb any rituals that might be taking place. You are welcome to camp at the shore, though you'll have to bring all your own supplies.

Buses run between the Minerva terminal in Quetzaltenango and Coatepeque (for the coast) passing San Martín every 30 minutes or so. The journey time is 40 minutes; the last returns from San Martín about 6pm.

Zunil and Fuentes Georginas

Ten kilometres south of Quetzaltenango is the traditional village of **ZUNIL**, a vegetable-growing market town surrounded by steep hills and a sleeping volcano. The plaza is dominated by a beautiful white colonial church with a richly decorated facade; inside an intricate silver altar is protected behind bars. The women of Zunil wear vivid purple *huipiles* and carry bright shawls – the plaza is awash with colour during the Monday market. Just below the plaza is a **textile co-operative**, where hundreds of women market their beautiful weavings. Zunil is also one of the few remaining places where **Maximón** (or San Simón), the evil saint, is still worshipped. In the face of disapproval from the Catholic Church, the Maya are reluctant to display their Judas, who also goes by the name Alvarado, but his image is usually paraded through the streets during Holy Week, dressed in Western clothes and smoking a cigar. Virtually any child in town will take you to his abode for a quetzal.

In the hills above, 8km from Zunil, sit the **Fuentes Georginas** (US$1.25), a spectacular set of luxuriant hot springs. Pick-up trucks from the plaza in Zunil are officially set at US$5 for the trip, no matter how many passengers hitch a ride – it's an exhilarating journey up a smooth paved road which switchbacks through magnificent volcanic scenery. The return trip is another US$5. Surrounded by fresh green ferns, thick moss and lush forest, the baths are sublime, and to top it all there's a restaurant and a well-stocked bar (with decent wine) beside the main pool. It's easy to spend quite some time here soaking up the scene, though in recent years the hot spring water that feeds the pools has cooled somewhat, perhaps due to a nearby hydroelectric power scheme. Rustic stone **bungalows** are available for the night (no phone; ❸) complete with bathtub, two double beds, fireplace and barbecue.

Buses to Zunil run from Quetzaltenango's Minerva Bus Terminal every half-hour or so, though some also pass closer to the centre of town, stopping beside the Shell gas station at 10 C and 9 Av in Zona 1. The last bus back from Zunil leaves at around 6.30pm. Shuttle-bus trips (US$5 return) organized by Adrenalina Tours (see overleaf) leave Xela for Zunil and Fuentes Georginas daily.

San Francisco El Alto

The small market town of **SAN FRANCISCO EL ALTO** overlooks the Quetzaltenango valley from a lovely hillside setting, and it's worth a visit for the view alone, with the great plateau stretching out below and the cone of Volcán Santa María on the horizon. Another good reason for visiting is the **Friday market**, possibly the biggest in Central America and attended by traders from every corner of

Guatemala – many arrive the night before, and some start selling by candlelight from as early as 4am. Throughout the morning a steady stream of buses and trucks fill the town to bursting; by noon the market is at its height, buzzing with activity.

The town is set into the hillside, with steep cobbled streets connecting the different levels. Two areas in particular are monopolized by specific trades. At the very top is an open field used as an **animal market**, where everything from pigs to parrots changes hands. The teeth and tongues of animals are inspected by the buyers, and at times the scene degenerates into a chaotic wrestling match, with pigs and men rolling in the dirt. Below this is the town's plaza, dominated by textiles. On the lower level, the streets are filled with vegetables, fruit, pottery, furniture, cheap comedores, and plenty more. These days most of the stalls deal in imported denim, but under the arches and in the covered area opposite the church you'll find a superb selection of traditional cloth. For a really good **photographic** angle and for views of the market and the surrounding countryside, pay the church caretaker a quetzal and climb up to the **church roof**. By early afternoon the numbers start to thin out, and by sunset it's all over – until the following Friday.

There are plenty of **buses** from Quetzaltenango to San Francisco, 16km away, leaving every twenty minutes or so from the Minerva terminal; the first is at 6am, and the last bus back leaves at about 5pm (45min).

Momostenango

A further 22km from San Francisco, down a paved road that continues over a ridge behind the town then drops down through thick pine forests, is **MOMOSTENANGO**, a small, isolated town and the centre of wool production in the highlands. Momostecos travel throughout the country peddling their blankets, scarves and rugs – years of experience have made them experts in the hard sell and given them a sharp eye for tourists. The wool is also used in a range of traditional costumes, including the short skirts worn by the men of Nahualá, San Antonio Palopó and the jackets of Sololá. The ideal place to buy Momostenango blankets is in the **Sunday market**, which fills the town's two plazas.

A visit at this time will also give you a glimpse of Momostenango's other feature: its rigid adherence to tradition. Opposite the entrance to the church, people make offerings of incense and alcohol on a small fire, muttering their appeals to the gods. The town is famous for this unconventional folk-Catholicism, and it has been claimed that there are as many as three hundred Maya **shamans** working here. Momostenango's religious calendar, like that of only one or two other villages, is still based on the 260-day *Tzolkin* year – made up of thirteen twenty-day months – that has been in use since ancient times.

As a visitor it's best to call on Momostenango for the market, unless you can coincide your visit with the start of the Maya new year or the fiesta on August 1. If you decide to stay for a day or two then you can take a walk to the *riscos*, a set of bizarre sandstone pillars, or beyond to the **hot springs** of Pala Chiquito, about 3km away to the north. The best place **to stay** is the *Hotel Estiver*, 1 C 4–15, Zona 1 (☎736 5036; ❷), which has clean rooms, some with private bathrooms, great views from the roof and safe parking. For **eating**, there are plenty of small comedores on the main plaza or try the one inside the *Hospedaje Paglóm*. There's a Bancafé **bank** at 1 C and 1 Av (Mon–Fri 9am–4pm) that accepts Visa, cash and travellers' cheques.

Buses run here from the Minerva terminal in Quetzaltenango, passing through Cuatro Caminos and (most) via San Francisco El Alto on the way every thirty minutes from 6am to 5pm (1hr 15min) and from Momostenango between 6am and 4pm. On Sundays, there are more services.

Totonicapán

Capital of one of the smaller departments, **TOTONICAPÁN** is reached down a road leading east from Cuatro Caminos. Surrounded by rolling hills and pine forests, the town stands at the heart of a heavily populated and intensely farmed little region. The valley has always held out against outside influence, for years shut off in a world of its own, and it's still a quiet place, ruffled only by the Tuesday and Saturday **markets**, which fill the two plazas. Until fairly recently a highly ornate traditional costume was worn here, but this has now disappeared and the town has instead become one of the chief centres of commercial weaving. To take a closer look at the work of local artisans, head for the town's visitor centre, the **Casa de la Cultura**, on 8 Av 2–17 (Mon–Sat 9.30am–5pm), which organizes good, but slightly pricey tours of the town (US$6–14; printed information available in English) and classes in weaving and wood carving (US$20–48 per person, depending on class size); the funds raised help benefit the community.

There are good connections between Totonicapán and Quetzaltenango, with **buses** shuttling back and forth every half-hour or so. Totonicapán is very quiet after dark, but if you want to stay, the best **hotel** is the *Hospedaje San Miguel*, a block from the plaza at 8 Av and 3 C (☎766 1452; ❷–❸): it's pretty comfortable and some rooms have bathrooms, but beware price rises before market days.

Huehuetenango

In the corner of a small agricultural plain, 5km from the Carretera Interamericana at the foot of the mighty Cuchumatanes mountain range, lies **HUEHUETENANGO**, capital of the department of the same name. Though Huehue is the focus of trade and transport for a vast area, its atmosphere is provincial and relaxed. Before the arrival of the Spanish, it was the site of one of the residential suburbs that surrounded the Mam capital of Zaculeu, and under colonial rule it became a small regional centre with little to offer other than a steady trickle of silver and a stretch or two of grazing land. The supply of silver dried up long ago, but other minerals are still mined, and coffee and sugar have been added to the area's produce.

Today's Huehuetenango has two quite distinct functions – and two contrasting halves – each serving a separate section of the population. The large majority of the people are *ladino*, and for them Huehuetenango is an unimportant regional centre far from the hub of things. Here the mood is summed up in the unhurried atmosphere of the attractive **plaza** at the heart of the *ladino* half of town, where shaded

walkways are surrounded by administrative offices. Overlooking it, perched above the pavements, are a shell-shaped bandstand, a clock tower and a grandiose Neoclassical church, a solid whitewashed structure with a facade that's crammed with Doric pillars and Grecian urns.

A few blocks to the east, the town's atmosphere could hardly be more different. Around the **market**, the hub of the Maya part of town, the streets are crowded with traders, travellers from Mexico and all over Central America, and the odd drunk. This part of Huehuetenango, centred on 1 Avenida, is always alive with activity, its streets packed with people from every corner of the department and littered with rotten vegetables.

Arrival, information and accommodation

Huehue is fairly small so you shouldn't have any problems finding your way around, particularly once you've located the plaza. You'll arrive at the chaotic, scruffy **bus terminal** halfway between the Carretera Interamericana and town. Minibuses make constant trips between the town centre and the bus terminal.

There's a **post office** at 2 C 3–54 (Mon–Fri 8am–4.30pm), a **Telgua** office at 4 Av 6–54 (7am–10pm) and several **Internet cafés**: try *Génesis* at 2 C 6–37 or *Mi Tierra* at 4 C 6–46 – both charge around US$1.25 an hour. Huehue also boasts a decent **language school** (see p.150).

Casa Blanca 7 Av 3–41 ⓣ & ⓕ769 0777. Modern mid-range hotel, built in colonial style. Many of the rooms downstairs have little natural light, but all have private bath and cable TV. There is a good restaurant and spacious garden. ❺

Hotel Central 5 Av 1–33 ⓣ764 1202. Slightly scruffy budget hotel, with largish rooms in a creaking old wooden building, plus a fantastic comedor. No singles or private baths. ❶

Hotel Mary 2 C 3–52 ⓣ764 1618, ⓕ764 7412. Centrally located with small but pleasant rooms with private shower, and loads of steaming hot water. ❷–❸

Hotel Maya 3 Av 3–55 ⓣ764 0369, ⓕ764 1622. Good-value place, with spacious if slightly spartan rooms, all with TV and bathroom. ❹

Hotel San Luis de la Sierra 2 C 7–00 ⓣ & ⓕ764 1103. Attractive modern hotel with en-suite rooms, all with cable TV; some have wonderful views of the mountains. There's ample parking and a fair restaurant. ❺

Hotel Zaculeu 5 Av 1–14 ⓣ764 1086, ⓕ764 1575. Something of an institution in Huehue, this long-running hotel has a selection of rooms – those in the old block tend to be a bit musty however, while those in the new block are more spacious (and pricey). All come with cable TV and private bath. In-house restaurant. ❹–❺

Todos Santos Inn 2 C 6–74 ⓣ764 1241. A decent, friendly budget hotel, though the rooms (some with private bath) do vary in quality – those upstairs are bright and cheery, others less well presented. The shared bathrooms are clean. Cheap rates for single travellers. ❷–❸

Eating, drinking and entertainment

Most of the better **restaurants** are in the central area around the plaza.

La Cabaña del Café 2 C 6–50. Logwood café with an excellent range of coffees (including cappuccino) and sandwiches (there's even roast beef), plus great cakes.

Café Jardín 3 C and 6 Av. Cheap, friendly place with a good US$2.50 set lunch, plus snacks and breakfasts.

La Fonda de Don Juan 2 C 5–35. Large, attractive place with gingham tablecloths, serving good (if slightly pricey) pizza, pasta and burgers.

Mi Tierra 4 C 6–46. Great little café-restaurant, set in a covered patio with a welcoming atmosphere. There's plenty of choice on the menu: *papas fritas*, fajitas, plus chicken and pork. Proper coffee is served and there's a no-smoking section. Also has Internet facilities and a good noticeboard.

Zaculeu

A few kilometres to the west of Huehuetenango are the ruins of **Zaculeu** (daily 8am–6pm; US$3), capital of the **Mam**, who were one of the principal pre-conquest highland tribes. The site includes several large temples, plazas and a ball court, but unfortunately it was restored pretty unsubtly by a latter-day colonial power: the

United Fruit Company, in 1946–47. The walls and surfaces were levelled off with a layer of thick white plaster, leaving them stark and minus the roof-combs, carvings and stucco mouldings that would have adorned the structures. Even so, Zaculeu does have a peculiar atmosphere of its own – surrounded by pines, and with fantastic views of the mountains, its grassy plazas make excellent picnic spots. There's a small **museum** on site (daily 8am–noon & 2–6pm) with examples of some of the unusual burial techniques used and some ceramics found during excavation.

The site is thought to have been a religious and administrative centre housing the elite, while the bulk of the population lived in small surrounding settlements or else scattered in the hills. Zaculeu was the hub of a large area of Mam-speakers, its boundaries reaching into the mountains as far as Todos Santos Cuchumatán. According to the records of the K'iche', a more powerful neighbouring tribe, they conquered the Mam some time between 1400 and 1475. Following the death of the K'iche' leader, Quicab, in 1475, the Mam managed to reassert their independence, but no sooner had they escaped the clutches of one expansionist empire than the Spanish arrived with a yet more brutal alternative.

Pedro de Alvarado dispatched an army under the command of his brother, Gonzalo, which was met by about five thousand Mam warriors. The Mam leader, Caibal Balam, quickly saw that his troops were no match for the Spanish and withdrew them to the safety of Zaculeu, where they were protected on three sides by deep ravines and on the other by a series of walls and ditches. The Spanish army settled outside the city and besieged the citadel for six weeks until starvation forced Caibal Balam to surrender.

To get to Zaculeu from Huehuetenango, take one of the **buses** that leave every thirty minutes close to the school from 7 Av between 2 and 3 calles – make sure it's heading for "Las Ruinas".

The Cuchumatanes

The largest non-volcanic peaks in Central America, the **Sierra de los Cuchumatanes** rise from a limestone plateau close to the Mexican border and reach their full height of over 3800m above Huehuetenango. This is magnificent mountain scenery, ranging from wild, exposed craggy outcrops to lush, tranquil river valleys. While the upper parts of the slopes are almost barren, scattered with boulders and shrivelled cypress trees, the lower levels are richly fertile and cultivated with corn, coffee and sugar. Between the peaks, in the deep-cut valleys, are hundreds of tiny villages, isolated by the enormity of the landscape.

Despite the initial devastation, the arrival of the Spanish had surprisingly little impact in these highlands and the communities here include some of the most traditional in Guatemala. A visit to the mountain villages, either for a market or fiesta (and there are plenty of both), offers one of the best opportunities to see Maya life at close quarters. In the late 1970s and early 1980s this was the scene of bitter fighting between the army and the guerrillas, a wave of violence and terror that sent thousands fleeing across the border to Mexico. Nowadays things are much calmer.

The most accessible of the villages in the vicinity, and the only one yet to receive a steady trickle of tourists, is **Todos Santos Cuchumatán**, whose horse-race fiesta on November 1 is one of the most interesting and outrageous in Guatemala. Mountain trails from Todos Santos lead to other villages, including the equally traditional pueblo of **San Juan Atitán**.

Todos Santos Cuchumatán

Spectacularly sited in its own steep-sided river valley, **TODOS SANTOS CUCHUMATÁN** is many travellers' favourite place in Guatemala. Though the beauty of the alpine surroundings is one attraction, it's the unique culture that is most memorable. The *traje* worn here is startling: the men wear red-and-white candy-striped trousers, black woollen breeches and pinstripe shirts, decorated with dayglo pink collars, while the women wear dark blue *cortes* and superbly intricate purple *huipiles*. It's the tradition and isolation that have made the village so attractive to visitors, photographers in particular, though you should be wary of taking pictures of people – particularly of children. Rumours persist locally that some foreigners steal babies, and a tragic misunderstanding led to the death of a Japanese tourist here in 2000.

The Todosanteros are some of the proudest of all Guatemala's Maya people – there is a distinctive swagger in the step of the men – and the **fiesta** (on November 1) is one of the most famous in the country, during which the village is taken over by unrestrained drinking, dancing and marimba music. The three-day event opens with an all-day horse race, and there is a massive stampede as the inebriated riders tear up the course, thrashing their horses with live chickens, their capes flowing out behind them. On the second day, "The Day of the Dead", the action moves to the cemetery, with marimba bands and drink stalls set up amongst the graves – a day of intense ritual that combines grief and celebration. By the final day of the fiesta, the streets are littered with bodies and the jail packed with brawlers. The Saturday **market**, although nothing like as riotous, also fills the village.

The village itself is pretty – a modest main street with a few shops, a plaza and a church – but is totally overshadowed by the looming presence of the Cuchumatanes mountains. Above the village – follow the track that goes up behind the *Comedor Katy* – is the small Maya site of **Tojcunanchén**, where you'll find a couple of mounds sprouting pine trees. The site is occasionally used by *costumbristas* for the ritual sacrifice of animals.

Todos Santos is home to two **language schools** (see p.150) where you can study Spanish or Mam; a percentage of the profits from both schools goes to local development projects.

Practicalities

Buses leave Huehuetenango for Todos Santos from the main bus terminal six times a day: at 5am, 7am, 10am, 1pm, 2pm and 3pm – get there early to mark your seat and buy a ticket. Some carry on through the village, heading further down the valley to Jacaltenango and pass through Todos Santos on the way back to Huehuetenango; ask around for the latest schedule.

Most places **to stay** are clustered close together just above the plaza past *Comedor Katy*. *Hotelito Todos Santos* (❷) has clean, functional tiled-floor rooms (two with bathroom); *Hospedaje Casa Familiar* (☎758 3283; ❶) has very basic but fairly clean wooden rooms and the views from the terrace café are breathtaking; while *Hotel Mam* has adequate rooms with warmish showers. *Hospedaje La Paz* (❶) and *Las Olguitas* (❶) are both extremely rough. Plenty of families rent out **rooms** too; try asking at the Spanish schools.

One of the best places **to eat** is *Comedor Katy*, where there's always something bubbling on the hearth; there's also good food at *Comedor Martita* next to *Hotel Mam*. The gringo-geared *Tzolkin* on the main street has decent breakfasts, sandwiches, pasta and pizza while the American-owned *Mountain Muse* (also known as *Rebecca's*) café-bookshop just below the plaza also has a decent menu. On the plaza there's a **post office**, and a Banrural **bank** (Mon–Fri 8.30am–5pm & Sat 9am–1pm) that will change travellers' cheques.

Though most of the fun of Todos Santos is in simply hanging out, it would be a shame not to indulge in a traditional **smoke sauna** (*chuj*) while here. Most of the guesthouses will prepare one for you. If you want to take a shirt, pair of trousers or *huipil* home with you, you'll find an excellent co-op selling quality weavings next to the *Casa Familiar*.

Walks around Todos Santos

The village of **SAN JUAN ATITÁN** is around five hours from Todos Santos across a beautiful isolated valley. Follow the path that bears up behind the *Comedor*

Katy, past the ruins and high above the village through endless muddy switchbacks until you get to the ridge overlooking the valley where, if the skies are clear, you'll be rewarded by an awesome view of the Tajumulco and Tacaná volcanoes. Take the easy-to-follow central track downhill from here past some ancient cloudforest to San Juan Atitán. There are two hospedajes (both ❶) if you want to stay, and morning **pick-ups** return to Huehue from 6am (1hr). Market days are Mondays and Thursdays.

Alternatively, you can continue west along the valley from Todos Santos to **San Martín** and on to **Jacaltenango**, a route which also offers superb views. There's a basic hospedaje (❶) in Jacaltenango, so you could stay the night and then catch a bus back to Huehuetenango in the morning. Some buses from Huehue also continue down this route.

Aguacatán

To the east of Huehuetenango, it's 22km to **AGUACATÁN**, a small agricultural town strung out along a very long main street, and the only place in the country where the Akateko and Chalchitek languages are spoken. Aguacatán's huge Sunday **market** gets under way on Saturday afternoon, when traders arrive early to claim the best sites. On Sunday morning, a steady stream of people pour into town, cramming into the market and plaza, and soon spilling out into the surrounding area. Around noon the tide turns as the crowds start to drift back to their villages, with donkeys leading their drunken drivers.

The traditional costume worn by the women of Aguacatán is unusually simple: their skirts are made of dark blue cotton and the *huipiles*, which hang loose, are decorated with bands of coloured ribbon on a plain white background. This plainness, though, is set off by the local speciality – the **cinta**, or headdress, in which they wrap their hair, an intricately embroidered piece of cloth combining blues, reds, yellows and greens.

Aguacatán's other attraction is the **source of the Río San Juan**, which emerges fresh and cool from beneath a nearby hill, making a good place for a chilly dip. To get there, walk east along the main street out of the village for about a kilometre, until you see the sign. From the centre it takes about twenty minutes.

Ten daily **buses** run from Huehuetenango to Aguacatán between 6am and about 4pm (1hr). The best **place to stay** (and eat at) is *Hotel y Restaurant San Juan* (☎766 0110; ❷–❸) two blocks north of the plaza, where there are clean tidy rooms with or without bath; they serve a mean *pollo dorado* here too. **Beyond Aguacatán** the road runs out along a ridge, with fantastic views stretching out below, eventually dropping down to the riverside town of **Sacapulas** an hour and a half away; presently there's only one bus a day heading this way, though there are regular pick-ups.

West to the Mexican border

From Huehuetenango the Carretera Interamericana runs for 79km to the Mexican border at **La Mesilla**. There are buses every thirty minutes between 5am and 6pm (2hr). If you get stuck at the border there's **accommodation** at the *Hotel Maricruz* (❷), a clean place with private bathrooms and a restaurant, or the cheaper *Hospedaje Marisol* (❷). The two sets of customs and *migración* are 3km apart, connected by shared (colectivo) taxis. At Ciudad Cuauhtémoc on the Mexican side you can pick up buses to **Comitán** (1hr 15min) and even direct to **San Cristóbal de Las Casas** (2hr 30min). Heading into Guatemala, the last bus leaves La Mesilla for Huehuetenango at around 5.30pm.

2.3

The Pacific coast

Beneath the chain of volcanoes that bounds the southern side of the highlands is a strip of sweltering, low-lying land some 300km long and 50km wide, known by Guatemalans simply as **La Costa Sur**. This featureless yet supremely fertile coastal plain – once a wilderness of swamp, forest and savanna – is today a land of vast fincas, scattered with uninteresting commercial towns and small, ramshackle seaside resorts.

The **Pacific coast** was once as rich in wildlife as the jungles of Petén, but while Petén has lain relatively undisturbed, the coast has been ravaged by development. Its large-scale agriculture – sugar cane, palm oil, cotton and rubber plantations – accounts for a substantial proportion of the country's exports. Only in some isolated sections, where mangrove swamps have been spared the plough, can you still get a sense of the maze of tropical vegetation that once covered it. The **Monterrico Reserve** is the most accessible protected area, a swampy refuge for sea turtles, iguanas, crocodiles and an abundance of bird life.

As for the archeological sites, they too have largely disappeared, though you can glimpse the impressive art of the **Pipil** around the town of **Santa Lucía Cotzumalguapa**. Here, a few small ceremonial centres, almost lost in fields of sugar cane, reveal a wealth of carvings, some of them still regularly used for religious rituals. The one site that ranks with those elsewhere in the country is **Takalik Abaj**, whose ruins are worth a detour on your way to or from Mexico, or as a day-trip from Quetzaltenango.

The main attraction should be the **beach**, but as nature has cursed the coast with mosquitoes and unpredictable currents, and man has added a scruffy assemblage of palm huts, pig pens and garbage, generally it's not. The hotels are also some of the country's worst, so if you're desperate for a dip and a fresh shrimp feast, it's best to visit as a day-trip from the capital or Quetzaltenango. The one exception to this rule is the nature reserve of **Monterrico**, which harbours a fairly attractive village and what may be the country's finest beach, with a superb stretch of clean sand.

The main route through the region is the **Carretera al Pacífico**, which runs from the border with Mexico at Tecún Umán into El Salvador at Ciudad Pedro de Alvarado. It's the country's swiftest highway and you'll never have to wait long for a bus. Venture off the Carretera al Pacífico, however, and things slow down considerably, and the bus services can be irregular.

Some history

Before the arrival of the **Ocós** and **Iztapa** tribes from the north, little is known of the history of the Pacific coast. By 1500 BC, however, these Mesoamerican tribes had developed village-based societies with considerable skills in the working of stone and pottery. Between 400 and 900 AD, the whole coastal plain was again overrun by Mesoamericans; this time it was the **Pipil**, who brought sophisticated architectural and artistic skills which they used in building ceremonial centres.

The first Spaniards to set foot in Guatemala did so on the Pacific coast, arriving overland from the north. Alvarado's first confrontation with the Maya happened here, in the heart of the lowlands, before the Spanish moved north to Quetzaltenango. Once established there, they dispatched a handful of Franciscans

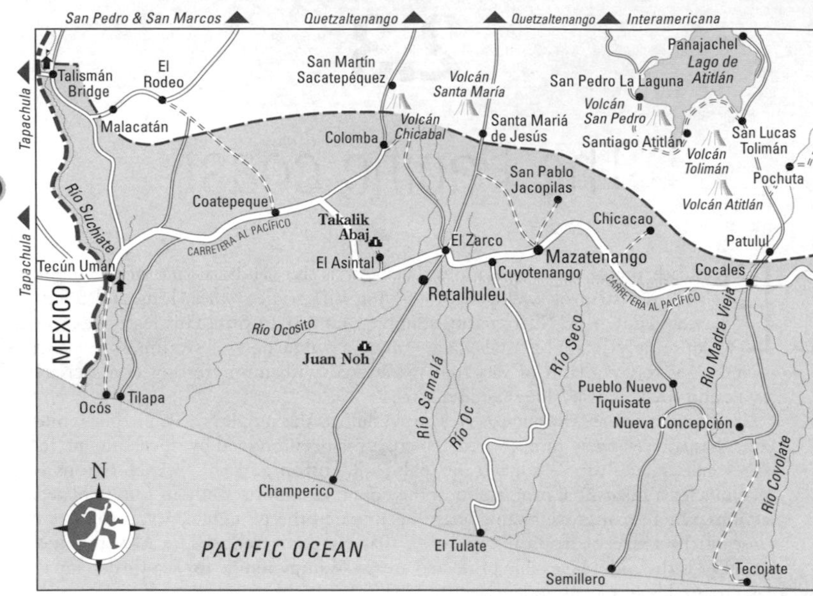

to convert the coastal population. In **colonial times**, the land was used for the production of indigo and cacao and for cattle ranching, never becoming anything more than a fairly miserable, disease-ridden backwater. It was only after **independence** that commercial agriculture began to dominate this part of the country.

Today this coastline is the country's most intensely farmed region, with coffee grown on the volcanic slopes and entire villages effectively owned by vast cotton- and sugar-cane-growing fincas. Much of the nation's income is generated here, and the main towns are alive with commercial activity and dominated by the assertive machismo of *ladino* culture. In the past, the highland Maya were forcibly recruited to work the plantations here, and today many thousands still come to the coast for seasonal work.

From the Mexican border to Cocales

The coastal border with Mexico is the busiest of Guatemala's frontiers. The northernmost of the two posts (open from 6am–9pm) is the **Talismán Bridge**, also referred to as **El Carmen**, where there's little more than some comedores and a few basic places to stay, plus the more upmarket *Hospedaje El Paso* (☎776 9474; ❹). There are regular buses to Guatemala City until about 7pm. If heading towards Quetzaltenango or the western highlands, take the first minibus to Malacatán and change there. On the Mexican side, over the bridge, a constant stream of minibuses and buses leaves for Tapachula (30 min).

Further south and leading directly onto the Carretera al Pacífico, the **Tecún Umán** crossing (open 24hr) is favoured by most Guatemalans and virtually all commercial traffic. It has an authentic frontier flavour, with all-night bars frequented by lost souls, contraband dealers, moneychangers and migrants. The *Villa Azul 2* on 3 Av (❹) and the *Hotel Don José*, 2 C 3–42 (☎776 8164; ❷), both with a/c , are two of the best hotels, but it's a much better idea to get straight out of town. There's a steady stream of buses to Guatemala City along the Carretera al Pacífico via

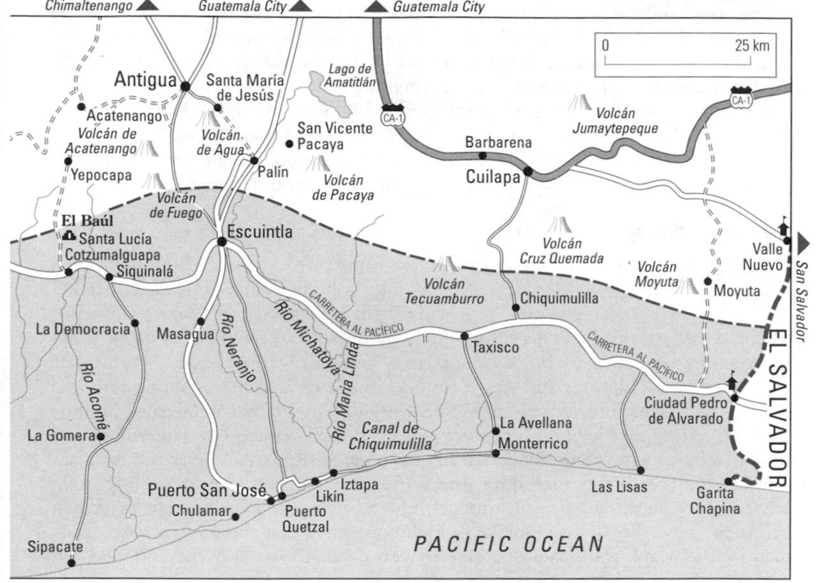

Retalhuleu. If you're Mexico-bound, there are very frequent bus services to Tapachula (40min) over the border.

Heading east from the Mexican border, **COATEPEQUE** is the first place of any importance you come to, a town that's in many ways typical of the coastal strip. A furiously busy, purely commercial centre, this is where most of the coffee produced locally is processed. All the action is centred on the **bus terminal**, from where buses run every twenty minutes to the two border crossings, and every thirty minutes to Quetzaltenango and Guatemala City. The best place to **stay** is the *Hotel Villa Real*, 6 C 6–57 (ⓣ775 1308, ⓕ775 1939; ❹), a modern hotel with tidy rooms, a restaurant and secure parking; or try the family-run *Hotel Baechli*, 6 C 5–35 (ⓣ775 1483; ❸), for something cheap and clean. There are two **banks** on the plaza; Bancafé has a Visa ATM and will change travellers' cheques.

Retalhuleu

About 40km beyond Coatepeque is the largest town in the region, **RETALHULEU**, usually referred to as **Reu** (pronounced "Ray-oo"). Set away from the highway and surrounded by the walled homes of the wealthy, Retalhuleu has managed to avoid the worst excesses of the coast and has a relaxed, easy-going air. It was founded by the Spanish in the early years of the Conquest and remains something of an oasis of civilization, with a plaza of towering Greek columns and an attractive colonial church. If you have time to kill, pop into the local **Museo de Arqueología y Etnología** in the plaza (Tues–Sat 8am–5pm, Sun 9am–noon; US$1.25), home to an amazing collection of anthropomorphic figurines, mostly heads, and some photographs of the town dating back to the 1880s. Within the plaza you'll also find the **post office** (Mon–Fri 8am–4.30pm) and three **banks**, including the Banco Agromercantíl with a MasterCard/Cirrus ATM and Banco Industrial with a Visa/Plus ATM.

Budget **accommodation** is in short supply in Retalhuleu. The cheapest recommendable place is the *Hotel América* at 8 Av 9–32 (ⓣ771 1154; ❸) where the clean rooms have fans and bathrooms. The best place in town is the modern *Hotel Posada de Don José*, 5 C 3–67 (☎771 0180; ❹), which has good a/c rooms and a large pool. Try the *Cafetería la Luna* on the plaza for good cheap **food**, or the restaurant at the *Posada de Don José* for a more substantial menu.

Virtually all **buses** running along the coastal highway stop at the Retalhuleu terminal on 7 Av and 10 C, a ten-minute walk from the plaza. There are buses to Guatemala City, the Mexican border and Quetzaltenango about every 30 minutes, plus regular buses to Champerico and El Tulate until about 6.30pm.

Takalik Abaj

The large site of **Takalik Abaj** (daily 9am–4pm; US$3.20) – whose name was changed recently from "Abaj Takalik" to offer a better translation of its K'iche' name meaning "standing stones" – provides firm evidence of an **Olmec** influence reaching this area in the first century AD. The remains of two large **temple platforms** have been cleared, but what makes a visit to this obscure site worthwhile are the carved sculptures and stelae found around their base, including rare and unusual representations of frogs and toads (monument 68) and an alligator (monument 66). Amongst the finest carvings is stela 5, which features two standing figures separated by a hieroglyphic panel that has been dated to 126 AD. Look out for giant Olmec-style heads too, including one with great hamster cheeks. In July 2002 archeologists unearthed a royal tomb, complete with jade necklace and mask belt below the observatory structure 7A, which confirmed that the site was later occupied by the Maya. You should be able to get a warm *agua* near the entrance, but there's no food available.

To **get to Takalik Abaj**, take a local bus from Reu 15km east to the village of El Asintal, from where you can walk (or take a pick-up) through coffee and cacao plantations to the site.

Champerico, Mazatenango and Cocales

Some 42km south of Retalhuleu, a fast highway runs to the beach at **CHAMPERICO**, which, though it certainly doesn't feel like it, is the country's third port. The town enjoyed a brief period of prosperity when it was connected to Quetzaltenango by rail, but there's little left now apart from a rusting pier. The dark sand **beach** is impressive for its sheer scale (though watch out for the dangerous undertow). Perhaps the best reason for visiting is the widely available and delicious fried shrimp and fish **meals**: try *Restaurant Monte Limar* or *Alcatraz* for fried shrimp and fish, or, for a treat, feast on paella or a shark steak at the *Hotel Miramar* (☎773 7231) at 2 C and Av Coatepeque, which also has a fantastic wooden bar and dark, windowless rooms (❷). Be warned it's not safe to wander too far from the busiest part of the beach – muggings have occurred in isolated spots here. **Buses** run between Champerico and Quetzaltenango every hour or so, and there are services every 30 minutes from Retalhuleu. The last bus for Retalhuleu leaves Champerico at 7pm.

Back on the highway, heading east, the next place of any size is the unremarkable town of **Cuyotenango**, where a side road heads off to the sweeping and almost undeveloped beach of **EL TULATE**. The surf is less dangerous here, and there's a handful of very simple fried fish 'n' shrimp shacks, but no hotels. Irregular buses head down to El Tulate from Cuyotenango from Reu and Mazatenango.

The next stop on the highway is **MAZATENANGO**, another seething commercial town which also has a quieter, calmer side centred on the plaza. Try *Cardinali's* at 10 C 4–36 for superb pizza and pasta, while the decent *Hotel Alba* (☎872 0264; ❹) offers clean rooms with bathroom and secure parking. About 30km beyond here is **COCALES**, a crossroads from where a road runs north to Santiago Atitlán, San Lucas Tolimán and Lago de Atitlán. The best bet is to take the first pick-up or bus for Santiago and catch a boat from there to other points on the lake. The last transport to Santiago Atitlán leaves Cocales at around 5pm.

Santa Lucía Cotzumalguapa and around

From Cocales, a 23km drive east brings you to **SANTA LUCÍA COTZUMALGUAPA**, another uninspiring Pacific town a short distance north of the highway. The main reason to visit is to explore the **archeological sites** that are scattered around the surrounding cane fields. You should bear in mind, though, that getting to them all isn't easy unless you have your own transport or hire a taxi.

As usual, the **plaza** is the main centre of interest. Santa Lucía's shady square is disgraced by one of the ugliest buildings in the country, a horrific green and white concrete municipal structure. In town, there are several cheap, scruffy **hotels** close to the plaza but the nearest half-decent place is *Hotel Internacional* (☎882 5504; ❸) just south of the main highway, which has clean rooms with fans. About 400m west of here the *Caminotel Santiaguito* (☎882 5435; ❻) is a slick motel with swimming pool and restaurant. For **food**, the *Comedor Lau* on 3 Av does reasonable Chinese meals, or there's a huge *Pollo Campero* on the north side of the square. Several **banks** will change your travellers' cheques: Banco Industrial on 3 Av has a Visa/Plus ATM.

Pullman **buses** passing along the highway will drop you at the entrance road to town, ten minutes' walk from the centre, while second-class buses go straight into the terminal, a few blocks from the plaza. Buses to the capital leave the terminal hourly until 4pm, or you can catch a bus from the highway.

Pipil sites around Santa Lucía Cotzumalguapa

A tour of the three **Pipil sites** around Santa Lucía can be a frustrating process, taking you through a sweltering maze of cane fields. Doing the whole thing on foot is certainly the cheapest way – children will approach you to act as your guide – but it's far easier to hire a taxi in the plaza; reckon on US$10 to visit all three sites. If you want to see just one of them, choose Bilbao, just 1km or so from the centre of town, which features some of the best carving. If you get lost at any stage, ask for "*las piedras*", as they tend to be known locally.

In 1880, more than thirty Late Classic stone monuments were removed from the Pipil site of **Bilbao**, and nine of the very best were shipped to Germany. Four sets of stones are still visible in situ, however, and two of them perfectly illustrate the magnificent precision of the carving, beautifully preserved in slabs of black volcanic rock. To **get to** the site, walk uphill from the plaza, along 4 Av, until you reach the Convento Las Hermanas where you bear left, following a dirt track along the side of a cane field. About 200m further on is a fairly wide path leading left into the cane for about 20m. This brings you to two large stones carved with bird-like patterns, with strange circular glyphs arranged in groups of three: the majority of the glyphs are recognizable as the names for days once used by the people of southern Mexico. In the same cane field, further along the same path, is another badly eroded stone, and a final set with a superbly preserved set of figures and interwoven motifs.

The second site is about 5km further afield in the grounds of the **Finca El Baúl**, reached by following 3 Av that heads north out of town. The hilltop site has two stones, one a massive half-buried stone head, with wrinkled brow and patterned headdress, possibly that of Huhuetéotl, the fire god of the Mexicans. In front of the stones is a set of small altars on which local people make animal sacrifices, burn incense and leave offerings of flowers. The next stones of interest are at the **finca** itself, a few kilometres further away from town, where the carvings include some superb heads, a stone skull, a massive jaguar and an extremely well-preserved stela of a ball-court player (monument 27) dating from the Late Classic period. Alongside all this antiquity is the finca's old steam engine, a miniature machine that used to haul the cane along a system of private tracks. As the finca has its own **bus service** you may be able to get a ride: buses leave from the Tienda El Baúl, a few blocks uphill from the plaza, four or five times a day, the first at around 7am and the last either way at about 6pm.

On the other side of town is the third site, at **Finca Las Ilusiones**, where another collection of artefacts and some stone carvings has been assembled in the **Museo Cultura Cotzumalguapa** (Mon–Fri 8am–4pm, Sat 8am–noon; US$1.25). Two of the most striking figures here are the pot-bellied statue (monument 58), probably from the middle Preclassic era, and a copy of monument 21 which bears three figures, the central one depicting a ball player. There are several other original items, including a fantastic stela, plus some more replicas, and thousands of small stone carvings and pottery fragments. To **get there**, walk east along the highway for about 1km, and follow the signs on the left.

La Democracia

The next town along the highway is Siquinalá, a run-down sort of place from where another branch road heads to the coast. Nine kilometres south along this road is **LA DEMOCRACIA**, home to a collection of archeological relics taken from the site of **Monte Alto** to the east of town and now displayed around the town plaza under a vast ceiba tree. These so-called "fat boys" are massive stone heads with simple, almost childlike faces, carved in Olmec style and thought to date from the mid-Preclassic period, possibly from as far back as 500 BC. Some are attached to smaller rounded bodies and rolled over on their backs clutching their swollen stomachs like stricken Teletubbies. Also on the plaza, the town **museum** (daily 8am–noon & 2–5.30pm; US$1.25) houses carvings, a wonderful jade mask, yokes worn by ball-game players, pottery, grinding stones and a few more carved heads.

Escuintla and south to the coast

Located at the junction of the two principal coastal roads from the capital, **ESCUINTLA** is the largest and most important of the Pacific towns. There's nothing to see here, but you do get a good sense of life on the coast – its heat, pace and energy, and the frenetic industrial and agricultural commerce that drives it. Below the plaza a huge, chaotic **market** sprawls across several blocks, spilling out into 4 Av, the main commercial thoroughfare, which is also notable for a mock castle that functions as the town's police station.

There are plenty of cheap **hotels** near 4 Av, most of them sharing in the general air of dilapidation; for a/c and secure parking head for the fair-value *Hotel Costa Sur*, 12 C 4–13 (☎888 1819; ❸). Among the **places to eat**, the best deal is at *Pizzería al Macarone*, 4 Av 6–103, which has inexpensive lunch specials and good ice cream. As for **banks**, there's a Bancafé with a Visa ATM at 4 Av and 12 C. There are also two **consulates** in town, Honduras at 6 Av 8–24, and El Salvador at 16 C 3–20.

Buses to Escuintla leave Guatemala City from the Zona 4 terminal, passing the Treból junction every 30 minutes until 7pm, returning from 8 C and 2 Av in Escuintla. For other destinations, there are two terminals: for places en route to the Mexican border, buses run through the north of town and stop by the Esso station opposite the Banco Uno (take a local bus up 3 Av); buses for the coast road and inland route to El Salvador are best caught at the main terminal on the south side of town, at the bottom of 4 Av (local bus down 4 Av). Buses leave every thirty minutes for Puerto San José and the eastern border and hourly to Antigua.

Puerto San José

South from Escuintla, an excellent smooth highway heads through acres of cattle pasture to **PUERTO SAN JOSÉ**, which, in its prime, was Guatemala's main shipping terminal. It's now been made virtually redundant by Puerto Quetzal, a container port a few kilometres to the east. Today both town and port are devoted to local tourism and what used to be rough sailors' bars pander to the needs of the day-trippers from the capital who fill the beaches at weekends.

The shoreline is separated from the mainland by the **Canal de Chiquimulilla**, which starts near Sipacate, west of San José, and runs as far as the border with El Salvador, cutting off all the beaches in between. Here in San José, the main resort area is on the other side of the canal, directly behind the beach. This is where all the bars and restaurants are, most of them crowded at weekends with big *ladino* groups feasting on seafood. The **hotels** are some of the worst value in the country, and cater to a largely drunken clientele – you could try *Casa San José Hotel*, Av del Comercio (Ⓣ776 5587; ❸), which has a pool and restaurant. **Buses** between San José and Guatemala City run every thirty minutes or so all day. From Guatemala City they leave from the terminal in Zona 4, and in San José from the plaza.

Monterrico

The setting of **MONTERRICO**, further east along the coast, is one of the finest on the Pacific coast, with the scenery reduced to its basic elements: a strip of dead straight sand, a line of powerful surf, a huge empty ocean and an enormous curving horizon. The village is scruffy, but friendly and relaxed, separated from the mainland by the waters of the Chiquimulilla canal, which weaves through a fantastic network of **mangrove swamps**. Mosquitoes can be a problem during the wet season, but Monterrico is still certainly the best place on the coast to spend time by the sea, though take care in the waves as there's a vicious undertow – lifeguards are on duty at weekends.

Arrival and information

The best way to **get to Monterrico** is via the coastal highway at **Taxisco**. From here, trucks and buses run along the 17km of paved road to **LA AVELLANA**, a couple of kilometres from Monterrico on the opposite side of the mangrove swamp, where boats (20min) shuttle passengers (US$0.40) and cars back and forth. There's a steady flow of traffic between Taxisco and La Avellana, the last bus leaving Taxisco at 6pm and La Avellana at 4.30pm – you'll find the latest schedules posted in the Proyecto Lingüístico Monterrico. Several direct **buses** run between La Avellana and the Zona 4 bus terminal in Guatemala City, taking around three hours; alternatively, get on any bus heading for Taxisco and change there. If you're travelling between Antigua and Monterrico there are several daily **shuttle-bus** services (US$7–10 each way) to La Avellena; tickets are bookable by any travel agency and most hotels.

Very regular buses also continue from Taxisco along the Carretera al Pacífico to the **border with El Salvador** at Ciudad Pedro de Alvarado until 5pm, just over an hour away. The border is a fairly quiet one, as most traffic uses the Valle Nuevo post to the north, but there are a few basic hospedajes and comedores on both sides of the border if you get stuck.

There are no **banks** in Monterrico, and the nearest in Taxisco had no ATM (but would change travellers' cheques) at the time of research. A new **language school**, the Proyecto Lingüístico Monterrico (see p.150), on the main drag, offers one-on-one Spanish tuition.

Accommodation

All Monterrico's **accommodation** is centred right on or just off the beach. Note that many places have reservation numbers in Guatemala City and others use cellular phones. Many places increase prices by about 20 percent at weekends, when it's also best to book ahead. Avoid the *Hotel Baule Beach* as regular thefts have been reported.

Café del Sol turn right at the beach, walk for 250m Ⓣ810 0821, Ⓦwww.cafe-del-sol.com. Good, friendly Swiss-Guatemalan-owned place with nine large accommodations – some beachside, others at the rear and a '*mirador*' room with sea views – with and without private bathroom. Tasty food and a small pool. ❹–❺

Eco Beach Place turn right at the beach, walk for

250m ⓣ611 6637, ⓔecobeachplace@hotmail.com. Next to the *Café del Sol*, this attractive guesthouse has large comfortable rooms (some sleep up to four); all but one have private bath. There's good grub, a nice lounge/bar area, a small pool and stunning Pacific vistas from the veranda. ❹

Hotel El Caracol turn left at the beach, walk for 120m ⓣ693 0430. Small place with two rooms with bathroom and fan, plus a pleasant 6-bed dorm (US$5 per person). The young Israeli-Canadian owners also offer body-board rental (US$3 per hour). ❸

Hotel El Mangle turn left at beach, walk for 300m ⓣ514 6517 or 490 1336. Ever-expanding, agreeable place with selection of small rooms, all with mosquito nets, fans, bathrooms and little terraces with hammocks. Garden area, small pool and beachside restaurant. ❸

Hotel La Palma at the end of the dock–beach road, on the right ⓣ705 4707 or 363 4905. Extremely clean French-American-run guesthouse with six doubles and one triple room, all with ceiling fans, around a little grassy patio. Excellent French food as well. ❸

Johnny's Place turn left at beach, walk for 150m ⓣ812 0409 or 611 0444. Popular travellers' destination with male and female dorms (US$4–5 per person) plus good-sized bungalows sleeping four. There are plenty of small bathing pools, a café-restaurant with ocean views and fairly priced tacos and pasta. ❷–❺

Pez de Oro turn left at beach and walk for 350m ⓣ204 5249 or 368 3684. Eleven very attractive cottages, all with good beds, nice wooden furniture, verandas and hammocks. The smallish swimming pool is shaded by coconut palms and there's an Italian restaurant with excellent pasta, fish, and wine by the glass. ❺

The town and Biotopo Monterrico-Hawaii nature reserve

Monterrico, like most places on the Pacific coast, is very quiet during the week but fills up at **weekends** with Guatemalans from the capital and language-school students from Antigua. Though the beach is far too expansive to get packed, the atmosphere tends to get raucous, with some of the more frenzied visitors ripping up and down the sands on their quadbikes.

Beach apart, Monterrico's other attraction is the **Biotopo Monterrico-Hawaii nature reserve**, which embraces the village, the beach – an important **turtle** nesting ground – and a large slice of the mangrove swamps behind, covering a total area of some 28 square kilometres (sadly, however, the reserve's protected status does not stop the dumping of domestic rubbish and the widespread theft of turtle eggs). The reserve encloses four distinct types of mangrove, with dark, nutrient-rich waters flowing between a dense mat of branches, interspersed with narrow canals, open lagoons, bulrushes and water lilies. The tangle of roots acts as a kind of marine nursery, offering small fish protection from their natural predators, while above the surface the rich vegetation and ready food supply provide an ideal home for hundreds of species of bird and a handful of mammals, including racoons, opossums, anteaters and armadillos, plus iguanas, caimans and alligators. The best way to explore the reserve is in a small *cayuco* (kayak); ask around at the dock for a boatman. The reserve's **visitor centre** (daily 8am–noon & 2–5pm; US$1), just off the beach between *Hotel Mangle* and the *Pez d'Oro*, has plenty of information about the environment (Spanish only). It also acts as an important sea turtle hatchery; while caimans, iguanas and freshwater turtles are also bred at the centre for release into the wild.

Eating and drinking

When it comes to **eating** in Monterrico you can either dine at one of the hotels on the beach – which can be pricey – or at one of the comedores in the village, the best being the *Divino Maestro*, where they do good *camarones al ajo*. However, perhaps the best food is at the Swiss-owned *Taberna El Pelícano* (closed Tues) just inland from *Johnny's Place* where pasta dishes are just US$3 and *ragout de pescado* costs US$8. By far the most lively bar is the beachfront *El Animal Desconicido* which hammers out an eclectic selection of rock and dance music and serves up a mean cocktail.

2.4

East to the Caribbean

The land to the **east of Guatemala City** is some of the most varied in the entire country, ranging from the cacti-spiked near-desert around the El Rancho junction to the permanently lush Caribbean coast. Although the coastal area was fairly densely populated in Maya times, it was largely abandoned until the end of the nineteenth century. Its revival was due to the arrival of the United Fruit Company, who cleared the land for the banana plantations that still dominate the area. Fruit-laden trucks thunder along the road to the coast, following the **Motagua valley**, a broad river corridor dividing two high mountain ranges. A couple of hours before you reach the coast, the route passes the ruins of **Quiriguá**, a small site with some of the finest stelae and carvings in the entire Maya world. At the end of the road is the faded, slightly seedy port of **Puerto Barrios** from where it's possible to cross the border into Honduras.

To the north of the Motagua valley is **Lago de Izabal**, a vast expanse of fresh water ringed by lonely villages and swamps, its shores home to a tremendous variety of wildlife (most of it threatened), including alligators, iguanas, turtles, toucans and manatee. The best base for exploring this region is sleepy **El Estor**, from where you can easily venture into the **Bocas del Polochic** nature reserve. Sailing towards the Caribbean from Lago de Izabal you pass through **El Golfete** lake and the towering, jungle-covered gorge systems of the **Río Dulce**. At the end of the river is **Lívingston**, a very funky coconut-and-ganja town, home to Guatemala's black Garífuna people.

Also included in this chapter are the **eastern highlands** – dry *ladino* territory, intermittently scarred by ancient, eroded volcanoes and hot, dusty towns. Though the scenery is superb, there is little for the traveller here, save the beautifully isolated **Volcán de Ipala**, with its stunning crater lake, and the curious holy town of **Esquipulas**, whose huge basilica – containing an image of the black Jesus – is the focus for Central America's largest annual pilgrimage.

The Motagua valley

Leaving the capital, the Caribbean highway passes through the hilly, infertile terrain of the upper **Río Motagua**. As you head further down the valley, the land rapidly becomes bleak, dry and distinctly inhospitable, until you come to the first place of any note: the **Río Hondo junction**. Here you'll find a waiting army of food sellers and a line of blue-and-red Pepsi-sponsored comedores. If you need refreshment, there are usually fresh coconuts for sale, too. The road divides here, with one arm heading south to Esquipulas and the three-way **border** with Honduras and El Salvador, and the main branch continuing on to the coast. There are a number of motels scattered around Río Hondo which, bizarre as it may seem, is viewed by middle-class Guatemalans as something of a weekend retreat, due to the presence of the large *Valle Dorado* waterworld park-motel (☎220 8840; ❻), close by at Km 146.

On down the valley the landscape starts to undergo a radical transformation: the flood plain opens out and the cacti and scrub are gradually overwhelmed by a profusion of tropical growth. It was this supremely rich flood plain that attracted both the Maya and the United Fruit Company, to the great benefit of both.

Quiriguá

Set splendidly in an isolated pocket of rainforest, surrounded by an ocean of banana trees, the ruins of **Quiriguá** (daily 7.30am–5pm; US$3.25) have some of the finest Maya carving anywhere. Only neighbouring Copán (see p.418) offers any competition to the magnificent stelae, altars and so-called "zoomorphs", covered in well-preserved and superbly intricate glyphs and portraits.

Entering the site beneath the ever-dripping ceiba, jocote, palm and fig trees, you emerge at the northern end of the **Great Plaza**. To the left-hand side of the path from the ticket office and new site **museum** (due to open in late 2004) is a badly ruined pyramid and, dominating the site at the southern end of the plaza, the untidy bulk of the **acropolis**. Liberally scattered amidst the luxuriant grass of the plaza are the finely carved **stelae** for which Quiriguá is justly famous. The nine stelae in the plaza are the tallest in the Maya world (the largest, stela E, rises to a height of 8m and weighs 65 tons), while their sides are all similarly covered with glyphs and portraits of the city's rulers, with Cauac Sky depicted on no fewer than seven (A, C, D, E, F, H and J). Two unusual features are particularly clear: the vast headdresses, which dwarf the faces, and the beards.

As you head down the path towards the acropolis you can just make out the remains of a **ball court** on your right, before you reach the other features that have earned Quiriguá its fame. Squatting at the base of the ruined acropolis are the **zoomorphs**: six bizarre, globular-shaped blocks of stone carved with interlacing animal and human figures – look out for the turtle, frog and jaguar. The best of the

△ Maya carvings, Quiriguá

The history of Quiriguá

The **early history** of Quiriguá is still fairly vague, but during the Late Preclassic period (250 BC–300 AD) migrants from the north established themselves as rulers here. Later, in the Early Classic period (250–600 AD), the centre was dominated by Copán, just 50km away, and doubtless valued for its position on the banks of the Río Motagua, an important trade route, and as a source of jade, which is found throughout the valley. It was during the rule of the great leader **Cauac Sky** that Quiriguá challenged Copán, captured its leader 18 Rabbit in 737, and was able to assert its independence and embark on an unprecedented building boom: the bulk of the great stelae date from this period. For a century Quiriguá dominated the lower Motagua valley and its highly prized resources. Under **Jade Sky**, who took the throne in 790, Quiriguá reached its peak, with fifty years of extensive building work, including a radical reconstruction of the acropolis. From the end of Jade Sky's rule, in the middle of the ninth century, the historical record fades out, as does the period of prosperity and power.

lot is zoomorph P, which shows a figure seated in Buddha-like pose, interwoven with a maze of other detail.

Practicalities

The **ruins** are situated some 70km beyond the junction at Río Hondo, and 4km down a turn-off from the main road. All **buses** running between Puerto Barrios (2hr) and Guatemala City (4hr) pass by. There's a fairly regular bus service from the highway to the site itself, plus assorted motorbikes and pick-ups. You shouldn't have to wait too long to get a ride back to the highway, or you can walk it in around forty-five minutes.

There are a couple of simple places to **stay** in the village of **QUIRIGUÁ**, just off the main highway 5km from the ruins; the village can be reached either by following the old railtrack (which is halfway between the ruins and the highway) west for 3km or heading back to the highway itself and getting a ride from there. In the village the *Hotel y Restaurante Royal* (☎947 3639; ❷–❸), alongside the former hospital for tropical diseases, is best choice, with large old rooms downstairs and modern rooms on the upper floor.

Puerto Barrios

Founded in the 1880s by President Rufino Barrios, the port of **PUERTO BARRIOS** soon fell into the hands of the United Fruit Company, who used their control of the railways to ensure that the bulk of trade passed this way. Puerto Barrios was Guatemala's main port for most of the twentieth century, and the Fruit Company were exempt from almost all tax. But in the latter years of the century a rapid decline set in, and the town has only seen an upturn in commerce after its port facilities were recently upgraded. Today the town appears pretty forlorn, with a smattering of strip clubs and poorly lit and badly potholed streets. The only reason most travellers come here is to get somewhere else: to Honduras via the border crossing at Corinto (see opposite), to Lívingston, or to Punta Gorda in Belize (see p.127) by boat.

Arrival and information

There's no purpose-built bus station in Puerto Barrios. Litegua **buses** (15 daily), which serve all destinations along the Caribbean Highway to Guatemala City, have their own terminal in the centre of town on 6 Av, between 9 and 10 C. All second-class buses, including hourly services to Chiquimula and four daily to Esquipulas, arrive and depart from an unmarked stop directly opposite, beside the railway tracks. **Taxis** seem to be everywhere in Barrios; drivers toot for custom as they drive through the streets.

There's no Inguat tourist office in town: check at the Litegua terminal for bus schedules and at the **dock** at the end of 12 C for boat departures to Lívingston and to Punta Gorda in Belize (daily boats at 10am and 2pm; US$15). If you're heading to Belize, clear **migración** (7am–8pm) first before you buy a ticket; the office is a block west of the dock on 12 C. The best **Internet** café is *Cafenet* at 13 C and 6 Av (daily 9am–9pm). There are plenty of **banks** in Puerto Barrios: Lloyds TSB is at 7 Av and 15 C, Banrural (with MasterCard ATM) is at 8 Av and 9 C and Banco Industrial (with Visa ATM) at 7 Av and 7 C. The **Telgua** office (daily 7am–midnight) is at the junction of 8 Av and 10 C and the **post office** is at 6 C and 6 Av.

Accommodation

Good budget **hotels** are not that plentiful in Puerto Barrios, and this is a very hot and sticky town, so you'll definitely want a fan, if not air conditioning.

Hotel Caribeña 4 Av between 10 and 11 calles ⓣ948 0384. Large place with good-value rooms (some with a/c) including doubles, triples and quadruples. The management is friendly and there's a quality seafood restaurant attached. ❷–❹

Hotel del Norte 7 C and 1 Av ⓣ948 0087. A historic Caribbean-style wooden hotel, with clapboard rooms that aren't especially comfortable, but there's a nice swimming pool, and the location, overlooking the Bay of Amatique, is magnificent. Best of all is the mahogany-panelled restaurant and bar – though the food doesn't match the decor. ❹ with bath, ❸ without.

Hotel Europa 2 3 Av and 12 C ⓣ948 1292. Clean, safe and friendly place, ideally located for the dock. All the good-value rooms have fan and private shower and there are good rates for single travellers. The almost identical *Hotel Europa 1* is at 8 Av and 8 C (ⓣ948 0127). Both ❷

Hotel Valle Tropical 12 C, between 5 and 6 avenidas ⓣ948 7084. Large new motel-style block with well-equipped (all have a/c, TV, bathroom and double bed) if plain rooms. Pool and restaurant. ❻

Eating, drinking and nightlife

For a cheap feed, there's an abundance of **comedores** around the market. For **fish and seafood** there's plenty of choice: try *Safari*, ten minutes north of the centre on the seafront at the end of 5 Avenida, which is good, if a little pricey, and serves huge portions. *La Caribeña*, 4 Av between 10 and 11 calles, does a superb *caldo de mariscos* (seafood soup). Meat-eaters won't do better than the *Rincón Uruguayo* (closed Mon), which excels at *parrilladas* – it's a ten-minute walk south of the centre at 7 Av and 16 C. Puerto Barrios also has more than its fair share of **bars** and **nightclubs**, offering the full range of late-night sleaze – a lot of the action is centred around 6 and 7 avenidas and 6 and 7 calles. Reggae and punta rock are the sounds on the street in Puerto Barrios, and you'll catch a fair selection at weekends in the *Canoa Club* on 5 Av and 2 C.

Overland to Honduras

To **get to Honduras** from Puerto Barrios, minibuses (every 30min; 6.30am–4.30pm) depart from the marketplace via the town of Entre Ríos (for *migración*) and on to the border (1hr). You may be asked for an unofficial "exit tax" (US$1–2) on the Guatemalan side and an entry fee for a similar sum from the Hondurans. Pick-ups leave the border to the village of **Corinto**, 4km away, from where buses depart for Puerto Cortés (every 90min; 3hr) via the pretty village of Omoa (see p.440). If you set out early from Puerto Barrios, you should get to San Pedro Sula (see p.433) by lunchtime and it's certainly possible to catch an afternoon flight on to one of the Bay Islands. San Pedro Sula is well connected with Puerto Cortés by Citul and other buses (every 30min 5am–7.30pm; 1hr 15min); the Citul terminal is located just across the plaza from the *migración*.

Lívingston, the Río Dulce and Lago de Izabal

At the mouth of the Río Dulce, and only accessible by boat, **LÍVINGSTON** not only enjoys a superb setting but also offers a unique fusion of Guatemalan and Caribbean culture in which marimba mixes with Marley. Along with several other villages in Central America, Lívingston provides the focus for the displaced **Garífuna**, or black Carib people, who are now strung out along the Caribbean coast between southern Belize and northern Nicaragua (for a brief history of the Garífuna, see p.118). To a lesser extent, the town also acts as a focal point for the Q'eqchi' Maya of the Río Dulce region.

Lívingston is undoubtedly one of the most fascinating places in Guatemala, and many visitors find the languid rhythm of life here hypnotic. The town is as popular with weekending Guatemalans as it is with international travellers, and offers a welcome break from mainstream Latino culture. Carib **food** is generally excellent and more varied than the usual comedor dishes, and Garífuna punta rock and reggae make a pleasant change from the standard merengue beat. While certainly not unaffected by the pressures of daily life in Central America, the general atmosphere is pretty chilled.

Lívingston is a small place, and you can see most of what there is to see in an hour or so. While there's not really that much to do in town itself other than relaxing in local style, a few places nearby are worth a visit. The local **beaches**, though safe for swimming, are not of the Caribbean dream variety, with the exception of the wonderful white-sand **Playa Blanca**, though this can only be visited on a tour. Sadly it's not safe to walk alone along the local beaches, as rapes and robberies have been reported.

The most popular trip out of town is to **Las Siete Altares**, a group of waterfalls some 5km to the northwest. Unfortunately, there have been sporadic **attacks on tourists** walking to these falls. The safest option is to hire a local guide or visit as part of a tour (see below).

Arrival and information

The only way to get to Lívingston is **by boat**, either from Puerto Barrios, the Río Dulce, Belize, or, occasionally, from Omoa in Honduras (see overleaf for more details). Boats arrive at the main dock on the south side of town; straight ahead, up the hill, is the main drag with most of the restaurants, bars and shops. The **migración** (daily 6am–7pm) is about 200m up the hill, on the left. For **changing money**, try either Bancafé (with Visa ATM) or Banrural, both on the main drag. The **Telgua** office (daily 7am–midnight) is on the right, up the main street from the docks, next door to the **post office**. There are several places with **Internet** access: try Buganet or Happy Fish on the main drag – rates are around US$2.50 an hour.

Exotic Travel (ⓣ947 0049, ⓔkjchew@hotmail.com), in the same building as the *Bahía Azul* restaurant, and Happy Fish (ⓣ902 7143), just down the road, are the best **travel agents** in town. The helpful owners can arrange **trips** (minimum six people) around the area, including visits to the lovely white-sand beach of Playa Blanca (US$10) and the Sapodilla Cayes off Belize (see p.129) for **snorkelling** (US$30). Several companies, including Exotic Travel, run morning boat trips up the Río Dulce (US$9 per person).

Scheduled **boats** leave for Puerto Barrios daily at 5am and 2pm (1hr 30min), supplemented by **lanchas**, which leave when full (roughly every 30min 6.30am–5.30pm; 30min). Boats also run to Punta Gorda in **Belize** on Tuesdays and Fridays at 7am (1hr) and to Omoa in **Honduras** when there are sufficient numbers (US$35 per person, minimum 6 people; 2hr 30min). Combined boat/shuttle bus tickets are sold by Exotic Travel to Antigua, Copán (both US$30), San Pedro Sula (US$35) and La Ceiba (US$45).

Accommodation

There are plenty of cheap **hotels** in town, though very little choice in the mid-range and luxury brackets. Book ahead on holidays, but at other times you should easily be able to find a bed.

Hotel California turn left just before the *Bahía Azul* restaurant. Clean hotel, offering reasonable if sparse rooms, most with private bath. ❷–❸

Hotel Casa Rosada about 400m left of the dock ⓣ947 0303, ⓦwww.hotelcasarosada.com. The ownership has recently changed but standards remain as high at this delightful hotel, with a harbourfront plot and lush, spacious grounds. The small, cheery wooden cabins are a little overpriced (and lack private bath) but do have charm. Excellent wholesome meals served as well. ❹

Hotel Doña Alida turn right immediately after the *Tucán Dugú*, then walk north 250m ⓣ947 0027. Welcoming owners and a selection of spacious modern rooms in a quiet cliffside location, with a little beach below. Rooms 10 and 11 both have excellent sea (and sunset) views. ❹

Hotel El Viajero turn left after the dock, walk for 200m. Friendly family-run place with cheap rooms, all with fan and some with private bath. There's a snack bar, too. ❷

Hotel Garífuna turn left off the main street towards the *Ubafu* bar and walk 250m ⓣ948 1091. Clean, secure locally owned guesthouse with good-value rooms, all with fan and private shower. ❷

Hotel Ríos Tropicales 200m up from the jetty ⓣ947 0158. Attractive hotel with pleasant wood-panelled rooms, some very spacious, with good beds and fans. Small sunny patio at the rear. ❹

Hotel Vista al Mar about 450m left of the dock ⓣ947 0131. Simple but attractive rooms in a wooden building, all with good fans and some with private bath. Run by amiable locals who also manage a little comedor. ❷–❸

Villa Caribe Tucán Dugú first on the right, uphill from the jetty ⓣ947 0072, ⓦwww.villasdeguatemala.com. Lívingston's only luxury hotel, with attractive modern rooms with balconies looking down from an elevated plot to the bay. Pleasant bar, swimming pool and lush gardens. Rooms start at just over US$100 per night. ❾

Eating and drinking

Lívingston is a great place to eat out. For local food, you must try the *tapado* (coconut-based fish soup) at *Tiburón Gato*, *Tilingo Lingo* or *Margoth*. Elsewhere, the restaurant in the historic Caribbean-style *Hotel Río Dulce* (on the left up from the jetty) has a superb menu, with plenty of fish and imaginative European cuisine; while *Buga Mama* just left of the jetty has good shrimp, fish and pasta. *Hotel Casa Rosada* (see above) also has great (mainly) vegetarian food – dinner here is US$9. The *Bahía Azul*, on the main street, is another popular place with an inexpensive menu (including *coco burguesa)* and an excellent terrace for watching Lívingston streetlife. For evening **entertainment** there are lots of groovy bars (*Ubafu* is usually the most lively), and the *Coco Bongo* club on the beach where you'll hear Jamaican reggae and pure Garífuna punta rock.

The Río Dulce

Another very good reason for coming to Lívingston is to venture up the **Río Dulce**, a truly spectacular trip that leads eventually to the town of the same name about 30km upriver. The total journey takes some two to three hours and can be organized through any of the travel agents in Lívingston.

From Lívingston the river leads into a system of **gorges** between sheer rock faces 100m or so in height. Clinging to the sides is a wall of tropical vegetation and cascading vines, and here and there you might see some white herons or flocks of squawking parakeets. Six kilometres from Lívingston there's a delightful river tributary, the **Río Tatín**, which most boatmen will venture up if you ask them, where there's a good guesthouse, the *Finca Tatín* (ⓣ902 0831, ⓔfincatatin@hotmail.com; ❷) with rustic dorms and private rooms with bathroom set in dense shoreside jungle and only reachable by boat. Run by hospitable Argentineans, there's excellent healthy food, kayaks for hire, walking trails and Spanish classes available.

Continuing up the Río Dulce for another kilometre or so, you'll pass an excellent place for a swim, where warm sulphurous waters emerge from the base of the cliff. Past here, the river opens up into the **Golfete** lake, surrounded by swampy lowlands, the north shore of which has been designated the **Biotopo de Chocón Machacas** (daily 7am–4pm; US$3.25), designed to protect the **manatee** – though the huge mammals are extremely timid and you'll be very lucky to see one. The reserve also protects the forest that still covers much of the lake's shore, and there are some specially cut trails where you might catch sight of a bird or two, or, if you've plenty of time and patience, even a tapir or jaguar. Heading on upstream, the river closes in again and passes the marina and bridge at the squalid town of **Río Dulce** (also known as Fronteras). This part of the Río Dulce is a favourite playground for wealthy Guatemalans, with boats and hotels that would put parts of California to shame. The area is also popular with European and North American yachties on account of its sheltered waters, stores and repair workshops. The road for Petén crosses the river here and the boat trip comes to an end.

Río Dulce town

The town of **RÍO DULCE** itself is little more than a truck stop, where traffic for Petén pauses before the long stretch to Flores. The town is actually formed out of older settlements, Fronteras to the north and El Rellano to the south, connected by a monstrous concrete road bridge. The road between them is lined with cheap comedores and stores, and you can pick up buses here in either direction.

As for **places to stay**, a good place for budget travellers is the lakeside Swiss-owned *Casa Perico* (Ⓣ909 0721; ❷) 1km northeast of the bridge, with dorm beds (US$5) and basic rooms (US$6.50 per person) along with a lively atmosphere and great food. Call them for a free lancha pick-up. Alternatively, *Hotel Backpackers* (Ⓣ208 1779, Ⓔcasaguatemala@guate.net) is a rival set-up right underneath the south side of the bridge with dorm beds (US$4), hammock space (US$2.50) and private doubles (❸). Owned by the nearby Casa Guatemala children's home, many of the young staff are former residents; it's a good place to pick up information about the Río Dulce region. On the north side of the bridge *Hotel Río Dulce* (Ⓣ930 3179; ❸), has clean neat doubles with fans. *Hacienda Tijax* (Ⓣ930 5505, Ⓦwww.tijax.com), two minutes by water taxi from the north side of the bridge, is a working teak and rubber farm with a pleasant lakeside plot and tasty, if slightly pricey food. There's a great canopy jungle walk, hiking trails and horse-riding, plus a swimming pool. Accommodation is either in basic rooms (❸), cabins (❹) or bungalows (❻).

As for **restaurants**, *Río Bravo*, on the north side of the bridge, is a good place to meet other travellers, eat pizza or pasta and drink the night away – you can also surf the **Internet** and make radio contact with most places around the river and lake from here. Just south of here *Bruno's* serves up international food and offers North American news and sports coverage – it's very popular with the sailing fraternity – they have Internet facilities here too. For cheap grub, there's a strip of pretty undistinguished comedores on the main road close to the bus stop. There are several **banks** in Río Dulce: Banrural has a MasterCard ATM and Banco Industrial a Visa ATM.

Moving on from Río Dulce, there are buses every thirty minutes or so to Guatemala City and to Flores via Poptún until around 6pm. If you're heading towards Puerto Barrios, take the first bus or minibus to La Ruidosa junction (every 30min) and pick up a connection there. Heading to El Estor, there are buses around the lakeshore every ninety minutes (1hr 45min) between 6am and 4pm. If you're heading for Lívingston via the Río Dulce gorge, the lancha **boat** captains will ambush you as soon as you step off a bus; boats (US$10 per person) leave when they have enough passengers until about 5pm. For a more leisurely cruise along the Río Dulce or to Finca Paraíso (both US$25 round trip) the *Shin-Tzu* catamaran, docked at *Tijax* (see above; Ⓣ493 0865) fits the bill nicely. There's a useful **website**

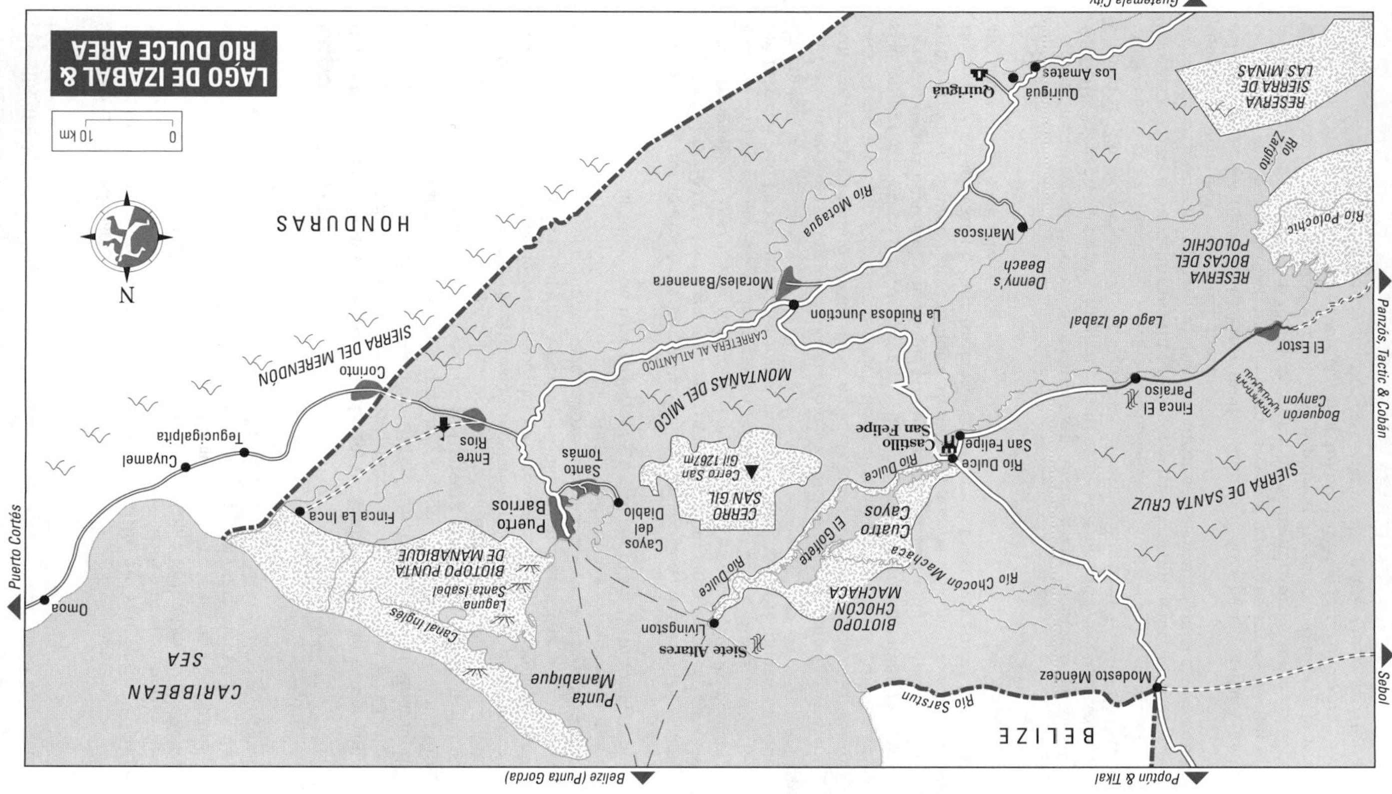
LAGO DE IZABAL &
RÍO DULCE AREA
0
10 km
N
Puerto Cortés
Omoa
CARIBBEAN
SEA
Cuyamel
Tegucigalpita
HONDURAS
SIERRA DEL MERENDÓN
Corinto
Finca La Inca
Canal Inglés
Laguna
Santa Isabel
BIOTOPO PUNTA
DE MANABIQUE
Entre
Ríos
Puerto
Barrios
Santo
Tomás
Punta
Manabique
Belize (Punta Gorda)
Cayos
del
Diablo
Livingston
Siete Altares
Río Dulce
CERRO
SAN GIL
Cerro San
Gil 1267m
MONTAÑAS DEL MICO
CARRETERA AL ATLÁNTICO
Morales/Bananera
La Ruidosa Junction
Río Motagua
El Golfete
BIOTOPO
CHOCÓN
MACHACA
Cuatro
Cayos
Castillo
San Felipe
Río Dulce
San Felipe
Río Chocón Machaca
Río Sarstun
BELIZE
Modesto Méncez
Poptún & Tikal
Sebol
Mariscos
Denny's
Beach
Quiriguá
Los Amates
Lago de Izabal
Finca El
Paraíso
SIERRA DE SANTA CRUZ
Boquerón
Canyon
El Estor
RESERVA
BOCAS DEL
POLOCHIC
Río Polochic
Río Zarquito
RESERVA
SIERRA DE
LAS MINAS
Guatemala City
Panzós, Tactic & Cobán

covering the Río Dulce region (@www.mayaparadise.com) with good links and listings.

Castillo de San Felipe

Looking like a miniature medieval castle, the **Castillo de San Felipe** (daily 8am–5pm; US$1.30), 1km upstream from the Río Dulce bridge, marks the entrance to Lago de Izabal, and is a tribute to the audacity of English pirates, who used to sail up the Río Dulce to raid supplies and harass mule trains. The Spanish were so infuriated by this that they built the fortress to seal off the entrance to the lake, and a chain was strung across the river. Inside there's a maze of tiny rooms and staircases, plenty of cannons and panoramic views of the lake.

Lago de Izabal

Beyond the *castillo*, the broad expanse of **Lago de Izabal** opens up before you, with great views of the highlands beyond the distant shores. Hotels in Río Dulce town, including the *Hacienda Tijax* and *Hotel Backpackers*, can arrange a tour around the lake with a local boatman, or you can easily explore the north shore along the road to El Estor on your own by bus. The **hot spring waterfall** (daily 8am–6pm; US$1.30) near the *Finca El Paraíso* (see below), 25km from Río Dulce and 300m north of the road, is one of Guatemala's most remarkable natural phenomena. Bathtub-temperature spring water cascades into pools cooled by a secondary flow of chilly fresh river water, creating a steamy, spa-like environment where it's easy to wallow away an afternoon hippo-style. Above the waterfall are a series of **caves**, their interiors crowded with extraordinary shapes and colours – made even more memorable by the fact that you have to swim by torchlight to see them (bring your own flashlight).

Two kilometres south of the hot waterfall on the lakeshore, the *Finca El Paraíso* (T949 7122; 5–6) has two rows of large, comfortable, but rarely occupied cabañas and a reasonable, if overpriced restaurant. The hotel enjoys a delightfully peaceful location and there's good swimming from the black-sand beach. **Buses** and pick-ups between Río Dulce and El Estor pass the hot springs and hotel hourly in both directions.

Continuing west along the lakeshore it's a further 7km to the **Boquerón canyon**, just 500m from the road but completely hidden. Near-vertical cliffs soar to over 250m above the Río Sauce, which flows through the bottom of the jungle-clad gorge, the riverbed dotted with colossal boulders. Villagers (including Hugo, a campesino-cum-boatman) will paddle you upstream in a canoe for a small fee. The return trip takes around thirty minutes, though it's possible to continue exploring Boquerón – which extends for a further 5km – on foot if you have sturdy footwear and don't mind a scramble.

El Estor

Heading west beyond Boquerón, it's just 6km to the sleepy lakeside town of **EL ESTOR**. Allegedly named by English pirates who came up the Río Dulce to buy supplies at "The Store" of Lago de Izabal, it's an easy-going, friendly place that was briefly energized in the 1970s when a vast nickel plant flourished just to the west, but quickly settled back into provincial stupor when the commodity price plummeted. Now locals are optimistic that the town can capitalize on the vast **eco-tourism** potential of the surrounding area.

There's not a lot to do in El Estor itself, although it does have a friendly and relaxed atmosphere, particularly in the warm evenings when the streets are full of activity. Don't miss the pool in the plaza, which harbours fish, turtles and small alligators. You could spend a delightful few days exploring the surrounding area, much of which remains untouched – you can rent **bikes** at 6 Av 4–26. For **tours**, try either *Café Portal* (T818 0843) on the east side of the plaza, Hugo at *Hugo's*

Restaurant, or Oscar Paz, who runs the *Hotel Vista del Lago*. All can arrange boats and guides to explore the surrounding countryside, plus fishing trips on the lake.

There's an excellent choice of good-quality budget **accommodation** in El Estor, though nothing in other price categories. The most atmospheric hotel is undoubtedly *Hotel Vista del Lago* (Ⓣ949 7205; ❸), a beautiful old wooden building by the dock, claimed by the owners to be the original "store" that gave the town its name; it offers small clean rooms with private bath, with those on the second floor boasting superb views of the lake. There's great accommodation too, on the lakeside just east of the plaza, where *Restaurant Chaabil* (US$6 per person) offers wooden rooms with hand-made beds and private bathrooms. Otherwise *Hotel Villela* at 6 Av 2–06 (❷) is a reasonable deal, with rooms, some with private shower, surrounding a pretty garden. Finally, a kilometre east of the centre, in a prime, tranquil lakeside plot, the bungalows at the *Hotel Ecológico Cabañas del Lago* (Ⓣ & Ⓕ949 7245; ❹) are comfortable, spacious and attractive – Hugo, the owner, will take you there if you drop in at his restaurant in the plaza.

There's not too much to get excited about when it comes to **food**, but *Restaurant Chaabil* is the fanciest place in town and has good seafood, while *Hugo's Restaurant* and *Café El Portal* score for comida típica – both are on the main plaza. For good inexpensive **breakfasts** or snacks head to the clean, friendly *Cafetería Santa Clave*, three blocks west of the plaza at 3 C 7–75.

Reserva Bocas del Polochic

Encompassing a substantial slice of lowland jungle on the west side of the lake, the **Reserva Bocas del Polochic** is one of the richest wetland habitats in Guatemala. The green maze of swamp, marsh and forest harbours at least 275 different species of bird, among them golden-fronted woodpeckers, Aztec parakeets and keel-billed toucans. It's also rich in mammals, including howler monkeys, which you're virtually guaranteed to see (and hear), plus rarely encountered manatees and tapirs.

You can **stay** next to the tiny Q'eqchi' village of **SELEMPÍM** on the edge of the reserve – accommodation is in a large, screened wooden house with bunk beds (US$12 per person per day, including three substantial meals) which provides villagers with employment. Locals also lead walking tours up into the foothills of the Sierra de las Minas and kayak tours of the river delta. The drawback is that there's no road to the reserve and you'll have to take a lancha to get there. There are occasional public lanchas for US$6 one way – check at the offices of Defensores de la Naturaleza (see below) but a private charter can amount to US$35 for a day-trip, or as much as US$75 to get to Selempím and back; obviously it's much cheaper if you can get a group together. The reserve is managed by Defensores de la Naturaleza, 5 Av and 2 C, El Estor (Ⓣ949 7237, Ⓦwww.defensores.org.gt), which organizes excellent **tours** into the heart of the refuge. To visit the zone nearest to El Estor, contact Hugo or Oscar in El Estor (see above), both of whom run good day-trip excursions.

The eastern highlands

The **eastern highlands** southwest of the capital have to rank as the least-visited part of Guatemala. The population is almost entirely Latinized, speaking Spanish and wearing Western clothes, although many are by blood pure Maya. The *ladinos* of this largely rural area tend to be drawn to cowboy culture and demonstrations of macho pride are not uncommon.

The landscape lacks the immediate appeal of the western highlands: the peaks are lower and the volcanoes less symmetrical. The region's towns are almost all pretty featureless and perennially hot and dusty, so you're unlikely to want to hang around for long. **Esquipulas** is worth a visit, though, for its colossal church, the most important pilgrimage site in Central America. It's also positioned very close to the border with Honduras and El Salvador, though if you're heading into Honduras, you're most likely to end up spending the night in **Chiquimula**, a dull, hot town that's the gateway to the ruins of Copán just over the border. Finally there's the spectacular crater lake on top of the **Volcán de Ipala**, an idyllic spot whose isolation adds to its appeal.

Chiquimula

Set to one side of the broad San José river valley is the town of **CHIQUIMULA**, an unattractive, bustling *ladino* stronghold – if you've just arrived from Honduras, things only get better from here. Most travellers who come here are on their way to or from the Maya ruins of Copán, just over the border in Honduras (see p.418), and though the town has long been an important transport terminal, there's little else of note save a massive ruined colonial church on the edge of town beside the highway.

Everything you're likely to need in Chiquimula is east of the plaza, off 3 C which leads towards the main highway. The **bus terminal** is at 1A C, between 10 and 11 avenidas, midway between the plaza and the highway. There are frequent **buses** from here to Guatemala City (every 30min 4am–5pm; 3hr 15min), Esquipulas (every 15min 5am–7pm; 1hr), Jalapa via Ipala (7 daily 6am–4pm; 2hr 30min) and Puerto Barrios (hourly; 3hr). For Copán, there are buses to the border at El Florido (every 30min; 1hr 30min). For **changing money** there's a branch of the Banco G & T Continental at 7 Av 4–75 (Mon–Fri 9am–7pm, Sat 10am–1pm). There's **Internet** access at Email Center at 6 Av 4–51 (daily 9am–9pm); the Telgua office (daily 7am–midnight) is on the corner of the plaza.

Of the town's **hotels**, *Pensión Hernández* at 3 C 7–41 (☎942 0708; ❷–❸) is an excellent selection with clean, simple rooms, all with fan and some with a/c and private bathrooms; it has parking, and a small pool too. A little further down the road, at 3 C 8–30, *Hotel Central* (☎942 6352; ❸) has five pleasant rooms all with private bath and cable TV. When it comes to **eating**, there are inexpensive comedores in and around the **market**, centred on 3 C and 8 Av, as well as *Magic Burger* on 3 Calle which is cheap and open late. *El Tesero*, 7 Av 4–40, serves pretty decent Chinese food at moderate prices while close by, *Bella Roma*, 7 Av 5–31, specializes in pizza and pasta.

The Volcán de Ipala

Reached down a side road off the main highway between Chiquimula and Esquipulas, the **Volcán de Ipala** (1650m) may at first seem a little disappointing – it looks more like a rounded hill. However, it's well worth heading for if looking for some peace. The chances are that if you visit on a weekday it should be pretty quiet (except for the hum of a diesel generator that extracts water). The cone is filled by a beautiful little **crater lake** ringed by dense tropical forest – you can walk round the entire lake in a couple of hours. The easiest route to the top is via a trail (built by Earth Corp volunteers) from the village of **El Chagüitón** south of the village of Ipala; it's a 2km climb to the visitor centre where you pay a US$1.30 entrance fee. Buses and pick-ups run from Ipala towards the village of Agua Blanca hourly; get off at **El Sauce** at km 26.5, from where it's an hour and a half to the summit via El Chagüitón.

The village of **IPALA** is connected by bus with Jutiapa to the south, Jalapa in the west and Chiquimula to the north. It's a pretty forlorn place with a few shops and few **places to stay**, the best of which is the *Hospedaje Pinal* (❷), which has good clean rooms with private bathroom.

Esquipulas

Southeast from Chiquimula a beautiful road heads through the hills, running beneath craggy outcrops and forested peaks before emerging suddenly at the lip of a huge, bowl-shaped valley, with the town of **ESQUIPULAS** below. The final town on the eastern highway, Esquipulas is the most important Catholic shrine in Central America, and is entirely dominated by the four perfectly white domes of its **church**, which are brilliantly floodlit at night. The rest of the town is a messy sprawl of cheap hotels, souvenir stalls and restaurants which have sprung up to serve the pilgrims who flock to the town year-round from all over Central America, creating a booming resort where people come to worship, eat, drink and relax, in a bizarre combination of holy devotion and indulgence. The principal day of **pilgrimage** is January 15, when even the smallest villages save enough money to send a representative or two, filling the town to bursting point.

As a religious shrine, Esquipulas probably predates the Conquest. When the Spanish arrived, the Maya chief surrendered rather than risk bloodshed; the grateful Spaniards named the town in his honour and commissioned the famed colonial sculptor Quirio Cataño to carve an image of Christ for the church. Perhaps in order to make it more appealing to the local Maya, he chose to carve it from balsam, a dark wood. Things really took off in 1737 when the bishop of Guatemala, Pardo de Figueroa, was cured of a chronic ailment on a trip to Esquipulas. The bishop ordered the construction of a new church, which was completed in 1758, and his body was buried beneath the altar.

Inside the church today there's a constant scurry of hushed devotion amid clouds of smoke and incense. In the nave, pilgrims approach the image on their knees, while others light candles, mouth supplications or simply stand in silent groups. The image itself is approached by a side entrance: join the queue to shuffle past beneath it and pause briefly in front before being shoved on by the crowds behind. Back outside you'll find yourself among swarms of souvenir and relic hawkers, and pilgrims who, duty done, are ready to head off to eat and drink away the rest of their stay.

Practicalities

Rutas Orientales runs an efficient half-hourly **bus** service between Guatemala City and Esquipulas; its office is on the main street at 11 C and 1 Av. There are also buses across the highlands to Ipala and regular minibuses to the borders with **El Salvador** (every 30min 6am–4pm; 1hr) and **Honduras** at Aguacaliente (every 30min 6am–5.30pm; 30min). If you want to get to the ruins of Copán, you'll need to catch a bus to Chiquimula and change there for the El Florido border post (see opposite). There's a **Honduran consulate** (Mon–Fri 8am–1pm & 3–5pm) in the *Hotel Payaquí*, beside the church. Banco Industrial has a branch with Visa ATM at 9 C and 3 Av, and there's also a Banco G & T Continental with a MasterCard ATM almost opposite.

When it comes to staying in Esquipulas, you'll find yourself amongst hundreds of visitors whatever the time of year. **Hotels** probably outnumber private homes but most budget places are grubby and bare. Prices are always negotiable, depending on the flow of pilgrims. Avoid Saturday nights, when rooms cost double. Many of the **budget** options are clustered together in the streets off the main road, 11 C. The family-run *Hotel Villa Edelmira* (❷–❸) is one of the best, or try *La Favorita* on 10 C and 2 Av (❷). For a touch more luxury, head for 2 Avenida, beside the church, where you'll find the *Hotel Los Ángeles* (☎943 1254; ❹) with modern rooms, and the *Hotel Esquipulao* (☎943 2023, ❹), a cheaper annexe of the *Hotel Payaquí* (☎943 1143; ❺), which has excellent rooms and a pool.

There are also dozens of **restaurants** and **bars**, most of them overpriced by Guatemalan standards. Breakfast is a bargain, however, and you shouldn't have to pay more than US$1.50 for a good feed. The *Hacienda Steak House*, a block from the plaza at 2 Av and 10 C, is a smart restaurant, while many of the cheaper places are on 11 Calle and the surrounding streets.

2.5

Cobán and the Verapaces

The twin departments of the **Verapaces** harbour some of the most spectacular mountain scenery in the country, yet attract only a trickle of tourists, perhaps because there's less obvious evidence of Maya tradition and costume than elsewhere. If you've time to spare, however, you'll find the highlands of **Alta Verapaz** astonishingly beautiful, with their fertile limestone landscapes and mist-soaked hills. The mountains here are the wettest and greenest in Guatemala – locals say it rains for thirteen months a year. To the south, the department of **Baja Verapaz** could hardly be more different: a low-lying, sparsely populated area that gets very little rainfall.

The regional hub and the capital of Alta Verapaz is **Cobán**, an attractive mountain town with some good accommodation and restaurants. Though a little subdued

once the rain really settles in, it's still the best base for exploring the area. To the northeast sit the natural bathing pools of **Semuc Champey**, surrounded by lush tropical forest and fed by the azure waters of the Río Cahabón, while directly north of Cobán the region around **Chisec** is opening up as a key ecotourism destination. In Baja Verapaz, the towns of **Salamá**, **Rabinal** and **Cubulco** are best seen during their fiestas, where costumes are worn and traditional dances performed.

The main **road** into the Verapaces climbs up from the El Rancho junction on the Carretera al Atlántico past the turn-off at La Cumbre, and skirts the Quetzal Sanctuary before arriving at Cobán – a journey made by frequent pullman buses. Most other roads in the region are unsealed and covered only by a limited service of second-class buses and pick-ups, so the going can be slow.

Some history

The history of the Verapaces is quite distinct from the rest of Guatemala. Long before the Conquest the local **Achi Maya** had earned themselves a reputation as the most bloodthirsty of all the region's tribes, and were said to sacrifice every prisoner that they took. So ferocious were the Achi that not even the Spanish could contain them by force. Alvarado's army was unable to make any headway against them, and eventually he gave up trying to control the area, naming it *tierra de guerra*, the "land of war". The church, however, couldn't allow so many heathen souls to go to waste, and under the leadership of **Fray Bartolomé de Las Casas**, they made a deal with the conquistadors. If Alvarado would agree to keep all armed men out of the area for five years, the priests would bring it under control. In 1537 Las Casas and three Dominican friars set out into the highlands, befriended the Achi chiefs, learnt the local dialects and translated devotional hymns. By 1538 they had made considerable progress and had converted large numbers of Maya. At the end of the five years, the invincible Achi were transformed into Spanish subjects, and the king of Spain renamed the province Verapaz (True Peace).

Since the colonial era the Verapaces have remained isolated and, in many ways, independent. All their trade bypassed the capital by taking a direct route to the Caribbean, along the Río Polochic and out through Lago de Izabal. The area really started to develop with the **coffee boom** at the turn of the century, when German immigrants flooded into the region to run fincas. The Germans quickly prospered and exported huge quantities of coffee back to Europe, only to be expelled during World War II, when the USA insisted that Guatemala remove the enemy presence. Today, the Verapaces are still dominated by the huge coffee fincas and the wealthy families that own them, and there are also hints of Germanic influence here and there. Taken as a whole, however, the Verapaces remain very much *indígena* country: Baja Verapaz has a small **Achi** outpost around Rabinal, and in Alta Verapaz the Maya population is largely **Poqomchi'** and **Q'eqchi'**. The production of coffee and, more recently, cardamom for the Middle Eastern market has cut deep into their land and their way of life, with many people being driven off prime territory and onto marginal plots. The northern, flat section of Alta Verapaz includes a slice of Petén rainforest, and in recent years Q'eqchi' Maya and landless mestizos from the south have expanded into this region, carving out sections of the jungle and attempting to farm marginal plots.

Market days in the Verapaces

Monday: Senahú, Tucurú.
Tuesday: Chisec, El Chol, Cubulco, Lanquín, Purulhá, Rabinal, San Cristóbal Verapaz, San Jerónimo.
Saturday: Senahú.
Sunday: Chisec, Cubulco, Lanquín, Purulhá, Rabinal, Salamá, San Jerónimo, Santa Cruz, Tactic.

Baja Verapaz

The main approach to both departments is from the Carretera al Atlántico, where the road to the Verapaz highlands branches off at the **El Rancho** junction. Beyond El Rancho this road climbs steadily into the hills, the dusty browns and dry yellows of the Motagua valley giving way to an explosion of greens as dense pine forests and alpine meadows begin to cover the mountains. Some 48km beyond the junction is **La Cumbre de Santa Elena**, where the road for the main towns of Baja Verapaz turns off to the west, descending into the **Salamá valley**, surrounded by steep hillsides and seemingly cut off from the outside world.

Salamá

At the western end of the valley is **SALAMÁ**, capital of the department of Baja Verapaz. The town has a relaxed and prosperous air and its population is largely *ladino*. There's not much to do other than browse in the Sunday market, though the crumbling colonial bridge on the edge of town and the old church, with its huge, gilded altars, darkened by age, are worth a look. The **fiesta** in Salamá runs from September 17 to 21.

The pick of the **hotels** is the *Hotel Real Legendario* at 8 Av 3–57 (☎940 0187; ❸), with very clean modern rooms, all with private bath, good beds and cable TV. For something cheaper, *Pensión Juárez* (☎940 0055; ❶-❷) is a good budget hotel at the end of 5 Calle, where some rooms have private bath. For **eating**, there are several places around the plaza: *El Ganadero* is the best restaurant and *Deli-Donus* scores for coffee and snacks. Hourly **buses** run from Guatemala City to Salamá (6am–4pm; 3hr 30min). There's also a steady shuttle of minibuses to and from La Cumbre, for connections with pullman buses between Cobán and Guatemala City.

Rabinal

Less than an hour west from Salamá, **RABINAL** is another isolated farming town dominated by a large colonial Baroque church. Here the proportion of *indígena* inhabitants is considerably higher, making both the Sunday market and the fiesta well worth a visit. Founded in 1537 by Bartolomé de Las Casas, Rabinal was the first of the settlements to be included in his peaceful conquest of the Achi nation. Sights are few in Rabinal itself, though the town's small **museum** (Mon–Fri 9am–4pm; free) beside the church is worth a visit, with exhibits on traditional medicinal practices, local arts and crafts, and the terrible impact of the civil war in the region. The hills around Rabinal are scattered with Maya ruins, including the remains of **Cahyup**, 3km northwest of the plaza, a forty-minute hike away.

Rabinal's **fiesta** (Jan 19–24) is noted for its dances. The most famous of these, a unique extended dance drama known as the "Rabinal Achi", re-enacts a battle between the Achi and the K'iche' tribes – it's performed annually on January 23. If you can't make it for the fiesta, the **Sunday market** is a good second-best – Rabinal's artesanía includes carvings made from the *árbol del morro* (calabash tree) and pottery.

The best budget **hotel** is the *Posada San Pablo* at 3 Av 1–50 (❶–❷), with spotless rooms, some with private bath; if it's full, try the *Hospedaje Caballeros*, 1 C 4–02 (❶). For an inexpensive **meal** try *Cafeteria Mishell del Rosario* on 1 Calle behind the church. Hourly **buses** run between Salamá and Rabinal (50 min) between 5am and 5pm.

Cubulco

Another forty minutes of rough road to the west brings you down to the isolated *ladino* town of **CUBULCO**, surrounded on all sides by steep, forested mountains. Cubulco is again best visited for its **fiesta**, this being one of the few places where you can still see the **Palo Volador**, a pre-Conquest ritual in which men throw themselves from a thirty-metre pole with a rope tied around their legs, spinning down towards the ground as the rope unravels, and hopefully landing on their feet. It's as dangerous as it looks: most of the dancers are blind drunk and deaths are not uncommon. The main action takes place on July 25. For a bed, try the basic *Hospedaje Pías* (❶) next to the large *farmacia* in the centre of town; there are several comedores next to the market. Hourly **buses** run between Salamá and Cubulco via Rabinal.

The Biotopo de Quetzal

Back on the main highway towards Alta Verapaz and Cobán, the road sweeps around endless tight curves below forested hillsides. Just before the village of Purulhá (Km 161) is the **Biotopo del Quetzal** (daily 7am–4pm; US$2.50), an 11.5-square-kilometre nature reserve designed to protect the habitat of the endangered bird. The forest is also known as the Mario Dary Reserve, in honour of a lecturer from San Carlos University who campaigned for years for a cloudforest sanctuary to protect the quetzal – he was murdered in 1981, after upsetting powerful timber interests. The reserve he instituted comprises steep and dense rain- and cloudforest, pierced by waterfalls, natural pools and the Río Colorado.

Paths through the undergrowth from the road complete a circuit that takes you up into the woods and around above the reserve headquarters (from where you can get maps). There a few quetzals hidden in the forest but they're extremely elusive. The **best time** to visit is at sunrise, just before or just after nesting season (March–June). A favoured feeding tree is the broad-leaved *aguacatillo*, which produces a small avocado-like fruit. Whether or not you see a quetzal, the forest itself, usually damp with a perpetual mist the locals call *chipi-chipi*, is well worth a visit: a profusion of lichens, ferns, mosses, bromeliads and orchids, spread out beneath a towering canopy of cypress, oak, walnut and pepper trees.

About 100m past the reserve entrance is the rustic *Hospedaje Ranchito del Quetzal* (☎331 3579; ❷), with very basic **rooms** with or without private bath; there's also a

The resplendent quetzal

The **quetzal**, Guatemala's national symbol, has a distinguished past but an uncertain future. The feathers of the quetzal were sacred from the earliest of times, and in the strange cult of Quetzalcoatl, whose influence spread throughout Mesoamerica, the quetzal was incorporated into the plumed serpent, a supremely powerful deity. To the Maya the quetzal was so sacred that killing one was a capital offence, and the bird is also thought to have been the *nahual*, or spiritual protector, of the Maya chiefs. When Tecún Umán faced Alvarado in hand-to-hand combat his headdress sprouted the long green feathers of the quetzal; when the conquistadors founded a city adjacent to the battleground they named it **Quetzaltenango**, the Place of the Quetzals.

In modern Guatemala the quetzal's image permeates the entire country, appearing in every imaginable context, as well as lending its name to the nation's currency. Citizens honoured by the president are awarded the Order of the Quetzal, and the bird is also considered a symbol of freedom, since caged quetzals die in confinement. Despite all this, the sweeping tide of deforestation threatens the existence of the bird.

The more resplendent of the birds, and the source of the famed feathers, is the male. The heads of males are crowned with a plume of brilliant green, the chest and lower belly is a rich crimson, and trailing behind are the unmistakeable oversized, golden-green tail feathers, though these are only really evident in the mating season. The females, on the other hand, are an unremarkable brownish colour. The birds nest in holes drilled into dead trees, laying one or two eggs at the start of the rainy season, usually in April or May. Quetzals also can be quite easily identified by their strangely jerky, undulating flight.

simple comedor here too. Quetzals are often seen in the patch of forest around the hotel. In a different league the *Hotel Posada Montaña del Quetzal* at Km 156.5 (☎331 0929, Ⓦwww.hposadaquetzal.com; ❺–❻) has attractive rooms and stone and timber bungalows with fireplaces and showers – plus a restaurant, bar and swimming pool. **Buses** from Cobán pass the reserve entrance every thirty minutes.

Alta Verapaz

Beyond the quetzal sanctuary, the main road crosses into the department of Alta Verapaz, and another 13km takes you beyond the forests and into a luxuriant alpine valley of cattle pastures, hemmed in by steep, perpetually green hillsides. The first place of any size is **TACTIC** – a small, mainly Poqomchi'-speaking town adjacent to the main road, which most buses pass straight through. The colonial **church** in the centre of the village, boasting a Baroque facade decorated with mermaids and jaguars, is worth a look, as is the Chi-Ixim chapel high above the town.

About 10km past Tactic is the turn-off for **San Cristóbal Verapaz**, a pretty town almost engulfed by fields of coffee and sugar cane, set on the banks of the Lago de Cristóbal. From here a rough road continues to **Uspantán** in the western highlands (see p.198), from where there are connections on to Santa Cruz del Quiché, Nebaj and Huehuetenango. Pick-ups leave San Cristóbal Verapaz every two hours or so for Uspantán, and there are two daily buses at 10.30am and 12.30pm.

Cobán and around

The heart of this misty alpine land and the capital of the department is **COBÁN**. It's not a large place: suburbs fuse gently with nearby meadows and pine forests, giving the town the air of an overgrown mountain village. When the rain settles in, Cobán can have something of a subdued atmosphere, and in the evenings the air is usually damp and cool. That said, the sun does put in an appearance most days and the town makes a useful base to recharge, eat well and sleep soundly – and also has some genteel cafés in which to sample some of the finest coffee in the world. In addition, Cobán is a hub for all kinds of **ecotourism** possibilities in the spectacular mountains and rivers nearby.

Arrival, information and getting around

The easiest way to reach Cobán is with Transportes Escobar Monja Blanca, one of Guatemala's best **bus** services, who operate half-hourly departures between Guatemala City and Cobán, a journey of four to five hours; their office is on the corner of 2 C and 4 Av, Zona 4. Leaving Cobán, buses to **local destinations** leave from different stops. From the main mercado terminal (a block north of the plaza) six daily buses run to Laguna Lachuá, three daily to Sayaxché and hourly to Chisec. For Lanquín, morning buses leave from outside the Dispensa Familiar store on 1 C just east of the plaza and afternoon buses from 3 C and 2 Av (next to the *Posada Don Matalbatz*). Six daily buses leave for El Estor from the Campo Fútbol 1km north of the plaza, but there have been **several robberies** on this route – check the safety situation first. There's also a daily shuttle bus to Tikal via Flores run by Semuc Tours at the *Hostal d'Acuña*, leaving at 6am, passing through Chisec, Candelaria and Saxyaché and arriving at Flores at 10am before continuing on to Tikal by 11.30am.

There is no Inguat office in town, but luckily the helpful staff at the *Hostal d'Acuña* (see p.252) more than adequately fill the **information** gap, run tours and have a good folder with maps and bus times; check out the useful noticeboard here too. Discovery Nature, inside the *Posada Don Juan Matalbatz*, also provide reliable information and run **tours**, including trips to Semuc Champey, and lagunas Lachuá and Sepalau. Another option is with the highly recommended Proyecto Eco Quetzal, at 2 C 14–36, Zona 1 (☎952 1047, Ⓔbidaspeq@guate.net), an adventure and cultural tour operator that takes visitors to remote and beautiful areas of the

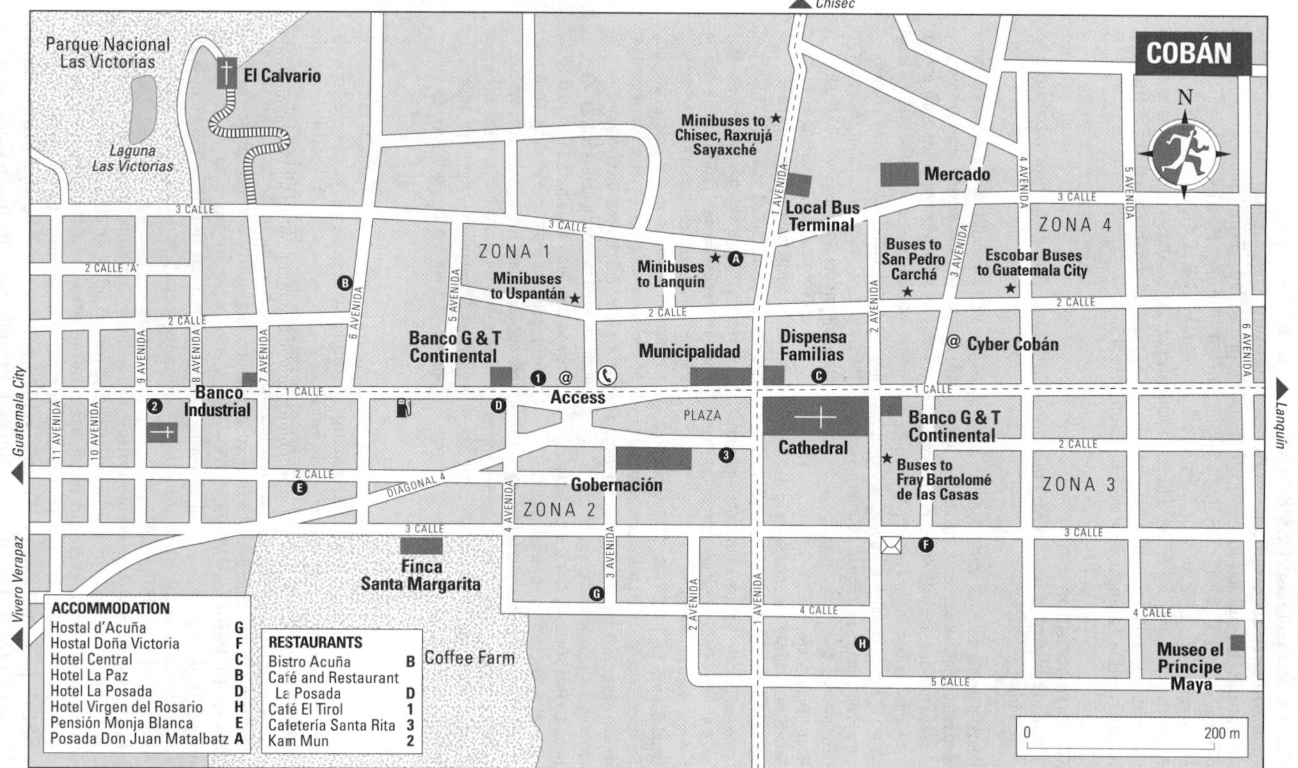
COBÁN
N
Parque Nacional Las Victorias
Laguna Las Victorias
El Calvario
Minibuses to Chisec, Raxrujá Sayaxché
Mercado
Local Bus Terminal
ZONA 1
ZONA 2
ZONA 3
ZONA 4
Minibuses to Uspantán
Minibuses to Lanquín
Buses to San Pedro Carchá
Escobar Buses to Guatemala City
Banco G & T Continental
Municipalidad
Dispensa Familias
Cyber Cobán
Banco Industrial
Access
PLAZA
Cathedral
Banco G & T Continental
Buses to Fray Bartolomé de las Casas
Gobernación
Finca Santa Margarita
Coffee Farm
Museo el Príncipe Maya
Chisec
Lanquín
Guatemala City
Vivero Verapaz
3 CALLE
2 CALLE 'A'
2 CALLE
1 CALLE
4 CALLE
5 CALLE
DIAGONAL 4
1 AVENIDA
2 AVENIDA
3 AVENIDA
4 AVENIDA
5 AVENIDA
6 AVENIDA
7 AVENIDA
8 AVENIDA
9 AVENIDA
10 AVENIDA
11 AVENIDA
0
200 m
ACCOMMODATION
Hostal d'Acuña G
Hostal Doña Victoria F
Hotel Central C
Hotel La Paz B
Hotel La Posada D
Hotel Virgen del Rosario H
Pensión Monja Blanca E
Posada Don Juan Matalbatz A
RESTAURANTS
Bistro Acuña B
Café and Restaurant La Posada D
Café El Tirol 1
Cafetería Santa Rita 3
Kam Mun 2

Verapaces. Trips using local Q'eqchi' guides include a three-day hike into the Chicacnab cloudforest (US$48), where quetzals are abundant.

For **Internet access** check out Access next to the *Café Tirol* on the north side of the parque. **Telgua** has its main office in the plaza (daily 7am–midnight); the **post office** is at 2 C and 2 Av (Mon–Fri 8am–4.30pm). **Banks** include Banco Industrial, 1 C and 7 Av, with Visa ATM and Banco G & T Continental, 1 C and 2 Av, with a MasterCard ATM. There's a **laundry**, La Providencia, at the sharp end of the plaza on Diagonal 4. Cobán is also a good base to **study Spanish**; recommended language schools are listed on p.150.

Accommodation

There are plenty of just-above budget and mid-range **hotels** in town, but nothing in the luxury bracket.

Hostal d'Acuña 4 C 3–17 ⓣ951 0482, ⓔcasadeacuna@yahoo.com. A superb place with excellent four-bed dorms (US$6 per person) and some small spotless rooms bordering the lush garden of a colonial house. Good food served on the veranda, and inexpensive tours offered. Highly recommended. ❸

Hostal Doña Victoria 3 C 2–38 ⓣ951 4213. Refurbished mansion decorated with antiques and artefacts and oozing character. The stylishly presented bedrooms all have private bath (though avoid the noise-prone streetside rooms). Café/bar and restaurant on site. ❺

Hotel Central 1 C 1–79 ⓣ952 1442. Vaguely Germanic-influenced design and clean, though darkish rooms with private bathrooms, set round a central garden. Comedor too. ❸

Hotel La Paz 6 Av 2–19 ⓣ952 1358. Safe, pleasant budget hotel run by a very vigilant *señora*. Some rooms have private bath. ❷

Hotel La Posada 1 C 4–12, at the western end of the plaza ⓣ952 1495, ⓔlaposada@c.net.gt. The finest hotel in town occupies an elegant colonial building with a beautiful, antique-furnished interior. The rooms, many with wooden Moorish-style screens (and some with four-poster beds), are set around two leafy courtyards and offer all the usual luxuries, though traffic noise can be a problem. There's also an excellent restaurant and café. ❻

Hotel Virgen del Rosario 2 Av 4–28 ⓣ952 1914. Excellent-value new place. The very comfortable spotless rooms here may have flowery bedspreads but all have cable TV and most have reading lights; towels are provided. ❷–❸

Pensión Monja Blanca 2 C 6–30 ⓣ951 1900 or 952 0531. Agreeably old-fashioned atmosphere and plenty of rooms, many with private bathroom. All choices are on ground level and set around two fecund courtyard gardens. Don't miss the Victorian-style tearoom for breakfast. ❸–❹

Posada Don Juan Matalbatz 3 C 1–46 ⓣ952 1599, ⓔdiscoverynat@intelnet.net.gt. Good, new colonial-style place with very spacious superior rooms/suites, some with bathtubs, and a few basic but clean budget rooms upstairs. Pool table, garden courtyard and tour agency. ❸–❺

The town

Cobán's heyday, when it stood at the centre of its own isolated world, is long gone. The elevated **plaza**, however, remains an impressive expanse, dominated by the cathedral, from which the town drops away on all sides. Check inside to see the remains of a massive, ancient church bell. A block behind, the **market** bustles with trade during the day and is surrounded by food stalls at night. Several blocks south you'll find an excellent collection of Maya artefacts and carvings inside the small **Museo El Príncipe Maya**, 6 Av 4–26, Zona 3 (Mon–Sat 9am–6pm; US$2), including shell necklaces, polychrome bowls and human figurines. Don't miss the eccentric flints or the main attraction: a stunning panel from a Cancuén altarpiece, embellished with 160 glyphs.

Life in Cobán revolves around **coffee**: the sedate restaurants, tearooms, trendy bars and overflowing supermarket serve it to the town's affluent elite, while the crowds that sleep in the market and plaza, assembling in the bus terminal to search for work, are migrant labourers heading for the plantations. For a closer look at Cobán's principal crop, take the guided tour offered by the **Finca Santa Margarita** (Mon–Fri 8am–12.30pm & 1.30–5pm, Sat 8am–noon; US$2), a coffee plantation just south of the centre of town at 3 C 4–12, Zona 2. The interesting tour (in English or Spanish) covers the history of the finca, examining all the stages of cultivation and production, and takes you on a walk through the grounds. You also get a chance to sample the crop and, of course, purchase some beans.

Likewise a short stroll from the town centre is the church of **El Calvario**, one of Cobán's most attractive sights. Head west out of town on 1 Avenida and turn right up 7 Avenida until you reach a steep cobbled path. You'll pass a number of tiny **Maya shrines** on the way up – crosses blackened by candle smoke and decorated with scattered offerings. There's a commanding view over the town from the whitewashed church, which has a distinctly pagan aura – Christian and Maya crosses hang from the roof inside hundreds of corn cobs (sacred in indigenous religion). Another place worth a look is the **Vivero Verapaz** (Mon–Sat 9am–noon & 2–4pm; US$1.25), a former coffee finca just outside town now dedicated to the growing of orchids, which flourish in these sodden mountains. The plants are carefully grown in a shaded environment, and a farmworker will show you around and point out the most spectacular blooms, which are at their best between November and January. You reach the nursery by leaving the plaza on Diagonal 4, turning left at the bottom of the hill, across the bridge and follow the road for 3km; taxis charge US$2.50.

Eating, drinking and entertainment

Eating in Cobán comes down to a choice between European-style restaurants and very basic, cheap comedores. In the latter, look out for *kaq' ik*, a terrific turkey soup. You'll find the cheapest food at the **market**, but as it's closed by dusk, head to the street stalls set up around the plaza. Central Cobán is pretty quiet at night, though there are some half-decent **bars**: *La Casona*, at 8 Av and 2 C, has live music and gets lively on Thursdays and weekends; *Bar Milenio* at 3 Av and 1 C also has live bands. Best of the **clubs**, *Keops*, 5 Av and 3 C, plays merengue and Latin dance. There are two **cinemas**: the CineTuria on the plaza, and the Cine Norte, on 1 Calle.

Bistro Acuña 4 C 3–17, Zona 2. Superb setting in a period home with rooms off a veranda and a garden; tables are candlelit at night. The menu is not cheap (a sandwich is US$5) but there are great pizzas, salads and pasta, and the breads and cakes are even better. Breakfast options include pancakes with fresh blueberries.

Café and Restaurant La Posada 1 C 4–12, Zona 2, inside *Hotel La Posada*. The smartest restaurant in town, with a stylish formal dining room, serving traditional Guatemalan specialities and international cuisine; there's always a daily special. The more relaxed café serves breakfasts, bagels and muffins.

Café El Tirol 1 Calle, on the north side of the plaza. Long-running place serving 52 different coffee possibilities, eight set breakfasts, hot chocolate, waffles and sandwiches. However the service here can be woefully lethargic. Closed Mon.

Cafetería Santa Rita 2 Calle, on the plaza close to the cathedral. This almost archetypal comedor with friendly service features filling *comida típica*; a good place to avoid all the trappings of all the other European-style cafés.

Kam Mun 1 C and 9 Av, Zona 2. Large, hygienic Chinese restaurant, with a solid line-up of economical choices.

San Pedro Carchá

A few kilometres east from Cobán, **SAN PEDRO CARCHÁ** has silver instead of coffee firing the economy and a stronger Mayan character. These days the two towns are merging into a single urban sprawl. Local buses between Cobán and Carchá leave from the terminal in Cobán and from the plaza in Carchá every 15 minutes. If you've an hour to spare, the **regional museum** (Mon–Fri 9am–noon & 2–5pm; US$0.75), beside the church, is worth a look. Alongside a collection of Maya artefacts are dolls dressed in local costumes and a mouldy collection of stuffed birds and animals, including the inevitable moulting quetzal. A little further afield, the **Balneario Las Islas** is a stretch of cool water that's popular for swimming. It's a couple of kilometres from the town centre: walk along the main street beside the church and take the third turning on the right, then follow the street for about 1km and take the right-hand fork at the end.

San Juan Chamelco

A few kilometres southeast of Cobán, easily reached by regular local buses from the terminal, **SAN JUAN CHAMELCO** is the most important Q'eqchi' settlement in the area. Many of your fellow bus passengers are likely to be women dressed in traditional costume, wearing beautiful cascades of old coins for earrings, and speaking Q'eqchi' rather than Spanish. Chamelco's focal point is a large colonial **church**, whose facade is rather unexpectedly decorated with twin Mayanized versions of the Hapsburg double eagle – undoubtedly a result of the historic German presence in the region. Inside the belfry is hidden the village's most significant treasure, a church bell that was given to the Maya leader Juan Matalbatz by the Holy Roman Emperor Charles V. The best time to visit the village is for its annual **fiesta**, on June 16.

Just outside Chamelco are the **Grutas de Rey Marcos** (daily 9am–5pm; US$3 including the services of a guide, plus hard hat and boot rental), a kilometre-long series of caves, though the tour only takes you a little way into the complex – you have to wade across an underground river at one stage to see some of the best stalactites and stalagmites, including one that's a dead ringer for the leaning tower of Pisa. The caves are a pleasant five-kilometre walk from Chamelco down a signposted road 150m west of the plaza; alternatively you can catch a pick-up from 0 C and 0 Av heading for the village of Chamíl. Just 500m from the caves is a great place **to stay**, *Don Jerónimo's* (ⓣ308 2255, ⓦwww.dearbrutus.com/donjeronimo; ❹ for full board), a vegetarian guesthouse/retreat in sublime countryside, run by a friendly, talkative American who has been living off the land here for more than twenty years.

Lanquín and Semuc Champey

Northeast of Cobán towards Sebol, a rough road (though it is being slowly paved) clings to slopes of a series of valleys, their precipitous sides patched with cornfields, but the level central land saved for the all-important coffee crop.

The road divides after 43km at the **Pajal** junction, three hours from Cobán, where a branch road heads down to **LANQUÍN**, 12km away, a very sleepy, modest Q'eqchi' village superbly sheltered beneath towering green hills. Don't count on practicing your Spanish here – the language has yet to gain much influence. Of the village's several **pensiones**, the good, cheap hospedaje-cum-store-cum-comedor *Divina Providencia* (❶) is the best, offering good grub, steaming hot showers and cold beers. The place that really packs in the travellers is the tremendous *El Retiro* (dorms US$4.50 per bed; doubles ❷), a ten-minute walk from the village along the road to Cahabón. This wonderful English-Guatemalan-owned lodge has an extensive grassy riverside plot and very attractive palm-leaf-thatched cabañas with mosquito screens, plus camping. There's great veggie food, a camp fire and a party vibe most nights, river tubing, and the owners run tours to sights in the region.

A couple of kilometres from the village on the road back to Cobán are the **Lanquín caves** (US$2.50), a maze of dripping, bat-infested chambers, stretching for at least 3km underground. An illuminated walkway complete with ladders and chains cuts through the first few hundred metres, but it's very slippery so take care. It's also well worth dropping by at dusk when thousands of bats emerge from the mouth of the cave and flutter off into the night.

Semuc Champey

The other attraction around Lanquín are the extraordinary pools of **Semuc Champey** (US$2.50, parking US$0.75), 10km to the south, which are a great deal more spectacular than the caves. There are a series of idyllic **pools** in which you can swim, formed by a natural staircase of turquoise waters suspended on a limestone bridge. The bulk of the Río Cahabón runs underground beneath this natural bridge, and by walking a few hundred metres upstream over a slippery obstacle course of rocks and roots you can see the aquatic frenzy for yourself. The river water plunges furiously into a cavern, cutting under the pools to emerge downstream. Don't leave your stuff unattended here. It's possible to spend the night at Semuc under a thatched shelter, or you could stay 1km back along the road to Lanquín at *Las Marías*, a basic new place with wooden rooms (❷) and dorms (US$2.50 per bed) and vegetarian cooking.

Pick-ups leave the plaza in Lanquín for Semuc on an irregular basis; or you can hire an *especial* return ride with a two-hour stay for around US$16 from the pick-up drivers in the plaza. Alternatively, tours are run from Cobán (see p.250), including the *Hostal d'Acuña*'s daily 7am shuttle bus (US$6 one way).

East to Cahabón

Beyond Lanquín the road continues 24km to **Cahabón**. From here, a very rough road heads south towards Panzós (see below), cutting high over the mountains through some of the finest, most verdant scenery in Guatemala. At the time of research there were no buses (only pick-ups) leaving Cahabón for the three-hour trip to El Estor (see p.242); check at *El Retiro* for the latest information.

The Polochic valley

If you're planning to head out towards the Caribbean from Cobán, or are simply interested in taking a short trip along Guatemala's back roads, then the **Polochic valley** is an ideal place to spend a day being bounced around inside a bus. However as there have been some **armed robberies** of buses recently, check the security situation first in Cobán before setting out.

The first two villages reached at the upper end of the lush V-shaped valley are **Tamahú** and **Tucurú**. High above Tucurú in the mountains to the north is the **Chelemá Reserve**, a large area of pristine cloudforest containing one of the highest concentrations of quetzals anywhere in the world. The forest is extremely difficult to reach; contact Proyecto Eco Quetzal in Cobán (see p.250), who can arrange accommodation with local families in the village of Chicacnab.

Beyond Tucurú the road plunges abruptly and cattle pastures start to take the place of the coffee bushes, while both the villages and the people begin to take on a more tropical look. Next comes **La Tinta** and then **Telemán**, from where a side road branches off north to **SENAHÚ**. Set back behind the first ridge of hills, Senahú is a small coffee centre set in a verdant, steep-sided bowl, and is an ideal starting point for a short wander in the Alta Verapaz hills. Three **buses** a day connect Cobán to Senahú. There are a couple of simple **pensiones** here, plus the *Hotel El Recreo Senahú* (☎952 2160; ❸) in the centre of the village, with twelve pleasant rooms. From here, you can trek to some nearby caves, the **Cuevas de Seamay**, used by Maya shamans for ceremonies, and on to Semuc Champey and Lanquín in a couple of days – ask for a guide at the *Hotel El Recreo Senahú*.

Continuing on down the Polochic valley you reach **PANZÓS**, the largest of the valley villages. Its name means "place of the green waters", a reference to the swamps that surround the river, swarming with alligators and bird life. In 1978, Panzós made the international headlines when a group of campesinos attending a meeting to settle land disputes were gunned down by the army and local police, though it's very peaceful today. Six daily buses from Cobán pass through the town en route to El Estor, while sporadic pick-ups leave Panzós for the uphill struggle to Cahabón, from where it's easy to continue to Lanquín and Semuc Champey. Beyond Panzós the road pushes on towards Lago de Izabal, passing a huge, deserted nickel plant, yet another monument to disastrous foreign investment, just before you come to El Estor (see p.242).

North towards Petén

Two routes head north from Cobán to Petén. Hourly buses run northeast until 3pm via the **Pajal** junction (see p.254) to the small isolated town of **Fray Bartolomé de Las Casas** where there are several pensiones – the best are the clean *Hotel Diamelas* and *Hotel Bartolo* (both ❷) – and a couple of banks. From Las Casas there's a steady flow of buses to Cobán, and also one daily to Poptún (see p.260) at 3am (5hr), plus pick-ups. A much quicker alternative route heads directly north via a smooth paved road past fields of cardamom and coffee, descending steadily in altitude to the small town of **Chisec** from where you can easily get to the spectacular **Lagunas Sepalau** and the huge cave of **Bombil Pek**. Both these routes meet up close to the small settlement of **Raxrujá**, which affords easy access to the ruins of **Cancuén.**

Raxrujá and the Candelaria caves

Some 18km west of Fray, **RAXRUJÁ** is little more than a few streets and some ramshackle buildings straggling round a bridge over the Río Escondido, a tributary of the Pasión, but it does function as a gateway to the extensive ruins of Cancuén and the Candelaria caves, and offers the only **accommodation** for miles around. First choice is the *Hotel Cancuén* (☎983 0720), on the edge of town down the road to Candelaria, with either basic simple rooms (❷) or spotless, excellent-value modern tiled rooms with TV and a/c (❸). For **food**, *Restaurant Tu Casa*, located next door, is a good choice with daily specials or, closer to the centre, try *Comedor Vidalia*. The Banrural (Mon–Fri 8am–5pm, Sat 9am–1pm) will cash travellers' cheques. **Buses** leave for Cobán at 3am, 4am, 8am, 1pm and 2pm, some via Chisec. Heading north to Sayaxché, it's mainly pick-ups, though there are daily buses at 7am, noon and 2pm.

The limestone mountains to the west of Raxrujá are full of caves. The most impressive are undoubtedly the **Candelaria caves**, 10km west, whose series of caverns stretches for around 18km and includes some truly monumental chambers such as the 200-metre-long "Tzul Tacca". Most of the caves are located on private property a short walk from the road and are jealously guarded by Daniel Dreux, who has set up the **Complejo Cultural de Candelaria** conservation area. Entrance to the complex, including a two-hour tour and a guide to the first cave system, costs US$3 per person, while a two-day tour by lancha covering 33km (only possible March–July) can also be arranged. Alternatively, contact one of the Cobán travel agents (see p.250). The complex has wonderfully atmospheric **accommodation** (☎710 8753, ⓔcuevascandelaria@aol.com; ❺ including all meals), but you can **camp** (US$2.50 per person) right opposite the entrance at the *Rancho Ríos Escondidos* (no sign).

Cancuén

North of Raxrujá is the large Maya site of **Cancuén**, where a huge Classic period palace has been unearthed. In 2000, newspapers across the world trumpeted the rediscovery of this ancient Maya city, lost for 1300 years, by an American-Guatemalan team of archeologists on the banks of the river Pasión. While the reality was very different – Cancuén had been discovered in 1907 and was even plotted on tourist board maps of the country – the sheer size of the ruins had certainly been underestimated, while new investigations revealed the site to be enigmatic in other ways. Uniquely, Cancuén seems to have lacked the usual religious and defensive structures characteristic of Maya cities and appears to have existed as an essentially secular trading city. For most of the twentieth century, the absence of soaring temple-pyramids led archeologists to assume that Cancuén was a very minor site, and it was ignored for decades. However, the vast amounts of jade, pyrite, obsidian and fine ceramics found recently indicate that this was actually one of the greatest trading centres of the Maya world, with a paved plaza (which may have been a marketplace) covering two square kilometres. Cancuén is thought to have flourished because of its strategic position between the great cities of the lowlands, like Tikal and Calakmul, and the mineral-rich highlands of southern Guatemala. The vast, almost ostentatious **palace** complex (structure L7–9) with 170 rooms and 11 courtyards, its sides adorned with dozens of life-sized stucco figures, is Cancuén's most arresting feature. Recent investigations at Cancuén have uncovered three stunning ball-court markers and two glyph-covered altar panels. At the time of writing, a camping area was under construction here and a visitor centre planned; call ⓣ902 3074 for up-to-date information.

To **get to** Cancuén, pick-ups (approximately hourly) leave Raxruhá for the *aldea* of **La Unión**, 12km to the north, where boatmen will take you by lancha (reservations ⓣ902 3074) for the thirty-minute ride along the Río Pasión to the site. It's also possible to travel via the village of La Isla, but connections here are not as good.

Chisec and around

Some 60km north of Cobán, **CHISEC** is a quiet, agreeable little place spread out along the highway. Though presently a fairly featureless place, Chisec has grown quickly in the last years as land-hungry migrants have moved into the region. It's one of the very few places in Guatemala not to have a church on its (huge) central plaza – many of its population are former guerrillas opposed to the influence of the Catholic Church. There are two **places to stay**, both about 800m north of the plaza, the best being *Hotel La Estancia* (ⓣ979 7748; ❸) with two floors of fairly plain but clean rooms, all with a/c and bathroom, a good comedor and a small swimming pool. On the other side of the road the *Hotel Nopales* (❷) is a decent budget place with bare, clean rooms. The best **food** is at the clean *Restaurant Bombil Pek* at the southern end of the village, with great breakfasts at *Cafeteria El Manantial* next to the Municipalidad (founded in 2002) on the south side of the plaza. Next door, Banrural issues Visa cash advances and will cash travellers' cheques, and you can surf the **Internet** at *Centro Electronico* just behind the bank.

Chisec makes the perfect base for visiting two remarkable natural attractions, the nearest being the "painted cave" of **Bombil Pek** some 2km north of town. There's a community-run guide office (daily 8am–3.30pm) beside the highway nearby, where you pay your entrance fee (US$3) and collect a flashlight; they also have **tubes** (US$2.50; best July–October) for river exploration for hire here. A guide then leads you along a delightful 40-minute hike through the *milpa* fields and forest, and down a steep slippery wooden staircase into the sinkhole and its vast 50m-high main cavern. Many ceramics have been found here and the cave is still used for Maya religious ceremonies. Your guide will then try to persuade you to squeeze through a tiny hole at the rear to a second, much smaller cave where the faded painted images of two monkeys (possibly representing the hero twins of the Popol Vuh) adorn the walls. From Chisec buses and pick-ups heading north along the highway pass the guides' office hourly.

The three exquisite jade lakes of **Lagunas Sepalau**, Chisec's other worthwhile attraction, are 9km from town along the road that heads west from the Municipalidad. Pick-ups run all day from the plaza and there's a bus at 11am. You'll be dropped off at the Q'eqchi' village of Sepalau where you pay a US$3 entrance fee. A local guide will accompany you to the lakes, 1km further away, with a lancha for paddling across the lake (and lifejackets). The first lake you come to, **Laguna Paraíso**, ringed by untouched dense jungle, is beautiful and peaceful, and makes the perfect spot for a swim. The second lake, called **Atsam'ja**, is much smaller, but the third and largest lake, named **Q'ekija**, a further kilometre down the track, is the most remarkable of all – a gorgeous blue-green colour, its near-vertical limestone sides backed by towering jungle. You'll almost certainly hear howler monkeys and see kingfishers, and perhaps toucans here.

Playa Grande and Laguna Lachuá

Northwest from Chisec, it's 80km on a mainly rough road to **PLAYA GRANDE**, the bridging point of the Río Negro. There's little traffic this way, mostly pick-ups. Most traffic from Cobán heads to Playa Grande via a turn-off on the main highway at the village of Bulbatz. Playa Grande itself is an authentic frontier settlement with cheap hotels, rough bars and brothels. If you need to **stay**, the best options are the basic but clean *Hospedaje Torre Visión* (❷) or *Pensión Reyna* (❶), while Banrural will change travellers' cheques.

The main point of interest in this area is the **Parque Nacional Laguna Lachuá** (US$5), a near-circular lake 4km off the main road east of Playa Grande. One of the least visited national parks in Central America, this is a beautiful, tranquil spot, with azure blue waters completely surrounded by dense tropical forest. Though it smells slightly sulphurous, the water is good for swimming, with curious horseshoe-shaped limestone formations by the edge that make perfect individual bathing pools. You'll see otters and an abundance of bird life, but watch out for mosquitoes. There's a large thatched *rancho* (shelter) with bunk beds (US$7) by the shore, or you can sling a hammock (available for rent), or camp. Fireplaces and wood are provided, though you'll need to bring food and drinking water.

Six daily minibuses and buses (plus pick-ups) leave **Cobán** for Playa Grande (4hrs) from the southwest corner of the bus terminal from the early morning. Coming south from Sayaxché, it's best to get off at Raxruhá and take another pick-up or truck from there.

Into the Ixcán

The Río Negro marks the boundary between the departments of Alta Verapaz and Quiché. The land to the west, known as the **Ixcán**, comprises a huge, swampy forest, which became the scene of bloody fighting in the civil war. The region has recently become a focus for *repatriado* settlement, with new villages being established by returning refugees who had fled to Mexico in the 1980s.

The journey further west across the Ixcán and into northern Huehuetenango is very arduous, along the worst roads in the country, even partly following a riverbed in the dry season. Allow around twelve hours to get from Playa Grande to Barillas; you'll probably have to switch from truck to bus to pick-up along the route.

2.6

Petén

The vast northern department of **Petén** occupies about a third of Guatemala but contains just three percent of its population. This huge expanse of swamps, dry savannas and tropical rainforest forms part of an untamed wilderness that stretches into the Lacandón forest of southern Mexico and across the Maya Mountains to Belize. Totally unlike any other part of the country, much of it is all but untouched, with ancient ceiba and mahogany trees that tower 50m above the forest floor. The area is also extraordinarily rich in **wildlife**: some 285 species of bird have been sighted at Tikal alone, including a great range of hummingbirds, toucans, blue and white herons, hawks, buzzards, wild turkeys and motmots (a bird of paradise). Beneath the forest canopy are many other species that are far harder to locate. Among the mammals are the massive tapir or mountain cow, ocelots, deer, coatis, jaguars, monkeys, plus crocodiles and thousands of species of snakes, insects and butterflies.

Recently, however, this position of privileged isolation has come under increasing threat. Waves of **settlers**, originally lured by offers of free land, have cleared enormous tracts of jungle, while oil exploration and commercial logging have cut new roads deep into the forest. The population of Petén, just 15,000 in 1950, is today estimated at perhaps 500,000. Various attempts have been made to halt the tide of destruction, but despite the fact that forty percent of Petén is officially protected by the **Maya Biosphere Reserve**, little is done to enforce this.

Natural environment aside, the Petén boasts an incredible number of Maya sites. The birthplace of **Maya civilization**, several hundred ruined cities have been mapped in the region, though most are still buried beneath the jungle. It's only relatively recently that archeologists have ascertained that Preclassic Maya culture first evolved in the Petén jungle at sites including Nakbé and Cival before peaking at the metropolis of **El Mirador** around 150 AD. Later during the Classic period (roughly 300–900 AD) the culture reached the height of its architectural, scientific and artistic achievement at **Tikal** and **Yaxhá**. At the close of the tenth century the cities were abandoned, probably due to a prolonged drought, and many of the people moved north to the Yucatán, where Maya civilization continued to flourish until the twelfth century.

By the time the Spanish arrived, tiny numbers of **Itzá**, a group of Toltec-Maya, had partially re-colonized the land around Lago de Petén Itzá. The forest proved so impenetrable however that it wasn't brought under Spanish control until 1697, more than 150 years after they had conquered the rest of the country. The Spanish had little enthusiasm for Petén however, and under their rule it remained a backwater. Independence saw no great change, and it wasn't until 1970 that Petén became genuinely accessible by car. Even today the network of roads is skeletal, and many routes are impassable in the wet season.

The twin lakeside towns of **Flores** and **Santa Elena** form the hub of the department. You'll probably arrive here, if only to head straight out to the ruins of **Tikal**, Petén's prime attraction, though the towns are also a key gateway for adventures to more distant ruins – **El Mirador**, **El Zotz** and **Nakbé**. Halfway between Flores and Tikal is the tranquil alternative base of **El Remate**. The caves and scenery around **Poptún**, on the main highway south, justify exploration; while down the other road south, **Sayaxché** is surrounded by yet more Maya sites. From Sayaxché you can set off **into Mexico** and the ruins of Yaxchilán via the road to Bethel.

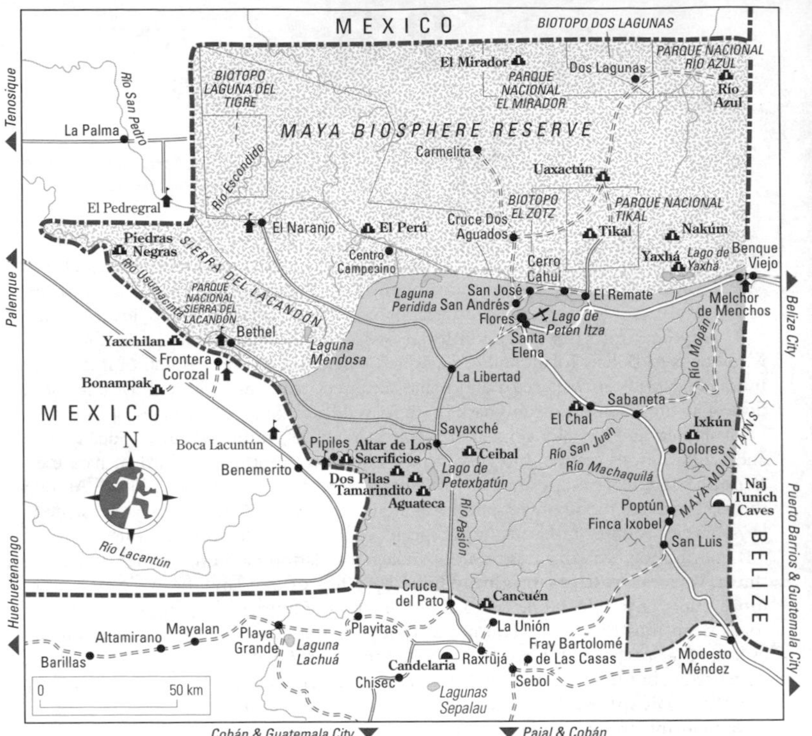

Getting to Petén

Many visitors arrive in Petén by bus or plane directly from **Guatemala City**. **By air** it's a short fifty-minute hop to Flores. A number of internal airlines fly the route daily and **tickets** can be bought from virtually any travel agent in the country; prices range between US$110 and US$140 depending on the airline. Demand is heavy and overbooking is common. **By bus** it can take anywhere between eight and ten hours. Numerous companies provide around twenty services a day from Guatemala City to Flores. If you don't want to do the 554-kilometre trip in one go, it's easy enough to do it in stages – the best places to break the journey are at **Quiriguá** (see p.234), **Río Dulce** (see p.239) and **Poptún** (see below).

Coming from the Guatemalan highlands you can reach Petén along the backroads **from Cobán** in Alta Verapaz, a long and adventurous route (see p.250). **From Belize or Mexico**, you can enter the country through Petén. From Belize you enter at the border town of Melchor de Mencos, while there are three routes from Mexico. But the most convenient and popular trip is from Palenque, skirting the ruins of Bonampak and Yaxchilán and crossing the Río Usumacinta at Frontera Corozal. All of these are covered on pp.277–279.

Poptún and around

Heading north from the Río Dulce (see p.239), the smooth paved highway to Flores cuts through a degraded landscape of small *milpa* farms and cattle ranches that was jungle a decade or two ago. Some 95km from Río Dulce, at an altitude of 500m, the first settlement of any interest is the small town of **POPTÚN**. For many travellers this dusty frontier settlement is the embodiment of rustic bliss and organic food – thanks to the proximity of the *Finca Ixobel* (see below). There's no particular reason to stay in the town itself, but you may well stop by to use a cybercafé (try *Servicio de Internet* next to the Fuente del Norte bus office) or banks (Bancafé has a Visa ATM). If you do get stuck here, **stay** at the friendly *Hotel Posada de los Castellanos* (☎927 7222; ❷), where you get hot water and a bathroom. The best food in town is at *La Fonda Ixobel*, which bakes good bread and cakes. For a more rural setting, head 6km north past the village of Machaquilá to the splendid cabañas of the *Villa de los Castellanos* (☎927 7541, ⓔecovilla@intel-net.net.gt; ❺, backpackers/students ❸), offering a comfortable base and good food for adventurous visitors to explore the forests, rivers and caves of central Petén. Carlos, the owner, is an excellent source of information – botanical, historical and logistical.

Finca Ixobel

About 4km south of Poptún, surrounded by aromatic pine forests in the cool foothills of the Maya Mountains, is the *Finca Ixobel* (☎410 4037, ⓦwww.fincaixobel.com), a working farm that also provides **accommodation**. The farm was originally run by Americans Mike and Carole DeVine, but on June 8, 1990, Mike was murdered by the army. This prompted the American government to suspend military aid to Guatemala, and after a drawn-out investigation which cast little light on their motives, five soldiers were convicted of the murder in September 1992. Others involved have managed to evade capture and their commanding officer, Captain Hugo Contreras, escaped from jail shortly after his arrest. Carole fought the case for years and remains at the finca.

Finca Ixobel is a supremely beautiful and relaxing place, where you can swim in the pond, walk in the forest, dodge the resident "attack" parrots and stuff yourself with delicious homegrown (mostly organic) food. Most people hang around way longer than they'd originally planned, some staying to work as volunteers. There are **hikes** into the jungle, horse-riding trips, tubing, 4WD jungle jaunts, and short excursions to nearby caves. Accommodation is either in attractive bungalows with two beds and a private bathroom (❹), regular rooms (❷) or **dorms** (US$3.75 per bed), and there's also camping and hammock space (US$3.50) and tree houses (❷). To get to the finca ask the bus driver to drop you at the gate (marked by a large sign), from where it's a fifteen-minute walk through the pine trees; after dark, it's safest to head for the *Fonda Ixobel* restaurant in Poptún and they'll call a taxi (US$2.25) to drop you off.

Flores

FLORES, the capital of Petén, has an easy pace and a sedate, Old-World atmosphere diametrically opposed to the commerce and hustle that typify most of Petén's towns. Its genteel cobbled streets, ageing houses and twin-domed church are set on a small island in Lago de Petén Itzá, connected to the mainland by a short causeway. It's small enough to explore in an hour or so and offers attractive places to stay, good restaurants and spectacular lake views. The frontier mentality lies just across the water in **SANTA ELENA**, a chaotic, featureless town which is dusty in the dry season and mud-bound during the rains.

The **lake** was a natural choice for settlement, and its shores were heavily populated in Maya times, with the capital of the Itzá, **Tayasal**, occupying the island that was to become modern Flores. Cortes passed through here in 1525, on his way south to Honduras, and left behind a sick horse that he promised to send for later. A horse-worshipping cult started as a result, and later visitors were sacrificed to the equine deity. Tayasal was eventually destroyed by Martín de Ursúa and an army of 235 in 1697. For the entire colonial period (and indeed up to the 1960s) Flores languished in virtual isolation, having more contact with neighbouring Belize than with the capital. Today, despite the steady flow of tourists passing through en route to Tikal, the town retains an urbane air.

Arrival and information

Arriving by **bus** from Guatemala City or Belize, most buses drop you a block or two from the causeway to Flores (though Linea Dorada buses continue over the causeway). The **airport** is 3km east of the causeway, a US$2 taxi ride into town. **Local buses** (every 10 minutes) cover the route but entail a time-consuming change halfway. Returning to the airport, local buses leave from the Flores end of the causeway every twenty minutes or so. Inguat has an **information** booth at the airport (daily 7am–noon & 3–6pm; ⓣ926 0533) and another office on the plaza in Flores (Mon–Sat 8am–4.30pm; ⓣ926 0669). There's also **CINCAP** (Mon–Fri 9am–noon & 2–6pm; ⓣ926 0718), a useful resource centre with detailed maps, books and leaflets. This is also the production office of *Destination Petén*, a free monthly listings and **information magazine**, available at most of the town's hotels and travel agencies.

Accommodation

Accommodation in Flores/Santa Elena has mushroomed in recent years and the sheer number of new **hotels** keeps prices competitive. There are several good budget places in Flores itself, making it unnecessary to stay in noisier and dirtier Santa Elena.

Flores

Butterfly Planet Hostel near the Linea Dorada office ⓣ926 0346, ⓔmartsam@itelgua.com. Right in the centre of town, with a multitude of dorm beds (US$3.75) and a couple of shared-bath rooms, opening onto a large courtyard. Guests have access to a kitchen and cheap beer. ❷

La Casa del Lacandón lakeshore, Calle Fraternidad ⓣ926 3591. One of the best-value hotels, overlooking the lake at the island's far side. Clean, tiled rooms, all with private hot-water bath, some with a/c. ❷–❸

Casazul close to the northern tip of the island ⓣ926 1138, ⓔreservaciones@corpetur.com. Stylishly converted colonial-style house, tastefully decorated in shades of blue. All rooms have private bath, fridge, a/c and TV; some have balcony. ❹

La Casona de la Isla Calle 30 de Junio ⓣ & ⓕ926 0593, ⓦwww.corpetur.com. An attractive citrus and powder-blue building, with modern rooms with clean, tiled hot-water bath, a/c, telephone and cable TV. Internet access, swimming pool and spectacular sunset views from the terrace restaurant/bar. ❺

Hospedaje Doña Goya north end of island ⓣ926 3538. Friendly, family-run guesthouse, offering clean, well-lit rooms, some with private hot-water bath and balcony, and excellent prices for single rooms. Breakfast available and there's a rooftop terrace with hammocks. ❸

Hotel Petén Calle 30 de Junio ⓣ926 0692, ⓕ926 0593, ⓦwww.corpetur.com. Modern hotel with rooms with private hot-water bath, fan, TV, a/c; and most have lake views. Small pool and lakeside restaurant has fabulous sunset views. Internet access for guests and kayaks for rent. ❺

Mirador del Lago I & II Calle 15 de Septiembre ⓣ926 3276. The best just-above-budget hotels in Flores, with well-furnished rooms with private hot-water bath and fan. Friendly management, and the restaurant has well-priced meals and a great lakeshore terrace. *Number I* is on the lakeshore and *No II* is across the street. ❸

Posada Tayazal Calle la Unión ⓣ & ⓕ926 0568, ⓔhotelposadatayazal@hotmail.com. Budget hotel with a selection of rooms, some with balcony and private hot-water bath. Prices and views increase as you head upstairs. ❷

Villa del Chef Calle la Unión ⓣ926 0926, ⓔenrico_ferrulli@yahoo.com. The best-value and most comfortable shared-bath budget rooms in Flores, with a small balcony and sitting area, above the restaurant of the same name. ❷

Villa del Lago southwest corner of island ⓣ & ⓕ926 0629, ⓔhotelvilladelago@itelgua.com. Modern, three-storey building with pretty, very comfortable rooms all with private hot-water bath, some with a/c and great views. ❹–❺

Santa Elena

Hotel Jade 6 Av. A backpackers' stronghold. Shambolic, but the cheapest place in town. ❶

Maya International on lakeshore ⓣ334 1818, ⓦwww.villasdeguatemala.com. Right over the lakeshore opposite Flores. Four-star hotel with good-sized rooms with private bath, TV, phone and a balcony. There's a reasonable restaurant and a pool. ❽

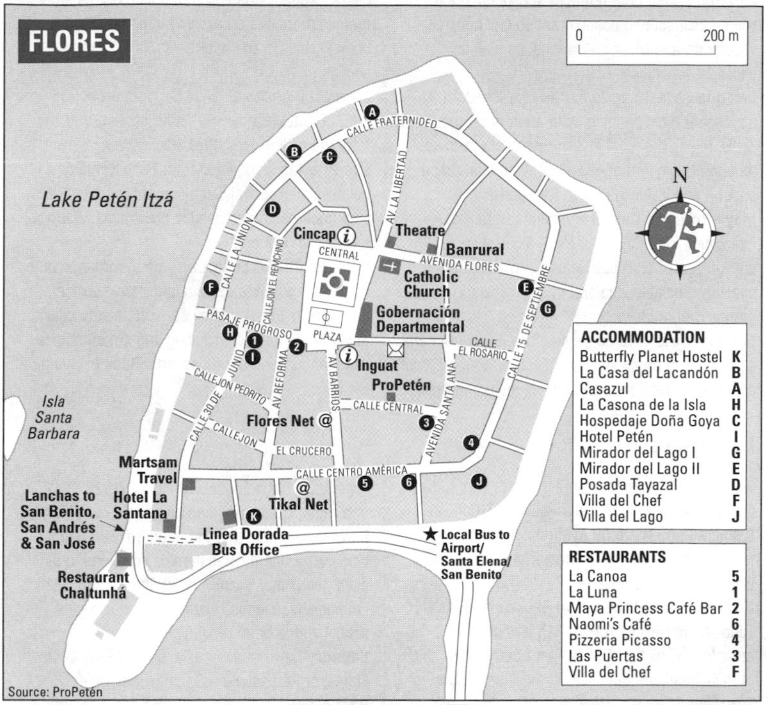

FLORES
0 200 m
N
Lake Petén Itzá
Isla Santa Barbara
CALLE FRATERNIDED
AV. LA LIBERTAD
CALLE LA UNION
CALLEJON EL REMCHINO
Cincap
CENTRAL
Theatre
Banrural
AVENIDA FLORES
Catholic Church
Gobernación Departmental
PASAJE PROGROSO
PLAZA
Inguat
ProPetén
CALLE EL ROSARIO
CALLE 15 DE SEPTIEMBRE
CALLEJON PEDRITO
AV REFORMA
AV BARRIOS
CALLE CENTRAL
AVENIDA SANTA ANA
CALLE 30 DE JUNIO
CALLEJON
Flores Net @
EL CRUCERO
CALLE CENTRO AMÉRICA
Martsam Travel
Hotel La Santana
Tikal Net
Lanchas to San Benito, San Andrés & San José
Linea Dorada Bus Office
Local Bus to Airport/ Santa Elena/ San Benito
Restaurant Chaltunhá
Source: ProPetén
ACCOMMODATION
Butterfly Planet Hostel K
La Casa del Lacandón B
Casazul A
La Casona de la Isla H
Hospedaje Doña Goya C
Hotel Petén I
Mirador del Lago I G
Mirador del Lago II E
Posada Tayazal D
Villa del Chef F
Villa del Lago J
RESTAURANTS
La Canoa 5
La Luna 1
Maya Princess Café Bar 2
Naomi's Café 6
Pizzeria Picasso 4
Las Puertas 3
Villa del Chef F
Causeway to Santa Elena (750 metres approx.)

SANTA ELENA
1 CALLE
1 CALLE A
2 CALLE
3 CALLE
SANTA ELENA
SAN BENITO
CALLE PRINCIPAL
4 AVENIDA
5 AVENIDA
6 AVENIDA
Avinsa Travel
4 CALLE (CALLE PRINCIPAL)
@ Tikal Net
Buses to Guatemala City & Poptún
Hotel Diplomatico
Bus Station
Banco Industrial (ATM)
Banco Agro Mercantil
4 CALLE A
Market
Buses to Belize
5 CALLE
ACCOMMODATION
Hotel Jade B
Maya International A
Airport, Tikal & Belize

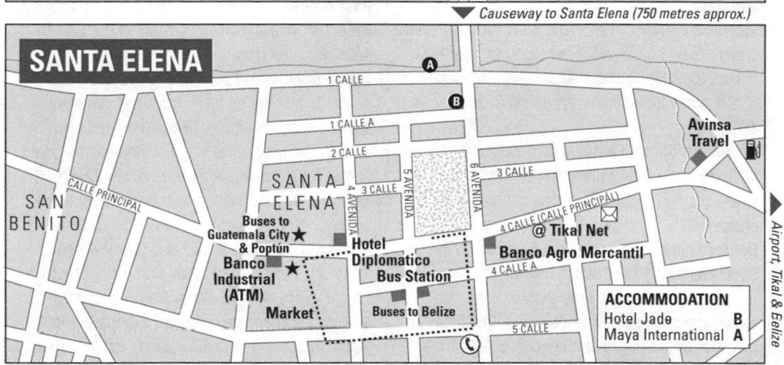

Eating and drinking

Flores unquestionably offers the best dining in Petén and there are a number of good restaurants, many with delightful lakeside views, though prices are a little higher than elsewhere in Guatemala. **Santa Elena** has a limited selection of comedores and not much else. Many restaurants serve **wild game**, often listed on menus as *comida silvestre*, such as *tepescuintle* (paca, a large relation of the guinea pig), *venado* (deer), or *coche de monte* (peccary, or wild pig). Virtually all this has been taken illegally from reserves.

La Canoa Calle Centro América. Popular, good-value place serving pasta, great soups, and some vegetarian and Guatemalan food, as well as excellent breakfasts.
La Luna Calle 30 de Junio. Set in a wonderfully atmospheric old building, with artwork on the walls, this is the most stylish restaurant in town, though it's not that pricey. Meat, fish, falafel and pasta – and it doesn't serve wild game.
Maya Princess Café Bar Avenida Reforma. An interesting international menu – Thai-style chicken, salad with basil leaves – plus daily specials. Sociable vibe and free movies shown at 4pm and 9pm daily.
Naomi's Café C 15 de Septiembre. Excellent café serving fresh bread and cakes and a range of local and international food and drinks, including pizza, pasta, cappuccinos and smoothies. Opens early for breakfast; there's an evening happy hour, also book exchange and book sales, and Internet access.
Pizzeria Picasso C 15 de Septiembre ⓣ926 0637. Great pizza served under cooling breezes from the ceiling fans; they also deliver.
Las Puertas signposted from Calle Santa Ana. Paint-splattered walls and live music as well as very good pasta and healthy breakfasts. Worth it for the atmosphere.
Villa del Chef C La Unión. A quiet, romantic little restaurant with tables on a lakeshore terrace (candlelit in the evenings) serving healthy cuisine at very good prices, including vegetarian choices like *pinchos*, and great desserts. Book exchange at the bar.

Listings

Banks Banco Agro Mercantil in Santa Elena, at the junction of the road to the causeway (Mon–Sat 8.30am–8pm) has a 5B ATM next door for MasterCard users. Banco Industrial (24-hour ATM) on 4 C has a Visa ATM.
Bike and motorbike rental Backabush Bike Tours, Av Barrios (ⓣ695 7481), has good mountain bikes for US$1.50 per hour, or take one of their excellent tours. For motorbikes (US$15 for 2 hrs) see Martsam Travel (below).
Car rental Budget, Hertz, Tabarini (with the widest choice; ⓣ926 0253) and Koka operate from the airport. Rates (including insurance) start around US$37 a day for a small car, around US$65 for a 4WD.
Communications Tikal Net, on C Centro América in Flores, and also C Principal in Santa Elena, where you can also make cheap international phone calls.
Doctor Centro Médico Maya, 4 Av near 3 C in Santa Elena (ⓣ926 0180), is helpful and professional, though no English is spoken.
Language schools San Andrés and San José (two attractive villages on the north shore of the lake) both have good Spanish schools. Official rates are all around US$175 a week for 20 hours of one-to-one lessons, food and lodging with a local family – expensive, but very few locals here speak English so you can progress quite quickly. In San Andrés, the Eco Escuela (ⓣ926 0718, ⓦwww.ecomaya.com) is the largest, longest-established school in Petén, while the Escuela Nueva Juventud (ⓣ711 0040, ⓦwww.volunteerpeten.com) is in a 70-hectare medicinal plant reserve and also offers environmental volunteer opportunities. In San José, there's the Escuela Bio Itzá (ⓣ928 8142, ⓔbioitza@guate.net), and also the newer Mundo Maya Ecological Spanish School (ⓣ928 8321, ⓦwww.mundomayaguatemala.com). In Flores itself, the Ixchel Spanish Academy (ⓣ926 3225, ⓔspanishacademy@martsam.com) is a new school with a good reputation.
Laundry Lavandería Amelia, behind CINCAP in Flores, or Petenchel on C Centro América.
Post offices In Flores, on Av Barrios, in Santa Elena C Principal, two blocks east of the Banco Agro Mercantil (Mon–Fri 8am–4.30pm).
Travel agents and tour operators Every hotel seems to be offering tours, but most can simply sell you minibus trips to Tikal or bus and plane tickets. The best travel agent in Flores is Martsam Travel, C Centro América (ⓣ & ⓕ926 3225, ⓦwww.martsam.com), where the owners speak English. They run a daily trip to Yaxhá (p.279) for US$20pp (minimum 2) and also offer overnight jungle trips to El Zotz, El Perú and many other sites. Explore, 4 Calle, Santa Elena (ⓣ926 2375, ⓦwww.exploreguate.com), are experts in trips to Ceibal (US$35), on the Río Pasión, and Aguateca and Dos Pilas (overnight US$140, including Ceibal) on Lago de Petexbatún. Eco Maya, C Centroamérica (ⓣ926 3202, ⓦwww.ecomaya.com) specialize in remote hikes to sites including Río Azul, El Mirador and Nakbé.
Voluntary work The language schools listed above always have some sort of programme for volunteers, including helping with women's groups, teaching children and environmental work. ARCAS (Asociación de Rescate y Conservación de Vida Silvestre), the Wildlife Rescue and Conservation Association (ⓣ926-2022,

Ⓦ www.rds.org.gt/arcas), set in 48 hectares of forest on the lakeshore, runs an inspiring rescue and rehabilitation programme for animals and birds. To volunteer you need to donate US$100 a week (the minimum stay required) and this covers food, lodging and transportation.

Around Flores and the Lago de Petén Itzá

At the **Skyway Ixpanpajul**, 10km from Santa Elena, just off the road to Guatemala City (daily 6am–6pm plus night tours; US$12), a network of suspension bridges and stone paths connects 3km of forested hilltops in a 9-square-kilometre private reserve. On the bridges, you can enjoy a monkey's-eye view of the canopy and there's an enormous *mirador* from where you can see virtually the whole of the Petén Itzá basin – and hear howler monkeys roaring in the background. Allow a few hours so you can take your time and see the trees and orchids. It's best to go in the early morning or after mid-afternoon or even at night (tours from Marstam Travel in Flores cost US$30), when wildlife (including coatimundi, marguey and snakes) really comes to life. Any Poptún-bound *microbus* will drop you at the entrance.

Another obvious excursion is a **trip on the lake**. Boatmen can take you around a circuit that takes in a *mirador* and small ruin on the peninsula opposite and the **Petencito zoo**, 3km east of Flores (daily 8am–5pm; US$2.50), a surprisingly well-looked-after collection of the local fauna, including jaguars and other cats, monkeys and macaws, housed in generally spacious enclosures in a hilly jungle setting on the lakeshore. A lancha to get there will cost around US$15 and for this price the boatman will wait for as long as it takes to have a look around. Slightly nearer, **Arcas**, an animal rescue centre (see "Voluntary work", opposite), is open to the public (daily 8am–5pm; US$2). Both these places can also easily be visited by bike, otherwise boatmen loiter with intent below the *Hotel Santana* in the southwest corner of Flores.

San Andrés and San José

Though accessible by bus and boat, the traditional villages of **San Andrés** and **San José**, across the lake from Flores, have until recently received few visitors. Sloping steeply up from the shore, the streets are lined with one-storey buildings, some fashioned out of palmetto sticks and thatch, some coated with plaster and tin-roofed, and others made from brightly painted concrete. Pigs and chickens wander freely. Just about the only outsiders are students at the villages' four **language schools** (see opposite). **SAN ANDRÉS** has the basic *Hotel Corina* (❷) on top of a hill behind the centre and 3km to the west you'll find the wonderful lakeside *Hotel Nitún* (Ⓣ201 0759, Ⓦwww.nitun.com; ❻ including transport from Flores), which offers spacious accommodation in thatched stone cabañas with private bathrooms; the restaurant serves superb healthy food. The hotel is also the base for Monkey Eco Tours (same contact details), who organize well-equipped expeditions to remote archeological sites.

Perched above a lovely bay, 2km east along the shore from San Andrés, **SAN JOSÉ** is even more relaxed than its neighbour. The village is undergoing something of a cultural revival: Itza, the pre-conquest Maya tongue, is being taught in the school, and you'll see signs in that language dotted all around. Take a look at the Catholic **church** where three sacred skulls are kept in a cabinet; they're paraded through the streets as part of a pagan ceremony on the Day of the Dead (November 1) each year. Beyond San José a signed track on the left leads 4km to the Classic-period **ruins of Motúl**. The site is fairly spread out and little visited (though there should be a caretaker about), with four plazas, stelae and pyramids.

Hourly **buses** leave from 5 C next to the market in Santa Elena to both villages, or you can take a shared **lancha** (US$0.75 to San Andrés, 25 min; US$1 to San José, 30 min) from the dock beside *Hotel Santana* in Flores.

El Remate

On the eastern shore of Lago de Petén Itzá, 30km from Santa Elena on the road to Tikal, the quiet and friendly village of **EL REMATE** offers a pleasant alternative to staying in Flores and makes a convenient base for visits to Tikal. **Getting to El Remate** is easy: all minibuses to Tikal pass through the village, or catch any bus heading for the Belize border and get off at the village of **Puente Ixlú** (also called El Cruce), from where it's a two-kilometre walk down the Tikal road. **Returning to Flores**, a few local buses and a swarm of minibuses from Tikal ply the route.

On the north shore of the lake, 3km along the road from the centre of El Remate, the **Biotopo Cerro Cahuí** (daily 6am–4.30pm; US$2.50) is a 6.5-square-kilometre wildlife conservation area comprising lakeshore, ponds and some of the best examples of undisturbed tropical forest in Petén. The smallest and most accessible of Petén's reserves, it contains a rich diversity of plants and animals, and is especially recommended for birdwatchers. There are hiking trails, a couple of small ruins and two thatched *miradores* on the hill above the lake; pick up maps and information at the gate where you sign in, close to the *El Gringo Perdido* hotel. There's lots to explore in the rich tropical environment around El Remate, including boat tours of the eastern end of the lakeshore operated by the *Casa de Don David*. Plenty of places also rent out canoes for a dollar an hour.

Accommodation and eating

Most of the **accommodations** listed below have a distinctive charm. As far as eating out in the area, there are a few simple comedores offering inexpensive Guatemalan **food**, and a couple of European-style restaurants; most of the hotels also provide meals. Accommodation options are listed in the order you reach them from Puente Ixlú.

Las Sirenas on the right ⓣ928 8477. Clean, comfortable rooms, some with private bath, in a wooden building with views of the lake. There's a café below and owner Beto Nuñez speaks English and offers guided tours. ❷

El Mirador del Duende high above the lake, reached by a stairway cut into the cliff ⓣ301 5576, ⓔmicuchitril@hotmail.com. An incredible collection of igloo-like whitewashed stucco cabañas decorated with Maya glyphs, plus space for hammocks and tents. Great terrace overlooking the lake and cheap vegetarian food. ❷

La Mansión del Pajaro Serpiente just below *El Mirador del Duende* ⓣ & ⓕ926 8498, ⓔpajaroserpiente@intelnett.com. American-Guatemalan-owned place that offers the best accommodation in the village, with wonderful thatched, two-storey stone cabañas in a tropical garden and smaller rooms, all with superb lake views. The honeymoon suite has its own pool. Good food is also available, and there's a small swimming pool. ❺

La Casa de Don David 300m beyond *La Mansión*, right on the junction ⓣ306 2190, ⓦwww.lacasadedondavid.com. Very well-run, spacious and secure accommodation in bungalows and rooms with private cold- or hot-water baths, set in grassy grounds that reach down to the lakeshore. The American-Guatemalan owners offer great information and filling meals, change money, arrange trips, and sell bus and shuttle bus tickets. ❹

Casa Roja 500m down the road to Cerro Cahuí on the right. Good budget deal right by the lake. Simple, well-constructed stick-and-thatch cabañas, plus camping and an inexpensive vegetarian restaurant. Kayaks for rent. ❷

Casa de Doña Tonita 800m down the road to Cerro Cahuí on the right. Four basic clapboard rooms, built high above the lake, with great views. The owner also runs a pleasant thatched-roofed restaurant next door with vegetarian food and snacks. ❷

Mon Ami 300m past *Dona Tonita's* ⓣ928 8413. Attractive rooms and bungalows with stylish, homely touches run by an inimitable Frenchman who has lived in Petén for over a decade. Also superb in-house restaurant with many Gallic dishes. ❸

El Gringo Perdido on the north shore, 3km from *Don David's* ⓣ & ⓕ334 2305, ⓔgringo_perdido@hotmail.com. Long-established place in a tranquil setting offering rooms with bath, a mosquito-netted bunk, good-value open-fronted cabañas and camping (US$3 per person); plus a restaurant. Guided canoe tours available. ❸

Tikal

Towering above the rainforest, **Tikal** is possibly the most magnificent of all Maya ruins. The site is dominated by five enormous temples, steep-sided pyramids that rise up to 60m from the forest floor, while around them are literally thousands of other structures, many half-strangled by giant roots and still hidden beneath mounds of earth. The site itself is deep in the jungle of the **Parque Nacional Tikal**, a protected area of some 370 square kilometres, on the edge of the even larger Maya Biosphere Reserve. The trees around the ruins are home to hundreds of species including howler and spider monkeys, toucans and parakeets. The sheer scale of the place is overwhelming, and its atmosphere spellbinding. Whether you can spare as little as an hour or as long as a week, it's always worth the trip.

Plane schedules are designed to make it easy to visit the ruins as a day-trip from Flores or Guatemala City, but if you can spare the time it's well worth **staying overnight**, partly because you'll need the extra time to do justice to the ruins themselves but, more importantly, to spend dawn and dusk at the site, when the forest canopy bursts into a frenzy of sound and activity. The air fills with the screech of toucans and the roar of howler monkeys, while flocks of parakeets and toucans wheel around the temples, and bats launch themselves into the night. With a bit of luck you might see a coati or a grey fox sneak across one of the plazas.

Arrival and information

Tourist minibuses meet flights from the capital and are operated by just about every hotel in Flores and Santa Elena, starting at 4am to catch the sunrise. In addition a **local bus** (Pinita) leaves the market at 1pm, arriving at Tikal about 2.30pm, then continuing to Uaxactún (see p.273), before returning to Santa Elena at 5am. If you're travelling from Belize to Tikal, get off at **Puente Ixlú** – the three-way junction at the eastern end of Lago de Petén Itzá – to change buses; there are passing minibuses all day long.

Admission to the national park (daily 6am–6pm) costs US$6.25. A **licensed guide** (US$40 for a 4hr tour) is a worthwhile investment if you can afford it; there's a desk in a visitor centre and many speak excellent English. The site also has a **post office**, and a **visitor centre**, with an overpriced café-restaurant and stalls selling film, postcards and books: Michael Coe's *Tikal: A Handbook to the Ancient Maya Ruins* is the best guide to the site, while *The Birds of Tikal* is useful for identifying some of the hundreds of species you might come across as you wander round. The **Museo Lítico** (daily 9am–4pm; free) is also located in the visitor centre, housing numerous poorly labelled stelae.

Between the *Jungle Lodge* and *Jaguar Inn* hotels (see below), the one-room **Museo Tikal** (Mon–Fri 9am–5pm, Sat & Sun 9am–4pm; US$1.25) houses some of the artefacts found in the ruins, including jewellery, ceramics, obsidian eccentric flints, the jade jewellery found in tumba 116 and the magnificent Stela 31, which shows the Tikal ruler Smoking Frog bearing a jaguar-head belt and a jade necklace. There's also a spectacular **reconstruction of Hasaw Chan K'awil's tomb**, one of the richest ever found in the Maya world, containing 180 worked jade items in the form of bracelets, anklets, necklaces and earplugs, and delicately incised bones.

Accommodation and eating

There are three **hotels** at the ruins, all of them fairly expensive and not especially good value. The best place is the *Jungle Lodge* (ⓣ476 8775, ⓕ476 0294, ⓦwww.junglelodge.guate.com; ❺/❼), which offers good bungalow accommodation with two double beds per bungalow, and a few small "budget" rooms with shared bath; there's also a restaurant and a pool. Next door is the overpriced *Jaguar Inn* (ⓣ926 0002, ⓦwww.jaguartikal.com; ❻), with nine bungalows with little verandas, a five-bed dorm (US$10 per person), hammocks with nets (US$5) and camping (US$3.25 per

The rise and fall of Tikal

According to the latest archeological evidence, the first occupants of Tikal arrived around 900 BC, probably attracted by its position above the surrounding seasonal swamps and by the availability of **flint** for making tools and weapons. The first definite evidence of buildings dates from 500 BC, and by about 200 BC the first ceremonial structures had emerged, including the first version of the **North Acropolis**. Two hundred years later, the **Great Plaza** had begun to take shape and Tikal was already established as a major site with a large permanent population. Despite development and sophisticated architecture, Tikal remained very much a secondary centre, dominated, along with the rest of the area, by **El Mirador**, the first Maya city-state about 65km to the north (see p.275).

The closing years of the **Preclassic** (250–300 AD) era were marked by the eruption of the Ilopango volcano in El Salvador, which smothered huge areas of Guatemala in a thick layer of volcanic ash. Trade routes were disrupted and the ensuing years saw the decline and abandonment of El Mirador, creating a power vacuum with bitter disputes between the cities of Tikal and Uaxactún. Tikal eventually won under the inspired leadership of Chac Tok Ich'aak (Great Jaguar Paw I), probably with the aid of the powerful highland centre of **Kaminaljuyú** – on the site of modern Guatemala City – which was itself allied with **Teotihuacán**, the ancient metropolis that dominated what is now central Mexico.

The victory over Uaxactún enabled Tikal's rulers to control much of central Petén for the next three centuries, developing into one of the most elaborate and magnificent of all Maya cities. This extended period of prosperity saw temples rebuilt, while the city's population grew to somewhere between 50,000 and 100,000, and its influence reached as far as Copán in Honduras.

In the middle of the sixth century, however, Tikal suffered a major setback. Already weakened by upheavals in central Mexico, where Teotihuacán was in decline, the city now faced major challenges from the east, where the city of **Caracol** was emerging as a regional force, and from the north, where **Calakmul** was becoming a formidable rival "superpower". In an apparent attempt to subdue a potential rival, Wak Chan K'awil, **Double Bird**, the ruler of Tikal, launched an attack (known as an "axe war") on Caracol and its ambitious leader, Yahaw to, **Lord Water**, in 556 AD. Despite capturing and sacrificing a noble from Caracol, Double Bird's strategy was only temporarily successful; in 562 AD Lord Water, backed by Calakmul, hit back in a devastating "star war", which crushed Tikal and almost certainly resulted in the capture and sacrifice of Double Bird. The victors stamped their authority over the humiliated nobles of Tikal, smashing stelae, desecrating tombs and destroying written records, ushering in an era

person), but no pool. Close by, the *Tikal Inn* (T926 1917, F926 0065, Ehoteltikalinn@intelgua.com; 6) is a better bet, with nice thatched bungalows, pleasant rooms and a glorious swimming pool. Alternatively, you can also camp or sling a hammock (US$4) or rent a tiny cabaña (US$13; sleeps two) at Tikal's **campsite**, complete with shower block. Hammocks and mosquito nets (essential in the wet season) are available for rent on the spot or from the *Comedor Imperio Maya* opposite the visitor centre. It's illegal to camp or sleep out among the ruins.

The three simple **comedores** at the entrance to the ruins, and a couple more inside, offer a limited menu of traditional Guatemalan specialities – eggs, beans, grilled meat and chicken. For a more extensive menu, there's a decent restaurant in the *Jungle Lodge*. Cold soft drinks are sold around the ruins by vendors.

The ruins

The sheer scale of the ruins at Tikal can at first seem daunting. The **central area**, with its five main temples, forms by far the most impressive section; if you start to during which Tikal was completely overshadowed by Calakmul. Another effect of this assault was to shift many smaller centres throughout Petén from Tikal's to Calakmul's influence.

Towards the end of the seventh century however, Calakmul's stranglehold had begun to weaken and Tikal gradually started to recover its lost power. Under the formidable leadership of Hasaw Chan K'awil, **Heavenly Standard Bearer**, who reigned from 682–723 AD, the main ceremonial areas were reclaimed after the desecration suffered. By 695 AD, Tikal was powerful enough to launch an attack against Calakmul, capturing and executing its king, Yich'ak K'ak or **Fiery Claw/Jaguar Paw**, and severely weakening the alliance against Tikal.

The following year, Hasaw Chan K'awil repeated his astonishing coup by capturing **Split Earth**, the new king of Calakmul, and Tikal regained its position among the most important of Petén cities. Hasaw Chan K'awil's leadership gave birth to a revitalized and powerful ruling dynasty: in the hundred years following his death Tikal's four main temples were built and his son, Yik'in Chan K'awil, or **Divine Sunset Lord** (who ascended to the throne in 734 AD), had his father's body entombed in the magnificent **Temple I**. Temples and monuments were still under construction until at least 869 AD, when Tikal's last recorded date is inscribed on Stela 24.

The cause of Tikal's final **downfall** remains a mystery, but what is certain is that around 900 AD almost the whole of lowland Maya civilization collapsed. It's probable that a number of factors took their toll, though a prolonged drought may have been the trigger. We do know that Tikal was abandoned by the end of the tenth century.

Little more is known of Tikal until 1848, when it was **rediscovered** by a government expedition led by Modesto Méndez. Later in the nineteenth century a Swiss scientist visited the site and removed the beautifully carved wooden lintels from the tops of Temples 1 and 4 – they are currently in a museum in Basel – and in 1881 the English archeologist Maudslay took the first photographs of the ruins. The site could only be reached on horseback and the ruins remained mostly uncleared until 1951, when the Guatemalan army built an airstrip, paving the way for a cultural invasion of archeologists and tourists. The gargantuan project to excavate and restore the site started in 1956, and involved teams from the University of Pennsylvania and Guatemala's Institute of Anthropology. Most of the major work was completed by 1984, but Temple 5 was restored in 2003 and thousands of minor buildings still remain buried in roots, shoots and rubble. There's little doubt that an incredible amount is still buried around the site – in 1996 a workman unearthed a stela (Stela 40, dating from 468 AD) while mowing the grass on the Great Plaza.

explore beyond this you can wander seemingly forever in the maze of smaller, **unrestored structures** and complexes. Compared to the scale and magnificence of the main area, they're not that impressive, but armed with a good map (the best is in Coe's guide to the ruins), it can be exciting to explore some of the rarely visited outlying sections. Whatever you do, Tikal is certain to exhaust you before you exhaust it.

From the entrance to the Great Plaza

From the entrance, a path leads past **Complexes Q and R**, twin pyramids built by **Chitam**, Tikal's last known ruler, to mark the passing of a *katum* (twenty 360-day years). Set to one side is a copy of the superbly carved Stela 22 (the original is now in the Museo Lítico). Bearing to the left after Complex R, you approach the **East Plaza**; in its southeast corner stands an imposing temple, beneath which were found the remains of several severed heads, the victims of human sacrifice. Behind the plaza is the **sweat house**, which may have been similar to those used by

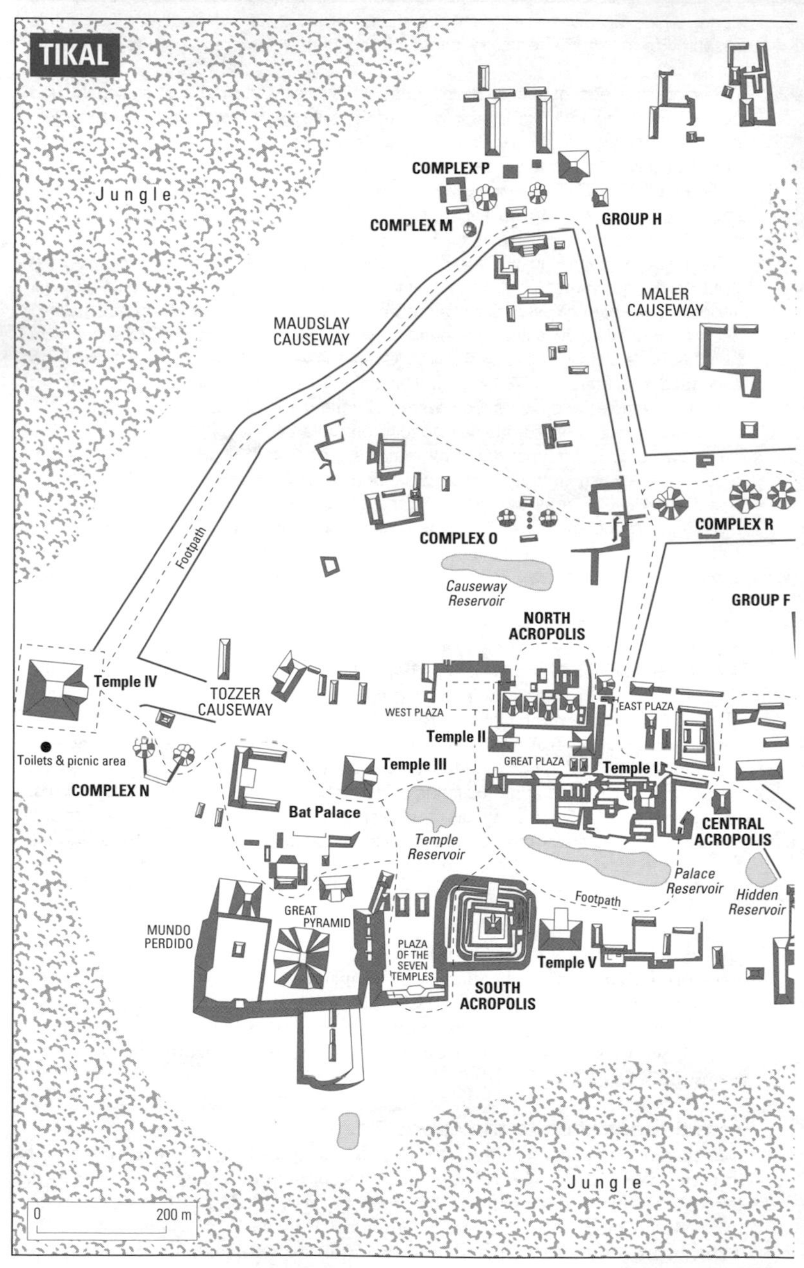
TIKAL
Jungle
COMPLEX P
COMPLEX M
GROUP H
MAUDSLAY CAUSEWAY
MALER CAUSEWAY
Footpath
COMPLEX O
COMPLEX R
Causeway Reservoir
NORTH ACROPOLIS
GROUP F
Temple IV
TOZZER CAUSEWAY
WEST PLAZA
EAST PLAZA
Temple II
Toilets & picnic area
Temple III
GREAT PLAZA
Temple I
COMPLEX N
Bat Palace
CENTRAL ACROPOLIS
Temple Reservoir
Palace Reservoir
Hidden Reservoir
Footpath
GREAT PYRAMID
MUNDO PERDIDO
PLAZA OF THE SEVEN TEMPLES
Temple V
SOUTH ACROPOLIS
Jungle
0
200 m

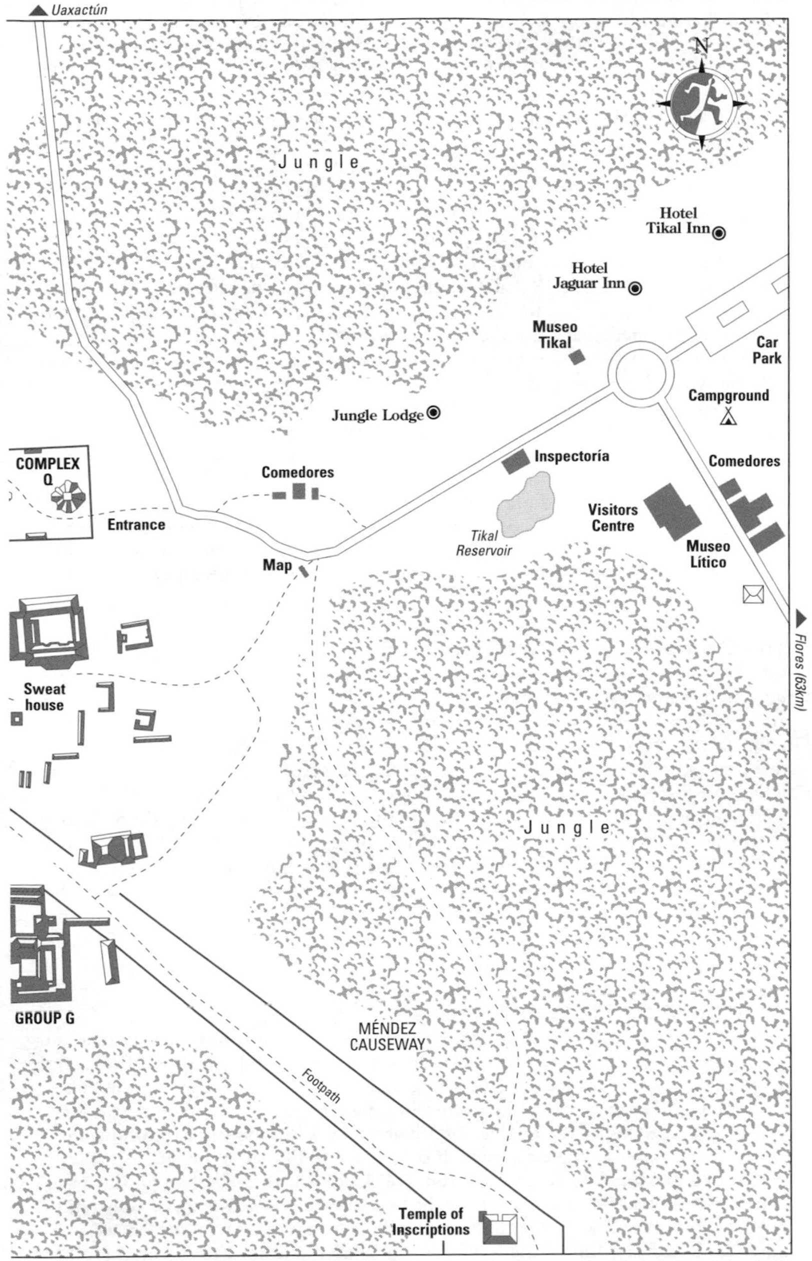
Uaxactún
N
Jungle
Hotel Tikal Inn
Hotel Jaguar Inn
Museo Tikal
Car Park
Campground
Jungle Lodge
Inspectoría
Comedores
COMPLEX Q
Comedores
Entrance
Visitors Centre
Tikal Reservoir
Museo Lítico
Map
Flores (63km)
Sweat house
Jungle
GROUP G
MÉNDEZ CAUSEWAY
Footpath
Temple of Inscriptions

highland Maya today. It's thought that Maya priests would take a sweat bath in order to cleanse themselves before conducting religious rituals.

From here a few short steps bring you to the **Great Plaza**, the heart of the ancient city. Surrounded by four massive structures, this was the focus of ceremonial and religious activity at Tikal for around a thousand years. Beneath the grass lie four layers of paving, the oldest of which dates from about 150 BC and the most recent from 700 AD. **Temple 1**, towering 44m above the plaza, is the hallmark of Tikal – it's also known as the Jaguar Temple because of the jaguar carved on its door lintel (now in a museum in Basel). This temple was built to contain the magnificent tomb of **Hasaw Chan K'awil** (682–721 AD) by his son and successor Yik'in Chan K'awil. The skeleton was found in the tomb at the temple's core, facing north and surrounded by an assortment of jade, pearls, seashells and stingray spines, the last a symbol of human sacrifice. There's a reconstruction of the tomb (tumba 116) in the Museo Tikal. Standing opposite, like a squat version of Temple 1, is **Temple 2**, known as the Temple of the Masks for the two grotesque masks, now heavily eroded, that flank the central stairway. As yet no tomb has been found beneath this temple, which now stands 38m high, although with its roof comb intact it would have equalled Temple 1.

The **North Acropolis**, which fills the whole north side of the Great Plaza, is one of the most complex structures in the entire Maya world. In true Maya style it was built and rebuilt on top of itself, and beneath the twelve temples that can be seen today are the remains of about a hundred other structures. As early as 100 BC the Maya had constructed elaborate platforms here supporting temples and tombs. Archeologists have removed some of the surface to reveal these earlier structures, including two four-metre-high Preclassic **masks**. In front of the North Acropolis are two lines of **stelae** with circular altars at their bases, all of which were originally painted a brilliant red.

The Central Acropolis and Temple 5

On the other side of the plaza is the **Central Acropolis**, a maze of tiny interconnecting rooms and stairways built around six smallish courtyards. The buildings here are usually referred to as palaces rather than temples, although their precise use remains a mystery. Possibilities include law courts, temporary retreats, administrative centres, and homes for Tikal's elite. Behind the acropolis is the palace reservoir, which was fed with rainwater by a series of channels from all over the city.

Further behind the Central Acropolis is the 58-metre-high **Temple 5**, whose commanding facade is now restored. It's now believed that the Temple was started in 600 AD and finished fifty years later by the ruler K'inich Wayan. A vertiginous wooden staircase (closed when it's been raining heavily) attached to the side of the temple accesses a slender upper level, just beneath the roof comb, from where you get a stomach-churning perspective of the Great Plaza and an ocean of jungle beyond.

From the West Plaza to Temple 4

Behind Temple 2 is the **West Plaza**, dominated by a large Late Classic temple on the north side, and scattered with various altars and stelae. From here the Tozzer Causeway – one of the raised routes that connected the main parts of the city – leads west to **Temple 3** (55m), covered in jungle vegetation. A fragment of Stela 24, found at the base of the temple, dates it at 810 AD. Around the back of the temple is a huge palace complex, of which only the **Bat Palace** has been restored. At the end of the Tozzer Causeway is **Temple 4**, at 64m the tallest of all the Tikal structures. Built in 741 AD, it is thought by some archeologists to be the resting place of the ruler **Yik'in Chan K'awil**, whose image was depicted on wooden lintels built into the top of the temple. Twin ladders, one for the ascent, the other for the descent, are attached to the sides of the temple. Exhausting as the climb is, one of the finest views of the whole site awaits, with the forest canopy stretching out to the horizon all around you, interrupted only by the great roof combs of the other temples.

The Mundo Perdido, Plaza of the Seven Temples and Temple of the Inscriptions

To the south of the Central Acropolis, reached by a trail from Temple 3, you'll find the **Plaza of the Seven Temples**, which forms part of a complex dating back to before Christ. There's an unusual triple ball court on the north side of the plaza, and to the east is the unexcavated South Acropolis. To the west, the **Mundo Perdido**, or Lost World, is another magical and very distinct section of the site with its own atmosphere and architecture. Little is known about the ruins here, but archeologists hope that further research in this area will help to explain the early history of Tikal. The main feature is the **great pyramid**, a 32-metre-high structure whose surface hides four earlier versions, the first dating from 500 BC. The top of the pyramid offers awesome views towards Temple 4 and the Great Plaza, though access is periodically closed when the stone steps are wet.

Finally, there's the **Temple of the Inscriptions**, reached along the Méndez Causeway from the East Plaza behind Temple 1. The temple (only discovered in 1951) is about 1km from the plaza. It's famous for its twelve-metre roof comb, at the back of which is a huge but rather faint hieroglyphic text.

The far north: Uaxactún, El Mirador and around

Away to the north of Tikal, lost in a sea of jungle, are dozens of other substantial **ruins** – unrestored and for the most part uncleared, but with their own unique atmosphere. Twenty-three kilometres north of Tikal, strung out by the side of a disused airstrip, are the village and ruins of **UAXACTÚN** (pronounced "Wash-ak-toon"). The village is a jumping-off point for the more remote sites of **El Zotz** and **Río Azul**, the bulk of whose temples are coated in an anarchic tangle of roots and shoots, with only the tallest roof combs visible. Dirt tracks go as far as Río Azul and El Zotz, offering the perfect destinations if you're in search of adventure and want to visit virtually untouched Maya sites. Further to the west, reached by tracks from the village of **Carmelita**, is the colossal Preclassic site of **El Mirador** and the ruins of several more formative cities, including Nakbé and Wakná. Excursions to these remote sites can be organized in Flores, or Carmelita itself.

Uaxactún

Substantially smaller than Tikal, the ruins at **Uaxactún** are thought to date from the same era. During the Preclassic period Uaxactún and Tikal coexisted in relative harmony, both being dominated by El Mirador, but by the first century AD, with El Mirador in decline, a fierce rivalry developed between Tikal and Uaxactún. The two finally clashed in 378 AD, when Tikal's warriors conquered Uaxactún, forcing it to accept subordinate status.

The overall impact of Uaxactún may be a little disappointing after the grandeur of Tikal, but you'll probably have the site to yourself. The most interesting buildings are in **Group E**, east of the airstrip, where three low reconstructed temples, built side by side, are arranged to function as an observatory. Viewed from the top of a fourth temple, the sun rises behind the north temple on the longest day of the year and behind the southern one on the shortest day. Beneath one of these temples the famous **E-VII sub** was unearthed, one of the oldest buildings ever found in Petén, once thought to date back to 2000 BC, though a much later date is now accepted. The original pyramid had a simple staircase up the front, flanked by two stucco masks, and post holes in the top suggest that it may have been covered by a thatched shelter. On the other side of the airstrip is **Group A**, a series of larger temples and residential compounds, some of them reconstructed, a ball court and some impressive stelae.

A **bus** from Flores passes through Tikal en route for Uaxactún at around 3pm; or take a **tour** from Flores (see p.264). **Staying overnight** you have two options: the welcoming *Campamento Ecológico El Chiclero* (ⓣ & ⓕ926 1095; ❷) offers clean rooms without bath, or you can camp or sling up a hammock for US$3. Owner Antonio Baldizón also organizes 4WD trips to Río Azul, and his wife Neria prepares excellent food. Otherwise *Aldana's* (❷) is friendly but very basic with wooden rooms, and camping at US$2 per person.

El Zotz

Thirty kilometres west of Uaxactún, along a rough track passable by 4WD, is **El Zotz**, a large Maya site set in its own nature reserve. To **get there** you can rent vehicles, supplies and equipment in Uaxactún, or take a tour from Flores. On foot, after about four hours – almost halfway – you come to **SANTA CRUZ**, where you can camp if necessary. At the site itself you'll be welcomed by the guards who look after the reserve headquarters. You can camp here and, with permission, use their kitchen and drinking water; remember to bring some food to share with them.

Totally unrestored and smothered by vegetation, El Zotz has been systematically looted, although there are guards on duty all year. Zotz means "bat" in Maya and each evening at dusk you'll see tens, perhaps hundreds of thousands of **bats** of several species emerge from a cave near the campsite. It's especially impressive in the moonlight, the beating wings sounding like a river flowing over rapids – one of the most remarkable natural sights in Petén.

Continuing beyond El Zotz, it takes about four and a half hours to walk to **Cruce dos Aguadas**, a crossroads village on a bus route to Santa Elena (bus leaves at 7am), where you'll find shops and the *Comedor Patojas*, where you can sling a hammock or camp. Northwards, the road goes to Carmelita for El Mirador and west towards El Perú (not passable in the rainy season).

Río Azul

The remote site of **Río Azul**, almost on the border where Guatemala, Belize and Mexico meet, was discovered in 1962. The city and its suburbs had a population of around five thousand and probably reached a peak in the Preclassic era. Although totally unrestored, the core of the site is similar to a small-scale Tikal, with the tallest temple (AIII) standing some 47m above the forest floor, surfacing above the treetops and giving magnificent views across the jungle.

Several incredible **tombs** have been unearthed here. Tomb 19 is thought to have contained the remains of one of the sons of Stormy Sky, Tikal's great expansionist ruler. Nearby tombs contained the bodies of warriors, dressed in clothing typical of Teotihuacán in central Mexico – further supporting evidence of links between Tikal and that mighty city. Extensive **looting** occurred after the site's discovery, with a gang of up to eighty men plundering the tombs and removing some of the finest murals in the Maya world once the archeological teams had retreated to Flores in the rainy season. Mercifully, despite its chamber being looted in 1981, Tomb 1's walls remain almost intact, and today there are two resident guards.

It's 95km north by **road** from Uaxactún to Río Azul, though it's only passable in the dry season, when it can be covered by 4WDs in as little as four hours, depending on conditions. **Walking** or on **horseback** it's four days each way – three at a push. Trips can be arranged through *El Chiclero* in Uaxactún or through a number of agents in Flores. Once you arrive at Río Azul you'll be welcome to **stay** at the guards' camp (bring some supplies).

El Mirador and around

El Mirador is perhaps the most exotic and mysterious of all Petén's Maya sites. Still buried in the forest, this massive city matches Tikal's scale, and may even surpass it. Rediscovered in 1926, it dates from an earlier period than Tikal, having flourished between 150 BC and 150 AD, and was almost certainly the first great city in the Maya world. It was unquestionably the dominant city in Petén, occupying a commanding position above the rainforest, at an altitude of 250m, and was home to tens of thousands of Maya. Little archeological work has been done here but it's clear that the site represents the peak of Preclassic Maya culture, which was far more sophisticated than was once believed.

The core of the site covers some sixteen square kilometres, stretching between two massive pyramids that face each other across the forest. The site's western side is marked by the massive **Tigre Complex**, made up of a huge single pyramid flanked by two smaller structures, a triadic design that's characteristic of El Mirador's architecture. The base of this complex alone would cover around three football fields, while the height of the 2000-year-old main pyramid touches 70m, equivalent to an eighteen-storey building and the tallest structure anywhere in the Maya world. In front of the Tigre Complex is El Mirador's sacred hub: a long narrow plaza, the **Central Acropolis**, and a row of smaller buildings. Burial chambers unearthed in this central section contained the bodies of priests and noblemen, surrounded by the obsidian lancets and stingray spines which were used to pierce the penis, ears and tongue in ritual bloodletting ceremonies. The spilling of blood was seen by the Maya as a method of summoning and sustaining the gods, and was clearly common at all the great ceremonial centres.

To the south of the Tigre Complex is the **Monos Complex**, another triadic structure and plaza, named after the resident howler monkeys. To the north the **León pyramid** and the **Casabel Complex** mark the edge of the site. Heading away to the east, the Puleston Causeway runs to the smaller East Group, the largest of which (about 2km from the Tigre Complex) is the **Danta Complex**. This is another triadic structure, rising in three stages to a height just below that of the Tigre pyramid, but with an even better view since it was built on higher land.

The area **around El Mirador** is riddled with smaller Maya sites, and as you look out across the forest from the top of either of the main temples you can see others rising above the forest canopy on all sides – including the giant Calakmul in Mexico. Among the most accessible are **Nakbé**, 12km south, the first known Maya city, first settled around 1000 BC with its 48-metre-high temple and huge stucco masks; **El Tintal**, around 21km southwest, which you'll pass on your way in from Carmelita; and **Wakná**, which was only discovered in 1998. The archeologist Dr Richard Hanson is campaigning hard to get the whole region protected; see Ⓦwww.miradorbasin.com for more background information.

Practicalities

Getting to El Mirador is a substantial undertaking, involving a rough 60km bus or pick-up journey from Santa Elena to the chicle- and *xate*-gathering centre of **Carmelita**, followed by two days of hard jungle hiking – you'll need a horse to carry your food and equipment. The journey is impossibly muddy in the rainy season, and is best attempted from mid-January to August; February to April is the driest period. The trip offers an exceptional chance to see virtually untouched forest, and perhaps some of the creatures that inhabit it. It's cheapest to get there independently by gathering some people together first (maybe in Flores) and heading for Carmelita and getting in touch with the Tursimo Cooporativa (if you speak Spanish contact them first on the community phone Ⓣ861 0366) who will then organize guides, packhorses, food, water and camping gear for you; there's more information at Ⓦwww.mostlymaya.com/carmelita. EcoMaya and Martsam Travel (see p.264) offer five-day **tours** (around US$330 per person for groups of four) from Flores, including guide, packhorse and digs in Carmelita. Bring some supplies for the guards, who spend forty days at a time in the forest, subsisting on beans and tortillas.

There are three daily **buses**, plus pick-ups from Santa Elena to Carmelita via San Andrés (see p.265) and Cruce Dos Aguadas (see p.274). There's basic but clean **accommodation** in Carmelita at the *Campamento Nakbé* (❷), 1.5km before the village, where the large thatched shelters have mosquito nets and hammocks, or, if you have your own tent, you can **camp** (US$2 per person). For a good feed, visit the *Comedor Pepe Toño* in the centre of the village, run by Brenda Zapata, who is a mine of information about the area and can introduce you to the local guides.

Sayaxché and around

Southwest of Flores, on a bend in the Río Pasión, the frontier town of **SAYAXCHÉ** makes an ideal base for exploring the surrounding forest and its huge collection of archeological remains. The town is the supply centre for a vast surrounding area that is being steadily cleared and colonized. The complex network of rivers and swamps that cuts through the forested wilderness here has been an important trade route since Maya times, and there are several interesting ruins in the area. Upstream is **Ceibal**, a small but beautiful site in a wonderful jungle setting; to the south is **Lago de Petexbatún**, on the shores of which are the small ruins of **Dos Pilas** and **Aguateca**. Both sites offer great opportunities to wander in the forest and watch the wildlife.

Sayaxché practicalities

Getting to Sayaxché from Flores is very straightforward, with four daily Pinita **buses** (5.30am, 11am, 2pm & 4pm; 1hr 30min) and very regular minibuses plying the fairly smooth 62-kilometre (mostly paved) road. A ferry takes you over the Río Pasión, directly opposite Sayaxché. **Hotels** in Sayaxché are on the basic side. The *Guayacán* (ⓣ926 6111; ❸), right beside the river, has clean functional rooms with private bath, and some with a/c, plus lovely sunset views from the terrace. The *Posada Segura* (❷), 250m right of the dock is cheaper but just as comfortable with decent, secure clean rooms, some with private bath and a good comedor. There are a few reasonable places to **eat**; best are the surprisingly stylish *El Botanero* on the second-left street after the dock where they have fish and shrimp and great cocktails, and the *Restaurant Yaxkin* (closes 8pm), where the portions are huge. You'll find plenty of **boatmen** eager to take you up- or downriver, though they tend to see all tourists as walking cash-dispensers and quote prices in dollars. Try Viajes Don Pedro (ⓣ & ⓕ928 6109), which offer **tours** of the area from their office on the riverfront. You can change **travellers' cheques** at Banora, a block up from the *Guayacán*.

Ceibal

The most accessible and impressive of the sites near Sayaxché is **Ceibal**, reachable either by land or river. It's easy enough to make it there and back in an afternoon **by boat**; haggle with the boatmen at the waterfront and you can expect to pay around US$50 (for up to six people). The boat trip is followed by a short walk through towering rainforest. **By road**, Ceibal is just 17km from Sayaxché. Any transport heading south out of town passes the entrance track to the site, from where it's an 8km walk through the jungle to the ruins.

Surrounded by forest and shaded by huge ceiba trees, **the ruins** are a mixture of cleared open plazas and untamed jungle. Though many of the largest temples lie buried under mounds, Ceibal does have some outstanding and well-preserved carving: the two main plazas are dotted with lovely **stelae**, centred around two low platforms. During the Classic period Ceibal was a relatively minor site, but it grew rapidly between 830 and 930 AD, apparently after falling under the control of colonists from what is now Mexico. Outside influence is clearly visible in the carving here: speech scrolls, straight noses, waist-length hair and serpent motifs are all decidedly non-Maya. The monkey-faced Stela 2 is particularly striking, beyond which is Stela 14, another impressive sculpture straight ahead down the path. If you turn right here and walk for ten minutes you'll reach the only other restored part of the site, set superbly in a clearing in the forest – an unmissable massive circular stone platform which was either an altar or observation deck for astronomy.

Lago de Petexbatún: Aguateca and Dos Pilas

A similar distance to the south of Sayaxché is **Lago de Petexbatún**, a spectacular expanse of water ringed by dense forest and containing plentiful supplies of snook, bass, alligator and freshwater turtle. The shores of the lake abound with bird life and animals (including howler monkeys) and there are a number of Maya ruins. **Aguateca**, perched on a high outcrop at the southern tip of the lake, is the furthest away from Sayaxché but the most accessible site, as a boat can get you to within twenty minutes' walk of the ruins. Extensive restoration work in still ongoing at this intriguing site, which is split in two by a natural chasm. The atmosphere is magical, surrounded by dense tropical forest and with superb views of the lake from two *miradores*. Currently there's no entrance charge and resident guards escort you around the temples, palaces and plazas, dotted with well-preserved stelae; they'll provide you with stout walking sticks (the slippery paths can be treacherous). A new visitor centre and café is under construction. The *Posada El Caribe* and *Chiminos* hotels (see below) run trips to all the sites in the area or you can book a tour in Flores (see p.264).

A slightly closer option is **Dos Pilas**, where some restoration is ongoing, buried in jungle west of the lake. Dos Pilas was the centre of a formidable empire in the early part of the eighth century, with a population of around ten thousand. The ruins are quite unusual, as the major structures are grouped in an east–west linear pattern. Around the central plaza are some tremendous stelae, altars and four short **hieroglyphic stairways** decorated with glyphs and figures. To get to **Dos Pilas** you have to trek 12km on foot (or by horse) from the *Posada El Caribe*, passing the small site of **Arroyo de Piedra**, where you'll find a plaza and two fairly well-preserved stelae.

It's a 45-minute speedboat trip from Sayaxché to the northern tip of Lago de Petexbatún, where you'll find the very friendly *Posada El Caribe* (Ⓣ928 6114, Ⓕ928 6168; ❻ full board), with clean, screened cabins and good food. Boat trips to Aguateca and horse trips to Dos Pilas can also be arranged. Three kilometres south of here on the western shore of the lake, the *Chiminos Island Lodge* (Ⓣ335 3506, Ⓕ335 2647, Ⓦwww.chiminosisland.com; US$88 per person including all meals) is a stunning alternative base, with six huge stylish, commodious bungalows all with wonderful viewing decks over the lake. There are some minor ruins in the patch of jungle around the hotel and the food is superb.

Routes to Mexico and Belize

There are a number of possible routes **into Mexico** from Petén, all of which offer a sense of adventure, a glimpse of the rainforest and involve shuttling between buses, boats and immigration posts. Getting to **Belize** is much more straightforward, with numerous daily buses connecting Flores with the border at Melchor de Mencos and good bus services onward.

Via Bethel or La Técnica to Frontera Corozal

The cheapest and most straightforward route to Mexico is via **BETHEL** on the Río Usumacinta, where there's a Guatemalan **migración** post. Five buses a day leave Flores for Bethel (5am, 6am, 8am, noon & 1pm; 4hr), passing the El Subín junction north of Sayaxché a couple of hours later. At Bethel it's relatively easy to find a lancha heading downstream (US$6; 30min) to Frontera Corozal.

Alternatively, it's usually possible to get off the bus, obtain your exit stamp in Bethel and continue on the same bus for a further 12km to the tiny settlement of **LA TÉCNICA**, where you can cross the Usumacinta (US$0.50) to Corozal on the opposite bank. At the time of writing there are no accommodation or other facilities in Técnica. Some agencies in Flores (see p.264) offer tickets direct to Palenque using this route (US$30 per person).

If you need to **stay**, Bethel itself is a pleasant village with some small ruins and an excellent eco-campamento here, the *Posada Maya* (☎801 1799) with comfortable rooms (❹), tents under thatched shelters (❷), and hammocks (❶) and a restaurant. It's located on top of a wooded cliff high above the river. Frontera Corozal, over the border, has a *migración*, plus comedores and two good places to stay: the comfortable *Escudo Jaguar* (❹) and *Nuevo Alianza* (❹) with hammock space, camping and clean cabins. Fairly regular buses and shared minibuses leave Frontera Corozal for Palenque until 3pm (4hr).

For further adventure, the spectacular ruins of **Yaxchilán** are 15km from Bethel, set around a great loop in the Usumacinta just over the border in Mexico; **hiring a boat** for the beautiful trip will cost around US$60 return, but you can usually hitch a return ride with others for around US$10. Even further downstream from Yaxchilán are the remote ruins of **Piedras Negras**, accessible only by boat. The *Posada Maya* in Bethel can arrange river transport but this costs around US$450 (for ten people and all meals).

From Sayaxché to Benemérito

This is not a popular route, as there are no regular boat services, only cargo barges (around US$10 per person); ask around at the dock for the next departure. Downriver from Sayaxché the **Río Pasión** snakes its way through an area of forest, swamp and small settlements to **Pipiles**, which marks the point where the rivers Salinas and Pasión merge to form the Usumacinta. All boats stop here at the *migración*, where you can get your exit stamp. Not far from Pipiles is the small Maya site of **Altar de los Sacrificios**, commanding an important river junction. This is one of the oldest sites in Petén, but these days there's not much to see beyond a solitary stela. Following the Usumacinta downstream you arrive at **BENEMÉRITO** in Mexico, a sprawling frontier town. There are basic hotels and restaurants in Benemérito and you can head on by bus to Frontera Corozal, and then by boat to Yaxchilán. **Buses** leave Benemérito for Palenque (4hr) at least seven times a day; make sure you stop at the **Mexican migración** for your tourist card.

El Naranjo to La Palma

A third (more expensive) route from Flores to Mexico runs along the mostly paved road to **EL NARANJO**, a rough place consisting of little more than an army base. There's a **migración** here, stores (offering poor exchange rates), comedores and basic hotels. As there are no longer any scheduled boats from El Naranjo down the Río San Pedro to La Palma, you may have to wait around for a day or so, and expect to have to pay US$20 for the four-hour ride. Boats pass Mexican **migración** after an hour. La Palma has good bus connections to Tenosique (last bus 5pm).

From Flores to Belize

The hundred kilometres from Flores to the Belizean border at Melchor de Mencos (2hr) takes you through another sparsely inhabited section of Petén. **Buses** and microbuses leave from the market place in Santa Elena about every 45 minutes. Alternatively, Linea Dorada/Mundo Maya operate two daily **express services** at 5am and 7am to Belize City (5hr; US$16) and on to Chetumal (8hr; US$23), leaving from their offices on C Principal in Santa Elena and in Flores. Though much more expensive than the public bus, this service is quicker and connects with services in Chetumal to Cancún.

Lago de Yaxhá

About halfway between Puente Ixlú and the border is **Lago de Yaxhá**, a shallow limestone depression ringed by dense rainforest and home to two isolated Maya sites: Yaxhá and Topoxté. The turn-off to the lake is clearly signposted. If you haven't travelled as part of a tour, you'll probably be faced with a sweltering two-hour walk to get there, though there is some traffic to and from the village of La Máquina, 2km before the lakes of Yaxhá and Sacnab, which is just to the east. Just before you reach the lakes you pass a **control post** where you may be asked to sign in. From here it's 3km to the site: head along the road between the lakes then turn left (signed) for Yaxhá.

Yaxhá (daily 6am–5pm; free), covering several square kilometres of a ridge overlooking the lake, is primarily a Classic-period city. The early history of the site is unclear, though the sheer scale of the ruins (in Guatemala only Tikal and El Mirador are larger) confirm it was undoubtedly a major player in the central Maya region. Restoration is ongoing, but most of the structures remain semi-buried in the dense forest. The ruins are spread out over nine plazas and around five hundred structures have been mapped so far. There are some substantial temple complexes: restoration is nearly complete at the **Acropolis Norte** and well advanced at the impressive **Grupo Maler**. The tallest and most impressive pyramid, the recently restored **Structure 216**, 250m northeast of the entrance, rises in tiers to a height of over 30m and gives spectacular views over the forest and lake. If you're not on a guided trip one of the guards will show you around for a small tip.

Topoxté, a much smaller site on an island close to the west shore of the Lago de Yaxhá, is best reached by boat from *El Sombrero* (see below). There's a four-kilometre trail to a spot opposite the island but you still have to get over to it – and large crocodiles inhabit the lake. The structures you see are not on the scale of those at Yaxhá, and date mainly from the Late Postclassic, though the site has been occupied since Preclassic times. Work is in progress to restore some structures.

If you want to **stay** nearby, the wonderful, solar-powered *Campamento El Sombrero* (ⓣ926 5229, ⓕ926 5198, ⓔsombrero@guate.net; ④), 200m from the road on the south side of the lake, has fine rooms in thatched wooden jungle lodges and space for **camping**; the Italian owner can arrange boat trips on the lake and horseback riding, and she'll pick you up from the bus stop if you've called in advance. There's another *campamento* on the far side of the lake, below Yaxhá, where you can pitch a tent or sling a hammock beneath a thatched shelter for free.

The unrestored **ruins of Nakúm**, another large site, are about 20km north of Lago de Yaxhá, though the road is periodically impassable. The most impressive structure is the residential-style palace, which has forty rooms and is similar to the North Acropolis at Tikal. There are two guards here who will show you where you can camp or put up a hammock. It's also possible to **walk to Tikal** in a day from Nakúm (around 25km), best done as part of a tour.

The border: Melchor de Mencos

Despite the differences between Guatemala and Belize, border formalities are fairly straightforward; you have to pay a small (illegal) departure tax on leaving Guatemala. **Moneychangers** will pester you on either side of the border and give a fair rate. On the Guatemalan side there's a **bank** (Mon–Fri 8.30am–6.30pm; no ATM or cash advances) just beyond the **migración**. By the riverbank just before the bridge is the recommended *Río Mopan Lodge* (ⓣ926 5196, ⓦwww.tikaltravel.com; ③). Owner Marco Gross knows Petén and its archeology extremely well and organizes amazing trips to remote Maya sites; you can also safely change money here. The cheap, sleazy hotels in the centre of Melchor are best avoided. Colectivo taxis (US$1.25pp) run to the settlement of Benque Viejo just over the border in Belize from where there are half-hourly **buses to Belize City** (3hr) via San Ignacio (20min).

Travel details

Buses

The main domestic and international bus routes from **Guatemala City** are covered in the box on p.174.

Antigua to: Chimaltenango (every 20min 5am–7pm; 40min); Guatemala City (every 15min Mon–Sat 4am–7.30pm, Sun 6am–8pm; 1hr); Panajachel (1 daily at 7am; 2hr 30min); Santa María de Jesús (every 30min; 30min).

Chichicastenango to: Guatemala City (every 20min 5am–5pm; 3hr); Quetzaltenango (8 daily; 2hr 30min); Santa Cruz del Quiché (every 20min; 30min).

Chiquimula to: El Florido for Copán (every 30min; 1hr 15min); Esquipulas (every 15min; 1hr); Guatemala City (25 daily; 3hr 15min); Ipala (7 daily; 1hr); Puerto Barrios (11 daily; 3hr).

Chisec to: Cobán (13 daily; 1hr 30min).

Coatepeque to: Guatemala City (every 30min; 4hr); Retalhuleu (every 30min; 50min); Quetzaltenango (every 30min; 2hr); Talismán and Tecún Umán (every 20min; 40min).

Cobán to: Cahabón (5 daily; 4hr); Chisec (13 daily; 1hr 30min); El Estor (6 daily; 8hr); Fray Bartolomé de Las Casas (6 daily; 6hr 30min); Guatemala City (31 daily; 4–5hr); Lanquín (7 daily; 3hr); San Cristóbal Verapaz (hourly; 45min); San Pedro Carchá (every 15min; 20min); Sayaxché (2 daily, plus 5 minibuses via Chisec; 4–5hr; Senahú (3 daily; 7hr); Tactic (hourly; 45min); Uspantán (2 daily; 5hr; plus minibuses). Shuttle buses also run from Cobán to: Flores (4hr 30min) daily at 6am via Chisec (1hr 30min), Candelaria (2hr) and Sayaxché (3hr) with connections on to El Remate and Tikal.

Cubulco to: Guatemala City via El Chol (1 daily; 9hr); Guatemala City via La Cumbre (5 daily; 5hr 30min); Rabinal (hourly; 30min); Salamá (hourly; 1hr 30min).

El Estor to: Cobán (8 daily; 8hr); Guatemala City (3 daily; 6hr); Río Dulce (9 daily; 1hr 45 min).

Escuintla to: Antigua (hourly; 1hr 15min); Ciudad Pedro de Alvarado, El Salvador (hourly; 2hr 30min); Guatemala City (22 daily; 1hr 15min).

Esquipulas to: Aguacaliente for Honduras (every 30min; 30min) and El Salvador (every 30min; 1hr); Chiquimula (minibuses every 15min; 1hr); Guatemala City (every 30min 2am–5pm; 4hr); Puerto Barrios (4 daily; 4hr).

Flores to: Belize City (2 direct daily; 5hr); Bethel (5 daily; 4–5hr); Chetumal (2 daily; 9hr); El Naranjo (7 daily; 4–5hr); Guatemala City (around 30 daily; 8–10hr); Melchor de Mencos (15 daily; 2hr); Poptún (every 30min; 1hr 30min), Río Dulce (around 30 daily; 3hr); Sayaxché (12 daily; 1hr 45min); Tikal (1 daily at 1pm; 2hr; plus innumerable private minibuses; 1hr); Uaxactún (1 daily; 2hr 45min).

Huehuetenango to: Aguacatán (10 daily; 1hr); Guatemala City (15 daily; 6hr); La Mesilla (26 daily; 2hr); Quetzaltenango (22 daily; 2hr); Todos Santos Cuchumatán (6 daily; 2hr 30min).

La Avellana to: Guatemala City (4 daily; 3hr 15min).

Panajachel to: Antigua (1 daily at 10.45am; 2hr 45min); Chichicastenango (5 daily Thurs & Sun, 1–2 daily at other times; 1hr 30min); Cocales (9 daily; 2hr 30min); Guatemala City (11 daily; 3hr 30min); Quetzaltenango (6 daily; 2hr 30min); Sololá (every 20min; 30min). There are also daily tourist shuttles to Antigua and on to Guatemala City, and shuttles to Chichicastenango on market days.

Poptún to: Flores (minibuses every 30min; 1hr 30min); Río Dulce (around 30 daily; 1hr 30min).

Puerto Barrios to: Chiquimula (12 daily; 3hr); Esquipulas (4 daily; 4hr); Entre Ríos for Honduras border (22 daily; 1hr); Guatemala City (15 daily; 5hr), passing Quiriguá (1hr 30min).

Quetzaltenango to: Chichicastenango (8 daily; 2hr 30min); Guatemala City (19 daily; 4hr); Huehuetenango (22 daily; 2hr); Momostenango (every 30min; 1hr 15min); Panajachel (6 daily; 2hr 30min); San Francisco El Alto (every 30min; 45min); San Pedro La Laguna (6 daily; 2hr 15min); Totonicapán (every 30min; 1hr); Santa Cruz del Quiché (10 daily; 3hr); Zunil (every 30min; 25min).

Rabinal to: Cubulco (hourly; 30min); Guatemala City via El Chol (1 daily; 8hr) and via La Cumbre (hourly; 4hr 30min); Salamá (hourly; 50min).

Raxrujá to: Cobán (5 daily; 3hr 30min–7hr); Sayaxché (3 daily; 2hr 30min).

Retalhuleu to: Champerico (every 30min; 45min); Cocales (20 daily; 50min); Guatemala City (18 daily; 4hr), Mazatenango (16 daily; 30min); Quetzaltenango (22 daily; 1hr 15min).

Salamá to: Cubulco (hourly; 1hr 30min); Guatemala City (hourly; 3hr 30min); Rabinal (hourly; 1hr).

Santa Cruz del Quiché to: Guatemala City (every 30min; 3hr 30min); Nebaj (7 daily; 2hr 45min); Quetzaltenango (10 daily; 3hr); Sacapulas (14 daily; 1hr 15min); Uspantán (7 daily; 3hr 30min).

Sayaxché to: Cobán (4 daily; 4hr–7hr depending

on route, plus minibuses via Chisec, 4hr); Flores (12 daily; 1hr 45min).
Talismán to: Guatemala City (12 daily; 5hr).
Tecún Umán to: Guatemala City (every 30min; 5hr); Quetzaltenango (17 daily; 2hr 30min).
Tikal to: Flores (1 daily, 2hr; plus minibuses, 1hr). Uaxactún (1 daily; 3hr).

Boats

El Naranjo to: La Palma in Mexico, no scheduled service.
Flores/San Benito to: San Andrés, boats leave when full, in daylight hours only (25min).
Lívingston to: Río Dulce (4–5 daily; 2hr); Puerto Barrios (2 ferries daily at 5am & 2pm; 1hr 30min; 6–10 speedboats daily; 30min); Omoa, Honduras (chartered trips only, minimum 6 people; 2hr 30min); Punta Gorda, Belize (Tues & Fri 7am, minimum 6 people; 1hr).
Puerto Barrios to: Lívingston (2 ferries daily at 10am & 5pm, 1hr 30min; numerous lanchas, 30min); Punta Gorda, Belize (daily at 10am & 2pm; 1hr 30min).
Sayaxché to: Benemérito, Mexico, a trading boat leaves most days (8–10hr).

Flights

From **Flores** four airlines fly to Guatemala City (7 daily; 50min), plus international services to Belize City (4 daily), Cancún (1 daily and three additional flights per week). You can also **charter** flights to Uaxactún, Dos Lagunas, El Naranjo, Sayaxché, Poptún, Río Dulce, Lívingston and to the Honduras border.

3

El Salvador

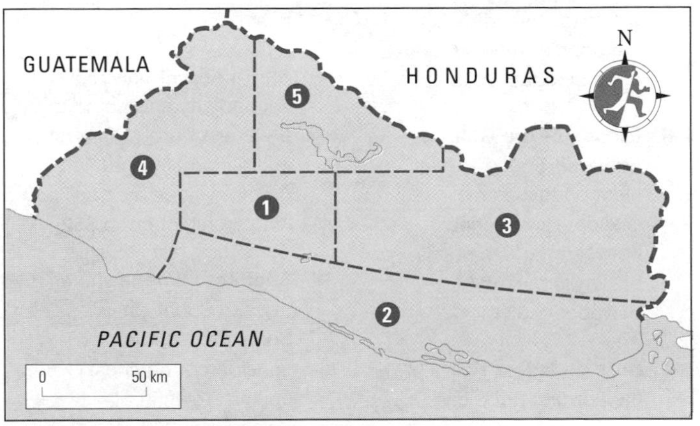

Highlights 284
Introduction and Basics 285
3.1 San Salvador and around 304
3.2 The Pacific coast 322
3.3 The east 333
3.4 The west 345
3.5 The north 360
Travel details 366

El Salvador Highlights

* **San Salvador** Experience the Jekyll-and-Hyde character and landscape of El Salvador's capital city. **p.304**

* **La Libertad beaches** Try out the surf or just bum around the Pacific beaches either side of the popular tourist base of La Libertad. **p.325**

* **Islands of the Golfa de Fonseca** Spend a quiet night on these tiny islands, sandwiched between the mountains of Honduras and El Salvador. **p.331**

* **Ruta de la Paz** Relive the horrors of the civil war in the haunting Museo de la Revolución Salvadoreña in Perquín. **p.341**

* **Bosque El Imposible** Once impossible to visit and now merely difficult, this pristine stretch of mountain forest is a haven for native wildlife. **p.347**

* **Santa Ana** El Salvador's second city and home to the finest Parque Central in the country, bordered on three sides by stunning architecture. **p.352**

* **Suchitoto** On the shores of Lake Suchitlán, Suchitoto is widely considered the finest colonial town in El Salvador. **p.360**

Introduction and Basics

The smallest and most densely populated country in Central America, El Salvador is chiefly remembered for the vicious **civil war** of the 1980s, when streams of harrowing news stories brought this tiny country to the attention of the world. For a decade, atrocity followed atrocity in a seemingly unstoppable sequence. Then in 1992, with both sides having fought each other to a standstill, **Peace Accords** were signed, and the attention of the world's press moved elsewhere, leaving behind a brutalized country faced with the immense task of rebuilding itself.

As a result, tourism in El Salvador has lagged behind that of its Central American neighbours. Despite its compactness and considerable natural beauty, many would-be visitors are deterred by the half-remembered headlines and the country's oft-exaggerated reputation for violence, danger and difficulty. Despite this, the rate of delinquency and violent crime has decreased significantly in recent years, though there remains an underlying distrust of the political process. The country's geographical position doesn't help, either: tucked into the Pacific underbelly of the isthmus, El Salvador is easily bypassed. Those that do make it here, however, are well rewarded by the sheer physical beauty of the place, with lush lowlands sweeping up through fertile hills and coffee plantations to rugged mountain chains. Almost every journey in El Salvador yields photogenic vistas of the majestic cones of towering **volcanoes**, while some of the secluded Pacific **beaches** are as fine as any in Central America.

As in Nicaragua, another country pulled apart by a decade of civil war, travelling in El Salvador brings you into contact with some of the most engaging and interesting people in the region. With a well-deserved reputation for hard work and business acumen, the predominantly mestizo Salvadoreños (or *guanacos*, as they're often affectionately described), live life with a vigour that's hard to match. That said, however, as the people here slowly find ways to come to terms with their brutal past and uncertain future, some residual suspicion of foreigners – particularly Americans – remains, and initial reactions to tourists can be, on occasion, cool. If you persist, however, and make an effort to speak Spanish, you will find that people begin to unbend and bring you into their lives. They may or may not be willing to talk about the civil war, but most prefer to look to the future with a sardonic humour, designed to lessen the travails of daily life, the corruption of politics and everything else that seems insurmountable.

Perhaps unsurprisingly, **tourist infrastructure** is at times sorely lacking. This is not the country for those who like everything on tap, and there's little luxury outside the cities, but for those with a spirit of adventure, El Salvador has plenty to offer. One feature particular to the country is its network of government-run tourist centres, or **turicentros** (see box p.290). Aimed more at locals than tourists, these provide bathing, eating and recreation facilities in areas of natural beauty, offering a convenient way to take advantage of them safely and comfortably.

Travelling around El Salvador is a lesson in humility. Contrasting with the vibrant colour and sweep of the landscape, the overwhelming evidence of the endemic **poverty** and social divisions that sparked the civil war in the first place hits you right between the eyes. As El Salvador enters its second decade of peace it remains a country painfully divided between haves and have-nots, and the full benefits of redevelopment projects and an improving economy have yet to trickle down to the majority of the population. From the muddy shanty towns of San Salvador to the broken-down shacks in the countryside, many people live in squalor, eking out a living selling fruit, sweets, household goods and sundry odds and ends on the street. In addition, the ever-growing population – at 6.5 million, the densest in Central America – is placing unprecedented pressure on the country's **natural resources**, with rampant deforestation a particular problem. In response to this, some of the last remaining tracts of pristine

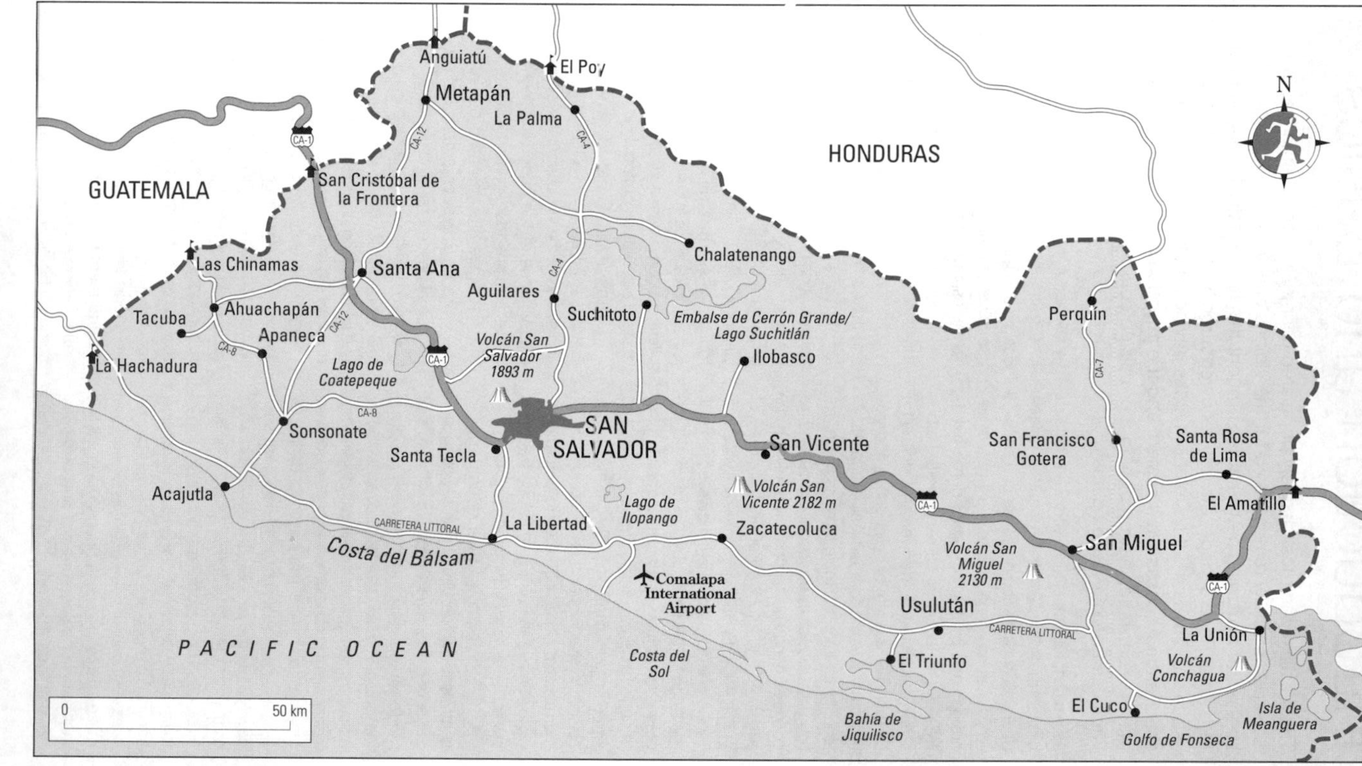
GUATEMALA
HONDURAS
N
Anguiatú
El Poy
Metapán
La Palma
CA-12
CA-4
CA-1
San Cristóbal de la Frontera
Chalatenango
Las Chinamas
Santa Ana
Aguilares
Suchitoto
Embalse de Cerrón Grande/ Lago Suchitlán
Perquín
Tacuba
Ahuachapán
Apaneca
CA-8
Ilobasco
La Hachadura
Lago de Coatepeque
Volcán San Salvador 1893 m
CA-7
Sonsonate
SAN SALVADOR
San Vicente
San Francisco Gotera
Santa Rosa de Lima
Santa Tecla
Acajutla
Volcán San Vicente 2182 m
Lago de Ilopango
El Amatillo
La Libertad
Zacatecoluca
CARRETERA LITTORAL
Costa del Bálsam
San Miguel
Volcán San Miguel 2130 m
Comalapa International Airport
Usulután
La Unión
PACIFIC OCEAN
Costa del Sol
El Triunfo
Volcán Conchagua
El Cuco
Isla de Meanguera
Bahía de Jiquilisco
Golfo de Fonseca
0
50 km

forest have been declared **national parks** to protect the valuable habitat and the animal species that live there. Access to such reserves is deliberately difficult, with permission often being needed in advance. Take the time and trouble to seek permission, though, and you will experience some of the finest natural surroundings in Central America.

Where to go

Despite a bad reputation, and a distinctly ugly central area, **San Salvador** is one of Central America's more pleasant capitals, with a thriving nightlife and facilities you won't find anywhere else in the country. For beaches, swimming and sun you don't have to stray too far from here, to the crater lake of Ilopango or, an hour's journey away, the Pacific coast. Also within easy reach are the small **Maya ruins** of San Andrés and Joya de Cerén which, although they pale visually in comparison to sites in Guatemala (El Salvador was at the furthest fringe of Maya culture) are nonetheless important. The World Heritage Site of **Joya de Cerén**, in particular, gives the most complete picture yet of what daily village life was like in Maya times.

Up and down the glorious sweep of the Pacific coast lie long, palm-fringed stretches of beach, the most beautiful being **El Espino**, **El Tamarindo** and **El Cuco**. Close to the capital are the famous **surf beaches** around **La Libertad**, while further east are the mangrove swamps of the **Bahía de Jiquilísco** and, near the border with Honduras, the idyllic islands of Meanguera and Conchagúita in the **Golfo de Fonseca**.

Further inland, the small city of **San Vicente** is an enjoyable base for trips to the volcano of Chichontepec and the lagunas of Apastepeque. The larger city of **San Miguel** hosts one of the biggest carnivals in Central America each November, drawing visitors from all over the country and beyond. In the northeast of the country, the **Ruta de la Paz** winds up through the poor but beautiful mountainous department of Morazán towards the moving war museum at **Perquín**, unmissable for anyone interested in El Salvador's recent history.

Western El Salvador is the most relaxing and perhaps most scenic part of the country, with the lovely old colonial city of **Ahuachapán** making a convenient entry point from Guatemala, and the laid-back city of **Santa Ana** as good a place as any to spend a few nights. In addition to the Maya ruins of **Tazumal** there are the exquisite **cloudforests of Montecristo and El Imposible**, bursting with exotic plants and wildlife. For climbers, the nearby **volcanic peaks** of Izalco, Volcán Santa Ana and Cerro Verde provide good hiking, while at their base is the **crater lake of Coatepeque**, whose deep blue waters are perfect for snorkelling, diving and swimming.

The north and east of El Salvador, though rough and wild, and less accommodating to travellers, hold a number of attractions. North of the capital **Suchitoto**, considered the finest colonial town in the country, stands above the glorious crater lake of Suchitlán, while **La Palma** and **Ilobasco** are famous for their artesanías, producing wooden handicrafts, pottery and hammocks.

When to go

The best time to visit El Salvador is during the **dry season** from November to February. Though temperatures reach a high of around 30°C – and in the coastal lowlands, the humidity means it feels much hotter – it's easiest to get around at this time and even the back roads are accessible. Towards the end of the dry season, in March and April, temperatures increase to around 34°C and, in the lowlands, it can feel unbearable. During the May to October **wet season**, the heat and humidity are temporarily relieved by short daily downpours, and the mountains around San Salvador see spectacular lightning storms. At this time travel can be difficult as remote mud roads become impassable, but for the most part the network of roads between the main population centres holds up well. Sometimes between September to November, El Salvador is affected by the tail end of **hurricanes** out in the Pacific; when this happens, as occurred during Hurricane Mitch in 1998, the rain can last for days, and cities begin to flood. Whatever the season, the climate is coolest in the **mountains**, where temperatures are moderated by altitude, being far fresher by day and cool at night.

Getting around

The best way to get around El Salvador is **by bus**. Short distances (the longest journey you're likely to take in one stretch, from San Salvador to La Palma for example, is around four hours), and relatively good main highways mean that the few **internal flights** that do exist are more trouble than they're worth.

Buses

Salvadoreño **bus** terminals are seemingly chaotic places, but once you get the hang of how to use them they're extremely efficient. Hundreds of companies operate buses to everywhere from everywhere every few minutes during daylight hours, although very few buses depart after dark. Buses are brightly painted, and have their route number and the name of their final destination emblazoned across the front. It makes sense to be aware of the route number that you need before travelling, as stating a mere destination can lead to you being bundled on to a bus without being informed that you have to change halfway. On back roads you may have to plan ahead a little to avoid getting stuck in the middle of nowhere for hours (or even overnight), but generally if you travel early in the day you'll have no problem reaching your destination. If roads are bad because of rain, everything gets delayed. Except for routes to the cities in the east there is only one **class** of bus, and everyone travels on it. It's much easier to cope if you have small bags; larger luggage gets thrown in a heap at the back or, occasionally, on the roof. Buses can be **hailed** at the side of the road and you can get off at virtually any point. You pay the driver's assistant and though a ticket is only occasionally issued, it should be retained. Buses are extremely **cheap**: a trip from San Salvador to Santa Ana (2hr 30min) costs just US$1.15, while San Salvador to Santa Rosa de Lima by fast bus (around 3hr 30min) will cost around US$2.20.

Virtually every town has departures to San Salvador; if you're trying to reach somewhere small from the capital, however, it's often quicker to go to the nearest major town and change. Heading **east** to San Miguel, Santa Rosa de Lima and La Unión the direct ("*directo*") buses are marginally more comfortable and make fewer stops, knocking about an hour off the standard journey. For more information about buses, contact the *Asociación de Empresaríos de Autobuses Salvadoreños* (*AEAS*) at their San Salvador office at C 27 Pte 1132, Colonia Layco (☎225 2661).

Taxis

Taxis in El Salvador are yellow, painted with black numbers and a "taxi" sign. They can be hailed anywhere on the street and tend to congregate in the main square and around bus stations in towns and cities. **Fares** should be agreed before you set off (be prepared to bargain). Expect to pay US$3–6 for most city trips, and anything upwards of US$30 for a half-day driving around the countryside (a good way to see some of the remoter spots if in a hurry). **Tipping** is not usual unless you've rented the taxi for the day.

Driving and hitching

Driving in El Salvador is relatively straightforward on the major roads and a perfect way to reach some of the more inaccessible beaches along the Pacific coast. There are **filling stations** in every town and at most

Overland routes to and from El Salvador

Crossing borders into El Salvador is a relatively stress-free experience. The main border crossings with **Honduras** are in the east at El Amatillo (see p.344), a busy crossing convenient for onward travel to Tegucigalpa, and the more relaxed crossing at El Poy (see p.365) in the northwest. The main border with **Guatemala** is at La Hachadura (see p.347) in the southwest, convenient for the Pacific beaches and used by international buses from Mexico. Another Guatemala crossing is at Las Chinamas (see p.351), just outside Ahunachapán, with regular connections to Guatemala City. The crossing at Anjiatú (see p.359) in the north near Metapán is the most convenient for Esquipulas in Guatemala. A smaller crossing at San Cristóbal (see p.357) is close to the city of Santa Ana, but has poor onward connections in Guatemala.

Finding your way around El Salvador's cities

Orientation in Salvadoreño cities is initially confusing but logical. Streets running north to south are **avenidas**; those running east to west are **calles**. The main avenida and calle will have individual names (along with a few of the others) and the heart of any city is at their intersection – usually, though frustratingly not always, at the Parque Central. North or south of this intersection avenidas are Norte or Sur, while east or west calles are Oriente or Poniente. Avenidas lying to the east of the main avenida are numbered evenly, rising the further out you go; west of the main avenida, the numbers are odd. Similarly, calles have even numbers south of the main calle and odd numbers to the north. Named avenidas/calles sometimes (though not always) change name either side of the intersection. A recent trend in San Salvador is the replacement of traditional street numbers with names honouring people of national historical note. This makes things more confusing as locals, taxi drivers especially, stick rigidly to the older names.

Addresses can be given either as the street name/number, followed by the building number, or as the intersection of two streets. So: "C 12 Pte #2330, Col Flor Blanca" is number 2330, Calle 12 Poniente in the district (*colonia*) of Flor Blanca, while "10 Av Sur y C 3 Pte" is the intersection of 10 Avenida Sur and Calle 3 Poniente.

major highway junctions, and no road is so long that you should have to worry about running out of fuel. However, some back roads become impassable at times during the rainy season, even to 4WD; ask locally about conditions before you set off. On a darker note, armed **hold-ups** of private cars on quieter roads are not unheard of, especially in the northern departments of Chalatenango. It will be automatically assumed that foreigners have something of value to steal, and it makes sense to have a sum of money set aside for handing over in the event of robbery. Keep an eye on the latest news and, if in doubt, seek police advice. In cities, thefts of cars, or items they contain do occur, and it's wise to leave your car in a guarded or locked car park. **Car rental** prices are on a par with those in the West: from US$40 a day for a small car to US$90 and upwards for a jeep. See p.318 for a list of **rental companies** in San Salvador. Take great care if driving on Sunday afternoons or public holidays as drink-driving-related road accidents tend to increase at these times.

Hitching is common in remote areas and around La Libertad, where the lack of regular bus services means that any passing vehicle is fair game. Pick-up services often operate here, working like buses, though you'll have to stand up in the back. Having said that, hitching carries obvious risks, and we do not recommend it. If you do hitch, it's polite to offer payment – about the same as the bus fare – for the journey.

Cycling

Cycling is a common way of getting around, and even the smallest of places usually has a repair shop. Mountain bikes, in particular, can take you to places that even the buses don't reach. The main highways, however, can be more than slightly nerve-racking for those on two wheels; you might want to consider putting them on top of a bus for sections of your journey. Unfortunately there are no formal places to **rent bicycles** from; your only option is to do a private deal with someone local.

Costs, money and banks

Though a dual-currency economy operated until recently, the **colón** (often called the peso) was officially phased out on January 1, 2003, and replaced by the **US dollar**. All US dollar notes and coins are now in free circulation, though anything over $20 is likely to send the shopkeeper running down the street in search of change. Colónes may still be quoted as prices in many areas, even though the payment is expected in dollars (US$1 = 8.75 colónes).

When travelling through smaller towns, be sure you have more than enough **cash** to get back to a big city again. **ATMs** are scarce and often non-existent outside of the largest population centres and payment by credit card is almost unheard of except in the top hotels and restaurants, where there is a commission charge of 5 percent. **Travellers' cheques** are becoming more widely recognized, but at present can only be changed in banks; in most cases you'll need to have your proof of purchase in order to change them. A few ATMs (*cajeros electrónicos*, mainly operated by Banco Agrícola, Banco Salvadoreño, Banco de Comercio and Banco Cuscatlán) accept foreign-issued Visa and MasterCards (Visa is more widely accepted) – though note that many machines charge a handling fee of around US$1.70. Opening hours for banks are 8.30 or 9am until 4 or 5pm, and some of them close for an hour at lunch from 1 to 2pm. Some banks in the larger cities also open between 9am and midday on Saturday. There are **casas de cambio** in San Salvador, Santa Ana and San Miguel (generally open daily 9am–5pm). **Moneychangers** can be found at borders, and along Alameda Juan Pablo II in San Salvador, but compare rates and make sure that you have some idea of the official exchange rate before handing any money over.

Costs

Though El Salvador is one of the more expensive Central American countries, day-to-day living is still, for foreigners at least, very cheap. A cup of coffee will cost US$0.25–60, while a soft drink will be US$0.60 and fresh juice US$1. Cigarettes are around US$1.50 a packet, while a meal in an ordinary café will set you back US$3–4.

In expensive hotels and restaurants, service charges and **taxes** are added to the bill automatically; room taxes are 13 percent while service charges are 7–10 percent. If you're spending less than around US$30/£17 a night for a room however, the tax is usually not charged. The **airport departure tax** is currently US$27.15, which must be paid in cash. There are usually no entry or exit taxes if entering or leaving the country by land, though citizens of the USA, Canada, Greece, Portugal and China will be obliged to pay US$10 for their tourist card. Some border crossings charge a small entry and exit fee of around $1, though most do not, and soliciting of illegal fees by customs officials is less common than in surrounding countries.

Information

The helpful government organisation Corporación Salvadoreña de Turismo, or **Corsatur**, at Av El Espino 68, Urb Madreselva, Sta Elena (Mon–Fri 8am–12.30pm & 1.30–5.30pm; ⊕243 7835, ⓦwww.elsalvadorturismo.gob.sv), has a useful bilingual guide, *Destination El Salvador*, giving an overview of what there is to see in the country. They can also provide information (Spanish only) on national parks and archeological sites, and details of local specialist tour operators. Privately-run information offices can be found in popular spots such as Suchitoto, while small towns like Apaneca and Perquín have kiosks that issue little more than photocopied pamphlets in

Turicentros

Most large, urban settlements in El Salvador are within a stone's throw of one of thirteen **turicentros**, public tourism centres designed to give city dwellers the opportunity to enjoy the natural beauty of the countryside in comfortable surroundings. There are three in the vicinity of San Salvador – Los Chorros (p.319), Apulo (p.320) and Parque Balboa (p.321) – but whichever city you find yourself in, one is never far away. Though facilities vary, most involve some kind of water-based diversion, be that in the form of swimming pools or natural lakes, along with ample provision of food and cabañas to escape the sun. Opening hours are between 9am and 5pm and there is usually a minimal entry charge of less than a dollar. For more information contact the Instituto Salvadoreño de Turismo, or ISTU (see opposite), who are responsible for administering the sites.

Spanish. The Instituto Salvadoreño de Turismo, or **ISTU**, C Ruben Darío, 9a–11a Av Sur, San Salvador (Mon–Fri 8am–4pm, Sat 8am–noon; ⓣ222 8000), is responsible for some of the national parks and the network of *turicentros* (see box opposite), though the staff will likely refer you to Corsatur.

Although El Salvador is gradually waking up to its own tourism potential, the concept of independent tourism is still in its infancy. If you have any questions, head for the largest and most expensive hotel, or strike up a conversation with a taxi driver. Alternatively, it might be possible to obtain information from municipal cultural centres (*casas de la cultura*), offices of the government-run culture development agency *Concultura*, or the city hall (*Alcaldía*).

Websites

Web resources for visitors to El Salvador are limited, but those sites that do exist are a good starting place for planning a trip.

ⓦ**www.cihuatan.org** Those with an interest in the archeology of El Salvador should check out this English-language site.

ⓦ**www.elsalvadormagazine.com** An online magazine with tourist information and arts and culture amongst the numerous subjects covered.

ⓦ**www.elsalvadorturismo.com** Colourful and informative site written in four languages and packed with tourist information.

ⓦ**www.hispanito.com/elsalvador** A fountain of information on tourism and current affairs, including a daily weather forecast.

ⓦ**www.surfelsalvador.com** Provides links to a host of El Salvador-based websites on a variety of subjects and of particular use to business visitors.

Accommodation

The widest choice of **accommodation** is, inevitably, in San Salvador. Elsewhere, choices are fewer, and usually narrower, though in the most popular places new hotels are beginning to open. Hotels on the coast and near the country's lakes are usually empty during the week but busy at weekends, and many hotels are busy around **Easter Week** and **Christmas** and/or at the time of a large festival; at these times it's worth reserving in advance. Always ask to see more than one room (when empty, hoteliers routinely show you the most expensive room) and, if you're staying for a few days, ask if there's the chance of a discount. Many hotels also have multi-bed rooms, which can cut costs a lot if you're travelling in a group. Beware that in some places, particularly at the coast, prices may be quoted for 12-hour periods rather than a full 24 hours. Check beforehand so that you don't end up paying twice what you expected.

Since dollarisation, accommodation prices have risen steadily. In **San Salvador** you'll need to pay at least US$20, often more, for a clean, secure, double room as the city's cheapest rooms are located in the worst and most dangerous part of town. The city's top-end establishments have everything you would expect of an international-standard hotel, with soft lighting, room service, cocktail bars and piped music swirling along carpeted corridors.

Outside the capital, top-of-the-range hotels are relatively few and far between, although there are a good number of comfortable places to stay. In general, expect to pay at least US$15 for an acceptable double room, rising to around US$20–25 with private bath and a/c.

Camping (and hammock-slinging) is possible on many beaches, but the only formal provision elsewhere is in the parks of Cerro Verde and Montecristo. Hiking in the mountains may also throw up some possibilities, but ask for local advice on safety in the area before you go, and get permission from the landowner. Note, too, that sudden downpours are common and, in the winter, can last for hours.

See p.36 for an explanation of the accommodation price codes.

Food and drink

Refined cooking is not one of El Salvador's strong points, although there are a few exceptions, with gourmet cuisine available in San Salvador and smart restaurants serving excellently prepared local dishes in the provincial cities. Most local people, however, eat in **comedores**, the ubiquitous café, where you can get a nutritious and substantial meal for around US$3–4. The cleanliness of these places varies, as does the quality of the food; if in doubt, choose one that's busy.

The main meal of the day is lunch – look out for **comida a la vista**, basically a cheap and cheerful set lunch served in a sort of school-canteen format, where you select meals from heated metal trays. Generally, unless it's a fiesta, people don't eat out a lot and places close relatively early, around 7–8pm. Only in the biggest cities, and mostly at weekends, will restaurants be full and stay open late.

A Spanish **menu reader** can be found on p.870.

What to eat

The mainstay of Salvadoreño food is the *pupusería*, serving **pupusas**, the cheap and filling national snack. These small tortillas are served piping hot and filled with cheese (*queso*), beans (*frijoles*), pork crackling (*chicharrón*) or all three (*revuelta*), and cooked on a hot plate. *Pupusas* are normally made from cornmeal (although the crispier ricemeal version is worth trying), and are served with optional hot sauce, tomato juice and/or *curtido*, a jar of pickled cabbage, beetroot and carrots. *Pupuserías* range from humble street-corner grills to huge, barnlike places filled with families at the weekends – most of them, however, only start serving in the late afternoon.

Other Salvadoreño **specialities** include *mariscada* (huge aquarium bowls of seafood in a creamy soup), *tamales* (meat or chicken wrapped in maize dough and boiled in a leaf), *ceviche* (raw, marinated fish), and *sopa de frijoles* (black or red bean soup – often a meal in itself). *Panes con pavo* are breadrolls filled with turkey and served with salad – many restaurants specialize in these alone – and *bocas* are small appetizers, often meat and/or pickles and vegetables, served with drinks or before a meal. At the coast *conchas* (cockles or any other seashells) are served raw with lemon juice, tomato, coriander and Worcester sauce.

There are US-style **fast-food** and **pizza** chains throughout the country. Fried chicken is particularly popular, and there is a branch of *Pollo Campero* in just about every sizeable population centre. **Chinese** and **Tex-Mex** restaurants are reasonably common too, as are **Italian** places in the larger cities, though their authenticity varies.

So far, El Salvador has not been struck by a cholera epidemic. If freshly cooked in front of you, **street food** is generally safe to eat, although there's a lot of dust and dirt in the air and hygiene standards are not always what they should be.

Drinking

Locally produced **coffee** is very good, usually drunk black and strong at breakfast and with an afternoon snack of tamales. In small villages it will be served *lista*, boiled up with sugar cane and surprisingly tasty. El Salvador's abundance of tropical fruits go to make delicious **juices** in the form of *jugos*, *licuados* and *frescos*. *Jugos* are pure juices mixed with ice, most commonly made of orange, papaya, pineapple and melon. *Licuados* (sometimes called *batidos*), blend the fruit juice with sugar, ice and sometimes milk, while *frescos* are a fruit-based, sweet drink, made up in bulk and served with lunch or dinner. Unless you ask otherwise, sugar will be added to *jugos* and *licuados*. *Horchata*, another favourite, is a rather heavy milk drink with a base of rice, sweetened with sugar and cinnamon. *Chaparro* is the Salvadoreño version of South American *chicha* and is officially illegal, though widely available. *Chaparro curado* is flavoured with fruit or honey.

The usual international-brand **soft drinks** are available, as well as local equivalents. Kolashanpan, billed as the national drink by its manufacturers, is a sickly-sweet, artificially-flavoured concoction reminiscent of Peruvian Inka Kola. **Water** is safe to drink in San Salvador only; elsewhere check that the water and ice used in drinks is purified. Bottled mineral water is available almost everywhere, as are bags of pure spring water, while most hotels provide drinking water. El Salvador produces four excellent **beers**, the most popular of which is Pilsener, followed by Regia and Suprema. Bahía, a crisp, clear beer similar to the Mexican brands, is new on the market. **Aguardiente** is a sugarcane-based liquor, produced under government control and sold through licensed outlets called *expendios*.

Opening hours, holidays and festivals

Opening hours throughout the country tend to vary. The big cities and major towns generally get going quite early in the morning, with government offices working from 8am to 4pm and most businesses from 8.30/9am to 5/5.30pm, with some closing for an hour at lunch. On **national holidays**, everything will be shut, with some businesses also closing on the day of local fiestas. **Archeological sites** are usually closed on Monday.

All towns and villages have their own **fiestas patronales** commemorating the local saint. The scope of these varies wildly, with some lasting only a day and some, like those at San Miguel (see p.336) and Sonsonate (see p.345) lasting weeks and encompassing a programme of arts and other events. Most commonly, the fiesta is a time for relaxation and holiday-making; large amounts of alcohol are consumed and towards the late evening things can get rather wild. Generally the last day will be the main event.

Public holidays

Jan 1 New Year's Day
Mar–Apr Easter (3 days)
May 1 Labor Day
Aug 3–6 El Salvador del Mundo
Sept 15 Independence Day
Oct 12 Columbus Day
Nov 1 Day of the Dead
Nov 2 All Saints' Day
Dec 25 Christmas Day

Local fiestas

Jan 8–15	Cristo Negro and Feria Gastronómica Internacional, Juayúa
Jan 12–21	San Sebastián, Cojutepeque
Jan 25–Feb 2	Virgen de la Candelaría, Sonsonate
1st week of Feb	Dulce Nombre de Jesús, Ahuachapán
3rd week in Feb	Dulce Nombre de María, La Palma
2nd Sun in May	Las Palmas, Panchimalco
July 1–26	Nuestra Señora de Santa Ana, Santa Ana
Aug 1–6	Fiesta al Divino Salvador del Mundo, San Salvador
Sept 12–14	Santa Cruz de Roma, Panchimalco
Sept 15	Independence Day, San Salvador
Nov 14–30	Virgen de la Paz, San Miguel
Nov 26	Nuestra Señora de los Pobres, Zacatecoluca
Dec 12	Virgen de Guadalupe, San Salvador
Dec 12–31	San Vicente Abad y Mártir, San Vicente

Communications

Letters from San Salvador generally take about one week to the US and nine or so days to Europe. The **main post office** in San Salvador (see p.318) is open Mon–Fri 8am–5pm and Sat 8am–noon; it offers a parcel service, but if you're sending anything of value it's better to use one of the **courier services**. The safest place to **receive letters** is at the *lista de correos* (window 14) of the main post office; alternatively some embassies (see p.318) hold mail addressed to their citizens. Post offices in smaller cities and towns keep the same hours as in the capital but aren't recommended as places to receive mail, while letters posted here take longer to arrive at their destinations.

Telecom, the recently privatized phone company, has newly renovated offices (all open daily 7am–6pm) in every town from where you can make local, long-distance and international calls. Offices in the larger towns also offer Internet services. Reverse charge (collect) calls can be made to the US and Canada, but not to the UK. A three-minute minimum call to Europe costs about

US$8, and direct-dial services are available to the US (AT&T, MCI, Sprint). The telephone code for the whole of El Salvador is ⓣ503.

Most public phones in El Salvador are now **cardphones**: either the yellow Telecom booths (with instructions in both Spanish and English) or the lime-green Telefónica booths (instructions in Spanish only). Both require prepaid cards which can be purchased at many stores, gas stations and the *Mister Donut* restaurant chain; the Telefónica card uses a unique number code which must be keyed in before use (don't insert the phonecard). You can make international calls from both types of cardphone (approximately $1.50 a minute to Europe), but it's cheaper to go to a Telecom office. There are also a limited number of red **coin-operated phones**, but they don't always work and you can't make international calls from them. Rates for local calls are the same as at Telecom offices.

Faxes can be sent from Telecom offices, and all hotels with a fax machine will usually send one for you, though at a considerable premium. Most towns now have places with **Internet** access, particularly around universities and in shopping malls. Connections are generally good and prices standard at around US$1 per hour, though often higher in hotels. In most large towns branches of Infocentros have the fastest connection (daily 9am–6pm).

The media

There are two main daily **national newspapers** in El Salvador: *La Prensa Gráfica* (ⓦwww.laprensa.com.sv) and *El Diario de Hoy* (ⓦwww.elsalvador.com/noticias). Both have full coverage of regional and international affairs – albeit from a very conservative standpoint – and the Friday and Saturday editions are good for arts and cultural events. *El Mundo* and *Diario Latino* are smaller afternoon papers with a moderate stance, while *Marca* is a more sensationalist, tabloid-style affair. The most left-wing of the dailies is *Co Latino*, while *Tendencias* is a liberal monthly magazine with in-depth analysis of political and social affairs. Daily papers are sold everywhere on the streets. The bigger hotels stock US newspapers and magazines, and the embassies have copies of papers from their respective countries.

There are seven national **television stations** and numerous cable channels showing programmes from South America, CNN and CNN en Español, and films. Over eighty **radio stations**, including Radio Venceremos (in the civil war the voice of the FMLN rebels), transmit pop, rock, Latin sounds and religious programming. The BBC World Service can be picked up in El Salvador on 15220, 12095 and 9915 kHz (shortwave).

Shops and markets

El Salvador produces a number of instantly recognizable **artesanías**, such as the brightly painted, naif-style wood and ceramics from La Palma, hammocks from Concepción Quezaltepeque, and interesting ceramics at Ilobasco. These are far cheaper in their place of manufacture, but the **Mercado Cuartel** and the **Mercado de Artesanías** in San Salvador both have an extensive selection of goods from across the country at reasonable prices; a number of more expensive shops around town also carry smaller selections. Hammocks can usually be found for sale in the Parque Central in San Salvador.

The outlets in the **malls** of San Salvador and San Miguel sell US clothing at US prices. For something a little more down to earth, local **markets** (open daily in most towns) sell clothing, fresh fruit, vegetables and much more besides. Most towns also have at least one **supermarket**.

Safety and the police

Historically, El Salvador has been considered one of the most dangerous places to travel in the Americas. After the signing of the Peace Accords in 1992, **street crime** and delinquency rose steadily, largely as a result of the Mara gang culture, introduced by returning exiles from the US, mixed with a large number of arms and munitions unaccounted for from the civil war. Under public

Emergency numbers

Police ☎121
Cruz Roja (ambulance) ☎222 7749 or ☎222 4054
Fire ☎271 2227

pressure to do something about the problem, successive governments have cracked down hard and all but eliminated the Mara, and the country today is no more dangerous than widely touristed places like Guatemala and Honduras. However, this does not mean that you should become blasé about security, and while the chances of being caught up in a violent incident are low, basic rules should be followed.

In the **cities**, very few people stay on the streets after dark, particularly in the centre, and the streets themselves are generally poorly lit. Intimidation and threat is usually more potential than actual, but do not walk around alone (this especially applies to women), and always take taxis after dark, even if you are only travelling a short distance. On the street don't flash large amounts of money or obviously expensive cameras, watches or jewellery. Try not to look too obviously lost and walk with confidence; if you think you've inadvertently strayed into the wrong part of town simply retrace your steps. The **civil police** are plentiful in San Salvador and other city centres, and a pilot **tourist police force** operates in the Zona Rosa and richer parts of the capital.

Bus hold-ups occasionally occur and there is nothing much you can do about it; keep a close eye on the latest news about various areas before you decide where to travel. Generally hold-ups are still comparatively rare and affect the local population far more than tourists; whatever happens, your life is far more important than anything you might be carrying. **Police checks** occur on some buses entering the capital. Don't be alarmed if you are asked to get off the bus to have your bag and body searched. Be polite and patient and have a copy of your passport ready for presentation.

Work and study

Unlike Guatemala and Costa Rica, El Salvador is not well equipped with **language schools**, although there are vague plans to set up schools in the more touristed areas like Apaneca and Panchimalco, with profits going to local communities – contact Corsatur (see p.290) to see how far things have progressed. The Academia Europea, 99a Av Nte #639, Col Escalón, San Salvador (☎263 4355 or ☎264 0237, ⓦwww.euroacad.edu.sv), has schools in all the country's major cities with private classes for US$12 per hour and group classes starting at US$50 for a thirty-hour course. Classes are aimed at business residents and accommodation isn't arranged. If you're looking to **teach English**, contact the Academia Europea directly, or check the listings for Academias de Idiomas in the *Yellow Pages*.

Of more lasting benefit may be **voluntary work**, particularly if you have specific skills. **CIRES** (Comité de Integración and Reconstrucción para El Salvador), C 2 Pte #2137 at 41a Av Sur, San Salvador (☎298 9410), is a non-governmental agency with a remit to set up development programmes in the wake of the Peace Accords. It works in fifty areas around the country, with national and international funding, on credit loans, agricultural co-operatives, housing, potable water schemes and primary health-care schemes, particularly for women and children; they are always interested to hear from foreigners with relevant medical, technical and administration skills.

History

The first settled peoples of El Salvador were the **Maya**, who had arrived in the territory from Guatemala by 1200 BC or earlier. By 500 BC they had developed several large settlements, the most important of which was Chalchuapa – close to present-day Santa Ana. A catastrophic eruption of Volcán Ilopango around 250 AD all but wiped out many of these settlements, forcing their inhabitants to flee north. Over the next two hundred years, during the early Classic period (300–900 AD), the land began to be repopulated, with important cities developing at San Andrés, Tazumal, Cara Sucia and, in the east, Quelepa. West of the Río Lempa the **Maya-Quiché** predominated, with the Chortí (Chortí being a dialect of Quiché) settling around Santa Tomas and Tejutla in what is today the department of Chalatenango. To the east of the river the **Lenca** – with linguistic links to the South American Chibchan group – developed in overall isolation from their neighbours.

Around 900 AD, when – for reasons still unclear – the Classic Maya culture began to crumble, these cities were abandoned. During the early Postclassic period (900–1200 AD), waves of Nahuat-speaking groups began to migrate south from Mexico. These settlers came to be known as the **Pipils**. New seats of power were built at Cihuatán, Tehuacán and Cuscatlán; unusually, the deserted Maya city of Tazumal was also reoccupied. The new settlers planted maize, beans, cocoa and tobacco, lived in highly stratified societies under a hereditary system of military rule, had highly developed arts and sciences, and worshipped the sun and the idols of Quetzalcoatl (man), Itzqueye (woman), Tlaloc (rain) and Mictlanteuctli (god of the underworld). Trade links with the west and north were strong, based on the exchange of cocoa, which was extensively cultivated.

Final waves of Nahuat-speakers arrived in the thirteenth and fourteenth centuries, threatening and occasionally displacing the already established communities. Chief among the new immigrants were the **Nonualcos**, who settled around what is now the city of Zacatecoluca, and the **Pokíomans**, who moved in around Chalchuapa.

The conquest of El Salvador

The first **conquistador** to set foot on El Salvador was Andrés Niño, who landed on the island of Meanguera in 1522. The Spanish returned in June 1524 when **Pedro de Alvarado**, commanding a force of around 250 Spanish troops and 5000 indigenous people, entered from Guatemala. The region was fertile and densely populated, with two rival city-states, Cuscatlán, more or less where the city of San Salvador now stands, and Tecpa Izalco, around the Sonsonate area. The Spanish called all this new territory **Cuscatlán**, a name which is still used today in presidential speeches to evoke national pride.

Defeating the Pipils at Acajutla and then at Tacuxcalco, Alvarado advanced up the Zapotitán valley to the city of Cuscatlán, only to find it deserted, its army having fled to the mountains. It is thought that the Pipil forces were up to twice as numerous as those of the Spanish, with the population of the territory as a whole put variously at between 130,000 and one million, leading Alvarado to report that the region would take time and effort to conquer. Not until April 1528 did a third Spanish force under **Diego de Alvarado** succeed in establishing the foothold of Villa San Salvador near present-day Suchitoto.

Once established, the Spanish almost immediately began to think about advancing east, motivated both by the search for riches and by the need to remain dominant to the rival group of conquistadors advancing up the isthmus from Panama under Pedrarias Davila. In

1530 Alvarado dispatched Luis de Moscosco from Guatemala to finalize the conquest of the east. Ten years later, despite a number of indigenous uprisings, the Spanish hold upon the territory was secure.

Colonial rule

The new territory never yielded the fabled riches of the mythical El Dorado, but the fertile lands provided wealth for those settled. The **encomienda** system was established, producing balsam and cocoa for export (the latter in response to an ever-increasing demand from Europe). Cattle also flourished – the indigenous farming method of slash and burn had created fertile pastures for grazing – providing a firm source of food and income. Predictably, the impact of the Spanish arrival was catastrophic for the indigenous inhabitants. Susceptible to European diseases, stripped of their land by the *encomenderos*, and forced into a new belief system, the indigenous population of El Salvador went into freefall. By the end of the sixteenth century at least half had perished.

The decline in the indigenous population left the Spanish *encomenderos* with insufficient labour. In the early years of the seventeenth century **black slaves** were imported, though this stopped in 1625 when two thousand slaves gathered in San Salvador, intent on rebellion. The plans came to nothing, but the slaves were henceforth considered too dangerous to use. Thereafter, the *encomienda* system was gradually abandoned, largely replaced by the end of the seventeenth century with a system of **peonage**. Work on the haciendas was rewarded by payment in vouchers, redeemable only in the hacienda shop, whose prices were set significantly higher than in the open market. Money for daily expenses, however, was advanced by the landowner, creating a debt that the worker, or "peon", was unable to repay and which, moreover, devolved upon his family and heirs.

Haciendas became enclosed, self-sufficient worlds; the workers were provided for, but in return became reliant upon the landowner for everything. Workers could get ahead by serving their patron in all areas, legal or illegal, while he in turn boosted his power by commanding such resources. Such patterns were to continue in Salvadoreño society in later years – not least in the private armies, raised by landowners, that developed into the death squads of the 1970s and 1980s.

From the early eighteenth century, landowners switched from the production of cocoa to that of *añil* (**indigo**). Although long cultivated, removal of protection measures in the European markets made it viable for large-scale production. Growing demand for the superior dye ensured that by the mid-1700s indigo had become the primary export crop. The principal beneficiaries of this were the hacienda owners and *comerciantes*, the middle men handling the sale and shipping of the crop.

By the end of the eighteenth century El Salvador was a rigidly stratified society, whose European elite consisted of the small number of Spanish-born Crown functionaries and priests and a few hundred Creole (Latin American-born) hacienda owners and *comerciantes*; these last two groups were allocated some responsibility in the management of local affairs on behalf of the Crown. Around half of all agricultural land was held in private haciendas, the vast majority of the population, mestizo and indigenous, cultivating maize at subsistence level.

Independence

The Salvadoreño Manuel José Arce was elected first president of the **Federal Republic of Central America** in April 1825. Beset by the deep divisions between Conservatives and Liberals, Arce attempted to unite the rival groups by force. Though himself a Liberal, he allied with the Conservatives of Guatemala resulting in almost

Anastasio Aquino and the indigenous rebellion

The most serious challenge to the nascent government of El Salvador came in 1833 with the indigenous uprising led by **Anastasio Aquino**. Ostensibly a protest against the practice of forced conscription among hacienda workers, the month-long rebellion was also a response to the instabilities in society generated by the new state of independence. In particular it focused resistance against a new decree stating that all land not in use should be converted into private property. The hacienda owners expanded their estates, while the indigenous and other groups living on subsistence agriculture found that much of the land needed for slash and burn cultivation had been transferred into private hands.

A worker on an indigo plantation near Santiago Nonualco, Aquino rebelled following the arrest and detention – and presumed conscription – of his brother by the hacienda owner. He and his followers, the so-called **"Army of Liberation"**, attacked army posts, releasing and arming the forced conscripts and sacked haciendas; according to legend the spoils from these were distributed among the poor. The well-disciplined forces of the rebellion were successful in early confrontations with government troops and at one stage looked capable of advancing on, and taking, San Salvador. Instead, Aquino chose to march on the nearby cities of Zacatecoluca and San Vicente, giving the government time to marshal its forces. On February 16 Aquino arrived in San Vicente and had himself crowned **"Emperor of the Nonualcos"** with a crown taken from the statue of San José in the Iglesia Nuestra Señora del Pilar.

He then returned to Santiago Nonualco where, on February 28, he was defeated by the resurgent government forces. Finally captured on April 23, Aquino was **executed** in San Vicente in July. His head was put on public display, a primitive act in accordance with the status of "primitive rebel" which the government accorded him.

immediate civil war, the first of a series of many to plague the five states during the short-lived union (it dissolved in 1839) and on into full independence. Between 1825 and 1876 El Salvador was in an almost perpetual state of turmoil as rival Liberals and Conservatives battled for power, assisted by like-minded groups from abroad. Not until the presidency of **Rafael Zaldívar** (1876–1885) did the country achieve any measure of stability.

A coffee oligarchy: 1860–1931

Commercial **coffee** production grew from 1860 onwards, fuelled by the collapse of the indigo market and the demand for coffee in Europe and North America. Other exports like sugar cane and beef also expanded, but coffee dominated and was seen as the best hope for the economy. Unusually, the boom was controlled domestically, with the creation of a **"coffee elite"** aided by government policy. In 1882, privatisation of lands worked under the communal *ejido* system displaced small-scale farmers and families dependent upon subsistence agriculture, concentrating land into fewer and fewer hands, and creating a tiny, powerful **oligarchy**. By the early twentieth century onwards, three-quarters of all land was held by less than two percent of the population.

Descended mainly from the original colonial European elite, the oligarchy monopolized coffee production and trade, extending its interests into other agricultural sectors, industry and finance. As the interests became more firmly entrenched, so did the oligarchy's willingness to take action to defend them, including forcing President Zaldívar from office in 1885. Private interests became the motivating force behind all governmental changes until a military coup in 1898.

The early twentieth century

The first decades of the twentieth century were a period of relative **economic stability**, but also deepening **social polarisation**. The elite dominated business and the state machine, working alongside a small, mainly urban, middle class. The vast majority, however, lived in the most basic of conditions, marginalized both in the countryside and, increasingly, in the urban centres. Despite regular elections, democracy existed in name only, with the bulk of the population denied access to both the political process and the coffee profits. Despair and anger at conditions was reflected in growing **violence**, in turn dealt with by increasing repression – of which the Guardia Nacional (National Guard), formed in 1912, soon became a highly feared instrument.

The surprise election of Liberal president **Pío Romero Bosque** in 1927 was a sign that things could change for the better. Vowing to make El Salvador a truly democratic society, Romero, to the alarm of the oligarchy, took steps to ensure that civil rights were observed for all. Romero's successor Arturo Arujo, winning what was possibly the first truly democratic election in 1931, vowed to continue on the same course.

1932 and "La Matanza"

Despite some initial success, Romero's and Arujo's plans for democratic consolidation were ended by international events. The **Wall Street Crash** in November 1929 and the Great Depression that followed were catastrophic for El Salvador. Virtually all (95 percent) exports were coffee, and once the market collapsed in 1929, so did the country's economy. Living conditions deteriorated appallingly amongst the landless poor and unrest both amongst the destitute masses and the elite grew. In December 1931 Arujo's brief period in office was ended by a **military coup**, engineered by the vice-president, General Maximiliano Hernández Martínez.

Repression meted out by the new government and their failure to deal with the poverty issue led to a Communist-led **rebellion**. On the night of January 22, 1932, thousands of campesinos armed with machetes – the majority indigenous – attacked military installations and haciendas in the west of the country, assassinating hundreds of civilians including government functionaries and merchants. The government had been aware of the plans days before the event, and it was rapidly quashed by the armed forces, the ringleaders being arrested and later executed.

Government repression reached unprecedented levels in the wake of the failed rebellion. The army, the police, the Guardia Nacional and the private forces of the hacienda owners engaged in a week-long orgy of killing. During **"La Matanza"** ("The Massacre"), as it became known, anyone suspected of connections to the rebellion, anyone wearing indigenous dress or anyone simply perceived to be guilty was shot. In some cases, whole villages disappeared. Exact figures have never been known, but the death toll is estimated at up to 30,000 people, although the government itself insisted that only 2000 were killed. For El Salvador's indigenous population, the effects of the massacre went far beyond the immediate death toll. As it became increasingly dangerous to be identified as *indio* (indian), traditional dress, language and customs largely disappeared.

Military government 1932–80

There followed an era of **military rule** as the oligarchy, desperate to defend its interests, handed political power to the army while retaining economic control. For the next fifty years the two groups worked together in a symbiotic relationship. Successive groups of **tandas** –

cliques of military officers – assumed power, felled by coups and counter-coups as factions within the military itself fought for supremacy. The economic business of state was handled by the oligarchy, who relied on the army to protect its interests. Depending on the faction in power, occasional limited **social reforms** were made, though the fundamental structures remained unchanged. A number of political parties were allowed to operate, but elections were a sham.

After World War II, economic interests diversified and during the 1960s and 1970s, some limited industrialisation also occurred. Needless to say, the profits and benefits deriving from this expansion remained firmly in the hands of the oligarchy, with social inequalities unchanged.

A downturn in export markets in the 1970s again led to a steep deterioration in conditions, with a subsequent increase in militant pressure for change. The elections of 1972, won by **José Napoleón Duarte**'s Christian Democratic Party (PDC), should have signalled a mandate for democratic change. The PDC advocated a peaceful road to reform, but the army had other ideas, installing its own candidate, **Colonel Arturo Molina**, as president. Duarte and other opposition leaders were exiled, the National University closed down, and trade union and reform activists persecuted and killed.

Repression continued throughout the 1970s with Molina's successor, **Carlos Humberto Romero**, winning rigged elections in 1977. Shortly afterwards, on February 28, news programmes around the world showed footage of the army firing upon unarmed civilians protesting in front of the San Salvador cathedral, killing as many as three hundred people. In 1979 the ineffectual Romero was himself deposed in a coup, replaced initially by a civilian military junta and then by a group of hard-line army officers in January 1980. The army accepted an offer from Duarte to form a provisional government on condition that certain reforms be introduced, yet repression continued, culminating in the **assassination of Archbishop Oscar Romero** on March 24, 1980 – a murder planned by serving army officer Roberto D'Aubuisson. Though preliminary reforms were implemented and agreement secured for a transfer of power to civilian hands, the cycle of extrajudicial violence continued.

The developments of the 1970s and continuing military domination had convinced many that change could only come through violence. Far-right paramilitary death squads waged campaigns of terror in the countryside and against those advocating reform. At the opposite end of the spectrum, left-wing guerrilla groups were mobilising and advocating radical change. Archbishop Romero's assassination was the point from where descent into civil war became inevitable.

The 1980s – Civil War

In October 1980 the formal integration of all left-wing guerrilla organisations led to the foundation of the Frente Faribundo Martí de Liberación Nacional, or **FMLN**. Three months later, in January 1981, the FMLN launched its first general offensive, gaining territory in the eastern and northern departments of the country and forcing the government into defensive action.

The newly installed Reagan administration in the White House was watching events in El Salvador closely. Paranoid about communist insurgency in the region, it pumped around US$1 billion in aid into the country to equip government forces, while aid channelled through covert sources is estimated to be at least a further US$500 million. The money flowed despite concerns over close connections between government security forces and the death squads. The **Mazote massacre** in December 1981 – when US-trained troops systematically murdered more than a thousand people – was first denied then ignored by both Salvadoreño and US authorities and only fully investigated in the early 1990s. Despite US support, the army was hampered by poor leadership and endemic corruption, unable to successfully confront the guerrillas' organised ambush tactics and targeted attacks against strategic infrastructure and economic installations. Army response, tending towards the blanket attack of large areas of "free fire" zones, rebounded most heavily upon the civilian population. Conservative estimates put the number of civilians put to death by right-wing death squads during the civil war at around eighty thousand and more than half a million fled the country as refugees.

Against a background of continued fighting, the promised transfer of power from military to civilian hands was completed, with **parliamentary elections** in 1982 and a new constitution introduced in 1983. In 1984 presidential elections brought Duarte to power on a mandate for continuing reform, although the FMLN continued to disrupt ballots from outside the political process. Sporadic attempts at peace talks foundered upon the seemingly irresolvable demands for fundamental changes in the role and structure of the army and for incorporation of the FDR (the political wing of the FMLN) into political life.

Incompetent and corrupt, Duarte was succeeded in 1989 by **Alfredo Cristiani**, candidate of the right-wing **ARENA** (Alianza Republicana Nacionalista) party founded by Roberto D'Aubuisson. Regarded internationally as a moderate leader, Cristiani began to unpiece economic reforms achieved over the previous decade. The response of the FMLN was to renew offensives against the government, most spectacularly during its **"final offensive"** of November 1989, when areas of major cities, including San Salvador, were occupied. In turn, the death squads and the military intensified their activities. Suspected FMLN sympathizers, trade unionists and Church activists were intimidated and assassinated. Thousands died when San Salvador and other cities were indiscriminately bombed by the air force and – in an incident that caused international outrage – six Jesuit priests, their housekeeper and her daughter were massacred in their rooms on the campus of the Universidad de Centroamérica on November 16, 1989.

Steps towards peace

By late 1989, an end to the fighting seemed a remote dream. Yet in April 1990, representatives of both the FMLN and the government, under the chairmanship of the UN, met in Geneva for the first of a series of **negotiations** that would lead to peace. This was achieved largely due to global changes: the end of the Cold War had reduced Central America's strategic importance, and both the US and USSR switched policy to an active encouragement of conflict resolution. Increasingly isolated and drawn into a military stalemate, both the government and the FMLN bowed to US and UN pressure to seek a negotiated solution.

A protracted negotiating process resulted in the **Chapultepec Accords**, signed on January 16, 1992, followed on February 1 by a formal ceasefire. The FMLN agreed to disengagement and demobilisation of its forces; the government to a reduction and purge of the armed forces. In addition, a number of civil institutions were to be created, including a new civilian police force (the PNC), a human-rights institution and a "Truth Commission". The UN set in place a resident observer mission (ONUSAL) to verify compliance within a set time limit. A land transfer programme, expected to transfer 10 percent of agricultural land to demobilized combatants and refugees, was inaugurated and a tripartite commission, including the government, workers and private sector, set up to formulate further social and economic policies. On December 15, 1992, the day the FMLN registered as a formal political party, the civil war was formally ended.

El Salvador at peace

Recovery from the civil war was slow, with many disaffected former combatants remaining on the fringes of society, unemployment soaring and the open circulation of black-market firearms. Delinquency, crime and violence ensued. The first postwar elections, held in March 1994, resulted in **Armando Calderón Sol** of the ARENA party assuming the presidency, beating the FMLN's Rubén Zamora. The new government pursued a neo-liberal, free-market economic policy and privatized large sectors of the economy. IMF loans were used to stabilize the currency and encourage growth in GDP.

On the downside, the cost of living rose, poverty increased and unemployment reached unprecedented levels, while large-scale privatisation further concentrated wealth in the hands of the elite. Public dissatisfaction increased with the government's perceived failure to comply with the Chapultepec Accords and with the amnesties granted to members of the military accused of committing human-rights atrocities. The profound divisions in society that had originally led to civil war grew wider than ever, and civil violence intensified.

Following its failure in the 1994 elections, the FMLN's fortunes were revived by impressive results across the country in the March 1997 municipal elections, winning the capital's prized mayoral seat. However, failure to build on these results allowed ARENA's **Francisco Flores** to triumph in the presidential elections of March 1999, though a low turnout of just forty percent highlighted the widespread contempt for the political process.

Hurricane Mitch hit the country in October 1998, killing 374 and making 56,000 people homeless. The government's response was slow, and much of the international effort was focused on harder-hit Honduras and Nicaragua. Infrastructure was destroyed, agricultural output badly damaged and disease spread across the affected areas, primarily the low-lying flood plain of the Lempa and San Miguel Grande rivers.

A report by the Universidad de Centroamérica (UCA), in March 2000, listed El Salvador as one of the most violent countries in Latin America, with widespread gang warfare, narco-trafficking and civil violence, and the small talk of the nation was littered with the term *delincuencia*.

Dollarization and after

On 30 November 2000, the Asamblea Legislativa approved the ARENA government's plan to **dollarize** the domestic economy – making El Salvador the third Latin American nation, along with Ecuador and Panama, to do so. The main thrust of dollarization was to create an attractive economic environment for foreign investment and a massive publicity campaign was launched across the country using the motto "Good for you, good for the country". For many Salvadoreños, however, the prospect of welcoming the "Yanqui" dollar reopened still-healing wounds, recalling the massive amount of US funding for the cruel right-wing government during the civil war. As veteran FMLN leader and 2004 presidential candidate Schafik Hándal put it: "After this, I wouldn't be surprised if they passed a law so that every 'señor' must now be called 'mister'". At about the same time, the government also announced its elaborately titled **Plan de Nación**, a public-private investment in public infrastructure totalling over 900 million dollars. Most of this money came from the sale of the state telecommunications company Antel, and will be devoted to building a new road network and developing Cutuco into the largest Pacific port in Central America.

El Salvador was again brought to the world's attention when a devastating **earthquake** ripped through the country on the morning of 13 January 2001.

Measuring 7.6 on the Richter scale, the earthquake killed over 1000 people and left more than 5000 injured; some 145,000 homes were destroyed and a further 120,000 were badly damaged. Two further earthquakes in the weeks that followed killed another 250 people and left tens of thousands more homeless. Hardest hit were the coastal areas, and for a country already struggling, the earthquakes represented a monumental disaster.

Despite early optimism from the FMLN, elections in March 2004 were once again won by the ARENA party. The FMLN had pledged to withdraw troops from Iraq, re-open diplomatic relations with Cuba and reinstate the colón, moves which prompted the Bush administration in Washington to warn of a potential souring of political, commercial and economic relations should they eventually triumph. The new president, pro US media mogul Tony Saca, has vowed to continue the policies of his predecessor Francisco Flores, promising that he would "govern for all". With over a third of the population living on less than $1 a day, and the country struggling to bounce back from a series of catastrophes, the people are hoping that ARENA's campaign slogan "The Best Is Still to Come" isn't another false promise.

3.1

San Salvador and around

Sprawling across the Valle de las Hamacas at the foot of the mighty Volcán San Salvador is the urban melee of **SAN SALVADOR**, El Salvador's mercurial capital. The city suffers from something of an image problem, with a crumbling centre of earthquake-damaged buildings that create a poor first impression, but out in the suburbs things couldn't be more different, with attractive parks and first-class facilities. Though development has been concentrated mainly in these suburbs, the old **centro histórico** has not been completely neglected. The plazas and parks here have been renovated, but plans to move the city's street traders into indoor markets have largely failed. Extra police have been deployed on the streets, and although much work remains to be done, the city is a more pleasant place to visit than just a few years ago. A stay here, however short, is probably inevitable, and many people find it easier to get used to the place and its diversions – restaurants, bars, shopping, cinemas – than they imagined.

San Salvador is a surprisingly green city as well, with a canopy of lush vegetation shrouding even the most unlikely of neighbourhoods, and a ring of mountains standing guard on the horizon. Dominating the skyline to the north is **Volcán San Salvador**, accessible via the town of **Santa Tecla**, 13km from the city, while in the hills to the south lies the extensive **Parque Balboa**, boasting vistas right across to the Pacific coast. Beneath the park to the east is the predominantly indigenous village of **Panchimalco**, with its splendid colonial church. Fifteen kilometres east of San Salvador sits the country's largest crater lake, beautiful **Lago de Ilopango**, with views on a clear day across to the peaks of Volcán Chichontepec (see p.335), whilst to the west are the natural gorge and pools of **Los Chorros**, a favourite weekend retreat. For those with an interest in archeology, the ruins of **Joya de Cerén** to the west are of international importance for their remarkable state of preservation, while those at **San Andrés** nearby are rather more traditional in form with pyramids and temples.

Some history

There has been a city in the vicinity of the present capital since around 1054, when the Pipils founded the city-state of **Cuscatlán** in the Zalcuatitán valley, stretching between what are today the towns of San Jacinto and Santa Tecla. Although the Spanish first arrived in the area in 1524, they did not succeed in establishing a settlement until 1528. This **Villa San Salvador**, to the south of where Suchitoto (see p.360) now stands, is thought to have been named after the day of Transfiguration of the Saviour of the World (El Salvador), the date of a conclusive victory against the Pipils. Outbreaks of cholera led to the settlement being moved to its present location in 1545, and the title of city was awarded in September 1546.

Rapid growth came only in the **late eighteenth century**, after San Salvador was named the first *intendencia* within the Reino de Guatemala in 1785, stimulating trade and commercial development. Growing pressure within the country and across the isthmus to break away from Spain was particularly evident here; Delgado's first call for independence was issued from San Salvador, and the city became the first capital of the **Central American Federation** in 1824. The city continued to grow slowly and steadily, becoming capital of the Republic of El Salvador in 1840.

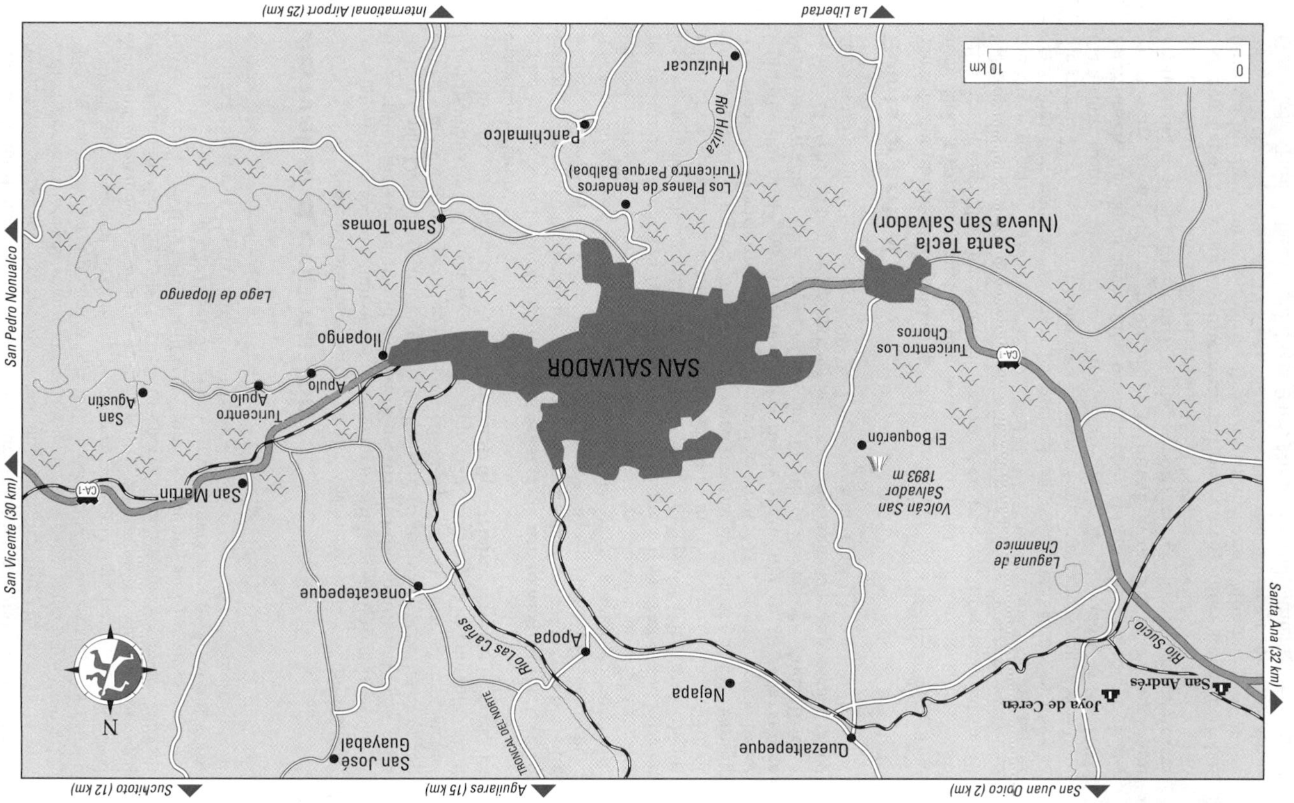

San Juan Opico (2 km)
Aguilares (15 km)
Suchitoto (12 km)
Santa Ana (32 km)
San Vicente (30 km)
San Pedro Nonualco
La Libertad
International Airport (25 km)
N
Quezaltepeque
San José Guayabal
Joya de Cerén
San Andrés
Nejapa
TRONCAL DEL NORTE
Río Las Cañas
Apopa
Río Sucio
Tonacatepeque
Laguna de Chanmico
Volcán San Salvador 1893 m
El Boquerón
San Martin
CA-1
Turicentro Apulo
San Agustin
Apulo
SAN SALVADOR
Ilopango
CA-1
Turicentro Los Chorros
Lago de Ilopango
Santa Tecla (Nueva San Salvador)
Santo Tomas
Los Planes de Renderos (Turicentro Parque Balboa)
Panchimalco
Río Huiza
Huízucar
0
10 km

A series of destructive **earthquakes** throughout the nineteenth and twentieth centuries levelled most of the centre and ensured that virtually nothing remains of colonial San Salvador; today, the oldest buildings date back only to around the end of the nineteenth century and many of these are in a sorry state. On October 10, 1986, in the midst of the civil war, another earthquake, measuring 5.4 on the Richter scale, destroyed around 60,000 houses and buildings, leaving six hundred dead and thousands homeless. As if this were not enough, the air force bombed areas of the city thought to be hotbeds of guerrilla support in November 1989, in response to the FMLN's "final offensive" on the country's major cities. Another massive earthquake in 2001 set the rebuilding programmes back several years, meaning the scars of both conflict and natural disaster are still very much in evidence.

Arrival and orientation

San Salvador's **central intersection** sits at the northwest corner of the Catedral Metropolitana, at the junction of the city's main **avenida** (called Avenida España to the north of the cathedral, and Avenida Cuscatlán to the south) and main **calle** (called Calle Delgado to the east and Calle Arce to the west). The heart of the capital – the **Centro Histórico** – is centred on a point just north of the Catedral Metropolitana and encompasses several important buildings and churches, along with the city's major markets. The **Terminal de Oriente** bus station marks its easternmost limits.

The business and residential districts **west and northwest** of the Centro Histórico are linked by the Alameda F. D. Roosevelt, which runs due west of centre to Plaza de las Américas, before changing its name to Paseo General Escalón, where it is fringed by wealthy residential districts. Many of the foreign embassies are located at the far end of the Paseo, as are a number of luxury hotels, banks and restaurants. The major **49a Avenida** crosses the Alameda 600m east of the Plaza de las Américas, then changes its name to Boulevard de los Héroes as it runs northeast, where it's lined with restaurants, bars and nightclubs and the Metrocentro/Metrosur shopping-mall complex. Just west of here lies the second major bus station, **Terminal de Occidente**. Alameda Manuel Enriqué Araujo branches southwest from the Plaza de las Américas, eventually changing to the **Carretera Interamericana** as it heads out of the city. North of this lies the **Zona Rosa**, a suburb of secluded houses, upmarket restaurants and nightclubs, supposedly aimed at tourists but more of a magnet for the local nouveau riche.

Points of arrival

San Salvador can be an **intimidating** city to arrive in for the first time, particularly after dark. If you have luggage, take a taxi and do not walk around the Centro Histórico at night. The international airport, **Aeropuerto Internacional de El Salvador**, is located at **Comalapa**, 44km from the city centre. The easiest way into the city is to take a **taxi**. Taxis Acacya (Ⓣ271 4937) have a booth at the airport open until well after the last flight has arrived and charge US$18 day or night to the capital. They also run a **colectivo** service (9am, 1pm & 5.30pm; US$3) from the airport to their office close to the centre at 19a Av Nte and C 3 Pte 1107. Alternatively, flag down any passing **bus** (numbers 14, 15 and 29 amongst others) for the city at the stop in front of the terminal on the highway (5am–8pm; 45min–1hr; US$0.50). To get back to the airport, services leave from the Acacya office at 6am, 7am, 10am and 2pm (about 1hr; US$3).

Depending on the company, **international buses** arrive either at the Puertobus terminal by the Centro Gobierno (from Guatemala and Honduras), or at the Terminal de Occidente, Blvd Venezuela in the southwest of the city (from Guatemala). Ticabus buses from Costa Rica, Nicaragua and Guatemala have their own terminal at C Concepción 121 in the Centro Histórico.

City transport

Learning to use San Salvador's **bus system** is essential – the heat, traffic and danger of some neighbourhoods makes walking long distances a bad idea. Luckily, bus services in the city are comprehensive, frequent and fast. Newer city buses are red and white or green and white, though these are vastly outnumbered by the legions of older buses and minibuses that ply the same routes and come in all shapes, colours and sizes. There's a **flat fare** of US$0.17 to anywhere in the city, which should be paid to the driver; minibuses are slightly more expensive (US$0.23) and you pay the driver's assistant, likely to be the one bundling you on board. There are some marked **stops** (*parada de buses*), generally outside large public buildings, shopping centres and so on. Otherwise look for groups of people waiting by the road; drivers will usually let you board at red lights and the minibuses tend to hoot anywhere along a route to alert you to their presence. Services trail off after around 7pm, finishing altogether at around 9pm – at which time you should be thinking of taking **taxis** everywhere in any case. City taxis ply the streets and wait around bus terminals, markets and major shopping areas. Fares should be settled before you get in – trips within the city cost US$3–6, depending on distance and time of day.

There are three main **bus terminals** serving urban and intercity routes. The centrally located Terminal de Oriente (☎221 5379) on Blvd del Ejército is a chaotic affair serving the north and east of the country as well as urban services #3, 5, 7, 8, 9, 28, 29, 34 and 42. Terminal de Occidente (☎223 5609) on Blvd Venezuela west of the centre is no less crazy, with services to the south and west of the country as well as urban routes #4, 27, 34 and 7C. The third, Terminal del Sur (no phone), runs limited intercity services to Zacatecoluca and Usulutan. Bus route information is available in Spanish only from AEAS (☎225 2661) at C 27 Pte 1132, Colonia Layco.

International buses for Tapachula (Mexico) and Guatemala depart hourly between 4am and 3pm from the Puertobus terminal, and they also have daily departures for Managua (5.30am) and San José (3am). Ticabus (☎222 4808) run a 6am bus to Guatemala and Tapachula, and a 5am bus to Panama City via Managua and San José daily. Other companies such as El Condor and Mermex run limited services to Guatemala and Tapachula from Terminal de Occidente, though these tend to be less comfortable and considerably more crowded.

For intercity and international bus routes, see "Travel details", on p.336.

Useful bus routes

#29 From Terminal de Oriente to Metrocentro via Centro Histórico.

#30B Along Blvd de los Héroes, up Alameda Roosevelt and part of Paseo Escalón, then turning west to run past the Zona Rosa.

#34 From Terminal de Oriente through Centro Histórico to Terminal de Occidente and out along the Carretera Interamericana, past the Mercado de Artesanías.

#44 Along Blvd de los Héroes, onto 49a Av Sur close to the Terminal de Occidente, past the Universidad de Centroamérica and out past the US Embassy to Santa Elena.

#52 Along Alameda Juan Pablo I, past Metrosur and on to El Salvador del Mundo (opposite the Telecom office), then up Paseo Escalón past the Galerías shopping mall.

#101A/B/C/D From Centro Histórico up Alameda Roosevelt to Plaza de las Américas, then on to Santa Tecla.

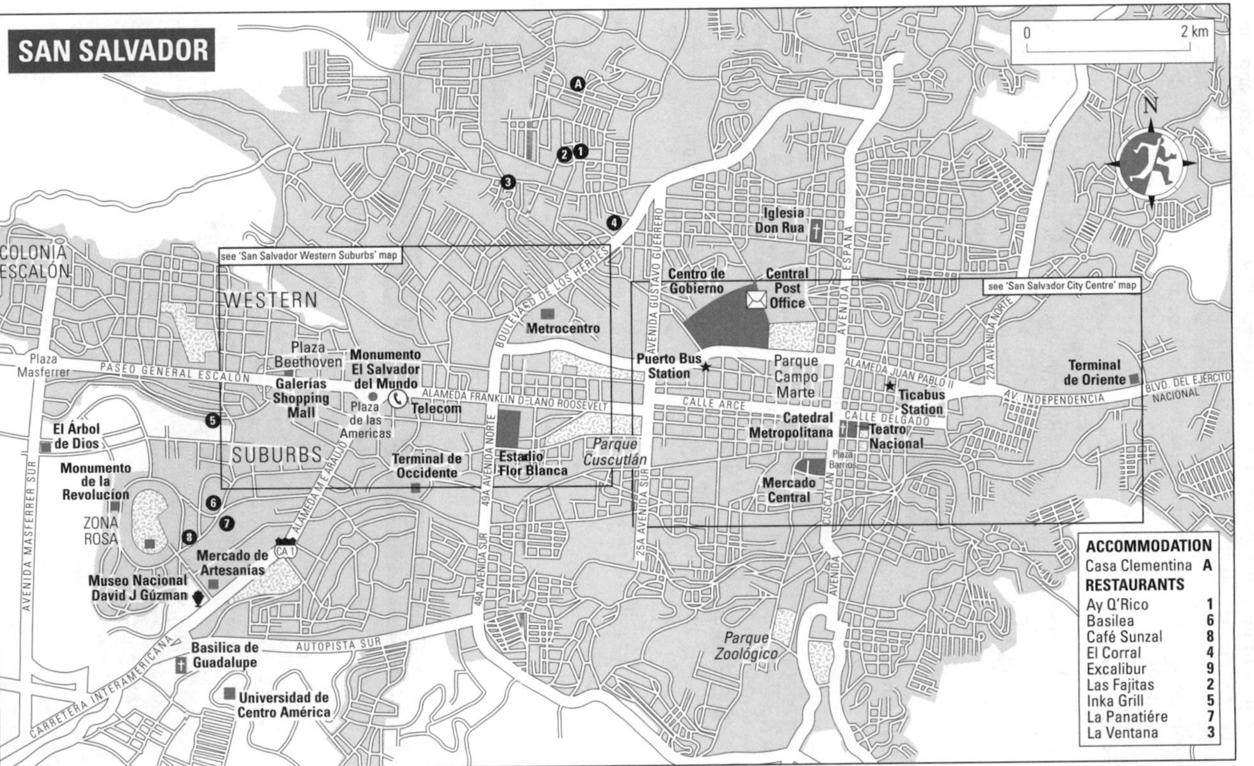

SAN SALVADOR
0 2 km
N
see 'San Salvador Western Suburbs' map
see 'San Salvador City Centre' map
COLONIA ESCALÓN
WESTERN SUBURBS
ZONA ROSA
Plaza Masferrer
PASEO GENERAL ESCALÓN
Plaza Beethoven
Galerías Shopping Mall
Monumento El Salvador del Mundo
Plaza de las Americas
Telecom
ALAMEDA FRANKLIN DELANO ROOSEVELT
BOULEVARD DE LOS HEROES
Metrocentro
El Árbol de Dios
Monumento de la Revolución
Museo Nacional David J Gúzman
Mercado de Artesanías
ALAMEDA M E ARAUJO
CA1
Terminal de Occidente
Estadio Flor Blanca
49A AVENIDA NORTE
49A AVENIDA SUR
AVENIDA MASFERRER SUR
CARRETERA INTERAMERICANA
AUTOPISTA SUR
Basilica de Guadalupe
Universidad de Centro América
Parque Cuscutlán
AVENIDA GUSTAVO GUERRERO
25A AVENIDA SUR
Centro de Gobierno
Central Post Office
Puerto Bus Station
Parque Campo Marte
CALLE ARCE
Catedral Metropolitana
Mercado Central
Plaza Barrios
AVENIDA CUSCATLAN
Iglesia Don Rua
AVENIDA ESPAÑA
ALAMEDA JUAN PABLO II
CALLE DELGADO
Ticabus Station
Teatro Nacional
Parque Zoológico
22A AVENIDA NORTE
AV. INDEPENDENCIA
BLVD. DEL EJÉRCITO NACIONAL
Terminal de Oriente
ACCOMMODATION
Casa Clementina A
RESTAURANTS
Ay Q'Rico 1
Basilea 6
Café Sunzal 8
El Corral 4
Excalibur 9
Las Fajitas 2
Inka Grill 5
La Panatiére 7
La Ventana 3
9 and Corsatur Office
Aeropuerto Internacional Comalapa (40 km)

Accommodation

Although prices in San Salvador are substantially higher than in, say, Guatemala or Honduras, the city's budget accommodation – most of it in or east of the Centro Histórico – is not generally conducive to peace of mind or a pleasant stay. The area **east of Plaza Barrios** and along C Concepción towards the Terminal de Oriente is distinctly unpleasant after dark, although we have listed the better hotels there. The **streets west of Plaza Barrios** are more sane, although dimly lit and virtually empty after nightfall. For peace of mind, it's worth investing a few dollars more to stay in the **western suburbs**, where you'll find some good-quality small hotels and guesthouses, as well as a selection of international-standard hotels where services (and prices) are everything you would expect in any capital city.

El Centro

American Guest House 17a Av Nte 119, between C Arce and C 1 Pte ⓣ222 8789, ⓕ222 3667, ⓔamericanguesthouse@hotmail.com. Dimly lit and rather gloomy rooms, but the service is friendly. Rooms, some oddly-shaped, come with a choice of private or shared bath, plus hot water and cable TV. International phone calls available and meals served at on-site café. ❹

La Frontera C 1 Pte Bis 1013, between 17a and 19a Av Nte ⓣ221 2435. Very spartan, but welcoming, secure and very cheap. Rooms are a bit dated, but are clean and some have en-suite bathrooms for a little extra cost. ❷–❸

Imperial C Concepción 659 ⓣ222 5169, ⓕ222 4920, ⓔhotelimperial@hotmail.com. The best within a cluster of overnight options near the Terminal de Oriente. The simple rooms are large and en-suite and there is a large courtyard for parking. Be aware that the surrounding streets are unpleasant after dark. ❹

León C Delgado 621, between 10a and 12a Av Nte ⓣ222 0951. Very basic but acceptable rooms with bath in a central location. Service can be poor, but prices are very cheap. Rooms on the lower floors or with fan are slightly more expensive. ❷

San Carlos C Concepción 121, between 10a and 12a Av Nte ⓣ222 8975. Clean and secure hotel, though given the nightmarish area the only reason to stay here is to catch an early Ticabus from the terminal below. Rooms at the back are rather quieter, those at the front subjected to constant noise from the main road. Drinking water and parking available. ❸

Villa Floréncia C 1 Pte 1023, between 17a and 19a Av Nte ⓣ221 1706. One of several similar hotels in the area behind the Puerto bus terminal. With large, bright, airy en-suite rooms, cable TV and communal seating areas, this is perhaps the best bet. ❹

Western suburbs

Alameda Alameda Roosevelt 2305, at 43a Av Sur ⓣ260 0800, ⓕ260 3011, ⓦwww.hotelalameda.com. Gracefully ageing and still affordable luxury hotel, with superbly equipped en-suite rooms, swimming pool, sauna, bars and restaurant, as well as its own private beach club on the Costa del Bálsamo beach Playa Flores de Libertad (see p000). ❻

Casa Clementina Av Morazán 34 at C Washington, Col Libertad ⓣ225 5962. Friendly, peaceful and secure with communal garden, TV, outdoor seating and breakfast included. Simply furnished but attractive en-suite rooms with fan. Recommended. ❺

Florida Pasaje los Almendros 115, off Blvd de los Héroes, Urb La Florida ⓣ260 2540, ⓕ260 2654. Air-conditioned hotel conveniently located for El Centro and the western suburbs, although the rooms are somewhat small. The roof terrace has nice city views. Breakfast included. ❺

Good Luck Av Los Sisimiles 2943, Pasaje 5, Col Miramonte ⓣ260 1655. Large, bright and very clean rooms with private bathrooms, cable TV and hot water. Parking facilities available. The hotel restaurant specialises in Chinese meals. ❺

Happy House Av Los Sisimiles 2951, Col Miramonte ⓣ& ⓕ260 1568. Friendly hotel, appearing slightly dilapidated from the outside, but rooms are large, clean and well-equipped, all en-suite with cable TV. This is the best choice at the price in this area. Internet access available at US$1 per hour and meals on request. ❹

Miramonte C Talamanca 2904, at Pasaje No 4, Col Miramonte ⓣ260 1880, ⓕ261 0536. Friendly hotel in a quiet neighbourhood, and a good place for a spot of self-indulgence, with a wide range of rooms of varying size, comfort and price – all have bath and cable TV; some also have balconies. Breakfast available on request. ❻

Occidental 49a Av Nte 171, between Alameda Roosevelt and C 1 Pte, Col Flor Blanca ⓣ211 4916. Good-sized but somewhat run-down dark rooms, with TV; some also have basic bathrooms. Service however is very friendly. Rooms at the front get very noisy from the traffic. ❹

Real Intercontinental Blvd de los Héroes, opposite the Metrocentro ⓣ 211 3333, ⓕ 211 4444, ⓔ sansalvador@gruporeal.com.sv. This landmark concrete monolith is the haunt of the rich and those travelling on expenses, with all the comfort and facilities you would expect of an international-standard hotel. ❾

Ximena's Guest House C San Salvador 202, Col Centro América ⓣ 260 2481, ⓕ 260 2427, ⓔ ximenas@navegante.com.sv. The only real "traveller's" hostel in the city, in a safe residential area close to bars and restaurants. There are dorms (US$5–7 per person) and a variety of rooms (some with private bath), plus a communal TV area, Internet access (US$2.50 per hour) and courtyard. English is spoken, and staff can help arrange tours. ❹

The City

Central San Salvador won't soon be winning any prizes for elegance, and the rough edge to life here can come as a shock to those used to the more tranquil atmosphere of other Central American cities. Smoky and neglected, **El Centro** is a vivid snapshot of Salvadoreño life and character, with whole swathes of the centre taken over by markets sprawling out of control in the **Centro Histórico**. Things get easier towards the modern, leafy suburbs of the **west**, with a number of parks, including **Parque Cuscatlán**, providing acres of green relief from the traffic and noise, and the **Paseo General Escalón** and the **Zona Rosa** offering cinemas, bars, clubs, shops and upmarket restaurants. The best museum in the city, commemorating those killed in the years of conflict, is based in the **Universidad de Centroamérica**, in the far southwest.

El Centro

Despite efforts by the authorities to rid **El Centro** of its traffic pollution, wall-to-wall street stalls and decaying buildings, little progress has been made in the past few years. That said, the parks, plazas and buildings in the **Centro Histórico** have received a generous makeover and some of the street sellers have been forcibly moved on, with varying degrees of success. It's not all doom and gloom though, and despite the slightly intimidating atmosphere of some areas there are a few sites of architectural interest that warrant a visit.

Centro Histórico

At the heart of the city is the rejuvenated **Plaza Barrios**, with trees giving some semblance of shade, and plaques commemorating the revolutionary FMLN soldiers and six Jesuit priests murdered at La UCA in 1989 (see p.315). The square's northern edge is dominated by the **Catedral Metropolitana**, its facade strikingly decorated with colourful contemporary murals by Salvadoreño artist Fernando Llort. The building dates back to 1888, but was severely damaged on a number of occasions, most recently by fire in 1951. Subsequent repairs were suspended by Archbishop Oscar Romero, who argued that funds should be diverted to feeding the hungry – his murder in March 1980 is widely perceived as the event that sent the country spiralling into civil war. After the archbishop's assassination, mourners carrying his body to its final resting place in a chapel beneath the cathedral were fired upon by government troops stationed on top of the surrounding buildings, and many were slaughtered as they tried to reach sanctuary inside the cathedral. Work resumed after the civil war and the building was finally completed in 1999.

On the western edge of the plaza stands the imposing bulk of the Renaissance-style **Palacio Nacional**, the seat of government until the devastating earthquake of 1986. The current building dates back to 1905, having replaced an earlier edifice destroyed by fire. Repairs to the damage caused by the 1986 earthquake are still underway, set back further by the 2001 quake – when the restoration is eventually finished, the building will house the national archives and a national history museum.

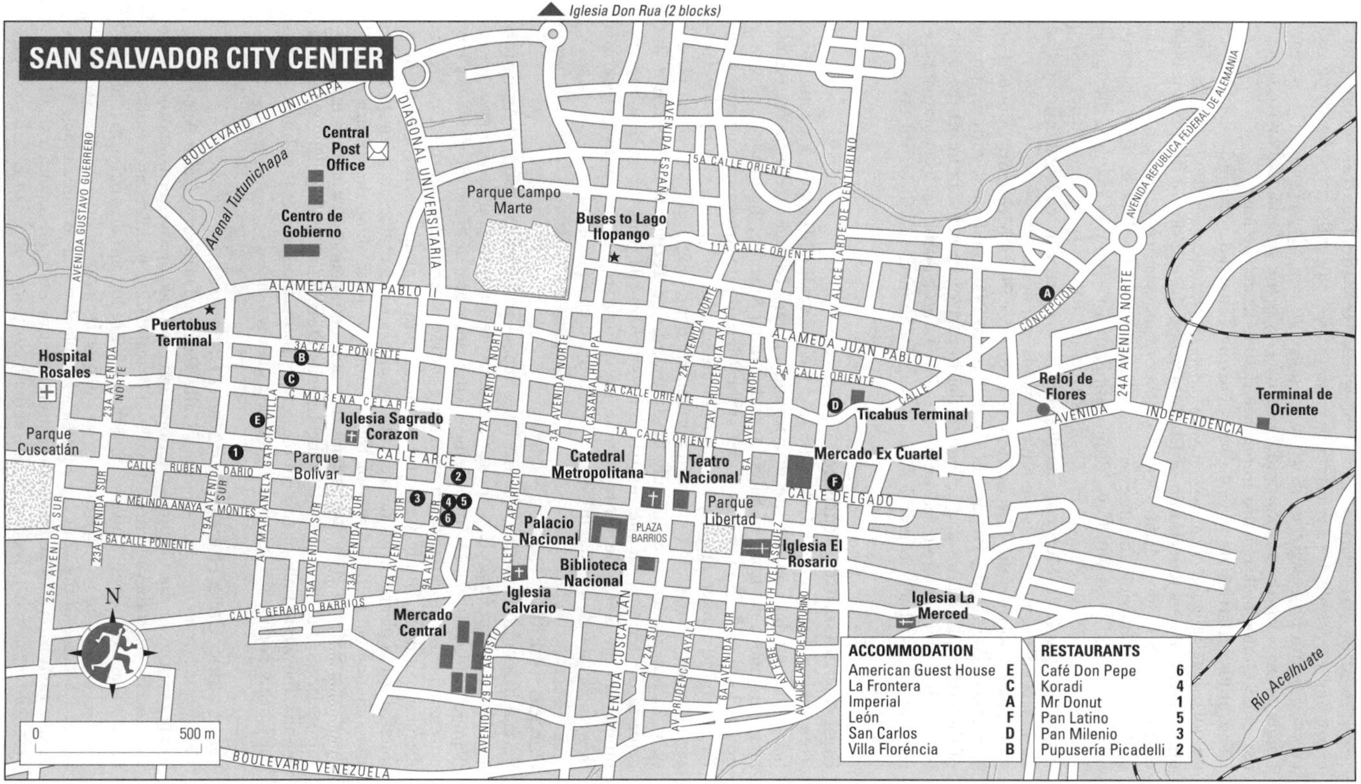

SAN SALVADOR CITY CENTER

Iglesia Don Rua (2 blocks)

Central Post Office
Centro de Gobierno
Parque Campo Marte
Buses to Lago Ilopango
Puertobus Terminal
Hospital Rosales
Parque Cuscatlán
Iglesia Sagrado Corazon
Parque Bolívar
Catedral Metropolitana
Teatro Nacional
Parque Libertad
Palacio Nacional
PLAZA BARRIOS
Biblioteca Nacional
Iglesia Calvario
Mercado Central
Iglesia El Rosario
Iglesia La Merced
Mercado Ex Cuartel
Ticabus Terminal
Reloj de Flores
Terminal de Oriente
Río Acelhuate
Arenal Tutunichapa

BOULEVARD TUTUNICHAPA
DIAGONAL UNIVERSITARIA
AVENIDA GUSTAVO GUERRERO
ALAMEDA JUAN PABLO II
AVENIDA ESPAÑA
15A CALLE ORIENTE
11A CALLE ORIENTE
AV ALICE LARDE DE VENTURINO
AVENIDA REPUBLICA FEDERAL DE ALEMANIA
24A AVENIDA NORTE
CONCEPCION
AVENIDA INDEPENDENCIA
5A CALLE ORIENTE
CALLE
3A CALLE PONIENTE
C MOSENA CELARIÉ
GARCIA VILLA
23A AVENIDA NORTE
7A AVENIDA NORTE
3A AVENIDA NORTE
AV CASAMA HUAPA
3A CALLE ORIENTE
2A AVENIDA NORTE
AV PRUDENCIA AYALA
6A AVENIDA NORTE
1A CALLE ORIENTE
CALLE ARCE
CALLE DELGADO
CALLE RUBEN DARIO
C MELINDA ANAYA MONTES
6A CALLE PONIENTE
19A AVENIDA SUR
23A AVENIDA SUR
25A AVENIDA SUR
AV MARIANELA GARCIA VILLA
15A AVENIDA SUR
13A AVENIDA SUR
11A AVENIDA SUR
9A AVENIDA SUR
AV LETICIA APARICIO
CALLE GERARDO BARRIOS
AVENIDA 29 DE AGOSTO
AVENIDA CUSCATLÁN
AV 2A SUR
AV PRUDENCIA AYALA
6A AVENIDA SUR
AV FEBE ELIZABETH VELASQUEZ
AV ALICE LARDE DE VENTURINO
BOULEVARD VENEZUELA

N

0 500 m

ACCOMMODATION	
American Guest House	E
La Frontera	C
Imperial	A
León	F
San Carlos	D
Villa Florência	B

RESTAURANTS	
Café Don Pepe	6
Koradi	4
Mr Donut	1
Pan Latino	5
Pan Milenio	3
Pupusería Picadelli	2

Southwest of Plaza Barrios is the sprawling **Mercado Central**, whose ever-expanding street stalls are a constant irritation to the city authorities. Anything and everything can be bought in its ruinous and cluttered alleys, even on a Sunday. Looming between the market and Plaza Barrios is the **Iglesia Calvario**, whose dark, neo-Gothic bulk remains impressive, despite its dereliction.

East of Plaza Barrios along C 4 Ote is **Parque Libertad**, previously the heart of colonial San Salvador, but now a slowly decaying relic of former glories. The unusual stained concrete church of **El Rosario** on the east side of the plaza is built over the tomb of José Matías Delgado, father of independence. Though somewhat dull from the outside, the interior is a smorgasbord of colour as light pours in through stained-glass windows, illuminating, in a rainbow of colours, the metal sculptures and contemporary designs that fill the church. The rather more traditional **Iglesia la Merced**, rebuilt from the original where Delgado first called for independence in 1811, is a couple of blocks southeast.

One block north of the El Rosario is the compact **Plaza Morazán**, bounded on its southern edge by the Renaissance-style **Téatro Nacional**. Built with the profits of the coffee plantations and reflecting the impact of French culture in the early twentieth century, the restored interior – all red plush, marble and decorative plasterwork – harks back to grander times. Regular musical and theatrical events are held here.

East of the Centro Histórico

Three blocks east from the theatre along C Delgado is the **Mercado Ex Cuartel**, a hangarlike building on the site of a former military barracks selling a reasonable range of handicrafts from El Salvador and Central America; the quality and selection of local crafts, however, is wider at the Mercado de Artesanías (see opposite). East from the market, the city begins to disintegrate rapidly, with earthquake-damaged buildings struggling to remain upright and depressing displays of abject poverty, as Av Independencia eventually heads towards the **Terminal de Oriente**. Just prior to the terminal, at the intersection with Alameda Juan Pablo II, is the city monument the **Reloj de Flores** – as its name suggests, a giant working clock in a flowerbed, though it frequently suffers from the theft of its hands.

Parque Infantíl

Several blocks north of the Centro Histórico, near the intersection of Av España and Alameda Juan Pablo II, is the forested **Parque Infantíl** (Parque Campo Marte) (9am–5pm; US$0.57). Despite being a busy departure and arrival point for city buses, it is also popular with lunching workers from the nearby Centro de Gobierno and for family weekend picnics. There's a children's playground here, forested tracks planted with native and medicinal species of tree, an open-air theatre and a monument to the heroes of 1890. Continue north along the eastern edge of the Parque and you come to perhaps the most commanding church in the city – and its largest functioning one – the **Iglesia Don Rua**. Built in the nineteenth century, the white bulk of the church towers above the surrounding houses and is particularly notable for its stunning stained-glass windows.

West along Calle Rubén Darío and Calle Arce

The two major commercial streets of **Calle Rubén Darío** and **Calle Arce** run in parallel west from the Catedral Metropolitana towards the western suburbs. In the Centro Histórico they're choked with stalls, wandering peddlers and traffic fumes. Head a few blocks west, however, and things begin to calm down. Further along C Rubén Darío is the recently made-over **Parque Bolívar**, of little interest save for a horseback statue of the liberator himself. One block west and three blocks south of Parque Bolívar on 17a Av Sur is the government printing press, with a small bookshop selling Spanish-language works on the history and culture of El Salvador. One block north of the Parque, on C Arce, is the nineteenth-century **Iglesia Sagrado Corazón**, complete with impressive stained-glass windows. C Arce ends a few blocks west of here, in front of the nineteenth-century **Hospital Rosales**, constructed in Belgium, transported in pieces and put together in the city.

South of the hospital, **Parque Cuscatlán**, a large expanse of green and shady walkways and grass lawns, offers respite from the heat and noise for office workers on their lunch break. At this point C Rubén Darío becomes the Alameda Roosevelt, heading out towards the richer western suburbs.

The western suburbs

From Parque Cuscatlán, **Alameda Roosevelt** runs west towards Blvd de los Héroes. This latter road is lined with fast-food restaurant chains, more upmarket restaurants and what is reputedly the largest shopping mall in Central America, the **Metrocentro/Metrosur** complex, three storeys of expensive boutiques, sporting-goods outlets selling mainly US brands at US prices and a couple of well-stocked, though pricey, souvenir shops. The bookshop on the second level of the Metrocentro has a decent selection of English-language fiction and general interest books, postcards and US magazines, and there's also an Internet café and food hall.

Alameda Roosevelt continues west to the **Plaza de las Américas**, isolated amid eight lanes of traffic. Here, surrounded by small grassy lawns and benches, stands the national symbol, the **Monumento El Salvador del Mundo**, a large plinth showing Jesus standing on top of the globe. The main **Telecom** office (with international telephone and fax services, plus Internet facilities) is also located here, as are a number of banks and fast-food outlets. From here, the road changes its name again, to **Paseo General Escalón**, lined with ritzy restaurants, banks and upmarket businesses. The Paseo continues west, passing **Plaza República de Argentina** (though most people use the old name of Plaza Beethoven), the **Galerías** shopping mall (including a good bookshop, cinema and Internet café) and the **British Embassy**, before reaching **Plaza Masferrer**, home to an enormous national flag and some good *pupuserías*. The **El Árbol de Dios** art gallery (Mon–Sat 9am–6pm; free), south of Plaza Masferrer, on Av Masferrer Sur at C 1 Mascota, has a large collection of paintings and sculptures by Salvadoreño artist Fernando Llort, renowned for his naif style. Beyond Plaza Masferrer are the rich suburbs of **Colonia Escalón** and **Lomas Verdes**, stretching high up onto the slopes of Volcán San Salvador.

Southwest along the Carretera Interamericana

Heading off from the Plaza de las Américas, the Interamericana runs through the southwest quarters of the city and out to western El Salvador. About 2km along this road is the **Mercado de Artesanías**, with a wide selection of handicrafts from all over the country. Good buys here include hammocks, painted wooden items from La Palma (see p.364) and bright hand-towels woven with Llort's paintings; prepare to bargain, although prices are around fifty percent higher than in the villages of origin. Just past the market, turn into Av la Revolución and a couple of hundred metres up stands the **Museo Nacional de Antropología "Dr David J. Guzmán"** (Tues–Sun 9am–4pm; US$1.50), named after an eminent Salvadoreño biologist and home to the nation's largest collection of cultural artefacts and anthropological displays, plus exhibits of modern Salvadoreño life and science. Perhaps the most important piece in the museum is the Monolito del Jaguar, a five-ton circular representation of a jaguar's head. Opposite the museum, the **Feria Internacional** is the site of regular, and very popular, international trade fairs and also has an open-air music venue that hosts a range of Latin music stars.

Av la Revolución continues uphill for another kilometre or so, into the heart of the leafy Col San Benito, ending in front of the **Monumento de la Revolución**, a vast, curved slab of concrete bearing a mosaic of a naked Goliath with head

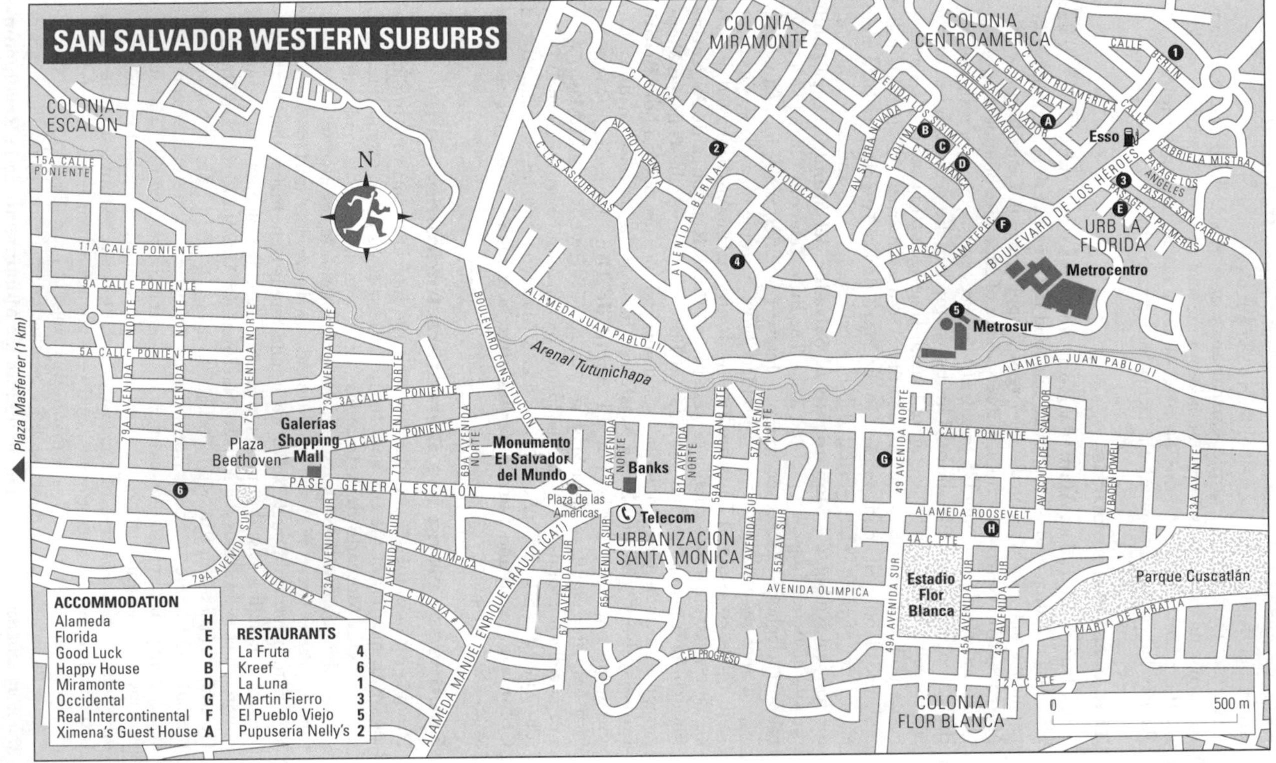

SAN SALVADOR WESTERN SUBURBS
N
COLONIA ESCALÓN
COLONIA MIRAMONTE
COLONIA CENTROAMERICA
URB LA FLORIDA
URBANIZACION SANTA MONICA
COLONIA FLOR BLANCA
Esso
Metrocentro
Metrosur
Galerías Shopping Mall
Plaza Beethoven
Monumento El Salvador del Mundo
Plaza de las Americas
Banks
Telecom
Estadio Flor Blanca
Parque Cuscatlán
Arenal Tutunichapa
BOULEVARD DE LOS HÉROES
BOULEVARD CONSTITUCION
ALAMEDA JUAN PABLO II
ALAMEDA JUAN PABLO III
ALAMEDA MANUEL ENRIQUE ARAUJO (CA1)
ALAMEDA ROOSEVELT
PASEO GENERAL ESCALÓN
AVENIDA OLIMPICA
AV OLIMPICA
AVENIDA BERNAL
AVENIDA LOS SISIMILES
AV SIERRA NEVADA
AV PROVIDENCIA
AV PASCO
C TOLUCA
C LAS ASCURANAS
C COLIMA
C TALAMANCA
CALLE LAMATEPEC
CALLE BERLIN
C CENTROAMERICA
CALLE
C GUATEMALA
CALLE SAN SALVADOR
CALLE MANAGUA
GABRIELA MISTRAL
PASAGE LOS ANGELES
PASAGE SAN CARLOS
PASAGE LA PALMERAS
15A CALLE PONIENTE
11A CALLE PONIENTE
9A CALLE PONIENTE
5A CALLE PONIENTE
3A CALLE PONIENTE
1A CALLE PONIENTE
4A C PTE
12A C PTE
79A AVENIDA NORTE
77A AVENIDA NORTE
75A AVENIDA NORTE
73A AVENIDA NORTE
71A AVENIDA NORTE
69A AVENIDA NORTE
65A AVENIDA NORTE
61A AVENIDA NORTE
59A AV SUR AND NTE
57A AVENIDA NORTE
49 AVENIDA NORTE
AV SCOUTS DE EL SALVADOR
AV BADEN POWELL
33A AV NTE
79A AVENIDA SUR
73A AVENIDA SUR
71A AVENIDA SUR
67A AVENIDA SUR
65A AVENIDA SUR
57A AVENIDA SUR
55A AV SUR
49A AVENIDA SUR
45A AVENIDA SUR
43A AVENIDA SUR
C NUEVA #2
C NUEVA #1
C EL PROGRESO
C MARIA DE BARATTA
0
500 m
Plaza Masferrer (1 km)
ACCOMMODATION
Alameda H
Florida E
Good Luck C
Happy House B
Miramonte D
Occidental G
Real Intercontinental F
Ximena's Guest House A
RESTAURANTS
La Fruta 4
Kreef 6
La Luna 1
Martin Fierro 3
El Pueblo Viejo 5
Pupusería Nelly's 2

thrown back and arms uplifted. Built to commemorate the revolutionary movement of 1948, the monument's location in one of the wealthiest areas of the city and overlooking one of its best hotels, the *Marriott*, is supremely ironic. East of the monument stretches the **Zona Rosa** entertainment district. Specifically aimed at tourists, the district's main drag, Blvd del Hipódromo, curves uphill and is lined with expensive restaurants, nightclubs and boutiques.

Heading further out along the Carretera Interamericana, on the left, is the elegant white mansion and lush gardens housing the Foreign Ministry and, where the road meets the Autopista del Sur, what is possibly the most beautiful church in San Salvador, the **Basilica de Nuestra Señora de Guadalupe**. Built after World War I and consecrated in 1953, the basilica is dedicated to the Virgen Morena, or Black Virgin, patroness of the Americas. Inside are beautiful stained-glass windows and a 1950s mural of the Virgin and angels over the altar.

La UCA and Jardín Botanico la Laguna

Stretching behind the basilica is the campus of the **Universidad de Centro América** ("La UCA"; also known as the Jesuit University), pleasantly laid out amid shady grounds. The moving **Centro Monseñor Romero** (Mon–Fri 8am–noon & 2–6pm, Sat 8am–11.30pm; free) at La UCA commemorates the assassinated Archbishop Romero along with the six Jesuit priests, their housekeeper and her daughter, who were murdered here by the security forces in November 1989. Volunteer students act as guides to the small museum, which houses clothing, photographs and personal effects of Romero and the priests, along with those of other human-rights workers killed during the years of conflict. There are diagrams and explanations of the campus massacre, as well as eyewitness descriptions of other low points during the war, such as the massacres at Río Sumpul (May 1980) and Mozote (December 1981). Outside, a small rose garden has been planted in tribute; the circle of six bushes is for the six priests, the white rose in the centre is for Monseñor Romero.

A short distance south of the university, the tranquil **Jardín Botanico la Laguna** (Tues–Sun 9am–5pm; US$1) sits incongruously at the edge of an industrial park and at the foot of old volcanic cliffs. The gardens contain plants from all over the world, set among shady trees and small streams, and are a good place to escape the city for an hour or two. Bus #101D or #44 will drop you off about five minutes' walk from the entrance.

Eating, drinking and entertainment

The best **restaurants** are concentrated in the western suburbs, catering to those with the money and time to indulge. The cheapest places to eat are the comedores in the Centro Histórico, although the richer suburbs occasionally throw up a few surprises – the **Plaza Masferrer** has a number of roadside eateries that stay open until quite late. Anywhere in the city, however, you're bound to stumble over a *pupusa* stall, whilst the markets and bus stations are full of stands selling cheap meals and snacks – always check out hygiene levels before indulging. The **Blvd de los Héroes** area is dominated by local and international fast-food chains, but also has a few good restaurants, while the **Paseo Escalón** and **Zona Rosa** are more cosmopolitan, with pricey international cuisine – book ahead at weekends.

Clubs and **bars** are likewise found mainly in the western suburbs, but there are also small pockets of expat and tourist nightlife, particularly in and around *Ximena's Guesthouse* and *La Ventana* bar in Col América, behind Blvd de los Héroes. For **listings**, keep a lookout for *Ke Pasa,* a free weekly entertainment guide available in bars and restaurants. *The Revue*, Guatemala's English-language magazine, also includes an El Salvador section and is widely available throughout the city.

Centro Histórico

Café Don Pepe C 4 Pte and 9a Av Sur. Sodas, juices, pastries and snacks served in a lively atmosphere. This is a popular lunch spot (US$3–5) and service can be a little slow at peak times; daytime only.

Koradi 9a Av Sur 225, at C 4 Pte. One of the few places catering to vegetarians, with soya burgers, wholewheat pizzas and great juices. Open in the daytime only; closed Sun.

Mr Donut C Arce and 21a Av Nte (and branches around the city). Nominally one of a chain of doughnut-and-coffee shops, though also serving excellent full breakfasts, lunches and light evening snacks. Sandwiches are a little expensive and generic, but ideal if you are in a hurry and don't have time to wait for Salvadoreño service.

Pan Latino C Arce at 9a Av Sur. A welcome break from the maelstrom outside, serving coffees, cakes, *tamales* and sodas. Take-away option available if you prefer your food *al fresco*.

Pan Milenio C Arce at 7a Av Sur (plus other branches throughout El Centro). Excellent cakes and pastries, and plenty of seating to relax and enjoy a coffee. Various sandwiches on offer, making this a very popular place for take-away food amongst workers.

Pupusería Picadelli C Arce, corner with 7a Av Sur. Basic *pupusería* but with plenty of special offers. Amongst the best value in the centre with a series of combo meals from as little as US$1.

Around Blvd de los Héroes

Ay Q'Rico Blvd Universitario 217. Popular among the local students for cheap daily menus (US$1.50–2) served with free beer. Also wide menu of seafood and poultry with a touch of Mexican.

El Corral Blvd de los Héroes corner C Sta Victoria. Steak house and traditional meals served in this large restaurant/bar. Live music at weekends when there is a US$6 cover charge, but a US$13 option includes entry, meal and entertainment.

Las Fajitas 39a Av Nte and Blvd Universitario. Colourful Mexican restaurant decorated with Chiapanecan cloths and serving up huge, spicy portions. Try the *brochetta* served standing vertically on a banana leaf. Take-away service available.

La Fruta Av Maracaibo 519 ☎260 1253. More than 200 juice combinations as well as breakfasts and lunches made from all natural ingredients. Evening meals available if you call in advance. Mon–Sat 9am–6pm.

La Luna C Berlin 228, Urb Buenos Aires ☎260 2921. Arty restaurant, theatre and nightspot serving a good range of vegetarian and meat dishes in the US$5–8 range.

Martin Fierro Pasaje Las Palmeras 123, off Blvd de los Héroes. Large restaurant specialising in grilled meat dishes, most with a Mexican twist. Live music most nights, with ample airy, covered seating.

El Pueblo Viejo Metrosur mall. Slightly above-average prices for generous portions of Salvadoreño food, steaks and seafood, plus live music at weekends. A popular place for lunch.

Pupusería Nelly's Av Bernal 210, north of Alameda Roosevelt between Blvd de los Héroes and Blvd Constitución. One of the city's best and friendliest places for a *pupusa* – try one made with cheese and *loroco* (a type of herb).

La Ventana C San Antonio Abad 2335, Col Centroamérica ☎226 5129. European-run restaurant and bar with an interesting selection of dishes (US$5–9) inspired by cuisines from around the world. Very popular at the weekends with expatriates, tourists and moneyed Salvadoreños. Daily until 1pm.

Paseo Escalón and the Zona Rosa

Basilea Blvd de los Héroes, Zona Rosa ☎279 0056. Seriously decadent but delicious food served up inside or on the quiet garden terrace with fountain. Dishes from all over the world include fabulous Maryland crab cakes; expect to pay US$10–17 per person.

Café Sunzal Av Las Magnolias 226, Zona Rosa ☎223 1433. International seafood and steak house with many dishes given a Latin twist. Imported beers and wines available as well as snacks from the grill.

Excalibur C Cortez Blanco, Pasaje 1 no.6, Madreselva, Antiguo Cuscatlán ☎257 8798. Housed in a dramatic medieval castle replica, you can dine on international cuisine here in a unique atmosphere. It's not cheap though, but the food is good if your wallet can take the shock.

Inka Grill 79a Av Sur Pasaje A, Col La Mascota. Popular Peruvian-style restaurant just up from the Zona Rosa. Andean specialities served in near-authentic surroundings, with replicas of Inca goods all around.

Kalpataru Av Masferrer 147 ☎263 1204. Slightly pricey but innovative vegetarian fare, including *pupusas* with unusual fillings like stir-fried broccoli and curried vegetables. Tienda Naturista and bookshop on site.

Kreef Paseo Escalón, at 77a Av Sur. German-style *bockwurst*, steaks and big sandwiches, though it's not cheap. The attached delicatessen is a favourite hangout for expats. Closed Sun evening.

La Panatiére Blvd del Hipodrómo 211 ⓣ223 6025. The coolest afternoon café in the Zona Rosa, and a good place to enjoy a leisurely cappuccino and pastry and watch San Salvador's rich kids at play.

Nightlife

Despite having the only identifiable nightlife scene in the country, visitors from Europe and the United States are likely to be disappointed by what is on offer. The entire population of the city appears to disappear at nightfall, and even in the Zona Rosa, the action takes place inside, rather than on the street. Many of the restaurants hereabouts have **live salsa/merengue** music and dancing at the weekends; two of the best are *El Corral* (see above), and *Quinto Sol*, 15a Av Nte and C 1 Pte, Col Centroamérica. *La Luna*, C Berlin 228, Col Centroamérica, and *La Ventana*, C San Antonio Abad 2335, are relaxed **bars** with a more European feel, popular with local professionals and foreigners. *El Arpa*, Avenida A 137, Col San José, is San Salvador's obligatory Irish pub, while *Los Celtas*, C San Antonio Abad at C Principal 2339, keeps the Scottish flag flying. Calle Lamatepec, off Blvd de los Héroes, also has a row of restaurant/bars that double as nightspots including *Eurobar*, and *Que Keres?*, at the junction with Av Los Sisimiles.

In the **Zona Rosa**, *Jungle Bar No More* has no cover charge, free beer between 8.30 and 10.30pm on Saturdays, and is patronised by a lively crowd. Blvd del Hipódromo, around C la Reforma, has a number of loud, street-side bars which start getting full from around 10pm; many, including *Karamba*, appeal to a younger, moneyed set. *Zone* and *Quest* are the only remaining discos along here. *Lapsus* **nightclub** on the Paseo Escalón plays local music and Euro-bop until late.

There are a couple of **cinemas** – including a huge Cinemark at Metrocentro and Galerías, and a multiscreen complex at Redondel Masferrer at the top of Paseo Escalón – and many others scattered around the city; the daily newspapers list programmes. *La Luna* (see above) shows a different film on video every weekday night, starting at around 7pm, while the Alianza Française (ⓣ223 8084) on 51a Av Nte 152 runs French film seasons.

Listings

Airlines Many of the airlines are based around the Alameda Roosevelt/Paseo Escalón districts. Aeromexico, Centro Comercial and C Loma Linda 26D ⓣ298 6226; Air France, Edificio Edim-Lama, Blvd del Hipódromo 645, Col San Benito ⓣ263 8192; Alitalia, Centro Comercial and C Loma Linda 26D ⓣ298 6226; American Airlines, Edificio La Centroamericana, Alameda Roosevelt 3107 ⓣ298 0777; Continental, Torre Roble Metrocentro, Blvd de los Héroes ⓣ260 8869; Copa, Alameda Roosevelt 2838 and 55a Av Nte ⓣ209 2699; Grupo Taca incorporating Aviateca, Lacsa, Nica and Taca, Edificio Caribe, Nivel 2, Paseo Escalón ⓣ267 8888; Iberia, Centro Comercial Plaza Jardin, Local C, C Santa Tecla at Av Olímpica ⓣ223 2600; Lufthansa, Fountainblue Plaza, Modulo B 1, 87a Av Nte ⓣ263 2850; Mexicana, *Hotel Presidente Marriott*, Av la Revolución, Col San Benito ⓣ243 3633; United Airlines, Centro Comercial Galerías, Local 14, Paseo Escalón 3700 ⓣ279 3900.

American Express 55 Av Sur, Edificio Credomatic, between Alameda Roosevelt and Av Olímpica (ⓣ245 3774); Centro Comercial la Mascota 1, Carretera Interamericana at C la Mascota (ⓣ279 3844) – take bus #101B (to Santa Tecla), which passes the building.

Banks and exchange Most banks ask for the original receipt when cashing travellers' cheques; an exception is Banco Hipotecario, at Av Cuscatlán between C 4 and 6 Ote and other branches around the city. The headquarters of most of the large national and international banks are along Paseo Escalón. You can get over-the-counter cash advances on Visa and MasterCard at most branches of Banco de Comercio and Banco Salvadoreño; a few also have ATMs.

Bookstores The bookshop in the Metrocentro mall has a selection of English-language books and some US magazines. Punto Literario, Blvd del Hipódromo 326, has English, French, German and Spanish literature. Centro Cultural La Mazorca, C San Antonio Abad 1447, Col El Roble, has a small range of Central American literature and political texts (Spanish only), while *La Ventana* restaurant (see p.316) has a small selection of political and social texts (in English and Spanish) and US magazines and newspapers.

Car rental Expect to pay around US$45 a day for a small car and up to US$120 a day for a Space Wagon or Jeep. Check that price includes insurance and that emergency assistance is available. Companies include: Avis, 43a Av Sur 127, Col Flor Blanca (Ⓣ261 1212), and at the airport (Ⓣ339 9268); Budget, C 1 Pte 2765 (Ⓣ260 4333); Hertz, C 9 Pte and 01 Av Nte, Col Escalón (Ⓣ264 2826), and at the airport (Ⓣ339 9481); Thrifty (Ⓣ339 9947) and National (Ⓣ339 9660) both have booths at the airport.

Embassies Most embassies are located in or around the Paseo Escalón and Zona Rosa districts – except for the US embassy, which is on the road to Santa Elena (take bus #44). British, C El Mirador and 89 Av Nte Edifico World Trade Center, Col Escalón Ⓣ209 6000; Canada, Alameda Roosevelt and 63 Av Sur Ⓣ279 4655; France, C 1 Pte 3718, Col Escalón Ⓣ279 4016; Germany, C 7 Pte 3972, Col Escalón Ⓣ247 0000; Israel, Alameda Roosevelt and 63 Av Sur Ⓣ211 3434; Italy, C La Reforma 158, Col San Benito Ⓣ223 4806; Japan, C Lomo Linda 258, Col San Benito Ⓣ224 4740; Spain, C La Reforma 164, Col San Benito Ⓣ257 5700; US, Blvd Santa Elena, Antiguo Cuscatlán Ⓣ278 1188.

Immigration office Ministerio del Interior, Centro de Gobierno, Alameda Juan Pablo I (Ⓣ221 2111; Mon–Fri 8am–4pm), is the place to get stamps, tourist cards and visas extended.

Internet access Internet outlets are opening (and closing) all the time, particularly around the University and in the shopping malls. Most operate between 9am–8pm, closing earlier at weekends and charging around US$1 per hour. Many hotels also have access though rates are considerably higher. There are several along Blvd Universitario at the corner of Blvd de los Héroes, and in the centre a cluster around the western end of C Arce between 23a and 17a Av Nte. Infocentros at 59a Av Sur at the corner with Alameda Roosevelt has a very fast connection.

Laundry Try Lavandería Lavapronto, C Los Sismiles 2944 (Mon–Sat 7am–7pm). An average load should cost US$2–3. Most hotels either provide a laundry service – though at a slightly higher price than the local *lavanderías* – or let you wash clothes in the laundry sink.

Libraries and cultural institutes La UCA has a very good library, while the Centro Cultural Salvadoreño (Mon–Fri 8am–noon & 2–5pm), opposite the Metrocentro on C los Sisimiles, has an ageing collection of Salvadoreño and English-language works. The Biblioteca Nacional is open to the public, but you have to show ID.

Medical care There's a 24-hour pharmacy at Farmacia Internacional, Edificio Kent, Local 6, Alameda Juan Pablo II at Blvd de los Héroes. Embassies have lists of recommended doctors in various fields, and the Medicentro at 27a Av Nte and C 21 Pte has a number of doctors specialising in different fields. Hospital Bautista El Salvador, 23 Av Nte 128 (Ⓣ222 5522) and Hospital Rosales, 25a Av Nte at C Arce (Ⓣ222 5866), provide emergency medical care.

Police The main station is in the Scottish castle-like building which occupies an entire block on 10a Av Sur at C 6 Ote (Ⓣ271 4422).

Post office Behind the Centro de Gobierno on Blvd Centro de Gobierno; look for the large building with UPAE on the side. The *lista de correos* (Mon–Fri 8am–5pm, Sat 8am–noon) is at window 12 in the main section. There are smaller offices in the lower level of the Metrocentro mall, by the Europa supermarket on Plaza Beethoven and on C Olímpico.

Telephone office Telecom, the French-owned former state phone company, has an enormous glass office at La Campana, Plaza de las Américas (take any bus heading for El Salvador del Mundo and get off by the monument).

Tour companies Organized tours start from around US$30 per person. Though these can save a lot of hassle, they can be rather rushed, whisking you on and off the tourist bus at a rapid rate. Bear in mind that rates increase per person for smaller groups. All (apart from El Salvador Divers) offer similar tours to archeological sites (primarily Joya de Cerén and San Andrés) and areas of scenic beauty (such as Bosque Montecristo and Cerro Verde), along with some activity trips. Amor Tours, 73a Av Sur at Av Olímpica (Ⓣ223 5131, Ⓕ279 0363); El Salvador Divers, C 3 Pte 5020-A, at 99a Av Nte (Ⓣ264 0961, Ⓦwww.elsalvadordivers.com), has diving trips along the Los Cóbanos/Los Remedios stretch of the Pacific coast and crater diving at Lake Coatepeque, plus PADI courses and equipment rental; Salvador Tours, Villas Españolas, local 3-b, Paseo General Escalón (Ⓣ264 3110, Ⓔsaltours@es.com.sv), run archeological and ecological tours across the country, plus surfing and beach trips; Ríos Aventuras (Ⓣ298 0335, Ⓔgrupotropic@navegante.com.sv) organise rafting on the ríos Paz and Lempa for minimum groups of four people.

Travel agents Plenty along the Alameda Roosevelt/Paseo Escalón for booking or changing flights.

Around San Salvador

San Salvador is an excellent transport hub, and within easy reach of the city are a number of destinations offering immediate relief from the heat and crowds. Head in any direction and in well under an hour you'll find lush, rolling countryside.

West of San Salvador: Los Chorros, Volcán San Salvador and Joya de Cerén

Heading **west**, the Carretera Interamericana runs 14km through light industrial and residential districts to the small, busy town of **Santa Tecla,** briefly the capital in 1854 and also known as Nueva San Salvador. Although considerably more relaxed than the capital, there is little reason to linger here. Six kilometres beyond, just off the highway is the *turicentro* of **Los Chorros** (daily 7am–5pm; US$0.90), beautifully situated in a natural gorge. Small waterfalls cascade through mossy volcanic slopes into a series of landscaped pools, suitable for bathing; there are public changing rooms and showers and a couple of comedores provide meals. Come on a weekday, unless you prefer your scenery with crowds. If you're in a group and feel brave enough to ignore the warnings about robbers, the surrounding hills provide pleasant walks. **Buses** for Los Chorros (#79) leave from 11a Av Sur and C Rubén Darío (every 15min; 40min); alternatively, take any Santa Ana bus from the Terminal de Occidente and ask to be dropped at the gate.

From Santa Tecla, a road heads north, up and around the heavily cultivated slopes of **Volcán San Salvador**, at 1960m the fifth-highest volcano in the country. Its summit is punctured by a 540m-deep crater, **El Boquerón**, containing a smaller cone created in the last eruption in 1917. You can get to the top by public transport and then either walk around the crater (about 2hr) or down the wooded slopes inside it. **Bus** #103 (hourly) and pick-ups run from 4a Av Sur and C Hernández in Santa Tecla to the top, with the last bus back down leaving in mid-afternoon. Bear in mind that **taxi** and pick-up drivers are reluctant to make the journey up to the crater in the afternoon, for fear of robbery – in any case, early morning is the best time to go, when the views from the summit are clearest. You can also walk up to the crater, though robberies have been reported; the police at the entrance may be willing to provide an escort for groups.

Joya de Cerén

Continuing west, the Carretera Interamericana runs through the flat and fertile Zapotitán Valley. Some 15km past Santa Tecla, a road branches off to the north and immediately splits at the Desvío del Opio; the left-hand fork here leads past the Maya site of **Joya de Cerén** (Tues–Sun 9am–4pm; US$2.85), designated a World Heritage Site by UNESCO in 1993. Known as the "Pompei of the Americas", the site houses the remains of a village destroyed in a volcanic eruption around 600 AD. Lava from this and subsequent eruptions buried the site under upwards of six metres of ash until its accidental discovery in 1976. The lack of any human remains suggests that the inhabitants had ample warning of the impending disaster.

The site itself is small and will disappoint those accustomed to the imposing Mayan edifices of Guatemala and Honduras. Its importance, however, lies in the wealth of detail provided about the daily lives of the Maya. Eighteen structures have been discovered, although only ten have so far been excavated, including houses, storage rooms and one believed to be used for religious rituals or communal events; not all are open to the public, however. Artefacts found at the site, including jars containing petrified beans, utensils and ceramics, as well as the discovery of gardens for growing a wide range of plants including maize, beans, agave and chilli peppers, have helped confirm a picture of a well-organized and stable society, relatively wealthy, and with trade links throughout the Central American isthmus. The ruins are housed under hangar roofs with cages around them preventing you from getting too close which, while protecting the ruins, seriously detracts from the experience.

A small museum at the site details the development of the Maya culture and outlines the course of excavations (Spanish-language only).

To get here from San Salvador, take bus #108 from Terminal de Occidente and get off just after crossing the bridge over the Río Sucio. If you wish to visit Joya de Cerén and San Andrés (see below) in the same trip, take #108 back towards San Salvador as far as the Desvío Opio, where you can intercept a #201 (en route from the Terminal de Occidente) to San Andrés.

San Andrés

Five kilometres west along the Carretera Interamericana stands another important Maya ceremonial centre, **San Andrés** (Tues–Sun 9am–4.30pm; US$2.85), set among rolling fertile agricultural land. San Andrés is one of the largest pre-Columbian sites in El Salvador, originally covering more than three square kilometres and supporting a population of about 12,000. The site reached its peak around 650–900AD, establishing itself as the regional capital for the settlements in the Zapotitán Valley, and was first excavated under the leadership of American archeologist Stanley Boggs in 1940.

Only sections of the ceremonial centre have been excavated and the remains of seven major structures are visible – sadly, they've been preserved using rather too liberal amounts of concrete. The **Acropolis** (or south plaza) forms the major part of the centre, a raised platform supporting a number of pyramids and annexes. Structure 1 on the south edge was a temple; on its north face are the remains of an altar. Access to these pyramids was restricted to the governing elite, whose living quarters lay along the northern and western edges of the Acropolis; the bases of two of these have been reconstructed. North of the Acropolis lay another plaza, used for markets and communal events. The largest pyramid (Structure 5) lies on the eastern edge of this plaza, but it has only been partially excavated. It is 13 metres high and dates from 600–900 AD, though ceramics found below it date from 750–250 BC and represent the oldest known artefacts associated with the site. Just behind the café, the **Obraje de Añil** (indigo works) was used in the extraction of indigo and demonstrates the importance of the dye in pre-Columbian times. You can wander freely around the site, which is also a popular spot for picnicking family groups at the weekends. A museum here (Spanish-language only) has a small replica of what the site would have looked like in its prime.

If in a group, it's possible to walk between San Andrés and Joya de Cerén. A path leads across the fields behind San Andrés, coming out about 4km northeast at an old railway track and abandoned station, just off the San Juan Opico road. From here it is another 3km or so to Joya de Cerén. From San Andrés you can also continue on to Santa Ana (see p.352) – buses (#201) can be flagged down on the highway – or return to San Salvador (same bus opposite direction).

East of San Salvador: Lago de Ilopango

Heading **east** from San Salvador, the Carretera Interamericana runs through a succession of dismal slums and dreary suburbs. A couple of kilometres past the domestic airport at Ilopango, a road branches south and winds down through scrubby hillsides, offering stunning views across **Lago de Ilopango**, to the mountains on the other side. The country's largest and deepest crater lake, Ilopango is a contrast of blue waters and dramatic, thickly vegetated cliffs tumbling into the water, surmounted to the east by the peaks of San Vicente volcano. Bus #15 runs from the corner of C 9 Pte and 1a Av Nte in San Salvador every half an hour or so.

On weekends, the city crowds pour in, most of them heading for the **turicentro** (daily 8am–5pm; US$0.80) at the poor, dusty hamlet of **APULO**, on the northern shore of the lake. It's a pleasant getaway with forested tracks, basic comedores, a swimming pool, changing rooms and a section of beach, although the water is slightly grimy. A number of small boats tout for custom here (US$12 per hour), and drifting around the Isla de Amor, Isla de los Patos and the Cerros Quemados (created in an 1880 eruption) is a pleasant way to spend an hour or so. From Apulo a road heads round the shore, past the grounds of the private Club Salvadoreño to the hamlets of **Corinto** and **San Agustín**; shortly before Corinto, where the road drops closer to the water's edge, there's access to small rocky **beaches** and cleaner stretches of water. If tempted to **stay** the night, the *Hotel Vistalago* (☎226 2315; ❻) sits about 2km above the lake, 500 metres from the highway on the access road. The views are notable, but the rooms – all with bath and a/c – are pricey.

South of San Salvador: Los Planes de Renderos

Heading **south**, a narrow, paved road clears the city surprisingly quickly and winds up to **Los Planes de Renderos**, a little-visited suburban area set in the hills around San Salvador. The air is much fresher here than in the city and the *mirador* lookout point affords superb views of San Salvador, the volcano and Lake Ilopango. Los Planes is also famous for its numerous *pupuserías*, including the barn-like *Pupusería Paty*, serving some of the best *pupusas* in El Salvador. Also worth a visit is *Casa de Piedra*, an open-fronted bar and restaurant with spectacular nighttime views of San Salvador – it's at km 8.5 on the Carretera Los Planes de Renderos.

Twelve kilometres from San Salvador is the **Parque Balboa**, a somewhat run-down *turicentro* (daily 8am–6pm; US$0.90; bus #12 from Av 29 de Agosto). About forty minutes' walk inside the park is the **Puerta del Diablo**, a split rock formation at the summit of the Cerro Chulo, with views to the coast and across to Volcán San Vicente volcano.

Just before the entrance to Parque Balboa, a road branches off to wind down to the coast; a turning after about 2km leads to the small town of **PANCHIMALCO**, dramatically set at the foot of the lush slopes of Cerro Chulo, with the Puerto del Diablo overlooking the town to the west. The area is inhabited by the Panchos, descendants of the Pipils, although traditional dress is rarely seen nowadays. The colonial church, built in 1725, is the oldest surviving church in the country, and there's a huge ceiba tree in the main square. Usually a sleepy, quiet place, things become livelier during the town's annual **festivals** (see p.293). Bus #17 runs regularly to the town from Av 29 de Agosto in San Salvador.

3.2

The Pacific coast

El Salvador's **Pacific coast** is a 300-kilometre sweep of sandy tropical beaches, dramatic cliffs, mangrove swamps and romantic islands. The **Carretera Littoral**, which runs along the entire coast, links the towns and villages here, and though public transport runs regularly to many places it's still worth renting a car for a few days to reach some of the more remote and beautiful beaches. While many of the beaches are being developed, don't expect the amenities of international resorts. Instead, the beauty of this part of the country lies in relaxing on clean, wide beaches or spending time in the relatively untouched fishing villages of the coast.

The region was very badly affected by the January 2001 **earthquake**, whose epicentre was located about 35km out to sea. Much of the rebuilding work has been completed, opening up many of the previously deserted beaches and resulting in an influx of weekend visitors. Devastation caused by the earthquake can still be seen however, especially in the poorest areas considered too remote or insignificant to warrant a rebuild.

The most accessible stretch of coast near San Salvador – and thus very crowded at weekends – is the **Costa del Bálsamo**. Located around the small fishing town of **Puerto La Libertad**, this stretch boasts some of Central America's best surfing beaches. To the east, the small city of **Zacatecoluca** acts as the main jumping-off point for the Salvadoreño playground of the **Costa del Sol**, home to the coast's most upmarket resort hotels. A little further down the coast are the green waterways and islands of the mangrove swamps of the **Bahía de Jiquilísco** and what many consider to be the finest beach in the country, **Playa El Espino**. Further east are the fine beaches of **El Cuco** and **El Tamarindo**, the former busy at weekends but delightfully deserted during the week. In the extreme east of the country is the faded port town of **La Unión**, from where you can catch early-morning lanchas to the tranquil **islands** of the Golfo de Fonseca.

The beaches west of Acajutla are best accessed via Sonsonate rather than along the coastal road, and are covered in "The west", beginning on p.345.

Puerto La Libertad and Costa del Bálsamo

Just 34km south of San Salvador, **PUERTO LA LIBERTAD** (often reduced by bus conductors to "El Puerto"), once a major port and still an important fishing town, has been reinvented as a tourist spot thanks to a lucky location between the beaches of the **Costa del Bálsamo** in the west and the **Costa del Sol** in the east. It's a popular place, particularly crowded at the weekends, when the hordes from the capital pour in to eat, drink and relax by the sea. La Libertad also has El Salvador's highest concentration of gringos, including a year-round community of international surfing bums who spend their time hanging out and waiting for the right break.

Arrival and orientation

Buses from San Salvador (bus #102) arrive in La Libertad at C Barrios, by the market, two blocks in from the sea and one block east from the Parque. Returning

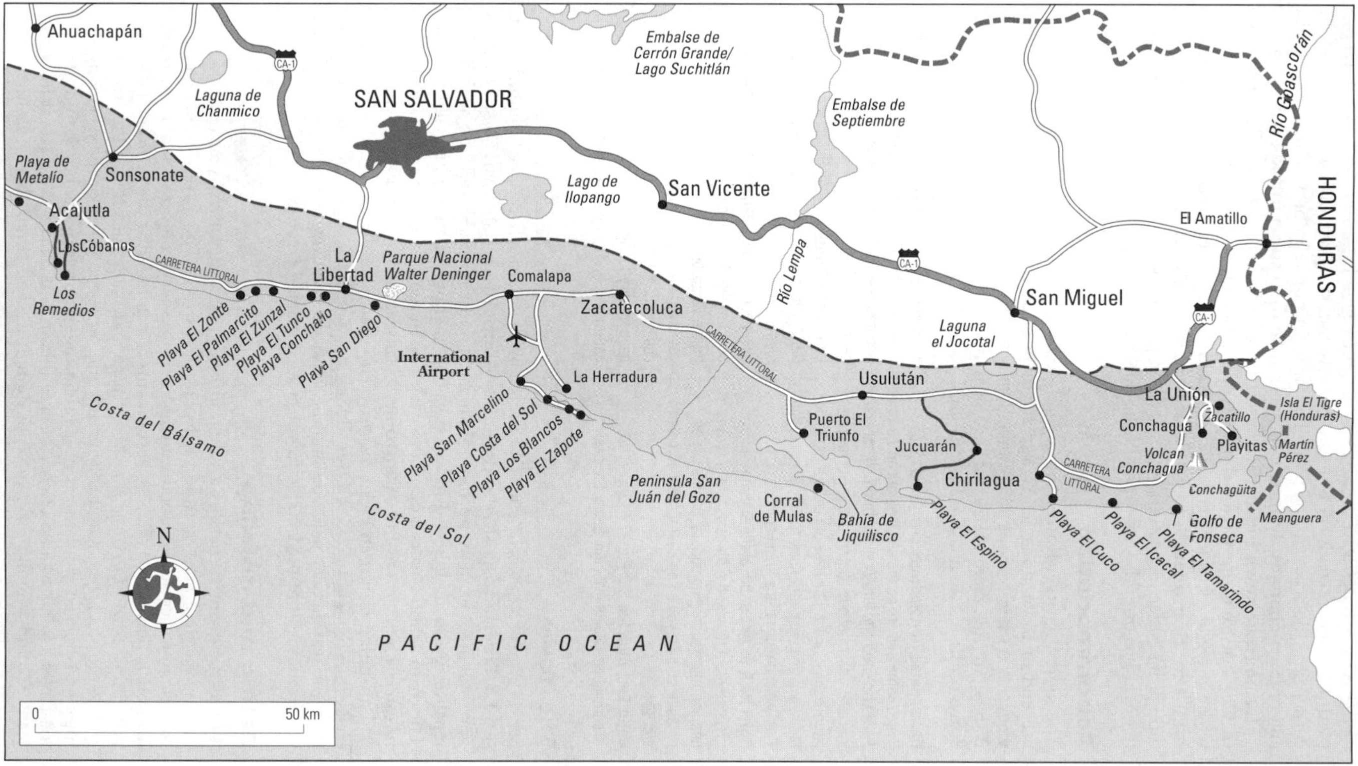

Ahuachapán
CA-1
Laguna de Chanmico
SAN SALVADOR
Embalse de Cerrón Grande/ Lago Suchitlán
Embalse de Septiembre
Río Goascorán
HONDURAS
Playa de Metalío
Sonsonate
Acajutla
LosCóbanos
Los Remedios
Lago de Ilopango
San Vicente
El Amatillo
CARRETERA LITTORAL
La Libertad
Parque Nacional Walter Deninger
Comalapa
Zacatecoluca
Río Lempa
San Miguel
Laguna el Jocotal
Playa El Zonte
Playa El Palmarcito
Playa El Zunzal
Playa El Tunco
Playa Conchalío
Playa San Diego
International Airport
La Herradura
Usulután
La Unión
Isla El Tigre (Honduras)
Zacatillo
Conchagua
Playitas
Martín Pérez
Costa del Bálsamo
Playa San Marcelino
Playa Costa del Sol
Playa Los Blancos
Playa El Zapote
Puerto El Triunfo
Jucuarán
Volcan Conchagua
Chirilagua
Conchagüita
Peninsula San Juán del Gozo
Corral de Mulas
Bahía de Jiquilisco
Playa El Espino
Playa El Cuco
Playa El Icacal
Playa El Tamarindo
Golfo de Fonseca
Meanguera
Costa del Sol
N
PACIFIC OCEAN
0
50 km

to the capital, buses leave from C 2 Ote just beyond the *turicentro*. The **Telecom** (with Internet access) is on C 2 Ote at 2a Av Sur; the **post office** is just round the corner near the access to the pier. The Banco Salvadoreño on C Barrios at the east end of town **changes dollars**, and there's a De Todo **supermarket** next door.

Heading east, town bus #540 runs every two hours inland to **Zacatecoluca** (p.326). To reach the **Costa del Sol**, take a bus or pick-up to Comalapa, from where there are frequent connections to the beaches. Heading west, a direct bus (#287) for **Sonsonate** leaves daily at 6am, with another leaving at around 1pm, though it's easier to head for San Salvador, get off at La Ceiba, and catch a more frequent bus from the other side of the dual carriageway.

Accommodation

The more upmarket **hotels**, some with their own pools, are generally at the western end of town along 5a Av Sur. If you're hoping to get a room on a holiday weekend, it's best to book in advance. The better cheap alternatives are listed below; if these are full, there are a couple of basic hotels around C 2 Ote and 1a Av Nte. Some of the restaurants also have rooms.

Hacienda de Don Rodrigo 5a Av Sur ⓣ335 3166. Same owners as the similarly priced *La Posada de Don Lito* further along the road, though this overnight option is slightly better. Rooms are large, ageing and a little over-priced, but handy for the beach and with hammock space for relaxation. The hacienda also has a small pool. ❻

Hotel Rick 5a Av Sur 30, at the end of C 4 Pte ⓣ335 3033. Friendly, if a bit basic, *Hotel Rick* is popular amongst visiting surfers. Rooms are all en-suite, though you'll pay a bit more if you want a/c. ❺

Hotel Surf Club Inn C 2 Pte 22 ⓣ346 1104, ⓔsurfclubinn@telemovil.com. Easily the best value in town with spacious en-suite rooms, all with a/c, cable TV, kitchen area and refrigerator. Supermarket and surf shop downstairs for all your beach needs. ❹

La Posada Familiar 3a Av Sur at C 4 Pte ⓣ335 3252. Very friendly and popular place with basic rooms, some with bath, that are just about the cheapest in town. Shared bathrooms are not the best though. A small comedor serves meals. ❷

Punta Roca opposite *Hotel Rick* ⓣ335 3261, ⓦwww.puntaroca.com.sv. Spacious, well-equipped a/c rooms with bath. Rooms sleep four, have an airy lounge area and a terrace with hammocks and great views along the bay. ❻

The Town

Set on a small bay, whose curve is bisected by the main wharf (*muelle*) jutting out to sea, **La Libertad** is a shabby, earthquake-damaged coastal town. Most of the old port buildings are now no more than shells and the roads could do with serious repair. Even so, La Libertad has an engaging energy and atmosphere all of its own. The main action occurs around the wharf when the fishing fleet comes in and sells its catch. There's a small **turicentro** here (daily 7am–5pm; US$0.90), with showers and changing rooms and a picnic area. The shady Parque Central sits two blocks back from the seafront; **C 2 Ote**, a block south of the Parque and one block back from the seafront, is where you find the **Casa de Cultura** (Mon–Sat 2–5pm), with an interesting, if limited, collection of pickled marine creatures.

Eating and drinking

The **dining**-out scene in La Libertad is a good one, unless you don't like fish (although there are a couple of decent *pupuserías*). The Salvadoreño speciality **mariscada**, a creamy seafood soup, is available everywhere and should be tried at least once. The more expensive **restaurants** are gathered at the seafront at the western end of town. *El Nuevo Alta Mar*, *Sandra* and *Karla*, all on C 4 Pte between 1a and 3a Av Sur, are all reasonably priced and serve the catch of the day along with meat and chicken standards, as well as offering glimpses of the beach from the dining tables. There's little to choose between them, but *Sandra* just edges it for a great *mariscada* and friendly service. Note though that all three also serve turtle eggs, which should certainly be avoided. The slightly more expensive US-owned *Punta Roca*, towards the far end of C 4 Pte, has a great sea view and a range of well-prepared fish and meat dishes along with a bar that gets lively at weekends. Further along, the restaurant *Vista al Mar* attracts a slightly more formal crowd, with an open terrace overlooking the sea. The **beach comedores** all serve fish, but at much lower prices. For huge juices and basic meals try *Comedor Paty*, in town on 2a Av Sur just down from the Parque.

Costa del Bálsamo

Strung out either side of Puerto La Libertad is the **Costa del Bálsamo**, a favourite for surfers and day-trippers from the capital. The coast takes its name from the now defunct trade in medicinal balsam that was once centred here. Though isolated balsam trees are still tapped on the mountainsides, the vast majority were cleared when tourism took over as the main source of income. **West** of La Libertad, the Carretera Littoral winds up around thickly wooded hills to palm-fringed and generally uncrowded beaches, during the week at least. Expensive beach clubs and exclusive restaurants litter the coast, but cheaper accommodation is available and surfing communities are in residence at most of them. To the **east** the beaches are more disappointing, infringed upon by the expansion of the town, with the exception of the glorious **Playa San Diego**, perhaps the best beach on this whole stretch of coast.

The beaches: east

Playa La Paz, the La Libertad town beach gets rather dirty, although the waves are good and surfers ride at the western end by the rocks. A short distance east of town, however, leads to much cleaner and welcoming expanses. The small and crowded beaches of **Flores** and **Obsipo** are within walking distance. There are a few huge seafood restaurants here, with meals fresh from the ocean, including *El Mirador del Pacífico* and *La Curva de Don Gere*, both of which have terraces with impressive ocean views, as well as *Fisherman's Beach Club*.

Five kilometres from La Libertad, the beautiful **Playa San Diego**, with its clean, white and seemingly endless stretch of sand, is deserted during the week except for a few fishermen. A turtle-nestling reserve has recently been set up here to help protect these endangered species, in an effort to reduce, if not eliminate, the collecting of eggs for restaurants. Bus #80 runs from 4a Av Sur in La Libertad to Playa San Diego every 30min, following a dirt road that turns off the Carretera Littoral a couple of kilometres from town at km33 to run parallel along the length of the beach. Views to the sea are blocked by the ranks of private homes behind locked gates, but if you get off the bus outside the *San Diego Beach* restaurant, there's a path just to the left of the nearby *Hotel Villa del Pacífico* that leads down to the sand. This is also the place to look for **accommodation**: the *Hotel Villa del Pacífico* (☎345 5681; ❺) has a/c rooms with bath, plus restaurant and pool set in manicured gardens right by the beach. The *San Diego Beach* restaurant (☎345 5678; ❻), a sort of decaying *turicentro* replica with pools and waterslides, has small, basic cabañas with private pool, both in a state of disrepair and vastly over-priced. Better cabañas are at *Cabañas Don Lito* (☎335 3166; ❺) on the main *ruta* just prior to the turn-off, run by the same owners as the *posada* in town.

A little further along the Carretera Littoral, past the turn-off for the beach, is the entrance to **Parque Nacional Walter Deininger**, an extensive stretch of dry forest, supporting a range of flora and fauna. Over half the park was destroyed by fire in 1986, and since then ISTU have been working on reforesting the area and encouraging the return of wildlife – check with their office in San Salvador (see p.291) about access to the park.

The beaches: west

West of La Libertad, the Carretera Littoral scales the forested mountainside passing access roads to a series of serene and generally uncrowded beaches. First up at km34 is **Playa Conchalío**, just outside town and very popular at weekends (there have been reports of robberies here, especially after dark, so be careful). *Hotel Los Arcos del Mediterraneo* (☎335 3490, Ⓦwww.hotelmediplaz@salnet.net; ❻) on the highway has large en-suite rooms, shielded from the traffic, all with cable TV and pool access. Further along the main road at km40.5 is **Playa El Majahual**, a pleasant expanse of sand, with a small waterpark with slides, some cheap comedores and a couple of hotels. Best is *Hotel Santa Fe* (☎278 1054; ❺), whose owner designed and named the hotel in honour of his favourite US city – look out for the guitar-shaped swimming pool. All rooms have private bath, and some also have air conditioning. Cheaper is *El Pacífico* (☎335 3464; ❹), though rooms are more basic and prices are often quoted for 12-hour periods.

Continuing west, at km42, is **Playa El Tunco**. The beach here is pebble strewn, but the crashing waves make it a surfer's favourite. A single road leads down from the *ruta* through the village, eventually terminating at the *Restaurante La Bocana*, which serves huge seafood platters and ice-cold beers. Just behind the beach are a couple of basic **places to stay**, the best being *Tortuga Surf Lodge*, offering comfortable but simple rooms in a pleasant setting (☎389 6185; ❸). The newest hotel here is the impressive *Roca Sunzal* (☎389 6126, Ⓦwww.rocasunzal.com; ❺, suites ❾), with a wide range of well-equipped rooms and two suites for up to six people. Some rooms have balconies and there's a good pool, though prices rise slightly at weekends.

Playa El Tunco merges with **Playa El Zunzal** (or Sunzal), a very popular surfing beach somewhat spoiled by the carelessly cemented frontage of the Club Salvadoreña. At the west end of the beach is the new *Café El Sunzal*, built into the rocks overlooking the beach, which serves excellent but pricey seafood and Salvadoreño cuisine, and is frequented by San Salvador's smart set. A few kilometres further on, **Playa El Palmarcito** is overlooked by the relaxing and comfortable *Atami Beach Club Resort* (you'll need to reserve ahead in San Salvador at 69a Av Sur 164, Col Escalón ☎223 9000; ❺). At km53, the small and uncrowded **Playa El Zonte** is another favourite among surfers; the *Horizonte Surf Resort* (☎737 8879; ❺) just back from the beach has clean cabins, some with a/c and hammock; there's also a small pool and nice gardens.

From La Libertad, local **bus** #80AB runs past Playa Conchalío to El Tunco and Zunzal (every 15min until 5.30pm); while bus #192 leaves every 30 minutes for Playa El Palmarcito and El Zonte.

Zacatecoluca

Heading east from La Libertad, the Carretera Littoral swings inland, running north of the international airport to the small city of **ZACATECOLUCA**. Its impressive whitewashed Moorish **Catedral Santa Lucía** is the only sight of note here, in front of which stands a monument to the city's most famous son, José Simeon Cañas, the man responsible for the abolition of slavery across Central America. The effect of the cathedral is somewhat diminished by the jumble of market stalls that strangle it on all sides, but if a priest is around he may let you climb the tower to see the marvellous views over the town and its volcano. Zacatecoluca was a pre-Columbian Nonualco city with about two thousand inhabitants when the Spanish first arrived. No records of conflict exist and in 1594, Don Juan de Pineda reported to the Spanish court that "there are three pueblos next to each other that are good, called San Juan and Santiago Nonualco and Zacatecoluca. In Zacatecoluca there is a corregidor who administers in the name of your majesty". In 1833, however, the indigenous revolt led by Anastasio Aquino from Santiago Nonualco posed a serious threat to the newly independent country. Supported both by local tribes and poor mestizos, and meeting with little effective resistance, Aquino at one point looked capable of marching on and taking the capital. Instead, his army contented itself with sacking Zacatecoluca before moving on to San Vicente, giving government forces time to regroup.

Apart from its big daily market, there's little of interest in Zacatecoluca except its proximity to the nearby beaches, but it's a pleasant enough place, with a couple of acceptable **hotels**. Just across the street from the bus terminal, *Hotel Primavera* (☎334 1346; ❷), at Av Juan Villacorta 23, has tidy rooms with bath and hammock and a small pool. Around the corner the *Hotel Brolyn* (☎334 1084; ❷–❸), C 7 Ote 25, is similar but slightly cheaper for standard en-suite budget rooms with fan and more expensive for rooms with a/c. **Bus** #133 runs every fifteen minutes from San Salvador's Terminal del Sur to Zacatecoluca, while bus #193 from Zacatecoluca runs all the way along the Costa del Sol.

The Costa del Sol

Due south of Zacatecoluca lies El Salvador's premier beach playground, the **Costa del Sol**, a fifteen-kilometre strip of palm-fringed beaches running between the ocean and the Jaltepeque Estuary. The clean expanses of sand here are good for swimming, and the place seethes with crowds at the weekends. From the highway, an access road runs the 20km south to the beginning of the beach strip and east along its length to La Puntilla at the end. Another road branches off 8km before the coast to the fishing town of **La Herradura**, from where boats can be rented to explore the estuary's mangrove swamps and small islands, some of them inhabited. **Buses** run down the Costa del Sol from Zacatecoluca, taking around an hour and a half to reach La Puntilla.

Behind the first beach along the strip, **Playa San Marcelino**, the rather plush *Costa del Sol Club* has swimming pools, sports facilities and a restaurant – try negotiating at the gate to be allowed in for the day. Some 3km east is **Playa Costa Del Sol**, where a *turicentro* (daily 7am–6pm; US$0.90) rents cabañas for the day (though not overnight) and has a couple of small restaurants. There's also some upmarket accommodation here at the *Izalco Cabaña Club* (☎264 1170, ⓔizalcocabanaclub@saltel.net; ❼) with a good *mariscada* in the restaurant and a nice pool if the ocean is too salty for your tastes. *Tesoro Beach Hotel* (☎334 0600; ❾) is equally good, located at the far end of the beach. A few kilometres further on, at kilometre 66, is **Playa Los Blancos** and the *Mini Hotel y Restaurante Mila* (no phone; ❸), the area's most reasonably priced hotel, with small but comfortable rooms and a swimming pool. At the far eastern tip of the Costa del Sol, **La Puntilla** has a number of comedores and cheap lodgings – you'll be approached as soon as you step off the bus. Lancha owners run trips from here across to the Isla de Tasajera, around the mangrove swamps of the Estero de Jaltepeque and up the Río Lempa, but you'll have to ask around.

Usulután and Bahía de Jiquilísco

East of Zacatecoluca, the Carretera Littoral crosses the Río Lempa at San Marcos Lempa before running through lush, green coffee country to the city of **USULUTÁN**, on the southern slopes of the volcano of the same name. Of little interest except as a transit point, the Carretera Littoral branches through the city, reforming again at its extremities. At the eastern fork, market stalls invade the tarmac and it is from here that buses arrive and depart. The westbound lane then takes the name C Grimaldi as it heads to the centre of town, passing through the neatly pruned Parque Central six blocks west of the bus station. Should you wish to **stay**, *La Posada del Viajero* (☎662 0217; ❷), close to the centre on C 6 Ote between 2a and 4a Av Nte, is clean and friendly.

About 20km southwest of Usulután, down a road lined with sugar-cane fields, is **PUERTO EL TRIUNFO**, a small village and port set on the shore of Bahía de Jiquilísco, separated from the ocean by the San Juan del Gozo peninsula. Formed by coastal mangrove swamps, the beautiful bay features 12km of waterways and a number of islands. Passenger boats cross to hamlets on the islands and to the village of

Corral de Mulas on the peninsula; if you miss these – they tend to leave early in the day – boats can be rented for a return crossing or for a few hours exploring the waterways around the smaller islands of Tortuga, Madre Sal, Los Cedros and San Sebastian. A long, fine sandy beach forms the ocean side of the peninsula; a road runs its length, branching off the highway at San Marcos Lempa. You can **camp** on the islands and the peninsula, and there is a small, basic and apparently nameless **hotel** (no phone; ❶) in Puerto El Triunfo, with a restaurant serving huge fish dishes.

The eastern beaches

East of Bahía de Jiquilísco are perhaps the best of the country's beaches, just isolated enough to remain peaceful during the week, if not always at weekends. The most famous of these sandy stretches is **Playa El Espino**, once delightfully deserted, though a newly paved road has resulted in a rash of development. **Playa El Cuco** further east is a popular spot for travellers avoiding the madness of the Costa del Sol. Beyond here things get quieter, and though transport is limited, the beaches are a real treat. **Playa El Tamarindo**, the most easterly of all, is arguably the most beautiful, a great golden curve around the Golfo de Fonseca, with views of the gulf islands and the hills of Honduras in the distance.

Playa El Espino

At the far eastern end of the Bahía de Jiquilísco is one of El Salvador's finest beaches, **Playa El Espino**. The once remote beach has been developed, with a 26km paved road from the Carretera Littoral opening it up to visitors, who come in droves. Around 16km from the turn-off, a *mirador* gives glorious views of the Bahía de Jiquilísco, though as you get closer to the town the extent of the development becomes more apparent. Still, if you can overcome the mob of hoteliers and restaurant owners keen to strip you of your cash upon arrival, there is still much to enjoy. The beach remains glorious and the water bathtub-warm. Should you wish to stay, *Hotel Restaurante Las Cabañas* (☎608 0701; ❺) is a good bet with basic but comfortable cabañas near the beach, though don't expect it to be quiet. Half a kilometre to the west, *Hotel Arcos del Espino* (☎608 0785; ❺) is slightly pricier but the beach nearby is not so busy. The best accommodation can be found at *La Estancia Don Luis* (☎608 0785; ❻), with excellent four-person rooms and a large pool; to reach it, take a left when the main road reaches the beach. All accommodation should be booked ahead at weekends. A whole host of comedores and basic restaurants sell similar fare, though prices for seafood are high and the quality isn't always the best. There's a slow and infrequent **bus** from Usulután (#351, 2–3 daily, last one back at 4pm; 1hr 30min–2hr) to the beach, though, obviously, things are much easier with your own transport.

Playa El Cuco

Thirty kilometres east of Usulután the Carretera Littoral turns south; at this junction, connecting buses head north to San Miguel (see p.336). As the road winds up through the mountains there are glorious views out across the valleys, before the road descends again towards the beaches. After passing the small, unexciting town of **Chirilagua**, 14km from the junction, a side road heads towards a beautiful beach, **Playa El Cuco**. The village of **EL CUCO** is rather ugly and dusty, with a facade of friendliness as locals try to herd you into substandard accommodation around the town. The beach itself, however, is fantastic, stretching seemingly endlessly into the distance, empty of tourists during the week. **Accommodation** in the town is limited to windowless concrete boxes, infested with mosquitoes at night and even at US$5 per person considerably over-priced. You're better advised to take the road that runs parallel to the beach at the entrance to town, where you'll find good quality hotels, most with beach access, though you may have to negotiate a price. First up *Villa del Mar* (☎619 9041; ⑤), with comfortable rooms and a large pool, though a definite tendency to overcharge foreigners. A little further along is the renovated *Hotel Leones Marinos* (☎619 9015; ④), with cabaña-style accommodation, including hammocks, set in shaded grounds around a pool and restaurant. Beyond here things get worse, though prices do not come down, until about 4km away you reach the luxurious *Trópiclub* (☎661 1800; ⑤), with its own restaurant and pool. Cabañas here take the names of Salvadoreño towns and are excellent value if you are in a small group. Playa El Cuco is accessible by direct bus (#320; 1hr 30min) from the terminal in San Miguel. The ride is one of the finest bus journeys in the country, with spectacular views of the valleys and the ineffable Volcán San Miguel; sit on the right side of the bus on the way to El Cuco for the best view.

Beaches further east

Beyond Chirilagua, the highway runs parallel to the coastline, passing a turn-off for the tidy little town of **Intipuca** before turning north again, around the western slopes of Volcán Conchagua and up to La Unión. All along this coast stand *salineras*, **salt farms** using traditional methods to extract the salt from the ocean water. The water is stored in shallow pools and allowed to evaporate slowly in the sun, before being harvested and collected in great mountains. Workers will be happy to sell you a huge bag for a very small fee. Buses from La Unión (#383) and San Miguel (#385) serve the coast road, passing all the beaches along the stretch. Some 5km past Intipuca, a side road leads to **Playa El Icacal**, 7km south. An untouched expanse of wide soft sand fringed by coconut palms, the beach has good swimming and makes a fine spot for a day of lounging. There's no accommodation, although a few comedores serve meals.

A few kilometres along the Carretera, another turn-off heads along the coast, past a series of beaches to the Golfo de Fonseca. **Playa Las Tunas** is the first beach that you encounter. There's a small village here with several restaurants and a couple of good accommodation options. *Hotel Restaurant Buenos Aires* (☎681 5581; ⑥), at the bend in the road a few yards pass the village entrance, is the cheapest in the area, with basic a/c rooms and good grilled fish served in the restaurant. Just beyond the bend, the new *Hotel Las Tunas* (☎681 5515; ⑦) is the best value of the pricier options on the 9km of coast to Playa El Tamarindo. All rooms have balconies with sea views and the pool, right on the edge of the beach, is superb. **Playa Torola** is the next beach, bounded by rocks at either end and with soft golden sand. *Torola Cabaña Club* (☎681 5435; ⑦) is an old favourite hotel here, and though rather over-priced in comparison to other nearby options, it has a magnificent terrace overlooking the beach where meals are served. **Playa Negras** a little further on is one of the better beaches on this stretch and the accommodation at *Hotel Playas Negras* (☎649 5097; ⑥) is amongst the cheapest you'll find, though the rooms are a little dark. The final beach, **Playa El Tamarindo**, is a few kilometres beyond the end of the tarmac, but it's well worth persisting along the dirt road to make it this far. The huge golden arc of sand, backed by uninterrupted palm trees, curves around the mountainous bay and remains deserted except for a few fishermen, even at weekends. In the bay the islands of the Golfo de Fonseca loom large, and in the distance the mountainsides of Honduras are clearly visible. The only accommodation here is at the *Tropitamarindo* (☎649 5082; ⑦), unfortunately rather pricey for what are little more than standard mid-range rooms. It's much better to stay at Las Tunas and commute, though be aware that the last buses back along the road leave around 4pm.

La Unión and Puerto Cutuco

The port town of **LA UNIÓN** sits in a stunning location on a bay on the edge of the Golfo de Fonseca. Faded since its glory days, La Unión's web of low white houses crumble a little further every day in the ferocious heat. The streets are rather

△ Waiting for the bus in Santa Rosa de Lima

depressing, and even the Parque Central swamped by dilapidated market stalls selling cheap merchandise lacks the character of other city squares. Redevelopment of **Puerto Cutuco**, virtually contiguous with La Unión, is underway, with plans to make it the largest Pacific port in Central America, perhaps reviving the fortunes and spirits of the inhabitants. Until then, the atmosphere around the town is unpleasant, with the main reason for passing through being a visit to the isolated islands of the **Golfo de Fonseca**. Eight kilometres west of La Unión is the junction with the Carretera Interamericana, which swings north to run 27km up to the Honduran border at **El Amatillo** (see p.344). There are no direct buses to the border from town; instead, take any of the frequent buses to Santa Rosa de Lima, or to San Carlos Desvío and change there.

Practicalities

The **bus terminal** is on C 3 Pte, 4a-6a Av Nte, two blocks northwest of the Parque Central. There's a **Telecom** on C 1 Ote at 5a Av Nte, two blocks east of the Parque. To **change money**, try either Banco Agrícola, C 1 Pte and Av General Cabañas, or Ahorromet Scotiabank, 1a Av Nte on the Parque. **Internet** access is available at *CINET Avila's* on C 1 Pte between Av 4 and 6 Nte, and *CIDEC* on the west side of the main plaza. Both charge US$1 per hour and close around 7pm.

The town's best **accommodation** option, the *Hotel Portobello* (☎604 4115; ❷–❹) on 4a Av Nte at C 1 Pte, has large, clean a/c rooms with bath, some with balcony, as well as rooms with fan and TV, but shared bathroom, for about half the price. *Hotel San Francisco* (☎604 4159; ❸), on C Gral Menéndez between 9a and 11a Av Sur, three blocks east of the Parque, has large, dark rooms, with a choice of a/c, fan, TV or a combination of the three.

The best **place to eat** is *Captain John's* at 3a Av Sur and C 4 Ote, with a pleasant outdoor terrace and a wide choice of fish steaks including marlin, sailfish and wahoo. *Restaurante Guadalajara*, C 1 Pte and 2a Av Sur, serves basic Mexican food and *comida a la vista*, while *Restaurante El Marinero*, C 3 Pte at Av Gral Cabañas, is the closest you'll come to a pavement café, with a large covered veranda from which to watch the street activity. For cooked breakfasts, try the cavernous *Restaurante El Viajero* next to the De Todo supermarket just off the Parque.

Islas del Golfo de Fonseca

Four delightfully secluded islands sit out in the Golfo de Fonseca under the stewardship of El Salvador. The smallest, **Zacatillo** and **Martín Pérez**, are uninhabited, but the two larger islands, **Conchagúita** and **Meanguera**, have settlements. Meanguera, in particular, is becoming a popular getaway and there is a small hotel here, the pretty *Hotel Isla Meanguera* (☎648 0072; ❷), with simple rooms with shared bath. There are no cars on the islands, but plenty of secluded coves to explore, as well as good swimming and boundless scope for hiking. Comedores in the village serve fresh seafood, delivered daily by a colourful fishing fleet that floats in the bay. For fantastic views of the surroundings, climb Cerro de Evaristo, the highest peak on the island.

The whole gulf region has long been associated with fables of the European **corsairs**, who made regular incursions along this coastline in the seventeenth and eighteenth centuries. Conchagúita was sacked by English pirates in 1682, who used it as a strategic base from which to attack ships sailing to Europe; the original inhabitants moved to the mainland and the island remained deserted until the 1920s, when settlers began moving back. In the centre of Conchagúita, on the Cerro del Pueblo Viejo, are the remains of a tiny pre-Columbian settlement; a path to the north of the ruins leads up to a large rock bearing engravings that some believe is a map of the gulf.

Morning ferries leave for the larger of the gulf islands from the port at La Unión, three blocks north of the Parque (US$2.50). Departures are in the early morning only (times change frequently, so check on arrival), and bear in mind that the only ferry back from Meanguera departs at 5am, so unless you plan to charter a private boat you will have to stay overnight. Local boatmen will take you across from La Unión, but at a price (US$70 per boatload), and there is little scope for negotiation.

Playitas and Conchagua

PLAYITAS, 8km southeast of La Unión, is a small fishing village whose main attraction is its proximity to the islands in the Golfo de Fonseca and its stunning views. On clear days, one can see across the gulf to the mainland of Honduras and, in the far distance, the mountains of Nicaragua. Islas Zacatillo and Martín Pérez (to the left looking out to sea) seem almost close enough to touch, while ahead and to the right are the larger Conchagúita and, beyond, the island of Meanguera. Local fishermen will take groups out to the islands from Playitas, but rates are high (about US$70 per boatload) and make sense only if you are in a large enough group and have missed the early-morning scheduled services from La Unión. To get to Playitas with your own transport from La Unión follow the signs out of town towards Puerto Cutuco; the road rapidly deteriorates as it heads down the coast and ends altogether in the village. Alternatively bus #418 traverses the route from the main terminal at La Unión.

Behind Playitas looms **Volcán Conchagua** (1243m), with beautiful views across the gulf to Nicaragua and Honduras. The friendly village of **CONCHAGUA**, sitting on its northern slopes, was founded by the inhabitants of Conchagúita at the end of the seventeenth century. The climate is fresher here, a pleasant relief from the heat of La Unión, and walks around the village give memorable views across the gulf. From Conchagua to the summit of the volcano, it's a strenuous walk of two or three hours. As in most remote parts of El Salvador, walking alone is not recommended.

3.3

The east

The rough and wild terrain of **eastern El Salvador** remained, in the main, unexplored territory for the pre-Columbian Pipils, who did not venture far beyond the natural frontier of the Río Lempa into this "land that smokes" of lofty volcanoes, hot plains and mountain ranges. Its Lenca inhabitants developed their society in isolation from the west, and it was only with some reluctance and difficulty that the Spanish conquered this frontier. Today, the wealth of the coffee plantations around the region's major cities, **San Vicente** and **San Miguel**, contrast cruelly with the rural poverty found elsewhere. Refugees from communities devastated by the civil war – eastern El Salvador saw the worst of the fighting – have in the last decade returned to try and pick up the pieces in this wild and beautiful area, but their struggle with poverty is painfully apparent. Travelling here, while difficult, is thought-provoking and moving; expect some reservation from locals whose resentment of US involvement in the civil war is still fresh (non-native Spanish-speakers will automatically be assumed to be *yanquis*).

The crumbling city of San Vicente, badly hit by the 2001 earthquake, makes a convenient base for hiking up the lofty peaks of **Chichontepec** and swimming in the **Laguna de Apastepeque**. Bustling San Miguel, the third-largest city in the country, is a transport hub, and a good place to recuperate from life on the road, with the largely unexcavated archeological site of **Quelepa** and the wetlands reserve of **Laguna El Jocotal** within easy reach. Buses head north from here to the tranquil mountain villages of the **Ruta de la Paz**, and the moving Museo de la Revolución Salvadoreña at **Perquín**. The nearby village of **Mozote**, scene of a horrific massacre, is a haunting place, where the weight of history bears heavily on its current inhabitants.

East to San Vicente

From San Salvador, the Carretera Interamericana edges its way east through industrial units, shanty towns and the grimy suburbs on the edge of the city. Buses from the Terminal de Oriente follow this route, first arriving at **COJUTEPEQUE** (bus #113), 32km from the capital. There's little to see here other than the shrine of the **Virgen de Fátima** of Portugal, a statue brought here in 1949. Housed at the top of the Cerro de las Pavas, about thirty minutes' walk from the centre of town, the shrine attracts worshippers from across the region, especially during the series of masses held in honour of Our Lady of Fatima on May 13. The summit also gives wonderful views over Lago de Ilopango.

Some 6km beyond Cojutepeque, a road branches north through beautiful rolling countryside to the small town of **ILOBASCO** (bus #111), noted for its brightly painted earthenware decorated with animals and everyday scenes. Most popular are the colourful reproductions of fruits and vegetables tied into bunches that, while mostly mass-produced, still retain an element of charm. Look out for the town speciality known as *sorpresas* (surprises) – detailed scenes of village life contained in small, egg-shaped shells. From here, a road runs 35km east to **SENSUNTEPEQUE**, a pleasant, quiet town (with a couple of hospedajes) set amid marvellous mountain scenery, though there is little actually to do unless you're here during the November fiestas – culminating on December 4 with the Día del Santa Bárbara. East of Cojutepeque on the Interamericana, a paved road leads off to the small village of **SAN SEBASTIÁN** (bus #110), famous for its hammocks and patterned cloth sheets and bedspreads. Several weaving shops around town will let you watch the goods being produced on simple wooden looms, but they may also pressure you into buying. Compare prices and bargain before handing over any money.

Further along the Carretera Interamericana, some 25km from Cojutepeque, a junction marked by ramshackle cane bus shelters gives onto the branch road for the attractive city of **San Vicente**, set in the Jiboa valley at the foot of **Volcán Chichontepec**. The approach is one of the most spectacular in the country; the road sharply descending to the valley floor on one side, while across on the other rises the conical bulk of the twin-peaked volcano, dwarfing everything in sight, including the white spires of the city nestling below.

San Vicente

SAN VICENTE was founded in 1635 by fifty local Spanish families in accordance with the 1600 Law of the Indies, which prohibited the Spanish from living among the indigenous people. It was this decree that brought violence to the city on February 16, 1833, when the forces of Anastasio Aquino, leader of the Nonualco indigenous uprising, arrived in the city. "Inebriated with alcohol and success", they removed the crown from the statue of San José in the Iglesia El Pilar (see opposite) and crowned Aquino "Emperor of the Nonualcos". The rebels then returned to Santiago Nonualco, some 30km away; here, Aquino was captured by government forces on April 23 and later sent back to San Vicente and hanged.

Today, San Vicente is a calm, low-slung city within a rich agricultural area producing sugar cane, cotton and coffee. It was attacked several times by guerrillas during the 1980s and an obvious military presence remains, with a huge sea-green barracks near the centre. Once one of the finest squares in the country, the central **Parque Cañas** was devastated by the earthquake in 2001, seriously damaging some of the city's finest monuments and completely demolishing the Alcaldía and southern side of the plaza. The centrepiece is the **Torre Kiosko**, an eye-catching openwork clock tower, though since the earthquake it stands rather lame and climbing atop it is no longer permitted. On the eastern edge of the Parque stands the rather bare city cathedral. Walk three blocks down its side, along C Daniel Díaz, and in the middle of the road is the original tempisque tree under which the city was founded. Two blocks south of the Parque on Av María de los Angeles is the **Iglesia El Pilar** (or Iglesia Nuestra Señora del Pilar, to give it its full name), built in 1769 and supposedly the oldest in the country. Due to earthquake damage it is no longer possible to enter the church building, but locals have set up an outdoor, though covered, temporary replacement. The statue of San José – complete with crown – stands in a glass case behind the altar as you walk in.

Military barracks take up an entire block between Iglesia El Pilar and the Parque; a walk west up the side of the barracks brings you to the extensive **market**, stretching over several streets. **Hammock** vendors can be found on most street corners – the hammocks, made in the surrounding villages, add a notable splash of colour to the town.

Practicalities

Buses coming from the highway run through the Parque, continuing on to the terminal a long way southeast of the centre. For the main square, get off as soon as you see the Torre Kiosko. Buses (#116) run to San Salvador every ten minutes, with the last leaving for the capital at 7pm. There are no direct buses to San Miguel; take a pick-up from the Parque the short distance to the Interamericana junction and then catch any San Miguel eastbound bus, which run every fifteen minutes from San Salvador. For phone calls the **Telecom** office is just off the corner of the Parque opposite the De Todo supermarket. The **post office** is on C 1 de Julio, one block south of the barracks. **Banks** include a Banco Hipotecario and Banco Agrícola on the Parque, and an Ahorromet Scotiabank on the corner of 1a Av Nte and C Quiñonez de Osorio. **Internet** access at Ciberworld, C 4 Pte (C Indalecio Miranda), costs US$0.75 per hour.

Accommodation in town is limited. On the Parque itself is the scruffy but amenable *Hotel Central Park* (☎393 0383; ❸). Rooms are a bit grim, though most have a/c and there's a pleasant communal balcony with views of the Parque. *Casa de Huéspedes el Turista* on C 4 Pte (C Indalecio Miranda) 15, one block southwest of the Iglesia El Pilar (☎393 0323; ❸), has simple rooms with fan, some en-suite. It's worth paying a bit more for a private bathroom as the shared ones do not always have guaranteed water.

Of the **places to eat**, easily the best bet is *Casa Blanca* at C Alberto de Merino 13 (daily 11am–9pm), two blocks east of El Pilar, with meat and fish dishes including *codorniz* (quail) served in a shaded garden. *Comedor Jacquelín*, on the Parque next to *Hotel Central Park*, has average *comidas a la vista*, in uninspiring surroundings. *Comedor Rivoly*, on Av María de los Ángeles, one block west of El Pilar, has good breakfasts and *comidas a la vista*, whilst *Restaurant Acapulco*, next to *Casa de Huéspedes el Turista*, serves pricey set lunches with salad and/or rice.

Around San Vicente

San Vicente is dominated by the towering bulk of **Volcán Chichontepec** (also known as Volcán San Vicente) to the southwest. Meaning "Hill of Two Breasts" in Nahuatl, the twin peaks rise to 2181m, making it the second-highest volcano in the country. It's considered dormant, with cultivated lower slopes and the steep summit left to scrub and soil. A number of **paths** lead up the slopes from both the village of **San Antonio** on the east side and from **Guadelupe** on the northwest flank. It's a stiff walk of at least two hours to the top from any of the trails, and good walking shoes, sun protection and lots of water are all essential. From the summit there are panoramic views north across the Jiboa valley, with San Vicente nestled at the bottom, and west across to Lago de Ilopango. **Buses** to San Antonio and Guadelupe leave every hour or so until mid-afternoon from San Vicente's market.

Laguna de Apastepeque, 3km northeast of the city (bus #156), is a small, well-maintained *turicentro* (daily 8am–6pm; US$0.90) set around a crater lake with clean blue water and shady banks. The good swimming makes this an extremely popular spot among families at weekends. Near Verapaz, 10km east of San Vicente, are the natural hot-springs **Los Infernillos**, used for years as a medicinal retreat because of their high sulphur content; buses leave all day for the village.

Eight kilometres from San Vicente on the road south to Tecoluca, the ruins of **Tehuacán** (Tues–Sun, irregular hours; US$2) lie on the eastern slopes of Chichontepec. A former Pipil settlement, the site covers an area of about three square kilometres, but there is very little to see. Excavations have uncovered the remains of a series of terraces oriented north to south, a central plaza and a pyramid, rather disappointing in comparison to sites in Mexico and Guatemala. Stone and earthenware artefacts taken from the site bear a clear resemblance to Mexican items from the same era, indicating the common heritage of the Mexican Toltecs and migratory Pipils.

San Vicente to San Miguel

Beyond San Vicente, the Carretera Interamericana continues through low mountains and coffee plantations before crossing the **Río Lempa**, 30km to the east. This formidable natural boundary once afforded the Lenca inhabitants of the eastern territories some measure of protection, first against the Pipils and then against the Spanish.

The first section of the highway gives bus drivers ample opportunity to fine-tune their high-speed cornering technique before crossing the mighty Lempa on the Puente Cuscatlán, which replaced the old bridge bombed by the FMLN in January 1984. The remains of the original bridge lie slumped in the river, a sobering reminder of El Salvador's recent history. At the village of Mercedes Umaña, about 45km from San Vicente, a road heads south to the rough town of **Berlín**, the scene of much activity during the war and today the location of an important geothermal power plant. From here, hourly buses run along a road around the **Volcán Tecapa** to the more pleasant town of **Santiago De María**, which has a couple of simple hotels. Halfway between the two towns is Alegría, from where paths lead up the volcano to the sulphurous crater lake **Laguna de Alegría**, an energetic walk of about one hour. This area is predominantly coffee-growing country, with plantations lining the slopes of the rolling mountains. From Santiago, buses run up to **El Triunfo** on the Carretera Interamericana, then continue on to San Miguel; from both Berlín and Santiago there are also regular connections south to Usulután.

Beyond El Triunfo the scenery changes: coffee pastures give way to dry plains dotted with the cones of volcanoes; to the south the land falls away to pasture lands and coastal mangrove swamps. A major crop in this area is *henequén* (sisal); fields of the distinctive, spiky grey-green plants line the highway into the distance.

San Miguel

Some 135km from San Salvador, the bustling, hot and flat city of **SAN MIGUEL** is the country's main trade centre. Modern and wealthy, with the sort of facilities you'll only find in the capital, it was a centre of arms trade during the civil war, though today the city's flat streets hum and rattle with more mundane forms of commerce. Despite being the birthplace of several national heroes, the city is surprisingly short on sights and attractions, and the best time to visit is during the November carnival, supposedly the biggest in Central America.

San Miguel hasn't always occupied such a position of prominence, and it has a turbulent history. Shortly after founding Villa San Salvador in 1528, the Spanish began to turn their minds to the territory east of Cuscatlán. Exasperated by the capture of an expedition led by Diego de Rojas by rival conquistador forces in 1530, Pedro de Alvarado dispatched **Luis de Moscoso** to finalize the conquest of the east. Around May 8, 1530, the day of San Miguel Arcángel, de Moscosco founded **San Miguel de Frontera**. Despite numerous ferocious uprisings, things

calmed down with the discovery of gold in the area, and city status was awarded in 1574. A fire in March 1586 destroyed much of the town, however, and it was moved the few kilometres to its present location at the northern base of the prodigious Volcán Chaparrastique. Initially the least important of the Spanish cities, San Miguel soon began to grow wealthy, at first on the profits of gold and trade, and then on the coffee, cotton and *henequén* grown on the surrounding fertile land, leading to the nickname "The Pearl of the East".

Though San Miguel sees few visitors, the city makes a good base for exploring the nearby Lenca archeological site of **Quelepa** and the wetland reserve of **Laguna El Jocotal**. A regional transport hub, San Miguel is also the starting point for buses to **La Unión** (bus #304), the stunning beaches of **El Cuco** (#320) and **El Tamarindo** (#385), and **Perquín** (#332) and the highland villages of the **Ruta de la Paz**.

Arrival and orientation

Most **buses** coming from San Salvador or points east and south of San Miguel arrive at the well-ordered main terminal on C 6 Ote between 8a and 10a Av Nte, four blocks (or ten minutes' walk) east of the centre. There is no official tourist information, but staff at the Alcaldía will help you with quick questions. The city is laid out in the usual quasi-grid system, with the main avenida (Av Gerardo Barrios/Av José Simeón Cañas) and the main calle (C Chaparrastique/C Sirama) intersecting at **Parque Gerardo Barrios** two blocks southwest of Parque Guzmán.

Accommodation

San Miguel's handful of more expensive **hotels** lie along Av Roosevelt (the Carretera Interamericana) to the west of town, about fifteen minutes' walk from the centre, and are listed from north to south. The majority of other choices cluster around the bus terminal, inevitably a rather sleazy area. Given its daytime bustle, San Miguel is very quiet at night, with empty, ill-lit streets, and after dark it's best to take one of the abundant yellow taxis – most journeys around the city shouldn't cost more than US$2–3.

In town

Casa de Huespedes C 1 Ote 506 ⓣ661 5612. A pretty little hotel with neatly presented and well-equipped en-suite rooms, all with a/c and cable TV. A little pricier than others nearby, but a definite step up in class and comfort. ❺

Hotel Caleta 3a Av Sur 601 between C 9 and 11 Pte ⓣ661 3233. Clean and quiet hotel, popular with travelling businessmen during the week. There's a small courtyard with hammocks, and some rooms have private bath. Staff can also help arrange surf trips to secluded beaches. ❸

Hotel del Centro C 8 Ote 505 at 8a Av Nte ⓣ & ⓕ661 5473. This very friendly, helpful and spotlessly clean hotel is the best of the cheaper options around the bus terminal. The comfortable rooms all have bath and TV, and there is ample room for parking. ❸

Hotel El Guanaco 8a Av Nte Pje Madrid ⓣ661 8026, ⓕ660 6403. Large hotel with big airy en-suite rooms all with a/c and cable TV. Meals served in the restaurant below. Located just behind the bus terminal. ❹

Hotel Migueleño C 4 Ote 610 ⓣ660 2737. Somewhat run down, but perfectly acceptable and extremely cheap. Rooms are large and en-suite with secure parking available. ❶

Hotel Terminal C 6 Ote ⓣ661 1086. Good-value, recently renovated rooms, some with balcony, opposite the bus terminal and handy for late arrivals. Rooms are en-suite with cable TV, a/c and telephone. Secure parking, restaurant service and new pool also available. ❹

Along Avenida Roosevelt

Hotel China House Av Roosevelt Km 137, near the Esso garage at the entrance to town ⓣ669 5029. Safe and secure hotel, set back from the main road, with its own parking. Rooms, arranged around a courtyard, are a bit run down but clean – all have TV and fan, and some have private bath. ❹

Hotel El Mandarín Av Roosevelt Nte 407 ⓣ669 6969, ⓕ669 7912. Luxury, San Miguel style. All rooms have bath, a/c, phone and TV, and there's an attached restaurant (open until 9pm). Has a bit

Nuestra Señora de la Paz

San Miguel's imposing cathedral, while rather disappointing inside, holds the cherished statue of **Nuestra Señora de la Paz**, the city's patroness. Accounts differ as to how she arrived in the city. One version claims that in 1683, San Miguel and San Salvador gathered together an army to fight the English pirates then attacking coastal villages and advancing inland. On seeing the massed forces, the pirates chose to retreat, leaving behind them a statue of the Virgin in the small port of Amapala, which was then taken to San Miguel. Another version has it that a fisherman, discovering a sealed casket on the beach, loaded it onto a donkey and began to walk to the city. The beast struggled on for fourteen days, before collapsing on the spot where the cathedral now stands. On opening the casket and seeing the contents, it was decided to build a temple to venerate the miraculous image. The statue was christened La Paz because of the cessation of bitter internecine fighting on her arrival.

Regardless of how she arrived, the statue's true moment of glory came during the eruption of Volcán Chaparrastique on September 21, 1787. On seeing a glowing river of lava advancing on San Miguel, the terrified citizens, praying to the Virgin to save them, took the statue to the door of the cathedral and presented her to the volcano. The lava changed course and the city was saved. In honour of these events, San Miguel holds two months of fiesta, beginning with the Virgin "descending" the volcano on September 21 and culminating in a procession through the streets, attended by thousands, on November 21. A more recent coda to the fiesta is the annual carnival held on November 29.

of a motel feel to it, but the pleasant pool shielded from the roaring traffic makes up for any shortcomings. Credit cards accepted. ❻

Hotel Milian's Av Roosevelt Nte at C 10 Pte ⓣ669 5053 ⓕ669 8064. Comfortable rooms with bath, a/c and cable TV. Ample secure parking and a great pool. The on-site restaurant serves meals and the hotel serves as an agent for the sale of international bus tickets.

Hotel Trópico Inn Av Roosevelt Sur 303 ⓣ661 1800, ⓕ661 1288. Large, modern, exclusive hotel with top-quality service and comfort. All rooms have TV, a/c, bath and phone. ❻

The City

The official centre of town, **Parque Barrios**, is overrun by an extensive market. It's a sprawling affair lined with narrow warrens filled with stalls selling all manner of food, clothes and other goods; if you're looking for souvenirs, you'd better to head to the Centro Comercial de Artesanías on Alameda Roosevelt between C 4 and 6 Pte. The heart of San Miguel however, is the shady **Parque David J. Guzmán** a block away to the northeast, named after the eminent nineteenth-century Migueleño biologist and member of the French Academy of Science. On the east of the Parque sits the **Catedral**, built in the 1880s. Despite a modern make-over the cathedral is still an impressive building, with a cast iron statue of Christ bearing his crown of thorns standing between two red-roofed bell towers. Inside it is rather bare, with the famed statue of **Nuestra Señora de la Paz** (see box opposite) above the altar. Just south of the cathedral is the **Antiguo Teatro Nacional**, a honey-coloured Renaissance-style building completed in 1909; performances occasionally take place here, particularly during fiesta time. On the south side of the square, the colonnaded Alcaldía, dating from 1935, is in serious need of renovation.

Of the few other minor sights within town, the most appealing is **Iglesia Capilla Medalla Milagrosa**, located at the western end of C 4 Pte where it joins 7a Av Sur. Set in pretty gardens, the church was built by French nuns working in the hospital that once stood next door. If a fan, the birthplace of Francisco Gavidia, one of El Salvador's most famous authors, is at the corner of C 6 Ote and Av Gerardo Barrios Nte; it's now a bookshop that occasionally sells town plans. Juan José Cañas, who penned the lyrics to the national anthem, was born on C 4 Pte between 1a and 3a Av Nte. A plaque marks the spot. A few houses further down at 205B, lies the derelict former home of David Guzmán.

San Miguel really comes alive in November for the **Fiestas Novembrinas**, particularly during **Carnival** on the 29th, whose music, fireworks and street dancing represent the climax of two months of celebrations for the festival of **Nuestra Señora de la Paz**, the city's patroness. A relatively modern affair, the carnival was instituted only in 1958, but has quickly grown to be the largest carnival in Central America (or so locals like to claim). If you're around during the festival look out for people wandering around holding large plastic iguanas aloft – the locals are nicknamed *garroberos* (iguana eaters) due to their penchant for the lizard's meat.

Eating and drinking

There are plenty of **places to eat and drink** in San Miguel. By day, there are a number of reasonable lunch places in town, especially in the area around the bus terminal, where cheap comedores and pastry cafés offer quick and simple meals. By night the focus shifts to the comedores and fast-food chains along Av Roosevelt between C 7 and 11 Pte. Local bakeries sell *tustacos*, a local speciality resembling a sweet tortilla.

La Barrita C 4 Ote, two blocks up from the cathedral. Well-prepared and reasonably priced meat and chicken dishes in an informal setting. Closed Sun.

Batyjugos Carlitos 1a Av Nte and C 4 Pte. Small homely café serving excellent snacks, lunches and coffee, plus extremely good papaya *licuados*. Prices are reasonable and service friendly.

Café Genesis C 4 Pte between 9a and 11a Av Nte. Colourful restaurant and *pupusería* specialising in Mexican dishes and *licuados*. Very popular with students from the nearby Universitario del Oriente (UNIVO).

Comedor Esmeralda 6a Av Nte between C 4 and 6 Ote. Good, basic breakfasts and *comidas a la vista*. One of a clutch of similar places in this former parking lot. Closed Sun.

El Paísa Av Roosevelt Sur opposite the *Hotel Trópico Inn*. Popular and reasonably priced Mexican food spot with outdoor tables. Portions are large and service is friendly, though a little slow at busy times.

El Patio C 4 Ote, other side of "UNIVO" from *Café Genesis*. A little more refined than *Café Genesis*, but still a student favourite and a great place for lunch. Snacks and *licuados* also available.

La Pema 5km from town on the road to Usulután ⓣ667 6055. El Salvador's most renowned restaurant. It's not cheap (around US$15–20 per head), but the huge servings of *mariscada*, a creamy soup with every conceivable type of seafood, and the bowls of fruit salad served as an accompaniment will mean you won't feel like eating again for a while. Come here and treat yourself. Tues–Sun 11am–5pm.

Pupusería Chilita C 8 Ote at 6a Av Nte. A barn of a neighbourhood *pupusería*, particularly popular at the weekends. Seating available on a breezy terrace at the back. The *pupusas* are good, but there's also a decent selection of *comidas a la vista*. Closed Sun. Open until around 9.30pm.

Pupusería El Paraiso Parque Guzmán. Well-prepared *pupusas* and *comidas a la vista* are dished out in a conveniently central location opposite the cathedral. Prices are low and quality is good. There is also a good selection of juices and *licuados* on offer.

Tipicos Shaddai C 4 Pte, opposite *Pizza Hut*. Wide selection of *minutas* and *licuados* at reasonable prices, served in a leafy courtyard away from the traffic and noise out on the street.

Listings

Banks BanCo, Banco Cuscatlán and Banco Salvadoreño (which gives Visa cash advances) cluster around the west side of the Parque and along C 4 Ote.

Internet Available at the Euro Cyber Café, part of the Academía Europea at Av Roosevelt 300 Sur (US$1 per hour) and the Academia Interamericana de Tecnología on 2a Av Nte near the cathedral (US$2.50 per hour).

Post office 4a Av Sur at C 3 Ote, south from the cathedral.

Shopping The Metrocentro on the Interamericana (also called Av Roosevelt) at the edge of town includes stores, banks, supermarkets, restaurants and a cinema; any bus heading south down Av Roosevelt will drop you outside. There's a Super Selectos supermarket on Av Roosevelt at C 11 Pte, and a Dispensa Familiar supermarket in town on Av Gerrardo Barrios at C Chaparrastique.

Telecom On the corner of Parque Guzmán next to the Alcaldía.

Around San Miguel

Threre's plenty to see in the environs of San Miguel, not least the protected **Laguna El Jocotal**, a breeding site for rare waterbirds, and the Lenca ruins at **Quelepa**. If you fancy a swim there is plenty of scope for getting wet with an **Aqua Park** (daily 9am–6pm; US$5.78; bus #324) at km 156 on the *ruta* and the invigorating **mineral pools** of El Capulín (bus #90 from San Miguel, get off at Moncagua). There's also a *turicentro* Altos de Cueva (9am–5pm; US$0.80; bus #29A), on the banks of the Río Grande, 28km towards San Salvador on the Carretera Americana.

Quelepa

A short distance along the highway, northwest of San Miguel, a road cuts off 1.5km to the pretty little village of **QUELEPA**. While there's nowhere to stay in town, the surrounding hillsides make for some great walking should you have time to spare. Beyond here lies the **Ruinas de Quelepa**, and though little of this predominantly Lenca site has been excavated the walk to it makes for an enjoyable half-day or so. The ruins are all that remain from a flourishing city that reached its peak between 625 and 1000 AD, from which period date its I-shaped pelota court and small pyramids. A jaguar-head altar, fragments of ceramics and other artefacts now in storage in San Salvador indicate that the inhabitants had trade links with cultures to the west, since most of the finds are in the style of – or possibly even from – Maya sites in Honduras and Mexico. The absence of Toltec-influenced artefacts also suggests that Quelepa was exclusively Lenca, rather than Pipil. Around forty structures have been identified at the site, amongst them a series of tombs. The friendly **Casa de Cultura** (Mon–Fri 9am–noon & 2–5pm) in Quelepa displays a collection of artefacts from the site – fragments of household utensils, ceramic figures and small ceremonial heads.

The **site** itself lies about 2km northeast of the village of Quelepa, between the Río San Estéban and a low range of hills. At first glance there appears to be nothing but fields of *henequén* and the odd herd of cows, but the small mounds in the fields are the remains of the pyramids, and close searching may bring to light the remnants of some walls. A nice way to return, if you don't mind getting your feet wet, is by wading up the shallow river all the way back to San Miguel. **Bus** #90 leaves Parque Guzmán in San Miguel frequently, dropping you off on the right of the highway, from where it is fifteen minutes' walk uphill to the village. Bus #90G, which runs directly to the village, leaves from the same place, but less often.

Laguna El Jocotal

About 18km southwest of San Miguel, just off Highway CA-2 on the road to Usulután, lies **Laguna El Jocotal**, a small wetland reserve supported by the World Wildlife Fund. This peaceful stretch of water, surrounded by reed beds with low hills in the distance, is the nesting and feeding ground for numerous species of birds seen year-round, including herons, terns and ducks. The best time to visit is in the early morning, when a warden is usually around the small dock to explain the conservation work, and you can rent a boat to explore the waterways. **Bus** #373 from San Miguel or Usulután passes the access road to the reserve. The lagoon is not well signposted from the road, so ask the bus driver to tell you where to get off. It's a walk of about ten minutes to the lakeshore, through a dusty village.

The Ruta de la Paz

North of San Miguel, the beautiful and sparsely populated mountainous department of Morazán experienced some of the war's worst atrocities, with massacres and bombing raids a regular occurrence. Much of the region is now encompassed by the so-called **Ruta de la Paz**, part of a major project to rebuild much-needed housing, schools and infrastructure, as well as to develop tourism in the region. The locals here all have a story to tell, though some are more willing to share their experiences than others. The main draw is the village of **Perquín** with its war museum, but the nearby town of **Mozote**, scene of a massacre that wiped out the village population, is worth a stop as well. Three **buses** leave San Miguel daily for Perquín (#332; 6.30am, 10am and 3pm, though times not rigidly observed; 3hr), Corinto, San Francisco Gotera and the small towns and villages between. It's easier to take one of the more frequent buses to Gotera (#328), and change there for Perquín.

San Francisco Gotera

North of San Miguel, Highway CA-7 runs 25km to **SAN FRANCISCO GOTERA** (usually called simply "Gotera"), a busy though beautifully located commercial town with streets choked by street vendors. The bus stops just after the dusty and ugly main square, with buses heading on to Perquín departing from the same place. There's no real reason to stay here, but if you do get stuck, the *San Francisco* (☎654 0066; ❶–❸), on Av Morazán at C 3 Pte, a block away from the bus stop, has a good range of rooms including en-suite doubles with cable TV and a/c. Bus #332A runs regularly north to Perquín and a pick-up service operates between 5am and 5.30pm. Two paved roads lead north from Gotera, the first towards

Cacaopera and Corinto, the second to Ciudad Segundo Montes, Arambala and Perquín.

Cacaopera and Corinto

The small village of **CACAOPERA**, 11km north of Gotera, takes its name from the Ulúa language, referring to the heavy cultivation of cacao in the area during colonial times. Indigenous culture and religion is still strongly adhered to in this region, and an excellent place to learn about it is the **Museo Guinakirika** ("community" in Ulúa) with fine exhibits on indigenous tradition and culture, as well as photos and arts and crafts. A highlight here is the colonial church dating back to 1660 (though heavily restored), with walls up to 5m thick. Adjacent is a bell tower with three huge bronze bells dating from 1772. The church is the focus of festivities from January 15–17, when the villagers dance in memory of the 8 *caciques* (priests) and the indigenous warrior deities Tupaica and Tumaica.

From Cacaopera, a road heads a little further northeast to the town of **CORINTO**, an important commercial hub in the region and home to a market on Wednesday and Sunday that attracts vendors from neighbouring Honduras. The main claim to fame of the town are the **Grutas del Espíritu Santo** (Tues–Sun 9am–4.30pm; US$2), a series of caves bearing pre-Colombian wall art located about 15 minutes north of the village on foot through some pleasant scenery. Though faint, the art is said to date back some 10,000 years. Should you need to stay in town, *Hotel Restaurante Familiar* (☎898 2844; ❷) is the only option. Corinto and Cacaopera can be reached on a day-trip from San Miguel (bus #327 from the main terminal).

Ciudad Segundo Montes, Arambala and Mozote

The second road north from Gotera begins to climb into the mountains, with *henequén* fields and cattle pasture giving way to pine forests and superb mountain vistas. After about 10km, the road passes the fringes of **Ciudad Segundo Montes**, a collection of new villages housing repatriated refugees and named after one of the six Jesuit priests assassinated by the military in 1989. Sympathetic visitors are welcome to tour the communities and talk with the residents, and staff at the reception office (closed Sun) in the main village – **San Luis**, on the highway – can explain local community projects (volunteer opportunities available). Dorm room **accommodation** is offered in San Luis (no phone; ❶).

Thirty-nine kilometres north of Gotera the road branches at the **Desvío de Arambala**, which forks east along a rough track to the village of **Arambala**. There is no public transport along this route, but hitching is common and pick-ups will take you for a small fee. Set amongst pine forests and extinct volcanoes, the village is a peaceful place, slowly rebuilding after a series of massacres that rocked the area during the civil war. Should you be looking, there is ample opportunity for volunteer work in the community if you ask around.

A few kilometres further on sits **MOZOTE**, scene of the country's most atrocious wartime massacre. The village, populated mainly by the elderly and the very young, was considered by the government to be a hiding place for FMLN guerrillas. In December 1981 the elite, US-trained Atlacatl army battalion attacked the village, killing some 1000 people, whose bodies were subsequently burnt or buried in mass graves. The few eyewitness testimonies to the events were ignored for years, and the bodies of the victims did not begin to be exhumed until 1992. Foreign groups are still working to uncover these mass-burial sites today and in some cases upwards of 85 percent of the bodies belong to children. Today, what remains of Mozote is virtually a ghost town, although families are slowly moving back. A moving **monument** to the victims features an iron sculpture of the silhouette of a family and a wall carrying the names of those killed. For a small fee (around US$4), local children will take you to the caves where the guerrillas were really hiding out, a pleasant rolling walk of 4 or 5km through forest and brush, where wildlife abounds. The caves themselves are not overly spectacular, but it was from here that **Radio Venceremos** ("We Will Triumph") was first broadcast, and as you look out over the surrounding countryside it is easy to see why it was never discovered by the army.

Perquín

The main paved section of road at the Desvío de Arambala begins its final climb to **PERQUÍN**, a small and, given its history, surprisingly friendly mountain town set in the middle of glorious walking countryside. During the war the town was the FMLN headquarters, and in later years where they broadcast Radio Venceremos to the nation. Attempts by the army to dislodge the guerrillas mostly failed, leaving the town badly damaged and deserted. Today, the "town that refused to die" has repaired most of its buildings, although the scars of war are evident everywhere, and nearly everyone has a horrendous tale to tell. Even so, there is today a sense of optimism and a determination to rebuild the community.

Perquín's main draw is the moving **Museo de la Revolución Salvadoreña** (Tues–Sun 8am–4.30pm; US$1.15), set up by ex-guerrillas in the wake of the 1992 Peace Accords. The curators travelled throughout the country collecting photographs and personal effects of those who died during the fighting, and notices request that visitors donate more in order to expand the collection. There is a succinct summary (in Spanish) of the process leading up to the armed struggle; displays of weaponry – including missile launchers, bombs and grenades – disabled after the signing of the Peace Accords; and examples of international propaganda aimed at bringing the events in El Salvador to the world's attention. Outside is the **bomb crater** left by a 1981 explosion and a mock-up of a guerrilla camp – the crude bent-wood and palm-leaf constructions offered little shelter but could be erected and dismantled quickly. Behind the museum lie the remains of the helicopter that was carrying Domingo Monterrosa (architect of the Mozote massacre) when it was shot down by the FMLN in 1984. The most moving exhibits are perhaps the anonymous transcripts of witnesses of the massacre, and drawings by refugee schoolchildren, depicting events as they saw them. A separate room contains the transmitting equipment and studio used by **Radio Venceremos**. Using subterranean sound rooms to evade detection, the station broadcast every afternoon throughout the war on a number of frequencies, transmitting the guerrillas' view of events, as well as interviews and music. After the peace accords, the station received an FM licence, and is now a commercial, mainstream station playing a mixture of Latin American sounds and US rock based in San Salvador – ironically, in offices rented from a member of the rival ARENA Party. To get to the museum, a rough road leads uphill from the corner of the Parque for about 200m.

Practicalities

If you **stay** in Perquín, *El Gigante* (☎680 4037; ❷), five minutes' walk from town back down the road to Gotera, has basic, windowless rooms with fan and shared bath. The more upmarket, American-owned *Hotel Perkin Lenca* (☎680 4046, Ⓔperkin@navegante.com.sv; ❻), 1.5km south of town, has solid wooden cabins with bath, hot water and hammocks, and an excellent restaurant and bar. Breakfast is included, and advance booking is recommended. A little further out of town, about 0.5km along the right-hand fork at Desvío la Tejera is the *Turicentro Cueva del Ratón* (☎680 4212; ❸). There's a pool here and two basic but rustic cabañas, and the friendly owner will help you to construct a fire under the stars. Back in town, **places to eat** are few and far between. The small comedores, *Las Colinas* just before the museum and *Café Perquín* off the main square, serve simple food and *comidas a la vista*. There's a small **tourist office** (Mon–Sat 8am–4pm; ☎680 4086) on the Parque that can provide you with a photocopied leaflet covering the Ruta de la Paz.

East to the Honduran border

East of San Francisco Gotera, a road continues through hot, low hills to **SANTA ROSA DE LIMA**, a messy but thriving place, with a large daily market, cheese industry and a well-maintained church. There's not much to do here, but it's a convenient stopover if you're crossing late from Honduras. The best of the few **places to stay** is *Hotel El Recreo* (Ⓣ664 2126; ❷) on 4a Av Nte between C Giron and C 1 Ote, which has clean rooms with bath, though it does get a little noisy. The basic but adequate *El Tejano* (Ⓣ664 2459; ❷), on C Giron between 6a and 8a Av Nte, is slightly cheaper, but has a 7am checkout. For **eating**, the very clean *Comedor Chayito*, at the corner of C Giron and C 1 Ote, does a good cheap *comida a la vista* (7am–6pm), while for something with a bit more kick try *Taquería Tex Mex* on Av G Arias between C 1 and 3 Ote. **Banks**, including Banco Cuscatlán, are clustered around the plaza at the centre of town. The **Telecom** is on C Giron, just down from the church.

Beyond Santa Rosa, the road continues for a further 10km before connecting with the Carretera Interamericana to run to the border at **EL AMATILLO**. Formed by the Río Goascoran, the border crossing is easy but busy, used by international buses and teeming with moneychangers and opportunistic beggars. On the Honduran side, buses leave regularly until late afternoon for Tegucigalpa and Jícaro Galán, 42km from the border; there are also direct buses to Choluteca, for onward connection to the Nicaraguan border along the Carretera Interamericana. A bank on the Salvadoreño side changes dollars and lempiras, though the rates are slightly better with the moneychangers. There is a US$2 fee to enter Honduras.

3.4

The west

The rich landscapes of western El Salvador in many ways offer a perfect introduction to the country. Soft mountain chains edge back from the valleys, dominated by the vibrant green expanses of coffee plantations from which the area gains its wealth. Spared from the most violent hardships of the conflict of the 1980s, the friendly towns and cities here have a relatively well-developed tourist infrastructure that makes travelling easier than in other regions as well.

The joy of this part of the country consists largely of soaking up the atmosphere. The Carretera Interamericana runs between San Salvador and the main city of the west, **Santa Ana**, but the main access route to the southern part of the region leads through the sweaty town of **Sonsonate** 65km west of the capital. From here, buses head off in several directions: down to the coast for the untouched beaches of **Los Cóbanos** and **Barra de Santiago**; on to the tranquil forest reserve at **Bosque El Imposible**; and northwest into the mountains. The mountain towns of **Apaneca** and **Juayúa**, and the nearby city of **Ahuachapán** are perfect for a few days relaxation, and are conveniently situated near the border with Guatemala. The larger, centrally located Santa Ana is a mellow contrast to the capital, while the peaks of **Cerro Verde**, **Volcán Santa Ana** and **Volcán Izalco**, the sublime crater lake of **Lago de Coatepeque**, and the pre-Columbian site of **Tazumal** are all close by. In the north of the region, near the Guatemalan border, the accommodating little town of **Metapán** gives access to the **Bosque Montecristo**, where hiking trails weave through unspoilt cloudforest amid some of the most remote and perfectly preserved mountain scenery in this part of the world.

Sonsonate and the southwest

SONSONATE, set in tobacco and cattle-ranching country, is a bustling, commercial place and transport hub that you'll invariably pass through when heading between the coast and the western highlands. There's little of tourist interest here, except during festival time – chiefly the **Verbena de Sonsonate** held at the end of January, when there's a host of music and drama performances, and the more colourful **Semana Santa**, when crowds flock to join the street processions and intricate pictures are drawn in coloured sawdust on the pavements. The city cathedral, once the pride of the city with its twin cupolas, was particularly badly hit by the 2001 earthquake, collapsing much of the structure, though repairs are underway.

Buses arrive at the main terminal 1.5km east of the centre. Following the road to the west leads you to the centre, but it's a long hot walk and it's easier to take bus #53C from outside the terminal straight to the Parque Central. Of the limited **accommodation** options in the centre, the reasonable *Hotel Orbe* (Ⓣ451 1517; ❸–❹) on Av Fray Mucci Sur and C 4 Ote, two blocks east of the Parque, has large rooms with private bath, some with a/c. The best option is the comfortable *Hotel Agape* (Ⓣ451 3192, Ⓕ452 4074; ❸), set in beautiful gardens on the outskirts of town, 2km along the road to San Salvador – take bus #53A or #53J from the crossroads by the bus terminal. There are a number of **restaurants** along this road, while in the centre a row of comedores on 4a Av Nte overlooks the river by an attractive white bridge.

Los Cóbanos and Los Remedios

Los Cóbanos, 25km due south of Sonsonate, is a favourite beach for Salvadoreño holiday-makers and generally crowded at the weekends. Although rather rocky, the pretty, gently curved beach makes a nice contrast to the palm-fringed expanses further down the coast. Walk round the headland at the west end of the small bay and you come to the quieter beach of **Los Remedios**. A couple of places have **cabañas** for rent: *Solimar* (☎451 0137; ④) is the nicest (although closed during the week), while *Mar y Plata* (☎451 3914; ④), set slightly back from the seafront, is slightly run down but a little cheaper. A number of small shacks serve fresh fish and other meals. **Bus** #257 leaves Sonsonate every hour for Los Cóbanos until early evening, and there are also occasional direct buses from San Salvador (#207); the last bus leaves the beach at 5pm.

Acajutla to Cara Sucia

Beyond Sonsonate, the major town on the coast is the port of **ACAJUTLA**, the site of Pedro de Alvarado's first encounter with the Pipils in 1524, but today a hot, decaying and distinctly edgy place; it's better to stay at Sonsonate. Acajutla lies 4km from the Carretera Littoral, which runs east towards Costa del Bálsamo (see p.325) or west a flat 45km or so to the Guatemalan border at La Hachadura, a beautiful journey with the slopes of the Cordillera Apaneca rising to the north and rolling pasturelands to the south. After 10km to the west, the highway passes the access road to **Playa de Metalío**, a quiet, palm-fringed beach whose beauty is somewhat marred by refuse washed up from Acajutla. More remote, **Playa Barra de Santiago** lies 15km further up the coast, across a small estuary by the fishing village of Barra de Santiago. A rough road leads the 7km from the highway to the estuary; one bus a day in the morning runs along it from Sonsonate. At the estuary, bargain with a fishing boat to take you across to the village and the beach.

A further 10km west, the dusty village of **Cara Sucia** lines the highway due east of the Río Cara Sucia. The nearby archeological site of Cara Sucia was a Maya settlement made wealthy by trade in salt, and initial excavations uncovered a number of structures including two pelota courts. Though there's not much to see today, it's a peaceful place for a picnic. There is no public transport to the site; from the crossroads 50m past the bridge at the village's end, take the road leading left, opposite *Comedor Nohemy*, for about twenty minutes until you reach the Cooperativa Cara Sucia buildings on the right; ask the guard to let you through and follow the track round the buildings, taking the right-hand fork to the ruins.

From Cara Sucia the highway continues the last few kilometres to **La Hachadura**, a busy border crossing used by international buses heading for Mexico. There's a small hospedaje on the Guatemalan side, and buses to Esquintla and Guatemala City.

Bosque El Imposible

The road leading right at the crossroads in Cara Sucia provides access to one of El Salvador's greatest hidden glories, the forest reserve of **Bosque El Imposible**, so called because of the difficulty of traversing the mountain tracks to get into it. Covering more than 31 square kilometres and rising through three climatic zones across the Cordillera de Apaneca, the reserve contains more than 400 species of trees and 1600 species of plants, some unique to the area. Birdwatchers may glimpse some of the more than 300 species, including the emerald toucanet, trogons, hummingbirds and eagles, while the park provides a secure habitat for a diverse range of animals, including anteaters, the white-tailed deer and ocelot, plus over 500 different species of butterfly.

Practicalities

Getting to El Imposible without a private vehicle is time-consuming; most of the San Salvador operators listed on p.318 run expensive tours here. There's a US$6 entry fee to enter the reserve, managed by a nongovernmental organisation, SalvaNatura (33 Av Sur 640, Col Flor Blanca, San Salvador; Ⓣ279 1515, Ⓕ279 0220, Ⓔsalvanatura@saltel.net) – you'll need to apply for written permission to visit at least one week in advance, and pay at the same time. When you reach the park the only money you may need to pay is if you wish to hire a guide (they hang around the entrance; be prepared to bargain). SalvaNatura also have a small office in the nearby village of **San Francisco Menéndez** (5a Av Nte 20; Ⓣ484 2090), the main point of access for the reserve, reached by a turning off the main highway 4km past Cara Sucia. Some pick-ups run from Cara Sucia to the entrance, but be prepared to leave early and also to haggle. There's another entrance to the park at the Desvío Ahuachapío turn-off from the Carretera Littoral, halfway between the Sonsonate–Acajutla road and Cara Sucia, and about 13.5km from the park itself.

This sector of the reserve is called **San Benito**, and there's a small community, **Caserío San Miguelito**, actually inside the park, with shops selling handicrafts and a comedor. The only **accommodation** near to the park is the new *Hostal El Imposible* (❻), located 500m from the entrance to the park. This consists of five comfortable cabañas, administered by SalvaNatura (see above), that should be booked well in advance through one of their offices.

The Cordillera Apaneca

Beginning at the northern edge of the Bosque El Imposible and stretching east for more than 70km from the Guatemalan border, the glorious mountains of the **Cordillera Apaneca** are covered in a patchwork of coffee plantations and acres of pine forest. The so-called "**Ruta de las Flores**" covers the area between the villages of Concepción de Ataco, 4km west of **Apaneca**, and **Nahuizalco**, and is named after the abundant white coffee flowers visible during May and the wild flowers that colour the hills and valleys from October to February. Further north **Juayúa** and **Apaneca** are peaceful and attractive mountain villages, coming to life at weekends when visitors escaping city life arrive. Both villages are surrounded by considerable natural attractions, the most well known of which, **Laguna Verde**, is an easy walk from Apaneca.

Nahuizalco and Juayúa

The population of the village of **NAHUIZALCO**, set on the southern edge of the range about 10km north of Sonsonate, is mostly descended from the region's indigenous peoples, although few wear traditional dress any longer. The town thrives on the manufacture of wicker, with workshops lining the main street. Some of the pieces are small enough to take home, and gentle bargaining is acceptable. There's also an intriguing daily **market** where fruit and vegetables are sold by candlelight once night falls.

Beyond Nahuizalco, the air cools and freshens as the road winds its way up into the mountains proper; there are superb vistas down to Sonsonate and across the plains to the coast. Five kilometres from Nahuizalco is **JUAYÚA** (pronounced "hwai-oo-a"), whose magnificent **Templo del Señor de Juayúa**, built in colonial style in 1957, houses the Black Christ of Juayúa, carved by Quiro Cataño, sculptor of the Black Christ of Esquipulas in Guatemala (see p.244). Consequently the town is something of a pilgrimage site, particularly during the January festival (Jan 8–15). Largely quiet during the week, the town sees an influx of visitors at weekends, when you should book ahead if you wish to stay. **Accomodation** is available at the *Casa de Huéspedes de Doña Mercedes* (Ⓣ&Ⓕ452 2287; ❹), two blocks southeast of the Parque at 2a Av Sur and C 6 Ote 3-6, a cheerful place with comfortable rooms, hot water and cable TV. The bathrooms, though shared, are very clean. *Hotelito Tecupán* (Ⓣ452 2781; ❹), on the Parque next to the Templo, has lovely large, homely rooms set around a floral courtyard with fountain. The attached restaurant is reasonably priced and does a good breakfast for US$2.50. Of the other **places to eat**, *Café Festival* on the Parque serves good coffee, cakes and breakfasts. Two kilometres outside of town, at the junction with the main carretera, *La Colina Parque* serves barbecued food in wooded gardens, with hammocks nearby so you can sleep off your excesses. If looking to **tour** the countryside, try Juayatur (Ⓣ452 2002), who can provide guides to local attractions including several nearby waterfalls. Tienda José on the main plaza is another good place to look for guides – ask for Doris. Expect to pay around US$5 per day for guides during the week, more on weekends.

Apaneca

A short leg further along the road from Juayúa stands another quiet and charming mountain town, **APANECA**, founded by Pedro de Alvarado in the mid-sixteenth century. The town retains an air of friendly tranquillity, despite being both popular with weekend visitors and home to one of the best-known restaurants in the country, *La Cocina de mi Abuela* (see below). During the week, you're likely to have the place – and the wonderful surrounding mountain scenery – to yourself. Along with visiting nearby **Laguna Verde**, other outdoor options include horse-riding tours; prospective guides usually gather around *La Cocina de mi Abuela*, charging around US$5 per person.

Laguna Verde

There's little to do in Apaneca itself, but it's an enjoyable and not too strenuous walk through woods and fincas to the **Laguna Verde**, a small crater lake 4km northeast of town. Fringed by reeds and surrounded by mist-clad pine slopes, the lake is a popular destination, and at the weekends you're likely to share the path with numerous families and groups of walkers.

From the highway on the edge of town, follow the dirt road to the right of the Jardín de Flores garden centre, which winds up and around the mountain, passing several fincas and a couple of small hamlets, overlooked by the weekend retreats of wealthy San Salvadoreños. An enjoyable shortcut is to walk up the dried-up stream bed through the woods, which links the bends of the road; this is more of a scramble and it's quite easy to get lost – ask directions from anyone you meet. The hamlet just above the lake, reached after about ninety minutes, has sweeping views on clear days; the white city sheltering in the valley below is Ahuachapán, while to the north is the peak of Cerro Artillería on the Guatemalan border. The grassy slopes around the lake make a good spot for a picnic and you can swim. Closer to town to the north, the smaller and less impressive **Laguna Las Ninfas** is an easy forest walk of about 45 minutes.

Practicalities

Apaneca is easily accessible by **bus** #249 from both Sonsonate (1hr 30min) and Ahuachapán (1hr). The **telecom office**, **post office** and a small **information kiosk** are in a row on the Parque, though the Alcaldía is often a better place to get information, with small printed leaflets available.

Increasing numbers of visitors has led to a boom in **accommodation** development, though you'll still need to book ahead on weekends. The best quality location is *Cabañas de Apaneca* (ⓣ453 0500, ⓔcabanasapaneca@navegante.com.sv; ❻), on the main road, home to twelve comfortable wood cabins set in lush gardens overlooking mountain slopes, along with a good on-site restaurant. The most affordable option is the *Hostal Rural Las Orquídeas* (ⓣ433 0061; ❹), a well signposted **hostel** at the north end of town with four clean, simple rooms with hot water; note that *Hostal Las Ninfas* no longer exists although the signs are still in place. The Swiss-owned *Hotel Belle Ville* (ⓣ433 0237; ❺), 2a Av Nte and C 5 Ote, makes a good mid-range option as rates include breakfast.

The best **restaurant** in town is *La Cocina de mi Abuela* (11.30am–5pm Sat & Sun only; ⓣ450 5203 ext 301), housed in a beautifully decorated colonial-era house and drawing wealthy San Salvadoreños and foreign residents alike. The nicest tables are on the covered veranda at the back, with scenic views allowing you to enjoy home-cooked specialities at surprisingly reasonable prices. Opposite, *Tipicos Texizal* serves huge tasty portions of local cooking at low prices. Alternatively, the *Restaurante Fonda Lamatepec*, near the *Cabañas de Apaneca*, also serves excellent, if pricey, Salvadoreño cuisine in a fine setting – fish fresh from Laguna Verde will set you back about US$8. Opening times however, are sporadic.

Ahuachapán and around

From Apaneca the road tumbles down 13km or so to the city of **AHUACHAPÁN**. This area, and the lands further north, are some of the oldest inhabited regions of El Salvador, due in large part to the extremely fertile soil. Artefacts found in the region date back to 1200 BC and the early Maya. Ahuachapán is also one of the oldest Spanish settlements in the country, made a city in 1862, and has generally been a place of quiet bourgeois comfort; two attacks by Guatemalan troops – in 1863 and 1864 – were both firmly rebutted. Like most towns in the area, its wealth grew from the coffee trade and the early twentieth-century British visitor Percy Martin noted: "The people as a whole seemed to me to be very well-to-do, and evidences of refinement and solid comfort were to be met with on all sides. . . I was also impressed with the absence of the usual number of drinking shops, of which I counted scarcely more than six in the whole town. The town is a quiet, sleepy and eminently peaceful place of residence where one might dream away one's life contentedly enough."

Today the city retains an air of peaceful charm, with tight streets and a quiet Plaza Central. The main industry is geothermal electricity generation, at one time supplying seventy percent of the country's power; consequently there are usually a number of European and Japanese technicians stationed here.

Arrival and information

Buses arrive at the terminal on Av Comercial, between C 10 and 12 Pte, eight blocks from the Parque Central. The terminal is a chaotic affair, choked by a rambling market growing uncontrollably beyond its allotted space. Confusingly, the Parque is not at the exact centre of town, but two blocks east of the intersection of the two main streets, C Gerardo Barrios and Av Francisco Menéndez. The latter and 2a Av Nte run parallel to each other from the bus terminal to the cathedral on the Parque. The **Telecom** is at C 3 Pte and 2a Av Sur by the Parque, while the **post office** is at C 1 Ote and 1a Av Sur. To **change money**, there are a cluster of banks at the corners of Av Francisco Menéndez and C Gerardo Barrios, and Banco de Comercio is on the corner of C 4 Pte and Av Francisco Menéndez. **Internet** access is available at the cybercafé (US$0.75 per hour) at 1 Av Sur and C 1 Pte, but the connection is extremely slow; *Infocentros* (US$1 per hour), a block further west at C 3 Pte is faster and closes half an hour later. There are two supermarkets, De Todo and Despensa Familiar, by the bus terminal.

Accommodation

Of the city's **accommodation**, *La Casa Blanca* (Ⓣ443 1505, Ⓕ443 1503; ❺), on 2a Av Nte at C Barrios a couple of blocks from the Parque, is good value, housed in a well-decorated colonial building with large, clean rooms, all with bath and TV. The restaurant is slightly overpriced but set around a relaxing courtyard. For those on a budget, *Hotel San José* (Ⓣ443 0033; ❹), on the little plaza two blocks west from the bus station, has clean, recently refurbished en-suite rooms, though some are a little dark. The nicest place to stay, however, is *Hotel el Parador* (Ⓣ443 0331; ❻), 2km out of town on the road to the Guatemalan border post. All rooms have bath, hot water and TV, and there's a restaurant and a small pool open to the public.

The City and around

Apart from its quiet, gently fading streets and the ever-expanding daily **market** around the bus station, the only things to see in Ahuachapán are its **churches**. The imposing white edifice of the **Iglesia Parroquia de Nuestra Señora de la Asuncíon**, on the Parque Central, dominates the centre of the city and acts as the focus for the annual fiesta in the first week of February. Dating from the 1950s, **El Calvario**, on C 6 Pte at 2a Av Nte, is home to a fine sculpture of a crucified Christ.

Immediately south of the city, the hump of **Cerro Ataco** is a safe and not too difficult climb of about two hours – follow 2a Av Sur out of town and pick any one of the small paths going up to the summit. The body of water visible to the northwest, off the road to Las Chinamas, is the **Lago de Llano**, a small, lily-fringed lake extensively fished by locals. It's a thirty-minute stroll along the main road from the centre of town to the lake, or you can catch bus #60 (regular departures from the market) to the rather depressing village of Las Brisas, 500m from the lake.

Some 5km east of town, near the hamlet of El Barro, are the **ausoles** (geysers) forming the basis of the local geothermal industry. The plumes of steam hang impressively over the lush green vegetation and red soil – particularly photogenic in the early-morning light. Access to the area is via the turn-off signed "Planta Geotérmica" on the road to Apaneca. The plant itself is off-limits, but locals will allow you access to their land for a small fee, from where you can get a better view.

Eating and drinking

Like most Salvadoreño provincial cities, Ahuachapán is not overly blessed with **places to eat**. All restaurants tend to close relatively early, around 7pm, except for the *El Parador* and *El Paso* restaurants – next to each other a kilometre or so north of town on the Las Chinamas road – both of which serve meat and seafood standards, and occasionally have live music at the weekends. In the centre, there's very little choice unless you are satisfied with *pupusas* and pizza. *Casa Grande* at 4a Av Nte 2 has plenty of character, with loud music blaring and a standard menu featuring some game specialities including venison (*venado*) and rabbit (*conejo*). *La Estancia*, housed in a rather run-down former coffee mansion on 1a Av Sur at C Barrios, has well-prepared standards at average prices, while *Mixta "S"*, 2a Av Sur by the Parque, is more of a fast-food place with simple meals, snacks and a selection of juices.

Tacuba

Fifteen kilometres west of Ahuachapán lies the quiet mountain village of **TACUBA** (bus #264), reached via a winding and scenic road with grand views of coffee plantations and Bosque El Imposible (see p.347). An important settlement existed here long before the Spaniards arrived, and the village retains strong folkloric traditions, although you'll only really notice these at fiesta time. There's not much to do in Tacuba itself, though it makes a fine base for exploring the nearby mountains and valleys. The excellent *La Cabaña de Tacuba* (Ⓣ417 4332; ❻), set amid beautifully cultivated gardens, offers a fine range of **accommodation**, including large double rooms and suites. The owner can supply information on nature trails and hiking in the area.

To Las Chinamas and Guatemala

From Ahuachapán, a reasonably good and very scenic road runs the 20km or so to the **Guatemalan border**, just past **Las Chinamas**. Local buses (#11AH) leave for the border every fifteen minutes, taking about an hour. International buses from Santa Ana also pass through at about 5.30am. There is no ticket office – stand on C 6 Pte more or less opposite the *Hotel San José* and flag them down. Buses run to Guatemala City from Valle Nuevo on the Guatemalan side.

Chalchuapa and Tazumal

Northeast from Ahuachapán, the road winds down through the last spurs of the cordillera onto a broad and scenic plain, running to **CHALCHUAPA**, which in addition to its faded but beautiful colonial church produces jade artesanías, including replicas of Maya artefacts. Chalchuapa's main draw is the archeological site of **Tazumal** (Tues–Sun 9am–5pm; US$3), located on the edge of town. The most important site in El Salvador, the ruins are – by comparison with sites in Honduras and Guatemala – rather small, although they do have their own, impressive, beauty. Tazumal is an easy trip from Ahuachapán (1hr) or Santa Ana (30min). **Bus** #218 drops passengers off at a small plaza a few blocks from the centre of town; from here, walk uphill for about four blocks and turn left at the sign.

What is now the town of Chalchuapa was the seat of power for a strong and thriving Maya population from 900 BC onwards. The inhabitants produced "Usulután" ceramics, key items of commerce in the Maya zone, and also controlled the trade in obsidian from Guatemala. This early society was literate – evidence suggests that they had both calendar and writing systems – and highly stratified, while artefacts indicate strong links with Olmec civilizations in Mexico.

The site as a whole was constructed in thirteen different stages over a period of 750 years, mostly during the Late Classic period (600–900 AD). Of the nine structures identified, only two remain in reasonable condition, with a third partially excavated; the rest have been destroyed by the expansion of the town. The central and largest structure – a fourteen-stepped ceremonial pyramid, influenced by the style of Teotihuacán in Mexico and sadly rather sloppily restored – dates back to the Classic period (300–900 AD); traces of a platform dating back to between 100–200 AD have been found beneath it. A number of smaller temples were originally attached to the main structure. At the base of its northern edge, a number of tombs (Late Classic period) have yielded artefacts such as Tiquisate ware from Guatemala, jade jewellery, items for religious rites and a flask containing powdered iron-oxide. The last was used for decorating a ceremonial stone *hacha* or head, used during games of pelota. The pelota court itself lay on the southern edge of the structure.

Tazumal as a Maya city was abandoned around the end of the ninth century, during the collapse of the Classic Maya culture; unusually, Pipils moved in and occupied the site. Structure 2, to the west of the main platform, is a Pipil pyramid dating back to the Early Postclassic period (900–1200 AD). The new residents also constructed another pelota court, to the northwest corner of the site. Tazumal was finally abandoned around 1200 AD, with the focus of settlement in the area moving towards the centre of the current town.

A **museum** (same hours; Spanish only) displays artefacts discovered during excavations. The nearby ruins of **El Trapiche** and **Casa Blanca** are currently being excavated and aren't yet open to the public.

Santa Ana

Self-possessed **SANTA ANA**, the second most important city in El Salvador, lies in a superb location in the Cihautehuacán valley. Surrounded by green peaks, with the slope of Volcán Santa Ana rising to the southwest, the gently decaying colonial streets exude a certain bourgeois complacency. Cooler and far mellower than San Salvador, and regarding itself as being above the unseemly commercial bustle of San Miguel, it's a good place to relax, admiring the handful of grandiose buildings or simply walking the streets soaking up the atmosphere.

Conquistadors passed through here soon after their arrival in El Salvador, discovering a Pipil town of about three thousand inhabitants. A Spanish settlement, however, was not founded until July 1569, when Bishop Bernardino de Villapando arrived en route from Guatemala. Commenting on the beauty and fertility of the area, he ordered work to begin on a church dedicated to **Nuestra Señora de Santa Ana**, the saint of the day of his arrival. Completed in 1576, this occupied the site of the present cathedral until it was destroyed in the early twentieth century to make way for the new building. The settlement grew relatively quickly: by 1770 the population was almost as large as that of San Salvador, with 589 Spanish and *ladino* families, and 138 indigenous families. Agriculture – particularly sugar cane and then coffee – and ranching contributed to the city's wealth. By the end of the nineteenth century Santa Ana was secure in its position as El Salvador's second city, and buildings reflecting the city's status, such as the theatre and cathedral, sprang up.

Today, the population is over 225,000, and Santa Ana retains an air of restrained, provincial calm that is generally only ruptured during the **July fiesta**, when a host of events bring the streets to life. Should you be looking for more active pursuits, the natural attractions of **Lago de Coatepeque**, the forest reserve of **Cerro Verde**, and the **Santa Ana** and **Izalco** volcanoes are all easy day-trips away.

Arrival and orientation

Buses arrive at the main terminal on 10a Av Sur between C 13 and 15 Pte, nine or so blocks southwest of the central district; city bus #51 runs to the centre from the terminal. As the terminal area is a bit chaotic, it's easy to get lost. Should you want to walk regardless, turn left out of the terminal amid the market and head uphill about 15 minutes to the centre. Buses for Metapán (#325) arrive and depart two blocks west of the main terminal, just up from the roundabout in front of the Despensa Familiar supermarket. International buses to and from Guatemala arrive and depart from C 25 Pte between 6a and 8a Av Sur. The Parque Central is at the intersection of C Libertad and Av Independencia.

Accommodation

Santa Ana's status as the country's second city is not reflected in its range of **accommodation**, although there are enough reasonably comfortable hotels and a couple of good budget choices. The area around 8a and 10a Av Sur has the highest concentration of cheap and basic places to stay, though wandering alone at night here is not recommended.

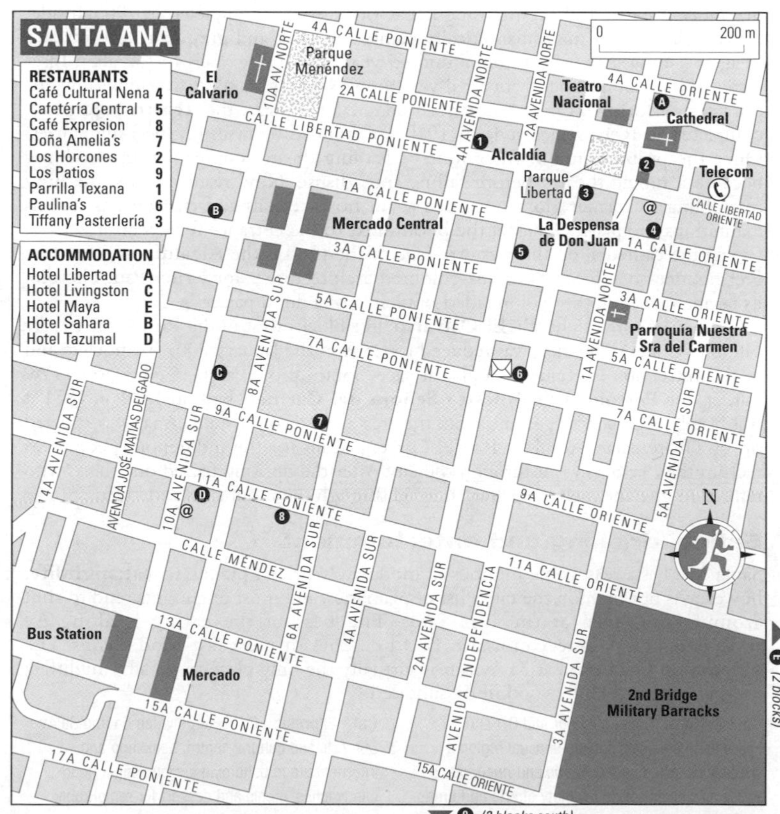

Hospedaje Tikal 10a Av Sur between C Méndez and C 11 Pte ⓣ440 4127. The better of a couple of bland, no-frills options on this street near the bus terminal. Little more than a bed in a room with fan and shared bathrooms, but if counting the pennies it's very cheap. ❷

Hotel Libertad C 4 Ote at 1a Av Nte ⓣ441 2358, ⓔjaval@navegante.com.sv. Great location right by the cathedral with gigantic, clean basic rooms with TV, some with bath. Free Internet for guests. Bring your own padlock for the doors. ❸

Hotel Livingston 10a Av Sur between C 7 and 9 Pte ⓣ447 4883. Safe and secure, with ample parking space and large, clean, well-equipped rooms, pleasantly furnished with cable TV and en-suite bathroom. ❹

Hotel Maya C 11 Ote at 11a Av Sur ⓣ441 3612. Good, secure place with motel-style rooms including baths. Rooms are furnished decently, but it's a long walk from the centre in a boring area. ❷

Hotel Sahara C 3 Pte between 8a and 10a Av Sur ⓣ & ⓕ447 9664, ⓔhotel_sahara@yahoo.com. The city's best, with a good selection of rooms with fan or a/c, telephone, cable TV and ample wardrobe space. The bar and on-site restaurant stay open until 10pm. ❺

Hotel Tazumal C 25 Pte and 10a Av Sur ⓣ440 2830. Large rooms in a gracefully ageing building complete with pretty courtyard. Service is amiable and all rooms are en-suite, some with cable TV, some with a/c. Very cheap at the price and the best budget option in the city. ❷

The City

Santa Ana's **Parque Libertad** is arguably the finest Parque Central in the country. The plaza itself is neatly laid out with a small bandstand, where people gather to sit and chat in the early evening, but it is the three buildings forming the north, east and west sides that really catch the eye. On the eastern edge of the Parque is the magnificent **cathedral**, an imposing neo-Gothic edifice completed in 1905. Inside, brick arches, rather unsympathetically painted in pink and grey, soar upwards and images – some dating back four hundred years – line the walls to the altar. Inset into the walls are plaques from local worshippers giving thanks to various saints for miracles performed. On the northern edge of the plaza, the **Teatro Nacional**, completed in Renaissance style in 1910, was funded by taxes on local dignitaries. Once the proud home of the country's leading theatre companies, the building became a movie theatre before falling into disuse. Now restored to something resembling its former glories, it once again hosts recitals and concerts, as well as exhibitions and plays. Check at the booth next to the entrance for upcoming dates. Facing the cathedral on the western edge of the plaza is the **Alcaldía**, another fine Renaissance-style piece of cream-coloured architecture – for writer Paul Theroux its facade possessed the "colonnaded opulence of a ducal palace".

Another important church, **El Calvario**, five blocks west of the Parque on 10a Av Nte by Parque Menéndez, was reduced to ruins in the January 2001 earthquake and its reconstruction continues at a glacial pace. South of the Parque Central, on 1a Av Sur, sits the **Parroquia de Nuestra Señora del Carmen**, built in 1822; in 1871 it was briefly occupied by peasants from the area around Volcán Santa Ana who, spurred on by Guatemalan president Rafael Carrera's calls for the indigenous peoples to reclaim their land, ran riot through the city. After the uprising fizzled out, those who refused to give themselves up were hunted through the mountains and killed.

Eating, drinking and entertainment

Santa Ana has a reasonable number of moderately priced **places to eat**; **nightlife**, however, is not high on the city's list of priorities, and most restaurants tend to shut around 8pm, even at the weekends. The best of the eating is along Av Independencia, where you'll also find branches of most fast-food chains. The **cinema** on C Libertad at 3a Av Sur is virtually the only place to go after nightfall; it shows standard Hollywood films, subtitled.

Café Cultural Nena 1a Av Sur and C 1 Ote. Fascinating little café serving unusual regional specialities including *chicharrón* and *nuegados de yucca* as well as selling a variety of arts and crafts.

Café Expresion C 11 Pte between 6a and 8a Av Sur. Arts and cultural centre, bookshop and Internet café in bohemian surroundings. Good sandwiches, meals and dessert for remarkably

cheap prices. Closed Sun.
Cafetéría Central 2a Av Sur between C 1 and 3 Pte. Good for large breakfasts and cheap lunches. Very basic *comida a la vista* available, along with excellent *pupusas*.
Doña Amelia's 6a Av Sur and C 9 Pte. Despite the gaudy neon sign outside, this is a quality restaurant with grilled meats and seafood on offer, including *mariscada*, hard to find away from the coast. Expect to pay US$8–16 per person.
Los Horcones next to the cathedral on Parque Libertad. The best views in the city, with seats on a rickety terrace facing the cathedral and plaza. Well-prepared standard dishes, and great juices.
Parrilla Texana C Libertad between 4a and 2a Av Sur. Meats served from the grill in a variety of combinations and forms. American diner–style decor and though not cheap, the portions are large and the food good.
Los Patios C 21 Pte between Av Independencia and 2a Av Sur. One of the smartest places in Santa Ana, serving tasty meals in a nice courtyard at reasonable prices. The restaurant does not have a sign, but when open it is easy enough to find.
Paulina's Av Independencia at C 7 Pte. Bar and restaurant with a variety of international meals and snacks served at low prices with a background of blaring music videos. Nicely furnished with jukebox and log tables and chairs.
Tiffany Pastelería C Libertad on the Parque. The best of a cluster of *pastelerías* on the Parque with a range of cakes and pastries. A great place for breakfast or a coffee.

Listings

Banks Cluster around 2a Av Nte behind the Alcaldía, and include the Banco de Comercio, Banco Agrícola, Banco Salvadoreño and Banco Hipotecario; Banco Cuscatlán is on the corner of C 3 Pte and Av Independencia.
Internet Widely available for US$1 per hour; try *Café Bautista*, 10a Av Sur between C 11 Pte and C Méndez (Mon–Sat 9am–noon & 2–6pm), or *Infocentros*, Av Independencia between C 9 and 11 Ote.
Market The original Mercado Central, on 8a Av Sur, C 1 and 3 Pte, burned down in 2000, but a temporary replacement operates on the same site.
Post office C 7 Pte between Av Independencia and 2a Av Sur.
Telecom C Libertad at 5a Av Sur, just down from the Parque Central.

Around Santa Ana: the three peaks

South from Santa Ana, the three **volcanic peaks** of Cerro Verde, Santa Ana and Izalco together form a concise, living example of geological evolution. The oldest, **Cerro Verde**, is now a softened, densely vegetated mountain harbouring a national park. **Santa Ana**, nominally active, has cultivated lower slopes giving way to a bare, lava-covered summit, whilst juvenile **Izalco**, one of the youngest volcanoes in the world, is an almost perfect, bare lava cone of unsurpassed natural beauty.

Parque Nacional Cerro Verde

From the El Congo junction, 14km southeast of Santa Ana, a narrow road winds up through coffee plantations, maize fields and pine woods to the **Parque Nacional Cerro Verde** (daily 7am–5.30pm; US$1), occupying the crater of the long-extinct volcano. This is the most accessible reserve in the country, and consequently you're unlikely to be able to walk the short trails in solitude, particularly at the weekends. The dense forest shelters numerous species of **plants**, including pinabetes and more than fifty species of orchid. **Mammals** such as armadillos and white-tailed deer are shy and hard to spot, though agoutis, which look like long-legged guinea pigs, are sometimes seen rummaging in the leaf litter. **Birds** are much more visible; hummingbirds and toucans are commonly seen, as is the shimmering green motmot (*torogoz*), El Salvador's national bird, recognisable by its long pendulous tail.

Cerro Verde is very well managed, with clear trails and lookouts over Volcán Santa Ana and, far below, Lago de Coatepeque. From the entrance gate a short track leads up to the car park, to the left of which is a small orchid garden. The main trail, the so-called **sendero natural**, leads from the top of the car park, looping clockwise through the reserve. Despite the weekend crowds this is an enjoyable walk of around 45 minutes through the green calm of the forest. Smaller trails branch off through the trees.

Three Sonsonate-bound **buses** (#248) a day run directly from Santa Ana to the car park, the last leaving the city in mid-afternoon (1hr 30min). The last bus from the car park leaves at 5pm and runs to El Congo only, from where you can pick up another service to Santa Ana or San Salvador. Alternatively, you could rent a taxi for a few hours. There are basic **cabañas** (no phone; ❶) by the car park, although you have to bring your own food and water; you can also **camp** – ask the wardens where you can pitch your tent.

Volcán Santa Ana

From a signed turn about ten minutes into Cerro Verde's *sendero natural*, a path branches down to the left, leading eventually to the summit of the **Volcán Santa Ana**, known also as "Lamatepec" or "father hill". The highest volcanic peak in the country at 2365m, Santa Ana is still considered active, although it hasn't erupted since the early twentieth century. The process of forestation is far less advanced here than in Cerro Verde, and the outlines of the volcano far starker.

The walk to and from the summit takes two or three hours each way. From the signed turn on the *sendero natural*, a downhill walk of about twenty minutes brings you to the Finca San Blas, beyond which the path begins to climb up through woodlands. After about 45 minutes, the gradient gets steeper, woodland cover gives way to rock and, towards the summit, lava. Three newer craters sit inside the larger older one – which takes about an hour to circumnavigate; there's a small, green sulphur lake at the bottom of the newest crater, spewing noxious fumes when the wind changes direction.

Volcán Izalco

Just below Cerro Verde on the road down is a stunning lookout west over the majestic **Volcán Izalco**, a bleak, black volcanic cone that startlingly contrasts the green slopes surrounding it. Beginning as a small hole in the ground in 1770, the volcano formed rapidly over the next two centuries as lava began to pour continuously from the earth. Clearly visible from the ocean, the volcano – known to sailors as the "lighthouse of the Pacific" – was used to navigate until its last eruption in 1966.

It's a steep **walk** of about three hours to the top, but locals advise against doing it alone. Local police will escort groups of five or more, leaving around 10.30am from the car park at the base. If you arrive later you may be able to convince them to take you up if your group is large enough. Beware of approaches from strangers and do not accept offers of help or guidance from anybody other than uniformed police officers. A marked trail leads from the lookout down for about thirty minutes to a saddle between the two volcanoes. From here it takes at least an hour to climb the completely bare slopes of volcanic scree to the summit.

Lago de Coatepeque

East from the El Congo junction (14km from Santa Ana), a winding branch road descends 3km to the stunning crater lake of **Lago de Coatepeque**, shadowed by three peaks. The bus ride descending the winding road towards the deep blue waters, fed by natural hot springs, passes a *mirador* (ask the driver to let you off here) from where there are panoramic vistas. It's a further 4km to the water's edge, the last 2km along a rough road. As much of the shore is bounded by private houses, access to the water is difficult. Boat rides are available at *Turicentro Rancho Alegre* (in reality little more than a pier and a comedor) and cost from US$3 per person for a half-hour trip, to US$15 per person for a full circuit of the lake, with prices based on a group of four.

Accommodation on the lake is limited. If on a budget, head for the *Amacuilco* (ⓣ441 6239, ⓔchucho289@yahoo.com; ❹), located on the main road at the entrance to town. It's a lovingly maintained **hostel** with some cabañas, dorm rooms (US$5–7 per person), café on a pier over the lake, a small pool and use of a canoe for US$3 an hour. Follow the road a little further round to reach the *Hotel Torremolinos* (ⓣ441 6037, ⓕ447 3020; ❺), with large, clean rooms, and a small private beach. They also arrange boat trips, but rates are much higher than at *Rancho Alegre*.

Bus #220 leaves Santa Ana every thirty minutes for the lake, running past the three hotels. If you're heading back to San Salvador, take the Santa Ana bus as far as El Congo then walk down the slip road to the main highway and catch any passing bus running from Santa Ana to the capital.

To San Cristóbal and the Guatemalan border

Beyond Santa Ana, the Carretera Interamericana heads northwest for 30km, through the small town of **Candelaría de la Frontera** and on through gentle, green rolling countryside to the Guatemalan border at **San Cristóbal**. There are frequent buses from Santa Ana (#36; 1hr) to the crossing, which is efficient and has no exit or entry charges. There aren't any banks at the border, but numerous moneychangers offer reasonable rates for dollars, colones and quetzales. On the Guatemalan side, buses run to Asunción Mita, with connections to Guatemala City.

From Santa Ana to Metapán

Leaving Santa Ana, CA-12 heads north through agricultural plains and badly deforested hills, becoming wilder after it passes through the dusty town of Texistepeque. Sixteen kilometres further on, at the hamlet of Desagúe, a dirt road leads 2km or so to serene **Lago de Gúija**, surrounded by low hills; Río Ostía, flowing through the lake, forms the border with Guatemala. On the **Las Figuras** arm of land – accessible on foot during the dry season – stretching out on the left side of the lakeshore are a number of faint pre-Columbian rock carvings; the area around the lakeshore was populated exclusively by indigenous groups until well into the seventeenth century. You can rent boats from here to the small island of **La Tipa** in the lake (US$15 per hour).

Ten kilometres beyond the lake the small, friendly town of **METAPÁN** is scenically situated on the edge of the mountains of the Cordillera Metapán-Alotepeque, which run east along the border with Honduras. Having survived a number of setbacks, including two devastating fires that nearly destroyed the town, Metapán was one of only four communities that supported Delgado's first call for independence in 1811, when rioting citizens opened the jail and attacked representatives of the Spanish crown. With low-set, gently whitewashed buildings, it is one of the more pleasant of Salvadoreño provincial towns, the market less unsightly than most and confined to the outskirts well away from the centre. At the Parque Central, the **Iglesia de la Parroquia**, completed in 1743, is one of El Salvador's finest colonial churches, with a beautifully preserved facade. Inside, the main altar is flanked by small pieces worked in silver from a local mine while the ornately decorated cupola features paintings of San Gregorio, San Augustín, San Ambrosio and San Géronimo. On the south side of the plaza, the colonnaded **Alcaldía** is an attractive building in its own right, watched over by two statues of jaguars symbolising the strength and suffering of the indigenous people of the department. The west side, rather bizarrely, is formed by a concrete-grey football stadium, a hideous construction that somewhat ruins the ambiance.

Practicalities

Buses arrive at the main terminal, five or six blocks from the centre. The street in front and slightly to the right of the terminal, C 15 de Septiembre, heads past the market and most of the hotels towards the centre. Turn right when you reach Av Benjamin Valiente. Metapán is blessed with a few decent **hotels**. The comfortable *Hotel San José* (☎442 0556; ❻), just to the right of the bus terminal as you leave, has comfortable rooms, all with bath and TV, plus a restaurant (open until 9pm). Best option in town is the friendly *Hotel Christina* (☎442 0044; ❹), on 4a Av Sur and C 15 de Septiembre, with a range of good, clean rooms with bath, hot water and TV. More basic and suitable for the tightest of budgets only is the *Hospedaje Central* (☎4032 0699; ❶) on 2a Av Nte at C 15 de Septiembre, with crumbling rooms, some with simple bath and all with fan.

For **eating**, *Antojitos La Nueva Esperanza* off the Parque on Av Benjamin Valiente has a wide menu including seafood and *comida a la vista*. *Chili Willy's* at C 5 Ote and 4a Av Nte serves a range of largely Mexican dishes, as well as good *pupusas*. Best for breakfast is *Pastelería La Exquisita* on C 15 de Septiembre around the corner from *Hospedaje Central*, selling cakes and sweets as well as a small selection of lunches. If you need to **change money**, there's a Banco Salvadoreño on the park and a Banco de Comercio at Av Ignacio Gomez and C 15 de Septiembre.

Around Metapán: Bosque Montecristo

The main reason for staying in Metapán is for access to the international reserve of **Bosque Montecristo**, jointly administered by the governments of El Salvador, Honduras and Guatemala. The reserve rises through two climatic zones centred on the **Cerro Montecristo** (2418m), at whose summit the borders of the three countries converge. The higher reaches of Montecristo, beginning at around 2100m, are home to an expanse of virgin **cloudforest**, subject to an average annual rainfall of two metres and 100 percent humidity. Orchids and pinabetes thrive in these climatic conditions, while huge oaks, pines and cypresses, some towering to over 20m, swathed in creepers, lichens and mosses, form a dense canopy preventing sunlight from reaching the forest floor. **Wildlife** abounds, with howler and spider monkeys the most visible mammals and jaguar and other large mammals hiding out. Birds including hummingbirds, quetzals, toucans and the regional endemic bushy-crested jay are more easily seen. The lower slopes of the reserve consist mainly of mixed pine and broadleaf forest cover, much of it secondary growth, replanted since the early 1970s – acute deforestation having provided the impetus for the creation of the reserve in the first place.

The park **entrance** is 5km from Metapán; after another 2km you come to the Hacienda San José, also known as the Casco Colonial, where the wardens are based and where you have to register. From here the road continues for another 14km before reaching **Los Planes** (1890m), 16km inside the park, where there's a **tourist centre**, comprising a well-organized recreation area with a small restaurant, camping area and the wonderful **Jardín de Cien Años** orchid garden. If **camping**, bring food and water.

From Los Planes a marked trail leads to **Punto Trifinio**, the summit of Cerro Montecristo, where the three countries meet. Walking straight to the summit will take around three hours; the path leads through the cloudforest, however, and you can branch off in any direction – bring warm clothing and good footwear. Trails also lead from just below Los Planes to the peaks of Cerro el Brujo and Cerro Miramundo.

Getting to Montecristo

The untouched beauty of the upper heights of Montecristo is due in large part to its remoteness; the only road in is a dirt track running northeast from Metapán. Most of the **tour operators** listed on p.318 can organize trips here; the more people in a group the cheaper it will be. If coming **independently**, the road from Metapán branches right off the highway just before the *Hotel San José*. Occasional pick-ups make the journey, though you'll have to come to a private arrangement;

ask around the market, though note that pick-up owners drive a hard bargain, regularly citing the poor state of the road as a reason for keeping their price high. Montecristo is managed by the National Parks and Wildlife Service (in Ilopango ⓣ227 0622; in Metapán ⓣ442 0475), and you'll need to get permission to enter it in advance from the Ministerio de Medio Ambiente in San Salvador (ⓣ223 0444). You're not allowed to enter on foot. Note that the cloudforest is closed to visitors from May to October, and that there's an entrance **fee** of US$3.

Crossing into Guatemala: north to Anguiatú

Regular buses (#211A; 30min) make the 13km trip from Metapán along CA-12 to **Anguiatú** and the **Guatemalan border** – the most convenient crossing if you're heading for Esquipulas in Guatemala (see p.244). Formalities here are straightforward, though if you're coming in the other direction note that the last bus to Metapán leaves at 6.30pm. There are no banks, but lots of moneychangers.

3.5

The north

North of San Salvador, hilly pastures and agricultural land give way to the remote, rugged and sparsely populated **Chalatenango** and **Cuscatlán provinces**, a region of poverty and pride, all but closed to outsiders. The Spanish found few natural riches to attract them this far north, and the wealth generated by the indigo and coffee plantations of the lowlands never reached here. Successive generations of campesinos have struggled to make a living in this harsh terrain, separated from the capital by both distance and mindset. The sustained underdevelopment of the area created fertile ground for dissent and support for the **FMLN**, who controlled large parts of the department of Chalatenango for significant periods during the 1980s. Both army and guerrillas struggled to take control, leaving communities devastated in their wake and refugees fleeing across the border to Honduras. The scars of this are still evident as villages struggle to repopulate and rebuild against a background of continuing economic hardship and marginalisation.

Understandably, then, the welcome extended to foreigners can be initially rather cool; tourism is not a widely understood concept and travelling here is neither easy nor comfortable. Incidences of car-jackings are higher than normal and you should also take great care if walking in the countryside around Chalatenango as the area has not been completely cleared of mines. A little common sense, however, along with persistence, does bring results. Quite apart from the breathtaking mountain views and clear blue skies, there are a couple of genuinely appealing places to see. Chief among them are the tranquil and friendly **Suchitoto**, considered to be the finest colonial town in the country, set on the shores of **Lago de Suchitlán**, and the mountain village of **La Palma**, with its cottage handicraft industry. The Pipil ruins of **Cihuatán**, though somewhat specialist in appeal, are an easy trip from the capital. In addition, the **Metapán Alotepeque** mountain range offers walking and hiking possibilities.

Suchitoto and Lago de Suchitlán

Despite virtual desertion during the civil-war years, the pretty colonial town of **SUCHITOTO**, 45km northeast of San Salvador, has undergone a social and cultural renaissance, resulting in its designation as a site of National Cultural Heritage in 1997. Set amid beautiful, rolling countryside, the town's height of glory came when the original Villa San Salvador was located near here in 1528. In the many years since the capital was relocated, life has generally been quiet, except during the 1980s, when the area became the scene of bitter fighting as the army struggled to dislodge the FMLN guerrillas from their mountain strongholds. Upwards of 90 percent of the inhabitants left the town, and the roads up and around Cerro Guazapo still bear the crumbling remains of the trenches and dugouts used by both sides, now quietly submerged beneath green vegetation.

Situated on a scenic ridge above the southern edge of **Lago de Suchitlán**, friendly Suchitoto – the Nahuatl name means "city of birds and flowers" – makes for a relaxing getaway from San Salvador. Boasting some of the finest standing examples of colonial architecture in the country, low red-tiled adobe houses stretch attractively along the town's streets. In the centre, the

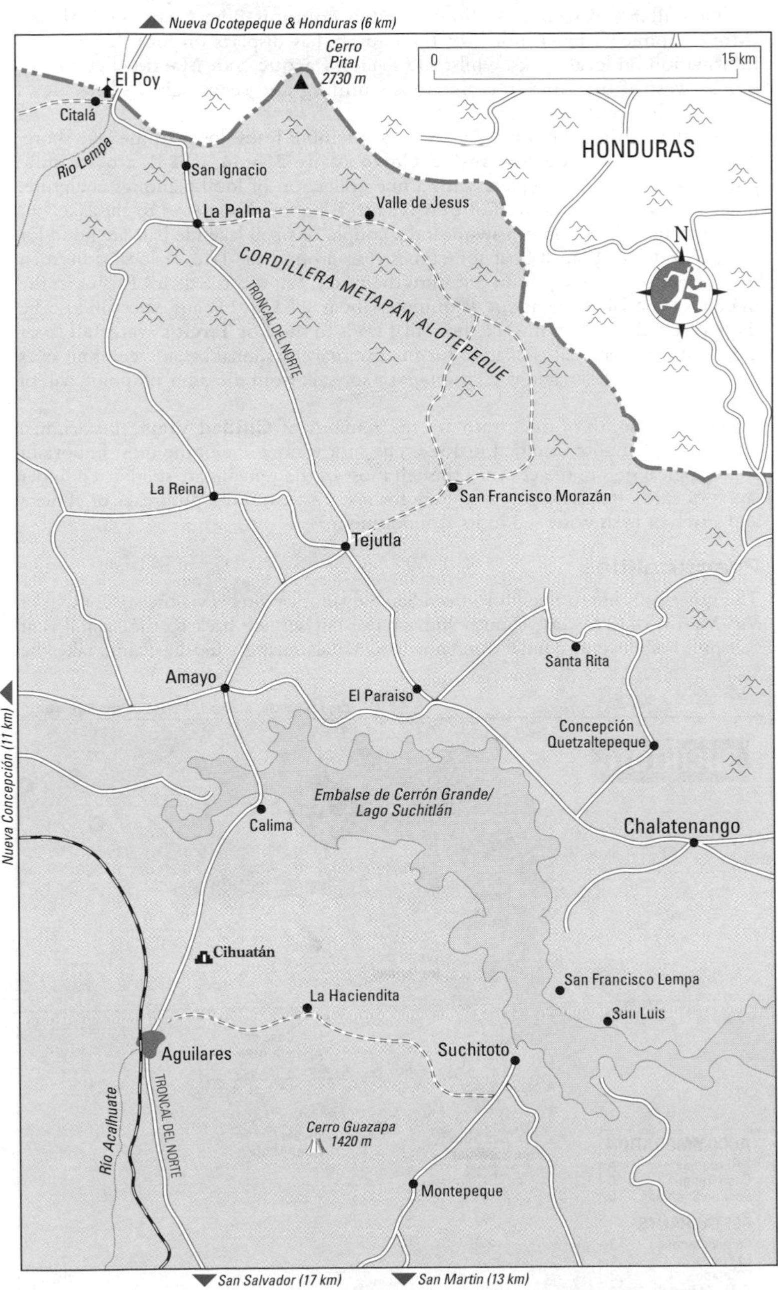
Nueva Ocotepeque & Honduras (6 km)
Cerro Pital 2730 m
0
15 km
El Poy
Citalá
Río Lempa
San Ignacio
HONDURAS
La Palma
Valle de Jesus
CORDILLERA METAPÁN ALOTEPEQUE
TRONCAL DEL NORTE
N
La Reina
San Francisco Morazán
Tejutla
Santa Rita
Amayo
El Paraiso
Nueva Concepción (11 km)
Concepción Quetzaltepeque
Embalse de Cerrón Grande/ Lago Suchitlán
Calima
Chalatenango
Cihuatán
San Francisco Lempa
La Haciendita
San Luis
Aguilares
Suchitoto
Río Acalhuate
TRONCAL DEL NORTE
Cerro Guazapa 1420 m
Montepeque
San Salvador (17 km)
San Martin (13 km)

whitewashed **Iglesia Santa Lucía** is worth a look, with a particularly fine wooden altar and strange hollow wooden columns. The **Casa de Cultura** (Mon–Fri; free), a block north of the church, has displays on local history and information on local walks, whilst the shaded **Parque San Martín**, a couple of blocks west of the church, commands stunning and seemingly endless views across the blue waters of the lake.

From the northeast of town, Av 15 de Septiembre leads down to the lake shore, passing the **Museo de Alejandro Cotto** (daily 2–5pm; US$4), a beautifully restored colonial house replete with a fine collection of local paintings, sculpture, indigenous artefacts and musical instruments. It's a few kilometres to the lake, but it's worth the trip as you can swim, and a couple of small lakeside bars are good for a relaxing drink. A small boat sometimes runs around the lake, or local fishermen may be persuaded to take you out onto the water. Trips to Isla de los Pajaros in the middle of the lake take about 40 minutes (boat US$10–15) and you can also be dropped off at a trail on the lakeshore that leads to the **Los Tercios waterfall** (boat US$4–6). The waterfall is of note for the unusual hexagonal basaltic columns over which the water flows and is 20 minutes or so walk from the drop-off point, half of it steeply uphill.

Some 8km south of Suchitoto are the remains of **Cuidad Vieja**, the original capital of El Salvador founded in 1528. The spot is now one of the most important archeological sites in the country, though most of the remains are still buried under layers of earth. It was a Spanish colony for just 17 years, until outbreaks of cholera and a lack of fresh water led to its abandonment.

Practicalities

The quickest route to Suchitoto from San Salvador by **bus** is via the small town of San Martín (#129 every 15min; 90min); the last service back to the capital is at 5.30pm. For onward connections north to Chalatenango and La Palma take the

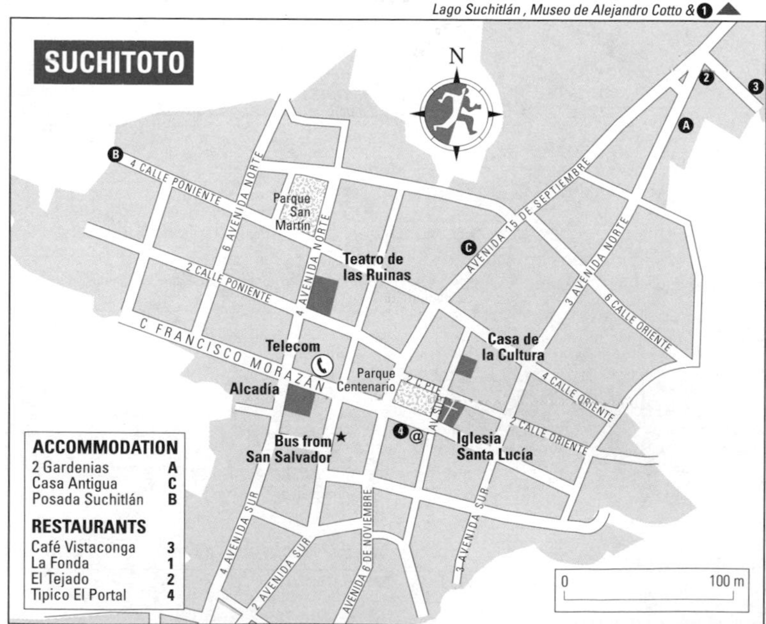

hourly bus #163 to Aguilares (1hr 30min) along the extremely rough but serviceable dirt road heading west. Internet is available at *Café Suchitoto* (US$0.75 per hour) on the main square, which also doubles as a fledgling tourist information centre. **Tours** of the lake and other attractions can be organised through *Casa Antigua* (see below).

More and more **accommodation** options are springing up as Suchitoto responds to increasing numbers of visitors. The most luxurious place is the *Posada Suchitlán* on C 4 Pte (Ⓣ335 1064, Ⓦwww.laposada.com; ❻), featuring well-furnished rooms set around small patios, a pool and a restaurant serving food until 9pm. The most popular traveller's haunt is *Casa Antigua* (Ⓣ & Ⓕ274 5267; ❹) on Av 15 de Septiembre 15, complete with a shady hammock-filled courtyard to go with basic doubles and dorm rooms (US$10 per person). Just as good is *2 Gardenias* (Ⓣ335 1868, Ⓔhostal2gardenias@hotmail.com; ❹) at 3a Av Nte 48, with an attached restaurant and bar serving reasonably priced food and drinks. Ten minutes from Suchitoto by car, at km34.8 on the Carretera San Martín, the renovated hacienda *La Bermuda* (Ⓣ226 1839; ❺) offers a small range of excellent accommodation set amid magnificent gardens complete with swimming pool; there's also some fine walking in the area.

For **eating**, *La Fonda*, at the northern end of town on Av 15 de Septiembre, serves well-prepared fresh fish and meat dishes, and has great views over the lake. At the intersection of 3a Av Nte and Av 15 de Septiembre, *El Tejado* also has memorable views along with a small menu of mainly grilled meats; there is also a pool should you fancy a dip (US$3 a day) and gardens with hammocks for sunbathing. *Café Vistaconga*, signposted just around the corner from *El Tejado*, is a friendly place with great lake views, live music on Saturday nights and tours arranged to surrounding attractions. There are also a couple of small comedores on the main plaza, as well as *Tipico El Portal*, a popular choice for local dishes.

Aguilares and Cihuatán

The main highway north, CA-4, or the **Troncal del Norte**, runs a bumpy 95km from San Salvador to the Honduran border at El Poy. Some 35km from the capital, the pleasant workaday town of **AGUILARES** has little more to offer than a relaxing snack in the garden at *Río Bravo* on the Parque Central. Archeology buffs, though, might want to pass through, as 4km to the north sit the ruins of **Cihuatán** (Ⓦwww.cihuatan.org). The ruins make up the most important Postclassic site in the country, but most of the buildings have yet to be excavated and there is very little by way of information.

Originally covering an area of around four square kilometres, Cihuatán (meaning "Place of Women" in Nahaut) was founded sometime after the first waves of Pipils (or Toltecs) began arriving in El Salvador in the tenth century and destroyed for reasons unknown around 1200 AD. Most of the completed excavations have been of the so-called West Ceremonial Centre, stretching west from the Río Acelhuate, where around twenty structures have been identified, including stepped pyramids and a pelota court bearing a clear Mexican influence. Administered by Concultura (Edificio A-5, Third Floor, Centro de Gobierno, San Salvador; Ⓣ221 4364), there are no set **opening hours** at the site. To visit, take a taxi from Aguilares (or a bus heading north on the highway) and ask the guard for permission to look round. All **buses** running from the capital to Chalatenango or La Palma pass through Aguilares.

Twenty minutes north of Aguilares, at km46.5 on the Troncal del Norte, is **La Hacienda de Colima** (Ⓣ309 3335; ❹), an ageing hacienda set in stunning surroundings. Run by the local village *co-operativa*, there is a choice of private and dorm accommodation, with shared bath set around a pristine courtyard. The views of Embalse Cerrón Grande and the nearby volcanoes are magnificent, and local guides are available should you want to explore the area. Birdwatchers will also be delighted by the thousands of waterbirds that use the Embalse, including seven species of heron, white pelicans, and vast flocks of ducks and waders. To get here, take any bus headed for La Palma or El Poy and ask the driver to let you off at the entrance.

Chalatenango and Concepción Quetzaltepeque

From Aguilares, the highway continues north 19km to a major road junction at **Amayo**, home to a collection of scrubby comedores and bus shelters. From here, paved highways run west to the small town of Nueva Concepción, and east through agricultural and pasture lands along the fringes of the lake to **CHALATENANGO**. An important commercial centre, Chalatenango has the rough-and-ready feel of a frontier settlement, an atmosphere enhanced by the raised wooden walkways fronting the buildings of the centre. During the early 1980s this was a stronghold of the FMLN, and though much of the town's physical damage has been repaired, a huge military garrison still looms over the central plaza. Despite a lawless reputation in recent times, things have calmed down considerably and the town is now a pleasant place to while away a few days doing nothing.

Buses arrive and depart from along 3a Av Sur, where you'll find branches of most banks. From here it's only a couple of blocks north to the Parque Central. There's no earthly reason to stay in Chalatenango but should you wish to, *Hotel La Ceiba* (☎301 1080; ④) is the best bet. From the Parque, take the road behind the Alcaldía downhill, before following it around to the right. Rooms are simple, but all are en-suite with cable TV, a/c and telephone, and there are nice views out over the forested mountainsides. To **eat**, try *Hamburguesas Comir* opposite Banco Cuscatlán on C 4 Pte for very basic *minutas* and snacks. Rather better is *El Rincondíto Chalateco* next to the army barracks, with *comida a la* vista and a choice from the menu.

Incongruously, Chalatenango lies in a beautiful setting, southeast of the La Peña Mountains and overlooking the distant Cerron Grande to the west. **Walks** in the surrounding hills are possible, but seek local advice and don't go alone; in addition to the threat of muggings, some of the surrounding areas were mined during the war and have yet to be cleared. Just outside town to the east is the **Agua Fria Turicentro** (daily 7am–5pm; US$0.90), with swimming pools filled by the nearby Río Armulasco. Twelve kilometres northwest of Chalatenango, the village of **Concepción Quetzaltepeque** is notable for its **hammock** industry. Workshops and homes around the village turn out colourful items in nylon and, less commonly, cotton and *mezcal* fibre for prices at about half those in San Salvador; the hammocks are also sold in the market at Chalatenango at roughly the same bargain rate.

La Palma

From the Amayo junction, Highway CA-4 begins its climb up into the mountains of the Cordillera Metapán Alotepeque passing through the small, unexciting town of Tejutla, before making the slow, winding ascent to the Honduran border. The tortuous bus journey is compensated for by the views, with pine-clad mountains falling away to either side, and distant, hazy ranges and volcanoes seeming to stretch on forever (for the best views sit on the left-hand side of the bus on the way to La Palma from Tejutla).

LA PALMA, supposedly named after the indigenous custom of building houses out of palms, is a sleepy mountain village founded in 1915 under the name Dulce Nombre de la Palma. The climate is cooler here and the calm is really only broken during the annual **fiesta of Dulce Nombre de María**, in the third week of February. The village is chiefly famous for its **artesenías**, which are sold all over the country – naif-style wooden and ceramic handicrafts and toys, brightly painted with representations of people, villages and farming life. This cottage industry, instituted by Salvadoreño artist Fernando Llort in the 1970s, is the economic mainstay of the village, with workshops lining the main road. Most sell their goods on the spot and are pretty relaxed about visitors turning up to watch the work; prices are somewhat cheaper than in San Salvador. On the main road through the village is the **gallery** of Salvadoreño artist Alfredo Linares (Mon–Sat 9am–noon & 1–4pm), displaying his fine watercolours and pen-and-ink representations of the area and its peoples. Prices for the originals are not particularly low, but postcards and prints are also sold.

North of La Palma are several fine **hiking trails**, including El Salvador's highest mountain, **Cerro Pital** (2730m), 10km away on the border. A rough road branches east just before La Palma to run to Las Pilas on the lower slopes of the mountain; a dirt road also leads up from the village of **San Ignacio** (see below). Hiking to the summit is an adventure of two or three days, for which you will need to be fully equipped – the owners of the *Hotel La Palma* are a good source of information on shorter walks and guides.

Practicalities

There is plenty of good-value **accommodation** in La Palma. At the southern entrance to town, the comfortable and rustic *Hotel La Palma* (☎335 9012; ❹) is supposedly the oldest functioning hotel in El Salvador. A rather over-priced restaurant serves all meals. Opposite, an unnamed *posada* (☎335 9129; ❶) is a fine budget option, with clean simple rooms in attractive surroundings, though the bathroom on the roof is a bit inconvenient. *Hotel y Restaurante La Montaña Paseo El Pital* (☎305 9344; ❺) is the most de luxe option, with large, modern double rooms with a/c, TV and bathroom, along with a swimming pool and bar terrace with magnificent mountain views. Where the road forks, taking the right fork uphill leads past *Posada Real* (☎335 9009; ❹) with reasonably priced standard rooms with cable TV and a small restaurant-cum-*pupusería*. Other **places to eat** include the rather pricey though tasty *La Estancia* restaurant, on the main road through the village, brightened up by colourful murals of rural life; *Del Pueblo* on the right-hand fork is a family-run establishment with bags of character and a good-value menu featuring mostly meats, though there is a small breakfast selection. **Internet** access is at the Centro Regional Rivas (daily 9am–6pm; US$1.25 per hour). From the main road, take a left at the Banco Cuscatlán and head downhill past the **post office** for four blocks.

To the Honduran border

The highway continues past La Palma to the Honduran border at El Poy, 11km away, a thirty-minute journey by bus. The village of **SAN IGNACIO**, 6km from La Palma and much quieter, also has a few craft **workshops** and two **places to stay**. In town, *La Posada de San Ignacio* (☎352 9419; ❷–❸) on the square has simple log cabins with shared bath, or rather better standard rooms with modern ceramic bathrooms. The four-star *Resort Hotel Entre Pinos* (☎335 9322, ⓦwww.hotelentrepinos.com; ❾) is on the highway, just before the village. The very comfortable rooms have bathrooms with hot water and great views, plus a restaurant, pools, bar, hiking trails, a small zoo and horseback-riding (US$7 per hour). Just short of El Poy, a road branching to the left crosses the Río Lempa and runs to the village of **CITALÁ**, 1km away. From here a daily bus leaves at 5am, running west along a rough but scenic mountain road to **Metapán**, for access to Bosque Montecristo (see p.358) and the Guatemalan border at Anguiatú, a journey of three to four hours. There's a basic *posada* (no phone; ❶) close to the centre of the village.

EL POY itself is a drab, dusty village with a collection of small comedores and general stores. Crossing the border here is straightforward and quick, with entry and exit windows next to each other in the same building; there is a US$2 entrance charge for Honduras, but no exit charges for El Salvador. Many trucks use this route, but private traffic is light; crossing early in the day is advisable. The last **bus** from the border for La Palma and San Salvador leaves at 4.30pm. On the Honduran side, buses run the 10km to Nueva Ocotepeque (see p.413) every forty minutes or so until 5pm, departing from just the other side of the gate that marks the beginning of Honduras.

Travel details

Buses

Set timetables for buses do not exist, but departures are frequent, every 15 minutes or so on popular routes, and every 30 minutes on less well-trodden ones. Buses are numbered, usually stating the destination as well; route numbers, along with estimated travel times, are given below.

Ahuanchapán to: Chalchuapa (#210; 1hr); Las Chinamas (#263; 1hr); Santa Ana (#210; 1hr 30min); Sonsonate (#249; 2hr 30min).

La Unión to: Conchagua (#382; 30min); Playitas (#418; 30min); San Miguel (#324; 1hr 30min); San Salvador (#304; 3–4hr); Santa Rosa de Lima (#342; 1hr 30min); El Tamarindo (#383; 1hr 20min).

Metapán to: Angiatú (#211A; 30min); Santa Ana (#235; 1hr 30min).

San Miguel to: El Amatillo via Santa Rosa de Lima (#330; 1hr 30min); Conchagua (#324; 1hr); Corinto (#327; 2hr); La Unión (#324; 1 hr); Perquín (#332; 3hr); Playa El Cuco (#320; 1hr); San Francisco Gotera (#328; 1hr); San Salvador (#301; 3–4hr), El Triunfo (#377; 1hr); Usulután (#373; 1hr).

San Salvador, Terminal de Occidente to: Ahuachapán (#202; 3hr 30min); Las Chinamas (#406; 4hr 30min); Desvío Opico para Joya de Cerén (#108; 1 hr); La Libertad (#102; 1 hr); Metapán (#201A; 3hr 30min); Playa Los Cóbanos (#207; 2hr 30min); Santa Ana via San Andrés (#201 1hr 20min–2hr); Sonsonate (#205; 1hr 30 min).

San Salvador, Terminal de Oriente to: Chalatenango (#125; 2hr 30min); Ilobasco (#111; 1 hr 20min); La Palma/El Poy (#119; 4hr 30min); San Miguel (#301; 3–4hr); San Francisco Gotera (#305; 3–4hr); San Vicente (#116; 1hr 30min); Santa Rosa de Lima (#306; 3–5hr); Suchitoto (#129; 1hr 30min); La Unión (#304; 3–4hr); Usulután (#302; 2hr 30min).

San Salvador, Terminal del Sur to: Usulután (#302; 2hr 30min); Zacatecoluca (#133; 1hr 30min).

San Vicente to: San Salvador (#116; 1hr 30min); Usulután (#417; 2hr).

Sonsonate to: Acajutla (#252; 30min); Ahuachapán (#249; 2hr 30min); Barra de Santiago (#285; 1hr 30min); La Hachadura (#259; 2hr); Izalco (#53A; 30min); La Libertad (#287; 1hr 30min); Nahuizalco (#53D; 30min); Playa Los Cóbanos (#257; 45min); Santa Ana (#209; 3hr); San Salvador (#205; 1hr 30min).

Usulután to: San Miguel (#373; 1hr); San Salvador (#302; 2hr 30min); El Triunfo (#363; 1hr); Zacatecoluca (#171; 1hr 30min).

Zacatecoluca to: Costa del Sol (#193; 1hr 30min); San Salvador (#133; 1hr 30min); Usulután (#171; 1hr 30min).

International buses

Santa Ana to: Guatemala City (hourly from 5.30am to 4pm; 4–6hr; buy ticket one day in advance from Melva International, C 25 Pte, 6a–8a Av Sur ⓣ440 1608).

San Salvador to: Managua (2 daily; 11hr); Panama (1 daily; 24hr); San José (2 daily; 18hr); Tapachula via Guatemala (15 daily; 6–10 hr); Tegucigalpa (3 daily; 7hr). For more details see main text (pp.306–307).

Honduras

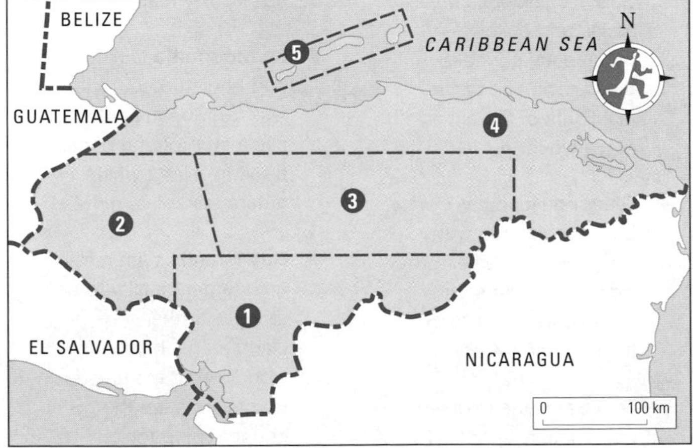

Highlights 368
Introduction and Basics 369
4.1 Tegucigalpa and the south 385
4.2 The central and western highlands 403
4.3 Olancho 426
4.4 The north coast and Mosquitia 432
4.5 The Bay Islands 460
Travel details 474

Honduras Highlights

* **Lago Yojoa** Dramatically surrounded by mountains, the shimmering Lago Yojoa is a bird-watcher's paradise. p.406

* **Copán Ruinas** Spectacularly preserved stelae and building ornamentation make these ruins one of the highlights of the entire Maya world. p.418

* **Olancho** Honduras's wild East is peppered with cloudforest reserves providing the most stunning and challenging hiking in the country. p.426

* **Tela** Set in the middle of three national parks, Tela is more than just a relaxed beach town. p.441

* **La Ceiba** The best nightlife in the country reaches a crescendo during the May carnival, when this seaside city goes party mad. p.446

* **La Mosquitia** Isolated and undisturbed, roadless La Mosquitia is literally a step off the beaten track to a land where nature still rules. p.455

* **Bay Islands** With a truly unique personality to go along with their Caribbean vibe, it is no wonder that the unique Bay Islands are the country's top tourist destination. p.460

Introduction and Basics

The original Banana Republic, a byword for corruption and poverty, Honduras is all too often rushed through by foreign tourists. Most head straight for the ruins of Copán, one of the finest Maya sites in the region. Some even miss that, in their haste to get to the palm-fringed beaches and clear Caribbean waters of the Bay Islands. Beyond these prime tourist sites, however, is a land of inspiring, often untouched natural beauty.

The second-largest country in Central America after Nicaragua, Honduras sprawls from the Atlantic to the Pacific coast, from Caribbean flatlands through the cooler mountainous interior, and south to the sun-baked shores of the Golfo de Fonseca. West to east, the forested highlands on the border with Guatemala give way to the vast, undeveloped savannas and wetlands of the Mosquitia. Ecotourism is a relatively new concept here, but more and more Hondurans are becoming aware of the role the country's extensive network of **national parks and reserves** plays in protecting irreplaceable natural resources. Almost a quarter of Honduran territory is protected, but a lack of funding and growing pressure on the land mean this status often exists more on paper than in reality. Nonetheless, the remoter reaches of the parks still host an astonishing array of flora and fauna, amid some of the finest stretches of virgin **cloudforest** and **tropical forest** in Central America.

Honduras's close alliance with the US, while preventing the bitter conflicts that beset its neighbours in the 1980s, has not alleviated the country's acute **social and economic problems**. After Nicaragua, this is Latin America's poorest nation, with levels of deprivation that can be disturbing to witness: just over half of Hondurans live in poverty and a quarter of the population is illiterate. Exacerbating the pressure on economic and environmental resources is a rapidly growing population, now approaching seven million, much of it absorbed by the ever-increasing shantytowns ringing the main cities.

Where to go

Though a visit to the capital **Tegucigalpa** is by no means essential, a stay here, however short, is made welcome by the presence of facilities and services you won't find elsewhere in the country. While on the small side, the city has a reasonable range of places to eat, drink and make merry. An hour on the bus from Tegucigalpa brings you to the peaceful mountain towns of **Santa Lucía** and **Valle de Ángeles**, with a profusion of local crafts and, a little further on, some excellent hiking close by in the cloudforest of **La Tigra**. To the south is the little-visited getaway of **Isla El Tigre**, becalmed in the warm waters of the Golfo de Fonseca and perfect for a few days spent doing nothing much at all.

If coming from Guatemala, you'll more than likely arrive in the western highlands close to the Maya ruins of **Copán**, one of the best-preserved archeological sites in Central America. It's an arduous trip from the capital, but there are some worthwhile places to break the journey, notably **Comayagua**, a couple of hours from Tegucigalpa, the former colonial capital, home to a wealth of historic churches and a couple of good museums. The equally charming colonial city of **Santa Rosa de Copán** also makes a logical destination on the way to or from Copán, while dusty **Gracias** benefits from its close proximity to the glorious **Parque Nacional Celaque**.

In the east of the country, the rugged, sparsely populated region known as **Olancho** is home to the rarely visited national parks of **La Muralla** and **Sierra de Agalta**. The latter contains the most extensive stretch of virgin cloudforest remaining in Central America. Heading towards the Caribbean you're almost certain to pass through Honduras's energetic second city, **San Pedro Sula**, the commercial centre of the country and a useful transport hub. Just an hour or so south of town is one of Central America's premier spots for ornithologists, the placid, fresh waters of **Lago de Yojoa**.

0
100 km
N
CARIBBEAN SEA
BELIZE
Punta Gorda
Golfo de Honduras
Roatán
Guanaja
Utila
Bay Islands (Islas de la Bahía)
Cayos Cochinos
Palacios
Las Marías
Brus Laguna
Río Plátano
Mosquitia
Puerto Lempira
Dulce Nombre de Culmi
GUATEMALA
Lívingston
Puerto Barrios
Puerto Cortés
Omoa
Tela
La Ceiba
Trujillo
Lago de Izabal
Corinto
San Pedro Sula
CA-13
CA-4
CA-20
CA-5
CA-39
La Entrada
El Florido
Copán
CA-11
Santa Rosa de Copán
Lago de Yojoa
Chiquimula
Santa Barbara
Esquipulas
Siguatepeque
Agua Caliente
Nueva Ocotepeque
Gracias
Comayagua
Catacamas
Juticalpa
CA-15
CA11-A
El Poy
La Esperanza
TEGUCIGALPA
Danlí
EL SALVADOR
Las Manos
SAN SALVADOR
El Amatillo
CA-1
NICARAGUA
El Espino
Isla El Tigre
Choluteca
PACIFIC OCEAN
Golfo de Fonseca

Frequent buses fan out from San Pedro to the **north coast**, with its pristine white beaches, clear warm waters and endless sun. **La Ceiba**, a vibrant city with a thriving nightlife, is the departure point for the **Bay Islands**, where world-class diving can be enjoyed in a location with a rich cultural mix. **Tela** and **Trujillo** are good-sized towns with great beaches, while the fishing village of **Omoa** moves at a quieter pace, and is increasingly popular with tourists wanting to kick back in the sun. For a glimpse of a different way of life, make for the friendly **Garífuna villages** dotted along the coast. Beaches aren't the only reason to hang around here. Within easy reach is the wetland reserve of **Punta Sal**, near Tela, sheltering a multiplicity of bird and marine life amid mangrove swamps and marshes. It requires a little more planning to get into the heart of **Pico Bonito**, a mountainous reserve near La Ceiba, but the effort is spectacularly rewarded. The jewel in the crown of Honduras's natural resources, however, is the biosphere reserve of the **Río Plátano** in **Mosquitia**. Encompassing one of the finest remaining stretches of virgin tropical rainforest in Central America, the region is largely uninhabited and a trip here really does get you off the beaten track.

When to go

As in much of Central America, the **climate** in Honduras is dictated more by altitude than by season. In the central highlands, the weather is temperate, pleasantly warm in the daytime and cool at night. It's hardly surprising that the Spanish focused their attention here, abandoning the flatlands and the northern coast, which can be unpleasantly hot at any time of year. While the Pacific and Caribbean coasts at least offer the relief of breezes and cooling rain showers, San Pedro Sula and other lowland towns can be positively scorching in summer.

Honduras's **rainy season**, known as "winter" (*invierno*), runs from May to November, though how much it will affect your trip depends on where you're travelling. In much of the country it rains for only a few hours in the late afternoon, though along the northern coast and in Mosquitia rain is a constant feature all year round. October and November are perhaps the only months you might want to avoid these parts: this is **hurricane season**, when heavy rains can cause serious flooding, washing away roads and cutting off all transport.

Getting around

There are a number of alternatives for **getting around** Honduras, depending on how fast you want to travel and where you want to get to. Buses are the cheapest way to go, but occasional flights cut down on the long, often tedious journeys through the country's mountainous terrain. Driving allows you to take things at your own pace and to reach the more remote areas that are rarely served by buses, while boats are the most atmospheric way of reaching the Bay Islands. There's also an extremely slow, cheap and uncomfortable weekly train service running along the north coast suitable for enthusiasts only.

Buses

Bus services in Honduras are well-organised with frequent departures from the main transport hubs of Tegucigalpa, San Pedro Sula and La Ceiba, backed up by networks of local services. On the longer intercity routes there's usually a choice of bus, with an increasing number of luxurious a/c express buses (*ejecutivos* or *lujos*) plus comfortable services with a few scheduled stops (*directos*); local buses are typically much slower, stopping whenever somebody hails them and cramming people on until they are hanging out of the doors. Timetables tend to be strictly observed, so plan ahead and double-check departure times if you want to avoid getting stuck. **Fares** are extremely low on most routes, at around US$0.80 an hour or less, though prices can triple on some of the really smart services – travelling between Tegucigalpa and La Ceiba can cost as much as US$18, depending on the service you choose. For intercity trips, it's worth buying a ticket well in advance, as you'll usually be issued with a seat number.

Taxis

Taxis operate in all the main towns, tooting as they cruise by anyone who looks remotely in need of a lift. Meters are nonexistent, so

Overland routes to and from Honduras

Honduras has land borders with **Guatemala**, **El Salvador** and **Nicaragua**, while a boat crossing runs weekly from Puerto Cortés to Placencia in **Belize**. Though it's possible to cross the border into Nicaragua via La Mosquitia, it's far easier to use the Las Manos (see p.399) or El Espino (see p.402) crossings in the southeast. Not far from here is the El Amatillo border (see p.400) with eastern El Salvador. The busiest border crossing with Guatemala is in the southwest of the country at Agua Caliente (see p.414), while the atmospheric border post of El Poy (see p.413) for La Palma, El Salvador, is close by. For tourists, the most frequently used crossing from Guatemala is at El Florido for Copán Ruinas (see p.424). A northerly border crossing to Guatemala at Corinto (see p.441) is currently very slow, though facilities are being developed.

always agree on a price before getting in. For safety reasons, it makes sense to use taxis to get around in the big cities at night. Expect to pay US$1.75–2.25 for a city ride in Tegucigalpa or San Pedro, while in smaller towns US$0.65 is the standard fare. For longer trips it can be worth hiring a taxi for a few hours, or even the whole day.

Driving and hitching

Renting a **car** is the simplest way to get to the more isolated national parks without having to rely on buses. Well-maintained highways connect the main cities, running between the north and south coasts and along the coasts themselves. There are also numerous dirt roads connecting the isolated villages of the highlands. Bear in mind, however, that these can be in quite appalling condition for large parts of the year, and at times completely impassable; check local advice on conditions before setting out. **Rates** start at around US$58 a day for a small car, US$90 for larger models and 4WDs, including insurance and emergency assistance. **Hitching** is very common in rural areas, and generally safe. Keep an eye out for pick-up trucks with lots of people in the back, and stick out your thumb. You're expected to offer payment at the end of the ride, usually the same as the bus fare.

Cycling

Cycling is a scenic way to travel around under your own steam, although negotiating the main highways can sometimes be a hair-raising experience. In the main tourist centres bikes can be hired (around US$4.50 a day), but in most places you'll need your own bike, preferably a mountain bike to cope with the terrain. Since bicycles are a common form of transport in rural areas, there are repair shops in most places, although it's wise to anticipate potential problems and come equipped with your own tools and spares.

Boats

A fast scheduled **boat** service – the *MV Galaxy II* – operates between La Ceiba and Roatán/Utila, running in both directions daily. An additional service to Utila – the *Utila Princess* – creates competition that keeps prices down to that island. Tickets are slightly cheaper than the airfare and the journey takes an hour to Utila (US$6.60) and two hours to Roatán (US$12.10). There are also unscheduled **cargo boat** departures for Mosquitia and Guanaja from La Ceiba and Trujillo – the only way to find out about these is to go to the dock and ask.

Planes

Internal **flights** are very affordable in Honduras, with all prices fixed by the government, and faced with a six- or seven-hour bus journey from Tegucigalpa to the north coast, you may prefer to fly. Flying is also the quickest way to reach the Bay Islands, and the most convenient way to get to the Mosquitia.

A small number of domestic airlines offer competitive fares, with frequent departures between Tegucigalpa and San Pedro Sula, La Ceiba and the Bay Islands. A one-way ticket between Tegucigalpa and San Pedro costs around US$45, whilst La Ceiba to Utila or Roatán is US$28 and La Ceiba–Palacios around US$40. There's a **departure tax** of US$2 for internal flights and US$27 for international flights.

Costs, money and banks

Honduras's currency is the **lempira** (L), which consists of 100 centavos. Coins come as 1, 2, 5, 10, 20 and 50 centavos and notes as 1, 2, 5, 10, 20, 50, 100 and 500 lempiras. For day-to-day living, Honduras works out extremely cheap for foreigners. At the current **exchange rate** of L17.9 to US$1 (L32 to £1), a cup of coffee typically costs around US$0.30, a soft drink around US$0.45 (L8) and fresh juice US$0.55 (L10). A meal in an ordinary café will be around US$2.50–3.30 (L45–60).

Honduras has a number of national **banks**, of which the biggest are Banco Atlántida, Bancahsa, Banco de Occidente and Ficensa. All of these change **travellers' cheques** – American Express is the most widely accepted brand, while Visa and Thomas Cook are also usually cashed without a fuss; other brands are frequently rejected, especially in more remote areas. When cashing travellers' cheques you will often be asked to show proof of purchase receipts.

Acceptance of foreign credit cards in ATMs can be a hit-and-miss affair. As a rule Visa is more widely accepted than other cards, but in any case if your PIN number is longer than four digits your card will be rejected. Visa cardholders can get cash advances in several banks, including Banco Atlántida; MasterCard holders will have much more of a problem – currently only Credomatic (with branches in Tegucigalpa, San Pedro Sula and La Ceiba) accepts this card. All debit cards, including Cirrus and Plus, are currently useless in Honduras except for the Visa debit card.

Banks in Tegucigalpa and San Pedro Sula are usually **open** Monday to Friday 9am to 4.30pm and Saturday 9am to noon; in smaller towns most shut for an hour at lunchtime and close up to an hour earlier in the afternoons.

Information

The helpful **Instituto Hondureño de Turismo**, in the Edificio Europa, Av Ramón Cruz and C República de México, Tegucigalpa (℡222 2124), can provide general **information** about where to go and what to see in the country. They also have booths at the Tegucigalpa and San Pedro Sula airports, and a free information service in the US (℡800/410-9608), as well as good links with the main tour operators and the luxury hotels. The office is also a good place to get hold of a copy of *Honduras Tips*, an invaluable local guide to what is going on throughout the country.

National parks and reserves are overseen by the government forestry agency, **COHDEFOR** (Apdo Postal #1378; ℡223 7703, ⓕ223 2653). If you intend spending much time in any of the parks, it's worth visiting their headquarters in Tegucigalpa for detailed information on flora and fauna. The office is a little difficult to find, just off the Carretera al Norte in Comayagüela. A large number of other private organisations are responsible for other national parks and reserves, though their roles are more administrative and they are likely to refer you to the Instituto de Turismo or private tour companies if you ask them for information.

Websites

Visitors to Honduras are relatively well-served by the Web, with a variety of **websites** aimed specifically at tourists.

ⓦ**www.honduras.com** The country's official website is unsurprisingly one of the best general websites on Honduras.

ⓦ**www.hondurasinfo.hn** Best for business-orientated visitors with the latest economic and political developments regularly updated.

ⓦ**www.hondurastips.honduras.com** The definitive guide to the country, also published as an irreplaceable monthly magazine (available free in hotels) detailing all the sights and latest developments of interest to tourists.

ⓦ**www.letsgohonduras.com** The website of the Instituto de Turismo makes for a good introduction to the main attractions and offers numerous organised tour packages.

ⓦ**www.travel-to-honduras.com** General site covering a range of subjects from business and tourism, to Spanish schools and volunteer work.

Accommodation

The choice of **accommodation** is widest in Tegucigalpa, San Pedro Sula, Copán and along the north coast, where there's a range of rooms to suit all pockets; outside these areas, the choice begins to narrow. Except in very remote regions, you'll always find a room, but don't count on it being particularly comfortable. Of the Bay Islands, Utila is the cheapest, with prices not much higher than on the mainland. Roatán has a few places catering to backpackers and a good selection of mid-range and luxury hotels, while Guanaja is geared heavily towards the luxury, all-inclusive, scuba-diving package holiday market.

On the mainland, expect to **pay** around US$5.50 per person for a basic, acceptable room outside the capital and big cities, more if you want a private bath. Paying US$10 and above will secure you a well-furnished room, with extras such as TV, a/c and hot water. A twelve percent tax is occasionally added to the bill; an additional five percent "tourist tax" is also added in some luxury places. Prices are higher in Tegucigalpa and San Pedro Sula: US$3 rooms do exist but are invariably located in the worst areas; decent budget rooms begin at around US$7 and mid-range at US$20, while those in the top hotels start at around US$85. That said, backpacker-style accommodation is beginning to spring up in some areas, including Tegucigalpa, generally representing excellent value for money and a relaxed ambiance. Normally the only time you need to reserve in advance is at Semana Santa or during a big local festival, such as the May Carnival in La Ceiba.

The only formal provisions for **camping** are found at Omoa, Copán Ruinas and in some of the national parks. Elsewhere, pitching a tent is very much an ad hoc affair. Tempting though they may seem, the north-coast beaches are **not safe** to be on after dark and camping is highly inadvisable. Elsewhere, if you intend to camp, make sure you ask permission from the landowner first.

See p.36 for an explanation of the accommodation price codes.

Food and drink

The range of **places to eat** in the big cities is wide and increasing all the time. Smart restaurants serving European, Latin American and Honduran cuisine abound in Tegucigalpa and San Pedro Sula, and the more touristy places, such as Copán and the Bay Islands, have a selection of excellent restaurants. Elsewhere, the choice narrows to comedores serving set lunches and dinners, consisting of the usual mix of beans, rice, tortillas and meat, and – very often – a Chinese restaurant. Although the authenticity of these is often questionable, portions are routinely big enough for two and they represent good value to the budget traveller.

A Spanish **menu reader** can be found on p.870.

What to eat

Honduran **specialities** worth trying include *anafre* and *tapado*. The former is a fondue-like dish of cheese, beans or meat, or a mixture of some or all of these. The latter is a rich vegetable stew, often with meat or fish added. North-coast cuisine has a strong Caribbean influence and fresh fish and seafoods feature heavily. *Guisado* (spicy chicken stew) and *sopa de caracol* (conch stew with coconut milk, spices, potatoes and vegetables) are dishes that should be tried at least once. *Pan de coco* (coconut bread) is often served with meals in the north and makes a delicious snack in itself; Tela in particular is famed for its coconut rolls, sold on the beach by women and children. Turtle eggs are widely sold on the coasts, but should obviously be avoided. Probably the most common street snack, sold all over the country, is the *baleada*, a white-flour tortilla filled with beans, cheese and cream; two or three of these constitute a decent-sized meal.

Drinking

Though there are a few venerable European-style cafés in the big cities serving fine **coffee**, most places serve up a weak brew made from poor-quality beans. **Fruit juices** are usually excellent, however, and available everywhere, most commonly in the form of *licuados* or *batidos* (blended with milk), or *frescos* (blended with water). Orange and other fruit juices are widely sold in cartons, but invariably have sugar added. Tap **water** is unsafe to drink; bottled, purified water is sold everywhere and many hotels supply it free to guests. The usual brands of **fizzy drink** are ubiquitous. Honduras produces five brands of **beer**, all of them made by the same company. Salvavida and Imperial are heavier lagers, Port Royal slightly lighter, and Nacional and Polar very light and quite tasteless. **Rum** (*ron*) is also distilled in the country, as is the Latin American rotgut, *aguardiente*. Imported European and South American wines are available in more expensive restaurants, though at a price. Adventurous connoisseurs of alcohol might wish to try *guifiti* in the Garífuna villages of the north coast, a distilled moonshine flavoured with cloves and tasting suspiciously like toothache tincture.

Opening hours, festivals and holidays

Business hours are generally Monday to Friday 9am to noon and 2 to 4.30 or 5pm, and sometimes from 9am to noon on Saturdays. Government offices work Monday to Friday 8.30am to 4.30pm, often with an hour's break for lunch. Government offices, post offices and many other businesses close on national holidays and the first Monday after an election. The major **public holidays** are listed in the box on above. All towns and villages have an annual **fiesta patronale** to commemorate the local saint. Some last only a day, some for a week or more, with a variety of events attracting people from far and wide. One of the largest is Carnaval in La Ceiba, more correctly known as **La Feria de San Isidro**. Held during the week leading up to the third Saturday in May, the festivities culminate in a street parade through the centre of the city, followed by performances of live music on sound stages until the early morning. The celebrations in San Pedro Sula in the last week of June, culminating on June 29 (a holiday in the city), and in Punta Gorda (Roatán), from April 6 to 12, celebrating the arrival of the Garífuna, are both worth making an effort to get to. The biggest festival of all, however, is that of the **Virgen de Suyapa** – patron saint of the country – in the first week of February, when pilgrims from around the country flock to Tegucigalpa to worship and celebrate.

Public holidays

Jan 1 New Year's Day
March/April Semana Santa: Thursday, Friday and Saturday before Easter Sunday
April 14 Day of the Americas
May 1 Labour Day
Sept 15 Independence Day
Oct 3 Birth of Francisco Morazán
Oct 12 Discovery of America
Oct 21 Armed Forces Day
Dec 25 Christmas Day

Communications

Letters posted from Honduras generally take around a week to get to the US and up to two weeks to reach Europe. Receiving letters via poste restante, however, is more hit and miss: mail may take weeks to work its way through the system, and there's always the chance it won't be given to you when it does arrive. The main **post offices** in Tegucigalpa and San Pedro Sula are open Monday to Friday 8am to 7pm and until 1pm on Saturdays; smaller offices open from Monday to Friday 8am to 5pm, with a lunch break, and on Saturdays until noon.

International phone calls are astronomically expensive from **Hondutel** offices (there's a branch in every town). A three-minute call to the US or Canada currently costs US$11.50, to Europe US$14.80 and to Australia or New Zealand US$18.20; it's also possible to make collect calls for a hefty fee. The branches in Tegucigalpa and San Pedro Sula are open 24 hours; elsewhere, offices are open daily from 7am to 9pm.

Unsurprisingly, given the rates, most travellers choose to avoid Hondutel when possible. A better bet is to visit cybercafés that offer

Useful phone numbers

☎**191** National phone operator
☎**192** Information
☎**195** Cruz Roja (Red Cross)
☎**197** International operator
☎**198** Fire brigade
☎**199** Police

Web phone calls, which cut international call rates to the price of surfing the Net, though line connections are notoriously crackle- and delay-prone. Though Hondutel have tried to make the practice illegal, it persists and connections are improving, though the service is generally only available for international calls.

Another alternative option is to purchase an **international calling card** from your home phone company before you travel. Once in Honduras, AT&T cardholders should dial ⓣ8000 123 for an operator, while MCI cardholders should dial ⓣ8000 121.

There are also **public phone** booths scattered around the major towns, which take 20 and 50 centavo coins; some also now accept Hondutel phonecards (L50 and L100). Local calls are very inexpensive, national calls cost L2 for a three-minute call. **Fax** services are available in most Hondutel branches (US$1.40 per page to send to North America, US$2.30 to the EU, US$2.45 to Australia or NZ), but rates are cheaper in cybercafés. Note that there are **no area phone codes**; the international country code for Honduras is ⓣ504.

Internet use has mushroomed in Honduras in the last few years, and many hotels and businesses are now on-line. There are also cybercafés in all the big cities and in most places where travellers congregate. Rates vary considerably: from US$0.55–1.35 per hour on the mainland, US$2–2.75 on Utila (where competition has drastically reduced rates over the last 12 months), to an astronomical US$10–12 on the other Bay Islands.

The media

There are six daily **newspapers** in Honduras, though all are owned by politicians, so don't expect dynamic investigative reporting – the Honduran papers overwhelmingly favour the opinions of their proprietors. *El Periódico*, *La Tribuna* and *El Heraldo* are published in Tegucigalpa, *La Prensa*, *El Tiempo* and *El Nuevo Día* in San Pedro Sula. Of these, *El Tiempo* is the most liberal, and has been regularly critical in the past of the activities of government and the armed forces. *La Tribuna* is also fairly moderate in its political stance; *El Heraldo* and *La Prensa* – which has the highest circulation at around 42,000 – are both conservative, with good international coverage. Though all the print media impose a certain level of self-censorship, particularly when reporting the actions of the armed forces and government, reporting standards are steadily improving.

There are two excellent **English-language** publications. The weekly *Honduras This Week* newspaper has in-depth coverage of Honduran events, as well as tourist and business information and a superb website (ⓦwww.marrder.com/htw). It's available from English-language bookshops in the capital and in the big hotels in Tegucigalpa, San Pedro Sula, Copán, La Ceiba and Roatán. *Honduras Tips* (ⓦwww.hondurastips.honduras.com) is an informative free **magazine**, geared to tourists, with useful hotel, restaurant, bar and nightlife listings, and transport information (including pretty accurate nationwide bus timetables), and you would do well to carry a copy with you. You'll find it in many hotels and guesthouses.

Honduras's airwaves are filled with over 150 **radio stations**, most in private ownership, which broadcast to some 3.5 million listeners weekly; Radio Honduras is the government-owned station. All the six terrestrial **television** networks are in private hands, with around one-third of households owning sets; there are also numerous cable networks broadcasting films, news and light entertainment from Latin America and the US. Programmes on US channels are usually in English with Spanish subtitles.

Shops and markets

While the **artesenías** available in Honduras may not be as wide-ranging or as colourful as those in Guatemala, there are a number of crafts that are instantly recognizable as Honduran. The range of **carved wooden goods**, particularly those produced around Valle de Ángeles is extensive, from simple bowls and dishes to elaborate chests and doors, while in the highlands and around Copán, **ceramics**, including replicas of Maya pottery and artefacts, are produced. On the north coast the speciality is cotton **hammocks**, along with **Garífuna** handicrafts, music and paintings. Good-quality

cigars are sold in Tegucigalpa, Santa Rosa de Copán and Copán, and a number of companies in Tegucigapla and San Pedro Sula sell high-quality **leather goods** at around half European prices.

For everyday goods, the general **markets** in every town usually provide a bewildering range of cheap clothing, food and household goods. More expensive boutiques and supermarkets are limited to Tegucigalpa, Santa Rosa de Copán and San Pedro Sula.

Safety and the police

Large parts of Honduras remain relatively safe for tourists, and travel in rural areas is generally an informative exercise in mutual trust and respect. In the cities however, **street crime** is a concern; pickpocketing and bag or jewellery snatches are predominantly opportunistic and can be prevented by exercising basic caution. While the centre of Tegucigalpa is reasonably safe at night, consider taking a taxi if it's late or you're on your own; Comayagüela, particularly around the market area, is not considered safe to walk around at all at night.

Government crackdowns on "Mara" culture have drastically reduced the amount of gang-related crime in reent years and the installation of tourist police in towns like Tela has had a positive effect on crimes aimed at tourists. However, common sense should still be exercised at all times: don't flash around money or valuables, and try to remain aware of where you are and how you are returning to your hotel.

The **police**, though now separate from the armed forces, are unlikely, overall, to be of much help if something does happen, but any incidents of theft should be reported for insurance purposes.

Work and study

Honduras is waking up to the demand for **language schools**, though it's by no means in the same league as neighbouring Guatemala, with just a few schools operating in Tegucigalpa, Copán and La Ceiba. Courses can be taken for any length of time you choose and always include the option of staying with a family. Schools generally also arrange cultural and social activities.

Opportunities for paid employment are few and far between in Honduras. Perhaps easiest to come by are jobs **teaching English** at one of the small language schools – try under listings for *Academias de Idiomas* in the yellow pages. On the other hand there are thousands of vacancies for **voluntary workers** (Honduras has more Peace Corps people than any other country in Latin America).

Language schools

La Ceiba

Centro Internacional de Idiomas Av San Isidro 12–13 (Ⓣ & Ⓕ440 1557, Ⓦwww.hondurasspanish.com). Small and friendly school offering weekly courses of four hours a day one-to-one tuition for US$220 with homestay, US$145 without. Air-conditioned classrooms; transfer credit is available from US universities.

Copán

Escuela de Español Ixbalanque a block and a half west of the Parque (Ⓣ651 4432, Ⓦwww.ixbalanque.com). Runs a one-week course for US$190 including homestay, twenty hours of tuition and afternoon activities.

Guacamaya one block north of the Parque (Ⓣ651 4553, Ⓦwww.guacamaya.com). Similar courses to the Ixbalanque school for $200 per week.

Tegucigalpa

Conversa Av República de Brasil 2419, Colonia Palmira (Ⓣ236 5170, Ⓦwww.world-wide.edu/honduras/conversa). Professionally run school with flexible study programmes – twenty hours of tuition plus homestay costs US$185 per week.

History

When the Spanish arrived in the sixteenth century, Honduras was populated by a number of different tribes. In the northeast – the Mosquitia, parts of the north coast and Olancho – were the **Pech** and **Sumu**, related to the South American Chibchans, while the north-central region was occupied by the **Tolupan**, migrants from possibly as far away as the present United States. Western Honduras was home to the **Maya**, while the **Lenca**, also believed to be descended from the Chibchans, inhabited the centre of the country. The **Pipils**, migrants from present-day Mexico, lived to the south, along the Golfo de Fonseca, with the Toltec-speaking **Chorotega**, also from Mexico, inhabiting the area around Choluteca.

Of these, it is the **Maya** about whom most is known. Archeologists believe that settlers began moving south into the Río Copán valley from around 1000 BC; construction of the city of **Copán** began around 100 AD. By the time of the founding of the royal dynasty in 426 AD, Copán exerted control as far north as the Valle de Sula, east to Lago Yojoa and west into what is now Guatemala. Home to the governing and religious elite, and supporting a total population of around 24,000, the city was the pre-eminent Maya centre for scientific and artistic development; today it is one of the world's foremost archeological sites. When, for reasons which are not entirely clear, Maya civilization began to collapse around 900 AD, Copán was abandoned, although the area it previously controlled remained inhabited.

Following the collapse of the Maya empire, the **Lenca** became the predominant group in Honduras, absorbing other indigenous cultures and settling in small, scattered communities, supported by subsistence agriculture and hunting and gathering. The Lenca established trade links as far north as Mexico and interacted peaceably with the Maya and Pipil.

Discovery and conquest

On July 30, 1502, on his fourth and final voyage, **Columbus** arrived off the island of Guanaja. Naming it the "Isla de Pinos" (Island of Pines), he then continued exploring the Central American coastline, accompanied by a Pech trader he had encountered coming from the direction of Guatemala. Sailing east along the coast, the fleet first stopped at Punta Caxinas, close to present-day Trujillo, where the first Catholic Mass in Latin America was held on August 14, 1502. Sailing on into harsh storms, the fleet rounded a cape where, encountering calmer waters, Columbus is reputed to have exclaimed "Gracias a Dios que hemos salido de estas honduras" (Thank God we have now left these depths), christening both the cape – Cabo Gracias a Dios – and eventually the country. Initially, however, the Spanish called these new lands Higueras, the name used by the indigenous groups they encountered.

Twenty years elapsed before the conquistadors returned to take possession of the new territory, the nominal conqueror being **Gil González Dávila**, who sailed up the Pacific coast from Panamá. In 1524, however, **Hernán Cortés** despatched his lieutenant **Cristóbal de Olid** to claim the whole of the isthmus on Cortés's behalf. Olid landed on the north coast in May 1524 and founded the first Spanish settlement, Triunfo de la Cruz on the Bahía de Tela; his own claims on the territory were abruptly ended by assassination later that year. Cortés himself, desperate to stamp his ownership on the new lands, left Mexico for Honduras in 1525, arriving on the north coast in the spring and ordering the founding of Puerto Caballos (now Puerto Cortés) and Trujillo. Aware that his absence from Mexico was undermining his position, however, Cortés returned there in April 1525. Five years later

Pedro de Alvarado, despatched from Guatemala, arrived to govern the territory. Under Alvarado, the city of San Pedro Sula was founded in 1536, and control of the inland regions was secured.

Lempira's rebellion

There was sporadic but persistent **resistance** to the Spanish advance by the indigenous groups they encountered, although the power of these was lessened by their geographical dispersal and the lack of a single powerful group. No significant threat to the Spanish was posed until **Lempira's rebellion** in 1536. A Lenca *cacique* (chieftain) from what is today Erandique in southwest Honduras, Lempira was a charismatic leader, popularly believed to be invincible. Persuading the tribes of the centre and western highlands to unite in rebellion, he amassed a force of up to 30,000 men, retreating with them to the natural mountain redoubt of Peñol de Cerquín. From here he signalled the outbreak of hostilities by killing three Spanish passers-by. The mass insurrection that followed was at first impossible for the Spanish to control; at one point Comayagua was burnt down and Gracias, San Pedro de Puerto Caballos and Trujillo besieged. Outright rebellion continued for three years, before the Spanish, having lured Lempira down to participate in peace talks, shot and killed him in 1539. With no leader at their head, Lempira's forces were easily overcome and the Spanish hold on the land assured.

The colonial period

With Honduras under control, the Spanish increasingly focused their attention on the interior of the country, in large part because of the inhospitable climate of the coastal settlements and their vulnerability to pirate attacks. Discovery of gold in the Valle de Comayagua in 1539, and of silver around Tegucigalpa over the following forty years, seemed to promise untold riches. The designation of Comayagua as capital in 1573 reflected the displacement of economic activity away from the coast.

For the indigenous inhabitants, the consolidation of Spanish power was catastrophic. Contemporary population records are notoriously inaccurate, but from an estimated 400,000 in 1524, the population probably fell to as low as 15,000 by 1571. Those who survived the diseases of the Old World were initially enslaved and shipped either overseas or into the mines. Social structures collapsed and communities were forcibly dispersed, with the highland tribes being most affected, since they had the greatest contact with the colonists. Incredibly, considering their impact, the number of colonists numbered fewer than 300 throughout the seventeenth century.

For the Spanish the steep **decline in population** was a severe hindrance to economic development. Though at their peak the mines provided a comfortable living for their owners, from the seventeenth century onwards the labour shortage made working deeper seams impracticable, and profits dropped sharply as a result. The depopulation of the countryside also hindered the development of a sustainable agricultural sector. *Encomienda*, the system of demanding labour and tribute from the indigenous population, theoretically ensured a supply of workers; in practice, labour scarcity meant that food production rarely rose above subsistence levels, capable only of supplying immediate local needs.

By the early 1800s, the Honduran economy was in crisis. Mining was virtually defunct and a series of severe droughts hit both agriculture and livestock. Society was sharply divided, with a thin layer of the relatively wealthy – state functionaries, merchants, a handful of mine- and hacienda-owners – above a poor mass of mestizos and indigenous peoples. A middle class was nonexistent and by independence in 1821,

Honduras still had no national printing press, newspapers or university.

Independence

News of **independence** from Spain reached Honduras on September 28, 1821. While the Liberals of Tegucigalpa celebrated, the Conservatives of Comayagua declared their intention of joining the American monarchy under the Mexican Agustín Iturbide. Following Iturbide's deposition, the provinces of Central America declared themselves an independent republic on July 1, 1823. In the civil war that almost immediately followed, the Honduran **Francisco Morazán** – Liberal and sometime soldier – succeeded in defeating Conservative forces in Guatemala and, elected president of the republic in 1830, tried to institute a series of far-sighted reforms in government, the Church, the judicial system and education. Opposed by Conservatives across Central America, his vision of the potential of a united republic was not enough to persuade even his own countrymen. There were sporadic uprisings and eventually civil war broke out again; Morazán failed to crush the Conservative-backed 1837 rebellion of Rafael Carrera in Guatemala, and – when Honduras and Nicaragua went to war against El Salvador – resigned in 1839. The Central American Republic was finished.

Rivalry in the newly independent **Republic of Honduras** between Liberals and Conservatives was as strong as ever, plunging the country into an almost permanent state of political and military conflict. The economy, too, was deeply unstable: subject to financial mismanagement by governments of both colours, lacking an export sector to secure foreign revenues and a national infrastructure to push growth, and undermined by flourishing corruption. The effects of this were clearly illustrated in the ill-fated venture to construct a national railway system. Sensing the opportunity to make a quick profit, British banks loaned a desperate government £6 million in 1867–70. Of this, only around £100,000 was ever received and barely 90km of track laid. The resulting debt – which over the next fifty years rose to £30m – was not fully paid off until 1953.

Marco Aurelio Soto and the Liberal reform

The man credited with beginning the modernization of Honduras was **Dr Marco Aurelio Soto**, a Liberal who was elected president in 1876. He and his successor Luis Bográn reformed the powers of judiciary and Church, professionalized the armed forces, and put communications and education infrastructures into place. What was created, in short, were all the elements, above a common language and religion, necessary to make Honduras a unified state capable of taking its place in the world. Recognizing the need to participate in the international economy, Soto also instigated agricultural reforms in order to develop the coffee and sugar cane industries for export.

Believing that foreign capital was the key to economic development, he encouraged **foreign investment** on extremely favourable terms, conversely laying the basis for the country's enduring economic problems. In the mining industry, for example, investors had an obligation to do little more than employ workers, while the government undertook to build roads, ports and any infrastructure necessary to get equipment in and the finished product out. At the El Rosario mine near Tegucigalpa – at one point the most productive mine in the western hemisphere – which accounted for 45 percent of the country's export income at the turn of the century, ninety percent of shares were in foreign (mainly US) hands.

The banana republic

The same thinking lay behind the development of the **banana industry** in the late nineteenth century, the industry that was to become the dominating factor in Honduras's future. More than happy to accept government concessions, which included exemption from customs duties and ownership of mineral rights, US fruit companies began to move into the rich agricultural lands of the north coast. Three companies – United Fruit, Vacarro Bros (later Standard Fruit) and the Cuyamel Fruit Company (bought out by United Fruit in 1929) – soon became dominant, all but wiping out small-scale producers. Further concessions, granted in return for promises to build railways, allowed the companies to steadily increase their holdings, which by 1924 amounted to two thousand square kilometres on the north coast and control of seventy percent of Honduras's total exports. Through expansion of interests, the companies also gained control of the country's railways, principal factories and major energy and telegraph companies, set up banks and acted as intermediaries in negotiations over foreign loans.

Political power and influence followed economic might. Cuyamel cultivated strong links with the Liberal Party, while United Fruit – whose support extended to instigating armed uprisings – bankrolled the Conservatives, now known as the National Party. A succession of weak and shortlived governments struggled to keep control in the face of the dominant interests of the fruit companies and, behind them, the United States, as the virtually autonomous north coast spun away from the impoverished centre and south.

The development of modern Honduras: 1932–1963

With the 1932 election of National Party president **Tiburcio Carías Andino** were laid the foundations for the modern state of Honduras. A virtual dictator for sixteen years until he was forced to step down in 1948, Carías strengthened the armed forces and cracked down on political opposition, the press and trade unions. Conversely, his economic austerity programme succeeded in balancing the economy and his authoritarian leadership forged a new national cohesion. His successor, **Juan Manuel Gálvez**, set up a central bank, a public service sector, and expanded the nascent export industry of coffee, sugar and light manufacturing.

This strengthened government was thus better placed to deal with the worst excesses of the banana companies, reflected in the **Banana Strike** of May 1954. Originating with Puerto Cortés dockers, the strike spread to 35,000 United and Standard Fruit workers, and then to workers in other industries. Ended by a settlement in early July, thrashed out between government, employers and unions, most demands went unrecognized. The two main achievements of the strikers, however – legitimization of labour unions and the drafting of an enduring framework of labour protection laws – made the strike a watershed in Honduran history.

A **coup** in October 1956 introduced the **military** as a new element into the hierarchy of power. Though civilian government resumed in 1957, with the election of Liberal Ramón Villeda Morales, a new constitution the same year gave the armed forces the right to disregard presidential orders they perceived to be unconstitutional, strengthening vastly the position of the military over the next twenty years.

Military influence – and the Football War

In October 1963 a second coup installed **Colonel Oswaldo López Arellano** as provisional president. Though elected constitutionally in 1965, López remained a ranking officer – eventually rising to Brigadier General – forging an unhealthily close alliance between the military and the National Party, in effect his personal political vehicle. During twelve years in power he decimated the Liberal opposition and reversed most of his predecessor's social reforms. Free-market economic policies led to an increase in unemployment and landlessness, while the profits which were creamed off government development projects fuelled unprecedented corruption. In an attempt to counter growing unrest over land, López introduced limited agrarian reform in 1967, in the shape of rural co-operatives, though these were far more acceptable to the fruit companies than the trade unions. Above all, however, his first period of office is remembered for one of the more bizarre conflicts in modern Central American history, the so-called "**Football War**".

On July 14, 1969, war broke out on the Honduras–El Salvador border. Ostensibly caused by a disputed result in a soccer match between the two countries, the conflict stemmed from tensions generated by a steady rise in illegal migration of campesinos from El Salvador into Honduras in search of land. In April 1969 the Honduran government gave settlers thirty days to return to El Salvador and began forced expulsions; sporadic violence broke out, with cynical manipulation of the situation in the press by right-wingers on both sides of the border.

In June, the two countries began a series of **qualifying matches** for the 1970 World Cup, the first of which, held in Tegucigalpa, was won 1–0 by Honduras. At the second game, won 3–0 by El Salvador, spectators at the San Salvador ground booed the Honduran national anthem and attacked visiting Honduran fans. The third and deciding match was pre-empted by the El Salvadorean army bombing targets within Honduras and advancing up to 40km into Honduran territory. After three days, around two thousand deaths and a complete rupture of diplomatic relations, the Organization of American States (OAS) negotiated a ceasefire, establishing a three-kilometre-wide demilitarized zone along the border. Tensions and minor skirmishes continued, however, until 1980, when a US-brokered peace treaty was signed. Only in 1992 did both sides accept an International Court of Justice ruling demarcating the border in its current location.

An experiment in democratic government, under Ramón Cruz in 1971–72, was marked by economic chaos and civil unrest, and ended abruptly with a second coup restoring López to power in December 1972. A new programme of industrialization, with the government responsible for investment and accumulation of capital, was – given the by now endemic corruption at senior levels of government, in the military and in business – a recipe for disaster. Millions of dollars of national and international loans and aid money were siphoned off to private bank accounts, and while limited agricultural reform succeeded to a degree in redistributing under-utilized land, it was not enough to contain rural unrest.

The "**Bananagate**" scandal, the payment of US$1.25m to government officials by United Brands (previously United Fruit) in return for reducing the taxes on fruit exports, eventually forced López to leave office in April 1975. Under his successors, **Colonel Juan Melgar Castro** (1975–78) and **General Policarpo Paz García** (1978–81), agrarian reform slowed to a trickle, repression of civil rights and freedom of speech increased, and corruption among military and government personnel grew to almost laughable levels. In a society sharply divided between rich and poor, almost seventy percent of rural households were unable to meet essential consumption costs, while five percent of the population controlled over half the land.

The lost decade – "USS Honduras"

Following the Sandinista revolution in Nicaragua in July 1979 and the election of Reagan to the US presidency in

November 1980, Honduras found itself at the centre of US geopolitical strategy – the "fourth border of the US", a state of affairs with which the government was only too happy to comply. The **elections** of November 1981, held under US diplomatic pressure, brought **Roberto Suazo Córdova** to power. Though a Liberal, Suazo was closely allied to the rabidly anti-Communist **Colonel Alvarez Martinez**, head of the police force (the FSP), then under military control, and later Commander in Chief of the armed forces. These two men allowed Honduras to become the focus for the US-backed Contra war in Nicaragua, accepting in return over US$1.5bn of direct economic and military aid from the US during the 1980s. US-funded training camps along the border were used on occasion to launch Contra attacks into Nicaraguan territory, while the Honduran army provided logistical support and participated in manoeuvres with the steadily growing numbers of US troops based in the country.

Domestically, the relationship between the military and government grew ever closer. **Human rights** violations rose alarmingly, with the army implicated in at least 184 "disappearances" of activists from labour organizations and peace movements. Forced conscription was common, and lengthy jail sentences were introduced for activities deemed subversive, including street demonstrations. In 1984, army officers, increasingly anxious over Alvarez's actions, forced him into exile. Though repression eased somewhat, the relationship between the military and government continued to be close, with corruption at senior levels in both institutions positively encouraged by the endless flow of dollars from the US.

Neo-Liberalism and Hurricane Mitch

Honduras's role as a geopolitical lynchpin diminished after Reagan left office and both the Contra war and the civil war in El Salvador were resolved. As the military became less obvious in day-to-day life, forced conscription was ended and most of the US troops stationed in Honduras were recalled, the country's endemic economic and social problems were thrown into stark relief.

National Party president **Rafael Leonardo Callejas** came to power in 1989 and introduced a neo-Liberal austerity programme, floating exchange rates, privatizing the state sector and cultivating foreign and private investment. Successful in the short term, particularly in forging relations with international lenders, the programme led to a sharp rise in poverty levels and failed ultimately to secure significant investment. Jurisdiction over legal and government affairs was slowly wrested back from the military by a resurgent judiciary, but monitoring groups reported that human rights abuses were still common. Callejas also failed to tackle the issue of corruption, and was himself formally indicted for misappropriation of public funds in 1994.

In 1993, the widely respected Liberal candidate, businessman-turned-politician **Carlos Roberto Reina**, was elected president. Faced with an economic recession and rapidly devaluing lempira, Reina put his claims to be capable of engineering moral renewal to the test by taking action on most overt cases of high-level corruption. He was not able, however, to prevent the economy sliding further into recession, or to halt a steadily worsening spiral of social instability. This last, fuelled by growing poverty and greater involvement with drug-smuggling between South and North America, affected the north coast in particular.

Reina's successor, Liberal **Carlos Flores Facussé**, took office in January 1998, after elections marred by allegations of corruption and vote-rigging on both sides. **Facussé** immediately set about trying to reduce Honduras's massive international debt, organizing a series of meetings with the IMF and

World Bank. Though Flores had been elected with a campaign pledge to reverse the cycle of deepening poverty and social despair through investment and a programme of national conciliation, he largely maintained the free-market economics of his predecessors. Corporation tax was slashed and sweeping privatization plans were proposed in an austerity package formulated to gain debt relief, while sales tax was hiked from 7 to 12 percent.

But just as these policies were being implemented, and before debt relief had been granted, **Hurricane Mitch** began brewing offshore in October 1998. The category-five hurricane first battered Guanaja, laying siege to the Bay Island for three days before ripping across mainland Honduras, unleashing colossal volumes of rainfall in an apocalyptic trail across the country. After causing landslides and storm surges that killed over a thousand people in the capital Tegucigalpa, Mitch pursued an erratic path back across Honduras, triggering devastating mud slides and floods in neighbouring Nicaragua and along the path of the Chamelecón and Ulúa rivers from the western highlands to San Pedro Sula. It's estimated that Mitch killed over 7000 people in Honduras, 4000 in Nicaragua and around 400 in Guatemala and El Salvador.

President Carlos Flores declared that Mitch had set Honduras back fifty years, and the world's media reported a cataclysmic picture of damage and devastation. These initial assessments came to seem over-pessimistic, however, as the nation – aided by teams from all over the world – steadily pulled itself together again, quickly patching up much of the key infrastructure. A year after the hurricane, all the main highways were open and most of the hundred bridges damaged by Mitch had been repaired or rebuilt, and tourists were returning.

Honduras today

Reconstruction aside, it quickly became clear that Mitch had seriously exacerbated the nation's fundamental weaknesses and inequalities. The **economy** remains critically weak and almost totally dependent on inward investment, which chiefly goes into the *maquila* garment-assembly factories of the north. This industry, dominated by Korean and US companies, enjoys tax-free status and pays notoriously poor wages, while technology companies opt to settle in the stable pastures of Costa Rica, where they can draw on a well-educated workforce.

Elections in November 2001 saw the end of Liberal Party rule, with Tegucigalpa businessman Ricardo Maduro leading the conservative National Party to victory with just over 50 percent of the vote. The main issue governing his presidency was the continued clean-up following Mitch and dealing with the escalating poverty and crime that had occurred as a result. His "zero-tolerance" approach to gang-related crime has had some success in reducing gang culture (his own son was kidnapped and killed in 2000), and the promotion of tourism has seen the instigation of special tourist police forces in areas once considered unsafe to visit. However, there have also been setbacks, corruption remains rife, and plans to build the first roads on the Bay Island of Guanaja, as well as a resort to rival Cancún, have been considered folly in certain circles.

4.1

Tegucigalpa and the south

Nestling in a mountain valley 1000m above sea level, Honduras's capital **Tegucigalpa** has a faded colonial charm and a refreshing climate. The historic core, home to many museums and churches, has something of a small-town feel to it, while wealthy suburbs and embassy districts spread out to the south and east. Across the Río Choluteca to the west lies **Comayagüela**, Tegucigalpa's shabbier, more industrial twin – together the two comprise the administrative **Distrito Central**. Although the nation's economic focus has long since shifted to San Pedro Sula, Tegucigalpa continues to function as the political and governmental centre of Honduras.

The city sights might keep you busy for a day or two, but it's worth planning a longer stay in the capital in order to venture out into the pine forests and mountain ranges that encircle the city. To the east, the colonial mining villages of **Santa Lucía** and **Valle de Ángeles**, both easily reached by local buses, evoke a time when this was a rough frontier, and rich seams of silver provided the wealth on which Tegucigalpa was built. Just a short distance further north is one of the country's most accessible cloudforest reserves, the **Parque Nacional La Tigra**.

South of Tegucigalpa stretches the stark, sun-baked coastal plain of the Pacific. Tourists are few and far between in this region, whose only real attraction is **Isla El Tigre**, a little-visited volcanic island set in the calm waters of the Golfo de Fonseca. The most likely reason for travelling here is to cross the border into Nicaragua or El Salvador; heading east into Nicaragua, you may well have to change buses in the regional capital, **Choluteca**, an appealing stopover thanks to its well-preserved colonial centre.

Tegucigalpa

Cluttered and crowded, **TEGUCIGALPA,** on first impression at least, is not the most welcoming of Central American capitals. Thick with traffic that at times obscures the city's dramatic mountainous backdrop, the winding narrow streets of the old centre meander haphazardly up the lower slopes of **Cerro Picacho**. Crumbling colonial buildings and decaying nineteenth-century mansions bear down on you while walking by, as do sidewalks choked with vendors, idlers and shoppers. That said, the city isn't completely without charms, and a stay of a few days will help you adapt to the pace of life. In terms of sights, there are several well-preserved colonial **churches**, in particular the eighteenth-century cathedral on the Plaza Morazán, a handful of national **museum and art collections**, and several small, well-patronized parks.

West of the old centre, the character of the city rapidly becomes more menacing as you approach the banks of the Río Choluteca. On October 29, 1998, ten-metre-high floods caused by **Hurricane Mitch** ripped through the river valley, tearing down buildings in a tide of devastation that killed upwards of a thousand people. Vast mud deposits and garbage still clog the banks and hundreds of vultures circle overhead in some of the worst scenes of urban decay in Central America. Cross one of the bridges and you're in **Comayagüela**, always a poor barrio but now distinctly threatening after dark. Save for the **market**, the only reason to pass through is to change buses.

Some history

Before the Spanish arrived, the Tegucigalpa valley was inhabited by Lenca groups settled along the Río Choluteca. Exactly when the conquistadors first arrived in the valley is unclear; records make no mention of the area until the 1560s, when silver deposits (Tegucigalpa means Silver Mountain in the Nahuatl language) were found in the hills to the east, around Santa Lucía (see p.396). The discovery of further deposits in the surrounding hills attracted growing numbers of settlers, who pushed the indigenous inhabitants out to what are now the outlying barrios of Comayagüela. **Real de Minas de San Miguel de Tegucigalpa** was founded on September 29, 1578, and in 1608 granted the status of alcaldía, with authority over a rash of mining settlements in the valley and surrounding hills. Town status came in 1768 and that of city in 1807, with profits from the silver mines aiding the construction of fine colonial churches and houses.

Its mining wealth and location at the centre of cross-country trade routes made Tegucigalpa an increasingly clamorous rival to the then capital, Comayagua. Following **independence** it was decided to alternate the seat of government between the two, a plan that was riddled with shortcomings but nevertheless staggered on until 1830, when parliament was permanently restored to Comayagua. Fifty years later, however, the Liberal President Soto shifted power back to Tegucigalpa, enraged by Comayagua's leaders' apparent dislike of his wife. In 1932, the city and its poor relation to the south, Comayagüela, were united under the title **Distrito Central**.

Since the late nineteenth century, when the economic focus of the country began to shift to the bountiful fruit plantations of the north coast, Tegucigalpa has become somewhat eclipsed by San Pedro Sula. In essence a chaotic small town grown large, the business of government remains the city's main industry. In the words of a local saying, "Tegucigalpa thinks, San Pedro works".

Arrival, information and orientation

Both international and domestic flights arrive at **Toncontín International Airport**, 7km south of the city. **Taxis** wait outside the terminal, but you can save a couple of dollars by walking 50m down to the highway and hailing one there; the journey to the centre should cost around US$2.80. City bus #24 ("Río Grande–Lomas") passes the airport frequently, running through Comayagüela and into the centre of Tegucigalpa in around forty minutes, depending on the traffic. At the airport there's a **bank**, a small **Hondutel** telephone office, a number of **car rental** agencies and the *Cyber City* **Internet café** (US$2 per hour) outside the arrivals hall. Tegucigalpa has no central **bus terminal**; each international or intercity bus line has its own terminal, most of them scattered around Comayagüela. The main exception is buses to and from Danlí/El Paraiso and the Nicaraguan border at Las Manos, which run from the Mercado Jacaleapa, Col Kennedy (see box p.395).

The helpful **Instituto Hondureño de Turismo**, in the Edificio Europa at Av Ramon Cruz and C República de México (Mon–Fri 8.30am–4.30pm; ⓣ222 2124 or toll-free in Honduras ⓣ800/222 8687, ⓔtourisminfo@iht.hn), provides maps of the country and major cities, as well as bilingual information on the country's main tourist attractions. For more detailed **maps**, try the Instituto Geográfico Nacional, C 15 off the Blvd de Comunidad Europea, Comayagüela (Mon–Fri 8.30am–noon & 2–4pm; ⓣ225 0752).

The heart of Tegucigalpa's **old city** is the pleasant Plaza Morazán; a number of interesting churches and museums, plus many hotels, lie within easy walking distance of the square. East from the centre, two major roads, **Av Jeréz** (which becomes Av Juan Gutemberg and then Av La Paz) and **Av Miguel Cervantes** (changing its name to Av República de Chile), run out through the richer suburbs and embassy district. Tegucigalpa's main artery, **Av 1** (later called Blvd de la Comunidad Europea), splits the city in two from north to south, running parallel to the Río Choluteca then continuing out past the airport to destinations south. Across the river, west from central Tegucigalpa, lies **Comayagüela**.

City transport

City buses are frequent and extremely noisy; they're generally old US school buses, though unfortunately not painted in the glorious colours seen elsewhere in Central America. Urban routes start running at around 6am and finish around 9pm.

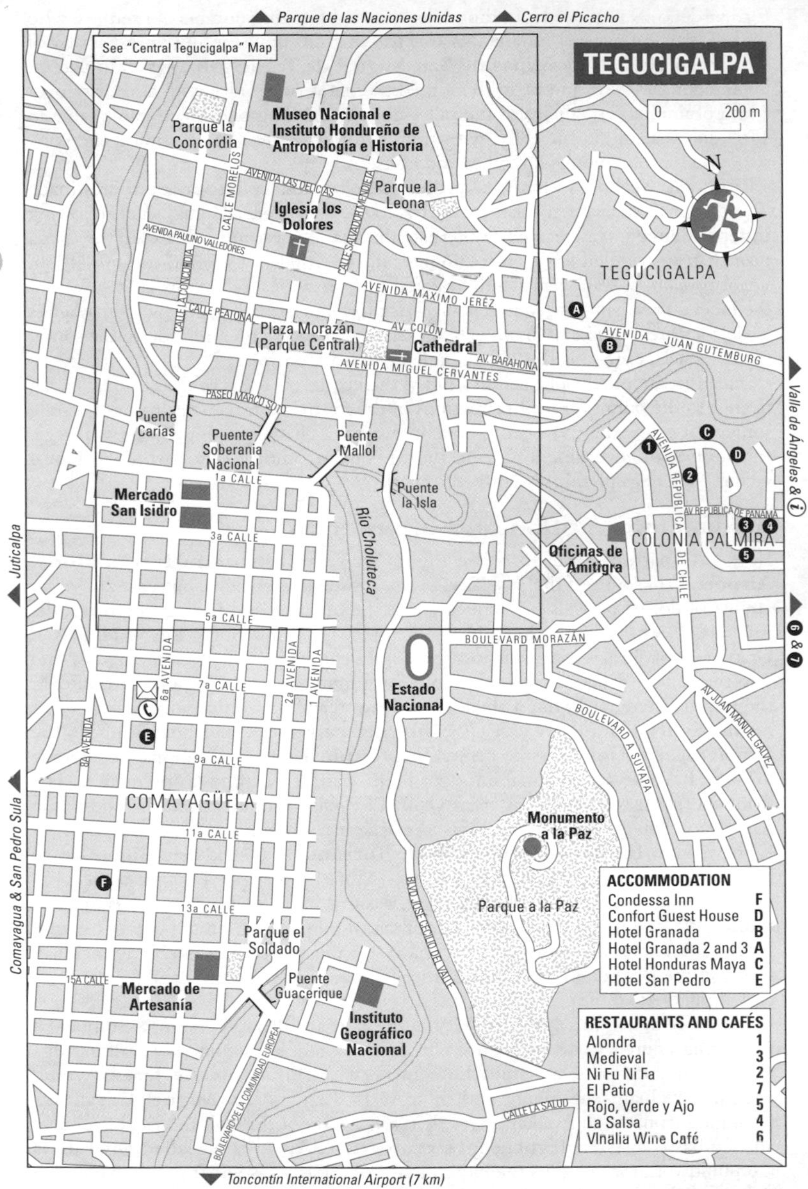

Route names and numbers are painted on the front and fares are extremely cheap (US$0.25 anywhere within the city), though none pass very close to the Parque Central. Any bus signed "San Miguel" (including the #21) runs past the US embassy and the tourist office along Av Juan Gutemberg.

Taxis come in a range of shapes and colours, but are easy to identify by the numbers painted on their sides. They announce their availability by incessant honking and are often shared, with passengers dropped off in turn. There are no meters but a trip in the city should be around US$2–2.50, a little more at night. **Colectivo taxis** gather at predetermined stops (*puntos*) and do not leave until they are full with passengers going to a similar area of the city. Though you may have to wait around a bit, they are cheaper than standard taxis, costing around US$0.45 per person.

Accommodation

The central and eastern parts of **Tegucigalpa** contain a reasonable range of upmarket **hotels** and pleasant, less expensive accommodation, convenient for museums, restaurants and enjoying the bustling evening streetlife. A nice alternative, though not particularly cheap, is to stay in one of the **B&B guesthouses**, which are mostly located outside the centre in the district of Colonia Palmira. Though Comayagüela contains a number of **budget** places, few travellers now stay there because of security concerns.

Tegucigalpa

Confort Guest House C 2 Col Palmira ⓣ & ⓕ 239 1197, ⓦ www.confortguest.com. Convivial guesthouse in a prestige location high above the city, with spacious, individually decorated rooms (all with TV), a small pool, secure parking and an attractive lobby filled with antique telephones and radios. There's also an apartment with kitchen available. Price includes breakfast ❻, apartment ❼

Hotel Boston Av Máximo Jeréz 321, between C El Telegrafo and C Morelos ⓣ 237 9411, ⓕ 237 0186. Spotlessly clean with all rooms en-suite, this is a decent-value hotel in a good location near the Iglesia Los Dolores. Prices have risen recently, but it still represents a good deal with an elegant communal TV area, inexhaustible supplies of hot water and free coffee. The large, old rooms at the front are nicer, despite the traffic noise. ❹–❺

Hotel Granada Av Juan Gutemberg at Av Cristóbal Colón ⓣ 237 2381, ⓔ hotelgranadategus@yahoo.com. Good budget option, with basic but clean rooms, some with bath, plus hot water and a communal TV area. Better rooms have TV and en-suite bathroom. Very good value and consequently always popular, but ask for a room away from the street. ❸

Hotel Granada 2 ⓣ 222 0597, ⓕ 237 0841; and **Hotel Granda 3** ⓣ 238 4438, ⓕ 237 0843 opposite each other on Subida Casa Martín, Barrio Guanacaste. Similar to – and just round the corner from – the original *Hotel Granada*. All rooms, including triples and quadruples, have private bath. You'll pay a little extra for a TV. ❸–❹

Hotel Honduras Maya C 3, Av República de Perú, Col Palmira ⓣ 220 5000, ⓕ 220 6000, ⓦ www.hondurasmaya.hn. This modern luxury hotel is something of a city landmark, its bold outline bedecked in Maya glyphs. The upper rooms have great views over the city, and facilities include a restaurant, café, large pool, souvenir shops, car rental and a travel agency. ❽

Hotel MacArthur Av Lempira 454, Barrio Abajo ⓣ 237 9839, ⓕ 238 0294, ⓔ homacart@datum.hn. Convenient for the centre and popular with business travellers; all rooms have hot water, fan and TV, while a/c is a slightly pricier option. There's a pool, secure parking and a small café serving expensive breakfasts. ❺–❻

Hotel Maya Colonial C Palace, just north of the Parque Central (no phone). A tumbledown old colonial building with dark, ancient rooms with en-suite bath. There is an air of faded charm, though, along with a good central location and basic comedor. ❷

Tobacco Road Av Jeréz ⓣ 222 4081, ⓔ tobacord@yahoo.com. Run by an American, this is the city's only backpacker hostel. A bohemian place with bar, coffee shop and bookstore, accommodation is in three- or four-bed dorms (US$4.50) with shared bath, and the price includes breakfast. Hot water, hammocks in the back and local tourist information available. ❶

Comayagüela

Condessa Inn Av 7 between C 12 and 13 (no phone). Basic, but clean, friendly and one of the best overnight options in the area. There's a small café and better rooms come with a/c and TV. ❷

Hotel San Pedro Av 6, C 8–9 ⓣ 222 8987. You'd hardly want to spend too long in this hotel – the ninety rooms with or without private bath are very basic – but it remains a popular choice with travellers because of its location close to the bus terminals. ❷

The city centre: Plaza Morazán and around

Plaza Morazán, Tegucigalpa's recently restored central square, is the centre of life for most people who live and work in the capital. Shaded by a canopy of trees, and populated by a plethora of street traders, it's an atmospheric, if not particularly peaceful, place to pass some time. A statue at the centre of the square commemorates the national hero **Francisco Morazán**, a soldier, Liberal and reformer who was elected president of the Central American Republic in 1830. The house where he was born, two blocks west on Av Cristóbal Colón, is now the **Archivo Nacional** (Mon–Fri 8.30am–4pm). On the east edge of the plaza, the blinding white facade of the **Catedral San Miguel**, completed in 1782, is one of the best preserved in Central America. Inside, look out for the magnificent Baroque-style gilded altar, and the baptismal font, carved in 1643 by indigenous artesans from a single block of stone. Three blocks east from here, on Av Paz Barahona, the **Iglesia**

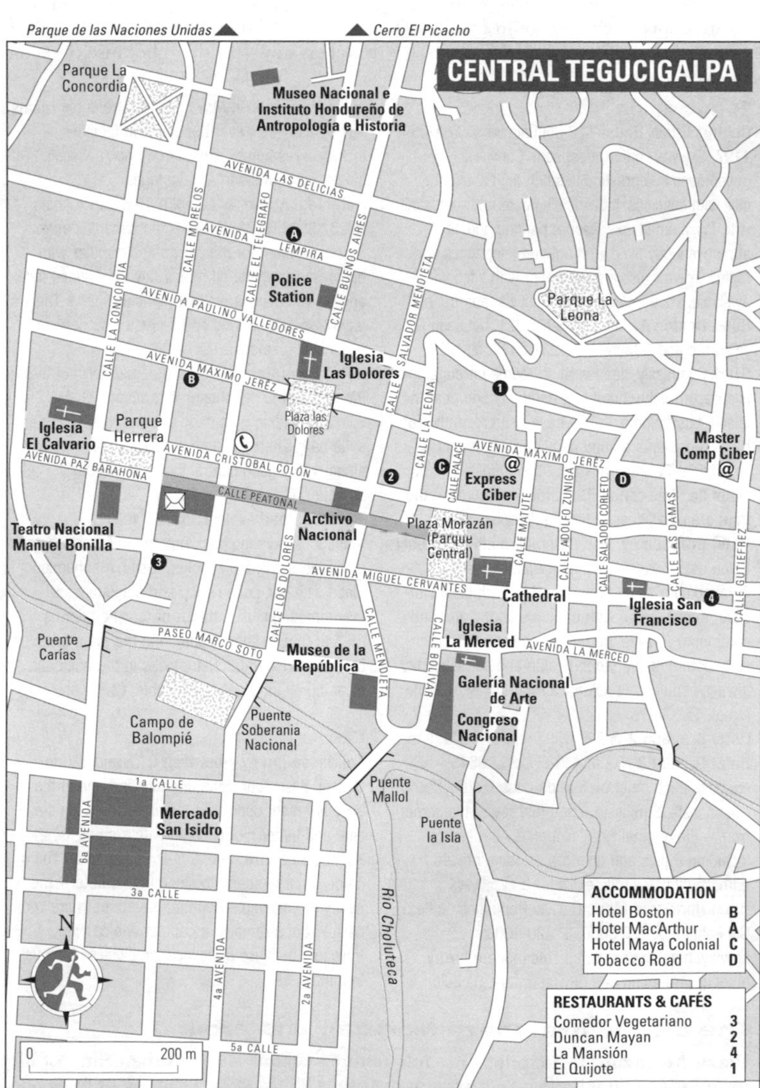

San Franciso is the oldest church in the city, first built by the Franciscans in 1592, although much of the present building dates from 1740.

Just to the south of the Parque Central, next to the Iglesia La Merced on C Bolívar, the **Galería Nacional de Arte** (Mon–Fri 9am–4pm, Sat 9am–1pm; US$1.10) is home to an extensive collection of Central American art. Displays on the ground floor range from prehistoric petroglyphs and Maya stone carvings to colonial paintings, while rooms upstairs are devoted to religious art and an ambitious collection of modern and contemporary Honduran art, featuring works by Pablo Zelaya Sierra, a leader of twentieth-century art in the country. Originally a Seventeenth-century convent and then the national university, the building's Neoclassical facade sits rather uncomfortably alongside the stained concrete hulk of the **Congreso Nacional**, the country's seat of government next door.

One block west of the Galería Nacional de Arte, at Paseo Marco Soto and C Mendieta, the late nineteenth-century presidential residence housed the **Museo Histórico de la República** from 1992 until 2000, though it has been closed for restoration since then, with no sign of opening in the near future. The museum building itself is still worth a quick look however – an egotistical lime-green palace overlooking the river.

West of Plaza Morazán

Running west from the plaza, the pedestrianized **Calle Peatonal** is lined with shops, cafés and innumerable street vendors. Walk west along here for twenty minutes or so, dodging the moneychangers, and you'll come to the small, shady **Parque Herrera.** On the west side of the Parque is the rather plain Iglesia El Calvario, start and end point of the city's Easter processions, while to the south stands the **Teatro Nacional Manuel Bonilla**. Completed in 1915, it was originally intended to honour Miguel de Cervantes; within the grey-stone Renaissance-style shell is an ornately plaster-worked interior, based on the Athenée Comique in Paris. Check the local press or ask at the box office for details of current shows.

A couple of blocks northwest from the central plaza and set on the small pedestrianized Plaza Los Dolores is the white, domed **Iglesia Los Dolores**, completed in 1732. Its Baroque facade is decorated with a representation of the Passion of Christ, featuring a crowing cock and the rising sun; inside, the elaborate gold altar dates from 1742. The plaza itself is crowded with cheap, shabby comedor stalls.

North of the centre

Two blocks west of the Iglesia Los Dolores, a right turn onto C Morelos and a fairly steep fifteen-minute walk brings you to the Villa Roy, an eighteenth-century mansion – formerly the home of President Lozano Díaz – that's now home to the **Museo Nacional e Historia de la República** (Mon–Sat 8am–4pm; US$1.10). Inside, a comprehensive exhibition covers the political, economic and social development of the republic, alongside a display of less interesting presidential artefacts. Five former presidential limousines from various administrations are on show in the car park, illustrating the increasing luxury with which the presidents have surrounded themselves. The **Instituto Hondureño de Antropología e Historia** below the villa has a small reference library with books and information on Copán and other archeological sites. A block west off C la Concordia is a welcome patch of green, the **Parque La Concordia**, dotted with replicas of Maya sculptures.

To the west, north of the Plaza Morazán, older suburbs – previously home to the wealthy middle classes and rich immigrants, now long gone – edge up the lower slopes of **Cerro El Picacho**. At the top stands the open-armed **Cristo del Picacho**, illuminated at night in a dazzle of coloured lights. Decent views can be had from the **Parque La Leona**, about twenty minutes' walk uphill from the centre along C Las Damas, but it's worth continuing (or catching a bus) up to the top, where the **Parque de las Naciones Unidas** commands a view across the whole of the city and valley beyond. There's ample space for picnicking and strolling among the trees, though the cramped zoo is best avoided. On Sundays **buses** run here every half-hour from behind Los Dolores church; on other days, take an El Hatillo bus from the Parque Herrera to the access road, from where it's about fifteen minutes' walk to the entrance.

South and east of the centre

East from the centre, **Av Máximo Jeréz/Juan Gutemberg** skirts the northern edge of **Colonia Palmira**, an upmarket district home to most of the capital's foreign embassies, luxury hotels, expensive restaurants and wealthy residences. The **US embassy**, a common reference point, lies along Av Juan Gutemberg about thirty minutes' walk from Plaza Morazán. Another city landmark, the modern **Hotel Honduras Maya**, can be found on the Av República de Chile, just south of Col Palmira, fifteen minutes' walk east from the centre. Continue past the hotel for about a kilometre and an overpass gives access to eastward-bound **Blvd Morazán**, Tegucigalpa's major commercial and entertainment artery – for some reason no city buses run along here. At its western end, the boulevard terminates at the **Estadio Nacional**, which hosts international and domestic soccer games. The vaguely Greek-temple-like structure visible to the south of here on the low Cerro Juana Laínez is the **Monumento a la Paz**, built to commemorate the treaty ending the 1969 Football War (see p.381). A road up to the monument starts from the fire station behind the stadium.

Comayagüela

The surging brown waters of the polluted Río Choluteca form a suitable border to Tegucigalpa's twin, **COMAYAGÜELA**, which sprawls away through down-at-heel business districts into industrial areas and poor barrios. There's little to see here and the workaday streets, invariably choked with traffic, have a much less relaxed feel than those of Tegucigalpa. At night there's an undeniably rough edge to the place, and even the inhabitants of Tegucigalpa prefer not to venture out here after dark.

San Isidro, the capital's main **market**, sprawls around Av 6 and C 1, just across the Puente Carías river bridge from C Morelos in Tegucigalpa. Stalls jostle for space along the narrow alleys and pavements, sometimes spilling over into the streets themselves, and buses crawl through the crowds, often only inches from the vendors. The atmosphere is hot and frenetic, with the smell of raw meat rising in hot weather. It's certainly a spectacle, but mind your possessions while walking around. About ten minutes' walk past the market, at the intersection with C 12, is the Banco Central de Honduras building; check in the newspapers for details of the occasional **exhibitions** hosted in the art gallery here. In the same building is the **Museo Numismático** (Mon–Fri 9am–noon & 1.30–4.30pm; free) with a collection of bank notes and coins from across the globe.

In the heart of Comayagüela, at Av 3 and C 15, is the small **Mercado de Artesanía**, housed in a rather gloomy building that never seems to get very busy. Stands sell handicrafts from around the country at prices lower than in Tegucigalpa's shops, although the selection isn't great.

Out from the city: the Basilica de Suyapa

Six or so kilometres east of the centre, the flat plains are broken by the monolithic white bulk of the **Basílica de Suyapa**. Built in colonial style in the 1950s to provide a new home for the **Virgen de Suyapa**, the patron saint of Honduras, the church's lofty, bare interior serves to highlight the striking blue stained-glass windows. According to legend, however, the Virgin has resisted all attempts to place her permanently in the new edifice, each time mysteriously returning to her original home, a simple chapel behind the church. The tiny 6cm-high statue of the Virgin was supposedly discovered in 1743 by two campesinos returning to Suyapa from working on Cerro del Pilingüín. Finding themselves still a distance from the village as dark fell, they decided to pass the night in the open air. After bedding down for the night, one of them noticed he was lying on something that felt like a stone and threw it to one side, without looking at it. Within a few minutes, however, the object had returned to the same place. The next day, the two carried the little statue down to Suyapa where, placed on a simple table adorned with flowers, the Virgin began to attract increasing numbers of worshippers. A certain Captain José de Zelaya y Midence built the chapel to house the statue in thanks for the recovery of his health.

You can see the statue behind the wooden altar in **La Pequeña Iglesia**, the much simpler, original eighteenth-century chapel, sheltered behind the Basilica. These days it is only moved to the new building temporarily, during the February festival of the Virgen de Suyapa, when thousands of pilgrims from across the country come to worship in a televised event accompanied by music and fireworks. City buses to Suyapa run regularly from the Mercado San Isidro in Comayagüela.

Eating, drinking and entertainment

Only San Pedro Sula can rival Tegucigalpa for the sheer variety of classy and upmarket **restaurants** that it boasts, but if staying in the centre you'll have to be prepared to travel to find them. The best restaurants are generally found in the eastern Colonia Palmira and along the Blvd Morazán, while the centre boasts cheap and cheerful café-style eateries and a few good-value restaurants.

City centre

Comedor Vegetariano Av Cervantes at C Morelos. Inexpensive vegetarian comedor with a slightly barren eating area. Bargain prices make up for the lack of atmosphere, though, with huge set meals, including soup, a daily special and dessert, costing around US$3. Closed evenings and Sun.

Duncan Mayan Av Cristóbal Colón, 2 blocks west of Parque Central. Busy barn of a place, popular amongst workers on their way home, with large helpings of local food, burgers and snacks from US$1.50.

La Mansión Av Miguel Paz Barahona. Great buffet-style restaurant, set around a quiet courtyard, serving inexpensive and tasty breakfasts and lunches.

El Quijote C Leona. One of the city's oldest restaurants, *El Quijote* has been in business for over 25 years. Great views of the Catedral and Parque Central go along well with an international menu, specialising in seafood and paella. An average meal with drink will set you back US$10–20. Closed Sun.

Colonia Palmira

Alondra Av República de Chile. The most elegant restaurant in town, patronized by the nation's elite, boasts an expansive, European-inspired menu, decent wine list, and a peaceful setting in a colonial mansion around a verdant garden. Relatively expensive (around US$18 a head), but a good choice for a splurge.

Medieval Av República de Panamá. Medieval-castle-style building, decorated with suits of armour, lion statues and frequent art displays from national artists. Decadent and pricey in the evening, there is a good-value lunch buffet (US$4.40) on weekdays that includes soup and a drink. Live music at weekends.

Ni Fu Ni Fa Av República de Chile. Argentinian-style *churrasqueria* with imported meat cuts have made this restaurant a big favourite with the Tegucigalpa in-crowd in a short space of time. Steaks are large and service is excellent. Expect to pay around US$10–15.

Rojo, Verde y Ajo Av 1 B off Av República de Panamá. A reasonably priced restaurant with an international menu heavy on Mediterranean cuisine. The English-speaking staff is friendly and portions are large enough for you to feel that you've spent your money wisely. Closed Sun.

La Salsa Av República de Panamá. Classy and civilised, this upmarket lunchtime restaurant is a favourite with local VIPs. Best dining is out on the terrace with views of the city and Cristo de Picacho monument. The menu features a wide variety of Honduran specialities. Closed evenings.

Boulevard Morazán

El Patio far eastern end of the Boulevard. Typical Honduran restaurant offering traditional dishes in massive, value-for-money portions – try El Conquistador, a breathtakingly huge steak. This is a great place to introduce yourself to homecooked Honduran cuisine.

Vinalia Wine Café behind the Jetstereo building on the Boulevard. Relaxed wine bar featuring light dishes, most with an Italian or Spanish twist. The atmosphere is distinctly arty, with live music most nights, a lounge for enjoying a wine from the extensive list, and a terrace perfect for a quiet coffee. Closed Mon.

Nightlife

Tegucigalpa has some of the best nightlife options in the country, but most **bars** in the centre are fiercely local hangouts, and as a visitor you may get an indifferent reception. In the centre, one of the best places to kick off an evening and meet other travellers is the bar at the *Tobacco Road* hostel (see p.389), known locally as *Café Tomás. Café Paradiso* on C Barahona is another central location, popular with local artists. For late-night revelry, move out to the trendy Colonia Palmira and Boulevard Morazán districts. *Taco Taco* on the latter behind *Wendy's* is a Mexican bar serving tequilas to a largely thirty-something crowd, while *Iguana Rana* further along is more of a sports bar with a rowdy atmosphere. *Vinalia Wine Café* (see above) is more formal, often with mellow live music accompanying your wine. Further out in the Centro Comercial Las Haciendas on Boulevard Suyapa, *El Trapo* is an international bar and hip hangout. **Clubbers** will find most of the action along boulevards Morazán and Juan Pablo II. The Egyptian-themed *El Nilo Ai Kip*, in the Furiwa building on Boulevard Juan Pablo II, is an exclusive disco open Wed–Sat and you'll need your passport to gain entry. Along Boulevard Morazán, *Hipa-Hipa* is an old favourite where a younger crowd dance to Latin sounds (Mon–Sat from 8pm) until the early hours. *Tropical Pat Disco* on Boulevard Miraflores is a typically Honduran place, though the incessant salsa and meringue beats may lead to an early night. If you have money to burn, *Casino Royale* at the *Honduras Maya Hotel* offers everything from roulette and blackjack to baccarat, though you'll need to prove you're not Honduran before you get in.

Listings

Airlines Air France, Galería la Paz 116, Av la Paz ⓣ237 0216; Alitalia, 4 Av & 9C, Col Alameda ⓣ239 4246; American Airlines, ground floor, Edificio Palmira, Col Palmira ⓣ232 1414; British Airways, Blvd Comunidad Europea ⓣ225 5102; Continental Airlines, Edificio Palic, Av República de Chile ⓣ220 0997; Copa, Floors 2–4, Edificio Europa, Col San Carlos ⓣ231 2469; Grupo Taca (Lacsa, Nica, Aviateca, Avianca), Edificio Interamericana, Blvd Morazán ⓣ239 0915; Iberia, Edificio Palmira, Col Palmira ⓣ232 7760; Isleña, Galería La Paz, Av La Paz ⓣ237 3410; Japan Airlines, Galería La Paz 312, Av La Paz ⓣ238 0425; KLM, Edificio Cicsa ⓣ232 6414; Lacsa, see Grupo Taca; Lufthansa, 2nd floor, Centro Comercial Plaza del Sol, Av La Paz ⓣ236 7560; Rollins, airport ⓣ234 2766; Sosa, airport ⓣ233 7351; Varig, Edificio Sempe, Blvd Comunidad Europea ⓣ225 5102.

American Express The local agent is Mundirama Travel Service, Edificio Cicsa, Av República de Panamá, close to the *Hotel Honduras Maya* (Mon–Fri 8am–noon & 1–5pm, Sat 8am–noon; ⓣ237 6111).

Banks and exchange Virtually all banks will change dollars and travellers' cheques. The Coin SA Casa de Cambio on C Peatonal may offer better rates for cash than the banks, whilst the moneychangers on the street invariably offer rates slightly better than the official one. Banco Atlántida, on the Parque Central and elsewhere, gives advances on Visa cards, whilst Credomatic, C Mendieta at Av Cervantes, gives advances on Visa and MasterCard.

Bookstores Metromedia, on C República de Colombia in Col Palmira, has a wide range of English-language fiction, nonfiction and travel, as well as used books, US newspapers and magazines. Shakespeare's Books, inside *Tobacco Road* (see p.389), has around 9000 secondhand books, mainly fiction, though they are unsorted. Librería Guaymuras, Av Cervantes at C Las Damas, is good for Spanish-language fiction and political, economic and social texts. The *Hotel Honduras Maya* and other luxury hotels have US newspapers and magazines, along with *Honduras This Week*.

Car rental Avis, airport ⓣ239 5712; Budget, airport ⓣ233 5161; Hertz, Centro Comercial Villa Real, in front of *Hotel Honduras Maya* ⓣ239 0772; Molinari, in front of *Hotel Honduras Maya* ⓣ239 7691, airport ⓣ233 1307; National, airport ⓣ233 4962.

Moving on from Tegucigalpa

Tegucigalpa is the transport hub of the nation, with regular **bus departures** for all the major towns and numerous smaller ones. Departures **south** to the Golfo de Fonseca, **north** to San Pedro Sula and **east** to Olancho are frequent and the roads good; buy tickets before boarding if taking an intercity bus. Destinations off the main highways – Copán, the west, and the north coast, for example – are generally reached by luxury service only, though this can be a welcome comfort on long journeys, whilst **flying** to the north coast is a suitable alternative. Leaving Tegucigalpa by bus can be bewildering; routes are generally operated by several companies, out of their own private terminals. The main companies are listed below, with terminal addresses, major destinations and phone numbers. Unless otherwise stated, all terminals are in Comayagüela. An (L) after the company name denotes a luxury service.

North coast destinations

Cotraibal Av 7 between C 11 and 12, Barrio Concepcion (☎237 1666). Trujillo (1 daily; 7.30am).
Cristina Av 8 between C 12 and 13, Barrio Concepcion (☎220 0117). La Ceiba (6 daily; 6.15am–3.30pm).
Etrusca C 12 between Av 8 and 9, Barrio Concepcion (☎222 6881). La Ceiba (4 daily; 7am–4pm).
Hedman Alas (L) Av 11 between C 13 and 14 (☎237 7143). La Ceiba (3 daily; 6am–1pm), San Pedro Sula (4 daily; 6am–4.30pm), Tela (3 daily; 6am–1pm), Saenz Primera, Centro Comercial Perisur (☎233 4229). San Pedro Sula (6 daily; 6am–6pm).
El Rey Av Centenario off C9 (☎237 6609). San Pedro Sula (every 40 minutes; 5.30am–6.30pm).
Viana (L) Boulevard FFAA (☎235 8185). La Ceiba (2 daily; 6.30am–1pm), San Pedro Sula (4 daily; 6.30am–6.15pm).

Central and western highlands destinations

Hedman Alas (L) Av 11 between C 13 and 14 (☎237 7143). Copán Ruinas (2 daily; 6am and 10am).
Norteños Barrio El Centro between C 6 and 7 (☎237 0706). Comayagua (hourly 6.30am–4.30pm).
La Sultana Av 8 between C 11 and 12 (☎237 8101). Santa Rosa de Copán (5 daily; 6am–11.30am).

Olancho destinations

Aurora C 8 between Av 6 and 7 (☎237 3647). Juticalpa (hourly; 5am–5pm).
Discovery Av 7 between C 12 and 13 (☎222 4256). Juticalpa (hourly; 6.15am–5pm).
Lineas Olanchanas (L) Behind the Hedman Alas terminal (☎237 4883). Juticalpa (3 daily; 7.30am–4.15pm).

Southern destinations

Dandy Servicio Barrio Villa Adela (no phone). Danlí (6 daily; 6.30am–5pm).
Discua Litena Mercado Jacaleapa (☎230 0470). Danlí (hourly; 6.30am–7.30pm).
Mi Esperanza (L) C 23 and 24, Barrio Villa Adela (☎225 1502). Choluteca (6 daily; 4am–6pm).

International destinations

King (L) Blvd Comunidad Europa, Barrio La Granja (☎225 5415). Guatemala and San Salvador (2 daily; 6am and 1pm).
Tica Bus (L) C 16 between Av 5 and 6, Barrio Adela (☎220 0590). Managua, San José and Panamé (1 daily; 9am).

Cinemas There are a few around the centre, with more modern complexes in the outer suburbs. All show first-run Hollywood movies, generally with subtitles. Closest to the centre are Aires Tauro on the Subida Casa Martín, off Av Juan Gutemberg, and Cine Variadades, C Mendieta at Av Cristóbal Colón.

Embassies Belize, ground floor of *Hotel Honduras Maya* (T & F 239 0134; Mon–Fri 9am–1pm); Canada, Edificio los Castaños, 6th floor, Blvd Morazán (T 231 4538, F 231 5793; Mon–Fri 9am–3pm); Costa Rica, Colonia El Triangulo (T 232 1768, F 232 1876; Mon–Fri 8am–3pm); El Salvador, 2 Av 205, Col San Carlos (T 236 8045, F 236 9403; Mon–Fri 8.30am–noon & 1–3pm); Guatemala, 4 C at Arturo López Rodezno 2421, Col Las Minitas (T 232 9704, F 231 5655; Mon–Fri 8.30am–3pm); Mexico, Av República de México 2402, Col Palmira (T 232 6471, F 231 4719; Mon–Fri 8–11am); Nicaragua, C11, Block M1, Col Lomas del Tepeyac (T 232 4290, F 231 1412; Mon–Fri 8.30am–1pm); Panamá, Edificio Palmira 200, Col Palmira (T 231 5508, F 232 8147; Mon–Fri 8am–1pm); UK, Edificio Palmira, 3rd floor, Col Palmira (T 232 0612, F 232 5480; Mon–Thurs 8am–noon & 1–4pm, Fri 8am–3pm); US, Av La Paz (T 236 9320, F 236 9037; Mon–Fri 8am–5pm).

Immigration Dirección General de Migracíon, Av La Paz near to the US Embassy (Mon–Fri 8.30am–4.30pm).

Internet access Widely available throughout the city. Express (daily 8am–8.30pm) on Av Máximo Jeréz, two blocks north of the cathedral, is well set up, while there are several more along the same road including Mastercomp, Centro Comercial, Av Máximo Jeréz – both charge around US$1.10 an hour.

Laundry Mi Lavandería, Av 2, C 3–4, Comayagüela, has coin-operated machines and a laundry service (Mon–Sat 7am–6pm, Sun 8am–5pm); Super Jet, Av Juan Gutemberg, just past the *Hotel/Restaurante Nankin*, offers a reliable laundry service and dry-cleaning (Mon–Sat 8am–6.30pm).

Library The Archivo Nacional is open to the public for reference use only, on production of a passport (Mon–Fri 8.30am–5pm); you'll need to be very specific about what you're after.

Medical care Contact your embassy for a list of recommended doctors. Emergency departments (24hr) at Hospital Escuela, Blvd Suyapa (T 232 6234), and Hospital General San Felipe, C La Paz by the Bolívar monument.

Photography Kodak on Av Cervantes by the central plaza and Konica on the C Peatonal have rapid and reliable developing service and sell film.

Police Go to the FSP office on C Buenos Aires, behind Los Dolores church, with any problems.

Post office C Peatonal at C El Telegrafo, 3 blocks west of the main plaza (Mon–Fri 8am–7pm, Sat 8am–1pm). Window 1 on the ground floor deals with the *lista de correos*.

Supermarkets Más Por Menos on Av la Paz, just past the river bridge, has a wide selection of canned and packaged goods and household items.

Telephone office First try the cybercafés for discounted international phone rates. Hondutel is at Av Cristóbal Colón at C El Telegrafo. Phone services operate 24hr, and reverse-charge calls to Europe are available. The fax office is open Mon–Fri 7am–5pm.

Travel agents Alhambra Travel (T 220 1700) in the *Hotel Honduras Maya* is quick, friendly and efficient.

Around Tegucigalpa

Tegucigalpa's excellent local transport links make for easy day-trips to a number of destinations in the surrounding countryside. Set in the pine-clad mountains to the east are the tranquil former mining villages of **Santa Lucía** and **Valle de Ángeles**, while to the north, charming **San Juancito** is a point of access for the cloudforest of **Parque Nacional La Tigra**. It is possible to visit the park in a day, but it's worth planning to spend at least a night there to fully enjoy the forest and wildlife. Finally, overland travellers may well make use of the Las Manos **border crossing**, the closest entry point into **Nicaragua** from the capital.

Santa Lucía

Twelve kilometres east of the capital, set amid the pine-clad mountain slopes so characteristic of the central highlands, **SANTA LUCÍA** is a legacy of the days when the riches to be gained from silver mining brought settlers to the area in droves. Built by the Spanish in the late sixteenth century, the fortunes of this archetypal colonial village – all whitewashed houses and red-tiled roofs set on a steep hillside – rose and fell with those of the mines. Its citizens' finest hour came in

1572, when King Felipe II, in gratitude at the stream of riches being produced, presented them with a carved wooden Crucifix. Now residing in the church, it's honoured annually during the fiesta of the **Cristo Negro** in the first two weeks of January. The scenic views from Santa Lucía, over the mountains and down to Tegucigalpa, make for a relaxed half-day or so spent ambling around the steep, cobbled streets and surrounding forest. **Buses** for Santa Lucía leave Tegucigalpa's Mercado San Pablo, Col Reparto, every thirty minutes until 6pm; the last bus back leaves around 5.30pm.

Valle de Ángeles

Beyond Santa Lucía, the road continues to rise gently amid magnificent scenery, winding through forests of pine laced with slender trunks reaching up towards clear blue skies. Eleven or so kilometres from Santa Lucía is **VALLE DE ÁNGELES**, another former mining town, now reincarnated as handicraft centre and scenic getaway for *capitalanos*. Perched on the edge of a valley and surrounded by wooded mountains, the town slumbers during the week in preparation for weekends when the tourists pour in. **Buses** from Tegucigalpa terminate a couple of blocks from the Parque Central outside a small **tourist information** office (Tues–Sun 8.30am–5pm). Everything in the town is only a few minutes' walk from here.

The town is chiefly noted for its quality, carved wooden goods – including bowls and household items, trunks and ornaments – but there is also a wide range of leather and ceramics. Numerous small shops around town sell crafts, and gentle bartering is possible if you're serious about buying. The covered **Mercado Municipal de Artesanías**, by the bus stop, offers an overview of the range and quality of handicrafts available, while Lessandra Leather, close to the bus stop, sells export-quality leather goods at decent prices.

Practicalities

Direct **buses** for Valle de Ángeles (1hr) leave Tegucigalpa every 45 minutes until 6pm from an open lot near the Hospital General San Felipe. To get there, follow Av Juan Gutemberg/La Paz past the Bolívar Monument and turn right at the Esso petrol station; the terminal is about 100m further along on the left, hidden down a side street. The last bus back to Tegucigalpa is at 5.30pm.

Although most visit Valle de Ángeles as a day-trip, there are a couple of **places to stay**. Northeast of the centre, *Posada de Ángel* (☎766 2233; ❺) boasts comfortable rooms, all with bath, set around a courtyard; the pool here is also open to day visitors (US$2.75). Ten minutes' walk north of town on the road to San Juancito, *Villas del Valle* (☎766 2534; ❸–❺) is rather better with a selection of fully-fitted cabañas and cheaper rooms, some with shared bath, set around pretty wooded gardens. Reservations for both places are recommended, even during the week. For **eating**, try *Restaurante Epocas* (closed Mon) on the Parque Central, which also functions as an antique shop; a range of excellently prepared Honduran dishes are served in the dark, candle-lit interior. Probably the best place to eat is *La Casa de las Abuelas* (closed Mon), located a block north of the Parque in a colonial mansion and serving local and international dishes until 10pm. **Internet** access (daily 8am–9pm; US$1.65 per hour) is at the Hondutel office behind the market in the southeast corner of town.

San Juancito

Heading north from Valle de Ángeles, a dirt road curves round the mountains, eventually linking up with the highway to Olancho – the tortuously slow progress of buses along this bumpy, winding route allows you plenty of time to gaze at the mountain scenery. **SAN JUANCITO**, 10km from Valle de Ángeles and set about a kilometre below the road down a bumpy turn-off, is a charming albeit shabby village of wooden houses set in the narrow Río Chiquito valley. Most visitors pass through quickly on their way to the cloudforest of Parque Nacional La Tigra, but this friendly little place makes for a pleasant stopover before returning to Tegucigalpa. The sole **accommodation** option is the *Hotelito San Juan* (☎766 2237; ❷), close to where Tegucigalpa buses stop; the affable owner also runs the nearby *pulpería*. More good home cooking can be found at the *Mesa del Minero* comedor above the village on the road to the park; its veranda offers great views across the valley and village.

Direct **buses** to San Juancito (2hr) leave from the Mercado San Pablo, Col Reparto in Tegucigalpa every morning at 10am and 3.30pm. It's also possible to reach the village from Valle de Ángeles: take any bus or pick-up heading for Cantarranas, all of which pass the turn-off road, from where it's a ten-minute walk. Returning to Tegucigalpa there's a bus daily at 6.30am, with a second supposedly departing at 1pm on Saturdays. Bus times on this route change frequently, so it's best to check locally.

Parque Nacional La Tigra

The oldest reserve in Honduras, **Parque Nacional La Tigra** (daily 8am–3pm; US$10) was given protected status in 1952 and designated a national park in 1980. Only 14km from Tegucigalpa, its accessibility and good system of trails make it a popular destination; by the same token, however, the diversity of flora and fauna is not as great as that found elsewhere. Previously owned by the El Rosario mining company, the slopes above San Juancito were almost completely denuded through heavy logging early in the twentieth century; the company also cut a road through the heart of the forest to provide easier access to Tegucigalpa, destroying much of the original cloudforest in the process. What can be seen in the central sections of the park open to visitors, therefore, is secondary growth and consequently most large mammals are absent. Nonetheless, parts of the park still shelter abundant oak trees, bromeliads, ferns, vines, orchids and other typical cloudforest flora, along with **wildlife** such as deer, white-faced monkeys and ocelots – though they tend to stick to parts of the park that are out of bounds to visitors. Early mornings are the best time for seeing some of the estimated 200 species of **bird** and park employees can usually tell you where to find quetzals. The well-laid **trails** across La Tigra provide some easy hiking, either on a circular route from the visitor centre or across the park between the two entrances; it's worth staying a couple of nights if you want to see everything in the park.

The trails

All the park's **trails** branch off the old logging road, which heads up from El Rosario, climbing 600m over a 2200m pass before descending to the western entrance at Jutiapa. The most pristine patch of forest is around the two highest peaks, **Cerro la Peña de Andino** (2290m), on the southern side of the park, and **Cerro El Volcán** (2270m), though both of these are out of bounds to visitors.

One of the more interesting routes, **La Cascada** branches left off the logging road about twenty minutes past El Rosario, and heads north, around the curve of the mountain, to a waterfall; about halfway the path passes the old mine workings of Peña Blanca. It takes around an hour to reach the waterfall along a mostly flat trail. From the waterfall follow the path signed for Jutiapa, which after a relatively strenuous half-hour rejoins the logging road. Turn left here and after a few minutes take another trail on the left, which curves downhill through the thick cloudforest canopy. Take your time to admire the gnarled tree limbs, hung with vines and bromeliads, above the carpet of spongy mosses. A gentle walk along here brings you out, around thirty minutes later, just above the Jutiapa entrance.

Practicalities

From San Juancito, a dirt track, accessible only by 4WD, winds up the mountainside to the abandoned mining village of **El Rosario**. Though only a couple of kilometres long, the track is very steep and exposed. On foot, it takes one hot hour to reach the **entrance** to the park. A further ten minutes' walk from the park entrance brings you to the wooden buildings of the mining company, perched above the road on a steep hillside. One of these houses the **visitor centre**, which has boards describing the geography and wildlife of the park; the friendly warden is usually around to answer questions and can provide trail maps. **Guides** (US$8.50 per day) are also available, though they only speak Spanish. **AMITIGRA**, a private organization based in Tegucigalpa at Edificio Italia, Av República de Panamá, Col Palmira (☎235 8494, ⓔamitigra@sigmanet.hn), run the park and can provide information. Theoretically you're supposed to contact them before you visit if you want to reserve space in the simple, clean **dormitory** in the former hospital building behind the visitor centre, but in practice this doesn't seem to matter. Dorm beds cost a hefty US$10 per night, though you can **camp** for US$3.50 per person. Nights can get very chilly, so bring a sleeping bag.

There is a second **entrance** on the western side of the park, reached via the village of Jutiapa, 17km east of Tegucigalpa. Though slightly easier to get to from the capital, this is a less popular entry point with very few facilities. To get there, take a **bus** from Av Colón (near the *Hotel Granada*) in the city centre to the village of Los Limones (4 daily; 1hr), from where it's a stiff five-kilometre uphill walk, passing through the village of Jutiapa (2km) on the way.

East to Nicaragua: Las Manos

The **Las Manos** border crossing, some 120km from Tegucigalpa, is the most convenient place to enter **Nicaragua** from the capital. Buses run regularly to the town of El Paraíso, 12km from the border, from where minibuses and pick-ups shuttle to the border every thirty minutes or so. With an early enough start, it's possible to reach Managua (see p.496) the same day.

Discua Litena runs six direct **buses** to El Paraíso (2hr 15min) daily, from its terminal at the Mercado Jacaleapa, Col Kennedy, in the southeast suburbs of Tegucigalpa, a fifteen-minute taxi ride from the centre. The same company also runs a more frequent service to the regional capital of **Danlí**, some two hours from Tegucigalpa, from where there are half-hourly buses to El Paraíso. Taxi drivers hawking for business may well tell you that no buses run to the border from El Paraíso, but this is not true. A service runs every 90 minutes or so. If you don't want to wait around, a taxi will cost you US$2.75.

The border post itself is a collection of huts housing the *migración* and customs officials. Both sides are open daily until 5pm and crossing is generally straightforward. There are no banks, but eager moneychangers accept dollars, lempiras and Nicaraguan córdobas. There's a US$0.50 **exit tax** to leave Honduras. On the Nicaraguan side, trucks leave every hour for Ocotal, from where you can pick up buses to Estelí and Managua.

Southern Honduras

South of the capital, the pine-clad mountain ranges drop down through rolling green pastures to the arid heat of the Pacific coastal plains. A world away from the clear air and gentle climate of the highlands, this region nonetheless has its own particular, stark beauty, defined by dazzling light and ferocious temperatures. Traditionally this is a poor region, and in recent years many of the campesinos and cattle ranchers who struggled to eke a living here have moved north to swell the barrios of Tegucigalpa and San Pedro Sula.

With relatively few attractions to make the journey worthwhile, tourists are scarce hereabouts. For a change of pace from the capital, however, the shrimping town of **San Lorenzo** and the colonial city of **Choluteca** both make convenient stopovers on the longer route to Nicaragua, and with time to spare, the island of **Isla El Tigre** in the Golfo de Fonseca is a perfect, deserted getaway.

The main transport junction in this part of the country is at the village of **Jícaro Galán**, at the intersection of Highway CA-5 and the Carretera Interamericana, some 100km south of Tegucigalpa. Buses heading in all directions stop here to exchange passengers before continuing **west** to the border with **El Salvador** at El Amatillo, 42km away, or **east** across the coastal plain to **Nicaragua**.

West to El Salvador

Seedy, steamy and hot **El Amatillo**, point of entry for El Salvador, teems with border traffic, extrovert moneychangers and opportunistic beggars. Crossing here is straightforward, however, with the border post open daily (6am–10pm). A bank on the El Salvadorean side changes dollars and lempiras, but you'll get slightly better rates from the moneychangers as long as you're careful.

The quickest way to El Amatillo by **bus** is to take an express service from Tegucigalpa to Choluteca, changing at Jícaro Galán onto the Choluteca–El Amatillo service. Over the border in El Salvador, buses leave for Santa Rosa de Lima – 18km away, and the closest place offering accommodation (see p.344) – and San Miguel (58km; see p.336) every ten minutes until around 6.30pm.

The Golfo de Fonseca: Isla El Tigre

Forty or so kilometres from Jícaro Galán, boats depart the fishing village of **Coyolito** for the volcanic **ISLA EL TIGRE**, whose conical peak rises sharply against the sky across the sparkling Golfo de Fonseca. So far, tourist development on the island has been minimal, and its beaches, calm waters and constant sunshine make for a perfect getaway. A road runs all the way around the island, giving access to some glorious deserted beaches and a couple of hotels. From the southern side of the island there are stunning views across the gulf to Volcán Cosiguina in Nicaragua, and in some places to Isla Meanguera and the mainland of El Salvador beyond. The island's peak can be climbed in a steep and very hot two- to three-hour walk; ask for directions to the start of the trail, about fifteen minutes' walk southwest of Amapala, the island's only town.

Previously the country's major Pacific port and now a decaying, nineteenth-century relic, **AMAPALA** was founded by special decree in October 1833. A brief stint as capital of the country in 1876 preceded a long slide into obscurity, exacerbated when port activities were transferred to Puerto de Henecán, further east along the coast, in the early twentieth century. Today the town is a sleepy place where nothing much happens, even during the annual **fiesta de Santa Cruz** on May 5. Wooden houses, some still brightly painted, cluster up the hillside from the main dock, a picture that's completed by a large, plain wooden church, a small Parque Central and an even smaller market building. The economy of both the town and the island is now based on agriculture and a tiny shrimp plant.

It takes four or more hours to walk the 18-kilometre road round the island. Transport is limited to taxis; drivers hang around at the end of the dock and charge US$16.50 for a one-way trip around the island. Around ten minutes east from Amapala is **Playa Negra**, a pretty, curving volcanic sand beach, with the secluded white-sand **Playa Gualora** fifteen minutes to the west; both beaches have accommodation. The most popular beach with locals is **Playa Grande**, a kilometre or so prior to Playa Negra; although there is no accommodation here, the beach is backed by palms and rows of comedores serving freshly barbecued fish.

Practicalities

To **get to the island**, you need to reach Coyolito; the turn-off is around 12km southeast of Jícaro Galán on the Carretera Interamericana, marked by a Dippsa fuel station; local buses wait on the highway to collect passengers for the slow but beautiful 30km journey through agricultural land and mangrove swamps to the village. There's a steady flow of **launches** (15 minutes; US$0.55) between Amapala and

Coyolito from 7am until late afternoon, although frequency tends to drop off after lunch; alternatively, fishermen can ferry you across to the island (US$5.50) and – if you're willing to bargain hard – through the mangrove swamps east of Coyolito to **San Lorenzo** (see below). Buses run between Coyolito and San Lorenzo every forty minutes between 5am and 4.20pm.

The best **place to stay** in Amapala is the *ApartHotel Victoria* (☎895 8543; ❸), three blocks inland from the dock and home to small apartments with two bedrooms, lounge area and bathroom. The unsigned *Hotel Internacional* (☎895 8539; ❷), at the end of the dock above a makeshift tourist office, has large, airy rooms and a balcony overlooking the water. A couple of streets back from the seafront, the *Hotel Ritz* (no phone; ❶) charges even less, but rooms are smaller and there's no view. For **eating**, look no further than the *El Faro Victoria* restaurant to the right of the dock, with a small menu that changes daily and tables overlooking the bay.

Outside town, the renovated *Hotel Playa Negra* (☎221 4223; ❻), set on rocks above Playa Negra, has a pool, restaurant and comfortable rooms, all with private bath, but you pay extra for a/c; they also organise packages including all food and transport from Tegucigalpa. For a more atmospheric location head for the *Villas Karissa* (no phone; ❺) on secluded Playa Gualora, where there's a selection of clean cabañas, each sleeping up to five people.

San Lorenzo

Just east of the Coyolito turn-off, dusty **SAN LORENZO** stretches for a couple of kilometres between the highway and the coastal mangrove swamps. A lively, friendly town, it makes for a reasonable stopover en route to or from Choluteca and Nicaragua. For **accommodation**, try the basic but clean *Perla de Pacífico* (☎881 3025; ❷), on the main street. All rooms come with fan, but only the more expensive ones have private bath. Down by the waterfront, just past the town's shrimp-packing plant, the *Hotel Miramar* (☎881 2039; ❺) has somewhat overpriced rooms, although the view from the restaurant over the mangroves and beyond to Nicaragua is memorable. The hotel also has a swimming pool open to non-residents. Beyond the *Miramar* stands a row of clean seafood **restaurants** open for lunch and dinner. On the waterfront, *La Maravilla* is known for its *sopa de pescado*, known locally as "sopa de viagra" because of the vast amount of supposedly aphrodisiac seafood that it contains.

San Lorenzo is served by **buses** every 40 minutes from Coyolito. They pull in at a terminal just off the main highway behind the huge market building. Services to Nicaragua and intercity services between Choluteca and Tegucigalpa stop at the fuel station on the main highway.

Choluteca

Honduras's fourth-largest city, with a population of slightly over 100,000, **CHOLUTECA**'s main attraction is its old colonial centre, one of the finest in the country. The municipal authorities spent years restoring the city's historic streets, and despite the ravages of Hurricane Mitch, the graceful buildings survived the mud and floods without too much damage. Most places of interest are grouped around the Parque Central, itself a pleasant place to enjoy the cooler evening air. Dominating the square, the imposing seventeenth-century **cathedral** is worth a look for its elaborately constructed wooden ceiling. On the southwest corner of the square is the birthplace of **José Cecilio del Valle** (22 Nov 1777), one of the authors of the Central American Act of Independence in 1821 and elected President of the Federation in 1834, though he died in Guatemala before taking office. His statue stands in the middle of the square. There are plans to turn this building into a municipal museum, though it has been closed to the public for some time. On the southern outskirts of town is the **Santuário de Esquipulas**, an imitation of the real thing in Guatemala, constructed by a local priest keen to bring the experience closer to the people. The sanctuary draws pilgrims from all over the country, and the extensive gardens are a pleasant place for a stroll.

Practicalities

While a convenient stopover, once you've seen the centre there's not much reason to hang about in the stifling Cholutecan heat. The main **bus terminal** is ten blocks northeast of the Parque Central, a twenty-minute walk or US$0.55 taxi ride. Buses run regularly along the Carretera Interamericana in both directions: west to El Amatillo and east to San Marcos de Colón for El Espino and the Nicaraguan border. There are also direct buses to Tegucigalpa from the Mi Esperanza terminal, just around the corner.

Should you need **to stay**, the *Hotel Pierre* (ⓣ882 0676; ❸–❹) on Av Valle, two blocks east of the Parque Central, is comfortable and conveniently located; rooms all have bath and TV, and some have a/c. A block nearer to the Parque Central along Av Valle, *Hotel Bonsai* (ⓣ882 2648; ❷–❸) is one of the better cheap hotels. The most basic rooms are little more than a bed with fan and shared bathroom, but there are also a/c rooms with private bath. Choluteca's water supply is contaminated, so choose where you eat very carefully. Most of the better hotels have their own private wells of clean water and are safe places to eat, especially *Café Frosty* at the *Hotel Pierre*. Apart from the hotel options, *Capri*, four blocks west of *Hotel Bonsai*, is a well-known pizza restaurant.

Routes to Nicaragua

From Choluteca, the Carretera Interamericana runs northeast along the valley of the Río Choluteca before beginning to ascend gently into the mountains. **San Marcos de Colón**, 110km from Choluteca, is a friendly little town, with basic accommodation – try the clean *Hotelito Mi Esperanza* (no phone; ❷), two blocks from the central square – and banks, though they'll only change cash dollars. Buses terminate here, and to get to **El Espino** and the border, 10km away, you need to take one of the frequent colectivo taxis (US$0.75). The border post itself (open daily 8am–5pm only) is quiet and straightforward, with moneychangers on both sides. On the Nicaraguan side, regular buses run to Somoto, 20km from the border, whilst buses direct to Tegucigalpa leave San Marcos at 5am and 4pm. In most cases it's quicker to take a bus to Choluteca and change there.

An **alternative route** to Nicaragua is to take Highway CA-3 from Choluteca, which swings south then east for the 38km to **Guasaule** (see p.524) on the Río Negro. Buses for Guasaule leave from the Mercado Nuevo in Choluteca, a few blocks east of the Parque Central, calling in at the bus terminal on the way; the journey takes about 45 minutes. There's regular transport from Guasaule on to Chinandega, León and Managua.

4.2

The central and western highlands

In their haste to reach the archeological site at Copán, or the palm-fringed beaches on the north coast, all many travellers see of the **central and western highlands** is the view from a bus window. To hurry through means missing much, though, as this is the heartland of the country, an expanse of rugged, pine-clad mountain ranges, split by fertile valleys and scattered with villages and a handful of colonial towns. The highlands are also home to the country's highest concentration of indigenous peoples, many of them descendants of those who fought with Lempira against the Spanish conquistadors.

From the capital, the Carretera del Norte (**CA-5**) highway offers the most direct route through the highlands to San Pedro Sula and the north coast. Along this road, the first place of interest is **Comayagua**, formerly the nation's capital and still boasting beautiful churches and other remnants of colonial architecture. Not far to the north lies Honduras's biggest lake, the vast blue **Lago de Yojoa** – an ornithologist's paradise, though Hondurans are more likely to come here for a weekend of fishing and boating. The western shore is much less developed than the eastern shore, but the **Parque Nacional Santa Bárbara**, and the coffee town of **Santa Bárbara** to the west, are worth a visit.

With a little patience, you can take a bus along the painfully slow route that branches west off the CA-5 at **Siguatepeque**. Huddled beneath the jungle-covered escarpment of the **Montaña de Celaque**, the cobbled town of **Gracias**, another colonial centre built on the wealth provided by silver mines, is a relaxing base for hikes in the pristine cloudforest reserve of the **Parque Nacional Celaque**. Beyond here the road improves and it's an easy trip northwest to the region's main town, **Santa Rosa de Copán**. Long the centre of the highland tobacco-growing industry, Santa Rosa is a supremely relaxing place to stay, and still unspoilt despite its growing popularity with tourists.

One of the chief attractions of western Honduras – and indeed of the country – is the ancient site of **Copán Ruinas**. Though a little smaller than the major Maya sites in Guatemala or Mexico, Copán is equally impressive, thanks to its wealth of fabulous carvings and its wonderful site museum, perhaps the best in the Maya region. From here it's only 12km to the Guatemalan border post at **El Florido**.

Comayagua

The conquistadors' first city and the capital of Honduras until independence, faded **COMAYAGUA** lies just 85km north of its rival, Tegucigalpa, at the northeast end of the fertile Comayagua valley. Today, the main reason to visit is the architectural legacy of the colonial period, in particular the dramatic cathedral overlooking the Parque Central. The first Spanish settlement was established here on December 8, 1537, and destroyed soon afterwards during the Lempira rebellion (see p.379). Swiftly rebuilt in 1539, Santa María de Comayagua, as it was first known, rapidly became wealthy thanks to the discovery of **silver** in the vicinity. King Felipe II of

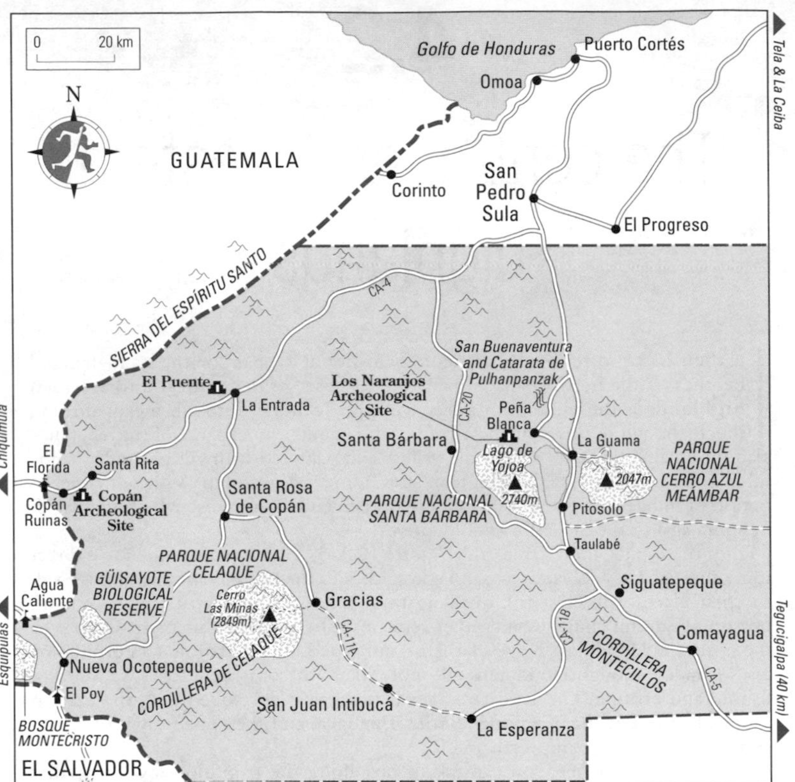

Spain bestowed on Comayagua the title of City in December 1557, and in 1573 it became the administrative centre for the whole of Honduras. Following independence, however, the city's fortunes began to decline, particularly after Tegucigalpa was designated alternate capital of the new republic in 1824, an ignominy compounded by the city's sacking and burning at the hands of Guatemalan forces during the civil war in 1827. Backwater status was sealed conclusively in 1880, when President Soto permanently transferred the capital to Tegucigalpa, supposedly because of the town's dislike for his wife. Although Comayagua is today a relatively rich and important provincial centre, its rivalry with Tegucigalpa has barely wavered over the centuries.

The Town

Most sights of interest are within a few blocks of the large **Parque Central**, graced by a pretty tiled bandstand, a fountain and a smattering of resident shoeshine boys. Few of the city streets are numbered, but the centre is relatively compact and orientation straightforward. On the southeast corner of the Parque is the **Catedral**, whose intricate facade consists of tiers of niches containing statues of the saints. More properly known as the **Iglesia de la Inmaculada Concepción**, it was the largest of its kind in the country during the colonial period, housing 16 altars, only four of which survive today. The Catedral is also home to the twelfth-century Reloj Arabe, one of the oldest clocks in the world. Formerly housed in the Alhambra in Granada, Spain, the clock was presented to the city by King Felipe II in 1582 and now resides in the cathedral's bell tower – the latter built between 1580 and 1708 and considered one of the outstanding examples of colonial Baroque architecture in Central America. Restoration work on the Catedral began in 2003 and is estimated to last three years, during which time the building will be closed to the public. However, some of the best colonial paintings have been moved across the road to the **Museo Colonial** (Mon–Sat 9am–noon & 2–4.30pm; L15). Housed in the Palacio Episcopal, the museum holds religious art, statues, chalices and documents from the city's churches, including Francisco Morazán's marriage license. The building was originally constructed for Comayagua's **university**, the first to be established in Central America, in 1678.

Two blocks north of the Parque Central, on the Plaza San Francisco, the **Museo Arqueológico** occupies a single-storey building that used to be the government palace (Tues–Sun 8.30am–4pm; US$1.10). The small but interesting range of exhibits include a pre-Columbian Lenca stela, polychrome ceramics and some terrific jade jewellery. The **Iglesia de La Caridad**, three blocks northwest of the Parque and completed in 1585, was built specifically for indigenous worshippers. At the back of the church is the country's only open-air chapel housing the "Señor de la Burrita", an image of Jesus on a donkey carried through the city during the Palm Sunday celebrations.

Two blocks east of the Parque Central is the **Caxa Real**, the former Governor's house and mint, perhaps the most important colonial building in the city. Years of fires, earthquakes and abandonment have taken their toll on the structure and only the facade still stands. Four blocks south from the Parque Central is another colonial church, the **Iglesia de la Merced**. Built between 1550 and 1558, though its facade dates back only to the early eighteenth century, this was the city's original cathedral, holding the Reloj Arabe until 1715, when the new cathedral was consecrated.

Practicalities

Highway CA-5 from Tegucigalpa passes 1.5km southwest of the centre, connected by a broad road known as "the Boulevard" (C Central). **Buses** between Tegucigalpa and San Pedro Sula drop passengers off on the highway at the top of the Boulevard, a US$0.50 taxi ride or twenty-minute walk from the Parque Central. Transportes Catrachos also run hourly buses to and from Tegucigalpa from a terminal five blocks south of the Parque. There are several **banks** on or just off the Parque Central, while **Hondutel** and the **post office** sit alongside each other on the street behind the cathedral. An extensive **general market** runs along Av 1 NO, C 2–3 NO, starting three blocks south of the cathedral.

The range of places to stay in Comayagua is quite narrow. Of the small number of **hotels** in town the most atmospheric place is *Casagrande*, two blocks south of the Iglesia La Caridad (Ⓣ772 0512, Ⓔcasagrande@honduras.com; ❺–❻), a beautiful colonial mansion with colonnaded courtyard and individually decorated rooms, filled with tasteful period furniture. *Hotel Norymax Colonial*, on C Central in front of the school (Ⓣ772 1703; ❸), is perhaps the nicest of several cheaper options along this road, with clean comfortable rooms and flower-filled balconies. At the northern end of town, just off the Boulevard, *Hotel Quan* (Ⓣ772 0070, Ⓔhquan@hondutel.hn) is a good alternative base, with a choice of either modern motel-style accommodation (❹) or less pleasant budget rooms (❷), some with private bath.

By far the best place in town to **eat** is the *Villa Real*, a block southeast of the plaza. Set in a beautifully restored colonial home, this stylish restaurant has an extensive menu, including pasta (US$4), grilled meats and fish dishes (US$6–7), plus a well-stocked bar. A popular option with local expats is *Hannemann's* on C Central, with an international menu heavy on Cajun-style food, while cheaper canteen-style service is available at *Comida Rapida Veneciana* a block east of the Parque Central.

Siguatepeque

North of Comayagua, the Carretera del Norte climbs across the pine-forested expanse of the Sierra de Montecillos before reaching **SIGUATEPEQUE**, about halfway between Tegucigalpa and San Pedro Sula. Meaning "town of beautiful women" in Nahautl, it's an attractive, garden-filled city with a refreshingly cool montane climate. The main focus is unsurprisingly the **Parque Central**, one of the nicest in the country, shaded by moss-covered araucaria and cypress trees. Northwest of the centre, **Bosque Calenterique** is an area of virgin forest, with towering pines and, on the highest slopes, a stand of Magay cacti that towers to over three metres in height. From here there is a magnificent view over the city. Just outside town to the south on the main highway is the privately owned **Jardín Rittenhouse** (8am–4.30pm; US$1.10), a mini-utopia laced with twisting paths, pools, bridges and an organic herb centre. In addition to its natural attractions, Siguatepeque is something of a hotbed of alternative therapies. The renowned herbalist Dr Waldemar (☎773 2828) resides here, while the **Hospital de Acupunctura** near Bosque Calenterique offers acupuncture, herbal medicines, sauna and massage (☎773 0305).

Accommodation in town is very cheap. *Hotel Versailles* (☎773 0157; ❷) on the eastern side of the Parque Central is a good budget bet with en-suite rooms including hot water, fan and TV. The finest hotel in town is the *Hotel Plaza San Pablo* (☎773 4020; ❹), three blocks southwest of the Parque, a modern, well-equipped hotel with a/c, secure parking and a restaurant. For **food**, the most upmarket option is *Steak House El Corral* a block south of *Hotel Plaza San Pablo*, with juicy cuts of meat served in a relaxed, romantic atmosphere. *Pizzeria Veneciana* two blocks west of the Parque is one of the longest standing restaurants in town, serving high-quality pizza. South of town on the main highway, *Atenciónes Maragarita* specialises in fresh fish from Lago Yojoa, including tilapia and bass.

Lago de Yojoa and around

Beyond Siguatepeque, the highway descends from the mountains and the air becomes appreciably warmer. Some 35km north sits the spectacular, sparkling blue **Lago de Yojoa**, a natural lake approximately 17km long and 9km wide. Its reed-fringed waters, sloping away to a gentle patchwork of woods, pastures and coffee plantations, are overlooked by the mountains of Cerro Azul Meámbar to the east and Santa Bárbara to the north and west. Both of these contain small but pristine stretches of **cloudforest** and are protected as national parks. The lake itself attracts over 400 species of **bird**, one of the highest concentrations in the country, along with small numbers of fishermen. In a previous incarnation in the 1960s, the lake was a magnet for sportsmen, who came to fish for the predatory **black bass**, introduced into the lake in 1954. Stocks of these depleted rapidly due to overfishing, but judicious management has succeeded in encouraging recent regrowth.

The lake is also a favourite with middle-class *Hondureños* at the weekends, when its peace and quiet is shattered by the buzz of jet-skis; during the week, however, the waters – and surrounding hotels – are virtually empty, making for a supremely relaxing base for a couple of days of rowing, birdwatching and exploring the surrounding countryside.

The eastern and northern shores

At **TAULABÉ**, the highway forks, with the CA-5 continuing up along the eastern shore of the lake. The main attraction here is the close proximity of some interesting **caves** (8am–5pm; US$0.55) at km140. Still not fully explored, over twelve kilometres of tunnels and caverns have so far been discovered, though only 400 metres have paths and lighting; local guides (US$1.75–2.25) hang around, but negotiate a price beforehand. Twenty kilometres north sits the small, unremarkable village of **Pitosolo** at the southeast tip of the lake. On the lakeshore 15km further north is the comfortable *Honduyate Marina* hotel (☎990 9386; ❼); watersports equipment, including fishing tackle, canoes and sailing boats, are available at the hotel and boat trips on the lake can be arranged.

Continuing north 7km the highway divides at **La Guama**, from where a dirt road (4WD required) runs east for another 5km to the entrance to **Parque Nacional Cerro Azul Meámbar** (daily 8am–4pm). Named after its highest peak, the blue-hued Cerro Azul Meámbar (2047m), this is one of the smaller reserves in the national network, with a core of untouched cloudforest. Anyone planning to hike here should be prepared for precipitously steep gradients in the upper reaches of the reserve, with sheer rockfaces, dense vegetation and tumbling waterfalls. Cerro Azul is managed by a private organization, PAG, based in Siguatepeque on C 3, Av 1–2 NO (☎773 2741); they can provide information on hiking and hiring guides. At the entrance, the park's **education centre** has cabins with bunks (❶), plus information on a number of short walking trails. There's no public transport to the park, but tours can be arranged through Angel Boesch (Ⓔaboesch@emb.hn) at the *Hotel Agua Azul* (☎991 7244; ❺), a little way north of La Guama along a paved road. The rustic cabins here enjoy a magical setting among wooded grounds sloping down to the waterside, and the restaurant's veranda has fabulous views across the lake; there's also a pool, and the hotel rents boats and organizes horse-riding on request.

The village of **Agua Azul**, just past the hotel, has some basic stores and a couple of comedores – the only eating places around here outside the hotels. Continuing along the road, it's 6km to the *Finca Las Glorias* (☎556 0461; ❻), another charming hotel; fishing trips and tours of the surrounding coffee finca are available. Four kilometres further on, the shabby, overgrown village of **Peña Blanca** is the commercial focus for the area. **Buses** running along the highway will stop at Pitosolo and La Guama if requested; there's an hourly service from the latter to Peña Blanca.

Two kilometres beyond Peña Blanca is the enjoyable *D&D B&B* (☎994 9719, Ⓔdndbrew@yahoo.com; ❷). The site's **microbrewery** represents your only chance to break the state monopoly on Honduran-brewed beers, with several varieties on offer for around US$1 a mug. If you decide to stay, there are six rooms for rent, as well as a pool and restaurant. To get here follow the El Mochito road (or take a colectivo taxi) until you pass a bridge over a small creek. A signed dirt road heads off to the right past a stone wall to the premises. A few kilometres from here, by the water's edge, is the archeological site of **Los Naranjos** (daily 8am–5pm; US$5), once an extensive Maya settlement. Most of the structures have been deliberately left unexcavated in an effort to protect them, though this will be of little comfort for disappointed visitors looking for a return on their entrance fee. There are, however, good, flat walking trails in the surroundings with good birdwatching opportunities.

Catarata de Pulhapanzak

North of Peña Blanca is one of the highlights of the region, the **Catarata de Pulhapanzak** (daily 8am–6pm; US$1.65, plus US$0.40 per person for camping), a stunning, 43-metre-high cascade of churning white waters on the Río Lindo. Claimed to be the prettiest waterfall in the country, the cascade is at its most dazzling in the early mornings, when rainbows form in the rising sun. A set of steep, wet steps on the right-hand side descends past several viewpoints to the riverbank at the bottom of the falls. The area immediately around the falls has been designated a public park, with comedores and a swimming spot. Right by the entrance, a grassy expanse is identified as the "ceremonial plaza" of a centre of Lenca culture believed to have been sited here, although no excavation has been carried out. The falls are an easy fifteen-minute walk from the village of **San Buenaventura**, 8km north of Peña Blanca; buses between El Mochito and San Pedro Sula run hourly passing through both Peña Blanca and Buenavista en route.

Santa Bárbara and the western shore

Back in Taulabé, the junction to the left leads onto Highway CA-20, which winds inland, separated from the western shore of the lake only by the green expanse of the Parque Nacional Santa Bárbara. Forty-five kilometres along this road is the colonial city of **SANTA BÁRBARA**. The city is a surprisingly sleepy place where handicrafts from the surrounding villages are sold, including reed baskets from La Arada, woven purses from Gualjoco and corn-husk dolls from Nueva Celilac. One of the best places to buy handicrafts is the **Empresa Comunitaria Yahamala** (Mon–Sat 8am–5pm, Sat 8am–noon) a couple of blocks southeast of the Parque Central. On the hillside overlooking the town, the ruins of the old colonial building known to locals as "**Castillo Bogran**" makes for a pleasant hike with great views at the summit. Should you wish to **stay**, the best and most central choice is the simple *Gran Hotel Colonial* (☎643 2665; ❹) two blocks east of the Parque, with en-suite rooms featuring hot water and TV. Santa Bárbara is served by regular **buses** from San Pedro Sula, Tegucigalpa and Comayagua, arriving and departing from the terminal two blocks west of centre.

The towering peak of the **Cerro Santa Bárbara** (2740m) forms a superb backdrop to the waters of the western shore of the lake. The peak is encircled by the dense, green cover of the **Parque Nacional Santa Bárbara**, consisting of virgin cloudforest, plus thick stretches of pine and mixed broadleaf forest on the lower slopes. The reserve is as yet relatively undeveloped for tourism and there are no facilities, though guides can by found by asking in the lakeside hotels.

La Esperanza to Gracias and Parque Nacional Celaque

South of the department of Santa Bárbara lie Lempira and Intibucá, the departments that make up the **western highlands** of Honduras, a beautiful landscape of pine forests, sparsely inhabited mountains and remote villages. These two departments contain the highest concentration of indigenous peoples in the country. Around La Esperanza particularly, look out for Lenca women wearing their typical coloured headdresses working in the fields, the traditional female role in Lenca society.

The drawback to travelling around here is the state of the roads: most are unsurfaced and can become impassable during the wet season. Private vehicles are infrequent, and public transport frustratingly slow and uncomfortable. If you're prepared to put up with the delays, however, you can take a cross-country route through La Esperanza to the colonial town of **Gracias** and the stunning cloudforest of the **Parque Nacional Celaque**, via the traditional village of **San Juan Intibucá**. Beyond Gracias the infrastructure begins to improve, and it's an easy journey on to Santa Rosa de Copán (see p.412).

La Esperanza

Three kilometres north of Siguatepeque a good paved road leaves the main CA-5 highway and heads 68km west to **LA ESPERANZA**; the route is served by buses every couple of hours until mid-afternoon. Centre of commerce and trade in the region and capital of the department of Intibucá, La Esperanza livens up during the colourful **weekend market**, when Lenca farmers from surrounding villages pour into town. While there's nothing of much interest to buy, it's worth hanging around to observe the intensive bartering and socializing that goes on. Should you need to stay, the centrally located *Hotel Alexandra* (☎783 1140; ❸) is a reasonable bet, with en-suite bathrooms and hot water. For a little more luxury, *Hotel Entrepinos* (☎783 0743; ❺) offers comfortable cabañas surrounded by pine trees. It's located 5km outside of town off the road to Siguatepeque.

San Juan Intibucá

A bumpy 52km north of La Esperanza, the village of **SAN JUAN INTIBUCÁ** is beginning to earn a place on the tourist trail thanks to a local *cooperativa* promoting the Lenca traditions of the area. Information about available tours and demonstrations are available from *Hotel Guanascos* in Gracias (see below) or *La Casa de Gladis Nolasco* a block from the Hondutel office on C Principal; options include participating in the roasting of coffee beans, hikes to nearby waterfalls and cloudforest, and observing the production of traditional handicrafts. Prices start from around US$1.10 for artesanía demonstrations to US$8.25 for a full-day guided hike. A variety of basic accommodation is provided by locals through the *cooperativa*, some with en-suite bathrooms and even hot water (❶). There are three daily pick-ups from La Esperanza (10am–4pm; 1.5 hours) and four daily from Gracias (6am–1pm; 1 hour) running to the town.

Gracias

Founded in 1536 by Spanish conquistador Juán de Chavez, **GRACIAS** lies in the shadow of the **Montaña de Celaque**, the peak that forms the centrepiece of the nearby **Parque Nacional Celaque**. Gracias is one of the oldest towns in Honduras, and it was here that the indigenous revolt was quashed in 1538 when the Spanish treacherously murdered the indigenous leader Lempira after promising him a truce. Lempira's betrayal is remembered during a weeklong festival from June 12–20. Today, Gracias is a hot, dusty place with little going on, but well located for day-trips to surrounding natural attractions. For a good view of the town's colonial buildings, including three churches in various states of disrepair, head up to **Castillo San Cristóbal** (daily 8am–5pm; free), a restored fort on a small hill, five minutes' walk above the western edge of town. The fort was built, but never ultimately used, to defend the area against Guatemalan troops during the nineteenth-century civil wars; inside its walls is the tomb of Juan Lindo, president of Honduras from 1847 to 1852. About an hour's walk south of Gracias are a set of natural **hot springs** (officially daily 8am–8pm, but access almost any time; US$1.50), with small purpose-built pools for bathing in the 36–39°C waters; a comedor at the site serves basic meals, snacks and drinks. The path at the southeast edge of town to the springs starts on the right just after the first river bridge on the road to La Esperanza, but it's easy to get lost, so ask directions along the way.

Practicalities

The **bus terminal** is an empty lot three blocks west of the Parque Central; buses heading west arrive and depart from here, while the 5am bus from La Esperanza stops at the southeast edge of town. Pick-up services supplement this bus route and are considerably faster, but it's still a long and uncomfortable ride. Regular buses to Santa Rosa de Copán depart throughout the day. Banco de Occidente, one block west of the Parque, changes dollars cash and travellers' cheques. **Hondutel** and the **post office** are next to each other, one block south of the Parque. **Internet** access is available at *Ecolem* (US$1.65) in front of the *Guancascos* hotel.

Best **accommodation** in town is at *Guancascos* (Ⓣ656 1219, Ⓔfronica@utopia.com; ❹), three blocks uphill (south) of the bus station. The spotless, en-suite rooms come with hot water and TV, and the owner is an excellent source for local information. The backpacker's favourite is *Hotel Erick*, one block north of the Parque (Ⓣ656 1066; ❷), which is basic but cheap and tidy. Most of the **eating** around town is comedor-style with basic, cheap menus. The restaurant at *Guancascos* draws most diners, serving a tasty *sopa de pescado* on a terrace with fantastic views. A block to the west, *Rinconcito Graciano* features meals made solely from natural, local ingredients, though service is indifferent.

△ Parque Nacional la Tigra

Parque Nacional Celaque

Containing one of the largest and most impressive expanses of virgin cloudforest in Honduras, **Parque Nacional Celaque** (US$2.75, plus US$2.75 per night) is best approached from Gracias. The focus of the park is the **Montaña de Celaque**, an escarpment that is the source of eleven rivers – Celaque means "box of water" in the Lenca language – and home to the highest peak in Honduras, the **Cerro Las Minas** (2849m). Thick forests coat the slopes of the escarpment, rising from pine and oak through to the cloudforest that covers the plateau.

The park entrance is 8km west of Gracias; take the dirt road that runs through the village of Mejicapa, 2km away, from where a marked track leads uphill to the entrance. Few private vehicles run along here, but the better hotels in Gracias can organise transport, costing upwards of US$10 one way if alone, to as little as US$2.75 if in a group. If walking, bear in mind that much of the route to the park is along the road and it can get very hot and dusty. From the entrance, a track leads for another 2km or so through the pine forest to the basic **lodge**, where there are bunkrooms and showers. Fresh drinking water is available here – and at stages throughout the hike – though if planning an overnight stay bring your own food supplies; last available food can be prepared by Doña Alejandrina at the lodge for a small fee. It can get cold at night and the trails can be slippy even when dry, so sleeping bags, decent boots and a change of warm clothing are essential. *Guancascos* in Gracias (see p.409) functions as an unofficial **information centre** for the park. As well as selling booklets and maps and renting some camping gear, they can also arrange lifts up to the lodge. They also run a small cabaña (price negotiable) near the park entrance, which should be booked at the hotel before departure.

Gentle rambles are possible through the woods surrounding the lodge, but a more adventurous option is the six-kilometre marked trail through the forest up to the peak of Cerro Las Minas. It's not necessary to hire a guide (US$20 per day) for this trail, though you'll need one if planning to undertake one of the more difficult treks on the southern slopes. In the upper reaches of the park much of the main trail consists of forty-degree slopes, so this is not a hike for the unfit. Plan on spending at least one night camping if the summit is your aim; there are two designated camping spots along the way.

The Trail to Cerro Las Minas

Starting behind the lodge, **the trail up Cerro Las Minas** follows a river for about five minutes, then crosses over twice and heads steeply uphill before running southwest along and up the slope of the mountain, through pine forest. After about an hour's walk, the track splits at approximately 1800m, with the right fork leading off to give glorious views of some waterfalls half an hour away, while the left fork leads to the first of the camping sites, **Campamento Don Tomás**, an hour and a half uphill. The shack that once housed bunkbeds here has been vandalised, so you'll need camping equipment if planning on staying.

From the campsite, the marked path traverses some scattered secondary growth, before heading very steeply upwards through thicker forest, levelling out on the plateau (2560m) two hours further on; **Campamento Naranjo** is at the edge of the plateau by a stream (drinkable), and has room for a few tents. Here the cloudforest proper begins, wrapped in a hushed, cathedral-like calm, and dripping wet at any time of year. Oaks and liquidambars loom overhead, draped in vines and bromeliads and banked by mosses and ferns. Thousands of years of geographical isolation has resulted in several endemic species of flora, including the abundant *Oreopanax limpiriana* and globus yew. Locals claim that the area is home to more quetzals than the whole of Guatemala, though you'll have to be patient to see one – they are often attracted to fruiting *aguacate* trees. From Campamento Naranjo to the peak is another two hours, much of it an easier climb, except for the last half-hour or so.

The ancient tree cover is more stunted at the summit, a result of almost continual cloud cover and temperatures that frequently drop below freezing.

Santa Rosa de Copán and southwest to the border

It's an easy ninety-minute bus ride 45km northwest from Gracias to **SANTA ROSA DE COPÁN**, a wonderfully preserved colonial relic built on the proceeds of the tobacco industry. Unusually for a town of this size, the majority of its streets are still cobbled, preserving an authentic colonial feel in spite of the town's unashamedly commercial outlook. Thus you'll find high-street boutiques lodged in red-roofed colonial mansions, and enclosed courtyards transformed into shopping plazas and malls.

Chosen as the headquarters of *La Real Factoria del Tabaco* (Royal Tobacco Factory) in 1765 because of the high quality of the crop grown in the region, the golden weed continues to play a role in the local economy. While the **Flor de Copán Cigar Company** maintains offices in the town centre – in the original Royal Tobacco Company building on C Centenario – their **cigar factory** is located 2km northwest of the town centre, about 300m after turning right out of the bus station. Around 30,000 hand-rolled cigars are produced here daily, and **tours** in Spanish are available (Mon–Fri 8.30am–noon & 2–4.30pm, Sat 7am–noon; US$2); you will not be admitted if you are wearing shorts or a skirt. Around eight blocks to the west is another mainstay in the local economy, the INAGINSA **coffee factory** (Mon–Fri 8.30am–noon & 2.30–5pm; free). A family-run business, tour guides are occasionally available but more than likely you'll be allowed to wander around on your own.

Back in the centre of town is the delightful, shady **Parque Contreras**, with a cathedral on its eastern side. **Calle Centenario**, lined with shops and restaurants, runs along the southern edge of the Parque, past the town **market** a couple of blocks east.

Practicalities

All **buses** arrive at a terminal just off the highway, about 2km northwest of the centre at the bottom of a long hill. It's a hard walk to the centre; other options into town include a taxi (US$0.70) and the yellow buses marked *urbanos* (US$0.15) running regularly to the Parque. **Hondutel** and the **post office** (Mon–Fri 8am–noon & 2–5pm, Sat 8–11am) are on the western edge of the Parque, with Banco Atlántida to the south. For **Internet** access, try the *Copanet* (daily 9am–9.20pm; US$0.55) at Plaza Savedra opposite *Hotel VIP Copán*. A town map can be purchased (US$0.85) at the Casa de Cultura two blocks south of the Parque, but for detailed **information** you're best off talking to the American owner of *Pizza Pizza*, who acts as an unofficial tourist information provider. Lenca Land Trails (ⓔlenca@hondutel.hn; based in the *Hotel Elvir*) offer a number of excellent tours, including trips to Parque Nacional Celaque, indigenous villages and nearby hot springs.

Accommodation

Santa Rosa has a wide range of **places to stay**, with the best of the budget accommodation clustered around Av 3 NE between C 1 and 2 NE.

Blanca Nieves Av 3 NE ⓣ662 1312. A decent budget option with friendly owners. Access is through a small shop, but rooms are neat and comfortable, those en-suite being larger than those with shared bathrooms and thus better value. ❷

Hotel El Rosario Av 3 NE ⓣ662 0211. Another decent budget option next door to *Blanca Nieves*, with a choice of en-suite and shared bathrooms. Rooms are clean, but some are a little dark and cell-like, and those with bathrooms are little more than a section of the same room portioned off with a shower curtain. ❸

Hotel Elvir C Centenario at Av 2 SO ☎662 0805, ⓔhotelelvir@hondudata.com. The most upmarket hotel in town, colonial-style rooms painted in traditional Copanecan colours with bath, TV, telephone and a/c as standard, as well as access to a pool, bar and restaurant. Lenca Land Tours (see opposite) operate from here, providing cultural tours to nearby villages. ❻

Hotel Mayaland opposite the bus terminal ☎662 0233. Conveniently located for transport, or if you are passing through and have an early bus, but a little way out from the centre. Rooms are modern and impersonal, but all en-suite with TV and telephone, though not all have a/c. Reliable hot water is a bonus. ❹

Eating and drinking

Santa Rosa's growing number of visitors has resulted in something of an **eating and drinking** boom. There are a variety of different types of cuisine on offer, as well as ubiquitous cheap comedores aimed mainly at the local market, although many of these provide excellent and filling food at rock-bottom prices. If looking to let loose after a hard week on the road, the most popular disco is *Luna Jaguar* (Wed–Sat 7pm–late) at the corner of C Centenario and Av 3 SE, playing a mix of Latin and international pop music. For a rowdier crowd, try *X tassi's* a block and a half south of the Parque along Av 1 SE.

Flamingos Av 1 SE, a block south of the Parque ☎662 0654. The most lauded restaurant in town, with a varied international menu that is predictably rather pricey. It's worth splashing out for a special occasion, and there's also a full bar. Closed Tues.

Lily's C Centenario a block west of the Parque ☎662 1733. Popular French restaurant with meals served on a pleasant patio courtyard. Locally produced cigars available at the bar.

Pizza Pizza 5 blocks east of the Parque along C Centenario. Great-value pizza and pasta, this was western Honduras's first pizza restaurant and is justifiably popular among the travelling community. Owner Warren Post is a mine of information on the area, and there is a book exchange and noticeboard. Closed Wed.

El Rodeo Av 1 SE, 2 blocks south of the Parque ☎662 0697. The best steaks in town, with huge slabs of meat served at very reasonable rates. However, the rows of animal heads adorning the walls may make you feel more like a salad.

The route to Nueva Ocotepeque and the border

From Santa Rosa de Copán, Highway CA-4 heads southwest through low valleys before climbing through the eastern flanks of the Cordillera de Merendón. **El Portillo**, a small, shabby roadside hamlet, marks the highest stretch of paved road in the country, at 2010m. Fifteen kilometres beyond the pass is **NUEVA OCOTEPEQUE**, the last town in Honduras before the border with both El Salvador and Guatemala, and served by several buses a day from Santa Rosa de Copán. Modern and unremarkable – it was founded after a flood destroyed the colonial village of Ocotepeque in 1934 – the town is redeemed by its setting at the base of the towering Cerro el Sillón (2310m). Most visitors pass straight through en route to El Salvador or Guatemala, but if you need **to stay** the best hotel in town is the *Internacional* (☎653 2357; ❸) at the corner of the Parque, excellent value for tidy, modern rooms, all with bath and cable TV. The Banco de Occidente, just up from the hotel towards the bus stop, changes dollars cash and travellers' cheques, but you'll get better rates for Guatemalan quetzales at the border.

Southeast of town lies the **Reserva Biológica la Fraternidad**, more often referred to as the **Bosque Montecristo**. Cerro Montecristo, at the centre of the reserve, is where the borders of El Salvador, Guatemala and Honduras meet. Access from the Honduran side is extremely difficult; the visitor centre and few tourist facilities that exist are reached through **Metapán** in El Salvador (see p.357).

The border: El Salvador and Guatemala

Buses run 10km south to the El Salvadorean border at **El Poy** regularly until late afternoon. El Poy itself is a drab, dusty little place but the crossing is straightforward as the migration windows are next to each other in the same building. There are no banks, but a profusion of moneychangers. For most nationalities there's no fee to enter El Salvador, though residents of Canada, USA, Greece and Portugal will be charged US$10 for their tourist card. El Poy has no **accommodation**, but there are basic hotel facilities in El Salvador at the village of Citalá, 1km away, and better places at San Ignacio, 5km from the border, and La Palma, the nearest town, 11km south of the border (see p.364). Buses to La Palma and on to San Salvador leave every thirty minutes until 4.30pm.

Some 18km west of Nueva Ocotepeque is the **Guatemalan** border crossing of **Agua Caliente** (open 6am–7pm). Buses make the thirty-minute trip to the border every half-hour or so until 6pm. There are no banking or accommodation facilities on the Honduran side. Over in Guatemala, minibuses leave every twenty minutes for Esquipulas (see p.244) until 6pm. There are six daily buses from the border, running every two hours between 7.30am and 3.30pm direct to San Pedro Sula (6hr); alternatively, take the first bus to Nuevo Ocotepeque and change buses there.

Copán and around

Set in serene, rolling hills 45km as the crow flies from Santa Rosa de Copán, **COPÁN** is one of the most impressive of all Maya sites. Copán's pre-eminence is not due to size – in scale it's far less impressive than sites such as Tikal or Chichén Itzá – but to the overwhelming legacy of artistic craftsmanship that has survived over hundreds of years. Not surprisingly, the site is heavily promoted by the Honduran government and tour operators, and now ranks as the second most visited spot in the country after the Bay Islands.

Copán Ruinas Town

The archeological site of Copán lies one kilometre south of the small town of **COPÁN RUINAS** – Copán to tourists, but Las Ruinas to locals, who use Copán for Santa Rosa de Copán – a charming place of steep cobbled streets and red-tiled roofs set among green hills. Despite the weekly influx of hundreds of visitors, which now contributes a large part of the town's income, it has managed to remain largely unspoilt and genuinely friendly. Many travellers are seduced by Copán's delightfully relaxed atmosphere, clean air and rural setting, and end up spending longer here than planned, studying Spanish, eating and drinking well, or exploring the region's other minor sites, hot springs and the beautiful countryside.

Arrival and information

Most **buses** enter town from the east, by a small football field, with some continuing up the low hill to the Parque Central; buses from Guatemala enter town from the west. Direct luxury air-conditioned Hedman Alas **buses** (Ⓣ651 4037) leave Copán for San Pedro Sula Monday to Saturday at 10.30am and 5.30pm, and 2.30pm on Sundays (2hr 45min), and continue on to Tegucigalpa. Two other bus companies, Gama and Casarola, also run less-expensive direct and non-direct services to/from San Pedro Sula; while slower local buses run every two hours to La Entrada, from where there are plenty of connections to San Pedro Sula and Santa Rosa de Copán. For travel around town and nearby sites (including the ruins), mini-motorbike taxis are cheap and efficient, charging US$0.30 for a typical journey. Roads around town are unnamed, but the town is small and you'll soon get your bearings.

There is a **tourist office** just off the Parque Central (Ⓣ651 4394, Ⓔinfo@copanhonduras.org; daily 8am–7pm), though consider checking out the excellent Ⓦwww.copanhonduras.org website before arriving. The **post office** is just off the Parque behind the museum; **Hondutel** is just south of the plaza.

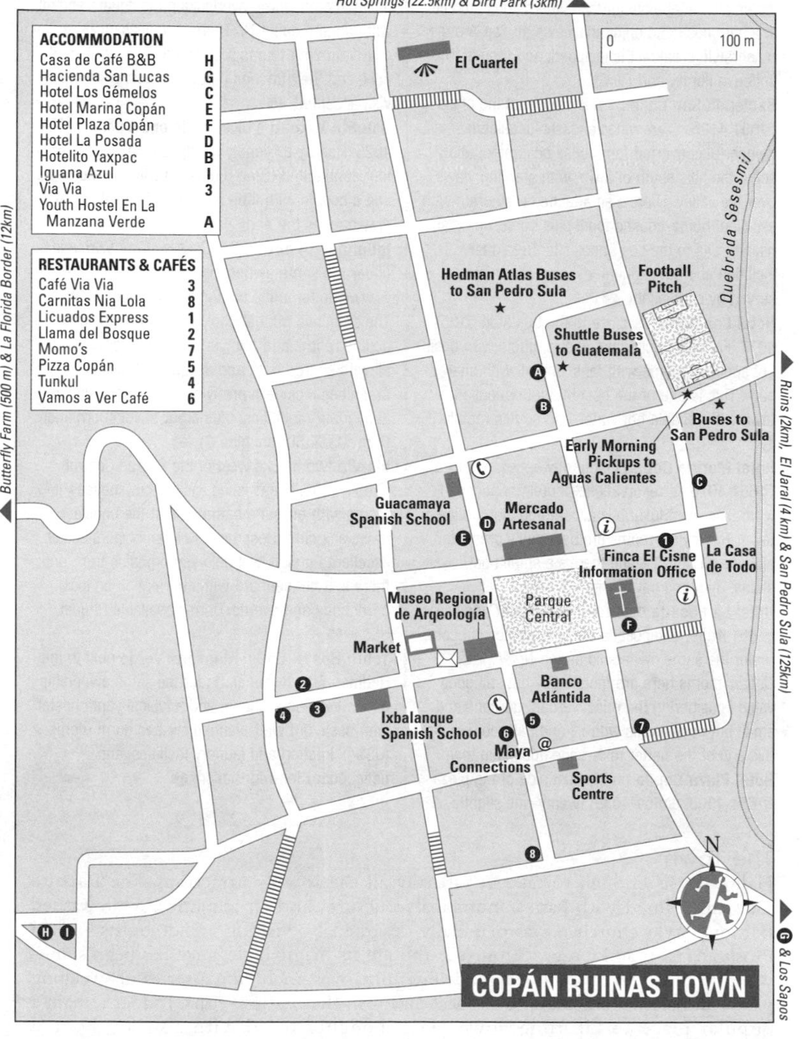

Accommodation

Many of the town's older **hotels** have undergone refits to attract the ever-expanding organized-tour market, while a swathe of new mid-range places help keep prices competitive. There's a clutch of pricier places along the streets north of the Parque, and several budget options, though the latter fill quickly so book ahead if arriving late in the day. Beware also of unofficial hotel representatives trying to shepherd you into hotels upon arriving (some may even board buses armed with a highly developed sales pitch).

Casa de Café B&B at the southwest edge of town, overlooking the Río Copán valley ⓣ651 4620, ⓦwww.todomundo.com/casadecafe. A charming place, with ten comfortable and airy rooms, all with wood panelling and nice individual touches, private bathrooms and steaming hot water, plus a fabulous garden where you could lie in a hammock and enjoy the views all day. A huge ranch-style breakfast is included, and there's free coffee, a library and TV. ❻

Hacienda San Lucas 1.8 km south of the plaza Ⓣ651 4106, Ⓦwww.haciendasanlucas.com. Wonderful converted farmhouse accommodation set in the hills south of town, with startling views over the valley. There's an attached restaurant with excellent home-cooked food, plus horse-riding and hiking trails to the Los Sapos site. Breakfast included and atmospheric evening meals are served by candlelight. ❼

Hotel Los Gémelos close to the bus stop Ⓣ651 4077. Friendly backpackers' stronghold with basic but spotless rooms with fans, and all with shared bath. This is one of the best budget options in town with reliable hot water, and so fills rapidly. ❷

Hotel Marina Copán just northwest of the plaza Ⓣ651 4070, Ⓔreservations@hotelmarinacopan.com. The most luxurious accommodation option in town. The stylish rooms are beautifully presented, all have a/c and TV, and there's a small pool, sauna, gym and bar on site. ❽

Hotel La Posada opposite *Hotel Plaza Copán* Ⓣ651 4059, Ⓔlaposada@hotelmarinacopan.com. Under the same ownership as the *Hotel Plaza Copán*, rooms here are more basic but still good value considering the price. Verdant gardens and small but cosy rooms with TV and bathroom make this one of the better mid-range options in town.

Hotel Plaza Copán on the east side of the plaza Ⓣ651 4508, Ⓕ651 4039. Twenty-one slightly pricey rooms, some overlooking the square and all with a/c and cable TV. There is a pleasant courtyard with fountain and small kidney-shaped pool, and the attached restaurant serves all meals. Visa accepted. ❻

Hotelito Yaxpac a block north of the plaza Ⓣ651 4025. Run by a friendly family, the *Yaxpac* features four simple and clean rooms, all with private bath and a couple with little balconies. The sole drawback is the early 8am checkout time. ❷

Iguana Azul next to the *Casa de Café B&B* (and under the same ownership) Ⓣ651 4620, Ⓦwww.todomundo.com/iguanaazul/index.html. The definitive budget choice, with three private double rooms and two very pleasant dormitories, all with shared bath and decent mattresses. Amenities include a pretty garden, communal area and laundry facilities, plus great travel information. Dorm US$4.50; doubles ❷–❸

Via Via two blocks west of the Parque Central Ⓣ651 4652. Great-value, simple but spotless rooms with en-suite bathrooms at the popular traveller's café. Hospitable Belgian owners speak excellent English, will help you organise trips, and there is a noticeboard with information on local attractions and events. Dorms available for just US$4. ❸

Youth Hostel En La Manzana Verde next to the Hedman Alas terminal. Under the same ownership as *Via Via* (same phone) and a typical youth hostel with basic but well-planned six-bed dorm rooms (US$4), kitchen and laundry facilities, and noticeboard for information. ❶

The Town

Half a day is enough to take in virtually all the town's attractions. The **Parque Central** – lined with banks, municipal structures and an attractive, whitewashed Baroque-style church – was originally designed by visiting archeologists Tatiana Proskouriakoff and Gustav Stromsvik, though its original elegance has been somewhat modified by grandiose remodelling initiatives, including a series of sweeping pillars and arches, unleashed by a local mayor in the last few years. It does remain a popular place to kill time however, its benches filled with cowboy-booted farmhands and camera-touting visitors in the late afternoon.

On the west side of the plaza, and somewhat eclipsed by the new sculpture museum at the ruins themselves, is the **Museo Regional de Arqueología** (daily 9am–5pm; US$2). Inside are some impressive Maya carvings from the Copán region, including the glyph-covered Altars T and U and **Stela 7**, discovered just 100 metres from the Parque Central in town, along with some remarkable intricately detailed eccentric flints – ornamental oddities with seven interlocking heads carved from obsidian. There are also two remarkable **tombs**, one containing the remains of a female shaman, complete with jade jewellery, an entire puma skeleton, the skull of a deer, and two human sacrificial victims. The other (10J-45) was constructed for an unknown, early Classic-period ruler of Copán and only discovered in 1992 during road-building work.

Just behind the museum (turn right beyond the post office), the tiny municipal **market** is worth a browse, while there's a wonderful view over the town and surrounding countryside from **El Cuartel**, the old military barracks up the hill five blocks north of the Parque Central. On the north side of the Plaza, the new **Mercado Artesanal** is a good place to check out local handicrafts, including dolls made from dried maize leaves, though there is little scope for bargaining and prices are often higher than from street vendors.

Copán's outskirts

A twenty-minute walk from the plaza, along the road to Guatemala, stands the **Enchanted Wings Butterfly House and Nature Centre** (daily 8am–5pm; $5.50), owned by an American enthusiast and his Honduran wife. Butterflies to look out for include the speckled brown "giant owl" and the scarlet-and-yellow "helicopter", two of the hardier species. Butterflies hatch in the morning hours, so it's best to time your visit accordingly. There's also a display of over 200 orchids, around a third of Honduras's native species, with the periods of February to April and July to August being the best time to see them flowering. On the other side of town, 3km north of the plaza, a **bird park** (daily 9am–5pm: $10) with macaws and toucans opened in early 2004. With walk-through aviaries and a stunning forest location, it's worth the hefty entrance fee. There is a nature trail, café, information centre explaining the relationship between the Maya and birds, and a natural pool for swimming.

Eating and drinking

Copán has a wide range of places to **eat** and **drink**, many of them catering specifically to the tourist market. Standards are usually very high, with generous portions and good service, and virtually all restaurants stop serving at 10pm. As for **nightlife**, many of the town's bars and cafés provide live music, especially at weekends. There are weekend discos in the local sports centre twice a month, while *Las Piscinas* on the road east out of town hosts pool parties and discos on Friday and Saturday nights, with entrance fee of around US$2.75.

Café Via Via two blocks west of the plaza. Belgian-owned establishment with a street-side terrace and leafy garden. Besides an array of sandwiches and good breakfasts – including pancakes and omelettes – there is a very reasonably priced fixed menu with vegetarian options, where nothing costs more than US$4.50. Frequent live music in the evenings.

Carnitas Nia Lola two blocks south of the Parque. This popular restaurant-bar serves large portions of delicious grilled and barbecued meats, plus vegetarian dishes, at reasonable prices. It's equally frequented as a drinking venue, with an early-evening happy hour and a good mix of locals and visitors.

Licuados Express one block east of the Plaza. Open by 6.30am, this little juice bar serves delicious *licuados*, juices and breakfasts to the town's early birds. Try the gourmet *licuados* – mocaccino or chocobanana are best – or tuck in to homemade cookies and bagels.

Llama del Bosque two blocks west of the Parque. Slightly old-fashioned restaurant with a reasonably priced menu including local breakfasts, meat and chicken dishes, *baleadas* and snacks.

Momo's one block south of the Parque. Fast becoming legendary for huge, bargain-priced meat dishes, this atmospheric log restaurant has an open-air barbecue where the food is cooked in front of you.

Pizza Copán opposite Hondutel. Popular with locals and tourists alike who come to indulge in delicious pizza and pasta. Take-away available, though be sure to check out the original stone sculptures, produced on site.

Tunkul Bar and Restaurant two blocks west of the Parque. Buzzing garden restaurant-bar with good food, including burritos, vegetarian dishes and a very popular garlic chicken, plus lively music and a happy hour (8–9pm).

Vamos a Ver Café one block south of the Parque. Busy Dutch-owned garden café, popular with travellers thanks to affordable and delicious homemade soups, sandwiches and snacks.

Listings

Banks Banco Atlántida on the Parque will change travellers' cheques, cash dollars and quetzales (at poor rates). The ATMs at both banks on the plaza accept Visa cards.

Book exchange Exchanges available at La Casa de Todo on the next corner from the *Hotel Los*

Gémelos, and at *Carnitas Nia Lola*.

Immigration The *migración* is on the west side of the Parque next to the museum (Mon–Fri 7am–4pm).

Internet There are several Internet cafés in town, including Maya Connections, just south of the plaza and La Casa de Todo (daily 8am–8pm). Rates are around US$1.25 an hour.

Language schools Copán is an excellent place to study, with two Spanish schools to choose between, though it's a more expensive learning centre than Guatemala – four hours of classes plus full family-based accommodation and meals costs US$190–200 a week. Guacamaya (ⓣ651 4553, ⓦwww.guacamaya.com), one block north of the plaza, is the older of the two schools and more expensive, though Ixbalanque (ⓣ651 4432, ⓦwww.lxbalanque.com), a block and a half west of the plaza, is also worth considering.

Laundry La Casa de Todo (see above) charges around US$0.90 for a normal load.

Shuttle buses Contact Monarcas (ⓣ651 4361), two blocks north of the plaza, for direct shuttles to Guatemala City and Antigua (US$25 per person).

Tour operators Go Native Tours (ⓣ651 4432, ⓦwww.lxbalanque.com), at the Ixbalanque language school and Yaragua Tours (ⓣ651 4147, ⓦyaraguatours@hotmail.com), half a block east of the plaza, both offer similarly priced tours. Trips include visits to the hot springs (see p.424; US$10 per person), horse-riding (from US$15 for 3hr), El Rubi waterfall (see p.424; US$17 though ask about security as attacks on tourists are not uncommon), and a spectacular local cave, the Cueva el Boquerón (US$40). Robert Gallardo at the butterfly farm (see overleaf) runs top-class birdwatching tours from around US$40 for a half-day.

Copán ruins

COPÁN RUINS lie 1.5km east of town, a pleasant fifteen-minute walk along a raised footpath that runs parallel to the highway, or US$0.40 in a mini-taxi from the Parque Central. Entrance to the site (daily 8am–4pm; US$10, including the Las Sepultras ruins, though access to the archeological tunnels is an extra US$12) is through the **visitor centre** on the left-hand side of the car park, where a small exhibition explains Copán's place in the Maya world. Inside the visitor centre there's a ticket office and a desk where you can hire a registered site **guide** (US$20 for a group of up to 10 people for 2hr) – an excellent investment if you want to get the most out of Copán. On the other side of the car park is a **cafeteria**, serving drinks and reasonable meals, and a small souvenir shop.

Opposite the visitor centre is the terrific **Museum of Mayan Sculpture** (daily 8am–4pm; US$5), arguably the finest in the entire Maya region, with a tremendous collection of stelae, altars, panels and well-labelled explanations in English. You enter through a dramatic entrance doorway, resembling the jaws of a serpent, and pass through a tunnel (signifying the passage into *xibalba*, or the underworld). Dominating the museum is a full-scale, flamboyantly painted replica of the magnificent **Rosalila Temple**, built by Moon Jaguar in 571 and discovered intact under Temple 16. A vast crimson and jade coloured mask of the Sun God, depicted with wings outstretched, forms the main facade of the temple. Other ground-floor exhibits concentrate upon aspects of Maya beliefs and cosmology, while the upper floor houses many of the finest original sculptures from the Copán valley, comprehensively displaying the skill of the Maya craftsmen.

From the museum it's a 200m walk east to the **warden's gate**, the entrance to the site proper, where your ticket will be checked and where there are usually several squabbling macaws to greet your arrival – these are tame and sleep in cages by the gate at night.

The Plaza Central and Gran Plaza

Straight through the avenue of trees from the warden's gate lie the **Plaza Central** and **Gran Plaza**, large, contiguous rectangular arenas strewn with the magnificently carved and exceptionally well-preserved stelae that are Copán's outstanding features. Initially, the visual impact of this grassy expanse may seem a little underwhelming: the first structure you see is **Stucture 4**, a modestly sized pyramid-temple, while the stepped buildings bordering the northern end of the plaza are low

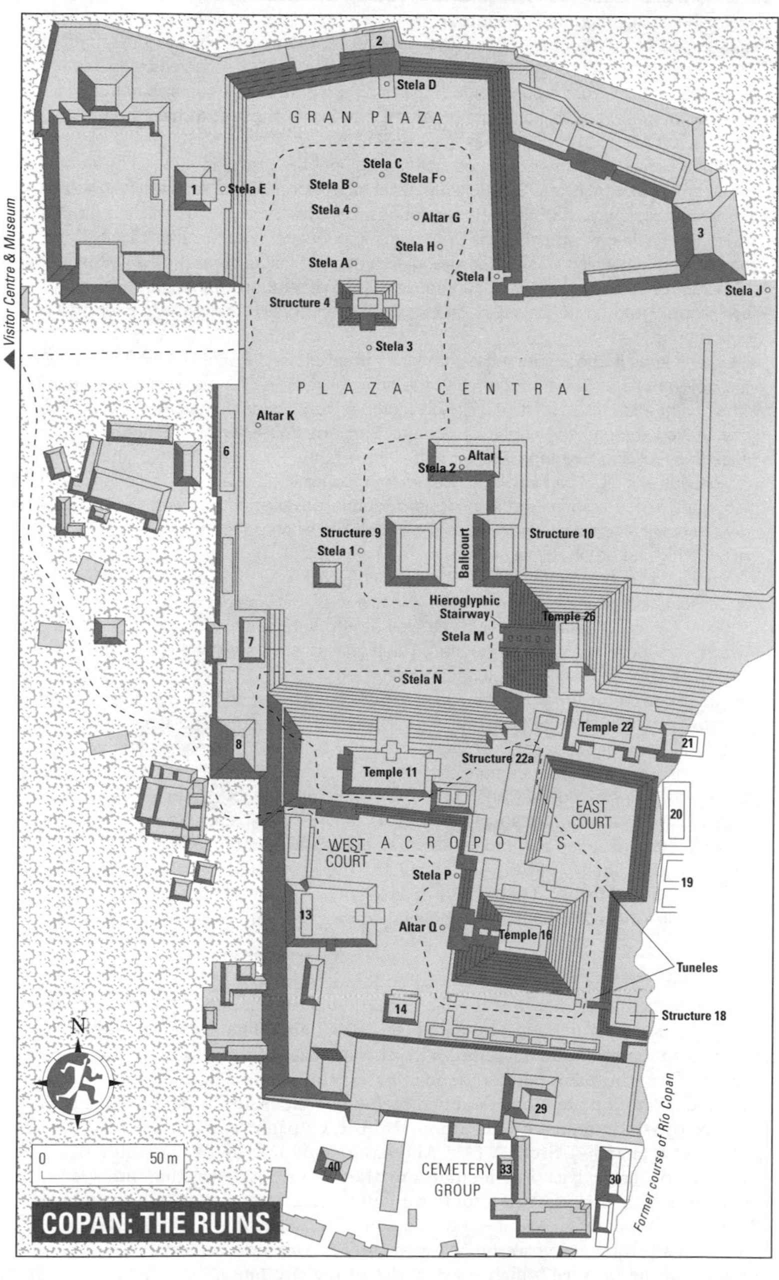

COPAN: THE RUINS
GRAN PLAZA
PLAZA CENTRAL
WEST ACROPOLIS
WEST COURT
EAST COURT
CEMETERY GROUP
Visitor Centre & Museum
Stela D
Stela C
Stela F
Stela B
Stela E
Stela 4
Altar G
Stela H
Stela A
Stela I
Stela J
Structure 4
Stela 3
Altar K
Altar L
Stela 2
Structure 9
Structure 10
Stela 1
Ballcourt
Hieroglyphic Stairway
Temple 26
Stela M
Stela N
Temple 22
Structure 22a
Temple 11
Stela P
Altar Q
Temple 16
Tuneles
Structure 18
Former course of Rio Copan
1
2
3
6
7
8
13
14
19
20
21
29
30
33
40
N
0
50 m

A brief history of the ruins

Once the most important **city-state** on the southern fringes of the Maya world, Copán was largely cut off from all other Maya cities except **Quiriguá**, 64km to the north in Guatemala (see p.234). Archeologists now believe that settlers began moving into the Río Copán valley from around 1400 BC, taking advantage of the area's rich agricultural potential, although construction of the city is not thought to have begun until around 100 AD.

Copán remained a small, isolated settlement until the arrival in 426 AD of an outsider, **Yak K'uk Mo'** (Great Sun First Quetzal Macaw), the warrior–shaman who established the basic layout of the city and founded a royal dynasty which lasted for 400 years. It's unclear whether he was from either Teotihuacan, the Mesoamerican superpower, or Tikal (which was under strong Teotihuacan influence at the time), but Yak K'uk Mo' became the object of an intense cult of veneration, first established by his son **Popol Hol** and continued by subsequent members of the dynasty over fifteen generations.

Little is known about the next seven kings that followed Popol Hol, but in 553 AD the **golden era** of Copán began with the accession to the throne of **Moon Jaguar**, who constructed the magnificent Rosalila temple, now buried beneath Temple 16. The city thrived through the reigns of **Smoke Serpent** (578–628 AD), **Smoke Jaguar** (628–695 AD) and **Eighteen Rabbit** (695–738 AD), as the great fertility of the Copán region was exploited and wealth amassed from control of the jade trade along the Río Motagua. These resources and periods of stable government allowed for unprecedented political and social growth, as the population boomed to around 28,000 by 760 AD, the highest urban density in the entire Maya region.

Ambitious reconstruction of the city continued throughout this era, using local andesite, a fine-grained, even-textured volcanic rock that was easily quarried and particularly suited to detailed carving, as well as the substantial local limestone beds, which were ideal for stucco production. The highly artistic carved-relief style for which Copán is famous reached a pinnacle during the reign of Eighteen Rabbit – whose image is depicted on many of the site's magnificent stelae and who also oversaw the construction of the Great Plaza, the final version of the ball court and Temple 22 in the East Court.

Following the audacious capture and decapitation of Eighteen Rabbit by Quiriguá's Cauac Sky, construction at Copán came to a complete halt for seventeen years, possibly indicating a period of subjugation by its former vassal state. The royal dynasty subsequently managed to regroup, however, flourishing gloriously, albeit briefly, once more. **Smoke Shell** (749–763 AD) completed the construction of the **Hieroglyphic Stairway**, one of the most impressive of all Maya constructions, in an effort designed to symbolize the revival. Optimism continued during the early years of the reign of **Yax**

and unremarkable. This part of the Great Plaza was once a public place, the stepped sides bordered by a densely populated residential area. The grandest buildings are confined to the monumental temples that border the southern section of the plaza, rising to form the Acropolis, the domain of the ruling and religious elite.

Dotted all around are Copán's famed **stelae** and altars, made from local andesite. Most of the stelae represent **Eighteen Rabbit**, Copán's "King of the Arts" (stelae A, B, C, D, F, H and 4). **Stela A** (731 AD) has incredibly deep carvings, although the faces are now eroded; its sides include a total of 52 glyphs, translating into a famous inscription that includes the emblem glyphs of the four great cities of Copán, Palenque, Tikal and Calakmul – a text designed to show that Eighteen Rabbit saw his city as a pivotal power in the Maya world. The one now standing in the plaza is a replica of the original which now resides in the site museum. **Stela B** (731AD) depicts a slightly oriental-looking Eighteen Rabbit, bearing a turban-like headdress

Pasah (763–820 AD), Smoke Shell's son, who commissioned **Altar Q**, which illustrates the entire dynasty from its beginning, and completed the final version of **Temple 16**, which towers over the site, around 776 AD. Towards the end of his rule, however, the rot set in: skeletal remains indicate that the decline was provoked by inadequate food resources created by population pressure, resulting in subsequent environmental collapse. The seventeenth and final ruler, **Ukit Took'**, assumed the throne in 822 AD, but his reign proved miserably inauspicious. Poignantly, the only monument to his reign, Altar L, was never completed, as if the sculptor had downed his tools and walked out on the job.

The site was known to the Spanish, although they took little interest in it. A court official, Don Diego de Palacios, in a letter written in March 1576, mentions the ruins of a magnificent city "constructed with such skill that it seems that they could never have been made by people as coarse as the inhabitants of this province". Not until the nineteenth century and the publication of *Incidents of Travel in Central America, Chiapas and Yucatán* by **John Lloyd Stephens** and **Frederick Catherwood** did Copán become known to the wider world. Stephens, the then-acting US ambassador, had succeeded in buying the ruins in 1839 and, accompanied by Catherwood, a British architect and artist, spent several weeks clearing the site and mapping the buildings. The instant success of the book on publication and the interest it sparked in Mesoamerican culture ensured that Copán became a magnet for archeologists.

British archeologist **Alfred Maudsley** began a full-scale mapping, excavation and reconstruction of the site in 1891 under the sponsorship of Harvard's Peabody Museum. A second major investigation was begun in 1935 by the Washington Carnegie Institute, which involved diverting the Río Copán to prevent it carving into the site. A breakthrough in the understanding not only of Copán but of the whole Maya world came in 1959 and 1960, when archeologists Heinrich Berlin and Tatiana Proskouriakoff first began to decipher **hieroglyphs**, leading to the realization that they record the history of the cities and the dynasties.

Since 1977, the Instituto Hondureño de Antropología e Historia has been running a series of projects with the help of archeologists from around the world. Copán is now perhaps the best understood of all Maya cities, and a series of **tunnelling projects** beneath the Acropolis have unearthed remarkable discoveries including the Rosalila Temple, buried beneath Temple 16, in 1989, which is now open to the public. In 1993, the Papagayo Temple, built by Popol Hol and dedicated to his father Yax K'uk Mo', was uncovered, and in 1998 further burrowing unveiled the tomb of the founder himself.

For those interested in finding out more, *Vision del Pasado Maya* by Fash and Fasquelle, available from the museums, is an excellent historical account of the site's history in Spanish.

that's intertwined with twin macaws, while his hands support a bar motif, a symbol designed to show the ruler holding up the sky. **Stela C** (730 AD) is one of the earliest stones to have faces on both sides and, like many of the central stelae, it has an altar at its base, carved in the shape of a turtle. Two rulers are represented here: facing the turtle (a symbol of longevity) is Eighteen Rabbit's father, Smoke Jaguar, who lived well into his eighties, while on the other side is Eighteen Rabbit himself. **Stela H** (730 AD) perhaps the most impressively executed of all the sculptures, shows Eighteen Rabbit wearing the latticed skirt of the Maize God, his wrists weighed down with jewellery, while his face is crowned with a stunning headdress.

The ball court and Hieroglyphic Stairway

South of Structure 4, towards the Acropolis, is the I-shaped **ball court**, one of the largest and most elaborate of the Classic period, and one of the few Maya courts still to have a paved floor. It was completed in 738 AD, just four months before Eighteen Rabbit's demise at the hands of Quiriguá; two previous versions lie beneath it. Like its predecessors, the court was dedicated to the great macaw deity, and both sloping sides of the court are lined with three sculptured macaw heads. The rooms that line the sides of the court, overlooking the playing area, are assumed to have been used by priests and members of the elite as they watched the game.

Pressed up against the ball court, protected by a vast canvas cover, is the famed **Hieroglyphic Stairway**, perhaps Copán's most astonishing monument. The stairway, which takes up the entire western face of the Temple 26 pyramid, is made up of some 72 stone steps; every block is carved to form part of the glyphic sequence – around 2200 glyph blocks in all. It forms the longest-known Maya hieroglyphic text, but, when discovered at the end of the nineteenth century, only the first 15 stairs were intact and well-meaning reconstruction efforts in the 1930s left the blocks so jumbled that their true meaning is unlikely to ever be revealed. What is known is that the stairway was initiated to record the dynastic history of the city: some of the lower steps were first put in place by Eighteen Rabbit in 710 AD, while Smoke Shell rearranged and completed most of the sequences in an effort to reassert the city's dignity and strength in 755 AD. At the base of the stairway the badly weathered **Stela M** depicts Smoke Shell and records a solar eclipse in 756 AD.

Adjacent to the Hierogylphic Stairway, and towering over the extreme southern end of the plaza, are the vertiginous steps of **Temple 11** (also known as the Temple of the Inscriptions). The temple was constructed by Smoke Shell, who is thought to have been buried beneath it, though no tomb has yet been found. At its base is another classic piece of Copán carving, **Stela N** (761 AD), representing Smoke Shell, with portraits on the two main faces of the stela and glyphs down the sides. The depth of the relief has protected the nooks and crannies, and in some of these you can still see flakes of paint – originally the carvings and buildings would have been painted in a whole range of bright colours, but for some reason only the red has survived.

The Acropolis

From the southwestern corner of the plaza, a trail runs past some original drainage ducts, beyond which stone steps climb steeply up the side of Temple 11 to a soaring cluster of temples, dubbed the **Acropolis**. This lofty inner sanctum was the reserve of royalty, nobles and priests; the political and ceremonial core where religious rituals were enacted, sacrifices performed and rulers entombed. The whole structure increased in size over four hundred years, the temples growing higher and higher as new structures were built over the remains of earlier buildings. A warren of excavated tunnels, some open to the public, bore through the vast bulk of the Acropolis to the Rosalila Temple and several tombs. From the summit of Temple 11, beside a giant ceiba tree (a tree held sacred to the Maya), there's a panoramic view of the site below, over the ball court and Great Plaza to the green hills beyond.

A few metres east of Temple 11 are the **Popol-Na** (Structure 22A), a governmental building distinguished by its interlocking weave-like brick patterns, and **Temple 22**, which boasts some superbly intricate stonework around the door frames. Constructed by Eighteen Rabbit, Temple 22 functioned as a "sacred mountain" where the elite performed religious blood-letting ceremonies. Above the door is the body of a double-headed snake, its heads resting on two figures, which in turn are supported by skulls. The decoration here is unique in the southern Maya region, with only the Yucatán sites such as Kabáh and Chicanna having carvings of comparable quality.

The East Court

Below Temple 22 are the stepped sides of the **East Court**, a graceful plaza that also bears elaborate carvings, including life-sized jaguar heads with hollow eyes which once held pieces of jade or polished obsidian. In the middle of the western staircase, flanked by the jaguars, is a rectangular Venus mask, carved in superb deep relief. Rising over the court and dominating the Acropolis, **Temple 16** is the tallest structure in Copán, a thirty-metre pyramid completed by the city's sixteenth ruler, Yax Pasaj, in 776 AD. In order to build Temple 16 Yax Pasaj had to build on top of the **Rosalila Temple**, though the new temple was built with extraordinary – and atypical – care so as not to destroy the earlier temple; generally, it was Maya custom to ritually deface or destroy obsolete temples or stelae. The temple served as a centre for worship during the reign of Butz'Chan (578–628 AD), or Smoke Serpent, Copán's eleventh ruler, a period that marked the apogee of the city's political, social and artistic growth, so the discovery of the Rosalila has been one of the most exciting finds of recent years. You can now view the brilliant original facade of the buried temple by entering through a short **tunnel** – an unforgettable, if costly (US$12), experience, as it may be sealed again in future years. The admission price does at least include access to two further tunnels, which extend below the East Plaza past some early cosmological stucco carvings – including a huge macaw mask – along with more buried temple facades and crypts including the Galindo tomb.

At the southern end of the East Court is **Structure 18**, a small square building with four carved panels, and the burial place of Yax Pasaj, in AD 821. The diminutive scale of the structure reveals how quickly decline set in, with the militaristic nature of the panels symptomatic of the troubled times. The tomb was empty when excavated by archeologists and is thought to have been looted on a number of occasions. From Structure 18 there's a terrific perspective of the valley, over the Río Copán, which eroded the eastern buildings of the Acropolis over the centuries until its path was diverted. South of Structure 18, the **Cemetery Group** was once thought to have been a burial site, though it's now known to have been a residential complex, and home to the ruling elite. To date, however, little work has been done on this part of the ruins.

The West Court

The second plaza of the Acropolis, the **West Court**, is confined by the south side of Temple 11, which has eight small doorways, and Temple 16. **Altar Q**, at the base of Temple 16, is the court's most famous feature and an astonishing monument of ancestral symbolism. Carved in 776 AD, it celebrates Yax Pasaj's accession to the throne on July 2, 763. The top of the altar is carved with six hieroglyphic blocks, while the sides are decorated with sixteen cross-legged figures, all seated on cushions, who represent previous rulers of Copán. All are pointing towards a portrait of Yax Pasaj which shows him receiving a ceremonial staff from the city's first ruler, Yax K'uk Mo', thereby endorsing Yax Pasaj's right to rule. Behind the altar is a small crypt, discovered to contain the remains of a macaw and fifteen big cats, sacrificed in honour of his ancestors when the altar was inaugurated.

Las Sepultras

Two kilometres east of Copán along the highway is the smaller site of **Las Sepultras** (daily 8am–4pm; entrance with the same ticket as for Copán), the focus of much archeological interest in recent years because of the information it provides on daily domestic life in Maya times. Eighteen of the forty-odd residential compounds at the site have been excavated, yielding one hundred buildings that would have been inhabited by the elite. Smaller compounds on the edge of the site are thought to have housed young princes, as well as concubines and servants. It was customary to bury the nobility close to their residences, and more than 250 tombs have been excavated around the compounds – given the number of women found in the tombs it seems likely that the local Maya practised polygamy. One of the most interesting finds – the tomb of a priest or shaman, dating from around 450 AD – is on display in the museum in Copán Ruinas town.

Around Copán

An uphill walk of a few hours out of town brings you to the small archeological site of **Los Sapos** (daily, no set hours; US$2). Dating from the same era as Copán, it is spectacularly set in the hills to the south of town. The site, whose name derives from a rock carved in the shape of a toad, is thought to have been a place where Maya women came to bear children, though unfortunately time and weather have eroded much of the carving. To get there, follow the main road south out of town, turn left onto a dirt track just past the river bridge and follow this as it begins to climb gently into the hills, past the *Hacienda San Lucas* (see p.416) which owns the site. The views across the tobacco fields of the river valley are beautiful, and there are plenty of spots for swimming along the way.

Pick-ups leave Copán regularly throughout the day for the peaceful town of **Santa Rita**, 9km to the northeast. At the river bridge, just before entering the town, a path leads up to **El Rubí**, a pretty double waterfall on the Río Copán, about 2km away. Attacks on tourists were commonly reported up until a few years ago, when, under local advice, people stopped visiting independently. The implementation of a new tourist police in the Copán area, coupled with the reported purchase of the site by a local gangster, may improve the security situation in the future, but you should always seek local information and, in any case, an organised tour may still be a better option.

Around 22km north of Copán are some **hot springs** (US$0.75), set in lush highland scenery dotted with coffee fincas and patches of pine forests. Once there you can either wallow around in man-made pools or head to the source via a short trail where cool river water and near boiling-hot spring waters combine. One way to get to the *aguas termales* is to hitch a ride on a passing pick-up, which are reasonably frequent from outside the *Hotel Paty* in Copán and also pass the bird park; expect to pay around US$1 for the ride, which takes about 50 minutes – but don't leave the springs any later than 3.30pm if you're planning to hitch back to Copán. Alternatively, speak to one of Copán's tour operators (see "Listings", p.417); Yaragua Tours can arrange a half-day pick-up trip at 2pm for US$10 per person for a minimum of four people.

A kilometre or so further north is the *agriturismo* centre at **Finca El Cisne** (ⓣ651 4695, ⓔfincaelcisne@copanruinas.com), a working finca involved in the production of cardaman, coffee and cattle. Tours involving you in the daily running of the centre as well as providing information on farming and agricultural practices in the region are well-organised and can be arranged through the Finca El Cisne office opposite La Casa de Todo in Copán Ruinas town. Day tours start from around US$35 including all meals, or you can stay over in comfortable rooms which include nocturnal visits to the hot springs (when they are closed to the public) from around US$70 per night.

Into Guatemala: El Florido

The Guatemalan border is just twelve kilometres west of Copán, and crossing here at the **El Florido** border post – usually busy with travellers coming to and from the ruins – is pretty straightforward, though it can be slow. There's no bank, but the ever-present moneychangers handle dollars, lempiras and quetzales at fairly good rates. Minibuses and pick-ups leave from the Parque in Copán Ruinas about every thirty minutes until around 4pm; there's also a fast shuttle bus to Guatemala City and Antigua (see "Listings", p.417 for details of tour operators). In recent years illegal charging of around US$2 both on the exit from Guatemala and the entrance to Honduras has become almost normal practice, despite clearly visible signs stating that the crossing is free. There is little you can do about it, and in most cases it's easier to just hand over the money. From the border, buses leave every thirty minutes (the last is at 4pm) for Chiquimula (1hr 15min; see p.244), 57km away down a smooth, newly paved road.

North to La Entrada and El Puente

Northeast from Copán the CA-11 winds its scenic way through lightly wooded mountains and fertile pasture to **LA ENTRADA**, a distinctly unlikeable junction town 55km northeast of Copán. Apart from it being a useful place to catch a bus to Santa Rosa or San Pedro Sula, La Entrada's only redeeming feature is its proximity to the small site of El Puente (see below); if you get stuck here, *Hotel San Carlos* (☎898 5228; ❹), at the junction of CA-11 and CA 4, is the best of the available **accommodation**, where rooms are at least comfortable and secure with en-suite bathroom and TV.

El Puente

Breaking the journey in La Entrada does give you a chance to visit the archeological site of **El Puente** (daily 8am–4pm; US$5); a signed turn on the CA-11 4km before La Entrada gives access to the site, 6km away. Opened in 1994, El Puente gets few visitors, which makes its location – amid the grassy fields flanking the Río Chinamito – all the more enjoyable, although after the glories of Copán, the scale of the site is inevitably disappointing.

Once a sizeable **Maya** settlement, dating back to the Late Classic period and under the authority of Copán, El Puente contains more than two hundred structures. To date, only a small number have been excavated, including religious buildings and structures for the use of the elite, built around what was the main plaza. The most important of these (Structure 1) is an eleven-metre-high, six-stepped pyramid, oriented east–west and thought to be a funerary temple; the long pyramid along its lower edge contains burial chambers. The small **museum** at the entrance to the park, about 1km from the restorations, has an informative exhibition on the site itself and on Maya culture in general.

There's no public transport to the site, but hitching is considered safe; traffic is more frequent in the mornings. A round-trip taxi fare from La Entrada will cost around US$10, including an hour at the ruins, while buses between Copán Ruinas and La Entrada pass the exit road to the site, from where you can hitch or take the long, hot walk.

4.3

Olancho

Stretching east of Tegucigalpa to the Nicaraguan border and north into the emptiness of Mosquitia, the sparsely populated uplands of **Olancho** are widely regarded as Honduras's "Wild East", an untamed frontier region with a not totally undeserved reputation for lawlessness. Traditionally the *Olanchanos* hold little respect for authority, and rebellion has played a major role in their history. The first Spanish settlers arrived in 1524, enticed to this mountainous region by Aztec tales of vast gold deposits, and immediately encountered resistance from the region's indigenous tribes. There was little peace for the next two hundred years as Pech, Lenca and other tribes periodically revolted against the Spaniards, who had set up slave camps to mine the rich gold deposits. The marauding presence of British pirates, who controlled the Caribbean coast to the north for most of the eighteenth century, further isolated Olancho, breeding an independent spirit and a distaste for governmental influence. Throughout the first forty years of the new Honduran republic there were bitter rebellions against Tegucigalpa, revolts that were only finally quelled in 1863 after a campaign of terror by President José Medina.

Since then Olancho has become one of the richer regions of Honduras, its wealth largely generated from exploitation of the huge forest reserves (much of it illegally logged) and cattle ranching (which has encroached into many of the national parks and reserves). A powerful local oligarchy, drawn from these industries and supported by military and police connivance, has led to environmental issues being given very peripheral priority, while activists opposing these interests have been threatened and killed.

Although Olancho makes up almost a fifth of Honduran territory, tourist attractions are few, and the high, forested mountain ranges interspersed with broad valleys often make travelling difficult and slow. However, these same ranges harbour some of the country's last untouched expanses of tropical and cloudforest: the national parks of **La Muralla** and **Sierra de Agalta** are awe-inspiring, while the smaller, more accessible reserve of **El Boquerón** offers ample opportunity for gentler hikes. Along the valleys, now given over to pastureland for cattle, are scattered villages and towns. Both **Juticalpa**, the department capital, and **Catacamas**, at the eastern end of the paved road, are good bases for exploring the region, while the isolated mountain settlement of **La Unión** acts as both gateway to La Muralla and a convenient stopover en route to the north coast.

Olancho's **climate** is generally pleasant, with the towns at lower altitudes hot during the day and comfortably cool at night; up in the mountains it can get extremely cold after dark. Once off the main highway, **travelling** becomes arduous, with the dirt roads connecting the remoter villages served by infrequent and invariably slow public transport.

Juticalpa and the east

Olancho's main **transport** artery, Highway CA-15, runs east from Tegucigalpa through mountain passes and across flat valleys to Catacamas, a journey of about four hours. Many people get no further than **Juticalpa**, the region's main centre, which makes a convenient base for expeditions into the national parks. North and east of Catacamas stretch the remote, impassable peaks of the Sierra de Agalta, part

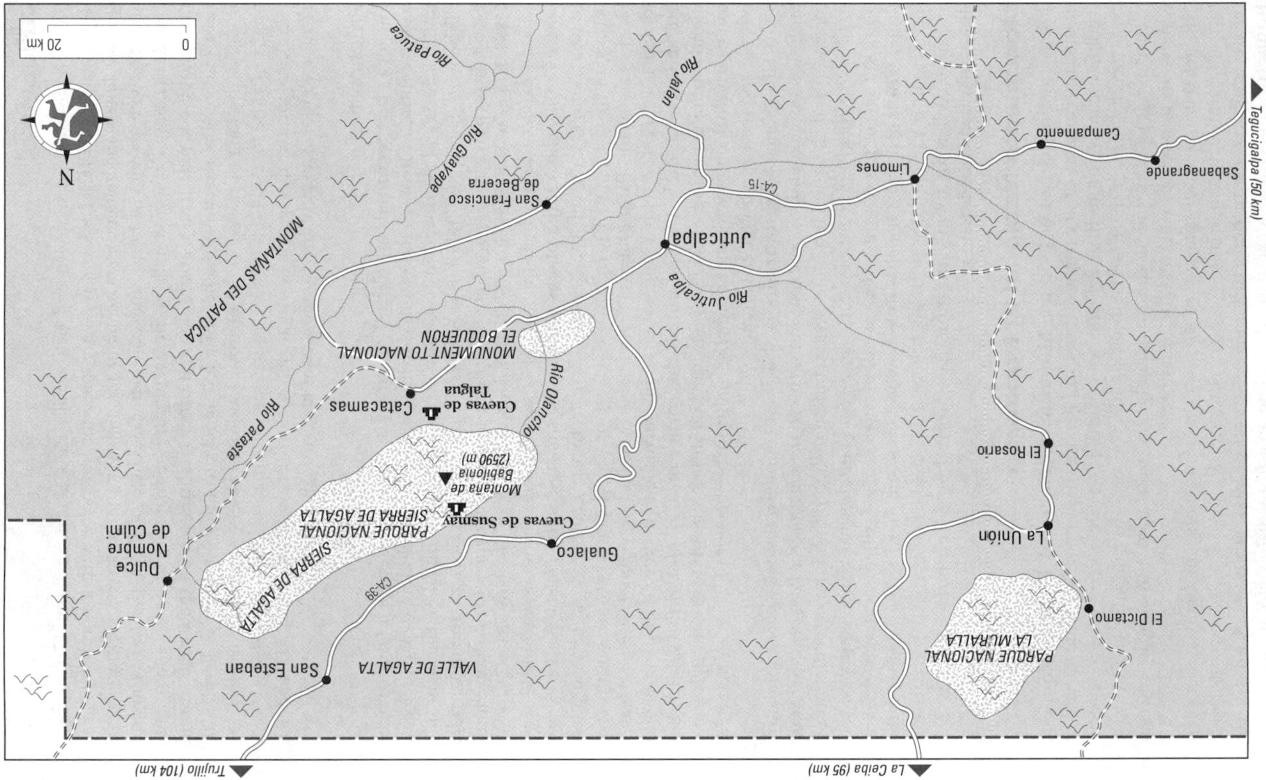

Trujillo (104 km)
La Ceiba (95 km)
Tegucigalpa (50 km)
N
0
20 km
Dulce Nombre de Cúlmi
San Esteban
VALLE DE AGALTA
CA-39
SIERRA DE AGALTA
PARQUE NACIONAL SIERRA DE AGALTA
Cuevas de Susmay
Montaña de Babilonia (2590 m)
Gualaco
Río Pataste
Catacamas
Cuevas de Talgua
MONUMENT TO NACIONAL EL BOQUERÓN
Río Olancho
MONTAÑAS DEL PATUCA
Río Patuca
Río Guayape
San Francisco de Becerra
Río Jalan
Juticalpa
Río Juticalpa
CA-15
Limones
Campamento
Sabanagrande
El Rosario
La Unión
El Dictamo
PARQUE NACIONAL LA MURALLA

of which is protected as the magnificent **Parque Nacional Sierra de Agalta**. Difficult to reach, the reserve is best approached from the north.

Juticalpa

Situated towards the southern end of the Valle de Catacamas, about 170km from Tegucigalpa, **JUTICALPA** is a thriving, pleasant little city with a number of reasonable hotels and restaurants. Capital of the department, its streets are busy night and day with provincial bustle and commerce. Centre of life is the leafy **Parque Banderas**, busy with food stalls in the evenings. The majority of hotels and restaurants, along with the banks, post office and other facilities, are on the streets around here. The general **market** stretches for a few blocks to the west, along C Perulapan. If you're thinking of hiking in the nearby cloudforest reserves it may be worth popping in to the local COHDEFOR office for information (daily 8am–4pm; ⓣ885 2253); it's located in a green house at the bottom of Av 7 between C 14 and 13, about two blocks west of the Empresa Aurora terminal.

Practicalities

Juticalpa's **bus terminals** are just off the highway on 1 Av SE, which leads straight to the centre, a fifteen-minute walk north. Local buses – including departures east to Catacamas and northwest to La Unión – run from the terminal on the right side of the road (facing town); Empresa Aurora's Tegucigalpa services use the other side. Good **Internet** access is available at either branch of *Serviciber* (daily 8am–8pm; US$1.10 per hour), both along C 2 within a few blocks of the Parque

Don't expect too much in the way of cosseted luxury in town, or indeed anywhere in Olancho. Of the **places to stay**, the smartest is the *Hotel Villa San Andrés* (ⓣ885 2405; ❺), just off the highway 2km from the centre, whose large spotless rooms all have a/c and TV. In town the best of the cheaper bets are within two blocks east of the Parque between Av 7 and 8, including *Apart Hotel La Muralla* (ⓣ885 1270; ❸–❹), with a range of tastefully furnished en-suite rooms, some with a/c and all with cable TV. Just around the corner on C 1 NO, is the similar, but slightly more expensive *Hotel Honduras* (ⓣ885 1580, ⓕ885 1456; ❹), though some rooms have balconies with the somewhat questionable benefit of views of the street outside and there is a buffet restaurant.

Juticalpa's range of **restaurants** is also pretty modest, though there's a healthy profusion of inexpensive comedores, plus the *Restaurante Tai Ka Lock* on the Parque for cheap and cheerful Honduran-style Chinese dishes. Behind the cathedral on Av 4, *El Nuevo Rancho* is more of a bar than a restaurant, but has a nice courtyard setting, and serves good sandwiches in addition to a few grilled meat and chicken dishes. For a genuine Olancho-style cowboy cook-up, head to *La Fonda*, on the highway near the entrance to town, where giant steaks and barbecued meats spit and sizzle. When the town's attractions have worn thin, the **cinema** at C 1, Av 2–3 shows subtitled US releases.

Monumento Nacional El Boquerón

Twenty kilometres east of Juticalpa, **Monumento Nacional El Boquerón**, one of the last remnants of dry tropical forest in Honduras, is home to a wide variety of wildlife including more than 250 species of bird. It's easily accessible as a day-trip from the city, though there are facilities should you want to camp. To see the forest properly, you need to follow the moderately strenuous track through the reserve, which cuts through a small patch of cloudforest.

To get there, you can take any of the buses running along the highway between Juticalpa and Catacamas, and get off at Puente Boquerón, a journey of about twenty minutes. From here, the reserve stretches back along the **Canyon de Boquerón**, a kilometre-deep natural rift. The area immediately around the bridge was flattened during Hurricane Mitch, but impressive gallery forest begins a few hundred metres from the road. Follow the track starting on the left-hand side of the **Río Olancho** – though it crosses over several times, so be prepared to wade – and after about a kilometre the path enters the gorge, eventually emerging onto the floodplain at the other side. From here it is around two more easy hours through level pastureland to the village of **LA AVISPA**. A daily bus leaves from here to Juticalpa, leaving around midday. Beyond the village, the path loops steeply uphill around Cerro Agua Buena (1433m) and through the **cloudforest** section; here you've the greatest chance of seeing elusive bird and animal life, since the trees are stunted and the vegetation less dense than in other reserves. One of the highlights is the mixed flocks of brightly coloured trogons and quetzals that feed together at fruiting trees. The reserve is also the only known Honduran location of the white-eared ground sparrow, fairly easily seen in the undergrowth. Beyond the cloudforest it's all downhill, the path emerging after a couple of hours on the highway at Tempisque, a few kilometres west of the main entrance. An early start would allow you to complete the walk in one day; alternatively, use the designated camping spots at the main entrance and at La Avispa – and don't forget food and water. It's an easy matter to flag down **buses** to Juticalpa or Catacamas along the highway.

Catacamas

CATACAMAS, situated midway along the Valle de Catacamas beneath the southern flanks of the Sierra de Agalta, is a much smaller version of Juticalpa, 41km away. Very few tourists come here – Catacamas marks the end of the paved road – which no doubt contributes to the affable, small-town charm of the place. It has a more spectacular setting than its larger neighbour: a short walk up to the **Mirador de la Cruz**, fifteen minutes from the centre on the northern side of town, gives superb views over the town and valley, and across to the Montañas del Patuca.

Perhaps the main reason for coming out this far is to visit the **Cuevas de Talgua** (daily 8am–4pm; US$5). Located 6km north of town on the banks of the Río Talgua, the caves are one of the country's foremost historical sites thanks to the discovery of a burial ground. Though the burial ground itself is out of bounds to visitors, the rest has recently been developed for tourists, with a small museum telling the tale of the finds and trails leading through the caves (guide US$0.25). To get there take the local bus from Catacamas to Talgua, leaving town at 6am and 11pm, though beware that the last return departs Talgua at 1pm. Alternatively, a taxi should cost around US$1.65.

Practicalities

Buses terminate four blocks south of Catacamas's Parque Central, a short walk away up a slight hill and dominated by a giant ceiba tree. The banks, post office and other essentials lie on the streets north of the Parque, while most hotels are to the south. For **Internet** access, *Servicentro* just off the southeast corner of the square has an inconsistent connection (US$1.40). Of the very limited **accommodation** available, *Hotel Colina*, 1 Av SW, just off the corner of the Parque (☎899 4488; ❸), is best, with reasonably comfortable rooms set round a courtyard, all with bath, TV and fans. Almost next door, the cheaper *Hotel Oriental* (☎899 4038; ❶–❷) has a selection of basic but orderly rooms, some with private bath. If looking for a bite to **eat**, *Restaurante Jardín Oriental* is the better of the two Chinese restaurants that stand side by side on the Parque, while *Vaquero's* on the east side of the Parque serves grilled meats in a slightly surly environment.

Parque Nacional Sierra de Agalta

Draped across the sweeping ranges of the Sierra de Agalta, the vast **Parque Nacional Sierra de Agalta** shelters the most extensive stretch of **virgin cloudforest** remaining in Central America. Since the establishment of the reserve in 1987, pressure on the land has remained acute, and large swathes of the lower forest of pine and oak have been cleared to provide pasture for ranching. Though there are signs that the environmental message is getting through – not least because the reserve is the watershed for the region and the source of the rivers Sico and Patuca, among others – the reserve's outskirts still receives little real protection. It's a different story in the higher reaches of the mountains, where the core of the reserve, Honduras's fourth highest peak, La Picucha, is so remote that both vegetation and wildlife have remained virtually untouched. Here a typical cloudforest of oaks, liquidambar and cedar, draped in epiphytes, vines and ferns, cover the higher slopes in a dense cloak, giving way, above 2000m, to an almost primeval dwarf forest, where the trees grow only to a height of around five metres.

This isolation ensures a protected, secure environment for a biologically diverse range of **animals and birds**, many of them extremely rare. Tapirs, jaguars, ocelots, opossums and three types of monkey are among the 61 recorded species of mammal, although you'll need a great deal of luck to spot them. More evident are the birds, of which more than four hundred species have been recorded, including 33 species of hummingbird. Along with longer **hikes** requiring the assistance of a guide (see "Practicalities", below), easier jaunts are available in the environs of the park. A series of eight waterfalls with a combined height of 150m, the **Chorros de Babilonia** can be accessed by car by a side road off the road from Gualaco to San Esteban; to reach the higher falls, a track leads from El Ocotal to the community of Planes de Babilonia. Alternatively a trip to the river caves at **Cuevas de Susmay** makes for an interesting day-trip, providing you have your own transport. Take the Jicalapa road from Gualaco to the village of Las Joyas de Zacate, from where a trail leads a kilometre or so through pasture and woodland to the caves. The pools are good for snorkelling, but the caves are large with unmarked trails, so don't venture too far or you may get lost.

Practicalities

The reserve's remoteness makes **independent access** difficult. There's no accommodation other than official camping spots, for which you'll need to bring all equipment and supplies. The easiest points of entry are along the northern edge of the Sierra, via the small towns of **Gualaco** and **San Esteban**, which you can reach off Highway C-39 between Juticalpa and Trujillo. Hiring a **guide** is pretty much essential for hiking on the difficult trails: ask at the COHDEFOR offices in Gualaco, San Esteban or Juticalpa, or call Turisol (☎988 4666). A daily bus to Trujillo, passing through both towns, leaves Juticalpa at 4am, and there are plenty of additonal pick-ups from the marketplace in Juticalpa if you ask around.

La Unión and La Muralla

Some 110km northwest from Juticalpa, **LA UNIÓN** is a pleasant mountain town and the most convenient point of departure for **Parque Nacional La Muralla**, 15km to the north. Its location, around halfway along a backdoor bus route between Tegucigalpa and La Ceiba, also makes it a possible stopover between the capital and the north coast. However, if you're considering travelling along this remote road it's essential you determine the current **security** situation first, as there have been regular hold-ups and robberies (of buses and private cars) in the last few years. Check in the COHDEFOR office in Juticalpa (see p.428) before you set out.

Accommodation in La Unión is basic, including *Hotel La Muralla* and *Hotel Karol* (both ❶). There are a couple of **comedores** around the Parque Central for meals. If you intend to visit La Muralla, first register at the **COHDEFOR** office (Mon–Fri 8am–5pm), three blocks from the Parque Central; the office can also help organize transport and guides into the park.

Parque Nacional La Muralla

La Muralla (daily 8am–4pm; free) takes its name from the appearance of the reserve when viewed from a distance – "the wall" of a high massif densely covered with leafy forest, forming an island of incredible biological diversity amid the surrounding low-level mountain ranges. Cocooned in the centre of the reserve is an extensive stretch of virgin cloudforest that, despite its remoteness, is more accessible to visitors than the Sierra de Agalta. The park's dazzling array of **birdlife** and its well-planned visitor facilities make a visit here very rewarding.

Forest cover in La Muralla ranges from pine woods at the level of the entrance (1400m) through to cloudforest from around 1800m. The mountains slope steeply, rising to the peak of **Las Parras**, at 2064m the highest point. For birdwatchers, quetzals, hummingbirds, kites and toucanets are among the species likely to be spotted; the aguacatillo tree in front of the visitor centre is a major food source for quetzals and they can sometimes be seen feeding there in the early mornings. More evasive are the white-tailed deer, jaguars, pumas, grey foxes and howler monkeys that inhabit the park.

It's possible to visit La Muralla as a day-trip from La Unión, although since wildlife-spotting is best done early in the morning, consider spending the night here. The shortest **trail**, El Pizote, swings from the visitor centre in a two-hour loop up through the damp hush of the cloudforest and back down again. Though steep, wet and slippery, this can be done unguided and benches are provided at the best points for birdwatching; guides are recommended, however, for greater understanding of what you're seeing. Longer trails run across the reserve to the **Cascada de Mucupina** (8hr return) and to **Monte Escondido**, a two-day hike.

Access to La Muralla is via the **visitor centre** at the southwest end of the reserve, about 15km north of La Unión on the road to El Díctamo village. Here you can pick up trail maps and information on wildlife; there are also dorm **beds** (US$5) (reservations through COHDEFOR in Tegucigalpa: ⓣ223 7703) and **camping space** (US$3), with two more camping spots further into the reserve. Bring plenty of food and water and some warm clothes.

4.4

The north coast and Mosquitia

A world away from the forested mountain ranges of the interior, Honduras's **north coast** stretches for 300km along the azure fringes of the Caribbean. A magnet for Hondurans and foreign tourists alike, most are drawn solely by the prospect of sun, sea and entertainment, which is provided in abundance by the coastal towns of **Tela**, **La Ceiba** and **Trujillo**, with their broad expanses of beach, clean warm waters, restaurants and buzzing nightlife. Dotted in between the main towns are a number of laid-back **Garífuna** villages blessed with unspoilt beaches, where a stay is likely to be more peaceful. **San Pedro Sula**, the region's major city and transport hub, provides amenities of a strictly urban kind.

When beach life loses its appeal, there are several natural reserves in the region to visit. The national parks of **Cusuco**, **Pico Bonito** and **Capiro y Calentura**, whose virgin cloudforest shelters rare wildlife, offer hiking for all levels of fitness; the wetland and mangrove swamps at **Punta Sal** and **Cuero y Salado** require less exertion to explore. Occupying the eastern corner of Honduras is the remote and undeveloped expanse of the **Mosquitia** (often spelt "Moskitia"), at whose heart

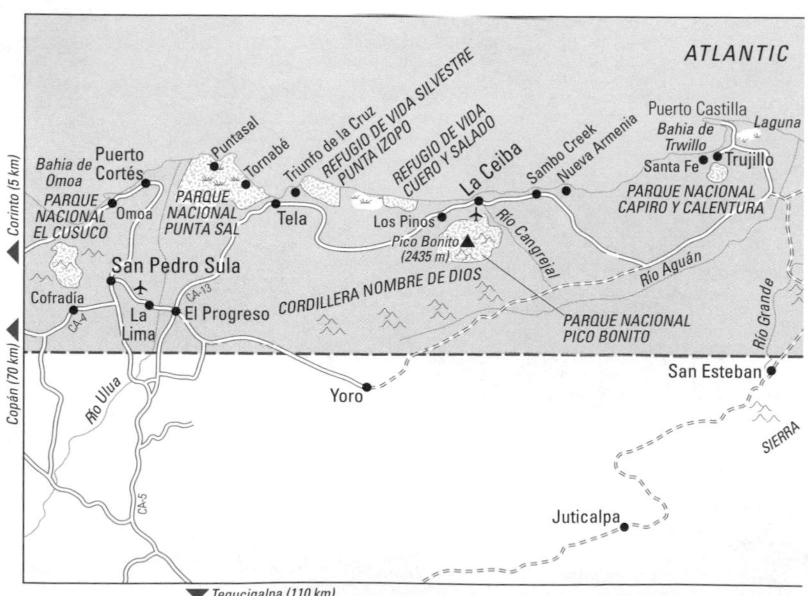

lies the **Río Plátano Biosphere Reserve**, an extensive swathe of virtually pristine tropical rainforest. Travelling here requires a spirit of adventure and the ability to lose track of time, but the effort it takes is well rewarded.

The two **dry** seasons – December through to April, and August to September – are the best times to visit the north coast. Temperatures rarely drop below 25–28°C, but the heat is usually tempered by ocean breezes. Outside the Mosquitia, **transport** is reasonably good, with frequent buses along the fast, paved highway that links the main coastal towns; as usual, reaching the remoter villages and national parks requires some forward planning.

San Pedro Sula

Honduras's second city and the country's driving economic force, **SAN PEDRO SULA** sprawls across the fertile Valle de Sula ("Valley of the Birds" in Usula dialect) at the foot of the Merendón mountain chain, just an hour from the coast. Flat and uninspiring to look at, and for most of the year uncomfortably hot and humid, this is a city for getting business done in rather than sightseeing. It's also the transport hub for northern and western Honduras, meaning a visit here is usually unavoidable, even if only to pass through. On a more positive note, in terms of **facilities** San Pedro rates alongside Tegucigalpa, with its own international airport, foreign consulates, and a wide range of hotels, restaurants and shopping outlets – indeed, thanks to its practical location and better transportation links, travellers sticking to the north of the country rarely need to make a visit south to the capital. If you do choose to stick around for a day or two, it's not difficult to organize a trip out to one of the country's finest cloudforest reserves, the nearby **Parque Nacional El Cusuco**.

One of the first Spanish settlements in the country, founded by Pedro de Alvarado in 1536, today's San Pedro bears almost no trace of its pre-twentieth-century incarnation. Burnt out by French corsairs in 1660 and virtually abandoned during a yellow-fever epidemic in 1892, the city struggled to maintain a population of more

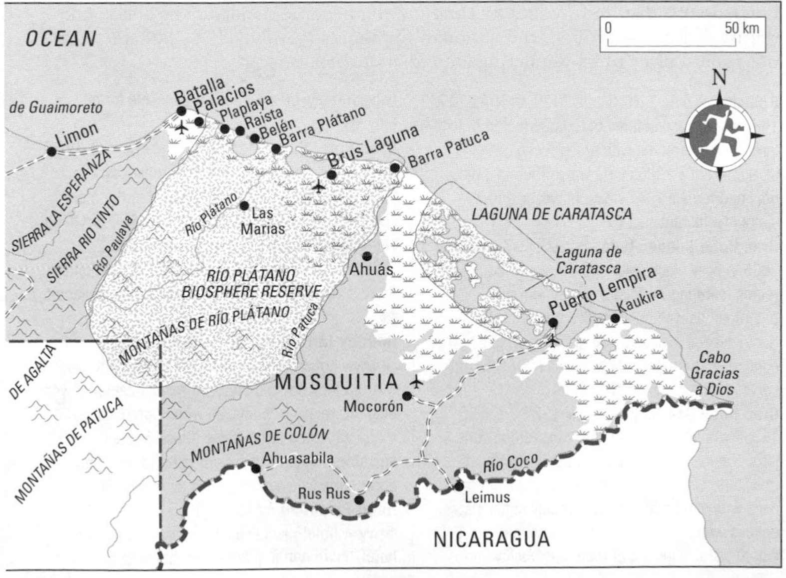

than five thousand, and today only a few wooden buildings remain as proof of its long past. Fortunes began to rise with the growth of the **banana** industry in the early twentieth century, when the city rapidly cemented its role as Honduras's commercial centre. With its outer reaches continuing to sprout factories, many of them foreign-owned, and a population now in the region of 600,000, San Pedro ranks as one of the fastest-growing cities in Central America.

Arrival and getting around

The **Aeropuerto Internacional Villeda Morales**, the point of arrival for both domestic and international flights, lies 12km southeast of the city. Hedman Alas buses run from the airport to the centre at 8am, 2.15pm, 4.30pm and 6.30pm, the first two services heading on to Copán Ruinas. **Taxis** charge around US$8 from the airport into town. Intercity and international **buses** arrive at their own separate terminals, most within a few blocks of each other in central San Pedro (see p.438 for addresses). **Train** enthusiasts may wish to take the five-hour train ride north to Tela, an enjoyable if slow ride. Services depart on Friday and Sunday at 6.30am, though you should be at the station – located two blocks east of the Parque Central along C 1 – earlier.

The bus terminals, many hotels and the main commercial area are close to the centre in the city's southwest sector. Running west from the Parque Central, C 1 is also known as the Blvd Morazán for the twelve blocks before it meets the **Av Circunvalación** ring road, which separates the city centre from San Pedro's wealthier residential districts; this is where many of the more upmarket restaurants are located. Beyond the Circunvalación, 1 Calle becomes Blvd los Próceres. Most of what you'll want to see in the city is within walking distance of the centre, but for reaching the Zona Viva, the abundant **taxis** are far more convenient than trying to get to grips with the complex bus system.

Accommodation

San Pedro's **accommodation** ranges from a spate of four- and five-star luxury hotels to sleazy, dollar-a-night dives. The best of the cheaper options are along Av 6. Expect to pay at least US$12 for an acceptable double room with bath in a secure hotel; double that, and TV and air conditioning become standard. The area south of the market can get rough, and although foreigners are unlikely to be targeted, it's not really a place to be wandering around after dark.

Bolívar C 2 & Av 2 NO ⓣ552 7129, ⓕ552 7135. This hotel has something of a dated feel to it, with large en-suite rooms with a/c and cable TV straight from a 1980s time warp. There's a nice pool and terrace downstairs, however, and a simple restaurant-bar. ❺

Gran Hotel Conquistador C 2 SO, Av 7–8 ⓣ552 7605. A cosy place, with small but well-equipped rooms featuring TV, telephone and en-suite bathroom, as well as attractive potted plants. Room service available and price includes a continental breakfast; the downstairs restaurant serves buffet lunches. ❺

Gran Hotel San Pedro C 3, Av 1–2 SO ⓣ550 1655, ⓔhotelsanpedro@hotelsanpedrosa.com. A large, rambling establishment popular with travellers. The choice of rooms ranges from basic ones with shared bath to reasonably spacious options with large beds, private bath, a/c and TV. Ask to see a selection of rooms as quality varies considerably. Internet access available for guests only. ❸–❹

Gran Hotel Sula C 1, at the Parque Central ⓣ552 9999, ⓦwww.hotelsula.hn. Venerable city landmark with an excellent location in the main square. The business-class rooms have everything you'd expect from the *Best Western* chain, including balconies with views over the city, and there's also a small pool, 24hr café and restaurant. ❼

Holiday Inn C 1, Av 10–11 ⓣ550 8080, ⓦwww.holidayinn.com/sanpedrosula. High tower luxury block set in a pleasant residential area, with elegant, relaxing rooms, all with huge beds and many with wonderful views. Glass-fronted elevators make for a dizzy ride up to the upper floors. Special weekend rates available. ❾

Hotel Ejecutivo Av 10 & C 2 SO ⓣ552 4361, ⓦwww.hotel-ejecutivo.com. Well-run mid-range hotel, located in a quiet residential area a

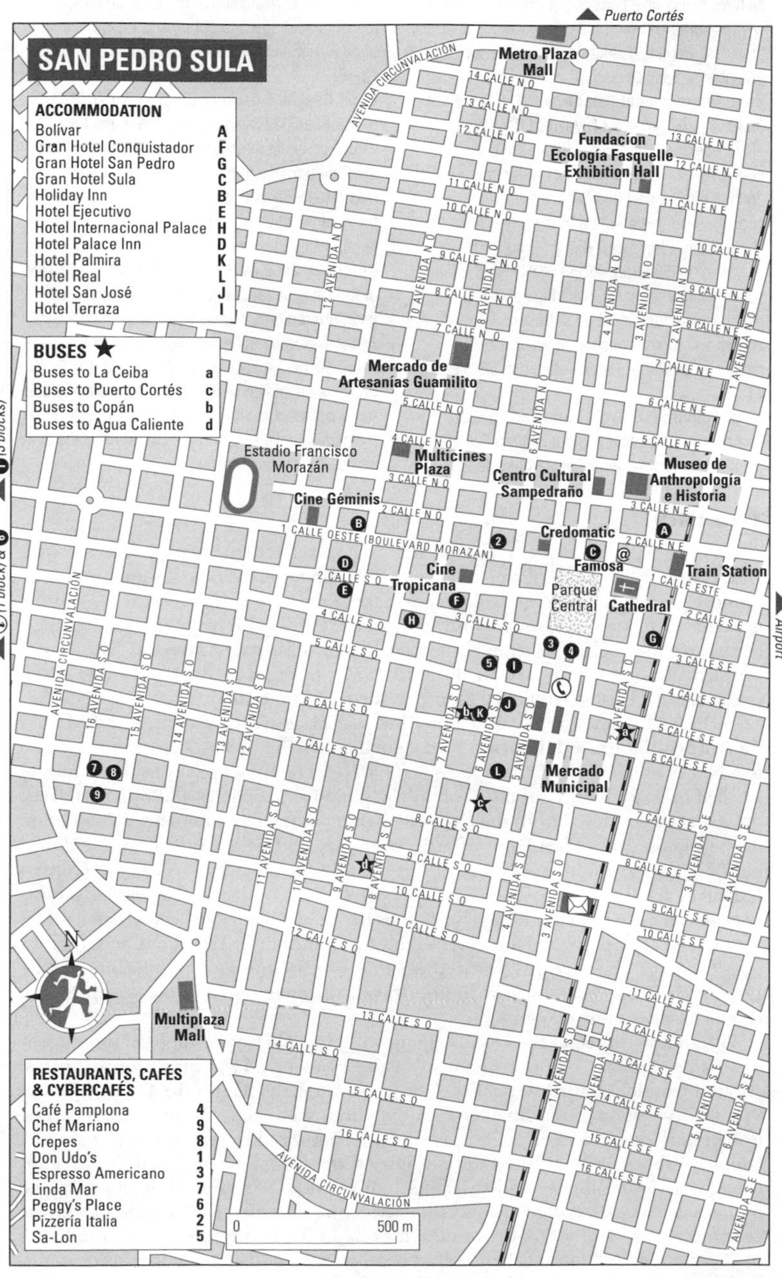
SAN PEDRO SULA
ACCOMMODATION
Bolívar A
Gran Hotel Conquistador F
Gran Hotel San Pedro G
Gran Hotel Sula C
Holiday Inn B
Hotel Ejecutivo E
Hotel Internacional Palace H
Hotel Palace Inn D
Hotel Palmira K
Hotel Real L
Hotel San José J
Hotel Terraza I
BUSES
Buses to La Ceiba a
Buses to Puerto Cortés c
Buses to Copán b
Buses to Agua Caliente d
RESTAURANTS, CAFÉS & CYBERCAFÉS
Café Pamplona 4
Chef Mariano 9
Crepes 8
Don Udo's 1
Espresso Americano 3
Linda Mar 7
Peggy's Place 6
Pizzería Italia 2
Sa-Lon 5
Puerto Cortés
Airport
(1 block) & 6
1 (3 blocks)
Metro Plaza Mall
Fundacíon Ecología Fasquelle Exhibition Hall
Mercado de Artesanías Guamilito
Estadio Francisco Morazán
Multicines Plaza
Cine Géminis
Centro Cultural Sampedraño
Museo de Anthropología e Historia
Credomatic
Famosa
Train Station
Cine Tropicana
Parque Central
Cathedral
Mercado Municipal
Multiplaza Mall
AVENIDA CIRCUNVALACIÓN
1 CALLE OESTE (BOULEVARD MORAZÁN)
1 CALLE ESTE
N
0
500 m

ten-minute walk from the centre. The large rooms all have two double beds, a/c, TV and bathrooms with powerful showers; the price includes a simple breakfast. Parking, laundry and room service available as well. ❻

Hotel Internacional Palace Av 8, C 3 SO ⓣ550 3838, ⓦwww.globalnet.hn/palace. This hotel offers upmarket accommodation at reasonable prices. All rooms have bath, hot water, a/c and TV, and the rooftop pool and bar are a good place to cool off. Small restaurant on the ground floor. ❺

Hotel Palace Inn Av 10 & C 2 SO opposite *Ejecutivo* ⓣ553 6383, ⓕ553 6384. Good-value option with large rooms including cable TV, telephone, a/c and en-suite bathroom. Internet access and room service from an on-site restaurant available. Rates reduced at weekends. ❺

Hotel Palmira C 6, Av 6–7 SO ⓣ557 6522. Ramshackle place that could do with a lick of paint, though conveniently located beside the Casarola bus terminal for Copán. There's a complicated pricing structure based on the presence and absence of fan, a/c, TV, and number of beds, but all-in-all rates are on the cheap side. ❸–❹

Hotel Real Av 6 between C 6 & 7 ⓣ550 7929, ⓔhotelreal2002@yahoo.com. One of the best-value options in the city conveniently located for the Citul terminal to Puerto Cortés. Beautifully decorated with local crafts and climbing plants in the communal courtyard, the en-suite rooms are large, with TV and a choice of fan or a/c. ❹

Hotel San José Av 6, C 5–6 SO ⓣ557 1208. One of the city's better budget hotels, offering clean, good-sized rooms, simply furnished if a little dark. All rooms are en-suite and have fans. ❸

Hotel Terraza Av 6, C 4–5 SO ⓣ550 3108. Fairly priced, safe and convenient for the centre and bus terminals. Rooms all have bath and hot water (some also have a/c), and the café downstairs serves decent breakfasts. ❸–❹

The City

San Pedro Sula's Parque Central, the large and recently re-paved **Parque Barahona**, is the focus of the city centre, teeming with vendors, shoeshine boys, moneychangers and general malcontents taking the air. Centrepiece of the Parque is a large fountain with bridges and bronze statues of washerwomen cleaning their clothes on the rocks. On its eastern edge, the colonial-style **Catedral Municipal** was actually only completed in the mid-1950s; facing it across the Parque is the unremarkable Palacio Muncipal, home to the city administration.

San Pedro has few tourist attractions, but one place worth visiting is the **Museo de Anthropología e Historia** (Wed–Mon 9am–4.15pm, Sun 9am–3pm; US$2), a few blocks north of the Parque at Av 3, C 4 NO. The museum's collection (mostly labelled in Spanish only) of pre-Columbian sculptures, ceramics and other artefacts, the majority recovered from the Sula valley, outlines the development of civilization in the region from 1500 BC onwards; weaponry and paintings from the colonial period continue the theme. While in the area, check out what's on at the **Centro Cultural Sampedrano**, C 3, Av 3–4 NO (ⓣ553 3911), which regularly hosts concerts and plays; the building also houses the public library. An even better venue is the new **Teatro Francisco Saybe**, the finest theatre in Honduras and a showcase for large productions; located on the Av Circunvalación, adjacent to the Universidad San Pedro Sula in the northwest of town, it's certainly worth a look should an interesting show be on.

With so little to see in the city, shopping will probably feature high on most agendas. San Pedro has a good selection of places to buy Honduran **handicrafts**. Around ten blocks northwest of the Parque Central, the **Mercado Guamilito**, Av 9, C 6–7 NO, is an indoor market with numerous stalls selling hammocks, ceramics, leatherwork and wooden goods; gentle bartering should get you better prices. A couple of shops on the Calle Peatonal, just off the Parque Central, sell similar stuff, though prices are higher and the range not as wide. For more shopping options, numerous malls are dotted around the city centre. **Danilo's**, a taxi ride out of the centre at Av 18 B, C 9 SO, is an outlet for one of the best leather-goods producers in the country, selling excellent-value bags, purses and belts, among other items. Finally, the vast general market, the **Mercado Municipal**, is between Av 4–5 SO and C 5–6 SO, though stalls spill onto the streets around for several blocks.

Eating, drinking and entertainment

As you'd expect in such a business-oriented city, there's a good selection of **places to eat** and a diverse range of evening entertainment. The more down-to-earth places can be found in the centre, while the stretch of Av Circunvalación south of C 1 – the so-called "**Zona Viva**" – is the place to go for upmarket restaurants, bars and clubs. After dark, the best bet for a **drink** in the central zone is *Johnny's*, next to the Mercado Municipal, an idiosyncratic spirits-only bar where locals go to shoot the breeze to the accompaniment of 1950s bebop. The real action though is out in the Zona Viva, with a group of bars around Av 16 getting very lively after dark. *Coco Grill* on Av 16 at C 9 is an open-air drinking den with loud music, bar snacks and regular drink offers. *Rancho's Grill* at the corner of Av Circunvalación and C 6 SO is another place where loud music plays day and night, if only to drown out the traffic noise on the outdoor seating. *Champs*, between Av Circunvalación and Av 15 SO, is a sports bar with pool table and TVs, which comes alive during big sporting events. **Clubbers** should head for either *Casa Criollas* (which includes a karaoke bar) or *Confetti's*, both on Av Circunvalación between C 14 & 15 NO, which play a combination of Latino pop and Euro dance.

Centre

Café Pamplona Parque Central. Always crowded with locals, this place has kitsch 1970s decor, an extensive menu, decent coffee and reasonable prices – but don't expect too much in the way of service. The conch soup is a delicious house speciality. Closes 8pm.

Café Skandia in the *Gran Hotel Sula* (see p.434). Air-conditioned and open 24hr, the *Skandia* is something of a San Pedro institution, offering reasonably priced sandwiches, light meals and snacks.

Espresso Americano just west of the Parque Central on C 3 SO. Modern *Starbucks*-style coffee house with good mochas, cappuccinos, and even frappaccinos to recharge your batteries.

Pizzería Italia C 1, Av 7 NO. Cosy little place serving good pizza (around US$4) and a small selection of pasta dishes (around US$5).

Sa-Lon Av 6, C 4-5 opposite *Hotel Terraza*. Reasonable-value Chinese and international menu with large portions for budget travellers. One portion of fried rice is easily big enough for two.

Zona Viva

Chef Mariano C 10 at Av 16 SO. Garífuna restaurant spread over 3 floors serving dishes with a Caribbean twist in colourful surroundings featuring beach and undersea scenes. Extremely popular for its authentic feel, vast menu and friendly service. Credit cards accepted.

Crepes Av 15 between C 8 & 9 SO. Huge variety of sweet and savoury crepes, with such imaginative combinations as guava with melted cheese and Hindu chicken, in addition to a selection of Colombian dishes and homemade soups.

Don Udo's C 1, Av 20 SO (☎553 3106). Considered one of the city's finest, this Dutch-owned restaurant offers a broad range of European and local dishes along with a reasonable wine list. Prices are not cheap, but worth it for a splurge; expect to pay from US$15 a head for a full meal with wine. Open evenings only Mon–Sat, along with Sun 10am–2pm for a less formal brunch.

Linda Mar C 9 at Av 16 SO. Homely seafood restaurant specialising in lobster, crayfish and conch dishes, though there's also a small selection of meats available. The house speciality for two people features a bit of just about everything on the menu for US$22.

Peggy's Place C 6 SO at Av 18. Log-cabin building housing a stylish bar-restaurant with a wide menu specialising in grilled meats; the hamburger combo plates are good value. There's also a palm-filled garden, and large TV playing major sporting events.

Listings

Airlines American Airlines, Av Circunvalación between C 5 & 6 ☎553 3506, airport ☎668 3246; Continental, Plaza Versalles, Av Circunvalación ☎557 4141, airport ☎668 3209; COPA, *Gran Hotel Sula* ☎550 5268; Iberia, Edificio Quiroz C 2, Av 1–2 ☎550 5311, airport ☎668 3218; Islea, Edifico Trejo Merlo, Av 7, C 1–2 ☎552 8322; Sosa, Av 8, C 1 SO ☎550 6545, airport ☎668 3223; Taca, Av Circunvalación & Av 13 NO ☎550 5270, airport ☎668 3333.

American Express Agencia de Viajes Mundirama, Edificio Martinez Valenzuela, C 2, Av 2–3 SO

Moving on from San Pedro Sula

As the main transport hub for northern Honduras, frequent **bus departures** leave San Pedro Sula for Tegucigalpa, Santa Rosa de Copán and all destinations along the north coast. Bus companies operate out of their own terminals, most of which are conveniently located within a few blocks of each other in the centre of the city. Companies are listed with their terminals, and departure destinations below. An (L) after the company name denotes a luxury service.

North coast destinations

Catisa Tupsa Av 2 at C 5 & 6 SO (☎552 1042). La Ceiba (12 daily; 5.30am–6pm; 3hr).
Citul Av 6 at C 7 & 8 SO, Barrio Lempira (☎553 0070). Puerto Cortés (11 daily; 5am–8.30pm; 1hr 15min).
Cotraibal Av 1 at C 7 & 8 (☎557 8470). Trujillo (5 daily; 6am–4pm; 6hr).
COTUC Av 1 at C 7 & 8 (☎557 3175). La Ceiba and Trujillo (every 45 minutes; 6am–4pm; 3–6hr).
Hedman Alas (L) C 3 NO at Av 7 & 8, Barrio Guamilito (☎553 1361). La Ceiba (4 daily; 6am–6pm; 2hr 30min); San Pedro Sula Airport (4 daily; 8.40am–6.30pm; 45min); Tela (3 daily; 10.10am–6.30pm; 1hr 30min).
Tela Express C 1/2 & Av 2 (no phone). Tela (5–7 daily; 8am–6pm; 2hr).
Viana (L) Av Circunvalación (☎556 9261). La Ceiba (2 daily; 10.30am–5.40pm; 2hr 30min).

Western highland destinations

Casasola Av 6 at C 6 & 7 (☎558 1659). Copán Ruinas (2 daily; 8am–2pm; 4hr).
Congolón Av 8 at C 9 & 10 SO (☎553 1174). Ocotopeque (5 daily; 6am–12.30pm; 5hr).
Gracianos C 6 at Av 7 & 8 (no phone). Gracias (1 daily; 2pm; 5hr).
Hedman Alas (L) C 3 NO at Av 7 & 8, Barrio Guamilito (☎553 1361). Copán Ruinas (2 daily; 9.50am–2.30pm; 3hr).
Toritos y Copanecos Av 6 at C 8 & 9 SO, Barrio Lempira (☎553 4930). Santa Rosa (7 daily; 7am–3.30pm; 2hr 45min).

Tegucigalpa and the south

Hedman Alas (L) C 3 NO at Av 7 & 8, Barrio Guamilito (☎553 1361). Tegucigalpa (4 daily; 5.45am–5.30pm; 3hr 30min).
Norteños C 6 at Av 6 & 7 (☎552 2145). Comayagüela (5 daily; 6.30am–6pm; 2hr 30min).
El Rey Av 7 at C 5 & 6 (☎553 4264). Tegucigalpa (6 daily; 6am–6pm; 4hr).
Viana (L) Av Circunvalación (☎556 9261). Tegucigalpa (3–4 daily; 6.30am–6.15pm; 3hr 30min).

International destinations

Hedman Alas (L) C 3 NO at Av 7 & 8, Barrio Guamilito (☎553 1361). Guatemala (1 daily; 9.50am; 8hr).
King Quality (L) C 6 at Av 7 & 8, Barrio El Benque (☎553 4547). San Salvador and Guatemala (1 daily; 6.30am; 8–15hr).
Ticabus (L) Texaco Monumento a la Madre (☎556 5149). Managua (1 daily; 5am; 8hr).

(☎553 1193, ⓕ557 9022).

Banks and exchange Banco Atlántida has a number of branches downtown, including one on the Parque Central, for exchange and Visa advances; Banco de Occidente, Av 6, C 2–3 SO, changes cash and travellers' cheques; Credomatic, Av 5, C 1–2 NO, advances cash on Visa and MasterCard. Lloyds TSB and Banet, 3 blocks west of the Parque along C 1, have ATMs that accept Visa.

Bookshops The cigar shop in the *Gran Hotel Sula* has a small assortment of English-language fiction, books on Honduras, and US magazines and newspapers.
Car rental Avis, Blvd Morazán 58 ⓣ552 2872; Budget, Aeropuerto Villeda Morales ⓣ566 2267; Dollar, Av 3, C 3–4 NO ⓣ552 7626; Hertz, airport ⓣ668 3157, *Holiday Inn* ⓣ550 4729; Molinari, airport ⓣ566 2580, *Gran Hotel Sula* ⓣ553 2639.
Cinemas There's a number of modern multi-screen cinemas – including the Multicines Plaza de Sula at Av 10 and C 4 NO; Cine Tropicana, at C 2, Av 7 SO; and the Cine Géminis, C 1, Av 12 NO – within easy walking distance of the centre; all show new US films and the occasional Latin American offering.
Consulates Belize, km5, road to Puerto Cortés (ⓣ551 0124, ⓕ551 1740); El Salvador, 6th floor, Edificio Rivera, C 3, Av 5–6 SO (ⓣ553 3604; Mon–Fri 9am–noon & 2–3.30pm); France, Av 9 at C 10 (ⓣ553 3560); Guatemala, C 8, Av 5–6 NO (ⓣ553 3560; Mon–Fri 8.30am–2pm); Italy, Edif La Constancia, Av 5 & C 2 NO (ⓣ552 3672); Germany, Av Circunvalación at Av 6 NO (ⓣ553 1244); Holland, Av 15 between C 7 & 8 NE (ⓣ557 1815); UK, Av 13, C 11–12 SO, No 62 (ⓣ557 2046; Mon–Fri 9am–noon).
Immigration Direcion General de Migración, Calle Peatonal, above the Moreira Honduras souvenir shop (ⓣ553 3728; Mon–Fri 8am–4pm).
Internet access There are countless cybercafés in town. Famosa in the mall at Av 2 NO has a good connection with webcams (Mon–Sat 8am–9pm; US$0.60 per hour). Another good central option is Blue.com, a block west of the Parque on C 1.
Laundry Lavandería Express, Av 9, C 3 NO (Mon–Sat 8am–5pm). Another central option is Lavafacíl at Av 7 and C 5 NO.
Medical care There's an emergency department at the Clínica Bendaña, Av Circunvalación, C 9–10 SO (ⓣ553 1618).
Police ⓣ552 3128.
Post office C 9, Av 3 SO (Mon–Fri 7.30am–8pm, Sat 7.30am–12.30pm).
Telephone office Hondutel, at C 4, Av 4 SO, is open 24hr; fax service is available 8am–5pm. American Food Co. opposite has Web phone-calling facilities with cheaper rates, though there is a bad delay on the line.
Travel agents and tours Agencia de Viajes Mundirama, Edificio Martinez Valenzuela, C 2, Av 2–3 SO (ⓣ550 7400, ⓕ557 9092), is an efficient place to book or change international air tickets, or try the reputable Transmundo de Sula, Av 5, C 4 NO (ⓣ550 1140). Mesoamérica Travel, C 8 at Av 32 NO (ⓣ557 8410, ⓦwww.mesoamerica-travel.com), is an excellent tour agency with trips to reserves including Punta Sal near Tela and Cusuco, the Bay Islands and Mosquitia. Maya Tropic Tours, based in the *Gran Hotel Sula* (ⓣ557 8830, ⓔinfo@mtthonduras.com), offers trips to Copán, Tela, Lago Yojoa and Omoa from around $75 per day.

Around San Pedro: Parque Nacional El Cusuco

Some 20km west of San Pedro in the Sierra del Merendón, the stunning **Parque Nacional El Cusuco** (daily 6am–5pm; US$15) supports an abundant range of animal and plant life, much of it rare and threatened. Though inevitably affected by the proximity of human settlement, Cusuco is still a joy to visit and not too difficult to reach from San Pedro. To see as much as possible, the best plan is to arrive in the afternoon, camp overnight and walk the trails early in the morning.

The lower reaches of the park have long been settled by humans and were heavily logged during the 1950s, contributing to disastrous floods during the 1970s. Here the mixed pine and broadleaf forest is secondary growth. At around 1800m the **cloudforest** begins, its dense oaks and liquidambars reaching 40m in some places, stacked over avocados and palms, all supporting mosses, vines, orchids and numerous species of heliconias, recognizable by the red or orange brackets holding the blossoms. Studies carried out in the park in the 1990s revealed the existence of at least seventeen species of plant hitherto unknown in Honduras.

Four **trails**, ranging between 1km and 2.5km, have been laid out among the lower sections of cloudforest (there is no access to the highest, steepest sections of the reserve), taking you through a hushed world of dense, dripping, multilayered vegetation. If you're incredibly lucky, you might spot the reserve's namesake, the *cusuco* (armadillo), as well as salamanders, monkeys and possibly even a jaguar. The reserve's dazzling range of birdlife includes quetzals, best spotted from April to June, along with trogons, kites and woodpeckers.

Practicalities

Cusuco is managed by the Fundación Ecologista Hector Rodrigo Pastor Fasquelle, whose office is at 12 Av NO between 1 & 2 C in San Pedro Sula (☎557 6598, ©fundeco@netsys.hn). Information leaflets are usually available, and they can also advise on getting to the reserve. The main point of **access** is via the small town of **Cofradía**, 18km southwest of San Pedro off Highway CA-4, the main road to the El Salvador/Guatemala border. From here, a dirt road continues for another 26km to the village of **Buenos Aires**, 5km beyond which you'll find the park **visitor centre**. Getting there independently is time-consuming: you need to take a westbound bus to Cofradía (buses to and from La Entrada or Santa Rosa pass through) and then wait for onward transport. Other options include renting a car – a 4WD can make the whole journey in about two hours, depending on the state of the road – or taking a tour from San Pedro (see "Listings", overleaf). The visitor centre has displays on the park's wildlife, trail maps and a camping site. Alternatively there is a small house for rent with kitchen facilities (reserve at the office; US$10 per person with a minimum of four).

The northwest coast: Puerto Cortés and Omoa

North of San Pedro Sula, Highway CA-5 runs through the flat agricultural lands of the Sula valley, amidst lush, tropical scenery. After 60km the four-lane highway reaches the coast at **PUERTO CORTÉS**, Honduras's main port, where the unstinting heat and dilapidated wooden buildings merely add to the rough-and-ready feel of the place. There's nothing here to entice you to stop, and you'll likely pass through only to change buses on route to Omoa, but if you do stay, *Hotel Formosa*, a block west of the centre (☎665 0853; ❷), is a good cheap option with all en-suite rooms, some with TV and a/c. There is little choice in terms of **places to eat**. Buffet meals are available at *Reposteria Plata* at Av 3 and C 2, popular with locals and open on Sundays when everywhere else is closed.

Three companies run **buses** between San Pedro Sula and Puerto Cortés, including the reliable Citul, who run the hour-long trip every thirty minutes between 6am and 6pm. The Citul terminal in Puerto Cortés is a block north of the main plaza at Av 4 and C 4 – if you're heading on to Belize or Guatemala, the **migración** (daily 8am–6pm; ☎665 0582 attended 24 hours) is conveniently close by at Av 5 and C 4, one block to the north. **Moving on** from Puerto Cortés, there are buses to Corinto, for **Guatemala**, every ninety minutes (8am–3.30pm; 4hr) and half-hourly connections to Omoa (1hr); buses leave from the Transportes Citral terminal on C 4 around the corner from the Citul terminal. It's also possible to travel from Puerto Cortés by fast skiff, the *Gulf Cruza* (☎963 8239 or ☎665 5556), to **Belize**, with weekly departures on Tuesdays at 11am from the old bridge at La Laguna, 3km south of the town centre. The journey to Belize City (US$75) takes around seven hours, with stops at Belizean immigration at Big Creek and at Placencia (4hr; US$50).

Omoa

Spreading inland from a deep bay at the point where the mountains of the Sierra de Omoa meet the Caribbean, the fishing village of **OMOA** has become increasingly popular in recent years, with travellers coming here for total rest and relaxation. Once a strategically important location in the defence of the Spanish colonies against marauding British pirates, today the village dozes lethargically under the heat of the Caribbean sun, with its one outstanding sight, the restored **Fortaleza de San Fernando de Omoa** (Mon–Fri 8am–4pm, Sat & Sun 9am–5pm; US$1.10), standing in mute witness to this colourful history. Now isolated amidst tropical greenery a kilometre from the coast, having been beached as the sea has receded over the centuries, the triangular fort was originally intended to protect the port of Puerto Barrios in Guatemala. Work began in 1759 but was never fully completed, due to a combination of bureaucratic inefficiency, problems with materials and labour shortage. The steadily weakening Spanish authorities then suffered the ignominy of witnessing the fortress being temporarily occupied by British and Miskito military forces in October 1779. A small museum on site tells the story of the fort and displays a selection of military paraphernalia including cannons and period weaponry.

The narrow village **beach**, lined with colourful fishing boats, offers stunning views west across the curve of the bay and the mountain backdrop. At weekends hordes of day-trippers turn up and it's often too crowded for comfort. Better **swimming** can be had by walking five minutes or so out of the village in either direction, while fifteen minutes around the headland to the east is a much wider and usually emptier expanse of beach.

Practicalities

Buses between Puerto Cortés to Corinto pass the southern end of the village at a crossroads. From here a road runs 2km to the beach where you'll find most of the action. Locals with pedal bikes traverse the road for a small fee, and some of the hotels offer free shuttle services. Rising numbers of foreign tourists have led to the opening of a handful of reasonably comfortable **places to stay**. Heading towards the beach from the highway, you'll come to the popular *Roli's Place* (Ⓣ658 9082; ❷), an excellent budget base with comfortable rooms as well as camping (US$2 per person), hammocks (US$2.50 per person) and dormitories (US$3.50 per person); they also have kayaks and bikes, a kitchen and laundry facilities. Turning right as you reach the beach, *Hotel Tatiana* (Ⓣ658 9182; ❸–❹) is a decent-value option with en-suite rooms; those with fan and TV are more expensive. Turn left on the beach for the most upmarket place in town, *Flamingos* (Ⓣ658 9199, Ⓕ658 9288; ❼), a huge pink edifice with chic rooms, all with bath and a/c, as well as a restaurant and bar. The best places for meals are the *champas* along the seafront, serving freshly caught seafood at very reasonable prices. Particularly recommended is *Jardín Romantico*, next to *Flamingos*, a wooden cabaña with a huge selection of fish dishes for around US$4.50.

Moving on from Omoa to **Guatemala** it's an excruciatingly slow and bumpy bus ride southwest to the town of **Corinto**, 2km from the border. Buses run hourly along this route, which is steadily being paved, but remains mostly in a poor state of repair. Corinto has its own **migración** (daily 8am–5.30pm) where you'll be charged US$1.80 for your exit stamp, though make sure that they do actually take the trouble to stamp it when you pay. Pick-ups shuttle to and from the border, from where you catch a minibus (every thirty minutes) over the Arizona bridge, along a new paved road which crosses the Río Motagua. Minibuses pass though the village of Entre Ríos, for Guatemalan *migración*, to Puerto Barrios, an hour from the Honduras border. Six daily buses run from Corinto, via Omoa, to Puerto Cortés from where there are onward connections to San Pedro Sula. More adventurous souls may be attracted by the slow train between Omoa and Tela or San Pedro Sula, with departures on Friday and Sunday only at 7am.

Tela and around

East of San Pedro, Highway CA-13 runs through fertile lowlands, past serried ranks of banana trees stretching for mile after endless mile. **La Lima**, 15km from San Pedro, is the definitive company town, headquarters for United Fruit ("Chiquita" brand) operations in Honduras. At **El Progreso**, a dusty town a further 15km east, the highway swings north to the Caribbean coast.

With its magnificent natural setting midway round the Bahía de Tela, surrounded by sweeping beaches, **TELA** has a near-perfect setting and is a magnet for

Hondurans and foreign backpackers alike. Today's Tela is a product of the banana industry. In the late nineteenth century United Fruit nominated what was then a backwater as its headquarters, and set about building a company town – Tela Nueva – on the west bank of the Río Tela; the old village became known as Tela Vieja. When the company removed its headquarters to La Lima in 1965, the town began to slip back into its former somnolence, although fortunes have been somewhat restored by the growth in tourism. In the past the town suffered from a reputation for unpredictability and violence, but a pilot tourist force of bilingual officers (now being imitated throughout the country) substantially cleaned up the town's image. Things can still get rowdy at weekends, but the wealth of fantastic natural reserves within minutes of the town – including **Punta Sal** – makes Tela well worth a visit whether you choose to partake in the nightlife or not.

Arrival and information

There are no direct buses between San Pedro and central Tela; buses to La Ceiba and Trujillo stop along the highway outside town, from where taxis (US$0.50) ferry passengers into the centre, five minutes away. Most local services, including the half-hourly buses to and from La Ceiba, use the terminal at Av 9, C 9 NE, near the market; buses to the surrounding villages use the terminal close by at Av 8, C 10 NE. Hedman Alas luxury services stop at the *Villas Telamar* (see opposite). A **train** runs to Puerto Cortés every Friday and Sunday at 1.45pm from the station three blocks south of the Parque Central.

Tela is one of the few Honduran towns with a **tourist information** centre (Mon–Fri 8am–6pm, Sat 8am–noon; ⓦwww.tela-honduras.com), located in the municipal building off the southeast corner of the Parque. For information on Punta Sal and other reserves in the area, stop in at **Prolansate**, C 9 and Av 3 NE (Mon–Fri 7am–noon & 1.30–5.30pm; ⓣ448 2042). **Hondutel** and the **post office** are next to each other at Av 4, C 7–8 NE, two blocks south of the Parque Central, and **Internet** access is widely available throughout town for US$1.10 per hour. To **change money**, Banco Atlántida sits just west of the Parque on C 9, the main drag. **Tours** to the surrounding area can be arranged through Garífuna Tours, off the southwest corner of the Parque along C 9 (ⓣ448 2904, ⓦwww.garifunatours.com), who run trips to Punta Sal and Punta Izopo (US$18 per person) as well as the EcoPass tour, encompassing visits to Punta Sal, Punta Izopo and Pico Bonito for US$58.

Accommodation

Given Tela's somewhat faded status, it's not surprising that many of the hotels are run down and uninviting. There are, however, a number of newer and better-value budget options for backpackers and some good mid- and high-range hotels. Many of the better places tend to get busy at weekends, when it pays to book ahead.

Boarding House Sara eastern end of C 11 ⓣ448 1477. Even though it's falling apart at the seams, cheap rates and welcoming English-speaking owners ensure this option is often full. Shared bathrooms only, but its beachside location is only a short stagger from the local disco. Reductions for longer stays. ❷

Cesar's Mariscos on the beach at Av 3 ⓣ448 2083, ⓦwww.hotelcesarmariscos.com. Located above the eponymous seafood restaurant, this pretty, upmarket hotel features spacious rooms, each uniquely decorated and many with balconies with sea views and hammock. Prices include a continental breakfast and free Internet access. ❺–❻

Ejecutivo's Aparthotel two blocks southwest of the Parque at C 8 ⓣ448 1076. Secure apartment-style accommodation with comfortable en-suite rooms, all with kitchen, TV and lounging area. A great bargain for those in a group. ❹

Gran Hotel Presidente Parque Central ⓣ448 2821, ⓔimpdetur@hondutel.hn. Old-style hotel with reasonable rates right in the middle of town. Rooms include cable TV, a/c, telephone and private bath, and there's also a pool and hot tub on site. ❺

Mango Hotel C 8, one block southwest of the Parque ⓣ448 0338, ⓦwww.mangocafe.net. A traveller's favourite under the same ownership as the *Mango Café*, cheaper rooms here come with fan while those a notch higher come with a/c and TV. Rooms are clean and there's a small communal terrace for meeting other guests, but overall prices are a bit high. ❸–❹

Maya Vista C 9, Av 10 ⓣ448 1497, ⓦwww.mayavista.com. Canadian-owned hilltop hotel, overlooking the ocean, with a selection of well-furnished, spacious rooms and attractive new apartments, some with full kitchen facilities and a/c, plus a great restaurant. Rooms ❹, apartments ❺

Posada del Sol C 8, opposite *Ejecutivo's* ⓣ448 1895. Rustic *posada* with pleasant, if basic en-suite rooms. There's an outdoor seating area in a nice garden, making this perhaps the best budget option in town. ❷

Tela two blocks west of the Parque on C 9 ⓣ448 2150. A rambling, green wooden edifice, with large clean rooms, somewhat dated in style but with plenty of character. All rooms are en-suite, though rates rise slightly for hot water and TV. Very popular with backpackers for its reasonable rates and friendly service. ❸

Villas Telamar Tela Nueva ⓣ448 2196, ⓦwww.telamar.com. Occupying what used to be executive housing for Tela Railway Company employees, this idiosyncratic piece of luxury has wooden houses spread across shady grounds, a stretch of beautiful beachfront, and facilities including a pool, tennis courts and nine-hole golf course. Accommodation is either in individual rooms or in villas sleeping up to fourteen people. ❼–❾

The Town

The centre of Tela, encompassing the **Parque Central** and main shopping area, lies about 2km north of the highway and two blocks from the beach. Five blocks west from the Parque Central, the **Río Tela** divides the old town from Tela Nueva. A fifteen-minute stroll covers practically everything there is to see, including the small **Museo Garífuna**, by the river on C 8 (Mon–Sat 8am–noon & 2–5pm, Sun 8am–11pm; free), containing lively exhibits covering all aspects of the Garífuna way of life, music and traditions, supplemented by a gift shop and the *Mango Café* (see see overleaf). However, it's the **beaches** that most people come for; those in Tela Vieja, though wide, are more crowded than the stretch of pale sand in front of the *Villas Telamar*. Even better beaches can be found along the bay outside town, where if you walk far enough you'll be able to find one entirely to yourself.

Eating, drinking and entertainment

Tela has an interesting mix of **places to eat**, with foreign-run restaurants catering to the steady flow of European and North American visitors competing with locally owned seafood places. One staple that shouldn't be missed is the delicious *pan de coco* (coconut bread) sold by Garífuna women and children on the beach and around town.

Tela has a thriving **nightlife**, at weekends at least, when the bars along C 11 behind the beach host crowds listening to salsa, reggae and mainstream dance music. In the small hours the focus turns towards the two *discotecas* at the eastern end of the beach. The first, *Las Brasas*, is more of a late-night bar with loud music and a dancefloor, while *Happy Port* in the unmarked building at the end of the tarmac is the main dancing venue, with frequent live music. Be aware though that things can get a bit rowdy at times, and walking along the beach alone after dark is not recommended. For a more tranquil drink, try either the *Delfín Telamar* at *Villas Telamar* (see above) on the beach or the *Mango Café* (see overleaf), which organizes regular evenings of Garífuna music and dancing.

Cesar Marisco's on the beach near the bridge at Av 3. A restaurant renowned for the quality of its seafood, in particular the *sopa de caracol* (conch soup; US$5). The outdoor eating area on the beach makes for a nice place to relax in the evening.

Luces del Norte C 11, Av 5 NE. Popular with foreign tourists, serving up a good range of seafood dishes, including a startling array of conch meals. Pleasant beachside surroundings mean you might want to spend a little time reading a title from the book exchange.

Mama Mia C 4, a block west of the Parque Central. Italian-owned pasta spot with some seafood and meat dishes along with a wide range of breakfast options. Cheap and cheerful: expect a decent portion if not *a la carte* dining. Doubles as a bar and Internet café.

Mango Café C 8, below Museo Garífuna. The most popular place in town amongst international travellers, *Mango*'s boasts a great riverside site to go along with wonderful service. The menu includes delicious Italian food, but be sure to try the Garífuna-style *tapado*, a wonderful seafood and coconut soup.

Maya Vista inside the *Maya Vista* hotel. A fairly expensive menu of well-executed meat and fish dishes, plus huge breakfasts. There's an engaging atmosphere most nights, and tables overlook the ocean.

Pizzería Rome Av 2 off C 9 near the bridge. Promotional offers on pizza and cheap pasta dishes mean this is a popular hangout for budget travellers looking to convert their money into as much food as possible. Free hotel delivery available.

Restaurante Casa Azul C 11, Av 6 NE. Snug place tucked into the ground floor of an atmospheric old house. The menu features a variety of Italian dishes, and there's also a small bar. A filling meal with drinks will set you back about US$9. Open nightly, save Tues, from 4pm.

Tuty's C 9, just off the Parque Central. A great breakfast spot, with excellent juices and a delicious array of sticky buns and sweet cakes. Closes 7pm.

Around Tela

Even if you're quickly bored with Tela itself, there are an abundance of places to visit in the nearby area. These include the **Garífuna villages** along the bay on pristine beaches on either side of town, along with the **Punta Sal** and **Punta Izopo** wildlife reserves, and **Lancetilla**, 5km south of town, probably the finest botanical reserve in Latin America. To get to any of these places, you can take taxis or rely on local buses, but renting a bike is probably the most enjoyable way to get around; ask at Garífuna Tours for rental information.

The Garífuna villages

The Garífuna villages of the north coast appear somewhat anomalous in the context of the rest of the country, but are an interesting getaway for a few hours at least, located on quiet and expansive stretches of beach. Heading **west** from Tela, a dirt road edges the bay between the seafront and the Laguna de los Micos, which forms the eastern edge of Punta Sal (see p.446). Seven kilometres along this road is the sleepy village of **TORNABÉ** and, beyond that, **MIAMI**, set on a fabulous stretch of beach at the mouth of the lagoon. Though Tornabé has a few brick-built houses, Miami is unique, consisting of nothing but traditional palm-thatched huts. Weekends are the best time to visit, when the villagers congregate to perform the traditional, haunting and melodic drum-driven rhythms of Garífuna music, in which the influence of Africa can be clearly heard. Accommodation in both towns is limited. Local families may rent out extremely basic rooms if you ask around, while the only formal overnight spot is Tornabé's *Puerta del Sol* (formerly *The Last Resort* ☎984 3964; ❺, cabin ❻), an idyllic getaway with small, comfortable, air-conditioned cabins and a decent restaurant; they also rent boats for exploring the lagoon and have a large family cabin. **Buses** run to Tornabé from the eastern end of C 10 in Tela every hour on the hour, with the last one back to town at 3.30pm. From Tornabé pick-ups run to Miami at 6.30am and 12.30pm Monday to Saturday, with returns at 8am and 2pm. A taxi from Tela to Tornabé will cost US$4.50.

Some 7km **east** along the bay from Tela, the village of **TRIUNFO DE LA CRUZ** occupies the site of the first **Spanish settlement** on the mainland. Cristóbal de Olid landed here on May 3, 1524, but the colony was abandoned within a few months and the area not resettled until the Garífuna began arriving at the end of the eighteenth century. There is some basic, room-only-style accommodation in town, as well as the luxurious and new *Caribbean Coral Inn* (☎994 9806; ❻) with plush cabin-style rooms (though none yet have a/c) and amenities including a gym and bar/restaurant. A couple of small restaurants serve good seafood – try *Jorge's*. The scenic walk along the beach from Tela takes around two hours, passing the smaller village of **LA ENSENADA** on the way, though it's not advisable – especially for women – to walk alone or to take anything valuable with you.

△ A beach on Roatán, Bay Islands

Intensive tourist development of this area is set to begin, with several luxury hotels in the pipeline.

Punta Sal and Punta Izopo

The **Parque Nacional Janette Kawas** (daily 6am–4pm; US$3), commonly known as **Punta Sal**, is a wonderfully diverse reserve encompassing mangrove swamps, coastal lagoons, wetlands, coral reef and tropical forest, which together provide habitats for an extraordinary range of animal, bird and plant life. Lying to the west of Tela, curving along the bay to the headland of Punta Sal, the reserve covers three lagoons: Laguna de los Micos, Laguna Tisnachí in the centre and the oceanfront Laguna El Diamante, on the western side of the headland. More then one hundred species of bird are present here, including herons and storks, with seasonal migratory visitors bumping up the numbers; animals found in the reserve include howler and white-faced monkeys, wild pigs, jaguars and, in the marine sections, manatees and marine turtles. **Boat trips** along the Río Ulúa and the canals running through the reserve offer a superb opportunity to view the wildlife at close quarters. Where the headland curves up to the north, the land rises slightly to Punta Sal (176m); a trail over the point leads to small, pristine **beaches** at either side.

It's possible to visit parts of Punta Sal independently by renting a boat in Miami to explore the Laguna de los Micos and surrounding area, though most people opt to join the trips organized by Garífuna Tours (see p.442). You could also hike the scenic eight kilometres from Miami to the headland along the beach. For **information** on the reserve contact Prolansate (see p.442) in Tela. Janette Kawas, after whom the reserve is named, was a former president of this nongovernmental organization and instrumental in obtaining protected status against intense local opposition. Her murder, in February 1995, has never been solved.

Jardín Botánico de Lancetilla

The extensive grounds of the **Jardín Botánico de Lancetilla** (Mon–Fri 7.30am–3pm, Sat & Sun 8am–3pm; US$5), 5km south of Tela, started life in 1925 as a United Fruit species research and testing station. Now managed by ESNACIFOZ, the reserve has grown into one of the largest collections of fruit and flowering trees, palms, hardwoods and tropical plants in Latin America. Within Lancetilla's boundaries are an arboretum, a still-functioning research station and a biological reserve – the last covers two-thirds of the total grounds and contains one of the only remaining stretches of virgin tropical wet forest on the Atlantic coast. The stability of the environment has also encouraged numerous species of bird to make their home here.

To **get to** Lancetilla, take the San Pedro highway for a couple of kilometres to the signposted turn-off south, from where it's a further 3km. Guided tours of the arboretum are available, and visitors are also free to wander at will along the marked trails; maps are available at the visitor centre. You need a whole day to visit the arboretum and then cross the reserves, through bamboo groves, to some small **swimming holes** on the Río Lancetilla. There's a **comedor** and a small **hostel** (US$8.75 per bunk) at the visitor centre; beds should be reserved on ⓣ448 0240.

La Ceiba and around

Some 190km east along the coast from San Pedro Sula, steamy **LA CEIBA**, the lively capital of the department of Atlántida, is the gateway to the Bay Islands. Though the town is completely bereft of architectural interest and its sandy beaches are strewn with garbage, it does at least enjoy a stunning setting beneath the steep, green slopes of the Cordillera Nombre de Dios. The city is bustling and self-assured by day, with a cosmopolitan mix of inhabitants including a large Garífuna community, but it's the night that's really celebrated in La Ceiba, when visitors and locals gather to sample the city's vibrant dance scene. Things really come to a head during La Ceiba's **Carnaval** in May, when 200,000 revellers descend on the town.

Ceiba, as it's generally known, owes its existence to the **banana** industry: the Vaccaro Bros (later Standard Fruit and now Dole) first laid plantations in the area in 1899 and set up their company headquarters in town in 1905. Although fruit is no longer shipped out through La Ceiba, the plantations are still important to the local economy, with crops of pineapple and African palm now as significant as bananas.

There are some good **beaches** just 10km or so outside town. Alternatively, with more time and a little planning – or the services of a tour operator – you can explore the cloudforest of the nearby **Parque Nacional Pico Bonito** or the mangrove swamps of the **Refugio Vida Silvestre**.

Arrival and getting around

Long-distance and local **buses** arrive at the main terminal, 2km west of the centre; taxis downtown, usually shared, charge US$0.50 per person. Those arriving by **air** will find themselves at the **Aeropuerto Internacional Golosón**, 9km from the centre, off the main highway west to San Pedro Sula. From the airport, a taxi into the centre costs US$4.50, or around US$3 if you flag one down on the highway, where you can also pick up buses heading into the city. The **ferry** to and from Roatán and Utila in the Bay Islands uses the Muralla de Cabotaje municipal dock, about 5km to the east of the city. There's no bus to the dock; taxis charge US$1.25 from the city centre.

Accommodation

Given La Ceiba's status as both a provincial and a party centre, there's a wide range of **places to stay**. The only problem will be in deciding whether you want to be near the centre, or closer to the nightlife along C 1. Prices inevitably tend to rise around Carnaval time in May, when reserving ahead becomes essential.

Amsterdam 2000 1 C, Av Barahona, Barrio La Isla ⓣ442 2292. Reasonable-value, Dutch-run hotel, just up from the beach, with adequate rooms, some with bath, and dorms ($5) with shared bath. Run down, but cheap enough for a brief stay. ❷

Dan's Hotel C 3, Barrio La Isla ⓣ & ⓕ443 4219. Very friendly and quiet family-run place in the Garífuna barrio of La Isla. Spotless rooms, all with bath, cable TV and a/c. The owners will cook breakfasts and other meals on request. ❹

Gran Hotel Paris Parque Central ⓣ443 2391, ⓦwww.granhotelparis.com. Upmarket hotel with an excellent location on the main plaza. The large, inviting rooms all come with a/c, phone and TV, and there's a pool, a quiet bar, restaurant and cybercafé. ❻

Hotel Alvarez Av Atlántida at C 4 & 5 ⓣ443 0181. Moderate selection of rooms with TV and fan in a characterful hotel featuring hand-painted wall murals; the dated reception area resembles a hangover from the seventies. ❷–❸

Hotel Colonial Av 14 de Julio, C 6–7 ⓣ443 1953, ⓕ443 1955. One of the smarter downtown places: all the rooms have bath, TV and phone, and facilities include a decent restaurant, a bar and, bizarrely enough given the heat, a sauna. ❹

Hotel Iberia Av San Isidro, C 5–6 ⓣ443 0100, ⓦwww.hoteliberia.com. Great value with huge, modern rooms, all en-suite with a/c and cable TV overlooking a central courtyard with fountain. There's also an Internet café and shops below. ❹

Hotel San Carlos Av San Isidro, C 5–6 ⓣ443 0330. Well-run and popular travellers' stronghold set in the heart of town, with a selection of simple but clean and safe rooms, all with fans. Located above a bakery, so you'll be woken by the scent of freshly baking bread. ❷

Posada del Puerto beachfront, off C 1 ⓣ440 0030. Very homely, friendly beachside guesthouse. All rooms have excellent-quality beds and pleasant decor, plus a/c and TV; there's also a guests' living room and kitchen, and a large restaurant, under the same management, next door. ❹

The City

Most things of interest to visitors lie within a relatively small area of the city around the shady and pleasant **Parque Central**, with its busts of Honduran historical heroes. The unremarkable whitewashed and powder-blue **Cathedral** sits on the

LA CEIBA
CARIBBEAN SEA
Dock
0
200 m
Hotel Partenon Beach
BARRIO INGLÉS
BARRIO LA ISLA
Parque Bonilla
Banco Credomatic
Market
Oficinas de Ferrocarril Nacional
FUCSA
Cinema
Parque Central
Cathedral
Stadium
Bus Station
Centro Internacional de Idiomas
1 CALLE
2 CALLE
3 CALLE
4 CALLE
5 CALLE
6 CALLE
7 CALLE
8 CALLE
9 CALLE
10 CALLE
12 CALLE
13 CALLE
14 CALLE
AVENIDA ATLÁNTIDA
AVENIDA REPÚBLICA
AVENIDA SAN ISIDRO
AVENIDA 14 DE JULIO
AVENIDA 15 DE SEPTIEMBRE
AVENIDA MIGUEL PAZ BARAHONA
AVENIDA PEDRO NUFIO
AVENIDA DIONISIO DE HERRERA
AVENIDA MANUEL BONILLA
ACCOMMODATION
Amsterdam 2000 B
Dan's Hotel C
Gran Hotel Paris H
Hotel Alvarez D
Hotel Colonial G
Hotel Iberia E
Hotel San Carlos F
Posada del Puerto A
RESTAURANTS & CAFÉS
Cafeteria Shalom 8
Caribeños 2
Centro Cultural Satuye 7
Cric Cric Burger 4
Expatriate's Bar and Grill 11
Flipper 5
Le Rustique 3
Masapán 9
Mesón del Puerto 1
Patty's Juices 6
Ricardo's 10
N
Megaplaza Mall
Airport, San Pedro Sula, Butterfly & Insect Museum

southeast corner, diagonally opposite the *Gran Hotel Paris*. Running north from the Parque almost to the seafront, Av San Isidro, Av Atlántida and Av 14 de Julio form the main commercial district, lined with shops, banks and a couple of supermarkets. For an interesting five-minute diversion, stroll a block west of the Parque to the **Oficinas de Ferrocarril Nacional**, planted with tropical vegetation and dotted with museum-piece train carriages, many dating from the days of the peak of the banana trade. The bustling main general **market,** sprawling along the streets around the decrepit old wooden market building on Av Atlántida, is likewise worth a look. For a more sanitized shopping experience, check out the vast new Megaplaza **mall** on the southern outskirts of town, where there's also a cinema, supermarket and restaurants. Nearby, about a kilometre south of the plaza, on the second floor of Casa G2 in Colonia El Sauce is a private **butterfly and insect museum** (Mon–Sat 8am–noon & 1–4pm; US$1.35) with over 12,000 butterflies and insects on display from 68 countries, though almost three-quarters are native species. Displays explain trapping procedures, and there are videos in English and Spanish.

Night action takes place along **C 1**, which runs parallel to the seafront. Nicknamed the "Zona Viva" due to its preponderance of bars and clubs, C 1 extends west from the old dock and over the river estuary into **Barrio La Isla**, a quieter residential district, mainly home to Garífuna, once it leaves the seafront. All the **beaches** within the city limits are, sadly, too polluted and dirty for even the most desperate to want to brave the rough water. Better by far is to head east to the much cleaner beaches a few kilometres out of town (see p.451).

Restaurants and cafés

The range of **restaurants** in La Ceiba is disappointing for such a big city, with most of the central choices being cheap comedor style, serving similar unhealthy menus of largely fried foods. Heading out to the beach things improve slightly, although prices are predictably higher.

Centre

Cafeteria Shalom inside a small mall on C 7, between Av Atlántida and Av 14 de Julio. Israeli-owned canteen serving some Middle Eastern food including falafel and kebabs. Open daily 7am–8pm.

Cric Cric Burger Av 14 de Julio, C 3. Good burgers, steak sandwiches and other snacks served to the accompaniment of very loud music. The side tables are a good place to watch comings and goings in the street.

Expatriate's Bar and Grill C 12, two blocks east of Av San Isidro. Airy, North American–owned thatched bar with excellent vegetarian dishes, grilled chicken and fish, and barbecued ribs. Welcoming atmosphere and popular with resident foreigners, so it's also a good source of local information. Closed Tues & Wed.

Flipper Av Atlántida at the corner of C 5. Good burgers, steak sandwiches and *minutas* as well as *comida a la vista* and *licuados.* Breakfasts available.

Le Rustique Moran building at the corner of C 5. Charming, tiny French eatery hidden away on a rooftop serving such specialities as onion soup and quiche. Closed Sun and Mon.

Masapán C 7, between Av La República and Av San Isidro. Consistently popular self-service cafeteria, open 24hours, with a cheap buffet of Honduran and American-style food.

Patty's Juices 14 de Julio, C 6–7. Friendly family-owned place ideal for delicious and inexpensive fresh juices, *licuados* and fruit salads.

Ricardo´s Av 14 de Julio. Boasting a good central location, this is one of the finest restaurants in the city. There's a wide selection of juicy steaks to go along with a salad bar, vegetarian and vegan options. It's not cheap though, and you won't get much change out of US$20 for a full meal and drink. Outdoor seating available. Closed Sun.

Zona Viva

Caribeños C 1, Barrio La Isla. Honduran-style restaurant close enough to the beach to feel the benefit of the breeze. Typical breakfasts and lunches served; try the delicious homemade Honduran tacos.

Centro Cultural Satuye 4 C, Av Herrera, Barrio La Isla. Light-hearted and informal Garífuna restaurant, with the sort of warm welcome and adventurous cooking that is synonymous with the Garífuna. Emphasis is on seafood dishes, usually with Caribbean spices and coconut added. Loud live music in the evening.

Mesón del Puerto on the seafront, just off 1 C, opposite *Caribeños*, Barrio La Isla. Excellent but pricey beachside restaurant with good service and a delicious menu of grilled meats. Take your pick of sitting indoors in the colonial decor of the air-conditioned dining room, or enjoy the sea breeze on the beach deck.

Nightlife

Not for nothing does La Ceiba have a reputation as the place to party. The **Zona Viva** hums most nights of the week, though weekends are really explosive, with a profusion of places to drink and get down. A hedonistic local crowd, plus a steady trickle of tourists and a growing number of resident expats have helped to create a buoyant atmosphere. The most exciting time to be in La Ceiba is during **Carnaval**, a weeklong bash held every May to celebrate the city's patron saint, San Isidro. Dances and street events in various barrios around town culminate in an afternoon parade on the third Saturday of the month. Led by a float carrying the Carnaval Queen, the parade moves slowly down the gaudily bedecked Av San Isidro. Bands on stages placed along the avenida then compete to outplay each other throughout the evening and into the early hours. The 200,000 or so partygoers who attend Carnaval every year flock between the stages and the clubs on C 1, where the dancing continues until dawn.

El Bacalao near the beach. Cool ocean breeze makes up for the lack of a/c at this basic drinking hole, popular with English-speakers for its cheap beers, raucous atmosphere and jukebox. It's no-frills, but if you're looking to drink until you drop it's the place to go.

Mango Tango 1 C. Tropical-style bar with weekend live music, well-stocked bar and selection of Honduran bar food. Singers and bands are welcome to perform.

El Mussol 1 C, 7 blocks from the bridge in Barrio La Isla. Probably the smartest club in the Zona Viva, with drink prices a little higher than in other venues. Beachfront bar, cocktail menu and video DJ, combined with an amazing set of disco lights, guarantee a late night.

Snake Bar on the beach around the corner from El Bacalao, Barrio La Isla. The only real beach bar in town, frequented by beach bums during the day, and dancers enjoying the sound of the waves during the evening.

Sur 1 C, near *Mango Tango*. Uruguayan-owned bar with a laid-back atmosphere and ambient background music. This is the place to come for a relaxing drink, where you can choose from the extensive cocktail menu and sit on the second-floor terrace. Tues-Sat only.

Listings

Airlines Atlantic at the corner of Av 15 de Septiembre and Av República (Ⓣ440 2343); Isleña (Ⓣ443 0179), Sosa (Ⓣ443 1399) and Taca (Ⓣ443 1912) are all on the Parque Central; all three also have ticket desks at the airport, as do Rollins Air (Ⓣ443 2177) and Cayman Airways (Ⓣ440 0863).

Banks Banco Ficahsa, just west of the Parque Central on C 8, will change travellers' cheques, while Credomatic, Av San Isidro, C 5–6, is the place for Visa and MasterCard cash advances.

Car rental Molinari, *Gran Hotel Paris* (Ⓣ443 2391, Ⓕ443 0055).

Cinema just east of the Parque Central on C 8, and two screens at the Cines Milenium in the Megaplaza a taxi ride south of town for the usual subtitled Hollywood fare.

Hospital Hospital Euro Honduras, C 1, Av Atlántida, Barrio el Centro (Ⓣ443 0244), is a modern and well-equipped private hospital, with a 24hr emergency clinic and English- and German-speaking staff.

Immigration Av 14 Julio, C 1–2 (Mon–Fri 8am–noon & 2–4pm; Ⓣ442 0638) on Parque Bonilla.

Internet access There are several cybercafés in La Ceiba, including the efficient Hondusoft (Mon–Fri 8am–8pm, Sat 8am–6pm) on the upper floor of the Centro Comercial Panyotti shopping mall at C 7 between Av Atlántida and Av 14 de Julio, with rates for US$1.25 an hour, plus Web phone facilities.

Language school Centro Internacional de Idiomas, Av San Isidro, C 12–13 (Ⓣ & Ⓕ440 1557, Ⓦwww.hondurasspanish.com), is a good Spanish school with a/c classrooms. Rates are

US$190 weekly for four hours of one-to-one tuition and homestay, including all meals.
Laundry Lavamatic Ceibeño, Av Miguel Paz Bahona between C 5 & 6.
Police ⓣ441 0795 or 199.
Post office Av Morazán and C 13, south of the Parque.
Telephones Hondutel, at Av Ramón Rosa, C 5–6, is open 24hr.
Travel agent Transmundo is centrally located opposite the Cathedral just south of the Parque.
Tour operators Several excellent companies arrange trekking trips to Pico Bonito and whitewater rafting on the Río Cangrejal: try La Moskitia Ecoaventuras, Parque Bonilla, Av 14 de Julio at 1 C (ⓣ442 0104, ⓦwww.honduras.com/moskita); Euro Honduras Tours, Av Atlántida at 1 C (ⓣ443 3874); or Ríos Honduras (ⓣ995 6925, ⓦwww.paddlehonduras.com).

Around La Ceiba

The broad sandy **beaches** and clean water at Playa de Perú and the village of Sambo Creek are easily reached day-trip destinations east of La Cieba. A trip to explore the **cloudforest** within the Parque Nacional Pico Bonito requires more planning, although the eastern edge of the reserve, formed by the Río Cangrejal, is still easily accessible, offering opportunities for swimming and whitewater rafting.

The beaches: Playa de Perú and Sambo Creek

Ten kilometres east of the city, **Playa de Perú** is a wide sweep of clean sand that's popular at weekends. Any bus running east up the coast will drop you at the highway-side turn-off, from where it's a fifteen-minute walk to the beach. About 2km past the turning for Playa de Perú, on the Río María, there's a series of **waterfalls** and **natural pools** set in lush, shady forest. A path leads from Río María village on the highway, winding through the hills along the left bank of the river: it takes around thirty minutes to walk to the first cascade and pool, with some muddy sections and a bit of scrambling during the wet season.

There are further deserted expanses of white sand at the friendly Garífuna village of **SAMBO CREEK**, 8km beyond Río María. You can eat excellent fresh fish at a couple of good **restaurants** in the village, including the expat-owned *Sambo Creek*; as the only place in town serving ice cream, it's a must-stop on hotter days. Olanchito or Jutiapa buses from La Ceiba will drop you at the turn-off to Sambo Creek on the highway, a couple of kilometres from the village; slower buses run all the way to the village centre from La Ceiba's terminal every 45 minutes.

Parque Nacional Pico Bonito

Directly south of La Ceiba, the Cordillera Nombre de Dios shelters the **Parque Nacional Pico Bonito** (daily 6am–4pm; US$6), a remote expanse of tropical broadleaf forest, cloudforest and – in its southern reaches, above the Río Aguan valley – pine forest. Taking its name from the awe-inspiring bulk of Pico Bonito (2435m) itself, the park is the source of twenty rivers, including the Zacate, Bonito and Cangrejal, which cascade majestically down the steep, thickly covered slopes. The park also provides sanctuary for an abundance of wildlife including armadillos, howler and spider monkeys, pumas and ocelot. The lower fringes are the most easily penetrable, with a small number of trails laid out through the dense greenery.

The easiest place to get into the park is via the *Lodge at Piço Bonito* (ⓣ440 0389, ⓦwww.picobonito.com; ⑨), a world-class **jungle lodge** with bungalow accommodation, gourmet cuisine, a pool and a sublime setting in the foothills of the forest reserve. To get there head for the village of **Los Pinos**, 12km from La Ceiba on the Tela highway, from where the hotel is signposted, 3km away up a dirt side-road. Trails from the lodge snake up through the tree cover to a lookout from where Utila is visible, and down to beautiful river bathing pools. Tour companies in La Ceiba operate day- and overnight trips to Pico Bonito from around US$40 per person (see above for a list of local companies).

Just below *Lodge at Pico Bonito* are a few further attractions. The Finca Mariposa **butterfly park** (Wed–Sun 8am–4pm; US$2), signposted 600m from the hotel, is home to more than forty species in a large, screened garden house; the surroundings feature small coffee and cacao plantations. Adjacent is a small **serpentarium** housing twenty snake species (same hours; US$1.35). A further 2km from the butterfly park, but better reached from a one-kilometre-long dirt road from Los Pinos, the small AMARAS **wildlife refuge centre** (ⓣ443 3824; US$2) takes in monkeys, big cats (including jaguars), macaws and parrots confiscated from traffickers and previously kept as pets, and where possible prepares them for release back into the wild – volunteers are needed and visitors welcome.

The **Río Cangrejal**, forming the eastern boundary of the park, boasts some of the best class III and IV rapids in Central America; **whitewater rafting** and **kayaking** trips are organized by some of the tour companies listed overleaf. There are also some magnificent swimming spots, backed by gorgeous mountain scenery, along the river valley. It's tricky to get to the river under your own steam, but you could contact the German-owned Omega Rafting (ⓣ440 0334, ⓦwww.omega-tours.hn), who run **cabañas** (US$3–6 per person) geared for ecotravellers on the banks of the Cangrejal – transport from La Ceiba, full board and a day spent either trekking, horse-riding or rafting costs US$50 per person. A similar outfit is run by Jungle River Rafting (ⓣ440 1268, ⓦwww.hondurasjungletours.net), who have a river lodge in the park with bar, restaurant and a choice of private and dorm accommodation (US$5–10 per person). They also boast the country's only high-wire zipline.

Refugio de Vida Silvestre Cuero y Salado

Thirty kilometres west from La Ceiba, the **Refugio de Vida Silvestre Cuero y Salado** (daily 7am–4pm; US$10) is one of the last substantial remnants of wetlands and mangrove swamps along the north coast. The reserve is home to a large number of animal and bird species, many endangered, including manatees, jaguars, howler and white-faced monkeys, sea turtles, hawks, along with seasonal influxes of migratory birds. Though nominally protected since 1987, the edges of the reserve are under constant pressure from local farmers wishing to drain land for new pastures.

The best way to see the reserve is to take a **guided tour** (US$5.50 for up to 7 people), not least because the guides know the spots where you're likely to see some wildlife. **FUCSA**, the body that manages the reserve, has an office in La Ceiba in the Edificio Ferrocarril Nacional, two blocks west of the Parque Central (Mon–Fri 8–11.30am & 1.30–4.30pm, Sat 8–11.30am; ⓣ443 0329, ⓔfucsa@laceiba.com). They run regular tours (US$11 per boat), which you'll need to book in advance. They also have a small **campsite** (US$1.35) at the reserve, and are in the process of constructing a visitor centre with basic accommodation.

To get to the reserve **independently**, catch an hourly bus (6.20am–3.30pm) from La Ceiba's terminal to the village of La Unión, 20km or so west. From here, you can either make your way on foot through the fruit plantations – it takes around an hour and a half to walk the 8km, travel by *burra*, a flat, poled railcar (locals charge between US$11–25, depending on numbers, to shunt you along the tracks), or take the train (US$10 return).

Trujillo and around

Perched above the sparkling waters of the palm-fringed Bahía de Trujillo, with the green backdrop of Cordillera Nombre de Dios rearing up behind, **TRUJILLO** immediately seduces the small number of tourists who make the 90km trip here from La Ceiba. Though you'd never guess it from the town's sleepy demeanour, this is an important city, capital of the department of Colón. All the elements for a relaxing stay are in place – warm, sheltered waters, clean beaches, and a good range of hotels and restaurants – and few people are in a hurry to leave.

The area around Trujillo was settled by a mixture of Pech and Tolupan groups when Columbus first disembarked on the American mainland here, on August 14, 1502. Trujillo itself was founded by Cortés's lieutenant, Juan de Medina, in May 1525, though it was regularly abandoned due to attacks by European pirates. Not until the late eighteenth century did repopulation begin in earnest, aided by the arrival, via Roatán, of several hundred Garífuna. In 1860, a new threat appeared in the shape of the US filibuster William Walker, who in June of that year briefly took control of the town; executed by firing squad in September 1860 by the Honduran authorities, he is buried in Trujillo's cemetery. The twentieth century has been distinctly less eventful, except for a severe battering at the hands of Hurricane Mitch, though few buildings in town were destroyed. There's often far more activity these days at **Puerto Castilla**, at the eastern end of the bay, the busy port through which passes the produce of the region's plantations.

Arrival and information

Buses enter Trujillo from the east, passing an airstrip, and terminating at a dusty terminal at the bottom of a hill. From here infrequent urban buses head up the hill to the Parque Central, or you can take a taxi (US$0.65). A sloping path from the Parque leads down to the seafront, which is lined with palm-thatched *champas*. Banco Atlántida on the Parque and Banco de Occidente one block west give Visa cash advances. **Hondutel** and the **post office** are next to each other three blocks south from the southeast corner of the Parque, and there's a small **migración** (Mon–Sat 8am–noon, 1–5pm; ⓣ434 4451) 1km southwest of the Parque in Barrio Cristales. **Internet** access is at *Café Internet* opposite the *Hotel Emperador* (Mon–Fri 8am–8pm, Sat 8am–6pm; US$2.65 per hour).

One kilometre south of town, up the hillside in the *Villas Brinkley*, **Turtle Tours** (ⓣ434 4431, ⓔinfo@turtletours.de) offer a range of tempting and moderately priced tours, including snorkelling excursions, canoe trips and city walks, plus five-day expeditions into the Mosquitia for US$375 per person. A **language school**, the Escuela de Idiomas Trujillo, is located close to the *migración* on the road to the Museo Rufino Galán (ⓣ434 4135); it costs US$195 per week for five hours of study daily and full family-based board and accommodation.

Accommodation

There's plenty of **accommodation** to choose from in the town centre, close to the restaurants and bars, though since Trujillo has never really featured on the tourist trail there are fewer rock-bottom cheapies than in La Ceiba or Tela. There are also a couple of excellent places in glorious settings just outside town, and you can **camp** at the *Campamento Hotel*.

Campamento Hotel & Restaurant on the beach 4km west of town ⓣ4991 3391. Comfortable wooden cabañas with a/c in an idyllic setting, scattered around extensive grounds reaching down to a private beach. There's also an open-air restaurant serving well-prepared seafood and other dishes, and safe camping (US$3 per tent) with access to a bathroom. ❺

Cristopher Colombus Hotel on the beach by the airstrip ⓣ434 4966, ⓕ434 4971. A large, green architectural curiosity, redeemed by its location and patronized by wealthy Hondurans, with facilities including a pool and tennis courts. ❼

Hotel Cocopando 1km west of centre in Barrio Cristales ⓣ434 4748. The town's best-value budget hotel, with a beachside setting, simple, clean rooms and a great comedor downstairs. Gets noisy at weekends when the neighbouring dance hall fires up. ❷

Hotel Colonial southern side of the Parque ⓣ434 4011. Well-situated hotel, with big beds and bath, a/c and TV in all rooms, though the downstairs ones are rather dark. ❹

Hotel Emperador by the market ⓣ434 4446. One of the town's nicest cheaper places, with clean rooms, all have bath, TV and fan, set round a courtyard. Service is friendly, but you won't be entrusted with a key. If interested in the area's history, ask for local academic Professor Cuevas, though he speaks only Spanish. ❷

O'Glynn three blocks south and one block east of the Parque ⓣ434 4592. Friendly place with simple, clean accommodation in the original hotel plus large modern rooms with a/c and TV in a new annex. ❹

Villas Brinkley 1km south of town ☎434 4444, ⓔbrinkley@hondutel.hn. One of the most pleasing hotels in Honduras, with a relaxed, welcoming ambiance and superb views from the terrace over the whole stretch of the bay and its glistening waters. There's a range of tastefully furnished rooms, all with bath and some with a/c and kitchen. The hotel also has a pool, and the restaurant is a good place to come for a meal even if you're not staying here. ❹–❺

The Town

The town proper stretches back five or so blocks south of the **Parque Central**, which is just fifty metres from cliffs overlooking the sea. On the north side of the square is a bust of Juán de Medina, who founded the town on 18 May 1525. Just along from here is the town's main attraction, the sixteenth-century **Fortaleza de Santa Bárbara** (daily 8am–noon & 1–4pm; US$0.55), site of William Walker's execution. Recently restored to incorporate a new museum, the low-lying fort hangs gloomily on the edge of the bluffs, overlooking the coastline it was singularly unsuccessful in defending against pirate attack. The museum charts the town's often colourful history, and has an exhibition room on Garífuna culture.

Much of Trujillo's charm lies in meandering through its rather crumbly streets, where the heat of the sun is alleviated by a constant breeze. Southwest from the centre, a couple of blocks past the market, is the **Cementerio Viejo**, where Walker's grave lies overgrown with weeds. Turn right past the cemetery and a ten-minute stroll brings you to the privately run **Museo y Piscinas Riveras del Pedregal** (daily 7am–5pm; US$1.65), an eccentric collection of rusty junk. Most of the orginal pre-Columbian ceramics once held here have been sold off, replaced with convincing replicas. Outside, the wheels of an American jumbo jet that crashed in the area in 1985 can be seen without having to part with the entrance fee. Behind the building are a couple of small, green-coloured swimming pools in which the brave may wish to bathe. Back at the Parque Central, walk west for ten minutes and you'll reach the **Barrio Cristales**, the site of the country's first mainland Garífuna settlement, founded in 1797. The Gari Arte shop here stocks Garífuna handicrafts and music tapes.

Trujillo's outstanding feature by far is its **beaches**, long stretches of almost pristine sand. The glorious sweep of the Bahía de Trujillo is as yet unaffected by excessive tourist development, and its calm, blue waters are perfect for effortless swimming. The beaches below town, lined with *champas*, are clean enough, but the stretches to the east, beyond the airstrip, are emptier. It's also possible to walk east along the beach to the reserve of **Laguna de Guaimoreto** or west to the Garífuna village of **Santa Fe** – see opposite.

Parque Nacional Capiro y Calentura

Directly above the town lies the dark green swathe of **Parque Nacional Capiro y Calentura** (daily 6am–5pm; free), the country's best example of a rare habitat known as "hurricane forest". The reserve's huge cedars and pines tower amid the thick canopy of ferns and flowering plants and vines, many of them used for medicinal purposes. Following the devastation wrought by Hurricane Fifi in 1974, much of the cover is secondary growth, but it still provides a secure habitat for howler monkeys, reptiles and a colourful range of birdlife and butterflies. You can walk into the reserve by following the dirt road past the *Villas Brinkley*, which winds, increasingly steeply, up Cerro Calentura to the radio towers just below the summit, a ten-kilometre walk, best done in the relative cool of early morning; alternatively, you could negotiate with a taxi driver to take you to the top and then walk down.

Eating, drinking and entertainment

The best **places to eat** are the informal *champa* bar-restaurants on the beach, where you can dine in the warm evening air, listening to the waves. The main cluster is on the beach below town – follow the ramp from the southwest corner of the Parque. There's another group to the east by the airstrip, about twenty minutes' walk away – note that it's not advisable to walk back along the beach after dark.

Later on in the evening, *Disco Horfez* and *Disco Truxillo* in the centre of town both heave at the weekends to Latin American rhythms, while *Black and White*, on the beach in Barrio Cristales, attracts a mainly Garífuna crowd.

Bahía Bar on the beach by the airstrip. Long-established, foreign-owned beach *champa* with a wide menu of seafood, good juices and sandwiches.

El Bucanero *Hotel Colonial* (see p.453). Decent menu with some good seafood options including, if you want to dine in style, lobster thermidor. Metamorphoses into a bar at night with happy-hour drink offers and something of a youthful ambiance.

Gringo's Bar next to the *Bahía*. Everything a tropical beachside bar should be, with well-cooked food, good breakfasts and an easy-going atmosphere.

Oasi's Restaurant southwest off the Parque. Clean and pleasant with a varied menu of pasta, seafood, pizza, meats, soups and a little bit of just about everything else you can think of. Guests are encouraged to sign the wooden beams of the walls and roof to register their opinions.

Perla del Caribe on the beach below town. New restaurant with seaside terrace and large, if slightly pricey, seafood menu. Most meals run US$8–10. Try the *ceviche mixta*.

Pizza Pantry two blocks southwest of the Parque. As well as reasonable pizza, the broad menu includes seafood, steaks and breakfasts.

Restaurante Lempira *Villas Brinkley* (see opposite). Feast on well-cooked European and Honduran dishes whilst admiring the fabulous views, then walk it all off on the stroll back to town. Moderately expensive, but worth every Lempira for the quality and ambiance.

Rogue's Galeria on the beach below town. Commonly referred to as "Jerry's", this engaging American-owned bar-restaurant features superb seafood and plenty of hammocks for daytime chilling. Also has a book exchange.

Around Trujillo

Expanses of white-sand **beach** stretch for miles around the bay from Trujillo, all clean, wide and perfect for swimming; don't take anything valuable with you, though, and don't venture onto them after dark. Walking east from town along the beach, for 5km or so, leads to the **Laguna de Guaimoreto**, a small reserve of mangrove swamps that is home to thousands of migratory birds, monkeys and other wildlife. Nearby on the beach, *Casa Kiwi* (ⓣ434 3050, ⓦwww.casakiwi.com; ❷) is a backpackers' refuge with dorms (US$2.75), camping space (US$1.65) and double rooms as well as hammocks, pool table and organised tours. To get there via public transport, take the bus from Trujillo to Punta Castilla, getting off when you see the sign just after crossing the bridge over the lagoon. A taxi will cost about US$4.40.

Fourteen kilometres **west** from Trujillo, the Garífuna village of **SANTA FE** is even more relaxed than Trujillo, though the beach isn't as attractive. Even so, it's worth a visit if only to sample the exquisite local seafood dished up by the *Comedor Caballero*, and there are also a couple of basic hotels (both ❷) in the village if you want to stay. A dirt road connects Santa Fe with Trujillo, travelled by three **buses** daily in either direction, or you could walk it in about two hours.

Taking a hot bath in the heat of the Caribbean may not strike everyone as an appealing thought, but a soak in the clean and very hot mineral waters of the **Aguas Calientes** springs (daily 7am–9pm; US$3), 7km inland from Trujillo, feels delightfully decadent. The experience can be topped off with a drink at the bar of the rather slick *Agua Caliente* hotel in the grounds (ⓣ434 4249; ❺). Any bus heading to Tocoa will drop you off at the entrance to the springs; buses stop running at around 6.30pm.

La Mosquitia

Honduras's northeast corner is made up of the remote and sparsely populated expanse of **La Mosquitia**. Bounded to the west by the mountain ranges of the Río

Planning a trip to Mosquitia

A number of companies, based in San Pedro, La Ceiba, Tegucigalpa and Trujillo (see the relevant sections for details), offer a variety of **tours** to Mosquitia. The advantages of an organized tour are that all the planning is done for you and you can count on being accompanied by knowledgeable guides. Travelling independently is by no means impossible, though, so long as you're prepared to go with the flow. **Transport** to and within the area is mainly by air or river: the main centres of **Puerto Lempira**, **Palacios**, **Brus Laguna** and **Ahuas** are connected to La Ceiba by regular flights, while launches ply the waterways connecting the scattered villages. **Accommodation** and facilities are basic; if you're making an independent trek, bring enough food with you for your party and guides. Finally, bear in mind that all schedules are subject to change and delay; transport on the rivers and channels, in particular, is determined by how much rain has fallen.

Air fares to the Mosquitia are standardized. From La Ceiba, a return ticket to Palacios costs US$85, to Puerto Lempira US$115, and to Brus Laguna US$100. Once in the Mosquitia, **boat** fares are relatively high, reflecting the need to import all fuel. Hiring a boat to get from the coast to Las Marías will cost at least US$120, even after bargaining hard, and not including food for the guides. Another alternative is to charter a boat from the pier in Trujillo to Palacios, though you'll need to be part of a group, or from La Ceiba. The captains of *El Corazon* and *Mr Jim* make the journey weekly (US$20 per person), but the trip takes 24 hours and there are no amenities on board. The cheapest way to get to Mosquitia is to take the **bus** from Trujillo to the village of Tocoa, a long and bumpy ride. From here pick-ups run to Batalla ($16 per person), where you can charter a boat across to Palacios. Progress by road is extremely slow however.

Plátano and Colón, with the Río Coco forming the border with Nicaragua to the south, this vast region comprises almost a fifth of Honduras's territory. With just two peripheral roads and a tiny population divided among a few far-flung towns and villages, entering the Mosquitia really does mean leaving the beaten track. There are no phones in the region, and all accommodation is extremely basic, often without electricity and with latrine-style toilets. Available food is limited to rice, beans and the catch of the day.

To the surprise of many who come here expecting to have to hack their way through jungle, though, much of the Mosquitia is composed of marshy coastal wetlands and flat savanna – likened by some to the landscape of South Carolina. The small communities of **Palacios** and **Brus Laguna** (formerly Brewer's Lagoon) are access points for the **Río Plátano Biosphere Reserve**, the most famous of five separate reserves in the area, set up to protect one of the finest remaining stretches of virgin tropical rainforest in Central America. **Puerto Lempira**, to the east, is the regional capital.

The largest ethnic group inhabiting the Mosquitia are the **Miskitos**, numbering around 30,000, who spoke a unique form of English until as recently as a few generations ago. There are much smaller indigenous communities of **Pech**, who number around 2500, and **Tawahka** (Sumu), of whom there are under a thousand, living around the Río Patuca.

Some history

Before the Spanish arrived, the Mosquitia belonged to the Pech and Sumu. Initial contact with Europeans was comparatively benign, the Spanish showing slight interest in the area, preferring to concentrate on the mineral-rich lands of the interior. Contact with Europeans intensified when the **British** began seeking a foothold on the mainland in the seventeenth century, establishing settlements on the coast at Black River (now Palacios) and Brewer's Lagoon (Brus Laguna), whose inhabitants – the so-called "shoremen" – engaged in logging, trading, smuggling and fighting the Spanish.

Britain's claim to Mosquitia, nominally to protect the shoremen, though their real reason was to ensure a transit route from the Atlantic to the Pacific, supposedly ended in 1786, when all Central American territories except Belize were ceded to the Spanish. In the 1820s, however, taking advantage of post-independence chaos, Britain again encouraged settlement on the Mosquito Coast and by 1844 had all but formally announced a protectorate in the area. Not until 1859 and the British–American Treaty of Cruz Wyke did Britain formally end all claims to Mosquitia.

The initial impact of mestizo Honduran culture on Mosquitia was slight. Since the creation of the administrative department of Gracias a Dios in 1959, however, indigenous cultures have become gradually diluted: Spanish is now the main language and the government encourages mestizo settlers to migrate here in search of land. Pech, Miskito and Garífuna communities have become more vocal in recent years in demanding respect for their cultural differences and in calling for an expansion of health, education and transport infrastructures.

Palacios, Brus Laguna and Ahuas

Sited on what was the British settlement of Black River, **PALACIOS** lies just west of one of the Río Plátano Biosphere Reserve's three coastal lagoons, Laguna Ibans. Served by regular flights to and from La Ceiba, this is frequently the starting point for organized trips to the Río Plátano Biosphere Reserve and a logical place for independent travellers to set out from. Adequate **rooms** (both ❷) can be had in the *Rio Tinto Hotel* run by local Don Felix Marmol, who is also the Isleña agent, or the *Jungle Lodge* by the airstrip, where the rooms are a little better.

Dotted along the Caribbean shoreline around Palacios is a cluster of interesting **Garífuna villages**, including **Batalla**, just to the west of town across the Palacios lagoon, and **Plaplaya**, about 8km to the east, where a **turtle project** has been established. Highly endangered giant leatherbacks, the largest species in the world (reaching up to 3m in length and 900kg in weight), nest in the beaches around the village between April and June. There's a resident Peace Corps worker stationed here to oversee the project, and volunteers are welcome. If you want to stay, *Sede's Hospedaje* (❶) is the cheapest, though *Yohanna's Hospedaje* (❷) is slightly more comfortable and the owner can also arrange boat trips. **Raistá**, the next coastal settlement, three hours' walk from Plaplaya, is a friendly Miskito village and also the base for a new **butterfly farm** (daily 8am–5pm; US$2.50, including tour), which exports exotic specimens to other parks in Honduras and North America. There's simple accommodation here (❶) and *Elma's Kitchen* nearby serves tasty, inexpensive meals. There are more rooms for rent in **Belén** (ask for Doña Mendelia), right next door to Raistá on the outer edge of Laguna Ibans, and in **Barra Plátano**, a two-hour walk east from Belén along the beach. Boats (*cayucos*) to the Río Plátano reserve and Las Marías can be hired in any of these villages, or from Palacios (US$120).

Thirty kilometres east along the coast from Palacios, on the southeastern edge of the Laguna de Brus, is the friendly Miskito town of **BRUS LAGUNA**. *Hospedaje El Tipico* (❶) on the waterfront has six basic rooms run by Joaquín Cruz, a good source of local information. He has a boat for hire and can arrange tours of the area. Regular **flights** connect the town with La Ceiba, and guides and boats can be hired for multiday trips, travelling up the Río Sigre (or Sikre) into the southern reaches of the Río Plátano reserve. **CANNON ISLAND** in the Laguna takes its name from the mid-eighteenth century English cannons that are dotted around the island. It is now the home of the luxury *Cannon Island Fishing Lodge* (Ⓔcabrera_yolanda@hotmail.com; ❾), set in tropical gardens, and offering superb tarpon and snook fishing. Fishing packages start at around US$150 including equipment.

A little under 40km inland from Brus Laguna as the crow flies is the Miskito village of **AHUAS**, scattered across the pine savanna (Ahuas means pine in Miskito). The village is only a kilometre from the Río Patuca, which forms the border of the Río Plátano reserve, and narrow cargo boats take passengers on the four-hour trip upriver to **Barra Patuca** on the coast. The town is extremely picturesque, with dwellings built out of wood and palm and, despite its isolation, extremely friendly. Rooms can be found by asking around near the airstrip.

The Río Plátano Biosphere Reserve

The **Río Plátano Biosphere Reserve** is the most significant reserve in Honduras, sheltering an estimated eighty percent of all the country's animal species. Visitors usually come here to experience the tropical rainforest; yet within its boundaries – from the Caribbean in the north to the Montañas de Punta Piedra in the west and the Río Patuca in the south – the reserve also covers huge expanses of coastal wetlands and flat savanna grasslands. Sadly, even international recognition of the importance of this diverse ecosystem, signalled by its World Heritage status, hasn't prevented extensive destruction at the hands of settlers: up to sixty percent of forest cover on the outer edges of the reserve has disappeared in the last three decades.

Getting to the heart of the Río Plátano reserve requires travelling up the Río Plátano, through savanna and secondary forest growth, to the small village of **LAS MARÍAS**, a Pech and Miskito settlement about seven hours upstream from the coast. There are three basic hospedajes in the village, *Hospedajes Tinglas*, *Martinez* and *Pagoda* (all US$3 per person), each serving meals, and plenty of prospective **guides** are available to help you explore the river and surrounding jungle for US$8–10 a day. The local guides have organized themselves into a rotation system, coordinated by the leader Martin Herrera, so that everyone gets some work once in a while. Unfortunately this means that individuals cannot be recommended and it's pot luck whether you get a good or a poor guide. A pleasant, if rather wet, trip is by *pipante* (pole-propelled canoe) five hours upstream to rock petroglyphs at Walpulbansirpi, carved by an unknown people. The journey itself is the main attraction, along channels too shallow for motorised boats to pass; in sections you'll be required to leave the boat and make your way through the undergrowth. *Pipantes* require three guides each, but carry only two passengers and cost US$25 (not including guides).

Upstream from the village begins the primary forest cover, pressing in against both banks of the river. Few experiences can match the initial impression of entering the **rainforest**, as towering trees – mahogany, tamarind, oak – reaching up to 50m or more, break through the dense canopy to the sunlight. Smaller in size are the forest's palms, ceiba and avocados, hung with vines and epiphytic ferns, whilst still closer to ground level are sprays of brilliantly coloured magnolias and lush ferns. Periodically shattering the cathedral-like calm are the raucous screams of troops of howler and spider **monkeys**, while tapirs, white-faced coatis, pacas, anteaters and squirrels are also hidden among the trees. Flashes of the brilliant plumage of **macaws**, **parrots** and **toucans**, a bright contrast against the dim light, are easier to come by.

Puerto Lempira

Capital of the department of Gracias a Dios, **PUERTO LEMPIRA** is the largest town in Mosquitia, with a population of 11,000. Set on the southeastern edge of the biggest of the coastal lagoons, Laguna de Caratasca, some 110km east of Brus Laguna, the town survives on government administration and small-scale fishing and shrimping. The best of the available **accommodation** is at the *Hotel Flores* (❹–❺) in the centre of town, where the small rooms all have a/c and bath; the *Hospedaje Modelo* (❷) opposite is basic but clean. Banco Atlántida, next to *Hotel Flores*, will change travellers' cheques and gives Visa cash advances. **Mopawi**

(Ⓣ898 8659, Ⓔmopawi@optinet.hn), the Mosquitia development organization, has its headquarters in the town, three blocks south of the main dock.

Puerto Lempira is hardly a transport hub, but the only traffic-frequented roads in Mosquitia lead west from here across the savanna to the village of Ahuasbila, an eight-hour drive, passing through Morocón and Rus Rus on the way. A side road shears off to Leimus on the Nicaraguan border; a truck leaves Puerto Lempira early each morning for Leimus, taking around five hours. There's a new Honduran **migración** post (daily 6am–8pm), but nothing on the Nicaraguan side, so you'll have to get your entry stamp in Puerto Cabezas.

4.5

The Bay Islands

Strung in a gentle curve less than 60km off the north coast of Honduras, the **Bay Islands** (**Islas de la Bahía**), with their clear, calm waters and abundant marine life, are Honduras's main tourist attraction. Resting on a coral reef, the islands are a perfect destination for cheap diving, sailing and fishing, while less active visitors can sling a hammock and relax in the shade on the many palm-fringed sand beaches. Composed of three main islands and some 65 smaller cayes, this sweeping 125km island chain lies on the **Bonacca Ridge**, an underwater extension of the Sierra de Omoa mountain range that disappears into the sea near Puerto Cortés. **Roatán** is the largest and most developed of the islands, while **Guanaja**, to the east, is an upmarket resort destination with some wonderful dive sites. **Utila**, the closest to the mainland, is a target for budget travellers from all over the world.

Even old hands get excited about **diving** the waters around the Bay Islands, where lizard fish and toadfish dart by, scarcely distinguishable from the coral; eagle rays glide through the water like huge birds flying through the air; parrotfish chomp steadily away on the coral; and barracuda and harmless nurse sharks circle the waters, checking you out from a distance. In addition, the world's largest fish, the **whale shark** (which can reach up to 16m in length) is a resident of the Cayman Trench, which plummets to profound depths just north of the islands. They are most frequently spotted in October and November, when dive boats run trips to look for them, but they can be encountered close to Utilan waters year-round.

The **best time to visit** the islands is from March to September, when the water visibility is good and the weather is clear and sunny; the rains start in October, while November and December are usually very wet, with squally showers continuing until late February. Daytime temperatures range between 25 and 29°C year-round, though the heat is rarely oppressive, thanks to almost constant east–southeast trade winds. **Mosquitoes** and **sandflies** are endemic on all the islands, and at their worst when the wind dies down; lavish coatings of baby oil help to keep the latter away.

Some history

The Bay Islands' history of conquest, pirate raids and constant immigration has resulted in a society that's unique in Honduras. The islands' original inhabitants were recorded by Columbus on his fourth and final voyage in 1502 as being a "robust people who adore idols and live mostly from a certain white grain from which they make fine bread and the most perfect beer". Post-Conquest, the indigenous population declined rapidly as a result of enslavement and forced labour. The islands' strategic location as a provisioning point for the Europe-bound Spanish fleets ensured that they soon became the targets for **pirates**, initially Dutch and French, and subsequently English. The Spanish decision to evacuate the islands, eventually achieved in 1650, left the way open for the pirates to move in. Port Royal, Roatán, became their base until the mid-eighteenth century, from where they launched sporadic attacks on ships and against the mainland settlements.

After the pirates left, Roatán was deserted until the arrival of the **Garífuna** in 1797. Forcibly expelled from the British-controlled island of St Vincent following a

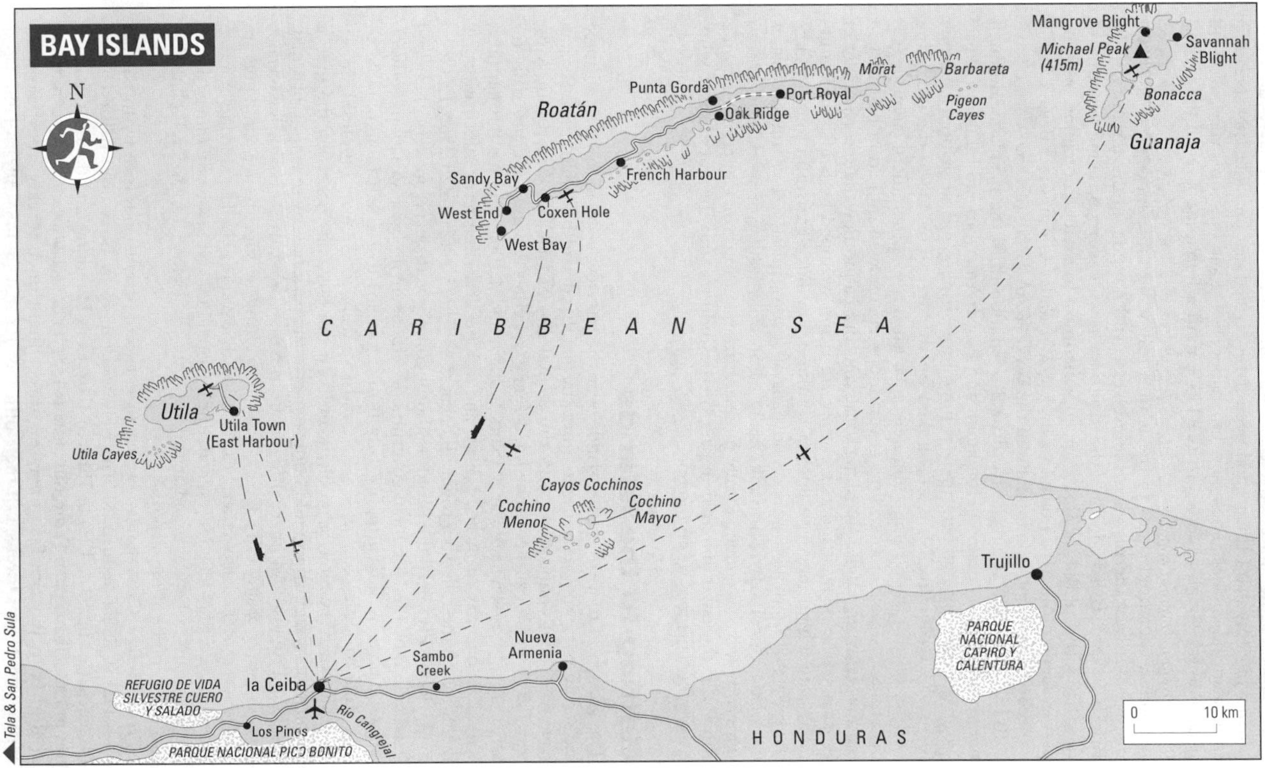

BAY ISLANDS

N

Mangrove Blight
Savannah Blight
Michael Peak (415m)
Bonacca
Guanaja
Morat
Barbareta
Pigeon Cayes
Punta Gorda
Port Royal
Oak Ridge
Roatán
French Harbour
Sandy Bay
West End
Coxen Hole
West Bay

C A R I B B E A N   S E A

Utila
Utila Town (East Harbour)
Utila Cayes
Cayos Cochinos
Cochino Menor
Cochino Mayor
Trujillo
PARQUE NACIONAL CAPIRO Y CALENTURA
Nueva Armenia
Sambo Creek
la Ceiba
REFUGIO DE VIDA SILVESTRE CUERO Y SALADO
Río Cangrejal
Los Pinos
PARQUE NACIONAL PICO BONITO
HONDURAS
0 10 km
Tela & San Pedro Sula

rebellion, most of the 3000-strong group were persuaded by the Spanish to settle in Trujillo on the mainland, leaving a small settlement at Punta Gorda on the island's north coast. Further waves of settlers came after the abolition of slavery in 1830, when white Cayman Islanders and freed slaves arrived first on Utila, later spreading to Roatán and Guanaja. These new inhabitants fished and built up a very successful fruit industry, which exported to the US – until a hurricane levelled the plantations in 1877.

Honduras acquired rights to the islands following independence in 1821, yet many – not least the islanders themselves – still considered the territory to be British. In 1852, Britain declared the islands a Crown Colony, breaking the terms of the 1850 Clayton–Bulwer Treaty, an agreement not to exercise dominion over any part of Central America. Forced to back down under US pressure, Britain finally conceded sovereignty to Honduras in the Wyke–Cruz Treaty of 1859.

Today, the islands retain their **cultural** separation from the mainland, although with both Spanish-speaking Hondurans and North American and European expats settling in growing numbers, there is ongoing reshaping and adaptation. A unique form of **Creole English** is still spoken on the street, but due to the increasing number of mainlanders migrating here, Spanish – always the official language – is becoming just as common. This government-encouraged migration has sparked tensions between English-speaking locals and the Latino newcomers, especially in Roatán, where many islanders feel they are being swamped by land-hungry outsiders with whom they have little in common. The huge growth in tourism since the early 1990s, a trend that shows no signs of abating, has also been controversial, as the islands' income, which traditionally came from fishing or working on cargo ships and oil rigs, is coming to rely more and more on tourism. Concern is growing too about the environmental impact of the industry and the question of who, exactly, benefits most from the boom.

Getting to the islands

The growth in tourism to the islands over the past few years means that all three are served by several daily flights from the mainland, and both Utila and Roatán have daily boat connections with the coastal city of La Ceiba (see p.446). Most travellers use the excellent scheduled **ferry services** leaving La Ceiba daily for Utila (1hr; US$7 one way) at 8.15am, 9.30am and 4.30pm and for Roatán (2hr; US$12.50 one way) daily at 11.30am and 4.30pm (for latest ferry information call the offices in the following towns: Roatán ⓣ445 1795, Utila ⓣ425 3166, La Ceiba ⓣ443 4633). **Flying** to the islands is also uncomplicated; tickets are very cheap and standardized by the Honduran government – there are no price variations between airlines. There are fifteen flights daily from La Ceiba to Roatán (30min; US$28), four daily to Utila (20min; US$28), and five daily to Guanaja (40min; US$34). Availability is very rarely a problem, and you can buy your tickets on the spot at the airport, though you should book ahead in the peak holiday seasons (Christmas, Easter and August). All internal flights from San Pedro Sula (1hr) and Tegucigalpa (1hr) stop over briefly in La Ceiba. Schedules change at short notice and flights are sometimes cancelled altogether; bear in mind that you may be late arriving or, more crucially, departing. The domestic **airlines**, Isleña, Taca and Sosa, have offices on the central square in La Ceiba and at the airport; another internal carrier, Rollins Air, also has an office at the airport.

From Belize City, the easiest way to get to the Bay Islands is to fly to Roatán with Taca (US$250 return). Alternatively, you can go by **boat** from Belize City or Placencia (see pp.39 & 123) to **Puerto Cortés** in Honduras, and then continue by bus to La Ceiba via San Pedro Sula (see p.433). There are also several **international flights** to Roatán: Taca operate a direct flight once weekly from Houston, Miami and New Orleans; call their office in Roatán (ⓣ445 1387) for the latest schedules.

Utila

Smallest of the three main Bay Islands, **UTILA** is a key destination for budget travellers, and one of the cheapest places in the world to **learn to dive** – and even if you don't want to don tanks, the superb waters around the island offer great swimming and snorkelling possibilities. Utila is still the cheapest of the Bay Islands, with a cost of living only slightly higher than that on the mainland, though prices are gradually rising. Life is laid-back, but interactions with locals can be cool and on occasion downright unfriendly, with many resenting the foreign-run dive schools that take the biggest share of the proceeds from the tourist industry. So while crimes against tourists are rare, the occasional verbal abuse isn't.

Arrival and information

All boats **dock** in the centre of **Utila Town** (also known as East Harbour), a large, curved harbour that's the island's only settlement and home to the vast majority of its 2000-strong population. The island's principal main road, a twenty-minute walk end to end, runs along the seafront from The Point in the east to Sandy Bay in the west. The airport is 3km north of Utila Town at the end of the island's other main road, **Cola de Mico Road**, which heads inland from the dock. The old dirt airstrip at The Point is no longer used for commercial flights.

However you arrive, you'll be met by representatives from the dive schools laden with **maps** and information on special offers. Many schools offer free accommodation during their courses, but it's worth checking out the various options before signing up. For more objective **information**, the Utila branch of BICA (Bay Islands' Conservation Association) has a visitor and information office near the *Bar in the Bush* off the Cola de Mico Road (Mon–Fri 9am–noon & 2–5pm; ⓣ425 3260). **Bikes** can be rented from Delco, next to Henderson's grocery store west of the dock, the *Mango Café* (see p.466) and other places around town – rates start at US$4.40 a day. Some locals use four-wheeled motorbikes to get around and occasionally pick up hitchers.

Accommodation

Utila has more than enough affordable guesthouses and hotels, and a profusion of rooms for rent; there's always somewhere available, even at Christmas and Easter. Most of the dive schools have links with a hostel, so that enrolling on a scuba course gets you a few free or discounted nights' accommodation. If you are thinking of staying longer to complete a lengthy dive course, many hotels give substantial discounts for long-term leases of rooms. Everywhere is within walking distance of the dock, and the accommodation listed below is in the order that you come to it. There are no designated places to **camp** except on the cayes.

East of the dock

Rubi's Inn two minutes' walk from the dock ⓣ425 3240, ⓔrubisinn@yahoo.com. Very clean, with airy rooms, some with a/c. Amenities include pleasant gardens with sea views, as well as use of a communal kitchen and swimming opportunities in the sheltered bay. ❹

Cooper's Inn five minutes' walk from the dock ⓣ425 3184. One of the best budget places on the island, with orderly, basic rooms (all with fans) and friendly management. There is use of a shared kitchen, shared bathrooms and restaurant. ❷

Sharkey's Reef Hotel behind *Sharkey's Reef Restaurant*, near the old airstrip ⓣ425 3212, ⓔhjackson@hondutel.hn. Set in a peaceful garden, the rooms here all have a/c, private bathrooms and cable TV, and some have kitchens. There's also a terrace with great views over the lagoon. ❺–❻

Tropical Sunset opposite *Sharkey's* ⓣ425 3190. A new overnight option with comfortable, modern rooms, some with sea views. Cheaper rooms come with a fan, while the more expensive ones boast a/c, TV and a balcony. There's also an on-site bar and restaurant. ❹–❺

Cola de Mico Road

Mango Inn five minutes' walk up the road from the dock ⓣ425 3335, ⓦwww.mango-inn.com. A beautiful, well-run place, timber-built in

Caribbean style and set in shady gardens. The range of rooms offered stretches from thatched, a/c bungalows to pleasant dorms. Also has a book exchange and laundry service, and the attached *Mango Café* is a lively spot (see p.466). Rates drop by at least half if diving with the Utila Dive Centre. Dorms US$10, rooms and bungalows ❺

Tony's Place opposite *Mango Inn* ⓣ425 3376. The simple but spotless rooms (with fan) here are amongst the best value on the island. The shared bathrooms are squeaky clean and the owner is friendly and informative. Hummingbird feeders attract birds, including the Canivet's Emerald, found only on the Bay Islands and a small area of adjacent Guatemala and Mexico. ❸

Jade Seahorse next to *Tony's Place* ⓣ425 3270. Unquestionably the most eccentric place to stay on the island. Run by an American artist and designed in his own unique style (see opposite), rooms are modern and well-equipped with minibar and tiled bathroom. ❼

West of the dock

Tropical Hotel opposite Hondutel telephone office (no phone). Very popular backpackers' stronghold, the small functional rooms all have fans and there's a communal kitchen. ❷

Seaside Inn opposite Gunter's Dive Shop ⓣ425 3150, ⓔhotelseaside@yahoo.com. Recently refurbished, the *Seaside Inn* contains an ample number of nondescript en-suite rooms, all with two double beds and some with a/c. There are also two apartments available for monthly rent. Internet access available. ❺

Margaritaville Beach Hotel ten minutes' walk west of the dock ⓣ425 3266. Tranquil seafront location well away from the main dock and handy for the beach. Large, airy rooms, all with private bath, and there's a hammock-filled terrace on site. ❹–❺

Blue Bayou at the end of the road (no phone). Simple en-suite rooms with fan make this an affordable and peaceful escape from the town with the coral reef right at your doorstep. If looking for a longer stay, there are two apartments with kitchen available for rent. ❸

Diving

Most visitors come to Utila specifically for the **diving**, attracted by the low prices, clear water and abundant marine life. Even in winter, the water is generally calm and common sightings include nurse and hammerhead sharks, turtles, parrotfish, stingrays, porcupine fish and an increasing number of dolphins. On the north coast of the island, Blackish Point and Duppy Waters are both good sites; on the south coast the best spots are Black Coral Wall and Pretty Bush. The good schools will be happy to spend time talking to you about the merits of the various sites.

Rather than signing up with the first dive school representative who approaches you, it's worth spending a morning walking around checking out all the schools. **Price** is not really a consideration, with the dozen or so dive shops all charging around US$199 for a three- to five-day PADI course; advanced and divemaster courses are also on offer, as are fun dives, from US$15. **Safety** is a more pertinent issue: for peace of mind, you should make sure that you understand – and get along with – the instructors, many of whom speak a number of languages. Before signing up, check that classes have no more than six people, that the equipment is well-maintained and that all boats have working oxygen and a first-aid kit. Anyone with asthma or ear problems should not be allowed to dive. All responsible schools will charge you US$3 a day insurance covering medical treatment in the event of emergency. Be aware that schools advertising discount rates may be cutting corners, as prices are already low and profits for the oldest schools minimal.

Recommended schools include the Utila Dive Centre (ⓣ425 3326, ⓦwww.utiladivecentre.com) on the road between the dock and the dirt airstrip, and its sister school Cross Creek (ⓣ425 3334, ⓔguests@utila-net.com); Gunter's Dive Shop (ⓣ425 3350, ⓔecomar@hondutel.hn), two minutes' walk west of the dock, which also rents out sea kayaks (US$5 per day); and Alton's (ⓣ425 3108, ⓔaltons@hondutel.hn), two minutes' walk west of the airstrip. Salty Dog's, a short walk west of the dock, has **underwater photography** equipment for rent, and many of the dive shops also rent out **snorkelling** equipment for around US$5 a day, free for divers.

It's important to bear in mind that the coral reef dies every time it is touched. BICA has been installing buoys at each of the sites to prevent boats anchoring on the reef and all the reputable schools will use these.

Swimming, snorkelling and touring the island

The best swimming near town is at the **Blue Bayou**, a twenty-minute walk west of the centre, where you can bathe in chest-deep water and snorkel further out; there's a US$1.50 charge to use the area, which also boasts a small sandy beach, food stand and a rickety wooden pier where you can sunbathe in peace away from the sandflies. Hammocks are slung in the shade of coconut trees and there's snorkelling gear available for rent (US$1.50 per hour). East of town, **Airport Beach**, at the end of the old dirt airstrip, offers good snorkelling just offshore (though access is more difficult), as does the little reef beyond the **lighthouse**. The old airstrip area has been slated for development as a resort centre, while the importation of ten bargeloads of white sand will create a new beach. The path from the end of the airstrip up the east coast of the island leads to a couple of small coves – the second is good for swimming and sunbathing. Five minutes beyond the coves, you'll come to the **Ironshores**, a mile-long stretch of low volcanic cliffs with lava tunnels cutting down to the water.

Another pleasant five-kilometre walk or cycle ride is along the Cola de Mico Road across the northern tip of the island to **Pumpkin Hill** and beach, passing the site of the new airport. The 82-metre hill, the eroded crest of an extinct volcano, gives good views over the island and across to the mainland and the dark bulk of Pico Bonito (see p.451). Caves in the side of the hill provide roosting for colonies of bats. Down on the beach, lava rocks cascade into the sea, forming underwater caves – there's good snorkelling here when the water is calm, though it's not safe to free-dive down into the caves. There are however some **freshwater caves** inland where it is safe to swim. To reach them, follow the road pass the airport until it becomes a dirt track, then take the first right and first left towards the island's power station. Just prior to here a red arrow points along a rocky track from where a ladder leads down to the cave pools. A second pool can be reached by crawling through a pitch-dark cave for several metres (you'll need a torch) before emerging into a large cavern littered with stalactites and stalagmites. Contact BICA before attempting this as they may provide you with a guide to ensure your safety.

The **Utila Iguana Station** (Mon, Wed & Fri 2–5pm; US$2.20), signposted from the road five minutes west of the dock, is a breeding centre for the endangered Utila spiny-tailed iguana, found only on the island and facing extinction. Guided tours explain the life cycle of the species. Finally, be sure to pop into the **Jade Seahorse** for a drink in the bizarre "Treetanic" bar (a boat-shaped tree house) and to walk around the grounds. Owned by a Californian artist, the hotel is a surrealistic mini-world, decorated with undersea mosaics, plastic fish, coloured marble and murals. The gardens of banana trees are filled with strange sculptures, tunnels and bottles of pyramids, adding to the feeling that you have stepped out of reality and into the mind of its creator.

The nearby cayes

Utila Cayes – eleven tiny outcrops strung along the southwestern edge of the island – were designated a wildlife refuge in 1992. **Suc Suc** (or Jewel) **Caye** and **Pigeon Caye**, connected by a narrow causeway, are both inhabited, and the pace of life here is even slower than that on Utila. Small launches regularly shuttle between Suc Suc and Utila (US$1), or can be rented to take you across for a day's snorkelling, if you have your own equipment. *Vicky's Rooms* on Suc Suc (no phone; ❷) offers basic **accommodation**, and there are a couple of reasonable restaurants, notably *Susan's Burgers*, and a good fish market.

Water Caye, a blissful stretch of white sand, coconut palms, pellucid water and a small coral reef, is even more idyllic given its absence of sandflies. Camping is allowed and a caretaker turns up every day to collect the US$1.35 fee for use of the island. To stay you'll need a tent, food, equipment for a campfire and water. Water Caye is also the venue for occasional full-moon parties and a spectacular annual two-day July rave, with European house and techno DJs, organized by Sunjam and the *Mango Inn*. **Transport** to the caye is organized during such events; at other times, dive boats will often drop you off on their way to the north coast for a small fee, or you can ask the owner of the *Bundu Café* (see below).

Eating

Lobster and **fish** are obviously staples on the islands, along with the usual rice, beans and chicken. With the tourists, however, have also come **European and American foods** – pasta, pizza, burgers, pancakes and granola. Since most things have to be brought in by boat, **prices** are higher than on the mainland: main courses start at around US$4.75, and beers cost at least US$1. For eating on the cheap, head for the evening stalls on the road by the dock, which do a thriving trade in *baleadas*. Note that many restaurants stop serving at around 10pm.

Bundu Café on the main street, east of the dock. A very popular travellers' hangout serving European-style breakfasts and lunches along with *lassi*-style milkshakes. Curry night on Thursdays and live music on Saturdays.

Captain Jack's five minutes' walk west of the dock. Dutch–Utilan-owned café-restaurant serving excellent-value lunches, including burritos and sandwiches, freshly squeezed orange juice, and delicious dinners such as fish cakes and grilled kingfish steaks. Don't be put off by the run-down building.

Cross Creek at the Point. Near-legendary Caribbean cooking from one of Utila's best chefs, served in a quiet spot beside the lagoon and majoring in flavoursome pan-fried fish and seafood. Menu changes daily and portions are enormous and cheap – around US$4 per main dish.

Mango Café *Mango Inn*. A popular place with an interesting selection of tasty, well-presented European food to go along with espresso drinks and a lively bar. The daily special, usually seafood, is great value, and the pizzas are generally considered the best on the island. Closed Mon.

Mermaid's two minutes east of the dock. Fast-food buffet with pizza, Chinese food and pasta at reasonable rates served under a breezy canvas roof.

Munchie's one minute west of the dock. The best breakfasts on the island, with a range of cooked food and fresh fruit, smoothies and *licuado*. Check out the Iguana Garden at the rear, a steep wall inhabited by a group of spiny-tailed iguanas.

La Piccola Kate's one minute west of the dock. The island's only specialist Italian restaurant boasts a wide selection of pasta, salads and daily specials including a free starter. Bread is homemade and many of the dishes are more imaginative than the standard Bolognese and pesto pastas that are sold elsewhere. Try the grilled aubergine and pesto starter.

RJs at The Point, beside the bridge. Popular with dive crews and students, with a gregarious atmosphere and excellent meat and fish barbecues. Get there early if you want a table, as it fills up quickly. Open Wed, Fri and Sun only.

Thompson's Bakery Cola de Mico Road. A great place to read, drink coffee and meet other travellers while sampling the good-value breakfasts or the range of daily baked goods including delicious johnny cakes.

Nightlife

Despite its tiny population, Utila is a fearsomely hedonistic party island. The hottest place in town for travellers is the *Coco Loco Bar*, just west of the dock, which draws a lively bunch with its extended happy hour and regular house, techno and reggae parties. *Casino*, by the dock, attracts a more local crowd with thundering reggae and a dash of salsa and merengue. During the rest of the week, the *Mango Café* is a popular spot for cheap beer and a quiet drink. Further along the Cola de Mico Road towards the new airport, the huge open-air *Bar in the Bush*, open on Fridays only, is the only late-night venue on the island, open until 3am, and often with live DJs. Note that drinking from glass bottles on the street is prohibited.

Listings

Airlines Tickets for Sosa and Rollins, covering domestic routes in Honduras, can be purchased in the captain's office by the dock. Isleña has an office two minutes' walk west of the dock.
Banks Banco Atlántida and Bancahsa, both close to the dock, change money and offer cash advances on Visa cards (Mon–Fri 8–11.30am & 1.30–4pm, Sat 8–11.30am); at other times try Henderson's store, just to the west.
Books The *Bundu Café*, on the main street, east of the dock, has a book exchange.
Doctor The Community Medical Center is two minutes west of the dock (Mon–Fri 8am–noon).
Immigration office At the port building (Mon–Fri 9am–noon & 2–4.30pm).
Internet access Numerous Internet cafés have sprung up along the coast road, but shop around as some still charge as much as US$5 an hour for connections that are no better or worse than those at the average going rate of US$2–2.50.
Post office In the large building at the main dock (Mon–Fri 9am–noon & 2–4.30pm, Sat 9–11.30am).
Telephones Many of the Internet cafés offer Web calls at good rates. Avoid the Hondutel office, next to the *migración*, as rates are extortionate.
Travel agents Morgan's Travel at the dock can help you with ferry and flight tickets.

Roatán

Some 50km from La Ceiba, **ROATÁN** is the largest of the Bay Islands, a curving ridged hump almost 50km long and 5km across at its widest point. Geared towards upmarket tourists, the island's accommodation mostly comes in the form of all-inclusive luxury resort packages, although there are some good deals to be found, especially in the **West End**. Like Utila, Roatán is a superb **diving** destination, but also offers some great hiking, as well as the chance to do nothing except laze on a beach. **Coxen Hole** is the island's commercial centre.

Arrival and getting around

Regular flights from La Ceiba and occasionally further afield land at the **airport**, on the road to French Harbour, 3km east of Coxen Hole – the main town on the south side of the island. There are information and hotel reservation desks, car rental agencies and a bank at the airport. A taxi to West End from here costs US$10, or you could walk to the road and wait for one of the public minibuses which head to Coxen Hole every 20 minutes or so (US$0.70) and change there. The **ferry dock** is in the centre of Coxen Hole. **Minibuses** leave regularly from Main Street here, heading west to Sandy Bay and West End (every 20min until late afternoon) and east to Brick Bay, French Harbour, Oak Ridge and Punta Gorda (every 30min or so until late afternoon); fares are US$0.70. However, if you really want to explore, you'll need to **rent a car** or **motorbike**: in addition to agencies such as Caribbean Rent-a-Car (☎455 5648) at the airport, Sandy Bay Rent-a-Car (☎445 1710) also has offices at Sandy Bay and West End, and rents out Jeeps (US$45 per day) and motorbikes (US$25 a day).

Coxen Hole

COXEN HOLE (also known as Roatán Town) is dusty and run down, and most visitors come here only to change money or shop. All of the town's practical facilities and most shops are on a hundred-metre stretch of **Main Street**, near where the buses stop. You'll find the headquarters of BICA (Mon–Fri 9am–noon & 2–5pm), who can help with tourist **information**, at the Cooper Building on the main street. Banco Atlántida has an ATM that takes Visa, and to change **travellers' cheques** you could also try Bancahsa. The **migración** and the **post office** are both near the small square on Main Street, while **Hondutel** is behind Bancahsa. HB Warren is the largest **supermarket** on the island, and there's a small and not too impressive general **market** just behind Main Street. **Internet** rates are lower here than the rest of the island, though still expensive; try Hondusoft, on the second floor of a small mall just up from the port (daily 9am–6pm; US$5 per hour).

Unless you've got an early ferry or flight, it's unlikely you'll want **to stay**. If you do, *Sarita* (☎445 1541; ❸), next to the dock, has basic rooms with TV and private bath. There are a number of cheap comedores, while *Qué Tal Café*, on Thicket Street, the exit road towards Sandy Bay, serves European-style breakfasts and snacks. Next door, Librería Casi Todo sells used **books**.

Sandy Bay

Midway between Coxen Hole and West End, **SANDY BAY** is an unassuming community with a number of interesting attractions. The **Institute for Marine Sciences** (Sun–Tues & Thurs–Sat 9am–5pm; US$3), based at *Antony's Key Resort*, has exhibitions on the marine life and geology of the islands and a museum with useful information on local history and archeology. There are also bottle-nosed **dolphin shows** (Mon, Tues, Thurs & Fri 10am & 3pm, Sat & Sun 10am, 1pm & 4pm; US$4), and you can dive or snorkel with the dolphins (US$100 and US$75 respectively; must be booked in advance on ☎445 1327). Across the road from the institute, several short nature trails weave through the jungle at the **Carambola Botanical Gardens** (daily 8am–5pm; US$3), a riot of beautiful flowers, lush ferns and tropical trees. Twenty minutes' walk from the gardens up Monte Carambola, the **Iguana Wall** is a section of cliff that's a breeding ground for iguanas and parrots. From the top of the mountain you can see across to Utila on clear days. Bordering the gardens is the **Tropical Treasures Bird Park** (Mon–Sat 10am–5pm; US$5, including guided tour), with toucans, parrots and scarlet macaws.

There are several places **to stay** in the area, though if you are looking for cheap rooms you're better off heading to the West End. The *Oceanside Inn* (☎445 1552; ❻), with large rooms and a good restaurant, is the best bet in town. Of the three dive resorts in the area, *Antony's Key Resort* (☎445 1003, Ⓦwww.anthonys-key.com; weekly packages from US$600) is tops; it's one of the smartest places on the island, with cabins set among the trees and on a small caye. If looking **to eat**, try *Rick's American Café*, set on the hillside above the road and serving giant burgers.

West End

With its calm waters and incredible sandy beaches, **WEST END**, 14km from Coxen Hole, makes the most of its ideal setting at the southwest corner of the island. From the beautifully sheltered, palm-fringed **Half Moon Bay** at the northern end of town, a sandy track runs a kilometre or so along the water's edge through the heart of the West End, past a plethora of guesthouses, bars and restaurants, geared towards independent travellers of all budgets. Thanks to the presence of a year-round community of sun worshippers and a rash of dive shops, the village retains a laid-back charm during the day whilst adopting a vibrant, party feel after dark. Nowhere else on Roatán will you get such an eclectic mix of people, attracted not only by the relaxed nature of the town, but also the unrivalled potential for watersports.

Practicalities

You can **rent cars** from Roatán Rentals, at the north of West End; nearby, Captain Van's rents out expensive bicycles (US$9), mopeds (US$29) and motorbikes (US$39). Though widely available, prices for **Internet** are overpriced and connections slow; Beach House (Mon–Fri 10am–10pm) opposite the entrance road from Coxen Hole is the cheapest at US$10, while the fastest connection is at King's Café further down the road, though they close at 6pm and charge US$12 per hour.

Most of the **accommodation** in West End and Half Moon Bay is charmingly individualistic, and heavy discounts are available during low season (April–July & Sept to mid-Dec), particularly for longer stays. There's a more than adequate range of **places to eat**, with fish, seafood and pasta featuring heavily on many menus, though prices are on the high side. **Drinking** can drain your pocket fast as well, so seek out the half-price happy hours featured at many of the restaurants and bars in town, some lasting until 10pm. The *Twisted Toucan*, halfway along the seafront, is typically the most happening place in town, save for Friday nights when *Foster's* hosts a weekly reggae jump-up.

Accommodation

Chillie's Half Moon Bay ⓣ 445 1214, ⓔ natives@hondutel.hn. Well set-up backpackers' choice, with dorm beds (US$15) and private rooms, a kitchen and camping (US$7.50) available. Also home to Native Sons Divers. ❺

Half Moon Bay Cabins Half Moon Bay ⓣ 445 1053. Luxurious and refined option with secluded cabins scattered around wooded grounds close to the water's edge; all have fan or a/c. There's also an expensive restaurant with silver-service and cocktail bar on site. ❻–❼

Mariposa Lodge on a side street half-way down the main beach road (no phone, ⓔ mariposalodge@yahoo.com). A good-value, quiet lodge with two apartments – complete with sundecks, kitchen and cable TV – plus small three-bed dorms (US$8.50). Extras include an on-site massage service ($35 for a full-body massage). ❺

Pinocchio's ⓣ 445 1481, ⓔ pinocchio69@bigfoot.com. A small, personable hotel, occupying a wooden building set on a small hill above the village. Rooms are clean and airy, if a little basic, but all with bath. The owners are a good source of information and there's a good restaurant downstairs (see below). ❺

Posada Arco Iris Half Moon Bay ⓣ 445 1264, ⓔ posadaarcoiris@globalnet.hn. Set in attractive gardens just off the beach, with excellent, imaginatively furnished and spacious rooms, studios and apartments, all with fridge and hammocks, and some with a/c. ❺–❻

Valerie's about 100m along West End, then up a signposted dirt track (no phone, ⓦ www.roatanonline.com/valeries. Venerable love-it-or-hate-it bohemian hostel set up with a profusion of quirky accommodation, including two trailer-style rooms, two apartments, a small house, a flat with hot tub and a large dorm (US$5 per person); guests can also use the kitchen. ❸–❺

Restaurants

Argentinian Grill Half Moon Bay. Argentinean-run restaurant with authentic *churrascos*, grilled

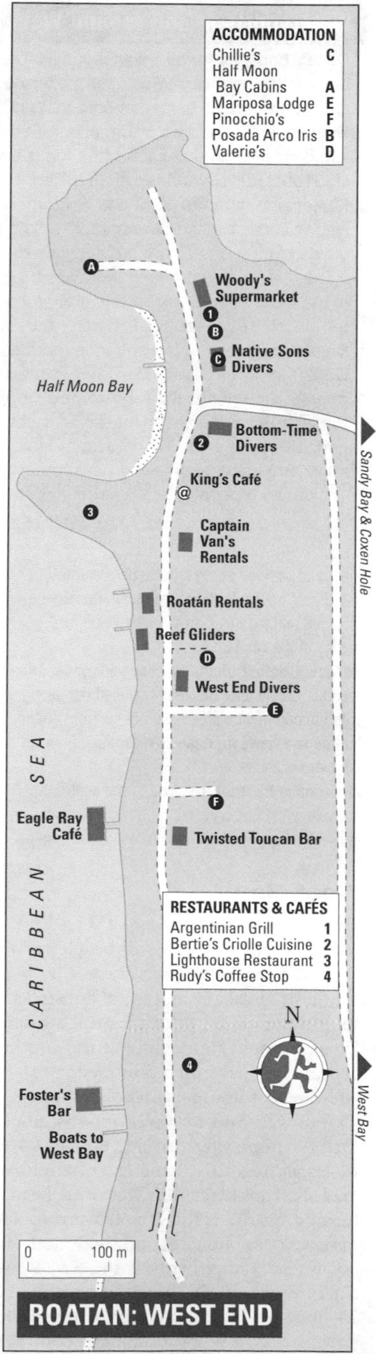

Watersports in and around West End

Diving courses for all levels are available in West End. Prices are officially standardized, with a four-day PADI open-water course costing around US$220, but it's worth asking around as some schools include basic accommodation, and sporadic price wars have been known to break out. Fun dives are set at US$25 a dive, though again substantial discounts are often on offer, with ten-dive packages set at around US$150. Recommended West End–based **schools** include West End Divers (ⓔreefglides@yahoo.com) and Bottom-Time Divers (ⓦwww.coconuttree.com), while Native Sons (ⓔnatives@hondutel.hn) is another good school, located at *Chilie's* hotel on Half Moon Bay. There are also two dive schools in West Bay (see below).

The reef lying just offshore provides superb **snorkelling**, with the best spots being at the mouth of Half Moon Bay and at the Blue Channel, which can be accessed from the beach 100m south of *Foster's* bar. You can also rent **sea kayaks** from the *Sea Breeze Inn*, close to the entrance road; expect to pay around US$12 for a half-day or US$20 for a full day. Underwater Paradise, based in the *Half Moon Bay Resort*, runs popular, hour-long **glass-bottomed boat** tours for US$18 per person, as well as a tourist **submarine** which, at US$200 per person, isn't cheap but makes for an unforgettable experience. Yush Tours at Half Moon Bay (ⓣ966 9643, ⓔkemrflowers@hotmail.com) offers snorkelling packages to reefs and shipwrecks from US$30 per boat (maximum 6 people) as well as fishing trips and dolphin tours.

meat and seafood at reasonable (by Roatán standards) prices. Portions are huge and service efficient, making this spot the best value for money in the West End.

Bertie's Criolle Cuisine at village entrance. Small menu of Creole specials, mainly grilled fish along with the odd meat dish. Prices are far from cheap, but the sea views from the terrace make it worth the extra expense.

Lighthouse Restaurant close to the seafront between West End and Half Moon Bay. Big portions of reasonably priced Caribbean food served up in friendly, diner-like surrounds.

Pinocchio's in the hotel of the same name. One of the finest restaurants in West End, with an eclectic range of creative, but fairly pricey European meat and fish dishes. Closed Wed. Open after 6pm.

Rudy's Coffee Stop The spot for legendary breakfasts including banana pancakes, omelettes, fresh coffee and juices. Opens early at 6.30am, so it's ideal for an early breakfast and a quick getaway. Closed Sun.

West Bay

Two kilometres southwest of West End, towards the extreme western tip of Roatán, is the stunning white-sand beach of **WEST BAY**, fringed by coconut palms and washed by crystal-clear waters. The beach's tranquillity has been mildly disrupted by a rash of cabaña and hotel construction, but provided you avoid the sandflies by sunbathing on the jetties, it's still a sublime place to relax and enjoy the Caribbean. There's decent snorkelling at the southern end of the beach too, though the once pristine reef has suffered in recent years from increasing river run-off and the close attentions of unsupervised day-trippers.

From West End, it's a pleasant 45-minute stroll south along the beach and over a few rock outcrops; alternatively you can take one of the small launches that leave *Foster's Restaurant* regularly – the last one returns around 7pm (9pm in high season). A dirt road also runs here: from West End, head up the road to Coxen Hole and take the first turning on the right. If you want to stay, the cheapest option is the basic *Keifito's Plantation* (no phone; ❺) on the waterfront, with plain over-priced rooms with fan and hot water. Rather better is the Swiss-owned *Bananarama* (ⓣ992 9679, ⓦwww.bananaramadive.com; ❻), home to comfortable little wood cabins with mosquito nets and 24-hour hot water. For something really luxurious, head for the *Island Pearl Resort* (ⓣ991 6955, ⓦwww.roatanpearl.com; ❾), which boasts stunning two-storey cottages equipped with kitchens and hot tubs, plus a gourmet restaurant set in a spacious beachside plot. The latter two hotels both have good in-house dive schools as well.

Northern Roatán

Leaving Coxen Hole, the paved road runs northeast past the small secluded cove of **Brick Bay** to **FRENCH HARBOUR**, a busy fishing port and the island's second largest town. Less run-down than Coxen Hole, it's a lively place **to stay** for a couple of days, with all the overnight options located right in the town centre. *Harbour View Hotel* (ⓣ455 5390; ❹) has reasonable rooms with bath and hot water, while the decadent *Fanstasy Island Beach Resort* (ⓣ455 5222; ❾) has luxury rooms, pool, a marina and opportunities for numerous watersports. The best place **to eat** is *Gio's*, by the Credomatic building on the waterfront, where you can dine on excellent but pricey seafood – the speciality is king crab – on an outdoor deck with a view of the harbour. Should you have time, stop by the town's private **Iguana Reserve** (daily 9am–5pm; US$1), home to more than 2800 specimens of four species; all the proceeds of the entry fee go towards the care of the animals. To get there follow the signs to the *Fantasy Island Resort* until you see signs leading to the centre.

From French Harbour the road cuts inland along a central ridge to give superb views of both the north and south coasts of the island. After about 14km the road reaches **OAK RIDGE**, an attractive fishing port with wooden houses strung along its harbour. There are some nice unspoiled **beaches** to the east of town, accessible by launches from the main dock, and other nearby communities can be reached by boat cruises through the mangroves. The best place **to stay** is the clean, pleasant *Hotel San José* (ⓣ435 2328; ❸–❹), on a small caye a short distance across the water from the main dock; launches run to the caye on demand (US$0.50).

About 5km from Oak Ridge on the northern coast of the island is the village of **PUNTA GORDA**, the oldest Garífuna community in Honduras. The best time to visit is for the anniversary of the founding of the settlement on April 12, when Garífuna from all over the country attend the celebrations. At other times it's a quiet and slightly dilapidated little port with no buildings of note. From the end of the paved road at Punta Gorda, it's possible to continue driving along the dirt track which runs east along the island, passing the turn-off for the secluded **Paya Beach** after around 1.5km. At this beach sits a secluded dive hotel, the all-inclusvie *Paya Bay Resort* (ⓣ435 2139, ⓦwww.payabay.com; ❾). A further 5km or so along is **Camp Bay Beach**, an idyllic stretch of white sand and coconut palms, though development is imminent. The road ends at the village of **PORT ROYAL**, on the southern edge of the island, where the faint remains of a fort built by the English can be seen on a caye offshore. The village lies in the **Port Royal Park and Wildlife Reserve**, the largest refuge on the island, set up in 1978 in an attempt to protect endangered species such as the yellow-naped parrot, as well as the watershed for eastern Roatán.

The eastern tip of Roatán is made up of mangrove swamps, with a small island, **Morat**, just offshore. Beyond is **Barbareta** caye, which has retained much of its virgin forest cover. The *Barbareta Beach Resort* here runs inclusive packages (ⓣ992 7725; ❾), with diving, windsurfing, hiking, mountain biking and fishing tours available. The reef around Barbareta and the nearby **Pigeon Cayes** offers good snorkelling; launches can be hired to reach these islands from Oak Ridge for around US$35 for a return trip.

Guanaja

GUANAJA, the easternmost Bay Island, was visited by Christopher Columbus in 1502, where he encountered the native Paya Indians and commented that he had "never tasted water sweeter" than that which ran through the brooks on the island. In more recent times, Guanaja was the most beautiful, densely forested and undeveloped of the Bay Islands, until Hurricane Mitch laid siege to it for over two days during October 1998, lashing the island with winds of up to 300kph. Though buildings have been patched up and reforestation projects implemented, the landscape will take decades to recover.

Guanaja is some 25km long and up to four kilometres wide, and is divided into two unequal parts by a narrow canal – the only way to get between the two sections of the island is by water-taxi, which adds both to the atmosphere and to the cost of living. The island is very thinly populated – most of Guanaja's 12,000 inhabitants live in **Bonacca** (also known as **Guanaja Town**), a crowded settlement on a small caye a few hundred metres offshore. It's here that you'll find the island's shops, as well as the bulk of the reasonably priced accommodation. The only other settlements of any substance are **Savannah Bight** (on the east coast) and **Mangrove Bight** (on the north coast). Note that sandflies and mosquitoes are endemic throughout the island, so arrive prepared to deal with them.

Arrival and information

Guanaja **airstrip** is on the larger, northern section of the island, next to the canal. Aside from a couple of dirt tracks there are no roads, and the main form of transport is small launches. All the airlines have associated **boats** that will take you across to Bonacca for a small fee, or alternatively you could hire a **water-taxi**, though high fuel costs are reflected in the fares. If you have pre-booked a resort on the island, representatives will invariably meet you at the airport. There are no scheduled **boat** services to Guanaja from the mainland, but regular cargo ships sail to the island from La Ceiba and other ports in Honduras. You can change dollars, travellers' cheques and get cash advances at Bancahsa, to the right of the dock (Mon–Fri 8–11.30am & 1.30–4pm, Sat 8–11.30am).

Accommodation

Most of the **hotels** on Guanaja are luxury all-inclusive dive resorts offering weekly packages. You'll also find a small number of mid-range hotels in Bonacca – though none are particularly good value for money.

Bayman Bay Club on the north side of the island ⓣ453 4191. Large, attractively furnished cabins set in plenty of space on a wooded hillside above a small beach. There's a treetop terrace with glorious views of the surroundings. Weekly packages, including dives and all meals, cost US$700–750 per person. ❾

Hotel Alexander on the main causeway, Bonacca ⓣ453 4393. Oceanfront hotel that is perhaps the best value on the island. All rooms come with a/c and cable TV, and there's a bar and restaurant on site. Three fully fitted apartments are available if you'd prefer to cater for yourself. ❺, apartment ❽

Hotel Miller halfway along the main causeway, Bonacca ⓣ453 432. Housed in a slightly run-down building, though the rooms are in reasonable condition; most have hot water and, for a little extra, a/c and cable TV. ❺

Island House Resort on the north side of the island ⓣ991 0913. A pleasant accommodation choice, this large house is run by a local dive instructor and is close to several expanses of beautiful beach. Rate includes full board. ❻

Posada del Sol on the south side of the island ⓣ237 4982, ⓔposadadelsol@aol.com. Another all-inclusive resort with stylish cabins scattered around sixty acres of property. Amenities include a pool, tennis courts, sea kayaks and snorkelling equipment. Dive packages from US$775 per person. ❾

Around the island

Wandering around Bonacca's warren of tight streets, walkways and canal bridges makes for an interesting half-hour or so – though government plans to eliminate the town's tiny waterways for new roads means the town may not be Honduras's closest match to Venice for much longer. Virtually all the houses in town are built on stilts – vestiges of early settlement by the Cayman islanders – with the main causeway running for about 500m east–west along the caye.

Though Guanaja's Caribbean pine forests were flattened by Mitch, there's still some decent **hiking** to be found outside of Bonnaca. A wonderful trail leads from

Mangrove Bight up to **Michael's Peak**, the highest point of the entire Bay Islands (412m) and down to Sandy Bay on the south coast, affording stunning views of Guanaja, Bonacca and the surrounding reef. Fit walkers can do the trail in a day, or you can camp on the summit, provided you bring your own provisions.

Some of the island's finest white-sand **beaches** lie around the rocky headland of **Michael's Rock**, near the *Island House Resort* on the north coast, with good snorkelling close to the shore. **Diving** is excellent all around the main island, but particularly off the small cayes to the east, and at Black Rocks, off the northern tip of the main island, where there's an underwater coral canyon. The **Mestizo Dive Site** was opened in 2002 to mark the 500th anniversary of Columbus's visit, with sunken statues of the explorer and national hero Lempira on a reef surrounded by genuine Spanish colonial artefacts, including a cannon. To get to these sites you'll have to contact one of the hotel-based dive schools: the *Island House Resort* usually has the best rates at around US$70 for two dives including equipment. **Fishing** and **snorkelling** can be arranged with local boatmen, who charge US$10–15 per trip. In many areas, however, the reef is close enough to swim to if you have your own snorkelling gear.

Eating and drinking

There are several **restaurants** in Bonacca, though most close on Sundays. Prices are generally steep as most of the supplies have to be shipped in from the mainland. In the centre of Bonacca itself, try *Pirate's Den* for fresh seafood with daily lunch specials and Friday barbecues. For Mexican food head to *Mexi-Treats*, located opposite the Banco Atlántida on the caye. *Best Stop*, next to the basketball court, is good for snacks, cakes and sticky buns, as well as a variety of fast food including hot wings, burgers and subs. The funkiest **bar** in town is *Nit's Bar*, just east of the main dock, where the clapboard walls shake to classic reggae sounds, while you'll find Guanaja's best margaritas at the air-conditioned *The End of the World* bar on Michael Rock Beach. The main disco on the island is *Pirate's Landing* at Savannah Bight, home to live DJs every night save Tuesdays.

Cayos Cochinos

Lying 17km offshore from the mainland, the **CAYOS COCHINOS** (**Hog Islands**) comprise eleven privately owned cayes and two thickly wooded islands – **Cochino Mayor** and **Cochino Menor**. The small amount of effort it takes to get to the islands is well worth it for a few days' utter tranquillity. Fringed by a reef, the whole area has been designated a **marine reserve**, with anchoring on the reef and commercial fishing both strictly prohibited. The US Smithsonian Institute, which manages the reserve, has a research station on Cochino Menor. On land, the island's hills are studded with hardwood forests, palms and cactus, while Cochino Mayor has a number of trails across its interior, and a small peak rising to 145m, where there is a lighthouse with glorious views.

Organized **accommodation** on the islands is limited to the *Plantation Beach Resort* on Cochino Grande (☎442 0974; ❾), which does weekly dive packages for around US$800, including all meals and three dives a day; they collect guests by launch from the Muralla de Cabotaje dock in La Ceiba on Saturdays (US$60 return). If you wish to make an independent visit, the *Princesa*, a 25-passenger boat (☎441 5986), runs from the same place at weekends only, with a day-trip including light lunch costing around US$65. Reservations should be made at least 48 hours in advance at La Ceiba's *Mango Tango Bar* (see p.450). It can be more rewarding, however, to stay in the traditional Garífuna fishing village of **CHACHAUATE** on Lower Monitor Caye, south of Cochino Grande. Here, the villagers have allocated a hut for visitors to sling their hammocks (US$4.50) and they will also cook meals for you. Basic groceries are available in the village, but there is no running water or electricity and toilets are in the form of latrines.

The only other way to the Cayos is to charter a boat from the Muralla de Cabotaje dock at La Ceiba (US$60–80 return for up to six people, but be sure to bargain hard), or from the Garífuna village of **Nueva Armenia** (around US$40 return for a charter), 40km east of La Ceiba. One bus a day runs to Nueva Armenia (2hr) from La Ceiba; more frequent buses to Trujillo, Tocoa and Olanchito all pass through Jutiapa, 8km inland from Nueva Armenia, from where you can hitch or walk.

Travel details

Mainland

Buses

The main domestic and international bus routes from **Tegucigalpa** are covered in the box on p.395 and from **San Pedro Sula** in the box on p.438.

Catacamas to: Juticalpa (hourly; 1hr).

Choluteca to: El Amatillo (hourly; 1hr 30min); Guasule (hourly; 45min); San Lorenzo (hourly; 45min); San Marcos (every 45min; 1hr 15min).

Comayagua to: Tegucigalpa (18 daily; 1hr 30min); Siguatepeque (18 daily; 1hr).

Copán to: La Entrada (10 daily; 1hr 30min); San Pedro Sula (5 daily; 3hr).

Gracias to: Santa Rosa de Copán (hourly until 6pm; 1hr 30min).

Gualaco to: Trujillo (1 daily; 6hr).

Juticalpa to: Catacamas (hourly; 1hr); Gualaco (1 daily; 2hr 30min); La Unión (1 daily; 4hr); San Esteban (1 daily; 4hr); Tegucigalpa (Empresa Aurora, 12 daily; 3hr).

La Ceiba to: Tegucigalpa (12 daily until 3pm; 7hr); Trujillo (12 daily until 4pm; 4hr).

La Entrada to: San Pedro Sula (every 30 mins; 1hr 30mins)

La Esperanza to: Gracias (1 daily; 4–5hr).

La Unión to: La Ceiba (1 daily; 7–8hr); Tegucigalpa (3 daily; 5hr).

Nueva Ocotepeque to: Agua Caliente (every 30min until 4pm; 1hr); El Poy (every 40min; 30min).

Puerto Cortés to: Corinto (5 daily; 4hr); Omoa (hourly; 1hr).

San Esteban to: Trujillo (1 daily; 4hr).

Santa Rosa de Copán to: Copán (2 daily; 3hr); La Entrada (8 daily; 1hr 30min); Nueva Ocotepeque (6 daily; 2hr); San Pedro Sula (every 30 min; 3hr; 3 direct services daily; 2hr 30min).

Siguatepeque to: La Esperanza (every 2hr until mid-afternoon; 2hr).

Tela to: El Progreso (every 30min; 1hr 30min); La Ceiba (every 30min; 2hr).

Trujillo to: La Ceiba (12 daily until 4pm; 4hr); San Pedro Sula (5 daily until 2pm; 6hr); Tegucigalpa via San Esteban and Juticalpa (1 daily at 4am; 10hr).

Flights

Brus Laguna to: La Ceiba (Rollins & Sosa; 3 weekly).

La Ceiba to: Ahuas (Sami; 5 weekly); Brus Laguna (Rollins & Sosa; 5 weekly); Palacios (Isleña; 1 daily Mon–Sat); Puerto Lempira (Isleña & Sosa; 7 weekly); Tegucigalpa (Taca, Sosa, Rollins & Isleña; 7 daily); Trujillo (Isleña & Rollins; 1–2 daily).

Palacios to: La Ceiba (Isleña & Rollins; 1–2 daily); Trujillo (Isleña; 1 daily Mon–Sat).

Puerto Lempira to: La Ceiba (Isleña & Sosa; 7 weekly).

San Pedro Sula to: Belize City (Taca, 1 daily); Cancún (Aerocaribe, 1 daily); La Ceiba (Isleña, 2 daily; Rollins, 3 daily; Sosa, 1 daily); Miami (Iberia, 2 weekly; American Airlines, 1 daily; Taca, 1 daily); Tegucigalpa (Taca, 2 daily; Isleña, 1 daily).

Tegucigalpa to: La Ceiba (Taca, Sosa, Rollins & Isleña; 6 daily); San Pedro Sula (Taca, 2 daily; Isleña, 1 daily).

Bay Islands

Flights

La Ceiba to: Roatán (Atlantic, 5 daily; Isleña, 7 daily; Sosa, 4 daily; Rollins Air, 4 daily); Utila (Atlantic, 2 daily; Rollins, Mon–Sat 2 daily; Sosa, Mon–Sat 2 daily); Guanaja (Atlantic, 2 daily; Isleña, Mon–Sat 2 daily, Sun 1 daily; Sosa, Mon–Sat 2 daily).

Boats

MV Galaxy runs daily between La Ceiba and Roatán (2hr; US$13) and Utila (1hr; US$12); *Utila Princess* runs two daily ferries to Utila from La Ceiba (1hr; 9am and 3pm).

5

Nicaragua

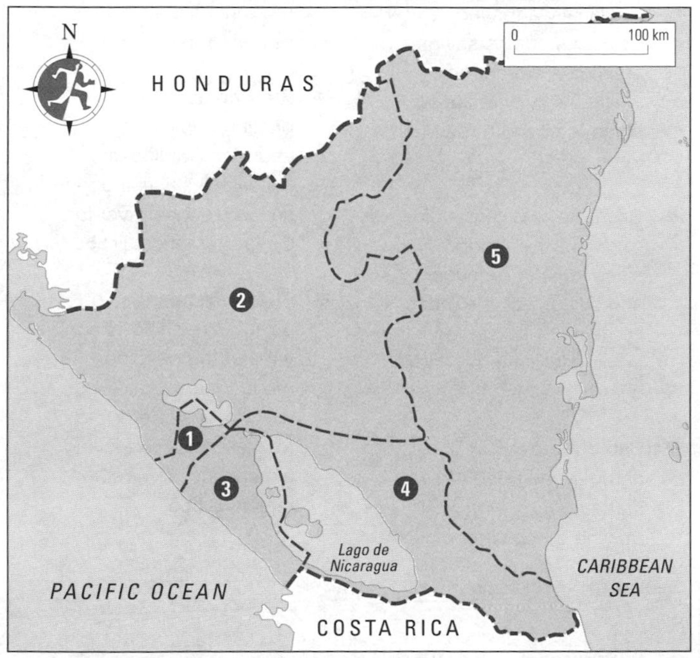

Highlights 476
Introduction and Basics 477
5.1 Managua and around 496
5.2 The north 516
5.3 The southwest 534
5.4 Lago de Nicaragua 550
5.5 The Atlantic Coast 560
Travel details 570

Nicaragua Highlights

* **Markets** Head to either Masaya or Mercado Roberto Huembes in Managua for the pick of Nicaragua's beautiful crafts. p.510 and p.535

* **León** León mightn't be as visually arresting as Granada, but it's still an artistically vibrant and intellectually stimulating place to spend a few days. p.516

* **Granada** One of the oldest Spanish-founded cities in Latin America and still one of the most beautiful, with alluring architecture and an easy charm. p.539

* **San Juan del Sur** The number-one beach town in the country with a thriving community of surfers, expats and locals. p.546

* **Isla Ometepe** Despite increasing tourist numbers, this island in the middle of Lago de Nicaragua still has a mysterious charm all of its own. p.551

* **Río San Juan** Sample pristine tropical forest, abundant wildlife and the ruins of El Castillo on the second longest river in Central America. p.556

* **The Corn Islands** Caribbean-island charm without the development. Little Corn, especially, offers one of the few real deserted-island experiences left in the region. p.565

Introduction and Basics

Wedge-shaped Nicaragua may be the largest country in Central America, but it is also one of the least visited. Even after more than a decade of peace, Nicaragua is synonymous in the minds of many with civil war; this reputation, when coupled with the dilapidated infrastructure of a country that has fought its way not only through a bloody conflict but also an American economic blockade, scares many off. Still, many travellers who spend any time there find – much to their surprise – that Nicaragua is their favourite country in the isthmus. Perhaps because it doesn't yet fully cater for the tourist experience, Nicaragua is an incorrigibly vibrant and individualistic country, with plenty to offer travellers prepared to brave the superficial obstacles of economic chaos, cracked pavements and crammed public transport.

Cuba aside, Nicaragua is unique in Latin America in having pulled off a bona fide **revolution** of the people. The revolution of 1978–79 and the civil war that followed in the 1980s, while ravaging the country, has also given it one of the most dramatic of recent histories. At times it seems that every Nicaraguan has both horrifying and uplifting personal stories to tell. And even though Nicaragua's long-suffering people would rather forget many aspects of the war, the country's political past continues to inform every minute of its present.

During the 1980s Nicaragua was the destination of choice in Central America for young, socialist-minded *internacionalistas* – foreign volunteer workers who came to the country to aid the Revolution by working in the education and health sectors. From 1996 onwards, the Alemán government discontinued many of the programmes that brought the *internacionalistas* to Nicaragua and tourism slumped, which was bad news for the country's hotel owners and tour operators. Recent years, however, have seen tourist numbers increase as part of the general upturn in interest in Central America.

In comparison with the Maya ruins of Guatemala or the national parks of Costa Rica, Nicaragua offers few traditional tourist attractions – almost no monuments or ancient temples remain, and earthquakes, revolution and war have laid waste to museums, galleries and theatres. For years the country has suffered from a chronic lack of funding, and high inflation and unemployment have also impoverished Nicaragua's infrastructure. However, no one visits Nicaragua and remains immune to the country's extraordinary landscape of **volcanoes** (17 in all), **lakes**, **mountains** and vast plains of **rainforest**. A smattering of **beaches** – the majority of them on the Pacific Coast – continues to attract the budget **surfing** and backpacking crowd, while culture and **the arts** are very much alive in Nicaragua, and it is here you can buy some of the best-value high-quality crafts in the isthmus.

More than anything, though, the pleasures and rewards of travelling in Nicaragua come from interacting with the inhabitants of the country's complex society. Its **people** are well-spoken, passionate, engaged and engaging – Nicaraguans tend to be witty and exceptionally hospitable. The best thing you can do to enjoy Nicaragua is to arrive with an open mind, some patience and a willingness to practise your Spanish.

Where to go

Most of Nicaragua's population lives in the hot, relatively dry and **fertile Pacific lowlands**, where much of the country's agriculture is centred. This region is also the political and cultural centre of the country – nearly everything thought of as being inherently Nicaraguan, whether food, music, dress or dance – comes from this area. Virtually every traveller passes through the capital, **Managua**, if only to catch a bus; but there's little to detain the tourist in the capital and many quickly make tracks for **Granada**, with its splendid lakeside setting and wonderfully atmospheric colonial architecture. The town

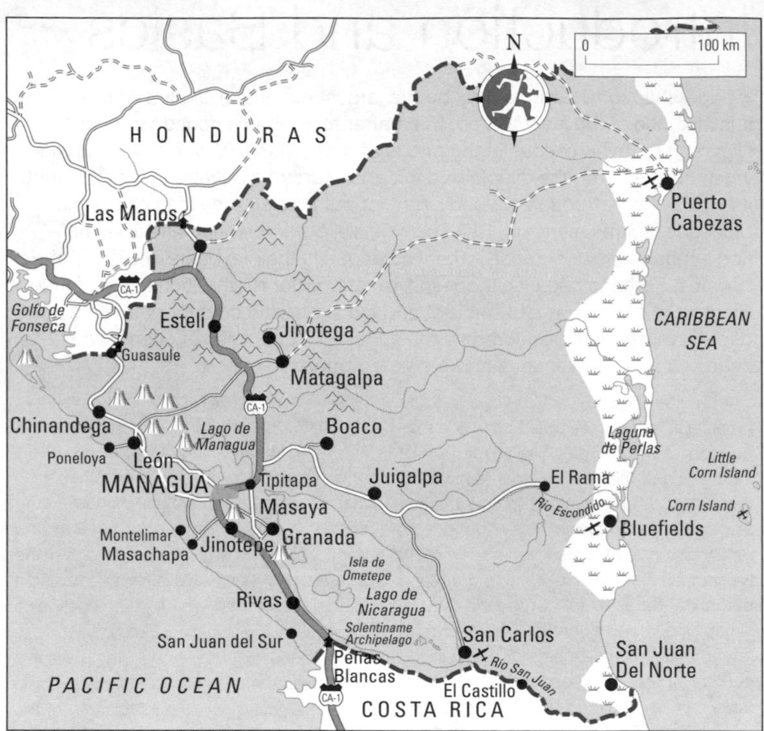

of **Masaya**, 26km southeast of the capital, is the arts-and-crafts centre of the country, and both Nicaraguans and foreign tourists descend upon its Mercado Nacional de Artesanía for some of the best crafts in Central America.

Ecotourism is beginning to have some impact in the **Lago de Nicaragua** area, with more and more travellers visiting Isla de Ometepe and the Solentiname Islands. Volcano-viewing and hiking are the attractions of Ometepe, with its thrilling twin volcanoes rising out of the freshwater lake. Further south in the lake, near the Costa Rican border, the Solentiname archipelago and the Río San Juan are some of the most pristine areas in Central America, where flora, fauna and a unique tradition of primitive naif painting prevail.

Nicaragua's mountainous **central region** is distinctly different, with a cooler climate and strikingly independent peoples. Much of the country's rich, mellow export-grade **coffee** is grown here, and farms dominate the scented landscape of blue-green pine-covered mountains. Hiking and birdwatching near the mountain town of **Matagalpa** are the main tourist attractions.

Physically cut off from the rest of the country, the Caribbean lowlands – called the **Atlantic Coast** in Nicaragua – actually make up nearly fifty percent of the country's landmass. Hot, humid and perpetually rainy, this area is sparsely populated and little-visited. Most of its inhabitants gain a living from fishing and subsistence agriculture. Politically and culturally distinct from the rest of Nicaragua, the region governs itself autonomously, regularly fighting tooth and nail with the central government. Descended from escaped African slaves and from the indigenous peoples (the Miskito, Rama and the Suma), the majority of Atlantic Coast inhabitants speak English – a legacy from the days when the area was a British protectorate. Food, dance, music and religion on the Atlantic Coast are West Indian rather than Spanish: rice-and-beans is cooked with coconut milk and the radio play is mainly reggae (mixed, bizarrely enough, with vintage North American country and western) in the hot and ramshackle jungle towns of **Bluefields** and **Puerto Cabezas**. The beautiful – and as yet unspoilt – **Corn Islands**, just off the coast of Bluefields, offer a welcome respite from the stresses of mainland life.

When to go

Nicaragua has two distinct seasons, the dry and the wet. The **rainy season** is called *invierno* (winter) and corresponds roughly with the Northern Hemisphere summer, from May to November. *Verano* (**summer**; December–April) is hot and often uncomfortably dry; dust covers everything, and the heat seems to rise to a kiln-like intensity. Fewer travellers come in the rainy season – which alone could be a reason for choosing to put up with the daily downpour. The seasons are most pronounced on the **Pacific Coast**, where rain often falls in the afternoons from May to November, although the mornings are dry. Influenced by the Caribbean trade winds, the **central mountain region** has sporadic rainfall all year, although it is drier in the "summer". Its climate is cooler year-round, with misty clouds covering its blue-green mountain summits. The **Atlantic Coast** is wet – very wet – year-round, and almost unbelievably hot and humid. As in the rest of the Caribbean region, September and October are the height of the tropical storm season.

Getting around

Finding your way around Nicaragua, whether on crowded school buses, sturdy old lake-boats, or in small planes, is at least half the fun of travelling in the country. Most journeys, with the exception of the trip to or from the Atlantic Coast, are relatively short and manageable. Public transport, especially buses, is geared toward the domestic population, and is very cheap.

Buses

Everywhere you go in Nicaragua you see packed **buses** careering down the highway, roof racks full of luggage and insides packed to the hilt. For the vast majority of Nicaraguans the bus is the only affordable way to travel, and despite the crush the service is good. The standard bus in Nicaragua is an old American or Canadian Blue Bird school bus – not uncomfortable, unless you have long legs. An increasing number of express minivans also service the more popular routes – they stop less frequently, have better suspension and are often driven by frustrated Formula One racers.

Managua is the **transport hub** of the country, and from here you can get virtually anywhere by bus. The most popular routes are Managua–Masaya–Granada; Managua–Rivas–San Juan del Sur; and, in the north, Managua–Leon and Managua–Matagalpa/Estelí. With some Spanish and a little fancy footwork you can get from almost any Nicaraguan town to another. Local services tend to be far less frequent and stop more often than "express" services between towns.

Most **intercity buses** begin running between 4am and 7am and the last buses

Overland routes to and from Nicaragua

The busiest route into and out of Nicaragua is the Peñas Blancas crossing (see p.543) at the southern **border with Costa Rica**. As such it can be a time-consuming process, especially when entering. Also in the south, the relatively remote and less congested Los Chiles river crossing is useful if travelling via San Carlos, with two scheduled boats per day (see p.558). The two main **border crossings with Honduras** in the north, meanwhile, are situated at El Guasaule (see p.524) and Las Manos (see p.530), with the latter providing easiest access to Tegucigalpa.

leave about 5 or 6pm. Fares are very cheap – most trips cost no more than US$1–2. If you are carrying luggage you may be charged half-fare – sometimes even full fare – for it. This is standard practice and there's no point arguing. Luggage that doesn't fit on the racks above the seats (although not all buses are fitted with these) is either put on the roof rack or at the back of the bus; the latter is a bit safer. You can tip the bus conductor a córdoba or two to keep an eye on it. Luggage is unloaded from the back door – try to watch proceedings to make sure your pack isn't stolen. Pickpocketing is also common – best to carry valuables in a money belt or inside pocket, and to keep any small backpacks on your front.

Departure times are frequent, usually every thirty minutes, or when the bus is full. **Bus stops** are never marked, but are usually located at the local market. You can flag down buses on the highway, but this means they'll probably be full and you'll have to stand. The conductor will collect your fare shortly after the bus departs, though he may not have change for big notes, in which case he'll take your money and return when he has collected enough fares to give you your change.

Taxis

Although you'll mostly see **taxis** in cities – many on their last legs although there are a fair amount of smart new imported Japanese models – they also make long-distance journeys. While a taxi from, say, Granada to Rivas, will cost several times the bus fare, it's still a good deal, especially if in a group, since drivers charge by the distance travelled rather than by the number of passengers. Another option is to hire a taxi to take you around for the day; this tends to be more expensive – at least double the price of a town-to-town journey, costing US$50 per carload or more. In all cases, negotiate the fare before getting into the cab.

Driving and hitching

Renting a car in Nicaragua is most reliable in Managua (for a list of companies, see p.511), although some of the more upmarket hotels in Granada and León may also be able to arrange car hire for you. You need a valid licence, passport and a credit card. Make sure you take out full-cover **insurance**, as road accidents in Nicaragua are on the increase. Throughout the country road signage is quite poor, and you'll need to ask directions frequently. Most roads are now paved, at least, although fuel remains expensive by Central American standards. As with other Central American countries, don't drive at night – it's less a question of crime than the lack of lighting disguising potholes, sudden deviations in the road, or even the road disappearing altogether, as well as cattle straying onto the highway.

Nicaraguans are a little surprised to see foreigners **hitching**, although it's common for locals to do so. You'll only see women hitching when accompanied by men, however, and it's wise to follow this rule as a traveller. You will be expected to pay for your lift, but usually no more than US$1–1.50, even for trips of a couple of hours. Competition for lifts out of Managua and other large towns is fierce: most hopefuls stand under a patch of shade on the highway just outside the city – if the competition is tough or drivers unresponsive they give in and take the bus.

Boats

For the many people who live around Nicaragua's numerous waterways and two large lakes, **boats** provide a vital link. Travellers, however, tend not to use boats much, since in most cases good bus or plane connections are also available. The longest boat journey in the country, from Granada on the west side of Lago de Nicaragua to San Carlos on the southeast corner of the lake, is a cheap, although slow (up to 14hr), way to cross this enormous inland sea. The Nicaraguan boat trip you're most likely to experience is the hour-long ride in a lancha – a medium-sized, motorized wooden craft – between San Jorge, near Rivas, and Moyogalpa on Ometepe island.

The trip from Managua and the Pacific lowlands to the Atlantic Coast can be made partly by boat, using either the slow public ferry or the high-speed *panga* (a large, motorized canoe carrying up to 20 people) that run from the hamlet of El Rama at the head of the Río Escondido to the coastal town of Bluefields. On the eastern side of the country nearly all travel is by boat along the complex network of rivers and lagoons of Mosquitia. All these services are private, and geared towards locals. Journeys are unscheduled, long and unpredictable, and you'll have to ask around in Bluefields and Puerto Cabezas for connections.

A ferry makes a weekly journey between Bluefields and the **Corn Islands**, though this 6- to 8-hour journey can be notoriously rough and many travellers opt to take a flight on the return leg. A twice-daily *panga* runs between **Corn Island** and **Little Corn Island** – the journey is great fun and takes about an hour, although you'll probably get wet.

Planes

Faced with a ten-hour bus trip followed by six hours on a slow river jungle-cruise, many people heading to Nicaragua's Atlantic Coast from Managua choose to **fly** at least one way. The private domestic airlines La Costeña and Atlantic Airlines operate reliable (and very scenic) flights between Managua, Bluefields and the Corn Islands for about US$120 return. Both operators offer similar prices, but La Costeña has a greater range and number of flights. While both companies fly to Puerto Cabezas in the northeast corner of the country (inaccessible by road for at least half the year), only La Costeña fly to San Carlos, near the border with Costa Rica, another relatively inaccessible location.

Costs, money and banks

Nicaragua's **currency** is the **córdoba**, written as C$ and divided into 100 centavos. Notes come in denominations of 100, 50, 20, and 10 córdobas although you may very occasionally spot a tiny 50 or 25 centavos note. Coins come in denominations of 5 and 1 córdobas, and 50 and 25 centavos. You'll learn quickly to get rid of the 100 and 50 notes, as in most places they're about as welcome as a stack of Russian roubles and no one – except maybe bus conductors – ever seems to have change.

Nicaragua is no longer as cheap as it used to be, although it's still one of the cheapest destinations in Latin America. The IMF and World Bank policies have had their effect, and **prices** have risen accordingly. In general bus transport, food bought at markets and some accommodation are still bargains; upmarket restaurant meals, petrol, car rental and more upscale hotel accommodation, especially in Managua, are surprisingly expensive. As a rule, the budget traveller in Nicaragua, staying in hospedajes, taking buses instead of taxis, and eating in markets or at food stalls, can get by on as little as US$10/£6 a day, although US$15–20/£10–12 is a more comfortable aim.

Banks and exchange

The banking system in Nicaragua is improving, though one of the main hassles of travelling around the country is the refusal of many banks to acknowledge the existence of **travellers' cheques**; which means that you'll always be carrying a huge wad of grubby córdobas with you. Both **Banco de América Central** and **Bancentro** – with branches in all major towns and cities – will change travellers' cheques, although at much poorer rates than cash.

Banks are usually open from 8.30am to 4.30pm and may close for an hour or more over lunch (12.30–1.30pm); many are also open on Saturday mornings. All will change US dollars, but no other currency.

To change travellers' cheques you can go to private currency-exchange houses, called **casas de cambio**, though at present these are only found in Managua. Changing cheques into dollars rather than córdobas incurs a fee of around US$4. The rate for changing dollar travellers' cheques at casas de cambio is slightly worse than the bank rate.

Credit cards such as Visa and MasterCard are accepted in some of the more expensive hotels and restaurants and you can often use them to pay for car rental, flights and tours. All branches of Bancentro and BAC advance cash on major cards. All in all, they're a better bet than travellers' cheques and you can also use them to withdraw money via Nicaragua's limited ATM network. Machines that accept foreign-issued cards can be found at the Plaza Inter shopping mall in Managua, outside the huge BAC headquarters in Managua, various Texaco garage forecourts throughout the country and in some banks in León and Granada. That said, you can't rely on ATMs alone and, especially out of the major centres, you'll have little alternative but to carry a decent amount of cash.

Moneychangers (*coyotes*) operate in the street, usually at the town market, but avoid changing dollars in the street – it's easy to get ripped off. If you must, avoid dealing with more than one person at a time, and watch out for sleights of hand (like replacing a US$100 bill with a US$1). Take a taxi after changing money.

The **exchange rate** at the time of writing was around 15.4 córdobas to the dollar, and is now relatively stable. Dollars are a very useful standby across Nicaragua (especially on the Atlantic Coast), and this will increase with the widespread acceptance of the dollar across Central America.

Information

There are **Intur tourist offices** throughout the country, and although the staff (in general only Spanish-speaking) are usually friendly and well intentioned, they can't offer much practical help; you're unlikely to come away with much more than a bunch of colourful leaflets. Ask for a copy of the quarterly *Between the Waves* magazine (free), a useful English-language publication geared towards expats and travellers. It's packed with articles on history, business, tourist activities and destinations within Nicaragua, often including up-to-date transport schedules. If Intur doesn't have it, you should be able to pick it up in selected restaurants, travel agencies, embassies and bigger hotels.

The only commercially available **map** of Nicaragua is the 1:755,000 sheet produced by Canadian firm ITMB Publishing/International Travel Maps. You can pick up a useful map of Managua in the city's Intur office although maps of other cities (save perhaps Granada) are usually very hard to come by.

Useful English-language **websites** include ⓦwww.guideofnicaragua.com, which has up-to-date information, maps and features on travelling in Nicaragua, and ⓦwww.intur.gob.ni, the official government tourist site. For more general information about the country visit ⓦwww.centralamerica.com/nicaragua, or try ⓦwww.lanic.utexas.edu/la/ca/nicaragua, a comprehensive portal with extensive links to almost every aspect of Nicaraguan society and culture.

Accommodation

Most travellers to Nicaragua find themselves at some point in a Nicaraguan **hospedaje** – a small, pension-type hotel, most often family-owned and run. Most are basic, though some, especially those in old Spanish colonial-style houses, are truly characterful places, with big rocking chairs ringing plant-filled patios and a lively family life going on around. As a rule, simple hospedajes still charge under US$5, although with inflation prices are moving into the US$5–10 range; most require payment in cash, usually in córdobas. Breakfast is not normally included in the price, and in most places you'll have to share a bathroom, though in only the most basic of hospedajes will you have to provide your own toilet paper and towel. More upmarket hospedajes occasionally offer the option of air conditioning; since electricity is so expensive this can double the price of the room. Nicaraguan units tend to be old and noisy and in most places a/c is not really necessary – you can get by with a ceiling fan.

Hotels tend to be fancier, with air conditioning, possibly cable television, and other services like tours and car rental. Outside Managua they're still fairly thin on the ground although definitely on the increase; Granada, León and San Juan del Sur have all seen a significant increase in upscale accommodation over the last few years.

Throughout the country **camping** is problematic, although not impossible; there is little tradition of camping in Nicaragua, and sandflies, mosquitoes, rain and theft are only a few of the deterrents to setting up a tent. If you're determined, the most promising areas in which to camp are beach towns like San Juan del Sur, Isla Ometepe and the Corn Islands.

See p.36 for an explanation of the accommodation price codes.

Food and drink

Nicaraguan **food** is based around the ubiquitous **beans**, **rice** and **meat** – and plenty of it. Everything is cooked with oil; even the rice is fried, often with a little onion and some finely sliced red chillies or small capsicums. If this sounds like gastronomic hell, take heart – *comida nica* grows on you and you may find yourself craving a plate of **gallo pinto** (beans and rice) once you've left the country. Homegrown Nicaraguan beef is also very tasty. In comparison with other Latin American countries **vegetarians** will have a fairly easy time of it in Nicaragua. Although the novelty does wane eventually, veggie food in the form of beans, rice, fried plantains, tortillas, cheese and eggs is almost always on the menu, even in the furthest reaches of the Atlantic Coast. Pizza (and to a lesser extent, pasta) is ubiquitous and vegetarian restaurants are even cropping up in the major towns. **Tropical fruit**, meanwhile, is cheap, plentiful and delicious; if you don't want to buy the fruit whole – the papayas are so huge it'd take you a week to eat them anyway – you can normally buy big, cheap plates of fruit salad or small bags of chopped fruit from bus terminals and markets.

A Spanish **menu reader** can be found on p.870.

What to eat

Nicaraguan meals are very much centred on meat, usually **chicken**, **beef** or **pork**, most deliciously cooked *a la plancha*, on a grill or griddle, and served spitting on a hot plate. **Seafood** is equally good: on the coast you'll be offered ocean fish such as snapper and bass, with freshwater fish on the menu around Lago de Nicaragua. Fish are usually served whole, deep fried and served with a rich tomato or garlic sauce. Weekends are traditionally the time to eat **nacatamales**, parcels of corn dough filled with either vegetables, pork, beef or chicken, which are wrapped in a banana leaf and boiled for a couple of hours.

On the Atlantic Coast the cuisine becomes markedly more **Caribbean**, and sweeter, spicier tastes invade the recipes. Although rice and beans is still a staple dish, you'll often find that the rice has been cooked in delicious mild coconut milk, and the fresh **coconut bread** is delicious. **Ron don** – "run down" – in local parlance "to cook" – is a stew of local yucca, chayote and other vegetables, usually with meat added, which is simmered for at least a day and traditionally eaten at weekends.

Throughout the country you'll see **ice cream** sellers pushing their Eskimo carts. Although the quality isn't great, the company produces an extraordinary range of homegrown flavours, embracing many local fruits and nuts, including chocolate with almonds, coconut, pistachio, star fruit, rock melon and mango. For the more exotic flavours you may have to go to an Eskimo shop or a supermarket.

Where to eat

Throughout Nicaragua **streetside kiosks** sell hot meals, usually at lunchtime. You'll soon become familiar with the plastic tablecloths, paper plates and huge bowls of cabbage salad set beside small barbecue grills. The food is generally well prepared and safe to eat: most Nicaraguans have their lunch this way, or in small **comedores** or **cafetines**, restaurants with ten or so seats that do a lunchtime *comida corriente*, a good-value set plate of meat, rice and salad. **Street vendors** sell a variety of snacks including nuts, popcorn and banana chips. In the early evening, small stalls open up in most towns on or around the central plaza selling cheap and filling fried foods with rice and salad.

Drinking

Nicaragua has two local brands of **beer**, Victoria and Toña, both lagers. Each has its aficionados, who refuse to drink the other. Victoria is the most common, and usually held up as the true national beer although it's actually fairly rough; Toña is smoother, darker and nuttier. You can buy them in cans, but to get them from your local shop you will need to exchange some "empties" – Nicaragua operates a strict recycling programme for beer bottles and with no empties to exchange you'll pay double the price.

Local Flor de Caña **rum** comes in dark and white, gold, old, dry and light, and is an excellent buy at just US$4–7. It's usually brought to the table with a large bucket of ice and some lemons, but you can mix it with soft drinks for something a little less potent.

Given Nicaragua's heat, it's just as well that there's a fascinating range of cold drinks, or **refrescos** (usually shortened to *frescos*), to choose from. These are made from a large range of grains, seeds and fruits, which are liquidized with milk, water and ice. *Cebada en grano* is a combination of ground barley and barley grains mixed together with milk and coloured pink – like most drinks it is flavoured with cinnamon and lots of sugar. *Pinolillo* is a maize drink with spices, served in large, carved, oval containers made from the seed of the jickory tree; the *semilla de Jicaroa* itself is made into a delicious drink that looks and tastes rather like chocolate. *Cacao* is also widely available, and often sold in small sealed plastic bags at traffic lights. Just about every fruit imaginable is made into a *fresco*, including watermelon, star fruit, papaya, rock melon (a small, local variety of melon) and oranges. During the rainy months, keep your eye out for *pitahaya* juice. Made from the fruit of a cactus, it's a virulent purple in colour and incredibly tasty. You can also eat the fruit raw, but be warned that you'll stain your hands and mouth a deep purple. Some drink stands and street vendors specialize in **raspados**, a cup full of ice scraped off a large block and topped with flavouring, anything from milk and chocolate to currants (*grosellas*).

Opening hours, festivals and holidays

Shops and **services** in Nicaragua still observe Sunday closing: otherwise you'll find most things open from 8am to 4pm. Some **museums** and **sites** close for lunch, normally shutting their doors between noon and 2, before reopening again until 4pm. Supermarkets, smaller grocery shops and the small neighbourhood shops called *ventas* generally stay open until 8pm. **Bars** and **restaurants** tend to close around 11pm, except for nightclubs and dance clubs – most of which are in Managua – which stay open until 2am or later.

Christmas and Easter are still the biggest **holidays**. At **Easter** especially the whole country packs up and goes to the beach: buses are packed, hotel rooms on the coast are at a premium, and flights to the Corn Islands are fully booked. **Christmas** and **New Year** are mainly celebrated in the home, and you'll find most things closed on December 25 and on January 1. The holiday marking the **Revolution**, on July 19, is still celebrated ardently by Sandinistas and is usually accompanied by parades and marches. In addition, each town in Nicaragua has its own **patron saint** and will observe the saint's day with processions and celebrations called Toro Guaco, when you might catch a glimpse of old customs inherited from the Aztecs mixed with mestizo figures like the masked *viejitos* (old ones –

Public holidays

January 1 New Year's Day
Easter week Semana Santa
May 1 Labour Day
July 19 Anniversary of the Revolution
September 14 Battle of San Jacinto
September 15 Independence Day
November 2 All Souls' Day (Día de los Muertos)
December 7 & 8 Inmaculada Concepción
December 25 Christmas Day

masks of old men and women worn by young and old alike). In all cases Nicaraguans love to dance, and you will probably see folkloric dances in the streets, usually performed by children.

Communications

The **mail** service in Nicaragua is fairly fast: though letters to Europe can take up to two weeks, they reach North America in about eight days. Theft from letters is an increasing problem, especially with mail sent into Nicaragua, so it's wise not to trust cash or anything valuable to the postal service. You can send **international mail** from any Nicaraguan town, although Managua, León and Granada have the best service. Mail sent from the Atlantic Coast will probably take the longest to reach the rest of the world.

Nicaraguan telephone company **Enitel** has an office in every town of any size throughout the country. While the phone service is more reliable than it used to be, calling out of the country can still be a hassle. There are virtually no coin-operated phones in Nicaragua and towns like Managua, León and Granada have new Publitel cardphones. **Cards** are available from Enitel offices and supermarkets and work by punching in a code, not magnetic strip. They can be useful for making **domestic** calls (and calls to neighbouring countries), although it's often easier, cheaper and more reliable to make calls from an Enitel office. Outside major towns, all telephone calls have to be placed at an Enitel office.

Calling abroad, you'll have to pay a visit to an Enitel office and wait in line with huge numbers of Nicaraguans. You can ask to reverse the charges or pay for your call afterwards in córdobas – tell the operator how long you wish to talk and they'll calculate the approximate cost for you. You'll then be sent to a numbered booth, where you wait for your call to be patched through – a sometimes frustrating process. Most Enitel offices are open long hours, from 7am until 8pm Monday to Friday, with reduced hours at weekends. Alternatively, many countries have **direct-dial** numbers that get you through to either a member-card operator (AT&T or Sprint) or your home country operator for a reverse-charge call. Calling Nicaragua from abroad, the **country code** is ⓣ505.

All that said, the **Internet** revolution is fast making conventional phones obsolete and Enitel faces stiff competition from the ever proliferating number of Internet cafés. While conventional calls to the UK cost a hefty US$4–5 per minute, Internet calls are priced as low as US$0.30 per minute, even cheaper to the USA. Using the Internet itself usually costs between US$1–2 per hour throughout the country, although rates often rise in smaller or more remote towns.

Fax machines are common in Nicaragua, although, except in Managua, Enitel does not provide a public fax service. If you stay at a mid-range or upmarket hotel you'll probably be able to send a fax abroad for a fee; otherwise – and especially outside Managua – you're out of luck.

The media

The Sandinistas were widely criticized for **censoring** Nicaragua's media during the 1980s, and though Nicaragua's press is now technically free, in 2000 the Alemán government introduced stringent new standards for journalists requiring them all to be university educated, professionally qualified and – the crux of the argument – government approved. Opponents say that these new conditions restrict the right to free speech.

Of the national **newspapers**, the most authoritative is *La Prensa,* founded in 1926. During the Chamorro years it was criticized for being too supportive of that government (Violeta Chamorro was on the editorial board, and her daughter was the paper's editor), though it now takes a slightly more independent line and attacks corrupt politicians irrespective of party allegiance – in the run-up to the 2001 presidential elections it was equally critical of all the candidates. The other widely available daily is the black-and-white *El Nuevo Diario*, which is leftist but more sensationalist and populist in tone.

The only **English-language publication** is the bi-monthly *Between the Waves* (see p.501). The Casa del Cafe in Managua sells a range of Spanish-language magazines including the Latin American edition of *Newsweek*. Foreign newspapers, even those readily available in other Central American countries, such as the *Miami Herald* or the *New York Times*, are virtually impossible to buy in Nicaragua.

Cable television is becoming increasingly widespread across Nicaragua, providing access to a range of international news, sports and movie channels. Many poorer Nicaraguans still get their news from the **radio**, while a number of FM stations pump out pop music, generally a mix of English and Spanish.

Safety and the police

Poverty and unemployment in Nicaragua have contributed to a rising crime rate. **Petty theft** is the most common form, especially on buses. Nicaraguans suffer from this as well as tourists, and locals take the usual precautions of not carrying anything valuable in an outside pocket, and spreading valuables and money over several pockets or purses; travellers should do the same. Opportunistic forms of theft aside, the only place where you need to worry about assault is in Managua. Here it's best not to walk around at night or to go out alone to bars, and be alert when leaving banks or casas de cambio, where thieves have recently targeted both foreigners and Nicaraguans. Never leave anything of value on the beach, even for a few minutes, as it is almost guaranteed to be stolen. Larger hotels will have safes where you can leave your passport and other valuables. **Women** should be wary of going out alone or even in a group at night – the chief threat is being harassed by drunken men spilling out of bars in groups.

The **police** in Nicaragua are generally reliable, except perhaps the traffic police (*policia de tránsito*), who are infamous for their opportunistic targeting of foreigners and who will take any chance to give you a fine (*multa*). To **report a crime** you must go to the nearest police station. If you need a police report for an insurance claim, the police will ask you to fill out a *denuncia* – a full report of the incident. If the police station does not have the *denuncia* forms, ask for a *constancia*, a simpler form, signed and stamped by the police. This should be sufficient for an insurance claim. Visitors to Nicaragua must carry their passport on them at all times. A photocopy is acceptable; police checks are not as common as they used to be. Keep passports secure in an inside pocket all the time, and keep a photocopy separately when travelling.

In an **emergency**, dial ☎128 for the Red Cross (*Cruz Roja*); ☎115 for fire (*bomberos*); ☎118 for police; or ☎119 in the case of a traffic accident.

Work and study

Gone are the heady days of the 1980s, when **internacionalistas** (foreign voluntary workers) came from Europe, North America and other Latin American countries to help the Revolution. Now, with the political shift to the right, *internacionalistas* come to Nicaragua in much reduced numbers. As overseas NGOs and aid agencies take over, it is becoming increasingly difficult to find good voluntary positions in Nicaragua. Most towns have a local IXCHEN **women's centre** (*casa de la mujer*), whose work is largely based on health, family welfare and community issues. Women are always welcome to visit and if your Spanish is good and you have some qualifications, they may be able to advise you regarding voluntary work.

Unless sponsored by an overseas government, agency or voluntary organization, opportunities for work are few, and what does exist is likely to be unpaid. In a country where unofficial unemployment figures hover around seventy percent, foreigners will only find casual work as **teachers** of English. Even so, the Nicaraguan government is strict in its immigration policy and to undertake any paid work you need a long-stay working visa; if you are sponsored by an overseas company they will probably take care of this for you. The address of Managua's *migración* office is given on p.512.

History

In comparison with its neighbours to the north, in Nicaragua you often get the impression that history didn't begin until the arrival of the Spanish. Few traces of Nicaragua's pre-Conquest history remain; certainly there are **no major monuments** of the likes of Tikal or Copán, and historians and archeologists are doubtful whether cities of equivalent size and complexity ever existed here, though modern Nicaragua retains aspects of its ancient history in its language, food and customs.

Events far to the north in Mexico determined the future of the country that would come to be called Nicaragua. After the fall of the Aztec city of Teotihuacán in 1000 AD, displaced **Mexica** (Aztec) migrated southward through the isthmus on the strength of a prophecy that they were to settle where they saw a lake with two volcanoes rising from the water – which they found in the striking form of Isla de Ometepe in Lago de Nicaragua.

Two groups of pre-Columbian peoples settled on the shores of the lake, roughly divided into the **Chorotegas** and the **Nahuas**, and collectively known as **Niquirano**. They were governed by chief **Nicarao**, a rich *cacique* (chief) from near present-day Rivas who came to be called Nicaragua by the Spanish, giving the modern country its name. In 1522 Nicarao welcomed **Gil González de Avila**, an intrepid explorer who had made his way to Nicaragua from Panama and Costa Rica, becoming the first Spaniard to arrive in the area. Nicarao allowed his people to be baptized and to mix interracially with the Spanish conquerors.

The inhabitants of central Nicaragua, the **Chontales**, **Matagalpas** and **Populucas**, were a different ethnic group, related to the Maya of Honduras, and offered far more resistance to the Spanish, though their language and peoples did not survive the Conquest. On the Atlantic Coast the pre-Miskito **Sumus** and **Ramas** (of whom little is known) made up the indigenous population. Nearly all the coastal peoples, except the Rama, mixed racially with the Afro-Caribbean population who came to its shores as freed or escaped slaves from British West Indian colonies.

The colonial era

Although the very first Spanish conquistadors glimpsed the eastern coast of Nicaragua as early as 1508, it was not until 1522, three years after Hernán Cortés landed on the coast of Mexico, that a Spanish expedition sailed up the Río San Juan into the Lago de Nicaragua. Two years later an expedition led by **Francisco Fernandez de Córdoba** founded the first cities, Granada and León, after suppressing local indigenous groups.

The story of colonial Nicaragua is a familiar one of exploitation of indigenous peoples and the country was used as a source of **slave labour** with many indigenous Nicaraguans being sent to work in the Peruvian mines. The Spanish did not make much of an effort to penetrate remote parts of the country or to establish other towns, and by the end of the 1500s León and Granada were still the only settlements. The country remained poor, the central mountains unexplored through fear of the fierce indigenous peoples who still lived there, while the Atlantic Coast was plagued by pirates. Not much would change in Nicaragua for nearly three hundred years.

Independence

By the beginning of the nineteenth century Spain had begun to lose its grip on power in Nicaragua. As in other New World colonies, in Nicaragua only *peninsulares* – those born in Spain – could hold positions of influence. Fuelled by the frustrations of the local-born elite, a revolt staged in 1811 in El Salvador ignited aspirations of independence throughout the region. Along with the other Central American countries, in 1821 Nicaragua gained independence from the Spanish Crown as part of the **Central American Federation**, before becoming a fully independent nation in 1838.

Following independence, the new republic of Nicaragua attracted the interest of the US, who believed that the Río San Juan and Lago de Nicaragua represented a possible route for transporting goods and passengers between the Atlantic and Pacific sides of the isthmus. In 1849, the American **Cornelius Vanderbilt**, in partnership with the Nicaraguan government, formed the **Accessory Transit Company**, ushering in a period of relative prosperity for the country. The company was granted exclusive rights to build a canal across the isthmus, and was also allowed to establish a transit route across Nicaragua along which passengers and mining equipment were moved during the Californian Gold Rush (the journey from the east to the west coast of the US by sea via Nicaragua was actually quicker than that across the US by land).

William Walker

William Walker was an ambitious and megalomaniacal – or just plain mad, depending on your interpretation – American adventurer. A native of Tennessee, schooled in law and journalism, Walker had vast political ambitions. The Liberals of León foolhardily handed him the chance to fulfil them by inviting him to Nicaragua to help them gain power over their arch-rivals, the Conservatives of Granada.

In 1855 Walker set foot on Nicaraguan soil and soon afterwards, with just sixty mercenaries, gained control of Granada – and, by default, the entire country. Walker installed a puppet government, though real power remained in his own hands. In 1856, alarmed by the situation, Costa Rica declared war on Walker, but an epidemic of cholera forced the Costa Ricans to withdraw. The same year Walker held a rigged election and declared himself President of the Republic. By making English the country's official language and **legalizing slavery**, Walker managed to alienate all Nicaraguans; Cornelius Vanderbilt, still a force in Nicaragua, was determined to have him out, and the other Central American countries, fearing Walker's activities might spark rebellions in their own territories, began plans to topple him.

Nicaragua paid dearly for the eventual overthrow of Walker, which came only with help from Guatemala and Costa Rica: many Nicaraguans lost their lives in the fighting, and as he retreated Walker ordered the beautiful colonial city of Granada burned. The final battle of 1856–57, in Rivas, near the Costa Rican border, would come to be known as the "**National War**". Intervention by the US forced the issue and on May 1, 1857, Walker and his remaining followers were escorted by marines out of Rivas and onto a ship back to the US.

Three years later, during a further bout of adventuring in Central America, Walker was captured by the British and handed over to Hondurans, who executed him in Trujillo.

The US invasion

For the next three decades, power seesawed, not always peacefully, between Liberals and Conservatives. Even so, the period from 1857 to 1893 was one of such unusual stability and prosperity that Nicaraguan historians often refer to it, somewhat nostalgically, as "**The Thirty Years**". This period coincided with the growth of what was to become Nicaragua's most important export: **coffee**, fuelled by Europe's and America's seemingly insatiable desire for the drink.

Despite the prosperity afforded the country by the coffee trade, at the beginning of the twentieth century Nicaragua's economy was dominated by the overwhelming presence of US companies, usually in alliance with Nicaraguan landowners – a pattern which was to characterize economic relations for most of the coming century. Angered when, in 1904, the US chose Panama for the site of the **Transisthmian Canal**, President José Santos Zelaya countered by inviting Germany and Japan to construct a rival canal across Nicaragua. Though this canal never left the drawing board, the subsequent worsening of relations with the US prompted a **civil war** in October 1909, with the nationalist Liberals and the US-friendly Conservatives again at each other's throats. In response, the US inaugurated a precedent in Nicaragua – and in the region as a whole – by landing four hundred US marines on the Caribbean coast. Zelaya resigned soon after.

From 1912 until 1933 the US kept a token number of troops in Nicaragua, more as a reminder of US influence than as any real military threat. Pro-US Conservatives held onto power until a further outbreak of unrest in 1926 prompted the US to send more marines, ostensibly to protect US citizens.

One of the opponents of the US presence in Nicaragua was **Augusto César Sandino**, a socialist who waged independent guerrilla activity, manned by his own personal army of peasants and workers. He eventually joined the Liberals' fight against the Conservatives and their US allies. In response to Sandino's activities – their excuse was the maintenance of "internal security" – in the first years of the 1930s the US took over the country's military and developed the Nicaraguan National Guard, which was to become such a significant force under the next political figure looming on Nicaragua's horizon – Somoza.

The Somoza years

The long era of **Somocismo**, or Somoza-family rule, began in 1934. In his role as head of the country's National Guard, **General Anastasio "Tacho" Somoza García** ordered the assassination of Sandino, by then the liberal candidate for the upcoming election. With Sandino dead, rigged elections were held and Somoza was sworn in as president of Nicaragua in 1937.

Educated in the US, where he attended a school run by the US marines, Somoza was also well-connected in Nicaragua through the kind of network of family influence that has always been so significant in Central American political life. Perhaps his privileged lifestyle and reliance upon his family's influence were responsible for Somoza's exceptionally cynical character; in any case, it was clear he had little sympathy for the majority of his compatriots. Indeed he ruled in typical Latin American strongman fashion as a *caudillo*, or dictator, as he ruthlessly pursued the enrichment of himself, his family and his coterie of associates. He cultivated the National Guard as his own personal army and gave it power far beyond the usual sphere of a military force, until it virtually controlled the radio stations, the postal services and even the health system.

Somoza remained in power through continuously rigged elections and re-elections, or appointments of puppet governments. In 1955 the Nicaraguan Congress amended the constitution to allow Somoza to be re-elected again. But by then political opposition was growing. Somoza's end came unexpectedly, both for him and the country, brought about by the independent action of **Rigoberto López Pérez**, a 27-year-old poet, who shot the dictator dead in the streets of León in 1956. The National Guard responded by shooting Pérez some fifty times.

As it turned out, little changed, despite Perez's dramatic action. Somoza's son, **Luis Somoza Debayle**, also US-educated, took the position of interim president. At the same time his younger brother **Anastasio "Tachito" Somoza Debayle** assumed command of the National Guard. Following in their father's footsteps, they stayed in power through manipulation of the constitution and electoral process. A long period of repression followed, during which dissidents were regularly tortured and imprisoned.

Opposition grew, however, and in the 1967 elections the Conservatives and Christian Social Party banded together to create the **National Opposition Union** (Unión Nacional Opositora, or UNO). Nonetheless, vote rigging and harassment of voters ensured Somoza's election as president. Luis Somoza died of a heart attack soon after and power was left concentrated in the hands of Anastasio Somoza – now both president and head of the National Guard.

Growing opposition

At a few minutes past midnight on December 23, 1972, Managua was rocked by an incredible seismic disturbance, causing the near total collapse of the city. By the time the ground stopped rumbling – just thirty seconds later – some 10,000 people were dead and about 50,000 families homeless.

Every Nicaraguan recognizes the **earthquake of 1972** as a national turning point. The earthquake was followed by the looting of the shattered shops of Managua's former commercial core, in which poor Managuans were joined by soldiers of the National Guard. Much of the emergency supplies sent from abroad were also intercepted by the Guard, acting on Somoza's orders, and then sold off to victims in the street. Businesses and homeowners were unable to claim compensation on damaged property because the Somoza-owned insurance companies refused to recognize their claims. All classes of Nicaraguans were appalled by the epic cynicism and greed behind Somoza's actions; by 1974 his personal wealth was estimated at some US$400 million. Even businessmen and the elite, both traditionally loyal to Somoza, deserted camp.

The **Frente Sandinista de Liberación Nacional (FSLN)**, named after Sandino, soon became a rallying point for dissidents. Founded in the late 1950s by law students at the National University in León as a Marxist-Leninist response to the dictatorship, by the early 1970s the FSLN had gained widespread support, especially in the countryside and among students.

The FSLN's first major success took place on December 27, 1974, when guerrillas raided the home of a government official and held several relatives of Somoza to ransom, gaining a US$1 million payout. The guerrillas fled abroad, and though the opposition was buoyed by the success of the rebels' audacity, in response Somoza stepped up the repression, surveillance, torture and murder of suspected dissidents.

Despite the fact that the Nicaraguan rebels were getting ready to strike and even the US was beginning to have reservations, the catalyst that began the Revolution was actually engineered by the dictator himself: on January 10, 1978, **Pedro Joaquín Chamorro**, opposition leader and editor of *La Prensa*, was assassinated by the National Guard, acting on Somoza's orders. Mass demonstrations and a general strike followed, crippling the country and galvanizing the opposition. Meanwhile, the US cut off the Somoza regime by suspending military aid.

The most dramatic event staged by the FSLN took place on August 22, 1978, when guerrillas stormed the National Palace while Congress was in session. After 2000 government members had been held hostage for two days, President Somoza was forced to meet the demands of the FSLN. A humiliation for Somoza, the audacity of the guerrillas once again inspired the population. By the end of 1978, demonstrations and outbreaks of fighting had spread around the country.

Revolution

In May 1979 – with Somoza more unpopular then ever and the economy in crisis – the FSLN launched its main offensive in Estelí and Jinotega. No longer merely a group of guerrilla insurrectionists bent on staging dramatic stunts, the **Sandinistas** were now a formidable fighting force: their influence had spread to the provinces, and their military strategy was centrally organized.

In June, a Nicaraguan **government-in-exile** was established in Costa Rica. Among the five-member governorship of the country were two people who would play key roles in the political future of Nicaragua – **Daniel José Ortega Saavedra** of the FSLN and **Violeta Barrios de Chamorro**, the widow of the assassinated *La Prensa* editor. By June the country was largely in the hands of the Sandinistas, although Managua remained under the control of Somoza and his National Guard. Isolated, Somoza was forced to resign and soon after boarded a plane to Miami. He eventually moved to Paraguay, where he was assassinated by South American leftist guerrillas in 1980.

Triumphant, the government-in-exile ceremoniously entered the city of León the day after Somoza's departure. A day later the FSLN forces entered Managua, and the Revolution was won, officially, on July 19, 1979. With the Revolution ended a long – perhaps even 500-year-long – era of feudalism in Nicaragua. However, the price had been high: around 50,000 were dead and over 120,000 had fled the country into exile.

The Sandinista years and the Contra War

As the 1970s became the 1980s, the challenge facing the **new Sandinista government** was enormous. The country's infrastructure was in ruins, but the mood of the country – among the leadership as well as the general population – was buoyant, even ecstatic.

First on the agenda for the Sandinistas was the resuscitation of the **economy**, severely damaged by Somoza's appropriation and by war. Foreign debts had to be renegotiated, loans secured, and economic aid directed. Somoza's properties were nationalized – some two thousand farms, accounting for twenty percent of Nicaragua's agricultural land.

Operating under emergency measures, the governing junta suspended all the mechanisms of Somocismo, including the constitution, presidency, Congress, and all courts. A new army, the Sandinista People's Army (**Ejército Popular Sandinista** or **EPS**), was formed along with a Sandinista-controlled police force. With the help of training by Cuban and Soviet armed forces, the EPS soon developed into the most powerful standing army in Central America.

Another task facing the Sandinistas was the construction of a civil society, which had never really existed in Nicaragua. In transforming the civil, military and judicial arms of Nicaragua, the Sandinistas made themselves ubiquitous, and within only a year of taking over the country they were in control of most aspects of Nicaraguan society.

The first democratic elections held under the Sandinistas, in 1984, were won by Daniel Ortega with a 67 percent majority. This was the first time most Nicaraguans had ever voted, and the first time since 1928 that the US did not have a hand in the electoral process. The Sandinistas were not universally popular, however, particularly in the **Atlantic Coast** region. Independent, traditionally suspicious of anyone of Spanish descent and not of a leftist bent, the Miskito, Rama and Creole peoples of the Atlantic Coast never really got behind the Revolution, especially after the Sandinistas made attempts to forcibly relocate indigenous groups and to impose leftist ideology upon them. Many coastal dwellers – the Miskito especially – were so disenchanted by the Sandinistas that they would make easy recruits in the civil war that was to come.

The main blow for the Sandinistas came in the form of **Ronald Reagan**'s election to the presidency of the US in November 1980. Convinced that Nicaragua's leftist policies and its friendship with Cuba and the Soviet Union meant the spread of Communism in the US's backyard, the Reagan administration **suspended aid** to Nicaragua in 1981 and thereafter waged an open campaign against the Sandinistas. The **Contra War** – "contra" being short for *contrarevolucionarios* – was launched with nearly $20 million of US military assistance. The troops, based in training camps in Honduras, were mostly made up of former National Guard soldiers who had fled the country on Somoza's departure, though they were soon joined by other groups, including Miskitos. Although it's true that sectors of the population were disgruntled with the Sandinistas, the presence of the universally hated ex-National Guard in the Contra forces caused most Nicaraguans to distrust the Contra movement.

By the mid-1980s the Contra War was causing widespread disruption in the country. What with open US support for the movement, as well as the ambivalent positions of Honduras and Costa Rica – both used as launching pads by the Contras – the Sandinistas felt increasingly isolated, and began to clamp down on political opposition. Revoking their promises for an open political society, they banned opposition in the media – including *La Prensa*, ironically an organ of dissent during the Somoza years – and prevented rival political parties.

Arguably it was the five-year-long **US trade embargo** that succeeded in strangling the Nicaraguan economy and undermining the Sandinistas. Within a few years, though, US support for the Contras was shaken by the **Irangate** scandal, during which it emerged that Oliver North was a lynchpin in a CIA scheme to sell weapons to Iran illegally, using the proceeds to fund the Contra activities.

The first serious initiative for peace in Nicaragua was taken by neighbouring Costa Rica's president, **Oscar Arias Sánchez**. The Arias Plan for peace in Central America, launched in February 1987, had the backing of the US and was signed by the presidents of five Central American republics. An initiative to stop conflict within Nicaragua and El Salvador, and to repair relations between Nicaragua and Honduras, the Plan was welcomed as the first serious attempt to solve by diplomatic means the political problems between nations in the region. In March 1988 the FSLN and the Contras signed a ceasefire agreement.

1990–1996: The Chamorro government

The **elections** scheduled for February 1990 were to be a test for the Sandinistas' staying power as a political force: opposition was gathering strength and in 1989 no fewer than fourteen political parties, with nothing in common except their opposition to the leftists, formed a coalition, the **National Opposition Union** (Unión Nacional Opositora, **UNO**), and appointed Violeta Barrios de Chamorro, then-publisher of *La Prensa*, as their presidential candidate. Head of a coalition of opposition forces that had the support of the US government and Nicaraguans living in Miami, **Doña Violeta**, as she is known in Nicaragua, had all the ingredients of a leader.

Ortega ran again for the Sandinistas, who adopted an anti-US stance, condemning the UNO as a puppet of US foreign policy. The UNO was fractured and disorganized, fighting what seemed to be, at least on the surface, a less charismatic campaign, which concentrated on promises of peace and reviving the national economy.

The international community and neighbouring Central American countries watched the elections carefully, expecting the Sandinista organizational know-how and showmanship to win through. Perhaps no one was more deeply shocked than Daniel Ortega when on February 25, 1990, Violeta Barrios de Chamorro emerged victorious with 55 percent of the vote against Ortega's 41 percent. Death had hit at nearly every family, and many people felt the Sandinistas had brought further hardship on the country by inviting the scrutiny of the US and the subsequent blockade. One way or another, Nicaraguans had decided it was time for a change.

Although there were extreme right-wing forces in her coalition, Violeta was seen as an acceptable moderate and with Chamorro's election victory came peace: the US lifted their embargo and cut off supplies to the Contras. After some delay, both sides were disarmed and plans were drawn up to re-integrate soldiers into society, a process that later came to grief as small bands of Contras and Sandinistas re-armed to fight for better conditions for veterans.

However you feel about their politics, the **achievements** of the Sandinistas were enormous. When they took over after Somoza's departure, about sixty percent of Nicaragua's population was illiterate. Literacy workers were dispatched to every corner of the country, armed only with a chalkboard and a gas lamp, and by the end of the Sandinista years the figure had been reduced to thirteen percent. They also transformed the role of women: several women led battalions into combat during the Revolution, and women made up about twenty percent of soldiers in the Sandinista army. Because the war effort ate up around half the national budget for many years, basic programmes in health education and culture were heavily reliant on foreign funding and international volunteers. As a result of this foreign influx, Nicaraguans are generally more aware of what is going on in the rest of the world than other Central Americans of similar background, and display a remarkable cosmopolitanism. In many ways, the Sandinistas effected a near-total transformation of Nicaraguan society.

With Chamorro's victory, the World Bank and the International Monetary Fund began negotiations to relieve Nicaragua's debt burden in exchange for a programme of **economic restructuring**. The honeymoon didn't last long, though, as the country was in a shocking state, the result of a drawn-out war, a crippling US embargo and falling production.

The new government's plan to halt inflation failed and the economic restructuring, without any of the cushioning in place under the Sandinistas, resulted in two paralyzing **general strikes**, which forced the government to alter much of its programme. Violeta Chamorro's inner circle, the members of the cabinet who effectively decided policy, managed to resolve the crisis by working with the Sandinista leadership during the months of the strikes; in doing so, they alienated the extreme right-wing element in the coalition, which wanted to crush Sandinismo once and for all.

To her credit, Violeta Chamorro managed to hold the government together during the six-year term, but during the **1996 election campaign** right-wing forces gathered around the former mayor of Managua, **Arnoldo Alemán**. His party, the Partido Liberal Constitucionalista (PLC), was a splinter group of the larger National Liberal Party (PLN), the political vehicle of Anastasio Somoza. The Sandinistas' chances of defeating the Liberals suffered a blow a year before the election when there was a damaging split in the party. A moderate faction led by ex-Vice President Sergio Ramirez broke away, leaving Sandinista leader Daniel Ortega in charge of the remnants. The result was that Alemán and the PLC won the election – narrowly and controversially – and formed another coalition government, this time more openly committed to the destruction of Sandinismo and more closely aligned with the Catholic Church and the US policy of global integration.

The Alemán government

Many Nicaraguans saw the **Alemán victory** as proof that the counter-revolutionary movement had not only won, but had welcomed Somocismo back into Nicaragua. In addition, many political neutrals were concerned that the Alemán administration would lead to **political cronyism** and **corruption** – failings of which his mayoral administration of Managua was frequently accused.

In 1998, the reputation of FSLN leader Daniel Ortega was severely tested by accusations of rape and sexual abuse made by his stepdaughter Zoilamérica Narvaez. Ortega disappeared from public office to fight the charges – which were never proven, although his stepdaughter continued to accuse him – but later returned to the political fray and began to exercise an even tighter grip over the FSLN. Meanwhile, President Alemán also strengthened his control over the governing PLC party, as allegations of fraud and corruption, along with doubts over his mental stability, began increasingly to be heard.

As if the life of most Nicaraguans was not already hard enough, in October 1998, **Hurricane Mitch** hit the region, causing massive flooding and landslides in central and northern Nicaragua. Many bridges, roads and villages were washed away, 500,000 homes were damaged and some 2500 people were killed. The hurricane also had a devastating impact on agriculture across the country, with widespread crop damage, while many towns were cut off for weeks by the intense flooding and burst rivers. The financial damage, though hard to calculate, ran into billions of dollars.

The new millennium

By the beginning of the new millennium, most statistics rated Nicaragua the second poorest country in the Americas, after Haiti, with two million Nicaraguans living on an income of less than a dollar a day. Foreign donor countries threatened to suspend aid for **post-Hurricane Mitch reconstruction** because of the uncertain distribution of foreign donations. And although the tourist and manufacturing industries showed signs of growth, the economy remained depressed, while two banks, Interbank and Bancafé, collapsed amid scandal and allegations of fraud that tainted both the FSLN and the PLC. As if this were not enough, an **earthquake**, with its epicentre in Laguna de Apoyo, killed six people in Masaya and damaged over 4000 homes; this was followed in October 2000 by persistent rains provoked by **Hurricane Keith**, which caused further widespread damage.

Politically, 2000 also saw some dubious horse-trading between the two leading parties, as the FSLN and the PLC worked together to create a new electoral law that excludes many small political parties from participating in the political process. The new law was put to test in the **municipal elections** in November 2000 when violence flared in parts of the north, as election results were severely delayed, despite it being clear that the Sandinistas had won in many areas, including the prized mayoral seat of Managua.

Support for the Sandinistas was still growing at the beginning of 2001, though the protest vote wasn't quite enough to re-instate the Sandinistas. The winner of the November presidential election was the PLC's **Enrique Bolaños**, a businessman who'd served as Alemán's vice president since 1996. Inaugurated in January 2002, the new president was in office for less than a year when his former boss was finally brought to book. In December of 2002, the National Assembly – with Bolaños leading the way – finally voted to strip Alemán of his immunity from prosecution; a few hours after the vote he was officially charged with defrauding the government of US$100 million.

The whole affair threatened to slide inexorably into farce when, in December 2003, Ortega shocked even the most cynical members of the media, his party and the Nicaraguan people by announcing his intention to form a pact with Alemán. With various US bigwigs openly trying to unite the fractured Liberal party against the Sandinistas in preparation for the 2004 municipal elections, Ortega explained that he and Alemán (of whom the US, unsurprisingly, had completely washed their hands) were uniting against what they considered US intervention. The pact never came to pass and the man who *Newsweek* recently listed as being among the world's "Super-Corrupt" was duly sentenced to twenty years in prison and fined US$17 million dollars.

While Bolaños has consistently made all the right noises about disavowing Alemán's corruption and pledging to clean up the government's act, his term in office has been marked by a steadily worsening economic situation. A central plank of his government's economic policy continues to be the aggressive promotion of **tourism** (currently the country's second largest source of income) and foreign investment, with an ambitious plan to increase visitor numbers to 800,000 by 2006.

Plans are also now in place to finally improve the country's woeful road network. Transport lies at the heart of another possible ray of economic hope: the long talked of **rail link** or "dry canal", between the Pacific and Atlantic coasts. Although the project has been embroiled in controversy from the start it seems that, pending the results of an environmental impact appraisal, work could begin on the project within the next two years. Opposition has been fierce, however, from both environmental and indigenous groups, who maintain such a link would lead to the destruction of natural resources and the obliteration of many indigenous communities.

Whether this international (and internationally funded) trade route will be the answer, or even part of the answer to Nicaragua's crippling economic problems remains to be seen. As do the dubious merits of entering into the proposed **Central American Free Trade Agreement**. Nicaraguan farmers are certainly not looking forward to the prospect of doing battle with subsidised American produce swamping the market. If the prospect of farmers going bankrupt en masse wasn't enough, Bolaños also has his work cut out with the ongoing **coffee crisis**. Revenue per ton of coffee exported from Nicaragua fell by more than forty percent between 1999 and 2000 and with low world prices continuing to put growers out of business, things reached a head in summer 2003 when 5000 unemployed coffee workers marched into Managua. Even the recent IMF/World Bank offer to cancel seventy percent of Nicaragua's external debt under the Highly Indebted Poor Countries Initiative comes with the condition that adherence to the dreaded "structural adjustment" policies will have to continue.

Try telling this to ordinary Nicaraguans, who've seen prices of basic commodities rise significantly over the past year in line with rising costs of fuel. In October 2002, the Nicaraguan Institute of Statistics and Censuses reported that sixty percent of the population (over 3 million people) were living below the poverty line with a million of those in extreme poverty. More than anything, the country's citizens want peace, justice and democracy, yet faced with this grinding poverty, rising unemployment, seemingly endemic corruption, continuing uncertainty over land ownership, increasing US meddling and worsening political instability, these dreams sadly seem more remote than ever.

5.1

Managua and around

Hotter than an oven and crisscrossed by anonymous highways, there can't be a more tourist-unfriendly capital than **MANAGUA**. Less a city in the European sense than a conglomeration of neighbourhoods and commercial districts, Managua offers few sights or cultural experiences of the type you can have in other Central American cities – in fact, most visitors are so disturbed by the lack of street names or any real centre to the city that they get out as fast as they can. Being a tourist in Managua does require some tenacity, but there *are* things to enjoy, and as Nicaragua's largest city and home to a quarter of its population, the city occupies a key position in the nation's economy and psyche.

Set on the southern shore of **Lago de Managua**, the city is low-lying and swampy, the flatness of its setting relieved only by the few eroded volcanoes and volcanic craters a few kilometres inland. It's also home to Nicaragua's few national museums and cultural organizations, most of them in the old **ruined centre**, whose historic cathedral is worth visiting, along with the Palacio Nacional, a museum of Nicaragua's culture and the home of its national library. Still, the reality is that there are few sights of interest, though the good news is that most of the city's modest attractions can be found within a few blocks of each other – an advantage in the draining heat.

Meanwhile, attempts are being made to establish a new commercial centre in the south along the **Carretera a Masaya**, just over the hill of Laguna de Tiscapa. A new Metrocentro shopping centre has opened here, along with hotels, restaurants, bars and cinemas, while the nearby district of **Altamira** boasts an increasing number of elegant restaurants and cafés serving tourists and the city's smart set. Another feature of post-earthquake Managua is the proliferation of *centros comerciales*, mostly low-slung North American–style **shopping malls**, with banks, supermarkets and secure parking.

Even if the city's tourist sights have been given a lick of paint (for the most part paid for by the Dutch, Austrian or Chinese governments), the majority of Managuans are still very poor. This begs a mention only because **street crime** is on the rise, and Managua has developed a reputation as a dangerous city. While Nicaragua remains one of the safest destinations in Central America, gang warfare is an increasing problem in Managua and certain parts of the city (Villa Revolución for example) are stamping grounds for *pandillas*, young thugs who won't think twice about robbing you, foreigner or local. While it's unlikely you'd be hanging around these areas anyway, tourists have also recently been robbed in broad daylight in barrio Martha Quezada so be on your guard. If you're alone it's advisable to take a taxi after dark rather than walking, even for short distances. Be careful also if travelling by private car or taxi on the Carretera Norte; it's advisable to keep your windows rolled up and doors locked.

Some history

Founded as a new capital city by the Spanish in 1858 as a foil to the warring political factions of León and Granada, from the beginning Managua was intended to represent the political middle ground. But the ground itself proved the problem: Managua sits smack on top of no fewer than eleven **seismic faults**, and the ground

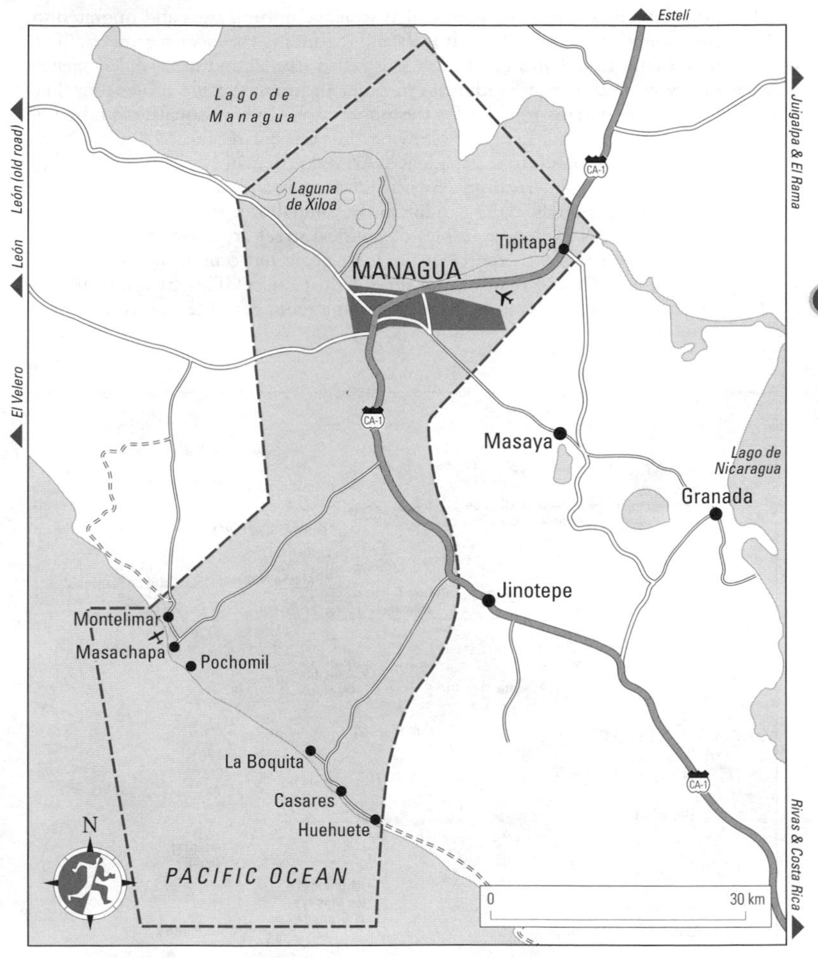

by the lakeshore is sandy and unstable. The earthquake of March 1931 destroyed most of the city, and what Managuans managed to rebuild was largely razed by a fire just five years later. Again the city was rebuilt, with modern commercial buildings of four or five storeys, wide streets, traffic lights and shops, only to be completely devastated by another **earthquake** on December 23, 1972. This one claimed over ten thousand lives and left many more homeless.

For a variety of reasons – the greed of the Somoza dictatorship, who intercepted foreign emergency aid and sold it to victims at inflated prices; the refusal of insurance companies (mostly Somoza-owned) to pay out disaster damages; and the subsequent **1978–79 Revolution** (when fighting caused further damage) – the **old centre** of Managua was never rebuilt. The Sandinista government wanted to rebuild the centre, using donated foreign funds, but this never happened and for many years "downtown" Managua remained a ruined shell of scruffy fields, skeletal ruins and old parking lots turned into graffiti-sprayed basketball courts, while squatters colonized the derelict spaces and constructed makeshift homes among the ruins.

During the Contra War many people fled violence in rural areas and migrated to Managua, creating new **neighbourhoods** and expanding the city's perimeter. (The wealthy still tend to live in neighbourhoods called *repartos* and *residenciales*; *colonias* were largely created by the Sandinistas in order to house specific professions, like teachers, and the barrios tend to be the poorer areas, where squatters and rural migrants try to eke out a living.) Following the war, during the 1990s, the city's mayor – and Nicaragua's future president – Arnoldo Alemán began the process of restoring the old centre, erecting expensive fountains and, unfortunately, having many of the famous murals of the Sandinista era painted over, thereby losing forever some of Latin America's best examples of political street art. Elected president in 1996, Alemán determined to resurrect the long-neglected central district, centred on an opulent new **Casa Presidencial** (Presidential Palace). This arrogant carbuncle is widely detested, and seen by Managuans as a reminder of the greed and mis-

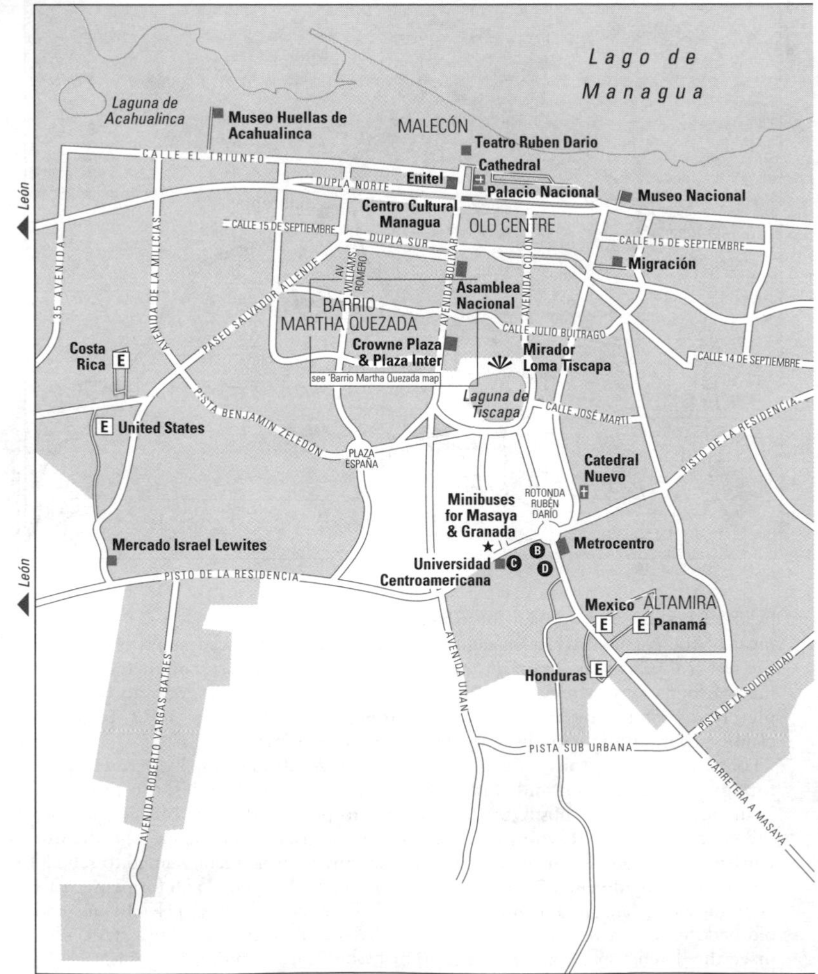

management that plagued them under Alemán's government and which eventually saw the former president jailed on corruption charges. Other parts of the area have also been re-landscaped with new plazas and fountains, though the old centre still lacks focus and few local people spend any time here, except on weekend evenings when they come to watch the music-and-light show in front of the old cathedral.

Arrival and orientation

The majority of travellers arrive in central Managua on the **international** Ticabus services from either Honduras or El Salvador in the north or from San José in Costa Rica to the south. Buses from within Nicaragua arrive at one of several crowded, noisy and generally chaotic **urban marketplaces** that also serve as bus terminals. For **drivers** Managua is a disconcerting city in which to arrive; the lack

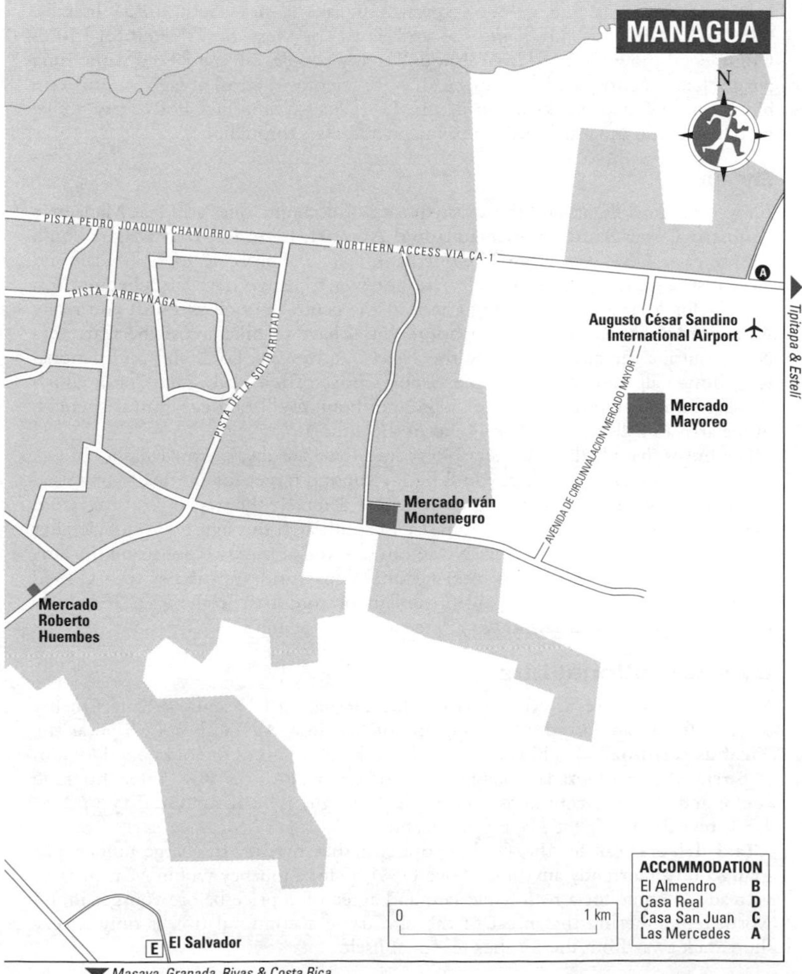

of a definable centre and landmarks – not to mention road signs or directions – makes driving into the city a stressful experience, especially coupled with zealous traffic cops, extensive roadworks and aggressive drivers.

The good news about arriving by air or bus is the abundance of **taxis**. If you know where you are going to stay, it's helpful to have the address given to you in terms of neighbourhood and distance from a well-known **landmark**; no one uses street addresses in Managua, and taxi drivers will find places by its relation to a well-known city fixture. Nevertheless, it's surprising how many taxi drivers are ignorant about the city's hotels and restaurants, especially within the travellers' locus of barrio Martha Quezada. Many taxi drivers haven't even heard of the Barrio itself – an indication of Managua's compartmentalised nature – and you'll have to describe its location, easily enough done by using the *Crowne Plaza* as a reference point. Distances are measured in metres as much as in blocks – in local parlance 100m is a city block or *cuadra*. Sometimes an archaic measure, the *vara*, is also used: one *vara* (a yard) is interpreted as roughly equivalent to a metre. To confuse the issue still further, many Managuans do not use the **cardinal points** in their usual form: in Managua north becomes *al lago* – towards the lake; *al sur* is south; *arriba* – literally, "up", is to the east; and *abajo*, "down", is to the west. So, "del Hotel Inter-Continental (now *Crowne Plaza*, although many people still use its old name) una cuadra [cien metros] arriba y dos cuadras [doscientos metros] al lago" means one block east and two blocks north of the *Hotel Inter-Continental*. For clarity, we've used blocks and the usual cardinal points in addresses throughout.

By air

All international flights and the vast majority of domestic ones arrive at Managua's **Augusto César Sandino International Airport**, 12km east of Managua. You'll have to pay a US$5 **entry fee**. The one bank there, Banpro, changes US dollars and gives cash advances at a reasonable rate but won't change travellers' cheques. You can pay for everything (including a taxi to the centre) in dollars, but if you really want **córdobas**, outside banking hours you'll have to hike across the Carretera Norte outside the airport and try the *Hotel Las Mercedes*. Local and international **telephone** calls can be made at the airport's **post office** (daily 7am–7pm), which also has limited Internet access for US$2 per hour. You'll find **car rental** agencies in the arrivals hall at the northern end of the airport.

The **buses** that ply the Carretera Norte into town are always crowded; should you manage to squeeze onto one, you'll be a tempting target for the many practised thieves operating on Managua's buses – taxis are definitely the way to go. A **taxi** from the arrivals gate into town costs around US$8, although this figure can double after dark; walking out to the Carretera Norte can save you at least two dollars on the fare.

When leaving, note that all international departures are subject to a US$32 **departure tax** that must be paid (in dollars or córdobas) at check-in. If you do leave by air, note also that you won't receive an exit stamp in your passport.

By international bus

Most travellers arrive in Nicaragua on the international Ticabus or King Quality services from San Salvador, Tegucigalpa or San José. All Ticabuses arrive at the **Ticabus terminal** (two blocks east and one block south of the old Cine Dorado) in barrio Martha Quezada, a neighbourhood just west of the Plaza Inter shopping centre and about as central as you get in Managua. The **King Quality** (☎228-1454) **terminal** is directly opposite Ticabus.

Taxi drivers wait for the Ticabus to arrive; they may try to charge innocents a **gringo fare** (currently anything above US$1.50 for a journey within Managua), so be ready to argue for a reasonable fare and agree on a price before you get in. It's worth remembering that most of the affordable accommodation is only a very short walk away from the Ticabus terminal itself.

By domestic bus

Buses from elsewhere in Nicaragua arrive at one of three city markets. Coming from Masaya, Granada, Rivas or other destinations in the **south**, you'll arrive at the **Mercado Roberto Huembes** near the Carretera Masaya on the southeastern edge of the city. A **taxi** from here to the centre should cost around US$2. Regular **express minivans** also run to and from Masaya and Granada from a small unmarked terminal on the highway opposite La UCA – all city taxi drivers will know how to find this terminal. Buses from the **north** and **east** – Estelí, Matagalpa, Jinotega, Ocotal, Somoto, Boaco, Chontales, San Carlos and El Rama – arrive at the terminal in the **Mercado Mayoreo** in barrio Concepción, near the airport. Buses from the **northwest** towns of León and Chinandega use the busy **Mercado Israel Lewites** in the southwest of the capital. No matter which market you arrive at, keep an eye on your belongings, especially at night. **Taxis** from Mayoreo to the centre will cost about US$2–3.

Information

The only place in Managua equipped to provide information is Managua's **Intur** office, one block west of the *Crowne Plaza* (Mon–Fri 8.30am–12.30pm & 1.30–5pm; ☎222-3333, ⓔpromocion@intur.gob.ni). Taxis will know it as the Ministerio de Turismo or, more simply, as the Turismo. If there's no one there, ask the security guard at the corner entrance to phone for you and someone will come and open the door. The staff are well-intentioned and some speak English, although they don't have much in the way of hand-outs. It's worth buying the excellent city map of Managua (US$2.50) from them, if available. You should also be able to pick up a copy of the free quarterly English-language magazine *Between The Waves* (also available in Managua's embassies and at selected hotels, restaurants, tourist offices, travel agencies and airports throughout Nicaragua), which has well-written features on travel, history, business and tourist activities as well as news, mini-guides for various towns and cities, and selected transport schedules.

City transport

Managua's heat and incoherent layout make it a disconcerting city for travellers to negotiate, and some form of transport is essential. **Buses** are the cheapest way to get around, but the abundant **taxis** are more straightforward to use and safer, particularly at night.

Buses

If your confidence and Spanish are up to it, it's worth taking the **bus** at least once, for an insight into how most Managuans live. While the bus service is incredibly **cheap** (US$0.20) and fairly comprehensive, the amazing crowdedness and notorious **pickpockets** – the two are obviously related – are a real deterrent. The crush makes it hard to avoid theft; keeping your money in an inside pocket or clutching your bag on your front are wise precautions, and avoid the rear of the bus if possible. A lack of bus route maps, signed bus stops, or destinations marked on the bus itself – buses are labelled only with numbers – make anything other than a simple trip hopelessly confusing. However, locals know the routes, and will help you find the right stop. You also need to signal to the bus to stop or it'll go flying past. It's also a good idea to have your money to hand before getting on. Services start at 5am and continue until 10pm, becoming less frequent from about 6pm onwards. For a rundown of the main city bus routes, see the box overleaf.

Useful bus routes

#108 Reparto Schick – Primavera
Carretera Norte, Migración, Mercado Oriental, Nueva Rotunda Santo Domingo, Máximo Jeréz, Altamira D'Este, Rotonda Centroamérica, Centro Comercial Managua, Mercado Huembes.

#109 Hospital Lenin Fonseca – Reparto Schick
Malecón, Teatro Nacional Rubén Darío, Centro Cultural, Palacio Nacional, Plaza Inter, Crowne Plaza, Hospital Bautista, Residencial El Dorado, Mercado Huembes.

#110 Seminario Nacional – Mercado Mayoreo
Las Piedrecitas, Siete Sur, Mercado Israel Lewites, UCA (Universidad Centroamericana), Rotonda Rubén Darío, Rotonda Santo Domingo, Altamira, Centro Comercial Managua, Mercado Huembes, Mercado Iván Montenegro.

#112 Centro Civico – Villa Libertad
Mercado Israel Lewites, Siete Sur, Las Piedrecitas, Museo Huellas de Acahualinca, Malecón, Teatro Nacional Rubén Darío, Carretera Norte, La Prensa, Mercado Iván Montenegro.

#113 Ciudad Sandino – Mercado Oriental
Las Piedrecitas, American Embassy, Montoya Statue, Martha Quezada, Plaza Inter.

#117 Americas II – Rotonda Rubén Darío
Carretera Norte, Mercado Iván Montenegro, Semáforos Rubenia, Mercado Huembes, Rotonda Centroamérica, Rotonda Universitaria, UCA.

#118 Refinería – Los Laureles
Las Piedrecitas, Siete Sur, Mercado Israel Lewites, Rotonda Güegüense/Plaza España, Martha Quezada, Plaza Inter, Ciudad Jardín, Semáforos Rubenia, Mercado Iván Montenegro.

#119 Refinería – Villa San Jacinto
Las Brisas, Linda Vista, Monseñor Lezcano, Rotonda Güegüense/Plaza España, UCA, Metrocentro, Los Robles, British Embassy, Mexican Embassy, Altamira, *Casa del Café*, Rotonda Centroamérica, Colonia Centro América, Mercado Huembes.

Taxis

Managua **taxis** are a plentiful mixture of spanking new imported models, impossibly battered imported models and a few heroic old Ladas that struggle around the city's streets. Taxis with red licence plates are officially registered and locals will tell you that these are safer and more reliable. Generally **cheap**, and with friendly, talkative drivers, they are always in good supply – as a tourist, taxis will honk at you as a matter of course, whether you want one or not. **Sharing** may sometimes save you a bit of money, and you could try flagging down an already occupied taxi if it seems to be going your way (equally, a taxi you're already in is highly likely to take other customers on board during your journey), though drivers will accept an additional passenger only if everyone is headed in vaguely the same direction. Fares are about US$1–1.50 per person, depending on distance. Drivers may be open to negotiation if you are in a group going to the same destination. Always agree on a fare **before** you get in.

Driving

Driving in Managua itself is not recommended. The city can seem like one endless freeway, with no street signs – confidence and a good city map are both essential. Should you get lost and find yourself in one of the various rough parts of the city, roll up your windows and lock the doors, especially at traffic lights. It's not safe to leave your car on the street, but most upscale hotels have secure **car parks**. For exploring outside of Managua, however, a car is a definite bonus; see p.511 for a list of **rental** agencies.

Accommodation

Site of the Ticabus terminal, the **barrio Martha Quezada**, a neighbourhood twelve blocks south of the old ruined city centre and just west of the *Crowne Plaza*, is the place for cheap, hospedaje-type **accommodation**, and also has some of the best hotels and guesthouses in Managua. Directions and addresses in the barrio use the local landmarks of the *Crowne Plaza*, the Ticabus terminal, and the Cine Dorado (now closed), west of the Ticabus terminal. During the Revolution years most foreigners stayed within this eight-by-five-block area and it became something of an international community. These days the barrio is definitely not the buzzing place it used to be, and there's not much to do on the hot, eventless streets except sleep, though there are still a number of good local **cafetines** and **restaurants**.

Accommodation in Martha Quezada is scattered in a two-block radius on either side of the Ticabus terminal. Arriving at the terminal, you will be met by touts, usually children, offering to take you to a hospedaje. They receive a percentage from the hotel owner for bringing people off the Ticabus and there's no harm in going with them, since you're under no obligation to stay if you don't like the hospedaje they take you to. There's no real concentration of hotels **elsewhere in the city**: several upscale airport-type hotels are located on the Carretera Norte near the international airport and near Metrocentro, and there are a few hotels in the residential neighbourhood of Bolonia, immediately south of barrio Martha Quezada. One or two other places can be found near the Universidad Centroamericana (UCA), towards the south of the city.

Barrio Martha Quezada and around

Apartamentos Los Cisneros one block north and one and a half blocks west of Ticabus ⓣ222-3535, ⓕ222-2828, ⓔpriscilacisneros@hotmail.com. The sole upmarket option in the heart of Martha Quezada, offering well appointed, self-contained two-person apartments with fridge, cooker, breakfast bar and optional fan or a/c. ❺

Casa Castillo one block west and one and a half blocks north of Ticabus ⓣ222-2265. Hospitable family-run hospedaje with English-speaking owner. Rooms are basic and rather dowdy but come with private bath; the ones right at the back and upstairs are larger and quieter. ❷

Casa Gabrinma one block south and half a block east of Ticabus ⓣ222-6650. Very welcoming and friendly guesthouse in a peaceful location. The immaculate rooms – all with roof fan – are set around a leafy inner courtyard, several of which are very large and one of which is set up specifically for families with kids. Recommended. ❹

Crowne Plaza formerly *Hotel Inter-Continental*, Av Bolívar ⓣ228-4151. The don of Managua hotels, this place is worth a look even if you can't afford to stay. Inside its Maya-pyramid-style, earthquake-proof walls are suitably luxurious rooms with all the facilities you'd expect, some with balconies offering stunning views of Lago de Managua and Volcán Momotombo. There's also a beauty parlour, several bars and a restaurant, and they'll change travellers' cheques. Rates start at US$140. ❾

Euro one block west and half a block south of Plaza Inter ⓣ222-4045, ⓦwww.hoteleuronic.com. New hotel with lots of varnished wood and gleaming tiles. Cable TV, a/c and hot water come as standard while the cheaper upstairs rooms are actually brighter and better value. There's also a suntrap of a swimming pool out back. Recommended. ❺

Los Felipe one and a half blocks west of Ticabus ⓣ222–6501, ⓔlosfelipe@ideay.net.ni. A world away from Martha Quezada's downtrodden listlessness, this friendly hotel has 27 clean and cute if slightly poky rooms nestled amid an urban jungle of tropical foliage. All come with private bath and TV, and there are Internet and laundry services available as well as a range of tours, a swimming pool and a restaurant. ❹

Hospedaje El Bambú one block east Ticabus (look for the bamboo door). Friendly Marie-Elena and family run a hospedaje with six rather dark rooms with fan and shared bath, set around a pleasant covered patio area. Meals on request. ❸

Hospedaje Quintana one block north and one block west of Ticabus ⓣ254-5487. For many years a popular place among *internacionalistas*, this spotlessly clean, family-run hospedaje has big rooms with fans, sturdy beds and zinc roofs. Some are windowless, so look before choosing. Laundry service available. They also run a slightly more expensive option around the corner with cooler, brighter rooms. ❷

Hospedaje Santos one block north and one and a half blocks west of Ticabus ⓣ222-3713. Sprawling, ramshackle hospedaje popular among travellers, with tons of atmosphere, funky art on the walls and an indoor patio with cable TV. Rooms, however, are dark and none too clean – try to get one upstairs, where ventilation is better. All have ceiling fan, and some come with private bath. ❷

Mansión Teodolinda one block south and one block west of the Intur office ⓣ228-1050, ⓦwww.teodolinda.com.ni. Sixty years of history lend this hotel a definite character. With their vintage wood-panelled ceilings, the self-contained rooms (which all come with built-in kitchen facilities) have a distinct 60s/70s feel. Recommended. ❼

Elsewhere in the city

El Almendro two blocks west and half a block south of Rotonda Rubén Darío ⓣ270-1260, ⓦwww.hotelelalmendro.com. Secluded behind high red-brick walls, this tranquil hotel offers lovely, bright, fresh a/c rooms with private bath, cable TV and tiled breakfast bar. Continental breakfast included. ❼

Casa de Huéspedes Sáenz Planes de Altamira #3, Carretera a Masaya, Altamira, one block from the *Hotel Princess* next to *La Piazzetta* restaurant ⓣ277-3733. Family-run guesthouse with spacious, clean rooms with TV, a/c, desk and private bath grouped around a leafy inner lounge with huge hammock. Special rates available for rentals longer than a month. Breakfast included. Reservations advisable. ❻

Casa Real two blocks west, two blocks south and half a block east of Rotonda Rubén Darío ⓣ278-3838, ⓦwww.hcasareal.com. Picturesque, mock-colonial hotel in quiet residential area with creeper-clad walls, colonnaded patio and peaceful, carpeted rooms with a/c, hot water, cable TV and the rare luxury of a hot tub. Breakfast is included and the staff is multilingual. ❽

Casa San Juan C Esperanza 560, behind the Universidad Centroamericana – known locally as "La UCA" ⓣ278-3220, ⓔsanjuan@cablenet.com. Welcoming mid-range guesthouse in a quiet neighbourhood. The spacious rooms, often rented by students, come with a/c, cable TV and private bath. Breakfast is included and other meals are available with advance notice. The hotel is popular, especially in January and August, so reserve in advance. ❺

Las Mercedes Km 11, Carretera Norte, opposite the airport ⓣ263-1011, ⓦwww.lasmercedes.com.ni. *Best Western* hotel catering for business travellers – the airport location makes it a useful stop if you're arriving late or leaving early. The comfortable, semi-detached cabin-style rooms have wooden ceilings and floors with TV, a/c and bath, and there's a reasonable on-site restaurant, plus bar, tourist information office, Internet access, laundry, tennis courts and swimming pool. ❽

The City

For the visitor, sprawling Managua can be thankfully divided into a few distinct areas. The **old ruined centre** on the lakeshore is the site of the city's tourist attractions, such as they are, including the few impressive colonial-style buildings that survived the 1931 and 1972 earthquakes, like the slowly decaying old municipal **cathedral** and the magnificently restored **Palacio Nacional**. **Lago de Managua**, which forms such a pretty backdrop to the old centre, is severely **polluted** from raw sewage and regular dumpings of garbage, chemical waste and mercury. The air doesn't seem any cleaner; winds from the lake blow dust around the city and old buses and taxis belch fumes into an increasingly crowded city.

Twelve blocks south from the old centre, most of Managua's hospedajes and restaurants are clustered in the **barrio Martha Quezada**. Just to the east, but

visible from everywhere, is the city's main landmark, the **Crowne Plaza**, formerly the **Hotel Inter-Continental** (not to be confused with the new *Inter-Continental Metrocentro* hotel at the Metrocentro shopping mall in the south of the city), whose white form, reminiscent of a Maya pyramid, sails above the city – it's about 1km south of the ruined old city centre, though you'll probably end up passing by it anyway as it stands at the junction of Av Bolívar, which runs north–south from the lake to Plaza España, and C Julio Buitrago, a major east–west thoroughfare. Many of the city's banks, airline offices and the well-stocked La Colonia supermarket can be found a further 2km south, around **Plaza España**. To the southeast of the city, a new commercial district has grown up along the **Carretera a Masaya** between the **Metrocentro** shopping centre and the upmarket suburb of **Altamira**.

The old centre

Most of Managua's "sights" are concentrated in the **old city centre**, completely levelled in the 1972 earthquake and until recently a haunting maze of fields, the concrete skeletons of buildings, burnt-out cars and impromptu basketball courts. Much of the old centre is now under redevelopment, with new plazas and monuments being constructed, and fairground rides and places to eat and drink springing up along the lake's edge. If you don't mind the heat, you can walk the twelve blocks from barrio Martha Quezada to the old centre, or take bus #109 north from the corner of Av Bolívar and C Julio Buitrago.

Plaza de la República

The centrepiece of the old centre is the recently renovated **Plaza de la República**. On the eastern side of the square stands the wrecked ash-grey Catedral Santiago de los Caballeros, known as the **Catedral Viejo**, an eerie monument to a destroyed city. Funds donated from foreign governments have enabled the cathedral to be re-roofed with a transparent fibreglass cap, and for cut stone to be laid on the formerly grass floor. Inside, birds fly through the ruined interior, where semi-exposed murals still line the walls, as do leaning stone angels and saints, some of them with their wings cracked. Though the cathedral is officially closed to visitors, the guard will usually allow you in for a few córdobas (a small extra payment is required to take photos). There's a colourful **music and choreographed fountain** display in front of the cathedral daily at 6pm – it's particularly popular at weekends when families, young couples and a large portion of Managua's street traders descend on the normally empty plaza. A newly erected, concrete **memorial** to FSLN founder **Carlos Fonseca** faces the cathedral from across the street, graced with a seemingly endless supply of fresh bouquets and fringed by a row of huge black and red flags.

Since its blue marble and cream stucco renovation it's hard to believe that the **Palacio Nacional** (Mon–Fri 8am–5pm, Sat & Sun 9am–4pm; US$2), next to the cathedral, was the scene of a cinematic **coup d'état**. On August 22, 1978, Sandinista commandos disguised as National Guard soldiers ran through these cool corridors and, in an audacious operation, captured the deputies of the National Assembly, effectively bringing to an end the rule of the dictator Somoza. This columned building was the seat of power during the long years of Somoza rule: the Colombian writer Gabriel García Márquez called it *el partenón bananero* – the banana parthenon. The Palacio is still a functioning government building but has had much of its interior turned into a **museum and art gallery**. Many of its walls are covered with colourful murals by foreign artists that run the gamut from Mexican Arnold Belkin's socialist-realist depiction of the Mexican and Nicaraguan revolutions to Russian surrealism. As well as rooms showing dark and derivative religious paintings, there is also a good display of Nicaraguan handicrafts, plus a few pre-Columbian artefacts. English-speaking guides are available. Upstairs is the new home of the **Rubén Darío National Library**, which has been beautifully furnished and decorated with funds donated by the government of China.

To the southwest of the Palacio National is a distinctive green building housing the **Centro Cultural Managua** (☎228-1006). The former home of the Gran Hotel, the low-slung, mock-colonial structure gives you a bit of an idea of how pre-earthquake Managua looked. The downstairs area hosts sporadic exhibitions and seminars, including the **Sábado de Artesanía**, a craft fair held on the first Saturday of each month. Prices are higher than in the outdoor Mercado Roberto Huembes (see p.511), but lower than in the *galerías* and art shops. The centre's upper floors house many of the country's arts organizations and it's worth going upstairs just to see the **historic photographs** lining the corridor. Some show Managua before the 1972 earthquake, an attractive city of palm trees and some colonial architecture; others, taken immediately following the quake, show crumpled buildings, crushed cars and gaping holes in the road – a sobering juxtaposition.

Sadly, the plaza's north side is home to the upstart salmon-and-mustard eyesore of the **Casa Presidencial**, finished in 2000. Constructed against the advice of eminent seismologists, the building is an unflattering monument to the style and substance of Arnoldo Alemán's vainglorious and corrupt presidency, and a pale imitation of the far more arresting Palacio Nacional opposite, whose style it apes, but singularly fails to match.

The lakefront

Perched like a huge white futurist bird 200m north of the Plaza de la República, near the swampy shores of Lago de Managua, is the **Teatro Nacional Rubén Darío**, Managua's main cultural venue. Foreign orchestras and dance troupes on tour perform here, along with Nicaraguan theatre groups. Check *La Prensa* or the window by the theatre's ticket booth for details of forthcoming events. If the building is open, it's worth going inside to see the massive chandeliers, marble floors and the stirring view out to the lake from the enormous second-floor windows. South of the theatre is the **Monumento a Rubén Darío**, a striking sculpted memorial to the iconic poet, restored in 1997. North of the theatre, a determined attempt has been made to transform the lakeshore boardwalk, or **Malecón**, with bars and food kiosks, plus a Ferris wheel and a couple of fairground rides. A well-maintained statue of Latin American liberator **Simón Bolívar**, sits in the middle of the nearby roundabout, guarding the shorefront's entrance. The area gets quite lively at weekends, though it's fairly deserted during the week except for stray kissing teenage couples. Just south of the Malecón is the vast **Plaza de la Fe Juan Pablo II**, a square whose central obelisk commemorates Pope John Paul II's two visits to Nicaragua. Like the Malecón, the plaza is rarely busy, and is also one of the fiercest suntraps in the city, though it looks better at night when floodlighting adds some definition to its vast expanse.

There are pleasant views to the north from the Malecón, where **Volcán Mombotombo** and little **Mombotombito** sit side by side against the horizon on the far shore of the lake, 50km away. Mombotombo's capacity for destruction is evoked in the **Museo Huellas de Acahualinca** (Mon–Fri 8am–5pm, Sat 9am–4pm; US$2), just west of the Malecón in barrio Acahualinca (take a taxi or bus #112), a rudimentary and under-funded affair but still worth a look for a glimpse into Managua's prehistory. On display are animal and human footprints from prehistoric nomads – preserved in volcanic ash, the footprints date back between 6000 and 10,000 years.

South of the old centre

Behind the *Crowne Plaza*, a path winds upwards to the **Laguna de Tiscapa**, a small and unremarkable lake in the centre of the city. The views of the city are excellent, however, stretching north to Lago de Nicaragua and the distant volcanoes and south beyond the new cathedral towards Masaya. The area around Laguna de Tiscapa is loaded with historical importance: the presidential palace used to be situated here and the large, silhouetted statue of Sandino marks the spot of the revolutionary leader's assassination. The Somoza regime also built torture chambers near the lake.

About 1km south of the laguna is Managua's biggest concentration of residential and commercial neighbourhoods. The main thoroughfare through this southern part of the city is the **Carretera a Masaya**, bordered to the west by the university area and to the east by residential and shopping districts; this is also where you'll find the **Metrocentro** shopping centre, which boasts shops, a food court, banks, a modern cinema and the *Inter-Continental Metrocentro* hotel. A short walk from Metrocentro, in the middle of a field, is the Catedral Metropolitana de la Purísima Concepción, known simply as the **Catedral Nueva**, a remarkably unorthodox piece of architecture whose roof resembles a collection of large concrete hand-grenades. The interior is rather stark, with a bleeding figure of Christ encased in glass being the only interesting feature.

A further 1km south from the Metrocentro along Carretera a Masaya is the embassy neighbourhood of **Altamira**, the focus for new commercial and hotel construction in the city, which has a number of hotels, cafés, Internet cafés and a good selection of international restaurants popular with the district's expat residents. A kilometre or so west of the Metrocentro, meanwhile, is the campus of the Universidad Centroamericana, or **La UCA**, as it's generally known, a tranquil place by Managuan standards (save for the annual student protests in December, when you'd be better off avoiding the whole, tear-gas-saturated area).

Eating and drinking

Wherever you walk in Managua – on the street, at the bus stop or even under a shady tree – you will find someone selling a drink or a *comida corriente*. Good, cheap food on the hoof is also easy to get in any of Managua's major **markets** – look out for *pupusas*, a Salvadorean concoction of cheese, tortillas, sauce and meat. You can also fill up on greasy, delicious food from any of the eateries down on Managua's **Malecón**. Hygienically speaking, the food is safe to eat, and you can get a decent meal for as little as a dollar. Managua also has a surprisingly cosmopolitan selection of **restaurants**: Chinese, Spanish, Mexican, Japanese, Italian, Peruvian, North American – even vegetarian. **Cafés** are thin on the ground, though, and the ones that do exist tend to be frequented by expats and wealthier Managuans.

Barrio Maria Quezada and around

Ananda next to the Montoya statue: from the Cine Dorado walk two blocks towards the lake then eight blocks west. An excellent vegetarian restaurant set around a covered patio and garden, this place is a veritable oasis amid Managua's concrete chaos. There's a varied menu including a good-value *plato del día*, reasonably priced fresh juices, nice bread and superb papaya milkshakes. A meal plus drink will cost you around US$3–4. Closed Mon.

Las Anclas one block north of Ticabus, opposite the *Quintana Anexo*. Friendly, family-run restaurant with bench-style tables and a good value, versatile menu featuring seafood and Nica favourites. They serve up one of the best plates of *gallo pinto*, tortillas, egg and cheese in the city.

Cactus Av Bolívar, opposite *Crowne Plaza* ⓣ 222-5256. Huge, Mexican-themed restaurant serving authentic cuisine. The service is good, and the tortilla soup comes highly recommended, as does the mouthwatering salsa served in little dishes on the side. Credit cards accepted but watch out for a hefty tax on your bill. Closed Mon and Tues.

Café Tonallí two blocks east and half a block south of Ticabus. Principally a bakery selling whole-wheat and specialist breads, and run by a women's co-op for the past decade, this wonderful little retreat has a few tables in its leafy garden where you can enjoy healthy dishes like veggie lasagne and pesto. It's also a great breakfast option with muesli, fruit, yoghurt, fresh coffee and croissants baked on the premises. Daily 7am–3pm. Closed Sun.

Las Cazuelas opposite *Hospedaje Santos*. Little restaurant with a nice atmosphere, red checked tablecloths and a huge menu serving local and international cuisine in the heart of barrio Martha Quezada. A meal will set you back around US$4–6. Its upmarket sister branch across the street, *Mariscos Las Cazuelas* (ⓣ 228-6090), deals primarily in pricey seafood although if your stomach's up for it, you can dine on brain and bull's balls soup for a mere US$4.

Comida Sara's opposite *Hospedaje Santos*. Despite the dilapidated exterior, *Sara's* is great for huge, dirt cheap (US$1–2) servings of simple, filling food; veggie soups and curries are best.

Mirna's one block west and south of the Ticabus terminal. Popular both with locals and travellers staying in barrio Martha Quezada, this small, family-run place has become something of an institution. They're open from 6.30am for típica or gringo breakfasts (7am on Sundays) and you can tuck into the *comida casera* buffet (US$2) from noon until 3pm.

Restaurante Corona de Oro three blocks south of the *Crowne Plaza* ⓣ 268-2263. The newly opened Managua branch of this Chinandega institution, with friendly, English speaking management and the kind of quality Chinese food they're already justly famous for up north. Chicken and meat dishes come in at around US$7, seafood double that price. Delivery service available.

Rincón Espanol one block west of Los Bomberos del Estadio ⓣ 266-3851. Catalan-owned restaurant that has been catering to upper class Managuans for nigh on five decades. The Spanish food is expensive (at around US$20, still within the range of most gringo pockets) but faultless while the service is almost embarrassingly attentive.

Altamira and around

El Astillero opposite *Valenti's Pizza*. Decent seafood restaurant with good selection of *ceviche* and other Peruvian delicacies such as *lomo saltado*; a main meal will set you back US$6–10. Also puts on regular live-music and promotional evenings.

Casa del Café one and a half blocks south from Monte de Los Olivos. If you can fight your way past the fleet of gleaming 4WDs parked outside, you'll find a boisterous crowd of wealthy Managuans and the odd traveller sipping coffee in this huge, chalet-style building dating from the 1850s. As well as wonderful cakes and pies – the *pastel de limón* is delicious – and the best coffee in town, they also serve gourmet sandwiches and soups (try the onion with Gruyère cheese) for US$3–4. You can buy Nicaraguan export-grade coffee and glossy magazines (in Spanish) downstairs.

Cocina de Doña Haydée Km 4, Carretera a Masaya, near the British Embassy (ⓣ 270-6160) and 250m east of Rotonda de Bello Horizonte (ⓣ 249-5494). Peerless *comida típica* served in a polished, upscale environment has given these two restaurants an enduring reputation, not least among expats. Despite the reputation, you can still order a full meal with dessert (don't miss the *Tres Leches)* and drinks for under US$10.

Don Pan one and a half blocks south of Monte de Los Olivos. The most renowned bakery in town with a modern café in front where you can enjoy their mouthwatering selection of croissants, pastries, banana breads and other sweet treats as well as fresh coffee, sandwiches, veggie tortillas and lentil soup. There's also a branch at Km 4 Carretera Norte.

La Hora del Taco one block north from Monte de Los Olivos, Los Robles ⓣ 277-5074. Stylish mid-range Mexican where you can eat traditional dishes like *mole* from funky, leather-topped tables. There's also a nice open-fronted upper level with a balcony and some great old photos of Pancho Villa and his compadres.

Il Borgo Antico one block south and 75m west of Rotonda Rubén Darío ☎277-5875. With its peaceful, secluded courtyard setting, hand-built, wood-burning pizza oven and authentic cuisine prepared by the owner's Italian mother-in-law, this friendly restaurant is probably the best of its kind in Managua. The menu features three different types of bruschetta, delicious Italian soups and an extensive, imaginative range of pizzas and pastas. A good feed with wine should set you back about US$15–20.

Paladar Colonia Los Robles, one and a half blocks east of *Hotel Colón*. Run by the same family which runs *La Sazón* and with a matching reputation, this is a slightly more stylish, upmarket version of its younger sister branch with similar opening hours. A meal costs a dollar or two more but the traditional home-style cooking is just as delicious and their *refrescos* are among the best in Managua; try the *Chia Tamarindo*.

Pizzeria Valenti's one block east of *Domino's Pizza*, house no. 6 ☎277-5744. The outside patio, an ice-cold mug of draught beer and one of Valenti's excellent thin-crust pizzas make this unpretentious place one of the best in Managua. It's also good value considering the area: a pizza and a beer will cost about US$5.

La Sazón two blocks west of Rotonda Rubén Darío. Packed with nearby office workers at lunchtime, this buffet-style eatery does some of the best *comida casera* in the city. A heaped plate with drinks will set you back less than US$4, but leave room for the delicious rice pudding, sold in little plastic cups. Mon–Fri 8.30am–2.30pm.

Sushi Itto Plaza Familiar No.11 & 12, Km 7.5 Carretera a Masaya ☎278-4886. It's a bit of a hike from town (you'll have to take a taxi unless you fancy walking along a motorway) but Nicaragua's very first sushi joint is already attracting a dedicated clientele. The extensive menu features both national and imported varieties for around US$1–2 a piece, as well as tempura and other Japanese staples.

Tre Fratelli Km 4.5 Carretera a Masaya ☎278-3334. Newly opened Managua branch of this San Francisco-based chain, specialising in California-influenced Italian fare. While a full meal with good Chilean wine will set you back US$15–20, the servings are huge, the service is attentive and the food (including gorgeous homemade bread) is delicious.

Nightlife and entertainment

Managua's nightlife has been given a shot in the arm with the return of some of the **"Miami Boys"**, businessmen and influential families who had fled revolutionary Nicaragua to settle in Miami. They've helped drive the demand for the new generation of upmarket bars, restaurants and discos which make up the new Zona Rosa nightlife hub, and unsurprisingly many of Managua's nightclubs are filled with the young and reckless teenagers of the Nica rich. Others have grandmothers and adolescents dancing to the same music. Most Nicas are fans of either rancho music (not unlike "country" – fairly unsophisticated and raucous) or merengue, but you can also hear plenty of salsa, disco and occasionally reggae. Women generally don't go out dancing without a male escort as it can be dangerous on the street at night. Beware of overcharging in the shadier places; while there have been reports of travellers being stung with outrageous bills and ending up in jail for non-payment, all the venues listed here should be OK.

Cinema is a popular diversion for rich Nicas and the large foreign population in Managua – at US$3 and up, most other Managuans can't afford the price of a ticket. There's a four-screen Cinemark complex in the Metrocentro shopping mall showing the latest Hollywood movies, usually in English with Spanish subtitles. Similar films can be found at the modern cinema complex in the Plaza Inter. The **theatre** scene in Nicaragua is small but active, and is particularly strong in children's theatre, puppetry and folk dancing – good news for non-Spanish speakers – while adult theatre tends toward the Brechtian style that has been such a dynamic part of the theatre tradition throughout Latin America. The nation's main venue is the **Teatro Nacional Rubén Darío**, recognized as one of the best theatres in Central America, with a main auditorium seating 1200 people, an exhibition space on the second floor, and an experimental theatre in the basement. Events are scheduled there most weekends and it's easy to get to, with bus #109 stopping right in front. Check the listings in *La Prensa* for details of performances.

Bar Shannon 50m from *Hospedaje El Bambú*. Established Irish-owned bar in the heart of barrio Martha Quezada. The clientele is a good mix of locals and travellers, and though you can't always bank on getting a Guinness they do sell London Pride. The owner can direct you to the popular late-night drinking and dancing spots on the fast-changing Managuan scene.

La Casa de Los Mejía Godoy Colonia Los Robles, two and a half blocks south of Shell Plaza el Sol, No.186 ⓣ270-4928. The brainchild of the famous Nicaraguan guitar-playing and songwriting brothers, Luis Enrique and Carlos Mejía Godoy, this is a cultural centre and bar rolled into one. Along with the live music, there's an art gallery, CD and bookstore to browse as well as a café-bar selling *comida típica*. One Wednesday a month, the bar plays host to traditional marimba sounds, young local musicians play on Thursday nights, and the brothers themselves normally perform on Friday and Saturday nights. Closed Sun and Mon.

La Cavanga on the northeast corner of the Centro Cultural Managua. A microcosm of Nicaraguan culture, this little bar plays traditional Nicaraguan music and is decorated with black and white photos of Old Managua and a few paintings by Ernesto Cardenal. It's one of the best bars in Managua, packed in the early evening with government workers and students.

Chamán half a block east of *Inter-Continental Metrocentro* hotel. One of Managua's clubs of the moment, catering to a younger crowd and with an emphasis on rock and alternative sounds as well as a bit of reggae and salsa. There's regular live music and the occasional rock-centric talent contests are worth a look. Cover charge is US$3/4 with one free drink.

Hipa Hipa Plaza Coconut Grove, half a block west and two blocks south of Distribuidora Vicky. Trendy club with three dancefloors which are regularly packed on weekends with a young, hedonistic crowd – including a good few gringos – grooving to salsa, merengue, hip hop, techno and *perreo*, a ragga-derived hybrid with a steamy Caribbean dance style to match. Cover charge is pricey at US$10.

Island's Taste two blocks east of Siemens, Km 6, Carretera Norte. The best Afro-Caribbean music venue and one of the best nights out in Managua, *Island's Taste* has a family ambiance, with kids and grandparents getting up for a dance. The fired chicken and cheap beer are a bonus. US$5 cover.

Jaro Kafé Cultural two and a half blocks south of the *Crowne Plaza*. Hip, hangar-like bohemian hangout with regular free live music and all-round quality sounds incorporating salsa, reggae, Brazilian, hip hop, rock, jazz and world music.

Monoloko 50 metres south of the Intur office. New rock-themed bar on the fringes of Martha Quezada, decked out with portraits of The Beatles, Hendrix, The Rolling Stones and, rather improbably, Oasis, with a soundtrack to match. On the food front, the speciality is Cocktail "*Vuelve A La Vida*" (Back To Life), a mix of squid, crab, oyster, shrimp and octopus.

El Quetzal in Col Centroamérica, in front of Registros Públicos. A barn-like, 70s-style dance joint complete with period mirrorballs where everybody gets up and dances into the small hours. Firmly off the tourist trail, with a neighbourhood atmosphere, cheap and filling Nicaraguan food and hot live salsa bands.

Ruta Maya 150m east from the Montoya statue ⓣ222-5038. Another cultural centre cum bar which plays host to a diverse cross-section of the city's musical and artistic talent and tends to attract an older, more sophisticated crowd. Seating is outdoors under a big marquee and traditional Nica food is also available. Gig tickets are usually priced in the US$3–4 range.

Shopping and markets

Managua's best shopping is to be found in its characterful and varied **markets**. The **Mercado de Mayoreo** in barrio La Concepción, near the airport, is divided into separate areas or buildings for different types of produce: onions, lettuces, seafood, eggs, chickens, plantains and so on, and you can get a cheap meal at the market café while waiting to board buses heading north. In contrast, the infamous **Mercado Oriental**, a few blocks southeast of the old centre, is a small, lawless city-within-a-city where you can buy just about anything, but need to keep a close eye on your pockets and an even closer eye on your back – any Nicaraguan will tell you that this is one of the most crime-ridden and dangerous places in the country. If you must go, take someone with you to watch your back and help carry your stuff. In the streets around the entrance to the market are several shops selling furniture and electrical goods. If you can carry it, it's worth buying a rocking chair here: beautifully made, they cost around US$25, and can be bought disassembled for carrying onto the plane.

Near the Carretera a Masaya in the south of the city, the **Mercado Roberto Huembes** is somewhat safer to wander around than the Oriental and has an excellent crafts section. You can find rocking chairs here, too, and some of the best hammocks in the world – everything from a simple net hammock, lightweight and perfect for the beach (US$5), to a luxury, two-person, woven cotton hammock with wooden separators and beautiful tassels (US$35). Products made of leather and skins are in abundance, but choose carefully as many of the species used are endangered. Traditional clothing is cheap, finely embroidered and perfect for the tropics. **Paintings** in the style of the artists' colony on the Solentiname Islands are available here, along with many fine pen-and-ink drawings and abstract works. You can buy Nicaraguan cigars (*puros*) as well as wicker products (*mimbre*) such as baskets, mats, chairs and wall hangings. Many of these crafts are produced using methods dating back to pre-Columbian times.

Markets apart, in these post-revolutionary days you can buy anything you want in Managua, and there are now plenty of large **supermarkets** along the Carretera Norte; the well-stocked La Colonia chain sells the largest selection of local and imported food including organic produce. You can also buy a lot of the basics at local *pulperías*, small shops set up in people's houses, which are never more than a couple of blocks away. **Fruit** and **vegetables** are cheapest at the weekend markets, when the growers come into town to sell their produce. Fresh produce tends to be more expensive elsewhere, unless you go to some of the bigger markets like the Oriental and the Mayoreo.

Listings

Airlines Air France, two and half blocks south of Rotonda Güegüense ⓣ266-2612 or 266-6615; Alitalia, four blocks west of Aval Card ⓣ266-6997; American Airlines, 250 metres south of Plaza España ⓣ266-3900; British Airways, in front of the old Hospital El Retiro ⓣ266-8268; Continental, Ofiplaza El Retiro Edificio no. 5, Suite 521 ⓣ278-7033 or 278-2836; Copa, Km 4.5, Carretera a Masaya, next to *La Piazzeta*, Edificio Carr ⓣ267-1894; GrupoTaca, Edif. Málaga, Plaza España ⓣ266-3136 or 266-5115; Iberia, Plaza España, Edificio Málaga ⓣ266-4296 or 266-4440; JAL, north side of Plaza España ⓣ266-3588; Lan Chile, four blocks west of Aval Card ⓣ266-6997.

Banks and exchange Central branches that exchange foreign currency include Banpro and Bancentro, both on the Carretera a Masaya near the *Hotel Princess*, and BAC (Banco de América Central), Plaza España. Both Bancentro and BAC offer advances on credit cards and will usually change travellers' cheques. ATMs which accept foreign cards (Visa, MasterCard and Cirrus) can be found by both the aforementioned banks and outside the basement floor of Plaza Inter, as well as in many Shell and Texaco garages and in the airport next to the tiny Banpro booth. The nearest bank to the hospedajes in barrio Martha Quezada is the Banpro, two and half blocks north of the old Cine Dorado.

Bookshops Hispamer, from UCA one block east, one block south and then one block east again. Largest selection of academic, fiction and non-fiction books (in Spanish) in Nicaragua. There's a small shelf of classic and modern English-language fiction, Oxford Uni Press editions designed primarily for English students but handy if you're hard up for something to read. Also sell a selection of mainly classical CDs and stationery.

Car rental Auto Express, two blocks north and twenty metres east of the *Crowne Plaza* ⓣ222-3816; Budget, one block west and one block south of the Montoya statue ⓣ266-6266; Hertz, Km 4, Carretera Sur, Edificio Caribe Motor de Nicaragua ⓣ266-8400 or *Crowne Plaza* ⓣ222-2320; Hyundai, Km 5, Carretera a Masaya ⓣ278-1249; Toyota, Casa Pellas, two blocks west of Gadala Maria ⓣ266-3620.

Embassies and consulates Canada, Calle El Nogal, no. 25, two blocks south of Los Pipitos (Mon–Thurs 9am–noon; ⓣ268-0433, ⓕ268-0437); Costa Rica, two blocks north and one block east of the Montoya statue (Mon–Fri 8am–1.30pm & 2–4pm, Sat 8am–noon; ⓣ266-5719, ⓕ268-7460, ⓔger_zun@yahoo.com); El Salvador, in Las Colinas, Pasaje Los Cerros, Av del Campo, Casa #142 (Mon–Fri 8am–2pm; ⓣ276-2134, ⓕ276-0712, ⓔembelsa@cablenet.com.ni); Guatemala, Km 11.5, Carretera a Masaya (Mon–Fri 9am–1pm; ⓣ279-9834, ⓕ279-9610, ⓔembanic@minex.gob.gt); Honduras, Reparto San Juan, one block south and one block east of Gimnasio Hercules, no. 312 (Mon–Fri 9am–2pm;

Ⓣ278-3043, Ⓕ270-4133); Panamá, Colonia Mántica, one block east of the main fire station, no. 93 (Mon–Fri 8.30am–1pm; Ⓣ266-8633, Ⓕ266-2224); USA, Cancilleria, Km 4.5, Carretera Sur (Mon–Fri 7.30–10am; Ⓣ266-6010 or 266-6012, Ⓕ266-3865).

Immigration office Departamento de Migración y Extranjeria, two blocks north of Los Semáforos de la Colonia Tenderí (Mon–Fri 8am–noon & 2–4pm; Ⓣ244-3989, Ⓕ249-2981).

Internet access *Internet Pioneer*, Level 3, Plaza Inter (US$2/hr); *Cyber C@fe*, one and a half blocks south of the *Crowne Plaza* (US$1/hr); *Cybe@Center*, Av Williams Romero, one block north of Cine Dorado (US$1/hr); *Kafe@Internet*, Av Willams Romero, one block north of the Cine Dorado (US$1/hr).

Libraries and cultural institutes Alliance Française, half a block north of the Mexican Embassy in Planes de Altamira (Mon–Fri 9am–12.30pm & 2–7.30pm, Sat 8am–12.30pm; Ⓣ267-2811, Ⓔalfmanag@cablenet.com.ni), holds French classes and workshops as well as film screenings, concerts and exhibitions.

Medical care The Hospital Bautista (Baptist Hospital) in barrio Largaespada, two blocks south and one and a half east of the Casa Ricardo Morales Aviles (Ⓣ249-7070 or 249-7277), is a good private hospital with an emergency department. Dr Enrique Sánchez Delgado, in Bosques de Altamira, Casa #417, two blocks east and half a block north of the Cine Altamira (Ⓣ278-1031), speaks English and German and charges around US$30 for a consultation. Natural medicines are available from Macrobiotica Internacional (Ⓣ266-6960; Mon–Fri 8.30am–5.30pm & Sat 8.30am–2pm), near barrio Martha Quezada on Calle 27 de Mayo, 150m from the Montoya statue.

Post office In the Enitel office (Mon–Fri 8am–4pm, Sat 8am–noon), three blocks west of the Catedral Viejo.

Supermarkets The two main chains are La Unión and La Colonia, which both sell everything you might possibly need, though at higher prices than in the markets. La Unión has branches in Centro Comercial Bello Horizonte and opposite La Iglesia El Redentor; La Colonia is in the Centro Comercial Plaza España and the Colonia Centroamérica Plaza de Compras.

Telephone office Enitel office three blocks west of the Catedral Viejo (daily 7am–9pm). *Cyber@Center*, on Av Williams Romero, has good (and cheap) Internet phone facilities, with a number of private, convenient, self-serve booths.

Travel agents Flights can be bought at the following places although if you're reconfirming a flight you'll have more luck at the individual airline office (see overleaf). Several of these companies also run organized tours (see p.515). Aeromundo, 75m south of Rotonda El Güegüense (Ⓣ266-8725, Ⓔaeromundo@ibw.com.ni); Continental Tours, one block south of Optica Matamoros, Plaza Fontain Blue, Módulo no. 4 (Ⓣ278-0708, Ⓔvcontour@cablenet.com.ni); Careli Tours, three blocks south of Plaza el Sol (Ⓣ278-25724); Munditur, Km 4.5, Carretera a Masaya (Ⓣ278-5716, Ⓦwww.munditur.com.ni); OTEC Turismo Joven, Calle 27 de Mayo, one and a half blocks west of Plaza Inter (Ⓣ222-2619, Ⓦwww.turismojoven.com); Tropical Travel, one block west and half a block north of Ciudad Jardín ITR (Ⓣ249-7548).

Out from the city

Beaches around Managua don't have the white sand and clear water of places like the Corn Islands or the beaches of San Juan del Sur and La Flor further south, but the water is warmer and they're easy to reach. Managuans visit on day-trips, particularly on national holidays, when the beaches – and public transport – get amazingly crowded, especially at Easter and Christmas: watch your belongings wherever you go.

The closest beaches to the city are **Pochomíl** and the nearby town of **Masachapa**, 3km beyond, around an hour and a half by hourly **bus** from the Mercado Israel Lewites. If you come by car there's a small fee (US$1) to enter Pochomíl, but once here you can settle in for the day, as there are restaurants all along the sand, and motorbikes and horses for rent. There are various accommodation options here if you fancy staying although the cheaper options aren't exactly enticing. The dowdy *Hotel de Playa Cabañas Del Mar* (Ⓣ269-0493; ❺) has large, gloomy and overpriced rooms with ancient a/c units and a cage-like restaurant. The fact that it's right next to where the old *Villa del Mar* now lies dormant and decaying makes it even more depressing. Double the price but light years removed in terms of comfort, design and value, the new *Hotel Vista Mar* (Managua ☎265-8099, Pochomíl ☎882-4716, Ⓦwww.vistamarhotel.com; ❼) offers mock-colonial, wooden tropical bungalows in immaculately landscaped grounds complete with extravagant swimming pools, fountains and even a wind-powered well pump. Budget travellers are limited to the clean but suffocating concrete boxes (with private bath and big spiders) at *Hospedaje Mar Azul* (❸) or the couple of insalubrious rooms at *Bar Milagros* (❷). There are several very basic hospedajes in nearby Masachapa, though it's more of a fishing village and its beach is not as clean as Pochomíl.

Southwest along the coast from Masachapa is the town of **Casares**, which has its own stretch of fairly rough, unshaded beach, and **Hueheute**, which is a bit rougher again. Near Casares is **La Boquita**, another area developed for tourism which charges a small entry fee and offers plenty of places to relax and eat. The beach here can be dangerous with large rocks hidden in the shallows, but the river mouth opening onto the beach provides a safe place to swim. The only place to stay is at *Hotel Palmas del Mar* (☎412-3351; ❺). There is a direct **bus** service from the Mercado Israel Lewites to La Boquita, but it's infrequent except on weekends and holidays; during the week, catch the bus to Diriamba and change there for La Boquita.

Montelimar resort

A short distance north of Pochomíl is the number-one resort in Nicaragua, **Montelimar** (☎269-6752, Ⓦwww.barcelo.com; ❾). Once the beach house of the dictator Somoza, it was turned into a resort by the Sandinistas and is now run by a Spanish company, though like many other properties nationalized during the Revolution, it's currently subject to an involved property dispute with Somoza's relations. Nicaragua's only five-star hotel, *Montelimar* has a relaxed atmosphere with a lovely private beach, four restaurants, four swimming pools, a small zoo and casino, and planned activities such as dance classes, horse-riding, tennis, windsurfing and volleyball. Most people come on a package, but you can book once you've arrived in Nicaragua. Prices are between US$120 and US$174 for a double room, including all meals, drinks and snacks.

El Velero

The hilly coast around **El Velero**, some 40km north of Managua towards León, is wilder than the beaches further south, punctuated by cliffs and peninsulas. A holiday village of sorts, El Velero is less frequented by day-trippers than Pochomíl or La Boquita, and consequently far more relaxed. Shady huts line the beachfront, along with showers, changing rooms and a number of food stands. The beach itself is excellent for swimming, and children can play safely in a rock pool at low tide. You can **stay** here at the holiday centre, originally set up for government workers, and still run by the Instituto Nicaragüense de Seguridad Social. Rooms (❹) have a/c and private bath and there's a restaurant and bar in the grounds. Call the INSS to make a reservation (Managua ☎222-6994, El Velero ☎311-5403). To get to El Velero, take a bus to León, alight at Puerto Sandino and take a camioneta. All in all, it's a three-hour journey from Managua.

Moving on from Managua

Even if you don't particularly want to go to Managua, it's virtually impossible to avoid, since almost all buses go to and from the capital. The main routes of interest to travellers are the **international** routes from Guatemala City, Tegucigalpa in Honduras, and San Salvador in El Salvador, operated by Ticabus (☎222-6094) and King Quality (☎228-1454) – all these services pass through Managua and you may well have to overnight here if you're travelling south to Costa Rica or Panamá. Transnica (☎268-3220) also run buses between Managua and San José (including a daily luxury service), departing from their main office, 50m east of Rotonda Santo Domingo. You can buy tickets from the small office opposite the Costa Rican Consulate on Calle 27 de Mayo.

The busiest **domestic** bus routes are those between the capital and the provincial cities, particularly León in the northwest and Granada in the south. Other main routes run to Matagalpa, Estelí, Masaya and Rivas, the last for connections to the Costa Rican border and the beach town of San Juan del Sur. Express buses also run on most routes from the Mercado Mayoreo – quicker but more expensive than normal buses. You can get most of the way to the Atlantic Coast by bus, a bone-jarring ten-hour trip from Managua to the port of El Rama, from where boats go upriver to Bluefields on the Caribbean. An alternate route is with a private bus company called Transporte Vargas Peña (☎280-4561 in Managua; ☎822-2930 in Bluefields), who provide bus transport to Rama and then a connection by launch to Bluefields: the company has one departure daily from the Mercado Iván Montenegro (9pm, arriving in Bluefields at 8am, with a one-hour wait in El Rama).

Barring international bus services, tickets for which usually need to be bought between one and three days in advance, you can't reserve tickets on any buses within Nicaragua. Buses leave when they become full, which is usually pretty quickly – every fifteen or thirty minutes, with less frequent services leaving every hour or ninety minutes. Don't worry about finding the right bus for your destination amid the chaos of Managua's terminals; more than likely an overenthusiastic tout will find you first and hustle you on to the nearest vehicle going your way. For a rundown of the main bus routes from Managua, see the box below.

Copa have direct, daily **international flights** between Managua and San José, as well as flights to and from Panamá. The main **domestic airlines** are La Costeña (☎263-2142/3/4, ⓦwww.flylacostena.com) and Atlantic Airlines (☎270-5355, ⓦwww.atlanticairlines.com.ni), which both run frequent and reliable scheduled

Bus routes from Managua

Destination	Departs from	Frequency	Duration
Chinandega	Mercado Israel Lewites	every 30min	2hr
Estelí	Mercado de Mayoreo	every 30min	3hr 30min
Granada*	Mercado Roberto Huembes	every 15min	1hr
Jinotepe	Mercado Israel Lewites	every 30min	2hr 30min
León	Mercado Israel Lewites	every 15–30min	1hr 30min
Masaya*	Mercado Roberto Huembes	every 30min	45min
Matagalpa	Mercado de Mayoreo	every 30min	3hr
El Rama	Mercado de Mayoreo	5 daily	10hr
Rivas	Mercado Roberto Huembes	every 25min	2hr 25min
San Carlos	Mercado de Mayoreo	5 daily	10hr
San José	Ticabus terminal	4 daily	9hr
San Salvador	Ticabus terminal	daily at 4.45am	12hr
Tegucigalpa	Ticabus terminal	daily at 5am	7hr
Guatemala City	King Quality terminal	2 daily	14hr
Tipitapa	Mercado de Mayoreo	every 15min	45min

*Regular express minibuses run to Masaya and Granada from an unmarked terminal on the highway opposite La UCA.

services, mainly to and from the Atlantic Coast (although only La Costeña fly to San Carlos). There are daily services to Puerto Cabezas and four flights weekly (Tues, Thurs, Fri & Sat) to Waspám on the northern Atlantic Coast; flights run to Bluefields several times a day, with two services daily to Corn Island. Advance reservations are essential. Both airlines have offices at the airport and agencies across the city.

Tours

Given the often erratic schedules of Nicaraguan transport, if you're short of time it's worth considering an **organized tour**, particularly to remote or difficult to reach areas like the Solentiname archipelago or the Río San Juan. In line with Nicaragua's overall efforts to make tourism the mainstay of the economy, Managua is home to a growing number of tour operators.

Careli Tours opposite El Colegio Pediagogico, Planes de Altamira ⓣ278-6919, ⓦwww.carelitours.com. Good for best-of-Nicaragua type packages as well as trips combining Nicaragua and Costa Rica, both lasting around a week.

Munditur Tours Km 4.5, Carretera a Masaya ⓣ278-5716, ⓦwww.munditur.com.ni. Run by the English-speaking and ever-helpful Richard Gaitán, Munditur is a family affair which has been going for nigh on forty years. As well as US$85 day-trips to Masaya, Granada and León Viejo, the company offer 5-day deep-sea fishing excursions to San Juan del Sur for around US$1500 all-inclusive.

Nicarao Lake Resort one block east of the traffic lights at the Military Hospital, Paseo Tiscapa ⓣ266-1018, ⓦwww.nicaraolake.com.ni. Corporate operator that owns various hotels throughout Nicaragua, and which concentrates on shorter one- to three-day tours to locations throughout the country.

Tours Nicaaragua Plaza Barcelona, Módulo no. 5, Reparto Serrano ⓣ278-0234, ⓦwww.toursnicaragua.com. Very professional company with an emphasis on ecotourism and cultural itineraries. The Lost Civilization package takes in sites throughout Nicaragua including Islas Zapatera and Del Muerto on Lake Granada and they also run a specialist birdwatching tour. Both trips last nine days, cost around US$2000 and are designed for groups although smaller two-person tours can also be arranged.

5.2

The north

Nicaragua's **north** is really two regions, divided by geography and climate as well as – to an extent – the character of their inhabitants. The **northwest** is largely an agricultural area, its hot, dry grassy plains given over to cattle farming, peanuts and cotton, and its horizons punctuated by dramatic volcanoes. Heading northwest from Managua, two roads lead to the colonial city of León and agricultural Chinandega, the only towns of any size in northwest Nicaragua. The only stop of any interest for visitors on the way to León is at the ruins of **León Viejo**, one of the very first Spanish settlements in Central America. Once the capital of Nicaragua, the city of **León** itself is of note mainly for its cathedral, the largest in Central America, though students of Nicaraguan politics and history will also find the city interesting for its role as the birthplace of the FSLN. Further northwest is the hot rural town of **Chinandega** and the **Cosigüina Peninsula**, along with a chain of volcanoes including **Volcán San Cristóbal**, at 1745m the highest in the country, and the smaller **Volcán Cosigüina**, perched on the end of the peninsula. Good beaches are scarce on this stretch of the Pacific Coast. **Poneloya**, a weekend and holiday destination for inhabitants of León, is wild and wave-raked and not really safe for swimming.

North of Managua the landscape is altogether different, with mountainous hillsides covered in bright-green coffee plants and cows grazing in cool alpine pastures. Set within a circle of mountains, the north has a more temperate climate and very productive soil, with plenty of tobacco plantations and an economy based on coffee, grains, vegetables, fruit and dairy farming. The 150km journey north from Managua to Estelí is one of the most inspiring in the country, as the Carretera Interamericana winds through the grassy Pacific plains, skirting the southern edge of Lago de Managua before climbing slowly into a ribbon of blue mountains.

Many travellers coming from the south notice a distinct difference in the people as well as the geography: northerners are poorer and more battle-hardened, and can sometimes seem less forthcoming than Nicaraguans in other areas. In both the Sandinista Revolution years and during the Contra–Sandinista struggles of the 1980s, this region, and particularly **Estelí**, its largest town, saw heavy fighting and serious bloodshed. Because of their staunchly leftist character and legendary tenacity, Somoza bore a particular grudge against the inhabitants of Estelí and waged brutal offensives on the city. Scars have not really healed, either on the bombed-out buildings that still dot the streets of Estelí or in people's minds, and the region remains a centre of unflappable Sandinista support.

León and around

The capital of Nicaragua until 1857, **LEÓN**, 90km north of Managua, is now a provincial city, albeit a vibrant, architecturally arresting and up-and-coming (at least in terms of tourism) one. A significant element in the city's healthy buzz is the presence of the **National University** (the country's premier academic institution) and its large student population, swelled by the ranks of young people studying at León's various other colleges and universities. The original León was founded by Hernández de Córdoba in 1524 at the foot of Volcán Mombotombo, where its ruins – now known as León Viejo (see p.523) – still lie. The city was subsequently

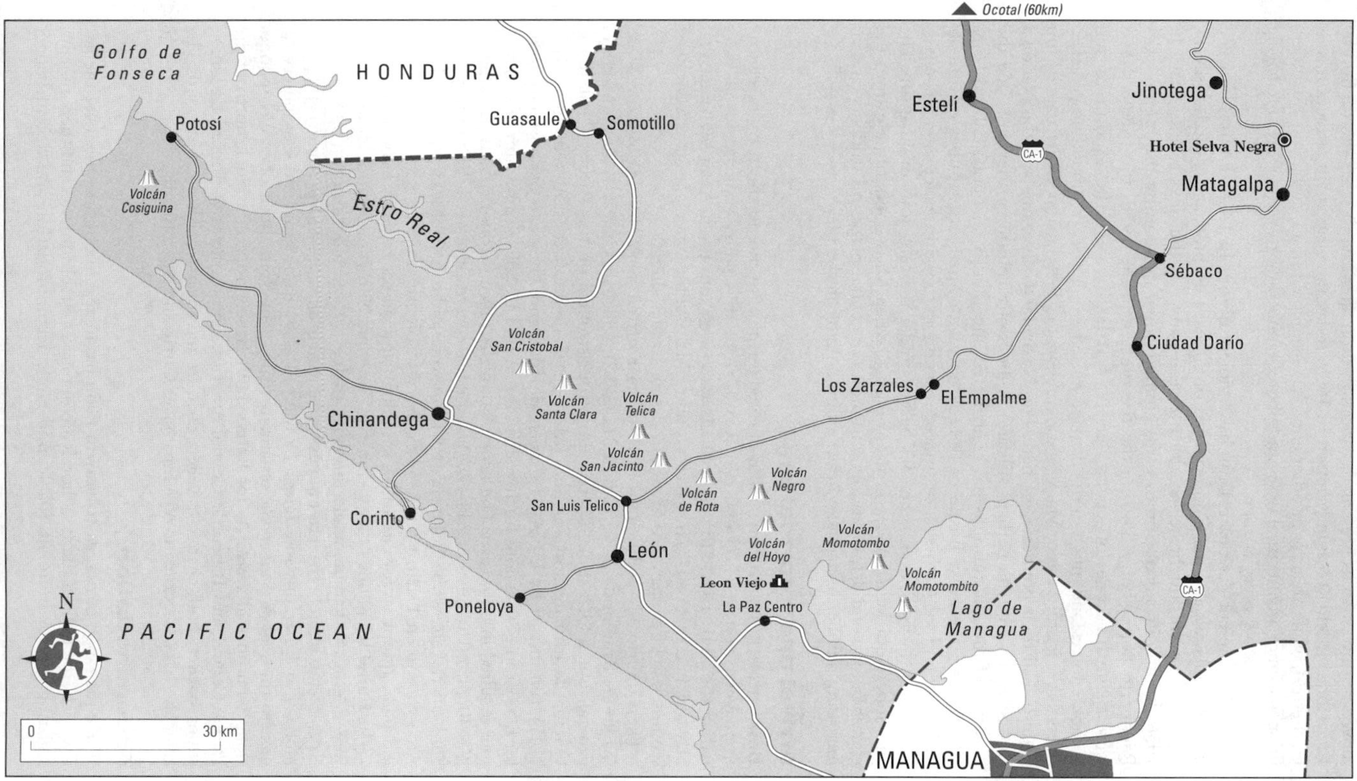

Ocotal (60km)
Golfo de Fonseca
HONDURAS
Guasaule
Somotillo
Potosí
Volcán Cosiguina
Estro Real
Estelí
Jinotega
Hotel Selva Negra
CA-1
Matagalpa
Sébaco
Ciudad Darío
Volcán San Cristobal
Volcán Santa Clara
Volcán Telica
Chinandega
Los Zarzales
El Empalme
Volcán San Jacinto
Volcán de Rota
Volcán Negro
San Luis Telico
Corinto
León
Volcán del Hoyo
Volcán Momotombo
Leon Viejo
Volcán Momotombito
Poneloya
La Paz Centro
Lago de Managua
N
PACIFIC OCEAN
0 30 km
MANAGUA

moved northwest to its present-day location soon after León Viejo's destruction by an earthquake and volcanic eruption in 1609. Today, the city's main attraction is its **Cathedral**, while an array of other churches – eighteen in all, displaying a wonderful spectrum of architectural styles and photographic opportunities – seem to spring up on practically every corner.

For all its present-day peace, León has a violent history. In 1824, tensions between the city's Liberals and the Conservatives of Granada erupted, and a total of seventeen battles were fought in the city over the course of the next twenty years. In 1956 the first President Somoza was gunned down in León by the martyr-poet Rigoberto López Pérez. During the Revolution in the 1970s the town's streets were again the scenes of several decisive **battles** between the Sandinistas and Somoza's forces, and much of the damage caused – bullet-scarred buildings, cracked sidewalks – is still visible. Many key figures in the Revolution either came from León or had their political start here. The **National University** and the National Law School were (and perhaps still are) hotbeds of revolutionary ferment, and the presence of these institutions has contributed enormously to León's Liberal bent. Whether it's the noisy bustle of the town's various markets, troupes of tourists milling around the Cathedral or students packing in to the Internet cafés, the city is in constant motion, even when it's baking under the ferocious midday sun. The atmosphere quickens further in the evenings, when Mass-goers tumble from the churches, food and drink vendors set up on the central plaza and students (and an increasing number of gringos) head out for a night on the tiles.

Arrival and information

Buses arrive at the anarchic, traffic-clogged terminal to the northeast of the centre, from where you can hop in a taxi (US$1; this fare is pretty standard for all rides within the city) or walk the eight blocks or so west into town. As in Managua, you may well find that your taxi driver has no real idea of the whereabouts of your chosen hotel, so be prepared to give your driver detailed directions.

There's a friendly and helpful Intur **tourist office** on Av Jose de la Cruz Mena (Mon–Fri 8am–noon & 2–5pm; ⓣ311-3782), which has a few leaflets, maps and general tour information. There's also a tourist office on the Parque Central, the Oficina de Información Turística (Mon–Fri 8am–noon & 2.30–6.30pm; ⓣ315-1217), run in part by UNAN's Escuela de Tourismo. They can organise city tours for US$10 and excursions further afield for around US$35, a minimum of two persons required in both cases. The Viajes Mundiales office (Mon–Fri 8am–12.30pm & 2–5.30pm; ⓣ311-5920 or 311-6920) is the place to reconfirm outbound **flights** or book air tickets, while Solentiname Tours, one and a half blocks west of Museo Archivo Rubén Darío (ⓣ311-3306, ⓦwww.solentinametours.com), is the best independent option for city tours, kayaking trips and packages to León Viejo.

The **Enitel** telephone office (Mon–Sat 7am–8pm, Sun 7am-5pm) is located on the west side of the Parque, while the **post office** is three blocks north, opposite the Recolección church. **Internet access** is incredibly cheap (US$1 per hour) and plentiful; Cyber Enter, opposite Iglesia La Merced (daily 8am–9pm) and Compuservice, next to the *Flor de Sacuanjoche* restaurant (daily 8am–9pm) both offer Web phones along with normal access. As for **banks**, both Bancentro, half a block north of the Parque Central, and Banco de Central America, next to the well-stocked La Unión **supermarket,** both change travellers' cheques and advance cash on credit cards. The latter also has a Credomatic ATM that takes Cirrus and MasterCard.

Accommodation

While the range of **places to stay** in León has increased considerably over the last few years, the bulk of the new hotels are upmarket establishments and there remains a glaring gap for more affordable, mid-range accommodation and decent budget options.

Avenida north of Mercado San Juan ☎311-2068. Popular budget option with basic but clean and bright rooms set around a leafy courtyard. Some with private bath, all with roof fan. ❷

Los Balcones two blocks east and one block north of the Parque Central ☎311-0250, Ⓔbalcones@ibw.com.ni. Immaculately restored colonial hotel whose upper rooms (complete with original wooden floors and shutters) are perhaps the most authentic and characterful in León. The house was originally owned by the English-speaking owner's great-grandfather and there's an old photo of the family in the foyer. A/c, hot water, private bath and Internet access available. Recommended. ❻

Casa Ivana around the corner from the Teatro Municipal ☎311-4423. Spartan, spacious rooms (private bath optional) in an atmospheric old house, perennially popular with foreign backpackers. The leafy courtyard and communal area with lived-in rocking chairs is an added draw. ❷

La Casona two blocks south of the Teatro Municipal ☎311-5282, Ⓔsidalgon@hotmail.com. Friendly new budget hostal with six basic rooms, some gloomier than others. In its favour are a sociable, comfortable living area, kitchen, laundry facilities and hammocks. ❷

Casona Colonial Guesthouse four blocks north of the Parque ☎311-3178. Peaceful, good-sized double rooms with bath, fan and comfortable beds in an old colonial house, somewhat crumbling but full of character. With its original high, sloping ceiling and faded majesty, Room No. 3 is especially atmospheric. Also offers an excellent breakfast (not included in rate). ❹

El Convento two blocks west and half a block north of the Parque Central ☎311-7053, Ⓦwww.hotelelconvento.com.ni. A lavishly restored seventeenth-century convent with peaceful rooms (all with a/c, phone, TV and private bath), León's flagship hotel also has walls lined with art and antiques including an altar from the Cathedral in the reception area, a grand dining room with surprisingly affordable food, and an immaculately maintained garden with fountain. ❽

Grand Hotel south side of the bus terminal; look out for the sign ⓣ315-1511, ⓔgrandhotel@ibw.com.ni. An oasis of verdant calm amid the chaos and squalor of the bus terminal area, this mid-range place offers quiet, relatively bright and cheerful rooms with optional a/c or fan, and cable TV. ❹

Guest House La Calle de los Poetas one and a half blocks west of Museo Archivo Rubén Darío ⓣ311-3306, ⓔrsampson@ibw.com.ni. Undoubtedly one of the best deals in the city, with four cool, quiet, tastefully furnished rooms (with fan and private bath) set around a pretty colonial courtyard and bordered by a large, rambling garden. Owner Rigo Sampson, a knowledgeable host, also runs a tour agency. ❸

Hostal Clínica half a block south of the Teatro Municipal, opposite *La Casona* ⓣ311-2031. Possibly the only hostal cum dental clinic in existence, this friendly family-run place offers decent rooms (some with private bath) around a pretty courtyard. The upstairs rooms (with foliage shadowed balcony) are the most desirable but negotiating the precipitous staircase after a few beers might present a problem. ❷

La Posada del Doctor four blocks north of the Parque Central, opposite the *Casona Colonial Guesthouse* ⓣ311-4343, ⓕ311-5986. Recently renovated, this colonial hotel offers good value for money with well-appointed, calming rooms (all with a/c, fan and private bath) and one of Nicaragua's few upmarket dorms (immaculate with six bunks and private bath; US$7), all set around a colourful courtyard. Lovely staff, laundry and kitchen facilities, and breakfast included. ❺

Vía Vía two blocks east and one and a half blocks north of the Mausoleo Héroes y Mártires ⓣ311-6142, ⓦwww.viaviacafe.com. León's answer to Granada's *Bearded Monkey*, this hip hostal is one of the few places in the city aimed directly at backpackers. Accommodation consists of a crumbling colonial dorm (US$3) and a few basic rooms with fan and shared bath. The candle-lit café (with pool table and open mic night every Tuesday) is probably its biggest draw, although there's also the requisite hammocks, book exchange, and even salsa and Spanish classes. ❸

The City

"León: ciudad heroica – primera capital de la revolución" say the street signs, and León certainly wears its FSLN heart on its sleeve. Although most of the old **Sandinista murals and graffiti** have been covered over there are still a few fine examples around town (the most famous being opposite the Mausoleo Héroes y Mártires, where a hat-wearing Sandino is depicted squashing a whey-faced Uncle Sam underfoot).

The Parque Central

The city's most obvious attraction is the colossal **Cathedral**, a cream-coloured structure of epic proportions towering over León from the heart of the city, the **Parque Central**. Begun in 1747, it took anything from seventy to a hundred years to build the Cathedral, depending on who you talk to. Inside the only things of interest are the large statues of the Twelve Apostles and the tomb of local hero **Rubén Darío**, Nicaragua's most famous writer and poet, guarded by a statue of a weeping lion. Masses are held daily at about 5pm and are worth attending, if only to people-watch.

The Parque Central is centred on a statue of **General Máximo Jeréz** guarded by four lions and visited by a constant stream of locals, street vendors and tourists. On the west side is one of the city's Sandinista strongholds, the decaying **Asociación de Combatientes Históricos Héroes de Veracruz** building, which now functions as a museum (8am–noon, 2–6pm & 8–10pm; by donation). FSLN combat veteran Dionísio Meza Romero supplies enthusiastic and knowledgeable explanations on the extensive collection of photos, articles and news clippings documenting the Revolution, its historical antecedents and its aftermath; he also gives Historical Revolutionary tours of León (9am & 3pm Mon–Sat; US$4). Enlivening the north side of the Parque is the grand **Casa de Gobierno** and the **Centro de Convenciones**, while on the northeast corner is the **Mausoleo**

Héroes y Mártires, a star-shaped monument dedicated to those who died fighting for freedom during the civil war, surrounded by a large mural colourfully detailing Nicaragua's history from pre-Colombian times to the ending of the civil war. If you value your hearing, avoid the Parque at the hours of 7am and noon when a ludicrously loud air-raid siren wails across the city, a throwback to the days when workers flocked in to León's booming cotton factories.

West and north of the Parque Central

Two blocks northeast of the Parque is one of Nicaragua's finest colonial churches, **La Recolección**,with a beautiful Mexican Baroque facade dating from 1786 and some fine mahogany woodwork inside. Followers of Nicaragua's other religion, poetry, might want to head for the **Parque Rubén Darío**, a block west of the Parque Central, which is home to a statue of the rather bored-looking poet dressed in suit and bow tie. A few blocks further west is the **Museo Archivo Rubén Darío** (Mon–Sat 9am–noon & 2–5pm, Sun 9am–noon; free, but donations appreciated), housed in a substantial León residence that was actually the house of Darío's aunt, Bernarda. Inside, the lovingly kept rooms and courtyard garden are home to wonderfully frank plaques narrating the story of Darío's tempestuous personal life and diplomatic and poetic career, along with many of his personal possessions and commemorative items, such as Rubén Darío lottery tickets. On the opposite side of the same block is the **Centro de Arte Fundación Ortiz-Guardián** (Tues–Sat 10.30am–6.30pm, Sun 11am–7pm; US$0.80), an expansive art gallery in two renovated colonial houses featuring an engrossing cross section of Latin American art, including pre-Hispanic and modern ceramics and some great monochrome photos of Nicaraguan rural religious festivals.

Two blocks north is the **Casa Rigoberto López Pérez**. Now a rather dowdy FSLN office, a plaque marks the spot where the young poet and revolutionary Rigoberto López Pérez assassinated the dictator General Somoza on September 21, 1956, before himself being shot some fifty times by the National Guard. Continuing in a revolutionary vein, the **Galería Héroes y Mártires** (Mon–Sat 9am–5.30pm; donations), half a block south and half a block east, houses wall after wall of simple, strangely moving black and white photos of Nicaraguans (men and women, young and old) killed fighting for the Sandinista cause. There's also a small craft shop attached, the proceeds of which go towards the gallery's upkeep.

South of the Parque Central

Three blocks south of the cathedral lie the ruins of **La Veinte Uno**, the National Guard's 21st garrison and scene of heavy fighting in April 1979. Oddly enough, the garrison now houses two different museums, which together go under the long-winded title of **Museo de Leyendas y Tradiciones General Joaquín de Arrechada (Antigua Cárcel de la Veinte Uno)** (Tues–Sat 8am–noon & 2–5pm, Sun 8am–3pm; US$0.30). One half of the building houses a bizarre collection of ghoulish figures from Nicaraguan folklore including a headless priest and a truly surreal display consisting of a wagon pulled by two stuffed oxen and driven by a Grim Reaper–style skeleton, apparently representing the legend of the "haunted oxcart". The other half of the building also centres on terror, albeit of the manmade variety, with a small collection of revealing black and white photos of the garrison both during and after the Somoza era. There's some text in Spanish documenting the torture and abuse that went on inside the garrison and you can also peer into the eerily empty prison cells at the rear of the building.

Subtiava

Four kilometres west of the city centre is the barrio of **Subtiava**, which long predates León and is still home to many of the city's indigenous population. It is also the site of one of the oldest churches in the country, the small adobe **parish church** of Subtiava. Recently renovated, the church is not always open (in theory the hours are Mon–Fri 8–11am & 2–4.30pm, Sat & Sun 8–11.30am), but worth a visit if you're catching a bus to or from the beach at Poneloya. One sight you can't miss in Subtiava – and indeed in all of León – in November and December is that of posses of young boys hammering away at snare drums while a huge **Gigantona** (a papier-mâché, Rio Carnaval–style figure of an elegant colonial-era lady, directed from underneath by a slightly older teenager) weaves among them. Traditionally, the boys are given a few córdobas for a recital of poetry, typically that of national bard Rubén Darío. The *Gigantonas* are judged during the festivities of La Purísima (a festival celebrating the Virgin Mary's conception) on 7th December with the best winning a prize.

Eating and drinking

León boasts a cosmopolitan and ever-increasing range of **places to eat and drink**, from the ubiquitous pizza joints and stalwart seafood restaurants to chic café-bars and bohemian hangouts. Most of the restaurants and pizza places close around 10pm while the trendier places stay open until the small hours, especially at weekends. The **nightlife** scene has also had a similar shot in the arm of late. For dancing, the long-established *Don Señor* (where a dress shirt is mandatory), on the corner opposite La Merced church, and *Discoteca Dilectus*, on the highway to Managua on the south side of the city, are the clubs of choice and the ones guaranteed to be packed at weekends (they can also get pretty full during the week). Things get going around 9pm and the playlist is the usual blend of salsa, merengue, pop, techno, hip hop and *perreo*, a lewd hybrid of ragga and hip hop beloved of young Nicas.

Café El Sesteo northeast corner of the Parque. The town's main café and the only one with al fresco tables, the atmospheric and open-fronted *El Sesteo* is a popular – if slightly expensive – place to eat, drink and people-watch. Skip their "famous" *cacao con leche*, however – not nearly as tasty as the menu would have you believe.

Guadalajara one block north of La Merced church. Delicious, good-value and well-presented Mexican food with bench-style tables. Try the quesadillas, a steal at US$1.50.

Jala La Jarra half a block north of the Teatro Municipal. Friendly, fashionable bar/restaurant in yet another old colonial house, strikingly re-done with chunky, antique-style wooden chairs and tables. The cocktails are worth a try and the *filete a la pimienta* comes highly recommended. Popular with locals on Sundays. Closed Mon.

El Matchico two and a half blocks north of the eastern edge of Parque Central. This French-owned bar is one of the hottest in town, not least because of its original interior design, quality music (Latin jazz, house and ambient techno) and mouthwatering crepes (US$5). Closest León has to a European pre-club style bar and correspondingly expensive (there's also a casino) but recommended nonetheless.

Los Pescaditos Barrio Subtiava, 4km west of the city. Perennially popular restaurant with a unique system of ordering your fish. The price is listed as "*segun tamano*", which means you pay according to size; you can handpick your dish from the freshly caught selection in the freezer. Alternatively, try the buttery *camarones con ajillo*, best washed down with a cold Victoria beer underneath the night sky.

Rincón Legal one block east and half a block south of Iglesia de la Recolección, opposite *Via Via*. A bohemian drinking den which wears its Sandinista colours proudly. The crumbling colonial walls are adorned with interesting Revolution-related photos and there's the added attraction of good music and a pool table in the back. Popular with locals.

Taquezal opposite the Teatro Municipal. Rustic, slightly fraying but very stylish and atmospheric café-bar with candle-lit tables and a good menu featuring decent vegetarian pasta dishes, Chinese food, wonderful iced tea with lemon and a fine selection of espresso drinks. Closed Sun.

White House Pizza opposite Iglesia de la Recolección ☎311-7010. With the tastiest and most professional pizza in town (a medium margarita will set you back about US$4), this chain does a roaring trade most nights. They'll also deliver to your hotel.

Around León: Poneloya and León Viejo

Day-trip destinations from León include the Pacific beach of **Poneloya**, due west of the city and easily reached by bus. The UNESCO World Heritage site of **León Viejo** is best reached in a car or taxi – a trip on public transport entails some fancy footwork to make the connections, and even then leaves you with a bit of a walk.

Poneloya

For monster Pacific waves, **Poneloya**, 20km west of León, is the most impressive beach in the country. The water here is notoriously dangerous, due to a combination of powerful waves and riptides, but it's the only beach within convenient reach of León, and many of the city's well-to-do residents have weekend homes here. Outside of peak times like Christmas and Easter, though, Poneloya seems rather run-down and forlorn, with restaurants closed and homes boarded up, and a rather bleak vista out to a sere Pacific. You really must take care if you **swim** here: waves come ashore with a supernatural force. Ask locals about riptides (*corrientes peligrosos*) before venturing into the water, and never swim alone. The smaller beach at **Las Peñitas**, at the south end of Poneloya, is much safer.

Most travellers come to Poneloya for the day and sleep in León – a good option, since **accommodation** in Poneloya is limited. Options include the *Hotel La Posada* at the entrance to the village (☎311-4812; ❸), where the clean, concrete rooms with bamboo roof come with a choice of fan or a/c, although you'll pay double for the latter. Across the road, the peeling wooden hulk of *Hotel Lacayo* (☎886-7369; ❷) is a bargain-basement option that has balconies on the beach but rather grotty beds and partition walls. Around 200m down the road is the famous *Restaurante Pariente Salinas*, a firm favourite with weekending Leónites and a good place for fresh seafood and snacks; try the *Lentejas Marinas* for a dollar. A two-kilometre walk in the opposite direction will take you southwards to *Las Peñitas* where *Mi Casita* (☎876-0873; ❸), a funky, friendly and good-value little hotel/bar with spartan rooms with wooden shutters, as well as a nice upstairs balcony and eccentric tree-stump tables in the bar area. Right at the end of the road where the Pacific curves round into an idyllic little bay lies the *Barco de Oro* (☎317-275, ⓔtortuga@ibw.com.ni; ❺), situated at the heart of the Las Peñitas fishing community. Formerly a nightclub frequented by Somoza, it's now a tranquil traveller's haven with pleasant rooms with rustic wooden beds and fan (one with a/c), and a lovely upstairs balcony for sunset watching. The French owner (who also speaks good English) works closely with the local community and can hook you up with one of the fishermen for a trip to the nearby **Isla Juan Venado**, a nature reserve (no camping) and turtle-nesting site. The cost of the island trip is US$40–60 for up to ten people, with the US$2 entrance fee being ploughed back into the community. Other activities on offer include sport **fishing** (with local fisherman Antonio Gonzalez; US$200 per day for up to three people), **horse riding** (US$5–10 per half-day) and **kayaking** (US$7 per half-day). While the bay is one of the safest and cleanest places to swim on the whole coast, note that it's dangerous to swim across to Salinas Grandes, not least because of stingrays and currents.

Buses to Poneloya (40min) leave León every 45minutes (until 6pm) from the Terminal Poneloya on C Darío, near the Subtiava church in barrio Subtiava (see opposite). A taxi will cost about US$5 each way – good value if you're in a group. The last bus returning to León in the evening is at 6.40pm.

León Viejo

Founded in 1524, the same year as Granada, **León Viejo,** 32km east of the modern city (daily 7am–6pm; US$0.30 admission which includes a guided tour in Spanish only; US$0.60 charge for vehicles) and now designated a UNESCO World Heritage site, was destroyed by an earthquake and volcanic eruption on December 31, 1609. Among the ruins excavated over the last thirty years or so, the cathedral is probably the most interesting. In November 2000, the graves of Nicaragua's first three bishops were uncovered inside and their remains are now interred in large coffins carved by Nicaraguan sculptor Federico Matus. Archeologists pulled off another major coup by unearthing the remains of Nicaragua's founder Francisco Fernández de Córdoba. His headless body (he was executed by his archenemy and original governor of Nicaragua, Pedrarias Dávila, whose bones were also located) was discovered amid the ruins of La Merced church. Other ruins belatedly revealed include the office where gold was melted down before being shipped back to Spanish coffers and the convent of the Mercedarios. León Viejo's setting also deserves mention, in view of the lake and under the looming shadow of Momotombo; the best view is to be had from the old fort, located to the east of the main ruins. The only way to get there comfortably is by car, either under your own steam or as part of a tour from León. Alternatively, the site – located in the remote coastal hamlet of Puerto Momotombo – is accessible through a local bus from **La Paz Centro** (a village about 60km north of Managua which you can reach via the frequent León–Managua service) although it's best to get an early start, as the last bus returns at 2pm.

Chinandega to the Honduran border

The first thing you notice about **CHINANDEGA**, 35km northwest of León, is its extraordinary heat. Set on a plain behind the looming form of Volcán San Cristóbal, the area's dry, kiln-like climate is ideal for cotton growing, the main economic activity, along with some groundnut cultivation and cattle farming. In Nicaraguan terms Chinandega is a fairly prosperous agricultural town. It's also home to the Flor de Caña rum distillery, Nicaragua's export-grade tipple, which sits on the outskirts of town.

Buses arrive at the market southwest of the centre, known as the **Mercado Bisne** – *bisne* being short for "business", as during the years of the Reagan-sponsored embargo much contraband came through here from **Corinto**, Nicaragua's main port, 21km west of the city on a sandy island reached by a bridge. (Corinto is still the only deepwater port in Nicaragua, and almost every molecule of shipping commerce passes through the town.). You can change travellers' cheques and dollars at Bancentro, on the opposite corner from the Shell garage. There's a very helpful Intur **tourist office** (8am–12.30pm & 1.30–5pm; ⓣ341-1935), next to the Costa Rican consulate in the Centro Commercial, one block north and half a block west of Banpro, where you can get info on climbing the nearby volcanoes.

Although you'll pay for the privilege, the most comfortable **place to stay** is *Los Volcanes*, Km 129.5, Carretera a Chinendega (ⓣ341-1000, ⓔhvolcan@ibw.com.ni; ❼). The luxurious rooms have cool, tiled floors and wood ceilings while the garden has great views of Volcán Cristóbal. A cheaper option is the very hospitable *Hotel, San José*, two and a half blocks north from the main banks (ⓣ & ⓕ341-2723; ❺), with immaculately clean, modern, quiet a/c rooms (although some are windowless) to the rear of a family home. For **eating**, Chinandega boasts one of the most authentic Chinese restaurants in Nicaragua: *El Corona de Oro*, one and a half blocks east of Iglesia San Antonio. It's open daily until 9pm for tasty oriental cuisine, most dishes coming in under US$5.

If you're heading to Guasaule and the Honduran border (see below) under your own steam, express **buses** from Chinandega run about every thirty minutes.

Guasaule and the border with Honduras

Most travellers experience **GUASAULE** from the safe capsule of the Ticabus, which whizzes you painlessly through this **border post**. Even if travelling by local transport, the process is relatively hassle free and shouldn't take more than half an hour in total. Be sure to take a few dollars, however: the **exit tax** is currently US$4, and it must be paid in US dollars (there is a branch of Bancentro in *migración* which will change money and is open 8am–8pm). Note that the post is open 24 hours but if you cross between noon and 2pm or after 5pm, you'll have to pay an extra US$4. It's about 1km between the Nicaraguan border post and the Honduran side, across an impressive new bridge funded by the Japanese. You can either walk it or take one of the bicycle taxis from Guasaule bus station. The fee for entering Honduras is currently US$2 (no matter the time you arrive; the post is also open 24 hours). From the border there's a direct bus to Tegucigalpa every two hours.

Leaving Honduras the fee is the same (US$2) although **entering Nicaragua** costs US$9 and again is **only payable** in US dollars. From the border a service departs for Chinandega – the nearest Nicaraguan town with acceptable accommodation – every thirty minutes or so, with a choice of minibus or ordinary bus. It's a long, boneshaking ride, however, on a road only blessed with tarmac at sporadic intervals. At Chinandega you can pick up an express bus on to Managua about every thirty minutes, or continue by bus to León (every 11min).

Estelí and around

At first sight **ESTELÍ**, the largest town in the north, can seem downtrodden and poor. It does have its poverty-stricken barrios, but it's also an engaging place and a hotbed of political activity. In Estelí, you can best get a sense of what the country must have been like during the Revolution and glimpse something of the vision that inspired so many people during the 1980s. The town continues to provide fierce support for the Sandinistas, and witnessed violent disturbances following the controversial delay in announcing the results of municipal elections in November 2000.

Although the war ended with the failure of the Sandinistas in the election of 1990, Estelí has been the scene of all-out fighting as recently as 1994. In what has become known as the **"one-day war"**, former Sandinista and Contra soldiers took up arms together to demand better conditions for veterans. At the same time they robbed a bank and their leader, "Pedrito El Hondureño", reportedly disappeared with the loot. The government responded by encircling the veterans in the centre of town with national police, soldiers and helicopter gunships. About a dozen veterans were killed along with two civilians. A further uprising in 1997 came to nothing.

More recently the town's government has been particularly successful in attracting **overseas aid** and Estelí is filled with the offices of international organizations working on projects as diverse as cooperative and organic farming, women's rights and the environment. In the early 1990s the town provided the location for the Ken Loach movie *Carla's Song*, the making of which no doubt funnelled a few córdobas into the local economy. Estelí's relatively rural setting also means that there are some attractive options for day-trips out from the city. **El Salto de Estanzuela** – a secluded waterfall within walking distance of the centre – makes for a great day out, while the wonderful **Miraflor nature reserve** is just under 30km away.

Arrival and information

Confusingly, Estelí now has **two bus terminals**. The shiny new Cotran Sur R.L. station at the southern entrance to town serves all destinations south of Estelí. The older station – located five minutes' walk to the north – serves all destinations north of Estelí including Ocotal, Somoto, Jinotega and the Honduran border, plus express buses to Managua, Masaya and León. The town is arranged on a narrow north–south grid, with most services clustered together in the small centre along C Transversal. Unlike almost anywhere else in Nicaragua, Estelí actually has streets with names, although in practice people still use the time-honoured system of locating places in terms of proximity to landmarks.

The Intur **tourist information office** (Mon–Fri 8am–noon & 1.30–5pm; ⓣ713-6799, ⓔesteli@intur.gob.ni), located one block north and three blocks west

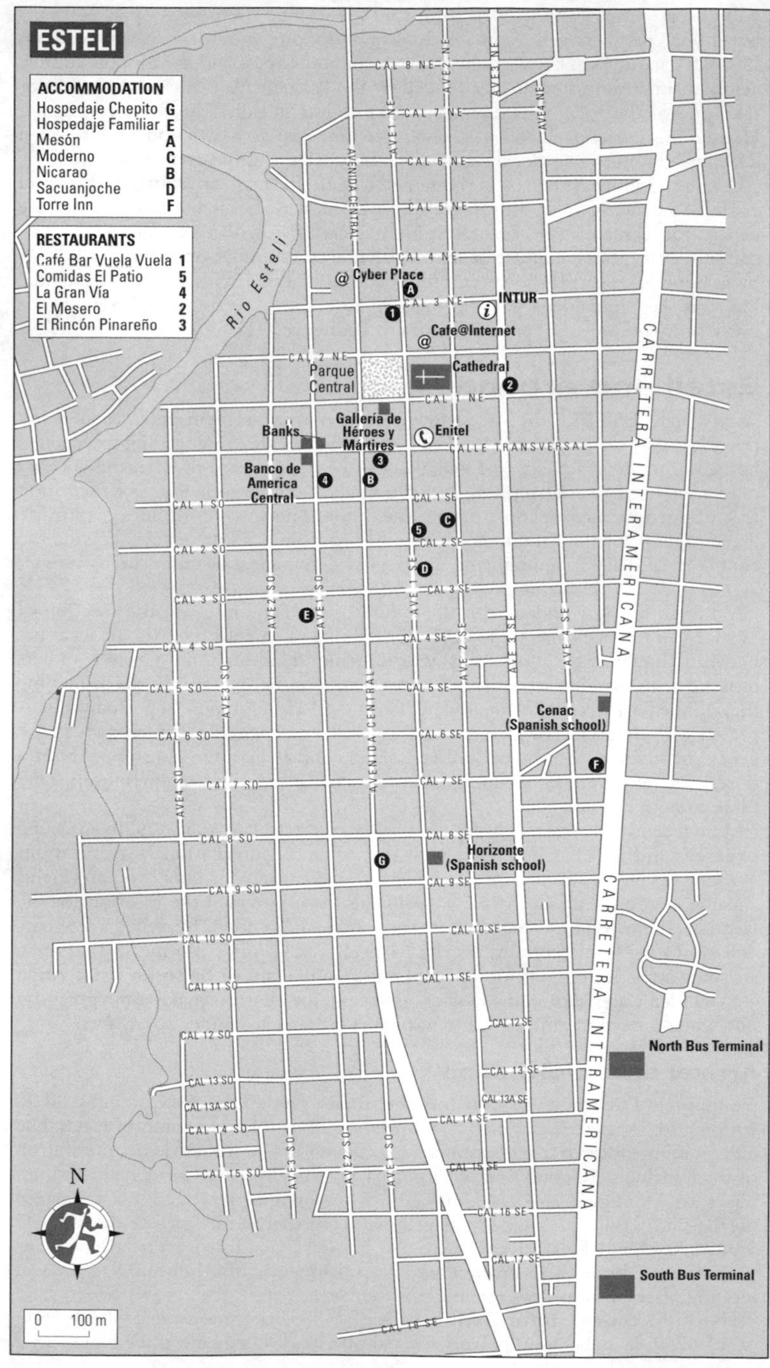
ESTELÍ
ACCOMMODATION
Hospedaje Chepito G
Hospedaje Familiar E
Mesón A
Moderno C
Nicarao B
Sacuanjoche D
Torre Inn F
RESTAURANTS
Café Bar Vuela Vuela 1
Comidas El Patio 5
La Gran Vía 4
El Mesero 2
El Rincón Pinareño 3
Rio Estelí
Cyber Place
INTUR
Cafe@Internet
Parque Central
Cathedral
Galleria de Héroes y Mártires
Banks
Enitel
Banco de America Central
CALLE TRANSVERSAL
AVENIDA CENTRAL
CARRETERA INTERAMERICANA
Cenac (Spanish school)
Horizonte (Spanish school)
North Bus Terminal
South Bus Terminal
N
0 100 m

of the Parque Central, has up-to-date bus timetables and details on visiting the various cigar factories located in town. The **post office** (Mon–Fri 7am–5pm, Sat 8am–noon) is located one block south and half a block west of the Parque; the **Enitel** office (Mon–Fri 8am–8pm, Sat 9am–5pm) is on C Transversal, one block south and one block east of the cathedral. **Internet access** can be found at Cyber Place on Av Central, one and a half blocks north of the Parque, and at Café@net on the north side of the Parque – both charge US$1.30 per hour and offer cheap international calls. There are three **banks** on the corner of Av 1 NE a block west of the Parque although Banco de América Central (Mon–Fri 8.30am–5pm, Sat 8.30am–noon) is the only one which changes travellers' cheques and advances money on credit cards.

Accommodation

Because Estelí sees quite a bit of gringo traffic in the form of aid workers, **hotels** tend to be a little more expensive than in other parts of the country and most of them are nothing to write home about. Like León, Estelí is also blessed with a 6am air-raid siren wake-up call (there's also one at midday) and if you really want a good night's sleep consider a room as far from the centre as possible.

Hospedaje Chepito southern end of Av Central ⓣ713-3784. Small, simple and dirt-cheap family-run hospedaje with camp beds and clean concrete floors catering for the budget traveller. Very popular with Nicaraguans. ❶

Hospedaje Familiar three and a half blocks south of the main banks ⓣ713-3666. Clean, basic rooms skirting a long patio with rocking chairs. A little overpriced, but the friendly proprietor's vegetarian menu includes natural fruit juices, fresh fruit breakfasts and homemade brown bread and yoghurt. Also offers good rates for weekly and monthly rental. ❸

Mesón one block north of the cathedral ⓣ713-2655, ⓕ713-4029. The *Mesón* has something of the feeling of a faded country inn, with a wood-panelled reception and friendly management – the rather scrappy courtyard has small wood and bamboo gazebos with tables, while the surrounding rooms, with private bath, TV and hot water, are cool, comfortable and quiet at night. ❸

Moderno two and a half blocks south of the eastern edge of the cathedral ⓣ713-2378, ⓕ713-4315. Clean, simple and homely rooms (hot water, TV, fan, desk and lamp) in a hotel with loads of panelled wood; one of the few places in town with real character. ❹

Nicarao Av Central, just south of C 1 SE ⓣ713-2490. Small hotel that's popular with gringos, possibly thanks to its covered patio where you can relax, dine on the excellent lunch specials (US$2.50) and write your postcards. Choice of budget or more attractive, comfortable rooms, all offering decent value. ❸–❺

Sacuanjoche three and a half blocks south of the cathedral ⓣ713-2482. Bright, fresh rooms with comfy beds, tiled floors, clean bath (no hot water) and varnished wooden ceilings around a pretty patio. Good value. ❷

Torre Inn two blocks from CENAC Spanish school on the Panamericana ⓣ713-6668, ⓔw.house@ibw.com.ni. Vaguely colonial-style hotel with clean, bright rooms (TV and hot water), swimming pool and restaurant. ❺

The Town

Although Estelí lacks the stunning mountain views of Matagalpa to the southeast, the centre of town is well kept and pleasant to wander around, and the climate refreshingly cool. Much of the pleasure lies in soaking up the atmosphere, particularly along Av Central, where shops' wares spill out onto the street and the windows display cowboy boots and the local farmers' favourite Western-style hats. The **cathedral** on the Parque has a rather austere facade, helping make it one of the least interesting in the country. The south side of the Parque is dominated by the **Centro Recreativo Las Segovias**, which puts on regular music and sporting events, particularly basketball. The **Casa de Cultura**, another cultural venue a block to the south, hosts art exhibitions, dancing and music events. Across the street, the **Artesanía Nicaragüense** has a reasonable selection of handicrafts, pottery, and cigars. On the same block is the tiny **Galería de Héroes y Mártires** (daily

△ Pepe Cabezan and La Gigantona, Subtavia, León

9am–4pm; donations), a moving and simple museum devoted to the Revolution and to the many residents of Estelí who died fighting in it (the women who work at the Galería are, for the most part, mothers and widows of soldiers who were killed).

To some extent a leftover from the Sandinista years, when *internacionalistas* flocked here, there are also two well-respected **language schools** worth considering in town. Horizonte, eleven blocks south of the far side of the cathedral (☎713-4117, ©horizont@ibw.com.ni), reportedly has the best teachers, and does courses for US$150 per week that includes accommodation with a local family. Slightly cheaper is CENAC, 300 metres north of the Shell station on the Carretera Interamericana (☎713-5437, ©cenac@tmx.com.ni), offering the same for US$140 per week. The Galería de los Héroes y Mártires also runs informal language classes based on learning about the area and the effects of the civil war.

Eating and drinking

Estelí's **eating** scene isn't in the same league as León or Granada but there are more than a few decent places scattered around town. There are few real bars as such, although clubbers are better catered for with a healthy selection of **discos**, most located far from the centre. *Disco Bar Tomcat* is the most conveniently situated, on the Interamericana opposite *Restaurante Cohifer No.2*; it's more relaxed than many other places and opens Thursday to Sunday. Keeping a similar timetable and playlist is *Las Calabasas*, 6km north from the centre. There's no dress code and the entrance fee is normally US$2, which you receive back in the form of drinks vouchers. Things heat up about 10pm and can go on till daybreak, a sharp and vibrant contrast with most northern clubs.

Café Bar Vuela Vuela one block north of the cathedral. Smart café/bar that's an NGO initiative with profits going towards helping disadvantaged youths back into the job market, and featuring a tasty, authentic range of Spanish tapas. Treats like gazpacho and papas bravas make this place a must, as does the healthy breakfast menu.

La Casita Finca Las Nubes at the southern entrance to town ☎713-4917. Idyllic, intimate café with rustic tables nestled amidst a lovingly tended garden. Part of a completely self-sufficient working farm, the *Casita* offers delicious homemade produce including organic coffee, yoghurt, cheese, jam and probably the best wholemeal bread in Nicaragua.

Comidas El Patio three blocks south of the cathedral. A pleasant stop-off for good-value breakfasts, snacks and lunches, enjoyed in the open air on tree-trunk tables. The yard also contains *Casa Italia*, a small Italian-run place with a good selection of veggie pastas, pizza and Italian wine; half a pizza and a couple of beers will set you back just under US$4.

La Gran Vía 20 metres south of the main banks ☎713-5465. Formerly *Café Palermo*, this busy restaurant now specialises in good, fairly expensive Chinese food (the US$2 lunch specials – served from 11am to 4pm – are much better value) although there's still a small selection of decent pasta dishes. Also does delicious flan and cheesecake for dessert. Closed Sunday.

Licuados Ananda one block south of the Parque next to the Casa de Cultura. The Estelí branch of this Managua restaurant has tranquil outdoor tables next to a strangely empty swimming pool. Great for breakfast and snacks (although the service can be slow) with a range of cheap, healthy vegetarian fare including yoghurt, muesli, *licuados*, tacos and *repochetas*.

El Mesero one block east from the back of the cathedral. One of the oldest restaurants in Estelí, the friendly *Mesero* cooks a reasonably priced selection of beef, chicken, pork and seafood dishes. Try the *Filete a la Jalapeña* for just over US$5.

El Rincón Pinareño one block south of the Parque ☎713-4369. Phenomenally popular, the *Pinareño* specialises in cheap, mouth-watering Nicaraguan fare with a Cuban bias. There's also a good range of tortillas (even a Mexican chorizo version) and daily specials.

Around Estelí: Miraflor and El Salto de la Estanzuela

The wonderful **Miraflor nature reserve**, 28km northeast of Estelí, is one of the country's least known but most worthwhile attractions and covers 206 square kilometres of forest, part of which is farmed by a group of agricultural co-ops. One of the project's main aims is to find sustainable ways in which farming and environmental protection can co-exist – over 5000 locals currently produce coffee, potatoes, milk, cheese and exotic flowers in and around the reserve, and the emphasis is firmly upon community-centred tourism. The reserve itself comprises several different climatic zones and ecosystems, ranging from savanna to tropical dry forest to humid cloudforest. To best appreciate this diversity it's advisable to stay for at least two or three days, either walking or horse-riding (US$6 per half-day for group of up to five people) between the zones and staying with different families each night. Guides can also take you to the reserve's waterfalls and caves, once inhabited by the ancient Yeluca and Cebollal mountain peoples. In terms of both flora and fauna, Miraflor is one of the richest reserves in the country with over 300 species of bird including quetzals, *guardabarrancos* (the national bird of Nicaragua) and *urracas*, a local type of magpie, as well as howler monkeys and reclusive mountain lions. There are also over 200 species of orchid.

Accommodation (❸) is available in either rustic cabins owned by local families or in the houses of the families themselves. Prices include three meals per day and the food is almost wholly organic; vegetarians are well catered for. To book a stay (or volunteer to help teach English), contact the offices of the UCA Miraflor, located on the street behind Estelí's stadium (Ⓣ713-2971, Ⓦwww.miraflor-uca.com). Fortunately, at least part of the reserve is served by public transport; full details can be obtained at the office.

El Salto de la Estanzuela

Another very worthwhile trip from Estelí is to **El Salto de la Estanzuela**, one of the few waterfalls in Nicaragua easily accessible on foot from a major centre of population. Located within the aegis of the recently created Reserva Natural Tisey-Estanzuela, it's a lovely two-hour walk through green, gently rolling hills – although it's also possible to drive right to the foot of the falls. The path begins just past the hospital at the southern entrance to town, by the *Kiosko Europeo*; follow the path for 4km or so until you see a sign for "Communidad Estanzuela"; go through the gate on the right-hand side and follow the path for another 1km. The falls themselves – 35m or so in height – are located at the bottom of a steep set of steps and are fairly spectacular, cascading into a deep pool perfect for swimming in. The only downside is the litter carelessly strewn around the rocks in front of the falls. Located within the same reserve is *La Posada del Tisey* (Ⓣ713-6213; ❶), a homely hideaway that ranks as one of the most authentic rural retreats in the country. The accommodation comprises rustic but clean wooden cabañas with healthy, organic meals for US$1. Nearby is **El Mirador**, one of the most spectacular viewpoints in all Nicaragua; on a clear day it's possible to see volcanoes as far away as El Salvador. If making the trip, call ahead as room is limited. You can catch a bus at the entrance to the reserve (by the aforementioned *Kiosko Europeo*) at 6.45am and 1.30pm daily, from where it's a ride of around 15km or so to the *Posada*. You can also take the same bus to the waterfalls although you'll have to get off where the road forks for Communidad Estanzuela.

Ocotal and the Honduran border

A dusty highway leads north from Estelí to **OCOTAL**, a pleasant, cool place located in a bowl of green mountains, and a useful stopover on the way to or from Honduras. **Buses** run between Ocotal and Estelí roughly every half an hour until 6pm; going in the other direction from Estelí, the last bus is at 4.40pm (there are also frequent express buses from Ocotal to Managua until 3.30pm). The bus terminal is on the highway 1km south from the town centre. The best **place to stay** is the *Hotel Frontera* (Ⓣ732-2668, Ⓔhofrosa@ibw.com.ni; ❷–❺), 1km north of town by the Shell station. All rooms have TV, a/c and bath with hot water, and there's also a bar, restaurant and swimming pool. The more expensive upper rooms have balconies with great views of the surrounding hills.

The main road snaking on northwards leads to the border post at Las Manos, a refreshing trip, with pine trees straggling across precipitous mountain ridges. Not quite as busy as the crossing at Guasaule, the crossing over is relatively painless. You'll have to fill out the usual form and pay the standard rate of US$2 (payable only in US dollars), although this fee doubles if you arrive at lunchtime (noon–2pm), at weekends or on public holidays. Note that while the post is open 24 hours, vehicles can only cross between 8am and 5pm. If entering Nicaragua, the process is the same although the cost is US$7 (US$9 outside normal hours and again payable only in dollars). At Honduran *migración* you'll be charged a flat rate of US$2, payable in either dollars or lempiras. If you're entering Honduras there are regular buses from Las Manos to the nearest town, El Paraíso, while two direct buses a day leave for Tegucigalpa (currently 9am and 2pm). Going from the border to Ocotal, buses leave every 15minutes until 6pm, while buses from Ocotal to Los Manos run roughly every half-hour until 4.40pm.

Matagalpa and around

Known as "La Perla del Septentrión" – Pearl of the North – **MATAGALPA** is spoken well of by virtually everyone in Nicaragua, principally, one suspects, because of its relatively cool climate: at about 21–25°C, it's considered *tierra fría* in this land of 30°C-plus temperatures. Located 130km northeast of the capital on the Carretera Interamericana, Matagalpa is a small, quiet town set among blue-green mountains covered in coffee plantations. Most visitors come here to visit the **Hotel Selva Negra** to the north, one of the country's premier tourist attractions.

Matagalpa's services, hotels and restaurants are spread out between the seven or eight blocks that divide the town's two principal parques. At the northern end of town, the **Parque Morazán** fronts the **Catedral de San Pedro**, dating from 1874. Unusually, the cathedral was constructed side on, with its bell towers and entrance facing away from the Parque. A large **Sandinista monument** showing three men firing guns stands on the east side of the Parque. Smaller **Parque Darío** in the south is the site of several hospedajes and restaurants. Two main thoroughfares, Av José Benito Escobar and Av Central, link the two squares.

The **Casa Museo Comandante Carlos Fonseca** (Mon–Fri 2–4pm; donations), 100m southeast of the Parque Darío, documents the life of a martyred local hero, gunned down by Somoza's National Guard in 1976, while the new **Museo del Café**, one and a half blocks south of Parque Morazán (Mon–Fri 8am–noon & 2–5pm, Sat 8am–noon; free), houses some interesting old photos of Matagalpa life and explanations of the coffee-growing process (in Spanish). The museum sells quality coffee and is also the brains behind Matagalpa's new Feria Nacional del Café (held in November), a festival celebrating the town's coffee expertise with seminars, talks and performances of local music. At the Tienda de Cerámica Negra, two blocks north of Parque Rubén Darío, you can buy examples of Matagalpa's typical artesanía, including the distinctive **black pottery** (*cerámica negra*) whose style indicates a link between the indigenous people of the Matagalpa area and the Maya – this type of pottery is otherwise found only in southern Mexico.

Practicalities

Buses arrive at Matagalpa's surprisingly civilised **bus terminal** and market, southwest of the city centre; it's about a ten-minute walk from the terminal to Parque Darío. The Intur **tourist office** (Mon–Fri 8am–12.30pm & 2–5pm; ⓣ612-7060) is two blocks north and half a block east of Parque Darío. The friendly and well-informed staff offers details about visiting coffee estates in the region, a trip known as the Ruta del Café. A number of **banks** sit on Av Central just south of Parque Morazán: Bancentro will change dollars and travellers' cheques. For phone calls head to **Enitel**, a block northeast of Parque Morazán (Mon–Fri 8am–7pm, Sat 9am–1pm).

If you have to spend the night in Matagalpa, the choice of **accommodation** isn't great but has improved significantly in the past year or so; many tourists still head out of town to stay at the *Hotel Selva Negra* (see below). The best-value options include the *Hotel Apante* on the east side of Parque Darío (☎612-6890; ❸), which offers tasteful, immaculate rooms with TV, colourfully tiled, hot-water bath and modern, comfortable beds. There's also an upstairs terrace with great views and Budget car rental facilities (from US$35 per day with one day free). The *Hotel Alvarado*, located just north of Parque Darío (☎612-2830; ❸), is another good choice, a family-run place above a *farmacia* with cute, wood-panelled rooms, the most desirable being on the top floor. The best-value **food** in town is to be had at *Antojitos de Maíz* (no sign on the door but look for the bamboo awning; closed Sun), one block north of Parque Morazán, with delicious traditional Nica fare at US$1–2 (the incredible-value Filete de Res comes highly recommended), *refrescos* for US$0.30 and very friendly, attentive service. Long-established local favourite *La Posada*, half a block west of Parque Darío, is the place for chicken, especially on weekends when it doubles as one of the most popular dancefloors in town.

The Selva Negra

North of Matagalpa, the **Selva Negra** is an area of dark blue, pine-clad mountains named by the area's German immigrants in the nineteenth century in emulation of their home country's Black Forest, which it strangely resembles. An amazing variety of wildlife flourishes in these pristine and sparsely populated tropical forests, including over eighty varieties of orchid, many birds (including the elusive, resplendent quetzal), and sloths, ocelots, margay, puma, deer and howler monkeys – all of which are more likely to be spotted here than anywhere else in the country. Due to its high altitude (around 1300m), the area has a spring-like climate and a refreshing mean temperature of 18°C. As well as the climate, travellers are attracted by the region's walking and wildlife-spotting opportunities. That said, you can't just head off into the mountains: much of the terrain is farmed or under coffee cultivation, and trails are virtually non-existent.

Because it offers an accessible route to the forest and mountains, nearly everyone who comes here stays in the **Hotel de la Montaña Selva Negra**, 10km from Matagalpa on the road to Jinotega (☎612-5713, Ⓦwww.selvanegra.com; ❺). An establishment of national repute, prices are high by Nicaraguan standards, but worthwhile, with accommodation in individually designed cabañas set in beautifully landscaped grounds; there's also a pricey restaurant on site serving traditional German fare like sauerkraut as well as local options and a hearty US$5 breakfast buffet on Sundays. At the time of writing, dorm facilities were in the works with rooms holding up to six people at a projected cost of US$10 per person. The various hiking trails snaking through the cloudforest in the hotel grounds are poorly marked and, in places, badly maintained; there's a real risk of getting lost so make sure you bring plenty of food and water. The trails are nevertheless fairly short and it's perfectly feasible to come up from Matagalpa early in the morning and pack most of them into a day's hiking; all you'll have to pay is the entrance fee of US$1.60. The hotel's owners, Eddy and Mausi Kuhl, come from a German family who arrived in Matagalpa in 1891 to grow coffee, and Eddy's finca still produces some of the best export-grade coffee in the country; the estate currently employs 250 workers, most of whom live nearby in specially built houses (there's even a school and health clinic on site). Worthwhile **tours** of the operation are run daily at 9am and 3pm (US$3 for guests, US$5 for visitors).

Jinotega

Set amid cool, lush mountains 34km north from Matagalpa, is the nondescript but pleasant town of **JINOTEGA**, famous for the coffee grown nearby. Many *internacionalistas* have been posted to Jinotega over the years, and the town has a generally friendly attitude toward strangers, though most travellers only stop here on day-trips from Matagalpa. It's worth coming to Jinotega simply for the ride, however, since the journey between here and Matagalpa is one of the most magnificent in the country, winding slowly up through misty green mountains, though the road is badly maintained. The climate here is significantly cooler than much of Nicaragua with low cloud and drizzle not uncommon; bring a sweater or light jacket.

There's a helpful Intur **tourist office**, half a block east of the Parque (Mon–Fri 8am–noon & 2–5pm; ⓣ632-4552), which offers info on the Ruta del Café, organises trips to the historic village of San Rafael del Norte and presents traditional music and dance on the last Thursday of each month. If you get caught in between buses and have **to stay**, the best-value option is probably *El Hotelito* (ⓣ632-2079; ❷), one block east of Banco Caley Dagnall, which comprises breezy, sunny rooms with mountain views and plywood-like walls. More upscale is *Hotel Café* (ⓣ632-22710, ⓕ632-4311, ⓔcafehtl@ibw.com.ni; ❻), one block east and half a block north of the Texaco garage, with plush a/c rooms (private bath and hot water) and continental breakfast. For **eating**, *Restaurante El Tico* (ⓣ632-2530), up by the bus station, comes highly rated for its cheap, melt-in-the-mouth steak and good service; they also serve the best *limonada* (fresh lemonade) in the north.

5.3

The southwest

The majority of Nicaragua's population lives in the fertile plain that makes up the **southwest** of the country. Bordered by Lago de Nicaragua to the east and the Pacific to the west, the area has been prized since pre-Columbian times for its agricultural potential. Studded by volcanoes – Volcán Masaya, Volcán Mombacho just south of Granada, and the twin cones of Ometepe's Concepción and Maderas – the southwest is otherwise a flat, low, grassy plain, ideally suited to cattle, and most of what is left of Nicaragua's beef industry is concentrated here, while coffee plantations can be found at higher altitudes. The area has always been at

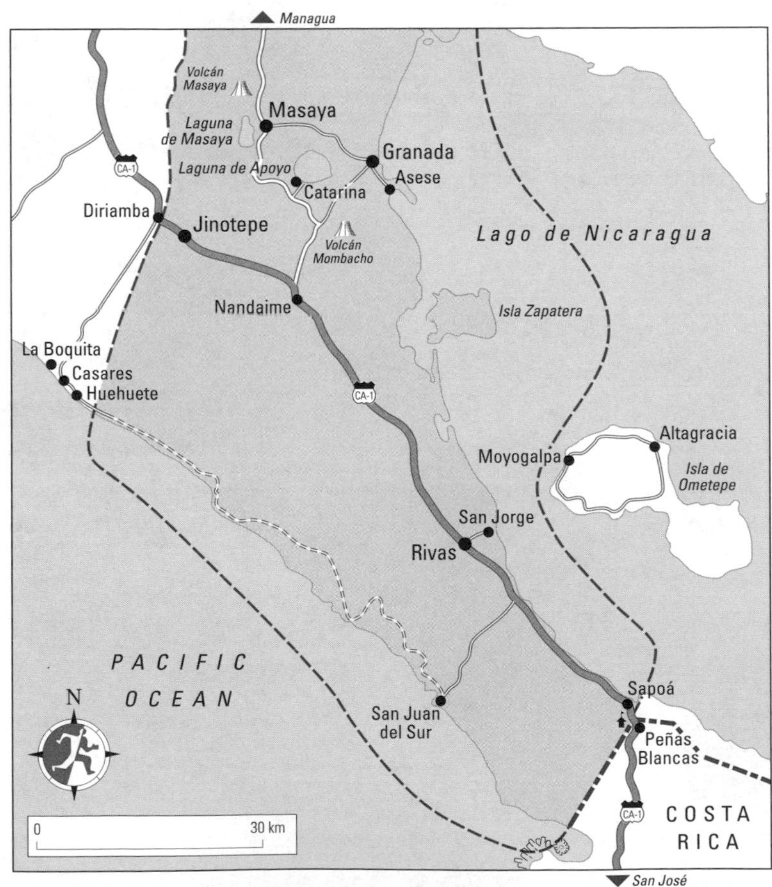

the hub of the economy and politics of the country, and many of Nicaragua's most prominent political families, including the Chamorros, come from here.

The region's only two cities of any size are Masaya, 29km south of Managua, and Granada, 26km further south. **Masaya**'s enormous craft market attracts virtually everyone who comes to Nicaragua, while the nearby **Parque Nacional Volcán Masaya** offers the most accessible volcano viewing in the country. With its fading classical-colonial architecture and lakeside setting, **Granada** is undeniably Nicaragua's most beautiful and popular city, and also makes a good base for exploring many nearby attractions including the **Isletas de Granada** and **Volcán Mombacho**. The road connecting Managua, Masaya and Granada passes through the picturesque "**Pueblos Blancos**", or White Towns – Nindiri, Niquinohomo, Masatepe, Catarina, Diria and Diriomo – small sleepy settlements boasting indigenous-influenced food, crafts, and traditions and fiestas inherited from the Chorotega and the Mangue groups of native Nicaraguans. Some 75km south of Granada, **Rivas**, the gateway to Costa Rica, is of little interest in itself, though many travellers pass through on their way south or en route to **San Juan del Sur**, the most pleasant beach town in Nicaragua, where surfing, swimming and seafood are the main attractions.

Masaya and around

Set between the Managua–Granada Highway and the hulking form of Volcán Masaya, **MASAYA**'s stirring geography would make it an attractive town to visit even if it weren't also the centre of Nicaragua's artesanía production and home to two colourful crafts markets. These are of quite recent provenance – only during the Sandinista years did Masaya and the Pueblos Blancos develop their crafts tradition into a marketable commodity – but Masaya is now by far the best place in the country to buy hammocks, rocking chairs, traditional clothing, shoes and other souvenirs. Many of the crafts on sale came originally from the indigenous barrio of **Monimbó**, and the district continues to churn out a sizeable proportion of the region's handicrafts. Monimbó still has its own chief (*cacique*), whose authority was recognized in law in 1991, though other signs of true indigenous culture are scarce, and Masaya's cultural affinities are expressed mainly in its crafts and at fiesta time.

The most exciting time to visit Masaya is on Sundays between mid-September and mid-December, when the town indulges in a ninety-day period of revelry known as the **Fiesta de San Jerónimo**. The beginning of the fiesta sees one of the most fascinating processions in Nicaragua, the **Torovenado**, when Monimbó's large gay population comes out in style, indulging in a spot of cross-dressing and ridiculing those in power, including the politicians of the moment. A more recent invention is the popular **Jueves de Verbena** festival, held every Thursday evening throughout the year, when a spirited celebration of indigenous culture, music, dance and gastronomy is held in the renovated Mercado Nacional de Artesanía, and locals, tourists and musicians dance, sing, eat and drink the night away.

Most visitors come here on day-trips from Managua or Granada – a sensible plan, since Masaya doesn't have a large range of hotels and the bus services are fast and efficient.

Arrival, information and accommodation

Buses from Managua's Mercado Roberto Huembes and from Granada arrive at the huge, dusty terminal next to Masaya's **main market**, to the east of town; it's a longish walk to the centre from here, so ask to be let off earlier, at the Iglesia San Jerónimo. Express minibuses between Managua and Masaya arrive at and depart from (every 15 minutes or so) the street in front of the small Parque San Miguel, three blocks east of the Parque Central.

There's a very useful **Intur** tourist office, staffed by local volunteers, in the **Mercado Nacional de Artesanía** (Mon–Fri 8am–4pm, Saturday 8am–noon;

☎522-7615). The Enitel office sits on the west side of Parque Central (Mon–Fri 8am–8pm, Sun 8am–noon), and the Bancentro next door offers an efficient dollar exchange and also changes travellers' cheques. There's an abundance of **Internet** cafés, including *Mi PC a Colores* next door to *Hotel Regis*, charging an hourly rate of less than US$1 along with dirt-cheap international calls.

Masaya isn't really the place to bed down for the night; pickings are slim and **hotels** are not used to catering for tourists. Run by a kindly elderly couple, the spotlessly clean *Hotel Regis*, one block east and half a block south of Iglesia San Jerónimo (☎522-2300; ❸), has cell-like, wood-panelled rooms with thin partition walls. Next door, the friendly *Hotel Central* (☎522-2867; ❸) competes on price and ambiance with brighter rooms (private bath optional) and cheaper breakfasts. Across the street, *Hotel Montecarlo* (☎522-2927; ❷) is probably the best of the lot: while the downstairs rooms are a bit poky, there's a lovely, big, wooden-floored room upstairs with balcony; ask if it's free.

The Town

Masaya is an attractive place to explore on foot: there's fairly little traffic in the streets and the heat is bearable. What little action there is in downtown Masaya takes place in the **Parque Central** where – with the help of Spanish finance – **La Parroquia de la Ascunción** has been renovated. It boasts images of various Central American saints inside, swathed in coloured satin and wilting gold lamé. More plain in its decor is the **Iglesia de San Jerónimo**, 600m north, the best example of colonial architecture in Masaya, despite its run-down condition. The statue of San Jerónimo on the altar depicts an old man wearing a loincloth and a straw hat, with a rock in his hand and blood on his chest, evidence of self-mortification.

Masaya's main attractions are its two **crafts markets**. The larger, located in the main market (open daily) next to the bus terminal, is the best place in Nicaragua to buy craft items, many of them produced in Masaya and nearby towns. Goods on sale include paintings, many in the naif-art tradition of the Solentiname archipelago, large, excellent-quality hammocks, carved wooden bowls and utensils, simple wood-and-bead jewellery, cotton shirts, straw hats, and leather footwear, bags and purses. Bargaining is accepted, and although prices are generally quoted in córdobas, traders will accept US dollars (small bills are best), though you may get change in córdobas. The mercado is an easy walk from the centre, but if the heat is getting you down, grab one of the many taxis or horse-drawn carriages, which will take you anywhere in town for about US$0.75.

The Mercado Viejo, or Old Market, has been converted into the grandly named **Centro Cultural (Antiguo Mercado de Masaya) – Mercado Nacional de Artesanía**, a pleasant mini-mall selling colourful pottery, carvings, bags, books and wall hangings. The prices are slightly higher than in the main market, but it has a nice atmosphere, a few cafés and is the site of the weekly **Jueves de Verbena** party night. Check out the giant wall map of the country, which shows the places in Nicaragua where crafts are produced. If your Spanish is up to it, ask about visiting artisans at work in their homes and workshops. Just a block to the east are a couple of artisan shops, Los Tapices de Luís and Rincón de las Artesanías, worth visiting, but again pricier than the market.

The **Laguna de Masaya** beckons on the western side of town, seven blocks from the Parque Central. Despite its crystalline and inviting appearance, the *laguna* is actually highly polluted with sewage effluent from the town. It's still worth the walk, however, as the Malecón here gives a stunning view of the smoking cone of Volcán Masaya (see overleaf).

Eating, drinking and nightlife

What it lacks in places to stay, Masaya makes up for in its tasty and cheap **eating** establishments. In the centre of town the best choice is *Restaurante Che-Gris*, just around the corner to the south of the *Hotel Regis*, which is renowned for its *brochettas* (meat on skewers), prawns in garlic sauce and chicken soup. *Comedor La Criolla*, a couple blocks north, offers a popular buffet with filling *comida típica* (plus rarities like *cannelloni*) for under US$2. Best of all, however, is the fabulous Mexican cuisine at *La Jorochita*, on Av Sergio Delgadillo, north of La Asunción (☎522-4831), where the waitresses are kitted out in traditional dress and you can dine off tacos and fajitas for about US$5. For nightlife, *El Delfín Azul*, opposite *Hotel Madera's Inn*, is open weekends until 3am.

Coyotepe

Three kilometres out of town on the road to Managua is the old fort of **Coyotepe**. Built on a hilltop by the Somoza regime to house political prisoners, the abandoned and decaying structure commands stunning views of Masaya, Laguna de Apoyo and the volcanoes of Masaya and Mombacho, and also offers an eerie reminder of the atrocities carried out here by Somoza's National Guard – bring a torch and you can poke around in the darkened and eerie dungeons. When Sandinistas stormed the fort during the Revolution, the National Guard responded by slaughtering all those inside. From Masaya, take any Managua-bound bus and ask to be let off at the entrance, from where a winding path leads up to the untended fort.

Parque Nacional Volcán Masaya

Just outside Masaya, the **Parque Nacional Volcán Masaya** (Mon–Sun 9am–5pm; US$4) offers a glimpse into the smoking cone of a volcano along with stunning long-distance views. Gazing warily down into the crater's precipitous, sulphurous depths, you can well imagine why the Spaniards considered this to be the mouth of hell itself. The large white cross above the crater marks the spot where Friar Francisco de Bobadilla placed his original cross in the sixteenth century, an attempt to exorcise the volcano's demonic presence. These days, the only dangers facing tourists are mortal ones; lone visitors should consider the transport provided by the ranger service (details below) as robberies hereabouts are not unheard of. Nor are eruptions: Volcán Masaya is known as one of the most active volcanoes in the world, erupting as recently as April 2001 when it rained rocks onto the parking area and spewed lava perilously close to it.

The **park entrance** lies between Km 22 and Km 23 on the Managua–Granada highway, about 4km north of Masaya. You can get off any bus between Managua and Masaya or Granada (except the express) at the entrance, from where you can either hike the fairly steep five-kilometre paved road up to the crater and back again or organise transport with a park ranger (US$2); ask at the centre detailed below. Alternatively, you could hire a taxi from Masaya. About 1.5 km from the park entrance, along the approach road, is the **Centro de Interpretación Ambiental** (Mon–Sun 9am–5pm), home to an exhibition outlining the area's geology, agriculture and pre-Columbian history, along with an interesting three-dimensional display of the country's chain of volcanoes. There are toilet facilities and you can stock up on cold drinks and water before the climb. There's also a shady picnic area nearby as well as a viewing point on a rickety boardwalk out the back.

For those interested in seeing the unique flora and fauna at closer range, the ranger service also offer cheap guided **tours** on two trails, Sendero Los Coyotes and Sendero de Las Pencas, as well as short trips to the extinct cone of Comelito and the subterranean Cueva Tzinancanostoc where you can view bizarre lava formations and a bat colony. Look out for the stunted bromeliads common to high-altitude volcanic areas as well as the famous *chocoyos del cráter*, small green parrots that have thrived in an atmosphere that should be poisonous. You're most likely to see them perching on the fence along the perimeter of the parking lot at the Centro de Interpretación Ambiental.

The Pueblos Blancos

Scattered within a fifteen-kilometre radius of Masaya are the "Pueblos Blancos" or White Towns – **Nindiri**, **Niquinohomo**, **Masatepe**, **Catarina**, **Diria** and **Diriomo** – small pueblos held dear all over the country as the embodiment of all things Nicaraguan (or, more precisely, all things from the country's Pacific zone). They get their name from the traditional whitewash used on the houses, **carburo**, which is made from water, lime and salt. The white buildings are pretty, but that said, there's not much more actually to see, few places to sample any cuisine and no handicrafts obviously on sale. Although each town has its own specific artisan traditions and fiestas, and local identity is fiercely asserted, to the visitor they seem remarkably similar, sleepy towns with a few hangers-out around nearly identical central squares. Niquinohomo was the birthplace of Augusto César Sandino, and the house in which he grew up is marked by a plaque opposite the Parque Central.

If you want to visit just one, **CATARINA** is the prettiest. The main draw is **El Mirador**, a magical lookout point at the top of the village that stares right down into the blue waters of the collapsed crater lake of **Laguna de Apoyo**, with Volcán

Masaya looming behind it. Restaurants, cafés and artesanía stalls have sprung up around the viewpoint. A regular local **bus** runs roughly every thirty minutes from Masaya's main bus terminal to Catarina. From Granada, buses to Niquinohomo pass through the town or alternatively you can take any Masaya or Managua bus and ask to get off at the Catarina turning, from where you'll need to take another short bus ride to the edge of the village.

Granada

Set on the western shore of Lago de Nicaragua some 50km southeast of Managua, **GRANADA** was once the jewel of Central America. The oldest Spanish-built city in the isthmus, it was founded in 1524 by Francisco Fernández de Córdoba, who named it after his hometown in Spain. During the colonial period Granada became fabulously rich, its wealth built upon exploitation: sited only 20km from the Pacific, the city was a transit point for shipments of **gold** and other minerals mined throughout the Spanish empire, with the help of indigenous slave labour. Laden Spanish galleons would sail from Granada across the lake, down the Río San Juan, out to the Caribbean and then to Europe. The wealth of the city also attracted traffic in the other direction: Granada's gold stores proved tempting to buccaneers and it was sacked several times by English and French **pirates**, until the Spanish built their **Castillo**, a fort on the banks of the Río San Juan (see p.553).

Granada's wealth and the generations of *criollos* – people of Spanish descent born in the New World – who made it their home contributed to its conservative character. The split between liberal León, the only other city of any size in the country, and conservative Granada developed as early as the eighteenth century, and persists to this day. At the beginning of the nineteenth century, feelings of rivalry between the two cities were ignited by Nicaraguan independence. With the departure of the Spanish, a power vacuum developed and the elite of León decided to fill it by inviting the troublesome American, **William Walker** (see p.488), to fight their cause. Walker attacked and captured Granada, from where he ruled the country for two years until being finally driven out. On his retreat from Granada, Walker ordered the city burned, and most of it subsequently fell into ruin (you can still see the black marks on the facade of the cathedral).

Granada never recovered its original splendour, though it's still the most architecturally arresting town in Nicaragua; the city's recent tourist boom has led to a large-scale restoration of the old colonial buildings, many of them newly re-painted in pastel shades. Today Granada is central to the Nicaraguan government's tourism ambitions, and a burgeoning network of foreign-owned bars, restaurants and hostels have sprung up to service the increasing number of visitors. The city also makes a good base from which to explore the lake, volcanoes, the Zapatera archipelago and Isla de Ometepe, while more adventurous travellers might head on to the Solentiname Islands and San Carlos (see p.555).

Arrival and information

Regular buses from Managua come into the **terminal** west of town, 700m from the Parque Central, from where you can walk or grab a taxi into the centre (expect to pay around US$1). Arriving from Rivas and points south, buses pull up at the **mercado**, a short walk southwest of the centre. Express **minivans** from Managua arrive at the small terminal half a block south of the Parque Central. If you're travelling from Costa Rica, the **Ticabus** for Managua will stop and let you off at its Granada office. The most exciting way to arrive, however, is by **boat** from San Carlos on the other side of Lago de Nicaragua (arrives Wednesday and Saturday; 12–14hr), as seemingly half of Granada comes out to watch the old boat dock. Although spread out, Granada can be explored comfortably on **foot**. **Horse-drawn taxis** are available, although the horses look thin and thirsty; a better bet are the **taxis** that line up in front of the *Hotel Alhambra* on the Parque Central.

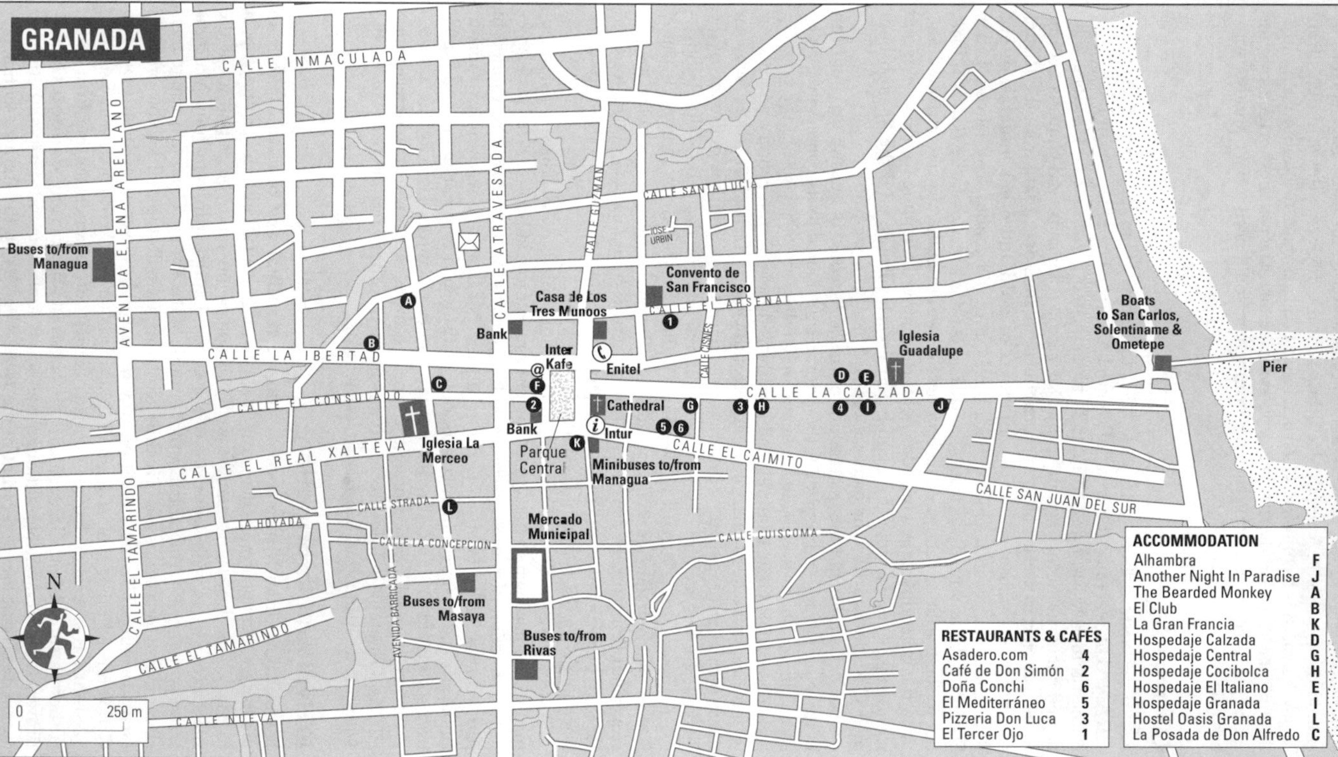
GRANADA
ACCOMMODATION
Alhambra F
Another Night In Paradise J
The Bearded Monkey A
El Club B
La Gran Francia K
Hospedaje Calzada D
Hospedaje Central G
Hospedaje Cocibolca H
Hospedaje El Italiano E
Hospedaje Granada I
Hostel Oasis Granada L
La Posada de Don Alfredo C
RESTAURANTS & CAFÉS
Asadero.com 4
Café de Don Simón 2
Doña Conchi 6
El Mediterráneo 5
Pizzeria Don Luca 3
El Tercer Ojo 1
Calle Inmaculada
Avenida Elena Arellano
Calle Atravesada
Calle Guzman
Calle Santa Lucia
Jose Urbin
Calle El Arsenal
Calle Cisnes
Calle La Ibertad
Calle El Consulado
Calle El Real Xalteva
Calle La Calzada
Calle El Caimito
Calle San Juan del Sur
Calle Cuiscoma
Calle Strada
La Hoyada
Calle La Concepcion
Avenida Barricada
Calle El Tamarindo
Calle Nueva
Buses to/from Managua
Casa de Los Tres Munoos
Bank
Inter Kafe
Enitel
Convento de San Francisco
Iglesia Guadalupe
Boats to San Carlos, Solentiname & Ometepe
Pier
Cathedral
Intur
Parque Central
Minibuses to/from Managua
Iglesia La Merceo
Mercado Municipal
Buses to/from Masaya
Buses to/from Rivas
N
0 250 m

All the **banks** in town change dollars; Bancentro, one block west of the Parque on C Atravesada, will change travellers' cheques, while Banco de América Central, on the south side of the Parque Central, has an ATM. The **post office** (Mon–Fri 8am–5pm, Sat 8am–noon), on C Atrevesada, has a reliable overseas mail service. The **Enitel** office is a block north of the cathedral, and there are **Internet** cafés (US$1–2 per hour) dotted around town; most popular is *Cafemail* next to the Casa de los Tres Mundos.

Accommodation

The range of **places to stay** in Granada has improved immeasurably over the past five years and renovation work continues apace. The city now boasts a comprehensive variety of accommodation options from budget hostels to upmarket hotels, with most of the newer places pitched at the upper end of the market.

Alhambra on the Parque Central ⓣ552-4486, ⓔhotalam@tmx.com.ni. Considered one of Nicaragua's finest hotels, this smartly designed, colonial-style establishment has rooms with a/c, TV, and bath with hot water, plus a swimming pool, bar and restaurant. Prices differ depending on which level you take a room – those higher up have better views over the Parque and are correspondingly more expensive. 6

Another Night In Paradise Calle La Calzada, on the corner opposite the Iglesia Guadalupe ⓣ552-7113, ⓔdonntabor@hotmail.com. Almost lives up to its name with a handful of very tasteful, bijou rooms (all with bath and fan), including a ground-floor double with its own private patio. Breakfast included. 5

The Bearded Monkey Calle 14 de Septiembre ⓣ552-4028, ⓦwww.thebeardedmonkey.com. Backpacker hangout in a renovated colonial house set around a large, verdant courtyard with hammocks, pool table, Internet access and TV. Accommodation consists of large, impersonal dorms (US$3 per person), loft rooms, single, double and triple rooms as well as a suite. There's also an industrious kitchen supplying healthy meat and vegetarian options and a small bar (with daily happy hour). 2

El Club corner of Calle de la Libertad and Avenida Barricada ⓣ552-4245, ⓦwww.elclub-nicaragua.com. Chic, friendly bar/restaurant (see p.543) with three original, luxurious, great-value rooms (all with funky mezzanine level); eleven more under construction as well as a swimming pool. Recommended. 5

La Gran Francia southeastern corner of the Parque Central ⓣ552-6000, ⓦwww.lagranfrancia.com. Newest of the colonial renovations, this centuries old and supposedly haunted building has been immaculately restored in an antique, vaguely Gothic style. Home to twenty rooms (six with balconies), all with a/c, hot water, telephone and TV, the building also boasts two bars, a lush courtyard and an upmarket but reasonably priced restaurant, all with period, religious-themed touches. 7

Hospedaje Calzada Calle La Calzada. Unpretentious, family-run hospedaje with clean, simple rooms, some with private bath. A good-value breakfast is available along with kitchen and laundry facilities and a ping-pong table. 2

Hospedaje Central Calle La Calzada ⓣ552-7044. The most colourful hospedaje in town, with murals, paintings and graffiti on most interior walls; guests are free to make their own artistic contributions. The sprawling accommodation consists of dorm beds (US$3–4 per person), basic but screened rooms with shared bath and two self-contained apartments (US$15/18). There's also a popular bar and restaurant serving "gringo" food. 3

Hospedaje Cocibolca Calle La Calzada ⓣ552-7223, ⓔcarlosgomezos@hotmail.com. Small but very popular hospedaje with homely and good-value rooms (all with private bath), the most desirable coming with a communal balcony and great views. Also has cooking facilities, Internet access and cable TV. 3

Hospedaje El Italiano Calle La Calzada ⓣ552-7047, ⓔitalianricky@latinmail.com. Bright and airy purpose-built new hotel with ten pleasant, pastel-painted rooms (all featuring bath, TV and a/c) grouped around a grassy courtyard. Also has bar and restaurant. Reservations recommended. 5

Hospedaje Granada Calle La Calzada ⓣ552-3716. Pleasant, quiet, family-run hospedaje with its own swimming pool and simple, clean rooms, some with private bath, all with fan. Great-value breakfasts. 3

Hostel Oasis Granada Calle Estrada, 100m north of Masaya bus terminal ⓣ552-8006, ⓔoasisgranada@hotmail.com. A self-proclaimed "backpacker's paradise", this brand new, imaginatively conceived hostel offers comfortable dorm beds (US$6) and private rooms in a restored colonial house. Also free Internet, laundry, bar and even a swimming pool. ❹

La Posada de Don Alfredo one block north of Iglesia La Merced ☎552-4455. A 177-year-old, German-owned colonial house restored in classic, wildly atmospheric style. Boasts a quaint courtyard and six huge rooms (some with private bath) with high ceilings and good beds, while the ebullient caretaker claims to serve the best breakfast in Nicaragua. He also has mountain bikes to rent for US$6 per day. ❹

The Town

Though Granada's stately air has been punctured somewhat of late by the influx of tourists, it remains one of Nicaragua's most relaxing cities, and a pleasant place to spend a few days. There are few "must see" attractions in the city itself, and most of the pleasure is simply in strolling the streets and absorbing the colonial atmosphere – be sure to take a peak through the opened front doors along Calle La Calzada to see the magnificent interior courtyards which adorn some of the houses.

At the centre of town sits the attractive, palm-lined **Parque Central**, where locals and visitors alike spend hours sitting under shaded trees. A few small kiosks sell snacks, while an ice-cream seller wanders around ringing his hand bell in search of trade. On the east side of the Parque is the large but disappointing **Cathedral**, built in 1712 and damaged when William Walker ordered the city burned; often closed to the public, it has a peeling off-white facade and a rusting tin roof. Contrasting the Cathedral are the city's captivating historic houses, many of which are ranged around the square and the **Plaza de la Independencia**, immediately to the north. The palatial red house with white trim on the corner of Calle La Calzada, across from the cathedral, is the **Bishop's Residence**, with a columned upstairs veranda typical of the former homes of wealthy Granadino burghers. About 50m north of the cathedral on the Plaza de la Independencia is the stately **Casa de los Tres Mundos** (previously the Casa de los Leones). Built in 1724, it has been restored and turned into a culture and music centre (daily 8am–6pm; free) with art exhibitions and informal arts rehearsals. Visitors can wander among its covered and open courtyards and maze-like corridors – the wooden panelling and staircases found within are rare in this concrete-and-adobe country.

Originally dating from the sixteenth century but rebuilt in 1867 after Walker's attack, the historic **Convento de San Francisco** (Mon–Fri 8.30am–5.30pm, Sat 8am–5pm; US$2), two blocks northeast of the cathedral, has been converted into one of Nicaragua's best pre-Colombian museums, housing many of the **petroglyphs** recovered from Isla Zapatera. Hewn from black volcanic basalt in about 1000 AD, these petroglyphs depict anthropomorphic creatures – half man, half lizard, turtle or jaguar – which probably had ritual significance for the indigenous peoples who inhabited the islands. It was also from the confines of this convent that in 1535 **Frey Bartolomé de las Casas**, apostle of the indigenous peoples of Central America, wrote his historic letter to the Spanish Court, condemning the Indians' mistreatment at the hands of the Spanish. The Convento also houses the city **library**: many of Walker's filibusters are buried in the catacombs in its basement.

A few blocks southwest of the Parque Central, activity picks up at the **market**, a few blocks of indoor and outdoor stalls surrounding the old green market building. You can grab a cheap bite here, including the likes of hot tamales and *gallo pinto*.

The lakefront

The **shoreline** is about 1km east of the Parque Central; head down the wide boulevard of Calle La Calzada and the wind picks up as the huge vista of the lake stretches across the horizon. The lakefront itself is pretty quiet, unless you happen to arrive as the boat from the other side comes in, when you can watch Granadinos meeting friends and family and see queasy passengers disembark as bananas, chickens and livestock are unloaded along the narrow dock. To the south a small park lines the lake, a few hundred metres beyond which is the entrance to the town's **Complejo Turistico**, a group of lakeside restaurants and bars, a narrow little beach and grassy areas – look for the strange little castle that marks the entrance. It's popular at weekends, but take care here after dark.

Eating, drinking and nightlife

Granada offers an increasingly cosmopolitan variety of places to **eat**, with Italian and Spanish food featuring prominently. Budget travellers can grab a quick but basic bite at the town market, and in the early evening a couple of small food stands open up on the Parque Central, selling cheap and filling meat and rice dishes. The city is often peculiarly dead **at night** (many restaurants are closed by 10pm), and most travellers in search of alcohol and company tend to head either to the candle-lit, bohemian confines of *La Fábrica* (one block south and one block west of the *Monkey*) or to the bars at the *Hospedaje Central* or *The Bearded Monkey*. Other worthwhile options include *Leidy Bar* in the centre of town, a disco/bar with wonderfully eccentric decor and a tiny dancefloor, rammed with locals on weekends. Also very popular with Granadinos is *Café Nuit*, a chic, verdant garden-bar opposite *La Fábrica*, and *El Regresso de la Pantera*, down at the Malecón. The latter is a rough around the edges place with a jam-packed dancefloor; gringo faces are rare, but if you're after an authentic local vibe this is the place.

Asadero.com towards the bottom of C La Calzada. Not an Internet café but a funky little restaurant with imaginative and varied meat and vegetarian platters for under US$4. A bulging visitors' book attests to many satisfied stomachs.

Café de Don Simón on Parque Central next to the BAC bank. Urbane little coffee shop with rustic alfresco tables and delicious breakfasts, popular with gringos. Daily from 6.30am.

El Club corner of Calle de la Libertad and Avenida Barricada. One of the hippest bars in the city, this stylish, Dutch-run hotel/bar (see p.541) attracts well-heeled Managuans as well as gringos and locals in the know. Good music, great food (including Italian *panini*, lasagna and homemade ice cream) and friendly hosts.

Moving on from Granada

Granada's location on the northern shores of Lago de Nicaragua makes it a gateway for **lake transport** to both Altagracia on Isla de Ometepe and San Carlos on the lake's southern shore. Tickets (US$4 to Altagracia, US$7 to San Carlos) are available on the day of travel between noon and 2.30pm from the dock office at the bottom of Calle La Calzada. The city also has good **bus** links to Managua, Masaya and Rivas (for connections to San Jorge, San Juan del Sur and Peñas Blancas). Buses for Managua depart from the terminal to the northwest of the centre; buses for Rivas, Nandaime and Niquinohomo use the small terminal in the market at the southern end of Calle Atravesada; and buses for Masaya depart from the even smaller terminal one block west of the southern end of Calle Atravesada. Express microbuses to Managua leave from yet another terminal half a block south of the Parque Central. All terminals are shown on the map on p.540.

Buses

Managua (every 15min; 1hr, express every 20min; 45min)
Masaya (every 25min; 45min)
Nandaime (every 25min; 1hr)
Niquinohomo (every 20min; 45min)
Rivas (8 daily; 1hr 30min)

Boats

Altagracia (Mon & Thurs at 3pm; 2hr 45min)
San Carlos (Mon & Thurs at 3pm; 12–14hr)

Doña Conchi one block along Calle El Caimito from *El Mediterráneo.* Very good Spanish food – slightly cheaper than *El Mediterráneo* – served in elegant, candle-lit surroundings and often accompanied by live Spanish music.

El Mediterráneo Calle El Caimito, two blocks from the cathedral ⓣ552-6764. Aesthetically conceived Spanish restaurant set around a romantic colonial courtyard dripping with atmosphere and serving imaginative Spanish meat and seafood dishes for US$10–12. Closed Mon.

Pizzeria Don Luca Calle La Calzada, opposite *Hospedaje Cocibolca.* Popular and unpretentious, with pleasingly authentic Italian food for under US$5. The homemade bread is delicious and the fiendishly hot *arrabiata* comes recommended. Closed Mon.

Los Portales opposite the Casa de los Tres Mundos. Open-fronted restaurant serving tasty Mexican and meat dishes for US$3–6.

Querube's in the heart of the market. Buzzing local lunch canteen where you can fill up on delicious *comida típica* for US$1.50, including drinks.

El Tercer Ojo Calle Arsenal, opposite the Convento de San Francisco. Deliciously different, vaguely bohemian tapas bar and upmarket deli rolled into one with fine cheeses, olives and bread on sale. The wine-fuelled happy hour (5–7pm) is a particularly happy time.

Around Granada

Although Granada is a convenient jumping-off point for trips to Ometepe and Solentiname (see p.551), there are a couple of worthwhile day-trips closer by. Granada's small Intur **tourist office** (Mon–Fri 8am–noon & 2–5pm; ⓣ552-6858) is on Calle El Caimito, opposite *La Gran Francia*, and stocks information on climbing local volcanoes and other attractions. For canopy **tours** head to Momobotour on Calle Atravesada, Módulo no. 2 (ⓣ552-4548, ⓦwww.mombotour.com). For **bike** hire, try The Biking Adventure/Gutiérrez Tours, one block east of the Parque Central (ⓣ850-7047, ⓦwww.nicaraguagutierreztours.com). They rent mountain bikes for US$12 per day and run bike tours to Volcán Mombacho – amongst other places – for US$39. Tierra Tour, on Calle Calzada, two blocks east of the cathedral (ⓣ862-9580, ⓔtierratour@yahoo.com), offer tours of the Isletas from US$15 per person, as well as city tours and trips to both volcanoes.

Isla Zapatera and the Isletas de Granada

About 20km south of Granada, in Lago de Nicaragua, **Isla Zapatera** is one of over three hundred and fifty islands scattered about the lake believed to have been formed from the exploded top of Volcán Mombacho. Many of the pre-Columbian artefacts and treasures you find in museums throughout the country came from this group of islands, which must have been of religious significance for the Chorotega-descended people who flourished here before the Conquest. At 52 square kilometres, Zapatera is the largest of the islands, skirted by attractive bays and topped by the much-eroded form of an extinct volcano. The island has been granted national park status, but that doesn't mean it's easy to get there. Unless you've got some nifty local connections, the only way to go is with a recognized travel agency, such as Tierra Tour in Granada, or Tours Nicaragua in Managua, which offers informed archeological excursions to the island (see p.515). Guides should be able to show you **El Muerto** (The Dead), a site chock-full of the remains of tombs, several **petroglyphs**, and the scant remains – a few grassy mounds and stones – of **Sozafe**, a site sacred to the Chorotegas. These remains apart, there's really very little to see, bar lovely views of the lake.

The alternative to a tour is to buzz round the **Isletas de Granada** in a hired lancha. Boatmen in **Puerto Asese**, a fifteen-minute drive or one-hour walk south of Granada, beyond the Complejo Turistico, charge around US$15 per hour for a boat for up to four people (be prepared to negotiate). You don't see much on the standard hour-long trip, so you may want to negotiate a two- or three-hour ride. Make sure the boat is covered, or take a hat and plenty of sunscreen – the sun out on the water is punishing. While many of the 300 islands are inhabited, the bulk of the accommodation consists of private holiday homes and your best bet for lodging is available at *Hotel La Ceiba* on La Ceiba island (☎882-2392; ❻), a venture operated by the Managua-based Nicarao Lake Resort (see p.515 for contact details). In addition to air-conditioned rooms with private bath, they also have four-person backpacker dorms (US$10 per person) and run their own boats to the island (US$15) from Puerto Asese. It's also possible to hire out an entire island – Isleta El Tempisque – for US$200 (this gets you two days and one night). The price includes accommodation with bed space for up to eighteen people, kitchen facilities, swimming pool, hammocks, fishing equipment etc. For more info call ☎279-9600.

Volcán Mombacho

Created in 1983, the Reserva **Nacional Volcán Mombacho** (Tues & Wed 8am–5pm for groups of ten or more, Thurs–Sun for the general public; US$8) was set up to protect and study the unique ecology of Volcán Mombacho, whose slopes are home to one of only two **cloudforests** (the other is at Volcán Maderas on Isla Ometepe) in Nicaragua's Pacific region. The cloudforest is able to grow here due to the volcano's height – its peak is frequently cloud covered – and the strong, cooling winds from Lago de Nicaragua. The reserve is run by the Fundación Cocibolca, whose interesting **research station and visitor centre** at the volcano's summit acts as the centre for the study and protection of the reserve's flora and fauna – which includes three species of monkey, 22 species of reptile, 87 species of orchid, 175 species of bird and some 50,000 species of insect. There's a well-marked **trail** around the four craters at the top of the volcano with signs explaining some of the reserve's unique flora and fauna. At the furthest point of the trail the views open out to provide a magnificent panoramic vista of Lago de Nicaragua, Granada, Las Isletas, Masaya and Laguna de Apoyo.

To get to the volcano take any **bus** from Granada bound for Rivas or Nandaime and ask to be let off at the turn-off for the park (at Intersection El Guanacaste; there's also a sign). From the turn-off it's a two and a half kilometre walk to the entrance, from where it takes two hours to walk to the top. Alternatively, you can take the "Eco-truck" to the summit – it leaves from the reserve entrance at 8.30am, 10am, 1pm and 3pm.

Rivas

Most travellers experience **RIVAS** as a dusty bus stop on the way to or from Costa Rica, San Juan del Sur, or Ometepe, unaware of the important role this unprepossessing town has played in Nicaraguan history. Founded in 1736, it became an important stop on the route of Cornelius Vanderbilt's Accessory Transit Company, which ferried goods and passengers between the Caribbean and the Pacific via Lago de Nicaragua – Rivas's heyday came during the California Gold Rush, when its languid streets were full of prospectors travelling with the Transit Company on their way to the goldfields of the western US.

Modern-day Rivas isn't actually such a bad place to get stuck in for a day. The colonial church on the **Parque Central** is worth a visit, primarily for a fresco featuring a maritime-themed depiction of Catholicism triumphing over the Godless communists. Also worth searching out is the **Museo de Antropología e Historia de Rivas** (daily 8am–5pm; US$1), situated five blocks west of the parque. Among the museum's highlights are recently unearthed artefacts of the local Nahua Nicarao people dating from the fourteenth to sixteenth centuries, prehistoric animal bones (thought to be from a mammoth), stuffed animals and even some dusty Latin 78rpm records from the turn of the early twentieth century. If feeling lazy, you can get around on town on a *papano* (bicycle taxis); they cost next to nothing and – potholes not withstanding – offer a surprisingly comfortable ride.

Practicalities

Rivas's ragged market and bus terminal, three blocks south and two blocks west of the Parque Central, is the **transport hub** of southern Nicaragua. From here you can catch buses north to Granada, Masaya and Managua; west to San Juan del Sur; and south to Peñas Blancas and the Costa Rican border. Bus stops in the market are not marked but everyone knows where buses depart – ask around. If headed to San Jorge (for Ometepe), it's best to get a **taxi** (US$1.50) as buses are infrequent and leave from the highway, a kilometre hike from the market. **Moneychangers** frequent Rivas's bus stops, looking for Costa Rican–bound or departing gringos and offering Costa Rican colónes, Nicaraguan córdobas and US dollars at rates more or less the same as at the border. In town, Banpro, two and a half blocks west of the Parque Central, will change dollars and there's an ATM in the Texaco garage near the entrance to town.

The town's **accommodation** selection isn't outstanding but there are a few decent options. The *Hotel Nicarao*, two blocks west of the Parque Central (Ⓣ453-3234, Ⓕ453-3120; ❻), is better than most, and its white, brick-walled rooms are equipped with private bath and either a/c or fan. For rock-bottom budget travellers, best bet is *El Primavera* (Ⓣ453-3298; ❷), near the Shell garage on the eastern edge of town next to the main highway. A quick, cheap **meal** can be picked up at any of the comedores on the Parque Central, where you'll find good chicken, pork or beef and rice dishes, and tamales. For seafood try the shiny new ranch-style *La Carreta*, one block north of the square, while *Chop Suey* – off the far south side of the parque – offers Chinese dishes alongside Nica favourites.

San Juan del Sur

You would never suspect it today, but in the mid-1800s the sleepy fishing village-cum-beach town of **SAN JUAN DEL SUR** was a crucial transit point on Cornelius Vanderbilt's trans-isthmian steamboat line, on which people and goods were transported to Gold Rush–era California. Boats would sail up the Río San Juan, disembark at Granada, and then continue by rail or carriage to San Juan del Sur, from where Pacific-going vessels would head north. A second age of glory arrived in the 1980s, as hordes of *internacionalistas* visited, making the town a well-known **holiday spot**.

Today San Juan del Sur is the most popular beach town in Nicaragua, at least with foreign travellers – European backpackers and American surfers together make up the biggest contingent. Located in a lush valley with a river running down to the town's beach, the setting is beautiful; the beach itself is a long wide stretch of fine dark sand running between two cliffs, with generally calm and shallow waters, suitable for swimming, and magnificent sunsets over the harbour. With excellent seafood restaurants and an increasing number of good places to stay, San Juan is the kind of town you could easily spend a few days in and it's experiencing yet another resurgence, with new hotels and restaurants springing up regularly. To the south are some beautiful and remote beaches, good for **surfing** or relaxing (although not necessarily swimming – the surf is rough).

Arrival and information

Buses leave Rivas every 45 minutes, and take 45 minutes to reach San Juan del Sur, pulling up outside the *Hospedaje Elizabeth* near the market. Almost as cheap (a mere US$1) and much quicker is a colectivo taxi, a fleet of which run regularly between the two towns. There's no tourist office in San Juan del Sur, but you can get **information** from *Casa Joxi* or *Maria's Bar* – the latter also rents out **bikes**. The **Enitel** office, two blocks south of *Hotel Estrella*, has an international phone service (Mon–Fri 8am–8pm, Sat & Sun 8am–5pm) and mail service (Mon–Fri 8am–noon, Sat 8am–1pm). You can also make cheap international calls at both *Cyber Leo* (one block back from the beach) and *Super Cyber* (follow the sign one block back from *Marie's Bar*); both charge the pretty standard hourly rate of US$2 for **Internet** usage. There's no bank in town, but many establishments take credit cards, travellers' cheques and dollars.

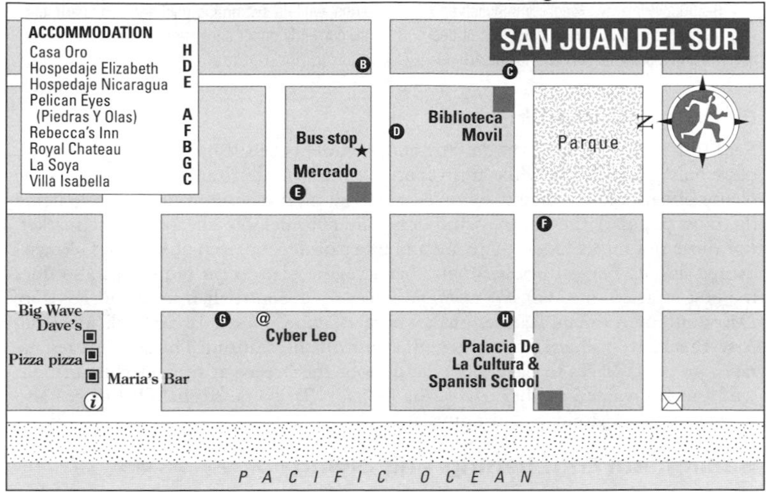

Accommodation

Like Granada, San Juan del Sur has witnessed a considerable expansion of tourist **accommodation**. There's everything from well-appointed hotels to surfer's dens with new arrivals at both ends of the market; the budget places are mainly located on the road to the beach from the bus terminal. Bear in mind that many places instigate price hikes in high season (Christmas and Easter) and on all weekends, during which time you're advised to reserve in advance. Consider avoiding the *Hospedaje Almendros*, as numerous travellers have recently reported missing cash and belongings.

Casa Oro one block behind the beach ⓣ458-2415, ⓔrockettom@hotmail.com. Friendly hostel offering dorms (US$5) as well as comfortable rooms with choice of a/c. Boasts a funky garden patio with hammocks, BBQ, kitchen facilities and a hot tub. ❸

Hospedaje Elizabeth 75m east of the market, opposite bus stop ⓣ458-2270. A ramshackle but friendly and raggedly charming guesthouse with twelve rooms (all have private bath). You can also pick up local maps here and rent bicycles. ❷

Hospedaje Nicaragua two blocks back from the beach. Small and easily missed hospedaje set back from the road with four spotless, well-maintained double rooms, all with fan, desk and private bath (shared shower). Offers relative quiet, privacy and very good value despite the rather hard beds. ❷

Pelican Eyes (Piedras Y Olas) one and a half blocks east from Iglesia Parroquial up a steep hill ⓣ458-2110, ⓔpelican@ibw.com.ni. Luxury, ecologically sound villas set in verdant hillside, many still under construction at time of writing. One option, *Casa Tranquila*, is an enchanting three-person cottage worth every penny of its US$126 price tag. You don't have to be a guest to use the breathtakingly situated bar, restaurant and swimming pool. ❾

Rebecca's Inn just off the northeastern edge of the parque ⓣ880-1476. Budget place with colourful, clean, wood-panelled rooms (fan and shared bath) and friendly service. ❸

Royal Chateau two blocks north from the park ⓣ & ⓕ458-2551. This colourful mock-colonial hotel offers pleasant rooms (some a/c, all private bath) around a huge garden planted with banana trees. The upstairs rooms come with a balcony perfect for sunset watching. ❹

La Soya on the eastern side of the block opposite *Marie's Bar* ⓣ458-2572, ⓔnestorpeterson@hotmail.com. *La Soya* offers four rustic, great-value brick rooms (with fan and shared bath) with seven more (as well as dorms) in the pipeline. The irrepressible owners serve up homemade Italian and Spanish food and plan on creating a garden/chill-out area with the emphasis on partying. ❷

Villa Isabella northwest corner of the Parque ☎458-2568, ✉jaxtraw2@aol.com. Stylish and very friendly American-owned hotel that prides itself on a personalised service. Rooms are immaculate with a/c, screened windows and huge baths, while a swimming pool and two apartments are currently under construction. ❻

Eating and drinking

Seafood is king in San Juan del Sur, and a whole baked fish, big enough for two, costs only US$6 or so, while fresh lobster comes in at around US$10. There are plenty of bars and restaurants serving seafood along the beachfront (*El Timon* being the most popular), though the same dishes are considerably cheaper in the market. For those not into seafood there are a number of decent alternatives: the German-owned *Maria's Bar* sells *wiener schnitzel* and veggie platters on request (it also does the best espresso in town), *Pizza Pizza* serves up decent Italian food and *Big Wave Dave's* humorous menu features quality burgers, good quesadillas and delicious "Big Arse Breakfasts"; all are situated together just off the seafront. The seafront restaurants are good places to have a beer and shoot the breeze at sunset, while gringos tend to congregate in either *Maria's* or *Ricardo's Bar* come **nightfall**; *Ricardo's* also screens films on Mondays and Thursdays.

Sailing, surfing, fishing and diving

The lack of conventional sights in San Juan del Sur means that most people are engaged either in sunning themselves on the beach or undertaking something more energetic in the azure sea beyond. **Surfing** is the most popular sport in town, and you can rent boards and arrange transport to some of the more remote beaches south of town by asking at *Maria's Bar*. San Juan del Sur is also a good spot for **sailing**. All-day cruises sailing south to Brasilito Beach can be arranged – again, ask at *Maria's Bar* – while water-taxis to the beach at Bahía Majagual (12km to the north), meanwhile, leave from the area in front of *Hotel Estrella* at 10am and 1pm daily, returning at 5pm (US$7). You can also travel there by taxi for US$10 one way, US$25 for Playa El Coco, another beach located to the south near La Flor. There's also good **deep-sea fishing** in this area and a number of companies organize trips; try Nicarao Lake Resort, a Managua-based company who operate from *Hotel El Pescador*. Dive Nicaragua (☎458-2505, ⓦwww.divenicaragua.com), next to *Hotel Villa Isabella* (with whom they offer dive/hotel packages), run NAUI and PADI courses (US$375 for full open-water certification) as well as snorkelling and water-skiing trips. San Juan del Sur Divers, 50m east of the Texaco garage (☎279-8628, ⓦwww.abucear.com), also offer fishing trips for US$20 per hour (minimum four hours) with full equipment, in addition to two tank dives for US$50 including all gear.

The **Refugio de Vida Silvestre La Flor**, 19km south of San Juan del Sur (US$10), is an excellent secluded spot to spend a night. It has good surf, a beautiful white sandy beach and a stand of shady trees, and there are more great empty beaches within walking distance. It's also a guarded reserve dedicated to protecting the sea turtles that nest there in large numbers between October and December. Mosquitoes and voracious sandflies are abundant – take repellent. To reach La Flor you'll either need to arrange private transport (taxis cost US$25 one way) or catch the once-daily bus that leaves San Juan del Sur in the mid-afternoon. There are a couple of tents at La Flor rented out on a first-come, first-served basis; otherwise, be prepared to string up a hammock.

South to Costa Rica

Crossing the border at **Peñas Blancas** can be a time-consuming process; don't be surprised if it takes up two hours. Local buses from Rivas go all the way to the border (the customs posts and duty-free shops at Sapoá, the old border post, now lie deserted); if you're leaving from San Juan del Sur, take the Rivas bus only as far as the highway and then catch a connecting bus – there's no need to go all the way back to Rivas. Buses pull up alongside a line of food stalls, in the middle of which you'll find the gateway to the customs post, built into the new seven and a half foot wall constructed by the Costa Ricans in an attempt to reduce illegal immigration. Officials are on hand at the gate to divest you of a US$1 municipal fee and supply you with the relevant forms. Fill them in and take these to the new customs building, where you'll be charged an exit tax that varies between US$2–4 (US dollars only) according to the day of the week and even time of day. To enter Costa Rica, you'll have to buy a tourist card (US$6) in the Nicaraguan *migración*. It's a 500m walk to the Costa Rican *migración* where you'll be charged a US$3 municipal fee and from where there is regular onward transport to San José. Going in the other direction, British citizens have to present a photocopy of their passport at Nicaraguan *migración*. Unfortunately you can't prepare this in advance as you need a copy of both the page with photo and official info as well as the page with your exit stamp from Costa Rica. There are photocopying facilities in the nearby duty-free facilities. You'll be charged a US$7/9 dollar entrance fee according to the time of day, again payable only in US dollars.

5.4

Lago de Nicaragua

Standing on the shore and looking out into its expanse, you can imagine the surprise of the Spanish navigators in 1522 when, nearly certain they were heading towards the long dreamed of route to the Pacific, they instead came upon **Lago de Nicaragua**. The lake – also known by its indigenous name, Cocibolca ("sweet sea") – is the largest **freshwater sea** in the Americas after the Great Lakes, and the tenth largest body of fresh water in the world. Over 177km long, about 58km wide and fed by forty rivers, the lake is not very deep (about 60m at its deepest point), though its waters can be rough.

Both Lago de Nicaragua and Lago de Managua were probably once part of the Pacific, until **volcanic eruptions** and earthquakes created the Pacific plain that separates the lakes from the ocean today. Fed by freshwater rivers over millennia, the lake water gradually lost its salinity, while the saltwater fish trapped in it evolved into some of the most unusual types of fish found anywhere on earth, including freshwater tarpon and swordfish. The lake is also visited by the **bull shark**, a voracious predator capable of moving between the ocean waters of the Caribbean and the fresh waters of the lake.

Crossing the lake can be quite an undertaking: Lago de Nicaragua is affected by what locals call a "short-wave phenomenon" – short, high, choppy waves – caused by the meeting of the Papagayo wind from the west and the Caribbean-generated trade winds from the east. Lake-going craft are notoriously thick-set and slow; the waves require them to advance slowly and in a zigzag pattern – one reason why lake crossings take so long. The lake's choppiness makes crossing it hell for those

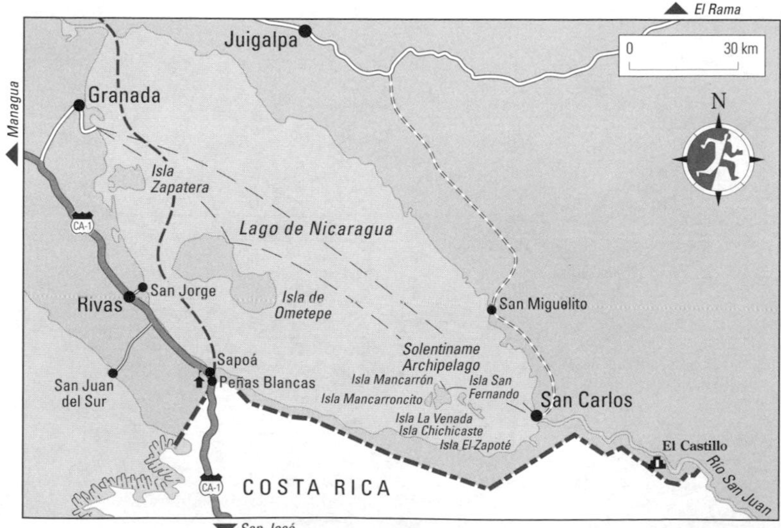

prone to seasickness, and there are occasional dangerous squalls, especially in November.

Travellers who have the patience to cope with erratic boat schedules (and preferably some Spanish, as settlements around the lake are few and isolated) are drawn by the area's unique **culture**. Many are captivated by the natural beauty of the **islands** dotting the southwest sector of the lake: twin-volcanoed **Isla de Ometepe** and the scattering of small islands known as the **Archipiélago de Solentiname**. Ernesto Cardenal, one of Nicaragua's best-known writers, lived for many years in Solentiname and the islands are also famous for their *pintores primitivos* – naif-style painters who depict lush landscapes in which jewel-coloured parrots and red jaguars poke their noses out of verdant jungles. In all, over 400 islands dot the lake, most of them inhabited and some used by well-to-do mainlanders as a place for holiday homes.

On its eastern edge the lake is fed by the 170-kilometre Río San Juan, which forms Nicaragua's southern border and runs out into the Caribbean. You can take a boat trip down the river to the remote **El Castillo**, an old Spanish fort on the banks of the Río San Juan, surrounded on all sides by pristine jungle and offering excellent opportunities for wildlife spotting. The Río San Juan and El Castillo are reached via the largest town on the east side of the lake, **San Carlos**, a muddy, bug-ridden town of little interest, used by travellers mainly as a transit point for exploring the river or travelling south to Costa Rica via Los Chiles.

Isla de Ometepe

"Va para la isla?" mainlanders ask you as you head to the San Jorge docks near Rivas to catch the boat to **ISLA DE OMETEPE**. And from the reverential way they say its name, you can tell Ometepe is considered a place apart from the rest of Nicaragua. There are dramatic views from the mainland of its two magical **volcanoes** rising steeply from the waters of Lago de Nicaragua, and on a clear day the view from the boat as you approach is truly spectacular. The higher and more symmetrical of the two cones is **Volcán Concepción**, Nicaragua's second highest volcano at 1610m. The dull mauve of Concepción's upper slopes, stripped of vegetation, contrasts sharply with the almost shining green of the farms, secondary forest and tilled fields on its fertile lower slopes. To the south is extinct **Volcán Maderas**, smaller (1394m) and less perfectly conical in shape, but clothed with precious **cloudforest**. On the latter volcano you're likely to spot rainforest **animals** such as the white-faced monkey (*carablanca*) and howler monkey (*mono congo*), while birdwatchers will want to keep their eyes out for green parrots (*loro verde*) and the commonly sighted blue-tailed birds called *urracas*.

Almost everyone who travels through Nicaragua comes to Ometepe, if only to sample the island's amazingly lush scenery and tranquil atmosphere. The island has an amazing **agricultural output**, owing to its unusually fertile volcanic soil, and is more prosperous than much of mainland Nicaragua. Most farms are smallholdings on the skirts of the volcano, growing citrus, bananas, coffee, cacao, watermelon and sesame, as well as dry-country products like tobacco and cotton. Towns on the island are well-kept, with schoolchildren and the occasional cow sharing the dusty graded roads with island traffic. **Walking**, **hiking**, **volcano-viewing** and **horse-riding** are really the only activities here, and many visitors come specifically to scale the smaller of the two volcanoes, Maderas.

Ometepe supports a population of 30,000 – quite large for an island of its size. Most people live around the foot of Volcán Concepción, which is where the two main towns, **Moyogalpa** and **Altagracia**, are found. A dirt and gravel **road** circles Concepción, though in the rainy season one stretch between Moyogalpa and Altagracia can become impassable, while another, very rough road (4WD only), goes about three-quarters of the way around Volcán Maderas.

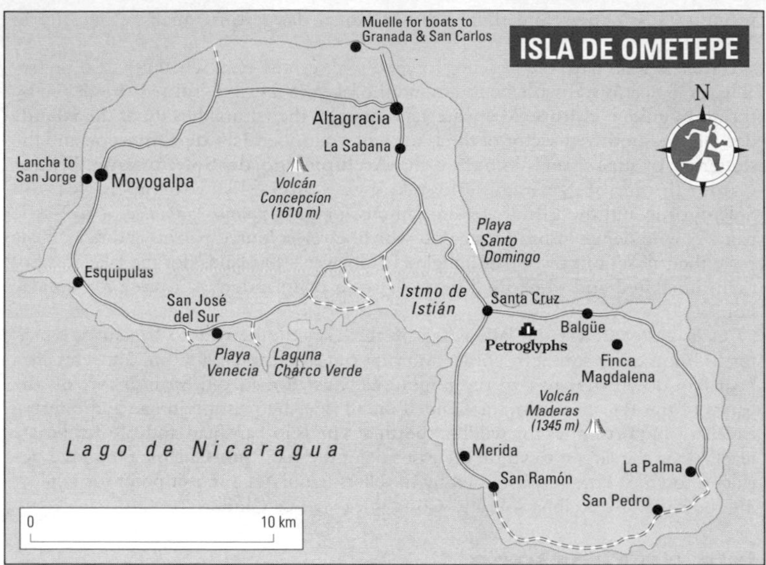

Some history

Ometepe's name comes from the Nahuatl language of the Chorotegans, the original inhabitants of Nicaragua, who called it Ome Tepetl – "the place of two hills". The island has probably been inhabited since the first migration of indigenous groups from Mexico arrived in this area, and a few stone sculptures and petroglyphs attest to their presence on the island – some can be easily seen if you go on a guided walk. It's not clear if there was any significant population on the island when Spanish farmers and cattle ranchers colonized Ometepe during the early 1600s. For hundreds of years Volcán Concepción was dormant, but one morning in 1804 the island's inhabitants woke up to find they had settled on an active volcano. Since then Concepción has erupted seven times, most recently in 1957: there has been no significant activity since. Still, the shadow of the volcano and its lava-scarred slopes looms everywhere on the island.

Island transport

The majority of travellers arrive in Moyogalpa on **ferry** or **lancha from San Jorge** on the mainland; there are twelve daily departures; itineraries change regularly, especially between the rainy and dry seasons, so it's best to check before travelling; call Exploring Omeptepe on the number opposite, or enquire at the Intur office in Granada. The recently introduced *Roman 1* catamaran runs three times a day and has cut the normal one-hour journey time in half. There are also two boats a week **from Granada** (currently Mon & Thurs at 3pm) to Altagracia, from where most travellers head straight for Moyogalpa, which offers a much better choice of hotels and services. A local bus service leaves Altagracia for Moyogalpa (last departure at 6.30pm). **Returning** to the mainland, you'll need to take an early-morning crossing if you want to travel on to Peñas Blancas on the Costa Rican border, though the 1.30pm crossing will still get you to Granada or Managua before buses stop running. Best to double-check the schedule the day before you plan to leave.

Getting around the island isn't too arduous. A dilapidated **bus** runs eleven times daily, shuttling between Moyogalpa docks and Altagracia, a journey of about an hour and a half along some pretty bad roads. Some of these buses go on to Playa Santo Domingo and Balgüe, on the northern side of Maderas, the jumping-off point for the *Finca Magdalena* and Volcán Maderas, although the usual fluctuating schedules means it's best to check on the ground. Sunday services for all buses are less frequent although the *micros* or minibuses that vie for tourist trade can be a good, if more expensive alternative; the more people you can muster for your journey the less you'll pay. You can also hire these drivers/minibuses for the day; beware, however, of these drivers telling you that the last bus has already left in order to get your custom. Another alternative is to rent a **jeep** from the *Hotel Ometepetl* for about US$60 for 24 hours; they also rent **motorbikes** for US$25 per 12 hours and **horses** for US$3 per hour. *Ometepetl* – in common with most hotels – also rent **bicycles** (US$8 per day). Given the relative lack of traffic, the ample tree cover and the fresh breezes off the lake, Ometepe is actually one of the best places in Nicaragua to do a spot of cycling even if the state of the roads takes a little bit of getting used to.

Moyogalpa

The largest town on the island, **MOYOGALPA** is set on the northwest side of Volcán Concepción. Lanchas from San Jorge arrive at the dock located at the bottom of the main street, a steep and narrow avenue lined with hardware stores, agricultural supply shops and the bulk of the town's accommodation. The occasional Land Rover can be spotted battling the town's streets, but most transport in town is by tractor or on rubber-wheeled, horse-drawn carts. There really isn't much to see or do in town and most travellers stay either because they've arrived on a late ferry, or they're catching an early one in the morning. If you're looking for a base from which to explore the island, tiny Playa Santa Domingo or even Altagracia are more inviting options. That said the island's best **tour agency**, Exploring Ometepe (Ⓣ836 8360, Ⓔometepeisland@hotmail.com), is located here, just up from the dock on the left. The outfit runs good-value excursions to the San Ramón waterfall and guided hikes up both Volcán Concepción and Volcán Maderas. The cost for the volcano trips is US$10 per person, with a minimum of three persons in the group.

Practicalities

Moyogalpa is home to many of Ometepe's services, lodgings and restaurants. There's no bank, but most shops, hotels and restaurants will **change dollars**. You can make calls and send mail from **Enitel** (Mon–Sat 8am–5pm) on the east side of the village. **Internet access** is available at *Cyber C@fe* about 350m up the main street from the dock on the right; it's situated inside the Arcia Comercial general store and costs US$2.50 per hour, although power cuts are common.

Most of Moyogalpa's **accommodation** is pretty basic. Moyogalpa's most upmarket place is the *Hotel Ometepetl*, opposite the docks on the right (Ⓣ459-4276; ❸), which has a number of box-like rooms and a few larger, brighter ones towards the rear (a/c optional). *Ometepetl*'s management is friendly, and there's a good bar, restaurant and 4WD rental service. *Hotel Casa Familiar* (Ⓣ4594240; ❷), a hundred metres or so further up, is another friendly option with private baths, spacious showers and a choice of a/c or fan; the knowledgeable owner can provide guides and organise tours. For something a little more gringo friendly, try the Moyagalpa branch of Granada's *Hospedaje Central* hostel (Ⓣ459-4262; ❸), two blocks north and one east of the dock, which has spacious doubles with optional a/c and bath, as well as dorms (US$2), a relaxing courtyard and a colourful bar/restaurant; the hostel is currently up for sale so it may well have changed by the time you read this.

There are a number of decent places in town **to eat**. *El Chele* (which also has pool tables), 50m uphill from the docks, and *Restaurante Ranchitos* on the main street both serve good, cheap local cuisine and are popular at weekends. As far as **nightlife** is concerned, assaults on people walking out to the nearby *Rancho Joaquín* make it an unattractive option although a new disco bar, *Johnny's Place*, has opened up on the other side of the dock.

Altagracia and Volcán Concepción

While there's very little to detain the traveller in **ALTAGRACIA**, a sleepy town set slightly inland from the lake on Ometepe's northeastern side, it's a more relaxed base from which to explore the island. The most attractive accommodation option is *Hospedaje y Restaurante Castillo* (☎552-8744, ⓔhotelcastillo@hotmail.com.ni; ❷), 100m south and 50m west of the **Parque Central**. It boasts basic but spotlessly clean rooms, some with private bath as well as a good restaurant, large hammocks and cheap Internet access. The Parque is nicely ringed by several pre-Columbian statues found on the island, while the **Museo de Ometepe** (daily 8am–5pm; US$1), off the west side of the park, houses a basic array of local archeological finds. The past, however, is brought to life much more vividly during the three-week-long fiesta of San Diego de Alcalá. If passing through on November 17 you may be lucky enough to see one of the highlights of the festival, the *Baile del Zompopo* or dance of the leaf-cutter ant. The locals set out from the church in a traditional procession through the streets, parading aloft an image of San Diego, the village's patron saint. Participants act out the distinctive dance with tree branches held aloft – representing the indigenous leaf-cutter ant – while moving to traditional drum rhythms.

The hike up **Volcán Concepción** starts from just outside Altagracia and takes around eight hours for the round trip. Much of the climb is extremely steep and it's a good idea to hire a guide – ask at the *Hospedaje Castillo*. Note that of the various trails leading to the volcano, La Sabana – often cited as the best access route – is actually one of the most daunting and its lack of tree cover can lead to heat exhaustion. La Concha is probably the best trail, cooler with more foliage.

Playa Santo Domingo

Stretching for more than a kilometre on the east side of the narrow isthmus separating Concepción and Maderas is the grey-sand **Playa Santo Domingo**. This is the only really swimming-friendly beach on the island (though the lake can be surprisingly rough at times), and many volcano-climbers and hikers spend a day soaking up some sun here. The beach is accessed from the main road circling Concepción, although the first kilometre or so of the road that forks off to Santo Domingo is in exceptionally bad condition (4WD essential).

Of the two mid-range **places to stay** on the beach, *Hotel Villa Paraíso* (☎453-4675, ⓔvparaiso@ibw.com.ni; ❸) is best. Rooms here are large, with fans and either shared or private bath, screened windows, lots of varnished wood and a windswept patio; they also offer the rustic luxury of small cabañas. The covered restaurant, overlooking the lake and bordered by hammocks, serves up delicious food including a selection of vegetarian dishes; try the cheese and bean crepe or the fish soup. Easily the most eccentric overnight option in the area is *El Zopilote*, an Italian-owned *finca ecológica* in the small village of El Madroñal exactly halfway between Balgüe and Playa Santo Domingo (ⓔeskobardemolition@yahoo.com; ❶). Along with spaces for camping, dorm accommodation is available in rustic thatched huts. Voluntary work opportunities are available and the finca also hosts occasional full-moon parties with DJs spinning Latin, reggae and drum'n'bass.

Volcán Maderas

The hike up the verdant forested slopes of dormant **Volcán Maderas** is less arduous than the steep climb up and down Concepción, though it can be a wet, muddy and slippery walk. The final stretch down into the crater is not for the faint of heart; the rocks are almost sheer and you'll have to use a rope provided by your guide. It takes about seven hours to get to the top and back down, so you need to set off early. Birds and howler monkeys can be heard (if not seen) all the way up, and the summit gives stunning views of Concepción and the lake. The crater itself is eerily silent and still, its lip covered by a mixture of dense, rainforest-like vegetation and a few bromeliad-encrusted conifers. **Guides** – a very good idea considering the ease with which you can stray off the path – can be hired from the *Finca Magdalena* for around US$15. Make sure you take plenty of water, sunscreen and perhaps a bathing suit; the clear water in the crater lagoon is good for a (chilly) swim. Note that even if you don't hire a guide from the finca, you'll have to pay them US$1.50 for an **entry permit**.

An unforgettable place to stay while having a crack at climbing the volcano is the supremely welcoming *Finca Magdalena* (Ⓣ880-2041, Ⓦwww.coop.cdc.com; ❶–❸), a huge old hacienda with bags of character and stunning views across the lake. Constructed in 1888, the finca was taken over by the Sandinistas and converted into a co-operative for the production of organic coffee. Although money from tourism now forms an important part of their income, the co-op (29 families in all) is still going strong today. Accommodation is in large dorm rooms with shared bath, box-like private rooms with partitions, or a private hut with shower. The large restaurant on the veranda serves hearty meals (as well as their own organic coffee, which you can also buy in bags) at very reasonable prices. If you're sitting out between four and five in the afternoon, you'll see the workers coming down from the hillside with their distinctive round wicker baskets slung over their shoulders, some stopping for a chat at the farm. To reach the finca, you'll need to take the slow and bumpy bus ride through the banana plantations from Altagracia to **Balgüe**, on the northern slopes of Maderas, from where it's a twenty-minute walk up a signposted path. The finca always sends someone to meet buses arriving in Balgüe after dark, since the path isn't lit and is very difficult to find at night.

If you have time, it's worth exploring the towns dotted around the lower slopes of Maderas. **Petroglyphs** are scattered over this part of the island: a group of them is located between the hamlets of Santa Cruz and La Palma – you'll need someone to show you where they are; ask at the *Finca Magdalena* for a guide (US$4). Another easy one-hour hike from the finca will take you to the pleasant, but extremely cold, **San Ramón waterfalls**; again, guides are available from the *Finca*.

The Solentiname archipelago

Lying in the southeast corner of Lago de Nicaragua, the **Solentiname archipelago** is made up of 36 islands of varying size which are becoming increasingly well known for their unspoilt natural beauty and remarkable **bird and animal life**. For a long time, though, it was the islands' colony of naif-art **painters** that brought fame to Solentiname. Priest and poet Ernesto Cardenal lived here for many years, writing and preaching liberation philosophy before becoming the Sandinistas' Minister of the Interior in the 1980s. His poetry and his promotion of the archipelago's primitive art and artisan skills brought Solentiname culture to the attention of the outside world, and it was Cardenal's work that led to the government declaring Solentiname a national monument in 1990.

The archipelago's largest islands are also the most densely inhabited: **Mancarrón**, **La Venada**, **San Fernando** and **Mancarroncito**. Most people stay on Mancarrón, where the islands' main hotel is located, and make trips to San Fernando and other nearby islands. Much of the **wildlife** in the area corresponds to that of northern Costa Rica, just over the border, and the dense jungles stretching from the eastern shore of Lago de Nicaragua to the Caribbean. The opulent birdlife includes parrots, macaws, egrets, storks and many kingfishers, while much of the islands' vegetation is pristine tropical forest.

Solentiname's **isolation** keeps all but the most determined independent travellers away, although tourist traffic in the form of organized tours is increasing. Travellers who give up trying to figure out the confusing and changeable boat schedules often come on a tour organized from Managua or Granada. There's absolutely nothing to do in Solentiname, except hunt out some of the *pintores primitivos*, if your Spanish is up to it. Make sure you bring plenty of córdobas with you – there's nowhere to change money on the islands. At the time of writing, there was also no telephone communication with the islands.

Practicalities: Mancarrón

Boats make the cheap (US$3–4) three-hour trip to Mancarrón (also calling at La Venada and San Fernando; note that the latter is often referred to as **Isla Elvis Chavarría**) from San Carlos twice a week, on Tuesdays and Fridays at noon and 2pm; going in the opposite direction, the boats leave on Tuesdays and Fridays at 4.30am, although the departure times change frequently and it's always best to check at the dock. Unless you come on a tour, this is currently the only way to get here by scheduled transport, although unscheduled private craft make the same trip, leaving constantly – ask around at the San Carlos docks. If time is an issue or you're travelling with a fair-sized group, you might want to use the high-speed services of Roberto Lennon Taylor (☎839-9257), who'll get you there in just over quarter of an hour for US$120. He also makes pricey journeys to Los Chiles, El Castillo, Isla de Ometepe and San Juan del Norte, amongst other destinations.

Nearly everyone who comes to Solentiname **stays** in the *Hotel Mancarrón* (in Managua ☎276-1910; ❹ including breakfast), an old tiled-roof building set in grassland on the island of the same name. Once there the hotel can fix you up with **boat tours** to nearby islands. Alternatively, you can stay at *Bueno Amigo* (❷), a clean, basic and friendly hospedaje located up the hill past the *Mancarrón*, where you can also buy meals for US$2.

Río San Juan

At 170km long, the mighty **Río San Juan** is one of the most important rivers in Central America, and played a key role in the discovery and subsequent history of Nicaragua. In colonial times it was the route by which the nascent cities of Granada and León were supplied by Spain and emptied of their treasure by pirates, though nowadays the river area has staked its economic hopes on the more genteel pursuit of **ecotourism**. The river is relatively pristine, and no settlement of any size exists along the riverbank other than remote and sleepy villages whose inhabitants make their living by fishing and farming. If you want to experience the tropical flora and fauna and don't mind being hundreds of miles from civilization of any kind, then a boat ride on the Río San Juan is worth the hassle of getting there. **Wildlife** is abundant along the river, and travellers who venture up- or downstream will certainly spot sloths, howler monkeys, parrots and macaws, bats, storks, caimans and perhaps even a tapir.

Most travellers see the Río San Juan from a boat en route between **San Carlos** on the eastern shore of Lago de Nicaragua and the old Spanish fort of the **El Castillo**, the only real tourist attraction in the area. Although, according to a treaty signed in 1858, the entire length and both shores of the river are deemed Nicaraguan territory, the southern bank of the river forms the border with Costa Rica and provides a constant source of wrangling between the two countries. Costa Rica has been pushing for the right to carry out armed navigation of the river and are apparently prepared to go to the International Court of Justice at The Hague to press their case. See p.714 for trips on the Costa Rican side.

The Río San Juan area is alarmingly **remote** and you have to be prepared to do battle with the elements. Little food and drink is available, not to mention consumer goods, whether it be batteries or toothpaste. There are good hospitals on the Costa Rican side, in Los Chiles and in Ciudad Quesada, but you should be prepared for any emergency. Apart from that, the **basics** you will need are a mosquito net, light raincoat, plastic bags for cameras and other mechanical equipment, sunglasses, repellent, sunscreen, a torch, good boots, a spare (dry) pair of shoes, matches, candles, bottled water, towels and a first-aid kit, including, if possible, a snakebite kit.

San Carlos

Sleepy, smelly and slatternly, **SAN CARLOS** has to be one of the most unprepossessing towns in the whole country. An air of apathy, if not downright stasis, pervades its ramshackle buildings and muddy streets. This could certainly be the fault of the fire that destroyed most of the town in 1984, or the climate of heat and torrential rain, but there appears to be a general lack of civic pride or willingness to treat the place to a splash of paint. If you're unlucky enough to arrive when they're suffering one of their plagues of greenfly-like insects (the locals do actually use the Spanish word *plaga*), a day or night here can be truly unpleasant. The people are friendly enough, but regardless you'll want to plant your connections so you won't have to spend the night here. Travellers come through San Carlos from Los Chiles in Costa Rica in order to make the lake trip to Granada, or to go to Solentiname. Increasingly, more determined **ecotourists** are coming through to pick up a boat to El Castillo and points further along the Río San Juan.

Getting to San Carlos

San Carlos can be reached by road, boat or air. The long, crowded and bumpy **bus** journey, which is erratic in the rainy season (always check that it's running), currently leaves Managua's Mercado Mayoreo bus terminal five times a day, taking nine or ten hours to reach San Carlos. If you plan on doing the heroic 300-kilometre **drive**, get your hands on a sturdy 4WD with high clearance. **Boats** leave for San Carlos from Granada on Mondays and Thursdays at 3pm, arriving in San Carlos at 3 or 4am the next day (check return times from San Carlos to Granada before travelling; the current schedule is Tuesdays and Fridays at 3pm). La Costeña **fly** from Managua to San Carlos once daily (check times in Managua), landing at the tiny, muddy field of an airstrip just north of town.

Practicalities

San Carlos's Banco de Finanzas will **change dollars**; there's also an **Enitel** office (Mon–Sat 8am–5pm, Sun 9am–5pm) and a separate **post office** (Mon–Fri 8am–noon &1pm–5pm, Sat 8am–1pm) but don't expect mail sent from here to get anywhere quickly. There's a small **Intur** tourist office, one block east and two blocks south of the main square (☎283-0301; Mon–Fri 8am–noon & 2–5pm), where you can get up-to-date info on Solentiname and points south on the Río San Juan.

San Carlos has a lot of transient traffic, which is reflected in the spartan decor and indifferent management style of its **hotels**. There's little to choose between the few vaguely acceptable and not overly bug-ridden, sinister or noisy places in town. The only place which offers even a modicum of comfort and cleanliness is *Hotel Cabinas Leyko*, two blocks west of the Parque (☎283-0354; ❸), with decent, if slightly damp wooden rooms with wall fan, screened windows (a must here) and shared bath. There's also a balcony with rocking chairs and lake views. The ramshackle *Hotel San Carlos* in front of the market (❷) is the place of choice for the local itinerant crowd with damp, musty, insalubrious and noisy rooms; their sole saving grace is the wooden porch right on the water. Rooms at the *Hospedaje Peña* (☎283-0298; ❶) are cramped and run down with granite-like mattresses, while the shared bathroom is an experience. At least there are good views of the lake from the upstairs rooms.

The best place **to eat** in town is probably *Restaurante El Mirador* inside the ruins of the old fort (worth a visit in itself), overlooking the southwestern end of the dock area. You can dine on chicken and seafood dishes in the US$3–4 range. *Restaurante y Bar Solentiname*, opposite *Hospedaje Peña*, is another decent option, clean and friendly with *Nica típica* like chicken in jalapeño sauce. Also worth a visit is the nearby *Restaurante Kaoma*: it looks like a seedy underground drinking den but dishes up good, filling meat, fish and vegetarian (on request) plates for US$2–3.

Crossing into Costa Rica

There are currently two boats per day leaving for **Los Chiles** in Costa Rica, departing at 10.30am and 1.30pm from the muelle (dock); note, however, that in common with most boats in this region and the Atlantic Coast, they'll only leave if and when full. You'll have to get your exit stamp from the customs office at the dock **before** departure and, as with every border post in Nicaragua, you'll pay US$2–4 depending on the time of day, payable in either dollars or córdobas. Coming the other way the charge is US$7–9 depending on the time of day. The actual border post is 3km before you reach Los Chiles; you get an entry stamp to Costa Rica at the Los Chiles muelle. Be aware that Costa Rican officials are rigorous in their checks on Nicaraguans in this area and there's always a chance that your boat will be sent back if you're travelling with Nicaraguans whose paperwork isn't satisfactory.

El Castillo

The full name of the Río San Juan's historic fort is La Fortaleza de la Limpia y Inmaculada Concepción, though everyone refers to it as **El Castillo**. Lying on a hillock perched beside a narrow stretch of the Río San Juan, the Castillo was built by the Spanish as a bulwark against the pirates who continually sacked Granada in the seventeenth century. The fort was more or less effective for over a hundred years, until the British finally took it in 1780, after which it was abandoned for nearly two centuries. The Nicaraguan Ministry of Tourism, with the help of funds from various overseas governments, has renovated and restored the low stone structure with an iron door and an access ramp, and has had several floors re-tiled. There's a library (closed at weekends) inside the walls with over a thousand books on the history of the castle and the Río San Juan area, plus a small **museum** (daily 8am–noon & 2–5pm; US$1) with dusty armaments of the period, information on the area's history and a few random artefacts found during the restoration of the castle. There's also a small **tourism office** just up from the dock (Mon–Sat 8–11am & 2–5pm), run by the Asociación Municipal de Ecoturismo El Castillo rather than Intur. They offer good-value horse-riding trips (US$10 for three hours) and walking tours in the nearby reserve.

Four **boats** a day leave San Carlos for El Castillo, a journey of about two and a half hours; the last returns at 2pm (5pm Sun). You can rent a *panga* (motorized dugout boat) in San Carlos for about US$160, holding up to eight people. Ask around at the docks and compare prices. The trip to and from the Castillo can be completed in a day, but if you want to hang around, the small and friendly village offers a few **accommodation options** and is a charming place to rest up for a few days, especially if you've been travelling hard and fast via San Carlos. The smart, friendly *Albergue El Castillo* (Ⓣ892-0174; ❺) offers simple but comfortable rooms with fans in a huge, wooden cabin-style hotel with balcony and great river views. Surprisingly perhaps, there aren't as many mosquitoes here as you might imagine and it's perfectly feasible to spend the night swinging in your hammock, contemplating the stars, the sheet lightning on the horizon and the occasional lonely flashlight in the darkness beyond. *Hospedaje Universal* (❶) is a basic, family-run concern with small, wood partition rooms and shared modern bath along with a newly built wooden balcony (with hammocks) right on the river. Another option is the *Monte Cristo River Resort* (Ⓔmcrr@cablenet.com.ni; ❻), 6km west of El Castillo (the boat from San Carlos to El Castillo usually stops there), where you can stay in luxury wooden cabins with TV, fridge and kitchen. If you really can't do without your upscale comforts there's also a hot tub and swimming pool as well as horses for hire, water-skiing facilities and sport-fishing trips.

Among the few **places to eat**, *Bar Restaurante Cafalito*, right on the dock, is the most convenient and the place where most travellers end up at night. The tables are upstairs on a lovely wooden open-air deck where you can dine on a whole fried fish for US$5 or shrimp in garlic sauce for a hefty US$8. Much cheaper is the easily missed *Soda Vanessa*, a few hundred metres along from the dock on the left. A couple of dollars will get you a decent plate of *comida típica*, a drink and even a serving of Vanessa's wonderful ice cream.

Beyond El Castillo: Reserva Biológica Indio Maíz

Downstream from El Castillo, heading out towards the Caribbean, the northern bank of the Río San Juan forms part of the 3000-square-kilometre **Reserva Biológica Indio Maíz**, the largest nature reserve in Nicaragua. The climate here is very wet and hot, with the vast expanses of dense rainforest sheltering many species, including the elusive manatee, jaguars, tapirs, scarlet macaws, parrots and toucans. The only real tourist infrastructure in the area is *Refugio Bartola* (Ⓣ289-7924, Ⓕ289-4154; ❻), a scientific research station which offers eleven rudimentary but comfortable wooden rooms, all with private bath and full board. There are also guided walking tours along the surrounding network of trails, boat trips along the Río Bartola and kayaks for hire. Save for these hiking opportunities, the usual way to see the Indio Maíz is from a boat on the Río San Juan – travelling toward the Caribbean, much of the left-hand bank of the river is the reserve. The pristine Indio Maíz vegetation stands in sharp contrast with the Costa Rican side, where agriculture and logging have eroded the forest. While you'll have to hire a private boat from El Castillo (at least US$30 one way) to get to the research station, it is possible to travel all the way down to **San Juan del Norte** on the Caribbean by cheap scheduled transport; boats leave from San Carlos for the 10hr journey on Tuesdays and Fridays at 5am. From there you just might be able to hitch a lift on a boat going up the coast. For such an adventure, however, you'll need a lot of time and even more cash; the scarcity of public transport beyond San Juan del Norte means that boat owners can pretty much name their price.

5.5

The Atlantic Coast

Nicaragua's **Atlantic Coast** is low-lying, soaked with mangrove swamps behind which loom near-impenetrable jungles – a vast region comprising about half of Nicaragua's total landmass. This area never appealed to the Spanish conquistadors' desire for fertile agricultural land and gold, and, further repelled by disease, endless jungle, dangerous snakes and persistent biting insects, the Spanish quickly made tracks for the more hospitable Pacific zone. As a result, Spanish influence has never been great along Central America's Atlantic seaboard, and it was left to other nations to fill that gap. English, French and Dutch buccaneers had been plying the coast since the late 1500s, and it was they who first made contact with the **Miskito**, **Sumu** and **Rama** peoples who populated the area, trading goods for fish and turtle meat. In return, the indigenous peoples gave the pirates safe harbour and welcomed them into their settlements. Nicaragua's fierce Miskito tribe (now thought to number about 70,000) came particularly under the influence of the English, and from 1687 to 1894 the Atlantic coast of Nicaragua and Mosquitia as a whole was a British Protectorate known as the **Miskito Kingdom**. Armed by the British, the Miskito became the terror of the Sumu and Rama, who were finally subjugated by the larger group. In turn, from the late 1500s until 1894, when Britain unceremoniously ceded Mosquitia to Managua, the British navy, merchants and privateers gained unlimited rights to fishing and other local products, and enjoyed safe conduct through the waterways of Mosquitia.

The **ethnicity** of the region today is complex. The Miskito, Sumu and Rama mixed with the slaves brought from Africa and Jamaica to work in the region's fruit plantations, and while many inhabitants are Afro-American in appearance, others have Amerindian features, and some combine both with European traits. For the most part black people from the Atlantic Coast call themselves Creoles; if they acknowledge having Spanish blood, or Spanish is their first language, they may call themselves mestizos. **English** is widely spoken on the Atlantic Coast, and English travellers may be surprised to be on the receiving end of a very warm welcome and some time-warp nostalgia for Britain.

During the years of the **Revolution** and the Sandinista government, the FSLN were met with suspicion on the Atlantic Coast. In part this was due to the area's traditional mistrust of the government in Managua, and also to a lack of sympathy with the Sandinista's revolutionary values. Nearly half the Miskito population went into exile in Honduras, while in the south a much smaller number made their way to Costa Rica. In 1985 the Sandinistas tried to repair relations by granting the region political and administrative autonomy, creating the territories **RAAN** (Region Autonomista Atlántico Norte) and **RAAS** (Region Autonomista Atlántico Sur), though this only served to stir up further discontent, being widely seen as an attempt to split the Atlantic Coast as a political force. In 2002, the Indigenous Council of Elders announced the creation of an independent "Communitarian Nation of Moskitia", with its own parliament and laws. At the time of writing, little seems to have come of this bizarre development, with more weight given to the belated codification, in 2003, of the 1987 autonomy law. Widespread celebrations were held with the announcement that regional institutions were finally going to be able to administer such departments as health, education and transport.

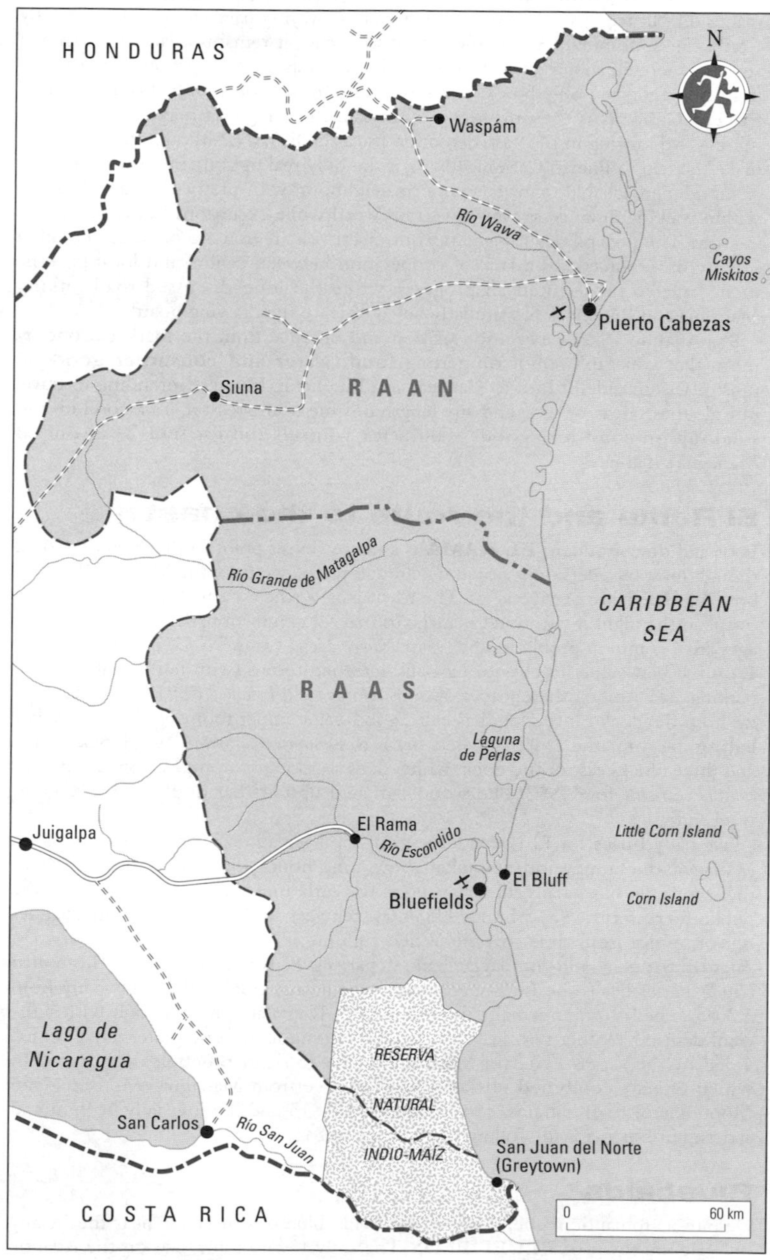
HONDURAS
N
Waspám
Río Wawa
Cayos
Miskitos
Puerto Cabezas
Siuna
RAAN
Río Grande de Matagalpa
CARIBBEAN
SEA
RAAS
Laguna
de Perlas
Juigalpa
El Rama
Río Escondido
Little Corn Island
El Bluff
Bluefields
Corn Island
Lago de
Nicaragua
RESERVA
NATURAL
INDIO-MAÍZ
San Carlos
Río San Juan
San Juan del Norte
(Greytown)
COSTA RICA
0
60 km

The only places in the area that attract visitors in any numbers are **Bluefields**, a raffish and rain-lashed Caribbean port town, and the **Corn Islands**, two small islands off Nicaragua's coast with sandy beaches, swaying palm trees, and a distinctly Caribbean atmosphere. As for the rest of the coast, it remains a largely unknown and impenetrable tangle of waterways and rainforests, to be approached with caution and negotiated only by experienced locals. In the northern half of the region, **Puerto Cabezas** is the only town of any size. The region's main industries are mining and logging in the vast, dense forests of the RAAN. Although few travellers make the trip to Puerto Cabezas (flying is the only real option), the town is actually more approachable than its southern neighbour, with pretty cliffs and beaches within walking distance as well as various worthwhile excursions in the surrounding area. The possibilities for ecotourism in this vast region are obvious, though a scarcity of resources and a lack of cooperation between central and local government have so far stymied all progress, while the long-discussed road linking Managua and Bluefields has similarly failed to leave the drawing board.

The Atlantic Coast's extreme isolation and distance from the market economy mean that you can't count on getting **food, water and consumer goods** in most places outside of Puerto Cabezas and Bluefields. If you're intending to travel outside these areas, or to spend any length of time in the region, it's a good idea to stock up on consumer goods – both for yourself and for trade – in one of Managua's markets.

El Rama and the route to the coast

Poor and downtrodden, **EL RAMA** is a major transit point to the Atlantic Coast, though most travellers only stop long enough to change from the Managua bus to a boat for Bluefields, or vice versa. The town is nevertheless a pleasant enough place to spend the night if you don't manage to make a connection, though water shortages are a common problem. The smart *Nuevo Hotel Oasis Del Caribe* (ⓣ817-0264; ❸) is the best-value hotel with pleasant, screened rooms (with fan), a balcony and parking area. Among the cheaper options, *Hospedaje El Viajero* (ⓣ817-0156; ❶), just up from the dock on the left, has basic, good-value upper rooms with balcony. For **eating**, head for the Dutch-owned *Bar Y Restaurante Caribbean*, two blocks north and three blocks east of the dock, which does seafood for around US$5 and decent *comida corriente* for US$2. The wood-panelled upstairs bar doubles as a disco at weekends.

Five daily **buses** for El Rama leave from the Mercado Mayoreo bus terminal in Managua; the bumpy journey takes about nine hours. In the opposite direction, there are eight buses daily, all departing in the early morning. Moving onwards, the public **ferry** service (5–7 hours; US$4.60) between El Rama and Bluefields goes out of service from time to time. When running it leaves Bluefields on Monday, Tuesday, Saturday and Sunday at 5am, departing El Rama at 1pm for the return trip. A better bet is the high-speed **panga** (2 hours; US$10) that runs daily from 5.30am. The last one normally departs from El Rama at 1pm, although with sufficient demand another may leave later in the afternoon. An easier alternative is provided by the Vargas Peña (in Managua ⓣ280-4561, in Bluefields ⓣ822-2930), which offers a combined bus-and-*panga* service from Managua (Mercado Iván Montenegro) to Bluefields, costing around US$15 and leaving daily at 9pm and arriving in Bluefields the following morning at 8am.

Bluefields

Despite its romantic name, there are no fields, blue or otherwise, near the steamy little lagoon town of **BLUEFIELDS**. The only town of any size on the Atlantic Coast south of Puerto Cabezas, Bluefields gets its name from a Dutch pirate, Abraham Blaauwveld, who holed up here regularly in the seventeenth century, and it has retained the fugitive charm of a pirate town, perched on the side of a lagoon at the mouth of the Río Escondido. For most of the year it **rains** torrentially, except in May, when there's a short dry season (although it often rains then too). During these downpours the town – already ramshackle – can look somewhat forlorn, an impression compounded by the unlikely and unceasing soundtrack of mournful American country & western blaring from the bars, restaurants and houses. The foul climate only adds to a definite sense of small-town suffocation and on weekends and at nights especially, the streets never feel like an especially safe place to be. Tourists are occasionally targeted for petty theft so watch your back and if you are out at night, don't stray from the centre of town.

Blufileños, as the town's inhabitants are called in Spanish, are mainly Creole, descended from Jamaicans. Both English and Spanish are spoken, although the English is heavily accented patois and takes some getting used to. There's a lot of activity in town, and most of it takes place on the street, where stalls sell batteries, tape players and other contraband goods from Costa Rica. Some examples of English colonial tropical architecture have survived the years: low-slung wooden buildings, bounded by grilled verandas, sitting alongside Caribbean-style cabañas – small wooden shacks painted in faded reds, greens and blues. You can't see the Caribbean from the town, and to get a sense of being at the ocean's edge you'll have to get a motorboat (*panga*) from the muelle over to the harbour and administrative hamlet of **El Bluff**, a collection of motley government buildings strung diagonally across the lagoon with the breezy open Caribbean at the end of a finger of land.

Hurricane Joan flattened Bluefields and the surrounding area in 1988, and there are still a few signs of the tremendous devastation. The town is occasionally plagued by electricity and water **shortages** – a good reason to bring a torch and batteries, as well as a few candles, and to stock up on bottled water when you can. Since 1995 Bluefields has received a shot in the arm in the form of the **URRACAN**, or Universidad de las Regiones Autónomos de la Costa Caribe Nicaragüense. The Bluefields campus is the largest of three on the coast – the others are in Puerto Cabezas and Siuna – and although most of the faculty are from the Atlantic Coast region, volunteer professors also come from abroad, mainly Canada and the United States. The small campus is located about 1km from the centre of Bluefields, up the hill that backs the town to the northwest.

During the last week in May, the streets of Bluefields are taken over by **¡Mayo Ya!**, one of the most exciting fiestas in the country. Derived from the traditional May Day maypole celebrations of the British, ¡Mayo Ya! features a mixture of reggae, folklore and indigenous dance that young Blufileños pair ingeniously with the latest moves from Jamaica.

Arrival and information

La Costeña and Atlantic Airlines **flights** from Managua land at the **airstrip**, 3km south of the town centre; remember to confirm your return flight as soon as you arrive. Taxis will take you into town for about US$0.50. The public **ferry** from El Rama arrives at the dock about 150m north of the town's Moravian Church. From the dock you can walk to all accommodation in Bluefields' "centre" – a three-block by three-block area where all the hotels, restaurants and services are concentrated.

The few streets in Bluefields are named. Calle Central is the main drag and runs north–south alongside the bay. The three streets running east–west are Avenida Reyes, Avenida Cabezas and Avenida Aberdeen. However, no one really uses these names, resorting to the usual method of directing from **landmarks**: the Moravian Church, the Mercado at the end of Av Aberdeen and the Parque to the west of town are the most popular ones.

In general, Bluefields is a dollar-friendly town – restaurants and hotels are only too happy to accept them. **Bancentro**, opposite *Hotel Central*, will change dollars

Mosquitoes and no se 'ums

Bluefields can feel like the mosquito capital of the world, at least at dawn or dusk, when clouds of the creatures descend on any inch of exposed flesh. You need to take precautions: use plenty of repellent and wear long sleeves and trousers (along with socks). **Malaria** is present in the region – see p.26 for precautionary details – and coils, a mosquito net and a sleeping bag offer useful protection as well.

As if that weren't enough, the **sandflies** that populate the coast are even more virulent than the mosquitoes. Known throughout English-speaking Central America as "no see 'ums", sandflies are seemingly immune to every repellent known to man except, bizarrely, Avon's Skin-So-Soft body oil. This is not normally available in Nicaragua, but locals in the know may have procured a supply.

into córdobas and also accepts travellers' cheques. A small Intur **tourist office** (8am–noon & 2–5pm; ☎822-0221) is located just off the southeast edge of the Parque, and there's a **post office** around the corner from the huge Lotería Nacional building (Mon–Fri 8am–noon & 1–5pm, Sat 8am–noon). You can make calls from the **Enitel** office (Mon–Sat 8am–7.30pm, Sun 9am–noon & 2–5.30pm), 50m east of the Parque, but the Internet revolution appears to have bypassed Bluefields; try at the University if desperate to log on.

Accommodation, eating and drinking

Lodging in Bluefields is underwhelming with gloomy, noisy, overpriced rooms the norm. The cheaper, more basic establishments attract a raffish local clientele – one reason why some places have a curfew of 10 or 11pm. The best deal in the centre of town is *Mini-Hotel Cafetin Central* (☎822-2362; ❹), which offers clean and compact if maddeningly noisy rooms with private bath, varying in quality but not price; ask to see a selection before choosing. *Casa de Urracan* (formerly *Hotel Tia Irene*; ☎822-0120, ⓕ822-2143; ❹), in barrio Pointeen, is another good choice with comfortable rooms boasting private bath and hot water. *Hotel South Atlantic No.2* (☎822-2265, ⓕ822-1219; ❻), adjacent to the Moravian Church, is the priciest place in the centre with private bath, a/c, TV and a gleaming upstairs "Sports Bar" with American football on TV and an extensive menu. A more peaceful night's sleep, meanwhile, can be had at *Hotel Aeropuerto* (☎822-2862; US$13), right by the airport, with large rooms, some dark and musty but some with wood panelling and windows leading onto a balcony with great views of the lagoon; ask to see a selection.

Unless you're into seafood, which is as plentiful and fresh as anywhere in Nicaragua, Bluefields doesn't offer a great deal of choice on the **eating** front. While the centrally located *Bar Y Restaurante Lobster Pot*, 75 metres south from the Lotería Nacional, and *Pesca Frita*, across from the market, offer reasonably priced fried fish and lobster in season, it's worth walking the few hundred meters south to *Bella Vista*, an atmospheric wooden building in a tranquil setting with great views right on the lagoon. The seafood is similarly priced and they also do some basic Chinese dishes. More upmarket is *Chez Marcel*, one block south of the Parque, which also specializes in seafood and accepts credit cards. Whatever else it is, Bluefields is certainly not short on nocturnal excitement. You'll probably hear the popular *Cima Karaoke Bar*, on the corner, 50m west of *Mini-Hotel Cafetin Central*, before you see it, a reggae and soca stronghold whose speakers blast into the street. *Four Brothers*, on the southwestern side of town (a short taxi ride), is the granddaddy of the Caribbean music scene in Bluefields and still commands a loyal, largely Creole crowd, while the young frequent the warehouse-like *Disco Blue Lagoon*, opposite the market, and *Disco Bacchus*, 50 meters south of the Parque.

The Corn Islands

Lying 70km off the Atlantic coast of Nicaragua, the **CORN ISLANDS** offer white beaches, warm, clear water, and even a bit of dreadlocked Rastafarian culture. Although there's not a lot to do, the islands are the epitome of relaxation – especially if travelling in Nicaragua is grinding you down – and the kind of place you come to for a couple of days and end up staying a week.

Like many parts of the Caribbean coast, during the last century both the larger **Corn Island** and tiny **Little Corn** (or La Islita) were a haven for **buccaneers**, who used them as a base for raiding other ships in the area or attacking the inland towns on Lago de Nicaragua. These days it's drug-runners who use the islands as part of the transportation route for US- and Europe-bound cocaine. The islands' other notable trade is in turtle flesh – officially legal, though conducted in a rather clandestine manner; a short walk along the bay in either direction from the main settlement will lead you past houses that are used to store large numbers of turtles on their backs awaiting slaughter. Despite these somewhat shady aspects to the islands' life, they're safe to visit and the beaches are lovely.

Most visitors stay on **Corn Island**, home to all the services and with a decent selection of hotels and restaurants. Easily reached by *panga* from the bigger island, **Little Corn** is extremely quiet, with no real tourist infrastructure – most people come on a day-trip, or stay only one night. Bring sunscreen, mosquito repellent, a flashlight, snorkelling equipment and an emergency roll of toilet paper. Both English and Spanish are spoken on the islands.

Corn Island

Corn Island is fairly heavily populated for an island of its size, with over six thousand inhabitants living on its ten square kilometres. The island is still recovering from the onslaught of **Hurricane Joan** in 1988 that destroyed much of the housing and flattened trees. Many of the hardest-hit buildings have been summarily patched up, but signs of the destruction remain.

It's possible to walk round the entire island in about three hours. **Brig Bay** (just south of the fish-processing plant) is very tranquil and has a small wreck just off the shore in front of the *Hotel Paraíso Club*. **Long Bay**, across the airstrip heading east, is quieter and less populated and there are plenty of places to swim in either direction. The southwest bay, **Picnic Center**, is a fine stretch of sand near a loading dock – it's the site of a huge party during Semana Santa, when crowds of people come over from Bluefields and the locals set up stalls to sell food and drink. Further around the island is the **South End**, where there's some coral reef good for snorkelling.

About 1.5km offshore to the southeast is the wreck of a **Spanish galleon** that lies in around 20m of clear water (given the islands' buccaneering past, it's likely that there are other wrecks in the area too). You can arrange **snorkelling** trips through the *Hotel Paraíso Club* (see p.567), or the Nautilus Ecotours dive center (☎285-5077), who also offer dives with boat, guide and complete equipment for US$55 per person, fishing trips, snorkel gear rental (US$4 per half-day) and bike rental (US$10 per day). Another option for an organised snorkelling trip is Dorsey Campbell (☎285-5059), who lives in the relaxed hamlet of Sally Peachy; if you can't get him on the phone, you'll probably find him in the vicinity of the *Pulpería Victoria*; US$10 (US$25 with boat) will get you equipment for as long as you want, plus Dorsey's formidable expertise and knowledge of the local coral and marine life.

Arrival, information and transport

The **passenger ferry**, a converted Sandinista gunboat, departs from the Bluefields dock to Corn Island on Wednesdays at 6pm; going in the opposite direction there are two boats a week, on Tuesdays and Sundays at 9am. The crossing can get very rough and takes anywhere between five and eight hours (US$10.50; buy your ticket before boarding from the office just off the dock). **Freight ferries** leave most days for Corn Island and will take a small number of passengers; ask around at the docks.

A better option, at least for those prone to seasickness, is to take the **plane**, not least because the hour-long flight from Managua gives an astounding perspective on the country as you fly over the volcanoes of Ometepe and across the perpetual green of the Atlantic Coast jungle, before the plane heads out over the Caribbean. La Costeña (☎263-2142) and Atlantic Airlines (☎270-5355) both fly several times daily to Bluefields from Managua (US$90 return) and between Bluefields and the Corn Islands (US$67 return), while La Costeña operate two flights daily from Managua to the Corn Islands (US$117) return. Both airlines have offices at Managua airport and on Corn Island, and also have booking agents across Managua. Flights land at the airstrip in the centre of the island. It's important to **confirm** your return flight once you arrive, particularly around Easter, when things get very busy.

From the airstrip it's five or ten minutes' walk to the beachfront at Brig Bay, where you'll find some hospedajes. If you have a heavy pack it's sensible to take a **taxi** (US$0.70 per person anywhere on the island, double that after 8pm). You can also **rent a car** for US$13 an hour (enquire at the *Paraíso Club* – see opposite) or a taxi for around US$8 an hour. When not being serviced, two local **buses** circle the island in opposite directions every forty minutes or so, commencing at 7am. They pass the airport before heading into town or out to the southwest bay where the ferry comes in.

There's no tourist office, but both the *Hotel Paraíso Club* and *Nautilus* (who also publish a free, rudimentary tourist map of the island) are good for **information**. The Caley Dagnall **bank** will change travellers' cheques but doesn't give cash advances on credit cards. It's best to come armed with plenty of dollars or córdobas. You can make **phone calls** (but not send mail; for this you need the *farmacia* cum *correo* opposite the airport, open 7am–9pm) at the **Enitel** office just round the corner from the *Fisher's Cave* restaurant (Mon–Sat 8am–noon & 1.30–4pm). The only **Internet access** on the island is provided by the *Paraíso Club*, who charge a monopolistic US$6.60 per hour.

Accommodation

Corn Island has some decent **hospedajes** and **hotels**, a number of which now have telephones, making it possible to reserve rooms; if you can't book in advance, come early if you want accommodation during the Easter period and expect to pay more. Another busy time is August 27, **Freedom Day**, which celebrates the abolition of slavery, an occasion for excess in a variety of forms and a large amount of crab eating – Picnic Center is the place to be for the party. Most of the hospedajes are scattered around the village and along **Brig Bay**, the beach area of the island. If you decide to opt for one of the places towards Southwest bay, be aware that many taxis refuse to drive on this road due to its poor condition, especially if the weather closes in and the roads become flooded.

Café del Mar on the beach, 50m or so south of *La Princesa de la Isla* Ⓦwww.cafedelmar-3js.com. This funky backpacker hangout offers cheap hammocks in a communal bamboo-and-mesh hut as well as camping space. The emphasis is squarely on chilling out with quality sounds at sunset, an open fire on the beach and good veggie food options. They also hire out body boards, organise fly fishing and run great-value two-day island-hopping tours (US$35 per person). ❶

Casa Blanca 100m south along the rough beach track skirting Brig Bay. Windswept, isolated hospodaje with clean, atmospheric little wooden rooms, fans and mosquito nets supplied. There are also pleasant verandas with hammocks but the latrine-style outside toilet (with precarious chicken-coop-style walkway) is an experience. ❸

Corn Island Dive Resort midway between Sally Peachy and South End ☎285-5100, Ⓔmant@caf.com.ni. Run by an American couple who offer two newly built, three-room wooden cabins (with a/c, private bath and hot water) right on the beach.

Breakfast included. They also offer five-day introductory PADI diving courses (US$275). ❻

Martha's B&B Southwest Bay, 50m south of Picnic Center ⓣ285-5136. Welcoming hosts Ellery and Martha Foster offer immaculate, modern if slightly overpriced rooms (with a/c and private bath) in a lovely, secluded grove of palms set back from the beach. Perfect if you're after something sedate and tranquil. ❻

Mini Hotel Morgan towards North End ⓣ285-5052. Although this place offers bright, pleasant rooms with TV, fan and choice of shared bath, its real attraction lies in the great-value, newly built two-storey apartments. The upstairs rooms are nicest: bright and fresh with a balcony, great views and sea breezes. ❺

Paraíso Club at the southern end of Brig Bay ⓣ285-5111, ⓕ285-5125, ⓔhotelparaiso@ibw.com.ni. Attractive thatched cabins with patio/hammocks set amid palm and banana trees. There's also Internet access, snorkelling equiment for hire, horse-riding tours, a laundry service and a pleasant restaurant under a large rancho – nice, but overpriced. ❻

La Princesa de la Isla Woula Point, between Brig Bay and Picnic Center ⓦwww.laprincesa.cjb.net. Corn Island's hidden gem with delightful rustic cottages, creatively constructed from old coral and rocks from the beach; the atmospheric restaurant serves authentic Italian cuisine (advance notice of 3 hours required). Highly recommended. ❻

Eating, drinking and nightlife

Seafood lovers are in for a treat on the islands as it's easy to get a good feed of **fish, prawns or lobster** for a reasonable price (US$5–10). Unfortunately Big Corn Island is also home to some of the slowest, most dithering service in Nicaragua; all part of the island's laid-back charm of course, but be prepared for a long wait. Although it's located in the northern Sally Peachy area, *Seva's* still holds the reputation as the best eatery on the island. It's not cheap but the food is consistently tasty; you can dine on fried fish for just under US$5, lobster or shrimp in tomato sauce for US$7. More central and vegetarian friendly is the popular *Nautilus*, a tiny café cum giftshop (another part of Nautilus Ecotours) with three tables located north of the dock. For breakfast (arrive early or you won't get a seat), you can feast on sourdough bread, homemade jam, yoghurt and freshly made crepes while main meals, including a delicious vegetable curry, come in at US$3. The biggest **disco** in town is the centrally located *Reggae Palace*, spinning reggae, soca and Garífuna music on weekends. If it's more of a local vibe you're after, try the *Sweet Corn Dance Hall*, at the back of the Sweet Corn Minimarket towards the South End area of the island.

Little Corn Island

Only three square kilometres in size, **Little Corn Island** (La Islita) lies about 7km northeast of its larger sister. Largely undeveloped and with a population of under 800, the island boasts lush palm trees and some beautiful **white-sand beaches**, good swimming, great snorkelling, diving and above all, plenty of peace and quiet – you can walk round and round the island and meet almost nobody else. Another bonus is the fact that there are no cars on the island; traffic consists almost solely of bikes, dogs and wheelbarrows. The regular *panga* leaves the small jetty at the northern end of Brig Bay on Corn Island at 10am and 4.30pm daily, returning from Little Corn at 7.30am and 2pm (one hour; US$5). The boat drops you off on the island's western side amid Little Corn's only real cluster of population and facilities, limited as they are. A concrete causeway serves as the main thoroughfare.

If you're going to work up the energy to do anything at all here, it's likely to be **diving** or **snorkelling**; the island has around nine square kilometres of glorious, healthy reef to explore. The *Casa Iguana*–masterminded, Aussie-run Dive Little Corn, located in a wooden hut right by the dock, is the only PADI scuba-diving shop in Nicaragua. As such, it has a comprehensive variety of guided dives and courses: a standard tank dive (from a dive-designed *panga*) costs US$50 while an Open Water Certification course comes in at US$295 including dives and equipment. A beginner scuba-diving course costs US$15, while snorkel gear is available to hire for US$5, kayaks for US$15 (per day).

Practicalities

There's a fair selection of **accommodation** considering Little Corn's size, much of it lacking electricity and running water but compensating with stunning vistas and first-rate tranquillity. Conveniently situated in the island's "village", 100m from where the *panga* lands, is *Bridgette's* (❸), with basic rooms and good-value meals. Also right by the dock is the *Hotel Los Delfines* (☎285-5239; ❺), a more upmarket option and the only place with electricity at night. Their comfortable, spacious bungalows come with fan or a/c, private bath and terrace. On the northeastern side of the island is the idyllically situated *Derek's Place* (❸), the island's chief backpacker hangout with small bamboo and coconut frond cabañas and dorms (US$5). There's also hammocks, camping space, and a secluded beach perfect for snorkelling. To get there, follow the path behind *Bridgette's* and walk for about thirty minutes (keep left when the path splits). On the eastern side of the island, on a bluff of land with great sea views, is the friendly US-owned *Hotel Casa Iguana* (no phone, ⓦwww.casaiguana.net), which has a selection of private cabins with veranda, hammock and private bath. They come in economy (❹) or deluxe (❻) models, all benefiting from the wonderful sea breeze blowing along the island's eastern side. They also serve communal dinners; if you're reserving in advance (a good idea in high season), let them know if you want veggie food. To get there, walk across the island from the village and turn right, a walk of about ten minutes.

For **eating**, *Elssa's Place*, on the "village" side, serves up cold beers and lobster for US$6. She also rents out hammocks for US$10 a night. For something a little more unique, head to the Italian-owned *Farm Peace and Love*, on the northeast side of the island near *Derek's*, where you can tuck into good-value treats like lobster *fettucini*, Italian salad and even homemade *focaccia*. The *Happy Hut*, meanwhile, is the place to skank to reggae of a weekend; it's located in the "village" by the beach.

The RAAN: northern Mosquitia

The **northern coast** of Nicaraguan Mosquitia is one of the most impenetrable and underdeveloped areas of the Americas. No roads connect the area with the rest of the country, and the many snaking, difficult to navigate rivers and lagoons, separated by thick slabs of jungle, prevent the casual traveller – or any non-local, for that matter – from visiting the area.

Bordered at its northern extent by the **Río Coco**, Nicaragua's frontier with Honduras, Mosquitia is dotted by small settlements of the indigenous Miskito peoples. Few of these hamlets show up on any map, but the region is far from empty. The area was highly sensitive during the war years of the 1980s, when Contra bases in Honduras continually sent guerrilla parties over the long river border to attack Sandinista army posts and civilian communities in Mosquitia and beyond. The Sandinistas forcibly evacuated many Miskitos from their homes, ostensibly to protect them from Contra attacks, but also to prevent them from going over to the other side.

Few travellers come to **Puerto Cabezas**, the only town of any size and importance in the area: getting around in these parts is difficult and as it's a region where people have very little money but a lot of guns, it's important to know what you are doing if you venture outside the port town. There are still isolated violent incidents (most recently during the 2001 elections) in the region involving re-armed former combatants although in large part they remain confined to the infamous Las Minas mining triangle, encompassing the towns of Siuna, Rosita and Bonanza. More than anywhere else in Nicaragua, services are poor, consumer goods nearly nonexistent, and food hard to come by. Make sure you bring plenty of córdobas and perhaps a few dollars too. A detailed map of the area, a compass, and emergency provisions as well as the usual mosquito repellent, sunscreen and first-aid kit, are all essential.

Puerto Cabezas

Small and scruffy **PUERTO CABEZAS** or **BILWI**, as the locals have named it in defiance of central governmental control (the name means "snake leaf" in the Mayangna-Sumo indigenous tongue), is the most important town north of Bluefields and south of La Ceiba in Honduras. Everyone seems to have come to this town of 30,000 people in order to do some kind of business, whether it be a Miskito fisherman walking the streets with a day's catch of fish dangling from his hand, a lumber merchant selling planks to foreign mills, or the government surveyors working on the all-season paved road through the jungle that may one day link the town with Managua. Nevertheless, there is real potential for tourism here and there's at least one organisation (AMICA) in town organising trips to the isolated communities and beauty spots located largely to the south. Given the friendly, and in general, welcoming nature of the inhabitants, it's a potential that will hopefully be realised one day, finance notwithstanding. The water at the local **beach** below the hotels can be clear and blue if the wind is blowing from the northeast although the townspeople usually head to Bocana beach a few kilometres away. Puerto Cabezas also serves as the base for YATAMA (Yapti Tasba Masraka Nanih Aslatakanka – which translates roughly as Children of the Mother Earth), a political party which fights for the rights of the indigenous Atlantic Coast peoples, and which is fiercely opposed to central government, whether Conservative, Liberal or Sandinista.

Practicalities

Most travellers arrive by **plane**. The daily La Costeña or Atlantic Airlines flight from Managua touches down at the airstrip 2km north of town, from where taxis will take you into the centre for about US$1. The town's few amenities are all scattered within a few blocks of the Parque Central, a few hundred metres west of the seafront. Although there's no Intur office, AMICA (Ⓣ282-2219, Ⓕ282-2325), four blocks south of the main square, run trips to the lagoon-side fishing village of Haulover, the long black-sand beach at Wawa Bar and the small community of Karata, most of whose members were displaced in Honduras and Costa Rica during the war but many of whom have now returned. There's an **Enitel** office (Mon–Fri 7am–8pm, Sat 7am–5pm, Sun 8am–5pm) at the southern edge of the Parque, and an adjacent Caley Dagnall **bank** that changes dollars and accepts travellers' cheques. Fairly cheap **Internet** access is available upstairs at CECOM, 50m south of El Cortijo.

The choice of **accommodation** comes as a pleasant surprise, especially if you've just arrived from Bluefields although affordable budget beds are in short supply. The good-value *Hotel Cortijo 1*, 100m north of the Parque (Ⓣ282-2340; US$20), has intimate, cool and comfortable wooden rooms (all with fan and private bath) strung along a delightful balcony, itself wrapped around a lush garden with resident parrots. They also have an impressive laundry service and do decent breakfasts with real coffee. Its charming and highly recommended sister hotel, *Hotel Cortijo 2*, located in the street behind running parallel to the sea (Ⓣ282-2223; US$27), is also great value, comprising large, seductive wooden rooms with private balcony and hammocks. There's also an amazing wooden jetty running right down to the beach. The managers of both hotels are friendly and helpful tourism students and a good source of local info. Fifty metres north of *Cortijo 1*, the friendly, ageing *Hotel Perez* (Ⓣ282-2362; US$16.60) boasts the novelty of carpeted floors and European-style glass windows; the best rooms, which you'll pay more for, are out back around the old wooden balcony.

As with most places on the Atlantic Coast, **eating** in Puerto Cabezas is geared towards seafood. The prepossessing *Kabu Payaska*, situated on a bluff 2km north of town, is an unforgettable place to enjoy fresh fish and bowls of seafood soup for around US$8; it's pricey but the glorious Caribbean views make for a memorable meal. In town, the *Disco Bar y Restaurante Miramar*, one block north and 75m east of the Catholic church, also has a small balcony with sea views, but it's not in the same league even if the lobster is cheaper. The reasonable Chinese food at *Dragon Chino* or *Disco Jumbo*, both in the main street leading northeast from the Parque, offer cheaper alternatives, with the latter also making its living from dancing; reggae, soca, salsa and calypso can be heard every night except Monday.

Travel details

Buses

The main domestic and international bus routes from **Managua** are covered in the box on p.514 and from **Granada** in the box on p.543.

Chinandega to: Guasaule (buses every 20min; 2hr 10min; minibuses every 20min; 1hr 30min); León (buses every 11min; 1hr 15min; minibuses every 30min; 45min); Managua (every 30min; 3hr; minibuses every 20min; 2hr).

Esteli to: León (buses 2 daily, one from each terminal; 2hr 30min; minibuses 3 daily; 2hr 30min); Managua (buses every 30min; 3hr; express buses 8 daily; 2hr); Matagalpa (buses every 30min; 1hr 50min; express buses 2 daily; 1hr); Masaya (express buses 2 daily; 3hr); Ocotal (hourly; 2hr 15min).

Jinotega to: Matagalpa (every 30min; 1hr 30min); Managua (every 90min; 3hr 30min).

León to: Chinandega (buses every 15min; 1hr 30min; minibuses every 30min; 45min); Estelí (buses 2 daily; 2hr 15min; minibuses 3 daily; 2hr); Managua (buses every 16min; 1hr 30min; express buses 10 daily; 1hr 15min; minibuses every 5/10min; 1hr 10min); Matagalpa (buses 2 daily; 3hr 20min; minibuses 3 daily; 2hr).

Matagalpa to: Estelí (every 30min; 1hr 45min); Jinotega (every 30min; 1hr 30min); Managua (every 30min; 3hr); León (2 daily; 3hr); Masaya (2 daily; 4hr).

Masaya to: Diriamba (every 30 min; 30min); Granada (every 30min; 30min); Managua (every 20min; 45min); Rivas (every 30min; 2hr).

Rivas to: Diriamba (10 daily; 1hr 30min); Granada (8 daily; 1hr 30min); Masaya (every 30min; 2hr); Managua (every 25min; 2hr 30min);

San Juan del Sur to: Rivas (every 45mins; 45mins).

Flights

La Costeña (Ⓣ 263-2142, Ⓦ www.flylacostena.com) and Atlantic Airlines (Ⓣ 270-5355, Ⓦ www.atlanticairlines.com.ni) both fly from Managua to Bluefields several times a day. On the other routes, La Costeña operate more flights with several a day to Puerto Cabezas and two daily to Corn Island. Atlantic fly twice a day to Puerto Cabezas although they only fly to Corn Island from Bluefields. La Costeña also operate daily flights between Managua and San Carlos. Advance reservations are highly advisable.

Boats

All boat services are subject to seasonal changes and cancellations at short notice due to weather conditions.

Altagracia to: Granada (Tues & Fri at 1.30am; 4hr); San Carlos (Mon & Thurs 6.20pm; 11hr).

Bluefields to: Corn Island (Wed 6pm; 5–8hr).

Corn Island to: Bluefields (Tues & Sun 9am; 5–8hr); Little Corn (*panga*) (daily at 10am & 4.30pm, returns at 7.30am and 2pm; 45min–1hr).

El Rama to: Bluefields (by ferry: Mon, Tues, Sat & Sun 1pm; 5–6hr; by *panga*: regular departures between 5am and1pm; 2hr).

Granada to: Altagracia (Mon & Thurs at 3pm; 2hr 45min); San Carlos (Mon & Thurs 3pm; 12–14hr).

Moyogalpa to: San Jorge (14 daily; 1hr).

San Carlos to: El Castillo (4 daily; 2–3hr); Altagracia (Tues & Fri 2pm; 11hr 30min); Granada (Tues & Fri 2pm; 12–14hr); Mancarrón (Tues & Fri noon and 2pm; 3hr).

San Jorge to: Moyogalpa (12 daily; 1hr).

6

Costa Rica

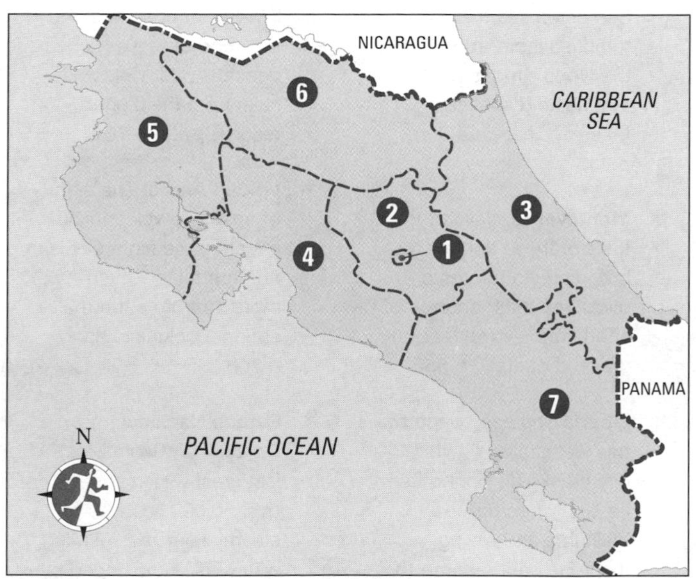

Highlights 572
Introduction and Basics 573
6.1 San José 594
6.2 The Valle Central and the Highlands 616
6.3 Limón Province and the Caribbean Coast 631
6.4 The Central Pacific and Southern Nicoya 650
6.5 Guanacaste 680
6.6 The Zona Norte 702
6.7 The Zona Sur 715
Travel details 725

Costa Rica Highlights

* **Whitewater rafting on the Pacuaré and Reventazón rivers** Adrenaline-fuelled nature spotting along jungle-fringed rapids. p.629

* **Desove at Tortuguero** See green sea turtles tumble ashore at one of the world's most important nesting sites for these ancient creatures. p.636

* **Monteverde** Walking the trails of these ancient, brooding cloudforests gives you a fair chance of spotting the extravagantly dressed quetzal. p.658

* **Liberia** The easy pace of this welcoming cowboy city cranks up during its fiestas, when rodeos, bullfights and roving marimba bands come to town. p.680

* **Parque Nacional Rincón de la Vieja** Hike to the summit of a volcano and take in the sulphur and brimstone of the bubbling mud pots. p.685

* **Sámara and Nosara** The low-key atmosphere and fine food of these Nicoya beaches offer welcome relief from the bigger resorts. pp.697–701

* **Volcán Arenal** The sight of an active volcano illuminating the night sky is unforgettable – even more so from a thermal spring, cocktail in hand. p.708

* **Parque Nacional Corcovado** Costa Rica's last great wilderness – over 40,000 hectares of steamy rainforest teeming with wildlife and ringed by pristine beaches. p.722

Introduction and Basics

In sharp contrast to the turbulent recent histories of Nicaragua, Guatemala and El Salvador, **Costa Rica** has become synonymous with stability and prosperity – Costa Ricans, or Ticos, enjoy the highest rate of literacy, health care, education and life expectancy in the isthmus. Unlike so many of its neighbours, the country has a long democratic tradition of free and open elections, no standing army (it was abolished in 1948) and even a Nobel Peace Prize to its name, won by former president Oscar Arias, a key architect in the peace plan that helped bring an end to regional conflicts in the 1980s.

In recent years Costa Rica has also become the prime **ecotourism** destination in Central America, if not in all the Americas, due in no small part to an efficient promotion machine that trumpets the country's complex system of national parks and wildlife refuges. Every year hundreds of thousands of visitors – mainly from the United States and Canada – come to walk trails through million-year-old **rainforests**, raft foaming whitewater rapids, surf on the **beaches** and climb the **volcanoes** that punctuate the country's mountainous spine. More than anything it is the enduring natural beauty that impresses. Milk-thick twilight and dawn mists gather in the clefts and ridges divided by high mountain passes; on the Pacific coast, carmine and mauve sunsets splash down into the sea like meteors; vaulting canopy trees and thick deciduous understoreys carpet large areas of undisturbed rainforest, and vestiges of high-altitude cloudforest offer glimpses into a misty, primeval universe, home to the jaguar, the lumbering Jurassic tapir and the truly resplendent quetzal.

One glib accusation you're almost certain to hear lobbed at the tiny nation is that it has no culture or history. It's certainly true that there are no ancient Mesoamerican monuments on the scale of Guatemala or Honduras, and just one percent of the population is of indigenous extraction, so you will see little native culture. However, anyone who spends some time in the country will find that Costa Rica's character is rooted in distinct **local cultures**, from the Afro-Caribbean province of Limón, with its Creole cuisine, games and patois, to the traditional *ladino* values embodied by the *sabanero* (cowboy) of Guanacaste. Above all, you're sure to be left with mental snapshots of *la vida campesina*, or rural life – whether it be aloof horsemen trotting by on dirt roads, coffee-plantation day-labourers setting off to work in the dawn mists of the Highlands, or avocado-pickers cycling home at sunset.

Where to go

Though everyone passes through it, hardly anyone falls in love with **San José**, Costa Rica's underrated capital. Often dismissed as an ugly urban sprawl, the city enjoys a dramatic setting amid jagged mountain peaks, plus some excellent cafés and restaurants, leafy parks, a lively university district and a good arts scene. The surrounding **Valle Central** is the country's agricultural heartland, and also home to several of its finest volcanoes, including the huge crater of Volcán Poás and the largely dormant Volcán Irazú, a strange lunar landscape high above the provincial capital of Cartago.

Though nowhere in the country is further than nine hours' drive from San José, the far north and the far south are less visited than other regions. The broad alluvial plains of the **Zona Norte** are often overlooked, despite featuring high-quality jungle lodges as well as active Volcán Arenal, which spouts and spews within sight of the friendly tourist hangout of Fortuna, affording arresting night-time scenes of blood-red lava illuminating the sky. Off-the-beaten-path travellers and serious hikers will be happiest in the rugged **Zona Sur**, home to Mount Chirripó, the highest point in the country. Further south, on the outstretched feeler of the Osa Peninsula, Parque Nacional Corcovado protects the last significant area of tropical wet

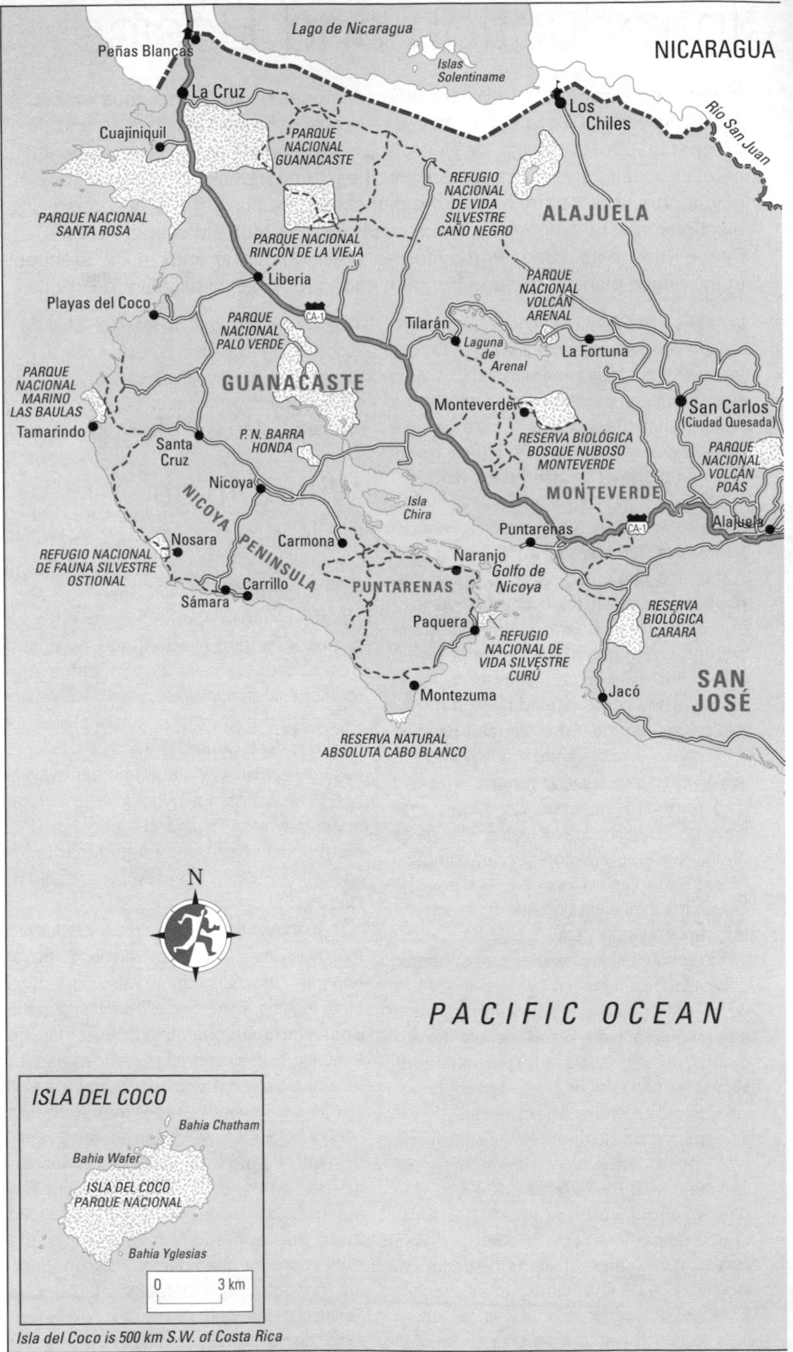

Lago de Nicaragua
NICARAGUA
Peñas Blancas
Islas Solentiname
La Cruz
Los Chiles
Río San Juan
Cuajiniquil
PARQUE NACIONAL GUANACASTE
REFUGIO NACIONAL DE VIDA SILVESTRE CAÑO NEGRO
PARQUE NACIONAL SANTA ROSA
ALAJUELA
PARQUE NACIONAL RINCÓN DE LA VIEJA
Liberia
PARQUE NACIONAL VOLCÁN ARENAL
Playas del Coco
CA-1
PARQUE NACIONAL PALO VERDE
Tilarán
Laguna de Arenal
La Fortuna
PARQUE NACIONAL MARINO LAS BAULAS
GUANACASTE
San Carlos (Ciudad Quesada)
Monteverde
Tamarindo
P. N. BARRA HONDA
RESERVA BIOLÓGICA BOSQUE NUBOSO MONTEVERDE
Santa Cruz
PARQUE NACIONAL VOLCÁN POÁS
Nicoya
MONTEVERDE
Isla Chira
NICOYA PENINSULA
Alajuela
Puntarenas
Nosara
Carmona
REFUGIO NACIONAL DE FAUNA SILVESTRE OSTIONAL
Naranjo
Golfo de Nicoya
Carrillo
PUNTARENAS
Sámara
RESERVA BIOLÓGICA CARARA
Paquera
REFUGIO NACIONAL DE VIDA SILVESTRE CURÚ
SAN JOSÉ
Jacó
Montezuma
RESERVA NATURAL ABSOLUTA CABO BLANCO
N
PACIFIC OCEAN
ISLA DEL COCO
Bahia Chatham
Bahia Wafer
ISLA DEL COCO PARQUE NACIONAL
Bahia Yglesias
0
3 km
Isla del Coco is 500 km S.W. of Costa Rica

6 COSTA RICA | Basics

forest on the Pacific coast of the isthmus and is probably the best destination in the country for walkers – and also one of the few places where you have a fighting chance of seeing some of the wildlife for which Costa Rica is famed.

In the northwest the cattle-ranching province of **Guanacaste** is often called "the home of Costa Rican folklore", and *sabanero* culture dominates here, with exuberant ragtag rodeos and large cattle haciendas. **Limón** Province, on the Caribbean coast, is the polar opposite to *ladino* Guanacaste and home to the descendants of the Afro-Caribbeans who came to Costa Rica at the end of the nineteenth century to work on the San José–Limón railroad – their language (Creole English), Protestantism and West Indian traditions remain relatively intact to this day.

Close to the **Pacific coast**, Monteverde has become the country's number-one tourist attraction, pulling in the visitors who flock here to walk trails through some of the last remaining cloudforest in the Americas and take the adrenalin-filled "canopy tours", the most popular of a growing range of adventure-tourism activities on offer throughout the country. Further down the coast is the popular beach of Manuel Antonio, with its picture-postcard ocean setting, plus the equally pretty, but far less touristed, beaches of Sámara and Nosara on the Nicoya Peninsula.

When to go

Although Costa Rica lies between 8° and 11° north of the equator, **local microclimates** predominate and make temperatures and weather unpredictable, though to an extent you can depend upon the **two-season** rule. The **rainy season** runs from about May to mid November, when you will have afternoon rains and sunny mornings. The **rains** are heaviest in September and October, but although they can be fierce, they will only impede you from travelling in the more remote areas of the country – the Nicoya and Osa peninsulas in particular – where dirt roads become impassable to all but the sturdiest 4WDs. In the **dry season** most areas are just that: dry all day, with occasional blustery northern winds blowing in during January or February and cooling things off. Otherwise you can count on sunshine and warm temperatures.

In recent years Costa Rica has been booked solid during the **peak season** – the North American winter months – when bargains are few and far between. The crowds peter out after Easter, but return again to an extent in June and July. During peak times you have to plan well in advance, faxing the hotels of your choice, usually pre-paying or at least putting down a deposit by credit card, and arriving armed with faxed confirmations and a set itinerary. Travellers who prefer to play it by ear are much better off coming during the rainy or **low season** (euphemistically called the "green season"), when many hotels offer discounts. The months of November, April (after Easter) and May are the best times to visit, when the rains have either just started or just died off, and the country is refreshed, green and relatively untouristed.

Getting around

Costa Rica's public bus system is excellent, cheap and remarkably regular, even in remote areas. However, getting anywhere by bus with a lot of baggage can be a problem; accordingly, many people travel light, leaving the bulk of their baggage somewhere secure (a San José hotel, for example) while on the road. Air-conditioned minibuses run daily transfers between most major tourist destinations and have become a useful, if expensive, time-saver. Car rental is more common here than in the rest of Central America, but it is very expensive.

Buses

Buses are by far the cheapest way to get around. The most expensive journey in the country (from San José to Paso Canoas on the Panama border) costs US$6, while **fares** in the mid- to long-distance range vary from US$2.50 to US$4. **Tickets** on most mid- to long-distance and popular routes are issued with a date and a seat number; you are expected to sit in the seat indicated. Make sure the date is correct; even if the mistake

Overland to and from Costa Rica

Costa Rica has several **land routes** to its neighbours, Nicaragua and Panama. The main northern border crossing with **Nicaragua** is at Peñas Blancas (see p.688) on the Interamericana highway. Further east, another crossing at Los Chiles (see p.709) involves a boat trip (and usually an overnight stay) to/from San Carlos on the shores of Lago de Nicaragua, although a bridge is planned.

The main route south into **Panama** is also on the Interamericana, at Paso Canoas (see p.724). On the Caribbean coast, Sixaola is a smaller crossing, while in the southern highlands, two little-used routes link San Vito with the border towns of Río Sereno and Cañas Gordas.

is not yours, you cannot normally change your ticket or get a refund. Neither can you buy return bus tickets on Costa Rican buses, which can be quite inconvenient, if heading to very popular destinations like Monteverde, Jacó or Manuel Antonio at busy times. In such cases, you'll need to jump off the bus as soon as you arrive and buy your return ticket immediately to assure yourself a seat.

San José is the hub for virtually all bus services in the country; indeed, it's often impossible to travel from one place to another without backtracking to the capital. Different companies have semi-monopolies on various regions; for a rundown of **destinations and routes**, including international services, see pp.611–615.

On the most popular buses, like the service to Golfito, it's advisable to **book in advance**, though you may be lucky and get on without a reservation. Services to popular tourist areas in high season – especially Monteverde – get booked up very fast, so again you should buy your ticket several days ahead of travel. For bus **timetables** check out Ⓦwww.costaricamap.com/ing/infotbuslocal.html.

Though most Costa Rican buses are pretty good, the best of the bunch – arguably the best in Central America – is Ticabus (Ⓦwww.ticabus.com), which runs the border routes from San José to Panama and Managua in modern air-conditioned buses.

Bus transfers

In recent years travellers have begun to make much use of the network of **air-conditioned minibuses** that connect most of Costa Rica's main tourist destinations. Although these cost five or more times as much as the public buses, they are significantly faster, more comfortable and will pick up and drop off at hotels. The main operator is Interbus (Ⓦwww.interbusonline.com), who have comprehensive coverage and charge US$25–40 for a mid- to long-range journey.

Driving

You have to exercise caution when **renting a car** in Costa Rica – companies have been known to claim for "damage" they insist you inflicted on their vehicle. Taking out full insurance is by far the best way to nip this in the bud. Renting a car through a Costa Rican travel agent or tour operator will cost you considerably less than doing it yourself. If you are travelling on a package, your agent will sort this out. Otherwise, go into an ICT-accredited travel agent in San José.

Car rental in Costa Rica is also expensive. Expect to pay about US$350 per week for a regular (non-4WD) vehicle, including insurance, and up to US$500 for 4WD. You will need a credit card, either MasterCard or Visa, which has sufficient credit for a US$1000 security deposit or the entire cost of the rental. There are car rental companies in most major towns and beach resorts; dropping your car off in another location normally entails a charge, but this might be waived for longer rentals.

It is imperative to take out full insurance, particularly on a non-4WD, as the conditions of the roads make it very likely that you will incur some minor damage. For a list of rental companies in San José, see p.609.

If you intend to drive in the rainy season (especially on the Nicoya Peninsula), or want to get to off-the-beaten-track places, you'll need to rent a **4WD**. (Indeed, due to the condition of the roads, some car rental companies refuse to allow their regular cars to be driven to Monteverde between May and November.)

In recent years a system of fines (*multas*) for infractions like speeding has been introduced in Costa Rica. The **speed limit** on the highways is either 75km/hr or 90km/hr; it's marked on the sidewalk or on signs. If you're caught speeding (and speed traps are common), you could find yourself paying up to US$150. (Tickets are paid at a police station or to your car rental company.) Fuel is positively cheap by European standards: about US$15 a tank on a mid-sized vehicle or about US$30 for a big 4WD.

Cycling

Costa Rica's terrain makes **cycling** a pleasure – indeed, it's easier to dodge the potholes and wandering cattle on a bike than in a car – and the range of places to stay and eat means you don't need to carry a tent. There is very little traffic outside the Valle Central, and Costa Rican drivers tend to be courteous to cyclists. Be warned, however, that if you cycle up to Monteverde, one of the most popular routes in the country, you're in for a slow trip: besides being steep, there's not much traction on the loose gravel roads.

San José's best **cycle shop** is Bicimania, at the corner of Paseo Colón and C 26. They have all the parts you might need, can fix your bike, and may even be able to give you a bicycle carton for the plane.

Planes

Costa Rica's two **domestic air carriers** offer a quite economical scheduled service between San José and many beach destinations and provincial towns. These can be very handy, saving many hours of bus travel better spent on the sand. **Sansa** (Ⓦwww.flysansa.com) is the state-owned domestic airline; **NatureAir** (Ⓦwww.natureair.com) is its commercial competitor. Both fly small, twin-propeller aircraft and service the same destinations. Of the two, NatureAir (which flies from Tobías Bolaños airport in Pavas, 7km west of San José) is more reliable and flies more frequently on some runs. Sansa (which flies from Juan Santamaría airport, 17km northwest of San José) is cheaper but less reliable. Both can be booked online, but make sure to reconfirm your flight in advance. Sansa also offers airpasses, with unlimited travel between selected dates. For a rundown of schedules, see p.613.

Costs, money and banks

Though prices have dropped from their peak of a few years ago, Costa Rica remains one of the most expensive countries in Central America. Some prices, especially for upper-range accommodation, are similar to those in the US, which never fails to astonish American travellers and those coming from the cheaper neighbouring countries. That said, with a little foresight you can still travel relatively cheaply.

Getting around Costa Rican towns

All Costa Rican towns of any size are intersected by an **Avenida Central**, which runs east–west, and a **Calle Central**, which runs north–south. From Avenida Central, parallel avenidas run odd numbers to the north and even numbers to the south. From Calle Central, even-numbered calles run to the west and odd numbers to the east. Avenidas 8 and 9, therefore, are actually quite far apart from one another, while calles 23 and 24 would be at opposite ends of the city. "**0**" in addresses is shorthand for "Central": thus Av 0, C 11 is the same as Av Central, C 11.

If you use street numbers as addresses, locals – and especially taxi drivers – won't have a clue where you are talking about. When possible use directions given in relation to local **landmarks**, buildings, businesses, parks or institutions, or according to the nearest intersection. People use metres to signify distance: in local parlance 100 metres equals one city block.

Currency, exchange and banks

The official currency of Costa Rica is the **colón** (plural colones). There are two types of **coin** in circulation: the old silver ones, which come in denominations of 5, 10 and 20, and newer gold coins, which come in denominations of 5, 10, 25, 50, 100 and 500. Public payphones do not yet take the new coins, and you will need the silver ones to make a call; otherwise they're interchangeable. There are **bank notes** of 1000, 2000, 5000 and 10,000. You'll often hear colones colloquially referred to as "pesos"; in addition, the 1000 is sometimes called the *rojo* (red). The colón floats freely against the US dollar, which in practice has meant that it devalues by some 10 percent per year; at the time of writing it was around 430 colones to US$1. Obtaining colones outside Costa Rica is virtually impossible: wait until you arrive and get some at the airport or border posts. US dollars are the unofficial second currency of Costa Rica and are accepted almost everywhere.

By far the easiest way to travel is with a **bank card**. Nearly all towns and resorts have at least one bank with an ATM accepting foreign cards. Many banks have machines that take Visa/Plus; the Banco Nacional's also take MasterCard/Cirrus, as do some others. Some machines will issue US dollars as well as colones. Getting money out can sometimes be a trial-and-error process and may require several attempts.

It's unlikely that you'll need to **exchange** US dollars for colones, as they are accepted almost everywhere. If you do, or if you are changing other currencies, such as sterling or euros, you'll find that the efficient and air-conditioned **private banks**, the majority of which are in San José (for addresses, see p.609), are much faster but charge scandalous commissions. The **state banks**, such as the Banco Nacional, are more reasonable but slow and bureaucratic.

Banking hours vary slightly from branch to branch but tend to be Monday to Friday 8.30am to 3.30pm for state banks and slightly longer for private ones (which are also sometimes open on Saturday mornings). You'll find **credit cards** especially useful in Costa Rica for making deposits for hotels via fax and for renting a car. In general, Visa and MasterCard are widely accepted, although retailers tend to accept only one or the other. In outlying areas, however, like the Talamanca coast, Quepos and Manuel Antonio and Golfito, some businesses may levy a six percent charge for credit card transactions; you may be better off taking plenty of cash.

Undeniably the safest way to carry money is to use **travellers' cheques**. These should be bought in US dollars only – Costa Rican bank staff will stare blankly at other currencies. However, do not expect to use travellers' cheques as cash except in mid- or upmarket hotels and guesthouses that regularly cater to foreigners.

Costs

The high cost of living is due in part to the **taxes** (16–25 percent) that are levied in restaurants and hotels, and also, more recently, to the International Monetary Fund, whose policies, aimed at restructuring the balance of payments deficit, have raised prices. Even on a rock-bottom **budget**, you're looking at spending US$25/£15 a day for lodging, three meals and the odd bus ticket. Campers and hardy cyclists have been known to do it on US$15/£10 a day, but this entails sleeping either in a tent or in somewhere pretty dire. You'll be far more comfortable if you count on spending at least US$20/£12 a day for accommodation and US$15/£10 for meals.

That said, **bus travel**, geared toward locals, is always cheap – about US$0.25 to US$1 for local buses, around US$4 or US$5 for long-distance buses (3hr or more). **Eating**, too, needn't be that pricey, and fruit, beer and cinema tickets will all seem very reasonable to visitors from most other countries. **Students** with ISIC cards may be entitled to some discounts at museums in Costa Rica. More useful is local student ID, available to visitors on language courses and other education programmes, which may get you discounts at museums and theatres.

Information

The best source of information about Costa Rica is the **Instituto Costarricense de**

Turismo, or **ICT**, Apartado 777, San José 1000, Costa Rica (Ⓣ506/223-1733 or 223-1090, Ⓕ223-5452, Ⓦwww.visitcostarica.com) – you can write to them from abroad, though it may take a while to receive a reply, and you'll probably just be given the same glossy brochures that are handed out at embassies.

You're better off visiting them in person at their office (see p.596) in the unprepossessing bunker underneath the Plaza de la Cultura in central San José, where the friendly, bilingual staff will do their best to answer any queries you may have. On request, they'll also give you a free country/city map, plus a very useful and comprehensive bus timetable with recent additions and changes corrected on the spot. The office can also provide a list of museums and their opening hours, details of many San José restaurants and nightclubs as well as a brochure produced by the Cámara Costarricense de Hoteles (Costa Rican Hotel Association) that gives contact details for a good many of the country's hotels. The small ICT booths at the three main entry points to the country – Peñas Blancas on the Nicaraguan border, Paso Canoas on the Panamanian border and San José's Santamaría International Airport – will probably be able to provide the map and the hotel brochure but not the timetables.

Apart from this, there are no official tourist offices outside the capital, and you'll generally have to rely on locally run initiatives, often set up by a small business association or the chamber of commerce, or hotels and tourist agencies. A number of San José–based **tour operators** can offer guidance when planning a trip around the country; see p.612 for details.

On the **Internet**, Ⓦwww.centralamerica.com, Ⓦwww.costaricanet.net, Ⓦwww.costaricabureau.com (the website of the Costa Rican Tourism and Travel Bureau) and Ⓦwww.costaricantourism.co.cr (the website of the Costa Rican National Chamber of Commerce) are all good sources of information and have links to thousands of Costa Rican websites. Weekly news on the country in English can be found at Ⓦwww.ticotimes.net, and Costa Rica's leading daily newspaper is online at Ⓦwww.nacion.co.cr.

Accommodation

Most towns in Costa Rica have a good range of places to stay, and even the smallest settlements have a basic pensión or hospedaje. Though prices are, in the main, higher than you'd pay in most other Central American countries, they're by no means exorbitant, certainly not when compared with the US or Western Europe. For an explanation of the accommodation **price codes** used in the *Guide*, see p.36.

Budget accommodation runs the gamut from the extremely basic, where your US$10–20 a night will get you little more than a room and a bed, to the reasonably well equipped, where for around US$20–30 a night you'll get a clean, comfortable en-suite room, a fan and possibly even a TV and phone. In the **middle and upper price range**, facilities and services are generally of a very good standard throughout the country. In this category, room rates – after a period of rapid inflation where some hoteliers decided they could charge pretty much what they liked – are thankfully coming down, although there's still some overcharging. With a bit of forward planning, however, you should be able to find somewhere decent for around US$35–55, even in the high season.

Out of season, it's well worth looking into some of the more upmarket rainforest lodges and beach resorts – the sort of places that have hot tubs, swimming pools, spas, gourmet restaurants and their own stretches of jungle – where you might be able to get yourself a night or two of luxury for as little as US$120–145.

When looking at prices, remember that not all hotels list the hotel tax (which stands at 16.39 percent including a 3 percent "tourist tax") in the published price. Be sure to check first.

Accommodation in coastal areas is often in **cabinas**, usually either a string of motel-style rooms in an annex away from a main building or hotel, or more often separate, self-contained units. They're usually – although not always – pretty basic, and most often frequented by budget travellers.

Few hotels, except those at the upper end of the range, have **double beds**; it's more common to find two or three single beds.

Single travellers will generally be charged the single rate, even if they are occupying a "double room" – though this may not be the case in popular beach towns and at peak seasons.

In the high season (Dec–April), and especially at Christmas, New Year's and Easter, you should **reserve** well ahead, especially for good-value hotels in popular spots, and for youth hostels. It's easiest to reserve a room with a credit card by **fax** or **email**.

Camping

Though **camping** is fairly widespread in Costa Rica, gone are the days when people could pitch their tents on just about any beach or field. You'll have a far better relationship with locals if you ask politely whether it is OK to camp nearby; if they direct you to a campsite, they are doing so not because they don't like the look of you, but in an attempt to keep their environment clean.

In the beach towns especially, you will usually find at least one well-equipped private campsite, with good facilities. Staff may also offer to guard your clothes and tent while you're at the beach. Alternatively, you might be able to find a hotelier (usually in an establishment at the lower end of the price scale) willing to let you pitch your tent in the grounds and let you use their showers and washrooms for a charge. Though not all national parks have campsites, the ones that do are generally good, with at least some basic facilities, and cost around US$2 per person per day. In some national parks, you may be able to bunk down at the ranger station.

When camping in Costa Rica never leave your tent or anything of value inside it unattended, or it may not be there when you get back. Never leave your tent open except to get in and out, unless you fancy sharing your sleeping quarters with snakes, insects, coati or toads. Finally, take your refuse with you when you leave.

Youth hostels

Costa Rica has a small network of eighteen good and reasonably priced **youth hostels**, affiliated with the Hostelling International organization. They cost around US$8–16 per night if you're an HI member, US$10–20 if not, and can be conveniently booked through *Hostal Toruma* in San José (see p.600) or by logging on to Ⓦwww.hicr.org. As with all accommodation in Costa Rica, bookings should ideally be made three months in advance, if you're coming in high season.

All eighteen hostels can be reached by public transport and follow conservation regulations based on the sustainable development principle. Most of them have a range of double, triple and family rooms and some offer a range of additional services, including Internet access, laundry and luggage storage. Bed linen, towels and soap are included in the price.

Food and drink

Eating out in Costa Rica can be pricey. Main dishes in restaurants can easily cost US$7–9, not including the service charge (10 percent) and the sales tax (15 percent). Tipping, however, is not necessary.

Where to eat

The cheapest places to eat in Costa Rica, and where most workers eat lunch, their main meal, are the ubiquitous **sodas**, halfway between the North American diner and the British greasy spoon. *Sodas* offer filling, set *platos del día* (daily specials) and **casados**, combinations of rice, beans, salad and meat or fish, for about US$3. Many *sodas* – at least in San José – are **vegetarian**, and in general vegetarians do quite well in Costa Rica. Most menus will have a vegetable option, and asking for dishes to be served without meat is perfectly acceptable.

Because Costa Ricans start the day early, they are less likely to hang about late in restaurants in the evening, and establishments are usually empty or closed by 10 or 10.30pm. Waiters tend to leave you alone unless they are called for. Non-smoking sections are uncommon, to say the least, except in the most expensive establishments, but in general Ticos don't smoke much in restaurants.

A Spanish **menu reader** can be found on p.870.

What to eat

Ticos call their cuisine **comida típica** ("native" or "local" food). Although simple, it's tasty, especially when it comes to interesting regional variations on the Caribbean coast (Creole cooking) and in Guanacaste (where many corn-based dishes survive more or less unchanged from pre-Columbian times).

The most common dishes throughout the country include rice, beans and some kind of meat or fish. The **casado** (literally, "married person") combines these and other ingredients, typically salad and fried plantain, to form a hunger-busting carbohydrate fix that is the classic campesino's lunch and budget traveller's staple. The ubiquitous **gallo pinto** ("painted rooster") is a breakfast combination of red and white beans with rice, sometimes served with *huevos revueltos* (scrambled eggs).

You will find excellent **fresh fish** in Costa Rica, two of the best of which are *pargo* (red snapper) and *corvina* (sea bass). *Ceviche* (raw fish in lime juice with coriander and peppers) is a speciality that is definitely worth trying as a refreshing starter or light main meal.

Obviously, **fresh fruit** is a must, and in any café, restaurant or *soda* you can order from a range of *refrescos*. Papayas, pineapple and bananas are all cheap and plentiful, along with some less familiar fruits like *mamones chinos* (a kind of lychee), *anona* (which tastes like custard) and *marañón*, whose seed is the cashew nut.

Drinking

Costa Rica is famous for its **coffee**, but most of the best blends are exported. Although you can buy the premium stuff in shops, very few cafés serve it. It's typical to end a meal with a small cup, traditionally served in a pitcher with heated milk on the side. It's good, although on the weak side; espresso fans will have to drink litres to satisfy their dependent cells. One of the highlights of Costa Rica is its **refrescos**, cool drinks made with milk (*leche*) or water (*agua*), fresh tropical fruit and ice, all whipped up in a blender. They are delicious; you can buy them at stalls or in bottles, though the latter tend to be sugary. You'll find **herb teas** throughout the country; those served in Limón are especially good. In Guanacaste you can get the distinctive corn-based drinks **horchata** and **pinolillo**, made with milk and sugar and with a grainy consistency.

Costa Rica has several local brands of lager **beer**, a must in the steamy tropics. Most popular is Imperial with its characteristic eagle logo, but Bavaria Gold is the best of the bunch, with a cleaner taste and more complex flavour; Bavaria also produce a decent dark beer. Pilsen and Rock Ice are other worthwhile tipples; of the local low-alcohol beers, Bavaria Light is the tastiest. Imported beers are available in many bars, restaurants and hotels.

There is an indigenous sugarcane-based spirit, **guaro**, of which Cacique is the most popular brand. It's a bit rough, but good with lime sodas or in a cocktail. For an after-dinner drink, try Café Rica, a creamy **liqueur** made with the local coffee.

Costa Rica has a variety of **places to drink**, from shady macho domains to pretty beachside bars, with some particularly cosmopolitan establishments in San José. The capital is also the place to find the country's last remaining **boca bars**, atmospheric places that serve *bocas* (tapas-style snacks) with drinks. **Gringo grottos** abound, especially in the beach towns, while in many places, especially port cities like Limón, Puntarenas and Golfito, there are the usual contingent of rough, rowdy bars, their seediness advertised by the giant Imperial placards parked right in front of the doors to block views of the inside.

In general, Sunday night is dead: many bars don't open at all, and those that do tend to close at around 10pm or so. Though Friday and Saturday nights are, as usual, the busiest, the best nights to go are often during the week, when you can enjoy live music, happy hours and other specials. Karaoke is incredibly popular, and if you spend much time in bars, you'll soon pick out the well-loved Tico classics. The **drinking age** in Costa Rica is 18, and many bars will only admit those with ID. A photocopy of your passport page is acceptable.

Opening hours, holidays and festivals

Though you shouldn't expect the kind of colour and verve that you'll find at fiestas in Guatemala, Costa Rica has its fair share of holidays and festivals, or **feriados**, when all banks, post offices, museums and government offices close. In particular, don't try to travel anywhere during **Semana Santa**, Holy (Easter) Week: the whole country shuts down from Holy Thursday until after Easter Monday, and buses don't run. Likewise, the week from Christmas to New Year's invariably causes traffic nightmares, overcrowded beaches and a suspension of services.

Provincial holidays, like Independence Day in Guanacaste (July 25) and the Limón Carnaval (the week preceding October 12), affect local services only, but nonetheless the shutdown is drastic: don't bet on cashing travellers' cheques or mailing letters if you're in these areas at party time.

Communications

Communicating by phone and email in Costa Rica is pretty straightforward in all but the most far flung of destinations. In urban areas phone coverage is pretty much total and, even in the most remote corners of the country, such as Corcovado, many hotels have access to mobile phones and sometimes satellite Internet link-up.

Costa Rica's privatized **postal system** is reasonably efficient, though you may have problems sending and receiving letters from remote areas. The most reliable place to send mail overseas from is San José's **Correo Central**, or main post office (see p.610), which is also the best place to collect post. In most cases – especially in Limón Province, where mail is very slow – it's probably quicker to wait until you return to San José and post mail from there. **Opening hours** for nearly all Costa Rica's post offices are Monday to Friday from 7.30am to 5 or 5.30pm. Those in San José and Liberia also have limited Saturday hours.

Public holidays

Jan 1 New Year's Day. Celebrated with a big dance in San José's Parque Central.

Feb–March (date varies) Ash Wednesday. Countrywide processions; in Guanacaste horse, cow and bull parades, with bullfights (in which the bull is not harmed) in Liberia.

March–April (date varies) Semana Santa (Holy Week).

March 19 El día de San José (St Joseph's Day). Patron saint of San José and San José Province.

April 11 Juan Santamaría Day. Commemorating the national hero who fought at the Battle of Rivas against the American adventurer William Walker in 1856. The biggest celebrations are in Alajuela, Santamaría's birthplace.

May 1 Labour Day.

June 20 St Peter's and St Paul's Day.

July 25 Independence of Guanacaste Day (Guanacaste Province only). Marking the annexation of Guanacaste from Nicaragua in 1824.

Aug 2 Virgin of Los Angeles Day. Patron saint of Costa Rica.

Aug 15 Assumption Day and Mother's Day.

Sept 15 Independence Day. Big patriotic parades celebrating Costa Rica's independence from Spain in 1821.

Oct 12 El día de la Raza (Columbus Day). Limón Province only, marked by Carnaval, which takes place in the week prior to October 12.

Nov 2 All Souls' Day.

Dec 25 Christmas Day.

Telephones

Instituto Costarricense de Electricidad (ICE), the Costa Rican state electronics company, provides international telephone, fax and Internet services via **RACSA**, its telecommunications subsidiary.

The easiest way to make an **international call** is to purchase a **phonecard** (*tarjeta telefónica*), available from most grocery stores, street kiosks and pharmacies. You'll need card number 199 (card number 197 is for domestic calls only), which comes in two denominations: 3000 colones (giving you 17 minutes of talk time to the US and 12 minutes to Europe) and 10,000 colones. To use, simply insert the card into a payphone, dial ⓣ199 and then ⓣ2 for instructions in English. Many payphones also accept credit cards. Note that, though the majority of public phones are now card operated, there are still some traditional coin-operated phones left but, as these only accept the old silver coins, they're not recommended for making international calls. You can **call collect** from any phone or payphone in Costa Rica; dial ⓣ09 or ⓣ116 to get an English-speaking operator. Phone, fax and directory services are also available at the San José Radiográfica office (see p.611).

The **country code** for the whole of Costa Rica is ⓣ506. There are no area codes and all phone numbers have seven digits.

Internet access

Most towns of any size in Costa Rica now have at least one **Internet café**, while places popular with tourists will usually have many more. Charges are low, usually US$1–1.50 per hour in major towns and around US$3–5 per hour in more remote areas, where they rely on satellite link-up.

Many Costa Rican hotels and businesses now have **email**. If you don't know an address, it's worth trying the hotel or establishment name, followed by @racsa.co.cr or @sol.racsa.co.cr – the most common suffixes for email addresses in Costa Rica.

The media

Though the Costa Rican **press** is free, it does indulge in a certain follow-the-leader style of journalism. Leader of the pack is the daily *La Nación*, voice of the (right-of-centre) establishment and owned by the country's biggest media consortium. It also comes with a useful daily pull-out arts section, *Viva*, with **listings** of what's on in San José – the classifieds are handy for almost anything, including long-term accommodation.

La República is no less serious, and geared more to business news. *Al Día* is the populist "body count" paper. Alternative voices include *El Heraldo*, a small but high-quality daily, and *La Prensa Libre*, the very good left-leaning evening paper. The weekly *Semanario Universidad*, the voice of the University of Costa Rica, certainly goes out on more of a limb than the big dailies, with particularly good coverage of the arts and the current political scene. You can find it on campus or in San Pedro.

Local **English-language papers** include the venerable and serious *Tico Times* (ⓦwww.ticotimes.net), which comes out on Fridays, and the *Central America Weekly*, intended for tourists, with articles on activities and holidays. Both can be a good source of information for travellers, and the ads regularly feature hotel and restaurant discounts. You can pick up recent copies of the *New York Times*, *International Herald Tribune*, *USA Today*, *Miami Herald*, *Newsweek*, *Time* and sometimes the *Financial Times* in the souvenir shop beside the *Gran Hotel Costa Rica* in downtown San José (Av 2, C 3/5) and at La Casa de Revistas on the southwest corner of Parque Morazán (C 7, Av 3). Elsewhere, they're difficult to find.

There are many commercial **radio** stations in Costa Rica, all pumping out the techno and house tunes-of-the-moment alongside salsa, commercials, and the odd bout of government-led pseudo-propaganda. Most Costa Rican households have a **television**, which shows wonderfully awful Mexican/Venezuelan *telenovelas* (soap operas) and some not bad domestic news programmes.

Safety and the police

Costa Rica is generally considered a very safe country, and what crime does exist tends to be **opportunistic crime** rather than violent. The main thing travellers have to worry about is pickpocketing and luggage theft, but if you take a few common-sense precautions you should get by unscathed.

In downtown areas, particularly in San José and Puerto Limón, you need to be wary at all times. Wear a money belt, and never carry anything of value – money, tickets or passport – in an outside pocket. **When travelling** on buses, either keep your bags with you or, if using the overhead compartments, keep an eye out for anyone hovering suspiciously, especially at bus stops – thieves have been known to pass bags out of bus windows to accomplices waiting outside. If possible try to store any bags you don't need for your trip in a hotel or guesthouse, although do make sure they're locked, have your name prominently written on them, and that you have left instructions for them not to be removed by anyone but yourself, under any circumstances. **Car theft** – both of cars and things inside them – also occurs. You should not leave anything of value in a parked car – even locked in the trunk – anywhere in Costa Rica, day or night.

In addition, keep copies of your passport, your air ticket and your travellers' cheques, plus your insurance policy at home; and, if possible, keep extra copies in your hotel. In Costa Rica you have to carry ID on you at all times – for foreigners this means **carrying your passport**. A photocopy of your passport – of the information-bearing pages and the page with your Costa Rican entry stamp – will do (the police understand tourists' reluctance to go about with their passports all the time), but if you are stopped and asked for ID, make sure you can produce the real thing – by going to your hotel, for example – in case the police demand to see it.

Emergency numbers

All emergencies ☎911
Police ☎117
Fire ☎118
Traffic police ☎222-9330 or 222-9245

Reporting a crime

If you have anything stolen you will need to report it immediately to the nearest police post. In San José the most convenient method is to head for the Organismo de Investigación Judicial (☎221-5337 or 221-1365) between Av 6 and 8 and C 15 and 19. In rural areas, go to the nearest **guardia rural** who will give you a report (you'll do better if you speak Spanish, or are with someone who does).

Any **tourist-related crime**, such as overcharging, can be addressed to the ICT in San José (see p.596).

National parks and reserves

Costa Rica protects 27 percent of its total territory under the aegis of a carefully structured system of **national parks**, **wildlife refuges** and **biological reserves** whose role in protecting the country's rich fauna and flora against the expansion of resource-extracting activities and human settlement has been generally lauded. In all, there are some 75 protected areas, which have established gradually over the past thirty years.

In total the parks and reserves protect approximately four percent of the world's total wildlife species and life zones, among them rainforests, cloudforest, *páramo* (high-altitude moorlands), swamps, lagoons, marshes and mangroves, and the last remaining patches of tropical dry forest in the isthmus. Also protected are areas of historical significance, including a handful of pre-Columbian settlements, and places considered to be of immense scenic beauty. Measures have been taken, too, to protect beaches where marine turtles lay their eggs, as well as a number of active volcanoes. An important, controversial and ongoing initiative is the establishment of the Mesoamerican Biological Corridor, a continuous strip of protected land from southern Mexico to northern Colombia, one of the most complex sustainable-development initiatives ever undertaken.

The **national parks**, which cover twelve percent of Costa Rica's protected land, provide more services and activities than the refuges and reserves, and tend to be more heavily touristed. That said, it's important to remember that none of the protected areas have been set up with tourists in mind – biologists, scientists and researchers make up a large portion of visitors. While we give information as to which **animals** inhabit the specific parks, bear in mind that you are in no way guaranteed to see them – although you'll probably see some of the more common or less shy ones, you'll be very lucky indeed to spot the larger mammals, such as the jaguar, ocelot or tapir. You are, however, guaranteed to spot plenty of the nation's incredibly rich and diverse birdlife.

Visiting Costa Rica's parks

All national parks have entrance **puestos**, or stations, where you pay your fee and pick up a map. Typically, the **main ranger stations**, from where the internal administration of the park is carried out, and where the rangers live, are some way from the entrance *puesto*. It can be a good idea to drop by the main station, where you can talk to rangers (if your Spanish is good enough) about local terrain and conditions, enquire about drinking water, and use the bathroom. In some parks, such as Corcovado, you can sleep in or camp near the main stations. Most parks now charge an **entrance fee** of US$6 per day. If you want to camp overnight in any park, you'll sometimes have to pay for all days of your stay.

Outside the most visited parks – Volcán Poás, Volcán Irazú, Santa Rosa and Manuel Antonio – **opening hours** are somewhat theoretical. Many places are open daily, from around 8am to 3.45pm, though there are exceptions – Manuel Antonio is closed on Monday and may be closed on Tuesdays in the future, while other parks may open a little earlier in the morning. Unless you're planning on camping or staying overnight, there's almost no point in arriving at a national park in the afternoon. In all cases, especially at the volcanoes, you should aim to arrive as early in the morning as possible to make the most of the day and, in particular, the weather (especially in the wet season).

The only central office where you can make reservations and get detailed, up-to-date **information** or buy **permits**, where required, is the Fundación de Parques Nacionales (Av 15, C 23/25, San José, ⓣ257-2239, ⓦwww.minae.go.cr/turismo/turismo.htm), who will contact those parks for which you need reservations, chiefly Santa Rosa, Corcovado and Chirripó (see the individual accounts in the *Guide* for more details). Other parks can be visited on spec.

Work and study

There are many **volunteer work and research projects** in Costa Rica, some of which include food and lodging. A good resource in the US for language study and volunteer work programmes is **Transitions Abroad**, a bimonthly magazine focusing on living and working overseas (visit ⓦwww.transitionsabroad.com or write to Dept TRA, PO Box 745, Bennington, VT 05201, USA). In Australasia, details of student exchanges and study programmes are available from the AFS, PO Box 5, Strawberry Hills, Sydney 2012, Australia (ⓣ02/9215 0077, ⓦwww.afs.org.au), or PO Box 5662, Level 3, 125 Featherstone Street, Wellington, New Zealand (ⓣ04/494 6020, ⓦwww.afsnzl.org.nz). UK residents should contact the Costa Rican Embassy (see p.21).

Study programmes and learning Spanish

There are so many **language schools** in San José that choosing one can be a problem: though you can arrange a place through organizations based in the US (see box, opposite), the best way to choose is to visit a few, perhaps sitting in on a class or two, and judge the school according to your own personality and needs. This method is not always possible in high season (Dec–April) when many classes will have been booked in advance, but at other times it should be no problem.

As with most things, you will pay more for a Spanish course in Costa Rica than in other Central American countries. Some of the language schools in Costa Rica are Tico-run; others are arms of international (usually

Costa Rica–based volunteer programmes

ANAI Aptdo 170–2070, Sabanillo ⓣ224-3570, ⓕ253-7524, ⓦwww.anaicr.org. Based in southern Talamanca, ANAI trains people to farm organically and manage forests sustainably. They also run volunteer programmes to help protect the Gandoca-Manzanillo Refuge and the turtles that come to the Caribbean coast each year (May–July), and offer work on ANAI's experimental farm (officially for a minimum of six months, but three-month stays can be arranged). Lodging and food included.

APREFLOFAS Aptdo 917-2150, San José ⓣ240-6087, ⓕ236-3210, ⓦwww.preserve-planet.org. Runs a host of wildlife preservation schemes and reforestation programmes around the country, and helps local communities set up sustainable eco-tourism projects. Minimum three months.

ASVO (Association of Volunteers for Service in Protected Areas), contact the director of International Voluntary Programmes ⓣ and ⓕ223-4989, ⓦwww.asvocr.com. Government-run scheme enabling volunteers to work in the national parks, helping guard protected areas, write reports and give environmental classes. Minimum one month.

DINADECO (Office of National Community Development) ⓣ235-0896, ⓕ253-1745, ⓔl.fallas@gobnet.go.cr. Costa Rican government institution that promotes citizen participation, family development, human-rights awareness and sexual equality. Foreigners are invited by the institution's International Cooperation Programme to get involved with individual development in small towns.

Genesis II Cloud Forest Reserve PO Box 655, 7050, Cartago ⓣ and ⓕ381-0739, ⓦwww.genesis-two.com. Accepts "physically-fit" volunteers for 4-week placements helping with reforestation and wildlife preservation projects in a Talamancan mountain reserve.

Humanitarian Foundation ⓣ837-5205, ⓔgnystrom@racsa.co.cr. Volunteers are placed in various programmes helping orphans, battered women, indigenous people and street children.

Monteverde Institute Aptdo 69–5655, Monteverde ⓣ and ⓕ645-5053, ⓦwww.mvinstitute.org. Volunteer projects in the Monteverde cloudforest including teaching, fieldwork on trails and other conservation efforts. Volunteers must know Spanish and commit for six weeks.

Volunteer programmes in the US & Canada

Caribbean Conservation Corps PO Box 2866, Gainesville, FL 32602 ⓣ1-800/678-7853, in Costa Rica ⓣ225-7516, ⓦwww.cccturtle.org. Volunteer research work on marine turtles at Tortuguero.

COTERC PO Box 335, Pickering, Ontario, L1V 2R6 ⓣ905/831-8809, ⓦwww.coterc.org. Canadian organization which recruits volunteers to work at the Caño Palma Research Station in Tortuguero, an educational resource centre set in a hundred acres of rainforest.

Global Service Corps 300 Broadway, Suite 28, San Francisco, CA 94133-3312 ⓣ415/788-3666, ⓦwww.globalservicecorps.org. Service programmes in Costa Rica.

Volunteers for Peace 43 Tiffany Rd, Belmont, VT 05730 ⓣ802/259-2759, ⓦwww.vfp.org. Volunteer projects in Costa Rica and other Central American countries.

North American) education networks. Whatever the ownership, instructors are almost invariably Costa Ricans who speak some English. In addition, school notice boards are an excellent source of information and contacts for travel opportunities, apartment shares and social activities. Most schools have a number of Costa Rican families on their books with whom they regularly place students for homestays.

History

Archeologists know little about the various people who inhabited Costa Rica until about 1000 BC, though it is known that the area was a corridor for merchants and trading expeditions between the Mesoamerican empires to the north and the Andean empires to the south. Excavations of pottery, jade and trade goods and accounts of cultural traditions have shown that the **pre-Columbian** peoples of Costa Rica adopted liberally from both areas. Although there is little of the monumental architecture associated with other Mesoamerican regions, excavations at Guayabo, east of San José, have revealed a very sizeable city which was continuously inhabited for over two millennia and perhaps had as many as seven or eight thousand inhabitants at various times.

When the **Spaniards** arrived in Costa Rica in the early sixteenth century it was inhabited by as many as 27 different groups or clans. Most clans were assigned names by the invaders, which they took from the *cacique* (chief) with whom they dealt. Many of these groups had affinities with their neighbours in Nicaragua to the north and Panama to the south. One of the most prominent in the archeological record were the Chorotegas, based in the Guanacaste area in the centuries immediately prior to Columbus. They built towns around a central marketplace, had a calendar, were active in trading fabrics, dyes and foodstuffs, and also developed a symbol-based written language. They also produced noteworthy sculpture, particularly in jade.

The arrival of the Spanish

On September 18, 1502, on his fourth and last voyage to the Americas, **Columbus** sighted Costa Rica, and four years later King Fernando of Spain despatched **Diego de Nicuesa** to govern what would become Costa Rica. From the start his mission was beset by hardship, beginning when their ship ran aground on the coast of Panama. Forced as a result to walk up the Caribbean shore, the expedition met native people who, unlike those who had welcomed Columbus tentatively but politely with their shows of gold, instead burned their crops rather than submit to the authority of the Spanish. This, along with the impenetrable jungles – and the creatures who lived in them – and tropical diseases, forced the expedition to turn back.

Next came **Gil González Davila** in 1521–22, who sailed from Panama, where Spanish settlements had already been established, up the Pacific coast, which offered safer anchorages. After being welcomed initially with gifts of gold, the expedition named the land Costa Rica (Rich Coast), but the indigenous peoples soon began a campaign of **resistance** that was to last nearly thirty years, employing guerrilla tactics, full-scale flight, infanticide, attacks on colonist settlements and the burning of their own villages. There were massacres, defeats and submissions on both sides, and although the land was named as part of the area of New Spain in 1540, it remained basically unsettled by the conquistadores at this time. Indeed, the Talamanca region remained an unexplored wilderness for centuries to come.

Early settlers

It seems more appropriate to discuss Costa Rica's *lack* of colonial experience, rather than a bona fide colonization. In 1562, **Juan Vásquez de Coronado** became the second governor of Costa Rica. Coronado has always been portrayed as the good guy, reputed for his favourable, if not benevolent, treatment of the indigenous peoples he encountered in his migration from the Pacific coast to the Valle Central. It was under his administration that the first settlement of any size or importance was established, and **Cartago**, in the heart of the Valle Central, became capital. During the next century settlers confined themselves more or less to the centre of the country; much of the settlement was under the infamous *encomienda* system, which saw soldiers and mercenaries granted parcels of land after their tours of duty. Rights to the land included rights to those already living on it, and the indigenous people in this situation became slaves and serfs, forced to work or surrender annual tithes of produce. The Caribbean coast was the haunt of buccaneers – mainly English – who put ashore and wintered here after plundering the lucrative Spanish Main; the Pacific coast saw its share of pirate activity, too, most famously when Sir Francis Drake put ashore briefly in the modern-day Bahía Drake in 1579.

This first epoch of the colony is remembered as one of **unremitting poverty**. Within a decade of its invasion, Costa Rica was notorious and widely disparaged throughout the Spanish Empire for its lack of gold. The land of the Valle Central was fertile, but there was uncertainty as to which crops to grow. Coffee had not yet been imported to Costa Rica, nor had tobacco, so it was to subsistence agriculture that most settlers turned. Lack of produce for trade with Spain meant a shortage of coinage, and settlers even resorted to adopting the cacao bean as currency at one stage. In 1719 the governor of Costa Rica famously complained that he had to till his own land. To make matters worse, Volcán Irazú erupted in 1723, nearly destroying the capital, which at this stage had only been joined by one other town of note: Cubujuquí, now Heredia. It has been argued, however, that the fact that settlers only barely eked out a living is what has made Costa Rica different to other Central American nations today: the comparative egalitarianism of modern Tico society can perhaps be partially ascribed to the fact that there was no development of a small landholding elite or "hacienda aristocracy".

Independence

The **nineteenth century** was the most significant era in the development of the modern nation state of Costa Rica. Initially, after Central America declared **independence** from Spain in 1821, freedom made little difference to Costa Ricans. Although status as a republic was granted in the summer of 1823, the news did not reach Costa Rica until well into the autumn, when a mule messenger arrived from Nicaragua to tell the astonished citizens of Cartago the news. A **civil war** promptly broke out among the inhabitants of the Valle Central, dividing the citizens of Alajuela and San José (which had been founded in 1737 as Villanueva de la Boca del Monte) from those of Heredia and Cartago. This struggle for power was won by the Alajuela–San José faction, and **San José** became the capital city in 1823.

Costa Rica made remarkable progress in the latter half of the nineteenth century, building roads, bridges and railways and filling San José with neo-Baroque, Europeanate edifices. Virtually all this activity was fuelled by **the coffee trade**, bringing wealth that the settlers just a century earlier could hardly have dreamed of. Beans were first imported from either Cuba or Jamaica in the early years of the century, and the crop flourished in the highland climate. The first Costa Rican coffee was blended with lower-grade Chilean beans, but when British merchant William Le Lacheur took a boatload of the stuff back to Liverpool, it went down a treat. Demand for Costa Rican coffee soared and lucrative trade with Britain ensued; today high-grade export coffee is still popularly known as *grano d'oro* (the golden bean). The nascent coffee bourgeoisie played a vital role in the cultural and political development of the country, and in 1848 the newly influential *cafetaleros* elected to the presidency their chosen candidate, Juan Rafael Mora. Extremely conservative and pro-trade, Mora came to distinguish himself in the battle against the American-backed filibusterer William Walker in 1856 (see p.488). His popularity didn't last, however, as he was harshly blamed for a devastating cholera epidemic that swept the country. The bourgeoisie resented his attempts to create a national bank, fearing for their coffee-fat wallets; he was removed from power and executed by his successor in 1860 after an unsuccessful attempt to regain control. A period of civil strife and military dictatorships followed, until the first somewhat democratic elections in 1889.

The twentieth century

The first years of the **twentieth century** witnessed a difficult transition towards real democracy in Costa Rica. Universal male suffrage had been in effect since the last years of the nineteenth century, but class and power conflicts still dogged the country, with several *caudillo* (authoritarian) leaders, familiar figures in other Latin American countries, hijacking power. But in general these figures ended up in exile, and neither the army nor the Church gained much of a foothold in politics.

With the election in 1940 of the Republican (PRN) candidate **Rafael Calderón Guardia**, a doctor educated in part in Belgium and a devout Catholic, came the social reforms and state support for which Costa Rica is still almost unique in the region. In 1941 Calderón established a new **labour code**, which reinstated the right of workers to organize and strike, and a social security system providing free schooling for all. Calderón also paved the way for the establishment of the University of Costa Rica, health insurance, income security and assistance schemes, and thus won the support of the impoverished and the lower classes and the suspicion of the governing Úlites. One of those less than convinced by Calderón's policies was the man who would come to be known as "Don Pepe", the coffee farmer **José María Figueres Ferrer**, who denounced Calderón and his expensive leftist reforms. Figueres soon formed an opposition party, ideologically opposed to the PRN, calling them "communists". After Calderón refused to accept an election defeat to his opponent Otilio Ulate, fighting around Cartago began on March 10, 1948, leading to the outbreak of the six-week **War of National Liberation**, in which each side was supported by other regional governments. Calderón rapidly capitulated once San José came under fire. Figueres, who took command of the ruling junta, wanted above all to engineer a complete break with the country's past and especially the policies and legacies of the Calderónistas. Seeing himself as fighting both communism and corruption, he not only outlawed the Popular Vanguard Party – formerly known as the Communist Party – but also nationalized the banks and devised a tax to hit the rich particularly hard, thus alienating the establishment. A **new constitution** in 1949 gave full citizenship to Afro-Caribbeans, full suffrage to women and abolished Costa Rica's army in an attempt to save resources and limit political uncertainty in the country. Don Pepe then handed power back to Ulate as promised; he was later elected president twice, in the 1950s and 1970s, having founded the PLN (Partido de Liberación Nacional), which remains the country's main leftist party.

The **1960s and 1970s** were a period of prosperity and stability in Costa Rica, during which the welfare state was developed to reach nearly all sectors of society. In 1977 the **indigenous bill** established the right of native peoples to their own land reserves – a progressive measure at the time, although indigenous peoples today are not convinced the system has served them well.

Storm in the isthmus: the 1980s

Against all odds, Costa Rica in the 1980s and 1990s not only saw its way through the serious political conflicts of its neighbours, but also successfully managed predatory US interventionism, **economic crisis** and staggering debt.

Like many Latin American countries, Costa Rica had taken out bank and government loans in the 1960s and 1970s to finance vital development. But in the early 1980s, the slump of prices for coffee and bananas put the country's current account in the red to the tune of millions. In September 1981, Costa Rica defaulted on its interest payment on these loans, becoming the first Third World country to do so, and sparking off a chain of similar defaults in Latin America that resonated throughout the 1980s and threw the international banking community into crisis. Despite its defaults, Costa Rica's debt continued to accumulate, and by 1989 had reached a staggering US$5 billion, one of the highest per capita debt loads in the world.

To compound the economic crisis came the simultaneous political escalation of the **Nicaraguan Civil War**. During the entire decade, Costa Rica's foreign policy and to an extent its domestic agenda would be overshadowed by tensions with Nicaragua on the one hand and with the US on the other. Initially, the Monge PLN administration (1982–86) more or less capitulated to US demands that Costa Rica be used as a supply line for the Contras, a right-wing insurgent group funded by the US, and Costa Rica also accepted military training for its police force from the US. Simultaneously, the country's first agreement for a structural adjustment loan with the International Monetary Fund (IMF) was signed. It seemed increasingly clear that Costa Rica was on the path both to violating its declared neutrality in the conflicts of its neighbours and to condemning its population to wage freezes, price increases and other side effects associated with IMF intervention.

In 1986, PLN candidate **Oscar Arias Sánchez** was elected to the presidency, and Costa Rica's relations with the US – and, by association, with Nicaragua – took a different tack. The former political scientist began to play the role of peace broker in the conflicts of Nicaragua, El Salvador and, to a lesser extent, Honduras and Guatemala, mediating between these countries and also between domestic factions within them. In October 1987, just eighteen months after taking office, Arias was awarded the **Nobel Peace Prize**, bringing worldwide attention to his tiny country.

Though Arias had gained the admiration of political leaders around the world, he proved to be less than popular at home. Many Costa Ricans saw him as diverting valuable resources and time to foreign affairs when he should have been paying attention to the domestic agenda, at a time when increasing prices caused by the IMF's economic demands meant that conditions in Costa Rica were not much improved.

The 1990s

In 1990, Rafael Calderón Fournier, son of Calderón Guardia, was elected to the presidency exactly fifty years after his father. He led the Partido Unidad Social Cristiana (PUSC), a rightist alliance and strong believers in a free-market economy. Ironically, one of his early acts was to declare a day of mourning for the funeral of Dad's nemesis, Don Pepe, who died a national hero that year. Problems compounded through Calderón's term in office: a devastating earthquake in 1991 caused much loss of life and structural damage in Limón Province, and the continuing influx of refugees from the less stable countries in the region placed great strains on the nation's economy and led to regrettable racial tensions.

Until 1994, elections in Costa Rica had been relatively genteel affairs, involving lots of flag-waving and displays of national pride in democratic traditions. The elections of that year, however, were probably the dirtiest to date. The campaign opened and closed with an unprecedented bout of mudslinging and attempts to smear the reputations of both candidates, tactics which shocked many Costa Ricans. The PLN candidate – the choice of the left, for his promises to maintain the role of the state in the economy – was none other than **José María Figueres**, the son of Don Pepe. During the campaign Figueres was accused of shady investment rackets and influence peddling. His free-market PUSC opposition candidate, Miguel Angel Rodríguez, fared no better, having admitted to being involved in a tainted-beef scandal in the 1980s. Figueres won, narrowly, though his term in office was plagued by a series of scandals. On a more positive note, in January 1995, a free-trade agreement was signed with Mexico to try to redress the lack of preference given to Costa Rican goods in the US market by the signing of NAFTA. Costa Rica's economy received a further shot in the arm in 1996 when computer hardware giant Intel chose the country for the site of its new factory in Latin America, creating thousands of jobs.

In February 1998, PUSC candidate **Dr Miguel Angel Rodríguez** was elected president, thus reinforcing the trend in Costa Rican politics for the past half-century, wherein power has been traded more or less evenly between the PLN and the PUSC. The new government committed itself to solving Costa Rica's most pressing problems, making improvements to the country's dreadful road system top priority, but financing this and other major public works by private investment. Increasingly, courting private money and catering to foreign interests became the order of the day. Rodríguez was succeeded in April 2002 by Abel Pacheco de Espriella, a psychiatrist also from the PUSC: the first time that party had been re-elected. One of the key issues Pacheco has faced is CAFTA, the Central American Free Trade Agreement that has alarmed anti-globalization movements worldwide and awoken widespread fear in Costa Rica of the definitive erosion of the advanced social system that has been in place in the country for the last half-century. Pacheco, the son of a banana farmer, was initially wary of the agreement, but finally added Costa Rica's name. At the time of writing, the agreement was under consideration by the US Senate. If passed, it would certainly mean the end of Costa Rica's nationalized insurance system, and two of the country's key export industries, bananas and coffee, would face heavy competition from the lower wages of other Central American countries. Plantation labour in Costa Rica costs as much as six times that of Honduras or Nicaragua.

The future

Costa Rica's economic future rides on a wave created in the past, a constant see-sawing between the price of the country's bananas and coffee on world markets and the amount it pays for imports. Still, the economy continues to grow, in large part fuelled by **tourism**, and the government is beginning to claw back the massive public-sector deficit through increased taxation, both on basic services like electricity and water, and on restaurant meals and hotel bills.

In recent years the government has managed to reduce the inflation rate, which is currently around nine percent, and **population growth** has slowed: necessarily so, for Costa Rica has the highest rural population density in Latin America, and there is tremendous pressure on land. This has led to an increase in social problems, particularly in San José; the country's legal and judicial institutions are doing their best to combat the most pressing of them, such as drug trafficking, domestic violence, child prostitution, and increasing crime and disorder.

The prognosis for the campesino, that now nearly forgotten former backbone of the country, is not good, as peasant agriculture becomes increasingly anachronistic in the face of the big banana, coffee, palmito and pineapple plantations. Furthermore, the burden of the welfare state in Costa Rica has become increasingly difficult for the state to carry. High external debts to service the country's respected system of social welfare mean that a staggering thirty percent of the government budget goes to interest payments to foreign banks. However, the nation's high literacy and life expectancy rates pay tribute to the relative success of the system over the last few decades and provide a strong platform for progress in the new century.

Despite the country's impressive system of national parks, the prognosis for **the environment** is blackened by the authorities' continuing strategy of attracting large hotel and development groups. Although tourism is a vital part of the nation's economy, other countries have found to their cost that summer visitors are notoriously fickle, and today's fashionable gated resort hotel can easily become tomorrow's five-storey white elephant. Treading the fine line between preserving Costa Rica's social system and creating a more stable economic foundation, and developing the tourist sector in a sustainable and sensible way seem to be the key challenges facing the nation in the early years of the third millennium.

6.1

San José

Sprawling smack in the middle of the fertile Valle Central, **SAN JOSÉ** has a spectacular setting, ringed by the jagged silhouettes of soaring mountains – some of them volcanoes – on all sides. That's where the compliments end, however, and you'll be hard pressed to find anyone, even a native *Josefino*, who has much good to say about the city's potholed streets and car-dealership architecture – not to mention the choking diesel fumes, kamikaze drivers and chaotically unplanned expansion. In the gridlocked centre things are wearingly hectic, with vendors of fruit, lottery tickets and cigarettes jostling on street corners, and thousands of shoe stores tumbling out onto the sidewalks.

In general, travellers talk about the city as they do about bank line-ups and immigration offices: a pain, but unavoidable. That said, if you've been travelling through the region, you'll find that compared to, say, San Salvador or Managua, San José is not only a reassuringly **safe** place (though street crime is rising) but also vibrant and cosmopolitan, with a sprinkling of excellent **museums**, some elegant buildings and landscaped parks, good cafés and the odd intriguing art gallery. Which is all to the good: most people find themselves spending some time here – the city is a major transportation hub, and many journeys across the country involve backtracking through the capital – learning to enjoy it, and even becoming perversely fond of the place.

Arrival

Arriving in San José is relatively stress-free: all the machinery to get you into town is well oiled, and there is less opportunistic theft than at other Central American arrival points. San José's compact, frenzied city centre is contained within about fifteen blocks running east–west, and four blocks north–south. To the west, the main approach is the four-lane **Paseo Colón**, lined with car rental agencies, upscale hotels and office buildings. The centre of town is bisected by the partly pedestrianized **Avenida Central**, a very pleasant place to stroll, while most commercial activity is concentrated in the streets between Avenida Central and Avenida 7. The nondescript **Plaza de la Cultura** is considered to be the centre of town.

Near the post office, in the streets immediately west of Calle 2, is the frantic and sometimes insalubrious **Mercado Central** area, four blocks west of which is the **Coca-Cola bus station**. The centre is subdivided into little neighbourhoods (barrios) that flow seamlessly in and out of one another: barrios **Amón** and **Otoya**, in the north, are the prettiest, lined with the genteel mansions of former coffee barons, while those further out toward San Pedro, **La California**, **Escalante** and **Los Yoses** are home to comfortable houses, the odd embassy and the *Toruma* youth hostel.

Further east, Avenida Central widens, heading out to the studenty suburb of San Pedro, home of the cool, leafy campus of the **University of Costa Rica** (UCR), one of the finest in Central America. The three or four square blocks surrounding the university are lined with some of the liveliest bars and restaurants in San José, though in most of them you'll feel more comfortable if you're under thirty.

Many of San José's residents live in the **suburbs** surrounding the city – many shopping malls and embassies are located in the eastern suburb of **Curridabat** and nearby **Escazú**, a mountain town to the north and west of San José.

By air

Most international flights arrive at the modern new terminal at **Juan Santamaría International Airport** (☎443-2622), 17km northwest of San José and 3km southeast of Alajuela (see p.589). The **ICT office** here (Mon–Fri 9am–5pm; ☎443-1535 or 443-2883) can supply maps and give advice on accommodation. There's also a **correo** (Mon–Fri 8am–5pm), an **ATM** machine (handily situated next to the departure-tax desk), and a **bank** (Mon–Fri 6.30am–6pm, Sat & Sun 7am–1pm), downstairs on the departure level; colones are not necessary for taxis, but you'll need them for the bus. If planning on flying out from San José following your trip, remember to save enough money to pay the departure tax (US$26). Visa credit cards (but not MasterCard) are accepted.

The best way to get into San José from the airport is by **taxi**, which takes about twenty to thirty minutes in light traffic and costs US$12–14 up until 9pm and then around US$20 after that. Official airport taxis are orange and line up outside the terminal. You'll have no problems getting a cab, as the drivers will stampede for your business when you're practically still in customs. Taxi drivers accept dollars as well as colones.

Alternatively, the Alajuela–San José **bus** (every 5min between 4.30am & 10pm; every 15min at other times) stops right outside the airport's undercover car park. Though it's much cheaper than a taxi, there are no proper luggage racks inside and the buses are nearly always full – you can just about get away with it if you're carrying only a light backpack or small bag. Drivers will indicate which buses are on their way to San José (a 30min journey) and which to Alajuela. The fare is 220 colones (US$0.50); pay the driver. The bus drops passengers in town at Av 2, C 12/14, where there are plenty of taxis around.

By bus

Most **international buses** from Nicaragua, Honduras, Guatemala and Panama pull into the Ticabus station, Av 4, C 9/11 (☎221-8954), next to the yellow Soledad church. Since buses can arrive at odd hours, you may want to take refuge at one of the 24-hour eating spots nearby on Av 2 before looking for a room. One of the cheapest is the *Casa del Sandwich* on the corner of C 9, and there's a taxi rank around the corner on Av 2 between C 5 and 9. Coming from Manugua on Transica, you'll arrive at the terminal at C 22, Av 3/5; taxis can be flagged down on Av 3.

The closest thing San José has to a **domestic bus station** is **La Coca-Cola** (named after an old bottling plant that used to stand on the site), five blocks west of the Mercado Central at Av 1/3, C 16/18 (the main entrance is on C 16). The name La Coca-Cola not only applies to the bus station proper – which is quite small and the arrival point for only a few buses, principally those from Jacó and Quepos – but also to the surrounding area, where many more buses pull in. Lugging your bags and searching for your bus stop around here makes it very hard not to look

Safety in San José

Although San José is a relatively safe city, there are dangers: mainly **mugging**, purse-snatching or jewellery-snatching. It's worth keeping a tight grip on your belongings around the Coca-Cola bus terminal – roughly from C 12 to 16 and between Av 1 and 3 – as well as around the Parque Central, Av 2, the Plaza de la Cultura and the Mercado Central. Other dodgy areas, day and night, include C 12 around Av 8 and 10, and Av 4 to 6 and C 4 to 12, just southwest of the centre. If **driving** in the centre of the city, keep windows rolled up so no one can reach in and snatch your bag.

Also, watch out when **crossing the street**, anywhere in the city: drivers can be aggressive and accidents involving pedestrians are common.

like a confused gringo, thus increasing the chances that you'll become the target of opportunistic theft: best to arrive and leave in a taxi. Be especially careful of your belongings around the **Tilarán and Monteverde bus stop** (C 12, Av 7/9): people waiting here for the 6.30am bus to Monteverde seem to be particularly at risk of attempted theft.

Information

San José's **ICT office** (Mon–Fri 9am–5pm; ⓣ223-1733 or 223-1090, ⓦwww.visitcostarica.com), underneath the Plaza de la Cultura at C 5, Av 0/2, has free maps, leaflets and hotel brochures, and booklets detailing the (ever-changing) national bus schedule. They also hand out the free monthly culture guide, which details concerts and festivals throughout the country.

In addition, the Sistema Nacional de Areas de Conservación (National System of Conservation Areas), or **SINAC**, runs a free phone line giving information in

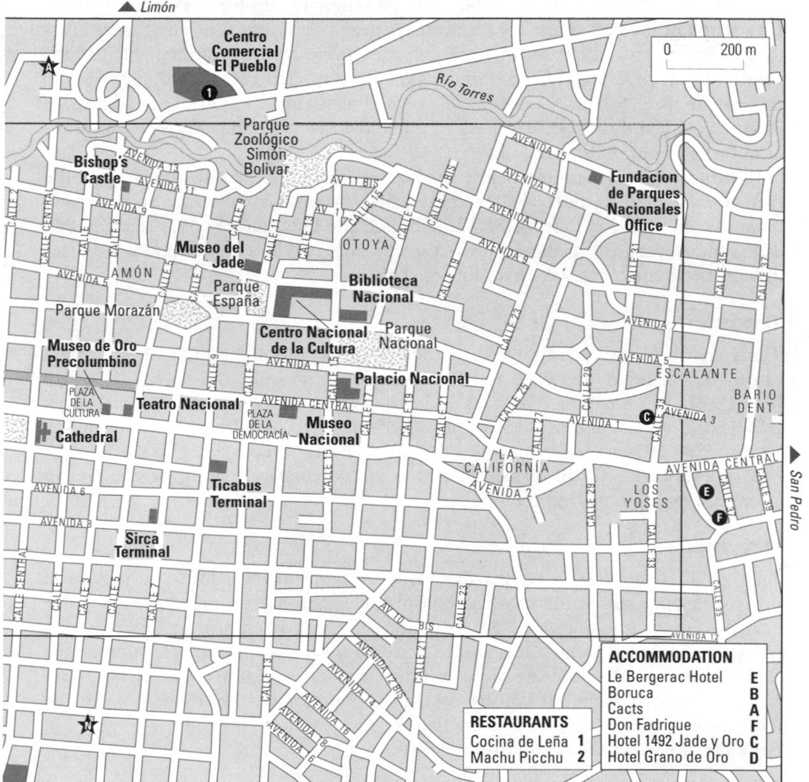

English and Spanish about Costa Rica's **national parks**: call ☎192 (Mon–Fri 8am–5.30pm). They can provide information on individual parks, particularly about transport and camping facilities. Basic information about opening hours, entrance tariffs and an explanation of the national parks system can be found at Ⓦwww.minae.go.cr. In San José you can get information, buy entrance tickets and make reservations for park shelters at the **Fundación de Parques Nacionales** office, Av 15, C 23/25, Barrio Escalante (☎257-2239, Ⓔazucena @ns.minae.go.cr).

City transport

Central San José is easily negotiated on foot, though buses are useful in the suburbs. The mountain town of **Escazú** is about twenty minutes' ride to the west, and the university suburb of **San Pedro** about ten minutes to the east. After 10pm the buses stop running and **taxis** become the best way to get around.

Buses

Fast, cheap and frequent buses connect the centre of the city with virtually all of San José's neighbourhoods and suburbs; they generally run from 5am until 10pm. **Bus stops** in the city centre area seem to change every year. Currently, most buses to San Pedro, Tres Ríos and other points east leave from the stretch of Avenida Central between C 9 and C 15. You can pick up buses for Paseo Colón and Parque Sabana (labelled "Sabana-Cementerio") at the bus shelters on Av 2, C 5/7. At some point, the city authorities are hoping to move the bus stops out of the centre proper in order to cut traffic and pollution.

All buses have their routes clearly marked on their windshields, and usually the **fare**, too. The fare is payable either to the driver or conductor when you board and is usually about 100 colones (US$0.25), though the faster, more comfortable *busetas de lujo* (luxury buses) to the suburbs cost upwards of 150 colones (US$0.40). Bus drivers or conductors always have lots of change.

Taxis

Taxis are cheap and plentiful, even at odd hours of the night and early morning. Licensed vehicles are red with a yellow triangle on the side, and have "SJP" ("San José Publico") licence plates. A ride anywhere within the city will cost US$1.50–2.50, and about double that to get out to the suburbs. The starter fare – about US$0.50 – is shown on the red digital display; make sure the meter is on before you start (ask the driver to *toca la maría, por favor*) or agree the fare in advance. Tipping is not expected.

Driving

Though it's a bad idea to **rent a car** for getting around San José, you may need one for driving out of the city. Cars should never be left on the street anywhere near the city centre, since they are guaranteed to be broken into or stolen. Secure **parqueos** (guarded parking lots) dot the city; some are 24-hour (there's one on the corner of A 0, C 19), but most close at 8 or 8.30pm. Some hotels, but by no means all, offer on-site parking. If you have to leave your car on the street, look for the local security guard (they carry truncheons); and pay him 300 colones to guard it. For a list of **car rental companies**, see p.609.

Accommodation

After a period of rapid growth – and high prices – in the hotel business during the 1990s tourism boom, San José is at last getting more quality hotel rooms, with fairer prices in all categories. Even the budget-to-moderate sector, previously the weakest category, has improved markedly with several new guesthouses and family-run hotels opening up, although rock-bottom hotels still tend, with a few exceptions, to be depressing cells that make the city seem infinitely more ugly than it is. The other recent major accommodation event in San José has been the arrival of international **hotel chains**, many of whose names (and generic facilities) – *Radisson*, *Holiday Inn* and *Best Western* – will be familiar to North Americans and Europeans.

If you're coming in **high season** (Dec–May), and especially over busy periods like Christmas and Easter, be prepared to reserve (and, in some cases, even pay) in advance – places that require payment in advance may give you a bank account number in Costa Rica for you to wire money to. Room **rates** vary dramatically between high and low seasons – the prices we quote are for a double room in peak season; expect to get substantial discounts at less busy times.

Though staying in one of the budget hotels in the **city centre** is convenient, the downside is noise and pollution – Avenida 2 and parts of avenidas 1, 3 and 5 can be noisy, but this is not a hard-and-fast rule, as the city authorities seem to like changing

CENTRAL SAN JOSÉ

RESTAURANTS & CAFÉS

Balcón de Europa	4
Café Bohemia	9
Café Digital	5
Café Mundo	1
Castro	11
Manolo's	7
Meridiano al Este	6
News Café	8
Tin-Jo	10
La Vasconia	3
Vishnu	2

ACCOMMODATION

Casa León	G
Casa Ridgway	I
Costa Rica Backpackers	H
Fleur de Lys	F
Hostal Toruma	E
Hotel Aranjuez	A
Hotel Rincon de San José	C
Kap's Place	B
Ritz	J
Santo Tomás	D

★ BUS STOPS

Nicaragua, Panama	A
Turrialba	B

Río Torres
Parque Zoológico Simón Bolívar
Fundacíon de Parques Nacionales Office
Alianza Francesa
Museo del Jade
OTOYA
AMÓN
Parque España
Parque Morazán
Biblioteca Nacional
Correo/Museo Postal
Mercado Central
Centro Nacional de la Cultura
Parque Nacional
Santa Teresita
Museo Ferrocaríl
Mas X Menos
Palacio Nacional
Teatro Mélico Salazar
PLAZA DE LA CULTURA
Museo de Oro Precolumbino
Cathedral
Parque Central
Teatro Nacional
PLAZA DE LA DEMOCRACÍA
Museo Nacional
ESCALANTE
BARIO DENT
Ticabus Terminal
Abandoned Railway Line
LA CALIFORNÍA
LOS YOSES
Sirca Terminal
Supreme Court
San Pedro
N
0 200 m
AVENIDA 15
AVENIDA 13
AVENIDA 11
AV 11 BIS
AV 11
AVENIDA 9
AVENIDA 7
AVENIDA 5
AVENIDA 3
AVENIDA 1
AVENIDA CENTRAL
AVENIDA 2
AVENIDA 4
AVENIDA 6
AVENIDA 8
AVENIDA 10
AVENIDA 12
CALLE 6
CALLE 4
CALLE 2
CALLE CENTRAL
CALLE 1
CALLE 3
CALLE 5
CALLE 7
CALLE 9
CALLE 11
CALLE 13
CALLE 15
CALLE 17
CALLE 17 BIS
CALLE 19
CALLE 21
CALLE 23
CALLE 25
CALLE 27
CALLE 29
CALLE 31
CALLE 33
CALLE 35
CALLE 37
CALLE 39

bus routes (the source of most street noise) every few years. The very cheapest rooms are in the insalubrious area immediately around La Coca-Cola, and while there are a couple of clean and well-run budget places here, the area is generally best avoided unless you've got an early bus to catch or are an aficionado of seedy hotels.

Not too far from downtown, in quieter areas such as **Paseo Colón**, **Los Yoses** and **barrios Amón** and **Otoya**, are a group of more expensive hotels, many in old colonial homes. There are also a number of decent hotels **in the suburbs**, particularly in Escazú to the west and, to a lesser extent, San Pedro in the east, both of which are just a ten- to fifteen-minute bus ride from downtown. Again, these tend to be a good deal quieter than the hotels in the centre of town.

Central San José

Boruca C 14, Av 1/3 ⓣ223-0016, ⓕ232-0107. Central, basic and rather charmless hotel in the Coca-Cola district with small, musty and dark rooms – it's very cheap and clean, though, and has a secure atmosphere and friendly family management. ❷

Cacts C 28–30, Av 3 bis ⓣ221-2928, ⓕ221-8616, ⓦwww.tourism.co.cr/hotels/cacts/cacts.htm. Recently expanded, *Cacts* now has 25 rooms, all with ceiling fans and TV and all but four with private bath. Its sunny roof terrace, tropical garden, swimming pool and hot tub add to its charm, and the friendly owners also run a travel agency and can help with tours and reservations. ❹

Casa León Av 6 bis, C 13/15 ⓣ222-9725. A good alternative if the *Costa Rica Backpackers* (see below) is full, this small guesthouse has dorms (US$10 per person in a mixed-sex dorm) and basic private rooms (US$15) with shared bath and kitchen – all spotlessly clean and good value. It also offers a laundry service and luggage storage. The house can be hard to find; look for it next to the train tracks and tell your taxi driver it's a *calle sin salida*.

Casa Ridgway C 15, Av 6 bis between Av 6/8 ⓣ & ⓕ233-6168 or 222-1400, ⓔfiends@racsa.co.cr. Near the Ticabus stop, this homely Quaker guesthouse is a good budget choice with several clean, single-sex dorms (US$10 per person), plus a few private singles (US$12) and doubles (US$24) with communal bathrooms. There's also a shared kitchen, laundry and luggage storage – note that alcohol is banned and there's a "quiet time" after 10pm. Reserve ahead in high season, and try not to arrive after 8pm except by prior arrangement.

Costa Rica Backpackers Av 6, C 21/23 ⓣ221-6191, ⓕ223-2406, ⓦwww.costaricabackpackers.com. A great place to meet fellow travellers, this is probably the city's best budget guesthouse, offering a mixture of single and mixed-sex dorms (US$9 per person) plus a few private double rooms (US$20). Facilities include a fully equipped kitchen, a garden with swimming pool, luggage storage, laundry service, a TV room, free Internet access and free parking.

Don Fadrique C 37, Av 8, Los Yoses ⓣ224-7583, ⓕ224-9746, ⓔfadrique@centralamerica.com. Upmarket but good-value hotel with restaurant, bar and tropical gardens, located in the former villa of Don Fadrique Gutierrez, early twentieth-century architect, general and philosopher. The hotel's halls are hung with Costa Rican art, and each of the twenty nicely furnished rooms comes with TV and private bath with hot water. Good low-season discounts. Breakfast included. ❼

Fleur de Lys C 13, Av 2/6 ⓣ223-1206, ⓕ257-3637, ⓦwww.hotelfleurdelys.com. Friendly hotel in an old San José house: each floor has a sunny, plant-filled atrium and each of its 31 prettily decorated rooms has TV and private bath. There's also a nice restaurant/bar. Convenient downtown location near Ticabus and Av 2, but still quiet, and good discounts in low seasoon. ❼–❽

Hostal Toruma Av 0, C 29/31 ⓣ & ⓕ224 4085, ⓦwww.toruma.com. Costa Rica's main HI hostel (see p.581), this beautiful establishment with Neoclassical exterior and high ceilings is a good place both to meet people and to make onward hostel, tour and travel reservations. Accommodation is in single-sex dorms (US$8 per person for HI members, US$10 for non-members – membership is available at the front desk) and a few singles (HI members $16, non-members $20), and there's also luggage storage, a safe, laundry, free Internet access and free parking. Book well in advance in high season. Non-smoking.

Hotel 1492 Jade y Oro Av 1, C 31/33 ⓣ256-5913 or 225 3752, ⓕ280 6206, ⓦwww.jade.co.cr. On a quiet stretch of Av 1, the *1492* has ten comfortably furnished rooms, some surrounding an elegant antique- and art-filled atrium, the others adjoining a small tropical garden. All have private shower and TV. The friendly staff can help with arranging tours. ❼

Hotel Aranjuez C 19, Av 11/13 ⓣ256-1825, from the US & Canada call toll-free 1-877/898-8663, ⓕ223-3528, ⓦwww.hotelaranjuez.com. Superb-value hotel in Barrio Aranjuez, a quiet area, but close to the centre. Rooms are arranged in converted houses that have been joined with communal sitting areas throughout, and there's a pretty garden around the back. The 23 rooms either have shared bath (❹) or private bath (❺) and TV, and a good buffet breakfast and free local phone calls and email are included. It's often full, so reserve ahead. Its small tourist office arranges tours to the *Laguna Lodge* in Tortuguero.

Hotel Grano de Oro C 30, Av 2/4 ⓣ255-3322, ⓕ221-2782, ⓦwww.hotelgranodeoro.com. Elegant converted mansion in a quiet area west of the centre, with 32 comfortable rooms and suites furnished in faux-Victorian style with wrought-iron beds and polished wooden floors – they're popular with honeymooners and older Americans. Several of the deluxe rooms have lovely private gardens, and there's also a new rooftop sun terrace with twin hot tubs. All rooms have cable TV, minibar, phone and fax, and an excellent breakfast is served in the highly recommended restaurant. ❽–❾

Hotel Rincon de San José Av 9, C 13/15 ⓣ221-9702, ⓕ222-1241, ⓦwww.hotelrincondesanjose.com. Formerly the *Edelweiss*, this recently revamped Dutch-owned hotel is situated in pretty Barrio Amón, with 27 clean rooms (all with cable TV), wooden floors and piping hot showers, plus the use of a computer and safe. The excellent *Café Mundo* restaurant is just across the street. Breakfast included. ❼

Kap's Place C 19, Av 11/13 ⓣ221-1169, ⓕ256-4850, ⓦwww.kapsplace.com. One of the very best budget choices around. Run by the unstintingly helpful Karla Arias (a bottomless source of information on all things San José), the hotel has fourteen comfortable, colourfully decorated en-suite rooms, two with a shared bathroom, a fully equipped communal kitchen plus a large two-floor apartment (with its own kitchen). It's got a great family-friendly atmosphere. Tours arranged on request. ❺

Le Bergerac Hotel C 35, Av 0 ⓣ234-7850, ⓕ225-9103, ⓦwww.bergerac.co.cr. For luxury without the price tag, this elegant and relaxing top-end hotel is a good bet. The eighteen spacious rooms all have cable TV, and some also have their own private gardens. A superb French restaurant, *L'Ile de France*, is prettily set next to an interior courtyard and there's a travel service which can help arrange tours. Continental breakfast included. ❺–❻

Ritz C 0, Av 8/10 ⓣ233-1731, ⓕ222-8849. Very clean and fairly large (25 rooms, a mixture of private and shared bathrooms) central hotel with its own tour service – it's popular with European travellers, and is a good place to meet other backpackers. Management is friendly and the communal areas are pleasant, though rooms are rather dark. Rooms with private baths are US$20, those without US$15. ❹

Santo Tomás Av 7, C 3/5 ⓣ255-0448, ⓕ222-3950, ⓦwww.hotelsantotomas.com. One of San José's best boutique hotels, located in quiet and elegant Barrio Amón, conveniently close to downtown. The hotel occupies an old mansion house decorated with burnished wood, Persian rugs and soft lighting. Rooms vary widely in size, character and price, though all have bath, TV and telephone. There's also a small swimming pool and hot tub, an excellent open-air restaurant, a travel service and free Internet access. ❼

San Pedro

La Granja off Av 0 in Barrio La Granja, San Pedro, 50m south of the *antiguo higuerón* – the site of a now disappeared tree which still serves as a local landmark ⓣ & ⓕ225-1073. Good-value eight-room guesthouse in a converted family house with a pretty garden, near the university, bars and restaurants. Most rooms have shared showers. Also has some cheap singles (US$15), a TV lounge, communal kitchen and laundry service. ❷–❸

Maripaz 350m southeast of the *antiguo higuerón* ⓣ & ⓕ253-8456, ⓔmaripaz@racsa.co.cr. Small (five rooms) B&B in the home of a welcoming Costa Rican family, located in a quiet and pleasant area close to the university and several language schools. Rooms come either with private (US$40) or shared bath (US$30).

Escazú

Casa de las Tias San Rafael de Escazú ⓣ289-5517, ⓕ289-7353, ⓦwww.hotels.co.cr/casatias.html. Set on a garden estate, this is a small, quiet, friendly and atmospheric place with just five individually decorated rooms complete with private bath and hot water. No under-12s allowed. ❼

Posada del Bosque Belo Horizonte de Escazú ⓣ221-7319, ⓕ257-3525. Very quiet, homely place, in large landscaped grounds, with comfortable no-smoking rooms with shared bath. The friendly owners can arrange tennis, swimming and horse-riding in the area. ❻

Posada El Quijote Bello Horizonte de Escazú ⓣ289-8401, ⓕ289-8729, ⓦwww.quijote.co.cr. Eight spacious rooms, all renovated in the style of a Spanish colonial manor and comfortably furnished with bath, hot water and cable TV. Breakfast is served in the lovely garden. ❻–❼

The City

Few travellers come to San José for the sights. A city of nondescript buildings, energized by an aggressive street life – umbrella-wielding pedestrians pushing through narrow streets, noisy food stalls, homicidal drivers – San José is certainly not a place that exudes immediate appeal. It has its diversions, however, with plenty of places to walk, sit, eat, meet people, go dancing and enjoy museums and galleries. It's also a manageable city: all the attractions are close together, and everything of interest can be covered in a couple of days. Of the museums, the exemplary **Museo de Oro Precolombino** and **Museo del Jade** are the major draws. The less-visited **Museo Nacional** offers some interesting archeological finds, while the **Museo de Arte y Deseño Contemporáneo** displays some of the most striking work in Central America. San José is also a surprisingly green and open city, with small, carefully landscaped parks and plazas punctuating the centre of town.

Around the Plaza de la Cultura

The **Plaza de la Cultura** cleverly conceals one of San José's treasures, the Banco Central–sponsored **Museo de Oro Precolombino**, or Pre-Columbian Gold Museum (Tues–Sat 10am–4pm; US$5; ⓦwww.museosdelbancocentral.org). The bunker-like underground space, though a touch gloomy, has been thoroughly revamped in recent years, and the gold on display is truly impressive – all the more extraordinary if you take into account the relative paucity of pre-Columbian artefacts in Costa Rica. The exquisitely delicate work on show is almost entirely the work of the Diquis, the ancient inhabitants of southwestern Costa Rica. Most of the pieces are small and unbelievably detailed, with a preponderance of disturbing-looking animals. Information panels (in English and Spanish) suggest that one of the chief functions of these portents of evil – frogs, snakes and insects – was to protect the bearer against illness, the Diquis believing that sickness was transmitted to people by spirits in animal form. In particular, the *ave de rapiña*, or bird of prey, seems to have been responsible for a multitude of ills: there are tons of them here – hawks, owls and eagles, differing only incrementally in shape and size. Look out, too, for angry-looking arachnids; jaguars and alligators carrying the pathetic dangling legs of human victims in their mouths; grinning bats with wings spread; as well as turtles, crabs, frogs, iguanas, armadillos, and a few spiny, unmistakeable lobsters.

San José's heavily columned, grey-brown **Teatro Nacional** sits on the corner of C 5 and Av 2, tucked in behind the Plaza de la Cultura. The theatre's marbled stairways, gilt cherubs and red velvet carpets would look more at home in Old Europe than in Central America, and remain in remarkably good condition, despite the dual onslaught of the climate and a succession of earthquakes. Even if you're not coming to see a performance, you can wander around the post-Baroque splendour, although you'll be charged US$3 for the privilege – another reason to come here for a show. The elegant attached café serves good coffee and European-style cakes.

Around the Parque España

On the north side of the **Parque España**, three blocks northeast of the Plaza de la Cultura, rises one of the few office towers in San José: the INS, or Institute of Social Security, building. This uninspired edifice is home to one of the city's finest museums, the **Marco Fidel Tristan Museo del Jade** (Mon–Fri 8.30am–3pm; US$2; ⓣ287-6034), home to the world's largest collection of American jade, much of it ingeniously displayed with subtle backlighting to show off the multicoloured and multitextured pieces to full effect. You'll see a lot of **axe-gods** – anthropomorphic bird/human forms shaped like an axe and worn as a pendant – as well as various ornate (and rather heavy-looking) necklaces and fertility symbols. The rich green colour of most (although by no means all) jade meant that it was particularly associated with agricultural fertility. Incidentally, the **view** from the museum windows is one of the best in the city, taking in the sweep of San José from the centre to the south and then west to the mountains.

Sprawling across the entire eastern border of the Parque España, the former National Liquor Factory, dating from 1887, today houses the Centro Nacional de Cultura, home to the cutting-edge **Museo de Arte y Diseño Contemporáneo** (Tues–Sun 10am–5pm; US$2). The museum's cosmopolitan, multimedia approach features works by artists from across Latin America, alongside the work of Costa Ricans, and it's definitely worth a visit to see what's going on in the arts in the Americas. There's also a theatre in the complex – a wander around during the day may offer interesting glimpses of dancers and musicians rehearsing.

Heading two blocks south from the Centro Nacional de Cultura brings you to the concrete **Plaza de la Democracía**, yet another of the city's soulless squares. Constructed in 1989 to mark President Oscar Arias's key involvement in the Central American Peace Plan, this expanse of terraced concrete slopes gently up towards a fountain and the impressive, fortress-like edifice of the **Museo Nacional** (Tues–Sat 8.30am–4.30pm, Sun 9am–4.30pm; US$2; ⓣ257-1433, ⓦwww.museocostarica.com), home to the country's most important archeological exhibitions. Highlights include petroglyphs, pre-Columbian stonework – the grinding tables and funerary offerings, in particular, show precise geometric patterns – and, in the Sala Arqueológica, wonderful anthropomorphic gold figures.

Centro Costarricense de la Ciencia y la Cultura

Near the Centro Comerical El Pueblo, a cluster of purpose-built shops, restaurants and bars at the north end of Calle 4, is the **Centro Costarricense de la Ciencia y la Cultura** (Tues–Fri 8am–4pm, Sat & Sun 10am–4pm; US$5). Located in a former prison, this complex devotes most of its space to the mildly interesting **Museo de los Niños** (Childrens' Museum), where Costa Rican kids can come to see interactive displays and learn about their country's history, culture and science. The complex also houses the **Museo Historico Penitenciario** (Penitentiary History Museum), which consists of a number of the original prison cells restored to their nineteenth-century condition, and some rather anodyne accounts of the country's penal history.

Around the Mercado Central

Northwest of the Parque Central and the commercial centre between Av 0/1 and C 6/8 is San José's **Mercado Central** (Mon–Sat 5am–5pm). Entering its labyrinthine interior you're confronted by colourful arrangements of fruits and vegetables, dangling sides of beef and elaborate, silvery ranks of fish. Shopping for fruit, vegetables and coffee here, as well as the Mercado Borbón one block north, is less expensive than in a supermarket, and it's also the best place in town to get a cheap bite – not only that, but the view from a counter stool is fascinating, as traders and their customers jostle for *chayotes*, *mamones*, *piñas* and *cas*.

The surrounding streets, which even in the daytime can look quite seedy, are full of noisy traders and determined shoppers. All this activity encourages **pickpockets**, and in this environment *turistas* stick out like sore thumbs. Take only what you need and be on your guard.

Two blocks east and one block north of the Mercado Central, in the Correo Central, C 2, Av 1/3, the **Museo Postal, Telegráfico y Filatelico** (Mon–Fri 8am–4pm; free) exhibits old relics of telegraphic equipment – of interest to buffs only.

Paseo Colón and Parque la Sabana

Clustered around the main entrance to La Coca-Cola, off C 16, shops selling women's underwear, cosmetics and luggage compete for space with a variety of cheap snack bars and drinks stalls. Two blocks south, however, the atmosphere changes, as Av Central turns into **Paseo Colón**, a wide boulevard of upmarket shops, restaurants and car dealerships. At the very end of the *paseo*, the solid expanse of green today known as **Parque la Sabana** was until the 1940s San José's airport, and is now home to the country's key art museum.

The bright white neocolonial edifice of the old air terminal in **Parque la Sabana** has been converted into the attractive **Museo de Arte Costarricense** (Tues–Sun 10am–4pm; US$5, Sun 10am–2pm free; ☎222-7734), with a good collection of mainly twentieth-century Costa Rican paintings. The **Salon Dorado** upstairs is remarkable: four full walls of bas-relief wooden carvings overlaid with sumptuous gold, portraying somewhat idealized scenes of Costa Rica's history since pre-Columbian times.

On the southwest corner of Parque la Sabana, across the road in the Ministry of Agriculture and Livestock complex, is the quirky natural science museum, the **Museo de Ciencias Naturales La Salle** (Mon–Fri 8am–3pm; US$1; ☎232-1306). Walk right in, and after about 400m you'll see the painted wall announcing the museum; the entrance is at the back. Displays range from pickled fish and snakes coiled in formaldehyde to some rather forlorn taxidermy exhibits – age and humidity have taken their toll.

Sabana Park itself makes a very pleasant spot for an afternoon stroll, with numerous shady trees surrounding its central lake and various colourful pieces of modern art dotted around. On Sunday afternoons it attracts hordes of local families who come to feed the resident geese and eat ice creams sold by the park's multitude of stalls. It's also probably the best place in San José to **jog**. Its cement track is usually full of serious runners in training, but you can run fairly safely all around the park in the day, although there have been reports of attacks on lone joggers at night. There's a small, dank changing hut, shower and lavatory beside the track, and you can leave your bag securely with the *señora* who takes the money (10am–4pm only).

San Pedro

First impressions of the student district of **San Pedro**, a couple of kilometres east of the city centre, can be off-putting, with Avenida Central (also known here as Paseo de los Estudiantes) lined by gas stations, broken-up sidewalks and dull malls as it passes through the area. Walk just a block away from the *paseo*, however, and you'll find a lively combination of university-student ghettos and elegant old residential houses, home to some of the city's best bars, restaurants and nightlife, catering to students, professors, residents and professionals.

Buses to San Pedro from the middle of town stop opposite the small **Parque Central**, centred on a monument to John F. Kennedy. Walking north from the square, through three blocks of solid *sodas*, bars, restaurants and abandoned railway tracks, you come to the cool, leafy campus of the **University of Costa Rica (UCR)**, founded in 1940 and now one of the finest universities in Central America, with a busy, egalitarian and stimulating atmosphere.

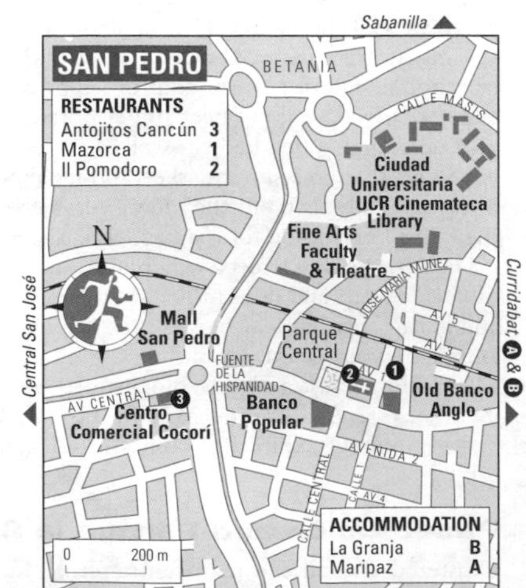

Eating

For a Central American city of its size, San José has a surprising variety of **restaurants**. Many of the best places are in the relatively high-income and cosmopolitan neighbourhoods around **San Pedro**, the **Paseo Colón**, and **Escazú**, but wherever you choose, eating out in San José can set your budget back on its haunches. The 23 percent tax on restaurant food (which includes a ten percent "service charge") can deliver a real death-blow, so it's cheapest to eat in the centre, at the *sodas* and snack bars, where the tax doesn't apply. A sit-down lunch of the *plato del día* at a **soda** will rarely set you back more than US$5, or for a quick sugar fix you could feast on *churros* dispensed over the counter. Healthier choices include *empanadas* and sandwiches to take out – combine this with a stop at one of the fruit stalls on any street corner and you've got a quick, cheap lunch. **Cafés** also abound: some, like *Giacomín*, have old-world European aspirations; others, like *Spoon*, are resolutely Costa Rican, with *Josefinos* piling in to order birthday cakes or grab a **coffee**. Of the major **ice-cream** chains, *Pops* is the best, with particularly good fruit flavours.

Working *Josefinos* eat their main meal between noon and 2pm, when *sodas* especially can get very busy. Many restaurants close at 3pm and open again for the evening. In the listings below we have given a phone number only for places where you might need to **reserve** a table.

Cafés and bakeries

Café Bohemia Teatro Salazar Popular, Av 2, C 0. Upmarket café adorned with historic photos of San José and filled with theatre-goers discussing the city's latest cultural offerings.

Café Parisienne *Gran Hotel Costa Rica*, Av 2, C 3/5. The closest thing in San José to a European street café, complete with wrought-iron chairs and trussed-up waiters, this is a wonderful place to sit and have coffee and cake on a sunny day watching the buskers and street-performers on the Plaza de la Cultura. It's also one of the few establishments in the city that does continental breakfast.

News Café Av 0, C 7/9. It's not cheap but it does make a good midtown pit stop and its balcony provides plenty of people-watching opportunities. Inside, the walls are adorned with pictures telling the story of the coffee-growing industry in Costa Rica.

Ruiseñor 150m east of the Automercado in Los Yoses. Upmarket – and expensive – restaurant with a pleasant outdoor terrace and old-fashioned, European-style service and atmosphere.

Zucchero C 33, Av 5/7. French-style treats – pastries, cakes and very good coffee – served up just north of Los Yoses in the quiet, residential Barrio Escalante.

Sodas

Castro Av 10, C 2/4. The 1970s fluorescent vinyl decor and the rough neighbourhood belie the treats inside. Definitely not a tourist haunt, this huge *soda* is where local families take their kids for a Sunday ice-cream treat (it's also got a play area) and to sample the excellent fruit salads.

Manolo's Av 0, C 3. On the main tourist drag, this is a popular late-night hangout. It's not cheap, but it is safe after hours and serves filling snacks from killer pastries to sandwiches. The slightly less expensive downstairs café is a great people-watching spot.

La Vasconia Av 1, C 3/5. Enormous menu featuring cheap breakfasts and lunch specials, including fairly cheap *ceviche* and *empanadas*. The place to go to get off the tourist trail and mingle with stressed office workers while looking at the thousands of photos of the national football team (some dating back to 1905) that adorn the walls.

Vishnu three branches at Av 1, C 1/3; Av 3 C1; Av 8, C 9/11. These cheery vegetarian *sodas* are an obligatory pit stop for anybody visiting San José, serving delicious *platos del día* with brown rice, vegetables and soups at very reasonable prices. The vegetarian club sandwich with chips will set you back a mere US$3, fruit plates with yoghurt around US$1.50.

Restaurants

Antojitos Cancún in the Centro Comercial Cocorí, 50m west of the Fuente de la Hispanidad roundabout, Los Yoses. Cheap, filling Mexican food, not wholly authentic, but good for late-night snacks and cheap all-you-can-eat buffets. There's also draught beer and an outside terrace where you can sit and watch the 4WDs whizz round the fountain, plus live mariachi on Fri and Sat from 10pm. Daily 11am–midnight.

Balcón de Europa C 9, Av 0/1 ☎221-4841. City landmark: the food, largely pasta and Italian staples, is nothing special, but the atmosphere is great. Sepia photos of the early days line the wood-panelled walls, along with annoying snippets of "wisdom". Monster cheeses dominate the dining room, as does the game strummer who serenades each table. Closed Sat.

Café Mundo Av 9, C 15, Barrio Otoya. Not quite what it was when it could justly have laid claim to the title of best restaurant in San José. It seems to be resting on its laurels slightly as shown by the sometimes less than stellar service. Still, the Italian-influenced food continues to delight, served amidst beautiful decor and a relaxed European atmosphere. The Caesar (US$5) and Niçoise (US$10) salads are large but a bit overpriced – if you're on a budget, go for the pizza, or just come for a cappuccino (US$2). At night the bar attracts a largely gay clientele. Closed Sat & Sun.

Cocina de Leña Centro Comercial El Pueblo ⓣ255-1360. Although some see this as an example of Tico food at its best – superbly prepared and served in faux rustic surroundings – others see it as a glorified *soda* selling overpriced staples to gullible tourists. The truth lies somewhere in between. It's certainly handy if you feeling like making a night of it in amongst the bars and discos of El Pueblo. Dinner for two costs around US$40.

Grano d'Oro Casa 251, C 3, Av 2/4 ⓣ253-3322. Upmarket restaurant with beautiful hacienda-style decor and a changing menu. Breakfast (from 6am) includes fresh fruit, eggs Benedict and banana macadamia pancakes. The salads are excellent – try the spinach, avocado and gorgonzola – while the main courses feature Costa Rican takes on international staples, such as filet mignon stuffed with tropical fruits. Amazing desserts, including *tiramisu* and piña colada cheesecake. Book ahead and bring plenty of funds.

Il Pomodoro San Pedro, 150m east of the entrance to UCR. One of the best pizza places in the city, with large pizzas – including a great vegetarian special – and cheap draught beer served in mugs and pitchers in a large and cheerful restaurant popular with the university crowd. Around US$20 for two.

Machu Picchu C 32, Av 1 ⓣ222-7384. A consistent San José favourite, and the only truly South American place in town (the velvet llamas on the walls help) – though the appetizers, including *ceviche* and Peruvian *bocas*, tend to be more interesting than the main dishes. Count on around US$30 for two with beer or wine. Closed Sun.

Mazorca 200m east and 100m north of San Pedro church. Macrobiotic restaurant just east of the entrance to UCR with homely, simple decor and menu (lunch is around US$5; takeaways are also available). The tasty bread, soups, peanut-butter sandwiches and macrobiotic cakes make a welcome change from greasy *arroz con pollo*. Closed Sun.

Meridiano al Este Av 0, C 21 ⓣ256-2705. Opposite the La California gas station (but don't let that put you off), this spot serves up good-quality international cuisine – pastas, steaks, pizzas and tapas – at reasonable prices and puts on nightly entertainment featuring everything from live music by local bands to poetry recitals and even comedy performances. It attracts a young, hip crowd.

Tin-Jo C 11, Av 6/8 ⓣ221-7605. Quiet, popular and fairly formal Asian restaurant offering a choice of Chinese, Indian, Indonesian, Thai, Burmese and (just to be sure) Japanese food. The lemongrass soup, bean-thread salad in lime juice and coconut milk curries are particularly good. Dinner with wine is roughly US$40 for two; skip the alcohol, or go for lunch, and you'll get away with half that.

Drinking and nightlife

San José's nightlife is gratifyingly varied, with scores of friendly **bars** and **live music** venues. Be aware, though, that prostitution is legal in Costa Rica and, in San José, very mainstream. Sex tourism is on the rise, and you'll find that many of the "bars" in downtown are, in reality, little more than pick-up joints for professional transactions. The cluster of casinos and bars on the Avenida Central between calles 5 and 11 that surround the notorious *Hotel Del Ray* fall mainly into this category: they are best avoided unless you want to spend every few minutes explaining why you're not interested in doing a little "business". Any time of day or night (most are open 24 hours), you'll find them full of scantily clad young ladies trying to attract the attention of the hordes of glassy-eyed gringos and Europeans that prop up the bars.

Most young *Josefinos*, students and foreigners in the know stay away from the centre of town and head, instead, to Los Yoses or San Pedro to drink. In **Los Yoses**, Av Central features a well-known "yuppie trail" of bars, starting roughly at the terribly fashionable *Cielo* and finishing at *Río*, a hugely popular American-style bar with an outdoor terrace. **San Pedro** is obviously geared toward the university population, with several very studenty bars. Many bars change character markedly come Friday or Saturday, when they host jazz, blues, upcoming local bands, rock and roll, or South American folk music. Ticos aren't known for burning the candle at both ends – with the exception of the university bars in San Pedro, most places close by 2 or 3am, earlier on Sunday.

It's worth experiencing one of the city's **discos**: even if you don't dance, you can watch the Ticos tear up the floor. *Terra U* is the place of the moment, while for traditional **salsa**, merengue, cumbia and soca try *La Plaza*, *Cocoloco* or *Las Risas*. **Cover charges** run to about US$4, though the big mainstream discos at El Pueblo charge slightly more than places downtown.

You need to be 18 to drink in Costa Rica. Even if you're well over age, if you look even remotely young, bring a photocopy of your passport as **ID**.

Bars and live music

Bar Jazz Café in San Pedro, next to the Banco Popular ⓣ253-8933. The best place in San José to hear jazz, with an intimate atmosphere and consistently good groups. The cover charge varies from US$5 to US$10, sometimes including a glass of wine, but is usually worth it. The music starts after 10pm.

Bar Río Boulevard Los Yoses. Extremely popular Los Yoses sports bar with a large terrace overlooking the main road. Inside, there are about eight TV screens (usually showing a mixture of eight different local and international football matches) and, at the back, a large dance area. Live music is staged on Tuesdays and some weekends. It serves a basic fast-food-style menu.

Caccio's 200m east and 25m north of San Pedro church. Insanely popular student hangout with guys wearing baseball caps and singing along to outdated songs – it's a great place to meet people, and the pizza and cheap cold beer are another bonus. Closed Sun.

Chelles Av 0, C 9. *Chelles* is a simple, brightly lit bar with football on the television, cheap beers and *bocas*, and 24-hour service, drawing an eclectic crowd of weary businessmen and late-night revellers.

Cielo Av 1, C 21. Across the street from *El Cuartel*, *Cielo* seems to have taken over from its great rival as the most popular bar with local *Josefinos*. From around 8pm every evening its two floors are packed with the city's youth (plus a smattering of tourists) discussing the day's events and, as the evening progresses, dancing their cares away.

El Cuartel de la Boca del Monte Av 1, C 21/23. Not quite as popular as it used to be, this well-established bar still packs them in on Mondays and, particularly, Wednesdays (when there's live music). At other times, it can feel a little dead. It also serves good food – lunch, dinner and *bocas*.

La Esmeralda Av 2, C 5/7. Landmark institution, being the headquarters of the union of mariachi bands, who whoosh by your table in a colourful swirl of sombreros and sequins before dashing off in a taxi to serenade or celebrate elsewhere in the city. Closed Sun.

Meridiano al Este Av 0, C 21 ⓣ256-2705. Not only is this one of the city's best new restaurants, it's also one of the best places to hear live music (as well as poetry recitals and comedy performances). The programme is constantly changing but Sunday is usually music night when you can hear the pick of the city's latest up-and-coming jazz and Latin performers.

Milano si Accende Av 11, C 3 bis. Self-consciously European-style bar serving Italian food and, on Mondays, playing European dance, electronica and chill-out music. Very comfortable sofas.

Las Risas C 1, Av 0/1. One of the best downtown bars, on three floors. The disco at the top is good, with a small dancefloor and lively young crowd. Bring ID – a copy of your passport will suffice — or the bouncers won't let you in. The cover charge of US$3 will usually get you two drinks or a tequila. Saturday is ladies' night.

Shakespeare Av 2, C 28. Quiet, friendly place that's popular with people popping in for a drink before seeing a performance at the adjacent Sala Garbo cinema or Laurence Olivier theatre. Also has occasional live jazz.

La Villa 150m north of the old Banco Anglo, San Pedro. Located in an atmospheric old house, frequented by students and "intellectuals" and plastered with political and theatrical posters, this is San José's best bar for beer and conversation, with Mercedes Sosa on the CD player, occasional live *peñas* and tasty *bocas*. Closed Sun.

Discos

Cocoloco El Pueblo. Smart, well-dressed clientele, small dancefloors, and the usual Latin techno-pop/reggae/merengue mix.

Déjà Vu C 2, Av 14/16. A mixed crowd – gay,

lesbian and straight – come for the hot and happening atmosphere, mostly house and techno with a few salsa tunes interspersed. There are two large dancefloors plus a quiet bar and a café. The neighbourhood is pretty scary though – take a taxi. Cover charge varies from US$3 to US$5, but drinks are cheap. Closed Sun & Mon.

Ebony 56 El Pueblo. Similar to *Cocoloco*, with several large dancefloors playing salsa and US and European dance music with the odd 1980s/90s pop hit thrown in. Currently the most popular of El Pueblo's glut of discos. Closed Sun.

Planet Mall Mall San Pedro. Apparently Central America's largest disco, it certainly has the same slightly soulless atmosphere common to many US and European mega-clubs. Still, it's wildly popular (if a little pricey at US$10) with the city's youth, playing a mixture of European dance and Latin rhythms.

La Plaza across from El Pueblo. Archetypical Latin American disco. Designed like a giant bull ring, the huge round dancefloor is packed with couples dancing to merengue and superb waiters who twirl in their truncated tuxedos when business is slack. There's also a bar with a big TV screen flashing out a steady diet of music and sport.

Terra U One block east of San Pedro church. San Pedro's most popular disco, making it one of the city's best venues for a weekend night out, with three open-air levels and a heaving dancefloor. Latin and Jamaican Dance Hall hits predominate, plus there's a TV screen showing music videos (when it's not showing highlights of football matches).

The arts and entertainment

Bearing in mind the decreasing financial support it receives from the national government, the quality of the arts in San José is very high. *Josefinos* especially like **theatre**, and there's a healthy range of venues for a city this size, staging a variety of inventive productions at affordable prices. If you speak even a little Spanish it's worth checking to see what's on.

Costa Rica's **National Dance Company** has an impressive repertoire of classical and modern productions, some by Central American choreographers, arranged specifically for the company – again, ticket costs are low. The city's premier venues are the Teatro Nacional, Av 2, C 3/5, and the Teatro Mélico Salazar, Av 2, C 0, where you can see performances by the **National Symphony Orchestra** and **National Lyric Opera Company** (June–Aug), as well as visiting orchestras and singers – usually from Spain or other Spanish-speaking countries. The Teatro Mélico Salazar also occasionally stages performances of traditional Costa Rican singing and dancing.

Going to the **cinema** in San José is a bargain, at around US$3–5 a ticket, though many venues have decamped to the suburbs – particularly to shopping malls, such as the Cinemark in Escazú's Multiplaza mall, which you can only reach by car or taxi. There are still a few good downtown cinemas left, however, several of which retain some original features, along with plush, comfortable seats. Most cinemas show the latest American movies, which are almost always subtitled. The few that are dubbed will have the phrase "hablado en Español" in the newspaper listings or on the posters. For Spanish-language art movies, head to Sala Garbo at A2, C 28.

For **details of all performances**, check the *Cartelera* section of the *Tiempo Libre* supplement in *La Nación* on Thursday and the listings in the *Tico Times*, which also distinguish between English- and Spanish-language films and productions.

Shopping and markets

San José's **souvenir and crafts shops** are well stocked and in general fairly pricey; it's best to buy from larger ones, run by government-regulated crafts co-operatives, from which more of the money filters down to the artisans. Items for sale include an abundance of pre-Columbian gold jewellery copies, Costa Rican liqueurs (Café Rica is best known), T-shirts with jungle and animal scenes, weirdly realistic wooden snakes, leather rockers and painted miniature ox-carts from the village of Sarchí (see p.621), walking sticks, simple leather bracelets, hammocks, and a vast array of wood carvings.

At the bottom of the Plaza de la Democracia, Av 0/2 and C 11/13, a long line of canvas-covered **artisans' stalls** sell hammocks, chunky Ecuadorean sweaters, leather bracelets and jewellery, mostly of the leather-and-bead type. You'll also find some Guatemalan textiles and decorative textile *molas* made by the Kuna peoples of Panama (see p.797), though all at steeper prices than elsewhere in the isthmus. Traders are low-pressure and friendly, and gentle bargaining is allowed.

La Casona C 0, Av 0/1. Large two-floor marketplace with stalls selling the usual local stuff along with Guatemalan knapsacks and bedspreads. Jewellery and Panamanian *molas* are the highlights, though quality at some stalls is pretty poor. Great for browsing, though.
Mercado Nacional de Artesanía C 22, Av 2 bis. One of the largest stocks of souvenirs and crafts in the country, featuring all the usuals: hats, T-shirts, Sarchí ox-carts, jewellery and woodwork, including snakes and walking sticks.
Plaza Esmerelda Uruca Pavas. Craft co-operative run by local artisans where you can watch cigars being rolled, necklaces being set and the ubiquitous Sarchí ox-carts being painted. Closed Sun.
Tienda de la Naturaleza Curridabat, 1km past San Pedro on Av 0. The shop of the private Fundación Neotropica, this is a good place to buy the posters, T-shirts and other paraphernalia painted by English artist Deirdre Hyde that you see all over the country. She specializes in the landscapes of tropical America and the animals who live there – her jaguars are particularly good.

Listings

Airline offices Alitalia, C 38, Av 3 ⓣ295-6870; American, Paseo Colón, C 26/28 ⓣ257-1266; Continental, C 19, Av 2 ⓣ296-4911; Copa, C 1, Av 5 ⓣ222-6640; Delta, at the airport ⓣ257-8946; Iberia, C 40, Paseo Colón ⓣ257-8266; Lacsa, C 1, Av 5 ⓣ222-9383; LanChile, Sabana Oeste ⓣ290-5222; Lufthansa, C 5, Av 7/9 ⓣ243-1818; Mexicana, C 1, Av 2/4 ⓣ295-6969; SAM, Av 5, C 1/3 ⓣ233-3066; Sansa, Av 5, C 1/3 ⓣ221-9414; TACA, C 1, Av 1/3 ⓣ296-9353; United Airlines, Sabana Sur ⓣ220-4844; Varig, Av 5, C 1/3 ⓣ290-5222.
Banks State-owned banks in San José include the Banco de Costa Rica, Av 2, C 4/6 (Mon–Fri 9am–3pm; Visa only) and Banco Nacional, Av 0/1, C 2/4 (Mon–Fri 9am–3pm; Visa only). Private banks include Banco Mercantil, Av 3, C 0/2 (Mon–Fri 9am–3pm; Visa only); Banco Metropolitano, C 0, Av 2 (Mon–Fri 8.15am–4pm; Visa only); BANEX, C 0, Av 1 (Mon–Fri 8am–5pm; Visa only); Banco Popular, C 1 Av 2/4 (Mon–Fri 8.30am–3.30pm, Sat 9am–1pm; Visa & MasterCard); and Banco de San José, C 0, Av 3/5 (Visa & MasterCard). There's an American Express office at C1, Av 0/1 (Mon–Fri 8.30am–5pm).
Bookstores Mora Books, Av 1, C 3/5, in the Omni building (ⓣ255-4136), has a good selection of secondhand English-language books, CDs, guide books, magazines and comics. Chispas, C 7, Av 0/1 (ⓣ223-2240), sells new and secondhand books, and has the best selection of English-language fiction in town. It also sells a good array of guide books and books about Costa Rica (in English and Spanish), plus the *New York Times*, *El País* and several English-language magazines. Lehmann, Av 0, C 1/3 (ⓣ223-1212), has a good selection of mass-market Spanish-language fiction and nonfiction, as well as lots of maps, children's books and a small (mainly secondhand) collection of English-language books. The Librería Internacional, with branches 300m west of *Taco Bell* in Barrio Dent (ⓣ253-9553) and in the Multiplaza Escazú (ⓣ298-1138), is the classiest of the lot, and has the best selection of international fiction; they also stock travel books and Spanish-language fiction, as well as books in English and German. Macondo, opposite the entrance to the library at the university campus in San Pedro, is probably the best bookshop in town for literature in Spanish, especially from Central America, as well as academic disciplines such as sociology and women's studies. Librería Universal, Av 0, C Central/1 (ⓣ222-2222), is strong on Spanish books, fiction, titles on Costa Rica (in Spanish), and maps of the country. Librería y Bazar Guillen at La Coca-Cola bus terminal is a good place to browse for reading material before leaving on a long trip – if you're away from the capital, you can order books from here by phone and the friendly owners will dispatch them to you by bus. 7th Street Books, C 7, Av 0/1 (ⓣ256-8251), has both new and used books; it's good on English literature and also has a wide selection of books and maps on Costa Rica in English and Spanish.
Car rental ADA, Av 18, C 11/13 ⓣ233-7733, ⓣ441-1260; Adobe, C 7, Av 8/10 ⓣ258-4242; Avis, at the airport ⓣ293-2222; Budget, Paseo Colón, C 30 ⓣ223-3284; Elegante, C 10, Av

13/15, Barrio México ⓣ257-0026; Europcar, Av 0, C 36/38 ⓣ257-1158, ⓦwww.europcar.co.cr; Hertz, at the airport ⓣ221-1818; Hola, in front of the *Best Western Irazú* on the airport highway ⓣ231-5666, ⓦwww.hola.net; National, at the airport ⓣ440-0085; Thrifty, C 3, Av 13 ⓣ258-5868; Tricolor, at the airport ⓣ440-3333.

Embassies and consulates Belize, 400m east of the Iglesia Santa Teresita, Rohrmoser ⓣ253-5598; Canada, C 3, Av 1 ⓣ296-4149; Colombia, 175m west of *Taco Bell*, in Barrio Dent ⓣ283-6861; El Salvador, Av 10, C 33/35, Los Yoses ⓣ256-4047; Guatemala, 100m north and 50m east of *Pizza Hut* in Curridabat ⓣ283-2557; Honduras, 300m east and 200m north of ITAN, in Los Yoses ⓣ234-9502; Mexico, Av 7, C 13/15 ⓣ280-5690; Nicaragua, Av 0, C 25/27 ⓣ222-2373 or 233-8747; Panama, C 38, Av 5/7 ⓣ281-2442; UK, 11th floor, Edificio Centro Colón, Paseo Colón, C 38/40 ⓣ258-2025; US, opposite the Centro Comercial in Pavas – take the bus to Pavas from Av 1, C 18 ⓣ220-3939.

Film processing San José is the only place in the country where you should try to get film processed. That said, it's expensive and the quality is low: best wait until you get home if you can. Bearing in mind these caveats, try Universal, Av 0, C 0/1, which only processes Fuji; IFSA, Av 2, C 3/5, which only processes Kodak; or Dima, Av 0, C 3/5, which processes both Kodak and Fuji.

Hospitals The city's public (social security) hospital is San Juan de Díos, Paseo Colón, C 14/16 (ⓣ257-6282). Of the private hospitals, foreigners are most often referred to Clínica Biblica, Av 14, C 0/1 (ⓣ257-5252; emergency and after-hours number ⓣ257-0466), where basic consultation and treatment (such as a prescription for a course of antibiotics) starts at about US$100. San José has many excellent medical specialists – your embassy will have a list – and private health care isn't expensive.

Immigration The Costa Rican *migración* (Mon–Fri 8am–4pm; ⓣ220-0355) is on the airport highway opposite the Hospital México; take an Alajuela bus and get off at the stop underneath the overhead walkway. Get there early if you want visa extensions or exit visas. Larger travel agencies listed on p.612 can take care of the paperwork for you for a fee (roughly US$10–US$25).

Internet access Most of the hotels and guesthouses in San José now offer Internet access, often for free but, should you find space at a premium, there are also plenty of Internet cafés in town. Expect to pay around 300 colones per half-hour (sometimes less). Many cafés also serve a range of drinks and snacks. Try *Café Digital*, Av 0, C 5/7, which also has a snack bar, a cigar shop and a balcony overlooking the Avenida Central; *Neotopia Cyber Café*, Av 1, C11; or *Internet Café Costa Rica*, Av 0, C 0/2.

Laundry Burbujas, 50m west and 25m south of the Mas x Menos supermarket in San Pedro, has coin-operated machines and sells soap; Lava y Seca, 100m north of Mas x Menos, next to Autos San Pedro, in San Pedro, will do your laundry for you, as well as dry-cleaning. Other places include Lava Más, C 45, Av 8/10, next to *Spoon* in Los Yoses; Lavamatic Doña Anna, C 13, Av 16; and Sixaola (one of a chain), Av 2, C 7/9. Many hotels and guesthouses also offer laundry service.

Libraries and cultural centres The Alianza Francesa, C 5, Av 7 (Mon–Fri 9am–noon & 3–7pm; ⓣ222-2283), stocks some French publications; the Quaker-affiliated Friends' Peace Center, C 15, Av 6 bis (Mon–Fri 10am–3pm; ⓣ221-8299), has English-language newspapers, plus weekly meetings and discussion groups. Other libraries/cultural centres include the Biblioteca Nacional, C 15, Av 3 (Mon–Sat 9am–5pm), and the Centro Cultural Costarricense-Norteamericano, 100m north of the Am-Pm supermarket in Barrio Dent (Mon–Fri 7am–7pm, Sat 9am–noon; ⓣ207-7500, ⓦwww.cccncr.com).

Pharmacies Clínica Biblica, Av 14, C 0/1 (open 24hr; ⓣ257-5252); Farmacia del Este, 100m south of San Pedro church (open until 8pm); Farmacia Fischel, Av 3, C 2; there are also many pharmacies in the blocks surrounding the Hospital Calderón Guardia, 100m northeast of the Biblioteca Nacional, in Barrio Otoya.

Post office The Correo Central (Mon–Fri 7am–5pm, Sat 7am–noon), C 2, Av 1/3, is two blocks east and one block north of the Mercado Central. They'll hold letters for up to four weeks (10 colones per letter; you'll need a passport in order to collect your post).

Sports The sports complex behind the Museo de Arte Costarricense on Parque la Sabana has a gym, an Olympic-size pool and a recently refurbished running track. The park itself has tennis courts and is as good a place as any for jogging, with changing facilities and showers – there are lots of runners about in the morning, though there have been reports of assaults on lone joggers in the evening and it's wise to stay away from the heavily wooded northeastern corner of the park. Parque de la Paz in the south of the city is also recommended for running and has a velodrome and a roller hockey rink; in San Pedro you can jog, swim and play basketball at the UCR campus. The Club Deportivo Cipresses (ⓣ253-0530), set in landscaped grounds 700m north of

La Galera in Curridabat, offers day membership for US$7, which gives access to weights, machines, pools and aerobics classes. The nearest public pool to San José is at Ojo de Agua, 17km northwest of town; you can get a bus there from Av 2, C 20/22 (15min).

Supermarkets The cheapest is Mas x Menos (open daily until 9pm), which stocks mainly Costa Rican brands of just about everything. There are several branches in San José, including one on Av 0 between C 9 and 11, and one on Av 0, 300m north of the church in San Pedro. Branches of the Automercado and the Am-Pm supermarket are springing up all over the place. A more upmarket option is the Muñoz y Nanne complex (open daily until 9pm), on Av Central in San Pedro, where you can buy US brands at high prices.

Telephone offices Radiográfica, C 1, Av 5 (daily 7.30am–9pm; ⓣ287-0087), is the state-run office where you can use directories, make overseas calls, and send or receive faxes – unfortunately, it charges a flat fee of US$3 for the use of its phones on top of the price of the call.

Moving on from San José

San José is the **transport hub** of Costa Rica, and home to most bus companies, all express bus services, flights and car rental agencies. Wherever you are in the country, technically you are never more than nine hours by road from the capital, with the majority of destinations being much closer than that. Eventually, like it or not, all roads lead to San José.

The tables on pp.612–615 deal with **express bus services** from San José. Regional bus information is covered in the relevant accounts in the *Guide*. As schedules are prone to change, exact departure times are not given here, though details are given where helpful in the accounts of the individual destinations; a full timetable is available free from the ICT office (see p.596).

Bus companies in San José

A bewildering number of **bus companies** use San José as their hub: the following is a rundown of their head office addresses and/or phone numbers, and the abbreviations that are used in the tables.

ATC	Autotransportes San José–San Carlos ⓣ255-4318 or 256-8914
BL	Autotransportes Blanco–Lobo, C 12, Av 9 ⓣ771-4744
BM	Buses Metropoli ⓣ530-1064
EA	Empresa Alfaro, C 14, Av 3/5 ⓣ222-2666
EG	Empresarios Guápileños ⓣ710-7780
EM	Empresa Esquivel ⓣ666-1249
EU	Empresarios Unidos ⓣ222-0064
ME	Transportes MEPE, Av 11, C 0/1 ⓣ257-8129
MO	Transportes Delio Morales, C 16, Av 1/3 ⓣ223-5567
MRA	Microbuses Rapiditos Heredianos, C1, Av 7/9 ⓣ223-8392
MU	MUSOC, C 16, Av 1/3 ⓣ222-2422
Nica	Nicabus ⓣ223-0293
PA	Panaline ⓣ256-8721
PU	Pulmitan, C 14, Av 1/3 ⓣ222-1650
SA	SACSA, C 5, Av 18 ⓣ551-0232
TC	Transportes Caribeños ⓣ221-2596
Tica	Ticabus, C 9, Av 4/6 ⓣ221-8954
TIL	Transportes Tilarán, C 14, Av 9/11 ⓣ222-3854
TJ	Transportes Jacó ⓣ223-1109
TRA	TRALAPA, C 20, Av 1/3 ⓣ221-7202
TRC	Tracopa-Alfaro, Av 18, C 2/4 ⓣ221-4214
TRN	Transnica ⓣ223-4242
TRS	Transtusa, Av 6, C 13 ⓣ556-4233
TU	TUASA, C 12, Av 2 ⓣ 442-6900
TUAN	Tuan ⓣ441-3781

International bus services from San José

Codes given under the "Co." column correspond to the relevant bus company (see box, overleaf). Advance purchase – at least a week in advance, particularly for Managua and Panama City – is necessary for all routes.

To	Frequency	Bus stop	Distance	Duration	Co.
David	1 daily	Av 3/5, C 14	400km	9hr	TRC
Guatemala City (overnight in Managua & El Salvador)	2 daily	Av 4, C 9/11	1200km	60hr	Tica
Managua	3 daily	Av 4, C 9/11	450km	11hr	Tica
Managua	3 daily	C 22, Av 3/5	450km	11hr	TRN
Managua	1 daily	C 0, Av 11	450km	11hr	Nica
Panama City	2 daily	Av 4, C 9/11	903km	18hr	Tica
Panama City	1 daily	C 16, Av 3–5	903km	18hr	PA
Paso Canoas (for Panama)	7 daily	C 14, Av 5	349km	8hr	TRC
Peñas Blancas (for Nicaragua & Santa Rosa NP)	5 daily	C 16, Av 3/5	293km	6hr	CA
Sixaola (for Panama)	2 daily	C 0, Av 9/11	250km	6hr	ME
Tegucigalpa (overnight in Managua)	2 daily	Av 4, C 9/11	909km	48hr	Tica

Tours

The Costa Rican tourist boom of the past ten years has led to a proliferation of **tour operators**, and wandering around the city you face a barrage of tour agencies and advertisements: if you want to shop around it could take some time to sort yourself out. The following is not a comprehensive list of tour operators in San José, but all those that we've listed are experienced and recommendable, offering a good range of services and tours. They're all licensed (and regulated) by the ICT.

There are scores of others – be especially wary of fly-by-night operators, of which there are plenty. You often see, for instance, posters advertising cheap "packages" to Tortuguero or to Monteverde, both for about US$80–100 – less than half the price of a regular package. These cut-price tours are not packages at all, and never worth the price: in some cases you will be responsible for your own transport, accommodation will be the most basic, and no tours, orientation or guidance will be given – something you can easily arrange on your own, for the same price or less.

Camino Travel C 1, Av 0/1 ⓣ234-2530, ⓕ225-6143, ⓦwww.caminotravel.com. Young, enthusiastic staff with high standards and a mainly European clientele. Experienced in both upmarket and independent travel, selling individual tours and booking good-quality accommodation from their range of countrywide contacts. Can also help with bus and transport information and car rental. Convenient downtown office.

Coast to Coast Adventures ⓣ280-8054, ⓕ225-6055, ⓦwww.coasttocoastadventures.com. Adventure sports specialists offering whitewater rafting, sea kayaking, hiking, mountain biking and canopy tours. Nine-day trips start at around US$1600 per person.

Costa Rica Expeditions C Central, Av 3 ⓣ257-0766, ⓕ257-1665, ⓦwww.costaricaexpeditions.com. This US-based firm is the longest-established and most experienced of the major tour operators, with superior accommodation in Tortuguero, Monteverde and Corcovado, a superlative staff of guides and tremendous resources. They offer whitewater rafting trips on the Pacuaré River for US$95 per person.

Costa Rican Trails Av 15, C 23/25 ⓣ221-3011, ⓕ257-4655, ⓦwww.costaricantrails.com. Small, friendly and very professional agency who will visit you in your hotel room to discuss their range of tailor-made and flexi-drive holidays in all price ranges. They're also experts in adventure sports, including rafting, scuba diving and motorbike tours.

Ecole Travel C 7, Av 0/1 ⓣ223-2240, ⓕ223-4128, ⓦwww.ecoletravel.com. Small agency, popular with backpackers, offering well-priced two-night tours to Tortuguero (US$205) and 3-day tours to Corcovado as well as whitewater rafting trips on the Pacuaré River. They also run boats from Moín docks near Puerto Limón to Tortuguero.

Expediciones Tropicales Av 11–13, C 3b ⓣ257-4171, ⓕ233-5284, ⓦwww.costaricainfo.com. Well-regarded agency, with knowledgeable guides, which runs the popular "Four-in-One" day-tour of Volcán Poás and nearby sights (US$79; 11hr), as well as a host of other trips from San José at competitive prices.

Horizontes Nature Tours C 28, Av 1/3 ⓣ222-2022, ⓕ255-4513, ⓦwww.horizontes.com. Highly regarded agency concentrating on rainforest walking and hiking, volcanoes and birdwatching, all with an emphasis on natural and cultural history. Specialists in mountain biking and horse riding, too.

Marbella Travel & Tours ⓣ & ⓕ219-3637, ⓦwww.marbellatours.com. Offer a range of one-day tours – San José city tours, coffee plantation tours, volcano tours, whitewater rafting, canopy tours, etc – for around US$70 each.

Serendipity Adventures Turrialba ⓣ556-2592, ⓕ556-2593, ⓦwww.serendipityadventures.com. Located near the Pacuaré and Reventazón rivers, the country's prime whitewater rafting destinations, this superior travel agency specializes in highly individual custom-made tours for self-formed groups with a sense of adventure. Serendipity make a point of searching out undiscovered parts of Costa Rica and, in addition to rafting, are experts in canyoning and rappelling and the only company in Costa Rica to offer hot-air balloon trips (US$900) to, among other places, Volcán Arenal. Tours are not cheap, starting at US$2000 per person for eight days.

Specops ⓣ232-4028, ⓦwww.specops.com. Adventure education group, comprising US Special Forces veterans and expert Costa Rican guides, specializing in white-knuckle thrills, jungle-survival courses, and adventure film and photography.

Domestic flights from San José

Sansa C 24, Paseo Colón/Av 1 ⓣ221-9414, ⓕ255-2176, ⓦwww.flysansa.com

To	Frequency	Duration
Barra del Colorado	1 daily	30min
Bahía Drake	2 daily	50min
Golfito	4 daily	45min
Nosara	2 daily	55min
Palmar Sur	2 daily	50min
Puerto Jiménez	3 daily	50min
Quepos	6 daily	30min
Sámara	2 daily	55min
Tamarindo	7 daily	40min
Tambor	2 daily	20min
Tortuguero	1 daily	35min

NatureAir Tobías Bolaños airport, Pavas ⓣ220-3054 or 296-1102, ⓕ220-0413, ⓦwww.natureair.com

To	Frequency	Duration
Barra del Colorado	1 daily	30min
Bahía Drake	2 daily	45min
Golfito	1 daily	1hr 10min
Liberia	4 daily	1hr 10min
Palmar Sur	2 daily	1hr 15min
Quepos	4 daily	25min
Sámara	1 daily	1hr 5min
Tamarindo	3 daily	50min
Tambor	2 daily	30min
Tortuguero	1 daily	50min

Domestic bus services from San José

In the table below, the initials in the "Co." column correspond to the bus company that serves this route; see the box on p.611 for a list of companies and telephone numbers. Where advance purchase is mentioned, it is advised, and strongly recommended in the high season (HS) or at weekends (WE; ie from Friday to Sunday). You need buy your ticket no more than one day in advance unless otherwise indicated. NP = National Park; WR = Wildlife Refuge; NM = National Monument.

Destination	Frequency	Bus stop	Distance	Duration	Co.	Advance purchase
Alajuela (and airport)	every 5min	Av 2, C 12/14	17km	35min	TU	no
Braulio Carrillo NP	*see* Guápiles					
Cahuita	4 daily	C 0, Av 11/13	195km	4hr	ME	yes (HS)
Caño Negro WR	*see* Los Chiles					
Cartago	every 5min	C 5, Av 18/20	22km	45min	SA	no
Chirripó NP	*see* San Isidro					
Corcovado NP	*see* Puerto Jiménez					
Golfito	2 daily	C 14, Av 3/5	339km	8hr	TRC	yes (3 days)
Guápiles	every 45min	C 0, Av 11/13	30km	35min	EG	no
Guayabo NM	*see* Turrialba					
Heredia	every 5min	C 1, Av 7/9 & Av 2, C12/14	11km	25min	TU/MRA	no
La Fortuna	12 daily	C16, Av 1/3	130km	4hr 30min	ATS	yes (HS)
Liberia	10 daily	C 24, Av 5/7	217km	4hr 30min	PU	no
Los Chiles	2 daily	C 12, Av 7/9	217km	5hr	ATS	no
Manuel Antonio NP	*see* Quepos					
Monteverde	2 daily	C 12, Av 7/9	167km	3hr 30min	TIL	yes (3–5 days)
Nicoya	6 daily	C 14, Av 3/5	296km	6hr	EA	no
Nosara	1 daily	C 14, Av 3/5	361km	6hr	EA	no
Playa Brasilito	2 daily	C 20, Av 3/5	320km	6hr	TRA	yes (WE)
Playa Coco	3 daily	C 24, Av 5/7	251km	5hr	PU	yes (WE)
Playa Flamingo	2 daily	C 20, Av 3/5	320km	6hr	TRA	yes (WE)
Playa Hermosa	1 daily	Av 5, C 20/22	265km	5hr	EM	no
Playa Jacó	5 daily	C16, Av 1/3	102km	2hr 30min	TJ	yes (WE)
Playa Junquillal	1 daily	C 20, Av 3/5	298km	5hr	TRA	no
Playa Panamá	1 daily	Av 5, C 20/22	265km	5hr	EM	no
Playa Potrero	2 daily	C 20, Av 3	320km	6hr	TRA	yes (WE)
Puerto Jiménez	2 daily	C 12, Av 7/9	378km	8hr	BL	yes
Puerto Limón	25 daily	C 0, Av 11/13	162km	2hr 30min	TC	no
Puerto Viejo de Talamanca	4 daily	C 0, Av 13	210km	4hr 30min	ME	yes
Puntarenas	15 daily	C 16, Av 10/12	110km	2hr	EU	no

Destination	Frequency	Bus stop	Distance	Duration	Co.	Advance purchase
Quepos	4 daily	C 16, Av 3/5	145km	3hr 30min	MO	yes (3 days)
Sámara	1 daily	C 14, Av 3/5	331km	6hr	EU	yes (WE)
San Carlos (Ciudad Quesada)	15 daily	C 12, Av 7/9	110km	3hr	ATS	no
San Isidro de El General	14 daily	C 0, Av 22/24	136km	3hr	MU	no
Sarchí	30 daily	Av 3, C 16/18	52km	1hr 30min	Tuan	no
Tamarindo	2 daily	C 14, Av 5	320km	6hr	EA	yes (WE)
Turrialba	17 daily	C 13, Av 6/8	65km	1hr 40min	TRS	no
Volcán Arenal	*see* La Fortuna					
Volcán Irazú	1 Sat & Sun	Av 2, C 1/3	54km	2hr	BM	no (but go early)
Volcán Poás	1 daily	Av 2, C12/14	55km	1hr 30min	TU	no (but go early)

6.2

The Valle Central and the Highlands

Despite its name – which translates literally as "Central Valley" – Costa Rica's **Valle Central** is actually an intermountain plateau poised at an elevation of between 3000 and 4000m. It's a largely agricultural region, with staggered green coffee terraces set amidst patchwork-quilt fields and loomed over by the blue-black summits of the surrounding mountains. Many of these are **volcanoes**, including the smoking Poás in the north and the precipitous Irazú in the east and, though there have been no real eruptions since Irazú blew its top in 1963, Poás and Irazú periodically spew light rains of fertile volcanic ash onto the surrounding farmland.

Although the area occupies just six percent of the country's total landmass, the Valle Central supports roughly two thirds of Costa Rica's population, containing the country's most fertile land as well as its four most important cities – San José (covered in the previous chapter) and the provincial capitals of **Alajuela**, **Heredia** and **Cartago**. The chief attractions for visitors, of course, are the volcanoes, especially **Volcán Irazú**, **Volcán Poás** and **Volcán Barva** and the surrounding national parks, but there's also good **whitewater rafting** on the Río Reventazón and Río Pacuaré near Turrialba, not to mention the oft-overlooked Monumento Nacional Guayabo, the country's most important archeological site.

Most people use San José as a base for forays into the Valle Central: although the **provincial capitals** each have their own strong identity, with the exception of Alajuela they have little to entice you to linger. If you do want to get out of the city and stay in the Valle Central, the nicest places are the lodges and inns scattered throughout the countryside.

Alajuela and around

Alajuela Province is vast, in Costa Rican terms at least, extending from **Alajuela** town, 20km northwest of San José, all the way north to the Nicaraguan border and west to the slopes of Volcán Arenal. The account below deals only with that part of the province on the south side of the Cordillera Central, spanning the area from Alajuela itself to the town of Zarcero, 59km to the northwest in the Highlands. **Parque Nacional Volcán Poás** is the area's principal attraction; the ride up to the crater gives good views over the whole densely populated and heavily cultivated province, passing flower-growing fincas, fruit farms and the occasional coffee field.

People also head out here to see the crafts factories at **Sarchí**, famous for its coloured wooden ox-carts; **Zoo-Ave**, the exceptional bird sanctuary and zoo just west of Alajuela on the way to La Garita; the **Butterfly Farm** at La Guácima; and the popular **La Paz Waterfall Gardens**.

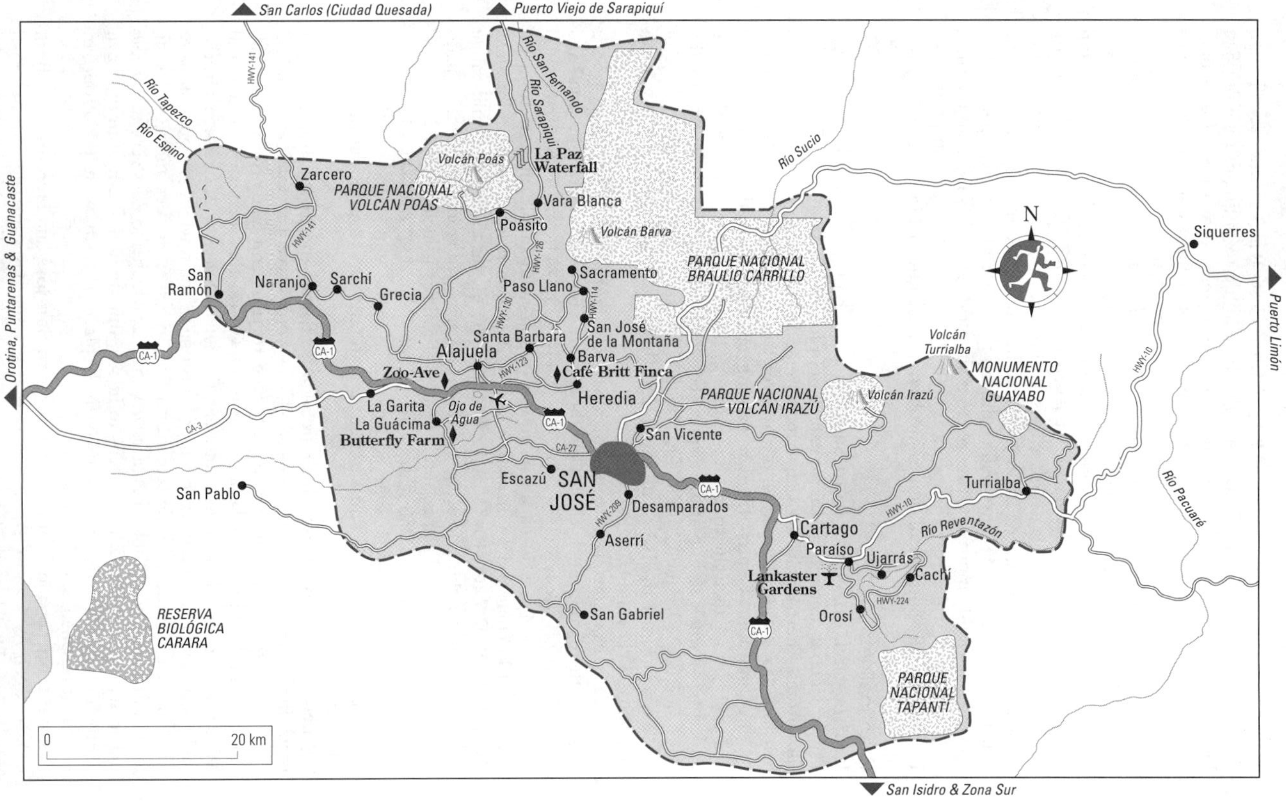

San Carlos (Ciudad Quesada)
Puerto Viejo de Sarapiquí
Puerto Limón
San Isidro & Zona Sur
Orotina, Puntarenas & Guanacaste
Río Tapezco
Río Espino
HWY-141
Río San Fernando
Río Sarapiquí
Volcán Poás
La Paz Waterfall
Zarcero
PARQUE NACIONAL VOLCÁN POÁS
Vara Blanca
Poásito
Río Sucio
Volcán Barva
HWY-126
N
Siquerres
San Ramón
Naranjo
Sarchí
Grecia
Sacramento
Paso Llano
HWY-114
PARQUE NACIONAL BRAULIO CARRILLO
HWY-130
San José de la Montaña
Santa Barbara
Alajuela
Barva
CA-1
Volcán Turrialba
MONUMENTO NACIONAL GUAYABO
HWY-10
HWY-123
Café Britt Finca
Zoo-Ave
Heredia
PARQUE NACIONAL VOLCÁN IRAZÚ
Volcán Irazú
La Garita
Ojo de Agua
La Guácima
Butterfly Farm
San Vicente
CA-3
CA-27
Río Pacuaré
Escazú
SAN JOSÉ
Turrialba
San Pablo
HWY-209
Desamparados
Cartago
Río Reventazón
Aserrí
Paraíso
Ujarrás
Cachí
Lankaster Gardens
HWY-224
San Gabriel
Orosí
RESERVA BIOLÓGICA CARARA
PARQUE NACIONAL TAPANTÍ
0 20 km

Alajuela

With a population of just 35,000, **ALAJUELA** is Costa Rica's second city. Though it was founded back in 1657, at first sight there's little to distinguish it from San José. Dig a little deeper, however, and you'll gain a sense of what San José would have looked like twenty years ago: there are fewer US chain stores, plus the city is much less congested – when walking down the street, it comes as a pleasant surprise to find yourself smelling bougainvillea rather than diesel. The city's few attractions, such as they are, are all less than a minute's walk from the Parque Central. Most impressive is the sturdy-looking whitewashed former jail that houses the **Juan Santamaría Cultural-Historical Museum**, Av 3, C 0/2 (Tues–Sun 10am–6pm; free), dedicated to Alajuela's most cherished historical figure, the drummer-boy-cum-martyr Juan Santamaría, who sacrificed his life to save the country from the American adventurer William Walker during the battle of 1856 (see p.488). The museum's curiously monastic atmosphere is almost more interesting than the small collection itself, which runs the gamut from mid-nineteenth-century maps of Costa Rica to crumbly portraits of figures involved in the battle of 1856.

Practicalities

Red-and-black Tuasa **buses from San José** arrive on C 8, four blocks west of the Parque Central, amongst an inhospitable confusion of bus stops, supermarkets and shoe stores. Alternatively, the beige-and-orange Station Wagon Alajuela bus from San José drops you off on Av 4, just west of Parque Juan Santamaría, two blocks south of the Parque Central. If you're **driving**, take the *pista* to the airport (General Cañas Highway), then the turn-off to Alajuela, 17km from San José – don't use the underpass or you'll end up at the airport. For getting around, **taxis** line up on the south side of the Parque Central. The Banco Nacional, C 2, A0, on the west side of the Parque Central, the Banco de San José, C 0, Av 3, and Scotiabank, C2, Av 3, can all change dollars and travellers' cheques.

Alajuela is a quieter place to stay than San José, and just 3km from the airport; although there's not much choice, the **hotels** are of good standard. The small and cheerful *Mango Verde* hostel, Av 3, C 2/4 (Ⓣ441-6330, Ⓕ441-7116, Ⓔmirafloresbb@hotmail.com; ❹), is an excellent budget option, with simple en-suite rooms, a communal kitchen and an attractive blue-walled courtyard. The friendly *Hotel 1915*, C 2, Av 5/7 (Ⓣ440-7163, Ⓕ441-0495; ❺), is the town's best mid-range option: the comfortable and attractive rooms are arranged around an interior patio with rocking chairs and plants, and a delicious breakfast is included. *Charley's Hotel* on Av 5, 200m north and 25m east of the Parque Central (Ⓣ & Ⓕ441-0115, Ⓔlilyhotel@latinmail.com; ❻), has eleven large, clean rooms with private bath and hot water, plus a TV lounge and kitchen. For details of accommodation around Alajuela, see opposite.

When it comes to **eating**, there are plenty of *sodas* and pastry shops, but not much in the way of gourmet cuisine. Still, you won't starve. Try *Soda Gallo Pinto*, C 2, Av 3/5, where you can get decent-sized tortillas and tacos for around 250 colones; the bustling *Soda Heladería* at Av 0, C6 on the corner of the Central Market or, for something a little different, the *Primer Sabor*, Av 3, C 2/4, a surprisingly good Chinese restaurant that represents one of the town's few concessions to international cuisine. A wide selection of sticky cakes, coffees and good-value lunchtime *casados* is available at *Ambrosia*, Av 5, C 2, which also does very reasonable Italian-style pizzas. *Bar La Troja*, a ten- to fifteen–minute walk south from the town centre along C 4, is the only vaguely lively place in town, with a rooftop bar, relaxed atmosphere and decent music.

Moving on, fast and frequent Tuasa **buses to San José** and **Heredia** leave from C 8 between Av 1 and Central (but note that some buses marked "Alajuela–San José" go via Heredia rather than direct to San José – check with the driver). All other buses depart from the loose collection of bus stops just south of Av 1 between

C 8 and 10, including regular services for Sarchí and La Guácima Abajo (for the Butterfly Farm). It's a confusing area, and the departure points are not well marked, so ask around to make sure you're waiting at the right place.

Around Alajuela

Twelve kilometres southwest of Alajuela, **La Guácima Butterfly Farm** (daily 8.30am–5pm, last tour at 3pm; US$15; Ⓦwww.butterflyfarm.co.cr) breeds valuable pupae for export to zoos and botanical gardens all over the world. The farm also has beautiful views over the Valle Central. In the wet season you should aim to get there early, as the rain forces the butterflies to hide, and the clouds obscure the view; on a sunny day, however, when the butterflies are active, it's a glorious sight. From Alajuela, **buses** (marked "La Guácima Abajo") leave from the area southwest of the main bus terminal; the Butterfly Farm is practically the last stop. Buses from San José (2hr) leave from Av 1, C 20/22, daily (except Sunday) at 11am and 2pm.

The largest aviary in Central America, **Zoo-Ave** (daily 9am–5pm; US$9; Ⓦwww.zooave.org), at Dulce Nombre, 5km northeast of La Garita, is just about the best place in the country to see the fabulous and many-coloured birds – especially macaws – that inhabit Costa Rica. The La Garita bus from Alajuela (15min) passes right by, leaving from the area southwest of the main terminal.

Accommodation around Alajuela

Around Alajuela a few luxurious, country-house-style **hotels** cater to a well-heeled clientele. *Orquideas Inn*, 5km outside Alajuela on the road to Poás (Ⓣ443-9346, Ⓕ443-9740, Ⓦwww.orquideasinn.com; ❼–❾), is a Spanish hacienda-style country inn with enormous rooms, landscaped gardens with pool, and attentive service. The super-luxurious *Xandari Plantation Inn*, 6.5km north of Alajuela (Ⓣ 443-2020, in the US 805/684-7879, Ⓕ442-4847, Ⓦwww.xandari.com; ❽), set high above the city, has 17 purpose-built "designer" villas, three swimming pools, a very good restaurant with commanding views of the town, and a full spa as well as its own private stretches of forest and coffee plantation (there are marked trails through both); low-season rates are good value (starting at around US$145) and airport pick-up is included. The *Siempreverde* lodge (Ⓣ449-5134, Ⓕ449-5035; ❺–❻), a small, comfortable four-room B&B, lies 8km north of Alajuela on the slopes of Volcán Poás, next to the lush surrounds of the Doka Coffee Estate (daily tours available; Ⓣ449-5152, Ⓦwww.dokaestate.com).

Parque Nacional Volcán Poás

PARQUE NACIONAL VOLCÁN POÁS (daily 8am–3.45pm; US$7), just 55km from San José and 37km north of Alajuela, is one of the most easily accessible active volcanoes in the world, with a history of eruptions that goes back 11 million years. Poás's last gigantic blowout was on January 25, 1910, when it dumped 640,000 tonnes of ash on the surrounding area. At the moment it is comparatively quiet.

You need to get to the volcano before the clouds roll in, which they inevitably do, as early as 10am, even in the dry season (Dec–April). Poás has blasted out three craters in its lifetime, and due to more or less constant activity, the appearance of the **main crater** is subject to change – it's 1500m wide and filled with milky turquoise water from which sulphurous gases waft and broil. Although it's an impressive sight, you only need about fifteen minutes' viewing and picture-snapping.

The park features a few very well maintained, short and unchallenging trails, which take you through a strange, otherworldly landscape, dotted with smoking fumaroles (steam vents) and tough ferns and trees valiantly holding up against regular sulphurous scaldings. Poás is also home to a rare version of cloudforest called dwarf or **stunted cloudforest**, a combination of pine-needle-like ferns, miniature bonsai-type trees, and bromeliad-encrusted cover, all of which has been stunted through an onslaught of cold (temperatures up here can drop to below freezing), continual cloud cover, and acid rain from the mouth of the volcano.

The **Crater Overlook trail**, which winds its way around the main crater, is only 750m long, along a paved road. A side trail (1km; 20–30min) heads off through the forest to the pretty, emerald Botos Lake, which fills an extinct crater and makes a good spot for a picnic. Named for the pagoda-like tree commonly seen along its way, the **Escalonia trail** (about 1km; 30min) starts at the picnic area (follow the signs), taking you through ground cover less stunted than that at the crater. A wide variety of birds ply this temperate forest, among them the ostentatiously colourful quetzal, the robin and several species of hummingbird. Although a number of large mammals live in the park, including coyotes and wildcats, such as the margay, you're unlikely to spot them. One you probably will come across, however, is the small, green-yellow **Poás squirrel**, which is found nowhere else in the world.

Getting to Volcán Poás

Most visitors get to the volcano on a pre-arranged **tour** from San José (approximately US$45 per person for a 4–5-hour trip, including return transport and guide – see p.612 for details of tour operators). All kinds of combination packages with other Valle Central sites exist: the "Four-in-One" tour organized by Expediciones Tropicales (Ⓣ257-4171, Ⓦwww.costaricainfo.com) is reasonably priced and very popular, and also takes in the La Paz Waterfall Gardens, Parque Nacional Braulio Carrillo and a boat ride on Río Sarapiquí (US$79 per person including breakfast, lunch and guide; 11hr). Alternatively, a Tuasa bus leaves daily at 8.30am from Av 2, C 12/14, in San José, travelling via Alajuela and returning from the volcano at 2pm (885 colones each way; 2hr). If you want to reach Poás before both tour buses and dense cloud cover arrive, you'll need either to drive or take a **taxi** from Alajuela (roughly US$30) or San José (US$45–50) – reasonably affordable if split between a group of people.

The park's **visitor centre** shows videos of the volcano and has a snack shop, which also serves hot coffee, though you're probably better off packing a picnic lunch. Make sure you bring a sweater and wet-weather gear with you in the rainy season. No **camping** is allowed in the park.

Accommodation near the park

If you want to get a really early start to guarantee a view of Poás's crater, there are plenty of places to stay in the vicinity, including a couple of comfortable **mountain lodges** on working dairy farms (though you'll need a car to get to them), and other, more simple and inexpensive places that can be reached on the daily bus to Poás. If you want to **camp**, the *Mountain View Campground* (Ⓣ482-2196; US$5 per tent per night), just before the *Chubasco* restaurant on the main road to Poás, has a pleasant garden site with hot showers.

Poás Volcano Lodge 6km from the small village of Poásito Ⓣ482-2194, Ⓕ482-2513, Ⓦwww.poasvolcanolodge.com. Set on a working dairy farm, the lodge has nine rustically furnished rooms (private and shared bathrooms), a very nice communal eating area with a sunken fireplace, extensive gardens including patches of forest (there are 3 marked walking trails) and can offer horse-riding tours of the nearby Braulio Carrillo National Park. Facilities include a basement games room and mountain bikes for hire. Meals (US$8–12) by arrangement. Poásito is 10km before the entrance to Poás on the main mountain road from Alajuela and San José – take a right fork towards Vara Blanca. ❻

La Providencia Ecological Reserve 1km from the park entrance on the slopes of Poás Ⓣ232-2448. Charming rustic cabinas on a working dairy farm near the top of Poás, with spectacular views. The owners prepare excellent local food, rent out horses for trots up the volcano (US$20 for 3 hours) and organize trout-fishing trips. ❺

Lo Que tu Quieras 5km before the park entrance Ⓣ482-2092. The least expensive option in the area, comprising three small cabinas with heated water and fireplaces, and a restaurant serving local dishes with huge picture windows and staggering views – stop for a drink on your way back from the volcano. Camping is permitted for a nominal fee. ❸

La Paz Waterfall Gardens

A fifteen-kilometre drive east of Poás is one of Costa Rica's newest and most popular attractions, the **La Paz Waterfall Gardens** (daily 8.30am–5.30pm; US$21; ⓦwww.waterfallgardens.com), an immaculate series of riverside trails linking five waterfalls on the Río La Paz. The trails are all set in a large colourful garden planted with native shrubs and flowers – there's also a large butterfly observatory and a hummingbird garden, which is home to sixteen different species. From the reception centre, visitors take one of several self-guided tours, which wind prettily through the site and along the river, where viewing platforms mean that at various points you're both above and underneath the waterfalls, the highest of which, **Magia Blanca**, crashes deafeningly down some 40m into swirling whitewater. The marked trails conclude at the top of the **La Paz Waterfall**, Costa Rica's most photographed cascade (it can also be seen from the public highway that runs over a large rickety bridge below).

There's currently no public transport to the gardens, and most people visit them as part of an organized tour from San José – Expediciones Tropicales (ⓣ257-4171, ⓦwww.costaricainfo.com) include La Paz as part of their "Four-in-One" highlights tour (US$79). You can stay at the gardens, however, at their recently opened, luxury *Peace Lodge* (ⓣ225-0643; ❽). The rooms all have hand-made canopy beds, stained-glass windows, balconies with views over the gardens, bathrooms and Jacuzzis. Staying at the lodge entitles you to access the gardens before and after official opening hours. If you're driving, take a right at the junction in Poásito towards Vara Blanca and, on reaching the village, take a left at the gas station and follow the well-marked signs for 5km.

Sarchí

Touted as the centre of Costa Rican arts and crafts, especially **furniture making**, the village of **SARCHÍ**, 30km northwest of Alajuela, is a commercialized place – firmly on the tourist trail but without much charm. Its setting is pretty enough, between precipitous, verdant hills, but don't come expecting to see picturesque scenes of craftsmen sitting in small historic shops: the work is done in factories. The **Sarchí ox-cart** is a kaleidoscopically coloured, painted square cart meant to be hauled by a single ox or team of two oxen. Moorish in origin, the designs can be traced back to immigrants from the Spanish provinces of Andalucía and Granada. Though full-scale carts (US$1000 plus) are, understandably, only rarely sold, smaller-scale versions (US$150–350) specially made for tourists are popular, as are Sarchí tables, bedsteads and leather rocking chairs (about US$85). Apart from the shops and factories, the only thing of interest is a bubblegum-coloured pink-and-turquoise **church**, which looks out from atop the hill in Sarchí Norte (see below).

Practicalities

Sarchí is a spread-out place, divided into two halves. Large *fábricas* line the main road from **Sarchí Sur**, in effect a conglomeration of *mueblerías*, to the residential area of **Sarchí Norte**, which climbs the hill. There are only a few **hotels**, of which the best is probably the small *Hotel Daniel Zamora* (ⓣ454-4596; ❺), on a side street opposite the football pitch in Sarchí Norte, which has clean rooms and hot water. For **lunch**, try *Restaurante Helechos* inside the Plaza de Artesanía, which serves decent Mexican food, or *La Finca* restaurant, to the right of the Mercado de Artesanía souvenir shop as you drive north out of town, which serves very good maize soup and grilled steak.

Local **buses** from Alajuela run approximately every thirty minutes from 5am to 10pm. Buses back (via Grecia) can be hailed on the main road. From **San José** an express service (1hr–1hr 30min) runs from La Coca-Cola every thirty minutes daily from 5am to 10pm; the return schedule is the same. You could also take the bus to

Naranjo from La Coca-Cola, every 25 minutes, and switch there for a local service to Sarchí – call the Tuan bus company for information (☎441-3781).

The Banco Nacional on the main road beyond the church **changes dollars and cheques**, as does a smaller branch in the Mercado de Artesanía. If you need a **taxi** to ferry you back and forth between Sarchí Sur and Sarchí Norte, or to Alajeula or Zarcero, they can be called on ☎454-4028 or hailed on the street.

Heredia and around

Heredia Province stretches northeast from San José all the way to the Nicaraguan border, skirted on the west by Hwy-9, the old road from San José to Puerto Viejo de Sarapiquí. To the east, the Guápiles Highway, Hwy-32, provides access to Braulio Carrillo and to Limón on the Caribbean coast. The moment you leave San José for **Heredia**, the provincial capital, the rubbery leaves of coffee plants spring up on all sides – the section of the province covered in this chapter is almost wholly given over to coffee production, and there are a number of popular "coffee tours", especially to the **Café Britt Finca** near Heredia town.

In the Valle Central, the province's chief attractions are dormant **Volcán Barva**, which offers a good day's climb, and the nearby **Rainforest Aerial Tram**, which allows you to see the canopy of primary rainforest from above, causing minimal disturbance to the animals and birds.

Heredia

Just 11km northeast of San José is the lively town of **HEREDIA**, boosted by the student population of the Universidad Nacional (UNA) at the eastern end of town. The town centre is prettier than most, with a few historical buildings, though a bit run-down. It's a natural jumping-off point for excursions to the nearby historical hamlet of **Barva** and to the town of San José de la Montaña, gateway to **Volcán Barva**. Many tourists also come for the **Café Britt Finca** tour, hosted by the nation's largest coffee exporter, about 3km north of the town centre.

Arrival and information

Buses leave San José for Heredia every 5–10 minutes from C 1, Av 7/9 (Tuasa), and from Av 2, C 12/14 (Microbuses Rapiditos Heredianos), and pull into Heredia at the corner of C Central and Av 4, a stone's throw south of the Parque Central. At night, **minibuses** leave San José hourly between midnight and 6am from Av 2, C 12/14. There's no tourist office in town. Banco Nacional, at C 2, Av 2/4, and Scotiabank, at Av 4, C 0/C 2, both have ATMs and change money and **travellers' cheques**. The **correo** (Mon–Fri 7.30am–5.30pm) is on the northwest corner of the Parque Central, while **taxis** line up on the east side of the Mercado Central, between Av 6 and 8, and on the southern side of the Parque Central.

Moving on from Heredia, **buses to San José** depart from C 0, Av 2/4 (about every 10min during the day). The town has no central bus terminal, but a variety of well-signed stops are scattered across town, mainly around the Mercado Central, from where most local buses leave.

Accommodation

Decent **accommodation** in downtown Heredia is pretty sparse, though it's unlikely you'll need to stay in town, since San José is within easy reach and there are also several resort-type hotels in the country nearby, including one of the finest in Costa Rica. Although all are accessible by bus, you'll find it handy to have a car once you're there.

△ Spider monkey

Heredia

Hotel America C Central, opposite the San José bus stop ⓣ260-9292, ⓕ260-9293. Clean, if soulless, rooms, some of them rather dark, though all have bathroom, fan, TV and hot water. Breakfast included. ❺

Hotel Ceus Av 1 ⓣ262-2628, ⓕ262-2639. Quiet hotel with spotless, but no-frills, rooms with private bathrooms and hot water. There's also a decent seafood restaurant. ❸

Hotel Valladolid C7, Av 7 ⓣ260-2905, ⓕ260-2912, ⓔvalladolid@racsa.co.cr. A slightly more upmarket choice with spacious, comfortable rooms, a roof terrace, Jacuzzi and sauna. ❼

Around Heredia

Chalet Tirol north of Heredia, well-signposted on the road to Los Angeles via San Rafael ⓣ267-6222, ⓕ267-6228. Incredibly kitsch hotel in lovely pine forest on the edge of the Parque Nacional Braulio Carrillo, with ten alpine chalets in a grassy clearing plus a reproduction Tyrol village church and a square complete with fountain. There's also a renowned gourmet French restaurant, and guided walking tours are available. ❼

Finca Rosa Blanca on the road between San Pedro de Barva and Santa Barbara de Heredia ⓣ269-9392, ⓕ269-9555, ⓦwww.finca-rblanca.co.cr. One of the best hotels in the country, like some giant white bird roosting above the coffee fields, with six themed suites and two villas, plus a gorgeous tiled pool which seemingly drips over the hillside. An excellent four-course dinner is served family-style round the large table in the fairy-tale hotel foyer. Horse-riding tours also available. Prices start at around US$175 and keep rising. ❾

The Town

Heredia's layout conforms to the usual grid system, centred on the quiet **Parque Central**, draped with huge mango trees and overlooked by the plain **Basílica de la Inmaculada Concepción**, whose unexcitingly squat design – "seismic Baroque" – has kept it standing through several earthquakes since 1797. North of the parque, the old colonial tower of **El Fortín**, "the Fortress", features odd gun slats which fan out and widen from the inside to the exterior, giving it a medieval look: you cannot enter or climb it.

East of the tower on Avenida Central, the **Casa de la Cultura**, an old colonial house with a large breezy veranda, displays local art, including sculpture and painting by the schoolchildren of Heredia. The **Mercado Central**, Av 6/8, C 2/4 (daily 5am–6pm), is a clean, orderly place, its wide aisles lined with rows of fruit and veg, dangling sausages and plump prawns.

Eating and drinking

Perhaps because of its student population, Heredia is crawling with excellent cafés, patisseries, ice-cream joints and the best vegetarian and health-food **restaurants** outside San José. **Nightlife** is low-key, restricted to a few local salsa spots, although several of the bars keep late hours. If you're young or studently inclined, head for the four blocks immediately to the west of the university, which is where you'll find the best **bars**.

Café Heladeria Azzura southwest corner of the Parque Central. Upmarket café with superior Italian ice cream, excellent *refrescos*, fresh sandwiches and real cappuccino and espresso.

Le Petit Paris C 5, Av 2/4 ⓣ262-2564. This French-owned oasis has tables set out in a small garden and serves delicious French cuisine. The lunch menu changes daily, and there's live jazz on Wednesdays. Expect to pay around US$10–15 for a full meal. Closed Sun.

Miraflores Disco y Taberna Av 2, C 2. This bar/disco is the town's most popular night spot. Latin and reggae beats predominate on the dance floor, and there's live music on Tuesdays.

Océanos C 4, Av 2/4. Nautically-themed bar decorated with an assortment of fishing paraphernalia and surfboards. It's very popular with students (partly because they pay a set 250 colones for their drinks) and, consequently, very full at weekends. It serves very good *bocas*.

Around Heredia

North and east of Heredia the terrain climbs to higher altitudes, reaching its highest point at **Volcán Barva**, at the western entrance of wild and rugged **Parque**

Nacional Braulio Carrillo. Temperatures are notably cooler around here, and the landscape is dotted with dairy farms and conifers. The towns here – **Barva**, **Santa Barbara de Heredia** and **San Joaquín de Heredia** – are the favoured residences of expats, but there's little to detain the visitor.

Rainforest Aerial Tram

The invention of American naturalist Donald Perry, the **Rainforest Aerial Tram** lies just beyond the eastern boundary of Braulio Carrillo (5km east of Río Sucio; Mon 9am–4pm, Tues–Sun 6am–4pm; US$49.50 per person; Ⓦwww.rainforestram.com). The product of many years' research, most of it carried out at nearby Rara Avis in the Zona Norte (see p.710), the tram was, when it opened in the mid-1990s, the first of its kind in the world (there are now two others: one near Jacó on the Pacific coast, the other on the island of Dominica). Twenty **overhead cable cars**, each holding five passengers and one guide, run slowly along the 3.6km aerial track, skirting the tops of the forest and passing between trees, providing eye-level encounters along the way. The ride, which takes around 1hr 30min, affords a rare glimpse of birds, animals and plants – including the epiphytes, orchids, insects and mosses that live inside the upper reaches of the forest – and, largely silent, it is less likely to frighten the animals. Don't come expecting to see particular animals, however, or you may be disappointed, although there are further opportunities for animal-spotting along the network of ground-level trails that traverse the park. Such has been the tram's success in recent years that it now operates its own jungle lodge with ten luxury bungalows, all with en-suite bathrooms and views of the forest. Room rates (US$95 per person) include unlimited tram rides and access to the trails as well as three meals a day.

Practicalities

Less than an hour from San José, the aerial tram turn-off is on the northeast border of the Parque Nacional Braulio Carrillo, 5.3km beyond the (signed) bridge over the Río Sucio, on the right-hand side; from the junction it's another 1.5km. To get there **by bus**, catch the Guápiles service from C 0, Av 11, which should drop you at the entrance, although you may have to ask the driver to stop. The return Guápiles–San José bus will stop when flagged down, unless full. Wear a hat, insect repellent, and bring binoculars, camera and rain gear.

Alternatively, and much more conveniently, you can organize a **tour** (US$65 per person) with the tram's San José office on C 7, Av 7 (Ⓣ257-5961, Ⓕ257-6053, Ⓦwww.rainforesttram.com), which includes transport to and from your hotel, a guided aerial excursion and hiking along the park's nature trails. Most San José travel agencies offer similar trips, albeit at a slightly higher price. There are also special early-morning birdwatching trips and torchlit night rides (until 9pm) – many canopy inhabitants only become active and visible in the dark – plus tours combining the tram with other regional attractions such as La Guácima Butterfly Farm or the Café Britt Finca.

North of Heredia to Volcán Barva

Set in a large verandaed house in landscaped coffee fields two kilometres north of Heredia, the **Museo de la Cultura Popular** (daily 8.30am–5pm; US$2) tries to give an authentic portrayal of nineteenth- and early twentieth-century campesino life. The kitchen has been preserved as it would have been on a coffee finca, and you can sample authentic food of the period, including *torta de arroz*, *pan casero* and *gallos picadillos*, although apart from this there's little to do other than to wander around the house and the carefully kept gardens.

The colonial village of **BARVA**, about 1km further on, is really only worth a brief stop on the way to Volcán Barva to have a look at the huge cream **Baroque church**, flanked by tall brooding palms, and the surrounding adobe-and-tiled-roof houses – though Barva was founded in 1561, most of what you see today dates from the 1700s. The village also boasts an excellent Mexican restaurant, *El Charro de Fofo*, which serves all the usual Mexican staples, like tortillas and refried beans, in a cheerful corner spot 300m south of the village's main square on the road to Heredia. **Buses** to San José de la Montaña (for the volcano) stop opposite the football field.

On the way north from Heredia to Barva, look out for the signs to the **Café Britt Finca**, 1km south of Barva (tours daily: May to mid-Dec 11am; mid-Dec to April 9am, 11am & 3pm; ⓦwww.coffeetour.com), the country's most important coffee exporter and producer of one of its best-known brands. Costumed guides take you through the history of coffee growing in Costa Rica, showing how crucial the crop was to the country's development, with a rather slick multimedia presentation and a thorough description of the process involved in harvesting the beans. Once you've toured the plantation, roasting factory and drying patios, it's back for a free tasting and, of course, the inevitable stop in the gift shop; they can pack and mail coffee to the US. The finca is signed from the road between Heredia and Barva and offers a pick-up from most San José hotels (US$30 including tour).

Parque Nacional Braulio Carrillo and Volcán Barva

The **PARQUE NACIONAL BRAULIO CARRILLO** (8am–3.45pm; US$7), 20km northeast of San José, covers 325 square kilometres of virgin rain- and cloudforest, though it's still little visited on account of its sheer size and lack of facilities. Most tourists experience the majestic views of cloud and foliage only from the window of a bus on their way to the Caribbean coast. Named after Costa Rica's third, rather dictatorial, chief of state, who held office in the mid-1800s, the park was established in 1978, mainly to protect the area from the possible effects of the Guápiles Highway that was then in construction between San José and Limón. Even when only seen from the highway, Braulio Carrillo's dense forested cover gives you a good idea of what much of Costa Rica used to look like about fifty years ago, when approximately three-quarters of the country's total terrain was virgin rainforest.

The park has three staffed ranger stations (*puestos*). Two are on the Guápiles Highway, one at Zurqui, just before the Zurqui tunnel some 23km from San José, and the other at Quebrada Gonzalez, 2km east of the Rio Sucio bridge. In theory, the San José–Guápiles bus should stop at both of these, but it's probably best to confirm this with the driver in advance. There are picnic facilities and well-marked trails leading from the *puestos* into the forest, but camping is not permitted and there's no accommodation within this section of the park.

The park's third *puesto* marks the entry point for trails up the dormant **Volcán Barva**, which has become an increasingly popular destination for walkers and climbers despite (or perhaps because of) the difficulty in reaching it. There's no public transport beyond the village of Sacramento, 3km from the entrance, and even if driving you'll have to cope with a very bad stretch of road just before you reach the volcano – you'll need a 4WD, even in the dry season. The **main trail** (3km; about 1hr) up Barva's slopes begins at the western edge of Braulio Carrillo and ascends through dense deciduous cover before reaching the cloudforest at the top. Along the way you'll get panoramic views over the Valle Central and southeast to Volcán Irazú; if you're lucky – bring binoculars – you might see the elusive, jewel-coloured quetzal (though these nest-bound birds are usually only seen at their preferred altitude of 3600m or more). It's easy to get lost on Barva. Take a compass, water and food, a sweater and rain gear; leave early in the morning to enjoy the clearest views at the top; and be prepared for serious mud in the rainy season.

Practicalities

Buses from Heredia to the hamlet of Sacramento leave daily at 6.30am, noon and 4pm. Buses back to Heredia leave at 7.30am, 1pm and (most conveniently, but on weekends only) 5pm. Otherwise, you'll have to get a taxi – ask in either of the restaurants mentioned below or try ringing local driver Lizandro Cascante (Ⓣ224-2400). From Sacramento it's a 3km walk up a steep track to the Barva *puesto*.

If you want to **stay** near the volcano, basic huts (US$2 per night) and camping facilities (reserve in advance on Ⓣ283-5906) are available at the Barva *puesto*. There are also a couple of surprisingly good places to spend the night in the hamlet of Guacalillo, 8km south of the volcano. *Hotel de Montaña El Portico* (Ⓣ237-6022, Ⓕ260-6002) has enormous, simply furnished rooms with private bath (❻) and attractive self-catering cabins (US$70 per night for up to 5 people), while the adjacent *Hotel Las Ardillas* (Ⓣ260-2172, Ⓔardillas@racsa.co.cr; ❻) has very pretty cabinas with wall hangings and fireplaces, and a wonderfully cosy restaurant. There's also a tiled spa with mud treatments, massage and hypnotherapy (US$20–50/hr).

If you want to stock up on energy before climbing, several **restaurants** in the area serve típico food, including the *Campesino*, about 3.5km beyond Paso Llano en route to Volcán Barva, and the *Sacramento*, another 500m further on. *Soda El Bosque* in Sacramento, a picturesque little café stuffed full of junk-shop objects collected by its owner, serves up traditional *gallos* with various toppings, as well as breakfast and *casados*.

Cartago and around

Cartago Province extends east of San José and south into the Cordillera de Talamanca, a region made fertile by deposits from Volcán Irazú. The section covered here is a heavily populated, farmed and industrialized region, centred on **Cartago** town, a major shopping and transportation hub for the southern Valle Central. The town itself is seldom used as a place to stay, however, and many of the area's attractions are usually visited on day-trips from San José.

It takes about forty minutes to reach Cartago on the good (toll) highway from San José. From Cartago there are road connections to Turrialba, on the eastern slopes of Irazú, and the Orosí valley, and south via the Interamericana over the hump of the Cordillera Central to San Isidro and the Valle de El General.

Cartago

CARTAGO, meaning "Carthage", was Costa Rica's capital for three hundred years before the centre of power was moved to San José in 1823. Founded in 1563 by Juan Vázquez de Coronado, the city, like its ancient namesake, has been razed a number of times, although in this case by **earthquakes** rather than Romans – two, in 1823 and 1910, practically demolished the place. Most of the fine nineteenth-century and fin-de-siècle buildings were destroyed, and what has grown up in their place – the usual assortment of shops and haphazard modern buildings – isn't particularly appealing. The highlight of the town is the **Iglesia de la Parroquía** (known as "Las Ruinas"), which sits on the eastern end of the concrete expanse of the Parque Central. Originally built in 1575, the church was repeatedly destroyed by earthquakes, but stubbornly rebuilt by the Cartagoans each time, until the giant earthquake of 1910 finally vanquished it for good. Only the elegantly tumbling walls remain, enclosing pretty subtropical gardens. From the ruins it's a walk of five minutes east to Cartago's only other attraction: the cathedral, properly called the **Basílica de Nuestra Señora de Los Angeles**, at C 16 and Av 2, rebuilt in a decorative Byzantine style after the original was destroyed in an earthquake in 1926.

Practicalities

SACSA run frequent local **buses** to Cartago from their San José terminal on C 5, Av 18/20 (after 8.30pm, buses leave from in front of the *Gran Hotel Costa Rica*), which head out of the city along Av 2 to C 19, then along Av Central and out through San Pedro – a journey of around 22km (30–45 minutes depending on the time of day). In Cartago buses sometimes do a bit of a tour of the town, stopping at virtually every block; wait to get off at the Parque Central. Like the other provincial capitals in the Valle Central, Cartago has no tourist office. The Banco de Costa Rica, Av 4, C 5/7, and Banco Nacional, C 1, Av 2, will change **travellers' cheques**, but it'll take a while. The **correo** (Mon–Fri 7.30am–6pm, Sat 7.30am–noon) is ten minutes from the town centre at Av 2, C 15/17. **Taxis** leave from the rank at Las Ruinas.

There's just one decent **hotel** in Cartago, the *Los Angeles Lodge* (Ⓣ591-4169, Ⓕ591-2218; ❺), on the square by the cathedral. Other accommodation in the town is frequented by commercial travellers and best avoided – in any case, getting stuck overnight in Cartago is an unlikely scenario, as there's a 24-hour bus service to San José. Of the town's few **restaurants**, the *Restaurant Los Angeles* (in the lodge) does good seafood, while the lively *Soda Apolo*, A 2, C 2, on the corner of the Parque Central, is a good source of solid, basic food. There are also plenty of pastry shops on the roads surrounding the Parque Central. To get back to **San José**, hop on whichever bus happens to be loading up in the covered area on Av 4, C 2/4. Buses leave every ten minutes between 5am and midnight, and about every hour otherwise.

Around Cartago

Dominating the landscape around Cartago, mighty **Volcán Irazú** is the area's most popular excursion. On the eastern slopes of the Cordillera Central, the small town of **Turrialba** is something of a local hub for watersports, with Ríos Reventazón and Pacuaré, two of the best whitewater rafting rivers in the country, nearby. Turrialba has also become a small centre for river kayaking – whitewater kayaking, in effect – with one or two specialist tour operators. The town is also the gateway to the **Monumento Nacional Guayabo**, the most important archeological site in Costa Rica.

Parque Nacional Volcán Irazú

The blasted-out lunar landscape of **Parque Nacional Volcán Irazú** (daily 8am–3.45pm; US$7) is dramatic, reaching a height of 3432m and giving fantastic views on clear days to the Caribbean coast. The inactive **Diego de la Haya crater** is a creepily impressive sight, its deep depression filled with a strange algae-green lake. Some 32km north of Cartago, the volcano makes for a long, but scenic, trip, especially early in the morning before the inevitable clouds roll in. Disappointingly, there is little actually to do in the park after you've seen the crater from the *mirador*, and there are no official trails, though it's possible to clamber along the scraggly slopes of a few outcroppings and dip into grey-ash sand dunes.

Practicalities

A visit to Irazú is strictly for day-trippers, since there's nowhere to stay in the park and camping is not allowed. Only one public **bus** runs to the park, leaving from San José's *Gran Hotel Costa Rica* at 8.15am on weekends and public holidays only – be there early in high season to make sure you get a seat – and picking up passengers at Cartago (from Las Ruinas) at 8.45am. The return fare is 1550 colones (US$3.75), which doesn't include the park entrance fee.

The bus pulls in at the crater parking area, where there are toilets and a **reception centre** offering information on the park and containing a snack bar serving *tamales*, cakes and hot drinks, as well as a small gift shop, which rents out waterproof ponchos (US$2) – it can get cold at the summit, so bring a sweater. The bus returns to San José at about 12.30pm. You can also get to Irazú on any number of half-day **tours** run by travel agencies in San José, which whisk you back and forth in a modern minibus for around US$35, not including the entrance fee.

Lankaster Gardens

Orchids are the main attraction at **Lankaster Gardens** (daily 8.30am–3.30pm; US$5), a tropical garden and research station 6km southeast of Cartago. While there are always some in bloom at any given time, the wet season (May–Nov) is less rewarding than the dry; March and April are the best months. To get to the gardens by **bus from San José**, take the Cartago service, get off at Las Ruinas, and change to a Paraíso bus. Get off when you see the *Casa Vieja* restaurant, about ten minutes out of town, and take the road off to your right, signposted to the gardens, then turn right again at the fork – a total walk of about 1km.

Turrialba and around

The pleasant agricultural town of **TURRIALBA**, 45km east of Cartago on the eastern slopes of the Cordillera Central, has sweeping views over the rugged eastern Talamancas, though there's little to keep you here long. Tourists are most likely to see it as part of a trip to the **Monumento Nacional Guayabo** or en route to a **whitewater rafting** or **kayaking** trip on the Reventazón or Pacuaré. Coast to Coast Adventures, Costa Rica Expeditions and Expediciones Tropicales all offer whitewater rafting day-trips on the rivers for around US$100 (see p.612). Many of the mountain-lodge-type hotels nearby have guided walks or horseback rides up dormant **Volcán Turrialba**, though the lack of trails means that the volcano is otherwise inaccessible to independent visitors. San José–Turrialba buses leave every hour between 5am and 10pm from C 13, Av 6/8.

Accommodation

Turrialba isn't really a tourist town, but it has some perfectly decent places to stay, from simple hotel rooms in town to picturesque mountain lodges in the surrounding countryside.

Hotel de Montaña Pochotel 8km from Turrialba towards Limón ⓣ538-151, ⓕ538-1212, ⓦwww.pochotel.com. Simple accommodation and traditional mountain fare in a stunning setting with volcano views in all directions. Camping also allowed. ❻

Interamericano southeast corner of Turrialba, near the old train station ⓣ556-0142, ⓕ556-7790, ⓦwww.hotelinteramericano.com. Basic, clean and very friendly with en-suite (US$25–30) and shared (US$20) bathrooms available, this is the best budget deal in town and an excellent place to meet other travellers. There's also a kitchen for guests' use, and the proprietor organizes kayaking and other tours. ❹–❺

Turrialtico Lodge 7.5km from Turrialba on the road to Limón ⓣ & ⓕ556-1111, ⓦwww.turrialtico.com. A cosy lodge with 14 wood-panelled rooms, all with private bath and hot water; some have balconies overlooking the gorgeous surrounding countryside. The excellent alfresco restaurant is renowned for its local specialities, which include barbecued meats and *pozol*, a tasty corn and pork soup. Tours to Irazú and the Río Reventazón are available. ❻–❼

Volcán Turrialba Lodge ⓣ273-4335, ⓕ273-0703, ⓦwww.volcanturrialbalodge.com. Quiet, modern and simply furnished farmhouse on the flanks of Volcán Turrialba (it advertises itself as "the only hotel with a volcano in its garden") whose 14 rooms all have woodburning stoves and private bath; diversions include ox-cart rides and horseback tours to Turrialba crater. You can arrange for a pick-up from San José, Cartago or Turrialba; otherwise you'll need a 4WD to get here over the badly rutted access road (call for directions). ❻

Wagelia Av 4, Turrialba, just beyond the gas station on the road from Cartago ⓣ556-1566, ⓕ556-1596. Small, clean and comfortable rooms with TV, fridge and phone, though it's popular and often full – ring in advance to reserve a room. ❼

Monumento Nacional Guayabo

The most important archeological site in Costa Rica, the **Monumento Nacional Guayabo** (daily 8am–3.45pm; US$7) lies 19km northeast of Turrialba and 84km from San José. Though interesting, don't go expecting something akin to the great Mayan and Aztec ruins of Mexico or Guatemala. In truth, there's not a great deal to see, the site's importance having more to do with the dearth of any other surviving contemporary structures. It was discovered by explorer Anastasio Alfaro at the end of the nineteenth century, but not excavated until the late 1960s. Guayabo belongs to the archeological-cultural area known as **Intermedio**, which begins roughly in the province of Alajuela and extends to Venezuela, Colombia and parts of Ecuador. Archeologists believe that Guayabo was inhabited from about 1000 BC to 1400 AD; most of the heaps of stones and basic structures now exposed were erected between 300 and 700 AD. The central mound is the tallest circular base unearthed so far, with two staircases and pottery remains on the very top.

Daily **buses** run to Guayabo from Turrialba (Mon–Sat at 11am & 5.15pm, returning at 12.30 & 5.30pm; Sun at 9am, returning at 4pm), though the inconvenient timetable means you either have not enough or too much time at the site. Alternatively, you could walk back to the main road, a four-kilometre downhill hike, and then intercept the bus that goes from the hamlet of Santa Teresita to Turrialba. It currently passes by at about 1.30pm, but you should double-check the times with the *guardaparques* or you might be left standing at the crossroads for 24 hours. **Driving** from Turrialba takes about thirty minutes; the last 4km is on a bad gravel road – passable with a regular car, but watch your clearance. **Taxis** charge around US$12 from Turrialba.

6.3

Limón Province and the Caribbean coast

Sparsely populated **Limón Province** sweeps south in an arc from Nicaragua down to Panama. Hemmed in to the north by dense jungles and swampy waterways, to the west by the mighty Cordillera Central and to the south by the even wider girth of the Cordillera Talamanca, Limón Province can feel like a lost, end-of-the-world place. Here you can watch gentle giant **sea turtles** lay their eggs on the wave-raked beaches of **Tortuguero**; snorkel coral reefs at **Cahuita**;

surf at **Puerto Viejo**; drift along the jungle canal from Tortuguero to **Barra del Colorado**, a major sports-fishing destination, or try animal- and bird-spotting in the many mangroves. The interior is criss-crossed by the powerful Río Reventazón and Río Pacuaré, two of the best rivers in the Americas for **whitewater rafting**.

Although Limón remains an unknown for the majority of visitors – especially those on package tours – it holds much appeal for ecotourists, having the highest proportion of protected land in the country. In addition, more than anywhere else in Costa Rica, the Caribbean coast exudes a sense of **cultural diversity** and a unique and complex local history. The only town of any size, **Puerto Limón**, is a lively, if jaded, port town, with a large (mostly Jamaican-descended) Afro-Caribbean population, and in the south, near the Panamanian border, live several communities of indigenous peoples from the **Bribrí** and **Cabécar** groups.

There are few options when it comes to **getting around** Limón Province. From San José to Puerto Limón you have a choice of just two roads, and from Puerto Limón south to the Panama border at Sixaola there is but one narrow and badly maintained route (not counting the few small local roads leading to the banana fincas). North of Puerto Limón there is no public land transport at all: instead, private lanchas ply the coastal canals connecting the port of Moín, 8km north of Puerto Limón, to Río Colorado near the Nicaraguan border. There are also scheduled **flights** from San José to Barra del Colorado. A good, frequent and quite reliable **bus** network operates in the rest of the province, with the most efficient and modern services running from San José to Puerto Limón and on to Sixaola. **English** is spoken widely along the coast, not just in Limón but also in Tortuguero, due to the many Miskito-descended people from Nicaragua.

It's very **wet** all year round, with a small dry spell in January and February. South of Limón, September and October offer the best chance of rain-free days.

Puerto Limón

Once the Caribbean coast's principal port, today **PUERTO LIMÓN**, 165km east of San José, has a somewhat neglected air. There has been little activity at the harbour since the big-time banana boats started loading at **Moín**, 8km up the headland toward Tortuguero, and to make things worse, the city was ravaged by the 1991 earthquake, which left a trail of wrecked buildings in its wake. All in all, the place does have some rough edges, and while the scare stories Highland Ticos gleefully tell of the place are a bit exaggerated, it's worth watching your back. Generally speaking, tourists come to Limón for one of three reasons: to get a boat to **Tortuguero** from Moín, to get a bus south to the **beach towns** of Cahuita and Puerto Viejo, or to join the annual Carnaval-like celebration of **El Día de la Raza** (Columbus Day) during the week preceding October 12.

Arrival and information

Of the two roads from the capital to Puerto Limón, the **Guápiles Highway** (Hwy-32) is one of the best maintained in the country (though that's not to say it's not without its fair share of potholes) and will get you to Puerto Limón in around three hours. The narrower and older Hwy-10, often called the **Turrialba Road**, runs through Turrialba on the eastern slopes of the Cordillera Central; it's considered dangerous and difficult to drive and carries very little traffic.

Arriving in Limón can be unnerving at night – it's best to arrive in daylight, if only to orientate yourself. Transportes Caribeños **buses** do the **San José–Limón** trip, running every half-hour from 5am to 7pm from C 0, Av 11, to the new Gran Terminal del Caribe on C 0, Av 15/17, where you can also pick up a bus to **Moín**. You should buy your ticket in advance if travelling to Limón for Carnaval, although extra buses are laid on during that period. Arrivals **from the south** – Cahuita, Puerto Viejo and Panama (via Sixaola) – terminate at the Transportes MEPE stop at C 3, Av 4, 100m north of the Mercado.

For **information**, you'll need to contact the San José ICT (☎223-1733), as there's no official tourist office in the entire province. The Banco de Costa Rica, on Av 2, C 1, will **change money**, as will Scotiabank, on Av 3, C2. The **correo** (Mon–Fri 7.30am–5pm, Sat 8am–noon) is at Av 2, C 4, though the mail service from Limón is dreadful – you're better off posting items from San José. There's **Internet access** at the *NetCafé* on Av 4, C 5/6. **Taxis** line up on the corner of Av 2, C 1. Note that during the El Día de la Raza Carnaval everything shuts for a week, including all the banks and the post office. Should you need **medical care**, head for Hospital Dr Tony Facio Castro (☎758-2222), at the north end of the *malecón* (sea wall), or the 24hr Red Cross centre on Av 1, one block south of the market.

Although Limón is not quite the mugger's paradise it's sometimes made out to be in the Highland media, standing on the sidewalk and looking lost is not recommended, nor is carrying valuables (most of the hotels we have listed have safes). As opposed to other Costa Rican towns, Limón's avenidas run more or less east–west in numerical order, starting at the docks. Calles run north–south, beginning with C 1 on the western boundary of Parque Vargas, by the *malecón*.

Accommodation

It's worth shelling out a bit for a **room** in Limón, especially if you're travelling alone – this is a place where the comfort and safety of your hotel makes a big difference to your peace of mind. If driving, it's certainly worth either booking a room

Carnaval in Limón

Though in the rest of the Americas **Carnaval** is usually associated with the days before Lent, Limón takes Columbus's arrival in the New World – October 12 – as its point of celebration. The idea was first brought to Limón by a local man named Arthur King, who had been away working in Panama's Canal Zone and was so impressed with that country's Columbus Day celebrations that he decided to bring the merriment home with him. Today **El Día de la Raza** (Day of the People) is basically an excuse to party.

The carnival features a variety of events, from Afro-Caribbean dance to Calypso music, bull-running, afternoon children's theatre, colourful *desfiles* (parades) and massive firework displays. Most spectacular is the **Grand Desfile**, usually held on the Saturday before October 12, when revellers in Afro-Caribbean costumes – sequins, spangles, fluorescent colours – parade through the streets to a cacophony of tambourines, whistles and blasting sound-systems.

at the *Hotel Acón*, one of only a few that have private parking, or storing your car in a guarded 24hr parking lot as opportunistic car theft is rife. In midweek the town's hotels fill up very quickly with commercial travellers; try to get to Limón as early as possible if you're arriving on a Wednesday or Thursday.

Staying **downtown** keeps you in the thick of things, and many hotels have communal balconies, perfect for relaxing with a cold beer above the lively street activity below. The downside of this is noise, especially at night. There's a group of quieter hotels outside town, about 4km up the road to Moín at **Portete** and **Playa Bonita**. A taxi up here costs less than US$2, and the bus to and from Moín runs along the road every twenty minutes or so. In all but the most upmarket places, avoid drinking the **tap water**.

Hotel prices rise by as much as fifty percent for **carnival** week, and to a lesser extent during Semana Santa, or Easter week. The least expensive times to stay are between July and October, and December to February, which (confusingly) are considered high season in the rest of the country. Limón has its share of dives, which tend to fill when there's a big ship in town. None of the places listed here is rock-bottom cheap. If this is what you're after, you'll find it easily enough, but always ask to see the room first and inspect the bathroom, in particular.

In town

Hotel Acón Av 3, C 2/3 ⓣ758-1010, ⓕ758-2924. Large, central hotel with rather gloomy, but well-equipped, rooms with TV, a/c and hot water. Private parking. ❺

Hotel Caribe Av 2, C 1, above the *Brisas del Caribe* restaurant ⓣ758-0138. Plain, but spacious, rooms with TV and fan, though they can be noisy at night. ❹

Hotel Miami Av 2, C 4/5 ⓣ & ⓕ758-0490. Friendly place whose clean rooms all have ceiling fans, cable TV and private bathrooms. ❹

Hotel Park Av 3, C 1, by the *malecón* ⓣ798-0555 or 758-4364, ⓔirlixie@sol.racsa.co.cr. The smartest option in town, popular with Ticos and travellers alike, so you'll have to book in advance. The most expensive rooms come with a sea view, slightly less expensive ones with a street view, and the cheapest, *plana turista*, no view at all. There's a good restaurant, too. ❺–❻

Hotel Teté Av 3, C4/5 ⓣ758-1122, ⓕ798-0470. Clean and well-cared-for hotel, with friendly staff – although nothing special, it's the best-value downtown option in this price range. Rooms on the street have balconies, but can be noisy; those inside are a little darker, but quieter. ❹

Portete and Playa Bonita

Cabinas Maeva Portete – look for the blue-and-white sign ⓣ758-2024. The best-value accommodation in Limón, with cute, yellow hexagonal cabinas nestling among palm trees, plus a beautiful pool and Neoclassical statues. ❹

Hotel Cocori Playa Bonita ⓣ795-1670, ⓕ795-2930. On the waterfront with clean, basic rooms (all with TV, some with sea views), a small restaurant and a swimming pool. Breakfast included. ❻

The Town

Fifteen minutes' walk around Puerto Limón and you've seen the lot – you may even spot one of the vultures that occasionally hang out on street corners. The partly pedestrianised **Avenida 2**, known locally as the "market street", is for all purposes the main drag, touching the north edge of Parque Vargas and the south side of the **Mercado Central**. The market is as good a place as any to start your explorations, and at times seems to be full of the entire town population, with dowager women minding their patch as thin men flutter their hands, clutching cigarettes and gesticulating jerkily. The *sodas* and snack bars here are good places to grab a bite.

Shops in Limón close over lunch, between noon and 2pm, when everyone drifts towards **Parque Vargas**, at the easternmost end of C 1 and Av 1/2, and the **malecón** to sit under the shady palms. A little shabby today, the park features a sea-facing mural by artist Guadalupe Alvarea depicting colourful and evocative images of the province's tough history. From here the *malecón* winds its way north – avoid it at night, as muggings have been reported.

As for other activities in town, forget **swimming**. One look at the water at the tiny spit of sand next to the *Hotel Park* is enough discouragement. There are few **day-trips** worth making from Limón. The trip up the canals to Tortuguero (see overleaf) takes three to five hours (with animal-spotting) one way, though it makes more sense to stay at least one night at Tortuguero, if doing this trip. A better possibility for a short boat trip is up the **Río Matina** from Moín – with a guide, you might be able to spot sloths, monkeys, iguanas and caimans. You could try the friendly and knowledgeable Bernardo R. Vargas (Ⓣ798-4322, Ⓕ758-2683), who also offers a packed one-day tour which takes in a walk in the rainforest at Aviarios del Caribe, the Parque Nacional Cahuita, a tour of local banana and coffee plantations and a city tour of Limón (US$40; 4–5hr).

Eating, drinking and entertainment

Limón has pretty good **food**, and variety too, but *Springfield* is the town's one authentic Creole restaurant, serving rice and beans cooked in coconut milk, jerk chicken and spicy meat stews. Inside the Mercado Central there's a host of decent *sodas* serving tasty *casados*. Outside Carnaval most people hang out with a beer in the evenings, but gringos in general and women especially should avoid most **bars** – especially those that have a large advertising placard blocking views of the interior. If you want to drink, stick to places like *Mares*, opposite the south side of the market, or *Brisas del Caribe*, next to the Parque Vargas. **Playa Bonita** is a great place for lunch or an afternoon beer, if you're tired of town.

In town

Brisas del Caribe Av 2, C 1, in the same building as the *Hotel Caribe*. Clean bar-restaurant with a good view of Parque Vargas. Except on nights when the sound-system is blasting, this is a quiet place to have a hassle-free coffee or beer. For food, there's a Chinese menu, as well as sandwiches, snacks and a good *medio casado* (half *casado*) for around US$2.

Park Hotel Av 3, C 1, by the *malecón*. The only restaurant in town where you feel you might actually be in the Caribbean – sea breezes float in through large slatted windows and all you can see is an expanse of blue sea and cloud. Excellent, though pricey, breakfast and standard Costa Rican fare.

Soda La Estrella C 5, Av 3/4. The best lunch in town: top marks for *soda* staples, excellent *refrescos*, coffee, snacks, basic plates and daily specials, all accompanied by cordial service.

Springfield north of the end of the *malecón*, across from the hospital. *The* place in Limón to get coconut-flavoured rice-and-beans with a choice of chicken, beef or fish (US$5). Try to arrive early, as the restaurant gets very full. Reggae-heavy discos are held on the outdoor dancefloor on weekends. Credit cards accepted.

Portete and Playa Bonita

Quimbambu Playa Bonita. Beach-bar with excellent, though pricey, fresh fish cooked to order. Live music at weekends.

El Ranchito in the *Maribú Caribe Hotel*, Portete. Peaceful and friendly poolside bar-restaurant high above the sea, offering excellent food and *refrescos*.

Moving on from Puerto Limón

Heading north to **Tortuguero**, shallow-bottomed private lanchas make the trip up the canal from the docks at Moín (3–5hr). It's best to arrive at the docks early (7–9am), although you may to be able to find boatmen willing to take you until 2pm. Expect to pay around US$50 each return for a group of four to six people; if you are travelling alone or in a couple, try to get a group together at the docks. Buses for **Moín** leave from the main bus terminal on C 0, Av 15/17, but the bus has no set schedule and only leaves when it's full (more or less every thirty minutes), so a taxi (US$2–3) may be a better option.

Buses to San José, run by Transportes Caribeños (see p.611), start running at 5am from the main bus terminal and continue hourly until 7pm. Prosersa (☎222-0610) also runs services from the main bus terminal to **Siquirres** and **Guápiles**, from where there are onward bus connections to the capital. Destinations **south of Limón** are served from the Transportes MEPE office (☎221-0524) at C 3, Av 4, 100m north of the Mercado Central, from where buses leave four times daily (from 7am until 6pm) to Cahuita (1hr) and five times (also from 7am until 6pm) direct to Puerto Viejo (1hr 30min–2hr). The **Sixaola** bus also stops in both places. Two buses (6am & 2.30pm; 2hr) go direct to **Manzanillo** village in the heart of the Gandoca-Manzanillo wildlife refuge, via Puerto Viejo.

Taxis line up on Av 2 around the corner from the main bus terminal: they'll do long-haul trips to Cahuita and Puerto Viejo (US$30–40), so if you're in a group, renting a taxi can be far more convenient than taking the bus.

Parque Nacional Tortuguero

Despite its isolation – 254km from San José by road and water, and 83km northwest of Limón – **PARQUE NACIONAL TORTUGUERO** is extremely popular with visitors. The park is one of the most important nesting sights in the world for the **green sea turtle**, which, along with the hawksbill, lays its eggs here between July and October. First established in the 1960s, Tortuguero covers a large area – 189.5 square kilometres to be exact – protecting not only the turtle nesting beach, but also surrounding forests, canals and waterways. Except for a short dry season during February and March, Tortuguero receives over 6000mm of rain a year, a soggy environment which hosts a wide abundance of species: fifty kinds of **fish**, caiman and **crocodiles**, numerous **birds**, including the endangered green parrot and the vulture, and some 160 kinds of **mammals**, several under the threat of extinction. It's the **turtles** that draw people here, however, and the sight of the gentle beasts tumbling ashore at night and shimmying their way up the beach to deposit their heavy load before limping back, spent, into the dark phosphorescent waves is truly moving.

The most popular way to see Tortuguero is on one of literally hundreds of **packages** that use the expensive "jungle lodges" across the canal from the village. These are usually two-night, three-day affairs, although you can certainly go for longer. Accommodation, meals and transport are taken care of, while guides point out wildlife along the river and canals on the way. The main difference between tours comes in the standard of hotels – check the reviews of the lodges on p.639 to help you choose. With a little planning, you can also get to Tortuguero **independently** and stay in cabinas in the village, which is a more interesting little place than initial impressions might suggest. Basing yourself here allows you to explore the beach at leisure – though the abundance of crocodiles and sharks means you shouldn't really swim – and leaves you in easy reach of restaurants and bars.

Getting to Tortuguero

The journey up the canals from Limón to Tortuguero is at least half the experience. Expect a three- or four-hour trip (sometimes longer) by lancha, depending upon where you embark – if on a package tour, it will probably be **Siquirres** on the Río Reventazón; if travelling independently, you'll find it easier to leave from **Moín**, near Puerto Limón. Either way you'll pass palm and deciduous trees, mirror-calm waters, and small stilt-legged wooden houses, brightly painted and poised on the water's edge – along, of course, with acres and acres of cleared land. Quite apart from the wildlife, the canal is a hive of human activity, with lanchas, *botes* (large canoes) and *pangas* (flat-bottomed boats with outboard motors) plying the glassy waters. Package tourists are disgorged at whichever of the lodges they are booked into.

If you're travelling **independently**, you ought to be able to find a boat at Moín willing to take you up the canal anytime from 6am until perhaps as late as 2pm (although it's best to set off early as the journey can take as long as five hours). You can arrange with your boatman when you would like to be picked up to return; it's really not worth going for the day – if you do, you'll have to make the return trip not later than 1.30pm to avoid getting stuck in the dark. Get a phone number from your boatman if possible, so you can call from Tortuguero village, if you change plans. The lanchas drop you at Tortuguero dock, from where you can walk to the village accommodation or take another lancha across the canal to the more expensive tourist lodges. If you haven't booked a hotel, be aware that accommodation in the village can fill up quickly during the turtle-nesting seasons (March–May & July–Oct).

Alternatively, you can do what the locals do and take the 9am bus from San José to **Cariari**, then switch to a bus for the **Geest banana plantation**, from where a boat goes to Tortuguero, leaving every day at around 1.30pm. It's a long journey, but the boat ride costs only US$10 each way, and if you're travelling alone it makes sense. The return boat to San José leaves daily at 7am.

If you come **by air** on one of Sansa's (Ⓣ221-9414, Ⓕ225-2176) or NatureAir's (Ⓣ220-3054, Ⓕ220-0413) daily flights, which leave early from San José (between 6–7am) and take approximately 35–50 minutes, you'll arrive at the airstrip some 4km north of the village. There are no taxis from here to the village, though the more upmarket lodges will come and pick you up; otherwise you'll have to walk.

The village

The peaceful village of **TORTUGUERO** lies at the northeastern corner of the national park, on a thin spit of land between the sea and the Tortuguero Canal. With its exuberant foliage of wisteria, oleander and bougainvillea, the whole place has the look of a somewhat dilapidated tropical garden. Tall palm groves and patchy expanses of grass are punctuated by zinc-roofed wooden houses, often elevated on stilts. This is classic Caribbean style: washed-out, slightly ramshackle and pastel-pretty, with very little to disturb the torpor until after dark.

A dirt path runs north–south through the village – the "main street" – from which narrow paths go off to the sea and the canal. Smack in the middle of the village stands one of the prettiest churches you'll see anywhere: pale yellow, with a small spire and an oval doorway. Nearby, the village's swanky new souvenir shop – complete with life-sized models of a leatherback and green turtle stationed outside – is very well-stocked with T-shirts, wooden souvenirs and cards. If the sun is getting to you, this is the place to pick up a hat or sunscreen. More souvenirs, albeit of slightly less authentic nature, are available at the purple Paraíso Tropical souvenir shop, which doubles as the village's NatureAir agent and sells tickets to San José.

Information

A display on the turtles' habits, habitat and history surrounds the **information kiosk** in the centre of the village. Officially, you should buy tickets for turtle tours here; the park rangers open the kiosk at 5pm, and this is a good time to find a local guide. In addition, Canadian naturalist and local resident Darryl Loth (Ⓣ709-8011,

Ⓕ709-8094, Ⓔsafari@racsa.co.cr), who runs the *Casa Marbella B&B*, as well as a small information office, can arrange tours, such as boat trips and hikes up Cerro Tortuguero (see p.641). At the north end of the village, there's also a **Natural History Museum** (daily 10am–5.30pm; US$1) run by the Caribbean Conservation Corporation (Ⓦwww.cccturtle.org), with a small but informative exhibition explaining the life cycle of sea turtles. You can watch a video explaining the history of turtle conservation in the area and, before you leave, you'll be invited to "adopt a turtle" for US$25, in return for which you'll receive an adoption certificate and information allowing you to track the migratory progress of your chosen beast on the Internet as it makes its purposeful way across the ocean.

Public **phones** are available at *Miss Junie's* restaurant, the Super Morpho supermarket by the football pitch and the Paraíso Tropical souvenir shop. There are no **bank** or money-changing facilities in Tortuguero – bring all the cash you'll need with you – and though there's a **correo** in the middle of the village, mail may take three or four weeks just to make its way to Puerto Limón.

Village accommodation

Staying at Tortuguero on the cheap entails bedding down in one of the independent **cabinas** in the village. **Camping** on the beach is not allowed, though you can set up tent at the mown enclosure at the **ranger station** (about US$2 per day) at the southern end of the village, where you enter the park. It's in a sheltered situation, away from the sea breezes, with water and toilets, but bring a ground sheet and mosquito net, and make sure your tent is waterproof.

Cabinas Aracari south of the information kiosk and football pitch Ⓣ798-3059. Clean, comfortable cabinas, all with private bath, cold water and fan, set in a beautiful tree-filled garden and run by a friendly local family. ❸

Cabinas Mary Scar east of the *pulpería*, before the beach Ⓣ220-1478. Two new cabins with private bathrooms, plus some older cabinas with shared bathroom – they're slightly gloomy, but very clean, and the bathroom is spick-and-span (and at just US$10 per person, something of a bargain). Family atmosphere, with simple meals (about US$3) cooked on request. ❷–❸

Cabinas Tortuguero south of the village, towards the entry to the national park Ⓔtinamon@racsa.co.cr. A good budget option, with five simple rooms (all en suite with fans) in a lovely garden and Italian food available on request (breakfast US$3, lunch or supper US$5). Canoes available for hire. ❷

Casa Marbella next to the information kiosk Ⓣ798-3059, Ⓦcasamarbella.tripod.com. Run by committed Canadian environmentalist Daryl Loth (an inexhaustible source of information on the flora and fauna of the area), this friendly B&B has four large, comfortable en-suite rooms. Breakfast is served on a small terrace overlooking the canal. Tours offered. ❹

Miss Junie's at the north end of the village, just before the Natural History Museum Ⓣ710-0523. Tortuguero's most popular cook (see p.640) is expanding her empire, hence the brand new restaurant next door and this refurbished complex of simply decorated, comfortable rooms all with private bath, hot water and fan. Excellent breakfast included in the price. ❺

The lodges

Staying at Tortuguero's **lodges**, most of which are across the canal from the village, has its drawbacks. Though convenient and, at the top end of the scale, rather luxurious, life as a lodger can be a pretty regimented affair, with guests shuttled in and out of the lodges with stop-watch-like precision, tour itineraries and meal times strictly adhered to and precious little nightlife. If you want to explore the village and the beach on your own, you have to get a lancha across the canal. Although this service is free, it's inconvenient and, outside the turtle-watching season, most lodges don't operate their boats at night. The lodges only rent rooms to independent travellers if they have space, which they rarely do owing to Tortuguero's perennial popularity; no official prices are posted for non-package rooms.

Tour operators to Tortuguero

A number of operators in San José and Limón offer **packages to Tortuguero**, some with accommodation (in the lodges) and meals included. Though you could usually fix things up more cheaply yourself, these save a lot of hassle, and many of them are very good value.

Costa Rica Expeditions C Central, Av 3, San José ⓣ257-0766, ⓕ257-1665, ⓦwww.costaricaexpeditions.com. The most upmarket and efficient Tortuguero packages, with accommodation at the comfortable *Tortuga Lodge* (from US$300 per person for a three-day, two-night package, including flights from San José). They also do trips to Barra del Colorado.

Ecole Travel C 7, Av 0/1, San José ⓣ223-2240, ⓕ223-4128, ⓦwww.ecoletravel.com. One of the longest-established companies going to Tortuguero and the best budget option, popular with students and backpackers – tours (from US$125 for two days and one night) start from Moín dock near Puerto Limón.

Grupo Mawamba at the *Mawamba Lodge* in Tortuguero, or in San José at C 24, Av 5/7 ⓣ293-8181, ⓕ239-7657, ⓦwww.grupomawamba.com. The best mid-range tour operator, providing superior, but affordable, packages staying at the *Mawamba Lodge*. The tours generally last three days (2 nights) and cost around US$260 per person, although longer stays can be arranged.

Riverboat Francesca Tours ⓣ226-0986, ⓦwww.tortuguerocanals.com. Good-value two-day, one-night tours of the Tortuguero canals for US$175. The price includes bus transportation from San José to Moín (where you embark for the canal tour), meals and lodging.

Jungle Lodge 1km north of the village, across the canal ⓣ233-0155, ⓕ233-0778. Friendly, comfortable and unpretentious lodge, set in its own gardens, with en-suite rooms, a good restaurant, games room, small disco, pool, free canoes and a lagoon. Good value. ❼

Laguna Lodge ⓣ225-3740, ⓕ283-8031, ⓦwww.lagunatortuguero.com. Extremely well-equipped lodge with riverside bar, pool, beach access and a new conference centre (which looks like a giant turtle as envisaged by Gaudí). The regime here is perhaps a little too strict to be truly comfortable, but the food and rooms are perfectly serviceable and the tour guides extremely knowledgeable – this is one of the only lodges to offer hiking trips through the jungle as well as canal tours. ❼

El Manatí 1.5km north of the village, across the canal ⓣ & ⓕ383-0330. Tortuguero's best budget lodge, this peaceful family-run affair has basic, but clean, rooms with private bath, hot water and fans, as well as several attractive two-bedroom cabinas. US$20 per person with breakfast included. ❺

Mawamba Lodge 1km north of the village ⓣ293-8181, ⓕ239-7657, ⓦwww.grupomawamba.com. Large, ritzy lodge where the well-organized facilities include a daily slide-show, environmentally friendly boats and round-the-clock cold beers. The cabina-style rooms have ceiling fans and private bathrooms; there's a large pool and Jacuzzi, and the village and the sea are just a short walk away. ❻

Pachira Lodge opposite the village ⓣ256-7080, ⓕ223-1119, ⓦwww.pachiralodge.com. Tortuguero's newest lodge, this luxurious establishment has spacious and attractive rooms in wood cabins, linked by covered walkways, with large en-suite, hot-water bathrooms, as well as a pool and imaginative tour options. ❻

Tortuga Lodge owned by Costa Rica Expeditions ⓣ257-0766, ⓕ257-1665, ⓦwww.costaricaexpeditions.com. The plushest lodge in the area, though it's furthest from the village, with exemplary (if slightly overattentive) service, excellent food, large, attractive en-suite rooms, a riverside pool and elegantly landscaped grounds with walking trails. ❼

Eating, drinking and nightlife

Tortuguero village offers good homely food, typically Caribbean, with wonderful fresh **fish**. The only disadvantage is that prices tend to be high: expect to pay up to twice as much for a meal as you'd pay in other parts of Costa Rica. For entertainment, the Centro Social La Culebra has a nightly **disco**, though the clientele can be a bit rough. *Bar Brisas del Mar* (known to the locals as *El Bochinche*) is better, with a large, semi-open-air dancefloor and a good sound-and-light system (when it's not visiting Limón). You can hear the sea from your table, and the atmosphere is low-key except on Saturday nights, when the lively weekly disco attracts a large local crowd and goes on well into the small hours.

Miss Junie's north end of village path, 50m before the Natural History Museum. The town's best restaurant offers solid Caribbean food – red beans, jerk chicken, rice, chayote and breadfruit, all on the same plate – by local cook Miss Junie, dished up with ice-cold beers.

Miss Miriam's adjacent to village football pitch. Cheerful and immaculate restaurant serving Caribbean food at very reasonable prices. Rooms available.

El Muellecito next to the *pulpería*. Tortuguero's best breakfast option, with tasty pancakes and fruit salad. Closes at 8pm.

Tropical Lodge Bar mid-village on the path to the national park entrance. Noisy and entertaining village bar with perfect sunset views over the river. Rooms with private bath, hot water and TV also available.

The Vine opposite the Jungle Souvenir Shop. Café, run by the owners of the souvenir shop, with good coffee, cheesecake and brownies. Closed during the rainy season.

Visiting the park

Most people come to Tortuguero to see the turtles laying their eggs, the so-called **desove**. Few are disappointed, as the majority of tours during laying **seasons** (March–May & July–Oct) result in sightings of the moving, surreal procession of the reptiles from the sea to make their egg-nests in the sand. Most turtles come ashore during the relative safety of night. Often dozens of turtles emerge from the sea at the same time and march up the sands to their chosen spots. Each turtle lays eighty or more eggs – the collective whirring noise of sand being dug away is extraordinary.

Although Tortuguero is by no means the only place in Costa Rica to see marine turtles nesting (they use the Pacific beaches, too), three of the largest kinds of endangered sea turtles regularly nest here in large numbers. Along with the **green** (*verde*) turtle, named for the colour of soup made from its flesh, you might see the **hawksbill** (*carey*), with its distinctive hooked beak, and the ridged **leatherback** (*baula*), the largest turtle in the world, which can easily weigh 300kg – some are as heavy as 500kg and reach 5m in length. The green turtles and hawksbills nest in the greatest numbers from July to October (August is the peak month); the leatherbacks come ashore from March to May.

Turtle tours, led by certified guides, leave at 8pm and 10pm every night from the village. If you're not going with an organized group from one of the lodges, you'll need to buy park entrance tickets (US$7) from the kiosk in the village, which is manned by park rangers from 5pm to 6pm every afternoon. There are more than a hundred certified guides in Tortuguero; they charge around US$10 for the turtle tour (roughly half the price of a lodge tour) and tend to hang around the ticket kiosk at 5pm in search of custom. Be sure to get there early as numbers are strictly limited. No more than 200 people are allowed on the beach at any one time. Visitors must wear dark clothing, refrain from smoking and are not allowed to bring cameras (still or video) or flashlights. Everyone must be off the beach by midnight.

During the day you can walk a single, generally well-maintained, self-guided trail (1km), the **Sendero Natural**, which starts at the entrance, just south of the village, and skirts a small swamp. As for that long, wild **beach**, you can amble for up to 30km south and enjoy crab-spotting or birdwatching, as well as looking for turtle tracks, which resemble the two thick parallel lines a truck would leave in its wake. Swimming is not a good idea, due to heavy waves, turbulent currents and sharks. Remember that you need to pay **park fees** to walk on the beach or along the trail.

Other activities around Tortuguero

Almost as popular as the turtle tours are Tortuguero's **boat tours** through the *caños*, or lagoons, to spot animals, including monkeys, caiman and Jesus Christ lizards, and birds, such as herons, cranes and kingfishers. Most lodges have **canoes** you can take out on the canal – a great way to get around, if you're handy with a paddle, but do stick to the main canal as it's easy to get lost in the complex lagoon system northwest of the village. In the south of the village, Ruben Aragón, 50m north of the ranger station, right by the water, rents traditional Miskito-style boats and canoes for about US$8 an hour, or US$15 with a guide-paddler.

It's also possible to climb **Cerro Tortuguero**, an ancient volcanic deposit looming 119m above the flat coastal plain 6km north of the village. A climb up the gently sloping side (90min round-trip) leads you to the "peak", from where there are good views of flat jungle and inland waterways. Ask at the village information kiosk or at the ranger station.

Cahuita village and Parque Nacional Cahuita

The tiny coastal village of **CAHUITA**, 43km southeast of Limón, is reached on the paved Hwy-36, which runs from Limón to Sixaola on the Panamanian border. Like other villages on the Talamanca coast, especially Puerto Viejo de Talamanca (see p.644) and Manzanillo (see p.647), it has become increasingly popular with backpackers and surfers for its laid-back atmosphere, walking opportunities and proximity to the highly regarded surfing beaches further south down the coast, along with the added appeal of great Afro-Caribbean food. Near the village, the **Parque Nacional Cahuita** was formed mainly to protect one of the only living coral reefs in Costa Rica; many people come here to **snorkel** and take rides in glass-bottomed boats. Though it's mainly wet all year round, the local "dry" season is between March and April, and from September to October.

Although tourism has undoubtedly brought prosperity to the village, it has also created problems – Cahuita has had its problems with drugs and opportunistic theft, and it's worth being cautious: lock your door and windows, never leave anything on the beach and avoid walking alone in unlit places at night. Nude or topless bathing is definitely unacceptable, as is wandering through the village in just a bathing suit. With a bit of common sense, though, most travellers really enjoy the community and atmosphere here.

Arrival and information

The easiest way to get to Cahuita from San José is by **bus** on the direct Transportes MEPE service (4 daily; 4hr), which goes on to Puerto Viejo. Taking a bus from San José to Puerto Limón (3hr) and then changing for Cahuita (4 daily) is only marginally less expensive than taking the direct bus and increases travelling time by at least an hour. In Cahuita buses stop at the central crossroads opposite *Sarafinas* bar-disco, which has a colourful and detailed map of the village painted on its exterior. Current timetables are posted in front of the Cahuita Tours office, 200m north along the village's main street.

Information

If you can find it, pick up a copy of the free *Costa Rican Caribbean Info Guide*, which unfolds into maps of the local area and a directory of accommodation and businesses in Cahuita. The only sources of visitor **information** in the village itself are the tour companies: Mr Big J's (☎755-0328), towards the Parque Nacional Cahuita *puesto* and beach, has a book exchange and laundry facilities; Cahuita Tours (☎755-0000) has public phones where you can make international calls; and Turistica Cahuita (☎755-0017) sells the *Tico Times*. There's **Internet access** at the

CyberNet Café in *Cabinas Palmar* (7.30am–10pm). There are no banks in town – the nearest are in Bribrí, 20km away, or Limón. Your best bet for **changing money**, travellers' cheques and obtaining cash advances on credit cards is the efficient cambio (7am–4pm) at *Cabinas Safari*; the Safari Supermarket changes cash only. The small police station (*guardia rural*) is on the last beach-bound road at the north end of the village; the **correo** next door (theoretically Mon–Fri 7.30am–5pm) keeps erratic hours, to say the least.

Accommodation

Though Cahuita is popular with budget travellers, it's not rock-bottom cheap. Groups get the best deal, as most **cabinas** charge per room and have space for at least three or four people. Though accommodation tends to be of the concrete-cell variety, standards are high, with fans, mosquito nets, clean sheets and bathrooms. Upstairs rooms are usually slightly more expensive, with sea breezes and maybe views.

The **centre of the village** has scores of options, the best of which are listed below – staying here is convenient for restaurants, bars and the national park. There's also accommodation in all price ranges along the long (3km or so) road that runs by the sea north along **Black-Sand Beach**. It's quieter here, and the beach is not bad, though women (even if travelling in groups) and those without their own car are better off staying in town, since a number of rapes and muggings have been committed along this road at night. You should **book ahead** on weekends during the Highland dry season (Dec–April).

Several **camping** options can be found in the vicinity, the nicest being at the Puerto Vargas ranger station in the national park (see opposite).

In the village

Cabinas Arrecife on the seafront just north of the police station ⓣ & ⓕ775-0081. A relaxed, backpacker-style atmosphere with hammocks slung up on the porch, cheap, simply furnished rooms and snorkeling gear for hire. ❹

Cabinas Jenny on the beach ⓣ755 0256. Beautiful rooms, especially the more expensive ones upstairs, with high wooden ceilings, sturdy bunks, mosquito nets, fans and wonderful sea views. Deck chairs and hammocks are provided, and there are good stout locks on all doors. ❹

Cabinas Sol y Mar towards Kelly Creek ⓣ755-0237, ⓔcabsolymar@hotmail.com. Small, basic rooms (with hot water) run by friendly locals, who also run the neighbouring *soda*; clean and safe. ❸

Hotel Kelly Creek beside the national park beach ⓣ755-0007, ⓦwww.hotelkellycreek.com. Four vast, wood-panelled rooms right by the park entrance, with mosquito nets and a good Spanish restaurant on site. ❺

Black-Sand Beach

Atlantida Lodge next to the football pitch on the road to Black-Sand Beach, about 1km from the village ⓣ755-0115, ⓕ755-0213, ⓦwww.atlantida.co.cr. The best of the village's pricier options: a friendly spot, with patio, pretty grounds, good security and the nicest pool in town (complete with Jacuzzi and poolside bar). The cool rooms are decorated in tropical yellows and pinks, with heated water, and there's free coffee and bananas all day. Bike rental also available. ❼

Bungalows Malu beyond the soccer field ⓣ755-0006. Five pretty, individual cabinas in a large tropical garden facing the sea, with an Italian restaurant on site. ❻

Cabinas Algebra 2km or so up the road to Black-Sand Beach ⓣ & ⓕ755-0057, ⓔalansa@racsa.co.cr. Attractive cabinas some distance from town, but the good *Bananas Restaurant* is on site; run by a friendly Austrian couple, who offer haircuts, laundry service and free pick-up from the village. ❺

Cabinas Iguana 200m south of *Soda Bambata* on a small side road ⓣ755-0005, ⓕ755-0054, ⓦwww.cabinas-iguana.com. Some of the best budget accommodation in town, with lovely wood-panelled cabinas on stilts, set back from the beach, and a main lodge with a big screened veranda, plus laundry service, book exchange and a small pool. The friendly owners also rent out two apartments and a three-bedroom house with kitchen. ❸

The village

Cahuita proper comprises just two puddle-dotted, gravel-and-sand streets running parallel to the sea, intersected by a few cross-streets along the way. Though it seems like anything nailed down has been turned into some kind of small business, you'll still see a couple of private homes among the haphazard conglomeration of signs advertising cabinas and restaurants. Few locals drive (bicycles are popular), so most of the vehicles you see kicking up the dust belong to tourists.

Cahuita's main street runs from the national park entrance at Kelly Creek to the northern end of the village, marked more or less by the football pitch. Beyond here it continues two or three kilometres north along Black-Sand Beach. At the central crossroads downtown, the small park, with its three small busts of Cahuita's founding fathers, is the focal point of the village, where locals wait for buses to San José and catch up on recent gossip. Opposite, *Coco's* disco and bar is *the* place to hang out at night; at weekends its breezy veranda is crammed full of partygoers and gaggles of young backpackers soaking up the atmosphere.

You can swim on either of the village's two beaches, although neither is fantastic: the first 400m or so of the narrow white-sand beach just south of town is particularly dangerous on account of riptides; **Black-Sand Beach** is littered with driftwood, although you can swim in some places. Sometimes called **Playa Vargas**, the beach south of Punta Cahuita in Parque Nacional Cahuita is better for swimming than those in the village. It's protected from raking breakers by the coral reef and is now patrolled by lifeguards; however, it's slightly awkward to get to (see below).

The principal daylight activity in Cahuita is taking a boat trip out to the park's coral reef to **snorkel** – try one of the town's three tour companies – or you can indulge off the beach at Playa Vargas. Though you can **surf** at Cahuita, Puerto Viejo (see overleaf) has better waves; Cahuita Tours and Turística Cahuita both rent out boards. Wherever you swim, either in the park itself or on Black-Sand Beach, don't leave possessions unattended, as even your grubby T-shirt and old shorts may be stolen. If you don't fancy snorkelling, Mr Big J's organizes **horse rides** along the beach and jungle hikes (US$20–30), and all of the tour agencies in Cahuita offer combined Jeep trips to local villages and nearby beaches (US$40).

Visiting the park

Parque Nacional Cahuita (daily 8am–5pm; "pay what you want" if entering at Kelly Creek; US$7 at the Puerto Vargas entrance, 4km south of Cahuita along the Limón–Sixaola road) is one of the smallest in the country, covering the wedge-shaped piece of land from Punta Cahuita back to the main highway from Puerto Limón to Sixaola and, crucially, the **coral reef** about 500m offshore. On land, Cahuita protects the littoral, or coastal, rainforest, a lowland habitat of semi-mangroves and tall canopy cover which backs the gently curving white-sand beaches of Playa Vargas to the south of Punta Cahuita and Playa Cahuita to the north. **Birds**, including ibis and kingfishers, are in residence, along with white-faced (*carablanca*) monkeys, sloths and snakes, but the only animals you're likely to see are howler monkeys, and perhaps coati.

The park's one **trail** (7km), skirting the beach, is a very easy, level walk, with a path so wide it feels like a road, covered with leaves and other brush, and a few fallen trees and logs. The Río Perzoso, about 2km from the Kelly Creek entrance, or 5km from the Puerto Vargas trailhead, is not always fordable. Similiarly, at high tide the beach is impassable in places: ask the ranger at the Puerto Vargas *puesto* about the *marea*, or tide, schedules. Walking this trail can also be unpleasantly humid and buggy: best to go in the morning.

Many **snorkellers** swim the 200 to 500m from Puerto Vargas out to the reef. Again, you should ask about currents, although the water here is calmer than at the beach next to Cahuita village. Camping facilities are available near the Puerto Vargas *puesto* entrance (US$2 per person).

Moving on from Cahuita

There are nine buses daily to **Limón**, where you can connect for **San José**, but if you're in a hurry to reach the capital it's faster and easier to take the direct non-stop service (4 daily; 4hr), run by Transportes MEPE. For **Puerto Viejo**, a local bus leaves Cahuita eight times daily, taking forty minutes (first bus at 6am, last at 7pm) and continuing on from Puerto Viejo to **Bribrí** and then **Sixaola** and the border.

Eating, drinking and nightlife

Cahuita has plenty of places **to eat** fresh local food, with a surprisingly cosmopolitan selection. As with accommodation, prices are not low – an evening meal starts at around US$5 – and service tends to be laid-back: leave yourself lots of time to eat. **Nightlife** in Cahuita revolves around having a beer and listening to music. At weekends the village's two discos, *Sarafinas* and *Coco's*, get very sweaty, with customers spilling out onto the street and cranked-up sound-systems playing on until the small hours.

Bar Hannia village centre. Small, friendly bar with cold beer and a relaxed atmosphere.
ChaChaCha next to Cahuita Tours. Fantastic gourmet cuisine – exotic salads, grilled squid, seafood and Tex-Mex – at very reasonable prices and served in a pretty setting with fresh flowers on the tables and fairy lights at night.
Chao's Paradise Black-Sand Beach. Groovy little joint serving up posh Creole cooking using the freshest ingredients.
Palenque Luisa village centre, opposite *Bar Hannia*. Good-value and popular restaurant with extensive menu, including *casados*, fish and Creole dishes, plus live calypso music on Saturday nights.
El Parquecito behind the village park. Best place in the village for breakfast, with fresh juices, pancakes and French toast.
Sobre Las Ollas at the northern end of the village, on the beach. Atmospheric and classy hangout with first-rate seafood – the lobster is delicious – and the sound of lapping waves in the background, though it's not cheap. Closed Tues.
Vista de Mar by Kelly Creek. Known to the locals as "El Chines", this barn-sized restaurant has a vast menu, featuring inexpensive rice-and-bean combos, fish and Chinese food. It's popular with backpackers, and can get very crowded.

Puerto Viejo de Talamanca and around

The 12km of coast between the languorous hamlet of **PUERTO VIEJO DE TALAMANCA**, 18km southeast of Cahuita, and **Manzanillo** village is one of the most beautiful stretches in the country. Though not spectacular for swimming, the **beaches** – Playa Chiquita, Punta Uva and Manzanillo – are the most picturesque on the entire coast; there's also plenty of accommodation, and it's livelier than Cahuita.

It's **surfing** that really pulls the crowds; the stretch south of *Stanford's* restaurant at the southern end of the village offers some of the most challenging waves in the country, and certainly the best on Costa Rica's Caribbean coast. Puerto Viejo's famous "**La Salsa Brava**" crashes ashore between December and March and from June to July. September and October, when La Salsa Brava goes away to wherever big waves go, are the quietest months of the year.

The **village** itself lies between the thick forested hills of the Talamanca mountains and the sea, where locals bathe and kids frolic with surfboards in the waves. It's a dusty little place in daylight hours, but it's reasonably well cared for, with bright hand-painted signs pointing the way to cabinas, bars and restaurants. The main drag through the centre, potholed and rough, is criss-crossed by a few dirt streets and an offshoot road that follows the shore. As in Cahuita, many Europeans and Americans have been drawn to Puerto Viejo and have set up their own businesses (you'll find plenty of places offering health foods and New Age remedies); and like Cahuita, most locals are of Afro-Caribbean descent. In recent years, Puerto Viejo's backpacker and surf-party culture has created a small **drugs scene**, though this is fairly low-key and shouldn't adversely affect your stay. Nevertheless, it's best to make sure your room is well secured at night, and to avoid wandering through the quiet fringes of the village alone in the small hours.

Arrival

All buses **from San José** to Puerto Viejo stop first in Limón and Cahuita (4 daily; 4hr 30min) and then go on to **Sixaola**, with the first one leaving San José at 6am and the last one at 3.30pm. The last bus back to San José departs at 4pm. Taking a bus from San José to Limón (every half-hour 5am–7pm) and changing there is only marginally less expensive, and will increase travelling time by an hour at least. Three buses daily go along the coast to **Manzanillo** (45min). If driving, be aware that the coast road south of Puerto Viejo is unpaved and very bumpy. As with Cahuita, the best way to negotiate Puerto Viejo's potholed, dirt-track streets is by bicycle. Several hire shops can be found in town, and many of the local hotels and cabinas also rent out bikes (US$3–4 per day).

Information

Puerto Viejo has no tourist information office, but as with Cahuita, the village's tour operators can give you advice and maps. The most helpful operator is **Puerto Viejo Tours** (Tues–Sun 8am–noon & 2pm–6pm; Ⓣ & Ⓕ750-0411, Ⓔpuertoviejotours@yahoo.com), opposite the bus stop on the seafront, which offers a wide range of tours, including rafting, horse-riding, snorkelling and birdwatching. They'll also change dollars and travellers' cheques, as will the nearby Comisaratio store. **Terraventuras Tours** (Ⓣ750-0426, Ⓔterraventuras@hotmail.com), on the main

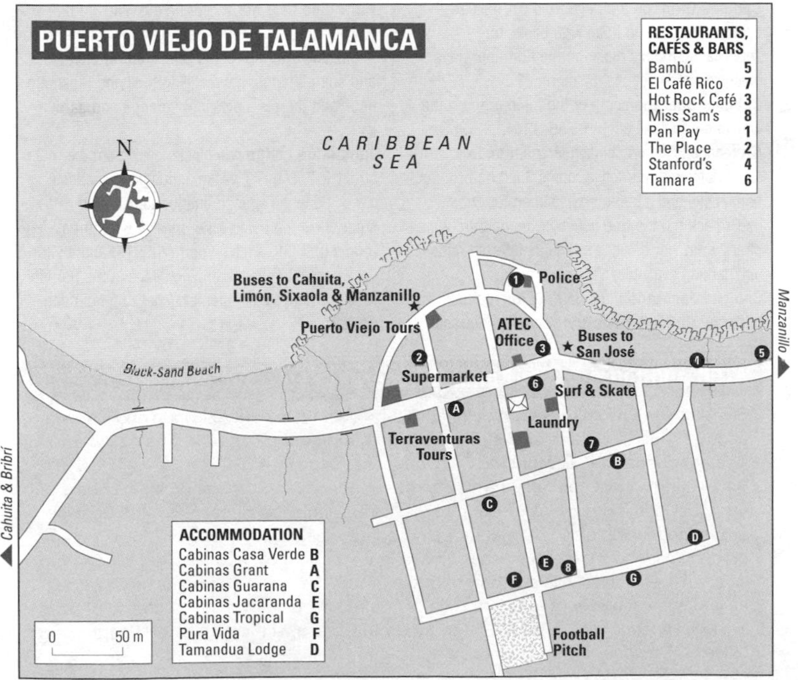

street, rents out snorkelling equipment at very reasonable rates, and **Surf & Skate** rents out surf and boogie boards and can organize surfing lessons. If you're interested in ecology, the proprietor of *Cabinas Tropical*, author and biologist Rolf Blancke (ⓣ750-0283, ⓔrblancke@racsa.co.cr), takes people out on excellent trips into the Gandoca rainforest (US$45 for a 12hr trip).

The **correo** (Mon–Fri 7.30am–6pm, Sat 7.30am–noon) is situated in the small commercial centre two blocks back from the seafront. A laundry service is next door. For film and other essentials, head for El Buen Precio **supermarket**, which has two public **phones**, as does the office of the ecotourism group ATEC, on the main road. Next to ATEC, there's an **Internet** café, *Video Mundo*.

Accommodation

Due to its rapidly increasing popularity, places to stay in and around Puerto Viejo have mushroomed and you shouldn't normally have any problem finding accommodation, although it's still best to reserve a room in advance during high season and surfing-season weekends (Dec–March, June & July). The vast majority of places to stay in the **village** are simple cabinas, some without hot water, while more upmarket establishments line the **coast** south of the village. You can **camp** on the beaches, but rock-bottom budget travellers usually forsake their tents for a little extra comfort.

Cabinas Casa Verde one block south of the main drag ⓣ & ⓕ750-0047, ⓦwww.cabinascasaverde.com. Fourteen fantastic-value cabinas, decorated with shell mobiles and pieces of washed-up coral, with very clean showers, ceiling fans, mosquito nets and space to sling hammocks. Bike rental and parking available. ❺

Cabinas Grant on the main road ⓣ750-0292. Spotless, locally run hotel with basic, but serviceable, rooms: those on the first floor have balconies and cost slightly more. ❹

Cabinas Guarana south of the main drag on the way to the football pitch ⓣ750-0244, ⓦgreencoast.com/cabinasguarana.htm. Excellent small hotel with attractive rooms, tiled bathrooms, hammocks and a communal kitchen for guests' use. Check out the tree house in the garden, which offers great views over the village. Internet access and parking available. ❺

Cabinas Jacaranda just north of the football pitch ⓣ750-0069. Basic, but very clean, budget option, with lively Guatemalan fabrics and a lush tropical garden. ❹

Cabinas Tropical on the eastern edge of the village ⓣ & ⓕ750-0283, ⓦwww.cabinastropical.com. Small, quiet and scrupulously clean hotel with five large, comfortable rooms and pet birds in the garden. ❹–❺

Pura Vida near the soccer field ⓣ750-0002, ⓕ750-0296. Popular budget hotel, which tends to fill quickly. The ten rooms (a mixture of private and shared baths) have ceiling fans and mosquito nets, and there's a pleasant veranda and garden. ❹

Tamandua Lodge two blocks back from the main street ⓣ750-0479, ⓔtamandua_lodge@racsa.co.cr. Recently opened budget hotel aimed squarely at the backpacker market with three rooms (US$20), a mixed dorm (US$15) and, by far the cheapest option, camping space in the garden (US$3). There's also Internet access and parking. ❸–❹

ATEC and tours to the Kéköldi Reserve

Skirted by the **Kéköldi Reserve**, inhabited by about two hundred Bribrí and Cabécar peoples, Puerto Viejo retains strong links with **indigenous culture**. The Associación Talamanqueña de Ecoturismo y Conservación, or **ATEC** (ⓣ & ⓕ750-0191, ⓦwww.greencoast.com/atec.htm), is a grassroots organization set up by members of the local community – Afro-Caribbeans, Bribrí indigenous peoples and Spanish-descended inhabitants. As well as being able to tell you where to buy locally made products, such as banana vinegar, guava jam, coconut oil, and jewellery made from coconut shells, seashells and bamboo, the group arranges some of the most authentic and interesting **tours** in Costa Rica. If you're spending even just a couple of days in the Talamanca region, an ATEC-arranged trip is a must – contact their Puerto Viejo office at least one day in advance.

Eating, drinking and nightlife

Puerto Viejo has a surprisingly cosmopolitan range of **places to eat**. Good, traditional **Creole food** is served at *Miss Sam's*, and ATEC can put you in touch with village women who cook typical regional meals on request. Although relatively quiet during the day, Puerto Viejo has a lively **nightlife**. If you're after a peaceful drink, one of the nicest spots in town is the spacious veranda in front of the Comisaratio store – buy your beer from the shop and drink it from the bottle as you watch the sun slide into the sea.

Bambú on the eastern edge of town. Beachfront reggae disco with good sunset views from its terrace, which gets absolutely packed on Mondays and Fridays; great fun.

El Café Rico opposite *Cabinas Casa Verde*. Dutch-run café with the best coffee in town, tasty sandwiches, crepes and breakfast. Nice rooms (❹), bike rental and laundry service also available.

Hot Rock Café on the main street, near ATEC. One of the town's more openly touristy places, it shows a movie to its largely American clientele at 7pm each night, usually followed by live music (Latin or reggae).

Miss Sam's three blocks back from the seafront. Wonderful Caribbean home-cooking at very reasonable prices. Often full at lunchtimes.

Pan Pay on the seafront near the police station. Popular breakfast spot and bakery with croissants, cakes and delicious Spanish tortillas.

The Place one block back from the bus stop. Attractive café specializing in vegetarian dishes and seafood, popular with tourists who are sick of rice, beans and pizza – try the tasty coconut-flavoured curries.

Stanford's just east of the main street. Restaurant and bar with a large outdoor disco where you can dance to the sound of reggae and waves crashing against the shore. Very popular at weekends.

Tamara on the main street, opposite the ATEC office. Good range of Caribbean, seafood and international dishes (pasta, pizza, etc) served up in a pleasant alfresco dining area.

South from Puerto Viejo to Manzanillo

The stretch south of Puerto Viejo, dotted by the tiny hamlets of **Playa Cocles**, **Playa Chiquita**, **Punta Uva** and **Manzanillo** (the main village), is one of the most appealing on Costa Rica's entire Caribbean coast. Palm trees lean vertiginously over small, empty beaches, while purples, mauves, oranges and reds fade into the sea at sunset, heralding the twilight mist that wafts in from the Talamancas. There's a low-key atmosphere, and excellent accommodation strung along the Puerto Viejo–Manzanillo road. Bus transport is infrequent, and you'll do best with a car, although you'll need a 4WD to negotiate the numerous potholes.

The little-visited, but fascinating, **Refugio Nacional de Vida Silvestre Gandoca-Manzanillo**, bordering Río Sixaola and the international frontier with Panama, incorporates the small hamlets of Gandoca and Manzanillo and covers fifty square kilometres of land and a similar area of sea. It was established to protect some of Costa Rica's last few **coral reefs**, of which **Punta Uva** is the most accessible. You can **snorkel** happily here. There's also a protected **turtle-nesting beach** south of the village of Manzanillo. **Playa Manzanillo** also has a large shelf of coral reef just offshore which teems with marine life and offers some of the best snorkelling in Costa Rica. The village itself is small and charming, with laid-back locals and a couple of great places to eat and hang out.

Accommodation

The stretch of coast from Puerto Viejo to Manzanillo offers more than 25 places to stay – mostly mid-range options, plus a couple of elegant boutique hotels and several self-catering places.

Aguas Claras Playa Chiquita ⓣ750-0180, ⓕ750-0386, ⓦwww.aguasclaras.net. The best self-catering option in the area, set in luxuriant gardens just 200m from the beach. Each of the brightly painted wooden chalets, which sleep up to 4 people, has mosquito nets, a sitting area, balcony with hammocks, clean bathroom, cold water, fully equipped kitchen and electricity. ❻

Almonds and Corals near Manzanillo ⓣ222-2024, ⓕ272-2220,

Ⓦ www.almondsandcorals.com. A sort of luxury tent lodge in a lush rainforest setting in the Gandoca-Manzanillo wildlife reserve. Each of the stilt-set tents contains comfortable furniture and has an adjoining bathroom. Restaurant, Jacuzzis, bike rental, tours and laundry also available. ❽
Cariblue Playa Cocles Ⓣ & Ⓕ 750-0057, Ⓦ www.cariblue.com. Luxurious individual cabinas, all with balconies and hammocks, in a nicely laid-out, jungle-ish setting with a very good Italian restaurant and a pool (with pool bar). ❽
Casa Camarona Playa Cocles Ⓣ 750-0151, Ⓕ 222-6184. Twenty rooms, all with private bathroom and a/c, set in a first-class location right on the beach. There's also an attractive restaurant and good artesanía shop. Breakfast included. ❼
La Costa de Papito Playa Cocles Ⓣ & Ⓕ 750-0080, Ⓦ www.greencoast.com/papito.htm. Ten bungalows with large bamboo beds and balconies, set in pretty gardens and run by an effusive New Yorker. Bike rental available. ❻
Miraflores Playa Chiquita Ⓣ & Ⓕ 750-0038, Ⓦ www.mirafloreslodge.com. Rustic, comfortable lodge opposite the beach, on an old cacao plantation with tropical flowers in the grounds. The decor is lovely, with Bribrí paintings, carvings and objets d'art. The upstairs rooms are brighter – with mosquito nets, mirrors and high bamboo ceilings – and there's an outside breakfast area. The owner has excellent contacts with local Kéköldi Bribrí communities and runs imaginative tours, including trips to Panama in a motorized dugout. ❺–❻
Pangea Manzanillo Ⓣ 224-2400, Ⓔ pangea@racsa.co.cr. Two beautifully decorated rooms, with private bath and breakfast included. Minimum 3-night stay. ❺
Shawandha Playa Chiquita Ⓣ 750-0018, Ⓕ 750-0037, Ⓦ www.shawandhalodge.com. Very chic French hotel comprising twelve large bungalows with enormous beds and gorgeous tiled bathrooms. Rates include breakfast. ❾
Villas del Caribe Playa Chiquita Ⓣ 750-0202, Ⓕ 750-0203, Ⓦ www.villasdelcaribe.com. Actually within the Kéköldi indigenous reserve, this hotel has very comfortable two-storey self-catering accommodation, with terrace, hot water, fan and organic garbage disposal. The grounds are right on the beach, with great sunset views. ❽

Eating and drinking

Big Breakfast Playa Cocles. Lodge café-bar offering a Caribbean-American menu (including free coffee), Internet access and happy hour from 5–7pm.
Elena's just beyond *Miraflores* lodge, 5km south of Puerto Viejo. This long-established *soda*-cum-restaurant serves succulent local fish and chicken dishes, as well as inexpensive lunchtime specials and snacks. The bar closes at 2am.
Maxis Manzanillo. Large upstairs restaurant with great views over the beach and renowned seafood, including lobster. Gets packed at weekends. Cabinas also available.
Selvin's about 8km south of Puerto Viejo. Long-established restaurant-bar dishing up beautifully cooked local fish (served with coconut-flavoured rice-and-beans at weekends).

Bribrí and the Panamanian Border

From a few kilometres north of Puerto Viejo the paved road (Hwy-36) continues inland to **BRIBRÍ**, about 10km southwest, arching over the Talamancan foothills with views of the green valleys stretching ahead to Panama. This is banana country, with little to see even in Bribrí itself, which is largely devoted to administering the affairs of indigenous reserves in the Talamanca mountains. Bribrí does, however, have one basic **place to stay**, *Cabinas El Mango* (no phone; ❶), a couple of simple **restaurants** and a Banco Nacional, which changes money and travellers' cheques.

The border and on into Panama

Sixaola–Guabito is a small crossing that doesn't see much foreign traffic, and for the most part formalities are simple, but you should get here as early in the morning as possible.

The Sixaola–Guabito border is open daily from 8am to 6pm Panama time (one hour ahead of Costa Rica). Tourists leaving Costa Rica need to buy a **Red Cross exit stamp** (around US$2 from the pharmacy in Sixaola); citizens of some nationalities may require a **tourist card** to enter Panama (valid for 30 days); the

Panamanian consulate in San José issues them, as does the San José office of Copa, the Panamanian airline (see p.609). Immigration requirements often change; check with the Panamanian consulate.

In Panama there's nowhere decent to stay before you get to Bocas del Toro (see p.823) – leave time to look for a hotel once you're there, and be aware that bus connections can be tricky.

6.4

The Central Pacific and Southern Nicoya

Although Costa Rica's **Central Pacific** area is less of a geographical or cultural entity than other regions of the country, it does contain several of its most popular tourist spots, among them the No. 1 attraction, the **Reserva Biológica Bosque Nuboso Monteverde** (also known as the Monteverde Cloudforest Reserve), draped over the ridge of the Cordillera de Tilarán. Along with the nearby **Reserva Santa Elena**, Monteverde protects some of the last remaining pristine cloudforest in the Americas.

The Central Pacific and Southern Nicoya are also home to some of the best-known **beaches** in the country, including some that are easily accessible from San José. Each offers a distinctly different experience. A former tiny fishing village near the southwest tip of the Nicoya Peninsula, popular **Montezuma** is surrounded by a series of lovely coves, perfect for sunbathing and hanging out. On the mainland coast, the rough water and huge waves at **Jacó** make it one of the best places to surf in the country. Further south, **Parque Nacional Manuel Antonio** has several extraordinary beaches, with white sands and azure waters.

With the exception of the cool cloudforest of Monteverde, the vegetation is Pacific lowland. The **climate** is tropical, hot and rather drier than in the south – about 33°C is a dry-season average. It's not that much cooler in the wet months, when Quepos and Manuel Antonio, in particular, often receive torrential afternoon rains.

Of the two **routes from the capital** to Puntarenas and points south, the main one is the Interamericana, which climbs over the Cordillera Central before dropping precipitously to the Pacific lowlands, levelling out at the town of Esparza, a few kilometres beyond which is the turn-off for Puntarenas. Buses to Jacó and Manuel Antonio take the slightly shorter old road via Atenas and Orotina. Visiting Monteverde is always a bit of an expedition. Although it is just 170km from San José, the roads along the final 35km or so are unpaved and in poor condition. In the dry season you can do it with a regular car, but in the wet you need 4WD.

Most people cross over to the southern **Nicoya Peninsula** from Puntarenas on the ferries to Naranjo or Paquera, but the new bridge across the mouth of the Río Tempisque has significantly shortened the drive. From Paquera there's public transport down to Tambor and Montezuma. From Naranjo you can continue south by car or north to Carmona and then up to Nicoya and Santa Cruz, but the roads aren't in great shape.

The Monteverde area

Though it's generally associated only with the cloudforest reserve of the same name, **Monteverde** is, properly speaking, a much larger area, straddling the hump of the Cordillera de Tilarán between Volcán Arenal and Laguna de Arenal to the east and the low hills of Guanacaste to the west. Along with the reserve, the area is home to the spread-out Quaker community of **Monteverde**, the neighbouring

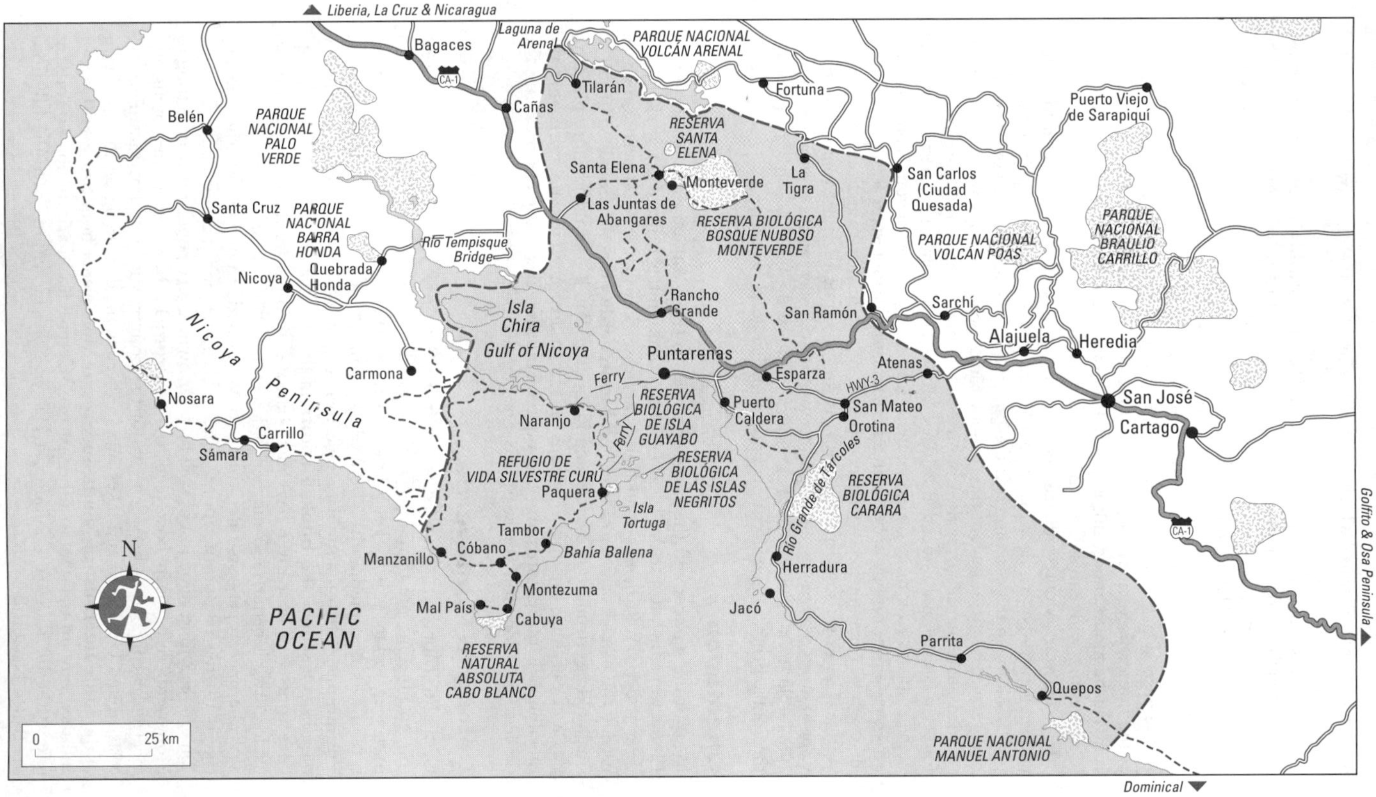

Liberia, La Cruz & Nicaragua
Golfito & Osa Peninsula
Dominical
Bagaces
CA-1
Laguna de Arenal
PARQUE NACIONAL VOLCÁN ARENAL
Tilarán
Fortuna
Cañas
Belén
PARQUE NACIONAL PALO VERDE
RESERVA SANTA ELENA
Santa Elena
Monteverde
La Tigra
San Carlos (Ciudad Quesada)
Puerto Viejo de Sarapiquí
Santa Cruz
PARQUE NACIONAL BARRA HONDA
Las Juntas de Abangares
RESERVA BIOLÓGICA BOSQUE NUBOSO MONTEVERDE
PARQUE NACIONAL VOLCÁN POÁS
PARQUE NACIONAL BRAULIO CARRILLO
Río Tempisque Bridge
Quebrada Honda
Nicoya
Rancho Grande
San Ramón
Sarchí
Alajuela
Heredia
Isla Chira
Gulf of Nicoya
Puntarenas
Atenas
Nicoya Peninsula
Carmona
Ferry
Esparza
HWY-3
San José
Nosara
RESERVA BIOLÓGICA DE ISLA GUAYABO
Puerto Caldera
San Mateo
Naranjo
Orotina
Cartago
Carrillo
Sámara
RESERVA BIOLÓGICA DE LAS ISLAS NEGRITOS
REFUGIO DE VIDA SILVESTRE CURÚ
Paquera
Isla Tortuga
Río Grande de Tárcoles
RESERVA BIOLÓGICA CARARA
Tambor
Cóbano
Bahía Ballena
Manzanillo
Herradura
Montezuma
Mal País
Cabuya
Jacó
PACIFIC OCEAN
RESERVA NATURAL ABSOLUTA CABO BLANCO
Parrita
Quepos
PARQUE NACIONAL MANUEL ANTONIO
N
0 25 km

village of **Santa Elena** – which has a cloudforest reserve of its own – and several other small hamlets.

The area's appeal stems in part from the **Reserva Biológica Bosque Nuboso Monteverde**, and also from the cultural and historical uniqueness of the Monteverde community, which was created in the early 1950s by a number of **Quaker** families. Hailing mostly from Alabama, where some of them faced jail for draft-dodging, the Quakers today are completely integrated into Costa Rican society. Many still make their living from dairy farming, producing the region's distinctive **cheese**, which is sold throughout the country. Abroad, the area is best known as the home of several pioneering **private nature reserves**. Of these, Monteverde is by far the most famous, although the less-touristed **Reserva Santa Elena** is just as interesting, with equally pristine cloudforest cover.

In recent years, Monteverde has become more popular than anyone ever imagined, and strict **rules** govern how many people can enter the reserve at any one time (see p.659). Although the cloudforest is the highlight of the area, the major drawcard for many travellers these days are the "canopy tours". These outings, which have mushroomed phenomenally over the country, take punters up into the high layers of the forest on ziplines and suspended bridges. Monteverde is one of the best places to do it: the emphasis is far more on excitement than biology, however you'll appreciate the ecosystem of the canopy in between adrenalin rushes. Monteverde is quite expensive, although you can find very good cheap lodging the further away from the entrance you go. The **rainy season** (May–Nov) is the best time to visit Monteverde if you want to avoid the crowds, although the weather can stay rainy and grey for days on end. Ideally, try to come at the beginning or end of the rainy season, when you get the double benefit of fewer visitors but reasonably good weather.

Orientation

Most of the services and the cheaper places to sleep, eat and drink are in **Santa Elena**, a major hub for the local farming communities centred on a triangle of three streets. From here, a road leads southeast 7km to the Monteverde reserve, passing the hamlet of Cerro Plano and **Monteverde** proper, essentially a group of smallholdings strung out over several kilometres. You'll find many more places to stay and eat along this route – many of which are very enticing, with only the metallic calls of bellbirds and the buzz of motorcycles and Jeeps breaking the silence. Five kilometres northeast of Santa Elena is the reserve of the same name.

Getting to Monteverde

Getting to Monteverde independently **from San José**, especially in the dry season, entails some pre-planning. Demand for the two daily buses is high, and you may need to buy your ticket a few days in advance. Once you arrive, buy your return ticket immediately. There's less demand for bus seats travelling from **Puntarenas**, and you should be able to get away with not booking. In the dry months you should also **book a room**; in the wet season you can just turn up. Give yourself at least three days in the area: one to get up there, at least one to explore (two is better), and another to descend.

All the major operators offer **tours** to Monteverde from San José; their advantage is a better rate on the more comfortable hotels and transport, but otherwise you can see Monteverde just as well on your own. A very popular way of getting to Monteverde is the "jeep–boat–jeep" transfer **from La Fortuna**, a time-saving and spectacular connection between two of the country's major attractions. The trip costs around US$15–20 and takes two to three hours depending on the condition of the roads. **Interbus** run shuttle services to Monteverde from San José (US$30) and then onward transfers to other parts of Costa Rica in a/c minibuses. You can reserve the Interbus a/c minibuses at *Pensión Santa Elena*, just down the hill from the Banco Nacional.

By car

Driving from San José to Monteverde takes about four hours via the Interamericana – two hours to the turn-off (there's a choice of three; see below), then another two hours to make the final mountainous ascent. One route, sometimes called the Sardinal route, takes the Interamericana north from Puntarenas towards Liberia, branching off at the **Rancho Grande** turning to Monteverde. Buses go a shorter route, continuing past Rancho Grande to the **Río Lagarto** turn-off – just before Río Lagarto itself – which is signed to Santa Elena and Monteverde. The least well-known route, which local *taxistas* swear is the best, is via **Las Juntas de Abangares**, a small town reached from a small road, labelled "145" on some maps, off the Interamericana. Once you've reached Las Juntas, drive past the main square, turn left and continue over a bridge; turn right, and follow the signs. The first 7km of this 37-kilometre road, via Candelaría, are paved, but have some spectacular hairpin bends – drive slowly. You can also reach Monteverde from **Tilarán**, near Laguna de Arenal. The road (40km) is often very rough, but provides spectacular views over the Laguna de Arenal and Volcán Arenal (see p.702).

Whichever route you take, you'll need **4WD** in the rainy season, when some agencies refuse to rent regular cars for the trip.

By bus

All **buses** arrive first in Santa Elena. Some then continue along the road to Monteverde, making their last stop at La Lechería (cheese factory). Most people arrive on one of the two direct services from **San José**'s Tilarán terminal (3hr 30min minimum, though it can often be more like 5hr, especially in the rainy season). Be particularly vigilant when waiting to board the bus – this service is a magnet for opportunistic thieves. When on the bus, keep everything with you if possible and valuables on your person. Note that taking the afternoon service from San José gets you to Monteverde after dark. From **Tilarán**, you can catch the 12.30pm bus (3hr), but in the rainy season, this may stop a few kilometres short of Santa Elena, leaving you with no option but to walk the remainder of the way. From **Puntarenas**, a daily bus leaves for Santa Elena at 2.15pm (3hr).

The **Santa Elena bus stop** is next to a church, at the top of the "triangle" near the Banco Nacional. From here, all amenities and many pensiones are no more than 100m away. The owners of pensiones and cabinas will come to the bus and try to entice you to their establishment; most are fine, so take your pick. If you are booked into one of the hotels on the road to the reserve, stay on the bus and ask the driver to drop you off, or, if you arrive on the bus from Puntarenas, arrange with your hotel to have a taxi meet you (US$5–6).

Moving on from the Monteverde area, buses to San José leave Santa Elena at 6.30am and 2.30pm daily, starting from the cheese factory in Monteverde. There's sometimes an extra service leaving at 2pm from Friday to Sunday; check the office beside the bus stop. For **Tilarán**, one bus leaves daily at 7am; for **Puntarenas**, the daily service departs at 6am. One bus leaves daily at 4.45am for the two-hour journey to **Las Juntas**, from where you can get to Liberia and points north in Guanacaste. If you're not a morning person, get the San José bus and ask to get off just after the bus turns onto the Interamericana, at the intersection for Chomes. From here, you can hail northbound buses to Liberia and elsewhere. Check timetables for all buses at the bus stop, where tickets are sold (Mon–Fri 5.45–11am & 1.30–5pm, Sat & Sun 5.45–11am & 1.30–3pm).

Accommodation

With the exception of a couple of pensiones on the road to Monteverde, the cheapest places to stay are in **Santa Elena**. All accommodation here is basic, but you'll get a bed and heated water at least, and almost certainly a warm welcome. Many small pensiones are run by locals and offer an array of services, from cooking

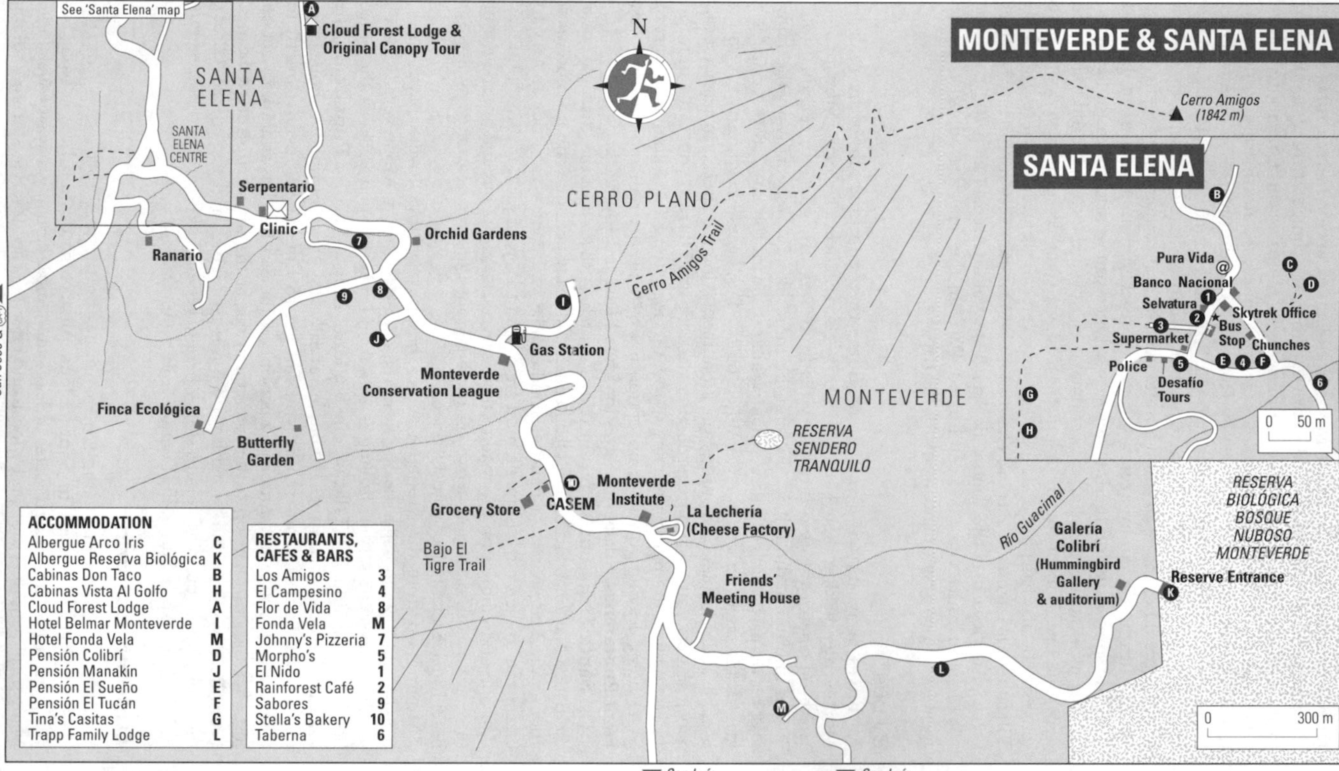
MONTEVERDE & SANTA ELENA
Reserva Santa Elena (5 km), Skywalk, Skytrek, Las Juntas (for Interamericana; 40 km) & Tilarán
See 'Santa Elena' map
Cloud Forest Lodge &
Original Canopy Tour
N
SANTA
ELENA
SANTA
ELENA
CENTRE
Serpentario
Clinic
Ranario
Orchid Gardens
CERRO PLANO
Cerro Amigos Trail
Cerro Amigos
(1842 m)
Gas Station
Monteverde
Conservation League
Finca Ecológica
Butterfly
Garden
MONTEVERDE
RESERVA
SENDERO
TRANQUILO
Monteverde
Institute
CASEM
Grocery Store
La Lechería
(Cheese Factory)
Bajo El
Tigre Trail
Friends'
Meeting House
Río Guacimal
Galería
Colibrí
(Hummingbird
Gallery
& auditorium)
Reserve Entrance
RESERVA
BIOLÓGICA
BOSQUE
NUBOSO
MONTEVERDE
San José & CA-1
San Luís
San Luís
0 300 m
SANTA ELENA
Pura Vida
Banco Nacional
Selvatura
Skytrek Office
Bus
Stop
Chunches
Supermarket
Police
Desafío
Tours
0 50 m
ACCOMMODATION
Albergue Arco Iris C
Albergue Reserva Biológica K
Cabinas Don Taco B
Cabinas Vista Al Golfo H
Cloud Forest Lodge A
Hotel Belmar Monteverde I
Hotel Fonda Vela M
Pensión Colibrí D
Pensión Manakín J
Pensión El Sueño E
Pensión El Tucán F
Tina's Casitas G
Trapp Family Lodge L
RESTAURANTS, CAFÉS & BARS
Los Amigos 3
El Campesino 4
Flor de Vida 8
Fonda Vela M
Johnny's Pizzeria 7
Morpho's 5
El Nido 1
Rainforest Café 2
Sabores 9
Stella's Bakery 10
Taberna 6

to laundry and horse hire. Many are convivial places to meet up and swap information with other travellers.

Hotels between Santa Elena and the entrance to the Monteverde reserve tend to be pricey, and are mainly used by tour groups and older, better-heeled tourists. While you'll certainly be comfortable in these places – large rooms, running hot water, orthopedic mattresses, even saunas and Jacuzzis are the norm – some travellers find the atmosphere a bit dour. You get little sense of a community, partly because Monteverde is not an obvious settlement, and many of the houses are set back in pasture, hidden from the main road.

Santa Elena

Albergue Ecológico Arco Iris up a side street just behind the *Pensión Santa Elena* ⓣ645-5067, ⓦwww.arcoirislodge.com. The best-value mid-range accommodation in the area, with well-decorated and spacious cabins in quiet landscaped gardens in a central location (❻); they also have cheaper rooms with bunk beds (❺), plus a family cabin. The delicious breakfast (US$5) with German bread, granola, fresh fruit, eggs and toast is unequalled.

Cabinas Don Taco 300m north of the Banco Nacional ⓣ645-5263, ⓦwww.cabinasdontaco.com. This pleasant hotel offers 8 standard rooms in the main building with shared balcony and 7 individual cabinas with private balcony, with fine views on a good day. Each cabina has a private bathroom with hot water, mini-refrigerator and TV. Hosts Ahias and Leyla are very welcoming. The price includes breakfast; laundry service and parking are also available. ❹

Cabinas Vista Al Golfo 300m west of the church ⓣ645-6321, ⓔvistaalgolfo@hotmail.com. One of the best budget options in Monteverde, with bright clean new rooms, some with bath, for only US$5 and US$10 per person. A breezy balcony gives fantastic views right to Puntarenas and the gulf of Nicoya, and there's a sociable shared kitchen and cheery owners who can organize tours. ❷

Pensión Colibrí town centre ⓣ645-5682. Simple, family-run accommodation in small rooms with shared bath and heated water. Although in the middle of town, it's a peaceful spot, with plenty of vegetation and a balcony to relax on. There are also en-suite rooms on offer, with cooked breakfasts and lunchtime *casados* also available (for a fee). The welcoming owners hire out horses, too. Good value. ❷

Pensión El Sueño town centre, 25m east of the supermarket ⓣ645-5021. Cosy, rustic wooden rooms right in the heart of Santa Elena; rooms in the main building have shared bath, while modern split-level en-suite rooms are available for around US$10 per person more. There's also a small lounge with leather rocking chairs for stargazing, a kitchen for guests' use and friendly *dueños*, who cook a good breakfast (included for en-suite guests, otherwise US$3). Good low-season discounts, but it's good value even in high season. ❷–❺

Pensión El Tucán 100m south of the Banco Nacional ⓣ & ⓕ645-5017. Located at the bottom of the "triangle" of streets, this is one of Santa Elena's more venerable budget lodgings, with small rooms with shared hot-water bathrooms above a decent restaurant. Classier rooms are set in cabins with private bath and balcony and cost double. Owners can book tours and transfers for you. ❷–❸

Tina's Casitas 300m west of the church ⓣ645-5641 or 820-4821, ⓦwww.tinascasitas.de. These simple and peaceful cabinas are the most tranquil budget option in Santa Elena. Decorated with rustic flair by the environmentally conscious owner, they surround a shared kitchen and have views of the gulf of Nicoya. Some rooms have private bathroom with hot water, and all make fine use of attractive natural wood for their furnishings. ❷–❹

Outside Santa Elena

Albergue Reserva Biológica de Monteverde at the entrance to the Monteverde reserve (contact the Monteverde Conservation League on ⓣ645-5122). Accommodation right in the reserve, though it's often packed with researchers and students – tourists have second priority. Reservations are essential, and you'll need to pay half your room cost 45 days in advance. It's dormitory accommodation, with bunk beds and shared bathroom, but there's an infectious environmental buzz about the place. A berth costs US$12 per person, US$27 with meals. ❹

Cloud Forest Lodge a kilometre or so up a turn-off 500m northeast of Santa Elena ⓣ645-5058. Set in forest high above Santa Elena, this secluded hotel is surprisingly low-priced for what's on offer. The well-appointed wood-panelled cabins all come with terraces with dizzying views over the Golfo de Nicoya. The hotel has its own 5km system of trails, plus a bar, restaurant, horse-riding tours and a 25 percent discount off the Original Canopy Tour, which is located here. It's best if you have your own transport, since it's a bit of a walk to Santa Elena or Monteverde. ❼

Hotel Belmar Monteverde Cerro Plano ⓣ645-5201, ⓦwww.hotelbelmar.net. The oldest of the area's many Swiss-style hotels, the perennially popular *Belmar* sits on the hillside above Cerro Plano two kilometres from Santa Elena and has great views of the bay from its restaurant and most of the rooms. There are two types of accommodation, which differ little except that the pricier rooms are somewhat larger and are equipped with a fan, rarely a necessity in blustery Monteverde. There's also a pool table on site. ❼

Hotel Fonda Vela Monteverde ⓣ645-5125, ⓦwww.fondavela.com. Set in quiet grounds fairly close to the reserve, the *Fonda Vela* has a lovely old-fashioned charm to it. It's expertly managed, with attentive staff, beautiful touches and a range of good-value rooms – plus a highly recommended restaurant. New rooms ("suites") aim for deluxe, with huge bathrooms and beautiful fixtures and furniture; they aren't much more expensive. Older rooms are more rustic and lack a fan or a/c, but have attractive wood-panelled walls and huge windows – most giving astonishing views, especially at sunset. ❽

Pensión Manakín Cerro Plano ⓣ645-5080, ⓦwww.manakinlodge.com. A sympathetically run family pensión, which backs onto forest, with some of the best budget rooms in the area, including bunk-bed accommodation (US$12 per person) and other rooms with shared or private (❺) bathroom. There's a cabin with a kitchenette, too, plus a small gym, laundry service and Internet access. Breakfast included. ❹

Trapp Family Lodge Monteverde ⓣ645-5858, ⓦwww.trappfam.com. This attractive wood-built establishment has nothing to do with *The Sound of Music* and is the closest hotel to the Monteverde reserve, being within easy walking distance. The whole place is clean, comfortable and well-priced; the rooms are light and airy, and you can contemplate the cloudforest from their large windows. The hotel itself is non-smoking, and there's also a decent restaurant for guests only. ❼

Santa Elena and around

The influx of tourists to the cloudforest reserves in recent years has transformed the little community of Santa Elena, with dozens of hotels, cabinas, and restaurants springing up in the formerly peaceful area. Enterprising individuals have set up a variety of other attractions in the zone, and they have been so successful that many people now visit purely to take one of the vaunted canopy tours, not even bothering to set foot in the reserves. Although the canopy tours are an undoubted thrill, to appreciate the area's wonderful wildlife, your best options are still the guided walks in the Monteverde or Santa Elena reserves. Twilight walks at other locations in the region also offer excellent spotting possibilities, while the plethora of butterfly gardens, serpentariums and similar sites offer a chance to observe the area's creatures at closer quarters. Some of these are fine facilities dedicated to the study and preservation of the region's biological inheritance, but others are more of the "put a lizard in an ice-cream carton and charge 'em eight bucks" variety.

Santa Elena itself is a place to hang out, gather information, and plan and arrange what you're going to see and do in the area. Although small, it has all the **practical facilities** a weary traveller could hope for. You'll soon have the place staked out: the centre of town is basically three streets in a triangle, which harbours a Banco Nacional at its northern apex with a Cirrus/MC/Visa/Plus ATM. Several spots offer **Internet access**, including Pura Vida, opposite the bank, which has a pretty reasonable connection and charges US$2 for an hour. Not too far off, *Chunches*, a café and shop, sells pricey secondhand paperbacks among other things and has a laundry service (as do most of the area's accommodations). There's also a reasonably well-stocked supermarket in town as well as a post office.

Outdoor activities and tours

Several agencies in town can organize a variety of tours and excursions. Next to the bus station, Skytrek (ⓣ645-5238, ⓦwww.skytrek.com) offers one of the most popular **canopy-style tours** (7.30am–3pm; 2hr 30min; US$40), zipping all comers along eleven high-tension cables suspended above the treetops. The longest of the pulley rides is an incredible 770m. Transportation to the site – 3km up the road to the Santa Elena reserve – is not included in the tour price, but can be arranged for a small extra fee. The same company owns the popular **SkyWalk** nearby (see p.660); combining the two on one ticket saves around US$10. Selvatura (Ⓣ645-5929, Ⓦwww.selvatura.com) are another reliable canopy-tour operator located opposite the bus stop; the Original Canopy Tour (Ⓣ645-5243, Ⓦwww.canopy-tour.com), based at the *Cloud Forest Lodge* (see p.655), is also reliable. Rates vary very little between companies; with student ID you can save US$10 or so.

The efficient and friendly Desafío Expeditions (Ⓣ645-5874, Ⓦwww.monteverde-tours.com), opposite the supermarket, specialize in **horseback tours** and care for the noble beasts very well. They offer a two-hour ride through forest and farmland (US$20) and a day-trip to the San Luís waterfalls that also involves some hiking (US$49); they can also organize bespoke horse tours of up to a week in different parts of the country as well as **canyoning trips** (US$49) that follow watercourses downstream, with rappel descents down waterfalls. Their transfer to La Fortuna (4–5hr) involves some scenic riding as well as the usual vehicle and boat transfer. Sabine's Smiling Horses (Ⓣ645-5051, Ⓦwww.horseback-riding-tour.com) is another recommended place to find a steed.

Monteverde is an important coffee-producing region, and you can learn about the coffee production process with the Cielo Verde **Coffee Tour** (Ⓣ645-5641, Ⓔtinas_casitas@hotmail.com), where you participate in each phase of the production of the black gold on a well-managed organic farm. Ask at *Tina's Casitas* (see p.655) for more information.

Wildlife exhibits

Just outside Santa Elena, on the road to the Monteverde reserve, the **Serpentario** (daily 9am–10pm; US$8/US$6 students; Ⓣ645-5238) is one of many wildlife showcases in the region, with a number of unnerving snakes in residence as well as a few other reptiles, all well displayed with information panels. Like many of the attractions in this area, the price has risen astronomically in the past couple of years, to the point where it's questionable value for money. If you go, it's worth visiting late in the afternoon, when the serpents tend to be a little more active. Nearby, the **Ranario** (9am–8.30pm; US$8/US$6 students; Ⓣ645-6320), signposted off the other side of the road, displays a fascinating array of colourful frogs and other amphibians. As with the snakepit, your ticket is valid for multiple entries, and in this case it's well worth making a visit during the day and one at night, as different species emerge from beneath their lilypads at different times of day. Both facilities include a guided tour in the price of admission.

Cerro Plano

The road from Santa Elena twists and turns six kilometres (ignore excitable signs proclaiming anything from seven to nine) to the Monteverde reserve entrance, offering some unforgettable views en route. Although easily walkable, the quantity of traffic can result in a mudbath or dustbath depending on the season. Hitching on the road is easy, and there are frequent buses to and from the reserve. Just over a kilometre from Santa Elena, the small settlement of Cerro Plano consists mainly of hotels, but down a signposted side road are a couple of other attractions.

The **Butterfly Garden** (daily 9.30am–4pm; US$8/US$6 students/US$3 kids; Ⓣ645-5512) provides an opportunity to walk among the different butterfly species from the varying climatic regions of Costa Rica. It's best to arrive between 10am and 2pm when the butterflies are most active, although the four butterfly farms and unimpressive natural history museum will likely only inspire the most devoted butterfly fans.

Nearby, the **Finca Ecológica**, a wildlife reserve and organic farm, is particularly worthwhile for its twilight walk (daily 5.30pm; 2hr; US$14; Ⓣ645-5554). Although it never strays too far from civilization, the informative guided tour gives you a good chance of seeing a variety of animals, including porcupines, armadillos, coatimundi, agoutis, grey foxes, and a marvellous variety of insects and roosting birds. Also in Cerro Plano are the **Orchid Gardens** (daily 9am–5pm; US$8); run by orchid enthusiast Gabriel Barboza, the gardens boast more than four hundred different species of orchid on show, including the world's smallest.

Monteverde village

Back on the main road, you'll soon come to the drawn-out settlement of **MONTEVERDE** proper, a seemingly timeless place, where milk cans are left out at the end of small dairy-farm driveways to be collected, modest houses sit perched above splendid forested views, and farmers trudge along the muddy roads in sturdy rubber boots. At the heart of the community is La Lechería, or **cheese factory**, which produces a range of European-style cheeses and, until the advent of tourism, was one of the area's main economic cogs. There's a shop where you can buy the produce (Mon–Sat 7.30am–4pm, Sun 7.30am–12.30pm), and you can see how the stuff's made on a two-hour tour (Mon–Sat 9am & 2pm; US$8; reservations on ☎645-5436). A little further on, the **Friends' Meeting House**, the centre for Quaker observance, welcomes interested visitors to participate in their meetings (Wed 9am & Sun 10.30am). The arts and crafts collective **CASEM** is an important spoke in this small community. Founded 20 years ago by eight women, it now has over 140 local artisans benefitting from its support.

Around the Monteverde community are two small reserves that offer small-scale rainforest walking experiences. The **Reserva Sendero Tranquilo**, a private reserve in the grounds of a local farm behind the cheese factory in Monteverde, offers informative guided tours (book on ☎645-5010; US$20 per person) through primary- and secondary-growth forest. The only part of the **Bosque Eterno de los Niños** (Children's Eternal Rainforest; part of the Reserva Santa Elena) that you are currently permitted to visit is the **Bajo El Tigre trail** (daily from 8am, last entrance at 4.30pm, reserve closes at dusk; US$5), a short, easy trek at lower elevations than in the cloudforest reserves; with great views out to the Golfo de Nicoya, sunsets from here can be spectacular. A good guided twilight walk focuses on the small creatures of the rainforest, although you may see one or two larger species (daily 5.30pm; US$15).

Reserva Biológica Bosque Nuboso Monteverde

The **RESERVA BIOLÓGICA BOSQUE NUBOSO MONTEVERDE** (daily 7am–4pm; US$12/US$6 students; ☎645-5122, Ⓦwww.cct.or.cr) is a large private reserve that protects the last sizeable pockets of primary cloudforest in Mesoamerica. Administered by the Centro Científico Tropical in San José, Monteverde Cloudforest Reserve, as it's known in English, is hugely popular with both foreigners and Ticos, who flock here in droves – especially during Easter week and school holidays – to walk the trails.

Few people fail to be impressed by the reserve's sheer diversity of **terrain**, from semi-dwarf stunted forest on the more wind-exposed areas to thick, bearded cloudforest vegetation, and some truly moving **views** of uninterrupted, dense green. The Monteverde reserve, which stretches over 105 square kilometres, supports six different **life zones**, or ecocommunities, hosting an estimated 2500 species of plants, more than 100 species of mammals, some 490 species of butterflies, including the rare blue morpho, and over 400 species of birds, among them the resplendent **quetzal** (best seen Jan–May). The cloudforest cover, however – dense, low-lit and heavy – makes it difficult to see animals.

Plant-spotting, however, is never unrewarding, especially if you take a **guided walk**, which will help you identify thick mosses, epiphytes, bromeliads, primitive ferns, leaf-cutter ants, poison dart frogs and other small fauna and flora. Serious rainforest walkers should plan on spending at least a day in the reserve; many people spend two or three days quite happily here.

Temperatures are cool: 15° or 16°C is not uncommon. Be sure to carry an umbrella and light rain gear. You should also bring binoculars, fast-speed film and insect repellent. It's just about possible to get away without **rubber boots** in the dry season, but you will most definitely need them in the wet. The reserve office rents both boots and binoculars out (US$1.50), as do some hotels.

Practicalities

A daily **bus** leaves Santa Elena twice daily for Monteverde (Mon–Sat 6.15am & 1pm, returning at 11am & 4pm; US$1); alternatively, a **taxi** will set you back US$6 per carload – try to get a group together to share. If you decide **to walk**, be aware that the road is uncomfortably dusty in the dry season, and that there's a surprising amount of traffic, though nearer the reserve it becomes quieter and gives good views over the area. At the entrance the **reserve office** is very well geared up for tourists, with a **visitor centre** where you can pick up maps and buy useful interpretive booklets for the trails. It also has a good souvenir shop and a small *soda*, which dishes out coffee, cold drinks and snacks, plus vegetarian *casados* at lunchtime. Also at the entrance, the **Galería Colibrí**, or Hummingbird Gallery (Mon–Sat 9.30am–4.30pm, Sun 10am–2pm), sells artwork and souvenirs and is an excellent spot to observe the many species of hummingbird that dart in to sup from the feeders hanging outside.

In an attempt to limit human impact on the reserve, a number of **rules** govern entrance to Monteverde. The reserve imposes a **quota**, with a maximum of 160 people allowed in the reserve at any given time, but serious birders, wildlife spotters and those who would prefer to walk the trails in quiet, should avoid the **peak hours** of 8–11am, when the tour groups pour in. An alternative is to book a ticket a **day in advance** – your hotel can reserve you a place for the following day – and get here by 5.30am (not earlier – it's still too dark), when, even though the visitor centre is closed, you are able to go on the trails. Bookings cannot be made any more than 24 hours in advance.

Albergue Reserva Biológica de Monteverde (see p.655) offers basic **accommodation** at the park headquarters, but it's often packed with researchers and students; in the reserve, three simple shelter facilities along the trails cater to overnight and long-distance hikers. These outposts, the closest of which is a two-hour hike from the reserve entrance, cost US$3.50–5 per person per night, plus the entrance fee for each day you're in the reserve. (For example, if you stay in the reserve for one night, you'll pay two days' entrance fees plus accommodation, a total of US$32). There's water, and simple cooking facilities are available, but you'll need to take your own food and a sleeping bag.

Walking in the park

Whatever sort of walk you go on in Monteverde – or anywhere else in the country, for that matter – it's worth realizing that you are more likely to be looking at plants, smaller animals and insects rather than staring into the eyes of pumas or tapirs. Bearing this in mind, the reserve itself runs excellent **guided walks**. Walks start at 7.30am sharp (or at 7.30am and 8am, if demand is high), last two to three hours and cost US$15 (plus the US$12 entrance fee). Ask in your hotel or call the reserve office a day in advance on ☎645-5122 to secure a place, since there's a maximum of just ten people – and make sure to arrive on time, too, or they'll set off without you. It might seem like a pricey tour, but the guides are informative and the experience supremely educational. The reserve's trails are walkable without a guide, although you'll see less. They are clearly marked, and you can get maps and interpretive booklets at the reserve office.

Another highly recommended way to experience another side of the rainforest – though not for those who are put off by the dark or by creepy crawlies – is the

night walk (US$13), which leaves at 7.30pm each evening – you don't have to book for this tour, but turn up at the reserve office by 7.15pm to buy a ticket. For US$2, the reserve can arrange round-trip transport from Santa Elena or your hotel; obviously this has to be reserved. The walk lasts two hours. If you're a serious bird-watcher, there are very worthwhile, five-hour walks devoted to that purpose; these leave at 6am and have to be reserved (2 person minimum; US$40–50). All walks include a **slide show**, during which you'll see some of the creatures you encountered in the reserve and many you did not, including the Monteverde golden toad, now feared extinct.

If you can't or don't want to go on the official tours, there are a number of excellent local **guides** who can show you the reserve and the entire Monteverde area. Check at the visitor centre.

Reserva Santa Elena

Though it's less touristed than the Monteverde reserve, the **Reserva Santa Elena** (daily 7am–4pm; US$9; ⓣ645-5390, ⓦwww.monteverdeinfo.com/reserve), 6km northeast of the village of Santa Elena, offers just as illuminating an experience of the cloudforest. Higher than the Monteverde reserve – it's poised at an elevation of 1650m – its three-square-kilometre area consists of mainly primary cover. Trails are steeper and more challenging, and there's a slightly higher chance of seeing quetzals in season. Established in 1992, it strives to be self-funding, assisted by donations and revenue from entrance fees, and gives a percentage of its profits to local schools. For maintenance and building projects it depends greatly on volunteers, usually foreign students.

Getting to the reserve from Santa Elena village entails an arduous 5km walk over a boulder-strewn road, much of it uphill. Fortunately, four daily buses make the trip (US$2/US$3 return), leaving in the morning from the Banco Nacional; the last bus back to town is at 3pm. **Jeep-taxis** (US$6) can be arranged by your hotel or can be picked up on Santa Elena's main street; the reserve can call a taxi to come and pick you up to take you back into town. There's a **visitor centre** at the entrance, with washrooms and an information booth where staff hand out maps of the twelve-kilometre network of trails. Highly recommended guided tours can be arranged for between one and four hours (about US$24, including entrance fee); the reserve also rents out boots and issues a succinct six-page leaflet discussing rainforests, cloudforests, epiphytes, seed-dispersal patterns and some of the mammals you might see in the reserve. Guided **nature walks** (US$15) are offered at 7.30am and 11.30am daily; night tours (US$15, inclusive of entrance fee) leave at 7pm daily. A line of hummingbird feeders have been strung along the entrance path, where you can watch these tiny, multi-coloured birds zooming in and out of nectar-dishes.

On the way up to the reserve, a different bird's-eye view of the forest can be had from the **SkyWalk** (daily 7am–4pm; US$15; ⓣ645-5238, ⓦwww.skywalk.co.cr), an impressive series of bridges and paths built by Fernando Valverde, a biologist from Monteverde and world authority on the construction of rainforest suspension bridges. Located 3.5km along the road towards the Santa Elena reserve, the Sky Walk consists of a network of suspension-style footbridges, stretching from the ground to canopy level between acres of virgin rainforest. Bridges provide some really spectacular views – but take waterproofs. If you're going to do the Sky Trek zipline tour, you can save US$10 by booking these together in Santa Elena (see p.657).

Eating, drinking and nightlife

There are several cheap *soda*-style eateries in Santa Elena, as well as a couple of classier options. Cuisine in many of the top-end **Monteverde** hotels is very good indeed, and most of them open their restaurants to the public. Menus are usually fixed, and meals are served at set times. Drop round in person to book for dinner and see what's on the menu. Being a Quaker community, there is not much **drinking** to be done in the Monteverde area, even in gringo-filled Santa Elena. Most restaurants do have alcohol on the menu, but you'll notice a definite whiff of temperance in the air. That said, there's usually atmosphere at *Los Amigos* bar down a side street opposite the church in Santa Elena, and later at *Taberna*, a lively *discoteca* a couple of hundred metres down the Monteverde road from the bottom of the Santa Elena triangle.

El Campesino Santa Elena, on the southern side of the triangle. Homely little place run by an expansive Tico and his young son. The decor is engagingly quirky, with legions of stuffed toys hanging from the ceiling, and the food focuses on steaks and seafood. Take the owner's recommendation for what's good that day; mains cost US$5–7.

Flor de Vida Cerro Plano. A quiet and relaxed vegetarian café and restaurant, offering snacks such as bagels as well as more substantial fare drawn from a range of continents. Main dishes such as vegetable stir-fries come in at US$5–7. A good lunch option, with views of the forest out the windows. Non-smoking.

Fonda Vela Monteverde, in the *Hotel Fonda Vela*. Two restaurants at the hotel of the same name – a fairly formal and intimate fireside restaurant and a larger, slightly less staid one – with lovely views out over the property and a varied (though fairly expensive) menu including good, generous breakfasts and succulent dinner specialities – try the chicken in white wine and almonds (US$11).

Johnny's Pizzeria Cerro Plano. One of the most popular restaurants in the area, both among tourists and locals, and it's not hard to see why, with superior cocktails, pizza (US$5–8) cooked in an open wood oven and superb service in a candlelit colonial decor. There's pasta, meat and fish on the menu, too, but everybody seems to come for the pizza. During the day you can sometimes see hummingbirds in the quiet garden.

Morpho's Santa Elena, opposite the supermarket. Comfortably the best food in Santa Elena proper, this upstairs restaurant is stylishly decorated, with bizarre hanging butterflies and wooden chairs that are easier on the eye than the back. Dishes such as *corvina al aguacate* (sea bass in avocado sauce), flavoursome steaks, and sumptuous desserts keep people coming back. There's an overpriced selection of Chilean wines, but mains are a steal at US$4–8. It's very atmospheric in the evening, though you'll wait for a table. Non-smoking.

El Nido Santa Elena, across from the Banco Nacional. The best of Santa Elena's *sodas*, this upstairs restaurant offers *casados* (US$3), a range of large and lip-smacking sandwiches (US$2.40) and tasty burgers that beat those at some of the more trendy eateries around. The *dueña* may come across grumpy at first, but has a heart of gold.

Rainforest Café Santa Elena, opposite the church. With a balcony overlooking the comings and goings of the town, this is the place to sit with a coffee or milkshake and relax. They also do slightly pricey, but tasty, sandwiches.

Sabores Cerro Plano, opposite the bullring. If cheese is not your go, a great way to sample the pure and natural dairy produce of this region is to treat yourself to the delights at this ice-cream parlour. The creamy fare with fresh tropical fruit or coffee flavours is quite delightful and can be covered with your favourite toppings.

Stella's Bakery Monteverde, opposite CASEM. Delicious strudel, brownies, sandwiches and coffee in a pleasant café-like atmosphere, although the owner is a touch surly. Daily 6am–5pm.

Around Monteverde: Tilarán

TILARÁN, 40km northeast of Monteverde, is a useful stop-off between Guanacaste to the west and the Zona Norte to the east. It's also about the best place in the country for **windsurfing** – the *Hotel Tilawa* (☎695-5050, Ⓦwww.hotel-tilawa.com; ❻), on the lakeshore east of town, can arrange rentals and lessons in this and kitesurfing. They also have a bar that brews its own beer and a choice of large rooms or equipped cabinas. There are a few other **places to stay** in Tilarán: try *Cabinas El Sueño* (☎695-5347; ❹), 150m from the northwest corner of the Central Parque, with good rooms with private bath and a nice patio, or *Hotel Naralit* (☎695-5393; ❹), for comfortable and spotless rooms. Tilarán has good **bus** connections with Cañas and the Interamericana, from where you can head on to Liberia and the Guanacaste beaches, or south to Puntarenas. There are two daily services to La Fortuna to the east (see p.702), a bumpy but beautiful trip along the shores of Lago Arenal that takes two hours. The bus station is 100m north of the Parque Central.

Puntarenas

Heat-stunned **PUNTARENAS**, 110km west of San José, has the look of raffish abandonment that haunts so many tropical port cities. What isn't rusting has long ago been bleached out to a generic pastel, and the town's cracked, potholed streets, shaded by mop-headed mango trees, are lined with old wooden buildings painted in faded tutti-frutti colours. Tourists come mainly to catch ferries across to southern Nicoya – there's little to see or do in the town itself.

Arrival and information

Scores of **buses** arrive from San José's Puntarenas terminal every day. The bus stop is on the corner of C 2 and Paseo de los Turistas, near the old train tracks and the old dock that juts out into the gulf. **Local services** from Manuel Antonio and Quepos arrive here, too, as do buses from Liberia and the daily service from Santa Elena, which arrives at about 9.30am.

The town lies on a long sandy spit, only a few blocks wide. The centre is just a few blocks northwest of the San José bus stop. Here, you'll find banks, the municipal market, and a slew of cheap hotels. The Banco de Costa Rica, Banco de San José and the Banco Nacional, virtually next to each other on the north shore near the docks area, offer **currency exchange** and have ATMs. Though it's easy enough to get around on foot, **taxis** scoot through the town, and can be flagged down. You can also wave down the buses that ply Avenida Central – the last stop is in front of the **ferry dock** at the western end of town. There's an **Internet café** and laundry, Millennium, at the point where Calle 17 meets the Paseo de las Turistas, which runs along the southern waterfront. The pride of Puntarenas is its local **museum** (Tues–Sun 9.45am–5.15pm), which gives a rundown on the archeology, biology and history of the region, focusing on the town's relationship with the sea that virtually surrounds it.

Accommodation

The **cheap hotels** around the docks are useful if you want to catch an early lancha to Paquera. It's not a great area at night, however. Wherever you stay, make sure your room has a fan that works.

Cabinas Arguedas Av 0, C 27/29 ⓣ661-3508. One of the city's better-value options, with unremarkable, but well-equipped, rooms with a/c and fridge. Parking and bike rental are also available, and it's but a short stroll to the car ferry terminal. ❹

Gran Hotel Imperial Paseo de los Turistas, C 0/2 ⓣ661-0579. Extremely handy for the bus station, this run-down hotel run by a quarrelsome family is housed in an old wooden building of some character. The rooms with private bath are spacious, dark and basic; some of those with shared bath have a dilapidated wooden balcony. Safe location, as the police station is across the road. ❹

Hotel Las Brisas Paseo de los Turistas, C 31/33 ⓣ661-4040, ⓔhbrisas@racsa.co.cr. A cheerful, friendly and clean waterfront hotel at the western tip of the peninsula. Rooms come with cable TV, phone and a/c; some have balconies looking out across the Golfo de Nicoya. There's also a swimming pool and a breezy café that offers Greek dishes among its meals. ❻

Hotel Tioga Paseo de los Turistas, C 17/19 ⓣ661-0271, ⓦwww.hoteltioga.com. One of the nicest downtown hotels, with an elegant atmosphere, extra-friendly management and several grades of a/c rooms – those on the sea-facing side have a balcony with the best views (❽). There's also a soothing interior courtyard and a pretty pool. Rates include breakfast in the cafeteria-style restaurant. ❻–❽

Moving on from Puntarenas

Though the new bridge across the Río Tempisque (see p.697) north of Puntarenas has made access to the Nicoya Peninsula easier, the ferries from the city are still popular among those heading to places like Montezuma on the peninsula's southern tip. The ferry port is at the northwestern tip of Puntarenas, a fifteen-minute walk from the centre. Regular buses run up and down Avenida Central from the centre (labelled "FERRY" on the front). There are three **ferry routes**: two cross to Paquera, run by Ferry Peninsular (daily: every two hours from 4am–10pm; 1hr; passengers US$0.80, cars US$14; ⓣ641-0118) and Tambor (four daily; 1hr; passengers US$1.50, cars US$11; ⓣ661-2084), and one runs to Playa Naranjo (6 daily; 1hr 15min; passengers US$1.50, cars US$11; ⓣ661-1069). Paquera is closer to the popular southern Nicoya destinations, and buses meet the boat and head onwards to Montezuma. If you're driving, it can be a slow old process buying tickets for **cars**; you're best off getting there more than an hour in advance, at least in high season. Park in the queue before going to buy your passage.

Two daily lanchas also run to Paquera; these speedier passenger-only boats leave from the dock by the market in the centre of town, departing at 11.30am and 4pm.

Buses leave at least every hour on the hour for **San José** from the San José bus terminal just off the Paseo de los Turistas on C 2. They arrive at San José's Puntarenas terminal and take about two hours, depending on traffic. Services to **Liberia** (7 daily; 3hr) and **Santa Elena** (daily; 3hr 30min) depart from here, too. For **Manuel Antonio**, take the Quepos service from the same place (4 daily; 3hr). This bus will also drop you off in Jacó.

Eating, drinking and nightlife

Food, even fish, is pricey in Puntarenas: you'll be lucky to get *casados* or *platos del día* for less than US$5. As usual the **mercado** is a good place to pick up a cheap meal and a *refresco*, although you should avoid drinking anything made with the local water. The beachside *sodas* and kiosks near the **old dock** are more appealing places to linger for a quiet drink or a seafood lunch.

The best **restaurants** in town are on the Paseo de los Turistas. *Aloha* is the most popular place in town for an evening drink, with an extensive and expensive menu, and nice breezy outdoor tables where you can sit looking out to sea. *Kimbo's*, between C 7 and C 9, is a lively and well-priced restaurant and bar, serving dishes such as *corvina* (sea bass) and beef stroganoff for around US$6. They also do cheaper fast food, and it's a popular spot with Tico tourists for a few drinks at night. *Gugas*, Avenida 2, C 0/1, is a relaxing unwalled bar and restaurant with friendly service and meat and fish dishes in a similar range. It's a block back from the waterfront not far from the bus station. *Soda Macarena*, at the bus stop, has cheap and delicious food, including all kinds of fruit plates and toasted sandwiches; try their "Churchills" – similar to a crushed-ice *granizado*, but made with ice cream.

The southern Nicoya Peninsula

The hour-long ferry trip across the Golfo de Nicoya from Puntarenas is soothing and slow-paced: the boat purrs through usually calm waters, passing island bird sanctuaries along the way. In the distance are the low brown hills of the Nicoya Peninsula, ringed by a rugged coastline and pockets of intense jungly green. Drivers can also cross further north over the new Tempisque bridge, funded by the Taiwanese government. It reaches the peninsula near the town of Puerto Moreno, but the poor roads south from here mean you'll save little, if any, time over the ferry if you're heading to Montezuma or Tambor.

Much of the southern peninsula has been cleared for farming and cattle grazing or, in the case of **Tambor**, given over to tourism development. Friendly **Cóbano**,

6km inland from Montezuma, is the main town in the southwest of the peninsula, with a gas station, correo, *guardia rural* and a few bars. There's also a Banco Nacional here, with a Cirrus/MC/Visa ATM, an important consideration as it's the only one in the area. Most tourists pass right through on the way to **Montezuma**, one of the most popular beach hangouts in the country, reached by a reasonable dirt road lined with cattle pasture on both sides. Those looking for surf and a quieter beach-side scene should head west to the waves of Mal País.

Montezuma and around

The popular beach resort of **MONTEZUMA** lies some 40km southwest of Paquera, near the southwestern tip of the Nicoya Peninsula. Some three decades ago a handful of foreigners fell in love with the place and settled here. Then it was just a fishing village, largely cut off from the rest of the country; nowadays it's totally devoted to tourism, with virtually every building offering gringo-friendly food, accommodation, or transfers and tours. That said, there's little large-scale development, and it's still basically a village.

What brings everyone here is the astounding beauty of the setting. Montezuma and the coast south to Cabo Blanco feature some of the loveliest coastline in the country: white sand, dotted with jutting rocks and leaning palms, and backed by lush greenery, including rare Pacific lowland tropical forest.

Arrival and information

From where you get off the bus, at the bottom of the hill, you can see pretty much the entire centre of "town", which consists of a beachfront road, and a short sloping

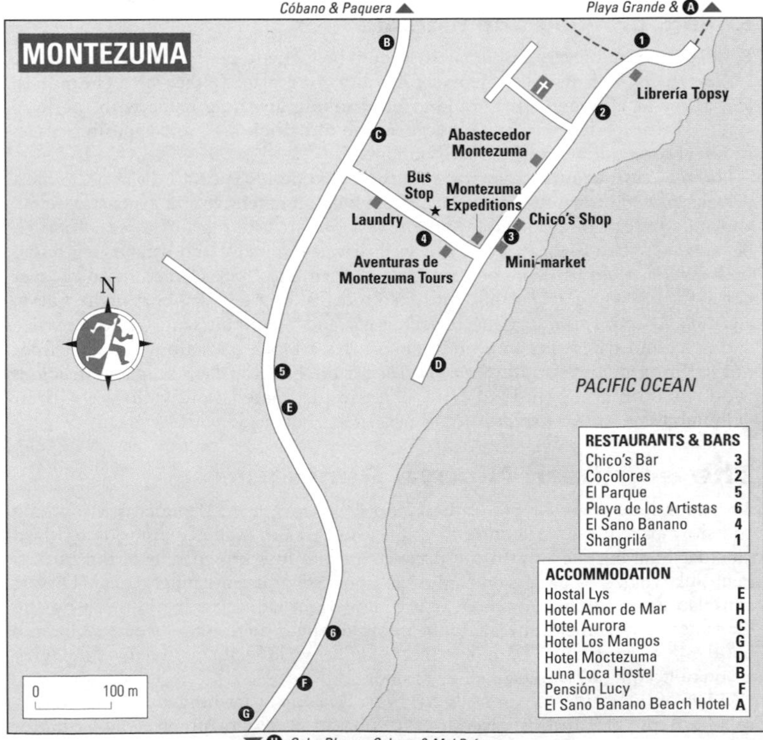

street leading up from it. At the top of this, a right turn takes you back up towards Cóbano, while a left leads south towards Cabo Blanco.

Nearly everyone in town claims to be able to fix you up with **tours**. On the main drag, the helpful multilingual people at Aventuras de Montezuma (Ⓣ & Ⓕ642-0050, Ⓔavenzuma@racsa.co.cr) have the largest range of tours, services and information in town, including trips to Isla Tortuga (US$40) and horse-riding on the beach and to local waterfalls (US$25). They have an Internet café and international phone service; they also arrange car and motorbike rental and sell tickets for NatureAir flights from Tambor to San José, as well as transfers.

In the centre of the village, the Montezuma Expeditions kiosk rents out bicycles and motorbikes, and offers full-day trips to Isla Tortuga (US$40, including breakfast and time for snorkelling); diving trips (US$90, including equipment rental); and four-hour horse-rides to waterfalls (US$25). They also arrange transfers to Cabo Blanco reserve and act as the local Sansa agent for flights to Tambor. The *Sano Banano*, adjacent to Aventuras de Montezuma, has an Internet café by its restaurant for US$3 per hour.

Chico's shop, next to the bar and grocery store of the same name, sells sunscreen, film, clothing and telephone cards, which you can use in the **telephones** outside (if the lines are working). There's a **laundry** next to the *Sano Banano*, while for nice **souvenirs**, head to El Jardín gift shop (in the hotel of the same name). For **newspapers** and a bookshop, try Librería Topsy, on the beachfront road. Dollars are accepted everywhere, and many places will accept travellers' cheques. Remember that the nearest bank and ATM is up the road in Cóbano.

A popular **return route to San José** involves taking a launch to just outside Jacó for US$30; from there you can get a cab to Jacó bus station and connect with the frequent San José–bound buses. Slower, but more convenient, is the Interbus service, which picks you up from wherever you're staying in the morning and gets you to San José in about six air-conditioned hours (US$35). You can book either journey at Aventuras de Montezuma.

Accommodation

There's a good range of places to stay in Montezuma. **Prices** are moderate, as the village still caters to a young, studenty crowd who can't afford the rates of, say, Manuel Antonio; even prices in some of the more upscale hotels drop in low season by about US$10–15. **Reservations** are useful in the dry season, especially at weekends, and are essential over Christmas and Easter. Most times, though, if you arrive on a late bus without a reservation, there is bound to be somewhere to stay, even if it's not your first choice.

Staying in the **village** is convenient, but can be noisy, due to the shenanigans at *Chico's Bar* and the odd car pulling in and out of the village. Elsewhere, it's wonderfully peaceful, with choices out on the **beach**, on the road that heads southwest to the Reserva Absoluta Cabo Blanco, and on the sides of the steep hill about 1km above the village.

Camping is prohibited on the beach; you would be better advised to stay at one of the organized camping sites between Montezuma and Cabuya, roughly 4km away on the road to the Reserva Natural Absoluta Cabo Blanco, where there are toilets, showers and barbecues.

Hostal Lys just south of the centre Ⓣ642-0642. A popular place to crash for budget travellers who aim on spending more time on the beach than indoors. Although basic, the rooms are scrubbed clean daily by the friendly owners, and the price is a winner, particularly considering it's right on the beach. ❸

Hotel Amor de Mar 600m southwest of the village on the beach, just across the bridge Ⓣ & Ⓕ642-0262, Ⓦwww.amordemar.com. Upmarket (for Montezuma) seafront hotel and well-managed by its German owners, this spot is set in pretty landscaped gardens on a rocky promontory, with hammocks swinging between giant mango trees. There's an attractive selection of rooms, with and without bathroom – those upstairs and facing the sea are best – and most come with veranda and ocean views. Good low-season discounts, and there's a small restaurant downstairs serving healthy breakfasts. 6–7

Hotel Aurora in the centre of the village, a block east and a block north of *Chico's Bar* ⓣ642-0051, ⓦwww.playamontezuma.net/aurora.htm. Pleasant, friendly and environmentally conscious hotel, with 16 varied rooms – the older budget rooms are good value (5), especially in low season, with fans, communal fridge, coffee- and tea-making facilities and shared bath. Upstairs rooms are a little more expensive (6), but still very good value; the new cabinas come with a/c and private bath with hot water. There's also an apartment with its own kitchen and terrace. Guests have use of a well-equipped kitchen. 5–6

Hotel Los Mangos about 500m down the road to Cabo Blanco ⓣ642-0076, ⓦwww.hotellosmangos.com. Expensive-looking, but slightly dark, bungalows (6), with hot-water showers and fan. The rooms, which come with or without bath (5), offer plenty of value; some have their own verandas complete with rocking chairs. There's also a pool, Jacuzzi, good restaurant and attractive grounds.

Hotel Moctezuma by the beach, in the centre of town ⓣ & ⓕ642-0058, ⓦwww.playamontezuma.net/ecotours/hotel.htm. Right in the thick of things in a potentially noisy location, this has two types of room, both of which offer value. In the main building, an old wooden affair with a spacious balcony overlooking the sea, there are simple, if gloomy, rooms with cold shower, fan and shared bathroom. The new annex across the street has brighter en-suite rooms with a small fridge. 4

Luna Loca Hostel 200m north of the village, on the road to Cóbano ⓣ642-0390, ⓦwww.playamontezuma.net/lunaloca.htm. Excellent backpacker hostel, peacefully set on the forested hillside, with a regular troupe of monkeys as visitors. There are three private rooms, but most beds are bunks in the clean dormitories, which are fronted by a sociable balcony. There's a shared kitchen, hot water, a TV lounge, and friendly atmosphere. Dorm beds are US$10 per night, which includes breakfast. 4

Pensión Lucy 500m south of the centre ⓣ642-0273. A Montezuma stalwart (though the government once attempted to have it torn down as it violates the *zona marítima*, which prohibits building on the first 50m of beach) containing clean and basic rooms with cold-water showers and a nice seaside veranda upstairs. There are also a couple of rooms with private bath. It's one of the village's best cheapie options, if a little quirky. The owner also offers a reasonable laundry service and runs an inexpensive eatery next door. 3

El Sano Banano Beach Hotel a 15min walk north of the village along the beach (your bags will be taken care of) ⓣ642-0638, ⓦwww.elbanano.com. A truly special place, one of the most characterful in the country, with secluded circular cabinas, all featuring beachfront balconies and outside showers (some also have kitchenettes). The newer split-level apartments, also with beach views, are perfect for families, and there's a lovely freeform swimming pool with a waterfall, sun terrace and beautifully landscaped gardens. You feel very close to nature, and you'll be grateful for a torch. Breakfast is included at the café in town. 7

The village and around

It's Montezuma's atmosphere, rather than its activities, that draws visitors, and other than hanging out and sipping smoothies, there's not much to do in the village itself. Despite the inviting palm-fringed white sand, **swimming** isn't very good on the beaches immediately to the north of Montezuma – there are lots of rocky outcroppings, some hidden at high tide, and the waves are rough and currents strong. It's better to head north along the lovely **nature trail** (1.5km; 30min), which dips in and out of several coves before ending at **Playa Grande**. There's reasonable swimming here, decent surfing, and a small waterfall at its eastern edge; some people also come here to sunbathe topless or nude, though this isn't particularly appreciated by local people.

Montezuma and its environs are laced with a number of **waterfalls**, the closest of which is about a one-kilometre walk down the road towards Cabo Blanco and then another 800m on a path through the dense growth (signed). Always take care with waterfalls, especially in the wet season, on account of **flash floods**, and under no circumstances try to climb them: many people have been injured – or even killed – in the attempt. Local tour operators lead **horse-rides** to falls that are otherwise difficult or impossible to reach on foot.

Isla Tortuga, off the coast of the peninsula near Curú, is a popular place to snorkel, swim safely in calm, warm and shallow waters, and sunbathe. Several companies in town organize day-trips for about US$40 per person.

The single most popular excursion in town, however, is probably to the **Cabo Blanco** reserve (see below) for a morning's walking. Although you can do this by tour, it's easy enough to reach by public transport or your own 4WD (or fully-insured 2WD in the dry season). If you like **mountain biking**, you could ride the 9km down to Cabo Blanco, walk the trails and bike back in a day. Mind the height of the two creeks en route, though, as you might not get through them on your bike at high tide.

Eating, drinking and nightlife

Just a few years ago all you could get to eat in Montezuma was fantastically fresh **fish**, practically straight off the hook; nowadays this is complemented by tourist favourites like vegetarian pizza, granola, mango shakes and paella, not to mention more exotic dishes. Eating three meals a day will set you back a few colones, though: Montezuma's accommodation may still be moderately priced, but food is on the expensive side. If you're staying somewhere with a kitchen, you can cut costs by grabbing food from the store in the centre of the village.

Nightlife in Montezuma centres around *Chico's Bar*, an interesting mix of local kids, who arrive packed in the back of pick-ups, and tourists guzzling from a surprisingly wide bar stock and shouting above the music. It closes at two, after which people tend to adjourn to the beach for some alfresco drinking. On Wednesdays, the action shifts to the *Shangrilá* in the grounds of the *Luz de Mono* hotel. More retiring types can take in the very popular nightly video shows (in English) at the *Sano Banano* at 7pm; you have to spend at least US$6 in the restaurant to get in.

Cocolores An excellent restaurant in a garden by the beach. The varied international menu includes a couple of vegetarian options as well as a toothsome coconut fish curry (US$6). The Lebanese salad (US$3.50) is another tasty choice, and the food is accompanied by homemade bread. Fine value for the quality on offer. Closed Mon.

El Parque Open *soda*-style eatery on the beach itself just south of the centre. Hearty portions of Costa Rican dishes, as well as burgers and sandwiches, sell for what, in Montezuma, are fairly reasonable prices.

Playa de los Artistas Rustic and inspiring beachside restaurant half a kilometre south of the village serving up some very classy Italian-inspired fish, steak and vegetable dishes. Splash out on an unhurried outdoor candlelit dinner and enjoy whatever's fresh and succulent on the frequently changing menu. There are usually several highly recommendable tuna and snapper choices; the average main course here will set you back US$10–12. Closed Sun.

El Sano Banano in the village. Excellent North American–style breakfasts and filling lunch and dinner specials – the fillet of fish (US$8) makes a good evening meal – plus crepes, vegetarian pizzas and vegetarian canelloni with spinach; organic produce is used where possible. If you have nothing else, try the incredible smoothies made with fresh fruit and yoghurt. They put on films in the evening – so you'll have to be early to get a seat.

Reserva Natural Absoluta Cabo Blanco

Seven kilometres southwest of Montezuma, the **Reserva Natural Absoluta Cabo Blanco** (Wed–Sun 8am–4pm; US$6; ⓣ642-0093, ⓦwww.caboblancopark.com), established in 1963, is Costa Rica's oldest protected piece of land. At over twelve square kilometres, Cabo Blanco occupies the entire southwest tip of the peninsula. The natural beauty of the area is complemented by its unique biodiversity, with pockets of **Pacific lowland tropical forest** of a type and mix that are found nowhere else in the country. Animals that live here include howler monkeys, plus sloths and squirrels. Agoutis and coati are common, as are snakes – so watch your step. Sea birds such as the brown booby nest down by the shore, using the islands off the very tip of the peninsula as their prime site, and you'll often see clouds of frigate birds hovering above.

You pay your entrance fee (US$6) at the ranger hut, where they'll supply you with a map of the trails, which also outlines the history of the reserve and species found in it. A **trail** (5km; 2hr) leads from here through tropical deciduous forest to **Playa Cabo Blanco** and **Playa Balsitas** – two very lovely, lonely (depending on the season) spots, though they're not great for swimming. Be wary of the high tide (*marea alta*) – ask the ranger at the entrance when and where you're likely to get cut off, if walking along the beach. It's very **hot**: 30°C is not uncommon, so bring a hat, sunblock and plenty of water. There's no real need to take a **guide** – ask at Aventuras de Montezuma in Montezuma, if you do decide you want one. No camping is allowed in the reserve, but there are places to stay in the village of Cabuya, a twenty-minute walk from the park entrance. One such place is *El Ancla de Oro* (ⓣ & ⓕ642-0369, ⓔlamont@racsa.co.cr; ❺), a welcoming place with accommodation in rustic cabins set among fruit trees with mosquito nets and fans; there are also self-catering bungalows available, as well as a restaurant.

Practicalities

The **roads** down to Cabo Blanco are bad; you'll need 4WD to get there yourself, except in the very driest time of year. Make sure there's full insurance on that rental car and watch the two creeks along the way – they're deep at high tide. An old, road-hardened **bus** rattles back and forth between Montezuma and Cabo Blanco five times daily, leaving from the side of Montezuma's *parqueo*, although it may not run in the rainy season if it has been very wet. **Jeep-taxis** make the trip from Montezuma to Cabo Blanco for US$10 per person.

Mal País and Playa Santa Teresa

Twelve kilometres southwest of Cóbano, the long surf beach of **Playa Santa Teresa** is luring increasing numbers of travellers as Montezuma becomes over-crowded. The beach, also accessible via a steep and bumpy road from Cabuya, is home to a straggly community that extends both ways along the oceanfront from where the Cóbano road hits the beach at the area's main landmark, *Frank's Place*. Turning left here takes you along the **Mal País** ("bad land") end of the strip, which is quieter and has a number of peaceful places to stay. The reason it's quieter is that there's better surfing at the other end of the beach in Santa Teresa, where there is a bigger concentration of cabinas, eateries and shops, as well as a couple of bars. Although the community is growing extremely rapidly, it remains a relaxed spot, with a mixture of expatriates, especially Italians, sharing the ample sand with the young surf crowd.

If you fancy learning how to ride a board, there are a few **surfing schools**, including Pura Vida (ⓣ640-0118), on the beach a couple of hundred metres north of the intersection. Nearby, Pacific Divers (ⓣ640-0187, ⓦwww.pacificdivers-costarica.com) run PADI courses and guided dives, although visibility usually isn't great. There are several places where you can hire horses to ride along the beach or up and over the jungle road to Cabo Blanco; one of these is Horse Tours and Bikes (ⓣ640-0209) at the Mal País end of the beach. No prizes for guessing the other line to their business. There are also a handful of **Internet cafés**, including one in the shopping annex, run by *Frank's Place*.

The relaxed gringo vibe at *Frank's Place* (ⓣ640-0096, ⓦwww.frankplace.com) makes it one of the most popular places to stay. The cheap rooms (❹) are decent, if a little dark, and the more upmarket ones (❻) come with private bath, a/c, kitchen and fridge. There's plenty of hanging-out space, with a pool, hammocks aplenty and a café-restaurant, which does aprés-surf stomach fillers such as *casados* for around US$3. Also on hand are an excellent range of intimate mid-range and upmarket hotels and cabinas; one of these is the forested *Blue Jay Lodge* (ⓣ640-0089, ⓦwww.bluejaylodgecostarica.com; ❼), south of the intersection, which has intimate, widely spaced bungalows that sleep up to three people. The best of the lot, a short walk up the hillside, have ocean views and plenty of wildlife going about its business around you; the price includes excellent hospitality and a generous breakfast. There's also a pool and a wholefood restaurant.

Camping is technically prohibited on the beach, but there are several sites regardless, including *Victor*, 500m south of the intersection, a simple place that costs US$2.50 per person. Mal País's large expat population means there's a wide choice of eating places: the *Piedra del Mar*, on the beach south of the junction, is a great place for a drink while watching the superb sunsets; it also does succulent seafood. At night things can get lively at *Bar Tabé*, just north of *Frank's*; there are also regular beach parties; check ⓦwww.malpais.net for more information.

Two daily **buses** run from Cóbano to Mal País and back; a taxi will set you back around US$13. Many of the hotels and cabinas can organize transportation for you.

Jacó

The thriving beach resort of **Jacó** makes no claim to being classy or exclusive: it's no more or less than a relaxed playground for tourists, surfers and *Josefinos*. As the closest beach to the capital it's a very popular weekend destination during the summer months. The long sand beach is reasonably clean and spacious, and swimming is possible, although the water isn't the cleanest and you have to watch out for riptides. It's patrolled in sections during the popular visiting periods. Jacó's nightlife is predictably hedonistic and sleazy, with young holidaymakers jostling for barspace with prostitutes and their clientele. Though there are numerous hotels and cabinas, it's wise to reserve in advance during the high season (Dec–April), especially at weekends.

Arrival, information and getting around

Jacó stretches along a three-kilometre main road, little more than a brash strip of shops, restaurants and hotels. Turning off from this main drag are a few streets that head for the sea but never quite make it, petering out in attractive palm groves or the beach. This is the **centre** of town, although many accommodation options are found to the north or the south of this little nucleus.

Buses leave for Jacó five times daily from San José's Coca-Cola bus terminal (3hr); four buses make the trip each day from Puntarenas (1hr 15min) and Quepos (1hr 15min). There may be extra services on holidays and holiday weekends, but if you intend to travel between Friday and Sunday, especially in the high season (Dec–April) or on public holidays, buy your ticket three days in advance. The bus stops at the extreme north end of the village at the Plaza Jacó mini-shopping centre, where the ticket office is also found, behind the Banco de Costa Rica. There are also the usual a/c minibus transfers available to destinations all over the country; a trip to San José or the airport costs US$21.

There are several banks on the main drag that take foreign-issued cards, including the Banco Nacional, which accepts Cirrus/MC as well as Visa/Plus; they also change travellers' cheques. There are several car rental agencies in town, including National, by the Banco Popular right at the centre of the strip, and Payless, at the northern end of town. Many places rent out mountain bikes, scooters, surfboards (about US$20 a day) and boogie boards (about US$10 a day). **Internet cafés** are in abundance; the *Centro Computacional*, between Calle Hicaco and Calle Las Brisas, is one, and *Mexican Joe's*, near the Banco Popular, is another. Most charge about US$0.75 per hour. There are several laundromats, including Aquamatic at the southern end of the strip. Of the many supermarkets, one of the best stocked is Mas X Menos, right in the middle of Jacó.

Locals advise against walking on the beach at night: **hold-ups** by knife-wielding characters have been reported. Otherwise walking around town, even at night, should be safe, especially since a special contingent of bike-riding police have taken to patrolling the streets. Part of their mandate is to crack down on the widespread use of recreational drugs, and snap searches are not uncommon.

Accommodation

Jacó's cheapest **cabinas** generally cater to weekending *Josefinos* or surfers. Much of the mid-range accommodation is self-catering. In general, be prepared to pay more than either the town or, in some cases, the accommodation, merits. You'll need to **reserve** at holiday times, like Easter and Christmas, and weekends, for any of the places listed below.

Jacó is well endowed with **campsites** – all charge about US$3 a night to pitch a tent and have showers, toilets and beach access. Sites include *Camping and Cabinas Mariott* (nothing to do with its hotel-chain namesake), set on level, clear grounds at the north end of town; the shaded *Camping Madrigal*, at the southern end of the beach; and the newer *Camping El Hicaco*, in the centre of town, with nice grounds dotted with picnic tables and plenty of shade.

Aparthotel Flamboyant in the centre, in front of the beach ⓣ643-3146, ⓕ643-1068, ⓔflamboya@sol.racsa.co.cr. Good-value, well-kept apartments sleeping two people, with hot water, kitchen and ceiling fans. There's a pool and Jacuzzi, and a good restaurant attached, plus it's right by the sand. ❻

Aparthotel Girasol on Calle Los Almendros, at the southern end of town ⓣ & ⓕ643-1591, ⓦwww.girasol.com. Spacious and luxurious tiled apartments on the beach, in grounds with a lovely swimming pool and lawned garden. They come equipped with cane-furnished lounge area, fan, a/c and a full kitchen, and sleep up to four. Service is friendly and there's secure parking. ❽

Cabinas Alice on the beach, towards the southern end of town ⓣ & ⓕ643-3061. Twenty-two super-clean cabinas set in beautiful beachfront grounds with little to disturb the peace except the crashing of waves. All cabins come with fan and hot water, while some also have a small kitchen plus fridge and a small terrace; the older and more basic cabinas are slightly cheaper. Good restaurant attached, and there's a swimming pool. ❺

Cabinas Roblemar on beachside Calle Bohío in the heart of town ⓣ643-3558. This central establishment has cabinas in a location right in the heart of town but is nonetheless fairly quiet. The rooms are on the small side but have comfortable large beds; each pair shares a simple kitchen and cold-water bathroom. ❹

Chuck's Cabinas on Calle Anita, near the beach at the northern end of town ⓣ643-3328. Unpretentious little place with a relaxed surfing vibe. There are simple rooms with cold-water bathroom as well as some dormitory accommodation available at a lower price (US$5 per person). You can also get repairs here for dings in your surfboard and advice on conditions. ❸

Hotel Best Western Jacó Beach north end of town ⓣ643-1000, ⓦwww.bestwestern.co.cr. Well-established resort hotel, refurbished to a good standard. It's not the cheapest place in Jacó, but it has lots of facilities, including a big clean pool, restaurant, casino and weekend disco, plus kayaking, sports-fishing and sailing lessons. Rooms are decorated in anonymous chain-hotel style, but are perfectly comfortable, and come with private bath, a/c and cable TV. All-inclusive rates available. ❽

Hotel Canciones del Mar ⓣ643-3273, ⓦwww.cancionesdelmar.com. Very appealing bamboo-framed beachfront hotel, with colourful and thoughtfully decorated apartments with full modern kitchen, patio and large beds. A big pool and hospitable welcome complete an attractive ensemble. Prices include breakfast, and there are worthwhile discounts for weekly and monthly stays. ❽

Hotel Mar de Luz in the centre, on the landward side of the main drag ⓣ & ⓕ643-3259, ⓦwww.mardeluz.com. Well-kept hotel set in landscaped grounds away from the road, with soothing, colourful modern apartments sleeping up to five and arranged around two large pools and an enclosed garden area. There's TV, a/c, microwave, and kitchenette in the rooms, plus a lounge, games area and a small library. Very family friendly. Credit cards accepted. ❻

Hotel Los Ranchos in the centre ⓣ & ⓕ643-3070. Arranged in attractive gardens around a pool, this welcoming hotel offers good value for single travellers and groups alike, with a variety of rooms and prices, from upstairs loft rooms (some with kitchenettes) to two-storey bungalows with kitchens sleeping two to four people. It's a pretty spot with a shaded balcony. ❺

Outdoor activities and tours

Jacó is very much a beach town; other than sunbathing, surfing and a little cautious swimming, there's little to do. Experienced **surfers** can rent boards at a number of competing places in town; ask at *Los Ranchos* hotel for advice and recommendations. Several people offer lessons; one of these is Gustavo Castillo, an experienced local surfer and teacher (Ⓣ643-3574). Renting a **mountain bike** (about US$10 a day) is useful for exploring the spread-out town. Some people rent **mopeds** (about US$35 a day) and head out onto the Costañera Sur highway to explore the 10km-long **Playa Hermosa**, 7km south of Jacó, another reputable surfing beach (see overleaf).

The biggest range of tours can be found at Jacó Adventures (Ⓣ643-1049, Ⓔjacoadventures@playajaco.com), 100m south of the *Restaurante Colonial*. Their day-long tours to **Manuel Antonio** (US$35) are popular, and they also run rafting trips on the **Río Savegre** (US$89) and **kayaking** and **snorkelling** tours for US$55; day-trips to **Isla Tortuga** (US$70) are another perennial favourite. Nearby, King Tours also offer many tours and all manner of bus transfers around the country.

Eating, drinking and nightlife

Inevitably, considering Jacó's holiday resort status, there's a wide choice of places to eat. There are many restaurants specializing in fresh seafood, and places to suit all budgets. Although it's much quieter off-season, the nights are usually pretty lively. For **drinking**, bar *Zarpe* at the north end of town is recommended for cold beer and good, if slightly pricey, Mexican *bocas*. *Bar y Restaurante Bohío*, right on the beach, is a great place for a sunset drink – check out the church-pew benches and tables under a ranch roof. They also do classy *bocas*, even if a bit pricey at US$3–4. The spacious *Onyx* bar, across the bridge in the northern section of Avenida Pastor Díaz, the main road, is an upstairs venue with several pool tables and a happy young tourist crowd socializing to pop and light dance music. The *Beatle Bar*, further north, isn't a bad place for an evening drink, but it becomes more of a pick-up venue for professional women later on. The most popular *discoteca* is the *Central*, on the beach on Calle Central, which charges US$2.50 at the door at weekends. Once it shuts, at 4 or 5am, late revellers head to *Pancho Villa's*, the bar/restaurant on the main road around the corner, to squeeze the last few drops out of the night.

Barco de Mariscos in the centre, on the main drag. Informal venue specializing, as its name suggests, in well-prepared fresh shellfish and fish dishes, the latter being fairly low-priced – around the US$6 mark. There's also a popular café and ice-creamery next door, under the same management.

Big Bamboo centrally located, on the main road. Recently opened spot that does some of the town's better and more interesting pizzas, as well as very tasty *empanadas*. They also deliver (Ⓣ643-3706), if the poolside terrace in your hotel is a little difficult to leave.

Casita del Maíz north end of town. One of Jacó's better *sodas*, popular with locals, with good *casados* made with fresh ingredients for US$3.

Chatty Kathy's opposite the Max X Menos supermarket. One of the best places in town for breakfast, this Canadian-owned upstairs café serves pancakes, cooked breakfasts and delicious cinnamon rolls, as well as light lunches.

Colonial on the main drag. Tastefully designed new bar/restaurant popular with travellers for drinks as well as main meals.

Gilligan's on the main strip. Quiet little restaurant, which offers but two or three daily specials, but enticing and delicious ones, with imaginatively prepared fish or chicken dishes often available for US$7–9.

La Ostra on the main drag. Long-established *marisquería* (seafood restaurant), set in a large quiet rancho next to a creek, that's good for both fish and shellfish. They do refreshing *ceviches* for US$3–6, as well as a range of fish dishes to suit all budgets, from *corvina* (sea bass) at around US$4 to lobster at considerably more. Service erratic but credit cards accepted.

Pacific Bistro at the northern end of the strip. The menu of this small, Asian-inspired restaurant focuses on salads and fish, which are of a superb standard and created with much flair by the owner/chef. If you see a tuna steak on the menu, don't pass it by or you'll miss a treat. Mains cost US$8–14 depending on what's on offer.

Sunrise at the northern end of the main road. The generous breakfasts on offer at this friendly and relaxed café are so tasty and popular that the owners shut at midday and head for the beach.

Moving on from Jacó

Buses for San José leave the bus stop at the north end of Jacó five times daily (3hr). It's also possible to continue to **Quepos** and the **Manuel Antonio** area; there are four buses daily that pass on their way from Puntarenas. Agencies in town organize transfers to San José (US$21) and other destinations in Costa Rica in air-conditioned minibuses.

Around Jacó

If brash and lively Jacó has dismayed you, worn you out, or you simply fancy a break for a few hours or days, there are some excellent, sparsely populated **beaches** but a short distance to the south. The first of these, **PLAYA HERMOSA**, is only 7km away, and offers a long stretch of darkish sand that has a tempting break for surfers. There's a line of places to stay and eat: *Cabinas Playa Hermosa* (Ⓣ643-2640; ❺) has very well-priced cabins with fans and a swimming pool, while *Jammin'* is a relaxed rasta restaurant with generous portions of surfer-friendly fare at the US$6–8 range for mains and less for sandwiches and snacks.

Further south is the long **PLAYA ESTERILLOS**, some 25km south. At its southern end (signposted Esterillos Este from the main road), the welcoming *Auberge du Pélican* (Ⓣ778-8105, Ⓦwww.aubergepelican.com; ❻–❼) has charming palm-shaded grounds and a/c rooms with wooden floorboards, attractive furnishings and decent bathrooms. With swimming pool, pool table, and a quality restaurant, this is a great place to relax. Breakfast included.

You can easily reach these places from Jacó by getting on a Quepos-bound bus and asking to be let off at the relevant point. In the case of Esterillos Este, you'll face a walk of just under a kilometre from the main road to the beach.

Quepos and Parque Nacional Manuel Antonio

The small corridor of land between the old banana-exporting town of **Quepos** and the little community of **Manuel Antonio**, outside the **Parque Nacional Manuel Antonio**, has experienced one of the most dramatic tourist booms in the country in recent years. The stunning, picture-postcard setting, with its spectacular white-grey sand beaches fringed by thickly forested green hills, is the main attraction, and there's also a huge variety of things to do – including walking the park's easy trails, whitewater rafting, ocean-cruising and horse-riding, to name but a few. The beauty of the area is due in part to the unique "*tómbolo*" formation of **Punta Catedral**, which juts out into the Pacific from the park. A rare geophysical phenomenon, a *tómbolo* results when an island becomes joined, slowly and over millennia, to the mainland through accumulated sand deposits. Other smaller islands, some of them no more than rocky outcroppings, straggle off from Punta Catedral and, from high up in the hills, watching a lavish sunset over the Pacific, it does seem as though Manuel Antonio is one of the more charmed places on earth.

That said, the huge tourist input has undeniably taken its toll on the whole area. The seven kilometres from Quepos town to the entrance of the national park is an unbroken line of hotels, whose construction has removed some of the pristine magic of the area, as has the sheer influx of people, which can reduce the park's main trails to conga-lines. The area isn't cheap, and in recent years, budget travellers searching for cheap beaches have headed instead to Montezuma or Tamarindo on the Nicoya Peninsula. Consequently, some hotels have had to drop their rates, and many places have gone from being overpriced to being merely expensive. You'll also need to take more precautions against **theft** than in the rest of Costa Rica. Never leave anything on the beach when you're swimming and, if you take the bus, don't let anyone handle your luggage. Wherever you stay, ensure your hotel room is locked at all times, and note that rental cars left on the street have become a favourite target.

Quepos

Arriving at the town of **QUEPOS** from San José, Puntarenas or Jacó, it's immediately apparent that you've crossed into the lush, wetter southern Pacific region. Vegetation is thicker and greener than up north, and you'll notice the proliferation of **sports-fishing** imagery – of all the sports-fishing grounds in Costa Rica, the Quepos area has the most variety, and many small tour agencies cater more or less exclusively to sports-fishers. The town itself, backed against a hill and fronted by a muddy beach, can look pretty ramshackle, but it's a friendly place, with plenty of hotels, bars and restaurants. More important, however, is its proximity to Parque Nacional Manuel Antonio and its beaches, 7km south.

Arrival and orientation

Buses leave San José's La Coca-Cola for Quepos eight times daily (at 6am*, 7am, 10am, noon*, 2pm, 4pm, 6pm* & 7.30pm*; those marked with an asterisk are express buses which take 3hr 30min, as opposed to the others, which take 5hr). At weekends, holidays and any time during the dry season, you'll need to buy your bus ticket for the Manuel Antonio service at least three days in advance, and your return ticket as soon as you arrive. All buses arrive in Quepos at the busy **terminal**, which doubles as the *mercado*, just one block east of the town centre. In addition to these two buses, Interbus's new **shuttle service** makes the trip between San José and Quepos (and Manuel Antonio) daily using air-conditioned Mercedes minibuses (US$25 each way). They leave San José at 9am and 1.30pm, returning from Manuel Antonio at 8.30am and 2.30pm, and will pick you up from your hotel at each end. For reservations, call ⓣ283-5573 in San José; book over the Internet at ⓦwww.interbusonline.com; or contact Lynch Tours in Quepos (ⓣ777-1170, ⓦwww.lynchtravel.com).

Due to the long drive and the condition of the roads, it's a good idea to **fly** from San José: this takes only fifteen minutes once in the air and, as Quepos residents like to point out, there are no potholes in the sky. There are ten flights a day run by Sansa and NatureAir; a one-way fare costs US$46–50, but the flights tend to get heavily booked up. The airstrip is about 5km north of town.

Information

To change **money and travellers' cheques**, head for the Banco Nacional, just northwest of the bus terminal; the attached ATM accepts Visa and MasterCard/Cirrus. Other banks also change travellers' cheques, as do Lynch Tours. The Banco de San José/Credomatic is the only place you can get cash advances on MasterCard, and is also open on Saturday mornings. Most businesses in town will change dollars.

The **correo** (Mon–Fri 8am–5pm) is at the eastern end of town. There's a plethora of places with **Internet access**, including *Internet Tropical*, in front of the *Hotel Malinche*, which also has an international phone service, plus good fruit *batidos* and toasted sandwiches; and *Quepos Internet Café*, opposite the soccer pitch, which has a happy hour and student discounts. There's a laundromat next to the *Mar y Luna* hotel in the centre. In the event of medical emergencies, Quepos has an excellent **hospital**, the Hospital Dr Max Teran (ⓣ777-0200), near the airport. There's car rental available in town at Álamo, by the soccer pitch.

Accommodation

Budget travellers will have a hard time in the Manuel Antonio area, especially in the dry season, when hotels are full and charging their highest prices. Most of the area's budget options can be found in Quepos, which is more economical overall than Manuel Antonio, both for accommodation and eating. Wherever you plan to stay, book well ahead in high season – as ever, things are cheaper and easier in the wet.

Cabinas Doña Alicia on the northwest corner of the soccer pitch ⓣ777-0419. Good budget choice: the rooms (with comfortable double beds) all sleep up to four people, apart from a few good-value singles, a rarity in Quepos. All have private bath (cold water only), there's parking around the back, and the friendly owners keep everything spotlessly clean. ❸

Cabinas El Cisne 200m north of the church ⓣ777-0719. Good-value rooms, with refrigerator, TV, small kitchen, fan or a/c, and nice folk running it. ❺

Cabinas Helen a block south of the mercado ⓣ777-0504. Clean cabinas in the back of a family home, with private bath, fridge, fans, small table and chairs, a small patio, parking and a laundry service. Secure, and recommended for those travelling with children. Good single rates, too. ❹

Hotel Kamuk on the western avenue ⓣ777-0811, ⓦwww.kamuk.co.cr. Clear, airy hotel belonging to the *Best Western* chain. There are two types of rooms; all have a/c, cable TV and phone; the more expensive ones have balconies and sea views. There's a bar and pool, and two good places to eat, a café and a restaurant. ❼–❽

Hotel Malinche just west of the mercado ⓣ & ⓕ777-0093. Modern, motel-style hotel with unremarkable but bright and comfortable a/c rooms with carpet, TV and balcony, and cheaper, older rooms with ceiling fans. Both have no hot water, but it's hardly missed in this climate. The upstairs rooms are better. The people who run the hotel are friendly, and can arrange good fishing charters. ❹–❻

Hotel Melissa just west of the mercado ⓣ777-0025. Darkish but clean and inoffensive budget rooms in a friendly central place, which has an upstairs balcony to observe the street in the afternoon heat. The rooms have their own small cold-water bathroom. Cheaper off-season. ❹

Outdoor activities and tours

There's a good range of **tours** in the Quepos area, while many of the upmarket hotels in town or on the road to Manuel Antonio have their own tour-service desk. Most day-trips include equipment rental and guides where necessary, along with lunch and/or snacks. Note that though you can theoretically visit **Bahía Drake and the Osa Peninsula** – including Isla del Caño just off the coast of Osa – from Quepos, it's far cheaper to get there from Palmar or Golfito (see p.719) in the Zona Sur.

In the town centre, the friendly and reputable **Lynch Tours** (ⓣ777-1170, ⓕ777-1571, ⓦwww.lynchtravel.com) is a good source of unbiased information. They can get you to Dominical, Corcovado and Bahía Drake either by bus or plane, and arrange transfers to nearly all parts of the country in air-conditioned Mercedes shuttle buses; they also arrange airport transfers (US$4) and handle plane-ticket sales and reservations. Their many local tours include horse-riding trips to a local waterfall (US$55), sports-fishing (US$450–1200 for a full day's offshore fishing), sea kayaking (US$65), whitewater rafting (US$70–98), rainforest canopy tours (US$65), and ever-popular daytime or sunset cruises, some specifically to see dolphins (US$65). Iguana Tours (ⓣ777-1262, ⓦwww.iguanatours.com), from their office by the soccer pitch, also run a variety of jungle tours and transfers.

Equus Stables (ⓣ777-0001, ⓔhavefun@racsa.co.cr), on the road to Manuel Antonio, can take you **horse-riding** on the beach – sunset is the time to go – and up into the mountains behind on a two-hour tour (US$35). As elsewhere in the country, it's worth having a look at how the horses are treated and stabled before you ride, since overwork and abuse of horses is fairly widespread and a thorny issue among travellers and riding outfitters.

There are several sport-fishing operators in town. Bluefin (ⓣ777-2222, ⓦwww.bluefinsportfishing.com) have three boats and charge US$600–850 for a full day's offshore charter. *Hotel Malinché* can set you up with a recommended local fisherman; Costa Rica Dreams (ⓣ & ⓕ777-0593) is another well-equipped outfit.

Moving on from Quepos

Buses to Manuel Antonio leave from the terminal at the *mercado* (15 daily; 20min) between 5.30am and 9.30pm; there are slightly fewer in the rainy season. The service **to San José** departs at 5am, 6am*, 8am, 9.30am*, noon*, 2pm, 3pm*, 4pm and 5pm* (those marked with an asterisk take 3hr 30min, the others 5hr). Buses **to Puntarenas** (3hr) leave at 4.30am, 7.30am, 10.30am and 3pm; the Puntarenas bus will also stop in Jacó (1hr 30min). When the condition of the road permits, buses also head southwards to Dominical and Uvita. **Taxis** line up at the rank at the south end of the *mercado*: the journey to Manuel Antonio costs US$3–5. If you're **driving**, you can get to San Isidro, Golfito and the Osa Peninsula, and other points in the Zona Sur via Dominical, 44km south of Quepos – although the road is usually in terrible condition and a sturdy 4WD is needed, it beats going all the way back to San José and taking the Interamericana south. For **plane** tickets and schedules to San José, visit Lynch Tours (see opposite).

Rafting outfitters Los Amigos del Río (☎777-0082) have an office between Quepos and Manuel Antonio (look for a large orange building on the left with inflatable rafts outside).

One of the most popular activities hereabouts are the **cruises** along the coast to Manuel Antonio. Sunset Sails (☎ & ℻777-1304; or book through Lynch Tours) offer dolphin-watching or sunset cruises (Dec–April only) in a classic wooden yacht, with stunning views of the coastline and offshore islands (4hr 30min; US$69); whales and sea turtles are sometimes spotted. Another popular excursion is to the Rainmaker Conservation Project, 22km north, where a series of hanging bridges give an opportunity to appreciate the jungle ecosystem; there's also an optional "canopy tour". Cost of the day's excursion is US$45–65 for a half-day.

Eating and drinking

As in other tourist towns in Costa Rica, head to the *sodas* frequented by locals for the cheapest meals – *Soda La Costa de Oro*, next to the Banco Popular, is the cheapest place in town, with fish *casados* for only US$2.50 and a busy lunchtime crowd of locals and tourists. As a rule, **fish** is predictably good – order grilled *pargo* or *dorado* and you can't go far wrong. *Café El Patio*, on the sea wall, has a real espresso machine and cakes – try the vanilla nut chill or iced raspberry mocha. *Parrilla Argentina*, next to the church, is the best place in town for juicy Argentinean-style steaks, cooked in the open by the generous chef. A big *bife de chorizo* costs US$11. *La Lanterna*, opposite the Banco Nacional, does excellent pizza as well as classy, if somewhat minimalist, Italian main courses using quality imported ingredients. These dishes come in at US$6–9, with pizza and pasta a little cheaper. One of the town's better bars is *Wacky Wanda's*, which usually has a cheerful mix of tourists and locals in air-conditioned comfort until fairly late at night.

Quepos to Parque Nacional Manuel Antonio

Southeast of Quepos, a 7km stretch of road winds over the surrounding hills, pitching up at the entrance to the Parque Nacional Manuel Antonio. This road is now the site of a tremendous number of hotels: the most exclusive – and expensive – are hidden away in the surrounding hills, reached by side roads, and the very best overlook Punta Catedral, which juts out picturesquely into the Pacific. Though there are some reasonably affordable places near the park entrance, and the occasional low-season discount, prices are high compared to the rest of the country.

La Buena Nota souvenir shop, on the road to Manuel Antonio between the *Hotel Karahé* and *Cabinas Piscis* (☎777-1002), functions as an information centre for the area, as well as selling camera film, foreign papers and magazines, and locally made handcrafted clothing, including some featuring *molas* (designs from the Panamanian Kuna peoples). There's **Internet access** in the unlikely setting of a restored railway car – brought all the way from northern Chile – in front of *La Cantina* restaurant across from the *Costa Verde* hotel.

The hotels below are listed in the order you encounter them from Quepos. All are well signed from the road. More than anywhere else, the choice is partial, each one representing the best value in its price range. Taking a **taxi** from Quepos to any of the hotels on the road to the park there's a set fare of around US$5. If you're going back to Quepos by taxi, it's cheapest to flag one down on the road. Fares are per person, and the driver may pick up a number of people along the way.

Accommodation

Cabinas Pedro Miguel ⓣ777-0035, ⓕ777-0279. One of the friendliest places in the area, Costa Rican–owned and managed, and home to the Escuela del Pacífico language school. The family rent *casitas*, backed up against the rainforest, with mosquito nets, kitchenette and basic furnishings. More upmarket bungalows are also available (❼). There's a small pool and a great cook-your-own restaurant. Low-season and midweek discounts are available, but book ahead. ❹

Hotel Plinio ⓣ777-0055, ⓦwww.hotelplinio.com. Good selection of rooms (though some are a bit dark), all well-screened and nicely decorated with Guatemalan prints – the highest rooms give spectacular sunset views which you can watch from the raised platform beds. The landscaped tropical gardens feature a pool and a 4km nature trail, with stupendous views from the top. There's a very good restaurant, too, a hospitable welcome, and off-season discounts. ❻

Hotel Mono Azul ⓣ & ⓕ777-1954, ⓦwww.monoazul.com. One of the best-value places in Manuel Antonio, with small but bright and clean rooms with fans, some new ones with a/c and a terrace, and, across the road, villas sleeping up to five. Lovely swimming pools and an excellent restaurant (see opposite) add further lustre. Book in advance. ❻

Hotel Las Tres Banderas ⓣ777-1284, ⓕ777-1478, ⓦwww.hoteltresbanderas.com. Situated in a quiet wooded area, this is one of the area's best and most welcoming hotels, though moderately priced. The large double rooms open onto a terrace or balcony looking out at the forest, while the even more spacious suites are furnished with kitchenette and sofa bed (❽). There's also a fully furnished apartment, a large swimming pool and a good restaurant sometimes serving tasty Polish specialities (non-guests must reserve). ❼

Hotel La Colina ⓣ777-0231, ⓦwww.lacolina.com. Located on the near-vertical incline locals call "cardiac hill", this lovely hotel offers rare, good-value mid-range rooms, all with private bath and a/c; if your legs are up to the stairs up the hill, you'll find apartments with a fantastic 180° view of the jungle and the sea (❽). The hotel also boasts one of the better restaurants in the area. There's a nice pool, too, and breakfast is included. ❻

Tulemar ⓣ777-0580, ⓦwww.tulemar.com. A great luxury hideaway, with fourteen beautiful octagonal bungalows, many with panoramic views over Punta Catedral, built on stilts and set into the hillside. All are luxuriously furnished with a/c, VCR and TV, phones and well-equipped kitchenettes, and come in at some US$275 during high season. There's also a large swimming pool and nature trails in the grounds. Breakfast included. Significantly cheaper off-season. ❾

Makanda-by-the-Sea ⓣ777-0442, ⓦwww.makanda.com. One of Manuel Antonio's best top-range choices, with a friendlier atmosphere than at some other luxury establishments in the area. Accommodation is in elegant villas, all with kitchenettes and outside balconies or terraces, set in quiet gardens with ocean views. Expect to pay about US$265 per night including taxes. No children under 16 admitted. Breakfast included. ❾

Hotel Si Como No ⓣ777-0777, ⓦwww.sicomono.com. Architectural award-winning complex set on a hill overlooking the Pacific and Punta Catedral – there are beautiful views from nearly every room. The hotel has solar-heated hot water, Jacuzzi, two pools, swim-up bar and waterslide, as well as a small cinema with nightly screenings (free to guests). Rooms (and prices) vary from well-appointed doubles (US$190 including tax) to fully equipped villas. The poolside *Rico Tico* grill serves excellent food, and breakfast is included. ❾

Hotel Costa Verde ⓣ777-0584, ⓦwww.costaverde.com. Friendly and professionally run hotel in a quiet area, with spacious rooms and studio apartments constructed from beautiful hardwood, rustic in feel but with all amenities and nice details such as decorative tiles and balconies with terrific ocean views. Reception is in a train carriage; the best-value rooms are in D block, looking out directly onto Punta Catedral and offering the most stunning views in Manuel Antonio. There's a separate a/c area for families, along with a restaurant, bar, and 3 swimming pools with stunning views. ❽

Albergue Costa Linda ⓣ777-0304. Friendly, backpacker-oriented spot. Dormitory rooms are pretty basic, with shared cold-water bathrooms, but there's a comfort-food restaurant as well as more upscale apartments (US$45–50). ❸

Cabinas Espadilla ⓣ777-2113, ⓦwww.espadilla.com. The nicest place in Manuel Antonio village, although slightly overpriced – the cabinas are better value for three or four people. Each airy room has large beds, private bath with hot water and kitchen, and fan or a/c, and the complex is set in attractive gardens with a nice pool. ❼

Hotel Vela Bar ⓣ777-0413, ⓕ777-1071, ⓔvelabar@maqbeach.com. Small and reasonably priced hotel offering basic, but pleasant, rooms with private bath and fan or a/c. There's also a small *casita* with kitchenette and lounge. Close to the beach and park. ❺

Eating and drinking

Eating in Manuel Antonio is notoriously expensive, and the area's few good-value restaurants, like *El Mono Azul* and *Mar y Sombra*, are understandably popular. The more upmarket hotels all have restaurants attached; some are very good, though most are expensive, or simply overpriced. Some restaurants in Manuel Antonio, including several of the best, close or have restricted hours in the rainy season – ask at *La Buena Nota* (see p.675) for information. For the more popular places – *Plinio*, *Karola's* and *Vela Bar* among them – you should call or stop by to make a reservation, especially at weekends and during high season.

Barba Roja next to the *Divisimar Hotel*, on the road to Manuel Antonio, about 2.5km from the park entrance. Friendly and perennially popular place for high-quality American cuisine, including burgers and desserts. Also a fine spot for a quiet drink while watching the sunset.

Café Milagro One of the best local places for breakfast (from 6.30am), with excellent locally roasted coffee and superlative cappuccino, pastries and cooked food served up in a pleasant environment.

Karola's near *Barba Roja*. Mexican cuisine, with burritos, seafood, vegetarian dishes and a macadamia nut pie that has entered local food legend. Closed Wed and in the low season.

Mar y Sombra Manuel Antonio village, 500m from the park entrance, on the beach. In a shady palm grove, this sprawling, cheap place is the most popular in the village. You can have a drink on the beach, and eat típico food including good *casados* (US$3), and there's a disco at weekends. Try the fried fillet of fish of the day, simply done in garlic and butter, with fried plantains and salad for US$5.

Plinio in the hotel of the same name ⓣ777-0055. Quite simply one of the best restaurants in the country, open for breakfast, lunch and dinner. There's a distinct Asian slant to the menu, with aromatic Thai soups, curries, stir-fries (mains US$8–10), and a selection of reasonable Chilean wine. There's a nice relaxed bar, too, with good music.

Rainforest Restaurant in *El Mono Azul* hotel. Generous and reasonably priced plates of well-cooked chicken, fish, hamburgers and sandwiches. There's also pizza and a nightly film, with a dinner-and-movie special for US$8 every night. Check out the shop next to the restaurant – all proceeds go to a local project run by children to preserve the rainforest and the habitat of the squirrel monkey.

Rico Tico Grill at the *Si Como No*. Poolside dining with a view over the ocean and superbly cooked food – try the succulent fish brochettes – only slightly marred by excessively obsequious service. Try an exceptional cocktail or chilled fruit drink. Breakfast is also good, with the added entertainment – if you're lucky and up early – of watching the squirrel monkeys and coatimundi that live in the trees in front of the restaurant.

Vela Bar Manuel Antonio village. The swankiest food in the village, with dishes (from around US$7) featuring good grilled fish, plus some vegetarian choices and paella.

Parque Nacional Manuel Antonio

By far the smallest park in Costa Rica's system, **PARQUE NACIONAL MANUEL ANTONIO** (Tues–Sun 7am–4pm; US$7; ⓦwww.manuelantonio.com),

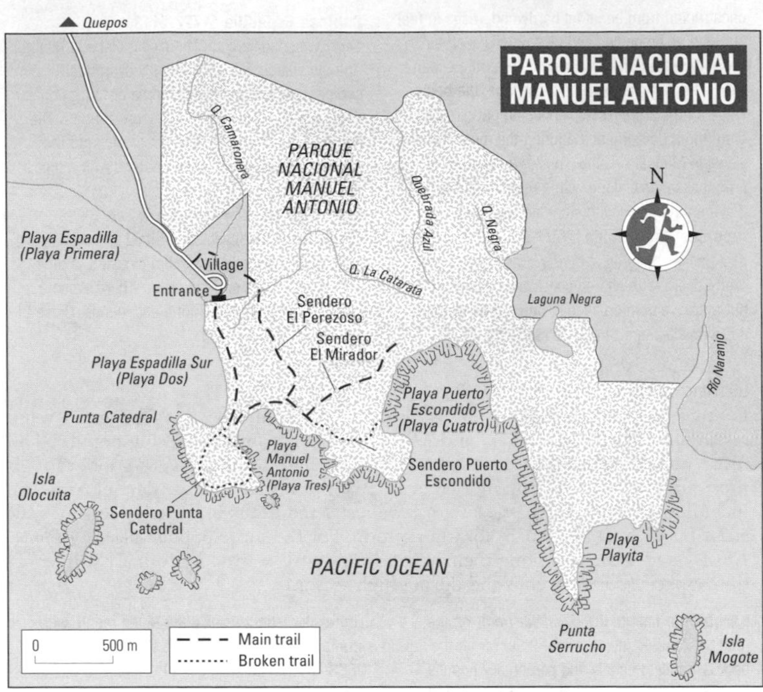

some 150km southwest of San José, fights it out with Parque Nacional Volcán Poás in the Valle Central for the title of the most popular national park in the country. It's hard not to appreciate the foresight that went into the establishment of the park in 1972: considering the number of hotels and restaurants sidling up to its borders, you can just imagine how developed the white sands would be today were they not protected. Even so, the park is suffering from the numbers it receives, and frequently reaches its quota of six hundred visitors in the park at any one time.

Covering an area of just under seven square kilometres, Manuel Antonio preserves not only the lovely **beaches** and the unique *tómbolo* formation of Punta Catedral, but also **mangroves** and humid tropical **forest**. Visitors can walk only on the coastal section of the park. The eastern mountain section is off limits to the public, and is regularly patrolled by rangers to deter poaching, which is rife in the area, and incursions into the park from surrounding farmers and campesinos.

This forest is one of the few remaining natural habitats for **squirrel monkeys**. Other **mammals** in the park – you're likely to see many of the smaller ones – include the racoon, coati, agouti, two-toed sloth and white-faced capuchin monkey. **Birdlife** is also abundant, including the shimmering green kingfisher, the brown pelican, which can often be seen fishing off the rocks, and the laughing falcon. Beware of the snakes that inhabit the park, draping themselves over the trails in imitation of jungle vines; you may not see them, but they're here.

The **climate** is hot, humid and wet, all year round. Though the rains ease off in the dry season (Dec–April), they never disappear entirely. The average temperature all year is 27°C, and it can easily go to 30°C and above.

Beaches in Manuel Antonio are known by a confusing number of different names, but because some are not safe for swimming, it's important to grasp which one is which. **Playa Espadilla**, also sometimes called Playa Primera, is actually outside the park, immediately north of the entrance. One of the most popular beaches in the country – it is very beautiful, with a wide stretch of smooth light-grey sand and stunning sunsets – it is also very dangerous, plagued by fast **riptides**. However, lots of people do swim here – or, rather, paddle and wade – and live to tell the tale, and now that there are professional lifeguards around, it's considerably safer than it used to be, in the dry season at least. Inside the park, swim at **Playa Espadilla Sur** (or Playa Dos), which is long and usually very calm, or at **Playa Manuel Antonio** (also called Playa Tres or Playa Blanca), which is immediately south of Punta Catedral, and more sheltered than the other beaches. Because of this, it's usually pretty crowded. The main entrance trail works its way along Playa Espadilla Sur until it reaches Playa Manuel Antonio (2.2km). From here, a circular trail, steepish in parts, takes you 1.5km up and down around Punta Catedral itself. It's far quieter than the main trail, and you'll get some very tranquil vistas over the ocean.

Practicalities

Buses from Quepos and San José drop passengers off 200m before the park entrance. If you're staying at a hotel between the park and Quepos, and want to go to either by **taxi**, it's cheaper to flag one down on the road rather than ringing from the hotel – you'll be charged a per-person fare, and the taxi may pick up more people. If you're driving, note that you'll be charged US$2.50 to leave your car at one of the supervised lots at the road loop at the end of Manuel Antonio village, or anywhere on the main street. The entrance hut is reached from the southern end of the beach – be prepared to get your feet a little wet reaching the path. There are no maps of the park available at the entrance, but it's pretty self-explanatory. There are toilets and showers at playas Dos and Tres. There have been problems with **theft** in Manuel Antonio, usually as a result of people leaving valuables (like cameras) on the beach: the rangers, who often sit at the picnic tables, might be able to look after your stuff, but ask nicely, as it's not actually part of their job.

Guided **tours** are available with park-accredited guides for US$15 per person. The guides are informative, speak English, and have sophisticated binocular devices to help in spotting animals. Ask at the park entrance, or ask your hotel to ring the park office to reserve a guide. Be aware that when you leave your car in the parking area in Manuel Antonio village you may be approached by "guides" offering their services at the same price as the official park guides. These so-called guides have been known to rob their clients while in the park; though it's more likely that they simply won't be able to show you anything you couldn't see with your own eyes, as they're not trained. If in doubt, the park-accredited guides carry photo ID. Take care if walking alone in the park: a number of robberies have been reported. Although rangers are often on patrol and can nearly always be found near Playa Tres, by law they can't deny entrance to the park to anyone, even suspicious characters.

6.5

Guanacaste

Guanacaste Province, bordered to the north by Nicaragua and hemmed in by mountains to the east and the Pacific Ocean to the west, is distinctly different from the rest of Costa Rica. Though little tangible remains of the dance, music and folklore for which the region is famous, there is undeniably something special about the place. Even though much of the **landscape** has come about essentially through the slaughter of tropical dry forest, it is still some of the prettiest you'll see in the country, especially in the wet season, when wide open spaces, stretching from the ocean across savanna grasses to the brooding humps of volcanoes, are washed in a beautifully muted range of earth tones, blues, yellows and mauves. Its **history**, too, is distinct: if not for a very close vote in 1824, it might have been part of Nicaragua, which would have made Costa Rica very small indeed.

Most tourists come for the **beaches**: specifically those where the **Nicoya Peninsula** joins the mainland (roughly two-thirds of the mountainous peninsula is in Guanacaste, with the lower third belonging to Puntarenas Province). Although beaches such as surf-crazy **Tamarindo** have long been favourite tourist destinations, quieter getaways like **Nosara** offer more space for contemplation, without losing anything except nightlife in exchange. Several beaches are also nesting grounds for **marine turtles**: giant leatherbacks haul themselves up the sand at Playa Grande, near Tamarindo, while **Parque Nacional Santa Rosa** is the destination for Olive Ridleys. An enormous number of hotels, some all-inclusive resort types, are being built on both coasts, and with the opening of the Liberia airport to international traffic, winter charter tourism has well and truly arrived. Inland, however, mass tourism is less evident. Here the dry heat, relatively accessible terrain and panoramic views make Guanacaste the best place in the country for **walking** and **horse-riding**, especially around the mud pots and stewing sulphur waters of **Parque Nacional Rincón de la Vieja** and through the tropical dry forest cover of Parque Nacional Santa Rosa. The only **towns** of any significance for travellers are the provincial capital of **Liberia**, and **Nicoya**, the main town of the peninsula. If you are overnighting on the way **to Nicaragua**, La Cruz makes a useful base.

Much of Guanacaste has long been put under pasture for cattle ranching, and a huge part of the region's appeal is the **sabanero** (cowboy) culture, based around the hacienda (ranch) and *ganado* (livestock). This dependence on cattle culture has its downside, however, and much of Guanacaste is now degraded pastureland. Although impressive efforts to regenerate former tropical dry forest are under way – at Parque Nacional Santa Rosa, for example – it is unlikely that this rare type of life zone will ever recover its original extent.

The province is significantly greener, and prettier, in the "wet" season (May–Nov), generally agreed to be the **best time** to come, with the added benefit of fewer travellers and lighter rainfall than in the rest of the country.

Liberia and around

The spirited provincial capital of **LIBERIA** has a distinctively friendly and free-thinking feel, its wide clean streets and blinding white houses the legacy of the

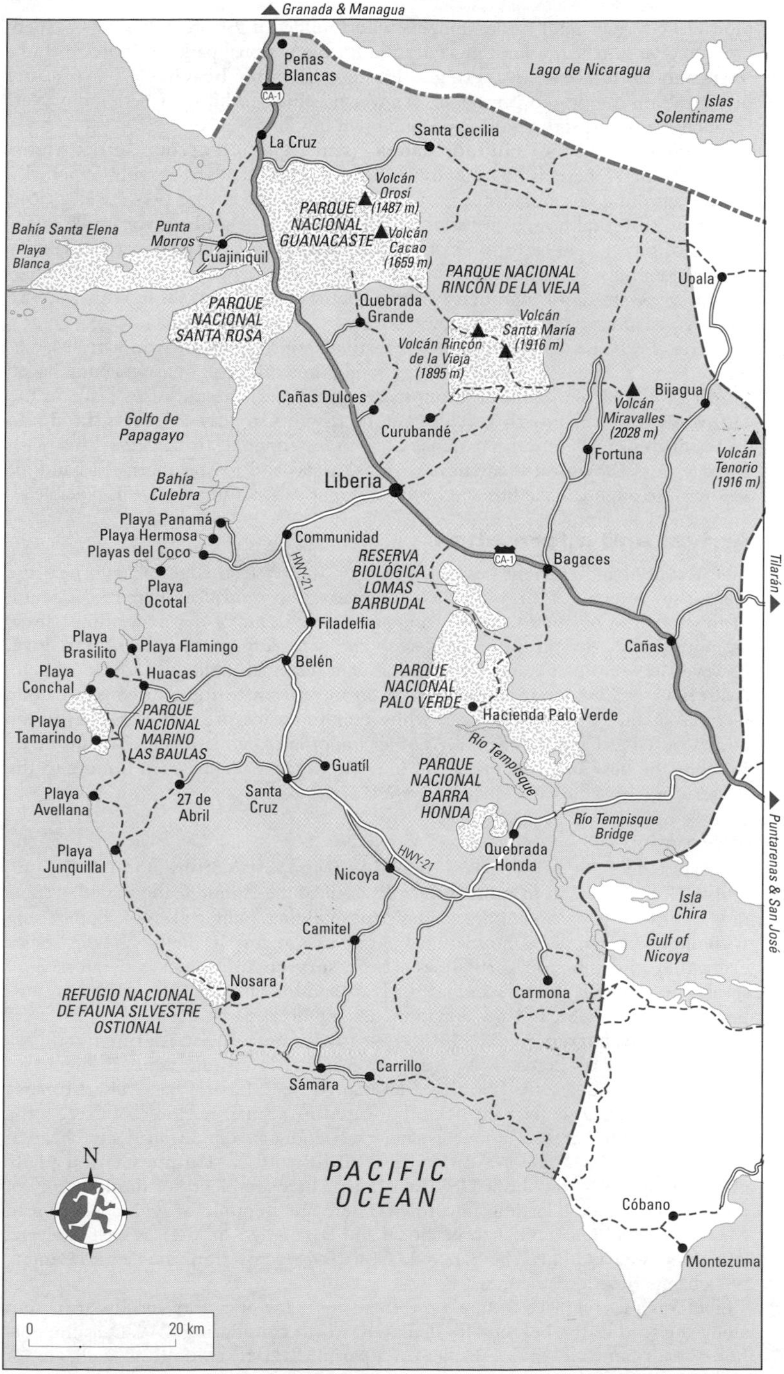

Granada & Managua

Peñas Blancas

CA-1

Lago de Nicaragua

Islas Solentiname

La Cruz

Santa Cecilia

Volcán Orosí (1487 m)

PARQUE NACIONAL GUANACASTE

Volcán Cacao (1659 m)

Bahía Santa Elena

Punta Morros

Playa Blanca

Cuajiniquil

PARQUE NACIONAL RINCÓN DE LA VIEJA

Upala

PARQUE NACIONAL SANTA ROSA

Quebrada Grande

Volcán Santa María (1916 m)

Volcán Rincón de la Vieja (1895 m)

Bijagua

Volcán Miravalles (2028 m)

Cañas Dulces

Curubandé

Golfo de Papagayo

Fortuna

Volcán Tenorio (1916 m)

Liberia

Bahía Culebra

Playa Panamá

Playa Hermosa

Playas del Coco

Communidad

HWY-21

RESERVA BIOLÓGICA LOMAS BARBUDAL

CA-1

Bagaces

Tilarán

Playa Ocotal

Filadelfia

Playa Brasilito

Playa Flamingo

Cañas

Belén

Playa Conchal

Huacas

PARQUE NACIONAL PALO VERDE

PARQUE NACIONAL MARINO LAS BAULAS

Hacienda Palo Verde

Playa Tamarindo

Río Tempisque

Guatíl

PARQUE NACIONAL BARRA HONDA

Playa Avellana

27 de Abril

Santa Cruz

Puntarenas & San José

Río Tempisque Bridge

Playa Junquillal

Quebrada Honda

HWY-21

Nicoya

Isla Chira

Gulf of Nicoya

Camitel

Nosara

Carmona

REFUGIO NACIONAL DE FAUNA SILVESTRE OSTIONAL

Carrillo

Sámara

N

PACIFIC OCEAN

Cóbano

Montezuma

0 20 km

pioneering farmers and cattle ranchers who founded it. At present most travellers use the town simply as a jumping-off point for the national parks of **Rincón de la Vieja** and **Santa Rosa**, an overnight stop to or from the **beaches** of Guanacaste, or a break on the way to Nicaragua. It's worth getting to know it better, however, for Liberia is perhaps the most appealing town in Costa Rica.

Sometimes called the "**ciudad blanca**" (white city) on account of its white-washed houses, Liberia is the only town in the country that seems truly "colonial". It has everything you might need for a relaxing stay of a day or two – well-priced accommodation (although not much choice), a very helpful tourist office and a couple of nice places to eat and drink. The nearby international airport delivers busloads of visitors to the western beaches, but Liberia happily remains unchanged: it's still the epitome of dignified (if somewhat static) provincialism, with a strong identity and atmosphere all its own.

Liberia also boasts several lively local **festivals**, one of which is in early March, when there's a lively ten days of parades, bands, fireworks, and bulls wreaking havoc on daring but alcohol-addled young locals. Most of the action takes place in the fairgrounds in the northwest corner of town. On July 25, **El Día de la Independencia** celebrates Guanacaste's independence from Nicaragua with parades, horseshows, cattle auctions, rodeos, fiestas and roving marimba bands. If you want to attend, make bus and hotel reservations as far in advance as possible.

Arrival and information

Liberia's clean and efficient bus terminal is on the western edge of town near the exit for the Interamericana – it's a ten-minute walk at most from here to the centre of town. At the bus station is an elaborately painted list of departure times: these are pure fiction, so you must check with the ticket office. Buses from **San José**, however, leave from and arrive at the Pulmitan terminal, a block southeast of here. **Addresses** in Liberia are most often given in relation to the church, the Parque Central, or the *gobernación*, a large white building across from the church on the corner of C Real and Av Central. Another important landmark is La Esquina de las Bombas, the busy intersection of the Interamericana with the road leading to the western beaches and with Liberia's Avenida Central.

Information

Liberia's faded, but helpful, **tourist office** (Mon–Sat 8.30am–noon & 2–5pm; ⓣ665-0135) is on C 1, five minutes' walk south of the Parque Central, with a small display of local *sabanero* culture in the same building. Staff will book hotels, help with directions and place international phone calls at cost. In the high season, especially, they also function partially as a **tour service**, using local operators. Staff speak some English and give unbiased advice and information. The office is a non-profit-making service, and any donations are appreciated.

The efficient **correo**, Av 3, C 8 (Mon–Fri 7.30am–6pm, Sat 7.30am–noon), is a bit hard to find: it's between Av 3 and Av 5 in the low-slung white house across from an empty square field bordered by mango trees. Liberia has a few **Internet cafés**: *Cybermania* (daily 8am–10pm), located in a small business centre on the north side of the Parque Central, is efficient, friendly, air-conditioned and cheap, as is the handy *Planet Internet*, on Calle Real just off the Parque Central (daily 8am–10pm). Both cost about US$1 per hour. There are plenty of **banks**, many of them on Av Central, leading into town. There are a couple of ATMs catering to MasterCard and Cirrus (Banco Nacional and Banco de San José), as well as several that accept Visa and Plus. The Banco de Costa Rica, across from the Parque Central, will change travellers' cheques.

Liberia is a useful place to hire a car; there are many operators, mostly strung out along the road to the beaches. It's definitely worth considering a 4WD, as the pot-holed roads can easily give a smaller car a pair of flat tyres in no time at all. Go for

full insurance regardless. Payless are one of the cheaper operators. Most hotels will arrange car rental for you; the rental companies will bring the car into Liberia, saving you a bus or taxi trip.

Accommodation

Liberia is a convenient place to spend the night, if you're heading north to the border or the beaches, and a likeable spot to spend a few days. At peak times it's worth booking a room, but you'll usually find something available even if you don't.

Hostal Ciudad Blanca Av 4, 200m south and 150m east of the *gobernación* ⓣ 666-3962. Spotless hotel in a noble building with a small breakfast terrace/bar, and twelve modern, a/c rooms with TV, private bath and ceiling fans. Popular with American travellers bedding down before heading out to the beach. Breakfast included. ❺

Hotel Las Espuelas on the Interamericana, a couple of kilometres south of town ⓣ 666-0144, ⓦ www.bestwestern.com. Much the better of Liberia's two representatives of the *Best Western* chain, this low, hacienda-style hotel offers standard a/c comfort; rooms come with phone and cable TV. There's a nice pool, a restaurant that does a decent slab of steak, and a bar with a pool table. ❼

Hotel Guanacaste Av 1, 300m south of the bus station ⓣ 666-0085, ⓦ www.hicr.org. Popular, HI-affiliated hostel, with a traveller-friendly cafeteria-restaurant. The rooms are simple, clean and dark; the doubles aren't great value (US$27) compared to the town's other options, but there are a few dorm places available (US$8). The hotel fills up quickly, so book ahead. If you have an HI card you get 15 percent discount; you might wangle a further 10 percent with student ID. The management organizes a daily transfer (US$20) to Rincón de la Vieja and sells bus tickets to Nicaragua. Visa and MasterCard accepted. ❹

Hotel Liberia C 0, 75m south of the Parque Central ⓣ 666-0161, ⓔ hotelliberia@hotmail.com. Well-established, friendly youth-hostel-type hotel located in a historic house – look for the jolly papaya orange exterior. The bare and basic rooms with shared cold-water bathroom are set around a sunny but bare courtyard: the newer rooms in an annex to the rear (❹) are better than the old ones and have their own bath, though they cost an extra US$4. Popular with vacationing foreigners and Costa Ricans alike – a reservation and deposit are required in the high season. The hotel staff also organize transport to Rincón de la Vieja. Visa accepted. ❷

Hotel Posada del Tope C 0, 150m south of the *gobernación* ⓣ & ⓕ 666-3876. Popular, cheap budget option in a beautiful historic house. The six basic rooms with fan and shared showers in the old part of the hotel are a bit stuffy, but clean; the more modern rooms across the street in a new annex with cable TV cost only slightly more and are set around a charming courtyard. The shared bathrooms aren't great, but there's plenty of character here, as well as friendly staff, parking, and a rooftop telescope for star-gazing. The manager runs transport to Rincón de la Vieja for US$10 per person return, as well as trips to Palo Verde and others. Visa and MasterCard accepted. ❷

The Town

Liberia's wide, clean streets are used more by cyclists and horsemen than motorists. It's pleasant to walk around in the shade provided by the mango trees, though in March and April watch out for the ripe fruit plopping down full-force at your feet. The town is arranged around its large **Parque Central**, properly called Parque Mario Cañas Ruiz. It's dedicated to *el mes del annexion*, the month of the annexation (July), celebrating the fact that Guanacaste is not in Nicaragua. Liberia's parque is one of the loveliest central plazas in the whole country, ringed by benches and tall palms that shade gossiping locals. Its **church** is startlingly modern – somewhat out of place in this very traditional town. About 600m away at the very eastern end of town, the colonial **Iglesia de la Agonía** is more arresting, with a mottled yellow facade like a pock-marked, washed-out banana. On the verge of perpetual collapse – it has had a hard time from those earthquakes – it's almost never open, but you could try shoving the heavy wooden door and hope the place doesn't collapse around you if it does give way. The town's most interesting street is **Calle Real** (marked as Calle Central on some maps). In the nineteenth century this street was the entrance to Liberia, and practically the entire thoroughfare has now been restored to its original – and strikingly beautiful – colonial simplicity. The tourist office houses the **Museo de Sabanero**, or Cowboy Museum (Mon–Sat 8.30am–noon & 2–5pm; donation appreciated), containing a small-scale display of objects from the big old ranch houses.

Eating, drinking and entertainment

Liberia has several **restaurants** that are particularly good for breakfast and lunch. Local treats include **natilla** (soured cream) eaten with eggs or *gallo pinto* and tortillas. For a real feast, try the various **desayunos guanacastecos** (Guanacastecan breakfasts): hearty food, made to be worked off with hard labour. For rock-bottom cheap **lunches**, head for the stalls in the bus terminal, *Las Tinajas*, or the town's various fried-chicken places.

For **drinking**, places like *Las Tinajas* and *Jauja* are good for a quiet beer. The town's main **disco**, *Kurú*, a couple of hundred metres west of the Interamericana down the road to the beaches, gets lively with salsa and merengue, especially on weekends and holidays. *Tsunami*, across the road and down a side street, is another reasonable choice. The main Saturday evening activity, however, involves the locals parading around the Parque Central in their finery, hanging out, having an ice cream, and maybe going to the movies at the Cine Liberia, located in the shopping mall a kilometre south of the main Interamericana intersection.

Restaurants and sodas

Cocina de José Av 2, C 4/6. The setting of this Tico restaurant is nothing to write home about – the small concrete terrace makes it look like a bus shelter – but the cuisine completely transcends its humbler surroundings. Juicy steaks come in at US$8–9, and the *tilapia* fillets are exquisite (US$6–8). You could start off with a hearty bean soup or the imaginative house salad.

Los Comales C Real, Av 3/5. A typical *soda*, very popular with locals for its generous portions of tasty rustic food, with *gallos pintos* costing a mere US$2, and *casados* US$3.

Jauja/Pizzeria de Beppe Av Central, C 8/10. One of the better restaurants in town, although very touristy. Large and tasty pasta dishes are a pricey US$6–7, pizzas are around US$7, and there are also typical steaks and fish dishes. It's all served in a pleasant and comfortable outdoor garden setting, although the big-screen TV can be off-putting.

Rancho Dulce C Real, Av 0/2. Small and lovable

Moving on from Liberia

Liberia is the main regional **transport hub**, giving easy access to Guanacaste's parks and beaches, the Nicaraguan border and **San José** (10 direct Pulmitan de Liberia buses daily; 4hr 30min). San José buses leave from the Pulmitan terminal, a block southeast of the main bus station, which serves all other destinations.

If you're heading for **the border**, take one of the hourly buses to La Cruz or Peñas Blancas (the border's official name; 1hr). Through buses from San José to Managua also stop here, although it can be tricky to get a seat; the *Hotel Guanacaste* can sell tickets (US$11 one way).

For **Parque Nacional Santa Rosa**, take a La Cruz or Peñas Blancas bus (hourly; 40min). You should take the earliest bus you can to give yourself time for walking, and ask the driver to let you off at Santa Rosa. You can also reach the park by colectivo taxi, shared between four or five people (US$15 per car); catch one at the northwestern corner of the Parque Central. Colectivo taxis can also be good value if you're heading for **Parque Nacional Rincón de la Vieja** or the lodges near Las Pailas ranger station (roughly US$25 for four people). Arguably the best way to get to Rincón de la Vieja is to travel with one of the various Liberia hotels – *Hotel Posada del Tope*, *Hotel Liberia* and *Hotel Guanacaste* – which arrange transport to the park. All services are open to the public, though hotel guests get first option.

The more northerly of Guanacaste's **beaches** are served by direct buses: for Playa Hermosa and Playa Panamá, five buses leave daily (1hr); for Playas del Coco, six leave per day (1hr). Heading south, six daily buses serve **Tamarindo** (1hr 30min–2hr); you can also easily get to **Santa Cruz** (hourly 5.30am–7.30pm; 1hr), from where you can hook up with buses to beaches further south. Buses for **Nicoya** leave on the hour from 5am to 7pm (2hr), and journeys to **Puntarenas** leave at 5am, 8.30am, 10am, 11am and 3pm (3hr).

Liberia's international **airport** to the west of town mostly deals with sunseeker flights from the United States and Canada, but there are also four daily flights to San José operated by NatureAir and Sansa. A cab to the airport should cost US$5; you can also jump off any westbound bus at the turn-off, but it's a twenty-minute walk from there to the terminal.

soda serving *casados* (US$3), sandwiches, *empanadas* and *refrescos*: great for a cheap lunch. You can sit at the tiny outdoor stools (if you have a small bottom) or tables. A reliable choice at any time of day.

Rincón del Pollo Av Central, 50m west of the Parque Central. A simple, open place where only three dollars will get you half a roast chicken served with tortillas and salad. They only serve soft drinks to accompany your meal, but don't object to you bringing takeaways.

Las Tinajas west side of Parque Central. The outdoor tables on the veranda of this old house make a good spot for watching the goings-on in the parque while enjoying a *refresco* or beer, the latter available on tap and served in chilled glasses. Basic *casados* and excellent hamburgers (US$3) are also served. There's regular live music; the place is basically the town's best bar.

Parque Nacional Rincón de la Vieja

The dramatically dry landscape of **PARQUE NACIONAL RINCÓN DE LA VIEJA** (daily 8am–4pm; US$6), northeast of Liberia, varies from rock-strewn savanna to patches of tropical dry forest and deciduous trees, culminating in the blasted-out vistas of the volcano crater itself. The land here is actually alive and breathing: Rincón de la Vieja last erupted in 1991, and rivers of lava still broil beneath the thin epidermis of ground, while **mud pots** (*pilas de barro*) bubble and puffs of steam rise out of lush foliage, signalling sulphurous subterranean springs. This is great terrain for **camping**, **riding** and **hiking**, with a comfortable, fairly dry heat – although it can get damp and cloudy at the higher elevations around the crater. **Birders**, too, will enjoy Rincón de la Vieja, as there are more than two hundred species in residence.

Getting to the park

The local dry season (Dec–March especially) is the best time to visit, as the hiking trails and visibility as you ascend the volcano are at their best. To make management of the forest more efficient, the park has been split into two sectors: **Sector Pailas** ("cauldrons") and **Sector Santa María**, each with its own **entrance** and ranger station. From Liberia most people travel through the hamlet of Curubandé, about 16km northeast, to the Las Pailas sector. The other ranger station, Santa María, lies about 25km northeast from Liberia. The **casona** that houses the ranger station here is a former retreat of US President Lyndon Baines Johnson, and, at more than 110 years old, is ancient in Costa Rican terms.

Both routes to the park are along stony roads, not at all suitable for walking. People do, but it's tough, uninteresting terrain, and it's really more advisable to save your energy for the trails within the park itself. Options for getting here from Liberia are covered in the box on overleaf; transfers run by hotels such as *La Posada del Tope* offer good value; **hitching** is also an option if you can find a truck driver making a delivery, possibly at one of the gas stations at La Esquina de las Bombas on the Interamericana at Liberia. Alternatively, you could **rent a car** (you'll basically need a 4WD) and stay in one of the upmarket tourist lodges such as the *Hacienda Guachipelín* or *Rincón de la Vieja Lodge* (see below).

To get to the **Las Pailas sector**, where most of the lodges are, take the Interamericana north of Liberia for 6km, then turn right to the hamlet of Curubandé – you'll see signs for the *Guachipelín* and *Rincón de la Vieja* lodges. A couple of kilometres before *Guachipelín* there's a barrier and toll booth, where you'll be charged US$1.75 to use the road. If you don't have your own transport, both lodges will pick you up from Liberia for an extra charge (US$10–25 return); they also offer **packages** from San José, with transport included. The **Santa María sector** and the *Rinconcito* lodge are reached by driving through Liberia's Barrio La Victoria in the northeast of the town (ask for the *estadio* – the football stadium – from where it's a signed 24km drive to the park).

Accommodation

There's a basic **campsite** near the Las Pailas *puesto*, and another slightly better equipped site at the Santa María *puesto* (US$2 per person), where there are lavatories and water for washing, though you should take your own cooking utensils, food and drinking water. If you have a sleeping bag, and ask in advance, you can also stay inside the musty bunk rooms in the Santa María ranger station (phone the ACG office at Santa Rosa for permission on ⓣ695-5598).

Buena Vista Lodge 31km northeast of Liberia ⓣ661-8158, ⓦwww.buenavistacr.com. A working cattle ranch – you can even ride with the cowhands if your horsemanship is up to it – with stupendous views over Guanacaste and some great trails through pockets of rainforest on the flanks of the volcano and up to the crater. Double rooms are housed in individual bungalows, many set around a small lake in which you can swim. A restaurant serves up wholesome meals, and there are reasonably priced horseback and hiking tours available. If you're driving here, a 4WD is recommended; alternatively, you can arrange to be picked up from Cañas Dulces (accessible from Liberia by bus). ❺

Hotel Hacienda Guachipelín 5km beyond Curubandé on the edge of the park ⓣ666-8075, ⓦwww.guachipelin.com. A working ranch, the historic *Guachipelín* looks every inch the old cattle hacienda, with comfortable doubles in the main house. Meals are extra and a little overpriced. There's a fantastic swimming pool, and breakfast is included in the price. Attractions include a nearby waterfall, mud pots and some well-marked trails; guides are available for a variety of tours, including riding and hiking to the volcano. Pick-ups from Liberia can be arranged for a fee. ❻

Rinconcito Lodge in San Jorge ⓣ666-2764, ⓔrinconcito@racsa.co.cr. The cheapest option close to the park, this farm is owned by a friendly family and has plain but good-value cabinas with cold-water shared or private bathroom. The owners are a good source of advice on local transport, guides and directions, and can also arrange horse-riding, guided tours and pick-ups from Liberia (about US$35 return per car). Meals available (breakfast US$3, lunch and dinner US$5). ❹

Rincón de la Vieja Lodge 5km northwest of *Guachipelín* and 3.5km from the Las Pailas park entrance; follow the signs ⓣ & ⓕ661-8198, ⓦwww.rincondelaviejalodge.com. Popular lodge with simple, rustic accommodation, including doubles with private bath and hot water (❻), and bungalows decorated in attractive *sabanero* style. (❼). There's a pool, reading area, and restaurant serving tasty and filling meals. Horse-riding, mountain-biking, a canopy tour and swimming in nearby waterfalls can all be arranged, and packages are available, with meals and some activities included. ❻–❼

Visiting the park

You can walk Rincón de la Vieja's **main trail** to Volcán Rincón's crater from either the Santa María or Las Pailas ranger stations. Whether on foot, horseback or a combination of the two, this is quite simply one of the best hikes in the country, if not *the* best. A variety of elevations and habitats reveals hot springs, sulphur pools, bubbling mud pots and fields of purple orchids, plus a great smoking volcano at the top to reward you for your efforts. **Animals** in the area include all the big cats, shy tapir, red deer, collared peccary, two-toed sloth, and howler, white-faced and spider monkeys. **Birders** will have a chance to spot the weird-looking three-wattled bellbird, the Montezuma oropendola, the trogon and the spectacled owl, among others.

From the Las Pailas *puesto* the summit is 7.7km away. Theoretically, if you start out early in the morning you could get to the top and back down before nightfall, but only if you don't mind rushing. The **summit** (1916m) of Rincón de la Vieja presents a barren lunar landscape, with a smoking hole surrounded by black ash and a pretty freshwater lake, Lago los Jilgueros, to the south. You can get hammered by wind at the top; bring a sweater and windbreaker. If you don't fancy the climb up the volcano, more gentle walks in the Las Pailas sector take you to fumaroles and mud pots, and you can also hike to two waterfalls, the *cataratas escondidas*. **Warning**: the trail is often closed due to low visibility or high winds, so it's definitely worth ringing ahead on ⓣ661-8139 to check conditions.

From the Las Pailas entrance, there's another very satisfying walk: a 6km circular trail that takes you around some highly unusual natural features, with bubbling mud pots and a mini-volcano as well as steaming vents that make for a highly atmospheric experience. Don't get too close: it's easy to be scalded, and be prepared to ford a couple of streams barefoot. Stop and look around every once in a while, as there's plenty of fauna on the forested sections of the trail. From Las Pailas, you can also walk to the Santa Rosa station (8km), where there's a simple campsite (US$2 per person).

Parque Nacional Santa Rosa

Established in 1971, **PARQUE NACIONAL SANTA ROSA** (daily 8am–4pm; US$6), 35km north of Liberia, is Costa Rica's oldest national park, having been established to protect an area of increasingly rare dry tropical forest. Today it's one of the most popular in the country, thanks to its good trails, great surfing (though poor swimming) and prolific turtle-spotting opportunities. It's also, given a few official restrictions, a great destination for **campers**, with a couple of sites on the beach.

Santa Rosa has an amazingly diverse topography for its size, ranging from mangrove swamp to deciduous forest and savanna. Home to 115 species of mammal – half of them bats – 250 species of bird and 100 types of amphibian and reptile (not to mention 3800 species of moth), Santa Rosa is of prime interest to biologists, attracting researchers from all over the world. Jaguars and pumas prowl the park, but you're unlikely to see them; what you may spot – at least in the dry season – are coati, coyotes and peccaries, often snuffling around watering holes.

The appearance of the park changes drastically between the **dry season**, when the many streams and small lakes dry up, trees lose their leaves, and thirsty animals can be seen at known waterholes, and the **wet months**, greener but affording fewer animal-viewing opportunities. From July to November, however, you may be able to enjoy the sight of hundreds of **Olive Ridley turtles** (*lloras*) nesting on Playa Nancite by moonlight; September and October are best. A maximum of twenty visitors are allowed access to the nesting area each day; reserve your place on ⓣ666-5051. Though too rough for swimming, the picturesque **beaches** of Naranjo and Nancite, about 12km down a bad road from the administration centre, are popular with serious **surfers**.

Santa Rosa's **La Casona** (Big House), one of Costa Rica's most famous historical sites, burned to the ground in May 2001, but it has been lovingly reconstructed. A beautiful wooden homestead, it has a small folkloric exhibition and a population of resident bats. A viewpoint up a path beside it gives a spectacular view of the Rincón de la Vieja volcanic peaks. A short *sendero natural* near the administration centre provides an easy introduction to some of the characteristics of the tropical dry forest.

Practicalities

Santa Rosa's **entrance hut** is 35km north of Liberia, signed from the Interamericana. After paying the park fee, pick up a map and proceed some 6km or so, taking the right fork to the **administration centre** (ⓣ666-5051, ⓕ666-5020), which also runs to Guanacaste and Rincón de la Vieja national parks. From here a rough road leads to the beaches; to drive these, even in the height of the dry season, you'll need a sturdy 4WD. The rangers discourage any driving at all beyond the main road; most people park their vehicle at the administration centre and walk.

If you're walking down to the beach, a ranger or fellow tourist will probably give you a ride, but on no account set out without **water** – a couple of litres per person, at least, even on a short jaunt. The easy-to-carry bottles of water with plastic handles sold at the gas stations on the road outside Liberia are particularly convenient – stock up before you come. You can also buy drinks at the administration centre.

Camping facilities at Santa Rosa are some of the best in the country. There are two sites, each costing US$2 per person, payable as you arrive at the administration centre. You only have to pay the park entrance fee for the day you arrive. The shady **La Casona** campground has bathrooms and grill pits, while **Playa Naranjo**, on the beach (and only open outside the turtle-nesting season), has picnic tables and grill pits, and a ranger's hut with outhouses and showers plus, apparently, a boa constrictor in the roof. Wherever you camp, watch your fires (the area is a tinderbox in the dry season), take plastic bags for your food, do not leave anything edible in your tent (it will be stolen by scavenging coati) and, of course, carry plenty of water.

You can also camp in another part of the park, the little-visited **Murciélago** sector, an area northwest of the main park, and accessed separately. It's a project to study the natural regeneration of former grazing land, and there's also a pretty beach that's safe for swimming. To get there, follow the Interamericana 10km past the Santa Rosa entrance, and take a left in the hamlet of Cuajiniquil.

Crossing the border into Nicaragua: Peñas Blancas

Peñas Blancas (7am–8pm daily), the main crossing point into Nicaragua, is emphatically a border post and not a town, with just one or two basic *sodas* and no hotels. Aim to get here as **early** as possible, as procedures are ponderous and you'll be lucky to get through the whole deal in less than ninety minutes. In addition, buses on both side of the border are far more frequent in the morning, and fizzle out completely by 5pm. Things are smoothest if you come with Ticabus – all passengers are processed together and are given priority. Both Costa Rican and Nicaraguan border officials are quite strict, and there are many checks to see that your paperwork is in order. Few travellers will need a visa for Nicaragua, but it's worth checking the current situation before leaving San José.

Exit stamps are given on the Costa Rican side, where there's a restaurant and a helpful, organized Costa Rican **tourist office** (6am–noon & 1–8pm).

Moneychangers are always on hand and have colones, córdobas and dollars. After getting your Costa Rican exit stamp, it's a short walk north to the barrier (see pp.548–549). If you're arriving from Nicaragua, the last San José–bound bus leaves at 3.30pm (5.30pm Fri–Sun), and the last Liberia bus at 5pm.

The Guanacaste beaches

Many of the **beaches of Guanacaste**, scattered along the rocky coastline from Bahía Culebra to Sámara on the west of the Nicoya Peninsula, are being aggressively developed for mass tourism. Most controversial is the fits-and-starts **Papagayo Project**, covering nearly the entire Bahía Culebra. Over the next fifteen years about fourteen thousand rooms are planned here, making it the largest tourist development in Central America (there are currently a total of just thirteen thousand hotel rooms in the whole of Costa Rica). That said, despite all the noise, the project seems to be permanently stalled. The **golf course** craze, however, shows no signs of abating. These pose a particular danger to the delicate environment, since golf courses require an enormous amount of water, which is often taken from wetlands, mangroves and other fragile habitats, never mind the fact that local people may have their water supply curtailed.

Despite the increasing development, the coast here has a lot to recommend it, not least **Parque Nacional Marino Las Baulas**, where droves of leatherback **turtles** come ashore to lay their eggs between October and February. If it's a good swim you want, however, best head down to **Sámara** or **Nosara** on the Nicoya Peninsula; if you want to learn to surf, resorty **Tamarindo** is the place.

It can take a long time to get to the Guanacaste coast from San José (4–5hr minimum, unless you fly) and in some places you feel very remote indeed. **Getting around** can take time, too, as the beaches tend to be separated by rocky headlands or otherwise impassable formations, entailing considerable backtracking inland to get from one to the other. Unless you're just going to one place, **bus** travel is tricky, although possible. By far the most popular option is to **rent a car**, which allows you to beach-hop with relative ease. Roads are not bad, if somewhat potholed – you'll do best with **4WD**, though this can prove expensive.

Playa Panamá and Playa Hermosa

Sheltered from the full force of the Pacific, the clear blue waters of **Bahía Culebra** on the **Gulfo de Papagayo** are some of the best for swimming and snorkelling in the country. The northernmost beach of the beautiful bay, **Playa Panamá**, with water gently lapping its grey volcanic sand, is still a nice quiet spot, although there is no shortage of upmarket resort hotels being built here, many of them by Italians. The all-inclusive gated *Occidental Costa Smeralda* (ⓣ672-0193, ⓦwww.occidental-hotels.com/costasmeralda; ❽) has a nice pool, good restaurant and efficient management; there's a two-night minimum stay.

Playa Hermosa, on the southern edge of Bahía Culebra and 10km north of the nearest beach to the south, Playas del Coco, is calm, clean and good for swimming. Small islets dot the bay, and despite a recent building boom in the area, in the wet season Hermosa can be wonderfully quiet. It's possible to go **diving** here; contact Diving Safaris (ⓣ672-0147, ⓦwww.costaricadiving.com) for trips or lessons.

If you want to **stay** on the beach, the popular and friendly *Hotel el Velero* (ⓣ672-1017, ⓦwww.costaricahotel.net; ❼) has split-level rooms with balconies and sea views in lovely gardens filled with birds and lizards. There's also a good restaurant and a small pool; a short path leads from the hotel down to the beach. It offers good value except in the month of December (❾). *Iguana Inn* (ⓣ672-0065; ❹) is a budget option a stone's throw from the beach, offering simple and colourful rooms with fan and small hot-water bathroom. There's also a swimming pool and a well-equipped shared kitchen. *La Finisterra* (☎672-0293, ⓦwww.finisterra.net; ❼) is a charming small hotel with a superb setting on the cliff at the southern end of the beach, offering warm hospitality, stunning sunset views, and an alluring international menu in its restaurant. The price includes breakfast, and there's a swimming pool. The best cheap eats in town are to be found at *Pescado Loco*, opposite the *Hotel Velero*; freshly caught fish costs US$5–6 and roast chicken US$3.

Five daily buses run from Liberia to Playa Hermosa and Playa Panamá. There's also a direct daily bus to the two beaches from San José leaving at an ungodly hour – 3.25am – and returning at 5am (5hr).

Playas del Coco

Thirty-five kilometres west of Liberia, with good road connections, **Playas del Coco** was the first Pacific beach to hit the big time with weekending Costa Ricans from the Valle Central. Its accessibility, budget accommodation and good restaurants make it a useful place for a couple of days' jaunt or, if you have a car, as a base to explore the better beaches nearby.

Playas del Coco is a popular **snorkelling** and **diving** centre: the staff at Rich Coast Diving (☎670-0176, ⓦwww.richcoastdiving.com), on the main road about 300m from the beach, speak English, organize snorkelling and scuba trips (US$50–80 for a two-tank dive) and rent out mountain bikes. Deep Blue Diving (☎670-1004, ⓦwww.deepblue-diving.com), in the precinct of the *Coco Verde* hotel, run similar trips.

Arrival and information

A direct **bus** (5hr) leaves San José for Coco three times daily at 8am, 2pm and 4pm, returning at 4am, 8am and 2pm. You can also get to Coco on six daily local services from Liberia (1hr). The town itself spreads out right in front of the beach, with a tiny **parquecito** as the focal point. The minimal services include a miniscule **correo** (Mon–Fri 7.30am–5pm) and public **telephones** on either side of the parquecito. The Banco Nacional, on the main road as you enter town, will change dollars and travellers' cheques and has a Cirrus/MC/Visa/Plus ATM. **Taxis** gather by the little park on the beach. There's **Internet access** at *Leslie's*, in the same building as *Cabinas Catarina* (see below). A good supermarket, Luperón, is next to the Banco Nacional.

Accommodation

Coco has lots of fairly basic **cabinas**, catering to weekending nationals and tourists. In the high season you should make sure to **reserve** for weekends, but you can probably get away with turning up on spec mid-week, when rooms may also be a little cheaper. In the low season bargains abound. There's **camping** (US$3) at *Chopin* (☎391-5998), on the road heading right 100m before the beach.

Cabinas Catarina 100m before you reach the parquecito ☎670-0156. The most basic budget cabinas in town, and a good deal. Each cabina has a private bath with cold water only, and the friendly management will let you do laundry and cook meals in the small kitchen. ❹

Cabinas El Coco on the beach, 200m north of the parquecito ☎670-0110, Ⓕ670-0167. Comfortable, clean and slightly overpriced cabinas right on the beach. The rooms at the front are best, but more expensive (❻); all come with private bath, and you have a choice of fan or a/c rooms. On weekend nights, noise from the nearby disco can be troublesome. ❹–❻

Cabinas El Dorado on the beach south of the parquecito ☎837-2726. Basic cabinas with cold showers and fan with the not inconsiderable benefits of being cheap as well as right on the beach. Those nearer the sea are a little airier, and have the advantage of being within earshot of the rolling waves. There's a bar and restaurant here, too. ❹

Hotel La Flor de Itabo on the main road coming into town, about 1km from the beach ☎670-0011, ⓦwww.flordeitabo.com. Tasteful, friendly and long-established hotel, decorated with lovely dangling shell mobiles and Guatemalan bedspreads. All rooms have private bath, a/c, hot water and TV; there are cheaper bungalows with fans only. There's also a fine on-site Italian restaurant, *Da Beppe*. ❻

Hotel Villa Flores on the road leading to the right before you reach the beach ⓣ670-0269, ⓦwww.hotel-villa-flores.com. Quiet and comfortable, this newly spruced-up hotel has bright, cheerful rooms each with firm mattresses, private bath, hot water and a/c. The deluxe rooms upstairs are furnished with dark wood; the large balcony up here is a fine place to contemplate the spacious grounds or catch sea breezes. Breakfast is included in the rates, as is the engagingly warm hospitality. There's also a pool, hot tub and small gym. ❻

La Puerta del Sol off the road leading to the right 100m before you reach the beach ⓣ670-0195, ⓕ670-0650. Friendly Italian-run retreat set in quiet gardens. The thoughtfully arranged complex has a pool and gym, and the rooms are furnished with a/c, phone and cable TV, and also have a small terrace and lounge area. Breakfast is included in the competitive rates, and the restaurant, *Sol y Luna*, serves Italian food of high quality. ❽

Vista Mar signposted turn 1km north of the village ⓣ & ⓕ670-0753, ⓔhvistamar@racsa.co.cr. A good-value and nicely maintained option by the beach, with eight spacious and pleasantly decorated rooms, either with shared or private bath with hot water, plus fan or a/c. There's a nice palm-fringed pool and a good restaurant serving Italian- and French-themed food. Breakfast included. ❻

Eating, drinking and nightlife

Coco has two very distinct types of **restaurants, sodas and bars**: those catering to nationals and those that make some sort of stab at cosmopolitanism to hook the gringos. There's usually lively nightlife, focused on the *Lizard Lounge* on the main street, an open bar with plenty of cocktails and shooters to get you in the mood, and moody bass beats. A little further up the street is *Banana Surf*, an upstairs bar with a balcony that opens late. At weekends, the *Cocomar discoteca* by the beach gets busy. A quietish, but atmospheric, bar is *La Vida Loca*, reached across a narrow foot-bridge 100m south of the park – look for the flashing cross.

Bar Coco opposite the parquecito. A popular place in a prime position. Good for seafood lunches and dinners or just a beer in the evening.

Papagayo on the main drag, 100m short of the beach. If it's fresh and available, you'll find it on the menu here: the town's best seafood restaurant is run by the family of the big shot of the local fishing fleet. The "catch of the day" will set you back US$7, while a gorgeous mixed platter comes in at US$15. The fish are prepared in a wide variety of styles, but the quality is always evident.

La Rana on the main road, 100m before the beach on the left. Serving burgers as well as Tico food at reasonable prices, this relaxing bar and restaurant is a pleasant place to dine, grab a snack or just chill out listening to music or catching up on the latest sporting events and news on the big screen.

Sol y Luna in the *Puerta del Sol* hotel. Expertly prepared Italian food in an attractive and intimate setting. The owners make a big effort to import the authentic ingredients, and there's also a decent wine selection. Mains are around the US$8–10 mark.

Tequila Bar on the main road, near the parquecito. Although it looks a little ramshackle, the Mexican food in this place is of high quality and good value, with filling plates starting around the US$5 mark. The key to the tasty dining is that the place is run by a Mexican, who'll give you a warm welcome.

Parque Nacional Marino Las Baulas

On the Río Matapalo estuary between Conchal and Tamarindo, **Parque Nacional Marino Las Baulas** (9am–4pm, open for guided night tours in season; US$6, including tour; ⓣ653-0470) is less a national park than a reserve, created in 1995 to protect the nesting grounds of the critically endangered **leatherback turtles**. Leatherbacks, which come ashore here to nest from October to February, have laid their eggs at **Playa Grande** for quite possibly millions of years, and it's now one of the few remaining such nesting sites in the world. The beach itself offers a beautiful sweep of light-coloured sand, and outside laying season you can surf and splash around in the waves, though swimming is rough, and plagued by crashing waves

△ The Pacific Coast, Costa Rica

and riptides. Despite its proximity to an officially protected area, someone seems to have given developers carte blanche to build at Playa Grande. What effect this will have on the millennia-old nesting ground of the turtles remains to be seen.

Around 200m from the park entrance, the impressive and educational **El Mundo de la Tortuga** exhibition (2–6pm, or until much later when turtles are nesting; US$5) includes an audio-guided tour in English and some stunning photographs of the turtles. You'll gain some insight into the leatherback's habitats and reproductive cycles, along with the threats they face and current conservation efforts. There's also a souvenir shop and a small café where groups on turtle tours are often asked to wait while a nesting turtle is located. It's open late at night – often past midnight – depending on demand and nesting times. There are two official entrances to Playa Grande, though **tickets** can only be bought at the southern entrance, where the road enters the park near the *Villa Baulas*. There are no bus services to the park. To **drive to Las Baulas**, take the road from Huacas to Matapalo, and turn left at the football pitch (a 4WD is recommended for this stretch during the wet season). Most people, however, visit the park by **boat** from Tamarindo, entering at the southern end rather than from the Matapalo road.

Playa Tamarindo

Stretching for a couple of kilometres over a series of rocky headlands, **Playa Tamarindo** is one of the most popular beaches in Guanacaste, attracting surfers and weekending Costa Ricans. Sprawling and occasionally snobby, **TAMARINDO** village, which has a sizeable foreign community, boasts a decent selection of restaurants, a lively beach culture and some nightlife, at least during high season. It's a popular place to learn to surf, but it is the least Costa Rican of places – locals are completely outnumbered by the tourist hordes. **Playa Langosta**, an excellent surf beach where you'll also find some of the area's classier hotels, lies a couple of kilometres to the south.

Arrival and information

You can **fly** into Tamarindo on NatureAir and Sansa (see p.613), both of which have offices in town; **buses** arrive by the village loop at the end of the road. This loop effectively constitutes Tamarindo's small centre and is surrounded by restaurants and populated by New Age jewellery-sellers. There are many banks in town, several with ATMs that accept international cards – the Banco Nacional, 500m north of the loop, is one, and will also change dollars, although you'll be hard pressed to find anywhere that doesn't accept them as currency. There are **public telephones** on the loop and several **Internet cafés** (costs are around US$2 per hour), including Tamarindo.Net at the junction north of the Tamarindo loop. You can wash clothes at Lavandería Mariposa by Iguana Surf. The Supermercado Tamarindo and Supermercado Pelicano sell basic foodstuffs. For **getting around** the area, and out to Playa Langosta, you could rent a scooter or a mountain bike from Tamarindo Rental Tours, among other places. There are several places to rent a car, including Budget, Payless and Economy.

Accommodation

Many of Tamarindo's **hotels** are very good, if expensive. You can **camp** at the dusty and mediocre *Camping Punta de Madero* (US$3) on the road to Playa Langosta, but the nicer beachside campsites have closed due to new government regulations. Playa Langosta's hotels offer a retreat from the sometimes hectic Tamarindo beachside scene, and are about a twenty-minute walk from the heart of the action.

B&B Sueño del Mar Playa Langosta ⓣ653-0284, ⓦwww.sueno-del-mar.com. Swing in a hammock on the ocean-facing veranda of this beautiful house, designed in Spanish-hacienda style with tiled roofs and adobe walls. The charming and luxurious rooms all come with pretty tiled showers, and rates (US$148, including taxes) include a tasty and filling breakfast. ❾

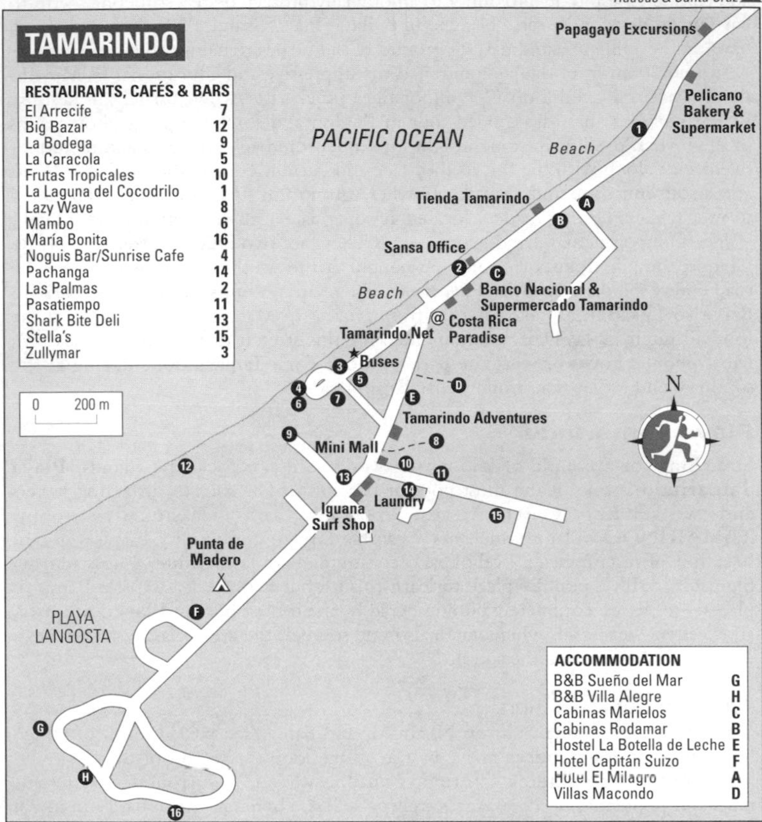

B&B Villa Alegre Playa Langosta ⓣ653-0270, ⓦwww.villaalegrecostarica.com. Relaxing Californian-owned B&B, set in a quiet location on the beach in Playa Langosta. The five rooms, which have large, comfortable beds, are themed on different countries and brightly decorated with exemplary taste. A generous breakfast is laid on and served on the veranda by the pool. A pair of villas, which sleep two to five and have their own kitchen facilities, are also available. ❽–❾

Cabinas Marielos Tamarindo ⓣ & ⓕ653-0141. Basic rooms, light and clean, with fan, cold water and the use of a small kitchen, in pleasant and colourful grounds set back from the main road. There are also rooms available with a/c, and a handful with hot-water bathrooms and fridge. The *dueña* is helpful and professional. ❺

Cabinas Rodamar Tamarindo ⓣ653-0109. Basic budget traveller's hangout, with dark cabinas in a motel-style compound set back from the main road. They have big beds, a cold-water bathroom and fan, and aren't bad for the price. Cheaper rooms are on hand with shared bathroom, but feel a little more spartan. It's friendly, and you can use the shared kitchen. ❸

Hostel La Botella de Leche Tamarindo ⓣ653-0944, ⓦwww.labotelladeleche.com. Excellent backpacker hostel offering comfortable bunk-bed accommodation in dorms. It's air-conditioned, sociable, and has a well-equipped communal kitchen and spick-and-span shared cold-water bathrooms. Designed with surfers in mind, you can rent and repair boards here, as well as arrange classes. It's very popular, and although the super-friendly *dueña* will do her utmost to squeeze you in, you'd be wise to reserve ahead. ❹

Hotel Capitán Suizo Playa Langosta ⓣ653-0075, ⓦwww.hotelcapitansuizo.com. Popular and upmarket Swiss-run hotel set in spacious, landscaped grounds on the beach. The cabina-style rooms all have a balcony or terrace, fridge, ceiling fans or a/c, bathtub, hot water and an outside shower. The palm-shaded pool is bigger than most, and the atmosphere friendly and relaxed. There's also a cocktail bar, beautiful beach views and a buffet breakfast. Prices in high season are US$145–170, including taxes. ❾

Hotel El Milagro Tamarindo ⓣ653-0042, ⓦwww.elmilagro.com. A long-time Tamarindo favourite, featuring nicely decorated cabinas with private bath (hot water) and either fan (❼) or a/c (❽). Some rooms are generously proportioned, with French windows opening onto flowered terraces. The poolside restaurant serves great food. Breakfast included.

Villas Macondo Tamarindo ⓣ & ⓕ653-0812, ⓦwww.villasmacondo.com. Quiet, welcoming spot offering excellent value, located up a dirt road to the left, just after taking the road towards Playa Langosta. The colourful cabinas come with comfortable beds, wooden ceilings and a little terrace, strung with hammocks; the more upmarket ones include cable TV, a/c and a fridge. There are also comprehensively equipped apartments (❽–❾) with one or two bedrooms. Guests have access to a kitchenette with gas stove, and the place is set around an enticing pool. Unsurprisingly, given the low prices, reserving ahead is in order. ❺–❻

Outdoor activities and tours

Swimming is not great around Tamarindo, as the waves are fairly heavy and there are riptides. Most people are content to paddle in the rocky coves and tide pools south of the town. Tamarindo's reliable, but relatively gentle, waves make it an ideal place to learn how to surf. The friendly and professional Iguana Surf (ⓣ653-0148, ⓦwww.iguanasurf.net) will almost certainly have you standing on a board by the end of your first class (around US$30 including board rental); their main office is 500m along the road to Playa Langosta. Tamarindo Adventures (ⓣ653-0108, ⓦwww.tamarindoadventures.net) is another popular school; Chica Surf (ⓣ827-7884, ⓔchicasurfschoolcr@hotmail.com) is an all-girls school and surf shop just off the loop in the centre of town. All of these places and more rent surfboards – typical prices are US$20 for a day's rental of a longboard, or US$100 for a week. You can also rent boogie boards, windsurfing equipment, and masks and snorkels.

The Las Baulas marine park begins just north of Tamarindo, and a popular boat excursion (2hr 30min) takes you around the river estuary, where you'll likely spot monkeys, birds and crocodiles among the different mangrove species. Many operators in town run this trip, which costs around US$40 per person. In leatherback nesting season (Nov to mid-Feb), you can head out on a **turtle tour** (about 2hr; US$30 per person); trips leave in the evening, the exact hour depending on the tide. Turtles also nest further south at Ostional wildlife refuge (see p.701). A trip there and back costs US$40. Many operators in town run these and other trips; one of the most professional and helpful is Costa Rica Paradise, also known as the Costa Rica Tourist Information Centre, just north of the turn-off to Playa Langosta (ⓣ653-0031, ⓦwww.crparadise.com). They'll also give you plenty of information about the town.

Eating, drinking and nightlife

Tamarindo has a large number of gringo-friendly restaurants, some of which are very good indeed. Fresh seafood is an obvious and delicious choice here, and a range of world and fusion cuisines are on offer. **Nightlife** focuses on the restaurants and bars – a couple of them with pleasant beachfront locations – in the centre of the village. *Las Palmas*, 200m north of the loop, is a trendy spot to unwind after a day in the surf and, cold drink in hand, watch the sun set. *Mambo*, on the circle, is a spacious place that is the place to be on Thursday and Friday night – later action focuses on *La Bodega*, a little to the south. On Saturdays, the scene shifts further south along the beach to *Big Bazar*, which has more of a dance music vibe.

Moving on from Tamarindo

Two daily buses run to and from San José, leaving Tamarindo outside the Tamarindo resort at 3.30am and 5.45am (5.45am and 12.30pm on Sun; 6hr), and six to **Liberia** daily, leaving from outside the Tamarindo Internet café on the loop. To head further south down the peninsula, take one of the six daily buses to Santa Cruz (1hr) and link up with buses to Sámara or Nosara from there. As always, bus timetables are likely to change. Continuing down the west coast of the peninsula is easier with your own transport. Interbus a/c bus services all over the country can be reserved through various agents in town.

There are eight to nine daily flights to San José run by NatureAir and Sansa (US$80 one way). Both have offices on the main road in the centre of town. The airstrip is located 2.5km north of town.

El Arrecife on the Tamarindo loop. A cheapish *soda* that offers pretty good value for these parts. Filling and flavoursome rice dishes cost US$4–5, while the old faithful, the *casado*, is US$4 and won't leave you peckish.

La Caracola just off the Tamarindo loop. Decorated with a cool beachfront vibe, this is the place to come for well-made cocktails, as well as Argentinean-style steaks (US$5–6), mouth-watering salads (US$4–5), or simpler *casados* (US$5). Relaxed atmosphere and top value for the quality and freshness presented. Closed Sat.

Frutas Tropicales Tamarindo. One of the few genuinely cheap places in Tamarindo. As the name says, there's plenty of tropical fruit in this little snack bar – try the fruit *refrescos*. Otherwise the menu is the usual *soda* fare, with *casados* (US$3.50) and hamburgers (US$3) both good bets. They also rent out a couple of cabinas (❹).

La Laguna del Cocodrilo at the northern end of Tamarindo ☎653-0255. Classy Mediterranean fare in a romantic setting in a palm-fringed garden (with resident crocodile) right on the beach. Starters, such as an exquisite tuna *carpaccio* (US$6), can be followed by fine seafood or steak mains (US$8–11), or more exotic offerings such as fried camembert in honey sauce, or chicken stewed in a spicy beer sauce. There's also a French bakery here to stock up on scrumptious picnic material.

Lazy Wave Tamarindo. This outdoor restaurant may look casual, but it dishes up some of the best cooking in the area, if not the country, with a very fairly priced menu (changes daily) distinguished by the delicacy and inventiveness of its ingredients and flavours. The bakery-patisserie is worth a visit, too.

María Bonita Playa Langosta ☎653-0933. Hospitable Caribbean-food restaurant 1.5km south of Tamarindo, serving favourites such as spicy chicken fillets (US$6) as well as some very juicy baked fish dishes. It's also a popular spot for a drink in these parts.

Noguis Bar/Sunrise Café on the Tamarindo loop. Casual café serving excellent breakfasts, with good breads, pastries and coffees – which you can either eat at the breezy seaside tables or take away – and fine meals such as fish tacos and fresh fillets.

Pachanga Tamarindo. Intimate, candlelit restaurant, tastefully decorated and with a short, French-influenced gourmet menu. An exquisite fish tartar (US$6) is one to watch out for, as is the snapper fillet (US$11), but do consider the changing daily specials – there's always something very enticing. Mon–Sat 6pm–10pm.

Pasatiempo Tamarindo, in the hotel of the same name. Perennially good and reasonably priced restaurant serving crowd-pleasers like Caesar salad (US$4), a wonderfully succulent blackened fish with greens, and chicken breast with mango stuffing (US$8). If nothing else, try the superlative fruit cocktails and a few nibbles. Live music twice a week in high season.

Shark Bite Deli Tamarindo, at the entrance to the Tamarindo resort. The best sandwiches in town: imaginative gourmet jobs that are guaranteed to please. There's also a book exchange here.

Stella's Tamarindo. One of the town's best restaurants, with good Italian pasta (US$4–7) and many fresh fish dishes cooked in excellent, inventive sauces. A large menu encompasses wood-oven pizzas and even – rare for Costa Rica – veal. Chicken stroganoff is a tasty choice, while a seafood platter for two is a must for that special romantic meal (US$27). Attractive open dining area. Main courses US$6–11. Closed Sun.

Zullymar on the Tamarindo loop. Unbeatable beachfront location – everybody seems to come here for a drink whilst watching the sun go down

– and good food, with main dishes for US$7–10. You can sit and watch the crabs scuttling across the sand while waiting; the service is slow. Once your tasty *corvina* or *dorado* arrives, however, you'll be inclined to forgive. There are cheaper pizzas served during the day only.

Nicoya

Bus travellers making connections between, say, Tamarindo and Sámara sometimes end up having to spend a night in **NICOYA**, the main settlement of the peninsula. And that's far from a penance; set in a dip surrounded by low mountains, it's a hot place, but undeniably pretty, with a lovely **Parque Central**, centring on a preserved white adobe church (earthquake-battered, structurally unstable and currently closed).

Practicalities

Eight **buses** a day arrive in Nicoya from San José, a journey of around six hours. Some take the slightly longer route via the road to Liberia, but most use the new Tempisque bridge (see box, below). Buses also arrive from a number of regional destinations, including Liberia (10 daily), Santa Cruz (16 daily), Sámara (3–6 daily) and Nosara (1 daily). Two buses head for Naranjo, from where you can catch the ferry to Puntarenas, or head further south towards Montezuma. Most buses arrive at Nicoya's spotless bus station on the southern edge of town, a short walk from the centre; the Liberia service pulls in across from the *Hotel Las Tinajas*.

The friendly *Hotel Jenny* (☎685-5050; ❹), 100m south of the Parque Central, is the cheapest **place to stay**, with old, basic rooms with a/c, TV and phone. The similarly priced *Hotel Las Tinajas* (☎685-5081; ❹), 100m northeast of the Parque Central, is nicer, with dark rooms inside the main building and lighter cabinas around the back. Good **restaurants** include the *Cafetería Daniela*, 100m east of the parque, for breakfast and pastries; the *sodas* by the parque (*El Nuevo Horizonte* is one of the best) for large *casados*; and, for Chinese food, the *Restaurant El Teyet*, across from the *Hotel Jenny*.

As usual, you'll find most **services** around the Parque Central, including the **correo** (Mon–Fri 7.30am–5.30pm) and the Banco de Costa Rica. The Banco Popular and Banco Nacional have ATMs that accept foreign-issued cards. **Taxis** line up by the parque, or call Coopetico (☎658-6226). There's an Internet café opposite the *Hotel Jenny*, just south of the Parque Central (US$0.70 per hour).

The Río Tempisque bridge

Opened in April 2003, the new Tempisque bridge connects the mainland with the Nicoya Peninsula from near Puerto Moreno, 17km from the Nicoya–Carmona road, and a point 25km west of the Interamericana on the mainland. Crossing here saves at least two hours in reaching places like Sámara. The bridge, 780m long, replaces a time-consuming ferry connection and was a US$26million gift to Costa Rica by the Taiwanese government. Costa Rica is one of some two dozen countries in the world that recognizes Taipei as the legitimate Chinese authority rather than Beijing. The bridge is partly held up by suspension cables, which are connected to towers that, at 80m, make the expensive present the tallest structure in the country.

Playa Sámara

By far the most peaceful and least developed of the beachside resorts on the Nicoya Peninsula, **Sámara**, 30km southwest of Nicoya, also boasts one of the nation's calmest swimming beaches. The long clean stretch of sand is protected by a reef about a kilometre out, which takes the brunt of the Pacific's power out of the waves. It's a great place to relax, and its distance from the capital makes it much quieter than the more accessible Pacific beaches, although the new Tempisque bridge means that many locals fear imminent overdevelopment.

Arrival and information

Sansa and NatureAir **planes** from San José arrive at the airstrip 6km south of town at Carrillo, from where 4WD taxis make the trip to Sámara for about US$6. The express **bus** from San José leaves daily at 12:30pm and 6:15pm, and arrives at Sámara some five hours later, stopping about 50m in front of the beach right at the centre of the village. The express bus **back to San José** leaves at 4am and 8.45am; there are also several daily buses **to Nicoya** (2hr).

You can buy tickets for some bus services from the Transporte Alfaro office (daily 7am–5pm) in the centre of the village, which also sells potato chips, suntan lotion and bottles of cold water; it's also home to the village's public **telephone**. Sámara's **correo** (Mon–Fri 7.30am–6pm) – a small shack really – 50m before the entrance to the beach, offers minimal services, and there is nowhere to change money (other than at the large hotels), although nearly everywhere accepts US dollars. A mobile ATM machine that accepts Cirrus/MC/Visa/ATM turns up in the village for much of the high season, but don't rely on it being there. Tropical Latitude, near the *Hotel Casa del Mar*, offers **Internet access** (daily 9.30am–5pm); for laundry, head for Lava Ya.

There aren't as many **tours** or other activities at Sámara as there are at other places on the peninsula, but Sámara Adventures (ⓣ656-0655), on the beachfront road just south of the centre, run a variety of fishing and watersports excursions, as well as wildlife-spotting trips to the Ostional reserve. Tío Tigre (ⓣ656-0098) will instruct you in the art of sea-kayaking and also run dolphin-watching cruises. Pura Vida (ⓣ656-0273) arrange dives and PADI courses. Apart from hanging around the beach here, plenty of people head six kilometres south to Playa Carrillo, an even more beautiful strip of palm-backed sand.

Accommodation

Staying in Sámara is getting pricier, with few cheap cabinas. Although during the low season most hotels can offer better rates than the ones listed here, at high-season weekends you should have a **reservation** no matter what price range. *Camping Coco*, on the beach, is clean and well run, with cooking grills, as is *Camping Playas Sámara*, at the north end of the beach, with toilets and showers (both US$3 a night).

El Ancla on the beachfront road 200m south of the centre ⓣ656-0254. Simply furnished rooms right on the beach, with cold-water bathroom and fan. Those upstairs are a mite hotter, but certainly a better option, as those downstairs feel dark and oppressive. Friendly *dueña* and good beachfront seafood restaurant. ❹

Aparthotel Mirador de Sámara first left as you come into town from Nicoya, 100m up the hill from the *Marbella* ⓣ656-0044, ⓦwww.miradordesamara.com. Huge apartments sleeping five to seven people, with large bathrooms, bedrooms, living rooms, kitchen and terrace, all with panoramic views over the town and beach. The bar is in an impressive tower with a wraparound view for watching the spectacular sunsets, and there's a small pool with nice wooden sundecks. Good low-season and long-stay discounts, but the price means it's better value for four or more people, rather than couples. ❽

B&B Casa Naranja town centre ⓣ & ⓕ656-0220. Owned by Suzanne, an energetic ex-chef from Paris, this small, central hotel has three rooms (one with a/c) in a modern building. The very fair price includes a good French breakfast, and the attached bar-restaurant-creperie is highly recommended. Visa accepted. ❹

Hotel Belvedere 100m down the road to Carrillo ⓣ & ⓕ656-0213, ⓦwww.samara-costarica.com. Wonderfully pleasant and excellent-value hotel. The ten rooms and two apartments come with either a/c or fan (the latter US$8 less), and all are brightly furnished in light wood, with mosquito nets and solar-heated water. There's also a Jacuzzi and swimming pool, and a good German breakfast is included. ❺

Hotel Giada about 100m before you come to the beach, on the left ⓣ656-0132, ⓦwww.hotelgiada.net. Small hotel set round a compact pool, with spotless banana-yellow rooms, good beds, overhead fans, private baths and tiled showers – the upstairs rooms are better for views and breeze. There's also a friendly Italian restaurant. ❺

Hotel Marbella first left as you come into town from Nicoya ⓣ & ⓕ656-0362. Fairly inexpensive hotel, with a tiny pool – for plunging rather than swimming – and ten rather dark, but brightly painted rooms, that come with either a/c or fan as well as cable TV. There's also an on-site restaurant. ❺

Eating, drinking and nightlife

Sámara has a couple of very nice places to **eat**, where you can also enjoy a cold beer by the lapping waves. **Nightlife** is quiet, except at weekends, where the dark *Tutti Frutti* disco on the beach gets going. It opens until 3am, and costs US$1 to enter. Much more pleasant, a little further north, *Las Olas* is a very relaxed open-plan beach bar with pool tables and cheery vibe. By far the most peaceful and stylish spot for a drink is *La Vela Latina*, south of the centre on the beach. Sit in rocking chairs as the friendly staff mix you one of their cracking daiquiris and be at peace.

Ananas as you enter town from Nicoya. Pleasant café serving incredibly tasty ice cream, fruit salads, juices, breakfasts and coffee-and-cake combinations. Open for breakfast, lunch and afternoon coffee only.

El Ancla on the beach. With a long menu of fish dishes and a pretty setting close to the water, this spot attracts plenty of holidaying Ticos, who know good seafood when they smell it.

Las Brasas town centre ⓣ656-0546. Two-level restaurant serving, among other things, Spanish dishes such as paella, or, of all things, an entire suckling pig (with advance notice). The fillet steaks (US$9) are very tasty, as is the guacamole, but the pasta dishes are nothing special.

La Casa de la Playa on the beach. Relaxing arty café and restaurant run by good people and serving healthy juices and salads, as well as fuller meals of seafood, including a tasty coconut curry (US$7) or grilled prawns.

Creperie Naranja town centre, in *Casa Naranja*. Authentic French and North African cuisine (the owner is a former Paris chef) served in a small outdoor garden lit with candles in the evening. The wide menu offers, among other things, savoury crepes (US$3.50), French favourites like duck *à l'orange* (US$5) and some incredible traditional cakes and desserts, flans, tartes and sweet crepes from US$3 to US$4 – pricey, but worth every penny.

Nosara and around

The pretty drive from Sámara 25km north to the village of **NOSARA** runs along shady and secluded dirt and gravel roads punctuated by a few creeks – it's bumpy, but passable, with a regular car in the dry season, but you'll need a 4WD in the wet. Local children like to erect "toll" booths to extract coins from passing motorists. The settlement itself is spread over a large area: the main concentration, properly called Bocas de Nosara, is set some 3km inland, between a low ridge of hills and the sea. Usually grouped together as **Playas Nosara**, the three beaches in the area – Nosara, Guiones and Pelada – are fine for **swimming**, although you can be buffeted by the crashing waves, and there are some rocky outcrops. Playa Guiones is the most impressive of the beaches: nearly 5km in length and with probably the best swimming, though there's precious little shade. The whole area is a great place to go beachcombing for shells and driftwood, and the vegetation, even in the dry season, is greener than further north. Some attempts have been made to limit development, and a good deal of the land around the Río Nosara has been designated a wildlife refuge.

In contrast to the busier Sámara, the vast majority of people who come to Nosara are North Americans and Europeans in search of quiet and natural surroundings. Much of the accommodation is slightly upmarket, and the owners and managers are more environmentally conscious than at many other places on the peninsula. A local civic association keeps a hawkish eye on development in the area, with the aim of keeping Nosara as it is, rather than having it become another Tamarindo or Montezuma.

Arrival and information

NatureAir and Sansa **fly** two to four times daily to Nosara from San José, on their way to Sámara, landing at the small airstrip. The San José **bus** comes in at the

Abastecedor general store. There isn't much to the village itself apart from a football field, a couple of restaurants and a gas station (the latter is little more than a shack, with no pumps to show what it is – gas is siphoned out of a barrel). The **correo** (Mon–Fri 7.30am–6pm) is next to the airstrip, and public **phones** are in front of the police station, next to the Cruz Roja. You can rent **bikes** at Souvenirs Tuanis in the ramshackle old house on the corner of the village. If it's long-term accommodation or taxis to the Ostional refuge you're after, check out their notice board. A useful listings website is Ⓦwww.nosara.com. Nosara's an easy place to get lost around, as signposting is erratic, but in reality, as the beachfront communities are divided into blocks, you won't stray too far from where you're trying to get to.

Accommodation

Accommodation around the beaches is of high quality, but there's not a lot to keep the budget traveller happy.

Blew Dog's Surf Club back from Playa Guiones Ⓣ682-0080, Ⓦwww.blewdogs.com. Popular and relaxed spot designed with surfers in mind. Accommodation comes in bungalows equipped with fan, fridge, and some with small kitchen. There's a restaurant serving gringo favourites and inevitably throbbing to the sounds of Bob Marley. ❺

Café de Paris south end of Nosara, at the entrance to Playa Guiones Ⓣ682-0087, Ⓦwww.cafedeparis.net. Well-appointed rooms set in bungalows arranged around the pool, all with private bath and hot water, and a choice of ceiling fans or a/c. Rooms range from standard doubles to suites with a/c, kitchen, fridge and a small rancho with hammocks. Internet access and a fine restaurant. ❻

Casa Tucan 200m east from Playa Guiones Ⓣ & Ⓕ682-0113, Ⓔcasatucan@nosara.com. Small, eight-room hotel, with brightly decorated rooms (some with kitchen), sleeping up to five people; all have private bath, hot water, fridge and fan or a/c. There's a good restaurant and bar, including a new juice bar, on the premises, and a swimming pool. Good low-season or long-stay discounts. ❼

Hotel Casa Romántica behind Playa Guiones Ⓣ682-0019, Ⓦwww.hotelcasaromantica.com. Clean and well-kept family-run hotel, right on the beach, with bright rooms, all with hot water, fridge and terrace (along with a family room sleeping five people). There's also a pool and a fantastic on-site restaurant. If you fly or take the bus, the owners will pick you up if you let them know in advance. ❻

Hotel Lagarta Lodge signposted from the village Ⓣ682-0035, Ⓦwww.lagarta.com. Set in a small private nature reserve, this lodge has excellent birdwatching and stunning coastal views – the rooms above the pool looking out onto the ocean have one of the best panoramas in the country. Rooms have private bath, hot water and fridges. A healthy buffet breakfast (not included) as well as other meals are also available. ❼

Hotel Playas de Nosara the hilltop, between playas Guiones and Pelada; follow the signs Ⓣ682-0121, Ⓦwww.nosarabeachhotel.com. Dramatically situated hotel on a headland overlooking the beach and pine-clad coastline. Its stunning design includes a 360-degree observation lounge that from afar makes the structure look like a mosque. The large, clean, cool rooms with fans are priced according to the quality of the view (not all rooms overlook the beach). Unfortunately, ongoing building works can make the place look like a construction site. There's a pool but, as yet, few other services. ❻

Eating and drinking

The Nosara area has experienced a mini-explosion of restaurants in the past few years. Many of them are very good, and prices are not as high as you might expect, given the area's relative isolation. There are a number of places in the **village**, most of them around the soccer field or on the road into town, though most of the better restaurants are huddled together near **Playa Guiones**, which is where the majority of tourists eat.

Bar-restaurant Tucan next to the *Casa Tucan* hotel. The menu features seafood in adventurous fruit-based sauces, lobster, chicken, pasta and steaks (all US$7–12), served in a pleasant rancho strung with inviting hammocks and coloured lights. A new juice bar offers "create-your-own" drinks.

Café de Paris at the southern entrance to Playa

Guiones. The brioche and *pain au chocolat* confirm this bakery as a bona-fide overseas *département* of France, while the pleasant poolside restaurant serves sandwiches and pizzas for lunch (US$4–9).

Giardino Tropicale south end of Nosara, on the road towards Sámara ☎682-0258. Superior-quality real Italian pizza cooked in a wood oven and served in a pretty plant-strewn dining area (US$6–9). Other well-crafted Italian dishes are also on offer; and you can opt to order for takeaway.

Gilded Iguana behind Playa Guiones. Upmarket gringo bar with Mexican food that attracts the local expats, and well-priced lunch specials, including filet of *dorado* (US$5) and fish and chips (US$3). Closed Mon, Tues & Sun.

La Luna just below the Playas Nosara hotels ☎682-0122. A lovable spot above Playa Pelada, with tranquil terrace tables overlooking the sea. The constantly changing menu always features a lip-smacking array of international dishes, many of them seafood-based. Highlights include the salads, as well as the homemade bread. Thai soups and curries are also enduringly popular, and the cheerful owners dream up some great desserts. Mains US$6–9.

Soda Vanessa in Nosara village. A typical *soda* with filling and well-prepared *casados* for under US$3, as well as other snack-style fare.

Refugio Nacional de Fauna Silvestre Ostional

Eight kilometres northeast of Nosara, Ostional and its chocolate-coloured sand beach make up the **Refugio Nacional de Fauna Silvestre Ostional**, one of the most important nesting grounds in the country for **Olive Ridley turtles**, which come ashore to lay their eggs between May and November. You can't swim here, though, since the water's too rough and is frequented by sharks.

If you're in town during the first few days of the *arribadas* – the mass arrivals of turtles to lay eggs that occur throughout the year, usually over the full-moon period – you'll see local villagers with horses, carefully stuffing their big, thick bags full of eggs and slinging them over their shoulders. This is quite legal: villagers of Ostional and Nosara are allowed to harvest eggs, for sale or consumption, during the first three days of the season only. Don't be surprised to see them barefoot, rocking back and forth on their heels as if they were crushing grapes in a winery; this is the surest way to pick up the telltale signs of eggs beneath the sand. It takes about fifteen minutes to drive the gravel-and-stone road from Nosara to the refuge; alternately you can bike it or take a taxi.

6.6

The Zona Norte

Costa Rica's **Zona Norte** ("northern zone") spans the hundred-odd kilometres from the base of the Cordillera Central to just short of the mauve-blue mountains of southern Nicaragua. Cut off from the rest of the country by a lack of roads, the Zona Norte has developed a distinct character, with independent-minded farmers and Nicaraguan refugees making up large segments of the population. Neither group journeys to the Valle Central very often, and many people of the north hold a special allegiance to, and pride in, their area.

Geographically, the Zona Norte separates neatly into two broad, river-drained plains (*llanuras*), which stretch all the way to the Río San Juan on the Nicaraguan–Costa Rican border. Less obviously picturesque than many parts of the country, the entire region nonetheless has a distinctive appeal, with lazy rivers snaking across steaming plains scarred by trails of blood-orange soil and flop-eared cattle languishing beneath the draped limbs of riverside trees.

Most travellers only venture up here to see the perpetually active **Volcán Arenal**, using the nearby town of **La Fortuna de San Carlos** as their base. To the east is the steamy **Sarapiquí** area, with its tropical forest **ecolodges** and research stations of **La Selva** and **Rara Avis**. Further north, the remote flatlands are home to the increasingly accessible **Refugio Nacional de Vida Silvestre Caño Negro**, which harbours an extraordinary number of migratory and indigenous birds.

The **climate** in the north is hot and wet, more so in the east than in the west near Guanacaste, where there is a dry season. There's a serviceable **bus** network, though if you're travelling outside the La Fortuna or Sarapiquí areas, you'd probably do better with a car. As for other facilities, the area around Volcán Arenal is best geared up for tourists, even boasting a couple of excellent five-star hotels. Between Boca de Arenal and Los Chiles in the far north, on the other hand, there is a real shortage of accommodation, though fuel and food are in good supply.

Volcán Arenal and La Fortuna

That the Arenal region attracts such huge numbers of tourists is largely due to the majestic **Volcán Arenal**, one of the most active volcanoes in the Western hemisphere. Just 6km away, **LA FORTUNA DE SAN CARLOS**, or **La Fortuna**, as it is more often called, was until recently a simple agricultural town but has changed beyond recognition. Nowadays, true to its name, it's booming, with visitors flocking to watch the lava ooze down the lip of the volcano like juice from a squashed fruit.

Despite being almost wholly geared to the tourist market, La Fortuna is still a likeable place, and the locals are patient and welcoming despite the large quantities of air-conditioned tour buses speeding through town. There's nothing to do except book tours, bed down and have a meal or a beer, and gaze at the volcano, looming 1633m above town. When you can see it, that is: it is shrouded in clouds for days at a time, and locals estimate that one in two visitors never actually get a glimpse of the summit or lava. One popular excursion is to La Fortuna's **cataratas** (waterfalls), just 6km from the south side of the church in town and an easy half-day trip, either hiking (make sure to wear sturdy, waterproof shoes) or on horseback. La Fortuna also has excellent bus connections, making it one of the main setting-off points for

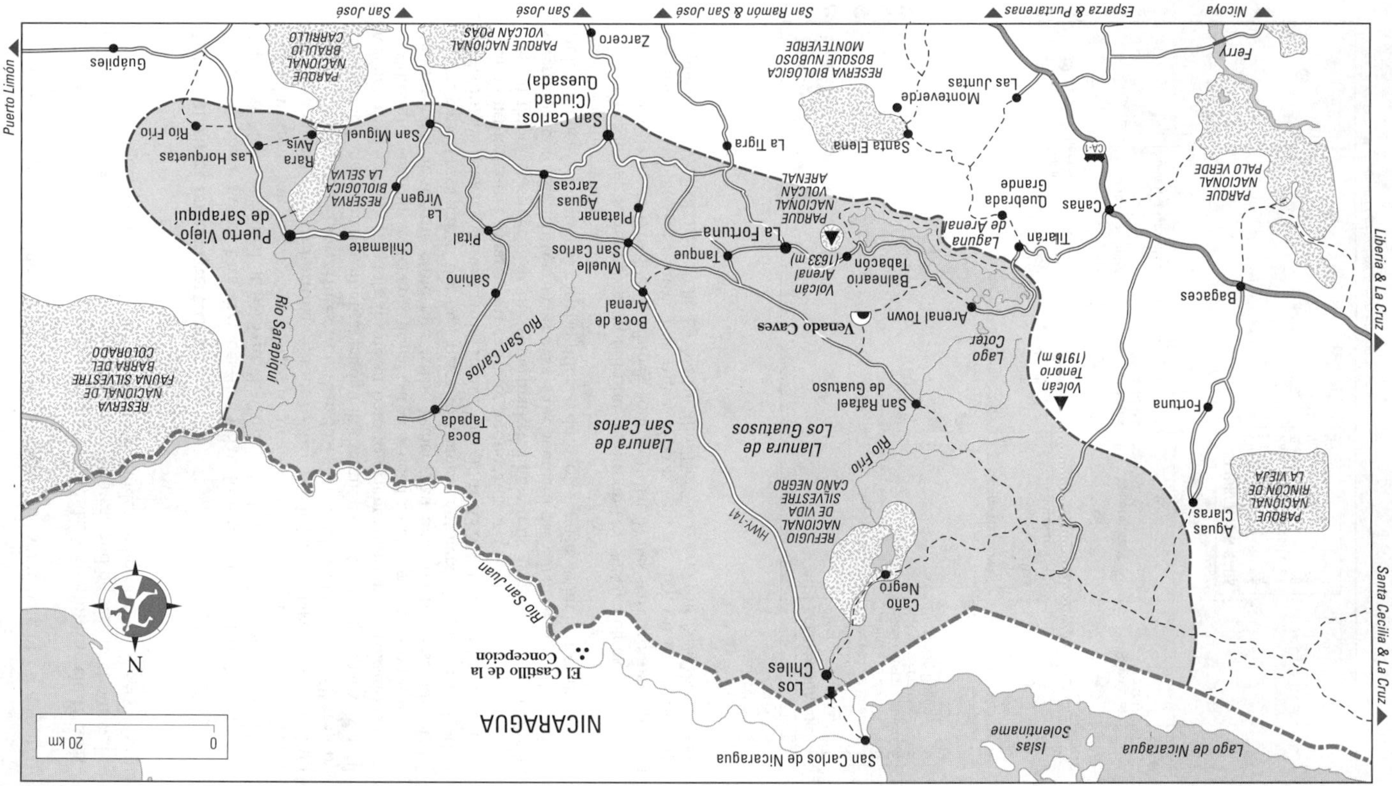

NICARAGUA
Lago de Nicaragua
Islas Solentiname
San Carlos de Nicaragua
Los Chiles
El Castillo de la Concepción
Río San Juan
0 20 km
N
Caño Negro
REFUGIO NACIONAL DE VIDA SILVESTRE CAÑO NEGRO
HWY-141
Aguas Claras
PARQUE NACIONAL RINCÓN DE LA VIEJA
Fortuna
Río Frío
Llanura de Los Guatusos
Llanura de San Carlos
San Rafael de Guatuso
Volcán Tenorio (1916 m)
Lago Coter
Boca Tapada
RESERVA NACIONAL DE FAUNA SILVESTRE BARRA DEL COLORADO
Río San Carlos
Río Sarapiquí
Venado Caves
Arenal Town
Boca de Arenal
Bagaces
Balneario Tabacón
Volcán Arenal (1633 m)
Sahino
Tanque
Muelle San Carlos
Tilarán
Laguna de Arenal
La Fortuna
Pital
Chilamate
Puerto Viejo de Sarapiquí
Cañas
Quebrada Grande
PARQUE NACIONAL VOLCÁN ARENAL
Platanar
Aguas Zarcas
La Virgen
RESERVA BIOLÓGICA LA SELVA
PARQUE NACIONAL PALO VERDE
CA-1
Santa Elena
La Tigra
Rara Avis
Las Horquetas
San Miguel
Río Frío
San Carlos (Ciudad Quesada)
Monteverde
Las Juntas
RESERVA BIOLÓGICA BOSQUE NUBOSO MONTEVERDE
Guápiles
Ferry
Zarcero
PARQUE NACIONAL VOLCÁN POÁS
PARQUE NACIONAL BRAULIO CARRILLO
Santa Cecilia & La Cruz
Liberia & La Cruz
Puerto Limón
Nicoya
Esparza & Puntarenas
San Ramón & San José
San José
San José

tours to the remote wildlife refuge of **Caño Negro** and something of a transportation hub for the region as a whole.

Note that as La Fortuna becomes increasingly popular, opportunistic **theft** is rising; never leave anything unattended, especially in a car, and be careful about walking around alone late at night. Also be wary of "guides" who offer their services on the street.

Arrival and information

There are three direct **bus** services from San José to La Fortuna, leaving the Atlántico Norte terminal at 6.15am, 8.40am and 11.30am. You could also take a direct bus from San José to San Carlos (Ciudad Quesada), where you can change for frequent buses to La Fortuna (40km; 1–2hr). From Tilarán, take either the 7am or the 12.30pm bus (3hr). Buses from San José, San Carlos and Tilarán all stop by the Parque Central, an ornamental garden in the middle of the village that was until recently the local soccer pitch. It's never hard to orient yourself: the volcano is west.

Although everywhere accepts dollars, if you need to change money, most hotels will do it for about the same rate as the Banco Nacional, on the east side of the central park. This bank is the best place to change travellers' cheques; it and other banks in town have MasterCard/Cirrus/Visa/Plus ATMs. Public phones can be found on the central square; you can buy phonecards at a couple of the tour agencies on the main street near the supermarket. These tour agencies are also among several places to offer **Internet access** – the standard price here is around US$1.20 an hour. There's a laundry that also offers a drop-off service 200m east of the central square, on the main road.

If you're looking to rent a car, you'll find Álamo (☎479-9090) a block west of the church and Poás (☎479-8027), a block south of that. Rates start around US$45 a day for a shoebox-size motor. The Aguas Bravas tour agency, on the main road opposite the football field, sells *La Nación*, the *Tico Times* and the *New York Times* –

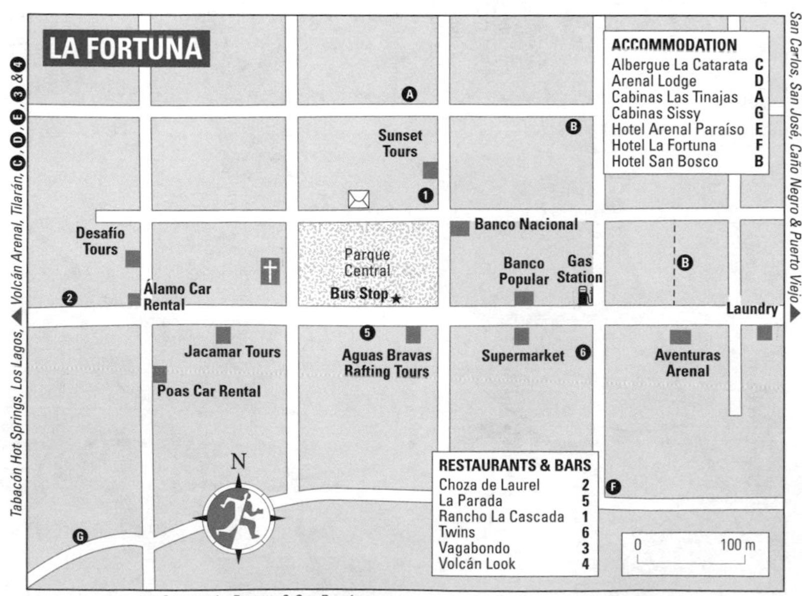

this is also the best place to **rent bikes** (around US$10/day for sturdy mountain bikes).

Taxis line up on the south side of the Parque Central – they rarely (if ever) use their meters, so agree a price before getting in and beware of overcharging, although most don't deviate from the standard rates. If in doubt, ask locals what they pay.

Accommodation

People with their own transport and a bit of money tend to stay in the **lodges** either on the road between La Fortuna and La Tigra/San Ramón, on the road linking La Fortuna and the Parque Nacional Volcán Arenal, or in one of the many pleasant hotels that border Laguna de Arenal. For the best views of the volcano, you're best off on the road to Arenal. Budget travellers tend to stay in town; most of the simple **cabinas** sprouting up all over town are pretty similar, with a few plain rooms and cold showers. Competition means that La Fortuna is also one of the few places in the country where you might encounter **hotel touts** as you stumble off the bus.

In La Fortuna

Cabinas Las Tinajas 100m north and 25m west of the central park Ⓣ479-9308, Ⓕ479-9145. Small complex of four clean, well-furnished and airy cabinas, equipped with cable TV, fan, and good hot-water bathroom. There are rocking chairs to while away time on the terrace, and the owners are very friendly: it all adds up to value for money. ❹

Cabinas Sissy 100m south and 125m west of the central park Ⓣ479-9256, Ⓕ479-9931. Basic budget travellers' hangout, friendly and clean, with a variety of rooms with fan and private or shared hot-water bathroom – some have cable TV. There's also a simple shared kitchen. You can camp here for US$4. ❷–❸

Hotel La Fortuna 75m south and 100m east of the central park Ⓣ479-9197. The town's original hotel has been recently refurbished and offers rooms that are clean, but simple, with fan, private bath and little else. The exterior rooms are airier – but expect to be woken early by traffic noise. Breakfast in the pleasant café/restaurant is included in the price, although you should be able to knock off a couple of dollars, if you forgo it. The cheerful staff can organize tours and transfers. ❹

Hotel San Bosco 100m northeast of the central park Ⓣ479-9050, Ⓦwww.arenal-volcano.com. Quiet hotel built around a garden on the north side of town. Rooms come with a/c and spacious hot-water bathroom, though they vary in price and size: if you don't like the first room you're shown, ask for another. The hotel's staff are friendly and informative, and there are excellent views of Arenal from the pool and hot tub, as well as from the terrace on the upper level. ❺

On the road to Arenal

Albergue Ecoturístico La Catarata 1km from La Fortuna, then 1.5km down a signed turn-off to the left Ⓣ479-9522, Ⓕ479-9168, Ⓔcatarata@racsa.co.cr. Situated in fertile farmland between La Fortuna and the waterfall, the nine rustic, but comfortable, cabinas all have fan and private bath with hot water. The restaurant serves simple local food made with organic produce from its garden, and a hearty, complimentary breakfast is served. A local initiative part-funded by the Canadian World Wildlife Fund, the ecolodge includes a butterfly farm, an experimental project to breed pacas and a medicinal herb farm. ❺

Arenal Lodge 16km west of La Fortuna and 2km up a side road, just after crossing the dam Ⓣ460-1881, Ⓦwww.arenallodge.com. Remote and leafy, this classy, peaceful retreat offers stunning views of the volcano and various types of accommodation, of which the refined "junior suites" offer the best value. Designed in old-time tropical luxury, with cane furniture, balcony with rocking chairs, and polished wooden floors, they also offer modern comforts such as fridge, microwave and coffee-making facilities. The on-site restaurant also has views, and the hotel can arrange any sort of tour or transfer – at a price. ❾

Hotel Arenal Paraíso 7km west of town Ⓣ460-5333, Ⓦwww.arenalparaiso.com. Attractive hotel with expensive-looking wooden cabinas, all with private bath with hot water (some also have fridges) and huge porches looking out directly onto the volcano. The more upmarket ones are further up the hill, with better views, and have a/c and a private balcony. The pool has a swim-up bar, and the price includes a fine breakfast buffet. ❼

Tours and activities around La Fortuna

Price competition between tour agencies in La Fortuna is fierce, but bear in mind that although you may save a few dollars by going with the cheapest agency, you could end up on a badly organized tour with under-qualified guides, or no lunch – get as many details as you can before you put down your cash. In general, it's worth going with a reputable tour operator, such as those listed below, and not with one of the freelance "guides" who may approach you, some of whom have been involved in serious incidents over the years.

By far the most popular excursion is the late-afternoon hike around **Volcán Arenal**, followed by a nighttime soak in the thermal pools at **Balneario Tabacón**, though few tours include the hefty admission fee (US$29; US$19 after 7pm) in their prices. The volcano hike involves a walk through rainforest, much of it uphill, and a final scramble over lava rocks – take care, as they're particularly sharp, and few guides carry a medical kit. Bring a torch, too. The actual sight of the volcano – if you're lucky enough to be there on a clear night when there's activity – is amazing. Scarlet rivers of lava pour from the top, and you can hear the crunch of boulders landing as they are spewed from the mouth of the volcano. You can, of course, visit the hot springs independently. Many visitors find simpler **Baldi Termae**, four kilometres west of La Fortuna, better value (US$14) than the ever-pricier Tabacón. There's nothing quite like relaxing in a hot tub, cocktail in hand, while watching the pyrotechnics unfold on high.

An increasing number of other activities are available in the area from sedate horseback rides or wildlife-oriented jungle walking to high-adrenalin whitewater rafting. **Horse rides** to the Catarata la Fortuna are an easy-paced traipse across farmland. Trips to the Caño Negro national park (see p.709) are an opportunity to see a vast array of bird and water life; there are inevitably several "canopy tours", and the recently constructed **Arenal Hanging Bridges** (☎479-9686, ⓦwww.hangingbridges.com) let you walk among the treetops in a private forest reserve near the dam across Lago Arenal. In another development, and to the concern of some environmentalists and vulcanologists, an Arenal cable car is now under construction that will no doubt give spectacular views of the volcano.

The "jeep–boat–jeep" transfer to Monteverde (see p.658) is a popular way of reaching the cloudforest and saves a lengthy and bumpy bus trip via Tilarán. The fastest cost around US$20 and take two to three hours, while more leisurely ones include a horseback segment.

Aventuras Arenal 150m east of the soccer pitch (☎479-9133, ⓦwww.arenaladventures.com). Professionally run trips, slightly less expensive than the likes of Sunset Tours, plus transport arrangements to just about anywhere in the country.

Desafío Tours ☎479-9464, ⓦwww.desafiocostarica.com. Located west of the church, this outfit are friendly, efficient and community-aware rafting specialists who run day-tours (US$65) on the Class IV Río Toro as well as trips in inflatable kayaks on the Arenal river (US$55). You can also take a demanding guided hike up Cerro Chato, the smaller volcanic peak clinging to Arenal's skirts (US$45). Their transfer to Monteverde includes a lakeside ride on well-loved horses (US$65), and they can sort out flights, tours and accommodation anywhere in the country.

Jacamar ☎479-9767, ⓦwww.arenaltours.com. Next to the *Lava Rocks* restaurant, this operator runs an Arenal night tour (US$25), trips to Caño Negro (US$50) and gentle rafting excursions on the Río Peñas Blancas. Their boat-and-taxi transfer to Monteverde costs US$19 and takes two and a half to three hours.

Sunset Tours ☎479-9801, ⓦwww.sunsettourcr.com. Located by the *Rancho la Cascada* restaurant, Sunset is pricier than other tour operators, but it has professional, well-qualified guides. Their volcano tours (US$22) include the entrance fee to the national park, but not to Balneario Tabacón. They have a good day-trip to Caño Negro (US$52), as well as taxi transfers to Monteverde (US$22).

Eating and drinking

Considering the number of tourists passing through, **restaurant** prices in La Fortuna are quite fair, catering for locals as much as visitors. The food is pretty much the same everywhere: the inevitable *casados*, *platos del día* and *arroz-con*-whatever. There's little evening activity to speak of, although *Twins*, a block east and half a block south of the central park, is a friendly, no-frills bar that keeps tourists and locals in late-night beer and karaoke, and *Vagabondo* (see below) has a large American-style bar and *discoteca* out the back that stays open pretty late most nights. At weekends, the *Volcán Look*, four kilometres west of town, is the liveliest *discoteca* in the area.

Choza de Laurel 200m west of the Parque Central on the main road. Very much on the tourist-bus circuit, this is nevertheless an atmospheric spot to eat, and one that delivers high-quality meals. The meat dishes, some of which are roasted slowly on a spit outside, are impressive both for tenderness and sheer size, although they aren't cheap – most mains are over US$8, and a cold beer costs double what you'd pay in most other places in town.

La Parada directly opposite the bus stop on the central park. This popular *soda* is a fine spot to sit and watch the world go by. Their *casados* are hardly inspiring, but they are big, filling and only US$2. There's also a variety of pizzas and enthusiastic staff.

Rancho La Cascada at the northeast corner of the park. You can't miss this cavernous thatched *palenque* hung with flags of diverse world nations. Although it's been a favourite tourist choice for a number of years now, the prices are still very reasonable and the quality good. Main courses, such as the house rice with prawns and vegetables, come in at US$3–4, while well-cooked steaks cost a little more, around US$8.

Vagabondo a kilometre west of town. This attractive open restaurant serves up very authentic Italian wood-fired pizzas in the US$6–8 range. There's a wide choice, good service and a relaxed atmosphere. Tucked away behind the restaurant is a large and convivial bar with pool tables that stays open late; the hospitable Italian owner also has some bright and cheerful cabinas here, as well as an interesting souvenir shop.

Moving on from La Fortuna

Despite its small size, La Fortuna has good bus connections, and with a little planning you can get from here to Guanacaste, Puntarenas, Monteverde and Puerto Viejo de Sarapiquí without backtracking to San José. For **Puerto Viejo de Sarapiquí**, take a bus to **San Carlos** (also called Ciudad Quesada;10 daily; 1–2hr), where you can pick up a service east to La Fortuna. Buses leave San Carlos for La Fortuna at 4.40am, 6am, 10am, 3pm and 5.30pm, but double-check these times before leaving. San Carlos is a pleasant regional town and not a bad place to spend a night, if you need. For **Monteverde**, there are two daily buses from La Fortuna to **Tilarán** (3hr), at the head of Laguna de Arenal, but most people take the "jeep–boat–jeep" transfer offered by various agencies. This saves time and a jarring ride; the trip across the lake is also spectacular. The Tilarán bus leaves at 8am and 5pm – if you take the later one you'll have to stay the night in Tilarán. You can connect in Tilarán with the Santa Elena service (for the Monteverde Cloudforest Reserve), which leaves at 12.30pm (3–4hr). Frequent local services connect Tilarán with **Cañas** and the Interamericana, where you can pick up buses north to **Liberia** and the beaches of **Guanacaste**, or south to **Puntarenas**. To get back to **San José** from La Fortuna, take the *directo* service (2 daily; 4hr 30min), which departs at 12.45pm and 2.45pm, or head to San Carlos from where you can connect with hourly buses to the capital.

For those **driving**, the roads are good, with the exception of a perennially difficult patch between La Fortuna and Arenal Town. La Fortuna's airport has been closed ever since a tragic plane crash in September 2000 on the side of the volcano necessitated one of the most hazardous recovery operations imaginable.

Parque Nacional Volcán Arenal

Though **Volcán Arenal** is one of the most active volcanoes in the Americas, whether you will see any lava flow depends very much on the weather. In the rainy season the spectacular night flows are very elusive, hidden by shrouds of mist and cloud. However, if nothing else you'll certainly hear unearthly rumbling and sporadically feel the ground shake – especially at night.

Volcán Arenal was afforded protected status in 1995, becoming part of the national parks system as the **Parque Nacional Volcán Arenal** (daily 8am–4pm; US$6). The park has some good **trails**, some of them across lava fields, while the four-kilometre "Tucanes" trail takes you to the part of the forest which was flattened by an eruption in 1968; you may also see some **wildlife** – birds (including oropéndolas and tanagers) and agoutis are particularly common. Although the park has a simple café, it's best to take a picnic lunch and plenty of water, if you intend to spend some time walking. Hiking any distance up the volcano's sides has always been energetically discouraged, and fences now stop you doing so. If you arrive on a cloudy or rainy day (which is most of the year, unfortunately) and can't see the summit, the park's visitor centre has video displays of the volcano's more spectacular activity.

You can't stay in or visit the park after dark except by taking one of the **night tours** which leave La Fortuna every evening at about 3–4pm. Most operators run them even when it's cloudy, in the hope that the cloud will lift or the opposite side of the volcano will be clear. None offers you a refund if you don't see anything, however, so you might want to wait for a clear evening before signing up. In addition, Aventuras Arenal (see p.706) run a sunset **boat tour** on which you can watch the action from Laguna de Arenal.

The **park entrance** is 12km from La Fortuna; look for the well-signed driveway off to the left. If you don't have your own vehicle, you can take a **taxi** from La Fortuna to the west side of the volcano (around US$35 return per car, including waiting time of a few hours), but unless you're in a large group, it's cheaper – and less bother – to take a tour. The **bus** from La Fortuna will drop you off at the entrance to the park and is much the cheapest option, though the return journey can be a bit tricky – unless you manage to connect with the bus coming from Tilarán or Arenal Town, your only option is to try to get a ride back with other park visitors. Hitching on the main road is also very easy.

The far north

The **far north** of the Zona Norte is an isolated region, in many ways culturally – as well as geographically – closer to Nicaragua than to the rest of the country and mostly devoted to sugar cane. Tourists come here to see **Refugio Nacional de Vida Silvestre Caño Negro**, a vast wetlands area and – at 192km from San José – one of the most remote wildlife refuges in Costa Rica. You can visit Caño Negro on a day-trip from the capital or on an excursion from La Fortuna or any of the larger hotels in the Zona Norte; getting there independently, as with everywhere in Costa Rica, is more complicated.

Los Chiles

Few tourists make it to **LOS CHILES**, a border settlement just 3km from the Nicaraguan frontier, and other than soaking up the town's end-of-the-world atmosphere, there's little to do, except perhaps try to rent a boat or horse to go to **Caño Negro**, 25km downstream on the Río Frío (see opposite). The only other reason you might come to Los Chiles is to cross the Nicaraguan border, although the majority of travellers still cross at Peñas Blancas, further west on the Interamericana. Two luxury **buses** per day run from C 12, Av 7/9, in **San José** to Los Chiles (5.30am & 3.30pm; 5hr), stopping at the small bus station. Also pulling in here are the almost hourly buses from San Carlos (Ciudad Quesada). Return buses to San José leave Los Chiles at 5am and 3pm, but be sure to check these times in advance.

Although Los Chiles has no official **tourist information**, everyone in town knows the current bus schedules and the times of the river-boat to the Nicaraguan border, though you'll need Spanish to ask around. Servicios Turísticos Caño Negro (☎471-1438), based at the *Cabinas Jabirú*, a block west and north of the bus station, can give some general tourist information and run trips to Caño Negro, Nicaragua, and local fishing excursions. You can **change dollars** and travellers' cheques at the Banco Nacional on the north side of the soccer pitch (Mon–Fri 8am–3.30pm); it also has an ATM accepting Visa/Plus/Cirrus/MasterCard.

Crossing into Nicaragua

Work has begun on a road bridge across to Nicaragua, but the project is constantly hit by delays. Currently, the only way to reach Nicaragua is by boat on the Río Frío: one to three daily services leave the docks in Los Chiles, with the time of departure depending on demand and tides. The journey to the small town of San Carlos de Nicaragua on the eastern lip of the huge Lago de Nicaragua (see p.557) takes just over an hour and costs $7. The Los Chiles *migración* officials are relatively friendly, and you may be able to confirm boat times with the groups of Nicas or Ticos who hang around the office.

If you need a visa for Nicaragua (few nationalities now do), you have to have done this in San José. Make sure that the **Nicaraguan border patrol**, 3km upriver from Los Chiles, stamps your passport, as you will need proof of entry when leaving Nicaragua.

You'll need some cash upon arrival in San Carlos; change a few colones for córdobas at the Los Chiles bank. From San Carlos it's also possible to cross the lake to **Granada** and on to **Managua**.

Refugio Nacional de Vida Silvestre Caño Negro

The largely pristine **Refugio Nacional de Vida Silvestre Caño Negro** (US$4), 25km west of Los Chiles, is one of the best places in the Americas to view huge concentrations of both migratory and indigenous birds, along with mammalian and reptilian river wildlife. Until recently its isolation kept it well off the beaten tourist track, though nowadays, more and more tours are visiting the area.

Getting to Caño Negro

Though most people come to the refuge on tours from La Fortuna, you can also get to Caño Negro **independently**. Driving is easy enough in the dry season, and two daily buses run there from Los Chiles, leaving year-round at 5am and 2pm (returning 7am and 6pm). You can also visit by tour from Los Chiles (see opposite) or La Fortuna. Alternatively, hire your own boat at the docks (US$60–100). In the latter case, make sure that you get taken right into the refuge – the entrance is marked by a sign poking out of a small islet at the mouth of the large flooded area.

If you take a tour, the **entrance fee** is included. If not, you should pay at the **ranger station** on the north side of the lake, provided you can find someone to collect the money. You can also **stay** at the ranger station (☎460-6484; $10) – call from the public telephone at Caño Negro to reserve – though facilities are variable. You may be able to buy a meal, but bring your own supplies just in case. There are also a handful of accommodation options in the village of Caño Negro. **Camping** is permitted in Caño Negro, but no formal facilities are provided and there's a charge of around US$4, payable to the ranger.

Unless you're an expert in identifying wildlife, the most rewarding way to enjoy the diverse flora and fauna of Caño Negro is to use the services of a **guide** who knows the area and can point out animals and other features of river life as you motor down to the refuge. If you come independently, ringing the ranger station in advance is the best way to arrange this. You could also ask around in the village of Caño Negro.

Puerto Viejo de Sarapiquí and around

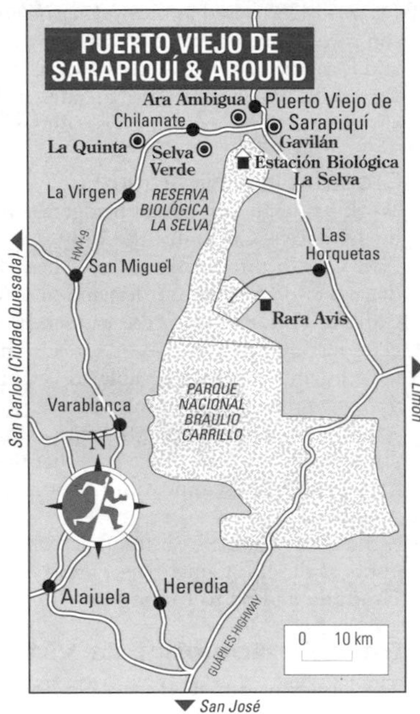

Steamy, tropical and carpeted with fruit plantations, the eastern part of the Zona Norte bears more resemblance to the hot and dense Caribbean lowlands than the plains of the north and, despite the toll of deforestation, still shelters some of the best-preserved premontane rainforest in the country. North by northwest from the Las Horquetas turn-off on the Guápiles Highway, the main road through the area makes a parabolic arc around the top of Parque Nacional Braulio Carrillo and stretches west to the village of San Miguel, from where Volcán Arenal and the western lowlands are easily accessible by road.

The region's chief tourist attractions are the biological research station **La Selva** and the ecolodges of **Rara Avis**, all of which offer access to some of the last primary rainforest in the country. The largest settlement, **Puerto Viejo de Sarapiquí**, is principally a river transport hub and a place for the banana, coconut, and pineapple plantation workers to stock up on supplies, prop their machetes at the bar and have a beer or two.

There are two options when it comes to getting **from San José** or the Valle Central to La Fortuna. The western route, which takes a little more than three hours, goes via Varablanca and the La Paz waterfall, passing the hump of Volcán Barva. This route offers great views of velvety green hills clad with coffee plantations, which turn, eventually, into rainforest. It's faster (1hr–1hr 30min), but marginally less scenic, to travel via the **Guápiles Highway**. The region receives a lot of **rain** – as much as 4500mm annually – and there is no real dry season (although less rain is recorded Jan–May), so wet-weather gear is essential.

Rara Avis

RARA AVIS, 17km south of Puerto Viejo de Sarapiquí and about 80km northeast of San José, offers one of the most thrilling and authentic ecotourism experiences in Costa Rica, featuring both primary rainforest and some secondary cover dating from about thirty years ago. Established in 1983, Rara Avis is both a tourist lodge and a private rainforest preserve, dedicated to the conservation, study and farming of the area's biodiversity. Its ultimate objective is to show that the rainforest can be profitable for an indefinite period, giving local smallholders a viable alternative to clear-cutting for their cattle. Rara Avis also functions as a **research station**, accommodating student groups and volunteers whose aim is to develop rainforest products – orchids, palms and so forth – as crops.

Rara Avis's **flora** is as diverse as you might expect from a premontane rainforest. The best way to learn to spot different flowers, plants, trees and their respective habitats is to go on a walk with one of the knowledgeable **guides**. Especially interesting plants include the stained-glass palm tree, a rare ornamental specimen, and the walking palm, whose fingertip- or tentacle-like roots can propel it over more than a metre of ground in its lifetime, as it "walks" in search of water. Orchids are numerous, as are non-flowering bromeliads and heliconias. A mind-boggling number of **bird species** have been identified, and it's likely that more have yet to be discovered. Among the more common **mammals** are monkeys, tapirs, ocelots and jaguars, though the last three are rarely seen.

Getting to Rara Avis

Because of its isolation you'll have to spend at least one night in the reserve, though two or three would be preferable. You'll need to reserve accommodation in advance, however you choose to arrive. If time is short, a **package** to Rara Avis that includes transport from San José may be worth considering (see p.612 for tour agents), but with a little planning it's perfectly possible – and more economical – to go on your own.

To get there **independently**, you need to take the Río Frío/Puerto Viejo de Sarapiquí bus from San José to the turn-off for the small village of Las Horquetas. From the junction, it's a five-minute walk to the **Rara Avis office** in the village (since all accommodation at the lodge must be pre-booked, they'll know you are coming). You'll then be loaded onto a tractor-pulled cart, which laboriously ascends the arduous final 15km of the journey. As the tractor for Rara Avis leaves daily at 9am, you have to take the 7am bus from San José. Make sure you get the express (*directo*) service via the Guápiles Highway (the bus via Heredia leaves thirty minutes earlier and takes the long western route to Puerto Viejo). It takes between an hour and ninety minutes from San José to reach the turn-off (*cruce*) for Las Horquetas – ask the driver to let you off.

If you come with your own transport, there's a car park at the office, where you can leave your vehicle. If you stay the previous night in La Fortuna, the twenty-minute taxi ride to the Rara Avis reception costs US$7–8; there are also several buses.

Getting to Rara Avis from Las Horquetas is at least half the fun, though not exactly comfortable. The uphill flatbed-tractor journey to the lodges takes two to four hours depending both on the condition of the road (actually, a muddy, rutted track) and on where you're staying. The pluses of this mode of transport include the sheer excitement – there's much multilingual cheering when the driver revs up the tractor and, squelching and spluttering, gets to the top of each slippery hill – and an exhilarating open-air view of the surrounding landscape, with plenty of time for toucan-spotting. Minuses include bumps and bruises, choking diesel fumes and a few worrying moments as the tractor slithers and slides up pitted hills.

If you miss the tractor, **horses** are available for hire from the villagers until about 1pm (US$25) – any time after that is pushing it, as the trip takes four hours, including walking the last 3km on a rainforest trail.

Leaving Rara Avis, the tractor departs at about 2pm, in time to catch the last bus for San José, which passes at about 6pm. If by chance you miss this bus, the Rara Avis office in Las Horquetas can arrange for a taxi (about US$25 per carload) to the Guápiles Highway, from where you can flag down a Guápiles–San José bus, which pass by hourly until 7pm.

Accommodation

There are three **places to stay** at Rara Avis (bookable on ⓣ253-0844 or 764-3131, ⓕ764-4187, ⓦwww.rara-avis.com). Rates include all meals, transport by tractor to and from Las Horquetas, and guided walks.

The main accommodation complex is the comfortable *Waterfall Lodge* (US$140 for a double, including taxes and meals). Set above a picture-perfect cascade, it has rooms with running hot water, private baths, spacious balconies with hammocks, and fantastic views of utterly pristine rainforest and the hot, flat lowland plains stretching towards the Caribbean. It's an idyllic place to stay; the only sounds heard at five or six in the morning are the echoing shrieks of birds and *monos congos* (howler monkeys). Meals, cooked by local women and served three times a day, are delicious. There's no electricity as such, apart from solar lighting and a generator for the kitchen. There's a telephone available for guests, but you'll need a credit card to use it.

About 500m away, *River-Edge Cabins* (US$160 for a double, including taxes and meals) is even more isolated and peaceful – if you stay here, though, you'll have to be unfazed by walking through the forest at night with only a torch or a lamp.

Five minutes from *Waterfall Lodge* is the centre's cheapest accommodation, *Las Casitas* (❽ – US$45 per person including taxes and meals), consisting of six rooms each sleeping four people in bunk beds. Facilities are comfortable enough, with shared bathroom, and the rate still includes all three meals and guided walks.

Rara Avis activities

Rara Avis has a network of very good **trails**. From the *Waterfall Lodge*, nine or so trails weave through fairly dense jungle cover. All of the trails are well marked and offer walks of thirty minutes to several hours, depending upon the pace. The guided walks are fun and informative, although guests are welcome to go it alone: you'll be given a map at the lodge receptions, but you should always let the staff know which trail you are following and about how long you intend to be. Rain gear is essential at all times.

Just below the *Waterfall Lodge*, a fifty-metre-high waterfall on the Río Atelopus plummets into a deep pool before continuing the river's slide down towards lower ground. **Swimming** in the icy-cold pool, shrouded in a fine mist, is a wonderful experience, and an alarm system has been installed to warn of any approaching floodwaters, an occasional hazard up here.

Estación Biológica La Selva

A fully equipped research station, **Estación Biológica La Selva**, 93km northeast of San José and 4km southwest of Puerto Viejo de Sarapiquí (Ⓣ766-6565; in San José Ⓣ240-6696, Ⓕ710-6535, Ⓦwww.ots.ac.cr), is probably the best place to visit in the Sarapiquí region, if you are a botany student or have a special interest in the scientific life of a rainforest. Like Rara Avis, it is also a superb birder's spot, with more than four hundred species of indigenous and migratory birds.

Though tourists are secondary to research at La Selva, visitors are welcome, either to stay at the centre, or take a guided walk during the day. The accommodation is booked up well in advance, and it's even worth reserving the walks beforehand, providing there is space. It's impossible to overstate La Selva's popularity, and in the high season it is sometimes booked months in advance, even for day-trips. Be sure to **reserve** way in advance by fax, if you are coming between November and April. Visiting in the low season (roughly May–Oct) is a safer bet, but even then you should call first.

La Selva's ground cover extends from primary **forest** – which represents sixty percent of the reserve's total area – through abandoned plantations to pastureland and brush, crossed by an extensive network of about 25 **trails** varying in length from short to more than 5km long and covering a total of nearly 60km. Most are in very good condition, clearly and frequently marked, though some are pretty rough, and many can get very muddy indeed. Only visitors staying at the complex are allowed to walk the trails unsupervised; day visitors will have to take one of the two daily guided walks. Tourists tend to stick to the main trails within the part of La Selva designated as the **ecological reserve**, next to the Río Puerto Viejo. These **trails**, the Camino Circular Cercano, the Camino Cantarrana and the Sendero Oriental, radiate from the river research station and take you through dense primary growth, the close, tightly knotted kind of tropical forest for which the Sarapiquí area is famous.

Practicalities

The least expensive way of getting to La Selva **from San José** is to take the 7am Río Frío/Puerto Viejo de Sarapiquí bus (marked "Río Frío"), which, if you ask, will drop you off at the entrance to the road leading to the station. Note, however, that it's a two-kilometre walk down the road from the junction. If you don't fancy the walk, continue in the bus on to **Puerto Viejo de Sarapiquí**, from where you can backtrack the four kilometres in a taxi for about US$2.50.

If you want to **stay** at La Selva, you *must* book in advance, by calling the office. The simple but comfortable student-residence-style **accommodation** at La Selva is overpriced (US$135 for two people), but it is the only way to gain access to the entire network of trails and it does help subsidize research. Researchers and students with scientific bona fides stay for considerably less. Rates include three meals a day, served in the communal dining hall, and one free guided walk per stay. Additional guided walks cost US$15 for guests. There are two daily guided walks at the complex, at 8am and 1.30pm. If you're just visiting, the walk costs US$26 and should be reserved beforehand. Led by highly-qualified guides, the walks are extremely informative and last more than three hours.

Puerto Viejo de Sarapiquí

Just short of 100km northeast of San José, **PUERTO VIEJO DE SARAPIQUÍ** (known locally as Puerto Viejo, not to be confused with Puerto Viejo de Talamanca on the Carribean coast) is an important hub for banana plantation workers and those who live in the isolated settlements between here and the Caribbean coast. It's a sleepy, humid place, with plenty of lazy jungle-outpost atmosphere, as well as a jumping-off point from which to visit the nearby rainforest lodges. There's not a great deal to do in the town itself, but Souvenirs Río Sarapiquí, on the main road just before the Banco Nacional, can arrange a variety of excursions, including boat trips on the river (US$15).

Numerous **buses** leave San José's Gran Terminal del Caribe for Sarapiquí; the **fast service**, via the Guápiles Highway and Las Horquetas, departs nine times a day from 6.30am to 6pm, completing the 97-kilometre trip in under two hours. Buses from San José to Sarapiquí **via Heredia** (ask the driver if you're unsure which bus you're on – there's nothing on the front indicating which route it takes) take more like three hours and leave at 6.30am, 1pm and 5.30pm, returning from Sarapiquí at 6am, 7.30am, 11am and 4.30pm.

Though most people choose to stay in one of the **lodges** in the countryside (see overleaf), they don't come cheap. Right by the football field on the main road in Sarapiquí, however, is *Mi Lindo Sarapiquí* (ⓣ766-6074; ❹), with clean and likeable rooms with fan and private bath above a good restaurant. Also on the main street is *El Bambú* (ⓣ766-6005, ⓦwww.elbambu.com; ❻), the plushest accommodation in town, with nicely decorated rooms (all with fans, colour TV and hot water), pretty potted tropical plants, a bar and restaurant set around the massive stand of bamboo that gives the place its name, a pool and a gym. The town has plenty of **sodas**: the lunchtime-only *La Sarapiqueña*, 50m south of *Mi Lindo Sarapiquí*, does good *gallos* and *pintos* for less than US$2. The Banco Nacional has an ATM that takes MC/Visa/Cirrus/Plus, plus there's a post office as well as a couple of supermarkets. Internet access is available at Internet Sarapiquí, 500m from the football field in the direction of the intersection of the main roads south and west (8am–10pm daily; US$1.20 per hour).

Accommodation around Puerto Viejo de Sarapiquí

Although La Selva and Rara Avis are the prime tourist destinations in this area, a number of very attractive **hotels** and **lodges** dotted around Sarapiquí allow you to experience something of the rainforest. In general, they're reasonably priced and accessible, and some offer **packages** from San José. If you're travelling by bus and the accommodation is west of Sarapiquí, you can either take the San José–Río Frío bus via Heredia, or get the fast bus to Sarapiquí and hop on one of the regular local buses heading towards La Virgen and Chilamate.

Gavilán Lodge 1km down a dirt road, 1km south of the Sarapiquí intersection ⓣ766-6743, ⓦwww.gavilanlodge.com. Very well priced, this tranquil place surrounds a sunny lawn by the Río Sarapiquí. There's a small Jacuzzi, and you can also cool off in the river. The cabin rooms are colourful, with fans and comfy beds as well as tiny hot-water bathrooms. Management is friendly, and there's a restaurant and shady lounge area. It's also a good passive birdwatching spot. ❺

Hotel Ara Ambigua 400m down a signed gravel road to the right, 1.5km from Sarapiquí ⓣ766-7101, ⓦwww.hotelaraambigua.com. Lovely rustic cottages, nicely furnished and impeccably clean. Rooms come with private bath, hot water and a/c, and are beautifully decorated with pastel shades and pictures of birds. There's a swimming pool, frog garden, and a few resident crocs; prices represent pretty good value. It's worth a visit for the tasty food – try the chicken brochettes – dished up by owners Lisbeth and Delfin in the pseudo-Baroque restaurant, complete with giant gold-painted wooden chandelier. ❹

La Quinta Lodge 7km west of Sarapiquí, and 5km east of La Virgen, 1.5km up a side road served by the occasional bus ⓣ761-1052, ⓦwww.quintasarapiqui.com. On the banks of the Río Sardinal, this comfortable lodge has 26 rooms, all with ceiling fans and hot water, set in bungalows scattered throughout the property and equipped with balconies and rocking chairs. Activities include swimming in the pool or river, exploring the lodge's own cultivated lands, its butterfly garden and the new on-site exhibition, "Jewels of the Rainforest". There's a pleasant outdoor restaurant, and biking, horse-riding and birdwatching can all be arranged by the cheerful staff. ❻

Selva Verde Lodge five kilometres west of Sarapiquí ⓣ766-6800, from the US ⓣ1-800/451-7111, ⓦwww.selvaverde.com. This upmarket and comprehensive rainforest lodge sits on two square kilometres of preserved forest alongside the Río Sarapiquí. While the jungle experience is somewhat sanitized, it's an undeniably relaxing and well-equipped resort, and the opportunities for spotting birds and monkeys are excellent. Accommodation is in large rooms in raised bungalows spaced among the trees; they are equipped with phone, fan and safe, as well as having a wide balcony. The rate (US$144 for a double in high season including taxes) includes full board at the restaurant's buffet. There are plenty of guided walks, horse rides, and other activities and facilities available. It's advisable to book well in advance. Children under 12 stay free. ❾

Moving on from Puerto Viejo de Sarapiquí

Puerto Viejo de Sarapiquí is a transport hub for the entire Zona Norte and eastern side of the country. From here it's possible to travel back to the **Valle Central**, either via the Guápiles Highway (1hr 30min or more) or via Varablanca and Heredia (3hr or more). You can also cut across country west to **San Carlos** (five daily; 2hr 30min) and on to **La Fortuna** (4hr) and Volcán Arenal, from where it's easy to continue, via Tilarán, to **Monteverde** and **Guanacaste**.

By river it's possible to continue north from Puerto Viejo along the Río Sarapiquí to the Nicaraguan border then east along the Río San Juan to Barra and Tortuguero on the Caribbean coast. You'll have to rent a private lancha to do this pleasant journey, which can take anywhere between four and seven hours (you're going upstream). It's fairly pricey, unless you're in a group of eight or so – about US$300 (8–10 maximum capacity). Ask at Souvenirs Río Sarapiquí or phone ⓣ766-6846.

6.7

The Zona Sur

Costa Rica's **Zona Sur** ("southern zone") is the country's least-known region, both for Ticos and for travellers, although tourism has begun to increase significantly in recent years. Geographically, it's a diverse area, ranging from the agricultural heartland of the Valle de El General to the high peaks of the Cordillera de Talamanca, most notably the mountain pass at Cerro de la Muerte ("Death Mountain") and **Cerro el Chirripó** – at 3819m one of the highest peaks in Central America. South of Chirripó, the cordillera falls away steeply into the river-cut lowlands of the Valle de Diquis around Palmar and the coffee-growing Valle de Coto Brus, near the border with Panama.

The chief draw is the **Osa Peninsula** in the extreme southwest, home to the **Parque Nacional Corcovado**, one of the country's prime rainforest hiking destinations, and the remote and picturesque **Bahía Drake**. More accessible, the **Playa Dominical** area of the Pacific coast is a surfing destination whose tremendous tropical beauty is beginning to attract increasing numbers of visitors (not to mention property developers). **Golfito**, the region's only town of any size, suffered from an unsavoury reputation for years after the pull-out of the United Fruit Company's banana operations in 1985, though its fortunes have improved since being made a tax-free zone for manufactured goods from Panama.

Despite the abundance of budget accommodation in the Zona Sur, you'll find yourself **spending** more than you bargained for simply because of the time, distance and planning involved in getting to many of the region's more beautiful spots, particularly around Parque Nacional Corcovado. Many people prefer to take a package rather than travel independently, and visitors who stay at the more expensive rainforest lodges often choose to fly in.

Climatically, the Zona Sur has two distinct regions. The first comprises the Pacific lowlands from south of Quepos roughly to the top of the Osa Peninsula, and the upland Valle de El General and the Talamancas, both of which experience a dry season from December to April. The second region – the Osa Peninsula, Golfito and Golfo Dulce – does not have so marked a dry season, and during the wettest part of the year, from around October to December, spectacular seasonal thunderstorms canter in from the Pacific. In the rainy season, some parts of Parque Nacional Corcovado become more or less unwalkable and local roads impassable.

Dominical

DOMINICAL, 44km south of Quepos (see p.672), probably represents the face of things to come along this stretch of the Pacific coast. Previously a secluded fishing village, it has, since the recent paving of the coastal road and the laying down of electricity and phone lines, begun to expand dramatically. A glut of new hotels, shops and restaurants have opened in the town, and the coastal areas to the south, still largely made up of unspoilt stretches of beach and rainforest (most of which are outside of protected parks and reserves), are rapidly being bought up by hungry property developers and hotel chains. The fear, expressed by many locals, that the area is destined to become the country's next Manuel Antonio – a once pristine area, now massively overdeveloped – seems about to be realized. Should the proposed paving of the Quepos–Dominical road go ahead as planned in the next few

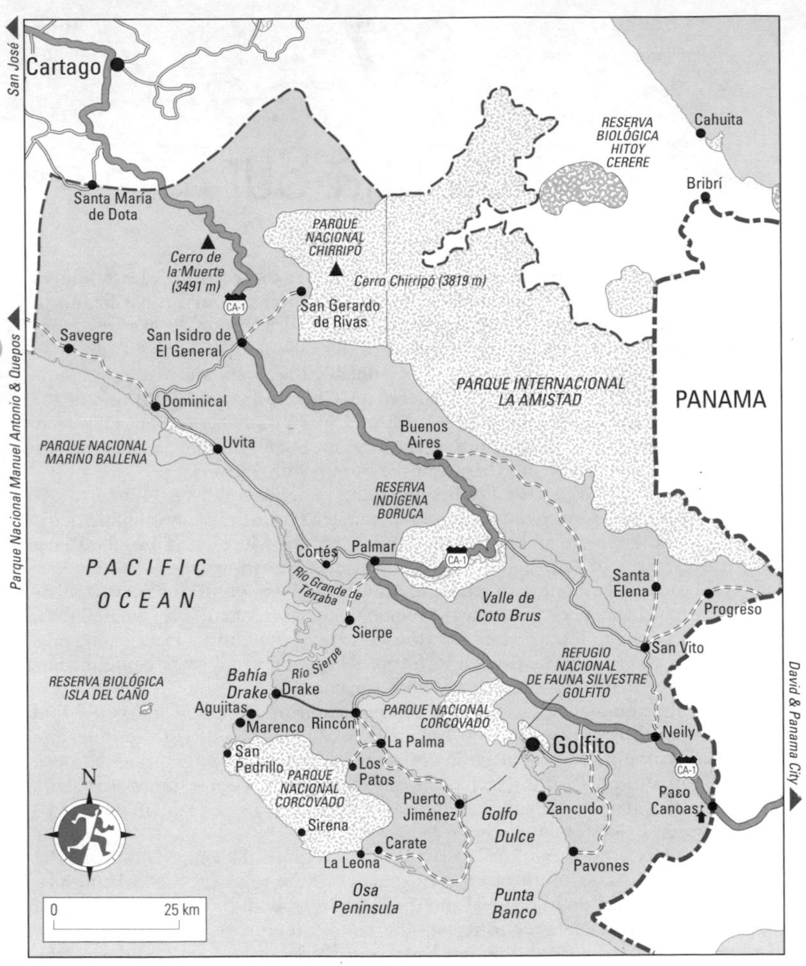

years, then the arrival of full-scale mass tourism, and all its attendant environmental problems, is surely only a matter of time.

As of now, Dominical stands just on the cusp of change. Despite its recent growth, the town is still relatively small scale with just a few dirt track roads, albeit lined with scores of (mainly American-owned) cabinas and budget hotels. Surfing is the big draw here with thousands of (again mainly American) visitors flocking every year to ride the big waves that crash on to the coast during the day before heading to the numerous beachfront bars to watch the postcard-perfect sunsets.

Dominical's growing status as a tourist destination has been confirmed by the opening of a smart new **tourist office** (Ⓔinfocenter@dominical.biz) in a purpose-built building at the northern edge of town. Here, you'll also find an **Internet café**, and, perhaps most significantly for the area's future, the offices of the Central Pacific Land Company. The tourist office can provide you with all the necessary details regarding local accommodation, board hire (the town is home to at least half a dozen surf schools), snorkelling (which is also very good in this area) and tours of the local area.

From San José the fastest route to Dominical is via the sleepy town of San Isidro de El General, on the Carretera Interamericana, from where there are reasonable bus connections. **From Guanacaste** and the Central Pacific, you'll do best to take the road south from Quepos, although be aware, if driving, that this is, as yet, unpaved and very bumpy. **Buses** from Quepos arrive at around 6.30am, 8.30am, 1.30pm and 3pm daily, and continue to San Isidro (2hr).

Accommodation in the Dominical area

The amount of **accommodation** in the Dominical area is growing all the time, which at least means there's plenty of choice. In the town itself most of it is budget and basic, catering mainly to the surfing community, but there are also a number of more upmarket places, usually owned by foreigners. The most expensive hotels include some wonderful hideaways, good for honeymooners, romantics and escapists. Aside from accommodation in the village, there's a string of hotels and self-catering lodges along the coast road towards Uvita.

La Cusinga Lodge 22km south of Dominical, past the Uvita Bridge Ⓣ & Ⓕ770-2549, Ⓦwww.lacusingalodge.com. One of the country's best ecolodges and one of the few places of this type to be owned and run by Ticos, *La Cusinga* occupies a gorgeous rainforest setting overlooking the Parque Nacional Marino Ballena, where humpback whales from the Arctic come each year to breed. Its seven cabinas have all been made on-site from the lodge's sustainable teak plantation and all the electricity is provided by solar and hydro power. Trails lead through the rainforest and down to a beautiful stretch of unspoilt beach. ❾

Hacienda Barú 1km north of Dominical, on the road to Quepos Ⓣ787-0003, Ⓕ787-0004, Ⓦwww.haciendabaru.com. Good-value, comfortable self-catering chalets set in a beautiful private reserve containing rainforest, mangrove and protected beach. Good for birders and orchid lovers – there are 250 varieties scattered around – plus there's a butterfly farm and a fixed canopy viewing platform on site; horse-riding tours and night tours are also available. ❻

Posada del Sol on the main street, 50 yards south of the *San Clemente Bar* Ⓣ & Ⓕ787-0085. Lovely hotel with four very good-value double rooms, all with private bath. ❺

Tortilla Flats on the beach Ⓣ787-0033, Ⓔtortflat@racsa.co.cr. Popular surfers' hotel with brightly decorated en-suite rooms and a beachfront bar where crowds gather every evening to watch the sunset. ❺

Eating and drinking

If you're self-catering, there are a couple of small **supermarkets** in Dominical itself (including one next door to the tourist office) plus another supermarket just outside town in the pink Plaza Pacifica mall. Of the village's **restaurants**, *El Rincon* serves excellent Italian-Argentinean food, and the *San Clemente Bar and Grill* has a Tex-Mex menu with a little Italian and Cajun thrown in. *Thrusters*, towards the beach on the left, is a large barn-like **bar** with TV, pool tables, darts board, table football and an extensive range of drinks.

Bahía Drake and around

BAHÍA DRAKE (pronounced "Dra-kay") is one of the most stunning areas in Costa Rica, with the blue wedge of Isla del Caño, a prime snorkelling destination, floating just off the coast and fiery-orange Pacific sunsets. The tiny hamlet of **AGUJITAS**, on the bay 10km south of **Drake** town, makes a good base for exploring the **Parque Nacional Corcovado**, which is situated on the southwest corner of the Osa Peninsula – the park's San Pedrillo entrance is within walking distance, and hikers can combine serious trekking with serious comfort at either end of their trip by staying at one of the upscale rainforest ecolodges that have sprung up around the park in recent years.

Like many other places in the Zona Sur, **getting to Bahía Drake** requires some planning. There are four choices: the tough way, hiking in from Corcovado; the cheap way, by bus from San José and then by boat along the Río Sierpe; the bumpy way, by 4WD along the gravel and dirt road between Rincón and the bay; and the luxury way, flying direct from San José to Bahía Drake, and taking one of the many **packages** offered by hotels in the area, which include transport to your lodge.

Travelling **independently**, you'll need to get a bus from San José to the banana processing town of Palmar Norte (7 daily; 5hr 30min), 120km southwest of San Isidro de El General; depending on what time you get in, you can then either bed down or get a local bus or taxi (about US$12) to **Sierpe**, where there are a few cabinas. In Sierpe you must find a **boatman** to take you the 30km downriver to Bahía Drake (2hr). You need someone with experience, a motorized lancha and lifejackets. Ask Sonia Rojas at the Fenix *pulpería* to help you find someone or try the riverfront bar of the *Hotel Oleaje Sereno* or the *Bar Las Vegas*, both of which are popular hangouts for boat captains. The going rate for a one-way trip to Drake is about US$20 per person or around US$65–85 per boatload (usually a maximum of 8 people); ask around for the best rates. If there's room, some hotel lanchas will take independent travellers – be sure to arrive early. The last lancha leaves at around 3.30pm, owing to fierce tides. If you want to make it to Drake from San José in one day, you'll need to catch the 5am bus.

Accommodation in and around Bahía Drake

Accommodation is clustered either in the tiny village of Agujitas, or on **Punta Agujitas**, the rocky point on the other side of the Río Agujitas. Virtually all the **ecolodges** listed below do a range of **tours**, from accompanied excursions to Corcovado to boat trips around Bahía Drake. The larger lodges are accustomed to bringing guests on packages from San José and can include transport from the capital, Palmar or Sierpe. The packages (and the prices we give below) usually include three meals a day – there are few eating options in Bahía Drake otherwise. Although hoteliers will tell you that you can't **camp** in the Drake area, people do – if you want to join them, pitch your tent considerately and be sure to leave no litter.

Bahía Drake Wilderness Resort Punta Agujitas Ⓣ & Ⓕ770-8012, in San José Ⓣ256-7394, Ⓦwww.drakebay.com. The most established lodge in the area, with rustic, comfortable cabinas or, if you want to rough it a bit, well-appointed tents – both options are well-screened. There's hearty local food, and the camp has its own solar-heated water supply, nighttime electricity, and excellent snorkelling and canoeing. It is quite expensive – around US$780 for three nights – although this does include air transfers from San José (and free laundry). ❾

Cabinas Jade Mar in the village Ⓣ384-6681, Ⓕ786-7366. One of the few village cheapies, and a good place to stay if you want to get a taste of local life, with extremely well-priced and pleasant, if basic, cabinas, kept very clean by the informative Doña Martha. All cabins have private bath (cold water only), and hearty meals are included in the price. Inexpensive tours to Corcovado and Isla del Caño are also available. ❻

Jinetes de Osa between Punta Agujitas and Agujitas Ⓣ385-9541, Ⓦwww.costaricadiving.com. One of the less expensive options in Bahía Drake, right on the area's main beach. There's an on-site PADI dive school; most guests come here on good-value dive packages (they organize trips to the Isla del Caño). Accommodation, some of it en suite, is simple, but comfortable, and rates include three meals a day. ❻

La Paloma Lodge Punta Agujitas Ⓣ293-7502, Ⓕ239-0954, Ⓦwww.lapalomalodge.com. Beautiful, rustic rooms in thatched hilltop bungalows, with private bath, balconies and hammocks – the airy, two-storey bungalows are best, being surrounded by forest and boasting spectacular views, particularly at sunset. *Pangas* (traditional canoes) are available for guests to paddle on the Río Agujitas behind the lodge, and there's also an attractively tiled swimming pool. Excellent service, with friendly and helpful staff. ❾

Poor Man's Paradise past Playa San Josecito Ⓣ771-4582, Ⓕ771-8841, Ⓦwww.mypoormansparadise.com. One of the most secluded lodges in what is, after all, a pretty secluded area, this spot enjoys a lush rainforest setting near a glorious stretch of beach. Cabinas with private and shared bathrooms are available, or you can camp for US$7. The thatched-roof restaurant serves good, filling meals. ❽

Rancho Corcovado on the beach, in front of Agujitas ⓣ350-4866, ⓕ786-7366. Good-value, family-run hotel with beautiful views over the bay and simple, clean en-suite rooms. Camping is permitted (US$6 per person), and rates include full board. Horse-riding tours are also available. ❺

Golfito

The former banana port of **GOLFITO**, 33km north of the Panamanian border, stretches for 2500m along the water of the same name (*golfito* means "little gulf"). The town's setting is spectacular, backed up against steep, thickly forested hills to the east, and with the glorious Golfo Dulce – one of the deepest gulfs of its size in the world – to the west. The low shadow of the Osa Peninsula shimmers in the distance, and everywhere the vegetation has the soft muted look of the undisturbed tropics.

Golfito's history is inextricably intertwined with the giant transnational **United Brands** company – locally known as "La Yunai" – which first set up in the area in 1938. United Brands built schools, recruited doctors and police, and brought prosperity to the area, but following fluctuating banana prices, a three-month strike and local social unrest, they eventually decided Golfito was too much trouble and pulled out in a hurry in 1985. The town died and gained a reputation for rampant unemployment, alcoholism, abandoned children, prostitution and general unruliness.

Today, at the big old *muelle bananero*, container ships are still loaded up with bananas processed further up towards Palmar Norte. This residual traffic (which includes US Navy and Coast Guard ships) in addition to tourism – Golfito is a good base for getting to the **Parque Nacional Corcovado** by lancha or plane – have helped revive the local economy. The real rescue, though, came from the Costa Rican government, which in the early 1990s established a **depósito libre** – or tax-free zone – in the town, where Costa Ricans can buy manufactured goods imported from Panama without the 100-percent tax normally levied. Ticos who come to shop here have to buy their tickets for the *depósito* 24 hours in advance, obliging them to spend at least one night, and therefore colones, in the town.

Golfito straggles for ages without any clear centre. The town is effectively split in two – by a division in wealth as well as architecture. In the north is the **zona americana**, where the banana-company executives used to live and where better-off residents still reside in beautiful wooden houses shaded by dignified palms. Here, you'll find the *depósito libre*, an unaesthetic outdoor mall ringed by a circular concrete wall. To the south, the **pueblo civil** (civilian town) is a tight nest of streets – hotter, noisier and more crowded than the zona. It's here you'll find the good-value hotels and *sodas*, as well as the lancha across the Golfo Dulce to Puerto Jiménez and the Osa Peninsula.

Arrival and information

Buses from San José leave Tracopa's terminal at 7am and 3pm for the eight-hour journey. Buy your return ticket (see box, overleaf) as soon as you disembark. You can also **fly** here with Sansa and NatureAir; the airstrip is in the *zona americana*. The Banco Nacional, opposite the Tracopa terminal, will change **travellers' cheques** and give cash advances on credit cards, but it's a tediously slow process. The **correo** is right in the centre of the *pueblo civil*, and an **Internet** café is on the main street next to the gas station. You can catch a **water-taxi** to Playa Cacao and other local destinations from the *muellecito* (ferry dock), just north of the gas station (US$4). Land-Sea Tours (ⓣ & ⓕ775-1614, ⓔlandsea@racsa.co.cr), on the waterfront at the southern end of the *pueblo*, organizes a wide range of tours, has a book exchange and is an excellent source of information.

Accommodation

Accommodation in Golfito comes in two varieties: swish places in the *zona americana*, catering to businesspeople and shoppers at the *depósito*, and decent, basic rooms in the *pueblo civil*.

Cabinas Playa Cacao Playa Cacao; no phone, ⓔ isabel@racsa.co.cr. Excellent budget accommodation just across the water from Golfito. The indigenous-style, thatched-roof cabinas are simply furnished, but very comfortable, with en-suite bathrooms and fans. The lovely owner, Isabel, will regale you with stories of her event-filled life in Costa Rica, Germany and the UK, in the communal dining area. Tours of the local mangrove swamps to see the crocodiles are also available for around US$40.

Esquinas Rainforest Lodge La Gamba, about 7km from Km37 on the Interamericana ⓣ & ⓕ 775-0901, ⓦ www.esquinaslodge.com. Friendly ecolodge run by the government of Austria as part of a model project combining development aid, nature conservation and rainforest research – all profits go to the local community. It's set in primary rainforest, with resident wildlife and on-site hiking and horse-riding trails. Wide range of packages available, plus a variety of tours, including ones to Corcovado and the Wilson Botanical Gardens. Fantastic meals are included in the room rate. ❾

Las Gaviotas at the southern entrance to town ⓣ 775-0062, ⓕ 775-0544, ⓔ lasgaviotas@hotmail.com. Well-equipped, if slightly shabby, resort with nice views over the gulf, plus the town's only swimming pool. The somewhat barrack-like (but very affordable) rooms all have private bath with hot water, a/c and cable TV. The waterside rancho restaurant serves great local seafood. ❻

Samoa del Sur on the main road between the *zona americana* and the *pueblo civil* ⓣ 775-0233, ⓕ 775-0573, ⓔ samoasur@racsa.co.cr. Fourteen spacious, though slightly gloomy, rooms on the waterfront, with a large and rather raucous boat-shaped bar-restaurant (it's the bar of choice for US marines on shore leave). ❹–❺

Moving on from Golfito

Buses to San José leave daily at 5am and 1pm – if you're getting the 5am bus you'll have to buy your return ticket in advance. There are also several daily flights to San José on Sansa and NatureAir. For **Corcovado** you'll need first to go to Puerto Jiménez, which can be reached either by lancha (daily at 11am; 1hr 30min; US$3) or small plane (about US$100 for up to 5 people) – contact the Alfa Romeo Aero Taxi office at the airstrip (ⓣ 755-1515, ⓔ taxicorcovado@racsa.co.cr).

The Osa Peninsula

In the extreme southwest of the country, the **Osa Peninsula** is home to an area of immense biological diversity, much of it protected by the **Parque Nacional Corcovado**. Few people fail to be moved by the peninsula's beauty: whichever direction you approach it from, you see what looks to be a floating island, an intricate mesh of blue and green, with tall canopy trees sailing high and flat like elaborate floral hats. Most visitors base themselves in the tiny, friendly town of **Puerto Jiménez**. From here, you could feasibly "do" the whole peninsula in four days, but this would be rushing it, especially if you want to spend time walking the trails and wildlife-spotting at Corcovado – better to allot five to seven days or more, if you want to explore Bahía Drake, too.

Puerto Jiménez and around

Although it's become increasingly touristy in recent years, **PUERTO JIMÉNEZ** – known locally simply as Jiménez – is still a relaxed, friendly place with plenty of cheap lodging and places to eat. You can also pick up the colectivo (a sort of open-back truck-taxi) from here to Carate, 43km southwest, or to Bahía Drake from where you can enter Corcovado (see p.722). Drivers shouldn't try reaching either destination in anything less than a 4WD at any time of year. Though the roads have been "improved" in recent years (making you wonder just how bad they were before), it's still a horrendously bumpy ride. The Carate drive, in particular, will involve the careful negotiation of at least half a dozen small (and in the rainy season not so small) rivers. Be aware that Puerto Jiménez is home to the only gas station on the entire Osa Peninsula, so be sure to fill up before you leave.

Arrival and information

There are two **buses** from San José via San Isidro to Jiménez (10hr), leaving the capital at 6am and noon and returning at 5am and 11am. A **lancha** for Jiménez leaves Golfito daily at 11am, returning at 6am, or you can **fly** in from San José or from Golfito.

The **Corcovado information office** (Oficina de Area de Conservación Osa; Mon–Fri 8am–noon & 1–4pm; ⓣ735-5036, ⓕ735-5276), which faces the airstrip, is staffed by friendly rangers, who can answer questions and arrange accommodation and meals at the park's *puestos*, if you haven't already done so (in most cases it's better to arrange this before you arrive; see p.723). For other tourist information, head to the small **tourist information office**, opposite the football pitch, which can provide details of tours to Corcovado and Bahía Drake. The helpful Osa Tropical (ⓣ735-5062, ⓕ735-5043, ⓔosatropi@racsa.co.cr), on the main road 50m north of the gas station, acts as the local NatureAir and Sansa agent; it also has an international phone and fax service and can make accommodation reservations. Banco Nacional, just north of the gas station, changes travellers' cheques and dollars. The correo, opposite the football pitch, has public phones and **Internet** access, as does the tourist office and *Café Net El Sol* on the main drag.

The **colectivo** to **Carate** goes twice daily (except Sundays) in the dry season at about 6am and 1.30pm; the one to **Bahía Drake** runs Monday to Friday at noon, but you'd do best to confirm the times locally. You could ask at the tourist office or at the El Tigre supermarket, its departure point. In the wet season it goes less often, about three days a week. The price is about US$10 per person one way; you can arrange to be dropped off and picked up if you're staying at any of the places en route – ask the driver. If you don't get a place on the truck, a number of local taxi drivers have **4WDs**; try Orlando Mesen (ⓣ735-5627; about US$60 return to Carate).

Accommodation

Jiménez's **hotels** are reasonably priced, clean and basic. Though it's best to reserve in the dry season, this may not always be possible, as phone lines sometimes go down. In the rainy season there are far fewer people about and you shouldn't need to book in advance. There are a few comfort-in-the-wilderness places between Jiménez and Carate around the lower hump of the peninsula, a couple of which make great retreats or honeymoon spots.

In Puerto Jiménez

Cabinas Agua Luna near the lancha pier ⓣ & ⓕ735-5393, ⓔagualu@racsa.co.cr. A range of comfortable waterfront accommodation, some of it quite smart, with cable TV, a/c and fridge. ❻

Cabinas Brisas del Mar on the waterfront, just east of the football pitch ⓣ735-5028. A choice of dorm-style rooms (US$10) or slightly more comfortable double rooms (US$40) in this basic backpacker complex overlooking the gulf. ❸–❺

Cabinas Oro Verde on the main street ⓣ735-5241. Nine very good-value, clean (albeit pretty basic) rooms right in the middle of town, with restaurant, laundry service and friendly owners. ❷

Cabinas Puerto Jiménez on the way into town from the Interamericana ⓣ735-5090. Quiet cabinas next to the water, with simple, spotlessly clean and nicely furnished rooms. They're well-screened, with bath and fan, though some can be dark – ask to see a few before you choose. ❷

Iguana Lodge follow the signs for 5km out of Jiménez to Playa Platanares ⓣ735-5205, ⓕ735-5436, ⓦwww.iguanalodge.com. Wonderful hotel run by very friendly US family with four two-storey cabinas in lovely gardens by the beach – all rooms face the sea and are attractively decorated. Rates include three delicious meals a day. ❾

Between Puerto Jiménez and Carate

The following are listed in order of their distance from Puerto Jiménez. The first, *Bosque del Cabo*, is 25km south from Jiménez. The last, the *Corcovado Tent Camp*, is right next to the park entrance. All are signed from the road and include three meals a day in their room rates.

Bosque del Cabo above Playa Matapalo, down a private road to the left off the Carate road Ⓣ & Ⓕ735-5206, Ⓦwww.bosquedelcabo.com. Wonderfully grand, eco-friendly lodge, with landscaped grounds and swathes of rainforest, run by a friendly American couple and offering ten luxurious hardwood and stucco cabinas (several with magnificent ocean views) plus two even more luxurious houses (which sleep up to 6). There's also a very good restaurant. Tours available. ❾

Lookout Inn just north of Carate, near the airstrip Ⓣ735-5931, Ⓦwww.lookout-inn.com. Six large rooms in a beach house set on rainforested hillside, with pool and beautiful ocean views. Informal and fun atmosphere; tours available. ❼

Luna Lodge set in the hills above Carate – call for a pick-up from the nearby Carate airstrip Ⓣ380-5036, Ⓦwww.lunalodge.com. Remote, tranquil and beautiful lodge with welcoming owners and staggering views over the surrounding virgin rainforest. Healthy home-grown food and yoga classes available. ❾

Corcovado Tent Camp about a 45min walk along the beach from Carate (book via Costa Rica Expeditions, see p.612). Twenty self-contained and fully screened "tent-camps" elevated on short stilts in an amazing beachside location, with bedrooms and screened verandas, communal baths and good local cooking. Very good value, with packages available (some including flights right to Carate), plus guided tours around Corcovado (US$38–68) and horse-riding. ❻

Eating and drinking

There's not much choice when it comes to **eating** in Jiménez, but you certainly won't starve. The most popular place in town (particularly with tourists and expats) is funky little *Juanitas*, which does reasonable Mexican food (including a very hot chile); it's a great place to hang out with a cool drink, even if you're not in the mood for food. Other good meeting places include *Restaurante Carolina*, on the main drag, which has a comida típica menu (and also rents out cabinas), and the *Agua Luna* hotel's very popular Chinese restaurant and bar overlooking the bay.

Parque Nacional Corcovado

Created in 1975, **PARQUE NACIONAL CORCOVADO** ("hunchback"), 368km southwest of San José (daily 8am–4pm; US$6), protects a fascinating and biologically complex area of land, most of it on the peninsula itself. It also covers one mainland area just north of Golfito, which may soon be made into a national park in its own right. It's an undeniably beautiful park, with deserted beaches, some laced with waterfalls, high canopy trees and better-than-average **wildlife-spotting** opportunities. Many people come with the express purpose of spotting margay, ocelot, tapir and other rarely seen animals. Of course, it's all down to luck, but if you walk quietly and there aren't too many other humans around, you should have a better chance of seeing some of these creatures here than elsewhere. To increase your chances, it's well worth investing in the services of a guide – the *puestos* have lists. A twelve-hour trek should cost about US$45.

Serious walking in Corcovado is not for the faint-hearted. The **terrain** includes beaches of packed or soft sand, riverways, mangroves, *holillo* (palm) swamps and dense forest, although most of it is at lowland elevations. Hikers can expect to spend most of their time on the beach trails that ring the outer perimeters of the park. Inland, the broad alluvial Corcovado plain contains the **Corcovado lagoon** and features the only sizeable chunk of tropical **premontane wet forest** (also called tropical humid forest) on the Pacific side of Central America. The Osa forest is as visually and biologically magnificent as any on the subcontinent: biologists often compare the tree heights and density here with that of the Amazon basin cover – practically the only place in the entire isthmus of which this can still be said.

The coastal areas of the park receive at least 3800mm of **rain** a year, with precipitation rising to about 5000mm in the higher elevations of the interior. This intense wetness, combined with a sunny respite, is ideal for the growth and development of the intricate, densely matted cover associated with tropical wet forests. There's a dry season (Dec–March), however, and the inland lowland areas, especially those around the lagoon, can be amazingly **hot**, even for those accustomed to tropical temperatures.

Practicalities

Unless you're coming to Corcovado with Costa Rica Expeditions and staying in their tent camp (see opposite) or in the nearby, similar *La Leona* tent camp, in the dry season, at least, you have to **reserve** in advance – this will include meals, camping space or lodging at the *puesto* of your choice (see below). The best way to do this is to fax the park's Puerto Jiménez office directly on ⓕ735-5276 or, if you're already in the country, visit the Fundación de Parques Nacionales in San José (see p.597), who will fax or telephone Corcovado on your behalf. You'll have to specify your dates and stick to them. It costs US$2 per night to camp at the *puestos*, or US$6 to sleep in the comfortable accommodation block at Sirena (plus US$2 reservation fee). You can either take **meals** with the rangers (US$3 for breakfast, US$6 for lunch and dinner – you pay in colones at the *puesto*) or bring your own food and utensils and use their stove. Food is basic – rice and beans or fish – but filling.

You should **bring** your own tent, mosquito net, sleeping bag, food and water, and plan to hike early – though not before dawn, due to snakes – and shelter during the hottest part of the day. Corcovado is set up so that the rangers at each *puesto* always know how many people are on a given trail, and how long those hikers are expected to be. If you are late getting back, they'll go looking for you. This gives a measure of security, but, all the same, take precautions. Incidentally, it's especially important when coming to Corcovado to brush up on your **Spanish**. You'll be asking the rangers for a lot of crucial information, and few, if any, speak English. If you're not fluent, bring a phrase book.

Puestos and routes through the park

The *pulpería* in the village of **Carate**, about 43km from Jiménez, sells basic foodstuffs; you can also camp here for a nominal fee. From here it's a nearly two-hour walk along the beach to the park entrance at **La Leona** *puesto*, although you can stop off for refreshment en route at the *Corcovado* and *La Leona* tent camps. It's then a sixteen-kilometre hike – allow six hours, as you have to wind along the beach, where it's slow going – to **Sirena**, the biggest *puesto* in the park, where you can stay in the simple lodge, exploring the local trails around the Río Sirena. If you're walking from Bahía Drake, you'll enter the park at **San Pedrillo** *puesto* and walk the 25km to Sirena from there.

The small hamlet of La Palma, 24km north of Puerto Jiménez, is the starting point for the walk to the **Los Patos** *puesto*, a twelve-kilometre hike, much of it through hot lowland terrain. You need to arrive at Los Patos soon after dawn; if you want to stay in La Palma and get up early, *Cabinas Corcovado* (no phone; ❷) is a good bet. The relatively new **El Tigre** *puesto*, at the eastern inland entrance to the park, is a good place to have breakfast or lunch with the ranger(s) before setting off on the local trails. To get there from Jiménez, drive 10km north and take the second left, a dirt track, signed to El Tigre and Dos Brazos.

All puestos have camping areas, drinking water, information, toilets and telephone or radio. Wherever you enter, jot down the details of the **marea** (tide tables), which are posted in prominent positions. You'll need to cross most of the rivers at low tide; to do otherwise is dangerous. Rangers can advise on conditions.

Walking the trails

The sixteen-kilometre trail from **La Leona to Sirena** runs just inland from the beach, which at least makes it easy to keep your bearings. If you can avoid anything untoward, you should be able to do the walk in five to six hours, taking time to look out for birds. En route, if you're lucky, you may be able to spot a flock of **scarlet macaws**, who roost in the coastal trees, and perhaps **monkeys** as well, particularly the white-faced capuchins, which are the most confident and inquisitive of the park's four breeds of monkey and thus the most likely to show themselves. Take lots of sunscreen, a big hat and at least five litres of water per person – the trail gets very hot, despite sea breezes.

The really heroic walk in Corcovado, all 25km of it, is from **Sirena to San Pedrillo** – the stretch along which you'll see the most impressive trees. It's a two-day trek, so you need a tent, sleeping bag and mosquito net, and you mustn't be worried by having to set up camp in the jungle. Fording the **Río Sirena**, just 1km beyond the Sirena *puesto*, is the biggest obstacle. The deepest of all the rivers on the peninsula, it has to be crossed with care and at low tide only: not only does it have the strongest out-tow current, but sharks come in and out in search of food at high tide. Get the latest information from the Sirena rangers before you set out.

The trail across the peninsula from **Los Patos to Sirena** is 20km long. You may want to rest at the entrance, as this is an immediately demanding walk, continuing uphill for about 6–8km and taking you into high, wet and dense rainforest – and after that you've still got 14km or so of incredibly hot lowland walking to go. This is a trail for experienced rainforest hikers and hopeful **mammal**-spotters: taking you through the interior, it gives you a reasonable chance of coming across, for example, a margay, or the tracks of tapirs and jaguars. That said, some hikers come away very disappointed, having not seen a thing. It's a gruelling trek, especially with the hot inland temperatures (at least 26°C, with 100-percent humidity) and the lack of sea breezes.

The **El Tigre** area, at the eastern inland entrance to the park, is gradually becoming more developed, with short walking trails being laid out around the *puesto*. These provide an introduction to Corcovado without making you slog it out on the marathon trails, and it can easily be covered in a morning or afternoon.

Paso Canoas and the Panamanian border

Duty-free shops and stalls lining the Interamericana announce the approach to **PASO CANOAS**. As you come into town, either driving or on the Tracopa or international Ticabus service, you'll pass the Costa Rican customs checkpoint, where everybody gets a going-over. Foreigners don't attract much interest, however; customs officials are far more concerned with nabbing Ticos coming back over the border with unauthorized amounts of cheap consumer goods.

To cross from Costa Rica into Panama, most nationalities need a **tourist card**, though UK citizens need only bring their passport. Tourist cards should be collected in advance from the **Panamanian consulate**, or from the office of Copa, Panama's national airline, in San José. Many people should also have a **visa** – Canadians, Australians and New Zealanders among them. You may also need a return ticket back to Costa Rica or an onward ticket out of Panama to another country (though the cheapest Tracopa bus fare will do), but bear in mind that immigration requirements frequently change, seemingly at whim, so always check with the Panamanian consulate before setting off.

The **migración** is on the Costa Rican side, next to the Tracopa bus terminal. You'll have to wait in line, maybe for several hours, especially if a San José–David–Panama City Ticabus comes through, as all international bus passengers are processed together. Arrive early to get through fastest. There's no problem **changing money**: there's a Banco Nacional on the Costa Rican side of the border and, beyond that, plenty of moneychangers. Note that you cannot take any fruit or vegetables across the border – even if they're for your lunch. They will be confiscated.

David, the first city of any size in Panama, is about ninety minutes beyond the border. Buses run from the Panamanian border bus terminal every hour or so until 5pm. From David it's easy to pick up local services, including the Ticabus to Panama City, which you can't pick up at the border.

Travel details

Buses

The main domestic and international travel routes from **San José** are covered on pp.611–615.

Alajuela to: La Guácima Abajo (4 daily; 20min); San José (every 5–10min; 20min); Sarchí (every 30min; 1hr); Volcán Poás (1 daily; 2hr); Zoo-Ave (every 30min; 15min).

Cahuita to: Puerto Limón (9 daily; 1hr); Puerto Viejo de Talamanca (8 daily; 1hr 30min–2hr); San José (4 daily; 4hr); Sixaola (4 daily; 2hr).

Cartago to: Paraíso (Mon–Fri every 10–20min); San José (every 10min; 40min).

Ciudad Quesada *see San Carlos*

Dominical to: Quepos (4 daily; 2hr); San Isidro (3 daily; 40min–1hr).

Golfito to: San José (2 daily; 8hr).

Heredia to: Paso Llano (3 daily; 1hr); San José (every 5–10min; 15min).

Jacó to: Puntarenas (4 daily; 1hr 15min); Quepos (4 daily; 1hr 15min); San José (5 daily; 2hr 30min–3hr).

La Fortuna to: San Carlos (6 daily; 1–2hr); San José (3 daily; 5hr); Tilarán (2 daily; 3hr).

Liberia to: La Cruz (14 daily; 1hr); Nicoya (10 daily; 2hr); Parque Nacional Santa Rosa (5 daily; 1hr); Peñas Blancas (6 daily; 2hr); Playas del Coco (6 daily; 1hr); Playa Hermosa (5 daily; 1hr); Playa Panamá (5 daily; 1hr); Puntarenas (5 daily; 3hr); San José (11 daily; 4hr 30min); Santa Cruz (14 daily; 1hr); Tamarindo (6 daily; 1hr 30min–2hr).

Los Chiles to: San Carlos (10 daily; 2hr 30min); San José (2 daily; 5hr).

Montezuma to: Paquera (6 daily; 1hr); Cabo Blanco (5 daily; 20min).

Nicoya to: Liberia (10 daily; 2hr); Nosara (1 daily; 2hr); Playa Sámara (3–6 daily; 1hr 30min); San José (8 daily; 6hr); Santa Cruz (16 daily; 40min).

Nosara to: Nicoya (1 daily; 2hr); Playa Sámara (2 daily; 40min); San José (1 daily; 6hr).

Palmar to: San José (7 daily; 5hr 30min); Sierpe (5 daily; 30min).

Paquera to: Montezuma (6 daily; 1hr); Tambor (6 daily; 40min).

Paso Canoas to: San Isidro (2 daily; 6hr); San José (6 daily; 9hr).

Peñas Blancas to: Liberia (6 daily; 2hr); San José (3 daily; 6hr).

Playas del Coco to: Liberia (6 daily; 1hr); San José (3 daily; 5hr).

Playa Hermosa to: Liberia (5 daily; 1hr); San José (1 daily; 5hr).

Playa Panamá to: Liberia (5 daily; 1hr); San José (1 daily; 5hr).

Playa Sámara to: Nicoya (3–6 daily; 1hr 30min); Nosara (2 daily; 40min); San José (2 daily; 5hr).

Puerto Jiménez to: San Isidro (2 daily; 5hr); San José (2 daily; 10hr).

Puerto Limón to: Cahuita (4 daily; 1hr); Manzanillo (3 daily; 2hr); Moín (6am–7pm every 30min; 25min); Puerto Viejo de Talamanca (5 daily; 1hr 30min); San José (every half-hour; 2hr 30min–3hr); Sixaola (1 daily; 3hr).

Puerto Viejo de Sarapiquí to: San Carlos (5 daily; 2hr 30min); San José (via Guápiles Highway, 7 daily; 1hr 30min–3hr; via Heredia, 4 daily; 3–4hr).

Puerto Viejo de Talamanca to: Cahuita (8 daily; 1hr 30min–2hr); Manzanillo (3 daily; 45min); Puerto Limón (4 daily; 1hr 30min); San José (4 daily; 4hr 30min); Sixaola (4 daily; 2hr).

Puntarenas to: Liberia (7 daily; 3hr); Quepos (4 daily; 3hr); San José (14 daily; 2hr); Santa Elena (1 daily; 3hr 30min).

Quepos to: Dominical (4 daily; 2hr); Jacó (4 daily; 1hr 15m); Puntarenas (4 daily; 3hr); San Isidro (2–3 daily; 3hr 30min); San José (9 daily; 3hr 30min–5hr).

San Carlos (Ciudad Quesada) to: La Fortuna (6 daily; 1–2hr); Los Chiles (10 daily; 2hr 30min); Puerto Viejo de Sarapiquí (5 daily; 2hr 30min); San José (14 daily; 3hr); Tilarán (1 daily; 4hr).

San Isidro to: Dominical (4 daily; 40min–1hr); Paso Canoas (2 daily; 6hr); Puerto Jiménez (3 daily; 5hr); San Gerardo de Rivas, for Chirripó (1 daily; 40min); San José (16 daily; 3hr).

San José to: Alajuela (every 15min; 20min); Braulio Carrillo (every 30min; 35min); Cahuita (4 daily; 4hr); Cañas (10 daily; 3hr 30min); Cartago (every 20min; 40min); David, Panama (1 daily; 9hr); Guatemala City, Guatemala (2 daily; 60hr); Golfito (2 daily; 8hr); Heredia (every 5–10min; 15min); Jacó (5 daily; 2hr 30min–3hr); La Fortuna (3 daily; 5hr); La Guacima Abajo (Mon–Sat 2 daily; 40min); Liberia (10 daily; 4hr 30min); Los Chiles (2 daily; 5hr); Managua, Nicaragua (7 daily; 11hr); Manuel Antonio (5 daily; 3hr 30min); Nicoya (8 daily; 6hr); Nosara (1 daily; 6hr); Palmar (7 daily; 5hr 30min); Paso Canoas (6 daily; 9hr); Parque Nacional Santa Rosa (4 daily; 6hr); Peñas Blancas (3 daily; 6hr); Playas del Coco (3 daily; 5hr); Playa Hermosa (1 daily; 5hr); Playa Junquillal (1 daily; 5hr); Playa Panamá (1 daily; 5hr); Playa Sámara (3 daily; 5hr); Puerto Jiménez (2 daily; 10hr); Puerto

Limón (25 daily; 2hr 30min–3hr); Puerto Viejo de Sarapiquí (via Guápiles Highway, 7 daily; 1hr 30min–2hr; via Heredia, 3 daily; 3–4hr); Puerto Viejo de Talamanca (4 daily; 4hr 30min); Puntarenas (14 daily; 2hr); Quepos (9 daily; 3hr 30min–5hr); San Carlos (14 daily; 3hr); San Isidro (16 daily; 3hr); Santa Cruz (5 daily; 5hr); Santa Elena (2 daily; 4–5hr); Sarchí (17 daily; 1hr 30min); Sixaola (4 daily; 6hr); Tamarindo (2 daily; 6hr); Tilarán (4 daily; 4–5hr); Turrialba (16 daily; 1hr 30min); Volcán Irazú (1 Sat & Sun; 1hr 30min); Volcán Poás (1 daily; 1hr 30min).

Santa Cruz to: Liberia (14 daily; 1hr); Nicoya (16 daily; 40min); San José (5 daily; 5hr); Tamarindo (2 direct daily; 1hr).

Santa Elena to: Las Juntas (2 daily; 2hr); Puntarenas (1 daily; 3hr 30min); San José (2 daily; 4–5hr); Tilarán (1 daily; 3hr).

Sarchí to: Alajuela (every 30min; 1hr); San José (17 daily; 1hr 30min).

Sierpe to: Palmar (5 daily; 30min).

Sixaola to: Cahuita (4 daily; 2hr); Puerto Limón (1 daily; 3hr); Puerto Viejo de Talamanca (4 daily; 2hr); San José (4 daily; 6hr).

Tamarindo to: Liberia (6 daily; 1hr 30min–2hr); San José (2 daily; 6hr); Santa Cruz (6 direct daily; 1hr).

Tilarán to: La Fortuna (2 daily; 2hr); San Carlos (1 daily; 4hr); San José (4 daily; 4–5hr); Santa Elena (1 daily; 3–4hr).

Turrialba to: Guayabo (2 daily Mon–Fri; 1hr+); San José (16 daily; 1hr 30min).

Boats

Golfito to: Puerto Jiménez (1 daily; 1hr 30min).

Naranjo to: Puntarenas (6 daily; 1hr 15min).

Paquera to: Puntarenas (14 daily; 1hr).

Puerto Jiménez to: Golfito (1 daily, 1hr 30min).

Puntarenas to: Naranjo (6 daily; 1hr 15min); Paquera (14 daily; 1hr).

Flights

Bahía Drake to: San José (4 daily; 45–50min).

Barra del Colorado to: San José (2 daily; 30min).

Golfito to: San José (5 daily; 45min–1hr 10min).

Liberia to: San José (4 daily; 1hr 10min).

Nosara to: San José (2 daily; 55min).

Palmar Sur to: San José (4 daily, 50min–1hr 15min).

Playa Sámara to: San José (3 daily; 55min).

Puerto Jiménez to: San José (3 daily; 50min).

Quepos to: San José (7–10 daily; 30min).

San José to: Bahía Drake (4 daily; 45–50min); Barra del Colorado (2 daily; 30min); Golfito (5 daily; 45min–1 hr 10min); Liberia (4 daily; 1hr 10min); Nosara (2 daily; 55min); Palmar Sur (4 daily; 50min–1hr 15min); Playa Sámara (3 daily; 55min); Puerto Jiménez (3 daily; 50min); Quepos (7–10 daily; 30min); Tamarindo (7–10 daily; 40–50min); Tambor (4 daily; 20–30min); Tortuguero (2 daily; 35–50min).

Tamarindo to: San José (7–10 daily; 40–50min).

Tambor to: San José (4 daily; 20–30min).

Tortuguero to: San José (2 daily; 35–50min).

7

Panama

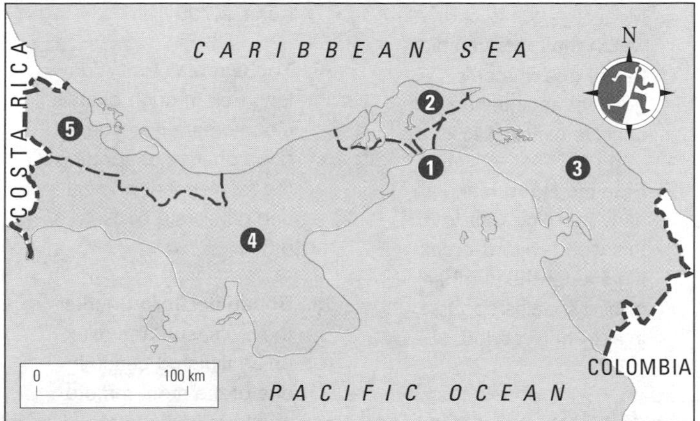

Highlights 728
Introduction and Basics 729
7.1 Panama City 747
7.2 The Canal and Colón Province 772
7.3 Eastern Panama: Darién and Kuna Yala 787
7.4 Western Panama 803
7.5 Bocas del Toro 823
Travel details 833

Panama Highlights

* **San Felipe** Wander around the cobbled streets of the old colonial city centre, visit the museums and the presidential palace and relax in a café. **p.754**

* **Panama Canal** Visit the Miraflores Locks and watch the massive ships transit one of man's greatest engineering achievements. **p.772**

* **Pipeline Road** Make an early-morning visit to this world-record-breaking site for the number of bird species spotted in a 24-hour period. **p.778**

* **Parque Nacional Darién** Explore the last great untamed wilderness in Central America by dugout canoe. **p.791**

* **San Blas Archipelago** Relax on palm-fringed islands of white coral sand and witness the traditional culture of the Kuna. **p.796**

* **The Quetzal Trail** A day-long trek through pristine cloudforest gives you a good chance of spotting the resplendent quetzal and other rare birds. **p.820**

* **Bocas del Toro** Snorkel the reefs, surf and relax on an isolated beach in one of the most remote and beautiful corners of the country. **p.823**

Introduction and Basics

Even before the construction of its famous canal, **Panama**'s strategic location at the wasp waist of the Americas and at the meeting place of the Atlantic and Pacific oceans made it one of the great crossroads of the world. A narrow, S-shaped isthmus that stretches some 750km between Costa Rica and Colombia, Panama remains a vital **thoroughfare** of international commerce. However, Panama is often only visited by travellers as an afterthought, neglected by would-be visitors, in part, because the land bridge to South America, the Darién Gap, remains virtually impassable and, in part, because the use of the US dollar and the relatively high level of economic development can make it a more expensive country to visit than other places in the region. But Panama suffers from a serious image problem, too. Although the last US troops have now left the country and the canal is in Panamanian hands, many outsiders still perceive Panama as a virtual colony of the US – a country artificially created in order to facilitate construction of the famous waterway – and its culture is sometimes seen as a desperately compromised imitation of North America. Yet while it is true that no other country in Central America has been so dominated by the US – indeed, Panama does owe its very existence to US intervention – in fact, the North American cultural influence, though strong, is but one among many. Spanish, African, West Indian, Chinese, Indian, European – all have contributed to a **compelling cultural mix**, creating the most cosmopolitan, open-minded and outward-looking society in Central America. At the same time, Panama is also home to some of the most unassimilated and culturally fascinating indigenous communities in the region – within 30km of Panama City's high-rise banking district the native Emberá continue to practise subsistence agriculture in the rainforest.

Those travellers who do make it down to Panama are surprised by the country's outstanding **natural beauty**. With 1600km of coastline on the Pacific and 1280km on the Caribbean, Panama boasts unspoiled beaches and coral reefs to match any in the region. And although it is Costa Rica that has achieved world renown as an **ecotourism** destination, Panama has little reason to envy its neighbour as far as pristine wilderness and ecological diversity are concerned. A biological bridge between continents, Panama supports an astounding degree of biodiversity, including over nine hundred bird species – more than in Costa Rica or in the whole of North America. More than half the country is still covered by dense tropical rainforest, and large areas are protected by a well-managed system of national parks and nature reserves.

The Panamanian government has finally begun to actively promote tourism and in most parts of the country the frequently applied moniker of "Central America's best-kept secret" no longer applies. Despite this progress, Panama's tourism industry is still relatively undeveloped, which means that in comparison to, say, Costa Rica, the **infrastructure** for visiting the protected wilderness areas is much more limited. But while this may put some people off, for others it simply adds to the sense of adventure. Moreover, wherever you travel in Panama, the reduced presence of a travellers' "scene" means you are likely to have much more direct contact with local people, an experience which, given the natural warmth and open-mindedness of most Panamanians and the fact that they have not yet become jaded with foreigners due to the impact of mass tourism, is undoubtedly one of the most rewarding aspects of any visit to this underrated and often misunderstood country.

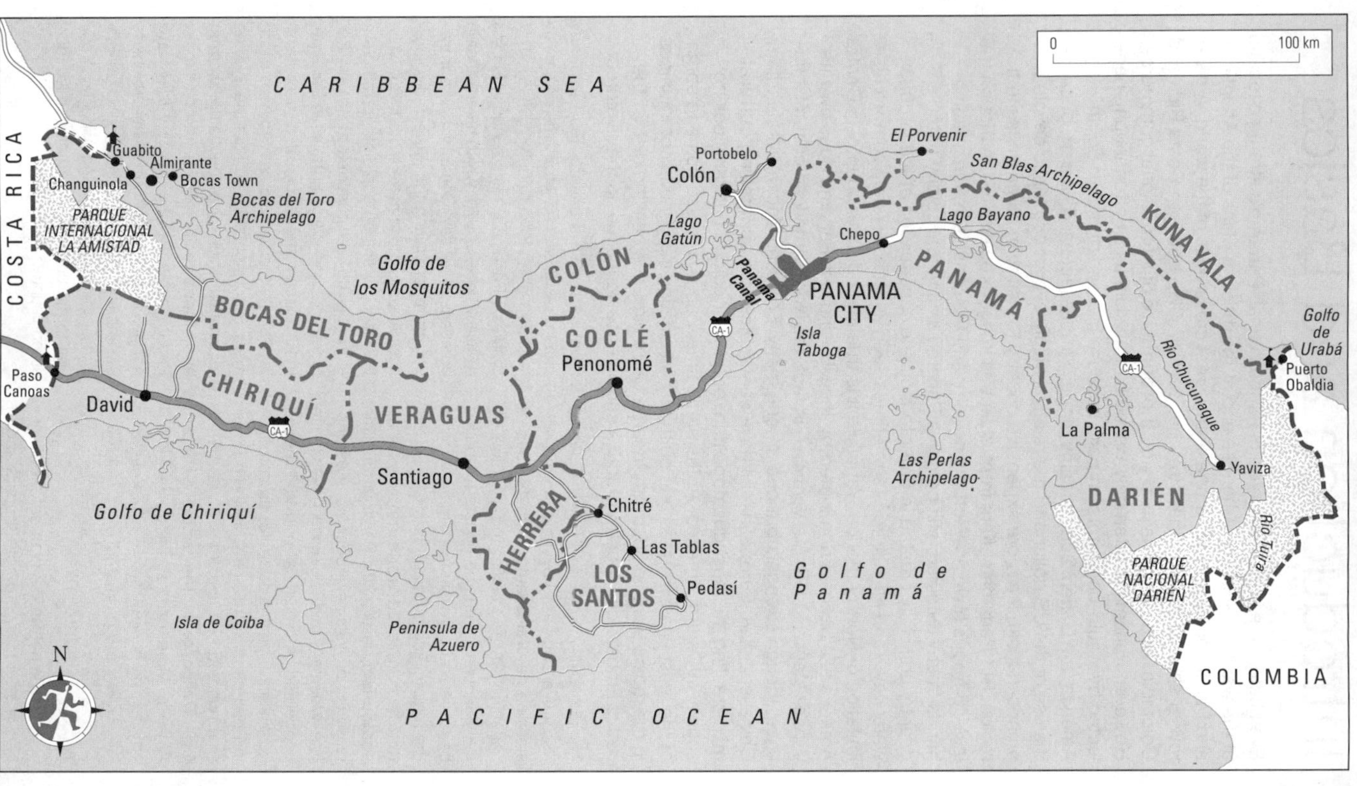
0
100 km
CARIBBEAN SEA
COSTA RICA
Guabito
Almirante
Bocas Town
Changuinola
Bocas del Toro Archipelago
PARQUE INTERNACIONAL LA AMISTAD
Golfo de los Mosquitos
BOCAS DEL TORO
CHIRIQUÍ
Paso Canoas
David
CA-1
VERAGUAS
Santiago
Golfo de Chiriquí
Isla de Coiba
Peninsula de Azuero
HERRERA
LOS SANTOS
Chitré
Las Tablas
Pedasí
COLÓN
COCLÉ
Penonomé
Lago Gatún
Colón
Portobelo
Panama Canal
PANAMA CITY
Isla Taboga
Chepo
El Porvenir
San Blas Archipelago
Lago Bayano
KUNA YALA
PANAMÁ
Río Chucunaque
La Palma
Las Perlas Archipelago
Golfo de Panamá
Yaviza
DARIÉN
PARQUE NACIONAL DARIÉN
Río Tuira
Golfo de Urabá
Puerto Obaldia
COLOMBIA
PACIFIC OCEAN
N

Where to go

Some two thirds of Panama's population live in the narrow corridor on either side of the canal, most of them in the capital, Panama City, or in the well-developed Pacific coastal plain west of the canal. The rest of Panama, east of the canal and north of the rugged mountain chain that runs like a spine down the length of the country, is heavily forested and sparsely inhabited, a virtual wilderness.

Cosmopolitan and contradictory, **Panama City** is the most exciting capital city in Central America, combining the intrigue and frenetic energy of its international banking centre with the laid-back street life of its old colonial quarter and the antiseptic order of the former US-controlled Canal Zone towns. Surrounded by some of the most accessible tropical rainforest in the Americas, it is also the best base from which to explore the rest of the country. Panama's best-known attraction for visitors, the monumental **Panama Canal** can easily be visited from the city – you can watch mighty ships being raised and lowered through the locks or, even better, take a cruise and transit it yourself. Also within easy reach from the capital are the colonial ruins and Caribbean coastline of the province of **Colón**. East of Panama City stretches **Darién**, the wild, rainforest-covered frontier between Central and South America. To the north, along the beautiful Caribbean coastline, **Kuna Yala** is the autonomous homeland of the Kuna, who live in isolation on the coral atolls of the San Blas Archipelago, accessible by light aircraft from the capital.

West of Panama City and the canal, the Carretera Interamericana to Costa Rica runs through the Pacific coastal plain, Panama's agricultural heartland. Densely populated in comparison with the rest of the interior and possessing a decent road network, this region lures travellers intrigued by the folkloric traditions and coastal nature reserves of the **Azuero Peninsula** and by the protected cloudforests of the **Chiriquí Highlands**, close to the Costa Rican border. The Caribbean coast west of the canal is virtually uninhabited except in the extreme northwest corner, in the remote archipelago of **Bocas del Toro**, probably the most popular part of the country among visitors thanks to its unspoiled rainforests, beaches, coral reefs, surfing hotspots and population of indigenous and West Indian–descended inhabitants.

When to go

Lying between seven and ten degrees north of the equator, Panama is set well within the **tropics**, and consequently temperatures are constant throughout the year at around 25°–32°C and vary only with **altitude**: the average temperature in the Chiriquí Highlands is about 19°C, but this is the only region in which you are ever likely to feel cold. **Humidity** is often very high. **Rainfall** varies markedly between the Pacific and Caribbean sides of the mountain chain that runs the length of the country: on the Pacific side, the annual average is about 1500mm, on the Caribbean, about 2500mm. The **best time to visit** Panama is during the dry season between mid-December and April, known as *verano* (summer), though this seasonal variation is really only evident on the Pacific side of the mountains. On the Caribbean side, rainfall is spread more evenly throughout the year, especially in Bocas del Toro where downpours are often a daily occurrence throughout the year. Though heavy, the rainstorms during the May–December rainy season – *invierno* (winter) – rarely last long in most of the country, and are no reason not to visit.

Panama is in the **Eastern Standard Time Zone**, five hours behind GMT and an hour ahead of Costa Rica.

Getting around

Travel within Panama varies as sharply as its geography. Although the **canal corridor** and the **western Pacific** region are covered by a comprehensive road network served by regular public transport, both **Eastern Panama** and **Bocas del Toro** are linked to the rest of the country by just a single road. Getting around these areas means relying on light aircraft and generally unscheduled boats.

Buses

Where there are roads, **buses** are the cheapest, easiest and most popular way to travel

Land and sea crossings to and from Panama

Panama has two land routes to Costa Rica: the main border crossing along the Carretera Interamericana is at **Paso Canoas** (see p.817), while the less frequented border outpost is at **Guabito** on the Caribbean coast (see p.832). Due to security concerns it is not recommended to cross overland to Colombia at this time (see p.800).

There are no regular passenger boat services between Panama and its neighbours; however, some travellers manage to find passage to Colombia aboard private yachts (see p.800).

around the country. Panama City is the hub of the network, with regular buses to Colón, Metetí in Darién, Almirante (for Bocas del Toro) and all the cities and towns of Western Panama.

Buses vary in comfort and size, from modern, air-conditioned Pullmans to smaller 'Coaster' buses and cramped, brightly painted old US school buses. Smaller towns and villages in rural areas are served by less frequent minibuses, pick-up trucks and flatbed trucks known as *chivas* or *chivitas*, converted to carry passengers. Most buses are individually owned, and even when services are frequent, **schedules** change all the time. The cities and larger towns have bus terminals, otherwise buses leave from the main street or square. You can usually flag down through-buses from the roadside, though they may not stop if they are full or going a long way.

Both Colón and David are also served by **express buses**, which are more expensive, more comfortable and faster than the normal service. The express bus to David and international buses to Costa Rica are the only ones worth **booking** in advance – in general, you can just turn up shortly before departure and you should get a seat. **Fares**, as elsewhere in Central America, are good value: the most you'll have to pay is US$20 for the overnight twelve-hour ride from Panama City to Almirante.

Driving and hitching

Driving in Panama is pretty straightforward: roads are fairly good and distances relatively short. **4WD** is rarely necessary except during the rainy season and in more remote rural areas, particularly Darién. Note, though, that even the paved major roads in the canal corridor and the west can be badly maintained. The main roads on the Azuero Peninsula are in good condition, however, as are the secondary roads to Cerro Punta, Boquete, El Valle and Almirante.

At around US$40 a day or US$200 a week (more for 4WD), **car rental** is reasonably cheap. It is also a good way of seeing the country, especially the canal corridor, areas close to Panama City and the Azuero Peninsula. All of the main rental companies are based in Panama City (see p.768), but some also have offices at the airports and in David. Always read the small print, make sure you are insured and check the car for damage before you accept it. **Petrol stations** are easy to find on major roads and in most towns – many are open 24 hours – but there are fewer in rural areas.

Given the often poor state of the roads and the rather frantic nature of the traffic, always remain alert to what is happening around you. In Panama City traffic is less chaotic than it first appears, but **parking and security** can be an issue. When driving through some of the rougher areas of Panama City – and in all of Colón – it's best to keep your doors locked and your windows closed. Most hotels in Panama have their own car parks, but when parking in the street doing so outside a bank or public building (where permitted) is often the safest option. Note that many rental companies will expect you to leave their vehicles in guarded car parks when unattended, especially at night.

Police **checkpoints** appear throughout the country, mainly on provincial borders, and normally you are only required to slow down. If the police ask you to stop, in most cases they will just want to know your destination and see your license.

Hitching is possible, but private cars are unlikely to stop for you on main roads served by buses. In more remote areas, it is often the only motor transport available, and there is little distinction between private vehicles and public transport – drivers will pick you up, but you should expect to pay the same kind of fares you would for the bus.

Cycling

Although riding a bike in Panama City is virtually unheard of, **cycling** is a popular way to get around in the west of the country, where roads are generally paved and traffic (away from the Carretera Interamericana) scarce, and towns usually have a shop offering parts and simple repairs. The stretch from the continental divide to Chiriquí Grande on the road from David to Almirante, in particular, is a cyclist's dream – some 40km downhill on a well-surfaced, little-driven road through rainforest-covered mountains that march down to the Caribbean. Other good roads for cycling include all those on the Azuero Peninsula and the roads to Cerro Punta and El Valle off the Interamericana.

Boats and ferries

Scheduled **ferries** run from Panama City to Isla Taboga and Isla Contadora as well as between Bocas del Toro and Almirante. **Motorized dugout canoes** are an important means of transport in Bocas del Toro, Darién and Kuna Yala; indeed, these boats are often the only way to reach islands or other remote areas. The only scheduled small boat services are the **water-taxis** in Bocas del Toro and Darién (between Puerto Quimba and La Palma). Otherwise, you'll have to either wait for somebody who is going your way, or hire a boat. The latter can be expensive, becoming increasingly economical the more people there are to share the boat, but it is often the most exciting way to get around. Hiring a motorized dugout canoe opens up unlimited possibilities for wilderness adventure – up jungle rivers to isolated villages or out to uninhabited coastal islands.

The occasional **boats and ships** running from Panama City along the Pacific coast of Darién (and sometimes continuing on to Colombia) sometimes take passengers, although they have no fixed schedule and are cramped, with little shelter from the baking sun. Similarly, some vessels run the length of Kuna Yala along the Caribbean coast from Colón, often continuing to Colombia, but both Kuna- and Colombian-owned ships are generally loath to take foreigners as passengers.

Planes

Cities and larger towns are served by regular flights by **Aeroperlas** (ⓣ315 7500, ⓦwww.aeroperlas.com), the principal domestic carrier, which also has regular flights to parts of Darién and Kuna Yala. **Turismo Aero** (ⓣ315 0439) also fly to parts of Darién as well as the Las Perlas islands. Other than Bocas del Toro and David, which are also served by **Mapiex Aero** (ⓣ315 0888, ⓦwww.aero.com.pa), some destinations are so close to Panama City that it's scarcely worth flying, but flights are generally inexpensive (the longest flight, from Panama City to Changuinola via Bocas, costs around US$60). The **early-morning flights** tend to be smoother due to the lack of thermals rising from the land, though with the unreliability of the airlines a planned, smooth early-morning flight could easily become a roller coaster of a mid-afternoon one. For those not used to travelling in light aircraft just tighten your seatbelt and read a book.

Trains

The **transisthmian railway** (ⓦwww.panarail.com), which runs alongside the canal between Panama City and Colón, offers an excellent way of seeing the canal and the surrounding rainforest. The only other train in Panama is the **banana railway** from Almirante in Bocas del Toro to the Costa Rican border, though this is intended for plantation workers and is much slower than making the same journey by road.

Costs, money and banks

Panama is the most economically advanced country in Central America and has the highest GDP per head (although income distribution is so polarized that poverty remains widespread). This, together with the use of the US dollar as the national currency, makes some **costs** higher than in other countries in the region.

Currency, exchange and banks

Panama adopted the US dollar as its currency in 1904, and has not printed any paper currency since. Dollars are referred to interchangeably as **dólares** or **balboas**. Panama does mint its own coinage: 1, 5, 10, 25 and 50 centavo pieces, which are used alongside US minted coins. Both US$100 and US$50 bills are often difficult to spend, for fear of forgeries or simply because change is difficult to come by, so it's best to make US$20 bills the largest you carry.

It is difficult to **change foreign currency** in Panama, and you should change any cash into US dollars as soon as you can. In Panama City there are Banco Nacional branches at the airport and on Via España in the El Cangrejo district, or you could try Panacambios, a casa de cambio also on Via España. Foreign banks will generally change their own currencies.

Travellers' cheques are the safest, if not the most convenient, way to carry your money and are easy to change so long as they are issued by major companies (Amex, Visa and MasterCard) and are in US dollars. The three major **banks** in Panama – Banco Nacional, Banistmo and Banco General – will all change these, as will some of the international banks in Panama City. Most banks are open from 8am to 3pm Monday to Friday, and from 9am to noon on Saturday; almost all branches now have **ATMs** as do many large supermarkets. Major **credit cards** are accepted in most hotels and restaurants in Panama City and the larger provincial towns. Visa is the most widely accepted, followed by MasterCard.

Costs

Though costs are low compared to Europe and North America, Panama – along with Costa Rica and Belize – is one of the more expensive Central American countries. Sticking to a tight budget you can just about get by on US$20/£11 a day. A **basic double room** will usually cost at least US$10/£5, and you will often have to pay twice that to get somewhere comfortable. Fortunately, **bus transport** is inexpensive – more or less US$1–1.50 an hour – and if you stick to basic local **restaurants** you can eat well on a dollar or two for each meal. Because of low taxes and import duties, imported consumer goods – electronics, clothing and the like – are often cheaper than in Europe or North America (see "Shopping" on p.739 for more on Panama's duty-free status).

Information

The best internal source of information in Panama is the Panamanian Tourist Institute, **IPAT** (Ⓦwww.visitpanama.com), which has its main office in Panama City (see p.750) and many provincial branch offices. Though the government is keen to promote tourism, the idea that some foreign visitors prefer independent travel to package tours is still a novelty to most IPAT workers. You can get some useful information at the Panama City office – advice, free maps, leaflets – but unless you go there with some fairly specific questions you may end up with little more than glossy brochures. The provincial offices vary, though even in the most rudimentary of them you should be able to find some useful information – a local map or brochures – and there is usually someone who speaks English. *The Visitor/El Visitante*, a free, twice-monthly **tourist promotion magazine** in English and Spanish available at IPAT offices, hotels and restaurants throughout Panama, lists attractions and upcoming events.

Panama's **national parks** and other protected natural areas are administered by the National Environment Agency, **ANAM** (Ⓦwww.anam.gob.pa). The main office in Panama City (see p.751) is in theory keen to promote ecotourism, though in practice they offer almost no information on visiting the parks. The ANAM regional offices, which administer the national parks directly, are generally more helpful, and they are an essential stop before visiting parks where permission is needed or if you want to spend the night in a refuge. Here, too, they are often unaccustomed to the idea of travellers visiting national parks independently, but they are usually very helpful. Several **tour operators** (see p.769) based in Panama City can also give you advice and information on visiting the rest of the country, though, of course, they will naturally do so in the hope of selling you a tour.

The only good **map** of Panama (1:800,000; available in specialist map shops) is produced by International Travel Maps (ⓦwww.itmb.com). In Panama large-scale maps are available at the Instituto Geográfico Nacional Tommy Guardia (Mon–Fri 8.30am–4pm) on Via Simon Bolívar, opposite the entrance to the University in Panama City. The best maps of Panama City are those offered by Delta (US$4) and Shell (US$7.50) at their petrol stations, though both are also available at tour agencies and shops throughout the city.

Websites

An increasing number of Panamanian businesses, government agencies and other organizations now have **websites**, and Internet addresses are given in the *Guide* where relevant. The following are just a few of the more useful general sites.

ⓦ**www.ancon.org** The website of the National Conservation Association, Panama's most influential environmental group, has excellent general information (in Spanish) on the country's national parks, ecology and endangered species, as well as scientific papers and information on voluntary work.

ⓦ**www.explorepanama.com** A comprehensive site providing information for tourists and those interested in living or working in Panama.

ⓦ**www.panamainfo.com** This general guide to tourism and business in Panama, in English and Spanish, has excellent links to a wide range of Panamanian websites.

ⓦ**www.pancanal.com** The official site of the Panama Canal Authority has plenty of information and news, a history of the canal and photographs, as well as live webcams at the Miraflores and Gatún locks.

ⓦ**www.thepanamanews.com** Panama's frequently updated online newspaper is a good place to keep up with the latest events.

ⓦ**www.visitpanama.com** The site of the Panamanian Tourist Institute, with information on attractions and links to hotels, airlines, tour agencies and other related sites.

Accommodation

Most areas of Panama offer a wide choice of places to stay, with an increasing number of hostels coming on the scene in recent years to ease the burden for budget-conscious travellers.

In general, the cheapest room, normally a double with private bath and air-conditioning, may **cost** US$15–20 a night, although **hostels**, most common in well-travelled spots like Bocas Town, Boquete, David, Isla Taboga and Panama City, will often put you up for under US$9. **Hot water** is rarely a necessity and is usually only available in more expensive places, except in the Chiriquí Highlands where it takes the place of a fan or a/c. In **Panama City** many hotels target business travellers and prices tend to be slightly higher, while at the very low end of the market some hotels cater largely to Panamanian couples – with hourly rates.

Outside of Panama City, you don't usually need to **book in advance**, except at weekends and during public holidays, fiestas and carnival, when many Panamanians escape the confines of the city for some serious rest and relaxation. During these times prices can double in certain hotels. The ten percent **tourist tax** charged on hotel accommodation is usually included in the quoted price and has been factored into our accommodation price codes. See p.36 for an explanation of these price codes.

Camping and places without hotels

There are no official **campsites** in Panama, but it is possible to camp in remote rural areas and national parks, though you should always ask permission or at least let local people know that you are doing so. Other than on uninhabited islands in Kuna Yala or deep in the wilderness, camping is never really necessary – even in the smallest villages there's almost always somewhere you can sling a hammock or bed down for the night in return for a few dollars. If you do camp, a hammock and a tarpaulin strung up against the rain are just as good as a tent. A **mosquito net** or mosquito coils (known as *mechitas* and widely available) in some places are essential.

Almost all the national parks have ANAM (see p.734) **refuges** where you can spend the night for US$5–10, though this fee is not always charged. They are usually pretty basic, with bunk beds, cooking facilities and running water.

Food and drink

Known as *comida típica*, **traditional Panamanian cooking** is broadly similar to what you will find elsewhere in Central America. Basic, filling meals based on rice and beans or lentils served with a little chicken, meat or fish form the mainstay, though *yuca* (cassava) and plantains are also important staples.

A Spanish **menu reader** can be found on p.870.

Where to eat

The cheapest places to eat are canteen-like **self-service restaurants**, serving a limited, but filling, range of Panamanian meals for a few dollars, which you will find almost everywhere. Larger towns usually have some more **upmarket restaurants** with waiter service where a main meat or fish dish may cost US$5–10, and in Panama City there is no shortage of expensive and exotic restaurants. There is often a five percent **tax** to pay on meals, and tipping – though always welcome – is only expected in more expensive places or where service has been particularly good. All towns have US-style **fast-food** places, but street vendors are less common than elsewhere in Central America.

In **remote areas** with no real restaurant, there is usually someone in the village who will be prepared to cook you a meal: try asking at the local shop, and bear in mind that it's best to let them know a few hours in advance. Large **supermarkets** in the major cities offer a good range of cold and hot snacks to either eat in or take out.

What to eat

Panama's national dish is **sancocho**, a hearty chicken soup with *yuca*, plantains and other root vegetables flavoured with coriander, closely followed by the ubiquitous **arroz con pollo** (chicken with rice). **Seafood** is plentiful, excellent and generally cheap, particularly *corvina* (sea bass), *pargo rojo* (red snapper), lobster and prawns – the latter are one of Panama's biggest exports. *Ceviche* – a cool, spicy dish of raw fish or seafood marinated in lime juice with onions and hot peppers – is a popular appetizer. Fresh tropical **fruit** is also abundant, but rarely on the menu at restaurants other than in juice form – you're better off buying it yourself in local markets.

Breakfast for most Panamanians is *fritura*, a combination of fried foods such as sausages, eggs, *patacones* (plantains fried and flattened then fried again), *tortillas de maiz* (smaller and thicker than elsewhere in Central America) and *hojaldres* (fried dough – much tastier than it sounds). Popular **snacks** include *carimañolas* or *enyucados* (fried balls of manioc dough filled with meat), *empanadas*, *tamales* (a mix of maize porridge, vegetables and pork or chicken wrapped in a banana-leaf parcel and boiled) and *patacones*.

The diverse **cultural influences** that have passed through Panama have also left their marks on its cuisine, especially in Panama City, where there are hosts of reasonably priced Greek, Italian, Chinese, Japanese and American restaurants. Elsewhere, almost every town has at least one Chinese restaurant, often the best option for **vegetarians** outside of Panama City. US influence is evident in the widespread availability of hamburgers, fries and hot dogs. Perhaps the strongest outside influence on Panamanian food, though, is the distinctive **Caribbean cuisine** of the West Indian populations of Panama City and the provinces of Colón and Bocas del Toro, which usually involves fish, seafood and rice, cooked in lime juice and coconut milk.

What to drink

Coffee is generally good in Panama, made espresso-style and served black. Weaker coffee is known as *café americano*. Otherwise, everyone drinks cold drinks, essential given the heat and humidity. The **drinking water** of Panama City is so good that it is known as the "Champagne of the Chagres", after the river from which it is drawn, and iced water, served free in restaurants as a matter of course, along with the tap water in all towns and cities except Bocas del Toro and remote areas, is perfectly safe. Known as **sodas**, bottled fizzy drinks are available everywhere. Cheaper and more refreshing, though, are **chichas**, delicious blends of ice, water and the juice of any one of a dozen tropical fruits, served in restaurants or, in paper cones, by street vendors everywhere (except, that is, in Kuna Yala, where *chicha* is a ceremonial alcoholic drink made from fermented sugarcane juice flavoured with coffee or cacao). *Batidos* are thick fruit milkshakes, often made with ice cream. Also popular are **pipas**, green coconuts containing a natural, sweet water that is said to cleanse the system, though in large quantities it acts as a diuretic. It's sometimes served ice cold from massive roadside fridges and drunk with a straw or, in Kuna Yala, hacked straight from the palm tree.

Beer is extremely popular in Panama; it's drunk as much for refreshment as for intoxication. Locally brewed brands include Panama, Löwenbrau, Atlas, Soberana and Balboa. Imported beers such as Budweiser. Heineken, Grolsch and Guinness are widely available in Panama City. When it comes to getting drunk, most Panamanians turn to locally produced **rum** – Seco Herrerano (known as *seco*), Carta Vieja and Abuelo are the most common brands – though imported whiskies and other spirits are widely available. **Wine**, mainly from Chile and California, is available in most towns, with the best selections found in the large supermarkets.

Opening hours, holidays and festivals

Business hours vary from establishment to establishment, but generally **banks** are open from 8pm to 3pm, Monday to Friday, and on Saturday morning. Businesses and government **offices** are usually open Monday to Saturday from 8 or 9am to 4 or 5pm, while **museums** generally open the same hours from Tuesday to Saturday, with some also opening on Sunday morning. Some close for lunch from around 12.30pm or 1pm to 1.30 or 2pm. **Shops** are usually open from Monday to Saturday from 9am to 6pm.

Panama has ten national **public holidays**, during which most government offices, businesses and shops close. Panama City and Colón also each have their own public holiday, and there is one public holiday for government employees only. When the public holidays fall near a weekend many Panamanians take a long weekend (known as a *puente*) and head to the beach or the countryside, so it can be difficult to find hotel rooms during these times.

Several of these public holidays coincide with **national fiestas** that continue for several days. **Carnival**, in February or March, lasts for four days and is the largest and wildest of these, celebrated with parades, drinking, water fights and dancing in Panama City and across the country, most colourfully in Las Tablas. As is the case with any such festivities anywhere in the world, take extra caution with your personal belongings as picking the pockets of tourists appears to be part of the celebrations. **Holy Week** (Easter) is celebrated with religious processions. In November, known as "El Mes de la Patria", the anniversaries of the first declaration of independence and of both independence days (from Spain and Colombia) are celebrated by a succession of drum-band parades.

In addition, **local fiestas** are held by every small town to celebrate its own anniversary and saint's day. The most vibrant of these are the **Fiesta of the Black Christ** of Portobelo on October 21, when up to 50,000 purple-clad pilgrims descend on that town (see p.783), and the numerous religious and folkloric fiestas of the towns and villages of the **Azuero Peninsula** (see p.808). In Kuna Yala, the Kuna celebrate their own independence day (the anniversary of the short-lived Dule Republic) in February, as well as several other dates throughout the year.

Public holidays

Jan 1 New Year's Day
Jan 9 Martyrs' Day (in remembrance of those killed by US troops in the 1964 riots)
Feb–March (date varies) Carnival
March–April (date varies) Good Friday
May 1 Labour Day
Aug 15 Foundation of Panama City (Panama City only)
Nov 2 All Souls' Day
Nov 3 Independence Day (from Colombia, 1903)
Nov 4 Flag Day (government holiday only)
Nov 5 National Day (Colón only)
Nov 10 First Cry of Independence
Nov 28 Emancipation Day (independence from Spain)
Dec 8 Mother's Day
Dec 25 Christmas Day

Communications

Other than in remote areas, Panama's **communications** network is good, with even most small towns having post and telephone offices as well as Internet cafés, making keeping in touch with home fairly easy.

Letters posted with the Correo Nacional (COTEL) cost US$0.35 to the US and Europe. They should reach either destination within a week or two, though have been known to take longer – it's best to post them in Panama City. Most post offices have an *Entrega General* (**Poste Restante** or General Delivery) where you can receive mail – in Panama City your correspondent must specify the post office zone: the most central is Zone 5, on Av Central/Via España. Post office **opening hours** are generally from 7am to 6pm Monday to Friday, 7am to 5pm on Saturday.

Panama's recently privatized telephone company is owned by Cable & Wireless. **Local phone calls** are cheap, and there's a wide network of modern payphones that take phonecards sold in shops and street stalls. You can make **international collect calls** from these via the international operator (☎106), and both AT&T (☎109) and MCI (☎108) can place collect or credit-card calls to the US. Hotels tend to overcharge for phone calls. Panama's **country code** is ☎507.

Mobile phones can be rented from the *Holiday Inn* (see p.753) and coverage is growing. Those areas currently served include Panama City, the Canal Zone, the Interamericana corridor, Bocas del Toro, Boquete and La Palma; mobile phone codes begin with a '6' or a '5'.

All major towns and cities as well as most smaller towns have **Internet cafés**; the rates are normally US$0.50/hr, but they can go up to US$2/hr in the more remote towns. Note that the "@" symbol is achieved by simultaneously depressing the Alt, 6 and 4 keys. Many Internet cafés also provide cheap international phone calls for about US$1.50 for the first minute and US$0.25 per minute thereafter.

Emergency numbers

Police ☎104
Fire ☎103
Tourist Police ☎270 2467

The media

For a small country, Panama has an impressive number of newspapers, and the **independent press** has flourished since the end of military rule in the early 1990s. *La Prensa*, *La Estrella de Panama*, *El Panama America* and *El Universal* are all serious broadsheets, while *Critica Libre* and *El Siglo* are the most popular tabloids. **La Prensa** (@www.prensa.com) is probably the most effective critic of the present government, has good international and sports sections and publishes entertainment listings. **The Visitor**, a free English- and Spanish-language magazine with a good entertainment listings section, is widely available. Other English-language publications available in the capital include the *Miami Herald*, *Newsweek*, *Time*, the *Economist* and the *Financial Times*.

Most Panamanian households have a **television**, as do most hotel rooms. There are five national television stations – channels 2, 4, 5, 13 and 21 – offering a mix of Latin American soap operas, sport, US sitcoms, movies and news, as well as a government educational channel, Channel 11. Cable and satellite television is also widely available – particularly in more upmarket hotels – featuring CNN, BBC World, and a plethora of US sport and entertainment channels. There's a wide variety of FM **radio stations**, especially in Panama City, and you'll seldom be out of earshot of a radio, blasting out anything from music and news to evangelical exhortations. Check ⓦwww.tvradioworld.com/region1/pnr, which lists the country's TV and radio stations, for further information.

Shops and markets

For many visitors, **shopping** is the main reason to come to Panama, and today people from all over Latin America and the Caribbean come here to buy consumer goods – electronics, designer fashion, jewellery – which are available here at a lower cost and in greater variety than elsewhere in the region. You can buy almost anything you might want in the bazaars and superstores of Panama City, often at a lower price than in Europe or the US, and the country is also home to the second largest duty-free zone in the world: the **Colón Free Zone**. Goods from all over the world are traded here in vast quantities, and though most business is in bulk, you can find good bargains (though you may have to pay duty when you return home).

Panama also produces some beautiful **handicrafts**. The most famous and exceptional are the **molas** – brightly coloured cotton cloths intricately decorated with abstract designs created by a system of reverse-appliqué – made by the Kuna people (see p.797). The *mola* has become something of a national symbol and are sold all over the country. The Emberá-Wounaan in Darién produce exquisite **carvings** in wood or *tagua* (a palm seed known as "vegetable ivory"), mostly of birds and rainforest animals, while the artisans of Western Panama, and in particular those of the Azuero Peninsula, produce a wide range of handicrafts including pottery, lurid fiesta masks, leatherwork, and straw sombreros. The brightly coloured dresses and fibre shoulder bags (*chacaras*) of the Ngobe-Buglé people also make beautiful and practical souvenirs. Sadly, the famous **Panama hats** are made in Ecuador.

Almost all these handicrafts are available in Panama City, in shops and in co-operative **artesanía markets**, but of course if you have the time it's much more rewarding (and cheaper) to buy them from the artisans themselves.

Safety and the police

Panama has something of an unjust reputation as a dangerous place to travel. Although **violent crime** does occasionally occur – indeed, most shops, banks and hotels have private armed guards – excluding certain areas Panama is far better than most countries in Central America. Nonetheless, you should take special care in **Colón** as well as in the El Chorillo and Santa Ana districts of **Panama City**. Late at night or when carrying luggage, it's common sense to take a taxi.

Outside of Colón and Panama City, the only other area where there is any particular danger is near **the Colombian border** in **Darién** and **Kuna Yala**. This wilderness frontier has long been frequented by Colombian Marxist guerrillas, bandits and cocaine traffickers, and several foolish travellers attempting to cross overland to Colombia have been kidnapped or killed – or have simply disappeared. It is still possible to visit the best areas of Darién in relative safety, including some parts of the national park, but until the general situation gets better, we recommend that you only travel here as part of an organized tour group specializing in the region or after having taken expert advice. If you are planning to travel to Colombia by sea, you should be aware that many of the boats that ply the coast are involved in smuggling.

If you are robbed, have a car accident or otherwise become the victim of a crime, report it immediately to the local **police** station, particularly if you will later be making an insurance claim. If treated respectfully, Panamanian police are generally honest and helpful. In Panama City the **tourist police** (*policia de turismo*) are better prepared to deal with foreign travellers and more likely to speak English – they wear white armbands and are often mounted on bicycles or mopeds.

Although by law you are required to carry your **passport** at all times, you will rarely be asked to present it except when in transit either by air or road; in fact, when walking around the towns and cities it may be better to carry a copy of your passport (including the entry stamp) – indeed, this is also what the tourist police recommend.

Work

Although Panama City teems with foreign workers, without a permit there are few opportunities for **work** in Panama. There are some English schools, but no shortage of teachers. With patience, luck or charm you may be able to find work crewing on a yacht, as a linehandler as it passes through the canal or even onwards to the Caribbean: for details see p.774. Finally, the environmental organization ANCON (Ⓣ314 0060, Ⓦwww.ancon.org) accepts volunteers to work on conservation programmes throughout Panama.

History

Perhaps no country in the world has had its history so thoroughly determined by geography as Panama. In prehistoric times this was a crucial land bridge in the migration routes by which the Americas were populated, and from the moment the conquistador **Vasco Núñez de Balboa** emerged from the forests of Darién to become the first European to look out onto the Pacific Ocean on September 25, 1513, the history of Panama has been the history of the route across the isthmus. Balboa claimed what he called the "Southern Ocean" in the name of the King of Spain, but received scant reward for his discovery – in 1519 his jealous superior **Pedro Arias de Ávila** (known as Pedrarias the Cruel), the first governor of what was by then known as Castilla de Oro, had him beheaded for his troubles.

In the face of appalling losses from disease in the first Spanish settlements on the Caribbean, Pedrarias moved his base across the isthmus to the more salubrious Pacific coast, where he **founded Panama City** in 1519. The new settlement became the jumping-off point for further Spanish conquests north and south along the coast, and, after the conquest of Peru in 1533, began to flourish as the transit point for the fabulous wealth of the **Incas** on its way to fill the coffers of the Spanish Crown. From Panama City, cargo was transported across the isthmus on mules along the paved Camino Real to the ports of Nombre de Dios and later Portobelo, on the Caribbean coast. A second route, the Camino de Cruces, was used to transport heavier cargo to the highest navigable point on the Río Chagres, where it was transferred to dugout canoes that carried it downriver to the coast. Once a year huge trade fairs lasting several weeks were held at Portobelo, when the Spanish royal fleet arrived to collect the gold and silver that had accumulated in the treasure houses of Panama and to trade European goods that were then redistributed across the Americas. The vast wealth that flowed across the isthmus was quick to attract the attention of Spain's enemies, and despite ever heavier fortification the Caribbean coast was constantly harassed by English and other European **pirates**. In the most daring attack, the English Henry Morgan and his men sailed up the Río Chagres and crossed the isthmus to ransack Panama City in 1671.

Though the city was rebuilt behind defences so formidable that it was never taken again, the raiding of the Caribbean coast continued, until finally in 1746 Spain rerouted the treasure fleet around Cape Horn. With the route across the isthmus all but abandoned, Panama slipped into decline, and settlement of the interior began to increase. While the Pacific coastal plain west of Panama City was settled by farmers, the forests of Darién and the Caribbean coast to the east provided a refuge for unsubmissive tribes and bands of renegade slaves known as *cimarrones*. Trade remained the dominant economic activity in Panama, with political power in the hands of the merchant class of Panama City – in contrast to other outposts of the Spanish Empire, where power resided with large landowners.

In 1821 Panama declared its **independence** from Spain, but retained its name as a province of Gran Colombia, which, with the secession of Ecuador and Venezuela, quickly became simply Colombia. Almost immediately, though, conflicts emerged between the merchants of Panama City, eager to trade freely with the world, and the distant, protectionist governments in Bogotá, leading to numerous half-hearted and unsuccessful attempts at independence.

The discovery of gold in California in 1849 sparked an explosion in traffic across the isthmus. Travel from the US east coast to California via Panama – by boat, overland by foot, and then by boat again – was far less arduous than the overland trek across North America, and thousands of "Forty-niners" passed through on their way to the goldfields. In 1851 a US company began the construction of a **railway** across Panama. Carving a route through the inhospitable swamps and forests of the isthmus proved immensely difficult – thousands of the mostly Chinese and West Indian migrant workers died in the process – but when the railway was completed in 1855, the Panama Railroad Company proved an instant financial success. Panama's importance as an international thoroughfare increased further, but the railway also marked the beginning of foreign control over the means of transport across the isthmus. Within a year, the first **US military intervention** in Panama – "to protect the railroad"– had taken place.

The French canal venture

In 1869 the opening of the first transcontinental railway in the US reduced traffic through Panama, but the completion of the **Suez Canal** that same year at last made the longstanding dream of a canal across the isthmus a realistic possibility. Well aware of the strategic advantages such a waterway would offer – the journey of a ship travelling from, for example, Boston to San Francisco would be reduced from 21,000km to just 8000km, if it could cross the continent through Panama rather than going around Cape Horn – Britain, France and the US all sent expeditions to seek a suitable route. It was the French, though, who took the initiative, buying a concession to build a canal from the Colombian government. In 1881, led by **Ferdinand de Lesseps**, the architect responsible for the Suez Canal, the Compagnie Universelle du Canal Interocéanique began excavations.

But despite de Lesseps' vision and determination, the "venture of the century" proved to be an unmitigated disaster. In the face of the impassable terrain – forests, swamps and the shifting shales of the continental divide – the proposed sea-level canal proved technically unfeasible, while yellow fever and malaria ravaged the workforce, killing as many as 20,000. In 1889 the Compagnie collapsed as a result of financial mismanagement and corruption, implicating the highest levels of French society in what an official described as "the greatest fraud of modern times".

But the dream of an interoceanic canal would not die. The US government, never keen on the idea of a canal controlled by a European power and convinced by its 1898 war with Spain of the military importance of a fast passage between the Atlantic and Pacific oceans, took up the challenge. President **Theodore Roosevelt**, in particular, was convinced that the construction of a canal across Central America was an essential step in pursuit of the control of all the Americas. At first the US favoured building a canal through Nicaragua, but the persuasive lobbying of Philipe Bunau-Varilla, a French engineer anxious to profit from the sale of the French rights and equipment, swung the crucial Senate vote in Panama's favour. A treaty allowing the US to build the canal was negotiated with the Colombian government in 1903, but the Colombian Senate refused to ratify it. Outraged that "the Bogotá lot of jackrabbits should be allowed to bar one of the future highways of civilization", Roosevelt gave unofficial backing to Panamanian secessionists who had long been seeking independence. The small Colombian garrison in Panama City was bribed to switch sides and a second force that had landed at Colón agreed to return to Colombia without a fight after its officers had been tricked into captivity by the rebels. On November 3, 1903, the **Republic of Panama** was declared and immediately recognized by the US, whose gunships standing offshore prevented Colombian reinforcements from landing to crush the rebellion.

Though it is true that Panama would never have come into existence as an independent republic without the involvement of the US, the independence movement was not wholly a US invention. The Panamanian merchant elite had good reason to seek independence – rule from remote Bogotá limited Panama's ability to trade and involved the country in Colombia's endless civil wars – and had attempted secession 33 times in the previous seventy years. The difference, in 1903, was the support of the US, and this, as the Panamanians were soon to discover, came at a high price.

The canal

A new **canal treaty** was quickly negotiated and signed on Panama's behalf by Bunau-Varilla. It gave the US "all the rights, power and authority... which [it] would possess and exercise as if it were sovereign", in perpetuity over an area of territory – the **Canal Zone** – extending five miles either side of the canal. In return, the new Panamanian government received a one-off payment of US$10 million and a further US$250,000 a year. These conditions were so favourable that even American Secretary of State John Hay had to admit they were "very satisfactory, very advantageous for the US and we must confess . . . not so advantageous for Panama". Panama's newly formed national assembly found the terms outrageous, but when told by Bunau-Varilla that US support would be withdrawn were they to reject it, the body ratified the treaty and work on the canal began.

It took ten years, the labour of 75,000 workers and some US$387 million to complete the task – an unprecedented triumph of sanitation, organization and engineering during which chief medical officer Colonel William Gorgas established a programme that eliminated yellow fever from the isthmus and brought malaria under control. The US engineers abandoned the idea of a sea-level canal, and instead constructed a series of locks to raise ships up to a huge artificial lake formed by damming the mighty Río Chagres, an obstacle the French had never been able to overcome. Together the engineers solved the problems that had defeated the French, excavating over 160 million cubic metres of earth and rock to create the largest concrete structure, earth dam and artificial lake that the world had ever seen. On August 15, 1914, the *SS Ancon* became the first ship to officially transit the canal, which was completed six months ahead of schedule.

An enormous **migrant workforce**, which at times outnumbered the combined populations of Panama City and Colón, was imported to work on the canal's construction, and many of these workers – Indians, Europeans, Chinese and above all West Indians – stayed on after its completion, transforming the racial and cultural make-up of Panama forever. They worked under what was effectively an apartheid labour system, where white Americans were paid in gold and the rest – the vast majority of whom were black – in silver. Dormitories, mess halls and even toilets and drinking fountains were set aside for the exclusive use of one group or the other, and despite the success of the sanitary programme, mortality amongst black workers was four times higher than among whites.

Meanwhile, though their economy boomed during the construction, Panamanians soon came to realize that in many ways they had simply exchanged control by Bogotá for dominance by the United States. The de facto sovereignty and legal jurisdiction that the US enjoyed within the Canal Zone made it a strip of US territory in which Panamanians were treated as second-class citizens, denied the commercial and employment opportunities enjoyed by US "Zonians". And the US agreement to guarantee Panamanian independence came at the price of intervention – inside and outside the Canal Zone – whenever the US considered it necessary to "maintain order", a right they exercised eight times between 1903 and 1936. Though the Panamanian government, largely controlled by a ruling elite known as the "twenty families", was ostensibly independent, in fact it was little more than a client of the US. "There has never been a successful change of government in Panama," one US official admitted in 1944, "but that the American authorities have been consulted beforehand."

Despite a new treaty limiting the US right of intervention in 1936, resentment of US imperialist control became the dominant theme of Panamanian politics and the basis of an emerging sense of national identity. Maverick politician **Arnulfo Arias Madrid** – a racist and Nazi sympathizer who later became one of Panama's most popular political figures – led demands for a further renegotiation of the canal treaty. But the US-backed Panamanian National Guard made sure that no president who challenged the status quo lasted long in office. Nevertheless, **anti-US riots** in 1959 and 1964 revealed the enduring popular resentment of US domination.

When Arnulfo Arias was deposed by the national guard after winning the 1968 elections, it appeared to be business as usual in Panama. But in fact the coup marked a turning point in Panamanian politics. After a brief power struggle, Lieutenant Colonel **Omar Torrijos** established himself as leader of the new military government. Described by his friend Graham Greene as a "lone wolf", Torrijos broke the political dominance of the white merchant oligarchy – known as the *rabiblancos*, or "white arses" – in his pursuit of a pragmatic middle way between socialism and capitalism. Over twelve years he introduced a wide range of populist reforms – a new constitution and labour code, limited agricultural reform, nationalization of the electricity and communications sectors, expanded public health and education services – while simultaneously maintaining good relations with the business sector, establishing the **Colón Free Zone** and introducing the banking secrecy necessary for Panama's emergence as an international financial centre. At the heart of Torrijos' popular appeal, though, was his insistence on gaining Panamanian control over the canal and his nationalistic opposition to US intervention in the country's affairs. After intensive negotiations Torrijos signed a new canal treaty with US president Jimmy Carter on September 7, 1977. Under its terms the US agreed to pass complete control of the canal to Panama by the year 2000, and in the meantime it was to be administered by the **Panama Canal Commission**, composed of five US and four Panamanian citizens. However, though a memorandum of understanding made it clear that the US had no right of intervention in Panama's internal affairs, the US retained the right to intervene militarily if the canal's neutrality was threatened, even after the year 2000.

Noriega and the US invasion

With his main aim accomplished, Torrijos formed a political party, the **Partido Revolucionario Democrático** (PRD), and began moving Panama towards free democratic elections, scheduled for 1984. In 1981, however, he died in a plane crash in the mountains of Coclé Province. Though the crash was officially an accident, many Panamanians now believe that there was some involvement by the **CIA** or by Colonel **Manuel Noriega**, his former intelligence chief. Whatever the truth, Noriega soon took over as head of the national guard, which he restructured as a personal power base and renamed the Panama Defence Forces (PDF), becoming the de facto military ruler in 1983. Although the 1984 elections gave Panama its first directly elected president in nearly two decades, Nicolás Ardito Barletta, who won amid charges of electoral fraud, was little more than a puppet of the US – and the real power in the country now lay in the hands of Noriega.

A career soldier, Panama's new military strongman had been on the US Army's payroll as early as the 1950s. When Noriega was promoted to intelligence officer by Torrijos in 1964, the US began to take a greater interest in him. After training at the US Army's notorious School of the Americas in the late 1960s, he was made chief of intelligence for the national guard in 1970 and became a key figure in the relationship between the US and Panamanian militaries.

In the early 1980s, Noriega assisted the US by supporting its interests in El Salvador, Honduras and, most importantly, Nicaragua. Whereas Torrijos had supported the leftist Sandinistas in Nicaragua's civil war, Noriega quickly became an important figure in covert US military support for the Contras, helping to funnel money and weapons to the guerrilla force.

Noriega, however, was also busy building his relations with the Colombian cocaine cartels in Medellín. Although this extracurricular activity was ignored by the US for years, the **Iran-Contra Affair** – in which the US government sold weapons illicitly to Iran and used the proceeds to fund the Contras – in 1986 brought the glare of the international press on Noriega. As the undemocratic nature of his regime and revelations about his involvement in drugs trafficking grew increasingly embarrassing for Washington, the US government in 1987 began a campaign to drive Noriega from power.

Economic sanctions were followed by Noriega's indictment on drug charges in the US in February 1988. After a US-backed coup attempt by dissident PDF officers failed in March 1988, the confrontation between Noriega and the US began to slide out of control. On December 20, 1989, US president George Bush launched "**Operation Just Cause**", and 27,000 US troops invaded Panama. They quickly overcame the minimal organized resistance offered by the PDF. Bombers, helicopter gunships and even untested stealth aircraft were used against an enemy with no air defences, and over four hundred explosions were recorded in the first fourteen hours. The poor Panama City barrio of El Chorillo was heavily bombed and burned to the ground, leaving some 15,000 homeless. Noriega himself evaded capture and took refuge in the papal nunciature before surrendering on January 5. He was taken to the US, convicted of drug trafficking and sentenced to forty years in a Miami jail, where he remains.

Estimates of the number of Panamanians killed during the invasion vary enormously – from several hundred to as many as ten thousand – largely because little care was taken in counting the dead, and many were quickly buried in mass graves. That the invasion was illegal, however, was clear – it was condemned as a violation of international law by both the United Nations and the Organization of American States, both of which demanded the immediate withdrawal of US forces. President Bush gave four reasons for the invasion: "to safeguard the lives of Americans, to defend democracy in Panama, to combat drug trafficking, and to protect the integrity of the Panama Canal Treaty". But the defence of democracy in Panama had scarcely been a US priority in the past, and Bush's concern with Noriega's extensive involvement in drug trafficking was also new. As director of the CIA in 1976, Bush had increased payments to Noriega – despite the CIA's detailed knowledge of Noriega's drug links. After the invasion the flow of drugs through Panama actually increased. The invasion was also in direct violation of the canal treaty provision prohibiting US intervention in Panamanian politics, and though one US soldier had been killed in the build-up to the invasion, this alone was scarcely sufficient reason to invade an entire country.

The real reasons for the US invasion remain unclear. Certainly Bush's desire to appear tough in the domestic political arena played a part, and the invasion set an important precedent for further US military interventions in the post–Cold War world. To many Panamanians, though, the reasons were all too familiar: reassertion of US control over Panama and its strategic waterway and the destruction of the PDF. Not that most Panamanians opposed the invasion: unlike Torrijos, Noriega was deeply unpopular, and almost all were relieved to see the back of him. But most were angry at the excessive use of force and felt humiliated by the reassertion of US dominance. Some likened Operation Just Cause to a brilliant cancer operation by a surgeon who had been pushing cigarettes to the patient for forty years.

After the invasion, the US installed **Guillermo Endara**, winner of elections annulled by Noriega in 1989, as president. In 1994, Endara, who had little national support, was defeated by Ernesto Perez Balladares, leader of the PRD – the party of both Torrijos and Noriega. After taking office, Perez Balladares implemented neoliberal economic policies – privatization of state-owned companies, reduction of public expenditure – aimed at meeting payments on the vast external debt that was the legacy of the Torrijos years.

The handover of the canal

In an interesting twist, the presidential elections of 1999 were contested between Martín Torrijos, son of the former military ruler, and the widow of Arnulfo Arias (the man Torrijos ousted in 1968), **Mireya Moscoso**, who won the election and presided over the handover of the canal. As the deadline for the handover and the closure of the last US military bases drew near, politicians in the US began to express doubts about the withdrawal, arguing that it threatened US strategic interests. When the port facilities at either end of the canal were sold to a Hong Kong–registered company, some even suggested this was part of a communist plot to take over the canal. But negotiations to maintain a US military presence as part of a multilateral anti-drugs base broke down, and on 31 December 1999 Panamanians celebrated the final victory in their struggle to gain control of the canal and establish **full independence**.

The US withdrawal was a mixed blessing for the Panamanian economy. Many jobs were lost with the closure of the bases and the loss of the US personnel's spending power, but the valuable real estate and infrastructure Panama inherited created huge economic opportunities. Some of these opportunities have been realized, with major infrastructure and investment programmes in the reverted areas, though critics say they have been handed over too cheaply to private business and political cronies rather than being used to provide housing for the poor. And like the ruins of a once powerful empire, some of the US bases are now dilapidated and abandoned.

The handover of the canal itself was seamless, and, so far, the waterway seems to be working as well under Panamanian control as it did under the US. The canal is now managed by the Autoridad del Canal de Panamá, which has widened the narrowest stretch, the Gaillard Cut, to accommodate two-way traffic of the largest Panamax vessels and begun dredging the huge Gatún Lake to increase its capacity for providing water to the locks. There are also proposals to build a new set of locks to accommodate the growing number of ships that are too big to transit the locks. **Relations with the US** remain complex, with an ongoing dispute over the US failure to clean up toxic chemicals (including depleted uranium shells) and unexploded ordnance from the bases and firing ranges.

Though the vast majority of Panamanians wish to move on from Panama's historical legacies, the political future of the country continues to be inextricably linked with its past, and in 2004 **Martín Torrijos**, son of previous leader Omar Torrijos, was elected *El Presidente* with 47 percent of the vote.

7.1

Panama City

If the world had to choose a capital, the Isthmus of Panama would be the obvious place for that high destiny.

Simón Bolívar, 1826

Few cities in Latin America can match the diversity, cosmopolitanism and sheer energy of **PANAMA CITY**: polyglot and postmodern before its time, in many ways it is closer in atmosphere to the mighty trading cities of Asia – Hong Kong or Singapore – than to anywhere else in the region. Situated on one of the great crossroads of the world, the city has always thrived on commerce, and its unique geographical position and the opportunities it presents have attracted immigrants from all over the globe. Though it is the undisputed political and social centre of Panama and home to almost half the country's population, Panama City's gaze is fixed firmly on the outside world, and its inhabitants pay scant attention to what they refer to rather vaguely as "the interior". Open-minded and outward-looking, the population is among the sharpest and most sophisticated in Central America.

With a spectacular setting on the Pacific bay of the same name, with the canal on one side and lush, forested mountains rising behind, Panama City encompasses some startling incongruities. On the southwest end of the bay stands the old city centre of **San Felipe**, a jumble of immaculately restored colonial buildings and crumbling ruins, while 4km or so to the northeast rise the shimmering skyscrapers of **El Cangrejo**, the modern banking and commercial district. Further east, amid the sprawling suburbs, stand the ruins of **Panamá Viejo**, the first European city to be founded on the Pacific coast of the Americas, while west of San Felipe the former US Canal Zone town of **Balboa** retains a distinctly North American character despite having been returned to Panamanian control in 1979.

Those who find the city's ceaseless commercial energy overwhelming, meanwhile, can always escape: to **Isla Taboga**, the idyllic "island of flowers" some 20km off the coast; along the **Amador Causeway** that juts out into the Pacific beside the canal; or into the **Parque Nacional Metropolitano**, the only tropical rainforest within the limits of a Latin American capital. Panama City is also a good base from which to explore the rest of the country – the canal, Colón and the Caribbean coast as far as Portobelo can all be visited on day-trips.

Some history

The first European city on the Pacific coast when it was founded by the **conquistador** Pedro Arias de Ávila (known as Pedrarias) on August 15, 1519, Panama quickly flourished as the base for further conquest along the Pacific and as the point of transit for the vast booty so accrued on its way to the treasure houses of Spain. By the mid-seventeenth century it had a population of some 10,000 and boasted some of the grandest constructions in the New World. The opulence of "Panama the golden" did not escape the notice of the **pirates** then ravaging the Spanish Main. In 1671 Henry Morgan captured the fort of San Lorenzo at the mouth of the Río Chagres, crossed the isthmus and descended on the city with a force of 1200 corsairs. After a bloody three-hour battle Morgan's desperate band

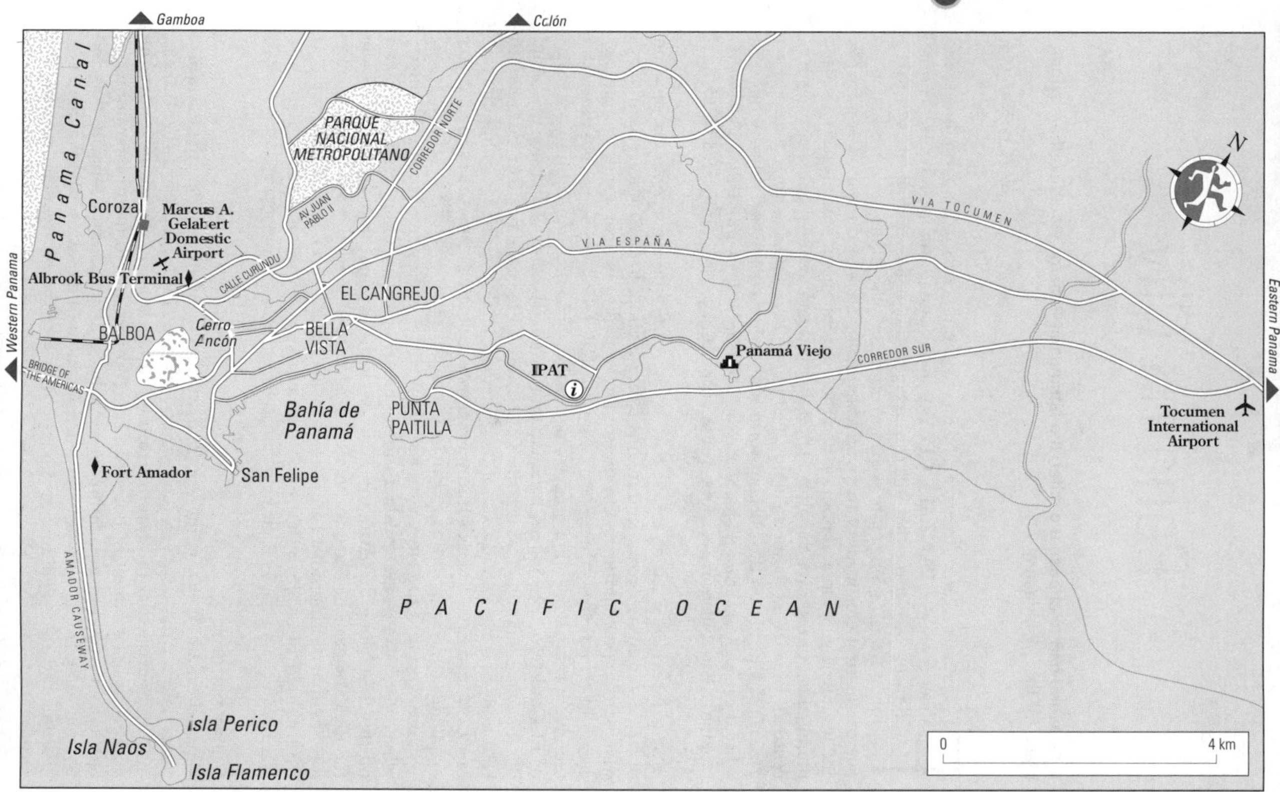
Gamboa
Colón
Eastern Panama
Western Panama
N
Panama Canal
Corozal
Marcus A. Gelabert Domestic Airport
Albrook Bus Terminal
PARQUE NACIONAL METROPOLITANO
CORREDOR NORTE
AV JUAN PABLO II
CALLE CURUNDU
VIA TOCUMEN
VIA ESPAÑA
EL CANGREJO
BALBOA
Cerro Ancón
BELLA VISTA
Panamá Viejo
CORREDOR SUR
IPAT
BRIDGE OF THE AMERICAS
Bahía de Panamá
PUNTA PAITILLA
Tocumen International Airport
Fort Amador
San Felipe
AMADOR CAUSEWAY
PACIFIC OCEAN
Isla Perico
Isla Naos
Isla Flamenco
0
4 km

defeated the much larger defending army and seized the city, already in flames after the defenders set light to its gunpowder magazines. They pillaged for three weeks before departing with 600 prisoners and a quantity of loot so vast that 175 mules were needed to carry it back across the isthmus. Known as **Panamá Viejo**, the ruins of Pedrarias' settlement still stand amid the sprawling suburbs of the modern city.

When the scattered survivors regrouped, they opted to rebuild the city on a rocky peninsula jutting out into the bay 10km to the west, a site deemed easier to defend and more salubrious than its swamp-bound predecessor. Founded in 1673 and today known as **San Felipe**, the new city was heavily fortified against pirate attack, protected by defences built at such enormous expense that the King of Spain was said to scan the horizon from his Madrid palace for a glimpse of the walls of Panama, saying that given the vast quantity of gold spent in their construction they should be visible from any point on earth.

Though it never matched the glory of its predecessor (and was all but destroyed by fires in 1737 and 1756), the new city slowly prospered, its fortunes rising and falling with the traffic across the isthmus. The decline brought about by the rerouting of the Spanish treasure fleet around **Cape Horn** in 1746 was arrested after **independence**, which made Panama free to trade with the world, and then reversed with the construction of the **transisthmian railroad** in 1855. The railroad, and subsequently the French and US canal construction efforts, brought immense prosperity and a wealth of new cultural influences that transformed the city and its population. But though the **canal** confirmed Panama City's importance as a global trading centre, it also restricted its development. Hemmed in to the west and northwest by the US-controlled Canal Zone, the city was only able to expand east along the coast, which it began to do very quickly from about 1920. The introduction of banking secrecy laws in the 1970s led to the rapid expansion of the financial services sector, boosted by a massive influx of narco-dollars from South America. Banking regulations were tightened enormously in the 1990s, but **El Cangrejo** remains a hive of intrigue and many of its luxury high-rise apartments stand empty, the astronomical rents paid by their fictitious occupants, providing a useful means of laundering money.

The **1989 US invasion** devastated the poor neighbourhood of El Chorillo and was followed by widespread looting, but the city recovered quickly, free of the economic sanctions imposed by the US on the Noriega regime. With the return of the last US military bases to Panamanian control at the end of 1999, vast amounts of real estate were made available. Many wealthy Panamanians have moved into homes in the former US-dominated suburbs of Albrook and Ancón, and a major infrastructure development programme is well under way in the reverted areas, counteracting to some extent the economic slowdown caused by the loss of the spending power of US servicemen and -women.

Arrival, information and city transport

Arriving in Panama City can be disconcerting, so unless you are travelling very light or are within walking distance of your hotel it's best to take a taxi. Spread out along the Bahía de Panamá, the city has no real centre, but once you've established your bearings it is relatively easy to find your way around. **San Felipe** and **El Cangrejo** are joined by **Avenida Central**, the city's main thoroughfare, which runs north from San Felipe through the district of Santa Ana then veers northwest, its name changing to **Via España** as it continues through the downtown districts of Calidonia, La Exposición and the residential neighbourhood of Bella Vista. Several other main avenues run parallel to Av Central: Av Perú, Cuba, Justo Arosemena and, along the seafront, Av Balboa.

Confusingly, many **streets** in Panama City have at least two names: Av Cuba, for instance, is also Av 2 Sur, and the road known universally as Calle 50 is also Av 4

Sur or Av Nicanor de Obarrio. We have used the most common names in the following accounts. Where we have given two roads for an address in our hotel and restaurant listings, note that the first indicates the street on which the place is located and the second refers to the nearest intersection.

By air

International flights arrive at Tocumen International Airport (☎238 4322), about 26km northeast of Panama City. There are several **car rental** offices here, a Cable & Wireless office with Internet access (daily 7am–9pm) and an **IPAT** office (☎238 4356, daily 8am–10pm) which has some basic tourist information, can book accommodation and will arrange a **taxi**, by far the best way to get into the city. These cost US$25 to hire individually or US$15 per person, if you share with another passenger, and they use the new Corredor Sur toll road (US$2.40). You can also take one of the frequent **buses** that run into the city and along Av Balboa to Plaza Cinco de Mayo and Plaza Santa Ana. Take any bus marked Tocumen, Pacora or Chepo from the stop across the main road outside; a ticket costs only US$0.70, but there's not much room for luggage.

Domestic flights arrive at Marcos A. Gelabert Airport (☎315 0241), better known as Albrook after the former US military airbase it occupies. All the domestic airlines have offices here, and there's also an IPAT information booth, an ATM and several car rental offices. A taxi into the city centre should cost about US$2–3; alternatively, occasional buses run to the SACA terminal at Plaza Cinco de Mayo.

By bus

International buses from Costa Rica and **domestic buses** from almost everywhere in the interior of Panama arrive and depart from the domestic bus terminal in Albrook, about 2km northwest of Calidonia, a massive, ultramodern complex that's easy to use and has shops, restaurants, Internet cafés and banks with ATMs. Buses heading into the centre of the city depart from well-marked stops outside; a taxi between the terminal and El Cangrejo or Bella Vista should cost about US$2. The only buses that do not arrive and depart from the Albrook terminal are those to Gamboa and elsewhere in the former Canal Zone, which leave from the bus terminal at Plaza Cinco de Mayo.

By sea

Irregular boats from Darién and Colombia dock at the **Muelle Fiscal** next to the Mercado Central on the seafront of Santa Ana. If you're heading for San Felipe, it's a short walk along the shore to the southeast. Otherwise, walk two blocks up the hill in front to Parque Santa Ana where you can catch a bus or hail a taxi to anywhere in the city.

Information

The main **IPAT** office (Mon–Fri 8.30am–4.30pm; ☎226 7000, Ⓦwww.visitpanama.com) is on the north side of the Atlapa Convention Centre on Av Israel, out in the suburbs east of El Cangrejo, but it's not really worth hauling yourself all the way out there for the limited information available. Though the staff do their best to answer specific questions and some representatives speak English, they tend to limit themselves to dishing out glossy brochures. For simple queries, you're better off asking at the IPAT booth on the corner of Via España and C Ricardo Arias in El Cangrejo, or at the international and domestic airports. Generally, you'll find tour companies (see p.769) a better source of information on the interior of the country, though of course they'll want to sell you a tour. The *Voyager International Hostel* (see p.754) is an excellent source of travel advice, though only for those staying there.

Panama's national parks and other protected natural areas are managed by the National Environment Agency **ANAM** (☎315 0855, ⓦwww.anam.gob.pa), in Edificio 804 at the former US military base of Albrook. Although promoting ecotourism is allegedly part of their policy, actually getting any information out of them is almost impossible – you're better off going to the regional offices or heading straight to the parks. The **Kuna General Congress** (☎316 1233) has an office on C Florida in Howard, where you can get general information on Kuna Yala and permission to stay in the *Nusagandi Nature Lodge* (see p.799).

City transport

Panama City's public **buses** are the cheapest way to get around town and are an exciting experience in their own right. Known as *diablos rojos* – red devils – the brightly painted former US school **buses** bounce along to the deafening combinations of reggae or salsa and the throaty roar of their huge chrome exhaust pipes. They cost just US$0.25 per ride, payable on exit, and go to almost every corner of the city between 6am and midnight. Most are individually owned, however, and there are no fixed **routes** or **schedules**: you just have to look for the destination painted on the windscreen. Plaza Santa Ana is the main hub where you can get buses to almost anywhere in the city.

Taxis are plentiful and inexpensive, with **fares** based on a zone system: US$1 plus US$0.25 for each zone boundary crossed and US$0.25 for each additional passenger. Most journeys within the city cost US$1–2, and none should cost more than US$3. IPAT-certified tourist taxis can be hired outside some hotels; these are generally larger cars driven by English-speaking drivers with some very basic tourist knowledge. They use set rates about four times greater than those of normal taxis. In both cases it's best to agree any fare in advance.

Accommodation

There are three main areas to stay in Panama City. A few budget travellers opt for the faded splendour of **San Felipe**, the city's old colonial centre, which offers low-cost accommodation in run-down hostels. The restoration of many of the area's historic buildings is making it more appealing, however, and with the opening of a number of lively bars and restaurants as well as an increased police presence it has become a popular nighttime destination. Nonetheless, some caution is still required when visiting this area after dark. Most upmarket hotels are in the safer neighbourhoods of **Bella Vista** and **El Cangrejo**, the hub of the city's nightlife, culture and commercial activity, which has some good mid-range and budget options. Between San Felipe and El Cangrejo, and with good access to both along the city's main arteries, the **Calidonia/La Exposición** area offers a wide choice of unexceptional modern hotels and pensions, including plenty of budget options and good mid-range deals. There's not much of interest in the area itself though, and here, too, you must be careful after dark.

San Felipe

Hospedaje Casa Grande C 8, Av Central. The bright yellow painted exterior belies the rather dark and shabby interior. The rooms are very basic with shared bathroom and some have balconies adorned with razor wire. Most rooms have partition walls that don't reach the ceiling and provide little in the way of sound-proofing or security. ❷

Hotel Herrera C 9, Parque Herrera ☎228 8994. Elegant, though decaying nineteenth-century Neoclassical building with balconies overlooking the park. Rooms are basic, and some of the furniture and mattresses seem almost as old as the building itself. Cheaper rates for shared bathroom, and more expensive rooms available with a/c and fridge. ❸

Calidonia/La Exposición

Hotel Centroamericano Av Equador, C Justo Arosemena ☎227 4555, ⓦwww.hotelcentroamericana.com. Modern and clean, if a bit dark, all rooms have basic bathrooms, a/c and TV. Service is friendly and the front rooms have balconies. ❸

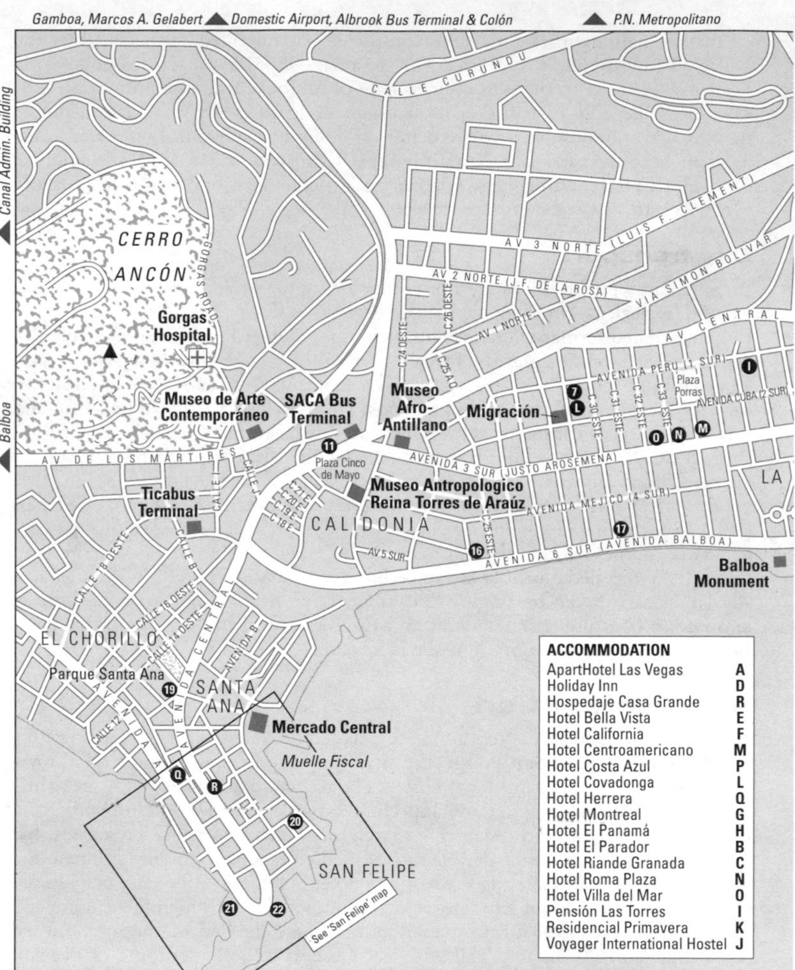

Hotel Covadonga C 29, Av Perú ⓣ 225 5275, ⓕ 225 4011. Modern and clean, with a good 24hr restaurant and a small rooftop swimming pool. Rooms have a/c, phone, cable TV and hot water. ❹

Hotel Roma Plaza Av Justo Arosemena, C 33 Este ⓣ 227 3844, ⓦ www.hotelromaplaza.com. Friendly and helpful, with good tourist facilities. Large, comfortable rooms with hot water, a/c, cable TV and fridge. The hotel also has a swimming pool, gym, bar, 24hr café and a good Italian restaurant. A little overpriced, but cheaper rates may be negotiated. ❻

Hotel Villa del Mar C 33 Este, Av Justo Arosemena ⓣ 225 8111. Opposite the *Hotel Roma Plaza*. Rooms with a/c, private baths. Although overall a bit run-down and rather cramped, the rooms are rather cheerful and the staff helpful. ❸

Pensión Las Torres Av Perú, C 36 ⓣ 225 0172. The upper floor of an incongruously elegant 1931 mansion on the corner above a cluster of restaurants. Entrance up the stairs, behind a row of small trees on C 36. Basic, clean rooms with TV and a/c. ❷

Bellavista/El Cangrejo

ApartHotel Las Vegas Av Eusebio A. Morales, C 49B Oeste ⓣ 269 0722,

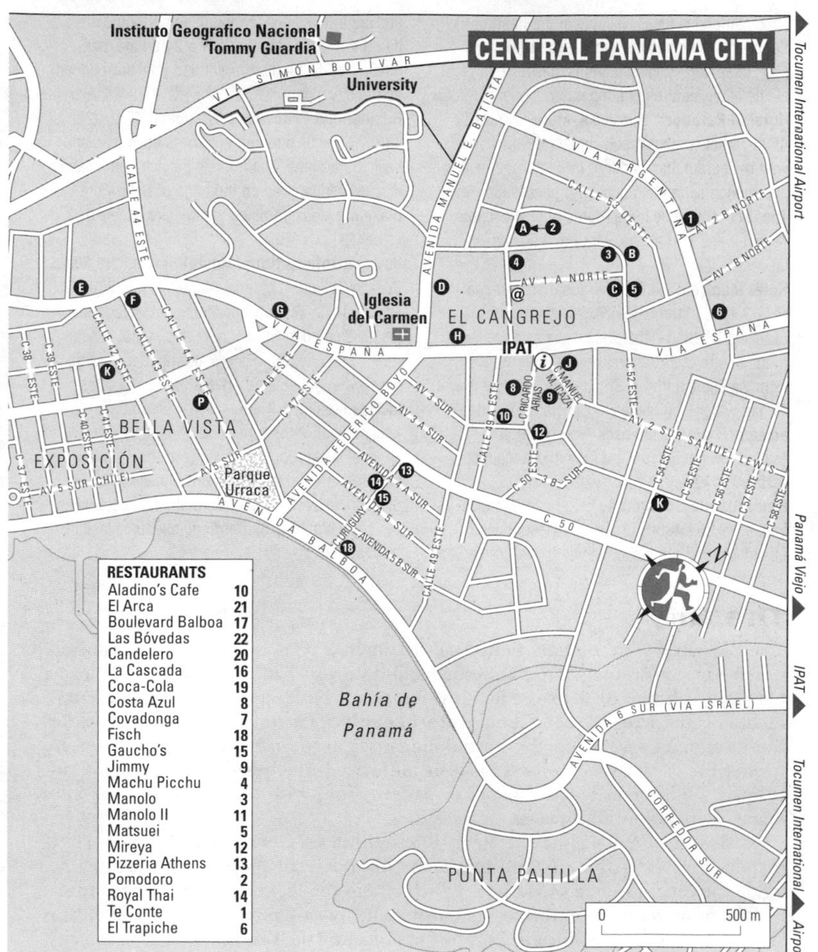

www.lasvegaspanama.com. Self-contained apartments with kitchen, bathroom, a/c, cable TV and phone, perfectly located two blocks from the centre of El Cangrejo. Smaller "mini-studios" with kitchenette also available. Good weekly and monthly rates. ⑥

Holiday Inn Ave Manuel Esponisa Batista ☎ 206 5555, www.holidayinnpanama.com. Mainly equipped for business stays. Well-equipped rooms and suites with the usual *Holiday Inn* essentials including writing desk, cable TV, quiet a/c, main telephone, second telephone in the bathroom, and iron. Excellent service, restaurant, bar, swimming pool, gym and helipad for those in a hurry. ⑧

Hotel Bella Vista Via España, Av Perú ☎ 264 4029. Unspectacular but reasonably priced rooms with a/c, cable TV, hot water and telephone. ③

Hotel California Via España, C 43 Este ☎ 263 7736. Large, modern and comfortable rooms with hot water, a/c, TV and telephone. ⑤

Hotel Costa Azul C 44 Este, Av Justo Arosemena ☎ 225 4703, hotelcostaazul@cwpanama.net. Small hotel with friendly service, Internet access, bar and parking. Bright, clean and spacious rooms with hot water, a/c and cable TV. ④

Hotel El Panamá C 49B Oeste, Via España ☎ 215 9000, www.elpanama.com. Formerly the *Hilton*, this five-star Art Deco–style hotel has plenty of character and is ideally located in the heart of El Cangrejo, with luxurious decor, large swimming pool, three bars, two restaurants, casino, gym, and all the other features of a top international hotel. ❾

Hotel El Parador C Eusebio A. Morales ⓣ214 4586, ⓔhelparador@cableonda.net. New hotel with restaurant, bar, parking, free Internet access and rooftop swimming pool with panoramic views. The excellent-value large rooms offer a/c, cable TV, hot water and phone, with most having balconies. ❺

Hotel Montreal Via España, Justo Arosemena ⓣ263 4422, ⓔhmontreal@cableonda.com. Excellent location – the closest in this price range to the centre of El Cangrejo – but a lot of noise from Via España traffic. Small, poorly lit rooms with TV, hot water (sometimes in the cistern), phone and a/c. Rooms at the back are quieter. Bar, rooftop swimming pool, parking and a modest restaurant. ❹

Hotel Riande Granada Av Eusebio A. Morales, Via España ⓣ264 4900, ⓦwww.hotelesriande.com. Luxurious international hotel with excellent service and central location, although some rooms are a bit on the small side. There's a 24hr café, bar, outdoor barbecue restaurant and pool surrounded by tropical plants. ❼

Residencial Primavera Av Cuba, C 42 ⓣ225 1195. Recently spruced up rooms have fans and basic bathrooms. The friendly service and location in a residential area on the edge of Bella Vista make it a pleasant place to stay and excellent value. ❷

Voyager International Hostel 8th and 3rd floors, Edificio Di Lido, C Manuel Maria Icaza ⓣ260 5913 or 636 3443, ⓦwww.geocities.com/voyagerih. Ideally located in El Cangrejo, this hostel boasts friendly and helpful owners, dormitories – some with a/c – and several private rooms. All rates include breakfast. There's also a communal kitchen (with 24hr supermarket nearby), laundry service, living room, large balcony, bag storage and free Internet access. A great place to meet other travellers and get information, especially on the city's nightlife. Can arrange cheap collection from airport. ❷–❹

The City

The old city centre of **San Felipe** (also known as Casco Viejo and occasionally Casco Antiguo) is the most picturesque and historically interesting part of Panama City and is home to many of its most important buildings and several museums, including the **Museo del Canal Interoceanico**. Crumbling colonial churches overlook quiet squares filled with monuments, and the narrow, cobbled streets are lined with ornate French- and Spanish-influenced nineteenth-century mansions, painted white or in faded Caribbean pastels, some with wrought-iron balconies draped with colourful flowers.

Northwest of San Felipe the steep, forested hill of **Cerro Ancón** offers commanding views of the city and marks the boundary of the former Canal Zone, while the canalside area of **Balboa**, which retains the feel of a US provincial town, makes an interesting contrast to the chaotic vitality of the rest of the city. Balboa is also the jumping-off point for visits to the peaceful **Isla Taboga**. North of the city, meanwhile, a stroll through the tropical rainforest of **Parque Nacional Metropolitano** offers an even more fundamental change of scenery. The modern-day commercial heart of the capital can be found in the neighbouring districts of **Bella Vista**, **El Cangrejo** and **Punta Paitilla**, where the majority of the city's banks, hotels, restaurants, shops and luxurious private residences can be found. Though offering little in the way of historical intrigue, the airy avenues of Bella Vista are an interesting contrast to the modern skyscrapers that comprise Punta Paitilla, with El Cangrejo, situated in between, offering a mixture of the two.

San Felipe

For centuries the heart of Panama City's social and political life, and still home to the presidential palace, the colonial city centre of **San Felipe** was declared a UNESCO World Heritage site in 1997 and is gradually being restored to its former glory after decades of neglect. Despite the upmarket restaurants and cafés that have opened up, however, San Felipe is still a poor, run-down neighbourhood with a relaxed but slightly seedy streetlife. Although ongoing restoration projects are making it a much more pleasant place to visit, they are not popular with the district's

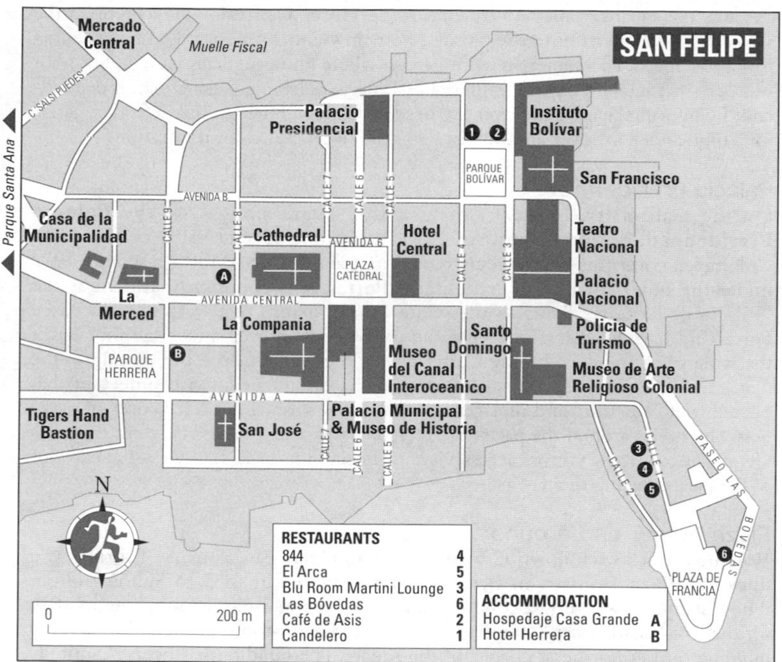

poorer residents, many of whom face eviction. Caution should be exercised when walking the streets at night, but the increased presence of tourist police makes it relatively safe during the day. The best way to see San Felipe is on foot, and **Plaza Catedral**, the main square, is a good place to start – you can reach it from the rest of the city by taxi or by walking down Av Central from Parque Santa Ana.

Plaza Catedral

Plaza Catedral, also known as Plaza de la Independencia – the proclamations of independence from both Spain and Colombia were made here – centres on a bandstand, ringed by benches shaded by trees and busts of eminent Panamanians. Flanked by white towers inlaid with mother-of-pearl, the classical facade of the **cathedral** looks out on the square from the west. It was built between 1688 and 1796 using stones from the ruined cathedral of Panamá Viejo (see p.760). Three of its bells were also recovered from its ruined predecessor, and reputedly owe their distinctive tone to a ring thrown by Empress Isabella of Spain into the molten metal from which they were cast. Southeast of the cathedral is the Neoclassical **Palacio Municipal**, whose small **Museo de Historia Panameña** (Mon–Fri 8.30am–3.30pm; US$1) offers a cursory introduction to Panamanian history that pales in comparison to its neighbour, the excellent **Museo del Canal Interoceanico** (Tues–Sun 9.30am–5.30pm; US$2; ⓦ www.museodelcanal.com.). The latter museum expounds clearly and in great detail the history of the transisthmian route, from the first Spanish attempt to find a passage to Asia to the contemporary management of the canal, with many photographs, video footage and historic exhibits including the original canal treaties. All displays are in Spanish, but most of the guides speak English. The museum has disabled access and a small shop selling modern and original canal memorabilia.

Across the square from the cathedral is the **Hotel Central**, built to replace the *Grand Hotel* and, in its time, the plushest hotel in Central America. The huge central patio was once a chandelier-lit palm garden where glittering balls were held, and it was here that jubilant crowds gathered in 1903 to celebrate Panamanian independence by pouring champagne over the head of General Huertas, the defecting garrison commander, for over an hour. In 2004 the hotel closed for restoration.

Palacio Presidencial

On the seafront two blocks north of the square along C 6, the **Palacio Presidencial**, originally built in 1673, was home to successive colonial and Colombian governors before being rebuilt in grandiose neo-Moorish style in 1922 under the orders of President Belisario Porras. It is commonly known as the "Palacio de las Garzas" due to the white Darién herons that were introduced by Porras and have lived freely around the patio fountain ever since. Rumour has it that when US president Jimmy Carter visited the palace before the signing of the new canal treaty his security team sprayed the building with a disinfectant that proved fatal to herons, and replacements had to be rushed in under cover of darkness. The streets around the palace are closed to traffic and pedestrians, but the presidential guards allow visitors access, via the checkpoint on C 4, to view the exterior of the palace during the day.

Plaza Bolívar and around

Walking a block back down C 6 and then two blocks east along Av B brings you out onto **Plaza Bolívar**, an elegant square dedicated in 1883 to Simón Bolívar, whose statue, crowned by a condor, stands in its centre. Bolívar came here in 1826 for the first Panamerican Congress, held in the chapter-room of the old monastery building on the northeast corner of the square. The building has been beautifully restored and the courtyard has a magnificent translucent roof so that events and exhibitions can be staged here. Although it is now the headquarters of the Ministry of the Interior, the parts of the building that are open to the public are well worth a visit. Next door stands the **church and monastery of San Francisco**, built in the seventeenth century but extensively modified since. The church is usually closed, but if you ask in the parish office on Av B, someone may be willing to open it up and show you around. Other than the carved wooden confessional dating to 1736 the interior is unspectacular, but the tower offers fine views across the city.

Just off the square to the south on Av B is the **Teatro Nacional**, designed by Genaro Ruggieri, the Italian architect responsible for La Scala in Milan. Extensively restored in the early 1970s, the theatre reopened in 1974 with a performance by Margot Fonteyn, the British ballerina and long-term Panama resident. Built to the most exacting acoustic standards, the splendid Neoclassical interior is richly furnished and decorated in red and gold, with French crystal chandeliers, busts of famous dramatists and a vaulted ceiling painted with scenes depicting the birth of the nation by Panamanian artist Roberto Lewis. Outside, it is a 200m walk from the parking lot at the end of Avenida B south along the seafront to the corner of Av A and C 1, past some immaculately restored nineteenth-century houses to the west and, overlooking the sea to the east, the ruined shell of the **Club de Clases y Tropas**. This recreation centre for Noriega's national guard was destroyed during the US invasion.

Plaza de Francia and around

A 100m walk south along C 1 brings you out onto the **Plaza de Francia**, enclosed on three sides by the seaward defensive walls and site of a monument dedicated to the thousands of workers who died during the disastrous French attempt to build the canal (see p.742). The centrepiece of the monument is an obelisk topped by a proud Gallic cockerel, which is ringed by busts of some of the key figures involved, including Ferdinand de Lesseps, the French diplomat who first conceived of the canal. There is also a plaque dedicated to Carlos Finlay, the Cuban doctor whose groundbreaking research on the causes of malaria and yellow fever was so important to the later success of the US canal. The Neoclassical **French Embassy** overlooks the square from the north, fronted by a statue of Mario Arosemena, a Panamanian politician who gave crucial support to the French venture. The elegant building to the east was formerly the Palace of Justice, badly damaged during the US invasion in 1989 and now home to the National Cultural Institute. In the colonial period the square was a military centre, and the vaults under the seaward walls served as the city's jails – built below sea level, they would sometimes flood at high tide, drowning the unfortunate prisoners within. Known as Las Bóvedas, some of the vaults have been restored: one houses a French restaurant that shares the same name (see p.766) and another a small art gallery. From the square, steps lead up to the **Paseo Las Bóvedas**, also known as the Esteban Huertas Promenade, which runs some 400m along the top of the defensive wall, all the way around the plaza and back to the corner of C 1 and Av A. Here, partially shaded by bougainvillea, courting couples seek refuge from busy city life, while Kuna gather to sell their handicrafts to passing tourists. From the sea wall you are afforded great views of the modern city and can see the ships in the bay waiting to transit the canal as well as the faded colours of the tenement slums of El Chorillo.

Along Avenida A

Two blocks west along Av A from the corner with C 1 stands the ruined **Church and Convent of Santo Domingo**, completed in 1678 and famous for the **Arco Chato** (flat arch) over its main entrance. Only 10.6m high, but spanning some 15m with no external support, it was reputedly cited as evidence of Panama's seismic stability when the US Senate was debating where to build an interoceanic canal. Unfortunately, the arch collapsed just after the centenary celebrations for Panama's independence in 2003. Although it's unclear why the arch collapsed, some say it was due to the disturbance caused by the estimated 20,000 people who descended on San Felipe for the celebrations, while others point to the area's extensive restoration. In the chapel next door, the absorbing **Museo de Arte Religioso Colonial** (Tues–Sat 9am–4.15pm; US$0.75) has a small collection of religious paintings, silverwork and sculpture from the colonial era. Four blocks west along Av A is the ruined shell of **La Compañía**, a Jesuit church and university completed only eighteen years before the Society's expulsion from all Spanish America in 1767. Only the walls and ornate facade still stand.

A block further west on the corner with C 8 is the **Church of San José**. Built in 1673, but since remodelled, the church is exceptional only as home to the legendary baroque **Golden Altar**, one of the few treasures to survive Henry Morgan's ransacking of Panamá Viejo in 1671 – it was apparently painted or covered in mud to disguise its true value. One block beyond San José, Av A emerges onto **Plaza Herrera**, a pleasant square lined with elegant nineteenth-century houses, some with wrought-iron balconies imported during the French canal construction. This was originally the Plaza de Triunfo, where bullfights were held until the mid-nineteenth century, but was renamed in 1922 in honour of General Tomas Herrera, whose statue stands in its centre. Herrera was the military leader of a short-lived independence attempt in 1840; he went on to be elected president of Colombia but was assassinated before taking office in Bogotá in 1854. Just off Plaza Herrera to the west stands **The Tiger Hand Bastion**, a crumbling and indistinct pile of masonry that is the last remaining section of the city's defensive walls on the landward side. The walls came to symbolize the class divide between wealthy San Felipe residents and the poorer neighbourhood of Santa Ana, and were largely dismantled in the mid-nineteenth century.

Santa Ana

Shaded by trees, the small green **park** in the centre of **Santa Ana** – a busy transport hub – offers an island of tranquillity from the swirling traffic. A few blocks to the west, under the shadow of Cerro Ancón, is the poor barrio of **El Chorillo**, which was devastated during the US invasion, leaving hundreds dead and thousands homeless. It has since been rebuilt, but the coloured concrete tenements that replaced the old wooden slum housing are already run down, and it remains a very dangerous neighbourhood even during the day. Just beyond Parque Santa Ana on Av Central, a right turn takes you down **Calle Sal si Puedes** ("get out if you can"), a steep, narrow street crammed with market stalls that runs two blocks down to the seafront and the covered **Mercado Central**, the lively food market. Southeast of the market is the **Muelle Fiscal**, from where occasional boats to Darién and Colombia leave (see p.800).

The area between the market and Av B is known as the **Barrio Chino** (Chinatown), the traditional centre of Panama City's large Chinese population, which began to arrive in the middle of the nineteenth century to work on the railway. The Chinese community is much more dispersed now, but the barrio retains a distinct Asian feel: there are Chinese supermarkets selling everything from dried shark fins to newspapers; restaurants where it is difficult to order unless you speak Cantonese; and, at the north end of C Juan Mendoza, an ornate gate that marks the official entrance to the barrio from Av Balboa.

The pedestrianized stretch of **Avenida Central** from Parque Santa Ana north as far as Plaza Cinco de Mayo is the liveliest and most popular shopping district in the city. Blasts of air conditioning and loud music pour from the huge superstores that line the avenue selling cheap clothing, electronics and household goods, as hawkers with megaphones attempt to entice shoppers inside. Nowhere is the sheer energy of the city and the enormous cultural diversity of its population more evident: stop for a while on one of the tree-shaded mosaic benches and you will see Hindus in saris, Kuna women in their traditional costumes, bearded Muslims in robes and skullcaps, *interioranos* in sombreros, Chinese, Afro-Antillanos and Latinos, all scrambling for bargains in the supercharged atmosphere of this postmodern bazaar. The area of Santa Ana west of Avenida Central and north of the Parque Santa Ana is a dangerous neighbourhood and caution should also be exercised when walking in the area to the east of Avenida Central from C 11 Este to C 23 Este.

Calidonia, La Exposición, Bella Vista and El Cangrejo

Ten blocks north, the pedestrianized section of Av Central ends as it emerges onto **Plaza Cinco de Mayo** and the maelstrom of traffic takes over again. In fact, this is two squares rolled into one: the first has a small monument to the volunteer firemen killed fighting an exploded gunpowder magazine in 1914 – the *bomberos* occupy a revered position in a city that has so often been devastated by fire. Opposite the monument a columned former railway station houses the **Museo Antropologico Reina Torres de Araúz** (Tues–Sun 10am–4pm; US$2), whose displays include the Salón de Oro, an exhibit of pre-Colombian gold objects, as well as another featuring carved stone statues from the ancient Barriles culture of Chiriquí. Behind the museum is a large, open-air **handicrafts market**. The second square, Plaza Cinco de Mayo proper, is a little further down, with a black, monolithic monument emblazoned with the nationalist slogan: "Ni limosnas, ni milliones, queremos justicia" ("neither alms, nor millions, we want justice").

Across the road, on the corner with Av Justo Arosemena, inside a small fenced garden stands a statue of **Mahatma Gandhi**, erected by the city's Hindu community and often garlanded in flowers. A block down Av Justo Arosemena on the corner with C 24 an unmarked wooden former church houses the **Museo Afro-Antillano** (Tues–Sun 9am–4pm; US$1), dedicated to preserving the history and culture of Panama's large West Indian population. It is very small, but its exhibits – featuring photographs, tools and furniture – give a good idea of the working and living conditions of black canal workers. There is also a small library and occasional events, including Afro-Antillano cookery courses and jazz festivals.

Beyond Plaza Cinco de Mayo, Av Central continues to the northeast, the city's main thoroughfare and still a busy shopping street as it runs through Calidonia and La Exposición. Two blocks away from Av Central on Av Cuba between C 29 and C 30, the **Museo de Ciencias Naturales** (Tues–Sat 9am–4pm; US$1) offers a basic introduction to Panama's geology and ecology, with many stuffed animals – look out for the pickled fer-de-lance, the venomous snake that killed the director of Panama's old zoo in 1931. A short walk south down C 30 brings you out onto Av Balboa on the seafront, and several blocks to the left, set in a small park shaded by palm trees, is the glorious **Balboa Monument**. Erected in 1913 with Spanish help, the likeness of Vasco Núñez de Balboa, the sixteenth-century explorer, stands atop a globe with a sword in one hand and a flag in the other, looking out in perpetual triumph on the southern ocean he "discovered".

As it continues northeast, Av Central changes its name to Via España and passes through the comfortable residential neighbourhood of **Bella Vista**. On the corner with Av Manuel E. Batista, the twentieth-century neo-Gothic wedding-cake **Del Carmen** church marks the beginning of **El Cangrejo**, the high-rise banking district and commercial heart of the city, centred on Via España between the church and Via Argentina, and on C 50. Most of the classier hotels and restaurants are here,

The Afro-Antillanos

Some five percent of Panama's population are **Afro-Antillanos** – descendants of the black workers from the English- and French-speaking West Indies who began migrating to Panama in the mid-nineteenth century to help build the railroad and canal. West Indians, largely from Jamaica and Barbados, formed the vast majority of the labour force in both the French and the US canal construction efforts, living and working in appalling conditions – most of the 20,000 workers who died during the French attempt were West Indians and, despite the vast sanitary improvements, mortality among black workers was four times higher than among whites during the US construction. Despite the racial discrimination – lower wages, poorer conditions, strict segregation – they faced in the US Canal Zone, many West Indians stayed in Panama City and Colón after the canal's completion, while others migrated to the banana plantations of Bocas del Toro. In Panama as a whole, they were widely considered second-class citizens or undesirable aliens. Populist politician Arnulfo Arias Madrid was an undisguised racist, and as president in 1940 pushed through a constitution that prohibited further immigration by blacks and denied the right to own property to those without an adequate knowledge of Panamanian history and the Spanish language. The inclusionary politics of the Torrijos regime eased discrimination: jobs in government and even business were made accessible to Afro-Antillanos and they became more widely accepted. Nonetheless, although more socially integrated than the black communities of several other Central American republics, they remain among the most marginalized sectors of the population.

More than a century after their arrival in Panama, the Afro-Antillanos maintain a vibrant and distinct **culture** whose influence is apparent in many aspects of contemporary Panamanian society. Many second- and third-generation Afro-Antillanos still speak English, or rather the melodic patois of the West Indies, and the street Spanish of Panama City and Colón is peppered with Jamaican slang. The Protestant churches they brought with them from the West Indies continue to thrive; heavily spiced Caribbean dishes have permeated Panamanian cuisine; and their music, from jazz in the 1950s through to "reggaespañol" – the compelling combination of Spanish lyrics and hardcore Jamaican dancehall rhythms that took Latin America by storm in the 1990s – is popular across the country.

as well as upmarket stores and shopping centres selling designer fashions and state-of-the-art electronics. This is also where much of the city's nightlife is concentrated, and it's safe to walk around at night.

Panamá Viejo

On the coast about 6km east of El Cangrejo stand the ruins of **PANAMÁ VIEJO**, the original colonial city founded by Pedro Arias de Ávila in 1519 and abandoned in 1671, after being ransacked by Henry Morgan and his band of pirates. Many of its buildings were dismantled to provide stones for the construction of San Felipe, and in recent decades much of the site has been built over as the modern city has continued to spread eastward. Despite this encroachment, a surprising number of the original buildings still stand, testimony to the skill of the Spanish masons who built them, and a walk among the ruins will give you a hint of the former splendour of the first European city on the Pacific Ocean.

To **get to Panamá Viejo**, either take a taxi (US$3–4) or catch any bus marked Panamá Viejo or Via Cincuentenario. If you're short on time and leaving Panama by air, you can see quite a lot of the ruins by asking your taxi driver to take the slow route to the airport via Panamá Viejo. The best place to start a visit is the new **museum** (Tues–Sun 9am–5pm; US$1.50; ⓣ224 2155, ⓦwww.panamaviejo.org) on Via Cincuentenario near the ruins, where exhibits explain to visitors the changes that have taken place since it was a tiny Indian village around 500 BC. Artefacts discovered during ongoing archeological excavations on display include nails and rusty swords, pottery and astonishingly well-preserved Sevillan tiles. The ruins are well marked with descriptions in English and Spanish.

The site

The ruins are spread out either side of Via Cincuentenario, with many trees still scattered among them, remnants of the forest that engulfed the site after its abandonment (some buildings still have gnarled roots embedded in their walls). The former **Plaza Mayor** is overlooked by the three-storey square stone tower of the **cathedral**, built between 1619 and 1629 to replace an earlier wooden structure, and flanked by the square **cabildo** (town hall) to the right and the well-preserved bishop's house to the left. Behind the cathedral, through the grounds of the National Sport Institute, you can still see the foundations of the **casas reales** – the royal treasury, customs house, court and governor's residence that together formed the centre of royal power in Panamá Viejo, originally separated from the rest of the city by a moat and wooden palisade. Returning to the cathedral and turning right brings you to the **church and monastery of Santo Domingo**, the smallest religious structure here but also the best preserved, with a tall buttressed tree growing inside. From here, Via Cincuentenario runs 400m north to the **Church of San José**, which survived the fire of 1571 and was the home of the famous Golden Altar, which escaped Morgan's notice and is now in the church of the same name in San Felipe (see p.757). Another 200m brings you to the **King's Bridge**, the beginning of the Camino Real, the treasure route across the isthmus to Nombre de Dios (see p.785). Be careful if walking alone in this area: the ruins are surrounded by poor barrios, and it's a long way from the tourist police who patrol the site.

The major ruins across the road from the cathedral are the **Church of La Compañía de Jesus** (Jesuits) and the **Church of La Concepción**, both of which had their respective monasteries, of which little now remains. Close by, on Via Cincuentenario, only one wall of the **Hospital de San Juan de Dios** still stands. As you walk east along Via Cincuentenario, after 100m you pass the remains of the **Monastery of San Francisco**, where the Franciscan monks were said to have been massacred by Morgan's men while tending to the wounded. Some 200m beyond are the crumbling remains of the **church and monastery of La Merced**, where Francisco Pizarro took communion before embarking on the conquest of

Perú in 1531. La Merced was considered the most beautiful church in the city and survived the fire in 1571 – Morgan used it as his headquarters – but its ornate facade was dismantled and moved to San Felipe, the cloisters are no more and the whole structure is sadly cut in two by the road.

The former Canal Zone

To the southwest of Calidonia and El Chorillo, Panama City encompasses the former Canal Zone town of **BALBOA**, administered by the US as de facto sovereign territory from 1903 to 1979. Panamanians who lived or worked here were subject to US law and many of the residents, known as Zonians, still maintain a distinct and somewhat exclusive transnational identity. Balboa retains many of the characteristics of a US provincial town; clean and well ordered, it stands in stark contrast to the chaotic vitality of the rest of the city. To the east the Canal Authority Building looks down on Balboa from the slopes of Cerro Ancón, a longstanding symbol of US power in the isthmus, now in Panamanian hands, while to the south is **Fort Amador**, a former US military base now being transformed into a massive luxury tourism development. Beyond the fort a **causeway** stretches 6km out to sea, between the bay and the canal approaches, linking the islands of Naos, Perico and Flamenco.

Cerro Ancón and Balboa

Along the border of the former Canal Zone runs Av de Los Mártires, named in honour of the 21 Panamanians killed by the US military during the riots of 1964 (see p.744). A sculpture by González Palomino, depicting three people climbing a flag pole, was erected here in 2004 as a tribute to the fallen; above it rises **Cerro Ancón**, a heavily forested hill crowned by a huge Panamanian flag that is visible throughout the city. From the entrance on Av de Los Mártires, it's well worth the twenty-minute walk up the steep path to the summit for the spectacular views of the city, the bay and the canal as far as the Pedro Miguel Locks, 10km away. Note that there have been muggings on the hill, so be wary – particularly if walking alone – but there is often a contingent of tourist police on hand. The small forest is surprisingly well preserved, and deer, agouti and iguanas are frequently seen, as well as plenty of birds. From the summit you'll have to return the way you came or take the longer fifty-minute walk down the road.

Just off the entrance on Av de Los Mártires is **Mi Pueblitos** (Tues–Sun 9am–9pm; US$1), a theme-park–style replica of the traditional villages of four of Panama's different ethnic groups: an early twentieth-century *interiorano* village, complete with church, telegraph office and barber's shop; an Afro-Antillano village with airy wooden houses on stilts painted in faded Caribbean pastels; a circle of Kuna palm and cane huts; and a few of the open-sided, raised platform huts of the Emberá, set amid lush forest. Although aimed primarily at Panamanians, it's actually less tacky than it sounds, and it's worth visiting if you are not going to see the real thing. Folk dances are performed on Friday evenings, and restaurants serve traditional food.

Some 200m east of the entrance to Cerro Ancón on Av de Los Mártires is a turn-off onto Gorgas Road, which winds round the side of Cerro Ancón to the Canal Authority Building in Balboa Heights, about twenty minutes away on foot. Just off Gorgas Road to the right, the **Museo de Arte Contemporáneo** (Tues–Fri 9am–5pm; US$1; ⓣ262 3380, ⓦwww.macpanama.org) has a small collection of modern art by obscure national and international artists, housed in a former Masonic temple of 1936. As you climb Gorgas Road, you'll pass the **Gorgas Military Hospital**, named after US military doctor William Gorgas, who did so much to reduce the death toll from malaria and yellow fever among the canal construction workforce. A formidable stone construction, the hospital now houses the Palace of Justice. As it continues around Cerro Ancón, the road's name changes to

△ Kuna hut, San Blas Archipelago

Heights Road, which is lined with several luxury villas set amid well-manicured lawns, including, at **107 Heights Road**, the residence of the Panama Canal Commission administrator.

Soon after, Gorgas Road reappears to the right (heading left will take you to the summit of Cerro Ancón) and winds down to the three-storey **Panama Canal Authority Administration Building** (daily 8am–11pm; free), a classic example of US colonial architecture built during the canal construction and still home to the principal administration offices. Inside, four dramatic murals by US artist William Van Ingen depict the story of the canal construction under a domed ceiling supported by marble pillars; here, too, are busts of Ferdinand de Lesseps, Theodore Roosevelt and Charles V of Spain. At the rear of the building, where a Panamanian flag now flutters, a broad stairway runs down to the **Goethals monument**, a white megalith with stepped fountains that represent the canal's different locks, erected in honour of George Goethals, chief engineer from 1907 to 1914 and first governor of the Canal Zone. Beside the monument is **Balboa High School**, whose ordinary appearance belies the dramatic events it has witnessed. It was here in 1964 that Zonians attacked students attempting to raise the Panamanian flag, triggering the **flag riots** that left 21 Panamanians dead. During the 1989 invasion the school was used as a detention camp for Panamanian prisoners, some of whom were allegedly executed by US soldiers. From here, the palm-lined El Prado Boulevard runs a few hundred metres down to **Stevens' Circle**. This is Balboa proper, the main residential area of the former Canal Zone, its solid white buildings with red-tiled roofs and immaculate lawns giving it a distinctively North American feel, and it is now home to the city's growing middle class.

Fort Amador and the causeway

From Balboa, Calle Amador runs towards the causeway through **Fort Amador**, a former US military base returned to Panama in 1996 that is being redeveloped as the centrepiece of the country's plans to promote tourism in the former Canal Zone. The complex will include luxury hotels and a marina as well as a "biodiversity exhibition centre" designed by acclaimed architect Frank Gehry. Construction of the centre started in February 2004, with completion scheduled for 2006. The administration centre, with models of the development, is already open to the public (Tues–Sun 10am–6pm; US$2 ⓦwww.biomuseopanama.com).

From Amador, a **causeway** (Calzada de Amador) runs out into the bay, linking the mainland with the tiny islands of **Naos**, **Perico** and **Flamenco**. Built during the canal construction with spoil from the excavation as a breakwater to prevent silting of the canal entrance, the causeway is a popular weekend escape for the city's residents, who come here to jog, swim, stroll, rollerblade or cycle (you can rent bicycles at the entrance; US$2.50/hr and proof of identification) and to enjoy the sea air and the view of the city on one side and the entrance to the canal on the other. In the early years of Panama City, the islands served as deep-water moorings for ships, and after the causeway's construction they together formed Fort Grant, heavily fortified for canal defence. The causeway remained a restricted area until 1989, contributing to the conservation of the islands' varied ecology. Some of the military installations can still be seen, including rails that once carried fifteen-inch guns.

On **Naos**, 2km along the causeway, the **Smithsonian Marine Exhibition Centre** (Tues–Sun 10am–6pm, Fri & Sat 10am–8pm; US$2; ⓦwww.stri.org), located at Punta Culebra, the site of an old artillery battery, offers an introduction to Panama's marine ecology, including an aquarium where you can stroke sea urchins, starfish and sea cucumbers. There is a small beach and swimming pool (daily 10am–5pm; US$5) as well as a strip mall of cafés and shops. The second island, **Perico**, is so small as to be indistinguishable from the causeway. Finally, **Flamenco** is home to the National Maritime Service, whose compound is closed to the public. The new Flamenco Marina and Shopping Centre (ⓦwww.fuerteamamdor.com), at the foot of the island, is the departure point for passenger ferries to Isla Taboga and for some ships embarking on canal transit tours; it's also a popular nighttime hangout thanks to its large number of bars, clubs and restaurants.

Parque Natural Metropolitano

A couple of kilometres north of central Panama City, the 2.65-square-kilometre **Parque Natural Metropolitano** is an unspoilt tract of tropical rainforest that's home to more than two hundred species of birds and mammals, such as titi monkeys, white-tailed deer, sloths and agoutis, in a slice of the former Canal Zone that reverted to Panamanian control in 1983. The park provides an excellent introductory experience to the rainforest environment, and it's possible to complete all of the main trails in just a few hours. You don't need a permit from ANAM to visit the park, which is officially open from 6am to 6pm, though there is nothing to stop you coming earlier and, as elsewhere, the best time to see wildlife, particularly birds, is early in the morning. The **park office** (Mon–Fri 8am–4pm, Sat 8am–1pm; US$2) and main entrance is on Av Juan Pablo II; some buses can drop you nearby or a taxi from El Cangrejo should cost about US$2. There is a small exhibition centre and library here, and three-hour **guided tours** can be arranged (US$2 per person; book in advance), though you can easily walk the park's five short **trails** without a guide. The best of these is the combined 3km La Cienaguita and MonoTiti trail, which leads to a *mirador* with fantastic views across the forest to the city.

Around Panama City: Isla Taboga

Twenty kilometres off the coast and about an hour away by boat, tiny **Taboga** is one of the most popular weekend retreats for Panama City residents, who come here to enjoy the island's clear waters, peaceful atmosphere and verdant beauty. Known as the "Island of Flowers" for the innumerable fragrant blooms that decorate its village and forested slopes, Taboga gets very busy on the weekends, particularly during the summer, but is usually quiet during the week.

The island was settled by the Spanish in 1524 and served as a deep-water port before such facilities were established on the mainland – it was from here that Francisco Pizarro set sail for the conquest of Perú. Frequent pirate raids led to the fortification of El Morro Island, opposite Taboga, which in the nineteenth century served as the headquarters of the Pacific Steam Navigation Company.

Taboga's one **fishing village** is very picturesque, with scrupulously clean narrow streets running between its whitewashed houses and dozens of gardens filled with bougainvillea and hibiscus. Most visitors head straight for one of the sections of **beach**, either right in front of the village or in front of the *Hotel Taboga* (to the right of the pier as you disembark), where the water is calmer and the view of Panama City magnificent. Despite what the hotel would have you believe, you don't have to pay to enter its part of the beach, though use of any of the *Taboga*'s facilities costs US$7, in return for which you'll be given tokens redeemable on drinks, basic food or other services in the hotel.

Behind the village, forested slopes rise to the 300m peak of **Cerro Vigia**, where a viewing platform on top of an old US military bunker offers spectacular 360-degree views. It's about an hour's climb through the forest to the *mirador* – follow the path some 100m up behind the church until you find a sign marked Sendero de los Tres Cruces, beyond which the trail is easy to follow. The other side of the island is home to one of the biggest brown pelican breeding colonies in the world and together with the neighbouring island of Uraba forms a protected **wildlife refuge**.

Snorkelling and diving are also popular activities on Taboga as marine life is abundant, particularly around El Morro. The *Hotel Taboga* and the *Kool Hostel* rent equipment, though for diving it is better to organize a trip with one of the dive companies in Panama City.

Practicalities

A visit to Taboga is worth it for the voyage alone. Slow passenger **ferries** leave from the Flamenco Marina at the end of the causeway, while the express service leaves from Muelle 18, via the car park to Muelle 19, in Balboa (2 daily from each dock between 8am and 10pm, returning between 3pm and 6pm, more frequently at weekends; 40min; US$8 return). There are plans to move all ferry services to Flamenco by the end of 2004.

There are three **places to stay** on the island. The family-oriented *Hotel Taboga* (ⓣ250 2122, ⓔhtaboga@sinfo.net; ❼) has comfortable rooms with a/c and TV, pool, tennis court, and snorkelling and scuba equipment for rent, but it's rather overpriced and has the feel of a 1950s holiday camp. Cheaper and more atmospheric, *Hotel Chu* (ⓣ250 2035; ❹) has basic rooms and communal bathrooms in a brightly painted wooden structure on stilts on the seafront. There's also a bar-disco, *El Galeon*, under the hotel, which is convenient if you want to stay up late drinking rum and dancing, but rather noisy if you don't. Travellers on a budget should head for *Kool Hostel* (ⓣ690 2545 or contact *Voyager International Hostel* in Panama City; ❷): after turning left from the pier, you'll find it on the top floor of the first red-orange house. The hostel offers small dormitories and private rooms with free breakfast and a communal kitchen; they can also arrange bicycle and snorkel rental.

The two hotels have **restaurants**; the *Chu* serves reasonable Chinese food and good seafood on a broad wooden balcony overlooking the sea, while the *Taboga* offers more varied and expensive international and Panamanian cuisine as well as a full buffet on the weekends. Opposite the church, *Aquario* serves good seafood dishes ranging from US$3–8.

Eating

Panama City's cosmopolitan nature is reflected in its **restaurants**: pretty much every cuisine in the world can be found here, from US fast food to Greek, Italian, Chinese, Japanese and French. Most of the more upmarket options are concentrated in **El Cangrejo** and **Bella Vista** – Via Argentina and Calle Uruguay have the widest selection, with many spots featuring outdoor tables that are good for people-watching – but you're never far from a range of good and inexpensive places to eat, and excellent **seafood** is widely available. Most restaurants in the city provide non-smoking areas and cartons to take home any leftovers. Cheap **takeout** meals are available from the Rey supermarket (open 24hr) on Via España, including half a rotisserie chicken US$2.50, potato salad US$0.70 and fruit salad US$0.80.

Bella Vista and El Cangrejo

Aladino's Café C 52 and Ricardo Arias opposite *Hotel Marriott*. Good range of tasty Lebanese and international food from about US$4 with a large mixed platter at US$10. Good service and popular with wealthy locals. Belly dancing Fri and Sat after 9pm.

Costa Azul C Ricardo Arias. Round-the-clock restaurant serving Panamanian cuisine that's popular with local office workers and features a large, slightly pricey menu, which includes good toasted sandwiches (US$2) and several sea bass dishes (US$8).

Fisch Av Balboa, C Uruguay ⓦwww.fischgrill.com. Stylish German-owned restaurant specializing in excellent fish and seafood dishes, including shark, grouper and sole, with live jazz most evenings and attentive service. Choose your fish, then select the cooking method and sauce, from garlic butter to creamy coconut (from US$6). There's also a range of salads and snacks (from US$4).

Gaucho's C Uruguay. Relatively expensive steakhouse, serving steaks from Argentina and the US (from US$15) and featuring some of the city's best service as well as delicious homemade bread.

Jimmy C Manuel M. Icaza off Via España. Good-value, extremely popular 24hr restaurant-cafeteria in the heart of El Cangrejo, with a wide choice of Panamanian food, from grilled meat and fish to sandwiches, pizza and strong coffee. Takeout available.

Machu Picchu C Eusebio A. Morales. Excellent seafood dishes, often with a Peruvian twist, accompanied by fine service, comfortable seating and a friendly atmosphere. Main courses from US$8.

Manolo C 49B Oeste, a block north from Via España. Offering a broad range of meats, fish and seafood as well as 12-inch pizzas (US$4), this spot retains its popularity despite the poor service and overpriced coffee.

Matsuei C Eusebio A. Morales, close to *Hotel El Parador*. Japanese restaurant with friendly service and a large menu that offers sushi, tempura, curries and teriyaki. Prices from US$9 to US$30 for a large sushi tray. Closed Sun lunch.

Mireya C 50 Este, a block south from the *Hotel Continental* on Via España. Small, inexpensive self-service vegetarian restaurant with a choice of hot dishes as well as a salad bar. Mon–Sat 6am–8pm.

Pizzeria Athens C 48E, C 50, behind the Delta petrol station. Very popular fast-food restaurant with harsh fluorescent lighting and phones on the tables for ordering. Not the best pizza, but very good Greek dishes, including *souvlaki*, *gyros*, roast aubergines (*berenjena*) and the inevitable Greek salad. About US$4–5 a head. Closed Wed. There's another branch on C 57 (closed Tues).

Pomodoro C 49B Oeste in *ApartHotel Las Vegas*. Extremely popular Italian place with a good atmosphere and outdoor seating in an enclosed tropical garden. Excellent pizza and pasta from US$5.

Royal Thai C Uruguay. Thai and Chinese food, with a smattering of vegetarian options; dishes run around US$6. Indoor and outdoor seating as well as cheaper takeout service. Daily 11am–11pm.

Te Conte Av Argentina. Smart café and *panadería* serving excellent coffee, cakes, pastries and savouries to eat in or take out. Also sells a wide selection of freshly baked bread.

El Trapiche Via Argentina. Slightly upmarket traditional Panamanian cuisine in a lively atmosphere, with three-course set lunches, tasty meat and fish dishes, and filling Panamanian breakfasts.

Santa Ana and Calidonia

Boulevard Balboa Av Balboa, C 31 Este. The spartan 1970s interior is livened up by the smart lunchtime crowd of local politicians and office workers, who come here to discuss work or grab a quiet moment away from their desks. Although specialising in toasted sandwiches (US$2), the large menu also includes a number of filling Panamanian dishes (from US$4).

La Cascada Av Balboa, C 24. Enormous, surreal and tatty open-air restaurant, with a huge 16-page menu consisting largely of meat and seafood fried in breadcrumbs or grilled to death. Tables lit with multicoloured mushroom lights are set around a 30ft-high waterfall that tumbles over artificial rocks to feed a moat filled with goldfish and floating plastic ducks. Starting at US$6, most meals are far too large and rather tasteless, but the restaurant still seems to attract a crowd.

Coca-Cola C 12, Av Central, on Plaza Santa Ana. Self-proclaimed "oldest restaurant in Panama" and something of an institution for the city's older residents, who gather to drink coffee, read the papers and discuss the news. Filling Panamanian standards for about US$3, plus it's particularly good for breakfast.

Covadonga C 29, Av Perú, next to hotel of same name. 24hr restaurant with reasonably priced Panamanian and international food and some delicious Spanish specialities. Good for breakfast.

Manolo II Plaza Cinco de Mayo. A tranquil haven from the bustle of Avenida Central, this Spanish-run place specializes in meats and seafood, including a delicious *sopa de mariscos*.

Amador and San Felipe

El Arca Between C1 and C2. With a delightful patio setting, as well as indoor seating in a modern glass-fronted interior, *El Arca* serves tasty, if pricey, international food and occasionally screens art-house movies on the patio wall.

Las Bóvedas Plaza de Francia ⓣ 228 8068. Exquisite French cuisine from about US$20 a head, served under the arched brick ceilings of one of the old colonial dungeons. Excellent service with live jazz (Fri & Sat). Reservations advisable. Closed Sun.

Candelero Parque Bolívar. Smart bar and restaurant serving Panamanian cuisine including excellent set lunches for $2 and evening meals Thurs to Sat for US$5. Popular for lunch with workers from the Presidential Palace and the Ministry of the Interior.

Flags Calzador de Amador. Vast, modern open-fronted complex with four restaurants (featuring Panamanian and Italian cuisine as well as "Texan grill" and sushi) and a bar area, with great views of Panama City across the bay. It's particularly popular at the weekend when the central stage plays host to live music, including local salsa bands.

Drinking, nightlife and entertainment

Panama City is very much a 24-hour city, whose residents like nothing better than to cut loose and eat, drink and dance into the early hours. Most of the upmarket places are around El Cangrejo, Amador and Casco Viejo, and once in a particular neighbourhood it's easy and relatively safe to walk between venues at night. Many restaurants double as bars, and there are several discos and nightclubs, playing a mixture of reggae, salsa, merengue, and US and Euro dance music. Cover charges tend to be high, but often include several (sometimes unlimited) free drinks. Be warned that many of the more upmarket nightclubs operate an unofficial, racist policy whereby black Panamanians are effectively refused admission. At the other end of the market are the cantinas and bars around Av Central: hard-drinking dives where women are rarely seen. The wildest nightspots are out in the Afro-Antillan ghetto of Río Abajo, but it is not a good idea to go there unless accompanied by locals. Check the papers as well as ⓦwww.thepanamanews.com and ⓦwww.prensa.com for entertainment listings, including live music and theatre.

Bella Vista and El Cangrejo

Bacchus C 49A Este, Via España. Rather exclusive nightclub with impressive lightshow and massive sound system pumping out booming rave music. Women sometimes admitted free during the week; can be difficult to get into on Friday nights, despite the US$10 cover charge.

Beer House Via España, Via Argentina. Appropriately named, lively drinking dive with loud salsa and merengue and a young crowd.

Liquid Discothèque America Airlines Building, Plaza New York Via, C 50 ⓦwww.liquidpanama.com. Only place in town with a decent-sized dancefloor. Plays a range of music from Europop to House for the over-25 crowd. Cover charge of US$8.

El Pavo Real C 51E, C 50. "English" pub with darts, pool tables and live music every night from 11pm, popular with expatriates and wealthy Panamanians. Expensive drinks and food, including the inevitable fish and chips (US$6).

Space Plaza Obarrio on Via Brazil, Via España. Panama City's most popular gay nightclub, playing a selection of English and international electronic music and featuring cabaret shows. Karaoke on Thursday, but Friday and Saturday are most popular. Cover charge of US$3.

Las Tinajas Av 2 Sur (C 51E), Av Federico Boyd ⓣ269 3840. Restaurant and bar serving traditional Panamanian food. Folk dance shows Tues & Thurs–Sat from 9pm. Reservations recommended; US$5 cover charge. Closed Sun.

Amador, San Felipe and Santa Ana

844 C 1. Trendy nightspot catering to a thirtysomething crowd, with sushi bar on the ground floor, modern, lively Latin beats played on the first floor, and chilled-out tunes on the second floor. Thurs to Sat from 7pm to late.

Balboa Yacht Club beside the canal just off Av Amador. A good place for a drink while watching ships pass under the Bridge of the Americas. Drop by, too, to ask about work as a linehandler on private yachts transiting the canal.

El Barko Calzador de Amador. Nibble on seafood or down a sangría while listening to the salsa beats and checking out Panama City's beautiful people, who come to this huge open-air nightclub on Isla Flamenco, at the end of the Amador Causeway, to see and be seen.

Blu Room Martini Lounge C 1. Popular first stop for people making a night of it in Casco Viejo; the music is Latin, and it can be selective over its clientele – so dress smart.

Café de Asis Parque Bolívar. Upmarket Casco Viejo bar-café whose relaxed atmosphere makes it a fashionable place for couples seeking some privacy; there are also tables outside in the square for those who prefer the fresh air.

Entertainment

Panama City isn't renowned for its love of high culture, but there are a couple of good theatres featuring national and international productions – check local press for listings. The Teatro Balboa, Stevens' Circle, Balboa (ⓣ228 0327), hosts jazz, folk dancing and theatre sponsored by the National Cultural Institute, while the splendid Neoclassical Teatro Nacional, Av B, Plaza Bolívar (ⓣ262 3525), hosts theatre and ballet performances. Cinema is far more popular, and there are many places where you can see the latest Hollywood blockbusters, in English with subtitles – *La Prensa* ⓦwww.prensa.com) lists current screenings – with prices starting at US$1.50.

Panamanians of all social classes love to gamble, and as well as the ever-present lottery-ticket sellers the city has several tax-free casinos, all located in the major hotels: try the Fiesta at *El Panamá* or the Crown at the *Hotel Continental*.

Cockfighting, a bloody but immensely popular spectacle throughout the country, can be seen at *Club Gallistico* (Mon, Sat & Sun; ⓣ221 5652; US$1) on the corner of Via España and Via Cincuentenario. Horse-racing meetings are held three times a week at the Hipódromo Presidente Remón, via José Agustín Arango (ⓦwww.hipodromo.com), out in the eastern suburbs. If you're looking for something a bit more active, you can play a round of golf at the championship Summit Golf course (ⓦwww.summitgolfpanama.com), 25 minutes from the centre of the city in the Canal Zone – but out of driving range of the ships, lest you be tempted.

Listings

Airlines Aeroflot, Unicentro Bellavista, Av Justo Arosemena, C 41 ⓣ225 0622 or 0497; AeroMéxico, Av 1B Norte, El Cangrejo ⓣ263 3033; Aeroperlas, Aeropuerto Marcos A. Gelabert ⓣ315 7555 or 7500 and at C 57 and Via España; Air France, C Abel Bravo, C 59 ⓣ223 0204; Alitalia, C Alberto Navarro ⓣ269 2161; American, C 50, Plaza New York ⓣ269 6022; Avianca, Edificio Grobman, C Manuel M. Icaza ⓣ223 5225 or 264 3120; Continental, Edificio Galerías Balboa, Av Balboa ⓣ263 9177; COPA, Av Justo Arosemena, C 39 ⓣ227 2672 (24hrs); Cubana, C 29, Av Justo Arosemena ⓣ227 2291; Delta, C53E, Marbella ⓣ214 8118; Iberia, Av Balboa, C 43 ⓣ227 3966; KLM, Av Balboa, C Uruguay ⓣ264 6395; LanChile, C 72 San Francisco ⓣ226 7119; Lloyd Aereo Boliviano, Edificio Bolivia, C 50 ⓣ264 1330; Lufthansa, C Abel Bravo, C 59 ⓣ223 9208; Mapiex Aero, Aeropuerto Marcos A. Gelabert ⓣ315 0344; Singapore Airlines, C 52 and Ricardo Arias ⓣ264 9855; TACA, Via Ricardo J. Alfaro ⓣ360 2094; Turismo Aero, Aeropuerto Marcos A. Gelabert ⓣ315 0439 or 0278/9; United, C Colombia, Av 45 ⓣ225 3087; US Airways, Av 1B Norte, El Cangrejo ⓣ263 3033.

American Express 9th Floor, Torre BBVA, Av Balboa (Mon–Fri 9am–12pm; ⓣ225 5858).

Banks and exchange Branches of the Banco Nacional de Panamá (BNP) (Mon–Fri 8am–3pm, Sat 9am–noon) and Banistmo (Mon–Fri 8am–3.30pm, Sat 9am–noon) across the city change travellers' cheques and allow cash withdrawals on credit cards – most have ATMs. Both banks have branches on Via España in the heart of El Cangrejo. The closest to San Felipe is the BNP on the corner of Av Central and C 17 Este. Foreign currency is more difficult to change – foreign banks will generally change their own currency, and there is a licensed exchange house, Panacambios (Mon–Fri 8am–4pm; ⓣ223 1800), Plaza Regency Building, Via España, opposite the Rey supermarket.

Bookstores Exedra Books, Via Brazil, Via España. Large modern bookstore with café and Internet access (Mon–Sat 9.30am to 9.30pm, Sun 11am to 8.30pm); Libreria Argosy, at the junction of Via Argentina with Via España, has a wide collection in Spanish and English; Gran Morrison department store on Via España sells a good range of English-language books on Panama.

Car rental Avis: C D, El Cangrejo ⓣ213 0555 or 278 9444, Marcos A. Gelabert airport ⓣ315 0434, Tocumen airport ⓣ238 4056; Budget: C 55, El Cangrejo ⓣ214 6806 or 263 8777, Tocumen airport ⓣ238 4069; Hertz: C 55, El Cangrejo ⓣ263 6511, Tocumen airport ⓣ238 4081; National: C 50, El Cangrejo ⓣ265 3333 or 2222, Tocumen airport ⓣ238 4144; Thrifty: Via España, C 46 ⓣ264 3085 or 2613, Tocumen airport ⓣ238 4955.

Cycling Rali-Carretero, Via España and Av Argentina (ⓣ263 4136, ⓦwww.rali-carretero.com), has a good range of spare parts, including Shimano, and a maintenance centre.

Embassies and consulates Canada, World Trade Center, C 58 ⓣ264 9731; Colombia, C 53 Este ⓣ223 6111; Costa Rica, Av Samuel Lewis ⓣ264 2980; Cuba, Av Cuba, Av Ecuador ⓣ227 0359; El Salvador, Ave Manuel Espinosa Batista ⓣ223 3020; Germany, World Trade Center, C 53 ⓣ263 7733; Guatemala, Via Argentina ⓣ269 3475 or 3406; Honduras, Av Balboa ⓣ264 5513; Israel, C Manuel M. Icaza ⓣ264 8022; Italy, Av Balboa ⓣ225 8948; Mexico, C 58 Av, Samuel Lewis ⓣ263 4900; Nicaragua, Quarry Heights, Amador ⓣ211 2113; Spain, C 33, Ave Perú ⓣ227 5122; UK, Torre Swiss Bank, C 53E ⓣ269 0866; US, Av Balboa, C 40 ⓣ207 7000.

Immigration office The *migración* is on the corner of Av Cuba and C 29 (Mon–Fri 8am–3pm). Come here to extend your visa or to get permission to leave the country if you have been in Panama for over three months – for the latter you will also have to visit the office of Paz y Salvo (Mon–Fri 8.30am–4pm) in the Ministerio de Hacienda y Tesoro on Av Cuba at C 35. At both offices it's best to arrive early; take a ticket and be prepared to wait.

Internet access There's a large number of Internet cafés throughout the city, especially in El Cangrejo on Via Veneto, C 49B Oeste, a block up from Via España opposite the entrance to *Hotel El Panamá*. Rates typically run around $0.50/hr. For the "@" symbol, simultaneously press the Alt, 6 and 4 keys, and always remember to sign out after accessing an email account.

Language Schools Berlitz, Av Balboa and C Anastasio Ruiz ☎265 4800, www.berlitz.com; ILERI, Via La Amistad, El Dorado ☎260 4424; Spanish Learning Center, off Via Argentina, El Cangrejo ☎213 3121, www.spanishpanama.com. Flexible scheduling – from crash courses to long-term tutoring by professional teachers – as well as home stay with families or in dormitory and good day-tours for students.

Laundry Most hotels have a laundry service, and there are cheap, coin-operated *lavamaticos* all over the city. Lavandería y Lavamatico Katty on Av 1a Norte, US$3 for wash and dry service (Mon–Sat 7am–7pm & Sun 8am–3pm). Dry cleaning service next door.

Medical care Centro Medico Bella Vista, Av Perú, C 39 ☎227 4022 (open 24hrs); Centro Medico Paitilla, Av Balboa, C 53 ☎265 8800. Hospitals include the Hospital National, Av Cuba C 38 ☎207 8100.

Office supplies Office Express on Via España, opposite Rey supermarket, has a large selection.

Pharmacy Farmacia Arrocha, Via España, C 49E (open 24hrs).

Photography Fujifilm, C Manuel M. Icaza, Via España, is one of many places that sells and develops print and slide film; Panafoto, C 50 and Av Aquilino de la Guardia sells a large range of camera equipment, film and binoculars.

Police Emergencies ☎104; tourist police ☎270 2467.

Post office The most central post office is on Av Central at C 34, opposite the Don Bosco church; there's another in El Cangrejo in the Plaza de la Concordia shopping centre on Via España (both open Mon–Fri 7am–6pm, Sat 7am–5pm). Mailbox next to *Voyager International Hostel* (see p.754) handles DHL, Fedex, TNT and UPS.

Shopping Supermercado Rey has 24hr stores throughout the city, including one on Via España. Modern shopping centres include El Dorado on Av Ricardo J. Alfaro, Los Pueblos at Albrook bus terminal and Multicentro on Av Israel.

Swimming pool Piscina Olímpica Adan Gordon, C31, Av Cuba, US$0.50.

Telephones Public phone booths throughout the city take US$5, US$10 and US$20 phonecards and some take coins. The main Cable & Wireless office (Mon–Fri 7.15am–6.30pm, Sat 7.30am–2.00pm) is in the Banco Nacional building on Via España. Calls cost US$0.10, US$0.25 and US$0.35 per minute for local, long distance and mobile calls respectively. Most Internet cafés offer cheap international calls for about US$0.25 per minute (US$1.50 for first minute).

Moving on from Panama City

Panama City is the **transportation hub** of the country, home to most bus companies, express bus services, and flights. **Domestic buses** – except for those bound for nearby Gamboa – depart from the Albrook terminal (see p.750). There's no need to **book** bus tickets in advance, unless it's for the express bus service to David or the international bus to San José. A short taxi ride away (about US$1) from the bus terminal, Albrook airport – officially known as Marcos A. Gelabert – is the departure point for all **domestic flights**. Most flights leave early in the morning; indeed, this is the better time to fly, as later in the day the thermals rising from the land buffet the light aircraft used on the routes. The only train station serving the city is at Corozal, 2km north of the bus terminal. Although the **transisthmian railway** (☎316 6070, www.panarail.com) is primarily a freight train and runs only to the Caribbean coastal city of Colón, an air-conditioned observation car offers tourists the chance to see the Panama Canal by rail. The train departs at 7.15am, arriving an hour later, and makes the return trip at 5.15pm (US$20 one way, US$35 return).

All of the main **tour operators** are based in Panama City, with specialist outfits eager to whisk you off on whitewater rafting adventures, diving trips, eco-tours or even surfing holidays.

Tourism companies

A number of operators in Panama City offer a range of **guided day-trips**, from historic city tours to canal transits, with a handful of specialist tour companies offering **adventure tours**, from multi-day trekking trips in Darién to diving excursions in the Caribbean.

Moving on from Panama City

All buses – with the exception of those to Gamboa, which leave from the terminal at Plaza Cinco de Mayo – depart from the modern Terminal de Buses in Albrook.

Destination	Frequency	Duration	Distance
Almirante	2 daily	12hr	574km
Chitré	hourly	4hr	251km
Colón	every 20min	1hr 30min	76km
Colón (express)	every 20min	1hr	76km
David	hourly	7hr	438km
David (express)	2 daily	5hr	438km
El Valle	every 30min	2hr 30min	134km
Gamboa	8 daily	45min	26km
Las Tablas	every 2hr	4hr 30min	283km
Meteti	7 daily	7–8hr	225km
Ocú	8 daily	4hr	228km
Paso Canoas	9 daily	9hr	494km
Paso Canoas (express)	2 daily	7hr	494km
Penonomé	every 20min	2hr 30min	150km
Santiago	every 30min	4hr	250km
Sona (for Santa Catalina)	every 20min	5hr	295km

International bus service from Panama City

To **San José, Costa Rica** Ticabus, Albrook ⓣ314 6385, ⓦwww.ticabus.com. One bus daily, 11am departure, 14–15hr; US$25 one way.

Domestic flights from Panama City

All flights leave from Marcos A. Gelabert domestic airport in Albrook. The only operators are Aeroperlas (ⓣ315 7500, ⓦwww.aeroperlas.com), Mapiex Aero (ⓣ315 0888, ⓦwww.aero.com.pa) and Turismo Aero (ⓣ315 0439). All internal flights (US$30–60) have maximum weight limits of 25lbs, which sometimes includes carry-on luggage; excess is charged at US$0.30–0.50 per pound.

Destination	Frequency	Duration	Operator
Bocas del Toro	4-5 daily	1hr	Aeroperlas, Mapiex Aero
Changuinola	4 daily	1hr 10min	Aeroperlas, Mapiex Aero
Chitré	3 daily	40min	Aeroperlas, Turismo Aero
Colón	2 daily	15min	Aeroperlas
Contadora	2 daily	15min	Aeroperlas
David	6 daily	1hr	Aeroperlas, Mapiex Aero
El Real	3 weekly	1hr	Aeroperlas
Garachiné	3 weekly	1hr 15min	Turismo Aero
Jaqué	3 weekly	1hr 10min	Aeroperlas
La Palma	3 weekly	1hr 25min	Aeroperlas
Sambú	3 weekly	1hr 20min	Turismo Aero
San Miguel	4 weekly	45min	Turismo Aero

To Kuna Yala: Daily to (30min–1hr 15min): El Porvenir, Río Sidra, Corazón de Jesús, Playon Chico, Tupile, Cartí, Ailigandi, Achutupo, Ustupo, Mulatupo and Puerto Obaldia. Flights are operated by Aeroperlas and depart from Marcos A. Gelabert domestic airport in Albrook. Be prepared for substantial delays and cancellations without warning, including the return leg.

ANCON Expeditions Edificio El Dorado, C Elvira Mendez ⓣ269 9415, ⓦwww.anconexpeditions.com. The highly professional commercial arm of the National Conservation Association offers Panama's best ecotours, with trips throughout the country and enthusiastic bilingual guides. From day-trips around the canal to week-long tours visiting some of the best natural environments in the country, some of which include stays at exclusive jungle lodges at Cana and Punta Patiño in Darién Province.

Aventuras Panamá ⓣ260 0044, ⓦwww.aventuraspanama.com. Established in 1994, the company runs whitewater rafting and kayaking trips in Chagres National Park and in Chiriquí. The rainy season, from June to December, is the best time for rafting, thanks to the higher water levels.

Canal and Bay Tours ⓣ314 1349 and 350 1353, ⓦwww.canalandbaytours.com. Partial canal cruises every Saturday and full transits once a month. Tours include food, drinks and entertainment and depart from Muelle 18 in Balboa.

Gamboa Tours Next to the *Holiday Inn*, Av Manuel E. Batista ⓣ269 1262, ⓦwww.gamboatours.com. Although it primarily arranges tours for those staying at the *Gamboa Rainforest Resort*, located 27km from Panama City in the Parque Nacional Soberanía, the company's day-trips, which include the Canal & City Tour and the Meet the Embera Indians Tour, are open to all. They can also arrange helicopter rental.

Margo Tours also called EcoMargo and Ecocircuitos C 51 ⓣ264 5339 or 4001, ⓦwww.margotours.com. Tours generally focusing on Panama's environment (among them 15-day Neotropical Ecology courses, birdwatching outings and three-day trips to *Burbayar* jungle lodge at Nusagandi), but also including historic tours of Casco Viejo and sea-kayaking trips down the Río Chagres.

Panamá Surf Tours 1st Floor, Sun Towers, Av Ricardo J. Alfaro, Bethania ⓣ236 8303 or 7069, ⓦwww.panamasurftours.com. A number of flexible surfing trips, with destinations around the country, including Bocas del Torro, Playa Santa Catalina and Playa Venao, led by local surfers.

Scuba Panamá Av 6 Norte, C 62A ⓣ261 3841, ⓦwww.scubapanama.com. Countrywide diving excursions, equipment sale and rental, and diving instruction. Diving trips range in length from a day to a week in locales on both sides of the isthmus – including the specialist "Two Oceans and the Panama Canal in One Day" for those looking to tick a few more boxes off on their diving checklist.

7.2

The Canal and Colón Province

Running 80km across the isthmus between the Atlantic and Pacific oceans, the **Panama Canal** is one of the greatest engineering feats of all time and, not surprisingly, the country's biggest visitor attraction, a sight that's easily explored on a day-trip from Panama City. Quite apart from its sheer magnitude, the canal also possesses an unexpected, rugged beauty. Though the corridor that surrounds this vital thoroughfare is home to almost two-thirds of Panama's population, for much of its length the canal cleaves a narrow path through pristine rainforest, large tracts of which are protected within **Parque Nacional Soberanía** and on **Isla Barro Colorado**. The former is one of the most accessible tropical rainforest preserves in Latin America, and both of them support an exceptional degree of biodiversity. The quiet town of **Gamboa** is the embarkation point for trips to the island, and it's also an easy 30-minute walk from here to the premier birding site of **Pipeline Road**. Soberanía and the larger, somewhat less accessible Parque Nacional Chagres also offer the opportunity to walk along the remnants of the partially cobbled **Camino de las Cruces** and the **Camino Real** – mule trains carved across the forested spine of the isthmus in colonial times to provide a convenient route by which Spain's accumulated treasures could be transported from Panama City to the Caribbean.

From 1903 to 1977 the strip of land that extends for five miles on either side of the canal was de facto US territory, an area known as the **Canal Zone**. The last US military bases closed at the end of 1999, when control of the canal was finally handed over to Panama, but the well-ordered society the US established in the Canal Zone still remains, in delicious contrast to the tropical disorder and vibrant Caribbean culture of **Colón** and the surrounding coast, whose inhabitants are descended from the workers brought in to build the waterway. Situated at the canal's Atlantic entrance, Colón is an infamously poor and dangerous – yet strangely compelling – city steeped in history, while the Caribbean coast of Colón Province offers a perfect antidote to its namesake city's sometimes depressing squalor. To the west, along the **Costa Abajo**, the formidable ruins of the colonial **Fort San Lorenzo** still guard the mouth of the Río Chagres amid untouched tropical rainforest; while to the northeast the **Costa Arriba** is an isolated region of pristine coral reefs and laid back fishing villages, much of which is protected by the **Parque Nacional Portobelo**, set around the ruins of the old Spanish ports of **Portobelo** and **Nombre de Dios**.

The Canal and around

Although Panamanians are keen to insist that their country is "much more than just a canal", the truth of the matter is that the **Panama Canal** remains the country's defining feature, the basis of its economy and the key to its history. Were it not for the US government's determination to build it, Panama might never have come into existence as an independent republic; nonetheless, it is also the root cause of

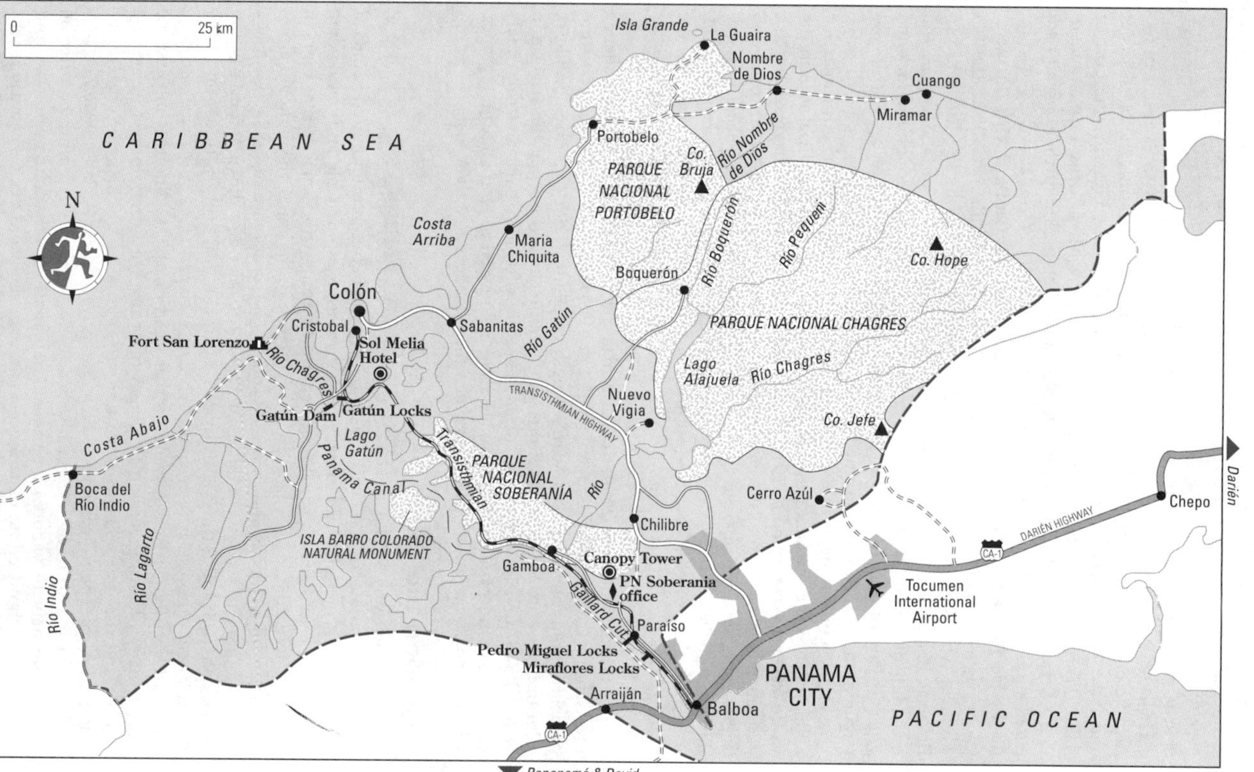

0 25 km
N
CARIBBEAN SEA
Isla Grande
La Guaira
Nombre de Dios
Cuango
Miramar
Portobelo
Co. Bruja
Río Nombre de Dios
PARQUE NACIONAL PORTOBELO
Costa Arriba
Maria Chiquita
Boquerón
Río Boquerón
Río Pequeni
Co. Hope
Colón
Cristobal
Sabanitas
Río Gatún
PARQUE NACIONAL CHAGRES
Fort San Lorenzo
Sol Melia Hotel
Río Chagres
Lago Alajuela
Río Chagres
Gatún Dam
Gatún Locks
TRANSISTHMIAN HIGHWAY
Nuevo Vigia
Co. Jefe
Costa Abajo
Lago Gatún
Panama Canal
Transisthmian
PARQUE NACIONAL SOBERANÍA
Río
Cerro Azúl
Boca del Río Indio
Chilibre
Chepo
Darién
DARIÉN HIGHWAY
CA-1
Río Lagarto
ISLA BARRO COLORADO NATURAL MONUMENT
Gamboa
Canopy Tower
PN Soberania office
Tocumen International Airport
Río Indio
Gaillard Cut
Paraíso
Pedro Miguel Locks
Miraflores Locks
PANAMA CITY
Arraiján
Balboa
PACIFIC OCEAN
CA-1
Penonomé & David

the US's deeply resented influence and interventions in national affairs. The struggle to establish control of the canal was central to the emergence of a Panamanian identity, and though after more than ninety years the waterway was finally handed over to Panamanian jurisdiction at midnight on December 31, 1999, its future remains one of the most controversial issues in Panamanian politics.

The canal's **configuration** is such that the Pacific entrance is 43.2km east of the Atlantic entrance. From the Bahía de Panamá on the Pacific side, the canal passes under the broad sweep of the Bridge of the Americas and alongside the port of Balboa, running at sea level some 6km inland to the **Miraflores Locks**, where ships are raised some 16.5m to Lago de Miraflores. About 2km further on, ships are raised another 10m to the canal's maximum elevation of 26.5m above sea level by the **Pedro Miguel Locks**, beyond which they enter the **Gaillard Cut** (formerly known as Culebra, but renamed in honour of Colonel William Gaillard, the US engineer who was responsible for its excavation). Described by the English Lord Bryce as "the greatest liberty ever taken with nature", Culebra was the deepest and most difficult section of the canal construction, a 13.6km cut through the rock and shifting shale of the continental divide. An enormous amount of excavation was required, and the work was plagued by devastating landslides.

After the confinement of the Gaillard Cut, the canal channel continues for 37.6km across the broad expanse of **Lago Gatún**, the largest artificial lake in the world when it was formed in 1913 by the damming of the Río Chagres. Covering 420 square kilometres, the lake is tranquil and stunningly beautiful; until you see an ocean-going ship appear from behind one of the densely forested headlands, it is difficult to believe that it forms part of one of the busiest waterways in the world. At the lake's far end ships are brought back down to sea level in three stages by the **Gatún Locks**, easily visited from Colón, after which they run 3km through a narrow cut into the calm Caribbean waters of Bahía Limón.

Since taking control in 2000, the Autoridad del Canal de Panamá has widened the Gaillard Cut to allow two-way traffic of "Panamax" vessels (the largest ships capable of transiting the locks, with a length of 294m, width of 32m and draft of 12m in fresh water), and in 2002 dredging commenced to deepen the navigation channel and increase the water-storage capacity of Gatún Lake and the canal's watershed output. The toll structure has also been revised to help increase revenues, which annually are now higher than when the US controlled the canal.

Exploring the canal

By far the best way to experience the canal is by **boat or ship** – passing through the narrow confines of the Gaillard Cut or weaving between the forested islands of Lago Gatún is the only way to truly appreciate its awesome scale and outstanding beauty. The easiest way is to take an **organized tour** with Canal & Bay Tours in Panama City (see p.771). A half-day, partial transit of the canal, through Miraflores and Pedro Miguel locks and into the Gaillard Cut, costs around US$100, while a full-day complete transit, continuing into Lago Gatún and down through Gatún Locks, costs US$150 – the company runs a partial transit every Saturday and a full transit once a month. Alternatively, ANCON Expeditions run excellent daily Panama Canal Jungle Boat Adventures that focus on the wildlife that inhabits the canal's many islands, including five types of primate, ospreys, sloths, toucans and iguanas, and also give you the opportunity to ride alongside the giant vessels transiting the canal. The tour includes lunch on a private island (US$99; see p.771).

The other way to travel the canal by boat is to get taken on as a **linehandler** on one of the private yachts that transit the canal – each yacht must take four linehandlers, who need no experience and are usually paid US$20–30 a day for the one- or two-day trip. The best way to find work is to visit the Panama Canal Yacht Club in Cristóbal, on the Caribbean side from where most transits commence, and talk with yacht owners; there's a notice board where you can offer your services, but direct contact is better. From the Pacific side try the Balboa Yacht Club, near the Bridge of the Americas, and the new Flamenco Marina at the end of the causeway.

Much of the canal can also be explored by **land**. A road served eight times daily by buses from the Panama City terminal on Plaza Cinco de Mayo runs 26km along the side of the canal, past the Miraflores and Pedro Miguel locks, to the town of Gamboa near Lago Gatún, passing the entrance to Parque Nacional Soberanía. This journey is described below; if time is short, you can easily find a taxi in Panama City to take you to Miraflores, wait for an hour or so and take you back for about US$15. The Gatún Locks, on the Caribbean side, can also be visited via Colón. The **transisthmian railway** (Ⓣ316 6070, Ⓦwww.panarail.com), which runs along the east side of the canal, was reopened for passengers in 2003 after being closed for more than a decade. Though still primarily for moving freight between Panama City and Colón, a passenger train is laid on for those working in Colón's Free Zone that incorporates an air-conditioned observation car exclusively for tourists. The train leaves from the station at Corozal, 2km north of Albrook bus terminal, for Colón at 7.15am and departs Colón at 5.15pm; the journey lasts one hour and costs US$20 one way or US$35 return and is an excellent way of seeing the canal and the surrounding rainforest.

Even experienced divers, jaded with the undersea wonders of the Caribbean and Pacific, should make an effort to **dive** in the Panama Canal. Huge amounts of machinery and entire villages were submerged by the rising waters of Lago Gatún, making for an unusual underwater attraction. Trips can be arranged through Scuba Panamá (see p.771).

The road to Gamboa

Those looking to visit the canal by land and explore other sites within the Canal Zone can hire a taxi or catch a bus for the 26km ride from Panama City to the sleepy town of Gamboa, which takes you past the Miraflores and Pedro Miguel lock complexes and runs alongside the Parque Nacional Soberanía. Buses leave hourly from the Plaza Cinco de Mayo (US$0.80), though if you want to stop at various points along the way you're better off hiring a taxi in the city (US$10–15/hr), which will enable you to stop at the Miraflores Locks, explore the Summit Botanical Gardens and Zoo or ride the aerial tram through the rainforest canopy at the *Gamboa Rainforest Resort*.

Miraflores Locks

The road to Gamboa leaves Panama City to the north through a series of former US military bases, known as the "reverted areas", which were handed over to Panama in the 1990s. One of these, Fort Clayton – once the nerve centre of US military operations throughout Latin America and the Caribbean – has been converted into an international university campus known as El Ciudad del Saber (the City of Knowledge). Opposite Clayton, 9km from Panama City, a side road leads a short distance to the **Miraflores Locks**, which raise and lower ships the 16.5m between sea level and Lago Miraflores in two stages, each using 197 million litres of fresh water, which flows through culverts 5m in diameter to fill each lock chamber in just ten minutes. Because of the extreme tidal variations in the Pacific, the first lock gates at Miraflores are the biggest in the whole system, each reaching 25m in height and weighing a colossal 730 tons. The gates open in just two minutes, and ships are guided through by electric locomotives known as mules, taking thirty minutes. The **new visitor complex** at the Miraflores Locks (daily 9am–5pm; free; Ⓦwww.pancanal.com) has several observation decks, a café and a restaurant, exhibition halls and shop, with guided commentary in English and Spanish when vessels transit the locks. The **best times** to see ships passing through are between 8 and 10.30am, when they come up from the Pacific side, and after 3pm, when they complete their descent from the Atlantic side.

Some 1.5km further up the road, the **Pedro Miguel Locks** raise ships to the level of Lago Gatún. There are no special facilities, but you can watch ships here, too. After the Pedro Miguel Locks, ships enter the Gaillard Cut, which cannot be seen from land. Instead, the road continues 1km to the small canal town of Paraíso, a little way beyond which on the left is the **French Cemetery**, which sits on the continental divide, one of the few remaining traces of the doomed French attempts to build a canal in the 1880s. There's not much to see other than the many small white crosses on the graves, in which a generation of France's finest engineers lie buried, but the place has the solemn atmosphere of a war cemetery. The road then climbs some 2km to the new German-built cable-stayed **bridge**, whose carriage-way towers some eighty metres above the canal and when completed in 2005 will provide a second link between the east and west of the country, easing congestion on the Bridge of the Americas. Three kilometres further on through dense rainforest the road forks: the road on the right cuts through the Parque Nacional Soberanía and travels another 9km to the Transisthmian Highway, which links Panama City with Colón, while the left-hand fork continues on to Gamboa. At the fork itself is the **Parque Nacional Soberanía office** (daily 8am–4pm; ⓣ232 7228), which provides information on the trails and, if arranged in advance, guides for larger groups. Officially, there is a US$3 charge for admission, but this is rarely requested.

Summit Botanical Gardens

Heading toward Gamboa from the fork, you'll pass the championship course at the Summit Golf Club (see p.768) and reach the **Summit Botanical Gardens and Zoo** (daily 8am–4pm; US$1). Established by the US in 1923, the gardens are home to more than fifteen thousand different plant species, including one of the world's largest collections of palm trees, spread throughout the landscaped grounds. Handed over to Panama in 1979, it's now a popular weekend destination for families from the capital, most of whom come for the zoo. Examples of most of Panama's large mammals are imprisoned here in the name of environmental education, including pumas, jaguars, ocelots and several species of monkey. The tapirs get a better deal thanks to funding from Houston Zoo for their new, spacious enclosure. There is also a captive breeding programme for the harpy eagle, Panama's endangered national symbol. Most have wild relatives in the surrounding forest, but your chances of seeing them are slim.

Gamboa

Continuing along the rainforest-flanked road for another 7km from the botanical gardens, the landscape begins to open up as it approaches the security cameras and razor-wire fences that protect the perimeter of "*El Renacer*" (the Reborn) low-security **prison**, which also marks where the canal channel emerges from the Gaillard Cut and follows the flooded bed of the Río Chagres into **Lago Gatún**. A one-way road and rail bridge crosses the Río Chagres before the road reaches **GAMBOA**, where the headquarters of the Canal Dredging Division are based. Today, Gamboa is something of a ghost town, as most canal workers now commute from Panama City, but many of its large wooden houses, built by the US in the 1930s, are now being purchased by eminent Panamanians and scientists with the aim of revitalising the small community. The **Smithsonian Tropical Research Institute** has a significant presence here, occupying a number of properties in the town, and their small dock is the jumping-off point for trips to Isla Barro Colorado (BCI), the principal site for their tropical research. Several hundred metres north of Gamboa is the entrance to Pipeline Road (Camino del Oleoducto), a 24km trail through the Parque Nacional Soberanía and one of the world's premier birding sites (see p.778). Amenities in the town are few at present, but they do include an ATM and a small shop. At the back of the town, one of the wooden houses has been restored and converted into *B&B Gamboa*. With four small dormitory rooms and a one-room apartment, the B&B is ideally located for access to the surrounding rainforest: be sure to contact the English-speaking owners, who will also rent you bicycles, in advance (☎213 3121, ⓦwww.spanishpanama.com; ❷).

Gamboa Rainforest Resort

Just outside of Gamboa, the *Gamboa Rainforest Resort* (☎314 9000, ⓦwww.gamboaresort.com; ❾) is the most ambitious of the new tourism developments to spring up around the canal in the wake of the US withdrawal. Set in the midst of the rainforest overlooking the Chagres at the point at which it flows into Lago Gatún, the massive hotel is rather overpriced, but it's worth visiting as a day-trip from Panama City for a ride on the **aerial tram** (daily 8.30am–4.30pm; US$35). Rather like a ski-lift transferred to the tropics, the tram climbs silently through the rainforest canopy for about 600 metres, offering a view of the forest ecosystem very different to what you see at ground level, plus a good chance of spotting wildlife, particularly monkeys and birds. At the summit an observation tower offers a spectacular panorama over the canal, the lake and the Río Chagres, winding lazily through dense vegetation. The ticket price includes guided tours of a butterfly house, an orchid nursery, a serpentarium (where some of Panama's most dangerous snakes are on display) and an aquarium with freshwater fish and reptiles. Also within the grounds of the resort, the *Restaurante Los Lagartos*, next to the small marina, serves excellent, if expensive, food, including a three-course lunch buffet with large plates for US$18. From the terrace over the lake, you get the chance to watch common slider turtles basking on floating logs, large peacock bass and the occasional spectacled caiman.

Isla Barro Colorado

As the waters of Lago Gatún began to rise after the damming of the Chagres, much of the wildlife in the surrounding forest was forced to take refuge on points of high ground that later became islands. One of these, **Barro Colorado** (BCI), administered by the Smithsonian Tropical Research Institute, is among the most intensively studied areas of tropical rainforest in the world. Though the primary aims of the reserve are conservation and research, you can visit by contacting the Smithsonian in the Panama City suburb of Ancón (☎212 8026, ⓦwww.stri.org) – call well in advance, as visitor numbers are strictly limited and the waiting list is very long, though there are sometimes cancellations. The four- to six-hour **tour** (daily except Monday and Thursday; US$70), conducted in English or Spanish by extremely knowledgeable guides, provides an excellent introduction to tropical rainforest ecology and the chance to see myriad species of bird, monkeys and tapirs. The outing, the fee for which includes lunch and the boat trip across the lake, starts promptly at 7.15am weekdays and 8am weekends from the pier in Gamboa.

Parque Nacional Soberanía

Stretching along the eastern flank of the canal, the 220-square-kilometre **Parque Nacional Soberanía** provides essential protection for the rainforest-covered watershed that is so vital for the canal's continued operation. Just half an hour from Panama City by road, Soberanía is the most easily accessible national park in Panama and is popular with local Panamanians and tourists alike, most of whom spend just a few hours exploring the park on one of the **trails**. All of the park's trails are well-signposted and pass over rugged terrain cloaked in pristine rainforest, offering reasonable chances of seeing monkeys and innumerable birds, or if you're lucky, large mammals such as deer or tapir. Entry to the park is US$3 per person, though there is not always a warden on hand to issue tickets.

The **Sendero El Charco**, the shortest and best-marked trail, begins a few kilometres beyond the Summit Botanical Gardens on the road to Gamboa, stretches for about 4km and takes about an hour to walk. The second trail, the old **Pipeline Road**, starts a few hundred metres outside Gamboa and holds the world record as the place in which the highest number of bird species were identified in a 24-hour period, the tally of 360 set by the Audubon Society in 1996. The trail stretches for 24km, ending on the shores of Lago Gatún, and so is too long to walk in a day.

The third trail is a remnant of the **Camino de las Cruces**, the colonial mule trail from Panama City to the now abandoned village of Venta de las Cruces, where cargo was transferred to boats and taken down the Río Chagres to the Caribbean. The trailhead is marked by an old cannon near the park office along the Gaillard Highway, which forks right off the Gamboa Road and cuts across to the village of Chilibre on the Transisthmian Highway from Panama City to Colón. The trail is still partially paved and runs about 10km through pristine rainforest to the banks of the Río Chagres, so you can either walk some distance down it and retrace your steps, or hire a boat in Gamboa to take you up the Chagres to Venta de las Cruces at the other end of the trail and walk back to the highway.

Just past Summit Gardens on the road to Gamboa, a right turn into the heart of Parque Nacional Soberanía takes you to the **Canopy Tower** (☎214 9724 or 264 5720, Ⓦwww.canopytower.com; ❾; advance booking required), a former US radar station that has been converted into one of Latin America's most unusual eco-lodges. The tower is basically a fifteen-metre-high aluminium tube topped by a large geodesic dome that has been stripped of all military equipment and refitted with brightly painted rooms and windows looking out onto the forest, though at US$130 for a basic room (with shared bathroom) they don't exactly go cheap. The tower also houses a communal dining room with hammocks and a small ecological library. At the top of the tower, an open-air gallery offers a panoramic, canopy-level view of the surrounding rainforest, the canal and the skyscrapers of Panama City. The *Canopy Tower* is hugely popular with birdwatchers, particularly in October and March when migrating hawks and vultures pass over in their thousands. The lodge's exclusive tours to the surrounding rainforest, including Pipeline Road, are led by some of the best bird guides in Central America, but will often incur an additional cost.

The Transisthmian Highway and Parque Nacional Chagres

From Panama City the **Transisthmian Highway** – the Transistmica – passes through the city's northern suburbs, over the continental divide and across the Río Chagres to Colón. East of the Transistmica as it crosses the Chagres is **Lago Alajuela**, an artificial lake formed after the completion of the Madden Dam in 1934 which provides forty percent of the water needed for the operation of the canal as well as all of Panama City's drinking water. The lake's watershed is protected by the **Parque Nacional Chagres**, 1290 square kilometres of mountainous rainforest comprising four different life zones that are home to more than three hundred species of bird, as well as several Emberá (see p.789) communities displaced by the flooding of Lago Bayano further east. It's relatively easy to visit the park as a day-trip from the capital: take any slow bus from Panama City to Colón and ask the bus driver to let you off 29km from Panama City at the turn-off for the lakeside village of **Nuevo Vigia**; then either walk the few kilometres to the village or wait for one of the irregular local buses. At Nuevo Vigia you can rent a motorized dugout canoe for about US$25, plus gas, to take you across the lake and up either the Río Pequeni or Río Chagres into the park. The Emberá communities of **San Juan de Pequeni** and **Parrara Puru** (at the mouth of the Chagres) both accept visitors and are keen to sell handicrafts (wood carvings and the like) which they produce to supplement the subsistence hunting and agroforestry which are the only other economic activities they are allowed to practise in the park.

When water levels permit you can also visit the park by **whitewater rafting** down the Río Chagres to the lake, an exciting one-day trip from Panama City, through level II and III rapids which are promoted as the "Chagres Challenge". The main operator is Aventuras Panamá (see p.771), though most Panama City tour agencies are able to book the trip.

It is still possible to walk along the remains of the **Camino Real** through the park to Portobelo (4 days) or Nombre de Dios (2–3 days), though this is only recommended if you have plenty of tropical wilderness experience – and be sure to inform ANAM in Panama City before any such outing. The trailhead is at the village of **Boquerón**, 12km off the Transistmica from a turn-off just beyond the one to Nuevo Vigia; you may be able to find a guide in the village to take you, but don't count on it. You'll need a good map, a compass, a machete, food and equipment to survive for several days alone in the rainforest.

Colón and around

In all the world there is not, perhaps, now concentrated in a single spot so much swindling and villainy, so much foul disease, such a hideous dung-heap of moral and physical abomination as in the scene of this far-fetched undertaking of nineteenth-century engineering.

James Anthony Froude, British journalist, 1886

Situated at the Atlantic entrance to the Panama Canal, with a population approaching 150,000, **COLÓN** represents the dark side of the Caribbean that never makes it into the holiday brochures and to most Panamanians its name is a byword for poverty, violence and urban decay. Although nineteenth-century British journalist James Anthony Froude never visited Panama's second city, claiming that his curiosity was less strong than his disgust, his opinion of Colón during the French canal construction was widely shared by his contemporaries and were he to visit the city today he would find little to change his mind. To a certain extent, Colón's reputation is not without reason – much of the city is a run-down slum, the streets strewn with rubbish and rife with violent crime. But despite decades of terminal decline, Colón retains the decadent charm of a steamy Caribbean port where pretty much anything goes, its former glory still evident in its many monuments and crumbling architecture. Moreover, if you can get past the initial hostility and suspicion, the people of Colón, mostly descendants of West Indians who came here to build the canal, are as warm and friendly as anywhere in the country, and they enjoy a lively street culture that helps offset the desperate poverty that most of them face. Most visitors to Colón come here solely to shop at the **Colón Free Zone**, a walled enclave where goods from all over the world can be bought at very low prices – the starkest possible contrast to the rest of the city, which these visitors avoid assiduously. Next to the Free Zone, a similar enclave known as Colón 2000 has been set up in the hopes of luring passengers from the many cruise ships that pass through the canal, but it has little to offer besides souvenir shops. Southwest of Colón, a road runs through the reverted area of Fort Davis to the **Gatún Locks**, where ships are raised and lowered between sea level and Lago Gatún, and on to **San Lorenzo**, an impressive colonial fortress overlooking the mouth of the Río Chagres.

Safety in Colón

Although sometimes exaggerated, Colón's reputation throughout the rest of the country for **violent crime** is not undeserved, and if you come here you should exercise extreme caution – mugging, even on the main streets in broad daylight, does happen. Don't carry anything you can't afford to lose, try and stay in sight of the police on the main streets, and consider renting a taxi to take you around, both as a guide and for protection. They charge about US$7 an hour. For those visiting nearby **Coco Solo** to enquire about boats to Colombia extra caution is required, as this small port can make even Colón feel like a welcome paradise.

Some history

Founded in 1852 on filled-in mangrove swamps as the Caribbean terminal of the transisthmian railway, Colón was originally named Aspinwall after one of the railway's owners. The Colombian authorities' insistence that it be called Colón, after Christopher Columbus, led to a long-running dispute that only ended because letters from the US addressed to Aspinwall never reached their destination. The railway brought many immigrants and a degree of prosperity to the town, and though it slipped into decline in 1869 when the completion of the transcontinental railway in the US reduced traffic across the isthmus, its fortunes revived with the initiation of the French canal construction in 1879. The French founded the neighbouring port enclave of Cristóbal, and vast quantities of men and material flowed through Colón, but it remained a poor, disease-ridden slum town famed for its depravity. Burned to the ground during an 1885 uprising led by **Pedro Prestan**, a Haitian rebel later hanged in front of huge crowds on Front Street, the city was rebuilt by the French and prospered again during the US canal construction effort. Colón's heyday came in the 1950s, when it was among the most fashionable cruise destinations in the Caribbean, but despite its role as Panama's main port and the success of the Free Zone (founded in 1949), the city slipped into gradual decline and the cruise ships stopped coming. Although the port and Free Zone continue to thrive, little of the money they generate stays in Colón, indeed many of the workers in these areas are bussed in from Panama City. In the face of urban poverty as extreme as any in Latin America and unemployment levels approaching fifty percent, it is little surprise that many have turned to **crime**, particularly drug trafficking, as a way to survive. In recent years cruise-ship traffic has increased dramatically with some 200,000 passengers arriving every year and it is not uncommon to have six huge cruise ships docked around Colón at any one time. So lucrative is this market that more facilities, including waste treatment, are being constructed here in the hope of turning Colón into an official cruise-ship port in an attempt to rival Miami. Unfortunately for the local population, the passengers are piled onto luxury buses and driven away in convoy on their day-trips, none of which include a city tour of Colón.

Arrival and information

The **bus terminal** is on the corner of Av del Frente and C 13. Buses arrive from and leave for Panama City every 20 minutes between 4am and 10pm, with buses to and from Portobelo running twice an hour from 5am to 8pm. If you arrive by **ship** from Kuna Yala, you'll come in at Coco Solo port, a US$3 taxi ride from the city centre. **Yachts** coming through the canal dock outside the Panama Canal Yacht Club in Cristóbal. France's Field, Colón's **airport**, is a short taxi ride outside the city: Aeroperlas has two **flights** a day between Panama City and Colón, used mainly by business people visiting the Free Zone, but you'd have to be in a real hurry to want to fly here, given the short distance between the two cities by land.

There is an **IPAT** office in Colón (Mon–Fri 8am–4pm; ⓣ441 9644), on Av Balboa close to C 9, but they don't have much information and will be very surprised to see you. The **post office** and a branch of the **Banco Nacional** are just around the corner on C 9; there are several more banks in the Free Zone.

Accommodation

There's a wide choice of **places to stay** in Colón, catering mostly to business people, and most of them would be seen as good value in any other city. If you are going to stay overnight, it's worth splashing out on a more expensive hotel with armed security and a restaurant so you won't have to go out at night.

Hotel Internacional Av Bolívar, C 11 ⓣ445 2930. Secure, with clean, spacious rooms with a/c, TV and hot water. Good restaurant and a rooftop bar. ⑤

Hotel Sotelo Av Guerrero, C 11 ⓣ441 7703. Small and dark, but with clean rooms with TV and a/c. There's also a bar, restaurant and casino. ⑤

New Washington Hotel Av Frente, C 2

Ⓣ441 7133, Ⓔnwh@sinfo.net. The best in town, in a recently refurbished historic building in elegant French style. The comfortable rooms have hot water, a/c and TV, while those at the front have balconies overlooking the sea. It's very secure and has a swimming pool, bar, restaurant, casino and parking. ❼

Pension Acropolis Av Guerrero, C 11 Ⓣ441 1456. Basic, with communal bathrooms; the best budget option in a moderately safe part of town. ❷

Sol Melia Hotel Fort Gulick Ⓣ470 1100, Ⓦwww.solmelia.com. The modern 300-room hotel is situated on a peninsula overlooking Lago Gatún, roughly 8km south of the city at Fort Gulick. This was once the site of the US Army's infamous School of the Americas, where various Latin American military officers underwent counterinsurgency training – a far cry from the luxury hotel that now stands here. The hotel has a vast swimming pool, large rooms with all the essential luxuries, restaurants and bars as well as surf kayaks for rent to tour the lake. ❽

The City

From the bus terminal, a left turn takes you north up dilapidated **Front Street** (Av del Frente), once the city's main commercial road, which runs along the waterfront of Bahía Limón. Most of the shops are closed and the elegant two- and three-storey buildings with pillared overhanging balconies are crumbling, their faded pastel paintwork covered in graffiti. Opposite the corner with C 8 is the abandoned **railway station**, built in 1909; beyond here the view of the bay is obscured by the shantytown settlement of La Playita, which is home to two hundred or so families of *precaristas*, as illegal urban squatters are known.

Just off Front Street on C 6, the **Colón Boxing Arena** was built in the 1970s to nurture the mass of local talent. The city has produced numerous world champions, the most famous of whom was "Panamá Al" Brown, the first Latin American world champion in the 1930s and one of the greatest boxers of all time. Four blocks down C 8 is the **cathedral**, built between 1929 and 1934 with high, neo-Gothic arches. Back on Front Street, it's six blocks north to the **New Washington Hotel**, built around 1850 to house railway engineers and rebuilt several times since. Famous guests have included Bob Hope, who entertained troops here during World War II, exiled Argentinean dictator Juan Perón and former British prime minister David Lloyd George. Inside a large palm-filled walled enclosure, the hotel's neo-colonial elegance, complete with chandeliers and ornate double staircase, is a reminder of Colón's former splendour. The seafront veranda is a good place to relax with a drink and watch the ships in the bay.

To the left of the hotel as you look towards the city is a small stone **Episcopal church** that was the first Protestant church in Colombia when it was built, for West Indian railway workers, in 1865. Seven blocks east along the seafront, a statue of Christ the Redeemer, arms outstretched, faces down **Av Central**, which is lined with monuments, including, on the intersection with C 2, a statue of Columbus with an indigenous girl, donated to Panama by Empress Eugenie of France in 1866.

Behind the bus terminal is the port enclave of **Cristóbal**, formerly part of the Canal Zone and still one of Latin America's busiest ports, handling more than two million tons of cargo a year. Apart from the yacht club (see overleaf) there's not much of interest here and most of the port is off-limits to visitors anyway.

The Colón Free Zone

The southeast corner of Colón is occupied by the **Free Zone** (Ⓦwww.colonfreezone.com), a walled city-within-a-city covering more than a square kilometre. This is the second biggest duty-free zone in the world after Hong Kong, with an annual turnover of more than US$10 billion. Thanks to an increase in cruise-ship traffic and stricter US immigration laws that deter Latin Americans shopping in Miami, the Zone is experiencing substantial growth. All manner of consumer goods are imported here and then re-exported across Latin America, and it is visited by thousands of businesspeople every week. The Free Zone is basically a forbidden city for Colón residents unless they work there, but you are allowed in if you present your passport at the gate. Inside, the contrast with the rest of Colón could not be greater – immaculate superstores line the Zone's clean, well-paved streets and the only smell is of money and expensive perfume. Most of the trade is in bulk orders, but you can buy individual items at low prices if you bargain hard or enlist one of the professional hagglers who tout their services at the entrance (they work for commission). Officially, what you buy must be held in bond and given to you at the airport as you leave the country.

Eating and drinking

Though there are several cheap **restaurants** in Colón serving the delicious local cuisine – usually seafood cooked to spicy Caribbean recipes – most are in dangerous parts of the city. In the evening you are better off eating in or near your hotel.

Café Nacional C 11, Av Guerrero. Popular, with good, inexpensive food and a convenient location, which is fairly safe during the day. Closed Sun.

Panama Canal Yacht Club on the seafront, inside the Cristóbal port enclosure. The open-air restaurant, serving decent seafood, is expensive, but the atmospheric bar, shaped like a ship's prow, is a good place to hang out if you're looking for work as a linehandler on a yacht transiting the canal or heading out into the Caribbean.

Restaurante Hotel Internacional on the ground floor of the hotel. Standard Panamanian and international food from about US$5, particularly good for breakfast. The rooftop bar (closed Sun), open to hotel guests only, is a good place to drink a sundowner and watch the ships lit up in the harbour at night while the city rages below.

Around Colón: the Gatún Locks

From Colón, a road runs 10km southwest to the **Gatún Locks**, where ships transit between Lago Gatún and Bahía Limón. The nearly two-kilometre-long locks, which raise and lower ships the 26.5m between the lake and sea level in three stages, are among the canal's most monumental engineering features. The **visitor centre** (daily 8am–4pm) has some photos of the locks during construction (their enormous size is most evident when viewed empty) and the viewing platforms get you much closer to the action than at Miraflores. The busiest times are in the morning between 9 and 11am and in the afternoon after 3pm. Here, you'll also get a good view of the lake, surrounded by dark, forest-covered mountains, and of the vast **Gatún Dam**. More than 2km long and 800m wide at its base, the structure was the largest earthen dam in the world when it was built in 1906 to dam the Río Chagres and form the lake.

Occasional **buses** from the terminal in Colón can drop you at the swing bridge – from where it is just a few minutes' walk to the locks' visitor centre – which crosses the canal when no ships are passing through (each transit takes about an hour). Alternatively, it is possible to hire a taxi in Colón (US$15–20 return). The road then forks, the left branch crossing the dam and following the west bank of the Chagres to the sea, then staggering along the **Costa Abajo** as far as the village of Boca del Río Indio. Costa Abajo is virtually undeveloped, with just a few fishing villages between the forest and the sea, and beyond Boca del Río Indio the coast is scarcely inhabited, stretching for 200km along the Golfo de los Mosquitos to Bocas del Toro. Taking the right fork, not on the bus route, takes you to **Fort San Lorenzo**, at the mouth of the Río Chagres.

Fort San Lorenzo

With a spectacular setting on a promontory above the Caribbean and overlooking the mouth of the Río Chagres, **Fort San Lorenzo** is the most impressive Spanish fortification still standing in Panama. Until the construction of the railway, the Chagres was the main cargo route across the isthmus to Panama City, and thus of enormous strategic importance to Spain. The first fortifications to protect the entrance to the river were built here in 1595, but the fort was taken by Francis

Drake in 1596 and, though heavily reinforced, fell again to Henry Morgan's pirates in December 1670. Morgan then proceeded up the Chagres and across the isthmus to ransack Panama City. Further fortifications were insufficient to prevent English admiral Edward Vernon from taking the fort again in 1740, but those that remain today, built during 1760–67, were never seriously tested, as by the time they were completed the era of the freebooters was coming to an end. The fort is well preserved, with a moat surrounding stout stone walls and great cannons looking out from the embrasures. It's an isolated place, surrounded by pristine rainforest, and the fort's view of the mouth of the Chagres and of the Costa Abajo can hardly have changed since the days of Drake and Morgan.

Fort San Lorenzo can only be reached by private car or **taxi** – you can rent one in Colón for about US$6 an hour. It's a drive of about forty minutes or so from the Gatún Locks, passing through dense rainforest and the former US training base of **Fort Sherman**, which until 1999 was home to the 17,000-acre US Army Jungle Warfare Training Center, used to train soldiers in combat for armed conflicts in Southeast Asia and Latin America.

Portobelo and the Costa Arriba

The **Costa Arriba**, stretching northeast of Colón, features beautiful beaches fringed by dense tropical forest, the historic towns of **Portobelo** and **Nombre de Dios**, and excellent diving and snorkelling in the **Parque Nacional Portobelo**. If you're heading here from Panama City, you can avoid Colón by getting off the bus at Sabanitas and catching a Colón-to-Portobelo bus.

Portobelo

Named by Christopher Columbus in 1502 after the magnificent bay on which it stands, **PORTOBELO** – "beautiful harbour" – was for centuries the most important Spanish port on the Atlantic coast of the New World, the northern terminus of the Camino Real. Today, it's a sleepy little town visited mostly by small groups of day-tripping tourists coming to explore the remains of the formidable fortifications built to defend the treasure fleets from pirate attack. The surrounding **Parque Nacional Portobelo** protects the region's dense rainforest, secluded sandy beaches and rugged coastline as well as stretches of coral reefs that are home to rare marine life and sunken treasure. On October 21 each year Portobelo explodes into life as thousands of purple-robed pilgrims descend on the town from across the country to pay homage to its patron saint, the miraculous **Black Christ**.

Portobelo was founded in 1597 to replace Nombre de Dios as the Atlantic terminus of the **Camino Real**, a year after the latter had been destroyed by Francis Drake. Set on a deepwater bay deemed easier to defend from the ravages of pirates,

The Black Christ of Portobelo

Without question the most revered religious figure in Panama, the **Black Christ** draws tens of thousands of pilgrims to Portobelo each year. But even as the icon inspires great devotion, the origins of the Black Christ still remain something of a mystery. Some say that it was found floating in the sea during a cholera epidemic, which disappeared after the Christ was brought into the town, others that it was on a ship bound for Colombia that stopped at Portobelo for supplies and was repeatedly prevented from leaving the bay by bad weather, sailing successfully only when the statue was left ashore. A small figure carved from black cocobolo wood with an agonized face and eyes raised to heaven, the Christ is reputed to possess miraculous powers. Every year on October 21 up to fifty thousand devotees, known as Nazarenos and dressed in purple robes, come to Portobelo for a huge procession that is followed by festivities that continue through the night – a wild and chaotic celebration of faith.

Portobelo was heavily fortified and for 150 years played host to the famous *ferias*, the grand trading events, when the Spanish treasure fleet came to collect the riches that travelled across the isthmus on mule trains from Panama City and to leave merchandise brought from Seville for distribution throughout the Americas. Unsurprisingly, the wealth concentrated in the royal warehouses here was an irresistible target for the **pirates** who scoured the Spanish Main. Henry Morgan ransacked the town for fifteen days in 1668 before moving on to San Lorenzo and thence to Panama City, and subsequent refortification was not enough to prevent the English admiral Edward Vernon from seizing Portobelo in 1739. Vernon destroyed the fortifications and, though they were rebuilt at enormous expense, the Spanish treasure fleet was rerouted around Cape Horn and the Portobelo *ferias* came to an end. The Spanish garrison left after independence in 1821, and with the establishment of Colón as Panama's principal Atlantic port, Portobelo slipped into the tropical indolence that characterizes it today.

The Town and ruins

Walking into Portobelo along the road from Colón brings you to the well-preserved **Santiago Battery**, constructed between 1753 and 1760 to the most exacting military standards of the day. From its stout battlements fourteen rusting cannons still look out to sea. Behind the battery the town itself begins, its ramshackle houses built on top of the ruins of the **Santiago de la Gloria Fort** and the many public buildings and merchants' houses destroyed by Vernon in 1739. The road leads onto the litter-strewn main square, flanked on one side by the colonial **Church of San Felipe**, built in 1776 and exceptional only as the home of the revered **Black Christ** (see overleaf).

Just off the square stands the two-storey **Casa Real de la Aduana** (daily 8am–4pm; US$1), the royal customs house, which has recently been restored with Spanish help and now houses a small **museum**. A massive, barn-like structure with solid walls of coral, the Aduana originally dates from the sixteenth century, but was rebuilt in its current form after being destroyed by Admiral Vernon. The biggest civil building in colonial Panama and an important symbol of imperial power, the Aduana stored treasure awaiting the arrival of the fleets from Spain and also housed a barracks and offices for royal officials. As well as a brief exhibition outlining the history of Portobelo, including a relief map of the town at the peak of its glory, the museum also has a display of the purple robes donated each year to the Black Christ, accompanied by some fascinating testimonies from the icon's devotees.

Looking out onto the bay behind the church, the **San Geronimo Battery** was built at the same time as the Santiago Battery and is equally well preserved, complete with cannons. Across the bay the twin batteries of **San Fernando** are also in good condition – it's easy to find someone in the town to take you across in a boat for a few dollars. Portobelo's most formidable defence, the **"Iron Castle" of San Felipe**, stood at the mouth of the bay on the opposite side, but was dismantled during the canal construction to uncover the basalt rock on which it was built – most of its stones were used to build the breakwater in Colón.

Practicalities

Buses for Portobelo leave from Colón; if you are coming from Panama City and want to avoid Colón, change at the Rey supermarket in Sabanitas, 14km before Colón. The small **IPAT** office (Ⓣ448 2073) in Portobelo, tucked away behind the municipal offices on the main square, keeps irregular hours. The only **accommodation** in the village itself is above the *Bar-Disco La Aduana* (❷), also on the main square, but the rooms are very basic and it gets very noisy at weekends. On the road towards Colón, *Coco Plum Eco Lodge* (Ⓣ448 2102, Ⓦwww.cocoplumpanama.com; ❺) has luxurious cabins with TV and a/c that sleep up to four people for US$50; dive operator Twin Oceans operate from here (Ⓣ448 2067, Ⓦwww.twinoceans.com). All are busy on weekends but charge less on weekdays. Several basic

restaurants in the village serve inexpensive fish and seafood cooked to local recipes with coconut rice – try the *Casa del Marisco* or *Restaurante Arith*. There are also a couple of more upmarket restaurants on the road towards Colón: *Restaurante El Torre* and *Restaurante Los Cañones*, both of which serve good seafood.

Parque Nacional Portobelo

The rugged coast around Portobelo is officially part of the **Parque Nacional Portobelo**, and although little is done for the area in terms of protection or administration (you don't need permission from ANAM to enter) it does have good **beaches** and some of the best **diving** and **snorkelling** on the Caribbean coast, including coral reefs, shipwrecks and, somewhere in front of Isla de Drake, the as yet undiscovered grave of Francis Drake, buried at sea in a lead coffin after he died of dysentery in 1596. Most of this area can only be reached by sea; you can either hire a boatman in town or go on an excursion with Twin Oceans (see opposite), who rent snorkelling and diving equipment as well as providing PADI-certified diving courses.

Isla Grande

Some 12km beyond Portobelo, a side road branches off the badly potholed paved road and runs a few kilometres to the tiny village of **La Guaira**, where launches can take you across to **Isla Grande** (US$1 each way), a hugely popular weekend resort for residents of Colón and Panama City. Though undeniably beautiful, friendly and relaxed, with some good beaches, Isla Grande is no more spectacular than other parts of Costa Arriba. It does, however, have better facilities – and higher prices. The best **swimming** beach is around the island to the right as you face the mainland; the beach round the other side is good for surfing. For **snorkellers**, there's plenty to see around the Christ statue in front of the village, though beware of the current beyond the reef and of passing boats.

Isla Grande has plenty of **places to stay**; head for the seafront path that passes for the main street. *Super Cabañas Jackson* (ⓣ448 2483; ❹), with small, box-like rooms, is one of the least expensive, while *Posada Villa Ensueño* (ⓣ320 6321; ❺) and *Cabañas Cholita* (ⓣ232 4561; ❺) have spacious cabins with a/c set around gardens. On the far side of the island, *Bananas Resort* (ⓣ263 9510, ⓦwww.bananasresort.com; ❽) boasts luxurious rooms, a restaurant, bar and the best beach on the island. During the summer and on weekends it's worth booking ahead, though on weekdays prices can be lower and you can turn up on spec. The island's **restaurants** mostly serve seafood (if you're feeling adventurous, try octopus cooked in coconut milk); seek out *La Cholita*, *Candy Rose* and *Villa Ensueño*, which are all very good. The **social centre** of Isla Grande is the seafront shack in front of *Super Cabañas Jackson*, where locals gather to drink beer, play dominoes and listen to loud reggae. There are three or four **buses** daily from Colón to La Guaira; the last one back to Colón leaves at 1pm (Mon–Sat) or 3pm (Sun).

Nombre de Dios

A further 23km beyond Portobelo along the badly potholed paved road is the small village **NOMBRE DE DIOS**, founded in 1520 and Portobelo's predecessor as the Atlantic terminus of the Camino Real. Almost nothing remains of the Spanish settlement destroyed by Drake in 1596, and it is difficult today to believe that in 1550 half the trade between Spain and the Americas passed through this tiny port. It is a charming village, though, friendly and laid-back, with the calm waters of Bahía de San Cristóbal in front and the lush forest descending like a curtain from the mountains behind. Of the beautiful deserted beaches close by, the best is **Playa las Damas**, which can be reached by walking an hour or so along the sands – you'll need to get one of the locals to show you how to wade across the sand bank in front of the Río Nombre de Dios. There are also plenty of good **snorkelling** spots (bring your own equipment). Several simple **restaurants** serve good fish and seafood, but there are no places to **stay**.

Beyond Nombre de Dios, the road staggers about 20km along the coast as far as the hamlet of Cuango, which has become a centre for illegal and highly destructive gold mining. The frontier of Kuna Yala is about 25km further along the coast, and you may be able to catch a lift from one of the boats that sometimes travel into the *comarca* from the village of **Miramar**, a few kilometres west of Cuango, though this trip is best done in the opposite direction (see p.798). There are three to four **buses** daily between Colón, Portobelo and Nombre de Dios; the last bus back usually leaves Nombre de Dios at 1pm, though it's worth checking with the locals in case it leaves earlier.

7.3

Eastern Panama: Darién and Kuna Yala

Sparsely populated by isolated indigenous communities and the descendants of escaped African slaves, the eastern third of Panama – some 19,000 square kilometres – is perhaps the last great untamed **wilderness** of Central America, the beginning of an immense forest that continues almost unbroken across the border into the Chocó region of Colombia and down the Pacific coast to Ecuador. This was the first region on the American mainland to be settled by the Spanish. Although they extracted great wealth from gold mines deep in the forest at Cana, they were never able to establish effective control over the region, hampered by the almost impassable terrain and by the fierce resistance put up by its inhabitants, and harassed at every turn by European pirates and bands of renegade African slaves known as *cimarrones*. The Scots also attempted to colonize the region (see p.795) in the seventeenth century, and although they actually managed to befriend the indigenous people, a combination of bad planning and fierce objections from Spain and England cut short their stay.

Although historically the whole of eastern Panama was referred to as Darién, today the area is divided into two distinct regions, separated by a low chain of forested mountains that runs the length of the Caribbean coast. The Caribbean side of these mountains is **Kuna Yala**, the autonomous *comarca* (territory) of the Kuna people, one of the most wildly beautiful and culturally fascinating parts of Panama. Here, some forty thousand Kuna live in isolation on the idyllic offshore islands of the **San Blas Archipelago**, from where access to the rest of the country is either by boat or plane.

The rest of eastern Panama is **Darién**, the almost impenetrable wilderness frontier between Central and South America, and the largest and most isolated province in Panama. Only one road penetrates Darién: known as the **Darién Highway**, it is an extension of the Carretera Interamericana, intended to connect the road systems of North and South America. But for the moment the 106km gap between the two – the **Darién Gap** – remains unbridged. Here, the vast forests remain largely undisturbed, one of the most pristine and biologically diverse ecosystems in the world and home to the semi-nomadic Emberá-Wounaan. Along the border with Colombia, the **Parque Nacional Darién**, the largest and most important protected area in Panama, protects huge swathes of these forests.

Eastern Panama has always been a wild frontier, a haven for rebels and renegades that defies effective government control. Today, drug traffickers, bandits and guerrillas have replaced the *cimarrones*, pirates and unsubmissive indigenous tribes of the colonial era, and in recent years, the situation has got markedly worse, with the vicious, decades-long Colombian **civil war** spilling over into Panama. The Marxist guerrillas of the Colombian Revolutionary Armed Forces (FARC) have long maintained bases close to the border in Darién, but now right-wing paramilitary groups backed by powerful landowners and drug traffickers have begun pursuing them, terrorizing isolated Panamanian communities they accuse of

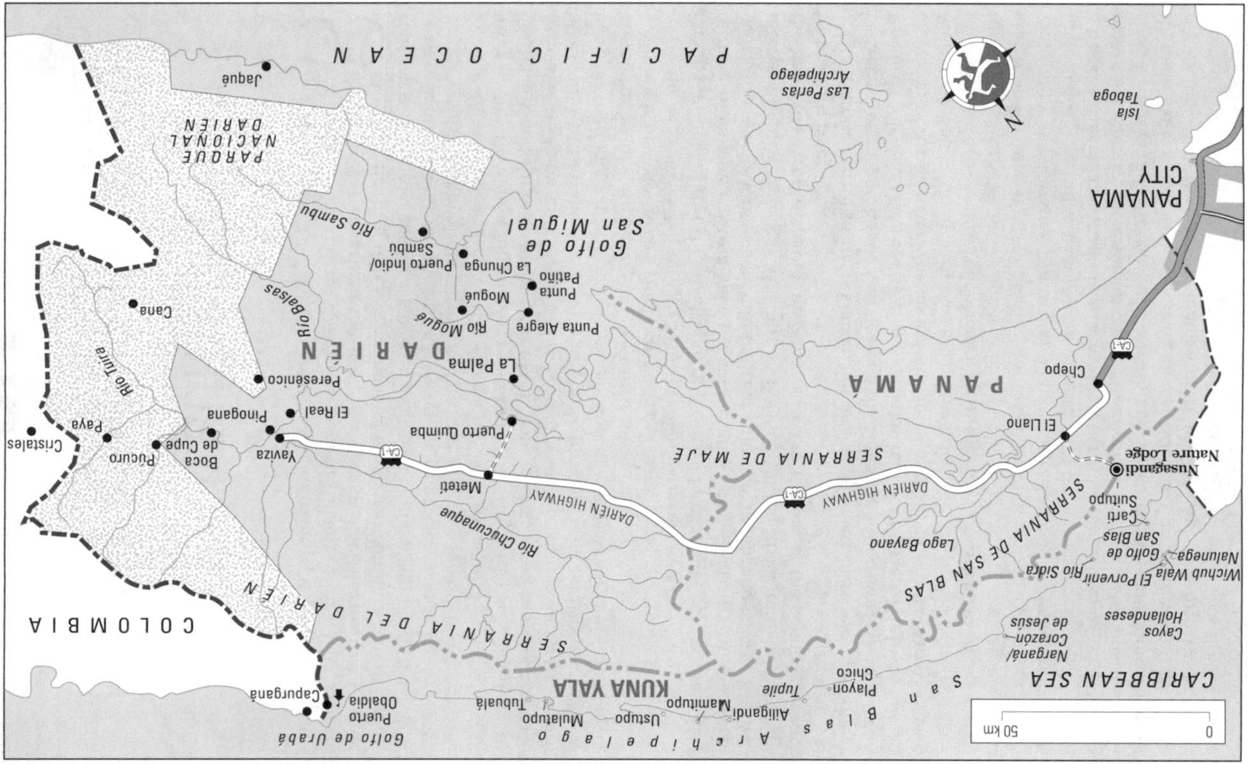

0 50 km
CARIBBEAN SEA
San Blas Archipelago
Golfo de Urabá
Puerto Obaldia
Capurganá
Playon Chico
Tupile
Ailigandi
Mamitupo
Ustupo
Mulatupo
Tubualá
KUNA YALA
Narganá/ Corazón de Jesús
Cayos Hollandeses
Wichub Wala
El Porvenir
Río Sidra
Nalunega
Golfo de San Blas
Carti Suitupo
Nusagandi Nature Lodge
SERRANIA DE SAN BLAS
Lago Bayano
SERRANIA DEL DARIÉN
COLOMBIA
Río Chucunaque
DARIÉN HIGHWAY
CA-1
Metetí
SERRANIA DE MAJÉ
El Llano
Chepo
PANAMÁ
Puerto Quimba
Yaviza
Boca de Cupe
Púcuro
Paya
Cristales
Pinogana
El Real
Peresénico
Río Tuira
La Palma
DARIÉN
Río Balsas
Cana
Punta Alegre
Río Mogué
Mogué
Punta Patiño
La Chunga
Puerto Indio/ Sambú
Golfo de San Miguel
Río Sambu
PARQUE NACIONAL DARIÉN
PANAMA CITY
Isla Taboga
Las Perlas Archipelago
Jaqué
PACIFIC OCEAN
N

harbouring the guerrillas. The paramilitaries have also been waging a brutal campaign against poor peasants in Colombia, driving floods of refugees across the border, only for them to be driven back by the Panamanian authorities. Thus, a climate of fear and suspicion reigns in parts of Darién and the eastern extreme of Kuna Yala, where remote villages have been abandoned and many locals fear to travel by river. Although large areas of the region can still be visited safely, including almost all of Kuna Yala and parts of the Parque Nacional Darién, actually crossing the frontier by land, always a risky adventure, would now be crazy and irresponsible.

Darién

With its mighty rivers, rugged mountain chains and vast, impenetrable rainforests, **Darién** is in many ways much closer to South America than to Central America, its incredible biological diversity matched only by the cultural diversity of its population, which is made up of three main groups: black, indigenous and colonist. Other than a few Kuna communities, the indigenous population of Darién is composed of two closely related but distinct peoples, the **Wounaan** and the more numerous **Emberá**, both of which are semi-nomadic South American rainforest societies. Recognizable by the black geometric designs with which they decorate their bodies, the Emberá-Wounaan have been migrating across the border from Colombia for the past two centuries. Only since the 1960s have they begun to settle in permanent villages and establish official recognition of their territorial rights in the form of a *comarca*, divided into two districts: the **Comarca Emberá Cemaco**, in the north, and the **Comarca Emberá Sambú**, in the southwest. The black people of Darién, descended from the *cimarrones* and released slaves, are known as **Dariénitas** or **libres** (the free) and are culturally distinct from the Afro-Antillano populations of Colón and Panama City (see p.759). The **colonists**, meanwhile, are the most recent arrivals, poor peasants driven off their lands in western Panama by expanding cattle ranches and encouraged to settle in Darién during the construction of the Darién Highway. Also known as **interioranos**, many colonists still wear their distinctive straw sombreros as a badge of identity and maintain the folk traditions of the regions they abandoned.

The **Darién Highway** was built in the 1970s and early 1980s to open up the region's supposedly empty lands to colonization and complete the last link in the Carretera Interamericana from Alaska to Tierra del Fuego. At present the road goes no further than Yaviza, 276km east of Panama City to the unbridged 106km "**Darién Gap**". Both governments are keen to complete the highway, but various factors have conspired to prevent this: the enormous expense; fears that a road link with Colombia would facilitate drug trafficking and the spread of foot-and-mouth disease from South America; and the opposition of environmentalists and indigenous groups. Sadly, the environmental consequences that this would evidently bring are all too apparent along both sides of the existing stretch of the highway, where illegal logging companies have plundered the land leaving behind low-grade cattle pasture. For the moment, the 5790-square-kilometre **Parque Nacional Darién** protects the exceptionally rich rainforests that stand in the highway's path along the border.

Given the **security concerns** affecting the border area, including parts of the national park and the Comarca Emberá Cemaco, a visit to **southwestern Darién** is a better option if you want to experience the ecology and culture of the region independently but without risking an encounter with armed groups. The provincial capital of **La Palma**, on the Pacific, is one base from which you can hire a boat to take you along the coast and up the Río Mogué to the community of **Mogué** or further south to visit the Comarca Emberá Sambú.

Visiting Darién

Several tour companies in Panama City (see p.769) run **tours** to Darién, ranging from short trips to two-week trans-Darién treks: ANCON Expeditions are the most experienced and have exclusive ecolodges in the national park at Cana and on the Pacific coast at Punta Patiño. It's easy enough to visit the region **independently**, although few travellers ever do. The national park can be reached on foot from El Real, and you can hire a motorized dugout canoe (although this can be expensive unless travelling in a group) in any of the region's towns to take you upriver into the forest and to visit indigenous communities. Most of the towns and small villages in Darién sell a good range of supplies, including machetes and pots and pans, as well as instant noodles. **Clothing** should include long pants and long-sleeved shirts, partly to keep the huge variety of insect life at bay, but also because it can get quite cool during the night. Do not wear anything that resembles army fatigues or has a camouflage pattern.

The Darién Highway

East of Panama City the **Darién Highway** is well paved as far as the busy cattle-ranching centre of **Chepo**, 53km away. Beyond here it's unpaved, getting worse the further east you travel, and is often impassable in the wet season. Some 18km east of Chepo, the highway passes through the quiet village of **El Llano**, where a side road leads up to the **Nusagandi Nature Reserve** in Kuna Yala (see p.799). Some 10km beyond El Llano, the highway crosses the peaceful **Lago Bayano**, surrounded by well-preserved rainforest. Formed in 1972 by the construction of the hydroelectric dam that provides most of Panama City's power, the lake is named after the king of the *cimarrones* who terrorized Panama's colonial rulers in the 1500s. After defeating several armies sent against him, Bayano was captured in 1555 and taken to Seville, where he lived out the rest of his years as an honoured prisoner of the Spanish king. Though the provincial border is still some 90km further east, beyond the lake you are, for all intents and purposes, in Darién. From the lake the highway rolls on for 196km through a desolate, deforested landscape, passing Emberá-Wounaan hamlets, with their characteristic open-walled houses raised on stilts, and tin-roofed colonist settlements before ending on the banks of the Río Chucunaque at Yaviza.

Metetí

Fifty kilometres before Yaviza the highway passes through **METETÍ**, a small roadside *interiorano* settlement that has grown in importance as an administrative and commercial centre in recent years as a result of the lack of security closer to the Colombian border. Metetí is the end of the road for most buses from Panama City, although a couple of buses a day usually go on to Yaviza. A side road leads some 20km down to **Puerto Quimba** on the Pacific coast, where scheduled **water-taxis** leave hourly across the Golfo de San Miguel to La Palma (45min; US$2.50), the provincial capital (see p.792). Pick-up trucks leave Metetí for Puerto Quimba every 45 minutes or so between 5.30am and 6pm. You can find **accommodation** at the *Motel Mi Felicidad* (no phone; ❷–❹). Metetí is also not a bad place to organize an expedition into the Comarca Emberá Cemaco to the north – you can probably find a guide and a motorized dugout canoe to take you down the Río Metetí to the Río Chucunaque, which forms the southern border of the *comarca* and runs parallel to the highway to Yaviza. Expect to pay about US$20 a day to hire a dugout canoe and much more (for petrol) if it's motorized.

Yaviza

Founded by the Spanish in 1638 as a garrison town to establish colonial control over the gold mines further up river, **YAVIZA** is the terminus of the Darién Highway. Beyond Yaviza, the only transport is by water, and the river port is always

Crossing the Darién Gap to Colombia

Though crossing the Darién Gap has always been a hazardous undertaking – and one of the most celebrated adventures in Latin America – given the present security situation we **do not recommend you attempt this trip**. Many travellers have disappeared or been killed attempting this in recent years, and at the very least you are likely to be robbed or kidnapped, even if you can find guides willing to take you (no easy task in itself, given that many of the villages in the region have been attacked or overrun by bandits and the inhabitants have fled). Moreover, it's also worth remembering that there is a **war** raging across the border in Colombia.

In 2004 the Panamanian authorities were not allowing civilians to travel beyond Boca de Cupe. Should the security situation in Darién improve, however, then before crossing you must first get permission from ANAM as well as the Colombian consulate in Panama City. (Make sure you have your exit permission from *migración,* if you have been in Panama for more than three months.) In Colombia you must register on arrival with DAS, the immigration agency.

busy with the plantain-laden Emberá dugout canoes from the upriver communities of the *comarca*, here to trade with the town's mostly black population. The town is also a good base for trips into the Comarca Emberá Cemaco, and a short distance from the Parque Nacional Darién office in El Real. Sadly, though, with the recent upsurge in **bandit** and **paramilitary incursions** from Colombia, Yaviza is today once more beginning to resemble a garrison town, with nervous, heavily armed policemen and the foreboding sound of military helicopters. You should let the police know of your presence and your plans when you arrive and ask their advice before you continue.

Buses from Meteti arrive and depart from beside the dock at the entrance to town. From here, the town's only real street runs down to a small square, just off of which the friendly *Hotel Tres Americas* has simple **rooms** (no phone; ❸). There's a basic **restaurant** next door and a few others on the main street, as well as shops where you can buy supplies.

Parque Nacional Darién

Covering almost 5800 square kilometres of pristine rainforest along the border with Colombia, **Parque Nacional Darién** is possibly the most biologically diverse region on earth – over five hundred species of bird have been reported here. Inhabited by scattered indigenous communities, the park contains the largest expanse of forest in Central America that has not been affected by logging, and it provides a home for countless rare and endangered species, including jaguars, harpy eagles and several types of macaw. Parts of the park are normally safe to visit, but the **security situation** can change rapidly, so it's a good idea to phone the park office in El Real, the launching point for trips into the park, or the ANAM office in Panama City (see p.751), in order to check on the current status before you plan to arrive.

To visit the park you should first head to the park office in the small town of **EL REAL**, about thirty minutes by boat down the Chucunaque and up the Río Tuira from Yaviza. There's no scheduled boat service, but if you go to the dock in Yaviza in the morning you can normally find one that will take you for about US$5 per person. These boats meet the Aeroperlas **planes** (☎315 7500) that arrive three times a week from Panama City at the El Real airstrip. In town, the *Hotel El Nazareno* (☎228 3673; ❷–❸) offers basic **accommodation**, but be warned this is the heart of cock-fighting country so don't expect a great night's sleep; you'll also find a few stores and a couple of simple restaurants – inform them in advance if you want an evening meal.

To enter the park you need permission from the ANAM **Parque Nacional Darién office** (daily 8am–4pm; ☎299 6183) in El Real. (The fee for park access is US$3 per day.) Check here, too, about the relative safety and accessibility of the park's **ranger stations**, all of which have basic lodges where you can stay for US$10 per night. One such outpost, **Rancho Frío**, is a three-hour walk through the forest from El Real, and it is normally safe to visit – the park office can provide a guide (US$10) to take you there. There are plenty of trails into the forest from Rancho Frío, including one through cloudforest to the peak of Cerro Pirre (1200m). A new private jungle lodge at **Peresénico**, on the banks of the Río Pirre at the edge of the national park and just a thirty-minute boat ride or three-hour hike from El Real, is planned for completion in 2005. Although the six thatched huts, each sleeping two with private bathroom, are primarily for the use of package tours booked through ANCON Expeditions (see p.771), the lodge may allow you to stay as an independent traveller, but contact their office in Panama City before setting off.

Be sure to bring food, bedding, mosquito repellent and nets or coils, and a water bottle and purifiers, even if you plan on staying at one of the ranger stations. Gifts for the park guards (such as food, drink, batteries and newspapers) are much appreciated.

Cana

Officially called Santa Cruz de Cana, the remote scientific station of **CANA** is the site of an important gold-mining town first established in the sixteenth century by the Spanish, who worked the lands here until they abandoned the region in the 1820s. At the beginning of the twentieth century, an English company took over the lease and constructed a twenty-kilometre-long railway from the mine through the jungle to the Río Tuira at Boca de Cupe. After twenty years the English left and the jungle began taking back the land; today, old secondary forest covers the area where up to sixteen thousand people once lived and worked. With the mining a distant memory, Cana is now one of the world's ultimate birding destinations, with a hit list of more than four hundred species, including several native to the nearby Cerro Pirre cloudforest. Frequently seen **birds** include the ornate hawk-eagle, scaly-throated leaf tosser, greenish-puffleg hummingbird, chestnut-mandibled toucan, beautiful treerunner, grey-cheeked nunlet and pairs of great currasows. In the cloudforests of Cerro Pirre, mixed flocks and ant swarms are common, the latter attracting many ant-thrushes and antpittas.

Even for the non-birder the place is stunning, with well-marked trails through the jungle, many of which still show evidence of the town's mining days, with rusting rails and locomotives visible in the undergrowth. Cana is reachable by a two- to three-day hike from Boca de Cupe, but you will have to get permission from ANCON Expeditions to stay here, as they manage the small jungle-lodge complex as a field station for their tours, which arrive here by small private plane.

La Palma and around

With a spectacular setting overlooking the broad mouth of the Río Tiura, with rugged, densely forested mountains rising on all sides, **LA PALMA** is the capital of Darién Province, a lively commercial and administrative centre that thrives despite its isolation. There's not much to do here, but it's a friendly place largely unaffected by the fear gripping much of Darién (though you should still register with the police on arrival) and a good base from which to hire a boat to the nearby islands of Boca Grande and Boca Chica, where fortifications built to protect the gold mine at Cana from pirates have been partially restored, or further south into the Golfo de San Miguel. By boat it is possible to visit the Emberá community of **Mogué**, **Reserva Natural Punta Patiño**, with its many life zones, or further south still into the **Comarca Emberá Sambú** and the relaxed local port town of Sambú – all of which are only accessible at high tide.

Practicalities

La Palma clings to a steep slope that runs down to the seafront, along which runs its only real street, a narrow strip of concrete lined with houses on stilts projected over the water. **Planes** arrive and depart for Panama City from the airstrip where Aeroperlas have a small office, while **boats** from nearby Puerto Quimba arrive on the dock below the main street. Tickets for the Puerto Quimba boats can be bought from the small booth in the main street, which is also a suitable place to enquire about hiring boats for the fifteen-minute trip to the islands of Boca Grande and Boca Chica as well as further south in the gulf. You'll also find small cargo boats that travel to Panama City, but these vessels are cramped, provide little protection from the baking sun and stop at many places along the way to load and unload their cargo.

The town has two clean and pleasant places to stay, both of which overlook the gulf. The elegant *Hotel Biaquirú Bagará* (☎299 6224; ❹) has several comfortable rooms with fan and private bathroom, while the *Pensión Takela* (☎299 6490; ❸) is more basic with a garish communal area. Along the main street there are several small **restaurants** serving basic, yet filling, Panamanian food, including the *Restaurante Regocijo*, whose neighbouring **bar**, the *Cantina Regocijo* provides much of the waterfront's pounding late-night reggae; a **telephone** office; a small unmarked shop with **Internet** access; and a **Banco Nacional** (Mon–Fri 8am–3pm, Sat 9am–noon), where you can change travellers' cheques, make Visa card cash withdrawals and drink free coffee.

Around La Palma

There is little to keep you in La Palma for more than a day, or indeed a few hours, unless you are waiting for passage on one of the small cargo boats that deliver and collect goods to and from the various towns and communities in Darién. The booth on the main street selling tickets for the Puerto Quimba boat is also the place to enquire about hiring a boat to travel south into the Golfo de San Miguel. An hour or so by boat is the Emberá community of **Mogué**, an ideal place to stay and learn about the unique culture of these indigenous people as well as a base to explore the surrounding secondary rainforest in pursuit of the rare harpy eagle.

Jutting into the gulf is a promontory that is the eastern limit of the 65,000-acre private **Reserva Natural Punta Patiño**, where several life zones support an outstanding array of birdlife and mammals. The lodge here, which is managed by ANCON Expeditions (see p.771), is a welcome place to relax after trekking through the steaming rainforest.

Mogué

From La Palma it's a fantastic two-hour boat trip (US$90 one way) through the Golfo de San Miguel, past forested islands and a wild coastline fringed with mangroves and deserted beaches, and up the Río Mogué to the small Emberá community of **MOGUÉ**. Accessible only at high tide, the village is an easy ten-minute walk from the riverbank and is the heart of a community, many of whose inhabitants are also dispersed throughout the surrounding rainforest. Like many Emberá communities in the area, the villagers are beginning to realise the financial benefits of tourism: they have built a large wooden platform on stilts with a palm-thatched roof (❸–❹) where visitors can relax and bed down for the night, either in a hammock, on a mattress or in a tent (provided). A small thatched-roof building has a shower and toilet for visitors' use only. Nearby, a small shop sells basic supplies and cold drinks; the community can arrange for someone to cook meals for you, too. The village makes for an excellent base to explore the surrounding rainforest, with a good chance of seeing the elusive **harpy eagle**, Panama's national bird and the most powerful bird of prey, whose call pierces the forest canopy. The walk to the nearby nesting site, which the community protects, takes about two hours with a guide (take plenty of water), passing through baking secondary forest where huge *cuipo* trees tower over the undergrowth covered with large colonies of beautiful, and harmless, golden orb spiders.

Reserva Natural Punta Patiño

Ten kilometres further along the coast from the mouth of the Río Mogué, the small fishing village of **Punta Alegre** makes for a good pit-stop on trips to Punta Patiño or elsewhere into the Comarca Emberá Sambú. Although there's not much to see or do in Punta Alegre, there is a small pensión above a bar where you can take a break from the hot sun and enjoy a cold drink. After another forty minutes by boat, you'll arrive at the **Reserva Natural Punta Patiño**, an expansive private reserve which contains many different types of forest, from primary to gallery, and is home to a whole host of birds, including the golden-headed manakin, bat falcon and white ibis, as well as spectacled caimans, large otter-like tayras and grey foxes. However, the large colony of capybaras that once inhabited the nearby swamps is in decline due to the local jaguar population's insatiable appetite for these huge web-footed rodents. To visit, contact ANCON Expeditions (see p.771), who arrange tours to and around the reserve, including trips to Mogué. They also manage eight private air-conditioned cabins that overlook an extensive coconut plantation as well as a lodge with commanding views over the Darién rainforest and the Golfo de San Miguel.

Sambú and Puerto Indio

It's an exciting one-day boat journey from La Palma up the tidal estuary of the Río Sambú to **SAMBÚ** and **PUERTO INDIO**, twin towns connected by a foot-bridge on the western boundary of the Comarca Emberá Sambú. Sambú is a trading town with a mixed population, while Puerto Indio is the capital of the *comarca*. The Emberá are keen to promote ecotourism, and this is a good place to find a guide and a motorized dugout canoe to take you upriver, deep into the *comarca* or downriver to the nearby Emberá community of La Chunga. Outside of Puerto Indio, the Emberá live in dispersed communities along the riverbanks, hunting, fishing and cultivating smallholdings that provide the only break in the otherwise pristine vegetation. Situated far from the Colombian border, the area around Sambú has rarely been blighted with the security problems found in other parts of Darién, and after spending just a short time among the generous and friendly population it's difficult to imagine you could feel safer elsewhere in Panama.

Although there's little to do here, a day spent chatting to the locals who congregate under the large mango tree next to the dock and outside the small shop next to the airstrip lends valuable insight into the simple and tough, yet rather inspiring, livelihoods of those inhabiting this culturally diverse and isolated community. Small cargo boats frequently stop here, and you can watch the locals unload their cargo of building supplies and petrol and then load the vessels with hardwood and empty soda bottles, as well as sacks of plantains and oranges brought downriver in small dugout canoes from the more isolated Emberá communities deep in the rainforest.

A superb fifty-minute journey by motorized dugout canoe through narrow, meandering rivers lined with mangroves and teeming with water birds will get you to the charming Emberá community of **LA CHUNGA**, where locals have constructed a number of traditional-style *casitas* – wooden palm-thatched structures with cane walls built on stilts – just outside the village for the sole use of visitors. All visitors are greeted by the community chiefs and offered a guide, whose role is to show you around, explain local traditions and ensure that your stay is an enjoyable one.

Practicalities

In Sambú the only place to stay is the *Hotel Chavéz* (no phone; ❷), next to the airstrip, with clean wooden rooms and shared bathroom. There's a restaurant next to

The settling of New Edinburgh

In one of the lesser known footnotes in the isthmus's history, in the late 1600s the Scots gambled their country's future on a **colony in Darién** in the hopes of transforming **Scotland** into a trading power to rival England. The chief proponent of the plan was **William Patterson**, the founder of the Bank of England, who formed the Company of Scotland in May 1695 to develop trade. Patterson declared Darién the objective – despite never having even been – and thanks to his glossy presentation depicting it as a veritable paradise, the company's directors duly agreed to go along with his plan. Interest in the company quickly reached fever pitch, with the Scots arriving in "shoals" to invest their entire, often meagre, fortunes in the venture. Soon, half the kingdom's wealth resided with the company.

A fleet of five ships and 1200 men set sail from Leith in July 1698, and within days many of the ships' supplies had spoiled and rations were cut, quickly demoralizing the crews. Once off the Spanish coast, however, the fleet caught the trade winds and sailed to the Caribbean, where they attempted to trade some of their goods and restock the ships. As luck would have it, their rather naïve choice of goods – wigs, shoes, stockings, thick cloth and bibles – found little demand in the tropics.

The fleet finally anchored in Caledonia Bay after four months at sea, and for five months the Scots worked hard to build **New Edinburgh**, disease, low rations and the tropical environment constantly conspiring against them. The only help they received came from the local Kuna, who, having despised their Spanish colonists, took rather a shine to the Scots and their tenacity. When the Scots' promised supply ships failed to materialize, morale began to ebb away, just as the rainy season started. With despair setting in and upon learning that England was forbidding anyone to assist them, the colony's council called it a day: after just ten months, the fleet set sail, most of their trade goods still rotting in the ships' hulls. Only one ship, the *Caledonia*, made it back to Scotland.

Unbeknownst to the first fleet, a second one had set sail just two months after they had abandoned the settlement – and this new group was no better equipped than the first, with trading goods of paper and bonnets. Finding the settlement abandoned, the second expedition soon encountered the same problems that had ruined the first and, worse, their presence drew the attention of the Spanish, based in Portobelo. Small **battles** soon broke out between the Scots, aided by the Kuna, and the Spanish. Six months after arriving in April 1700, the Scots finally surrendered to the Spanish force and, thanks to the respect bestowed on them by the Spanish governor, they were allowed to evacuate with full military honours. None of the ships made it back to Scotland.

The venture crippled Scotland financially, leaving the many subscribers to the company penniless and the kingdom at the mercy of rival England. Several years later, in 1707, England agreed to compensate all those who had subscribed to the company in return for the creation of a joint kingdom of England and Scotland.

the small dock, plus a number of small shops selling a good range of supplies, including pots and pans as well as tinned foods and instant noodles, should you intend to travel upriver to some of the many isolated communities.

There are no scheduled **boat** services to Sambú, but if you ask around in La Palma you may be able to find a cargo boat that will take you in return for a contribution to fuel costs. You may have to wait for several days, and the boats are often crammed full of cargo with little shade to offer relief from the scorching sun. The quickest – and often cheapest – way to reach Sambú is by light **aircraft** from Panama City. Turismo Aero (☎315 0439 & 0278/9) fly here three days a week, often via Garachiné. Remember to confirm your return flight at least an hour before the scheduled departure at the large red house a block behind the *Hotel Chavéz* – and be prepared for a delay.

If you decide to head on to La Chunga, you will need to hire a boat in Sambú: try the friendly Raul Cabrera (☎299 6090), who speaks very clear Spanish and lives near the airstrip; for US$50 he will take you to La Chunga, introduce you to the heads of the community and take you back to Sambú the following day. Be sure to travel at high tide, otherwise you'll have to traipse through knee-high mud to dry-ish land, and then walk through the jungle for 1km before crossing the small river to the community. In the village there's a fire pit where visitors can cook their own food, but it's easy enough to get someone to prepare some food for you: try the local shop, where the wife of Ricardo Cabrera (no relation to Raul), the English-speaking community chief, will be happy to cook for you (US$2).

The cost to stay in the community is US$45 per person, but group discounts are available. Although this may seem steep for the relatively basic accommodation, which includes a bamboo bed with mattress, sheets, mosquito net, towel and candle, the community gets very few visitors and are basically opening up their entire community to you, as well as providing you with a guide to show you around and ensure you are well looked after.

Kuna Yala

Stretching some 375km along the northeastern Caribbean coast of Panama from the Golfo de San Blas to Puerto Obaldía, **Kuna Yala** is the autonomous *comarca* of the Kuna (or Dúle), the only region in the country populated and governed exclusively by indigenous people. Although their territory includes the narrow strip of land between the sea and the peaks of the Serrania de San Blas, almost all the Kuna live on the **San Blas Archipelago**, a chain of coral atolls that runs the length of the forested coastline like a string of pearls. The Kuna like to say that there is an island for every day of the year – in fact, there are slightly more, some forty of which are inhabited, with populations ranging from several thousand to single families living on narrow sandbanks that are all but submerged at high tide. The untamed beauty of its forested coastline, palm-fringed islands, coral reefs and bountiful marine life make Kuna Yala a good destination for a beach holiday, though transportation can be difficult and there are few facilities. The real appeal, though, is the opportunity to witness the unique culture and lifestyle of the Kuna themselves.

Some history

Historians still argue over whether the **tribes** the Spanish first encountered on the coasts of Darién were Kuna, but it is clear that by the mid-sixteenth century the Kuna were migrating into Darién from the great Atrató swamp in present-day Colombia. Gradually driven onto the north coast by war with the Spanish and with the Emberá, their historic rivals, they began moving to the relative safety and isolation of the islands in the nineteenth century. A treaty signed with the Spanish in 1787 guaranteed a measure of independence, but in the early twentieth century the authorities of newly independent Panama initiated efforts to "civilize" the Kuna, sending police and missionaries to the islands. This twin assault on Kuna culture and autonomy and the exploitation of their natural resources by outsiders provoked an explosive reaction. In 1925 the Kuna rose up in what they still proudly refer to as **"the Revolution"**, killing or expelling the Panamanian police garrison and declaring an independent republic. The government sent a punitive expedition, but a US warship standing offshore prevented further bloodshed – the Kuna had sent representatives to Washington to request assistance before the uprising – and a settlement was made by which the Kuna recognized Panamanian sovereignty in return for a degree of autonomy. Protracted negotiations in the decades after the revolution led to the final recognition of Kuna Yala as an independent self-governing *comarca* in 1952. No non-Kuna can own land or property in the territory, and the

Kuna culture

Fishing is the mainstay of the traditional Kuna subsistence economy, but they also cultivate food crops in forest clearings on the mainland and collect coconuts to sell to Colombian trading ships. Kuna society is regulated by a system of highly participative **democracy**: every community has a *casa de congreso* where the *onmakket*, or congress, meets regularly. Each community also elects a *sahila*, usually a respected elder, who attends the Kuna General Congress twice a year. The General Congress is the supreme political authority in Kuna Yala, and it in turn appoints three *cacique*, who represent the Kuna politically and culturally in the national government. Colonial missionaries struggled in vain to Christianize the Kuna, and though some of the Christian sects that have made so much headway elsewhere in Latin America have now established a foothold in Kuna Yala, most Kuna cling to their own **religious beliefs**, based above all on the sanctity of Nan Dummad, the Great Mother, and on respect for the environment they inhabit. The Kuna also have a rich tradition of **oral history**, and the ritual interpretation of their past by poet-historians plays an important part in decision-making and in maintaining their collective identity. Though Kuna men wear standard Western clothes, **Kuna women** wear gold rings in their ears and noses and blue vertical lines painted on their foreheads; they don headscarves and bright bolts of trade cloth round their waists, their forearms and calves are bound in coloured beads, and their blouses are sewn with beautiful reverse-appliqué designs known as **molas**. Depicting everything from fish and birds to complex abstract designs and even political slogans, *molas* are the most popular souvenir for visitors to Kuna Yala and are on sale all over Panama.

It would be wrong to consider Kuna culture as entirely traditional and unchanging – indeed, its very strength comes from the Kuna's ability to absorb those aspects of the outside world that suit them and adapt them to their needs. The Kuna have travelled the world as sailors, many worked in the US bases, and thousands work and study in Panama City and Colón. Of course, this integration with the outside world poses some problems – egalitarian traditions are gradually being eroded and some resources, particularly lobster, are being overexploited to satisfy market demand. But if their history is anything to go by, the Kuna are likely to find ways of resolving these problems without losing their culture and their identity.

Kuna General Congress is responsible for all administration in accordance with the Kuna's own constitution – a degree of political autonomy far greater than that of any other indigenous people in Latin America.

Visiting Kuna Yala

Although the Kuna are generally keen to promote **tourism**, they are determined to control its development and limit its negative impacts. When in Kuna Yala, particularly in the more remote areas, it is important to remember that you are a guest of the Kuna and must abide by their laws. Always ask **permission** from the local *sahila* when you visit a particular town or wish to stay on an island, and ask before **photographing** anybody (expect to pay about US$0.25 per photo, more for group shots). The Kuna are particularly sensitive about the *casas de congreso* and the cemeteries on the mainland – never enter or photograph these without permission. During your visit make sure you respect the Kuna's sometimes strict **social codes** – full or partial nudity and public displays of affection, for example, are frowned upon on the more densely populated islands. Note that some islands charge a **fee** for visitors, and most will assign a **guide** to take you around.

Nearly every **tour company** in Panama City (see p.769) organizes trips to Kuna Yala, some to exclusive resort hotels. Although such tours are often the best way to visit, it is easy to visit the *comarca* independently. The few islands with any organized tourist **facilities** are concentrated in the western end of the archipelago in the

Golfo de San Blas. Here, you can stay in basic guesthouses or small hotels where meals and boat trips – to other islands, beaches and snorkelling spots, or into the forests of the mainland – are included in the price. Away from these islands the possibilities for adventure are endless – there's no reason why you shouldn't fly to any of the other islands or mainland communities where, once you have received permission from the *sahila*, you can find a family to stay with and rent a boat to take you around. You can also – again, with permission – get a boatman to drop you on one of the many uninhabited islands to camp, though you will need to bring all your own food and water. If you are planning any kind of **long stay** in Kuna Yala, you need permission from the Congreso General Kuna office in Panama City (☎316 1233), Calle Florida, in Howard.

By air

The easiest way to reach Kuna Yala is by **plane**. Almost all the forty or so inhabited islands and the twelve mainland communities have airstrips close by, but only eleven are served regularly by Aeroperlas (☎315 7500, Ⓦwww.aeroperlas.com), from Marcos A. Gelabert domestic airport in Albrook. Flights cost between US$32 and US$40 one way. The airstrips are often bigger than the islands themselves and so are necessarily located on the mainland; a small arrival and departure fee is charged, usually added to the cost of your accommodation. If you need to return to Panama City on a specific day, you should book in advance – though this is still no guarantee that the plane will arrive on time or indeed turn up at all. Flying between islands is very difficult as the flights rarely hop between them; it's also worth bearing in mind that most of the small airstrips have no facilities at all.

By sea

You can reach the islands and travel between them by boat, though the large wooden dugouts used by the Kuna tend to have very small motors so progress is rather leisurely. In addition, several Kuna-owned trading ships travel between Coco Solo port near Colón (see p.779) and the islands, but they are generally unwilling to carry outsiders, as are the Colombian ships from Turbo or Cartagena that tramp up and down the archipelago trading basic goods for coconuts. You may be able to get them to take you between islands, but remember that this is a wild coast, and many of the ships that pass along it are involved in smuggling. If you can get on one, they are the least expensive way to travel throughout the archipelago – the three- to five-day trip from Coco Solo to Puerto Obaldía, on the Colombian border, won't cost you more than US$30, meals included.

Smaller wooden boats from the village of **Miramar** on the Costa Arriba in Colón Province (see p.786) occasionally travel to the islands around El Porvenir to deliver fresh fruit and vegetables. Though it's not really worth trying to come into Kuna Yala this way – you don't really want to hang around in Miramar waiting for a boat – it's an exciting way to return from the islands: the boats all pass by the *Hotel San Blas* in Nalunega (see p.801), and are usually happy to take passengers back to the Costa Arriba for about US$10. The archipelago is also popular with **private yachts**, and you may find one that's prepared to take you to Colombia via the islands – try asking around at the Panama Canal Yacht Club in Cristóbal or at *Voyager International Hostel* in Panama City (for more on travelling to Colombia by yacht, see p.800).

On foot

You can **walk** into Kuna Yala across the Serrania de San Blas from the village of El Llano, 70km east of Panama City on the Darién Highway, a two-day journey passing through the pristine Nusagandi Nature Reserve (see opposite). There are plenty of other adventurous walking routes across the Serrania from the coast of Kuna Yala to the tributaries of the Chucunaque, which you can then descend by dugout canoe to reach the Darién Highway, but for these you will need guides.

Nusagandi Nature Reserve

The semi-abandoned road that runs some 47km from El Llano on the Darién Highway across the Serrania de San Blas to the coast is the **best land route** into Kuna Yala, and is easy to follow without a guide. Built in the 1970s as part of General Torrijos' planned "conquest of the Caribbean", the road originally extended to the coast opposite the island of Cartí, bringing a wave of colonists to the borders of Kuna Yala, who cleared the forest for agriculture and cattle ranching. The Kuna General Congress acted swiftly in response to this threat to the territorial and ecological integrity of the region, establishing a **nature reserve** covering some thousand square kilometres – the first such reserve in Latin America to be set up and administered by an indigenous people. Today, the road is usually passable by 4WD as far as the park guard station and **nature lodge** at **Nusagandi**, 27km from El Llano.

Visiting the reserve

About fifteen kilometres from the highway on the way to Nusagandi is the new *Burbayar Lodge* (☎264 1679 & 654 0952, Ⓦwww.burbayar.com), where a package tour of two days and one night costs US$150 per person and includes all meals, transportation from Panama City and guided tours throughout the reserve in search of the 400 species of bird that inhabit it as well as outings to nearby caves and local indigenous communities. Visits to the lodge can also be booked through tour operators in Panama City (see p.769).

From here, the road deteriorates as it continues on to *Nusagandi Nature Lodge*, where you can stay with **permission** from the Congreso General Kuna in Panama City (see p.751). The fee is US$5 per day to visit the reserve, plus US$10 per night to stay in the Nusagandi lodge. It's a short, but rough, drive from El Llano to Nusagandi, if you have your own vehicle, or about six hours on foot – you may be able to hitch, but don't count on it. Perched just over the continental divide, **Nusagandi** has excellent views of the jagged, forest-covered ridges that march down to the Caribbean, and on clear days you can see the islands laid out in the shimmering waters of the Golfo de San Blas. Set amid the pristine forests, the run-down **nature lodge** has dorms, with a communal bathroom and a kitchen – you should bring all the food you need, plus a little extra for the park guards. The forest around the lodge is rich in wildlife, particularly toucans and various species of monkey. **Trails** pass waterfalls and *miradores*, and the knowledgeable park guards are usually happy to act as guides.

Beyond Nusagandi, the 20km road down to the **coast** is impassable to vehicles but easy to follow on foot. It's a tough walk (6–8hr) through pristine forest, longer if you stop to observe the wildlife, so you should leave early in the morning. For the last two hours the road levels out as it reaches the narrow coastal plain where the Kuna farms are concentrated, but even here you are unlikely to see another soul. The only place where the road is difficult to follow is after it crosses a bridge over the Río Cartí Grande – you should veer left here. An hour beyond the bridge you emerge at the coast beside the Cartí airstrip, where you can find a boat to take you over to Cartí or one of the other islands.

The islands

Set just off the Punta de San Blas on the northern tip of the gulf, the island of **EL PORVENIR** is the administrative capital of Kuna Yala and home to the airport for the nearby islands of **Wichub Wala**, **Nalunega** and **Ukuptupu**, which are those best prepared to receive visitors. You can **stay** here at the *Hotel El Porvenir* (no phone; ❼), where all meals and various boat trips are included, but there's little reason to do so – apart from the airstrip, the Kuna-controlled *gobernación*, and a small beach, there's nothing much to the place. The hotels on Wichub Wala and Nalunega send boats to meet arriving planes, and you are better off heading onto one of these straight away.

On **Nalunega**, the *Hotel San Blas* (☎290 6528; ❻) is the biggest and longest established on the islands. Fenced off from the village with its own stretch of beach, it offers a choice of basic rooms in a modern concrete building or cooler sand-floored cabins on the pleasant beach in front. Bathrooms are shared. The owner, Luis Burgos, and several of the staff speak some English, and snorkelling equipment is available to rent. On **Wichub Wala** the pleasant *Kuna Niskua* (☎225 5200, ⓔiguabi@hotmail.com; ❼) has pleasant rooms in the midst of the community. On nearby Ukuptupu, *Cabañas Ukuptupu* (☎299 9011; ❼) occupies the former Smithsonian marine research station, built on a tiny semi-submerged coral outcrop with cool, well-built rooms connected by walkways over the sea. Rates in these three hotels are good value when you consider they include three decent meals a day, usually with fish and sometimes lobster, and boat excursions to pristine beaches, busy Kuna communities or into the forests of the mainland. The most popular excursion is to **Achutupu**, or Dog Island, where a wrecked Colombian cargo boat just off shore makes for excellent snorkelling.

Crossing into Colombia

Although at present it's no longer safe to enter Colombia overland via the Darién Gap (see p.791), it is still possible to cross the border to Panama's southern neighbour by other methods, including as a passenger on a private yacht, by foot from Puerto Obaldía at the eastern tip of Kuna Yala or on the cargo boats that tramp down the Pacific coast. However, be aware that all these options pose an element of danger and the Chocó region of Colombia south of Panama is one of the most dangerous in South America.

Frequently, **private yachts** carry passengers between Colón and the Colombian city of Cartagena on an informal basis. This adventurous trip takes three or four days, passing through the San Blas Archipelago, and should cost about US$200 per person plus food – about the same as a flight to Cartagena. *Voyager International Hostel* in Panama City (see p.754) usually has up-to-date information on which yachts are carrying passengers on this route, and you can always ask around at the yacht clubs in Cristóbal (Colón) or Balboa (Panama City).

You can also enter Colombia **on foot via Puerto Obaldía**, a remote border outpost at the far southeastern extreme of Kuna Yala, served by light aircraft from Panama City. It has a basic pensión and a couple of restaurants. After going through customs and *migración*, you can walk or take a motorboat down to Capurgana, a small fishing village and incipient holiday resort on the Colombian coast. From Capurgana boats head across the Gulf of Urabá to Turbo, where you must register with DAS, the Colombian agency that deals with immigration, and you can catch one of the regular light aircraft flights to Medellín and Cartagena.

On the **Pacific side**, occasional boats from the Muelle Fiscal in Panama City run down the coast of Darién to **Jaqué**, 90km due south of La Palma (20hr), and sometimes continue to Juradó and Bahía Solano in Colombia (3 days), from where there are onward flights to Quibdó, Medellín and Turbo. You can get an exit stamp from the *migración* at the dock in Panama City, but you should check on entry requirements with the Colombian consulate there.

Be warned, though, that the whole border area is busy with **guerrilla and paramilitary activity**: the police garrison at Puerto Obaldía has been attacked several times; the naval base at Juradó was destroyed by guerrillas in 1999, leading most of the town's population to flee to Panama; and Turbo is at the centre of Urabá, one of the most violent regions in Colombia.

Cartí, Río Sidra and the Cayos Holandeses

One of a cluster of densely populated islands close to the mainland and roughly 10km south of El Porvenir, **CARTÍ** is a busy community where about 1500 Kuna live crammed onto a tiny patch of land. There's a small, basic *dormitorio* (❸) and a cafeteria serving basic meals, and if you stay here, you'll be living in the midst of the community. Although there's no beach, you can easily hire a boatman to take you out during the day. There is a **museum** (US$2), however, which has a collection of Kuna arts and crafts, including examples of the miniature carved dugout canoes used in funeral ceremonies. Cartí's **airstrip** is on the mainland, where the path down from Nusagandi emerges onto the coast.

Some 10km east of Cartí is the community of **RÍO SIDRA**, where you'll find *Cabañas Robinson* (ⓣ299 9058 & 9007 & 9028; ❹–❻), the best budget option and one of the nicest places to stay in the archipelago. The owner and host, Arnulfo Robinson, has cabins on three small yet beautiful islands, some with hammocks and others with beds. Mr Robinson is constantly travelling between the islands to cook and entertain his guests; when his islands are full he can come at any time of the day, so it is worth taking some snacks and water with you. All of the islands have **soft coral beaches** and reefs for snorkelling, and one of the islands, Isla Naranja Chica, has a small Kuna community living on it who are happy to interact with visitors. The community of Río Sidra is served by a small airstrip on the mainland, ten minutes by boat from the densely populated island that shares the same name and is home to Mr Robinson's family – it's also a place to get basic supplies including purified water and cold sodas.

About 20km northeast of Río Sidra, the outlying chain of islands known as the **CAYOS HOLANDESES** are amongst the most pristine and beautiful in the archipelago and are an excellent spot for snorkelling. To reach them, you'll have to arrange for a boat to come and fetch you at the end of your stay – it takes about two to three hours from El Porvenir. Sea conditions can be rough, though, and you may have to pay up to US$50 to persuade someone to take you.

Narganá, Corazón de Jesús and Isla Tigre

For some Kuna the twin islands of **NARGANÁ** and **CORAZÓN DE JESÚS**, 40km east of El Porvenir, are a nightmare vision of what the future of Kuna Yala might be like if the *uaga burba* – the spirit of the outsiders – continues to spread. Few women here wear traditional dress; the buildings are mostly of concrete rather than cane and palm; there is a **Banco Nacional** but no *casa de congreso*; and whereas most communities do not allow missionaries onto their islands, here five different Christian sects compete for possession of the islanders' souls. In some ways, this makes it an interesting place: the front line in a long-standing cultural struggle. However, continuing on to nearby **ISLA TIGRE**, by motorized dugout canoe, makes for a much better place to stay. Here the traditional Kuna culture remains and the beaches, coral reefs and nearby deserted islands remain in pristine condition, thanks to the caution exercised over any excessive development. You can **stay** at the *Cabañas Tigre* (ⓣ229 9006; ❸), where hammocks slung in cane and thatch huts on the beach provide the accommodation; the owner will provide meals at an extra cost, though there are a few simple **restaurants** in the community.

Ailigandi and Achutupu

Some 60km further along the coast towards Colombia, the island of **AILIGANDI** is an important regional centre with a population of some two thousand, many of whom are Baptists. You can **stay** at the *Hotel Ikasa* (ⓣ224 8492; ❹), a simple, clean concrete construction with a basic restaurant, or you may be invited to stay in someone's home. There's also a small communal **restaurant**. Once again, there is plenty of scope for excursions, and the island is also home to the **Hogar Cultural Kuna**, where woodcarving, pottery, weaving and *mola* design are taught.

Served by its own airstrip on the mainland, but only 10km east of Ailigandi, the island community of **ACHUTUPU** is home to the *Dolphin Island Lodge* (Ⓦwww.dolphinlodge.com). Established as a non-profit venture by the local community, the lodge provides some of the most plush accommodation within San Blas. The internally decorated cane and thatch cabins, set along the narrow beach, have comfortable beds and private bathrooms. Meals, tours and flights are provided as part of the package deals that are sold through tour operators in Panama City (see p.769).

7.4

Western Panama

A region of unspoilt surf-fringed beaches, sleepy rural towns and cool mist-swathed highland cloudforests, Western Panama is divided in two by the rugged **Cordillera Central**, which begins not far west of the Panama Canal and runs some 400km to Costa Rica. North of the mountains, the undeveloped Caribbean coast is covered in dense rainforest and inhabited by isolated indigenous groups. South of the mountains, the drier and more fertile coastal plain is largely deforested and heavily settled. This agricultural heartland is known as **el interior** (its inhabitants are known as *interioranos*), the homeland of *ladino* (people of indigenous and European descent) rural culture.

Before the arrival of the Spanish, this Pacific coastal region was home to the most sophisticated **indigenous societies** in the country, and it was here that the conquistadors met the fiercest resistance, especially that led by Urraca, a chieftain whose likeness now decorates the one-cent coin. These societies were gradually defeated and either assimilated or driven into the infertile highlands – where their descendants, the **Ngobe-Buglé**, still live – while the forests were cleared for agriculture and cattle ranches.

The region's towns – **Penonomé**, **Chitré**, **Las Tablas**, **Santiago** and **David** – are little more than pleasant provincial market centres not necessarily worth a visit in their own right and the surrounding agricultural lands scarcely match the untamed wildernesses found elsewhere in the country. Even so, several places are worth checking out as you head west towards Costa Rica or Bocas del Toro. Close to Panama City, a series of spectacular Pacific **beaches** and the cool mountain resort town of **El Valle** are the most popular weekend destinations for those after some respite from the confinement of city life, while slightly further west near Penonomé the remnants of the pre-Columbian societies that dominated the region can be seen at **Parque Arqueológico el Caño**. South of the Interamericana, the **Península de Azuero** is a fascinating agricultural region famed for its religious fiestas, in which early Spanish folk traditions survive almost unchanged. In addition, although the peninsula is largely deforested, the surrounding coastline has been left mostly untouched and is home to a rich and varied marine ecology. Divers and snorkelling fanatics prize the rarely visited coral reefs surrounding **Isla Iguana Wildlife Reserve**, while at **Isla Cañas Wildlife Reserve**, to the south, sea turtles arrive every year in the thousands. In the far west, near the Costa Rican border, the Cordillera Central rises to its highest peaks in the **Chiriquí Highlands**, a beautiful region of dense cloudforests, idyllic mountain villages and extinct volcanoes, including **Volcán Barú**, the country's tallest peak.

West from Panama City

West of Panama City, the **Interamericana** runs along a narrow plain squeezed between the Pacific and the slopes of the Cordillera Central. The landscape becomes noticeably more arid as you travel west – deforestation and El Niño have made the crescent formed by the coastal plains of Coclé and Herrera provinces the driest region in Panama, and the sugar-cane fields depend on irrigation water from the rivers that run down from the mountains to the north. At the border of Coclé Province, 23km beyond Aguadulce and 213km from Panama City, the road forks at

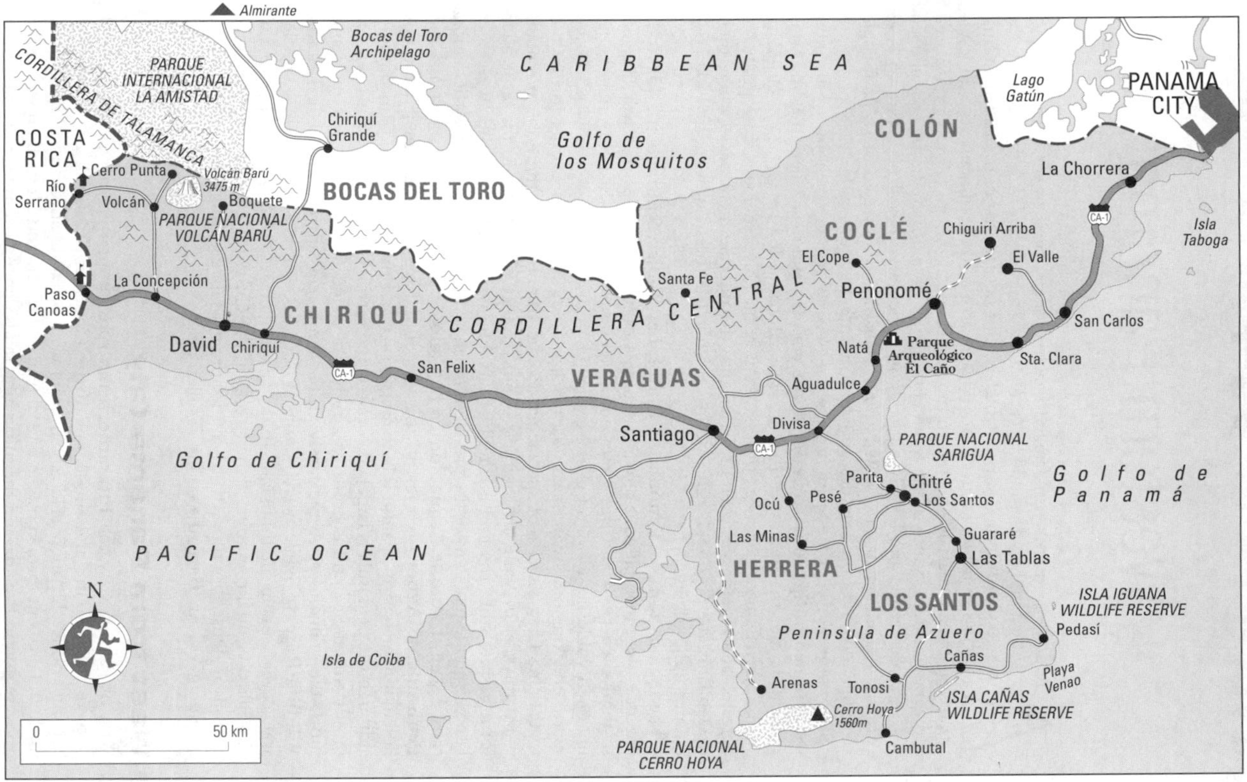

CARIBBEAN SEA
PACIFIC OCEAN
Golfo de los Mosquitos
Golfo de Chiriquí
Golfo de Panamá
Bocas del Toro Archipelago
Almirante
COSTA RICA
CORDILLERA DE TALAMANCA
PARQUE INTERNACIONAL LA AMISTAD
Volcán Barú 3475 m
PARQUE NACIONAL VOLCÁN BARÚ
BOCAS DEL TORO
CHIRIQUÍ
CORDILLERA CENTRAL
VERAGUAS
COCLÉ
COLÓN
HERRERA
LOS SANTOS
Península de Azuero
PANAMA CITY
Lago Gatún
Isla Taboga
Isla de Coiba
PARQUE NACIONAL SARIGUA
ISLA IGUANA WILDLIFE RESERVE
ISLA CAÑAS WILDLIFE RESERVE
PARQUE NACIONAL CERRO HOYA
Cerro Hoya 1560m
Parque Arqueológico El Caño
Río Serrano
Cerro Punta
Volcán
Boquete
Paso Canoas
La Concepción
David
Chiriquí
Chiriquí Grande
San Felix
Santiago
Santa Fe
El Cope
Penonomé
Chiguiri Arriba
El Valle
San Carlos
Sta. Clara
La Chorrera
Natá
Aguadulce
Divisa
Ocú
Las Minas
Pesé
Parita
Chitré
Los Santos
Guararé
Las Tablas
Pedasí
Playa Venao
Cañas
Tonosi
Cambutal
Arenas
CA-1
N
0
50 km

Divisa: the Interamericana continues west to Santiago, the capital of Veraguas Province, while Carretera Nacional turns south into the Península de Azuero.

Beaches along the Carretera Interamericana

From Panama City, the Interamericana crosses the Bridge of the Americas, which soars 1600m across the mouth of the canal, and passes through the satellite town of La Chorrera, home to Panama's notorious "Traumalandia" high-security prison, as it heads west towards the province of Coclé. For 50km beyond the village of Bejuco, 29km west of La Chorrera, the coast is lined with some of the most beautiful and popular Pacific **beaches** in Panama, all just a few kilometres from the highway and accessible by taxi or local buses. From east to west **playas Gorgona and Coronado** are the most fashionable weekend destinations for the wealthy residents of Panama City, while **Playa San Carlos** is the most popular with surfers.

Playa Santa Clara, 30km east of Penonomé, is probably the loveliest – a seemingly endless stretch of white sand lapped by usually calm waters. The beach is 1.5km from the Interamericana, but there is a local taxi (Ⓣ606 9084) and a phone at the junction. There are two **restaurants**, *Las Veraneras* (daily 10am–9pm), which serves decent fish and seafood, and *El Balneario*, which also serves seafood, rents small palm-thatched huts and allows camping (US$5); contact either spot for advice on renting horses from locals. *Cabañas Veraneras* (Ⓣ993 3313, Ⓦwww.lasveraneras.com; ❻) has a large number of cabañas, the smallest ones, with shared shower, accommodate four people and overlook the beach, while the largest has a kitchen, a/c and BBQ area, and sleeps up to ten people.

El Valle

Just beyond San Carlos, 96km west of Panama City, a twisty road climbs up into the cordillera to **EL VALLE**, a small village set in an idyllic fertile valley that was once the crater of a volcano, now long extinct. At 600m above sea level, El Valle is comparatively cool, and the surrounding countryside is good for walking or horseback-riding. Renowned for its flowers – particularly its **orchids** – the area is a popular retreat for Panama City residents at the weekend. Otherwise, it's a peaceful place, where most people still get around by bicycle or on horseback, and the only noise is that of lawnmowers and of hummingbirds buzzing among the flowers.

The village and around

Spread out along Avenida Principal, the elongated heart of El Valle is where most of the village's amenities can be found, along with signposts pointing the way to all local attractions, most of which are located on the outskirts of the village. The daily **market**, in the centre, draws the biggest crowds, especially at its height on Sundays, when locals pour in to sell their fruit, handicrafts (including carved soapstone, traditional earthenware pottery and woven baskets) and flowers. Nearby, a small **museum** (Sun 10am–2pm; US$0.25), run by nuns and housing exhibits on local history and folklore, stands next to the twin-towered church of San José. Beyond the church a side road leads to the less-than-impressive **thermal baths** (daily 8am–noon & 1–5pm; US$1), by the Río Anton, which are reputed to have medicinal powers. Next to the antenna-topped Cable & Wireless building on Av Principal, a rocky 1km road leads up to **El Nispero**, a plant and orchid nursery with a small zoo (daily 7am–5pm; US$2) where you can see monkeys, ocelots and the celebrated golden frog that is native to the area. Cages are cramped, though, and some of the animals look pretty miserable.

Across the bridge over the Río Guayabo at the east end of Av Principal, the road forks three ways. A thirty-minute walk up the right fork takes you up to **El Chorro Macho** (daily 6am–5pm; US$2.10), a 35-metre waterfall set amid the forest of a private ecological reserve; for another US$2 you can also use the delightful natural swimming pool in the river. The reserve also operates exciting cable rides through the forest canopy, the so-called **Canopy Adventure** (ⓣ983 6547), costing US$42.50 for just over an hour or US$10 for a quick traverse over the river. The left fork from the bridge leads to the smaller **Las Mozas** waterfall, while a fifteen-minute walk along the centre fork leads to a group of **petroglyphs**. Carved on a huge white rock and highlighted with chalk and charcoal, the petroglyphs are pre-Columbian abstract designs, including spirals and anthropomorphic and zoomorphic figures; nobody knows when or by whom they were carved, let alone their significance. Further afield, innumerable trails climb up into the **cloudforests** of the surrounding mountains, which are excellent for birdwatching – try following the path up behind the petroglyphs to the peak of **La India Dormida**, the mountain ridge that looms over the valley to the west and whose silhouette resembles the sleeping form of a legendary Indian princess.

Practicalities

Buses pull in at the covered market on Av Principal, which acts as the town's unofficial bus terminal, although most buses will stop upon request. Buses from Panama City arrive every thirty minutes between 7.30am and 6.30pm, and minibuses arrive every 45 minutes from San Carlos, a twenty-minute trip. There's a small **IPAT** office (Wed–Sun 8.30am–4.30pm; ⓣ983 6474), in a kiosk next to the market, but the owner of *Artesanías Don Pepe*, which sells excellent maps of the area (US$2), is also an excellent source of local information.

You'll find most of the accommodation in El Valle scattered along Av Principal. *Restaurante Santa Librada* (ⓣ983 6376; ❷–❸), with rooms of varying sizes and levels of comfort, is the town's best budget option, although the *Motel Niña Delia* (ⓣ983 6110; ❸), with small, en-suite rooms, is also good value and has a pleasant patio and garden. Moving up the scale, *Hotel Don Pepe* (ⓣ983 6425; ❺) has large, modern en-suite rooms, Internet access and helpful service, while the luxurious *Hotel Los Capitanes*, C El Ciclo (ⓣ983 6080, ⓦwww.panamainfo.com/loscapitanes; ❼), boasts spacious, well-furnished rooms set amid beautiful grounds. A new adventure-orientated resort, *Crater Valley*, C El Gaital (ⓣ983 6942, ⓦwww.crater-valley.com; ❽), has large rooms sleeping four to six people and organizes rafting, hiking, climbing and mountain-biking outings.

Some of the town's **restaurants** only open their doors at weekends, but of those that are open daily the *Santa Librada*, on the main street, is one of the best and serves very good típica food. *Restaurante Don Pepe* has a large menu of Panamanian food and offers filling breakfasts. For basic, filling and inexpensive meals, try the restaurant inside the covered market. Opposite the museum, *Pinocchio's* serves decent pizza, roast chicken and ice cream. On the higher end, the restaurant at the *Los Capitanes* serves good international cuisine, with main courses from about US$10.

The **Banco Nacional** has an ATM on Av Principal, by the turn-off for El Nispero. If you're not staying at the *Hotel Don Pepe*, you can log onto the **Internet** at the local library. You can rent **bicycles** (US$2/hr) from the *Hotel Don Pepe* and **horses** (US$3.50/hr) from Iñes (ⓣ622 4374), who has a little kiosk near the *Hotel Campestre*, about ten minutes' walk out of town to the northeast. In both cases, you'll probably get a better price on weekdays.

Moving on from El Valle, you can either take a direct bus to Panama City or a minibus to San Carlos, where you can flag down buses heading in either direction along the Interamericana.

Penonomé and around

Founded in 1581 as a *reducción de Indios* – a place where conquered indigenous groups were forcibly resettled so as to be available for labour service – and briefly the capital of the isthmus after the destruction of Panamá Viejo, the lively market town of **PENONOMÉ** was named after Nomé, a local chieftain cruelly betrayed and executed here by the Spaniards after years of successful resistance. Now the capital of the province of Coclé, Penonomé doesn't have much to see apart from its small museum, though it makes a good enough base for exploring the surrounding area, including Chiguiri Arriba, with its hiking trails and spectacular views, and the pre-Columbian site of the Parque Arqueológico El Caño.

From the bus terminal on the Interamericana, Penonomé's busy commercial main street, called both Via Central or Avenida J. D. Arosemena, runs a few hundred metres to the **Plaza 8 de Diciembre**. Featuring a statue of Simón Bolívar and the inevitable bandstand, the square is flanked by several government buildings and an unspectacular **cathedral**. From here, head two blocks down Calle Damían Carles, take a right and continue for two blocks and you'll arrive at the blue-and-white painted **Museo de Historia y Tradición Penonomeña** (Tues–Sat 9am–4pm, Sun 9am–1pm; US$1). Expected to reopen after renovations at the end of 2004, the museum has some good pre-Columbian ceramics decorated with abstract designs and colonial religious art. The streets around the market bustle with campesinos from local villages selling agricultural produce (and spending much of the proceeds in the town's many bars).

Practicalities

Buses from Panama City arrive at the **terminal** at the intersection of Via Central and the Interamericana every twenty minutes or so, and when you're ready to move on it's easy to flag down any through bus going east or west along the Interamericana. Opposite the bus terminal, *Hotel Dos Continentes* (Ⓣ997 9325; ❹) makes for good-value **accommodation**, with clean, spacious a/c rooms, while rooms at the friendly *Residencial El Paisa* (Ⓣ997 9242; ❸), just off the plaza on Av Manuel Amador Guerrero, are cramped and slightly stuffy.

Of the town's several **restaurants**, the best is at the *Hotel Dos Continentes*, which is popular and particularly good for breakfast. There are several restaurants called *Gallo Pinto*, each with menus as original as their name – opt for the one opposite *El Paisa*. On the Interamericana, *Las Tinajas* is a reasonably inexpensive, self-service place, while *Parillada El Gigante*, also on the Interamericana, offers pizza and grilled meat. The **post office** is on C Damían Carles, and you'll find a **Banistmo** on Av J. D. Arosemena, which has an ATM and changes travellers' cheques.

Chiguiri Arriba

From the market area in Penonomé, *chivas* (flatbed trucks converted to carry passengers) head off to villages scattered in the folds of the cool, forested mountains that rise to the north. Of these potential destinations, **Chiguiri Arriba**, 29km away to the northwest, makes an easy day-trip (1–2 *chivas* daily; leaving about 10am, returning in the afternoon; 1hr 20min; US$1.50), with plenty of good hiking trails, spectacular views and a thirty-metre waterfall nearby – local children will happily guide you there for a small tip. Some 2km before the village is *La Posada del Cerro La Vieja* (Ⓣ983 8900 or 223 4553, Ⓕ264 5378; ❽), a luxurious **eco-resort** set amid beautiful gardens and a private forest reserve. Rates include all meals and guided excursions, on foot or horseback. The resort can also arrange longer trips across the mountains to El Valle or down through pristine rainforest to the Caribbean coast by trail and motorized dugout canoe along the Río Indio, though there's no reason – with a little Spanish, a local guide and the right supplies and equipment – why you can't do this independently.

El Caño Archeological Park and Natá

Some 25km west of Penonomé on the Interamericana, the **Parque Arqueológico El Caño** (Tues–Sat 9am–4pm, Sun 9am–1pm; US$1) is the most impressive pre-Columbian site in Panama – that's not saying very much, though, as compared with the Mayan wonders elsewhere in Central America there's very little to see. An important ceremonial site from 500 to about 1200 AD, El Caño later became a cemetery that was still in use after the Conquest, but the hundreds of stone statues that formed what was described as the "Temple of the Thousand Idols" were illegally decapitated by US archeologist Hyatt Verril in the early twentieth century, and the best of their zoomorphic and anthropomorphic heads are now in New York. Often plagued by mosquitoes, the site consists of several funeral mounds, one of which is excavated and open to view, and lines of headless standing stones. A small **museum** displays ceramics and lesser stone statues, but otherwise there's nothing to delay you for more than half an hour. To reach the site from the marked turn-off on the Interamericana, walk ten minutes to the village of El Caño, beyond which it's another 25 minutes' walk.

Several kilometres west of the El Caño turn-off, **NATÁ** was founded by Gaspar de Espinoza in 1522 as the forward base for the Spanish conquest of what was then known as Veragua. The indigenous forces led by Urraca relentlessly attacked the site until their defeat in 1556, and Natá became an agricultural centre supplying the now long-abandoned gold mines on the Caribbean coast. Today, Natá is a quiet backwater, notable only for the **Church of Santiago Apóstol**, built in 1522 and quite possibly the oldest church on the American mainland still in use. Set on the main square about five minutes' walk from the highway, it boasts a fine Baroque facade and an intricately carved colonial altar.

The Península de Azuero

Jutting out into the Pacific Ocean like the head of an axe (or adze, which is what *azuero* means), the largely deforested **Península de Azuero** was one of the earliest regions of Panama to be settled by Spanish colonists and is considered the cradle of Panamanian rural tradition and folklore. Predominantly given over to cattle ranches and smallholdings, the landscape here is dry and scrubby, dotted with small villages little changed from colonial times, its well-paved roads often blocked by herds of cattle being led to market by cowboys on horseback. In many ways, visiting the Azuero is like going back to seventeenth-century rural Spain – the peninsula's Spanish heritage is clearly evident in the traditional handicrafts and folk costumes, and above all in the vibrant religious **fiestas**.

Between fiestas, the principal towns of **Chitré** and **Las Tablas** are sleepy market centres where little happens, but the historic town of **Los Santos** and the eerie desert landscape of the **Parque Nacional Sarigua**, both near Chitré, make interesting excursions. Further south, meanwhile, the peninsula's rich coastal ecology is well preserved. Deserted white-sand beaches surround the small town of **Pedasí**, which is the jumping-off point for trips to the nearby **Isla Iguana Wildlife Reserve**, an offshore island ringed with coral reefs that is one of the best places for snorkelling or scuba diving on the Pacific coast of Panama. The rarely visited **Isla Cañas Wildlife Reserve**, further west, is an excellent place to observe nesting sea turtles. The mountainous western half of the peninsula, scarcely penetrated by roads, is home to the **Parque Nacional Cerro Hoya**, among the most beautiful and remote national parks in Panama, accessible only by boat or by a long, unpaved road from Santiago.

Chitré

The capital of Herrera Province and the largest town on the peninsula, **CHITRÉ** is a quiet market centre where life is conducted at a leisurely pace. Although the small museum is the only thing to see here, the town, as the peninsula's main transport hub, makes for a good base for exploring. Chitré centres on the Parque Unión, with the usual bandstand, benches and trees. The square is flanked on one side by the **cathedral**, which was built mostly in the eighteenth century and remodelled in the late 1980s, with an impressive vaulted wooden roof. The cathedral faces down Av Herrera – walk down a block and turn left on C Manuel Correa and you'll

Fiestas in the Península de Azuero

The Península de Azuero is famous throughout Panama for its many **religious fiestas**, usually honouring a particular patron saint. Many date back almost unchanged to the days of the early settlers, and represent the most obvious expression of the region's Spanish heritage. Religious **processions** are accompanied by traditional music, fireworks and costumed folk dances which are as **pagan** as they are Catholic. Listed below are just a few of the major events; every village and hamlet has its own fiesta, and there's almost always one going on somewhere – IPAT in Los Santos has good information on all these.

Jan 6 Fiesta de Reyes and Encuentro del Canajagua in Macarcas.

Jan 19–22 Fiesta de San Sebastian in Ocú.

Feb (date varies) Carnaval in Las Tablas (and everywhere else in the country).

March/April (date varies) Semana Santa, celebrated most colourfully in La Villa de Los Santos, Pesé and Guararé.

Late April Feria International del Azuero in La Villa de Los Santos.

June (date varies) Corpus Christi in La Villa de Los Santos.

June 24 Patronales de San Juan in Chitré.

June 29–30 Patronales de San Pedro y San Pablo in La Arena.

July 20–22 Patronales de La Santa Librada and Festival de la Pollera in Las Tablas.

Aug 15 Festival del Manito in Ocú.

Sept 24 Festival de la Mejorana in Guararé.

Oct 19 Foundation of the District of Chitré, in Chitré.

Nov 10 The "First Cry of Independence" in La Villa de Los Santos.

reach the **Museo de Herrera** (Tues–Sat 8am–noon & 1–4pm, Sun 8–11am; US$1), three blocks away. Set in an elegant colonial mansion, the museum has a collection of pre-Columbian pottery from the surrounding area and a good display on local folklore and customs, featuring traditional masks, costumes and musical instruments.

Practicalities

Buses from Panama City pull in at the **terminal** on the southern outskirts of town, about ten minutes' walk from the centre. The **IPAT** office for the entire peninsula is in neighbouring Los Santos (see overleaf). The best **hotel** in the centre of town is the *Rex* (☎996 4310; ❹) on Parque Unión, which has comfortable rooms with TV and a/c as well as an Internet café. The *Hotel El Prado* (☎996 4620 or 6859; ❸), on Av Herrera near the cathedral, and the *Hotel Santa Rita* (☎996 4610; ❸), just around the corner on C Manuel Correa, are both similar, with small, clean rooms and a choice of fan or a/c; the former has a balcony overlooking the street, which makes it a good place for watching fiestas.

The *Meson del Rex*, in the *Rex* hotel, is the best **restaurant** in town, its Spanish ownership evident in its red-checked tablecloths and excellent, reasonably priced cuisine. Also on the square, the open-air *Restaurante El Aire Libre* has a limited menu but great breakfasts, while the self-service *Restaurante Estrella #2*, on the corner opposite the cathedral, offers cheap and filling típica meals in a large room with ceiling fans. The **Banistmo** is on the corner of C Manuel Correa and Av Perez. The **post office** (Mon–Fri 7am–6pm) is a block down Av Perez, and there's **Internet access** at *Hotel Rex*.

Moving on from Chitré, buses to Las Tablas, Santiago and to villages in the interior of the peninsula leave from the **terminal**, while buses to Los Santos (every 10min; 10min) can be flagged down at any of the stops on the main streets in town.

Around Chitré: Parque Nacional Sarigua

Ten minutes north of Chitré, the village of **La Arena** is famous for its pottery, sold on the roadside by the potters themselves. Four kilometres further north, just before the village of **Parita**, a signposted side road leads into **Parque Nacional Sarigua**, eighty square kilometres of salt flats ringed by dense mangroves, forming one of the strangest landscapes in Panama – a harsh, arid marshland entirely devoid of vegetation due to occasional flooding by high tides. The salt flats have existed for thousands of years, but deforestation and sea winds that carry salt further inland are causing them to expand, threatening the livelihoods of local farmers. Not that the flats support no life at all – the area provides an excellent breeding ground for shrimp, which are farmed commercially and attract numerous wading birds. Indeed, archeological remains suggest that these marine resources provided the basis for Panama's oldest known human settlements – pottery, graves and arrowheads from between 5000 and 1500 BC have been found in the area, as well as mounds of discarded shells.

To reach Sarigua, take any bus heading north from Chitré, get off before Parita and walk 4.5km along the marked dirt road heading east or catch the irregular minibus from Chitré to the village of Puerto Limón, 1.5km from the park. There's a rangers' station at the entrance to the park and a small **visitor centre**, as well as a viewing tower (daily 8am–4pm), where you'll be charged the US$3 entrance fee.

Several other small wildlife reserves are found along this stretch of the coast, including **Playa El Aguilito**, about 6km southeast of Chitré past the airport, due south of Parque Nacional Sarigua and one of the best places in Panama for observing migrating birds. The best time to visit is in the morning, though the baking sun and fierce winds that occur in the afternoon are an experience in themselves. For information on other reserves in the areas, go to the ANAM office (Mon–Fri 8am–4pm; ☎996 7619) on the road to Los Santos.

La Villa de Los Santos and Guararé

South of Chitré, just across the Río La Villa and east of Carretera Nacional, **LA VILLA DE LOS SANTOS** – often referred to simply as Los Santos – is where the first Panamanian declaration of independence from Spain was made on November 10, 1821. A small, quiet town, Los Santos comes alive twice a year: to commemorate the "Cry of Independence" on November 10, and during the eight-day rum-fuelled fiesta of Corpus Christi in late May or early June.

The **IPAT** office (Mon–Fri 8.30am–4.30pm; ☎966 8013) on Parque Bolívar, the centre of the town, is fairly helpful, with plenty of information on the peninsula. Also on the parque, the **Museo de la Nacionalidad** (Tues–Sat 8am–4pm, Sun 9am–noon; US$1) has a small collection of colonial religious art and documents relating to the independence declaration. The building – an eighteenth-century house where the declaration was signed – is actually more interesting than its contents. Just off the parque, the **Church of San Atanacio**, built in the eighteenth century, features several intricately carved Baroque colonial altars.

From Los Santos the road continues 20km south to Las Tablas, passing through the small town of **GUARARÉ**. It's worth stopping here for the **Museo Manuel F. Zarate** (Tues–Sat 8am–4pm, Sun 8.30am–noon; US$1), behind the church on the main square, which has a fascinating exhibition on the folklore and fiestas of the peninsula, featuring masks, costumes, old photographs and a fine collection of *polleras*, the painstakingly embroidered, colonial-style dresses characteristic of the peninsula. A local teacher and musician, Manuel Zarate was dedicated to conserving the rich folk traditions of the Azuero, and in 1949 he began the "La Mejorana" National **Folkloric Festival**, a competition of traditional music, dance and costumes from across the country that is celebrated annually on September 24 in Guararé.

△ Rainforest waterfall

Las Tablas

LAS TABLAS was founded in the seventeenth century by refugees fleeing by sea from Panamá Viejo after its destruction by Henry Morgan and his band of pirates. The settlers dismantled their ships to build the first houses, hence the town's name: Las Tablas means "the planks". Turn up at any other time of year, and it's almost impossible to believe that this quiet colonial market town hosts the wildest **carnival** celebrations in Panama, but for five days in February the place is overwhelmed by visitors from all over the country who come here to join in the festivities. The town divides into two halves – **Calle Arriba** and **Calle Abajo** – that fight a pitched battle with water, paint and soot on streets awash with a seemingly endless supply of Seco Herrerano, the peninsula's vicious firewater. The fiesta of **Santa Librada** in July is less raucous, but just as colourful, and includes the **pollera fiesta**, which celebrates the peninsula's embroidered colonial-style dresses. Produced in the town, these dresses are something of a national symbol.

Practicalities

Buses from Panama City arrive at the Shell station a few blocks from the square, while those from Chitré pull into the Parque Porras. The best **place to stay** is the *Hotel Zafiro* (☎994 8200; ❹) on Parque Porras, which has modern rooms with a/c and TV, plus a balcony overlooking the square that makes it good, though noisy, at fiesta time, when prices go up. If you want to come here for carnival, you're better off trying to stay in Chitré, though even there accommodation is booked up well in advance.

The popular *Los Portales*, one block up Av B. Porras, is one of several basic **restaurants** on and around the square. A block away, *Jardín Praga* is also good and has a massive dance hall that is the centre of things on Friday and Saturday nights. **Banks** include the Banistmo on the square and the BBVA one block away on Av B. Porras. If you're heading into **Cerro Hoya** (see p.814) from this side of the peninsula, you should get information and permission from ANAM (Mon–Fri 8am–4pm; ☎994 6676) on the outskirts of town on the road to Pedasí; note that you don't need permission to visit Isla Iguana and Isla Cañas. **Moving on** from Las Tablas, hourly buses for Pedasí and Tonosí leave from the square and along Av B. Porras.

Pedasí and around

From Las Tablas, a road runs 42km south through cattle country to **PEDASÍ**, a friendly, uneventful little village best known as the hometown of ex-President Mireya Moscoso (1999–2004) and as the jumping-off point for **Isla Iguana**, just off the coast. **Places to stay** are on the main street: the long-established *Residencial Moscoso* (☎995 2203; ❸–❹) has comfortable rooms with a/c and TV and less expensive ones with shared bath and fans, while the better *Hotel Dim* (☎995 2303; ❹) has large, well-ventilated rooms and a charming garden with hammocks and a patio under a palm-thatched roof. Pedasí's **restaurants** include the *Angela*, on the main street, and *Centenario*, just off the main square, both of which serve inexpensive típica staples; *JR*, also on the main street, is a small restaurant where an ex-chef of the famous *Hotel El Panamá* cooks and serves excellent French food. The **IPAT** office (daily 8am–6pm), on the left as you enter the village from the north, is very helpful, and they also have **Internet access**. The only bank in town is the BNP (Mon–Fri 8am–3pm, Sat 9am–noon), which has an ATM. **Diving** trips and **snorkelling equipment** rental can be arranged through *Buseo de Azuero* (closed Wed) next to the IPAT office. **Buses** from Las Tablas and along the coast to Cañas via Playa Venao pass along the main street. In addition to those on Isla Iguana, there are several other good **beaches** near Pedasí – Playas La Garita, El Toro, El Arenal and Punta Mala – some of them within walking distance of town; taxis are on hand, too, if you want to head for those further afield.

Isla Iguana

Some 7km off the coast of Pedasí lies **Isla Iguana**, an uninhabited wildlife reserve surrounded by the most extensive **coral reefs** in the Bahía de Panamá. The reefs are composed of twelve different types of coral and teem with more than 540 species of fish, making Isla Iguana one of the best sites for **snorkelling** and **diving** in the country. The island has white-sand beaches, crystalline waters and a colony of some five thousand magnificent frigate birds, though, despite its name, iguanas are scarce – their meat remains a local delicacy. Between May and November you may see **whales**, and even the most inexperienced angler has a good chance of catching big game fish.

You can **hire a boat** to take you to the island from **Playa El Arenal**, a short taxi ride or thirty-minute walk from Pedasí down a signposted and paved road, past the IPAT office, where the staff will happily arrange this for you. Fishermen charge US$40 per return trip (25min each way) – on the weekends, you may find other visitors to share the cost. You should take all the food and drink you need. There is a visitor centre (open daily) on the island with toilets and showers, and you can **camp** (US$3) on the island or sling a hammock under a makeshift shelter on the beach – take plenty of drinking water and arrange for a boat to collect you the next day.

Playa Venao

Thirty kilometres west of Pedasí, the black-sand **Playa Venao** is great for **surfing**. There's an international competition here every November – come any other time, though, and you'll not find it crowded. The grotty *Jardín Vista Hermosa* (☎995 8107) serves inexpensive seafood and rents very basic concrete **cabañas** on the beach that sleep up to three people for US$14 a day. If you eat at the restaurant, however, they don't mind if you camp. A few kilometres east of Playa Venao, a signposted steep dirt road cuts south off the highway and leads to *Resort Playa Playita* (☎996 6551 or 639 2968; ❻), an extremely pleasant place closely managed by its energetic English-speaking owner. The small resort, situated around a sandy bay, is ideal for swimming, relaxing in a hammock or snorkelling (gear for rent), though for those more interested in wildlife there is an iguana pen, hummingbird area and many large birds including ostriches and rheas roaming freely throughout the grounds. Accommodation consists of several immaculate cabins, each sleeping four; camping in the resort is also allowed (US$5). Fishing trips can be arranged (US$30/hr), too, and the resort's seafood restaurant will be happy to cook your catch.

Isla Cañas Wildlife Reserve

Separated from the mainland by dense mangrove swamp, **Isla Cañas** is the most important **sea-turtle nesting site** on Panama's Pacific coast, its 14km-long beach frequented by four of the world's eight species of sea turtle. Though archeological evidence suggests that people have been coming to the island to hunt turtles and harvest their eggs for many centuries, it was only settled in the 1960s. The settlers, who now number some 400, have cleared most of the land for crops, but the eggs have always been their principal source of income. Since 1988, the hunting of turtles has been prohibited and a co-operative has been established to control the harvest. Members watch over the beaches at night and collect the eggs as soon as they are laid, keeping 80 percent for sale and consumption and moving the rest to a nursery where the turtles can hatch and return to the sea in safety. The reserve was officially established in 1994, protecting the mangroves as well as the marine life, and the turtle population has made a dramatic recovery since. Come here between May and January and you will almost certainly see green, hawksbill or Olive Ridley turtles laying their eggs at night – the latter sometimes arrive in massive **"arribadas"** of several thousand in one night between August and November, a truly magnificent sight. From December to March there's a good chance of seeing the leviathan-like leatherback turtle, which can weigh over 800 kilos.

Given the popularity of the similar Parque Nacional Tortuguero in Costa Rica (see p.636), it's surprising that there is as yet almost no tourist development at Isla Cañas; so, if you make it down here, you will almost certainly have the place to yourself. The island is also very beautiful by day – you can hire a horse and ride along the endless white sand or get one of the locals to take you through the mangroves in a small boat.

Practicalities

To **reach Isla Cañas** take a bus heading for the village of **Cañas** from Pedasí or Tonosí and tell the driver you want to go to the island – the port is down a side road a few kilometres from the village but buses go there on request. **Small boats** wait at the port to take people to the island (US$0.50 per person), slipping through channels cut in the mangroves to reach it, though at low tide you may have to wade through mud to get there. Once on the island, head for the ANAM office (☎995 8002) to pay the US$3 **visitors' charge**.

The co-operative that manages the turtles – the Cooperativa Isleños Unidos – has three rustic but clean **cabañas** (❷) with outside bath and mosquito nets. The mosquito nets are absolutely essential, as is insect repellent. The co-operative also has a small **restaurant**, although you should let them know in advance if you want to eat. For a small tip (a few dollars should suffice), the co-operative will assign a staff member to take you out on the beach at night to see the turtles – they may even let you eat an egg or two, freshly laid and still warm. **Buses** to Pedasí and Tonosí from Cañas normally come down to the port to collect passengers.

Tonosí and Parque Nacional Cerro Hoya

From Cañas the road continues 25km west to **TONOSÍ**, a small town set in a green valley ringed by mountains. Although you'll find several basic **restaurants** and a couple of pensiones, there's no reason to stay here unless you get stuck on your way to Isla Cañas. **Buses** to Las Tablas cut through the mountainous interior rather than following the coast via Pedasí. West of Tonosí the southwestern tip of the peninsula is covered by **Parque Nacional Cerro Hoya**, pretty much the last remaining slice of natural forest on the Azuero. Rainforest-swathed mountains rise from pristine beaches to heights of more than 1500m, encompassing five distinct life zones. The park's existence is challenged by settlers anxious to continue logging and clearing land for cattle ranching on its eastern fringes, and partly as a result ANAM is keen to promote ecotourism so locals can enjoy some of the economic benefits of conservation.

To visit the park you must first visit ANAM in Las Tablas (see p.812) for permission and information; they may also be able to help with transport. There are two routes into the park. **From Tonosí** you can get into the park by renting a boat from the nearby coastal village of **Cambutal** to take you to **Cobachón**, a coastal settlement just outside the park boundaries where you can camp near the ranger station or arrange to stay with local families. The easier approach, however, is by bus **from Santiago**, 98km along the west coast of the peninsula to the village of **Arenas**, where the park rangers will charge you the US$3 entrance fee and should be able to arrange transport by boat further down the coast to **Restingue**, another ranger station set on a beautiful beach with a network of trails into the surrounding forest. There's a basic refuge, with cooking facilities, where you can stay for US$5, but you'll need to bring a sleeping bag and all your own food supplies.

Santiago and the route west

The easiest way to continue west from the Azuero is to return to the Interamericana at **Divisa**, though it's possible to cut across the interior – via Pesé, Las Minas and Ocú – from Chitré. From Divisa, the Interamericana continues 36km west to **SANTIAGO**, Panama's fourth biggest city and a busy market centre, though it's an incorrigibly dull and provincial place, with little reason to stay except to break a journey.

Practicalities

Buses to Panama City and Chitré arrive and leave from the terminal on C 10, which links the Interamericana with Av Central in the city centre, while through buses heading for David pull in at the service station close to the *Hotel Gran David* on the Interamericana. The *Gran David* (☎998 4510; ❸) is the most convenient **place to stay**, with comfortable rooms set around a central garden with a swimming pool and a good restaurant. There's little reason to venture into the city, as there are several other places to eat on this stretch of the Interamericana, as well as a large mall development based around a branch of the BNP bank with ATM and La Galería complex that contains a cinema and shops.

West to David

From Santiago, the Interamericana continues west into the rich agricultural province of Chiriquí. A large area of the forested slopes of the Cordillera Central to the north and the Caribbean coast beyond is recognized as the **Comarca Ngobe-Buglé**. Commonly but erroneously referred to as the Guaymi, the Ngobe and Buglé (or Bokata) are two closely related peoples who together form the largest indigenous group in Panama. Recognizable by their women's brightly coloured dresses, the Ngobe-Buglé travel widely throughout the provinces of Chiriquí and Bocas del Toro to work on the farms, ranches and banana and coffee plantations – migrant wage labourers on the rich lands that once belonged to their ancestors.

David and around

The only one of three Spanish settlements founded in the area in 1602 to survive repeated attacks from indigenous groups, **DAVID** developed slowly as a marginal and remote outpost of the Spanish Empire – as late as 1732 it was overrun and destroyed by British-backed Miskito groups raiding from Nicaragua. Only as settlement of Chiriquí increased in the nineteenth century did David begin to thrive as a market and transportation centre. Today, despite being a busy commercial city – the third largest in Panama – and the focus of Chiriquí's strong regional identity, it retains a sedate provincial atmosphere. Hot and dusty, with unexceptional modern architecture spread out on a well-planned grid (the only surviving feature of the original colonial settlement), David has few attractions, but it's a good place to break a journey between Panama City and Costa Rica, Bocas del Toro or the Chiriquí Highlands – the last can be visited as a day-trip, though if you have the time, it's much better to stay up in the cool mountain towns of Boquete or Cerro Punta.

Arrival and information

Aeroperlas and Mapiex Aero **flights** from Panama City and Bocas del Toro arrive at the **airport**, about 5km out of town, a US$2 taxi ride away. Both Mapiex Aero (☎721 0841) and Aeroperlas (☎721 1195 or 1230) have offices at the airport and the latter also has an office just off the parque on C A Norte next to the *Hotel Puerto Del Sol*. **Buses** from Panama City, Almirante, Boquete, Cerro Punta and Paso Canoas, and TRACOPA international buses from San José all leave from the terminal on Av Cincuentenario. If you're heading to San José or by express bus to Panama City, you should buy a ticket in advance. There's a self-service restaurant, *America*, in the terminal and a left-luggage office that's open until 8pm. If you're heading for Costa Rica and need a visa, the **Costa Rican consulate** (☎774 1923) is on the outskirts of town on Cs B and C Sur and Av Este, while if you need a Panamanian visa extension or permission to leave the country, the **migración** (Mon–Fri 8am–3pm; ☎775 4515) is on Calle C Sur.

Accommodation

Accommodation in David is probably the best value in the country. There's a broad range, mostly in the city centre.

Hotel Alcalá Av 3 Este, C D Norte ☎774 9018. Clean and comfortable rooms with a/c, TV and hot water; some have balconies. ❺

Hotel Gran Nacional C A Sur, Av Central ☎775 2221. Recently refurbished, this expensive but good-value establishment is by far the grandest place in town, with immaculate, modern rooms featuring a/c, phone and TV. There's also a bar, pool, casino, and three restaurants. ❻

Hotel Iris Parque Cervantes ☎775 2251. Small, clean and comfortable rooms with a/c, TV and hot water, plus there's a café and communal balcony overlooking the square. ❹

Hotel Occidental Parque Cervantes ☎775 4068 or 8340, Ⓕ775 7424. Good-value and spacious a/c rooms – those at the front of the building are brighter and share a balcony overlooking the square. ❹

Pensión Fanita C B Norte, C 5 Este ☎775 3718. A large, ramshackle wooden house that unintentionally resembles a Wild West bordello. The floors are bowed and the rooms rather dingy, but you can have one for under US$3. ❶

The Purple House Hostel C C Sur, Av 6 Oeste ☎774 4059. Located in the quiet suburbs, close to the city's new commercial centre, with dormitories and private rooms, this well-managed hostel has helpful owners who often meet the buses from Costa Rica. On site, there's a kitchen, cable TV, lockers, good tourist information, laundry service, free Internet access, a patio and parking. The hostel will also arrange discounted trips to Boca Brava, 50km away, where there's good snorkelling and pleasant beaches. ❷–❸

The Town

David centres on **Parque Cervantes**, a good place to relax with a freshly squeezed sugar-cane juice and get your shoes shined in the shade of its immense trees. Three blocks southeast of the parque down C A Norte on the corner with Av 8 Este, the **Museo de Historia y Arte José de Obaldía** (Mon–Sat 8.30am–4.30pm; US$1) has a small but intriguing collection focusing on local history and culture, ranging from pre-Columbian artefacts and colonial religious art to relics from the Coto War with Costa Rica and photographs of David in the early twentieth century. The building is a beautiful colonial mansion that was home to successive generations of the distinguished Obaldía family – José was the founder of the province of Chiriquí, and later generations included presidents of both Colombia and Panama.

Eating, drinking and entertainment

There are plenty of good-value **restaurants** in David, several of which double as nightspots at the weekends. Otherwise, entertainment generally revolves around the city's many bars and pool halls, and a few discos – including *La Taverna* and *La Boom*. You can catch the latest Hollywood blockbusters at the modern **cinemas** at the *Gran Nacional* hotel and the Chiriquí Mall on the Interamericana.

BBQ Marco Av 6 Oeste, C N Norte. Open-fronted restaurant in the quiet suburbs serving tasty grilled Mediterranean food, with some vegetarian options, popular with both locals and tourists.

Café El Fogón Av 1 Oeste, C B Norte. Reasonably priced típica food that's popular with the locals, especially at lunchtime, and served in a friendly atmosphere.

Café Java Juice Plaza Florencia, Av Francisco Clark. A bit out of the way (it's close to the turn-off to Boquete), but the fantastic juices – made from local fruits such as mango and strawberry – and tasty snacks served in a relaxed atmosphere with outdoor seating make it worth a visit.

MultiCafe C A Norte, Av 3 Este. Modern self-service restaurant with a/c and parking that attracts a busy weekend crowd. Meals rarely cost more than US$3 and include beef stew and fried chicken – both served with lots of rice and plantains.

Restaurante Hotel Nacional Av Central, C A Sur. Comfortable dining with a menu consisting largely of meat, fish and pizza. There's nothing remarkable about the food at US$5–6, but it's a step up from típica food and the cable TV, tuned to either films or football, helps you endure the slow service.

Listings

Banks Banco Nacional (Mon–Fri 8am–3pm, Sat 9am–noon) is on Parque Cervantes; Banistmo (Mon–Fri 8am–3pm) is a block away on the corner of Av Cincuentenario and C Central.

Car rental Budget (☎775 5597) and Thrifty (☎721 2477) can be found at the airport.

Hospitals Hospital Chiriquí, on C B Sur, Av 4 Oeste, and Hospital Mae Lewis, on the Interamericana, are both open 24hrs and have English-speaking doctors.

Internet access There are several Internet cafés close to Parque Cervantes and one opposite the Romero supermarket on C F Sur.

Laundry Lavandería Panamá (Mon–Sat 7am–7pm), two blocks south of the parque on Av 3 Este.

Pharmacy The Romero supermarket on C F Sur has a 24hr pharmacy.

Post office A block north of the parque on C C Norte (Mon–Fri 7am–6pm, Sat 7am–5pm).

Shopping Ferreteria Romero, C Central, Av 3 Este, sells a small range of snorkelling, camping and fishing equipment; Chiriquí Mall on the Interamericana has a selection of modern shops; Super 99 and Romero supermarkets on C F Sur are open 24hrs.

Telephone A Cable & Wireless office (daily 8am–4.30pm) is on the corner of Av Cincuentenario and C C Norte.

On to Costa Rica

From David the Interamericana continues west 56km to the Costa Rican border at **PASO CANOAS**, passing through the saddle-making town of La Concepción, from where a side road heads up to Volcán and Cerro Punta (see overleaf). The **migración** at the border is open around the clock, plus there's an **IPAT** office (daily 6am–midnight; ☎727 6524) and a **Banco Nacional** where you can change travellers' cheques. Moneychangers will change Costa Rican currency. After passing through *migración* and customs (a formality unless you have anything to declare) you simply walk across the border, though queues for both can be long if international buses are passing through. If you're coming the other way, PADAFRONT **buses** for David (every 10min between 5am and 6pm; 1hr 20min) and Panama City (9 daily; 7–9hr) depart from just beyond the border.

The Chiriquí Highlands

North of David rise the slopes of the **Cordillera Talamanca**, home to **Volcán Barú**, an extinct volcano that at 3475m is the country's tallest peak. These are the **Chiriquí Highlands**, a region of cloudforest-shrouded peaks, fertile valleys and mountain villages. The cool, temperate climate and stark scenery give the highlands a distinctly alpine feel, an illusion reinforced by the influence of the many European migrants who have settled here since the nineteenth century. Sadly, their agricultural success poses a grave threat to the survival of the region's spectacular **cloudforests**, which have been cleared at a devastating rate over the past fifteen years. Large areas are now protected by **Parque Nacional Volcán Barú** and **Parque Internacional La Amistad**, whose cloudforests are home to some of the country's most endangered **wildlife**, including jaguars, pumas, tapirs, harpy eagles and resplendent quetzals, and whose trails offer some of the best hiking in Panama.

Two roads wind up into the highlands on either side of Volcán Barú. The first runs from La Concepción through the town of **Volcán** to **Cerro Punta**, the highest village in Panama and the best base for visiting the cloudforests. The second climbs to **Boquete**, an idyllic coffee-growing town which has become a popular resort and is the best place from which to climb Volcán Barú. The trail that runs between the two, around the back of the volcano through the cloudforests, can be walked in a day. Plans to build a road between Volcán and Boquete through the cloudforest in 2004 were quashed – though more for political than environmental reasons, so the threat still looms.

The road to Cerro Punta

From La Concepción a silky smooth 45km road to Cerro Punta winds up into the mountains through a lush valley with excellent views of the plain and the Golfo de Chiriquí before emerging at Hato de Volcán. Usually known simply as **VOLCÁN**, the small town creeps along the road, without a real centre, on a broad plateau at the foot of Volcán Barú. Volcán is a resort in its own right, with some good **trails** in the surrounding hills, including one to the protected Chiriquí lakes, but you're better off pushing on to Cerro Punta or **Guadelupe**, if you want to visit the Parque Nacional Volcán Barú. Should you choose **to stay** in Volcán, the *Hotel Dom Tavo* (☎771 5144; ❺), on the main street, has comfortable rooms, a nice garden and Internet access, while the *Motel California* (☎771 4272; ❹), a US-style motel with hot water that's close to the crossroads, is another option. Along the main drag, you'll find several **restaurants**, as well as a Banistmo, with an ATM. Click on Ⓦwww.volcanbaru.com for additional local information.

Cerro Punta

Set almost 2000m above sea level in a bowl-shaped valley surrounded by densely forested mountains, **CERRO PUNTA** is the highest village in Panama. In the eighty or so years since it was settled, agriculture has expanded so rapidly that the town now produces some eighty percent of all the vegetables consumed in Panama. This agricultural boom has come at the expense of the surrounding forests, however, and the local population is just beginning to face up to the consequences of deforestation, soil erosion and excessive pesticide use.

Despite these problems, the village, frequently swathed in cloud, and surrounding fields are still undeniably beautiful, filled with abundant flowers and buzzing with hummingbirds. The spectacular scenery, together with the cool, crisp mountain air (it even gets cold at night – a rare luxury in Panama) makes Cerro Punta a perfect base for **hiking**, and the pristine cloudforests of La Amistad and Volcán Barú are both within easy reach. These parks are perhaps the best places in all of Central America to catch a glimpse of the elusive resplendent quetzal, particularly in the dry season between January and April. Another worthwhile destination is the **Finca Dracula Orchid Farm**, which is home to one of the most extensive orchid collections in Latin America. The farm is about five minutes' walk beyond *Los Quetzales Lodge and Spa* in the hamlet of Guadelupe, which is 3km north of Cerro Punta. Visits can be arranged through the lodge (see below).

Practicalities

Everything in Cerro Punta is spread out along the main road from David and a side road leading towards Parque Internacional La Amistad. **Buses** from David pull up on the one main street. There are a couple of **places to stay**: the *Hotel Cerro Punta* (☎771 2020; ❺), on the main road, has clean, comfortable rooms with good views, while the friendly *Pensión Eterna Primavera* (no phone; ❹), on the road towards La Amistad, has five overpriced and musty rooms. A few kilometres before Cerro Punta, *Hostal Cielito Sur* (☎771 2038, Ⓦwww.cielitosur.com; ❻) is a stunning place to stay. Set amid beautiful grounds, the four immaculate rooms, some with kitchens, are decorated with traditional Panamanian artwork. The price includes a substantial breakfast.

In Guadelupe, *Los Quetzales Lodge and Spa* (☎771 2182, Ⓦwww.losquetzales.com; ❸–❻) has pleasant rooms in a chalet-like building and a cramped, but clean, dormitory (US$12), plus a large lounge with a log fire in the main building that's a great place to relax. The lodge, which can organize tours with horses and guides into the parks, also has three self-catering cabañas in the cloudforest at which you can watch quetzals and up to ten different species of hummingbird from your balcony – an amazing experience, if a bit steep at about US$100 a night. All of the above have hot water. All buses to and from Cerro Punta collect and drop off passengers in Guadelupe – just let the driver know that's where you want to go.

The *Hotel Cerro Punta* has a reasonable **restaurant** with meals from about US$5, and there are several places in the village where you can get inexpensive típica meals and excellent *batidos* – creamy milkshakes made with local strawberries and blackberries. In Guadelupe, *Los Quetzales* has a bakery and pizzeria downstairs and a restaurant upstairs; nearby, the *Refresceria La Canelita* is good for coffee and snacks, but also has more substantial seafood and chicken, though sadly rarely cooked with any locally grown vegetables. Alternatively, especially for those with a sweet tooth, buy some crackers or bread from a local shop and a pot of homemade jam, produced from berries and fruit grown in the surrounding hills, from one of the roadside stalls.

Parque Internacional La Amistad

Covering 4000 square kilometres of rugged, forested mountains on either side of the border with Costa Rica, **Parque Internacional La Amistad** forms a crucial link in the "biological corridor" of protected areas running the length of Central America. Encompassing some nine life zones, the park supports an incredible biodiversity, including more than four hundred different bird species, making it the most important park in Panama after Darién. Although almost all of the Panamanian section of the park is in Bocas del Toro, it is only accessible from the Pacific side of the country.

To **get to the park** from Cerro Punta, walk or take a minibus to **Las Nubes**, several kilometres away down a potholed, but well-signposted, side road. There's a permanently staffed **park office** here, where you must pay the US$3 admission charge; they also have an exhibition centre and a **refuge** (US$5 per night) – bring your own food and, ideally, a sleeping bag, as it gets cold at night. There are three well-marked **trails**, with *miradores* offering excellent views of the four highest mountains in Panama (at least before the cloud descends) and a 55m waterfall, but though it teems with birds, the forest immediately around Las Nubes is secondary growth. The area was heavily deforested in the early 1980s when one of Noriega's cronies established an illegal cattle ranch here – the park office was his holiday home – and is only just beginning to recover. Longer trails lead into the virgin cloudforest further away, but you'll need to get one of the park guards to guide you, which they're usually happy to do.

The quetzal trail to Boquete

From Guadelupe a partially paved road winds 6km up the western slope of Volcán Barú to **Respingo**, a park guard station at the entrance to **Parque Nacional Volcán Barú**, where the US$3 admission fee is rarely charged. There's a clean refuge with shared bath (❷), and you can camp. From Respingo the **quetzal trail** runs around the northern flank of the volcano to Boquete, a four- to six-hour hike, mostly downhill, through spectacular cloudforest. For the first hour or so the trail plunges down a steep valley and can be difficult to follow, so if unsure, you should get one of the park guards to guide you as far as a point known as La Victoria, beyond which the trail is easy to follow. It runs along the Río Caldera and eventually becomes a track before emerging at **Alto Chiquero**, another park guard station. From here, it's another hour's walk to the tarmac road above Boquete, where you can hitch or walk the last few kilometres into town – take a left turn when you reach the tarmac. If you don't wish to lug all your gear along with you on the trail, consider staying in David, leaving the bulk of your luggage at the hotel or hostel, and taking an early-morning bus to Cerro Punta from where you start the trail and, upon arrival in Boquete, catch a bus back to David – this journey can also be broken with an overnight at Cerro Punta or Boquete or indeed both. Note that walking the trail in the other direction, from Boquete to Cerro Punta, involves some steep climbs.

Boquete

Set in the tranquil Caldera Valley 37km north of David at just over 1000m above sea level, **BOQUETE** is the biggest town in the Chiriquí Highlands, the centre of coffee production and a popular weekend resort for the residents of David. The slopes surrounding the town are dotted with coffee plantations, flower gardens and orange groves, rising to rugged peaks that are usually obscured by thick cloud that descends on the town in a constant fine mist known as *bajareque*. Only when the cloud clears, most often in the morning, can you see the imperious peak of Volcán Barú, which dominates the town to the northwest. Throughout the year, particularly in the dry season, the town is often subjected to very fierce winds, especially in the afternoon.

Arrival and information

Buses from David arrive and depart from the Parque Central, and *transporte urbana* **minibuses** head up to the surrounding hamlets from the streets around the parque – taking one of these and then walking back to town is a good way to see the nearby countryside. IPAT has a **tourist information centre** (daily 9.30am–6pm) and café overlooking the town at **Alto Boquete** on the road towards David. Although few speak English, the staff members are reasonably helpful, offering maps and basic information on walks in the countryside around Boquete. It's worth coming up here to enjoy the panoramic views, but otherwise you can get better advice from the hotels in Boquete mentioned below.

There's a **Banco Nacional**, on the main road a block south of the parque, which changes travellers' cheques and has an ATM. The **post office** and **telephone**

office (Mon–Fri 7am–6pm, Sat 7am–5pm) are both on the main square, while high-speed **Internet access** is available at *McNet* in *Aparta-Hotel Kalima Suites* opposite *Pensión Marilós*.

Accommodation

There are plenty of **places to stay** in Boquete and the ones listed below are signposted from the main street– all have hot water and tend to fill on the weekends and over public holidays when prices can double.

Hostal Mozart 3kms up the Volcancito road, just before the IPAT office ⓣ720 3764. This brightly decorated house features a terrace with stunning views overlooking the Pacific, a large garden and secure cabins with private bathrooms – all guarded by the friendly dog. Excellent breakfast. ❹

Hotel Panamonte on the way out of town to the north ⓣ720 1324, ⓦwww.hotelpanamonte.com. The most luxurious accommodation in Boquete, in an elegantly restored wooden building, with pool, a good restaurant, spa, a beautiful garden and charming staff. ❼

Hotel Rebequet Av B. Porras, opposite the *Pensión Marilós* ⓣ720 1365. Clean and comfortable en-suite rooms set around a small courtyard, plus communal kitchens. ❺

Pensión Marilós Av B. Porras ⓣ720 1380. Similar to, but slightly cheaper than, the *Hotel Rebequet*. Rooms have shared bathrooms, plus there's a book exchange and cooking facilities. ❹

Pensión Topas Av B. Porras ⓣ720 1005, ⓔschoeb@cwpanama.net. Six rooms decorated with Tintin murals, set around a nice garden and small pool with views of the volcano. Camping in the garden is also permitted for a fee. The helpful and knowledgeable European owners can arrange guided excursions and horse hire. Good breakfast (US$3). ❹

Pensión Virginia Parque Central ⓣ720 1260. Charming, if slightly dilapidated, accommodation with friendly owners. ❹

The Town and around

The town itself is a charming and – except during the annual *Feria de las Flores y el Café* (usually held in January) when the town is packed – peaceful place, spread out along the road that comes in from David and around two squares, the **Parque de las Madres**, decorated with flowers, fountains and a monument to motherhood, and the **Parque Central**, which bustles with activity during the weekend market. Sadly, recent developments have put Boquete's unique charm under threat. Foreign investment has flooded the area in recent years, seeing the construction of an all-inclusive luxury condo targetting retirees from the US and the clearing of cloud-forest to make way for golf courses, all of which has helped push land prices beyond the reach of most locals and prompted fears that the town is being turned into a kind of tropical theme park for foreigners.

The real attraction of Boquete, however, is walking or riding in the surrounding countryside. As well as the climb to the summit of the volcano – a strenuous day's walk or a couple of hours' drive – there are plenty of less demanding walks you can make along the narrow country lanes, with well-signposted attractions. One of these, heading out of town to the north towards the hamlet of **Alto Lino**, takes you past the **Café Ruiz** coffee-processing plant (ⓣ720 1000, ⓦwww.caferuiz.com), where you can take three-hour **coffee tours** (Mon to Sat; 9am; US$14) or shorter thirty-minute tours of the roasting plant (on demand; US$4). Chiriquí River Rafting, Av Central (ⓣ720 1505, ⓦwww.panama-rafting.com), offers **whitewater rafting** trips, classes II to IV, from US$75 to US$105. *Hotel Panamonte* (see above) offers good, but often pricey, trips. Most hotel managers will offer advice on tours. Most hiking trips in the area don't require a guide, although don't stray from the paths when in the cloudforest.

Cafés and restaurants

Bistro Boquete Av Central. Lively hangout with smart airy interior and a small yet inviting menu of international food (US$4–10), which may well ensure your return. The inside is smoke free, but there are tables outside – though a little bit close to the road for most people's comfort.

Java Juice Av Central. Its walls swathed in old coffee sacks, this friendly café serves up excellent value food, including burgers, salads, shakes and sandwiches – as well as plenty of vegetarian options – from US$1. It's good place to get local information on tours, plus there's Internet access.

Pizzeria La Volcánica Av Central. Small restaurant, popular with the locals, dishing up good-value pizza.

Restaurante Hotel Panamonte just north of the town. Relatively expensive, but excellent, breakfast, lunch and dinner, served in plush surroundings.

Santa Fe Bar & Grill Just over the Río Caldera bridge. Unremarkable food, but the riverside setting is extremely pleasant.

Volcán Barú

Boquete's biggest attraction is undoubtedly the ascent of **Volcán Barú**, the soaring extinct volcano that is Panama's tallest mountain. A 22-kilometre road winds up the mountain through spectacular scenery to the peak, from which on rare clear days both oceans can be seen. Along the way, the road passes coffee plantations, tended by Ngobe labourers, which soon give way to majestic cloudforest, whose tall trees are bearded with lichen and covered with orchids and bromeliads. As you climb, the views of the Caldera Valley, the plains around David and the islands of the Golfo de Chiriquí open up, the air becomes cooler, and the cloudforest gradually gives way to stunted, elfin forest and, finally, to bleak, high-altitude páramo. Surrounded by seven long-extinct craters and crowned by a cluster of telecommunications aerials, the **peak** is often shrouded in cloud, but don't let this dishearten you – even in the depths of the rainy season the cloud breaks every so often to reveal the sight of at least one of the oceans as well as the forest-covered mountains marching west to Costa Rica. Outside of the mid-December to April dry season, your best chance of experiencing the view is to be on the peak at dawn – to do so, you'll need to camp out or walk all night. That said, even if the view is partially obscured, it's still a worthwhile climb.

The first 6km of the road is paved, after which it becomes a rough track passable only with a customized 4WD. To **walk** to the summit, it's best to get a *transporte urbana* minibus or a taxi (US$4–5) to the end of the tarmac, beyond which it's a steep and strenuous four- to six-hour hike and another six hours or so back to Boquete, unless you catch another minibus on the way down. If you're very lucky, you might be able to hitch a ride on a truck heading to one of the farms on the lower slopes or catch a telecommunications vehicle – the latter is highly unlikely, but if your luck is in, be prepared to pay US$40. If you're on foot, it's a long day's walk: take waterproof clothing and plenty of food and water, as there is none available on the hike. Trails lead down the other side to Volcán and Cerro Punta, but they are difficult to follow without a guide. You can **camp** on the grassy plateau just below the peak, but it gets very cold at night and there is rarely any water available.

7.5

Bocas del Toro

Isolated on the Costa Rican border between the Caribbean and the forested slopes of the Cordillera Talamanca, **Bocas del Toro** – usually called simply "Bocas" – is one of the most remote and beautiful provinces in Panama. Until the road across the cordillera from the province of Chiriquí was built in the early 1980s, Bocas del Toro was completely cut off from the rest of Panama and could be reached only by sea, air or via Costa Rica. From the volcanic slopes of the Cordillera Talamanca down to the Caribbean, most of the mainland is still covered by rainforest, apart from a narrow coastal strip where bananas are cultivated. Offshore, the **Bocas del Toro Archipelago** is home to an ecosystem so complex and well preserved that it has been described by biologists as "the Galapagos of the 21st century". This exceptional natural diversity is matched by the equally unusual make-up of the region's population. While the inland forests are still populated by indigenous groups – Ngobe-Buglé, Naso and Bribrí – the islands are dominated by the descendants of **West Indian** migrants, and English, or rather Guari-Guari – Jamaican patois embellished with some Spanish and Ngobere – remains the lingua franca.

Long one of the best-kept secrets in Central America, in recent years Bocas has started to attract more and more visitors. Indeed, thanks to its growing reputation and easy accessibility from Costa Rica, you're likely to see more travellers here than anywhere else in Panama. Fortunately, although a tourism boom is well under way in the islands, it has yet to change the friendly, laid-back approach to life adopted by most of the inhabitants. What's more, the pristine beauty of the archipelago's ecosystems – tropical forests, mangroves, deserted beaches, extensive coral reefs and crystalline waters teeming with rare marine life – is largely protected by the **Parque Nacional Marino Isla Bastimentos**. The only drawback is the unpredictable weather: the dry season is much less clearly defined than in the rest of the country and bright sunshine frequently gives way to torrential tropical rain with alarming rapidity, often lasting for many hours and, on occasion, days.

Most visitors head straight out to the islands and the provincial capital, **Bocas del Toro** – also referred to as Bocas Town or just plain Bocas – which is the best base from which to explore the archipelago. Only those heading to Costa Rica usually visit the coastal banana zone and its main town, **Changuinola**.

Some history

Christopher Columbus explored the coast of Bocas del Toro as he searched for a route to Asia during his fourth voyage in 1502, and many of the place names date from his visit – islas Cristóbal and Colón were named in his honour, Isla Bastimentos was where he took on supplies, Isla Carenero where he careened his ships when they needed cleaning or repairs. During the colonial era the Spanish had little success in taming the many warring indigenous tribes that populated the mountainous interior, and European pirates often sheltered in the calm waters between the province's many offshore islands. By the nineteenth century, English ships from Jamaica were becoming frequent visitors, arriving in search of hardwoods from the mainland forests and turtles, and in 1826 the town of Bocas del Toro was founded by West Indian migrants on stilts above a mangrove swamp.

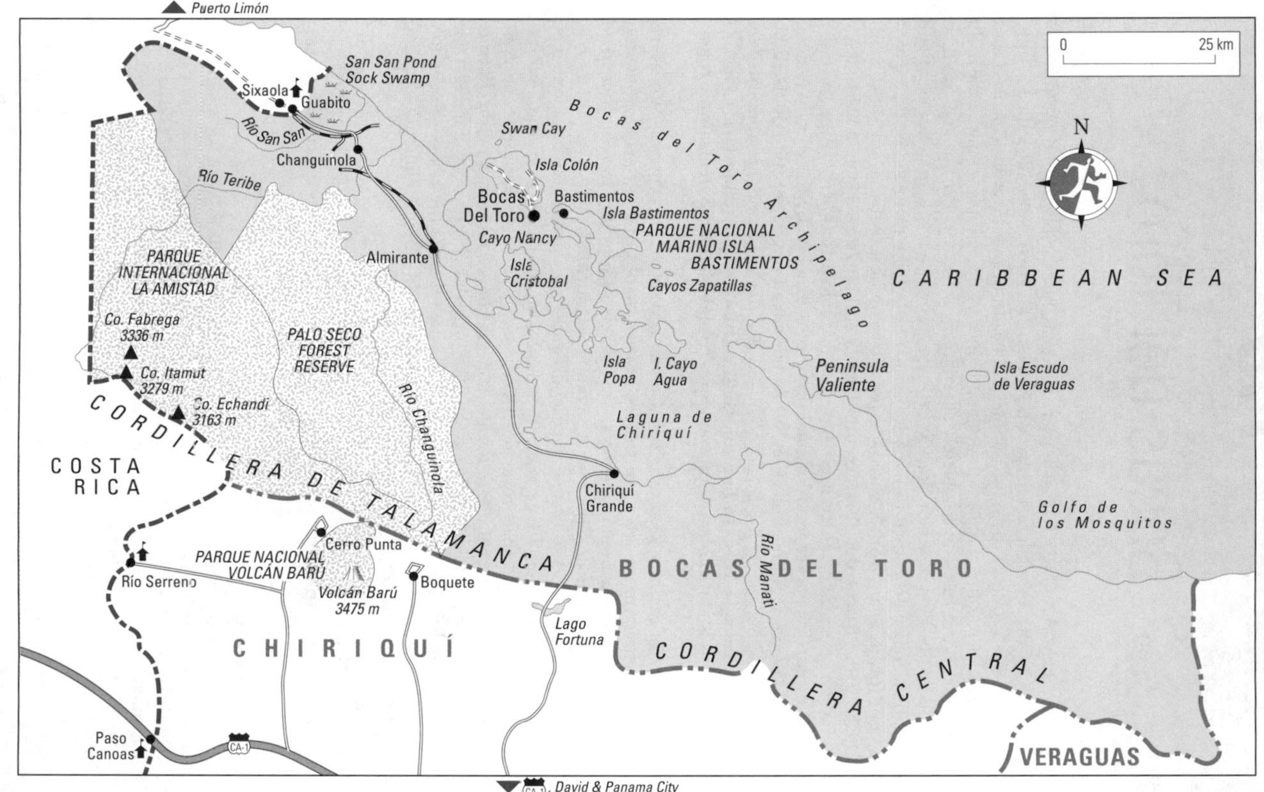
Puerto Limón
0 25 km
N
San San Pond
Sock Swamp
Sixaola
Guabito
Río San San
Changuinola
Río Teribe
Bocas del Toro Archipelago
Swan Cay
Isla Colón
Bocas
Del Toro
Bastimentos
Isla Bastimentos
PARQUE NACIONAL
MARINO ISLA
BASTIMENTOS
Cayo Nancy
Almirante
Isla
Cristobal
Cayos Zapatillas
CARIBBEAN SEA
PARQUE
INTERNACIONAL
LA AMISTAD
Co. Fabrega
3336 m
Co. Itamut
3279 m
Co. Echandi
3163 m
PALO SECO
FOREST
RESERVE
Río Changuinola
Isla
Popa
I. Cayo
Agua
Peninsula
Valiente
Isla Escudo
de Veraguas
Laguna de
Chiriquí
COSTA
RICA
CORDILLERA DE TALAMANCA
Chiriquí
Grande
Golfo de
los Mosquitos
Cerro Punta
PARQUE NACIONAL
VOLCÁN BARÚ
Río Serreno
Volcán Barú
3475 m
Boquete
BOCAS DEL TORO
Río Manatí
Lago
Fortuna
CHIRIQUÍ
CORDILLERA CENTRAL
Paso
Canoas
CA-1
VERAGUAS
CA-1, David & Panama City

Isolated from the rest of the country and plagued by malaria and yellow fever, the settlement developed slowly until the arrival of US banana companies towards the end of the century. Concentrated on the islands of the Bocas del Toro Archipelago, the banana plantations brought a measure of prosperity and encouraged further settlement by West Indian migrants, many of whom came here after working on the French canal construction. By 1895 bananas from Bocas accounted for more than half of Panama's export earnings, and Bocas Town boasted five foreign consulates and three English-language newspapers.

Early in the twentieth century, however, the banana plantations were repeatedly devastated by crop disease, leading the fruit companies to move production to the mainland around Changuinola, and the islands reverted to the tropical indolence that characterizes them today. The region's isolation from the rest of Panama only ended in 1981, when the road across the isthmus from Chiriquí to Chiriquí Grande was completed. In the past few years, the development of tourist facilities has accelerated enormously. Huge areas of the archipelago have been bought by foreign speculators who are dividing it up into lots for the construction of luxury hotels and holiday homes, and the regional economy is dominated by US interests in a way not seen since the banana era began in the late 1800s. Certainly, the tourism boom has revived the local economy, generating much needed employment and income for local residents, and for now the region appears to be coping well with the boom in tourism. Nonetheless, much concern still exists over how well this will be sustained in the future.

Chiriquí Grande and Almirante

From the village of Chiriquí, 14km east of David on the Interamericana, a spectacular road runs across the continental divide, crossing the Fortuna hydroelectric dam and through the pristine forests that protect its watershed, to the small town of **Chiriquí Grande** on the shore of the Laguna de Chiriquí. Until recently, this was the end of the road and the jumping-off point for the islands, but in 2000 the road along the shore of the lagoon to Almirante was completed, linking the coastal banana strip around Changuinola to the rest of Panama for the first time. Boats to the islands now leave from Almirante and Changuinola, so there's no reason to stop in Chiriquí Grande.

Some 50km beyond Chiriquí Grande, **ALMIRANTE** is a ramshackle port town of rusting tin-roofed houses propped up on stilts over the calm waters of the Caribbean. The town, which serves as the export terminal for the Changuinola banana industry, is the best place for those coming via David to catch a **water-taxi** to the islands of Bocas del Toro. **Buses** to Almirante pick up and drop off passengers either at the town's small bus station or on the outskirts beside the main road; in either case, it's a short taxi ride (US$0.50) or about a ten-minute walk to the port.

Buses for Changuinola, where you can get connections for the border, leave from the terminal close to the port. Adjacent to the terminal is the train station, from which a banana-workers' train runs to the border each morning – it's not really meant for tourists, but you might be able to persuade them to let you on for the ride. **Water-taxis** to Bocas del Toro leave every 30 minutes or so until about 6.30pm; the trip takes half an hour. If you arrive by bus, touts from the water-taxi companies will lead you to the port – the services are exactly the same, though you should check which company is leaving first before you buy a ticket. The *Palanga* runs to the islands four days a week. Although cheap (US$1), the ferry takes two hours to get there, making it only worth using if you have a car (from US$15).

There's no reason to stay in Almirante unless you miss the last boat and get stuck on your way to the islands. If you do, you can find secure, if pretty basic, **accommodation** at the unmarked *Hotel San Francisco* (☎758 3779; ❹), above the De La Rosa supermarket across the main street from the bus terminal. Several no-frills **places to eat** can be found near the bus terminal and the water-taxi dock.

Bocas Town and around

Situated on the southeastern tip of Isla Colón, the provincial capital of **BOCAS DEL TORO** is by far the best base from which to explore the islands, beaches and reefs of the archipelago. Bocas Town, which is connected to the rest of the island by a narrow causeway, is also a charming place in its own right, with rickety wooden buildings painted in faded pastels and a friendly and laid-back, mostly English-speaking, population. The fact that there's nothing much to see here is hardly a problem – after a hard day in the sea and sun there's no better place to chill out with a cool drink while the sun sets behind the forest-covered mountains of the mainland.

Arrival, orientation and information

As Bocas Town is small, with most activity concentrated on the seafront, it's easy to find your way around. The **ferry** from Almirante docks at its southern end, while scheduled **water-taxis** arrive and depart from the Taxi Maritímo dock – unscheduled water-taxis to the various islands and beaches also dock here, or they can be hailed from anywhere on the seafront. **Flights** with Aeroperlas (Ⓣ757 9341) and Mapiex Aero (Ⓣ757 9841) land at the small airstrip four blocks from the main street. Though everything in the town is within easy walking distance, **taxis** may become a necessity when the rain starts pelting down (US$0.75 per journey).

The **IPAT office** (Mon–Fri 8.30am–4.30pm, Sat & Sun 9am–4pm; Ⓣ757 9642), housed in a grand new building, is one of the most helpful in Panama and worth a visit if you're going to be spending a few days in the area. As well as providing tourist information, they also have toilets, **Internet access** and a well laid-out exhibit on the history and ecology of the archipelago. Detailed **maps** of the area are available from most shops for US$2. **ANAM**'s local office can give you permission to camp within the Isla Bastimentos Marine Park and may also be able to help organize a visit to see turtles laying their eggs (between May and September). Information on many of the hotels and tour operators in Bocas can be found on the **website** Ⓦwww.bocas.com.

For other practical matters, there's a **Banco Nacional** (Mon–Fri 8am–2pm, Sat 9am–noon), where you can change travellers' cheques and use the ATM, a small **post office** in the Palacio Municipal, as well as a Cable & Wireless **telephone** office (Mon–Fri 8am–noon & 1–4pm). **Bicycles** (US$1–1.50/hr or US$8/day) and mopeds (US$5/hr or US$20/day) can be rented from several places around town, while a large range of groceries can be purchased, albeit at higher prices than on the mainland, at one of the several **supermarkets**. During your stay be sure to drink **purified water**, as the tap water is not potable.

Accommodation

There's a good range of accommodation in Bocas, with more and more foreign-owned places opening up. Things can fill up pretty quickly on weekends and during holidays, but you should always be able to find somewhere to stay. Young touts meet the planes and water-taxis and for a small tip will help you find somewhere in your price range; alternatively, you can ask at the IPAT office.

Bocas Inn Av H, C 3 Ⓣ757 7600, Ⓔbocasinn@anconexpeditions.com. Airy wooden structure on the seafront run by ANCON Expeditions, primarily as a field station for their tour groups, but independent travellers are also welcome. Clean, comfortable rooms with bathroom and a/c – those at the front share a large balcony with hammocks overlooking the bay – and there's a small bar and good environmental library for guests. Breakfast included. ❻

Casa Max Av G, C 5 Ⓣ757 9120, Ⓦcasamax.netfirms.com. Small, friendly place with clean, cheerfully painted rooms with balconies, comfortable beds and a homely feel. Pleasant patio area to relax and a vivarium stocked with examples of the local poison-dart frogs, plus good advice from the Dutch owners. Free coffee and fruit in the morning. ❹

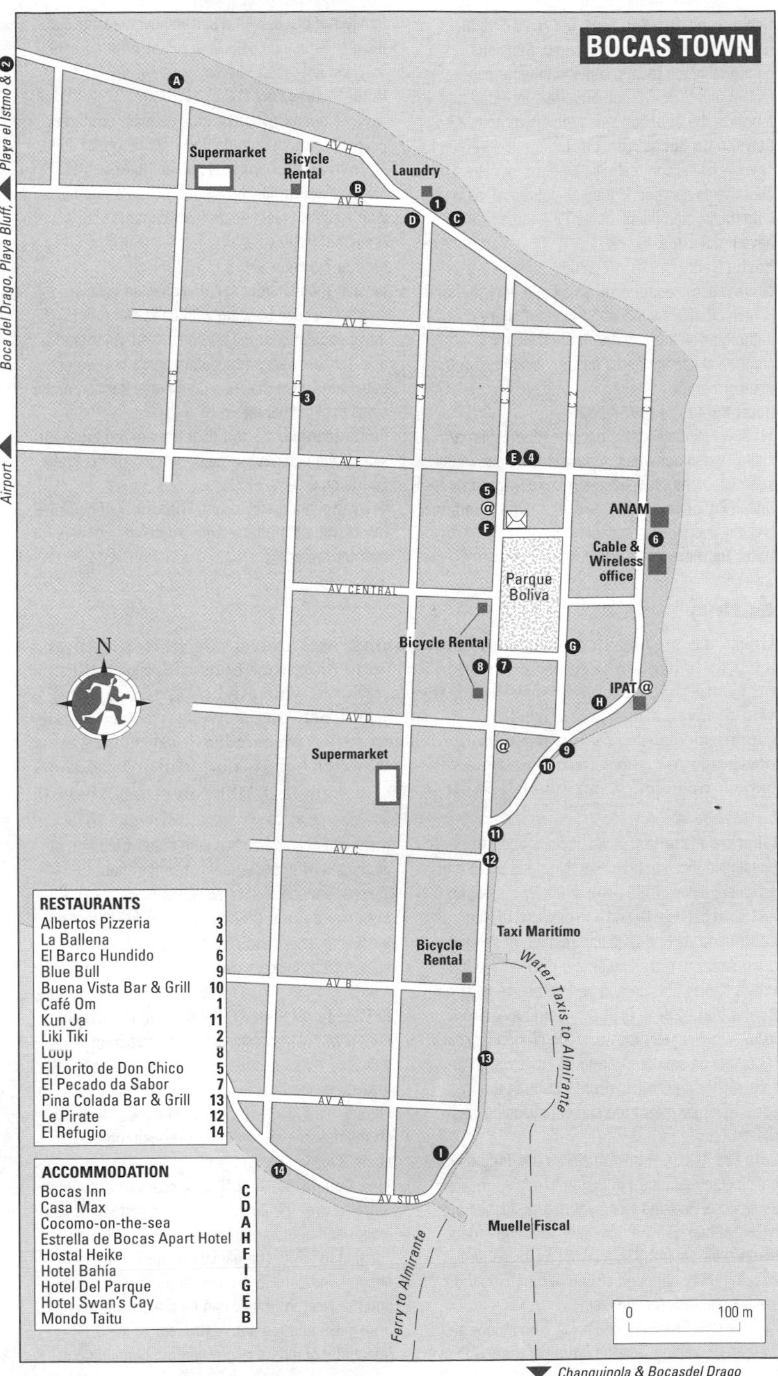
BOCAS TOWN
Boca del Drago, Playa Bluff, Playa el Istmo & 2
Airport
Supermarket
Bicycle Rental
Laundry
AV H
AV G
AV F
AV E
AV CENTRAL
AV D
AV C
AV B
AV A
AV SUR
C 6
C 5
C 4
C 3
C 2
C 1
ANAM
Cable & Wireless office
Parque Boliva
Bicycle Rental
IPAT
Supermarket
N
Taxi Maritímo
Bicycle Rental
Water Taxis to Almirante
Muelle Fiscal
Ferry to Almirante
0
100 m
Changuinola & Bocasdel Drago
RESTAURANTS
Albertos Pizzeria 3
La Ballena 4
El Barco Hundido 6
Blue Bull 9
Buena Vista Bar & Grill 10
Café Om 1
Kun Ja 11
Liki Tiki 2
Loop 8
El Lorito de Don Chico 5
El Pecado da Sabor 7
Pina Colada Bar & Grill 13
Le Pirate 12
El Refugio 14
ACCOMMODATION
Bocas Inn C
Casa Max D
Cocomo-on-the-sea A
Estrella de Bocas Apart Hotel H
Hostal Heike F
Hotel Bahía I
Hotel Del Parque G
Hotel Swan's Cay E
Mondo Taitu B

Cocomo-on-the-Sea Av H, C 7 ⓣ757 9259, ⓦwww.panamainfo.com/cocomo. Spacious, comfortable a/c rooms, some with verandas looking out to sea. Large breakfast included and tours can be arranged using their own boat. ❻
Estrella de Bocas Apart Hotel C 1 ⓣ757 9011, ⓦwww.bocas.com/estrella. Modern rooms and apartments set around a small courtyard, all with large beds, tiled floors, cable TV – the apartments have fridges, too. ❺–❽
Hostal Heike C 3 ⓣ757 9708, ⓦwww.bocas.com/heike. Small and very friendly hostel, offering rooms with fans that share clean bathrooms with hot water. There's also a communal kitchen and a balcony overlooking the main street. ❷
Hotel Bahía C 3 ⓣ757 9626, ⓦwww.hotelbahia.biz. Spacious rooms with a/c, cable TV and hot water in an imposing early twentieth-century wooden structure – formerly the United Fruit Company HQ – with a large communal balcony overlooking the seafront. ❺
Hotel Del Parque C 2 ⓣ757 9008. Friendly, family-run place, with a balcony overlooking the main square and cool, clean rooms offering cable TV, good hot-water showers and a/c. ❺
Hotel Swan's Cay C 3 ⓣ757 9090, ⓦwww.swanscayhotel.com. The most upmarket place in town, built in the local architectural style, but with an incongruously opulent interior and elegant, well-furnished a/c rooms – it's popular with wealthy weekenders from Panama City. Breakfast included. ❽
Mondo Taitu Av G, C 5 ⓣ757 9425, ⓦwww.mondotaitu.com. Ramshackle yellow-painted wooden building with basic fan rooms that's popular with the surfing crowd. All rooms and dormitory accommodation share hot-water bathrooms, plus there's a communal kitchen and a small cocktail bar. ❷
Punta Manglar a short boat trip around the west side of the peninsula – book through Bocas Water Sports on C 3 ⓣ757 9541, ⓦwww.puntamanglar.com. Purpose-built eco-dive resort with comfortable wooden cabins on stilts over the water. ❻

Eating

Bocas has an excellent choice of **restaurants**, with everything from Indian and Thai to Italian and Lebanese on offer, including numerous budget options, though be aware that opening hours are rather erratic. As you might expect, seafood is widely available here, with lobster, conch and octopus as well as other locally caught specialities tasting particularly delicious when prepared to local recipes using coconut milk and Caribbean spices. The tap water here is not drinkable, so don't expect free iced water when you sit down for a meal as you would elsewhere in Panama.

Alberto's Pizzeria C 5. A spacious open-fronted building in the "suburbs" serving good pizza and spaghetti dishes (US$4–10). Friendly atmosphere and good service. Open 5–11pm, closed Sun.
La Ballena Av E, C 3. Italian restaurant serving great seafood, pizzas and meat dishes (about US$8). Tables outside and an impressive wine list.
Buena Vista Bar & Grill C 1. Set in a seafront location, this eatery draws visiting Americans with US sports on satellite TV and US-style burgers, sandwiches and salads (from US$5). In the evening larger meals are served, including ribs. Closed Tues.
Café Om Av H, C 4 next to *Bocas Inn*. Probably the only Indian restaurant in Panama, this spot, with its slow service and wobbly furniture, dishes out excellent curries with rice, naan and homemade chutney for about US$6, as well as juices and wraps (US$4). Although closed at lunch, they do serve breakfast. Closed Wed.
Kun Ja C 3. Chinese restaurant, with indoor and waterfront seating, serving large portions of tasty meat and seafood dishes with either fried rice or in chop suey or chow mein style for about US$4. Takeout service is also available.
El Lorito de Don Chicho C 3. Locals seldom eat anywhere other than at this busy spot, which serves tasty, inexpensive, self-service Panamanian food.
El Pecado da Sabor C 3. Not to be missed, the chef here cooks an eclectic combination of delicious Thai, Lebanese and Mexican dishes made with the finest local and imported ingredients (US$3–10). The best tables are those on the rickety balcony that overlooks the main street. Closed Sun and Mon.
Pina Colada Bar & Grill C 3, near ferry terminal. Situated over the lapping surf, this restaurant has indoor and outdoor seating as well as a bar stocked to party. The genial Colombian manager ensures the service is some of the best in town, and the western music can be a welcome break from salsa and reggae. At the rear of the restaurant stands a large vivarium containing a

number of snakes, so while you tuck into your superb mango chicken (US$8) or excellent burger with homemade coleslaw and bread (US$5) you can pity the pythons and their meagre meals of baby rat.

El Refugio Av Sur. The building's rather rickety, but it houses the only restaurant in town where you can watch the sun set over the mainland from the water's edge. Quiet atmosphere and good seafood and meat dishes from US$7.

Drinking and nightlife

Several restaurants double as **music** and **drinking venues** in the evening, plus there are a few good **bars** where you can relax with a cold Balboa Ice or a cocktail. On the weekends, many locals head to *Discoteca El Encanto* on the seafront of C 3 to dance the night away to pounding reggae beats.

El Barco Hundido C 1, beside the Cable & Wireless office. Locally known as the Wreck Deck, this spot is the most popular hangout for locals, tourists and surfers alike who come here to drink cold beer (US$1) until the early hours. A DJ performs most nights, playing a repetitive mix of modern R&B, Eighties pop and the ubiquitous Bob Marley. Opens at 7pm and gets lively after 9pm.

Blue Bull C1, inside Starfleet. Laid-back seafront bar serving cold beer and excellent cocktails, with happy hour from 6–7pm and live calypso music at weekends.

Liki Tiki Playa El Istmito, Feria del Mar. Large American-run beachfront bar and restaurant with volleyball court that's about a twenty-minute walk out of town from the main street. Closed Mon and Tues.

Loop C 3. Also called the Pool Bar, this friendly local hangout has pool tables and stays open throughout the early hours.

Le Pirate C 3. Seafront restaurant serving indifferent fish and seafood – it's more popular as a bar, especially for sundowners.

Around Bocas Town

The islands, cays and mainland waterways surrounding Bocas Town offer wide-ranging opportunities for relaxing on pristine beaches, visiting Ngobe-Buglé villages and diving near unspoilt coral reefs teeming with tropical fish. A quick bus or cab ride away, the **beaches of Isla Colón** are easily accessed from Bocas, while nearby **islas Carenero** and **Bastimentos** both boast locales favoured by visiting surfers. Most visitors, however, make a point of exploring the **Parque Nacional Marina Isla Bastimentos**, a renowned marine park of rainforests, mangroves and coral reefs that stretches across a series of islands in the archipelago.

The easiest way to visit the marine park, as well as the other spots around Bocas Town, is with one of the area's **tour companies** (see overleaf). A number of agencies offer day-trips to beaches and snorkelling spots in and around the park, typically costing US$15–30 per person and including a stop at a restaurant for lunch (US$6–10). The more expensive tours often provide free cold drinks and snorkelling equipment. Alternatively, you can hire a boat in Bocas Town or Bastimentos: with a group of four or more people this could work out cheaper than an agency tour and also means you can decide exactly where you want to go. Prices vary according to the distance involved, the size of the boat, the power of the motor and your negotiating ability. Note that though a boat with a small motor may seem good value, you could end up spending most of the day chugging to and from your destination rather than in the water snorkelling or lying on the beach; in addition, be sure to check whether the boat has lifejackets. A typical day's excursion might include a visit to the **Cayos Zapatillas** in the morning, lunch and snorkelling at Crawl Cay, and an afternoon on Red Frog Beach. Boatmen and agencies also take trips round the side of Isla Colón to Starfish Bay, Boca del Drago, and on to **Swan Cay**, a small, yet towering, coral island off the north coast that is an important nesting site for birds, including brown boobies and the rare red-billed tropic birds.

Endless possibilities exist for boat excursions **further afield**: east around the Peninsula Valiente to the **Isla de Escudo de Veraguas**, which aficionados consider

Tour companies in Bocas del Toro

ANCON Expeditions Av H, C 3, at *Bocas Inn* ⓣ757 9600, ⓦwww.anconexpeditions.com. Excursions to the marine park and into the forests on the mainland. They're slightly more expensive than other operators, but they are the most organized, have good boats and are the only tour company in town with experienced naturalist guides.

Bocas Water Sports C 3 ⓣ757 9541, ⓦwww.bocaswatersports.com. Professional and well-established US-run outfit offering diving, kayaking and snorkelling outings as well as equipment rental.

J&J and Transparente Tours C 3 ⓣ757 9915. Run by experienced locals, this long-established company runs regular trips into the marine park, along with other customized trips. They also rent out snorkelling gear.

Starfleet C 1 ⓣ757 9630, ⓦwww.explorepanama.com/starfleet. Canadian-owned company with a friendly, professional team offering diving and snorkelling excursions on a ten-metre catamaran and full PADI open-water diving courses (about US$205).

Taxi 25 C 1, next to the Cable & Wireless office ⓣ757 9028. Well-established local tour company specialising in day tours, with three trips a day to different destinations starting at 9.30am for US$15 per person.

one of the best **diving** spots in the whole Caribbean, or up one of the rivers into the **rainforests** of the mainland to visit isolated Ngobe-Buglé communities. A trip down the **Changuinola channel** may result in the sighting of laughing falcons and crab-eating raccoons, although every thirty minutes the peace is interrupted by the speeding water-taxis. Alternatively, you can head to Dolphin Bay, where you have a good chance of seeing the rather shy bottle-nosed **dolphins** that live there year-round. Be aware that bad weather may result in a change of itinerary or even cancellation and that beyond the main islands the sea can get very rough.

Surfing tours to Bocas can be arranged through Panama Surf Tours (see p.771), but most surfers just turn up with their boards, seek local advice, find a water-taxi and head out. The main season is between December and March, with many excellent and varied surfing spots in the area. Although none are within walking distance of Bocas, the town is nonetheless the best place to use as a base. The main hotspots include Carenero, off the northeast tip of Isla Carenero; Dumpers, just north of Boca del Drago; Paunch, on the northeastern tip of Isla Colón; Red Frog Beach, on Bastimentos; and Silverbacks, between Bastimentos and Carenero. The first three mentioned here break over reef, so wear booties, and even when the weather is overcast wear plenty of sunscreen.

Elsewhere on Isla Colón

From Bocas Town, a dirt road runs across a narrow isthmus to Isla Colón and forks after about 1.5km – one branch heading across the centre of the island to Boca del Drago, about 14km away on the north coast, the other 8km up the east coast towards Bluff Point. The latter road passes **Playa Bluff**, a beautiful long, white-sand beach that is visited by turtles between May and September. The surf here can be powerful and the currents strong, so be careful and don't swim alone

BOCA DEL DRAGO is a small fishing community set on a broad horseshoe bay with calm waters perfect for swimming and a narrow beach fringed with palm trees and patches of mangrove and coral. You can stay here at *Cabañas Estefani* (ⓣ626 7245, ❸), which has two cosy self-catering cabins; the *Yarisnori* restaurant next door (closed Tues) serves simple, delicious seafood. A **bus** runs to Boca del Drago from the square in Bocas Town several times daily (US$2); alternatively, you can hire a **taxi** in Bocas to take you to either Boca del Drago (US$20) or Playa Bluff (US$16) and pick you up again later. Otherwise, the best way to get around the island is to rent a **bicycle** in Bocas Town.

Isla Carenero

Although just 200m across the water from Bocas Town, tiny Isla Carenero receives few visitors, with those who do come mostly here to surf or dine at one of the restaurants. To get here, catch a water-taxi (US$1) or one of the dugouts with small outboards (US$0.20) from Bocas direct to your destination. On the westward side a narrow concrete path goes as far as the small marina; here, the island is rather run-down and wooden houses on stilts stand over the partially waterlogged and heavily littered ground. The eastern side is accessed by a sandy path with small bridges over the many drainage channels, though more pleasant than the west of the island it's hardly pristine. **Accommodation** options on the eastern side include *Buccaneer Resort* (☎757 9042, Ⓦwww.bucaneer-resort.com; ❽), which has excellent suites and raised, octagonal bungalows with palm-thatched roofs accessed by a series of wooden boardwalks as well as a good restaurant and bar, and *Hotel Tierraverde* (☎757 9900, Ⓦwww.hoteltierraverde.com; ❻), which offers pleasant rooms with a/c, hot water, DirectTV and balcony. Close to the Carenero reef break, the *Mukundu Surf Camp* (☎628 7012; ❶–❷) occupies a wooden building over the water with basic accommodation and a balcony strewn with multicoloured hammocks. For great seafood, head to *Pargo Rojo*, or if you're in the mood for excellent grilled meat try the *Sunset Grill*; water-taxis from Bocas Town will take you directly to their seafront locations.

Bastimentos

Situated outside the national marine park on the western tip of **Isla Bastimentos**, the small fishing community of **BASTIMENTOS** is not really set up for tourism, making it a good place to stay if you want a more relaxed Caribbean experience than that provided by Bocas Town. Regular **boats** run from the water-taxi terminal in Bocas Town to Bastimentos (US$2 per person), where it's easy to find a boatman who'll take you on excursions into the park or elsewhere in the archipelago. An undulating concrete path acts as the community's main thoroughfare, snaking its way along the coastline, overlooked by wooden stilted houses rising out of the steep green hillside. **Accommodation** on the island includes *Hostal Bastimentos* (☎757 9053; ❸–❹), behind the friendly *Roots* restaurant; *Pelicanos* (☎757 9830; ❹), to the east of the town, with comfortable rooms, a bar and a good restaurant with a terrace over the water, plus a friendly owner who can arrange tours; the popular *Sylvia Guest House* (☎757 9442; ❷), which is basic, but friendly and good value; and *Tio Toms* (☎757 9831; ❸), over the water with simple rooms and great breakfasts. Near the eastern tip of the island, just outside the park boundaries, the luxurious and secluded *Al Natural Resort* (☎757 9004, Ⓦwww.bocas.com/alnatura.htm; ❾) has stylish, rustic cabañas with solar-powered lighting and rainwater showers; transport to and from Bocas Town and three meals a day are included in the price.

Parque Nacional Marina Isla Bastimentos

Most visitors to Bocas come to explore the pristine beauty of **Parque Nacional Marina Isla Bastimentos**, a 130-square-kilometre reserve that encompasses a range of virtually undisturbed ecosystems that include rainforest, mangrove and coral reef. Deserted white-sand beaches and extensive reefs support an immense diversity of **marine life**, including dolphins, sea turtles and a kaleidoscopic variety of fish – a veritable paradise for snorkellers and divers. Foreign visitors to the park are supposed to pay a US$10 entrance fee, but this is only charged at Playa Larga and on the Cayos Zapatillas (see overleaf).

Some of the best **beaches** in the archipelago are on the eastern side of Isla Bastimentos, which faces the open sea. These beaches all have powerful surf, which can make swimming dangerous, and are best visited by boat when the sea is calm. The most popular and easiest to reach, **Red Frog Beach** is an idyllic stretch of sand that takes its name from the tiny, but abundant, bright-red poison-dart frogs (don't touch!), which inhabit the forest behind the beach and are found nowhere else in the world. It's a ninety-minute walk to Red Frog Beach from Bastimentos village down an often muddy track. By far the better way to get there is by boat: from the small dock on the south side of the island it's a fifteen-minute walk through the jungle to the beach (at the dock, pay the US$1 entry fee to the people who maintain the trail). A couple of beaches further east is Ola Chica, or **Polo Beach**, a longer and more secluded beach, partially protected from the surf by reefs – a spear-fishing hermit who has lived here alone for about thirty years often cooks up his catch for visitors (US$5 for all you can eat).

Further east – a muddy three-hour walk from Bastimentos village – the fourteen-kilometre stretch of **Playa Larga** is an important nesting site for **sea turtles** between May and September. There's an ANAM ranger station here where you may be charged the US$10 park entrance fee, and a basic refuge where you can **camp** for another US$10: you'll need to stay overnight if you want to see the turtles coming up to lay their eggs. You should get permission from the ANAM office in Bocas Town before coming here.

Southeast of Bastimentos island, but still within the park, are the **Cayos Zapatillas**, two idyllic coral-fringed islands where notorious English pirate Henry Morgan is supposed to have buried his loot – though treasure-seekers have so far failed to find it and his curse is supposed to hang over anyone who does. The Zapatillas are excellent for snorkelling, but you must pay the park admission fee (US$10) at the ANAM station on the southern island or just visit the nicer northern island, where **camping** is also possible with permission from ANAM in Bocas Town.

Changuinola and the Costa Rican border

Back on the mainland, the road to the border runs 29km west from Almirante through seemingly endless banana plantations to **CHANGUINOLA**, a typically hot and uninteresting banana town where almost everyone works for the Chiriquí Land Company ("the Company" – successor to United Fruit), which owns most of the surrounding land. **Buses** from Almirante and the border at Guabito arrive at the terminal, which is usually busy with workers heading to the banana fincas, known by numbers rather than names. Buses to Guabito leave every thirty minutes, taking twenty minutes to reach the border. **Water-taxis** to Bocas del Toro take an hour and leave every thirty minutes from the dock near Finca 60, on the outskirts of town, travelling through the narrow Changuinola channel into the Bay of Almirante. There's no reason to stop here unless you get stuck between Costa Rica and Bocas, but if you do end up **staying** here, everything you might need can be found along the main road that runs alongside the terminal, including the a/c *Hotel Carol* (☎758 8731; ❸), a **Banistmo** and several **restaurants** – the one in the bus station is good and inexpensive, while the *Chiquita Banana*, opposite, is more upmarket.

Crossing the border

From Changuinola the road runs 16km to the border with Costa Rica at **GUABITO**, where there's little more than a few shops selling consumer goods to Costa Rican day-trippers. The **migración** is open daily from 8am to 6pm Panama time (which is one hour ahead of Costa Rica); from here, it's a short walk across a bridge to Costa Rica, where you can change currency in the town of **Sixaola** (see p.648).

Travel details

Buses

Almirante to: Changuinola (every 30min; 45min); Panama City (2 daily; 12hr).
Boquete to: David (every 15min; 1hr).
Cañas to: Pedasí (1–2 daily; 2hr); Tonosí (1 daily; 1hr).
Cerro Punta to: David (every 20min; 2hr 30min).
Changuinola to: Almirante (every 30min; 45min); David (8 daily; 5hr); Guabito (every 30min; 20min).
Chiguiri Arriba to: Penonomé (1–2 daily; 1hr 20min).
Chitré to: Las Tablas (every 10–15min; 30min); Los Santos (every 10min; 10min); Panama City (hourly; 4hr); Santiago (every 45min; 1hr 20min).
Colón to: La Guaira (3–4 daily; 2hr); Nombre de Dios (3–4 daily; 2hr); Panama City (every 20min; express 1hr, local 1hr 30min); Portobelo (15 daily; 1hr).
David to: Almirante (every 45mins; 3hr); Boquete (every 25min; 1hr); Cerro Punta (every 20min; 2hr 30min); Changuinola (8 daily; 5hr); Panama City (12 daily; 7hr; 2 express buses daily; 5hr); Paso Canoas (every 10min; 1hr 20min); San José, Costa Rica (1 daily; 7hr 30min).
El Valle to: Panama City (every 30min; 2hr 30min); San Carlos (every 45min; 20min).
Gamboa to: Panama City (8 daily; 45min).
Guabito to: Changuinola (every 30min; 20min).
La Guaira to: Colón (3–4 daily; 2hr).
Las Tablas to: Chitré (every 10–15min; 30min); Panama City (every 2hr; 4hr 30min); Pedasí (hourly; 45min); Tonosí (hourly; 2hr 30min).
Los Santos to: Chitré (every 10min; 10min).
Metetí to: Panama City (7 daily; 7–8hr); Puerto Quimba (every 45min; 30min); Yaviza (1–2 daily; 2–3hr).
Nombre de Dios to: Colón (3–4 daily; 2hr).
Panama City to: Almirante (2 daily; 12hr); Chitré (hourly; 4hr); Colón (every 20min; express 1hr, local 1hr 30min); David (hourly; 7hr; 2 express buses daily; 5hr); El Valle (every 30min; 2hr 30min); Gamboa (8 daily; 45min); Las Tablas (every 2hr; 4hr 30min); Metetí (7 daily; 7–8hr); Ocú (8 daily; 4hr); Paso Canoas (9 daily; 9hr; 2 express buses daily in evening; 7hr); Penonomé (every 20min; 2hr 30min); San José, Costa Rica (1 daily at 11am; 15hr); Santiago (every 30min; 4hr); Sona (every 20min; 5hr).
Paso Canoas to: David (every 10min; 1hr 20min); Panama City (9 daily; 9hr; 2 express buses daily in evening; 7hr).
Pedasí to: Cañas (1–2 daily; 2hr); Las Tablas (hourly; 45min).
Penonomé to: Chiguiri Arriba (1–2 daily; 1hr 20min); Panama City (every 20min; 2hr 30min).
Portobelo to: Colón (15 daily; 1hr).
Puerto Quimba to: Metetí (every 45min; 30min).
San Carlos to: El Valle (every 45min; 20min).
Santiago to: Chitré (every 45min; 1hr 20min); Panama City (every 30min; 4hr).
Tonosí to: Cañas (1 daily; 1hr); Las Tablas (hourly; 2hr 30min).
Yaviza to: Metetí (1–2 daily; 2–3hr).

Water-taxis

Almirante to: Bocas del Toro (every 30min; 30min).
Boca del Drago to: Bocas del Toro (4 daily; 10min).
Bocas del Toro to: Almirante (every 30min; 30min); Boca del Drago (4 daily; 10min); Changuinola (8 daily; 1hr).
Changuinola to: Bocas del Toro (7 daily; 1hr).
La Palma to: Puerto Quimba (hourly; 45min).
Puerto Quimba to: La Palma (hourly; 45min).

Flights

Bocas del Toro to: Changuinola (2 daily; 20min); David (Mon–Fri 1 daily; 55min); Panama City (4 daily; 1hr).
Changuinola to: Bocas del Toro (2 daily; 20min); David (Mon–Fri 1 daily; 30min); Panama City (4 daily; 1hr).
Colón to: Panama City (2 daily Mon–Fri; 15min).
David to: Bocas del Toro (1 daily Mon–Fri; 50min); Panama City (6 daily; 1hr); Changuinola (1 daily Mon–Fri; 30min).
Panama City to: Achutupu (1 daily; 1hr 10min); Ailigandi (1 daily; 50min); Bocas del Toro (4–5 daily; 1hr); Cartí (1 daily via Corazón de Jesús; 45min); Changuinola (4 daily; 1hr 10min); Chitré (3 daily; 40min); Colón (2 daily Mon–Fri; 15min); Contadora (2 daily; 15min); David (6 daily; 1hr); El Porvenir (1 daily; 25min); El Real (3 weekly; 1hr); Garachiné (3 weekly; 1hr 15min); Jaqué (3 weekly; 1hr 10min); La Palma (3 weekly; 1hr 25min); Río Sidra (1 daily; 45min); Sambú (3 weekly; 1hr 20min); San Miguel (4 weekly; 45min).

Contexts

Contexts

Wildlife 837–843

Ecotoursim 844–849

Books 850–862

Wildlife

Be it the sinuous spotted jaguar, the technicolour macaw or the yellow-beaked toucan, tropical animals are more colourful and fabulous than their temperate-zone cousins, and nowhere is this more true than with the life forms of Central America.

The immense **geographical diversity** of the Central American isthmus accounts for the vast number of its resident animals, birds, insects and reptiles. And within each species you can observe an enormous variety, according to locality and **habitat**. For example, the freshwater turtles that inhabit mangrove streams are quite different from their larger sea-going cousins, and you won't see a jaguar on the dusty agricultural plains of northwest Nicaragua. Meanwhile, the harpy eagle seems to be locally extinct in Guatemala, but is thought to be alive and well in the matted density of the rainforests of Panama's Darién Gap (specifically the Punto Patiño reserve), Panama being the only country in the isthmus with a healthy population of these birds with thighs the size of a man's waist and claws as big as a grizzly bear. You may encounter rare squirrel monkeys, delicate and savant-faced, which are endemic to a small wedge of the Pacific coast of Costa Rica. Similarly, Guatemala's bizarrely fluffy ocellated turkey can be seen only in the jungles of Petén.

The animals of the isthmus do have in common a general **genealogy** – many can be described as mixtures of temperate-zone (North American) and tropical (South American) fauna. Some of the animals you are more likely to see – because of their abundance and diurnal activity – look like outsize versions or variations of temperate-zone mammals: the agouti or paca (*tepezcuintle*), a large water-rodent, for example, or the mink-like tayra (*tolumuco*), which may flash by you on its way up a tree. The Neotropical river otter (*nutria*) is a friendly creature, although extremely shy. The coati (or coatimundi if it is a lone male; *pizote* in Spanish) looks like a confused combination of a raccoon, domestic cat and an anteater. There's also a tropical raccoon (*mapache*) that looks like its northern neighbour, complete with eye mask.

Despite its reputation as a wildlife haven, Costa Rica does not have Central America's most diverse vertebrate fauna – that honour goes to Guatemala. Nor does it have the richest avifauna, an honour which falls to Panama with 940 recorded species including eleven endemic varieties (the country's Parque Nacional Soberanía – specifically the 28km stretch of Pipeline Road or *Camino de Oleoducto* – currently holds the world record for the number of species spotted in 24 hours, an incredible 360). Costa Rican insects and birds are certainly numerous, however, with 850 species of birds (including migratory ones) – more than the US and Canada combined. Costa Rica is also home to a quarter of the world's known butterflies – more than in all Africa – about 3000 types of moth, and scores of bees and wasps. Despite all this abundance, you may spot a quetzal more easily in, say, the central mountains of Nicaragua, which are sparsely populated and undertouristed, and where there are still plenty of nesting sites remaining.

Nowhere in Central America – even in Costa Rica's or Belize's national parks – should you expect to see the larger (and shyer) mammals as a matter of course – the tapir, jaguar and ocelot are particularly elusive. Many of the more exotic mammals that inhabit the isthmus are either nocturnal, endangered, or made shy through years of hunting and human encroachment. Although encounters do occur, they are usually brief, with the animal in question fleeing in a haze of colour and fur or dipping quietly back into the shadows from which it first emerged. That said, however, it's quite likely that you'll come into (usually fleeting) contact with some of the smaller and more abundant mammals.

Birds

Bird life, both migratory and indigenous, is abundant in Central America and includes some of the most colourful birds in the Americas: the quetzal, the toucan and the scarlet macaw. The most famous bird of Central America is without doubt the brilliant green and red resplendent **quetzal**. With a range historically extending from southern Mexico to northern Panama, the dazzling quetzal was highly prized by the Aztecs and the Maya. In the language of the Aztecs, *quetzali* means, roughly, "beautiful", and along with jade, the shimmering, jewel-coloured feathers were used as currency in Maya cities. The feathers were also worn by Maya nobles to signify religious qualities and social superiority, and formed the headdress of the plumed serpent Quetzalcoatl, the Aztec over-god. Hunting quetzals is particularly cruel, as it is well known that the bird cannot (or will not) live in captivity, a poignant attribute that has made it a symbol of freedom throughout Mesoamerica.

The male in particular, which possesses the distinctive feather train, up to 1.5m long, is still pursued by poachers. The quetzal is further endangered by the destruction of its favoured high-altitude cloudforest habitat. These days the remaining cloudforests – particularly Monteverde and the mountains of Cartago in Costa Rica; the Biotopo del Quetzal in Guatemala's Baja Verapaz; and the Volcán Barú and La Amistad national parks in Panama – are among the best places to try to see the birds (March–May especially), although they are always difficult to spot, in part due to shyness and in part because the vibrant green of their feathers, seemingly so bright, actually allows them to blend in well with the wet and shimmering vegetation in which they live.

The increasingly rare **scarlet macaw** (*lapa*), with its liberal splashes of red, yellow and blue, was once common on the Pacific coast of southern Mexico and Central America; they can also be found in the rainforests of Belize (where the Belize Zoo has a conservation project aimed at protecting the remaining 300 birds), and in the Darién National Park in Panama.

Parakeets are still fairly numerous and are most often seen in the lowland forested areas of the Pacific coast. You're also likely to see chestnut-mandibled and keel-billed **toucans** (*tucanes*), with their ridiculous – but beautiful – banana-shaped beaks. The chestnut-mandibled is the largest; their bills are two-tone brown and yellow. Keel-billed toucans have the more rainbow-coloured beaks and are smaller, which is sometimes taken advantage of by their larger cousins, who may drive them away from a cache of food or hound them out of a particular tree.

In the **waterways** and **wetlands** of the isthmus, most birds, at least in winter, are migratory species from the north, including herons, gulls, sandpipers and plovers.

The most common bird, and the one you're likely to come across hiking or riding in cattle country, is the unprepossessing grey-white **egret** (*garça*). Of the commonly found **raptors**, the laughing falcon (*guaco*) has the most distinct call, which sounds exactly like its Spanish name. The "laughing" bit comes from a much lower-pitched variation, which resembles muted human laughter. The shrunk-shouldered **vulture** (*zópilote*) is the one bird that almost everyone will see at some point, hanging out opportunistically on the side of major highways waiting for rabbits and iguanas to be thumped beneath the wheels of passing vehicles.

Mammals

Central America's **mammals** range from the fairly unexotic (at least for North Americans and Europeans) white-tailed deer (*venado cola blanca*) and brocket deer (*cabra de monte*), to the lumbering, antediluvian Baird's tapir (*danta*) and the semi-sacred jaguar (*jaguar/tigre*). Now an endangered species, the **jaguar** is endemic to the New World tropics and has a range from southern Mexico to northern Argentina. Although it was once common throughout Central America, especially in the lowland forests and mangroves of coastal areas, the jaguar's main foe has long been man, who has hunted it for its valuable pelt and because of its reputation among farmers as a predator of calves and pigs. It is easily tracked, due to its distinctive footprint. Incredibly, the hunting of jaguars for sport was allowed to continue into the 1980s, although it was at least hampered by the fact that it is illegal to import jaguar pelts into most countries, including the United States.

Though you would be phenomenally lucky (or unlucky, depending on how you see it) to come across a jaguar in the wild, one of the sorriest sights you may come across is a jaguar caged in a hotel or private zoo, where it can do little but pace back and forth. Considered sacred by the Maya, the jaguar is a very beautiful mid-sized cat, nearly always golden with black spots, and very rarely a sleek, solid black. They feed on smaller mammals such as agoutis, monkeys and peccaries, and may also eat fish and birds.

Not to be confused with the jaguar, the **jaguarundi** is a small cat, also very rarely seen, that ranges in colour from reddish to black. Little-studied, the jaguarundi has short legs and a low-slung body, and is sometimes mistaken for the *tayra*, or tropical mink. All the cats have been made extremely shy through centuries of hunting. The one exception, which does not yield a big enough pelt, is the small, sinuous-necked **margay** (*tigrillo*), with its complex black-spotted markings and large, inquisitive eyes. It has been known to peek out of the shadows and even sun itself on the rocks in open view. The **ocelot** (*manigordo*) is similar, somewhere between the margay and jaguar in size, but is another animal you are very unlikely to see. Of all the cats, the sandstone-coloured **mountain lion** (*puma*) is said to be the most forthcoming. It's a big animal, and although not usually aggressive toward humans, it should be treated with respect.

Along with the jaguar, the **tapir** is perhaps the most fantastical beast inhabiting the Neotropical rainforest. Rather homely, with eyes set back on either side of its head, the tapir looks like something between a horse and an overgrown pig, with a stout grey-skinned body and a head that suggests an elephant with a short trunk. Their antediluvian look comes from their prehensile snout, small ears, and delicate cloven feet. Vegetarian creatures weighing as much as 300kg, they are extremely shy in the wild, largely nocturnal, and stick to densely forested or rugged land: consequently they are very rarely spotted by casual rainforest walkers. The tapir has proved to be very amiable in captivity, and is certain to be unaggressive should you be lucky enough to come upon one in the wild. Like the jaguar, its main foe is man, who hunts it for its succulent meat. Nowadays the tapir is protected to a degree, particularly in some of the national parks of Costa Rica and Panama.

The **peccary** (*saíno*), usually described as a wild pig or boar, comes in two little-differentiated species in Central America: collared or white-lipped. They can be menacing when encountered in packs, when, if they get a whiff of you – their sight is poor so they'll smell you before they see you – they may clack their teeth and growl a bit. The usual advice, especially in Costa Rica's Corcovado National Park, where they travel in groups as large as thirty, is to climb a tree. However, peccaries are not on the whole dangerous and in captivity have proved to be very affectionate, rubbing themselves against you delightedly at the least opportunity.

One of the oddest animals is the tropical **anteater** (*hormiguero*), which you may well see vacuuming an anthill at some point. Top of the list for gregariousness – and sometimes noise – are the several species of **monkey** which inhabit the tropical lowland forests of the region. Most people can expect to at least hear, if not see, the **howler monkey** (*mono congo*), especially in the lowland forests: the male has a mechanism in its thick throat by which it can make sounds similar to those of a gorilla. Their whoops are most often heard at dawn or dusk. The **white-faced** or capuchin (*carablanca*) monkey is slighter than the howler, with a distinctly humanoid expression on its delicate face. This, combined with its intelligence, often consigns it to being a pet in a hotel or private zoo. The **spider monkey** (*araña*) takes its name from its spider-like ability to move through the trees employing its five limbs – the fifth one is its prehensile tail, which it uses to grip branches. The **squirrel monkey** (*mono tití*) is found mainly in and around Manuel Antonio National Park on Costa Rica's Pacific coast, and in parts of Panama. Their delicate grey and white faces have long made them attractive to pet owners and zoos, and consequently they have been hunted to near-extinction in Costa Rica.

Two types of **sloths** (*perezosos*) live in the trees of the hotter regions of the isthmus: the three-toed sloth, active by day, and the nocturnal two-toed sloth. True to their name, sloths move very little during the day and have an extremely slow metabolism. They are excellently camouflaged from their main predators, eagles, by the algae that often covers their brown fur. In the first instance, at least, they are very difficult to spot, then, when you're used to the familiar hairy clump, you begin to notice them more often.

Amphibians and reptiles

If you spot nothing else during your time in Central America, you'll almost certainly see a **frog** or a **toad**. Though they may look vulnerable, many tropical frogs and toads protect themselves by secreting poison through their skin. Using some of the most powerful natural toxins known, the frog can directly target the heart muscle of the predator, paralyzing it and causing immediate death. As these poisons are transmittable through skin contact, you should never touch a rainforest frog (conversely the frogs can also absorb toxic substances such as DEET through their own skin, another reason not to handle them). Probably the best-known, and most toxic, of the frogs, is the colourful **poison dart frog**, usually quite small, and found in various combinations of bright red and blue or green and black.

The chief thing you'll notice about the more common frogs is their size: they're much stouter than temperate-zone frogs. Look out for the gaudy **leaf frog** (*rana calzonudo*), star of many a frog calendar. Relatively large, it is an alarming bright green, with orange hands and feet and dark-blue thighs. Its sides are purple, and its eyes are pure red to scare off potential predators.

Travelling along isthmus waterways, in most places you will see **caimans** sunning themselves on riverside logs, and massive **crocodiles** lolling on the mudflats. The crocs look truly fearsome, and usually confine themselves to fresh water – although the reefs off the Belize coast are home to some American salt-water crocodiles.

Pot-bellied **iguanas** are the most ubiquitous of the region's lizards. Despite their dragon-like appearance, they are very shy, and if you do spot them, it's likely that they'll be scurrying away in an ungainly fashion.

Central America is also home to a vast array of **snakes** (*serpientes*, *culebras*). Many of them are non-venomous, but it's worth knowing about a few of the ones that are in case you have a (statistically very unlikely) encounter. Bear in mind, though, that snakes are largely nocturnal, and for the most part at least as wary of you as you are of them. Of all the snakes it is the **bushmaster** (*cascabela, matabuey*) that inspires the most fear. A viper whose range extends from southern Mexico to Brazil, it is the largest venomous snake in the Americas – it can reach a size of nearly 2m. The most aggressive of snakes, it will actually chase people if it is so inclined. The good news is that you are extremely unlikely to encounter one, as it prefers the sort of dense, precipitous and mountainous territory tourists hardly ever venture into.

Once solely the inhabitant of rainforests, the **fer-de-lance** viper (*terciopelo*) has now adapted quite well to cleared areas, grassy uplands, and even some inhabited stretches, although you are far more likely to see them in places which have heavy rainfall (like the Caribbean coast) and near streams or rivers at night. Though it can reach more than 2m in length, the **terciopelo** (as it is most often called, in English or Spanish) is well-camouflaged and very difficult to spot, its grey-black skin with a light crisscross pattern resembling a big pile of leaves. Along with the bushmaster, the terciopelo is one of the few snakes that may attack without provocation.

Considering the competition, it's not hard to see why the **boa constrictor** (*boa*) wins the title of most congenial snake. Often with beautiful semi-triangular markings, largely retiring and shy of people, the boa is one of the few snakes you may see in the daytime. Although they are largely torpid, it is not a good idea to bother them. They have big teeth and can bite (though they are not venomous) but are unlikely to stir unless startled. If you encounter one, either on the move or lying still, the best thing is to walk around it slowly, giving it a good 5m berth.

Insects

The many climates and microclimates of Central America support an enormous diversity of **insects**, of which **butterflies** (*mariposas*) are the most flamboyant and sought-after. Active during the day, they can be seen, especially from about 8am to noon, almost anywhere in the region. Most adult butterflies take their typical food of nectar – usually from red flowers – through a proboscis. Others feed on fungi, dung and rotting fruit. Best known, and quite often spotted, especially along the forest trails, is the fast-flying **blue morpho**, whose titanium-bright wings seem to shimmer electrically.

The **lantern fly** (*machaca*) emits an amazingly strong mint-blue light, like a mini lightning streak – if you have one in your hotel room you'll know it as soon as you turn out the light. The **ant** kingdom is well represented, especially in the humid forests. Chief among the rainforest salarymen are the **leaf-cutter ants**, who work in businesslike cadres, carrying away bits of leaf to build their distinctive nests. Endemic to the Neotropics, carnivorous **army ants** are often encountered in the forest, typically living in large colonies, some of more than a million individuals. They are most famous for their "dawn raids", when they pour out of a hideaway, typically a log, and divide into several columns to create a swarm. In this columnar formation they then go off in search of prey – other ants and insects – which they carry back to the nest to consume.

Marine life

Of all the Central American marine areas, Belize's barrier reef and the Bay Islands of Honduras are probably the best places to spot sea life, whether while diving, snorkelling, or taking a boat trip. Belize, in particular, is home to a particularly rich concentration of marine life. The Caribbean **coral life** on the reef and in the Bay Islands is second to none in Central America, with oysters, the distinctive neon pink chalace sponge, the tentacled fire coral, and the apartment sponge – a tall thin tube with small holes stacked neatly through it.

Among the Caribbean coast's marine mammals, the friendliest has to be the sea cow or **manatee**, elephantine in size, good-natured and well-intentioned, not to mention endangered. Manatees all over the Caribbean are declining in number, due to the disappearance and pollution of the fresh or saltwater riverways in which they live. You may come across them in the coastal areas of Belize. In Costa Rica your only reasonable chance of seeing one is in the Tortuguero canals in Limón province, where they sometimes break the surface. At first you might mistake it for a tarpon, but the manatee's overlapping snout and long whiskers are quite distinctive.

Five species of **marine turtle** nest on Central America's shores. Nesting takes place mostly at night and mostly in the context of *arribadas*: giant invasions of turtles who come ashore in their thousands on the same beach (or spot of beach) at a certain time of year, laying hundreds of thousands of eggs. Greens, hawksbills and leatherbacks come ashore on both coasts, while the Olive Ridley comes ashore only on the Pacific.

The strange blunt-nosed **loggerhead** can sometimes be seen in Belize, although they are still hunted for food there and so their numbers are in decline. The **green turtle**, long prized for the delicacy of its flesh, has become nearly synonymous with its favoured nesting grounds at Tortuguero in northeast Costa Rica. In the 1950s it was classified as endangered but, thanks in part to the protection offered by areas like Tortuguero, is making a comeback. Some greens make herculean journeys of as much as 2000km to their breeding beaches, returning to the same stretch year after year. *Arribadas* are most concentrated in June and October.

The **hawksbill** (*carey*), so-named for its distinctive down-curving "beak", is found all over the tropics, often preferring rocky shores and coral reefs. It used to be hunted extensively on the Caribbean coast for its meat and shell, but this is now banned. Poaching does still occur, however, and you should avoid buying any tortoiseshell that you see for sale. Capable of growing to a length of 5m, the **leatherback** (*baula*) is the largest reptile in the world. Its "shell" is actually a network of bones overlaid with a very tough leathery skin. Though it nests mostly on the Pacific beaches, it also comes ashore on the Caribbean coast.

The **Olive Ridley** (*lora, carpintera* – also called the Pacific Ridley) turtle nests on Pacific beaches, particularly on their protected grounds at Playa Nancite in Santa Rosa National Park and Ostional near Nosara on Costa Rica's Nicoya Peninsula, as well as Refugio de Vida Silvestre La Flor near San Juan del Sur in southern Nicaragua. They come ashore in massive *arribadas* and, unusually, often nest during the day.

The **black river turtle** and the **snapping turtle**, about which little is known (except that it snaps), also inhabit rivers and mangrove swamps, and may occasionally be spotted on the riverbanks.

Though **dolphins** (*delfines*) and **whales** thread themselves through the waters of the Pacific coast, it's rare to see them, as they usually remain many miles offshore. **Sharks** (*tiburones*) can be found on both coasts, and though the vast majority of species are harmless, it's wise to ask around before going for a swim.

Ecotourism

Global **tourism** is a multi-billion-dollar industry. With some 567 million international tourists per year – set to rise to 1.56 billion by the year 2020 – the industry was worth around US$463billion in 2002, a figure representing 10 percent of the world's GDP. Tourism can play an important role in maintaining indigenous cultures, and also provides an invaluable source of foreign currency for many Central American countries. Along with these benefits, though, there are some detrimental consequences, including disruptive effects environmentally, socially, culturally, and even economically.

Though notoriously difficult to classify, **ecotourism** is estimated to account for as much as forty percent of the Central American market. Through sheer numbers alone, such tourism is bound to have an impact, even on societies sufficiently developed to be able to absorb it. Of course, many of the relatively undisturbed areas that appeal to the ecotourist are located in those societies that are *least* able to absorb the impact.

Since the term was coined a decade or so ago, the **rationale** behind ecotourism has been that money dispensed by visitors from developed nations could be channelled successfully into protecting the natural resources they come to visit. By enabling local people to earn more by protecting their environment and encouraging visitors to come to it, both sides are able, theoretically, to benefit. In the words of the London-based Economics for Environment Consultancy, all natural resources have a "rent", or scarcity value. Local management of the resource and the capturing of this rent in the form of visitor fees, can be used to control the number of people visiting the resource, and allows for greater flexibility in determining and funding the best method of protection. This protection should be in line with local customs and traditions, and the evolution of the local society itself.

Codes of conduct

Though well-meaning, ecotourism **codes of conduct** can seem preachy and presumptuous. Still, in any attempt to define the term, or to go any way towards understanding its aims, it's useful to know what the locally accepted guidelines are. The Asociación Tsuli, the Costa Rican branch of the Audubon Society, has developed its own short code of conduct, called **Environmental Ethics for Nature Travel**:

1 Wildlife and natural habitats must not be needlessly disturbed.

2 Waste should be disposed of properly.

3 Tourism should be a positive influence on local communities.

4 Tourism should be managed and sustainable.

5 Tourism should be culturally sensitive.

6 There must be no commerce in wildlife, wildlife products or native plants.

7 Tourists should leave with a greater understanding and appreciation of nature, conservation and the environment.

8 Tourism should strengthen the conservation effort and enhance the natural integrity of places visited.

Definitions

Ecotourism is a tricky term to **define**. It is often seen in relation to what it is not: package tourism, wherein visitors have limited contact with nature and with the day-to-day lives of local people. But as more and more organizations and businesses hijack the eco prefix for dubious uses, the authentic ecotourism experience has become increasingly difficult to pin down. For some, ecotourism is a way of assuring themselves that they are a better tourist, and that they are giving something back. Others point to the fundamental **contradiction** between attempting to protect an area whilst encouraging large numbers of people to visit it – at heart, perhaps, the best way to be an ecotourist is not to be a tourist at all. Lying somewhere between these different views is the argument that if people are going to travel, they may as well do so in a low-impact manner that minimizes destruction of the visited environment and promotes cultural exchange.

One of the best attempts to put forward a workable definition has been made by **ATEC**, the Talamancan Ecotourism and Conservation Association in southwest Costa Rica, which seeks to promote "socially responsible tourism" by integrating local Bribrí and Afro-Caribbean culture into tourists' experience of the area, as well as giving residents pride in their unique cultural heritage and natural environment. They say: "Ecotourism means more than bird books and binoculars. Ecotourism means more than native art hanging on hotel walls or ethnic dishes on the restaurant menu. Ecotourism is not mass tourism behind a green mask. Ecotourism means a constant struggle to defend the earth and to protect and sustain traditional communities. Ecotourism is a cooperative relationship between the non-wealthy local community and those sincere, open-minded tourists who want to enjoy themselves in a Third World setting and, at the same time, enrich their consciousness by means of significant educational and cultural experience."

A case study: Costa Rica

Along with Belize, **Costa Rica** has become virtually synonymous with ecotourism in Central America and is widely regarded as being at the cutting edge of worldwide conservation strategy, an impressive feat for a small, cash-strapped Central American nation. At the centre of its internationally applauded conservation effort is a complex system of national parks and wildlife refuges protecting a full 25 percent of its territory. These statistics are used with great effect to attract tourists, the vast majority of whom still come to see the country's remarkably varied tropical flora and fauna.

However, for years the country has been in danger of being overwhelmed by its own popularity, attracting over 1,032,000 visitors annually – the population of the country itself is only 3.8 million. Not surprisingly, what most concerns biologists nowadays is how much damage is being caused by so many feet tramping through the rainforests.

In **Manuel Antonio National Park**, on Costa Rica's Pacific coast, visitors can walk seaside trails, one of which circles the stunning Punta Cathedral, jutting out into the sea. As ecotourism experiences go, it's a soft option, easily reachable and sandwiched between beautiful beaches. Here the **squirrel**

monkeys, an endangered species, have become too used to people. Ecotourists walking Manuel Antonio's trails complain about them behaving "as if they were in a zoo", begging for food and being cheeky, or alternately hiding from the stress of having, on popular holidays like Easter, literally hundreds of people trudge through their habitat. Rangers at Manuel Antonio talk openly of the "psychological pressure" large numbers of visitors put on some animals. When the squirrel monkeys began to display symptoms of neurosis, officials took the decision to shut the park on Mondays, to give the animals a rest.

Monteverde and **Santa Elena**, two small farming communities high in the mountains of the Cordillera Central, are home to two reserves that together protect one of the last sizeable pristine pieces of **cloudforest** (high-altitude rainforest) in the Americas. In recent years increasing tourism has transformed the communities, and flotillas of tourist buses rattle up and down the muddy roads connecting the towns to the reserves. In the high season, the Monteverde administrators have had to set a 100-visitor-a-day ceiling in order to preserve the ecological integrity of the reserve. Both communities have resisted paving the 40-kilometre stretch of road which links them with the Carretera Interamericana, in an attempt to avoid a day-tripper culture where visitors would be bussed up to the reserve for the day and then back down to their beach hotels, spending little money but having the maximum impact on the local environment.

It could be argued that an underdeveloped country in need of foreign currency shouldn't complain about being too popular, especially when the type of tourism it has developed is so very "green". But Costa Rica highlights what some observers criticize about the concept of ecotourism – at least in Latin America – that it represents not so much an act of environmental altruism but is merely part of an imperialist, bourgeois agenda: wealthy First World ecotourists can console themselves that they are saving the environment, but what about the 38 percent of Costa Rica's population who live in poverty and without access to land? Many tropical biologists have concluded that, in sum, if you love the rainforest, it would be better to stay at home and donate money to conservation organizations rather than travelling abroad to tramp through the forests and change local economies with the influx of your dollars. Ask any national park or private reserve administrator in Costa Rica about this and their response is nearly uniform – "People are going to come anyway. You can't stop them. Our job is to make sure the tourism is managed properly."

It's a delicate balance. Many powerful vested interests are lined up to log, mine and prospect for minerals in Costa Rica. There's also increasing tension between MINAE, the government body charged with looking after the national parks, and the tourist office (ICT), who are responsible for raising visitor numbers. The head of MINAE recently threatened to close the national parks to all visitors unless the ICT provided more money for their upkeep. As the country with the highest population density in Central America, there is also tremendous pressure on land, and parks are regularly invaded by squatters. All in all, though, there's no doubt that the financial success of ecotourism has guaranteed the survival of many natural places. All you have to do is look at the land *not* protected by the reserves – the lowlands around Monteverde, for example, which have now been almost completely cleared for pasture.

Ecotourism around Central America

While there may be no lack of genuine enthusiasm for ecotourism across Central America, sadly in many cases a lack of money means that numerous wildlife, nature and marine reserves across the region have little real existence except on paper. Political turmoil during the 1980s and the grinding problems of poverty mean that – with the notable exception of Costa Rica – questions of environmental preservation and sustainability have until recently been largely neglected.

Honduras, for example, has an extensive national network of parks and reserves, many of which were designated protected areas only in 1987. Some, like Celaque in the central highlands and Cusuco near San Pedro Sula, are extremely well-managed and have ensured the protection of irreplaceable tracts of virgin forest and fragile ecosystems. Others exist as little more than lines on maps, and given the government's lack of resources, local people's need for land, and the, at times, illegal activities of large landowners, there's little realistic chance of changing this situation.

In **El Salvador**, a nascent network of national parks is now in existence. Perhaps the most advanced – in terms of a comprehensive project for both environmental protection and community development – is the Bosque Montecristo, part of the El Trifinio International Biosphere, administered jointly by the governments of El Salvador, Honduras and Guatemala. The work carried out here places as much emphasis on the local indigenous communities as on environmental protection. Similar developments can be seen in **Panama**, whose Nusangandi Nature Reserve in Kuna Yala was the first reserve in Latin America to be set up and administered by an indigenous people.

Since the mid-1980s the number of foreign tourists visiting **Belize** each year has grown from fewer than 100,000 to well over 500,000. Given Belize's abundant natural resources – the second-largest barrier reef in the world, tropical forest, Maya ruins – the promotion of tourism has been founded on "greenness" and sustainability. Marine, wildlife and archeological reserves have been established, with local groups encouraged to take an active part in developing and maintaining ecotourist facilities. In Central America and the Caribbean, Belize is seen as having paved the way in creating a locally controlled industry that benefits both cultural traditions and the environment.

Certainly the country has benefited, with at least 15 percent of its GDP now derived from tourist revenues. Underneath the surface, however, things are less than rosy, with growing disquiet about the nature of so-called ecotourist development and fears that the industry is now spiralling beyond the control of Belizeans. Significant environmental damage has been sustained by the country's reef system, while a deliberate marketing of the country as a "green" destination has created a demand – with cruise ships alone expected to bring a million passengers within a decade – which it's thought can only be met by more and larger tourist developments, funded, if not managed, by foreign capital. The proposals to regenerate Belize City's waterfront were a case in point, having been drawn up initially under the sponsorship of US aid. The resulting (and still expanding) Tourism Village – a kind of cruise line terminal cum shopping mall primarily designed to transfer tourists from the cruise ships to scheduled tours – has obvious appeal to tourists, but in reality is of little benefit to Belizean residents, who still have to put up with decaying infrastructure and increasing poverty and crime.

Given that the cruise line company which owns the village gets to keep most of the landing fee, much of the income is leaked away. That said, twenty percent of the fee does go to PACT (The Protected Areas Conservation Trust), which ploughs the money back into infrastructure and development projects in protected areas and local communities. There are also the obvious immediate economic benefits for the tour guides, operators and Maya sites and reserves which the tourists pay to enter, again merely underlining the irony in the fact that the sheer volume of visitors puts unprecedented pressure on the environment, yet at the same time allows income for protected areas which might otherwise be left open to slash-and-burn agriculture. With yet more cruise ship associated developments on the way, however, including a fourteen-acre seafront site earmarked as a parking and turning site for tour buses, the pretence of any kind of eco- or sustainable tourism in Belize City rings ever more hollow.

New initiatives: the way forward

In recent years Mario Boza, prominent conservationist and a founder of Costa Rica's national parks system, has advocated a strategy of **macro-conservation**. Shifting the emphasis from individual country projects in favour of linking together chunks of protected land across national borders, he argues, will allow the creation of larger protected areas for animals that need room to hunt, like jaguars and pumas. Even more importantly, these initiatives will allow countries to make more effective joint conservation policies and decisions.

Macro-conservation **projects** include the Mesoamerican Biotic Corridor (all of Mesoamerica), El Mundo Maya (Belize, El Salvador, Guatemala, Honduras and Mexico), Si-a-Paz (Nicaragua and Costa Rica) and Parque Internacíonal La Amistad (Costa Rica and Panama). The largest conservation project undertaken in the western hemisphere, the **Mesoamerican Biotic Corridor**, which began life as the Paseo Pantera (Path of the Panther) is an interesting example of ecological cooperation between the Central American governments. When completed it is hoped this green corridor will allow unimpeded migration, north and south, of a wide range of animal, bird and marine life. In some species this could be the answer to long-term survival (jaguars, for instance, need about 100 square kilometres in which to roam). While the project benefits from US$100million dollars in international backing, part of the strategy is to implement a tightly controlled ecotourism program, with tourist dollars helping to pay the green corridor's way. Mario Boza is even heading a plan to extend the concept to the whole of the Americas, in effect creating a continuous line of protected areas from the Arctic to southern Chile.

Arguably, however, the most revolutionary change in conservation management, and the one likeliest to have the biggest pay-off in the long term, is the shift towards **local initiatives**. Some projects are truly local, such as the tiny grassroots organization TUVA on Costa Rica's Osa peninsula, which oversees the selective logging of naturally felled rainforest trees, or the ecotourism co-operative of Las Delicias on Costa Rica's Nicoya Peninsula, which provides professional guides to take tourists into Central America's largest underground caves, and the UCA Miraflor nature reserve near Estelí in Nicaragua, where tourists can walk between the various climactic zones, staying with different local families each night. Another initiative, even more promising in terms of how it affects the lives of many rural-based Central Americans, is the creation of "buffer zones" around some national parks. In these zones campesinos and other smallholders can do part-time farming, are allowed restricted hunting rights, and receive education as to the ecological and economic value of the forest. Locals may be trained as nature guides, and campesinos may be given incentives to practise non-traditional forms of agriculture and ways of making a living which are not so harmful to the environment.

In the Talamanca region of Costa Rica, ATEC (source of the "ecotourism definition" offered on p.844) takes tourists on tours of the local **indigenous** Kéköldi reserve. The Bribrí indigenous guides take outsiders into the local villages, on treks through the rainforest pointing out traditional medicinal uses of many plants, and demonstrate how many local products such as banana vinegar, guava jam and herbal teas are made. All tour fees go back into the local community. In the department of La Mosquitia, Honduras, the **Pech** indigenous people live in small villages near the headwaters of the Río Plátano, within the protected lands of the 5000-square-kilometre UNESCO Biosphere Reserve of the same name. Their income is supplemented by offering guide services and by selling miniature wooden carvings of *pipantes* (dugout canoes) and small bags of packaged cocoa. Some tour operators are taking tourists on multi-day jungle excursions in the area, and a fair portion of this revenue goes directly into the pockets of the indigenous Pech, Miskito and Garífuna communities visited.

Despite the problems outlined above, there's no question that ecotourism is the most effective way of preserving the natural environment while allowing it to pay its way. At present, though, the onus falls on eco-minded visitors to make sure their dollars are going to the right place. Probably the most positive sign for the future is the growth in community-based projects, a step forward in the development of an economically viable industry that's committed to protecting the stunning landscapes, wildlife and cultures of Central America.

Books

The following is a list of the books that proved most useful – or enjoyable – in the preparation of this guide. General books are listed first, followed by individual sections on each country. Publishers are given in the format UK/US; where only one publisher is listed, this covers both the UK and US, unless specified. The book symbol marks titles that are particularly recommended.

Central America

History, politics and society

Peter Dale-Scott and Jonathan Marshall *Cocaine Politics: Drugs, Armies and the CIA in Central America* (University of California Press). Polemical but well-researched exposé of CIA involvement in cocaine trafficking and political oppression in Central America in the 1980s. Reveals the truth behind the Iran–Contra scandal and gives the lie to the rhetoric of the war on drugs.

James Dunkerley *Power in the Isthmus* and *The Pacification of Central America* (Verso). Detailed accounts of Central American politics (excluding Belize) offering a good overview of events up to the early 1990s, particularly the region's civil wars. Well researched with plenty of statistics and charts, though the style is factual rather than flowing.

In Focus (LAB/Interlink Books). An excellent series of country guides giving concise, highly readable accounts of the people, politics and culture of each nation. Titles are currently available covering Costa Rica, Guatemala, Belize and Nicaragua.

Ralph Lee Woodward Jr *Central America: A Nation Divided* (Oxford University Press, o/p). More readable than Dunkerley, and probably the best general summary of the Central American situation, despite its daft title.

Travel and impressions

★ **Simon Calder** *The Panamericana* (Vacation Work). Prolific writer, broadcaster and veteran backpacker Calder travels the entire Carretera Panamericana – the Pan-American Highway – from the Texas border to Yaviza in Panama. An enormously funny and candid guide to the road and places just off it.

Glen David Short *An Odd Odyssey: California to Columbia by Bus and Boat, Through Mexico and Central America* (Trafford). Intrepid Aussie Short gives a slightly different perspective to an oversubscribed genre, bypassing the baggage of American writers with a lively, occasionally gung-ho yet down to earth and honest account encompassing chunks of historical and political context, and breathing life into eccentric character sketches.

Thomas Gage *Travels in the New World* (University of Oklahoma Press). Unusual account of a Dominican friar's travels through Mexico and Central America between 1635 and 1637, including some fascinating insights into colonial life as well as some great attacks on the greed and pomposity of the Catholic Church abroad.

Aldous Huxley *Beyond the Mexique Bay* (Flamingo, UK, o/p). Huxley's travels, in 1934, took him from Belize through Guatemala to Mexico, swept on by his fascination for history and religion, and sprouting bizarre theories on the basis of everything he sees. There are some great descriptions of Maya sites and indigenous culture, with superb one-liners summing up people and places.

★ **John Lloyd Stephens** *Incidents of Travel in Central America, Chiapas, and Yucatán* (Dover). Stephens was a classic nineteenth-century traveller. Acting as American ambassador to Central America, he indulged his own enthusiasm for archeology; while the republics fought it out among themselves he was wading through the jungle stumbling across ancient cities. His journals, told with superb Victorian pomposity, make great reading. Some editions include fantastic illustrations by Catherwood of the ruins overgrown with tropical rainforest.

Ronald Wright *Time among the Maya* (Abacus/Henry Holt, o/p). A vivid and sympathetic account of travels from Belize through Guatemala, Chiapas and Yucatán, meeting the Maya and exploring their obsession with time. The book's twin points of interest are the ancient Maya and the violence of the 1970s and 80s, subjects which are covered with superb historical insight, while a lengthy bibliography offers ideas for further reading. Certainly one of the best travel books on the area.

Archeology and Maya civilization

★ **Michael Coe** *The Maya* (Thames & Hudson). Now in its sixth edition, this clear and comprehensive introduction to Maya archeology is the best on offer. Coe has also written several more weighty, academic volumes. His *Breaking the Maya Code* (Penguin/Thames & Hudson), a very personal history of the decipherment of the glyphs, owes much to the fact that Coe was present at many of the most important meetings leading to the breakthrough.

Joyce Kelly *An Archaeological Guide to Northern Central America* (University of Oklahoma Press). Detailed and practical guide to 38 Maya sites and 25 museums in four countries; an essential companion for anyone travelling purposefully through the Maya region of Central America. Kelly's star ratings – based on a site's archeological importance, degree of restoration and accessibility – may affront purists but it does provide a valuable opinion on how worthwhile a particular visit might be.

Simon Martin and Nikolai Grube *Chronicle of the Maya Kings and Queens: Deciphering the Dynasties of the Ancient Maya* (Thames & Hudson). Extravagantly illustrated and academically rigourous Mayan history focusing on the pivotal city-states, their rules and the relations between them. The timelines are a useful resource and the work is one of the most authoritative of recent years, if perhaps a little too in-depth for beginners.

Mary Ellen Miller and Karl Taube *The Gods and Symbols of Ancient Mexico and the Maya: An Illustrated Dictionary of Mesoamerican Religion* (Thames & Hudson, o/p). A superb modern reference on ancient Mesoamerica, written by two leading scholars. Taube's *Aztec and Maya Myths* (British Museum Press, UK) is a perfect short, accessible introduction to Mesoamerican mythology.

Linda Schele and David Freidel These two authors, both in the forefront of the "new archeology" which has fuelled Maya studies since the 1960s, have been personally responsible for decoding many of the glyphs. While their writing style, which frequently includes "re-creations" of scenes inspired by their discoveries, is controversial, it has nevertheless inspired a devoted following. *A Forest of Kings: The Untold Story of the Ancient Maya* (Quill, US), in conjunction with *The Blood of Kings*, by Linda Schele and Mary Miller, shows that far from being governed by peaceful astronomer-priests, the ancient Maya were ruled by hereditary kings, lived in populous and aggressive city-states, and engaged in a continuous entanglement of alliances and war. *The Maya Cosmos* (Quill, US), by Schele, Freidel and Joy Parker, is a more difficult read, but continues the examination of Maya ritual and religion in a unique and far-reaching way. *The Code of Kings* (Shribner, US), written in collaboration with Peter Matthews and illustrated with Justin Kerr's famous "rollout" photography of Maya ceramics, examines the significance of the monuments at selected Maya sites in detail. It's her last book – Linda Schele died in April 1998 – and now a classic of epigraphic interpretation.

Robert Sharer *The Ancient Maya* (Stanford University Press). Classic, comprehensive and weighty account of Maya civilization, now in a completely revised and much more readable fifth edition, yet as authoritative as ever. Required reading for archeologists, and a fascinating reference for the non-expert.

Wildlife and the environment

Catherine Caulfield *In the Rainforest* (o/p). Still one of the best introductory volumes to the rainforest, dealing in an accessible, discursive fashion with many of the issues covered in the more academic or specialized titles. Much of the book is directed at the Amazon, but could easily be transposed to Panama, Guatemala or Costa Rica – the author turns a wry eye on Costa Rica's cattle-ranching culture, as well as providing an interesting profile of the farming methods used by the Monteverde community.

Alan Forsyth *Tropical Nature: Life and Death in the Rain Forests of Central and South America* (Touchstone Books, US). Another great primer for the uninitiated. Forsyth brings his subject to life without dumbing down the book's academic gravitas, and the chapters are sufficiently concise and self-contained to allow casual browsing as well as serious study.

Steve Howell and Sophie Webb *The Birds of Mexico and Northern Central America* (Oxford University Press). The result of years of research, this tremendous work is the definitive book on the region's birds. Essential for all serious birders.

John C. Kricher *A Neotropical Companion* (Princeton University Press). Subtitled "An Introduction to the Animals, Plants and Ecosystems of the New World Tropics" and containing an amazing amount of valuable information for nature lovers. Researched mainly in Central America, so there's plenty that's directly relevant.

Belize

History, politics and society

Rosita Arvigo with Nadia Epstein *Sastun: My Apprenticeship with a Maya Healer* (Harper). A rare glimpse into the life and work of a Maya *curandero*, the late Elijio Panti of San Antonio, Belize. Rosita Arvigo has ensured the survival of many generations of accumulated healing knowledge, and this book is a testimony both to her perseverance in becoming accepted by Elijio Panti and the cultural wisdom of the indigenous people. Arvigo has also written and co-authored several other books on traditional medicine in Belize, including *Rainforest Remedies*.

Gerald S. Koop *Pioneer Years in Belize* (Country Graphics, Belize). A history of the Mennonites in Belize, written in a style as stolid and practical as the lives of the pioneers themselves. A good read nonetheless.

Assad Shoman *Thirteen Chapters of a History of Belize* (Angelus Press, Belize). A long-overdue treatment of the country's history written by a Belizean who's not afraid to examine colonial myths with a detailed and rational analysis. Primarily a school textbook, but the style will not alienate non-student readers. Shoman, active in politics both before and since independence, also wrote *Party Politics in Belize*, a short but highly detailed account of the development of party politics in the country.

Ann Sutherland *The Making of Belize: Globalization in the Margins* (Bergin and Garvey, US, o/p). A recent study of cultural and economic changes in Belize, based on the author's experiences as a visitor and her observations as an anthropologist. The result is an enjoyable mixture of academic research, anecdotal insights and strong, even controversial, opinion; Sutherland reserves her strongest criticism for conservationists, whom she castigates as "ecocolonialists [who] totally disregard the interests of the Belizean people".

Archeology

Byron Foster (ed) *Warlords and Maize Men – A Guide to the Maya Sites of Belize* (Cubola, Belize). An excellent handbook to fifteen of the most accessible sites in Belize, compiled by the Association for Belizean Archeology and the Belize Department of Archeology.

Fiction, poetry and autobiography

Zee Edgell *Beka Lamb* (Heinemann). A young girl's account of growing up in Belize in the 1950s, in which the problems of adolescence are described alongside those of the Belizean independence movement. The book also explores everyday life in the colony, describing the powerful structure of matriarchal society and the influence of the Catholic Church. *In Times Like These* (Heinemann) is a semi-autobiographical account of personal and political intrigue set in the months leading up to Belize's independence.

Zoila Ellis *On Heroes, Lizards and Passion* (Cubola Productions, Belize). Seven short stories written by a Belizean woman with a deep understanding of her country's people and their culture.

Emory King *Belize 1798* (Tropical Books, Belize). Rip-roaring historical novel peopled by the characters involved in the Battle of St George's Caye. King's enthusiasm for his country's history results in the nearest thing you'll get to a Belizean blockbuster, yet it's based on meticulous research in archives on both sides of the Atlantic. Wonderful holiday reading.

Various *Shots from the Heart* (Cubola Productions, Belize). Slim anthology of the work of three young Belizean poets: Yasser Musa, Kiren Shoman and Simone Waight. Evocative imagery and perceptive comment relate experiences of a changing society. Musa's *Belize City Poem* (published separately) is a sharply observed, at times vitriolic, commentary on the simultaneous arrival of independence and US-dominated television on Belizean society.

Wildlife

Les Beletsky *Belize and Northern Guatemala – the Ecotraveller's Wildlife Guide* (Academic Press, UK). Although other, specialist wildlife guides may cover their subjects in more detail, this is the only reasonably comprehensive single-volume guide to the mammals, birds, reptiles, amphibians and marine life of the region. Helpfully, the illustration of each creature is given opposite its description, avoiding confusing page-flicking.

Alan Rabinowitz *Jaguar* (Arbor House, UK). Rabinowitz was instrumental in establishing Belize's Jaguar Reserve in 1984. This is an account of his experiences studying jaguars for the New York Zoological Society in the early 1980s and living with a Maya family in the Cockscomb Basin, Belize.

Guatemala

History, politics and society

Jim Handy *Gift of the Devil* (South End Press). The best modern history of Guatemala, concise and readable, with a sharp focus on the Maya population and the brief period of socialist government. Don't expect too much detail on the distant past, which is only explored in order to put the modern reality into some kind of context, but if you're interested in the history of Guatemalan brutality then this is the book to read, as it sets out to expose the development of oppression and point the finger at those responsible.

Rigoberta Menchú *I, Rigoberta Menchú – An Indian Woman in Guatemala* and *Crossing Borders* (Verso). Momentous story of one of Latin America's most remarkable women, Nobel Peace Prize winner, Rigoberta Menchú. The first volume is a horrific account of family life in the Maya highlands, recording how Menchú's family were targeted, terrorized and murdered by the military. The book also reveals much concerning Quiché Maya cultural traditions and the enormous gulf between *ladino* and indigenous society in Guatemala. The second volume documents Menchú's life in exile in Mexico, her work at the United Nations fighting for indigenous people and her return to Guatemala. An astounding tale of a woman's spirit, courage and determination.

Víctor Perera *Unfinished Conquest* (University of California Press). Written by a Guatemalan, this is a superb and extremely readable account of the civil war, and also has comprehensive coverage of the political, social and economic inequalities affecting the country. Immaculately researched, the book's strength comes from its extensive interviews with Guatemalans and its incisive analysis of recent history.

The Popol Vuh The great poem of the Quiché, written shortly after the Conquest and intended to preserve the tribe's knowledge of its history. It's an amazing swirl of ancient mythological characters and their wanderings through the Quiché highlands, tracing their ancestry back to its beginning. The best version is translated by Dennis Tedlock and published by Touchstone in the US.

★ **Jean-Marie Simon** *Eternal Spring – Eternal Tyranny* (W.W. Norton). Of all the books on human rights in Guatemala, this is the one that speaks with the greatest clarity, combining the highest standards in photography with crisp text. If you want to know what happened in Guatemala over the last twenty years or so there is no better book.

Travel and impressions

Stephen Connely Benz *Guatemalan Journey* (University of Texas Press). One of the best travelogues on Guatemala. Lucidly written and strong on insight and astute observation as well as historical context, the book documents the fate of the country's dispossessed through a series of perceptive snapshots.

Marcos McPeek Villatoro *Walking to La Milpa: Living in Guatemala with Armies, Demons, Abrazos and Death* (Moyer Bell Ltd). A deeply felt, naïvely charming account of lay missionary Villatoro's and his wife's two-year stint in the small northern village of Poptún. While Villatoro eschews political comment for the simple joys and tragedies of everyday life, the turbulent political climate of the time forms a shadowy, ever present backdrop.

Daniel Wilkinson *Silence on the Mountain: Stories of Terror, Betrayal and Forgetting in Guatemala* (Houghton Mifflin). Part historical narrative, part personal travelogue and part public testimony, Wilkinson's book succeeds in giving a voice to those who suffered most during Guatemala's brutal civil war.

Fiction and poetry

Miguel Angel Asturias *Hombres de Maíz* (Macmillan). Guatemala's most famous author, Nobel Prize-winner Asturias's fiction is deeply indebted to Guatemalan history and culture. *Men of Maize* is generally regarded as his masterpiece, classically Latin American in its magic realist style, and bound up in the complexity of indigenous culture.

John Curl *Ancient American Poets* (Bilingual Press). English translation of the only known ancient Maya poetry in existence. While references to Catholicism place the verse in the early colonial period, themes of love, nature and ritual centre it in a deeper, more elemental context.

Gaspar Pedro Gonzales *A Mayan Life* (Yax Te' Press, US, o/p).

Absorbing story of the personal and cultural difficulties affecting a K'anjobal Maya from the Cuchumatanes mountains. The conflict between indigenous and *ladino* values becomes acutely evident as the central character seeks a higher education. Rich in ethnological detail and highly autobiographical, the book claims to be the first novel ever written by a Maya writer.

Ana Maria Rodas *Poemas de la Izquierda Erotica* and *El Fin de los Mitos y los Sueños.* Guatemala's foremost female journalist and the first to explore feminist themes in her poetry. Although these works have been translated in the past, you might have more luck trying to pick up a used copy of *Ixok Amar-Go: Central American Women's Poetry for Peace*, an anthology featuring contributions from Rodas and edited by the late Zoe Anglesey.

Art and archeology

William Coe *Tikal: A Handbook to the Ancient Maya Ruins.* Superbly detailed account of the site, usually available at the ruins. The detailed map of the main area is essential for in-depth exploration.

Peter D. Harrison, Colin Renfrew and Jeremy A. Sabloff *The Lords of Tikal: Rulers of an Ancient Maya City* (Thames & Hudson). Possibly the most comprehensive, engaging and approachable overview of Tikal, based on Harrison's three decades plus of excavation and research but also taking into account recent advances in the translation of Maya hieroglyphics.

Carmen L.Pettersen *The Maya of Guatemala: Life and Dress* (o/p). The definitive work on Maya dress (*traje*) with sixty intimate, meticulous watercolours documenting the subtle variations in indigenous dress among different Guatemalan towns.

Jim Pieper *Guatemala's Folk Saints: Maximón/San Simón, Rey Pascual, Lucifer and Others* (University of New Mexico Press). Engrossing study balancing academic enquiry with fascinating and beautifully conceived photos of Guatemala's weird and wonderful folk art.

El Salvador

History, politics and society

Charles Clements *Witness to War* (Bantam Press, o/p). Fascinating account of a year spent by a volunteer US doctor working in the guerrilla zone of Guazapa in the early 1980s, offering a vivid portrayal of how the civil war affected a specific area – and by extension suggesting what conditions were like across the border in El Salvador.

Mark Danner *The Massacre at El Mozote* (Vintage, US). Meticulously researched account of one of the most barbaric and shocking chapters in the country's history. Danner's courageous investigation serves as perhaps the most compelling indictment of Reagan-era foreign policy currently in print.

Larry Dowell, Mark Deinner *El Salvador* (Norton, o/p). Evocative and compelling collection of photographs taken during 1986, sharply delineating the progress of the civil war and its impact.

Rysard Kapuscinski *The Soccer War* (Granta, UK). While it also includes other key revolutions of recent history, buy this book for Kapuscinski's inimitable account of the so-called "Soccer War", when existing tensions exacerbated by a series of qualifying matches for the 1970 World Cup dragged Honduras and El Salvador into a short-lived but fully fledged border war.

Fiction and poetry

Wilfredo Argueta *War Child Morazan, El Salvador* (Re'De Arte, US). Intense, vividly imagined verse documenting Argueta's painful, revelatory adolescence in a rural community ravaged by civil war.

Roque Dalton *Taberna y Otras Lugares* and *Poemas Clandestinas*; *Pobrecito Poeta que era Yo*. Perhaps the most famous El Salvadorean poet, Dalton was also a journalist and revolutionary, and in constant open conflict with successive governments. Born in 1935, he was imprisoned and exiled on various occasions, but always returned to the land of his birth. He was a member of the People's Revolutionary Army (ERP) in the early 1970s, along with founder members of the FMLN. After differences of opinion led to his departing the movement he was assassinated on ERP orders in May 1975 near Guazapa; his death remains a landmark in Salvadorean literary history and still remains unsolved. *Taberna y Otras Lugares* and *Poemas Clandestinas* are both collections of poetry, while *Pobrecito Poeta que era Yo* is a novella.

Salarrué *Eso y Más*, *Cuentos de Barro* and *La Espada y Otras Narraciones*. Born Salvador Salazar Arrué in 1899, Salarrué is one of the most widely known El Salvadorean writers. His short stories and novellas focus on the lives and realities of campesinos and non-metropolites.

Honduras

History, politics and society

Tom Barry and Kent Norsworthy *Honduras: A Country Guide* (LAB/Resource Center). Concise but comprehensive study of contemporary political, economic and social affairs, with some historical background.

Jack R. Binns *The United States in Honduras, 1980–1981: An Ambassador's Memoir* (McFarland & Company). While this book's warts-and-all diary format can be heavy going at times, the momentum of events carries the narrative, providing both a unique window on a turbulent period in Honduran history and an insight into the inner workings of US diplomacy.

Susan C. Stonich *The Other Side of Paradise: Tourism, Conservation and Development in the Bay Islands* (Cognizant Communication Corp.). Well-researched account of tourism's detrimental consequences on both the land and the people, written within the historical context of the islands.

Travel and impressions

Archie Carr *High Jungles and Low* (University Press of Florida). Spirited account of Carr's involvement in a mahogany expedition through the Honduran highlands, written with the kind of infectious enthusiasm missing from many modern-day travelogues.

Peter Ford *Tekkin a Waalk along the Miskito Coast* (Flamingo Press, o/p). In the mid-1980s Ford gave himself the task of walking along the Caribbean coast from Belize to Nicaragua, resulting in this nice tale, with snippets of information on Garífuna history and contemporary development.

Fiction

Paul Theroux *The Mosquito Coast* (Penguin). Well-known tale of the collapse of a man in the steaming heat of Mosquitia. Though entertaining, Theroux only touches on a remote corner of Honduras and the novel does little to enlighten the reader about the country as a whole. The movie, with Harrison Ford and Helen Mirren, was filmed in Belize.

Guillermo Yuscarán is the pen name of expatriate Willam Lewis, a long-time resident of Honduras. His novels and short stories, illustrating contemporary Honduran life, can be bought (in Spanish and English; Nuevo Sol, Tegucigalpa) in bookshops in Tegucigalpa and San Pedro Sula.

Specialist guides

William L. Fash *Scribes, Warriors and Kings* (Thames & Hudson). The definitive guide to the ruins of Copán, lavishly adorned with drawings, photographs and superb maps.

Cindy Garout *Diving the Bay Islands* (Aqua Quest, US, o/p). Glossy book with lots of great photos outlining the best places to dive off all the islands. Consider it essential if you're going to spend much time diving here.

Nicaragua

History, politics and society

Gioconda Belli *The Country Under My Skin* (Bloomsbury). An account of graduation from ignorance and innocence to political and sexual awakening, utterly different from Omar Cabezas' book (see below) but just as compelling. The famous Nicaraguan poet and novelist bares her soul in this memoir, recounting her incredible journey from domestic drudgery to jet-setting Sandinista diplomacy.

★ **Omar Cabezas** *Fire from the Mountain: The Making of a Sandinista* (Jonathan Cape, o/p). A brutally frank, blackly comic and deeply human account of Cabezas' transformation from student activist to active guerrilla. His writing takes on an almost elemental quality at times and this account offers a wonderful insight into that rich vein of irreverent yet self-deprecating humour that often characterises Nicaraguans.

Hazel Plunkett *Nicaragua in Focus* (LAB/Interlink). Part of the excellent In Focus series, this well-written, succinct, reasonably up to date and inexpensive overview of Nicaraguan society incorporates history, politics, economy, environment and culture. An ideal introduction, with informed suggestions for further reading.

Holly Sklar *Washington's War on Nicaragua* (South End Press). A dissection of US policy on Nicaragua in all its ugly manifestations. Covers the Iran–Contra affair, the years of political double talk that undermined regional attempts to broker peace, the drug running, gun running and espionage that sought to destabilize the Sandinista regime, and the whole saga of the often clandestine US support for the Contras. A fascinating book.

Various *Sandino's Daughters: Testimonies of Nicaragua Women in Struggle* (Rutgers University Press, o/p). Interviews with Sandinista women who participated at various levels in the struggle to liberate Nicaragua and later worked for the creation of a new and just society. First published in 1981, it's one of the most popular books written about that period.

Travel and impressions

Edward Marriott *Wild Shore* (Picador, UK). The author follows the Río San Juan from the Atlantic coast to Lago de Nicaragua in search of the bull shark – the only shark able to live in both fresh and salt water – and the fishermen who make their living from hunting it. The result is an intriguing blend of natural and social history in which the bull shark emerges as one of the few constants in Nicaragua's turbulent history, and a symbol of survival in a country where exploitation has become a way of life.

★ **Salman Rushdie** *The Jaguar Smile, A Nicaraguan Journey* (Picador, Viking Penguin). The result of a three-week trip to Nicaragua at the height of the Sandinista era in the mid-1980s, Rushdie was impressed – or seduced – by the Sandinista achievement. The real charm of this slim narrative is Rushdie's witty portrait of cosy Managuan political society.

Fiction and poetry

Ernesto Cardenal *The Cosmic Canticle* (Curbstone Press). Thirty years of work went into this narrative poem and mythic song – an epic work spanning the whole of Latin American history.

Rubén Darío *Cuentos Completos* (Fondo de Cultura Enconimica); *Azul Cantos de Vida y Esperanza* (Espasa-Calpe); *Poesia* (Alianza). In Nicaragua, Darío is perceived more as a national hero than a writer, and as a kind of reference point in the national psyche. In his own work he was, like so many Latin American authors, a versatile writer, writing stories and essays as well as poetry, for which he remains best known.

Francisco Goldman *The Ordinary Seaman* (Grove Press, US). Dark and depressing book about the fate of several Nicaraguan men contracted to work on a freighter. Their salvation from the wreck of post-Sandinista Nicaragua turns out to be a rotting hulk in Brooklyn harbour. Flight, exile, death and bittersweet memories form an enormous part of Nicaragua's culture since the revolution, and this book captures much of it.

Sergio Ramírez *To Bury Our Fathers* (Readers International, o/p). A fictional re-creation of events during the Sandino era, this labyrinthine tale from the revered novelist and former Sandinista vice-president dextrously weaves together the constituent parts of both Nicaragua's tragic modern history and its indomitable character. At times vaguely reminiscent of a darker García Marquez, with the often surreal series of events based on real incidents.

Costa Rica

History, politics and society

Tjabel Daling Costa *Rica in Focus: A Guide to the People, Politics and Culture* (LAB, Interlink). The most authoritative and up-to-date country guide currently available, entertainingly illustrated with bits of Costa Rican life, such as billboards and labels. The text offers an especially clear-eyed cultural and social analysis.

Marc Edelman and Joanne Kenen (eds) *The Costa Rica Reader* (Grove Atlantic, US, o/p). The best single title for the general reader, with chronologically arranged essays by respected historians – academic in tone but not inaccessible. See especially Chilean sociologist Diego Palma's essay on current Costa Rican politics and class conflict, which punctures the picture of Costa Rica as a haven of middle-class democracy.

★ **Paula Palmer** *What Happen: A Folk History of the Talamanca Coast* (San José, Ecodesarrolos). The definitive – although now dated – folk history of the Afro-Caribbean community on Limón Province's Talamancan coast. Palmer first went to Cahuita in the early 1970s as a Peace Corps volunteer, later returning as a sociologist to collect oral histories from older members of the local communities. Great stories and atmospheric testimonies of pirate treasure, ghosts and the like, complemented by photos and accounts of local agriculture, foods and traditional remedies. Available in English and Spanish (in Costa Rica only).

Travel and impressions

Allen M. Youn *Sarapiquí Chronicle: A Naturalist in Costa Rica* (Smithsonian Institution Press, o/p). Lavishly produced book based on entomologist Allen M. Young's twenty years' work in the Sarapiquí area, featuring a well-written combination of autobiography, travelogue and natural science, centring on the insect life he encounters.

Art and archeology

Between Continents, Between Seas: Precolumbian Art of Costa Rica (Harry Abrams, US, o/p). Produced as a catalogue to accompany the exhibit that toured the US in 1982, this is the best single volume on Costa Rica's pre-Conquest history and craftsmanship, with illuminating accounts of the lives, beliefs and customs of its pre-Columbian peoples as interpreted through artefacts and excavations. The photographs, whether of jade pendants, Chorotega pottery or the more diabolical of the Diquis' gold pieces, are uniformly wonderful.

Fiction and poetry

Fabián Dobles *Ese Que Llaman Pueblo* (San José, Editorial Costa Rica). Born in 1918, Dobles is Costa Rica's elder statesman of letters. Set in the countryside among campesinos, this title is a typical "proletarian" novel.

Carmen Naranjo *Los perros no ladraron* (1966), *Responso por el niño Juan Manuel* (1968), *Ondina* (1982) and *Sobrepunto* (1985). In keeping with a tradition in Latin American letters, but unusual for a woman, Naranjo has occupied several public positions, including Secretary of Culture, director of the publishing house EDUCA and ambassador to Israel. Her novel *There Never Was Once Upon a Time* (Latin American Literary Review Press, US) is available in English.

Wildlife and the environment

Les Beletsky *Costa Rica: Ecotraveller's Wildlife Guide* (Academic Press, o/p). This readable wildlife and natural history handbook is a good compromise between a guidebook and a heavy field guide. The text is accompanied by photos and drawings; the plates showing species with photos of their typical habitats are particularly useful. Includes detailed information on about 220 bird, 50 mammal and 80 amphibian and reptile species.

Daniel H. Janzen *Costa Rican Natural History* (University of Chicago Press). The definitive reference source, with accessible and continuously fascinating species-by-species accounts. The introduction is worth reading, dealing in a cursory but lively fashion with tectonics, meteorology, history and archeology. Illustrated throughout with gripping photographs and available in paperback, but still doorstep-thick.

F. Gary Stiles and Alexander F. Skutch *A Guide to the Birds of Costa Rica* (Helm Field Guides/Cornell University Press). You'll see guides all over Costa Rica clutching well-thumbed copies of this seminal tome, illustrated with colour plates to aid identification. Hefty, even in paperback, and too pricey for the amateur, but you may be able to pick up good secondhand copies in Costa Rica.

Philip J. De Vries *The Butterflies of Costa Rica and Their Natural History* (Princeton University Press). Much-admired volume, really for serious butterfly enthusiasts or scientists only, but illustrated with beautiful colour plates so you can marvel at the incremental differences between various butterflies.

Panama

History, politics and society

John Lindsay-Poland *Emperors in the Jungle: The Hidden History of the US in Panama* (Duke University Press). A well-researched exposé of US involvement in Panama from the days of canal construction all the way through to their final withdrawal. Includes detailed accounts regarding the 1989 invasion, plans to create a new canal using atomic weapons, chemical weapons testing and the still unresolved issue of contamination.

David McCullough *The Path Between the Seas: The Creation of the Panama Canal* (Simon & Schuster, US). Compelling and authoritative account of the epic struggle to build the Panama Canal. Detailed and well researched, it nonetheless reads like a novel.

John Prebble *The Darién Disaster* (Pimlico, UK). A detailed if somewhat dated account of the short-lived Scottish dream to establish a colony on the isthmus of Panama to control the trade between the East and West at the end of the seventeenth century. The venture quickly collapsed through incompetence, obstruction from the British government and opposition from Spain, ultimately crippling the Scottish economy.

John Weeks and Phil Gunson *Panama: Made in the USA* (LAB). Detailed exploration of the unanswered questions behind the US invasion of Panama in the context of the turbulent history of US–Panamanian relations and the struggle for control of the Canal.

Travel and impressions

Graham Greene *Getting to Know the General* (Vintage/Random House). Fascinating personal reminiscences regarding the author's unlikely friendship with General Omar Torrijos, dictator of Panama from 1968 to 1981.

Fiction

Douglas Galbraith *The Rising Sun* (Picador, UK, o/p). Tour de force of historical fiction set during the disastrous Scottish attempt to establish an independent colony in Darién during the late seventeenth century.

John Le Carré *The Tailor of Panama* (Sceptre/Ballantine Books). Fast-moving spy thriller by the great master of the genre, set in Panama on the eve of US military withdrawal. Its satirical depiction of Panama as a murky world of intrigue and corruption, populated by ambiguous characters, caused great controversy when it was first published.

Specialist guides

Robert S. Ridgely & John Gwynne *A Guide to the Birds of Panama* (Princeton University Press). The definitive ornithological guidebook for Central America – also covers Honduras, Nicaragua and Costa Rica – though it's bulky and expensive.

Language

Language

Language

There's a bewildering collection of languages across the Central American isthmus, numbering well above thirty in all; fortunately for the traveller, there are two that dominate – English, primarily in Belize, the Bay Islands of Honduras, and the Atlantic coast and Corn Islands of Nicaragua, but spoken to some extent all along the Caribbean coast; and Spanish everywhere else.

English

Belizean English may sound familiar from a distance and, if you listen to a few words, you may think that its meaning is clear. Listen a little further, however, and you'll realize that complete comprehension is just out of reach. What you're hearing is, in fact, **Creole**, a beautifully warm and relaxed language, typically Caribbean and loosely based on English, with elements of Spanish and indigenous languages. A similar dialect, Guari Guari, is spoken in the Panamanian province of Bocas del Toro. Written Creole, which you'll come across in Belizean newspapers, is a little easier to get to grips with. There's an active movement in Belize to formalize the language, and a dictionary is currently in production. Luckily, almost anyone who can speak Creole can also speak English.

To get a taste of the language on the streets in Belize, here are some simple phrases. For more, get hold of a copy of *Creole Proverbs of Belize*, usually available in Belize City.

- Bad ting neda gat owner. – Bad things never have owners.
- Better belly bus dan good bikkle waste. – It's better that the belly bursts than good victuals go to waste.
- Cow no business eena haas gylop. – Cows have no business in a horse race.

In the Bay Islands of Honduras things are much simpler. English is English rather than Creole, and immediately understandable, albeit spoken with a unique, broad accent. Influenced by Caribbean, English and Scots migrants over the years, local inflexions turn even the most commonplace of remarks into an attractive statement. English, however, is slowly being supplanted by Spanish as the language heard on the street, as growing numbers of mainlanders make the islands their home.

Spanish

Those new to the region can take heart – **Spanish**, as spoken across Latin America, is one of the easier languages there is to learn and even the most faltering of attempts to speak it is greatly appreciated. Apart from the major tourist areas in Guatemala, Costa Rica, and in some parts of Panama and Honduras,

English is not widely spoken; taking the trouble to get to know at least the basics of Spanish will both make your travels considerably easier and reap countless rewards in terms of reception, appreciation and understanding of people and places.

Overall, Latin American Spanish is clearer and slower than that of Spain – gone are the lisps and bewilderingly rapid, slurred, soft consonants of the old country. There are, however, quite strong variations in accent across Central America: Guatemalan Spanish has the reputation of being clear, precise and eminently understandable even to the worst of linguists, whilst the language as spoken in Honduras – thick and fast – can initially bewilder even those who believed themselves to be reasonably fluent. Nicaraguans in particular take great pleasure in fooling around with language, creating new words, pronouncing certain letters differently and employing different grammar. There are enough Nicaragnismos – words and sayings particular to Nicaragua – to fill a 275-page dictionary. As far as pronunciation goes, the "s" is often dropped from word endings and the "v" and "b" sounds are fairly interchangeable.

For the most part, the rules of **pronunciation** are straightforward and strictly observed. Unless there's an accent, words ending in d, l, r and z are **stressed** on the last syllable, all others on the second last. All **vowels** are pure and short.

A somewhere between the "A" sound of back and that of father.

E as in get

I as in police

O as in hot

U as in rule

C is soft before E and I, otherwise hard; cerca is pronounced "serka".

G works the same way – a guttural "H" sound (like the ch in loch) before E or I, a hard G elsewhere; gigante is pronounced "higante".

H is always silent.

J is the same sound as a guttural G; jamón is pronounced "hamoan".

LL sounds like an English Y; tortilla is pronounced torteeya.

N is as in English, unless there is a tilde (accent) over it, when it becomes NY; mañana is pronounced "manyana".

QU is pronounced like an English K.

R is rolled, **RR** doubly so.

V sounds like a cross with B, vino becoming beano.

X is slightly softer than in English, sometimes almost like SH, so that Xela becomes "sheyla"; between vowels in place names it has an H sound – México is pronounced "May-hee-ko".

Z is the same as a soft C; cerveza is pronounced "servesa".

Formal and informal address

For English speakers one of the most difficult things to get to grips with is the distinction between formal and informal address – when to use it and to whom and how to avoid causing offence. Generally speaking, the third-person "**usted**" indicates respect and/or a non-familiar relationship and is used in business, for people you don't know and for those older than you. Second-person "**tú**" is for children, friends and contemporaries in less formal settings. (Remember also that in Latin America the second-person **plural** – "vosotros" – is never used, so "you" plural will always be "ustedes"). In day-to-day exchanges, genuine mistakes on the part of an obviously non-native speaker will be well received and corrected with good humour.

One idiosyncrasy is the widespread use of "**vos**" in Central America. Now archaic in Spain, it is frequently used in place of *tú*, as an intimate form of address between friends of the same age. In most tenses, conjugation is exactly the same as for *tú*. In the present indicative, however, the last syllable is stressed with an accent (*tú comes/vos comés*); in "-ir" verbs in this tense, the final "i" is kept instead of changing to an "e" (*tú escribes/vos escribís*). In commands, the vos form drops the final "r" of the infinitive, replacing it with an accented vowel (*tú come/vos comé*). Take your lead from those around you – if you are addressed in the "*vos*" form it is a sign of friendship which should be reciprocated; on the other hand it is sometimes seen as patronizing to use it with someone you don't know well.

Nicknames and turns of speech

Nicknames are very common in Central America, used in both speech and writing and for any situation from addressing a casual acquaintance to referring to political candidates. Often they centre on obvious physical characteristics – *flaco/a* (thin), *gordo/a* (fat), *rubio/a* (blond).

Often, these nicknames will be further softened by **diminution** – the addition of the suffix *-ito* or *-ita* at the end of nouns and adjectives, a trend used sometimes with a passion in everyday speech. You are quite likely to hear someone talk about their *hermanito* for example, which translates as "little brother" regardless of respective ages, whilst *mí hijita* ("my little daughter") can as easily mean a grown woman as a child.

Also very common are **casual street addresses**, used lightly in brief encounters and to soothe transactions. Heard in virtually every country are *(mí) amor* – used in much the same way as "love" in England and also between friends – as is *jóven* or *jovencito/a*, young one. More specific to each country (often but not always between men) are terms used to make casual questions or remarks less intrusive. *Papa* (literally "father") is used daily in Honduras, for example as in "*¿Qué hora tiene, papa?*" (What time is it?), whilst the Nicaraguans use *primo* (cousin). Panamanian men regularly address each other as *compadre*, often abbreviated to *compa*. In Nicaragua, the local term (a fond one) for foreigners is *chele/a*.

Politesse

Verbal courtesy is an integral part of speech in Spanish and one that – once you're accustomed to the pace and flow of life in Central America – should become instinctive. Saying *Buenos días/Buenas tardes* and waiting for the appropriate response is usual when asking for something at a shop or ticket office for example, as is adding *Señor* or *Señora* (in this instance similar to the US "sir" or "ma'am"). The response when thanking someone for a service is more likely to be *para servirle* (literally "here to serve you") rather than the casual *de nada* ("you're welcome"). The *tss tss* sound is commonly employed to attract attention, particularly in restaurants. In this very polite culture shouting is frowned upon.

On meeting, or being introduced to someone, Central Americans will say *con mucho gusto*, "it's a pleasure", and you should do the same. On departure you will more often than not be told *¡que le vaya bien!* ("may all go well") a simple phrase that nonetheless invariably sounds sincere and rounds off transactions nicely. In rural areas, especially, it is usual to greet even complete strangers met on the path with *!Adiós, que le vaya bien!* Don't be surprised if you're greeted with "*Adiós*", as this can mean both hello and goodbye.

Phrasebooks and dictionaries

It's worth investing in a good **phrasebook** and **dictionary** before you go. One of the best specifically Latin American dictionaries is the University of Chicago *Dictionary of Latin-American Spanish* (Pocket Books). Alternatively, HarperCollins produce the best general range of pocket dictionaries and grammars, which include many Latin American terms. The *Rough Guide to Mexican Spanish* can also prove extremely useful.

Words and phrases

Basics

yes, no	**sí, no**	open, closed	**abierto/a, cerrado/a**
please, thank you	**por favor, gracias**	with, without	**con, sin**
where, when	**dónde, cuando**	good, bad	**buen(o)/a, mal(o)/a**
what, how much	**qué, cuanto**	big, small	**gran(de), pequeño/a**
here, there	**aquí, allí**	more, less	**más, menos**
this, that	**este, eso**	today, tomorrow	**hoy, mañana**
now, later	**ahora, más tarde**	yesterday	**ayer**

Greetings and responses

hello, goodbye	**¡hola!, adios**
good morning	**buenos días**
good afternoon/ night	**buenas tardes/noches**
How do you do?	**¿Qué tal?**
See you later	**Hasta luego**
sorry	**lo siento/ disculpeme**
Excuse me	**Con permiso/ perdon**
How are you?	**¿Cómo está (usted)?**
Not at all/ You're welcome	**De nada**
I (don't) understand	**(No) Entiendo**
Do you speak English?	**¿Habla (usted) inglés?**
I don't speak Spanish	**(No) Hablo español**
What (did you say)?	**Mande?**
My name is...	**Me llamo...**
What's your name?	**¿Como se llama usted?**
I'm English	**Soy inglés(a)**
...American	**americano(a)**
...Australian	**australiano(a)**
...Canadian	**canadiense(a)**
...Irish	**irlandés(a)**
...Scottish	**escosés(a)**
...Welsh	**galés(a)**
...New Zealander	**neozelandés(a)**

Numbers and days

1	**un/uno/una**
2	**dos**
3	**tres**
4	**cuatro**
5	**cinco**
6	**seis**
7	**siete**
8	**ocho**
9	**nueve**
10	**diez**
11	**once**
12	**doce**

13	**trece**
14	**catorce**
15	**quince**
16	**dieciséis**
20	**veinte**
21	**veintiuno**
22	**veintidos**
30	**treinta**
40	**cuarenta**
50	**cincuenta**
60	**sesenta**
70	**setenta**
80	**ochenta**
90	**noventa**
100	**cien**
101	**ciento uno**
200	**dos cientos**
201	**dos cientos uno**
500	**quinientos**
1000	**mil**
1999	**mil novecientos noventa y nueve**
2000	**dos mil**
100,000	**cien mil**
1,000,000	**un millón**

first	**primero/a**
second	**segundo/a**
third	**tercero/a**
fifth	**quinto/a**
tenth	**decimo/a**

Monday	**lunes**
Tuesday	**martes**
Wednesday	**miércoles**
Thursday	**jueves**
Friday	**viernes**
Saturday	**sábado**
Sunday	**domingo**

Needs – hotels and transport

I want	**Quiero**
Do you know...?	**¿Sabe...?**
I'd like....	**Quisiera... por favor**
I don't know	**No sé**
There is (is there)?	**Hay (?)**
Give me... (one like that)	**Deme... (uno asi)**
Do you have...?	**¿Tiene...?**
...the time	**...la hora**
...a room	**...un cuarto**
...with two beds/ double bed	**...con dos camas /cama matrimonial**
It's for one person (two people)	**Es para una persona (dos personas)**
...for one night (one week)	**...para una noche (una semana)**
It's fine, how much is it?	**¿Esta bien, cuánto es?**
It's too expensive	**Es demasiado caro**
Don't you have anything cheaper?	**¿No tiene algo más barato?**
Can one...?	**¿Se puede...?**
...camp (near) here?	**¿...acampar aquí (cerca)?**
Is there a hotel nearby?	**¿Hay un hotel aquí cerca?**
How do I get to...?	**¿Por dónde se va a...?**
Left, right, straight on	**izquierda, derecha, derecho**
Where is...?	**¿Dónde está...?**
...the bus station?	**...el terminal de bus?**
...the train station?	**...la estación de ferrocarriles?**
...the nearest bank	**...el banco más cercano** (ATM is **cajero automático**)
...the (main) post office?	**...el correo (central)?**
...the toilet	**...el baño/sanitario**
Where does the bus to... leave from?	**¿De dónde sale el camión para...?**
What time does it leave (arrive in...)?	**¿A qué hora sale (llega en...)?**
What is there to eat?	**¿Qué hay para comer?**
What's that?	**¿Qué es eso?**
What's this called in Spanish?	**¿Cómo se llama este en español?**

A Spanish menu reader

While menus vary by country and region, these words and terms will help negotiate most menus.

Basic dining vocabulary

Almuerzo	Lunch
Carta (la)	Menu
Cena	Dinner
Comida típica	Typical cuisine
Comida corriente	Cheap set menu, usually served at lunchtime
Cuchara	Spoon
Cuchillo	Knife
La cuenta, por favor	The bill, please
Desayuno	Breakfast
Plato del día	Plate of the day
Plato fuerte	Main course
Plato vegetariano	Vegetarian dish
Tenedor	Fork

Frutas (fruit)

Cereza	Cherry
Chirimoya	Custard apple
Ciruela	Plum
Durazno	Peach
Frutilla	Strawberry
Guayaba	Guava
Higo	Fig
Limón	Lemon
Manzana	Apple
Maracuyá	Passion fruit
Mora	Blackberry
Naranja	Orange
Pera	Pear
Piña	Pineapple
Pitaya	Cactus fruit
Plátano	Banana
Tomate de arból	Tree tomato
Tamarindo	Tamarind
Toronja	Grapefruit

Legumbres / verduras (vegetables)

Aguacate	Avocado
Alachoafa	Artichoke
Arvejas	Peas
Cebolla	Onion
Champiñón	Mushroom
Coliflor	Cauliflower
Curtida	Pickled cabbage, beetroot and carrots
Espinaca	Spinach
Frijoles	Beans
Frijoles volteados	Refried beans
Gallo pinto	Mixed rice and beans
Hongo	Mushroom
Lechuga	Lettuce
Lentejas	Lentils
Maíz	Corn/maize
Menestra	Bean/lentil stew
Palmito	Palm heart
Patata	Potato
Papas fritas	French fries
Pepinillo	Gherkin
Pepino	Cucumber
Tomate	Tomato
Zanahoria	Carrot

Carne (meat) y aves (poultry)

Bistec	Steak	**Jamón**	Ham
Carne	Beef	**Lechón**	Suckling pig
Carne de chancho	Pork	**Lomo**	Steak
Cerdo	Pork	**Pato**	Duck
Chicharrones	Pork scratchings, crackling	**Chumpipe**	Turkey
Chuleta	Pork chop	**Res**	Beef
Conejo	Rabbit	**Ternera**	Veal
Cordero	Lamb	**Tocino**	Bacon
Filete	Steak	**Venado**	Venison

Menudos (offal)

Chunchules	Intestines	**Lengua**	Tongue
Guatita	Tripe	**Patas**	Trotters
Hígado	Liver		

Mariscos (fish) y pescado (seafood)

Anchoa	Anchovy	**Erizo**	Sea urchin
Atún	Tuna	**Langosta**	Lobster
Calamares	Squid	**Langostina**	King prawn
Camarón	Prawn	**Lenguado**	Sole
Cangrejo	Crab	**Mejillón**	Mussel
Ceviche	Seafood marinated in lime juice w/ onions	**Ostra**	Oyster
Concha	Clam; scallop	**Pargo Rojo**	Red snapper
Corvina	Sea bass	**Trucha**	Trout

Cooking terms

A la parilla	Barbequed	**Duro**	Hard boiled
A la plancha	Lightly fried	**Encebollado**	Cooked with onions
Ahumado	Smoked	**Encocado**	In coconut sauce
Al ajillo	In garlic sauce	**Frito**	Fried
Al horno	Oven-baked	**Picante**	Spicy hot
Al vapor	Steamed	**Puré**	Mashed
Apanado	Breaded	**Revuelto**	Scrambled
Asado	Roast	**Saltado**	Sautéed
Asado al palo	Spit roast	**Secado**	Dried
Crudo	Raw		

Bebidas (drinks)

Agua (mineral)	Mineral water
con gas	sparkling
sin gas	still
sin hielo	without ice
Arguardiente	Sugarcane spirit
Aromática	Herbal tea
hierba luisa	lemon verbena
manzanilla	camomile
menta	mint
Café	Coffee
Café con leche	Milk with a little coffee
Cerveza	Beer
Cola	Fizzy drink
Gaseosea	Fizzy drink
Horchata	Milky, cereal-based drink sweetened with cinnamon
Jugo	Juice
Leche	Milk
Licuado	Fresh fruit milkshake
Limonada	Fresh lemonade
Raspados	Ice shavings with sweet topping
Refresco	Generic term for cold soft drinks
Ron	Rum
Té	Tea
Vino blano	White wine
Vino tinto	Red wine

Food glossary

Arroz	Rice
Aciete	Oil
Ajo	Garlic
Ajillo	Garlic butter
Arroz	Rice
Azúcar	Sugar
Chile	Chilli
Galletas	Biscuits
Hielo	Ice
Huevos	Eggs
Mantequilla	Butter
Mermeleda	Jam
Miel	Honey
Mixto	Mixed seafood/meats
Mostaza	Mustard
Pan (integral)	Bread (wholemeal)
Pan de coco	Coconut bread
Pimienta	Pepper
Queso	Cheese
Sal	Salt
Salsa de tomate	Tomato sauce

Soups

Caldo	Broth
Caldo de gallina	Chicken broth
Crema de espárragos	Cream of asparagus
Sopa de caracol	Spicy conch stew
Sopa de frijoles	Bean soup
Sopa del día	Soup of the day

Bocadillos (snacks)

Empanada	Cheese/meat pastry	**Salchichas**	Sausages
Hamburguesa	Hamburger	**Sanwiche**	Sandwich
Nacatamales	Corn-dough parcels filled with vegetables, pork, beef or chicken	**Tamale**	Ground maize with meat/cheese wrapped in leaf
Patacones	Fried green plantains	**Tortilla**	Toasted maize pancake
Pupusa	Small, thick tortilla filled with cheese, beans or pork and topped with salad	**Tortilla de huevos**	Omelette
		Tostada	Toast

Postres (dessert)

Ensalada de frutas	Fruit salad	**Piñonate**	Candied papaya
Flan	Crème caramel	**Torta**	Tart
Helado	Ice cream	**Tres Leches**	Cake made with three varieties of milk
Pastel	Cake		

Glossary

Abastecedor A general store that keeps a stock of groceries and basic toiletries.

Aguacero Downpour.

Aguardiente Raw alcohol made from sugar cane.

Aguas Bottled fizzy drinks: Coca-Cola, Sprite etc.

Ahorita Right now (any time within the coming hour).

Alcalde Mayor.

Aldea Small settlement.

Ayuntamiento Town hall/government.

Barranca Steep-sided ravine.

Barrio Neighbourhood, area within a town or city; suburb.

Biotopo Protected area of national ecological importance, usually with limited tourist access.

Bomba Gas station.

Cabaña Literally a cabin, but can mean anything from a palm-thatched beach hut to a US-style motel room. Usually applies to tourist accommodation.

Cacique Chief. Originally a colonial term, now used for elected leaders/figureheads of indigenous *comarcas* in Panama.

Camioneta Small truck or van, or in Guatemala a second-class bus.

Campesino Peasant farmer, smallholder, cowboy.

Cantina Local, hard-drinking bar, usually men-only.

Carretera Interamericana Transnational highway that runs 24,400km from Alaska to Tierra del Fuego, broken only by the Darién Gap between Panama and Colombia.

Carro Car, equivalent of *coche*.

Case de cambio Currency exchange bureau.

Chac Maya god of rain.

Chicle Sapodilla tree sap from which chewing gum is made.

Chiquillos Kids; also *chiquititos, chiquiticos*.

Chorreador Sack-and-metal coffee-filter contraption, still widely used.

Churrigueresque Highly elaborate, decorative form of Baroque architecture (usually found in churches).

Classic Period during which ancient Maya civilization was at its height, usually given as 300–900 AD.

Colectivo Shared taxi/minibus, usually following fixed route. Can also be applied to a boat – *lancho colectivo*.

Colonia City suburb or neighbourhood, often seen in addresses as "Col".

Comedor Basic restaurant, usually with just one or two things on the menu, always the cheapest place to eat. Literally "dining room".

Conquistador "One who conquers": member of early Spanish expeditions to the Americas in the sixteenth century.

Convento Convent or monastery.

Cordillera Mountain range.

Corriente Second-class bus.

Creole Of mixed African/Caribbean and European descent; also refers to the English patois spoken in Belize and Caribbean towns throughout the region.

Cuadra Street block.

Descompuesto Out of order.

Don/Doña Courtesy titles (sir/madam), mostly used in letters or for professional people or the boss.

Efectivo Cash.

Ejido Communal farmland.

Evangélico Christian evangelist or fundamentalist, often a missionary. Name given to members of numerous Protestant sects seeking converts in Central America.

Feria Fair (market).

Finca Ranch, farm or plantation.

Finquero Coffee grower.

Gambas Buttresses; the giant above-ground roots that some rainforest trees put out.

Garífuna People of mixed African and Amerindian descent, with a unique language and strong African heritage, who live on the Caribbean coast between southern Belize and Nicaragua.

Gaseosa Fizzy drink.

Gasolinera Gas station.

Glyph Element in Maya writing and carving; roughly the equivalent of a letter or numeral.

Gringo/Gringa Any white-skinned foreigner, particularly North Americans. Not necessarily a term of abuse.

Guaca Pre-Columbian burial ground or tomb.

Hacienda Big farm, ranch or estate, or big house on it.

Henequén Fibre from *agave* (sisal) plant, used to make rope.

Hospedaje Very basic pensión or small hotel.

Huipil Maya women's traditional dress or blouse, usually woven or embroided.

I.V.A. Sales tax.

Indígena An indigenous person; preferred term among indigenous groups, rather than the more racially offensive *índio:* indian.

Invierno Winter (May–Oct).

Jornaleros Day labourers, usually landless peasants who are paid by the day, for instance to pick coffee in season.

Juego de pelota Ball court.

Ladino A vague term – applied to people it means Spanish-influenced as opposed to indigenous, and at its most specific defines someone of mixed Spanish and indigenous blood. It's more commonly used simply to describe a person of "Western" culture, or one who dresses in "Western" style, be they of indigenous or mixed blood.

Licuado Fresh blended fruit juice, made with water or milk.

Malecón Seafront promenade.

Maya Indigenous people who inhabited Honduras, Guatemala, Belize and southeastern Mexico from the earliest times, and still do. Although they also lived in El Salvador, there are none left there today.

Mestizo Person of mixed indigenous and Spanish blood, though like the term *ladino* it has more cultural than racial significance.

Metate Pre-Columbian stone table used for grinding corn.

Migración Immigration office.

Mipla Maize field, usually cleared by slash-and-burn farming.

Mirador Look-out point.

Miskito Native American group living along the area of the Caribbean coast of Honduras and Nicaragua known as the Mosquitia (often spelt "Miskita").

Muelle Jetty or dock.

Natural An indigenous person.

Neotrópicos Neotropics: tropics of the New World.

Oriente East; often seen in addresses as "Ote".

Palacio Mansion, but not necessarily royal.

Palacio de gobierno Headquarters of state/federal authorities.

Palacio municipal Headquarters of local government.

Palapa Palm thatch. Used to describe any thatched/palm-roofed hut.

Paseo A broad avenue; also the traditional evening walk around the plaza.

Pelota Ball, or ball court.

Pensión Simple hotel.

Peón Farm labourer, usually landless.

Personaje Someone of importance, a VIP, although usually used pejoratively to indicate someone who is putting on airs.

Planta baja Ground floor – abbreviated PB in elevators.

Plateresque Elaborately decorative Renaissance architectural style.

Poniente West; often seen in addresses as "Pte".

Popul Vuh The Quiché Maya's epic story of the creation and history of their people.

Postclassic Period between the decline of Maya civilization and the arrival of the Spanish, 900–1530 AD.

Preclassic Archeological era preceding the blooming of Maya civilization, usually given as 1500 BC–300 AD.

Pullman Fast and comfortable bus, usually an old Greyhound.

Pulpería General store or corner store. Also sometimes serves cooked food and drinks.

Quiché Largest of the Guatemalan Maya groups, centred today on the town of Santa Cruz del Quiché.

Rancho Palm-thatched roof; can also mean a smallholding.

Redondel de Toros Bullring, used for local rodeos.

Refresco Drink, usually made with fresh fruit or water, sometimes fizzy drink, although this can also be called a *gaseosa*.

Sabanero Cowboy.

Sacbe Maya road, or ceremonial causeway.

Sierra Mountain range.

Soda Costa Rican cafeteria or diner; in the rest of Central America it's usually called a comedor.

Stela Freestanding carved monument. Most are of Maya origin.

Tecún Umán Last king of the Quiché Maya, defeated in battle by the conquistador Alvarado.

Temporada Season: *la temporada de lluvia* is the rainy season.

Terreno Land; small farm.

Tienda Shop.

Típico/típica Literally "typical". Used to describe food or, in Guatemala, the multi-coloured textiles geared to the Western customer.

Traje Traditional costume.

Verano Summer (Dec–April).

Rough Guides

advertiser

small print and

Index

A rough guide to Rough Guides

In the summer of 1981, Mark Ellingham, a recent graduate from Bristol University, was travelling round Greece and couldn't find a guidebook that really met his needs. On the one hand there were the student guides, insistent on saving every last cent, and on the other the heavyweight cultural tomes whose authors seemed to have spent more time in a research library than lounging away the afternoon at a taverna or on the beach.

In a bid to avoid getting a job, Mark and a small group of writers set about creating their own guidebook. It was a guide to Greece that aimed to combine a journalistic approach to description with a thoroughly practical approach to travellers' needs – a guide that would incorporate culture, history and contemporary insights with a critical edge, together with up-to-date, value-for-money listings. Back in London, Mark and the team finished their Rough Guide, as they called it, and talked Routledge into publishing the book.

That first *Rough Guide to Greece*, published in 1982, was a student scheme that became a publishing phenomenon. The immediate success of the book – with numerous reprints and a Thomas Cook Prize shortlisting – spawned a series that rapidly covered dozens of destinations. Rough Guides had a ready market among low-budget backpackers, but soon also acquired a much broader and older readership that relished Rough Guides' wit and inquisitiveness as much as their enthusiastic, critical approach. Everyone wants value for money, but not at any price.

Rough Guides soon began supplementing the "rougher" information about hostels and low-budget listings with the kind of detail on restaurants and quality hotels that independent-minded visitors on any budget might expect, whether on business in New York or trekking in Thailand.

These days the guides – distributed worldwide by the Penguin Group – offer recommendations from shoestring to luxury and cover more than 200 destinations around the globe, including almost every country in the Americas and Europe, more than half of Africa and most of Asia and Australasia. Our ever-growing team of authors and photographers is spread all over the world, particularly in Europe, the USA and Australia.

In 1994, we published the *Rough Guide to World Music* and *Rough Guide to Classical Music*, and a year later the *Rough Guide to the Internet*. All three books have become benchmark titles in their fields – which encouraged us to expand into other areas of publishing, mainly around popular culture. Rough Guides now publish:

- Travel guides to more than 200 worldwide destinations
- Dictionary phrasebooks to 22 major languages
- History guides ranging from Ireland to Islam
- Maps printed on rip-proof and waterproof Polyart™ paper
- Music guides running the gamut from Opera to Elvis
- Restaurant guides to London, New York and San Francisco
- Reference books on topics as diverse as The Weather and Shakespeare
- Sports guides from Formula 1 to Man Utd
- Pop culture books from *Lord of the Rings* to Cult TV
- World Music CDs in association with World Music Network

Visit **www.roughguides.com** to see our latest publications.

Rough Guide credits

Text editors: Stephen Timblin and Jeff Cranmer
Layout: Katie Pringle
Cartography: Manish Chandra, Rajesh Chhibber, Animesh Pathak
Picture research: Mark Thomas
Proofreader: Diane Margolis

....

Editorial: London Martin Dunford, Kate Berens, Helena Smith, Claire Saunders, Geoff Howard, Ruth Blackmore, Gavin Thomas, Polly Thomas, Richard Lim, Lucy Ratcliffe, Clifton Wilkinson, Alison Murchie, Fran Sandham, Sally Schafer, Alexander Mark Rogers, Karoline Densley, Andy Turner, Ella O'Donnell, Keith Drew, Andrew Lockett, Joe Staines, Duncan Clark, Peter Buckley, Matthew Milton; **New York** Andrew Rosenberg, Richard Koss, Hunter Slaton, Chris Barsanti, Steven Horak, Amy Hegarty, Anne Lise Sorensen
Design & Pictures: London Simon Bracken, Dan May, Diana Jarvis, Mark Thomas, Jj Luck, Harriet Mills; **Delhi** Madhulita Mohapatra, Umesh Aggarwal, Ajay Verma, Jessica Subramanian
Production: Julia Bovis, John McKay, Sophie Hewat
Cartography: London Maxine Repath, Ed Wright, Katie Lloyd-Jones, Miles Irving; **Delhi** Manish Chandra, Rajesh Chhibber, Jai Prakesh Mishra, Ashutosh Bharti, Rajesh Mishra, Animesh Pathak, Jasbir Sandhu, Karobi Gogoi
Cover art direction: Louise Boulton
Online: New York Jennifer Gold, Cree Lawson, Suzanne Welles, Benjamin Ross; **Delhi** Manik Chauhan, Narender Kumar, Shekhar Jha, Rakesh Kumar
Marketing & Publicity: London Richard Trillo, Niki Smith, David Wearn, Chloë Roberts, Demelza Dallow, Kristina Pentland; **New York** Geoff Colquitt, Megan Kennedy
Finance: Gary Singh
Manager India: Punita Singh
Series editor: Mark Ellingham
PA to Managing Director: Julie Sanderson
Managing Director: Kevin Fitzgerald

Publishing information

This third edition published October 2004 by
Rough Guides Ltd
80 Strand, London WC2R 0RL
345 Hudson St, 4th Floor,
New York, NY 10014, USA
Distributed by the Penguin Group
Penguin Books Ltd,
80 Strand, London WC2R 0RL
Penguin Putnam, Inc.
375 Hudson St, NY 10014, USA
Penguin Books Australia Ltd,
487 Maroondah Highway, PO Box 257,
Ringwood, Victoria 3134, Australia
Penguin Books Canada Ltd,
10 Alcorn Avenue, Toronto ON
M4V 1E4 Canada
Penguin Books (NZ) Ltd,
182–190 Wairau Road, Auckland 10,
New Zealand
Typeset in Bembo and Helvetica to an original design by Henry Iles.

Printed and bound in China

896pp includes index
A catalogue record for this book is available from the British Library

ISBN 9-78184-353-288-0

3 5 7 9 8 6 4

Help us update

We've gone to a lot of effort to ensure that the third edition of **The Rough Guide to Central America** is accurate and up to date. However, things change – places get "discovered", opening hours are notoriously fickle, restaurants and rooms raise prices or lower standards. If you feel we've got it wrong or left something out, we'd like to know, and if you can remember the address, the price, the time, the phone number, so much the better.

We'll credit all contributions, and send a copy of the next edition (or any other Rough Guide if you prefer) for the best letters. Everyone who writes to us and isn't already a subscriber will receive a copy of our full-colour thrice-yearly newsletter. Please mark letters: "**Rough Guide Central America Update**" and send to: Rough Guides, 80 Strand, London WC2R 0RL, or Rough Guides, 4th Floor, 345 Hudson St, New York, NY 10014. Or send an email to **mail@roughguides.com**.

Have your questions answered and tell others about your trip at **www.roughguides.atinfopop.com**.

Acknowledgements

Editorial acknowledgements

The editors would like to thank all of the authors for their dedication and hard work; Katie Pringle for her patience and first-rate typesetting; Katie Lloyd-Jones, Jasbir Sandhu and Manish Chandra for their mapmaking expertise; Mark Thomas for his eagle-eyed photo-researching; Julie Bovis and Simon Bracken for their tireless production work; Diane Margolis for her outstanding proofreading; Hunter Slaton and Richard Koss for their ingenious assistance; and Andrew Rosenberg for overall direction.

Author acknowledgements

Peter Eltringham: Once again, Peter would like to thank everyone – from archeologists to zoologists – who provided help and support during the research in Belize. I'm going to be seeing many of you soon to thank you personally. Selecting just a few of you for inclusion here is a difficult task, so I'll just say a special thank you to John Pirie and Rob Coates for giving their time to research some remote places and enabling me to better understand Belizean culture. And *muchas gracias* to those special people who've swiftly and expertly answered my emailed queries as I was writing: Marty Casado and Peter Jones on Ambergris Caye, Ellie Dial and Laura Godfrey in Placencia, Bruno and Melissa Kuppinger in Toledo, and Anabel Ford in California and Cayo.

Joe Fullman: Thanks to Karla Arias for all her help in San José, Geinier Guzman for his knowledge of the Pacific Coast, Jim Dobbins for walking the mean streets of Tortuguerro with me, Greg Ingram for translating, driving and generally being a great companion, and most of all to Nic Mainwood for being wonderful, reading through my stuff and learning enough Spanish to understand what *Te Amo* means.

Brendon Griffin: Thanks firstly to Frika, for enduring my absence yet again. To Ting and especially Keith for braving Bluefields and the potholes of Big Corn. Peter, Toby and Joe for invaluable help and info with Basics and Contexts. Anry Luis Rodriguez and Rigo Sampson, Arle Morales and the wonderful staff at Finca Magdalena, David Thomsen for delicious bread and an insight into the Sandinista era, Louis and Esther Ketelaars, David for a generous dinner on Big Corn, Jane in San Juan Del Sur, Lucrecia and family, Ellen and Marco Snoek, Richard Gaitan, and all Intur staff, especially in Chinandega and San Carlos, and the indefatigable Mario Sanchez Ramirez upstairs in the Managua office.

Toby Nortcliffe: My sincere thanks go to Marco and his team – especially Abdiel, Alvaro, Benny, Hernán, Ivan, Jacqueline and Melanie. In Panama City my thanks go to Abdiel and Mike at the hostel, Jim Malcolm and Penny Walsh at the British Embassy, as well as Joseph Ennis. In David, I would like to thank Andreá and José. On birding matters my appreciation goes to Bob "Sean" Scanlon. Finally, for their lifelong assistance in all things travel, thanks to Will Waddington and Bill Fischer.

Paul Smith: Thanks to Thomas Taylor (massive help!!) and Bob Dale (great beer!) in Honduras, Thilo Knecht in El Salvador, Mum, Dad, Joe and Carol for their love and support, Thomas Kohnstamm for starting the process and Stephen Timblin for his patience and hard work in taking over the editing.

Iain Stewart: My thanks to everyone that helped me in Guatemala, particularly Lorena Artola, Migdalia de Barillas, Nancy Mejía and Marlon Laz of INGUAT, Philippa Myers, Deedle and Dave at the lake, José Manuel Briz, Tom of Xelapages and Patrick and Pieter in Xela, Don David in El Remate and Peter Eltringham.

Andy Symington: Many thanks to all the obliging folk in Costa Rica who gave generously of their time and information during the research process, and also to all the people involved in the planning and editing stages at Rough Guides. I am as ever grateful to family and friends for their support and understanding, and particularly to Martin Davies for his excellent company despite getting off so lightly.

Reader letters

Many thanks to all the readers who took the time to write to us with comment and updates. They include:

John Alexander, Karl Andersson, Karin Anna, Scott Arneman, Hendrik S. Bakker, K. Behr, Roy and Audrey Bradford, Martine Bruin, Rachel Bullet, Lorraine Burchell, M. Butter, Chris Callard, Ben L. Campbell, Geoffery Clover, Francis and Maite Coke, Richard Counts, Damon Crowhurst, Sarah Curtis, Alison and Dana Doncaster, Sara Down, Anthony Downing, R. Drenth, Nina Esakov, Scott Espie, Linda and Mike Fender, Nick Felten, Mike Haaijer, Marc Hamel, Woflgang Huber, Sam Hussain, Andrew van Isterson, Anton Jansen, Gerard Kohl, Tania Kurland, Andrew van Iterson, Gerard Kohl, Tania Kurland, Bo Lanner, Simon Loft, Oliver Marshall, Ted Mau, Kevin McGrath, Bradley Meacham, Martin Mowforth, Elizabeth Nutter-Valladares, Jaime O'Drisceoil, Emil Olsson, Susan Pot, Baltasar Rodil, Peter Schreiner, Claudia Senecal, James Smith, Ellen Anne Teigen, Jens Vogt, Anna Williams, Monika Woltering, Hakan Yazici.

Photo credits

Cover credits

Main front Guatemalan cowboys at bar © Corbis
Small front top picture Toucan © Alamy
Small front lower picture Textiles © Alamy
Back top picture Bus, Solola, Guatemala © Robert Harding
Back lower picture Arco de Santa Catarina, Antigua © Corbis

Colour intro

Boat on Lago Atitlán © Jamie Marshall
La Paz waterfall © Darrell Gulin/Corbis
Detail of lemons and traditional cloth © Sue Carpenter/Axiom
Tree frog © David A. Northcott/Corbis
Tikal © Robert Francis /South American Pictures
School of fish, Ambergris Caye © Stephen Frink/Alamy
Young girl at Carnaval, Puerto Limón © Ian Cumming/Axiom
Close-up of flowers © Darrell Gulin/Corbis
Walking up the Columbia River, Belize © Ian Cumming/Axiom
Antigua © Jamie Marshall
Sololá, Guatemala © Peter M. Wilson

Things not to miss

Caye Caulker sunset © J. Sparshatt/Axiom
Parque Nacional Corcovado © Ian Cumming/Axiom
Cathedral in León © Jason P. Howe/South American Pictures
Keel-billed toucan © Gavirel Jecan/Corbis
Lago de Atitlán © Iain Stewart
Volcán Arenal © Jevan Berrange/South American Pictures
Bay Islands © Robert Francis/South American Pictures
Woman in traditional *pollera* dress © Mike Harding/South American Pictures
River kayaking © David Samuel Robbins/Corbis
Tikal © Robert Francis/South American Pictures
Antigua © Chris Sharp/South American Pictures
Pelican at dawn © Robert Francis/South American Pictures
Civil War monument, Mozote © Jason P. Howe/South American Pictures
Copán © Chris Sharp/South American Pictures
Flor de Cana rum © Royalty-Free/Corbis
Snorkelling along Lighthouse Reef © Kevin Schafer/Corbis
Coffee fields © Tony Morrison/South American Pictures
Monteverde cloudforest © Britt Pyer/South American Pictures
Tree-covered hills, Chiriquí Highlands © Danny Lehman/Corbis
Lago Yojoa © Laura Ferguson/South American Pictures
Sandinista mural, León © Robert Francis/South American Pictures
Finca El Paraíso © Iain Stewart
Panama Canal © Mike Harding/South American Pictures
Belize Zoo © Tony Morrison/South American Pictures
River travel in La Mosquitia © William Grey/Travel Ink
Santa Ana © Jason P. Howe/South American Pictures
Mountain Pine Ridge Forest Reserve © Chris Sharp/South American Pictures
San Salvador © Jason P. Howe/South American Pictures

Black & Whites

Semana Santa, Antigua © Jenny Acheson/Axiom (p.4)
Caye Caulker © Doug McKinlay/Axiom (p.8)
Beach hut in Palcencia © Chris Sharp/South American Pictures (p.48)
Fly-fishing in Belize © Owne Van Der Wal/Corbis (p.75)
Pine forests and waterfalls, Macal Valley © Charlotte Lipson (p.102)
Semana Santa, Antigua © Doug McKinlay/Axiom (p.134)
Close-up of masks © Jamie Marshall (p.191)
Maya ruins, Quiriguá © Chris Sharp/South American Pictures (p.235)
San Salvador's Catedral Metropolitana © Jason P. Howe/South American Pictures (p.284)
Buses in Santa Rosa de Lina © Robert Francis/South American Pictures (p.329)
Maya ruins, Copán © Robert Francis/South American Pictures (p.368)
View to El Picacho, Parque Nacional la Tigra © Robert Francis/South American Pictures (p.410)
Beach on Roatán © Robert Francis/South American Pictures (p.445)
Masaya's market © Robert Francis/South American Pictures (p.476)
Pepe Cabezan and La Gigatona © Jason P. Howe/South American Pictures (p.527)
Rancher herding cattle © Martin Rolers/ Corbis (p.572)
Spider monkey © Rebecca Whitfield/South American Pictures (p.623)
Pacific Coast, Costa Rica © Chris Caldicott/Axiom (p.692)
Male quetzal © Michael & Patricia Foqden/Corbis (p.728)
Traditional hut © Tony Morrison/South American Pictures (p.762)
Waterfall in Panamanian rainforest © Danny Lehman/Corbis (p.811)

Index

Map entries are in **colour**

A

Acajutla (ES)....................347
accommodation..............36
- in Belize 54
- in Costa Rica 580
- in El Salvador................291
- in Guatemala..................142
- in Honduras 373
- in Nicaragua..................482
- in Panama.....................735

Achutupu (P)..................802
Actun Tunichil (B)..........107
Agua Azul (H)................407
Aguacatán (G)...............224
Aguilares (ES)................363
Agujitas (CR).................717
Ahuachapán (ES) 349
Ahuas (H) 458
AIDS..............................27
Ailigandi (P)...................801
airlines
- in Australia and New Zealand 18
- in North America...........13
- in the UK and Ireland.........16

airpasses.........................33
Alajuela (CR) 618
Almirante (P) 825
Altagracia (N) 554
Altun Ha (B)......................84
Amapala (H) 400
Ambergris Caye (B)...88–94
amoebic dysentery 28
Anguiatú (ES) 359
ANTIGUA (G) 180–190
Antigua 182
- accommodation...............183
- arrival 182
- bars 188
- cafés 186
- Casa Popenoe 185
- Catedral de San José.......184
- clubs 188
- information....................183
- La Merced.....................186
- Las Capuchinas...............185
- listings........................189
- Museo de Arte Colonial....185
- Palace of the Captains General 184
- Parque Central...............184
- restaurants...................186
- restaurants...................187
- San Francisco.................185
- Semana Santa 181
- transport 183
- Volcán Pacaya 186

Apaneca (ES) 348
Apulo (ES) 320

B

Bacalar Chico (B)............93
Bahía de Jiquilísco (ES)..327
Bahía Drake (CR) 717
Barro Colorado (P)........777
Barton Creek Cave (B)..107
Barva (CR)......................625
Bastimentos (P).............831
Bay Islands (H).....460–473
Bay Islands...................461
BELIZE 47–132
Belize 50
BELIZE CITY (B) 66–76
Belize City 68–69
- accommodation...............70
- arrival 67
- bars 73
- Bliss Centre for Performing Arts 72
- Coastal Zone Museum 71
- House of Culture..............72
- Image Factory, the 71
- information....................67
- listings........................74
- Marine Terminal 71
- Maritime Museum.............71
- Museum of Belize.............71
- music 73
- National Handicrafts Center 71
- restaurants....................72
- St John's Cathedral 72
- Swing Bridge 71
- Tourist Village.................71
- transport 75

Belize, northern 77–98
Belize, northern........78, 90
Belize, south 115
Belize Zoo (B) 99
Belmopan (B) 101
Benque Viejo (B) 112
Bermudian Landing (B)...85
Bethel (G) 277
Biotopo de Quetzal (G)..249
bites and stings 28
Blue Creek (B)...............130
Blue Hole, the (B)............98
Bluefields (N)........562–564
Bocas del Toro province (P) 823–832
Bocas del Toro province.....................824
Bocas del Toro town (P) 826–829
Bocas del Toro town....827
Bombil Pek (G)..............257
books...................850–862
Boquete (P) 820
Bosque el Impossible (ES) 347
Bosque Montecristo (ES)...........................358
Braulio Carrillo (CR) 626
Bribrí (CR) 648
Brus Laguna (H)...........457
buses 33

C

Cabo Blanco (CR).........667
Cacaopera (ES).............342
Cahal Pech (B)..............106
Cahuita (CR).........641–644
camping 37
Cana (P) 792
Cancuén (G) 256
Candelaria caves (G).....256
Caño Negro (CR) 709
Cara Sucia (ES).............347
Caracol (B) 111
Cartago (CR) 627
Cartí (P) 801
Catacamas (H) 429
Catarata de Pulhapanzak (H).........407
Catarina (N)..................538
Caye Caulker (B)......94–98
Caye Caulker.................95
Cayo District (B) 99–114
Cayo District 100
Cayo Holandeses (P) 801
Cayos Cochinos (H)......473
Ceibal (G) 276
Celaque (H) 411
Cerro Hoya (P) 814
Cerro Punta (P) 818

Cerros (B)........................79
Chagres, Parque Nacional (P)...............778
Chajul (G).......................201
Chalatenango (ES)........364
Chalchuapa (ES)...........351
Champerico (G).............228
Changuinola (P)............832
Chichicastenango (G)......................193–196
Chichicastenango........194
Chiguiri Arriba (P)..........807
Chimaltenango (G)........192
Chinandega (N).............524
Chiquimula (G).............244
Chiriquí Grande (P).......825
Chisec (G)....................257
Chitré (P).......................808
cholera...........................28
Choluteca (H)................401
Coatepeque (G)............227
Cobán (G)............250–253
Cobán..........................251
Cobán and the Verapaces.................246
Cocales (G)..................228
Cockscomb Basin Wildlife Sanctuary (B).............121
Cojutepeque (ES)..........334
Colón (P)..............779–782
Colón Province (P).......773
Comayagua (H)....403–405
Comayagüela (H)..........392
Community Baboon Sanctuary (B)...............85
Conchagua (ES)............332
consulates, Central American, abroad........21
Copán (H)............414–423
Copán Ruinas town (H).......................414–418
Copán Ruinas town.....415
Copán, ruins of (H)......................418–423
Copán, ruins of............419
Corazon de Jesús (P)...801
Corcovado (CR).............722
Cordillera Apaneca (ES)............................348
Corinto (ES)..................342
Corinto (G)....................237
Corn Islands (N)...565–568
Corozal (B).....................77
Costa Arriba (P)............783
Costa del Bálsamo (ES)............................325
Costa del Sol (ES).........327
COSTA RICA........571–726
Costa Rica...........574–575
Costa Rica, Carribean coast of 631
Costa Rica, Central Pacific.......................651
Costa Rica, northern 703
Costa Rica, southern...................716
Costa Rica, Valle Central......................617
costs 31
in Belize 53
in Costa Rica 577
in El Salvador...................289
in Guatemala....................141
in Honduras 373
in Nicaragua.....................481
in Panama........................733
Coyotepe 537
crime 43
in Belize 58
in Costa Rica 584
in El Salvador...................294
in Guatemala....................147
in Honduras 377
in Nicaragua.....................486
in Panama........................739
Crooked Tree (B).............83
Cruce dos Aguadas (G) 274
Cubulco (G)...................248
Cuchumatanes, the (G).......................222–224
cycling............................35

D

Dangriga (B).........116–118
Dangriga......................117
Darién (P).............789–796
Darién Highway (P) 790
Darién, Parque Nacional (P)................791
David (P)...............815–817
David 816
Dominical (CR).............715
dengue fever..................26
diarrhoea........................27
drink: see eating and drinking
driving......................19, 34

E

eating and drinking
in Belize 55
in Costa Rica 581
in El Salvador...................291
in Guatemala.......................42
in Honduras 374
in Nicaragua.....................483
in Panama........................736
ecotourism...........844–849
El Amatillo (ES) 344
El Amatillo (H) 400
El Boquerón, Monumento Nacional (H) 428
El Caño Archeological Park (P) 807
El Castillo (N) 558
El Cuco (ES)..................328
El Cusuco, Parque Nacional (H) 439
El Espino (H) 402
El Estor (G)....................242
El Florido (H) 424
El Mirador (G)................275
El Naranjo (G)................278
El Porvenir (P) 799
El Poy (ES) 365, 413
El Puente (H).................425
El Rama (N)...................562
El Remate (G)................266
EL SALVADOR 283–366
EL Salvador..................286
El Salvador, eastern.....333
El Salvador, northern ...361
El Salvador, Pacific coast of 323
El Salvador, western....346
El Tulate (G)...................228
El Valle (P) 805
El Velero (N) 513
El Zotz (G) 274
email 39
embassies, Central American abroad 21
Escuintla (G)..................230
Esquipulas (G)...............244
Estación Biológica La Selva (CR) 712
Estelí (N) 525–529
Estelí 526
exchange rates 31

F

festivals
in Belize 56
in Costa Rica 583
in El Salvador...................293
in Guatemala....................144
in Honduras 375
in Nicaragua.....................484
in Panama........................737

flights
from Australia and New Zealand.........17
from the UK and Ireland.....15
from the US and Canada....12
online agents.........11
food: see eating and drinking
Flores (G).............261–265
Flores.........263
Fort San Lorenzo (P).....782
Fuentes Georginas (G)...218

G

Gales Point (B).............116
Gamboa (P).................776
Garífuna, history of.......118
Gatún Locks (P)...........782
glossary...................874–76
Glover's Reef (B)...........121
Golfito (CR).................719
Golfo de Fonseca (H)....400
Golfo de Fonsceco, islands (ES)...............331
Gracias (H)...................409
Granada (N)..........539–544
Granada.......540
Green Hills Butterfly Ranch (B)..................101
Guabito (P)...................832
Guanacaste (CR)...680–701
Guanacaste (CR)..........681
Guanaja (H)..........471–473
Guararé (P)...................810
Guasaule (N)................524
GUATEMALA........133–282
Guatemala............136–137
Guatemala, eastern.....233
Guatemala, Pacific coast of.............226–227
GUATEMALA CITY (G)............161–175
Guatemala City.....162–163
accommodation...............165
arrival.........162
bars.........171
cafés.........170
Casa Mima.........168
Cathedral.........167
cinemas.........171
clubs.........171
information.........164
Jardín Botánico.........168
Kaminaljuyú.........170
listings.........172
Mercado Central.........167
Museo Ixchel.........169
Museo Miraflores.........170
Museo Nacional de Arqueología y Etnología.........169
Museo Nacional de Arte Moderno.........169
Museo Nacional de Historia Natural.........170
Museo Popol Vuh.........169
orientation.........162
Palacio Nacional.........167
Parque Aurora.........169
Parque Central.........167
restaurants.........170
Teatro Nacional.........168
Torre del Reformador.........168
transport..........164, 173–175
Zona 1.........167
Zona 1.........166
Guatemalan Western Highlands (G).....178–179

H

Half Moon Caye Natural Monument (B).............98
health.......................26–30
hepatitis..........................27
Heredia (CR)................622
history
of Belize.........61–65
of Costa Rica...........588–593
of El Salvador...........296–303
of Guatemala...........151–160
of Honduras.............378–384
of Nicaragua.............487–495
of Panama...............740–746
HIV.................................27
Hog Islands (H)............473
Hol Chan Marine Reserve (B)...................92
HONDURAS.........367–474
Honduras.....................370
Honduras, central and western highlands of..............404
Honduras, north coast of.............432–433
Hopkins (B)..................119
Huehuetenango (G).......220
Huehuetenango...........220

I

Ilobasco (ES)................334
Independence (B)..........126
Indian Church (B)............82
Indian Creek (B)...........126
insurance........................25
Internet..........................39
Intipuca (ES).................329
Isla Cañas (P)...............813
Isla Colón (P)................829
Isla de Ometepe (N)......................551–554
Isla de Ometepe (N).............................552
Isla el Tigre (H).............400
Isla Grande (P).............785
Isla Iguana (P)..............813
Isla Taboga (P).............764
Isla Tigre (P)................801
Ixcán, the (G)...............258
Ixil triangle (G)......198–201
Iximché (G)...................193

J

Jacó (CR).............669–672
Jacotenango (G)...........190
Jaibalito (G)..................211
Jardín Botánico de Lancetilla (H).............446
Jinotega (N)..................532
Joya de Cerén (ES).......319
Juayúa (ES)..................348
Juticalpa (H).................428

K

K'umarkaaj (G).............197
Kuna Yala (P)........796–802

L

La Amistad (P).............819
La Avispa (H)................429
La Ceiba (H).........446–451
La Ceiba.....................448
La Chunga (P)..............794
La Democracia (G)........230
La Ensenada (H)..........444
La Entrada (H)..............425
La Esperanza (H)...........408
La Fortuna de San Carlos (CR)........702–708
La Fortuna de San Carlos......................704
La Hachadura (ES)........347
La Libertad (ES)............322
La Mesilla (G)...............224
La Milpa (B)....................83
La Muralla (H)...............430

La Palma (ES) 364
La Palma (P)..................792
La Paz Waterfall
Gardens (CR) 621
La Selva (CR)................712
La Técnica (G)...............278
La Tigra, Parque
Nacional (H) 398
La Unión (ES)................329
La Unión (H).................430
La Villa de Los
Santos (P) 810
Lago Coatepeque (ES)...356
Lago de Atitlán
(G).......................201–212
Lago de Atitlán.............202
Lago de Ilopango (ES)..320
Lago de Izabal (G) 242
Lago de Izabal (G)........241
Lago de Nicaragua
(N).......................550–559
Lago de Nicaragua 550
Lago de Petén Itzá (G)..265
Lago de Petexbatún
(G) 277
Lago de Yaxchá (G) 279
Lago de Yojoa (H)...406–408
Laguna Chicabal (G) 217
Laguna el Jocotal (ES)..341
Lagunas Sepalau (G) 257
Lamanai (B).....................82
Lancetilla, Jardín
Botánico (H) 446
language 863–876
language schools
Guatemala 149
Honduras 377
Lankaster Gardens
(CR) 629
Lanquín (G) 254
Las Baulas, Parque
Nacional Marino (CR)..691
Las Chinamas (ES) 351
Las Marías (H)...............448
Las Sepultras (H) 423
Las Tablas (P)................812
Laughing Bird Caye (B)..126
León (N) 516–522
León.............................519
León Viejo (N)...............523
Liberia (CR) 680–685
Liberia..........................683
Lighthouse Reef (B) 98
Limón Province
(CR) 31–650
Limón Province 631
Little Corn Island (N).....567
Lívingston (G)................238
Los Chiles (CR).............708
Los Cóbanos (ES).........346
Los Manos (H) 399
Los Planes de
Renderos (ES)...........321
Lubaantun (B) 130

M

Macal River (B)..............107
Macal River 109
mail 38
malaria 26
MANAGUA (N)......496–515
Managua..............498–499
accommodation 503
Altamira 507
arrival 499
Barrio Martha Quezada 505
beaches, nearby 512
Catedral Viejo 505
Centro Cultural Managua ...506
cinema 509
information 501
Laguna de Tiscapa 507
listings 511
markets 510
Museo Huellas de
Acahualinca 507
nightlife 509
Palacio Nacional 506
Plaza de la Republica 505
restaurants 507
shopping 510
Teatro Nacional Rubén
Darío 506
tour companies 515
transport 501, 513–515
Managua, around (N)...497
Mancarrón (N) 555
Manuel Antonio (CR).....677
maps 23
Masaya (N) 535–537
Masaya........................536
Matagalpa (N) 531
Maya Centre (B)............121
Mazatenango (G) 228
media
in Belize 57
in Costa Rica 584
in El Salvador 294
in Guatemala 146
in Honduras 376
in Nicaragua 485
in Panama 738
medical help 29
medical resources...........30
Melchor de Mencos (G)..279
Mennonites 81
Metapán (ES) 357
Meteti (P)......................790
Miami (H)......................444
Miraflor (N) 529
Mogué (P) 793
Momostenango (G).......219
money 31
Monkey Bay Wildlife
Sanctuary (B) 100
Monkey River (B) 126
Montelimar (N) 513
Monterrico (G)..............231
Monteverde (CR)..650–661
Monteverde 654
Montezuma (CR) 664
Montezuma 664
Monumento Nacional
El Boquerón (H).........428
Monumento Nacional
Guayabo (CR) 629
Mopan River (B) 108
Mosquitia (H)........455–459
Mosquitia.............432–433
Mountain Pine Ridge
(B).......................108–111
Mountain Pine Ridge...109
Moyogalpa (N) 553
Mozote (ES) 342

N

Nahuizalco (ES)............348
Nakúm (G)....................279
Narganá (P) 801
Natá (P) 808
Nebaj (G)......................199
New Edinburgh,
history of (P)..............795
NICARAGUA 475–570
Nicaragua....................478
Nicaragua, Atlantic
Coast of..,..................561
Nicaragua, north 517
Nicaragua, southwest..534
Nicoya (CR)..................697
Nicoya Peninsula 651
Nombre de Dios (P) 785
Nosara (CR) 699
Nueva Ocotepeque (H)...413
Nusagandi Nature
Reserve (P)................799

O

Ocotal (N).....................530
Olancho (H) 427
Olive Ridley turtles
(CR) 701

Ometepe (N).........551–554
Omoa (H).......................440
Orange Walk (B).............80
Osa Peninsula
(CR) 720–724

P

Palacios (H)...................457
Panajachel (G)......203–207
Panajachel (G)..............204
PANAMA...............727–833
Panama 730
Panama Canal
(P).......................772–779
Panama Canal..............773
PANAMA CITY
(P).......................747–771
Panama City.........752–753
accommodation................751
arrival 749
Balboa...............................761
bars 766
Bella Vista 759
casinos...............................767
Cerro Ancon........................761
Church of San José..........757
cinemas 767
cockfighting 768
discos 766
drinking 766
El Cangrejo 759
Fort Amador.......................763
handicrafts market............758
Hotel Central.....................756
information.........................750
Isla Taboga.........................764
listings...............................768
Museo Afro-Antillano 758
Museo Antropologico
Reina Torres de Araúz...758
Museo de Art
Contemporáneo 761
Museo de Arte Religioso
Colonial 757
Museo de Ciencias
Naturales 759
Museo de Historia
Panameña 755
Museo del Canal
Interoceanico.................755
nightlife 766
Palacio Presidencial..........756
Panama Canal Authority
Administration Building...763
Panamá Viejo 760
Parque Nacional
Metropolitano 764
Plaza Bolívar 756
Plaza Catedral 755
Plaza de Francia 756
restaurants 765
San Felipe 754
San Felipe.........................755
Santa Ana 758
Smithsonian Marine
Exhibition Centre 763
Teatro Nacional.................756
theatre...............................767
tour companies.................769
transport 749, 751, 769
Panama City, greater
(P)...............................748
Panama, eastern..........788
Panama, western 804
Panchimalco (ES)..........321
Panzós (G) 255
Parque Nacional Braulio
Carrillo (CR)................626
Parque Nacional
Cahuita (CR)......641–644
Parque Nacional
Celaque (H) 411
Parque Nacional Cerro
Cazul Meámbar (H)....407
Parque Nacional Cerro
Hoya (P) 814
Parque Nacional
Chagres (P) 778
Parque Nacional
Corcovado (CR) 722
Parque Nacional
Darién (P) 791
Parque Nacional El
Cusuco (H)..................439
Parque Nacional Janet
Kawas (H)...................446
Parque Nacional La
Amistad (P).................819
Parque Nacional La
Muralla (H)..................430
Parque Nacional La
Tigra (H) 398
Parque Nacional Manuel
Antonio (CR)..............677
Parque Nacional Manuel
Antonio (CR).............678
Parque Nacional
Marina Isla
Bastimentos (P) 831
Parque Nacional Marino
las Baulas (CR) 691
Parque Nacional Pico
Bonito (H)..................451
Parque Nacional
Portobelo (P) 785
Parque Nacional Rincón
de la Vieja (CR) 685
Parque Nacional Santa
Rosa (CR)...................687
Parque Nacional
Sarigua (P) 810
Parque Nacional Sierra
de Agalta (H) 429
Parque Nacional
Soberania (P) 777
Parque Nacional
Tortuguero (CR)..636–640
Parque Nacional Volcán
Arenal (CR)................708
Parque Nacional Volcán
Irazú (CR) 628
Parque Nacional Volcán
Masaya (N)................538
Parque Nacional Volcán
Poás (CR)...................619
Pasa Canoas (CR) 724
Paso Canoas (P) 817
Pedasi (P).....................812
Peñas Blancas (CR)......688
Peñas Blancas (N) 548
Peninsula de Azuero
(P) 808–814
Penonomé (P) 806
Perquín (ES) 343
Petén 260
phones 38
Pico Bonito (H).............451
Placencia (B).........123–125
Placencia.....................124
Playa del Coco (CR) 690
Playa Grande (G) 258
Playa Hermosa (CR) 689
Playa Panamá (CR).......689
Playa Samára (CR)........697
Playa Tamarindo
(CR) 693–697
Playa Venao (P).............813
Playitas (ES).................332
police 44
in Belize 58
in Costa Rica 584
in El Salvador....................294
in Guatemala.....................148
in Honduras 377
in Nicaragua......................486
in Panama.........................739
Poneloya (N) 523
Poptún (G)....................260
Portobelo (P) 783
public holidays
in Belize 56
in Costa Rica 583
in El Salvador....................293
in Guatemala.....................144
in Honduras 375
in Nicaragua......................484
in Panama.........................737
Pueblos Blancos (N) 538
Puerto Barrios (G).........236
Puerto Cabezas (N).......569
Puerto Cortés (H)..........440
Puerto Cutuco (ES).......329
Puerto El Triunfo (ES)....327

Puerto Indio (P)............794
Puerto Jiménez (CR).....720
Puerto La Libertad (ES)..322
Puerto Lempira (H)........458
Puerto Limón
(CR) 632–636
Puerto Limón................633
Puerto San José (G) 230
Puerto Viejo de
Sarapiquí (CR)............713
Puerto Viejo de Sarapiquí and around................710
Puerto Viejo de
Talamanca (CR)..644–647
Puerto Viejo de Talamanca.................645
Punta Gorda (B)............127
Punta Gorda (B)...........128
Puntarenas (CR)............662

Q

Quelepa (ES).................340
Quepos (CR).........673–675
Quetzaltenango
(G).......................212–217
Quetzaltenango............213
Quetzaltenango, central 215
Quiriguá (G)..................234

R

RAAN, the (N) 568
Rabinal (G) 248
rabies 28
Rainforest Aerial Tram
(CR) 625
Rara Avis (CR)...............710
Raxrujá (G) 256
Refugio de Vida Silvestre
Cuero y Salado (H).....452
Refugio Nacional
de Fauna Silvestre
Ostional (CR)..............701
Refugio Nacional de Vida
Silvestre Caño
Negro (CR) 709
Refugio Nacional de
Vida Silvestre Gandoca-
Manzanillo (CR)..........647
Reserva Biológica
Bosque Nuboso
Monteverde (CR)........658
Reserva Biológica Indio
Maíz (N)......................559
Reserva Natural Absoluta
Cabo Blanco (CR)......667
Reserva Natural Punta
Patiño (P) 794
Reserva Santa Elena
(CR) 660
Retalhuleu (G) 227
Reu (G)..........................227
Reversa Bocas del
Popochic (G)..............243
Rincón de la Vieja (CR)...685
Río Azul (G)...................274
Rio Bravo Conservation
Area (B) 83
Río Cangrejal (H)...........452
Río Dulce (G).................239
Río Plátano Biosphere
Reserve (H) 458
Río San Juan (N)..556–559
Río Sidra (P)..................801
Rivas (N)........................545
Roatán (H) 467–471
Roatán, West End........469
Ruta de la Paz (ES).......341

S

Sacapulas (G) 198
St Margaret's
Village (B) 115
Salamá (G) 248
Samára (CR)..................697
Sambú (P) 794
San Andrés (ES)............320
San Andrés (G) 265
San Andrés Itzapa (G)...190
San Antonio (B).....110, 130
San Carlos (N)...............557
San Cristóbal (ES).........357
San Francisco
el Alto (G) 218
San Francisco
Gotera (ES)................341
San Ignacio (B) 103–106
San Ignacio 105
San Ignacio (ES) 365
SAN JOSÉ (CR)....594–615
San José..............596–597
accommodation................598
arrival 594
bars..................................606
cafés 605
central San Jose..............599
Centro Costarricense de la
Ciencia y la Cultura.......603
dance 608
discos 606
information........................596
listings..............................609
live music..........................606
Marco Fidel Tristan
Museo de Jade 602
markets.............................608
Mercado Central...............603
Museo de Arte
Costarricense 604
Museo de Arte y Diseño
Contemporáneo 603
Museo de Ciencias
Naturales La Salle 604
Museo de Oro
Precolombino 602
Museo Nacional................603
Parque España 602
Plaza de la Cultura 602
restaurants........................605
San Pedro 604
San Pedro 604
shopping...........................608
sodas 605
Teatro Nacional.................602
theatre..............................608
tour operators...................612
transport 597, 611–615
University of Costa Rica...604
San José (G) 265
San Juan Atitán (G).......223
San Juan
Chamelco (G).............254
San Juan Cotzal (G)......201
San Juan del Sur (N).....546
San Juan del Sur 547
San Juan Intibucá (H) ...409
San Juan La
Laguna (G) 210
San Juancito (H) 397
San Lorenzo (H) 401
San Marcos de
Colón (H) 402
San Marcos La
Laguna (G) 210
San Martín
Sacatepéquez (G) 217
San Miguel (ES)....336–340
San Miguel 337
San Pedro (B)..................88
San Pedro Carchá (G)...253
San Pedro La Laguna (G)....208–211
San Pedro Sula (H) 433–439
San Pedro Sula 435
SAN SALVADOR
(ES).....................304–318
San Salvador................308
accommodation................309
arrival 305
Basilica de Nuestra Señor
de Guadalupe...............315
cafés 315

Catedral Metropolitana.....310
Centro Monseñor Romero.....315
El Centro.....310
El Centro.....311
history.....304
Jardín Botánico La Laguna.....315
listings.....317
Mercado Central.....312
Mercado des Artesanías...313
Metrocentro.....313
Museo Nacional de Antropología.....313
nightlife.....317
Palacio Nacional.....310
Parque Infantíl.....312
Parque Libertad.....312
Plaza Barrios.....310
restaurants.....315
Teatro Nacional.....312
transport.....307
Universidad de Centro América.....315
western suburbs.....314
Zona Rosa.....315

San Salvador, around (ES).....305

San Sebastián (ES).....334

San Vicente (ES).....334

Santa Ana (ES).....352–355

Santa Ana.....353

Santa Antonio Palopó (G).....207

Santa Bárbara (H).....408

Santa Catarina Palopó (G).....207

Santa Cruz (G).....274

Santa Cruz del Quiché (G).....196

Santa Cruz La Laguna (G).....212

Santa Elena (CR).....656

Santa Elena (G).....261

Santa Elena (G).....263

Santa Fe (H).....455

Santa Lucía (H).....396

Santa Lucía Cotzumalguapa (G)....229

Santa María de Jesús (G).....190

Santa Rita (B).....79

Santa Rosa (CR).....687

Santa Rosa de Copán (H).....412

Santa Rosa de Lima (ES).....344

Santa Tecla (ES).....319

Santiago (P).....814

Santiago Atitlán (G).....207

Santiago Sacatepéquez (G).....192

Sarapiquí (CR).....710–714

Sarapiquí.....710

Sarchí (CR).....621

Sareneja (B).....80

Sarigua, Parque Nacional (P).....810

Sayaxché (G).....276

Seine Bight (B).....122

Selempím (G).....243

Selva Negra (N).....532

Semuc Champey (G)....254

Senahú (G).....255

Sensuntepeque (ES).....334

Shark-Ray Alley (B).....92

Shipstern Nature Reserve (B).....80

Sierra de Agalta (H).....429

Siguatepeque (H).....406

Sittee River (B).....120

Sixaola (CR).....648

Soberania, Parque Nacional (P).....777

Solentiname archipelago (N).....555

Sololá (G).....202

Sonsonate (ES).....345

Spanish language guide.....865

study abroad
in Belize.....59
in Costa Rica.....586
in El Salvador.....295
in Guatemala.....148
in Honduras.....377
in Nicaragua.....486
in Panama.....739

Suchitoto (ES).....360

Suchitoto (ES).....362

T

Tactic (G).....250

Tacuba (ES).....351

Takalik Abaj (G).....228

Tamarindo (CR)....693–697

Tamarindo.....694

Taulabé (H).....406

taxis.....34

TEGUCIGALPA (H).....385–396

Tegucigalpa.....388
accommodation.....389
arrival.....387
Basilica de Suyapa.....392
Catedral San Miguel.....390
central Tegucigalpa.....390
Comayagüela.....392
Galería Nacional de Arte...391
history.....386
Iglesia San Francisco.....390
information.....387
listings.....394
Museo Nacional e Instituto Hondureño de Antropología e Historia..391
nightlife.....394
Plaza Morazán.....389
restaurants and cafés.....393
transport.....387, 395

Tegucigalpa, around (H).....386

Tela (H).....441–444

Tikal (G).....267–273

Tikal.....270–271

Tilarán (CR).....661

Tobacco Caye (B).....118

Todos Santos (G).....222

Tonosi (P).....814

Tornabé (H).....444

Tortuguero (CR)...637–640

Totonicapán (G).....219

tour operators
in Australia and in New Zealand.....18
in North America.....14
in the UK and Ireland.....17

Transisthmian Highway (P).....778

transport.....33
in Belize.....51
in Costa Rica.....576
in El Salvador.....288
in Guatemala.....139
in Honduras.....371
in Nicaragua.....479
in Panama.....731

travel agents
in Australia and New Zealand.....18
in North America.....13
in the UK and Ireland.....16

Trifuno de la Cruz (H)....444

Trujillo (H).....452–455

Turneffe Islands (B).....98

Turrialba (CR).....629

turtles, Olive Ridley (CR).....701

Tzununá (G).....211

U

Uaxactún (G).....273

Uspantán (G).....198

Usulután (ES).....327

Utatlán (G).....197

Utila (H).....463–467

Uxbenka (B).....130

V

vaccinations....................26
Valle de Angeles (H)......397
Verapaces, the
(G).......................246-258
Verapaces, the 246
visas................................20
Volcán (P).......................818
Volcán Agua (G)............190
Volcán Arenal
(CR)....................702–708
Volcán Barú (P).............822
Volcán Barva (CR).........626
Volcán Cerro Verde
(ES)............................355
Volcán Chichontepac
(ES)............................335
Volcán Concepción
(N)..............................554
Volcán de Ipala (G)........244
Volcán Irazú (CR)..........628
Volcán Izalco (ES).........356
Volcán Maderas (N).......554
Volcán Masaya (N)........538
Volcán Mombacho (N)..545
Volcán Poás (CR)..........619
Volcán San Salvador
(ES)............................319
Volcán Santa Ana (ES)....36
Volcán Santa Maria
(G).............................217
volunteer work: see work

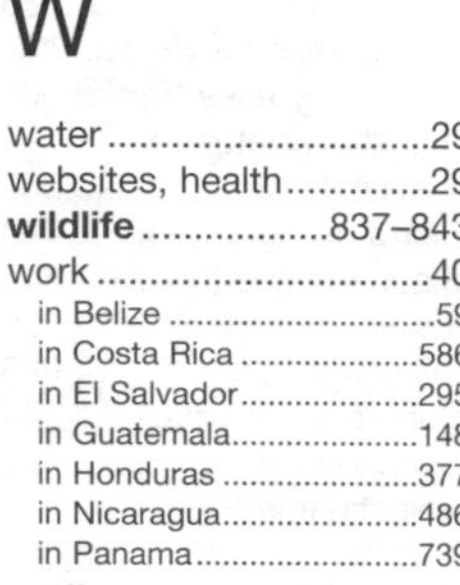

W

water..............................29
websites, health.............29
wildlife..................837–843
work................................40
in Belize..........................59
in Costa Rica..................586
in El Salvador.................295
in Guatemala...................148
in Honduras.....................377
in Nicaragua....................486
in Panama.......................739

X

Xunantunich (B).............112

Y

Yaviza (P).......................790
youth hostels..................37

Z

Zacatecoluca (ES).........326
Zaculeu (G)...................221
Zunil (G)........................218

I INDEX